Vital Statistics
of the United States

Births, Life Expectancy, Deaths, and Selected Health Data

Third Edition, 2008

Vital Statistics
of the United States

**Births, Life Expectancy, Deaths,
and Selected Health Data**

Third Edition, 2008

Edited by
Mary Meghan Ryan

Published in the United States of America
by Bernan Press, a wholly owned subsidiary of
The Rowman & Littlefield Publishing Group, Inc.
4501 Forbes Boulevard, Suite 200
Lanham, Maryland 20706

Bernan Press
800-865-3457
info@bernan.com
www.bernan.com

Copyright © 2008 by Bernan Press

ISBN-13: 978-1-59888-268-1
ISBN-10: 1-59888-268-6
eISBN-13: 978-1-59888-296-4
eISBN-10: 1-59888-296-1

ISSN: 1549-8603

∞™ The paper used in this publication meets the minimum requirements of American National Standard for Information Sciences—Permanence of Paper for Printed Library Materials, ANSI/NISO Z39.48-1992. Manufactured in the United States of America.

CONTENTS

LIST OF TABLES

PART A: BIRTHS

PART B: MORTALITY

PART C: HEALTH

DETERMINANTS AND MEASURES OF HEALTH

LIST OF FIGURES

INTRODUCTION

Until 1993, the federal government published *Vital Statistics of the United States* in several thick-bound volumes. These volumes offered comprehensive data on births, deaths, marriage and divorce, and can currently be found in libraries. However, there was nothing comparable published between 1993 and 2004, when the first edition of the present volume was published by Bernan Press. However, in the interim, the Centers for Disease Control and Prevention (CDC) and its National Center for Health Statistics (NCHS) continued to compile much of this information as periodical reports and news releases, which were available electronically on their Web site. A summary of these data can also be found in the *Statistical Abstract of the United States*, compiled by the U.S. Department of Commerce and published by Bernan Press. These circumstances gave Bernan Press the motivation to bring together a comprehensive collection of birth, death, and health statistics into a single volume called *Vital Statistics of the United States*. The 2008 volume is the publication's third edition.

The third edition is presented in a new streamlined format. There are three parts: births, mortality, and health. Each part is preceded by a figure that calls attention to noteworthy trends in addition to highlights of data found in the tables. Within each part, there are numerous tables and additional figures. Notes and definitions appear at the end of each section.

Part A: Births provides preliminary data for 2006 and final data for 2005 and earlier years on many aspects of natality, including birth and fertility rates, number of children, births to unmarried women, maternal health, methods of delivery, other characteristics of mothers, medical visits by pregnant women, and infant health status. The data were obtained from the National Center for Health Statistics.

Part B: Mortality focuses on deaths and death rates, according to a number of medical, demographic, and social characteristics. Especially detailed are the tables on causes of death, which are shown by age, sex, Hispanic origin, race, and (to a lesser extent) state of residence. Death rates are also given by marital status and level of educational attainment, and special tables are provided for infant mortality. These tables were obtained from the National Center for Health Statistics, with most information coming from *Deaths: Final Data for 2005*. Other sources included *Deaths: Preliminary Data for 2006* and *Health, United States, 2007 with Chartbook on Trends in the Health of Americans*.

Part C: Health, offers a collection of statistics concerning health and disease. While health is not a traditional component of vital statistics, there are connections between health status and birth and death statistics. For example, a person analyzing death rates from cancer may also be interested in a table on the incidence rate of cancer. This chapter shows selected data on several topics, including determinants and measures of health, use of addictive substances, ambulatory care, inpatient care, health personnel, health expenditures, and health insurance. Data were obtained from different surveys conducted by the National Center for Health Statistics and the Census Bureau.

It is of interest to view some of the vital statistics for the United States in the context of international experience. Tables I-1 to I-2, which comprise the international comparisons tables shown on the following pages, compare selected vital statistics for various regions and countries. Data are provided for life expectancy and infant mortality. Among 37 selected countries, life expectancy in the United States ranked 26th for both males and females in 2003. Hong Kong had the longest life expectancy for males at 78.5 years and the second longest for females at 84.3 years. Japan ranked first in life expectancy for females at 85.3 and second for males at 78.4 The United States ranked 29th in infant mortality in 2004, tied with Poland and Slovakia. Romania had the highest rate of infant mortality at 16.8 per 1,000 live births while Singapore had the lowest at 2.0 per 1,000 live births.

Table I-1.   Life Expectancy at Birth and At 65 Years of Age, According to Sex, Selected Countries, Selected Years, 1980–2003

(Number.)

Country	Male								Female							
	1980	1990	1995	2000	2001	2002	2003	2003 (rank)	1980	1990	1995	2000	2001	2002	2003	2003 (rank)
At Birth																
Australia	71.0	73.9	75.0	76.6	77.0	77.4	77.8	5	78.1	80.1	80.8	82.0	82.4	82.6	82.8	6
Austria	69.0	72.2	73.3	75.1	75.6	75.8	75.9	18	76.1	78.8	79.9	81.1	81.5	81.7	81.6	15
Belgium	70.0	72.7	73.4	75.1	75.4	75.6	75.9	18	76.8	79.4	80.7	81.4	81.1	81.7	81.7	13
Bulgaria	68.5	68.3	67.4	68.5	68.6	68.9	68.9	34	73.9	75.0	74.9	75.1	75.4	75.6	75.9	35
Canada	71.7	74.4	75.1	76.7	77.0	77.2	77.4	7	78.9	80.8	81.1	81.9	82.1	82.1	82.4	9
Chile	—	71.1	71.8	72.6	72.7	72.9	72.9	29	—	76.9	77.8	78.6	78.7	78.9	79.0	30
Costa Rica	71.9	74.7	74.0	75.4	75.6	76.2	76.2	16	77.0	79.1	78.6	80.2	79.9	81.0	81.0	19
Cuba	72.2	74.6	75.4	74.7	74.7	74.7	75.4	24	—	76.9	77.7	79.0	79.2	79.2	79.8	28
Czech Republic[1]	66.8	67.6	69.7	71.7	72.1	72.1	72.1	30	73.9	75.4	76.6	78.4	78.5	78.7	78.7	32
Denmark	71.2	72.0	72.7	74.5	74.7	74.8	76.5	13	77.3	77.7	77.8	79.3	79.3	79.5	79.9	27
England and Wales	70.8	73.1	74.3	75.6	76.0	76.2	76.5	13	76.8	78.6	79.5	80.3	80.6	80.7	80.9	20
Finland	69.2	70.9	72.8	74.2	74.6	74.9	75.1	25	77.6	78.9	80.2	81.0	81.5	81.5	81.8	11
France	70.2	72.8	73.9	75.3	75.5	75.8	75.9	18	78.4	80.9	81.8	82.7	82.9	83.0	82.9	5
Germany[2]	69.6	72.0	73.3	75.0	75.6	75.4	75.7	23	76.1	78.4	79.7	81.0	81.3	81.2	81.4	16
Greece	72.2	74.6	75.0	75.6	76.1	76.4	76.5	13	76.8	79.5	80.3	80.6	80.7	80.7	81.3	17
Hong Kong	71.6	74.6	76.0	78.0	78.4	78.6	78.5	1	77.9	80.3	81.5	83.9	84.6	84.5	84.3	2
Hungary	65.5	65.1	65.3	67.4	68.1	68.4	68.4	35	72.7	73.7	74.5	75.9	76.4	76.7	76.7	34
Ireland	70.1	72.1	72.9	73.4	74.7	75.2	75.8	21	75.6	77.6	78.4	79.1	79.7	80.3	80.7	22
Israel	72.2	75.1	75.5	76.7	77.1	77.5	77.5	6	75.8	78.5	79.5	81.1	81.6	81.4	81.7	13
Italy	70.6	73.6	74.9	76.6	76.7	76.8	76.8	12	77.4	80.1	81.3	82.5	82.8	82.9	82.5	7
Japan	73.4	75.9	76.4	77.7	78.1	78.3	78.4	2	78.8	81.9	82.9	84.6	84.9	85.2	85.3	1
Netherlands	72.5	73.8	74.6	75.5	75.8	76.0	76.2	16	79.2	80.9	80.4	80.5	80.7	80.7	80.9	20
New Zealand	70.0	72.4	74.4	76.3	76.3	76.3	77.0	10	76.3	78.3	79.7	81.1	81.1	81.1	81.3	17
Northern Ireland	68.3	72.1	73.5	74.8	75.2	75.6	75.8	21	75.0	78.0	78.9	79.8	80.1	80.4	80.6	23
Norway	72.3	73.4	74.8	76.0	76.2	76.4	77.1	9	79.2	79.8	80.8	81.4	81.5	81.5	82.0	10
Poland	66.0	66.7	67.6	69.7	70.2	70.4	70.5	32	74.4	76.3	76.4	77.9	78.3	78.8	78.8	31
Portugal	67.7	70.4	71.6	73.2	73.5	73.8	74.2	27	75.2	77.4	78.7	80.0	80.3	80.5	80.5	25
Puerto Rico	70.8	69.1	69.6	71.1	71.4	71.6	71.8	31	76.9	77.2	78.9	80.1	80.3	80.5	80.6	23
Romania	66.6	66.6	65.5	67.8	67.7	67.4	67.7	36	71.9	73.1	73.5	74.8	75.0	74.8	75.1	36
Russian Federation	61.4	63.8	58.3	59.2	59.1	58.9	58.6	37	73.0	74.4	71.7	72.4	72.3	72.0	71.8	37
Scotland	69.0	71.1	72.1	73.1	73.3	73.5	73.8	28	75.2	76.7	77.7	78.6	78.8	78.9	79.1	29
Singapore	69.8	73.1	74.2	76.1	76.4	76.5	77.4	7	74.7	77.6	78.6	80.1	80.3	81.1	81.8	11
Slovakia[1]	66.8	66.6	68.4	69.2	69.6	69.8	69.9	33	74.3	75.4	76.3	77.4	77.7	77.7	77.8	33
Spain	72.5	73.3	74.3	75.7	76.1	76.1	76.9	11	78.6	80.3	81.5	82.5	82.9	83.5	83.6	3
Sweden	72.8	74.8	76.2	77.4	77.6	77.7	77.9	4	78.8	80.4	81.4	82.0	82.1	82.1	82.5	7
Switzerland	72.8	74.0	75.3	76.9	77.4	77.8	78.0	3	79.6	80.7	81.7	82.6	83.0	83.0	83.1	4
United States	70.0	71.8	72.5	74.1	74.4	74.5	74.8	26	77.4	78.8	78.9	79.5	79.8	79.9	80.1	26
At 65 years																
Australia	13.7	15.2	15.7	16.9	17.2	17.4	17.6	4	17.9	19.0	19.5	20.4	20.7	20.8	21.0	4
Austria	12.9	14.3	14.9	16.0	16.3	16.3	16.3	19	16.3	17.8	18.6	19.4	19.8	19.7	19.9	13
Belgium	13.0	14.3	14.8	15.5	15.8	15.8	15.8	22	16.9	18.5	19.1	19.5	19.7	19.7	19.7	15
Bulgaria	12.7	12.9	12.8	12.8	13.1	13.1	13.8	32	14.7	15.4	15.4	15.4	15.8	15.8	15.9	34
Canada	14.5	15.7	16.0	16.8	17.1	17.2	17.4	6	18.9	19.9	20.0	20.4	20.6	20.6	20.8	6
Chile	—	14.6	14.9	15.3	15.4	15.4	15.4	28	—	17.6	18.1	18.6	18.7	18.8	18.7	27
Costa Rica	16.1	17.1	16.7	17.2	17.1	17.8	17.7	3	18.1	19.3	18.6	19.6	19.4	20.5	20.0	12
Cuba	—	—	—	16.7	16.8	16.8	16.9	12	—	—	—	19.0	19.3	19.3	19.3	22
Czech Republic[1]	11.2	11.6	12.7	13.7	14.0	14.0	13.9	30	14.3	15.2	16.0	17.1	17.2	17.4	17.3	31
Denmark	13.6	14.0	14.1	15.2	15.2	15.4	15.5	27	17.6	17.8	17.5	18.3	18.4	18.3	18.6	28
England and Wales	12.9	14.1	14.8	15.8	16.1	16.3	16.5	18	16.9	17.9	18.3	19.0	19.2	19.2	19.4	21
Finland	12.5	13.7	14.5	15.5	15.7	15.8	15.8	22	16.5	17.7	18.6	19.3	19.6	19.6	19.6	18
France	13.6	15.5	16.1	16.7	16.9	17.0	17.1	8	18.2	19.8	20.6	21.2	21.3	21.4	21.4	3
Germany[2]	13.0	14.0	14.7	15.7	16.0	16.2	16.1	20	16.7	17.6	18.5	19.4	19.6	19.7	19.6	18
Greece	14.6	15.7	16.1	16.3	16.7	16.7	16.8	13	16.8	18.0	18.4	18.3	18.6	18.7	18.9	24
Hong Kong	13.9	15.3	16.2	17.3	17.7	17.8	17.9	2	13.9	18.8	19.5	21.5	22.1	22.0	21.7	2
Hungary	11.6	12.0	12.1	12.7	13.0	13.1	13.0	35	14.6	15.3	15.8	16.5	16.7	17.0	16.9	32
Ireland	12.6	13.3	13.6	14.6	15.0	15.3	15.7	25	15.7	16.9	17.3	17.8	18.2	18.6	18.9	24
Israel	14.4	15.9	16.0	16.9	17.2	17.3	17.3	7	15.8	17.8	18.0	19.3	19.8	19.7	19.7	15
Italy	13.3	15.1	15.8	16.5	16.5	16.6	16.6	17	17.1	18.8	19.6	20.4	20.4	20.6	20.6	8

— = Data not available.

[1]In 1993, Czechoslovakia was divided into two nations, the Czech Republic and Slovakia. Data for years prior to 1993 are from the Czech and Slovak regions of Czechoslovakia.

[2]Until 1990, estimates refer to the Federal Republic of Germany; from 1995 onwards, data refer to Germany after reunification.

Table I-1.   Life Expectancy at Birth and At 65 Years of Age, According to Sex, Selected Countries, Selected Years, 1980–2003—*Continued*

(Number.)

Country	Male								Female							
	1980	1990	1995	2000	2001	2002	2003	2003 (rank)	1980	1990	1995	2000	2001	2002	2003	2003 (rank)
Japan	14.6	16.2	16.5	17.5	17.8	18.0	18.0	1	17.7	20.0	20.9	22.4	22.7	23.0	23.0	1
Netherlands	13.7	14.4	14.7	15.3	15.5	15.6	15.8	22	18.0	18.9	19.0	19.2	19.3	19.3	19.5	20
New Zealand	13.2	14.7	15.6	16.7	16.7	16.7	17.1	8	17.0	18.3	19.1	20.0	20.0	20.0	20.1	10
Northern Ireland	11.9	13.7	14.4	15.3	15.7	15.9	16.1	20	15.8	17.5	18.0	18.5	18.7	18.9	19.1	23
Norway	14.3	14.6	15.1	16.0	16.1	16.2	16.7	16	18.0	18.5	19.1	19.7	19.8	19.7	20.1	10
Poland	12.0	12.7	12.9	13.6	13.9	14.0	13.9	30	15.5	16.9	16.6	17.3	17.6	17.9	17.9	30
Portugal	12.9	13.9	14.6	15.3	15.6	15.6	15.6	26	16.5	17.0	17.8	18.7	18.9	19.0	18.9	24
Puerto Rico	—	—	—	—	—	—	—	—	—	—	—	—	—	—	—	—
Romania	12.6	13.3	12.9	13.5	13.5	13.0	13.1	34	14.2	15.3	15.4	15.9	16.1	15.8	15.9	34
Russian Federation	11.6	12.1	10.9	11.1	11.1	10.9	10.7	36	15.6	15.9	15.1	15.2	15.3	15.1	14.9	36
Scotland	12.3	13.1	13.8	14.7	14.9	15.1	15.2	29	16.2	16.7	17.3	17.8	18.0	18.1	18.2	29
Singapore	12.6	14.5	14.6	15.8	16.0	16.0	17.0	10	15.4	16.9	17.3	19.0	19.2	19.2	19.7	15
Slovakia[1]	12.3	12.2	12.7	12.9	13.0	13.3	13.3	33	15.4	15.7	16.1	16.5	16.8	17.0	16.9	32
Spain	14.8	15.4	16.0	16.6	16.8	16.8	16.8	13	17.9	19.0	19.8	20.4	20.7	20.7	20.7	7
Sweden	14.3	15.3	16.0	16.7	16.9	16.9	17.0	10	17.9	19.0	19.6	20.0	20.1	20.0	20.3	9
Switzerland	14.4	15.3	16.1	16.9	17.2	17.5	17.5	5	17.9	19.4	20.2	20.7	21.0	21.0	21.0	4
United States	14.1	15.1	15.6	16.3	16.4	16.6	16.8	13	18.3	18.9	18.9	19.2	19.4	19.5	19.8	14

—— = Data not available.

[1]In 1993, Czechoslovakia was divided into two nations, the Czech Republic and Slovakia. Data for years prior to 1993 are from the Czech and Slovak regions of Czechoslovakia.

[2]Until 1990, estimates refer to the Federal Republic of Germany; from 1995 onwards, data refer to Germany after reunification.

NOTE: Rankings are from highest to lowest life expectancy (LE) for the most recent year available. Since calculation of LE estimates varies among countries, comparisons among them and their interpretation should be made with caution. Countries with the same LE receive the same rank. The country with the next lower LE is assigned the rank it would have received had the higher-ranked countries not been tied, i.e., skip a rank.

Table I-2.   Infant Mortality Rates and International Ranking, Selected Countries and Territories, Selected Years, 1960–2004

(Number per 1,000 live births.)

Country[1]	1960	1970	1980	1990	2000	2001	2002	2003	2004	International rankings[2]	
										1960	2004
Infant Deaths per 1,000 Live Births[3]											
Australia	20.2	17.9	10.7	8.2	5.2	5.3	5.0	4.8	4.7	5	20
Austria	37.5	25.9	14.3	7.8	4.8	4.8	4.1	4.5	4.5	24	18
Belgium	23.9	21.1	12.1	6.5	4.8	4.5	4.4	4.3	4.3	11	16
Bulgaria	45.1	27.3	20.2	14.8	13.3	14.4	13.3	12.0	11.7	30	36
Canada	27.3	18.8	10.4	6.8	5.3	5.2	5.4	5.3	5.3	15	24
Chile	120.3	82.2	33.0	16.0	11.7	8.3	7.8	7.8	8.4	36	33
Costa Rica	67.8	65.4	20.3	15.3	10.2	10.8	11.2	10.1	9.0	33	34
Cuba	37.3	38.7	19.6	10.7	7.2	6.2	6.5	6.3	5.8	23	27
Czech Republic	20.0	20.2	16.9	10.8	4.1	4.0	4.2	3.9	3.7	4	8
Denmark	21.5	14.2	8.4	7.5	5.3	4.9	4.4	4.4	4.4	8	17
England and Wales	22.4	18.5	12.0	7.9	5.6	5.4	5.2	5.3	5.0	9	23
Finland	21.0	13.2	7.6	5.6	3.8	3.2	3.0	3.1	3.3	6	6
France	27.5	18.2	10.0	7.3	4.4	4.5	4.1	4.0	3.9	16	9
Germany[4]	35.0	22.5	12.4	7.0	4.4	4.3	4.2	4.2	4.1	22	11
Greece	40.1	29.6	17.9	9.7	5.9	5.1	5.1	4.8	4.1	25	11
Hong Kong	41.5	19.2	11.2	5.9	2.9	2.7	2.4	2.3	2.5	26	2
Hungary	47.6	35.9	23.2	14.8	9.2	8.1	7.2	7.3	6.6	31	28
Ireland	29.3	19.5	11.1	8.2	6.2	5.7	5.0	5.1	4.9	18	21
Israel[5]	31.0	18.9	15.6	9.9	5.4	5.1	5.4	4.9	4.5	20	18
Italy	43.9	29.6	14.6	8.2	4.5	4.7	4.5	4.2	4.1	29	11
Japan	30.7	13.1	7.5	4.6	3.2	3.1	3.0	3.0	2.8	19	3
Netherlands	17.9	12.7	8.6	7.1	5.1	5.4	5.0	4.8	4.1	2	11
New Zealand	22.6	16.7	13.0	8.4	6.3	5.6	6.2	5.2	5.7	10	26
Northern Ireland	27.2	22.9	13.4	7.5	5.1	6.1	4.7	5.2	5.5	14	25
Norway	18.9	12.7	8.1	6.9	3.8	3.9	3.5	3.4	3.2	3	5
Poland	54.8	36.7	25.5	19.3	8.1	7.7	7.5	7.0	6.8	32	29
Portugal	77.5	55.5	24.3	11.0	5.5	5.0	5.0	4.1	4.0	35	10
Puerto Rico	43.3	27.9	18.5	13.4	9.9	9.2	9.8	9.8	8.1	27	32
Romania	75.7	49.4	29.3	26.9	18.6	18.4	17.3	16.7	16.8	34	37
Russian Federation[6]	—	—	22.0	17.6	15.2	14.6	13.2	12.4	11.5	—	35
Scotland	26.4	19.6	12.1	7.7	5.7	5.5	5.3	5.1	4.9	13	21
Singapore	34.8	21.4	11.7	6.7	2.5	2.2	2.9	2.5	2.0	21	1
Slovakia	28.6	25.7	20.9	12.0	8.6	6.2	7.6	7.9	6.8	17	29
Spain	43.7	28.1	12.3	7.6	3.9	3.4	4.1	3.6	3.5	28	7
Sweden	16.6	11.0	6.9	6.0	3.4	3.7	3.3	3.1	3.1	1	4
Switzerland	21.1	15.1	9.1	6.8	4.9	5.0	5.0	4.3	4.2	7	15
United States	26.0	20.0	12.6	9.2	6.9	6.8	7.0	6.9	6.8	12	29

—— = Data not available.

[1]Refers to countries, territories, cities, or geographic areas with at least 1 million population and with complete counts of live births and infant deaths according to the United Nations Demographic Yearbook.

[2]Rankings are from lowest to highest infant mortality rates (IMR). Countries with the same IMR receive the same rank. The country with the next highest IMR is assigned the rank it would have received had the lower-ranked countries not been tied, i.e., skip a rank. Some of the variation in IMRs is due to differences among countries in distinguishing between fetal and infant deaths.

[3]Under 1 year of age.

[4]Rates for 1990 and earlier years were calculated by combining information from the Federal Republic of Germany and the German Democratic Republic.

[5]Includes data for East Jerusalem and Israeli residents in certain other territories under occupation by Israeli military forces since June 1967.

[6]Excludes infants born alive after less than 28 weeks gestation, of less than 1,000 grams in weight and 35 centimeters in length, who die within 7 days of birth.

PART A:
BIRTHS

BIRTHS

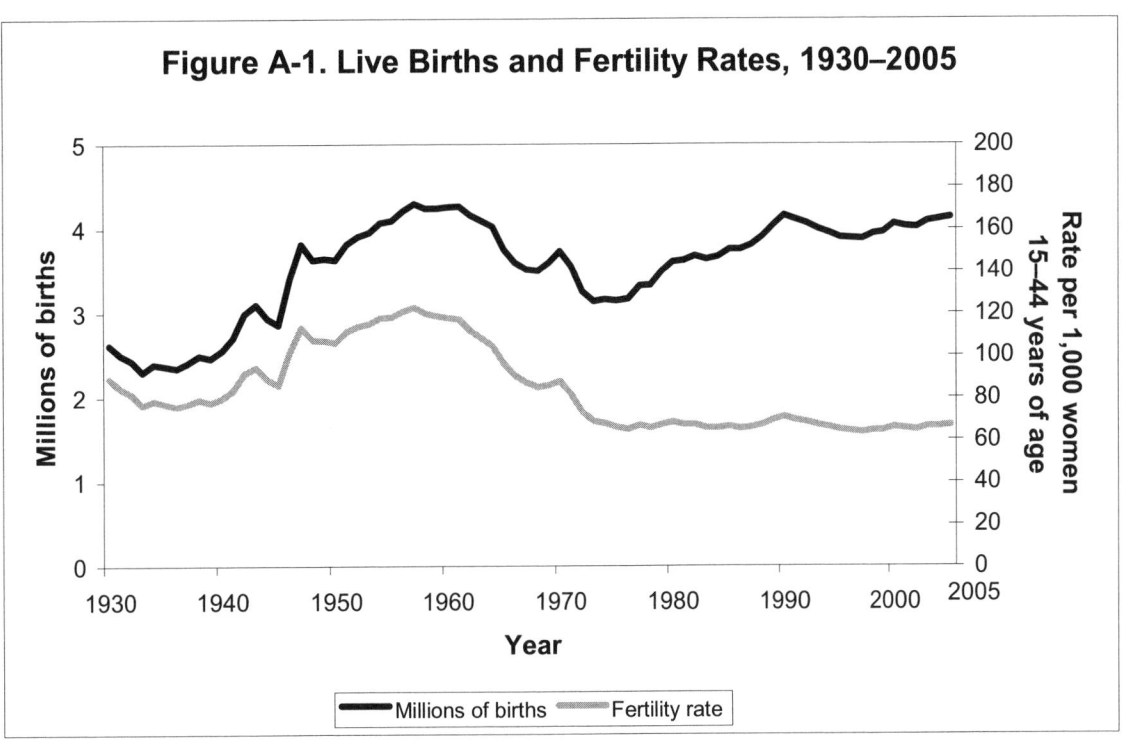

Figure A-1. Live Births and Fertility Rates, 1930–2005

HIGHLIGHTS

- In 2005, there were 4,138,349 registered births in the United States, about 0.6 percent more than in 2004, and the highest number since 1990. Whites accounted for 78 percent of total births while Blacks accounted for 15 percent of total births. Nearly 6 percent of births were to Asian and Pacific Islanders and only 1 percent to American Indian and Alaskan Natives. (Table A-1)

- The birth rate for women in their forties has more than doubled since 1981. For women age 40–44 years old, it has increased every year since 2000 and it rose from 8.9 to 9.1 births per 1,000 women between 2004 and 2005. (Table A-6)

- Childbearing by unmarried women reached a record high of 1,527,034 births in 2005, up 4 percent from 2004.

From 2002 to 2005, the number of births to unmarried women increased 12 percent. (Table A-25)

- The twin birth remained steady in 2005 at 32.2 per 1,000 live births after increasing every year from 1985 through 2004. The birth rate for triplets and higher order multiples declined again in 2005 to 161.8 per 100,000 live births. From 1980 until 1998, this birth rate increased rapidly, rising from 37.0 to 193.5 per 100,000 live births. (Table A-53)

- Since 1991, teenage birth rates have declined significantly. From 1991 to 2005, the birth rate for teenagers 15–19 years of age declined by 34 percent. Although teenage birth rates vary considerably by state, they tend be lowest in states in the North and Northeast and the highest in the South and Southwest. (Table A-57)

3

Table A-1.   Live Births, Birth Rates, and Fertility Rates, by Race, Selected Years, 1940–2005

(Number, live births per 1,000 population in specified groups.)

Year	Number					Birth rate					Fertility rate				
	All races[1]	White	Black	American Indian or Alaska Native	Asian or Pacific Islander	All races[1]	White	Black	American Indian or Alaska Native	Asian or Pacific Islander	All races[1]	White	Black	American Indian or Alaska Native	Asian or Pacific Islander
Registered Births, Race of Mother															
1980[2]	3,612,258	2,936,351	568,080	29,389	74,355	15.9	15.1	21.3	20.7	19.9	68.4	65.6	84.7	82.7	73.2
1981[2]	3,629,238	2,947,679	564,955	29,688	84,553	15.8	15.0	20.8	20.0	20.1	67.3	64.8	82.0	79.6	73.7
1982[2]	3,680,537	2,984,817	568,506	32,436	93,193	15.9	15.1	20.7	21.1	20.3	67.3	64.8	80.9	83.6	74.8
1983[2]	3,638,933	2,946,468	562,624	32,881	95,713	15.6	14.8	20.2	20.6	19.5	65.7	63.4	78.7	81.8	71.7
1984[2]	3,669,141	2,967,100	568,138	33,256	98,926	15.6	14.8	20.1	20.1	18.8	65.5	63.2	78.2	79.8	69.2
1985	3,760,561	3,037,913	581,824	34,037	104,606	15.8	15.0	20.4	19.8	18.7	66.3	64.1	78.8	78.6	68.4
1986	3,756,547	3,019,175	592,910	34,169	107,797	15.6	14.8	20.5	19.2	18.0	65.4	63.1	78.9	75.9	66.0
1987	3,809,394	3,043,828	611,173	35,322	116,560	15.7	14.9	20.8	19.1	18.4	65.8	63.3	80.1	75.6	67.1
1988	3,909,510	3,102,083	638,562	37,088	129,035	16.0	15.0	21.5	19.3	19.2	67.3	64.5	82.6	76.8	70.2
1989	4,040,958	3,192,355	673,124	39,478	133,075	16.4	15.4	22.3	19.7	18.7	69.2	66.4	86.2	79.0	68.2
1990	4,158,212	3,290,273	684,336	39,051	141,635	16.7	15.8	22.4	18.9	19.0	70.9	68.3	86.8	76.2	69.6
1991	4,110,907	3,241,273	682,602	38,841	145,372	16.2	15.3	21.8	18.3	18.3	69.3	66.7	84.8	73.9	67.1
1992	4,065,014	3,201,678	673,633	39,453	150,250	15.8	15.0	21.1	17.9	17.9	68.4	66.1	82.4	73.1	66.1
1993	4,000,240	3,149,833	658,875	38,732	152,800	15.4	14.6	20.2	17.0	17.3	67.0	64.9	79.6	69.7	64.3
1994	3,952,767	3,121,004	636,391	37,740	157,632	15.0	14.3	19.1	16.0	17.1	65.9	64.2	75.9	65.8	63.9
1995	3,899,589	3,098,885	603,139	37,278	160,287	14.6	14.1	17.8	15.3	16.7	64.6	63.6	71.0	63.0	62.6
1996	3,891,494	3,093,057	594,781	37,880	165,776	14.4	13.9	17.3	14.9	16.5	64.1	63.3	69.2	61.8	62.3
1997	3,880,894	3,072,640	599,913	38,572	169,769	14.2	13.7	17.1	14.7	16.2	63.6	62.8	69.0	60.8	61.3
1998	3,941,553	3,118,727	609,902	40,272	172,652	14.3	13.8	17.1	14.8	15.9	64.3	63.6	69.4	61.3	60.1
1999	3,959,417	3,132,501	605,970	40,170	180,776	14.2	13.7	16.8	14.2	15.9	64.4	64	68.5	59.0	60.9
2000	4,058,814	3,194,005	622,598	41,668	200,543	14.4	13.9	17.0	14.0	17.1	65.9	65.3	70.0	58.7	65.8
2001	4,025,933	3,177,626	606,156	41,872	200,279	14.1	13.7	16.3	13.7	16.4	65.3	65	67.6	58.1	64.2
2002	4,021,726	3,174,760	593,691	42,368	210,907	13.9	13.5	15.7	13.8	16.5	64.8	64.8	65.8	58.0	64.1
2003	4,089,950	3,225,848	599,847	43,052	221,203	14.1	13.6	15.7	13.8	16.8	66.1	66.1	66.3	58.4	66.3
2004	4,112,052	3,222,928	616,074	43,927	229,123	14.0	13.5	16.0	14.0	16.8	66.3	66.1	67.6	58.9	67.1
2005	4,138,349	3,229,294	633,134	44,813	231,108	14.0	13.4	16.2	14.2	16.5	66.7	66.3	69.0	59.9	66.6
Race of Child															
1960[3]	4,257,850	3,600,744	602,264	21,114	—	23.7	22.7	31.9	—	—	118.0	113.2	153.5	—	—
1961[3]	4,268,326	3,600,864	611,072	21,464	—	23.3	22.2	—	—	—	117.1	112.3	—	—	—
1962[3,4]	4,167,362	3,394,068	584,610	21,968	—	22.4	21.4	—	—	—	112.0	107.5	—	—	—
1963[3,4]	4,098,020	3,326,344	580,658	22,358	—	21.7	20.7	—	—	—	108.3	103.6	—	—	—
1964[3]	4,027,490	3,369,160	607,556	24,382	—	21.1	20.0	29.5	—	—	104.7	99.8	142.6	—	—
1965[3]	3,760,358	3,123,860	581,126	24,066	—	19.4	18.3	27.7	—	—	96.3	91.3	133.2	—	—
1966[3]	3,606,274	2,993,230	558,244	23,014	—	18.4	17.4	26.2	—	—	90.8	86.2	124.7	—	—
1967[5]	3,520,959	2,922,502	543,976	22,665	—	17.8	16.8	25.1	—	—	87.2	82.8	118.5	—	—
1968[3]	3,501,564	2,912,224	531,152	24,156	—	17.6	16.6	24.2	—	—	85.2	81.3	112.7	—	—
1969[3]	3,600,206	2,993,614	543,132	24,008	—	17.9	16.9	24.4	—	—	86.1	82.2	112.1	—	—
1970[3]	3,731,386	3,091,264	572,362	25,864	—	18.4	17.4	25.3	—	—	87.9	84.1	115.4	—	—
1971[3]	3,555,970	2,919,746	564,960	27,148	—	17.2	16.1	24.4	—	—	81.6	77.3	109.7	—	—
1972[3]	3,258,411	2,655,558	531,329	27,368	—	15.6	14.5	22.5	—	—	73.1	68.9	99.9	—	—
1973[2]	3,136,965	2,551,030	512,597	26,464	—	14.8	13.8	21.4	—	—	68.8	64.9	93.6	—	—
1974[2]	3,159,958	2,575,792	507,162	26,631	—	14.8	13.9	20.8	—	—	67.8	64.2	89.7	—	—
1975[2]	3,144,198	2,551,996	511,581	27,546	—	14.6	13.6	20.7	—	—	66.0	62.5	87.9	—	—
1976[2]	3,167,788	2,567,614	514,479	29,009	—	14.6	13.6	20.5	—	—	65.0	61.5	85.8	—	—
1977[2]	3,326,632	2,691,070	544,221	30,500	—	15.1	14.1	21.4	—	—	66.8	63.2	88.1	—	—
1978[2]	3,333,279	2,681,116	551,540	33,160	—	15.0	14.0	21.3	—	—	65.5	61.7	86.7	—	—
1979[2]	3,494,398	2,808,420	577,855	34,269	—	15.6	14.5	22.0	—	—	67.2	63.4	88.3	—	—
1980[2]	3,612,258	2,898,732	589,616	36,797	—	15.9	14.9	22.1	—	—	68.4	64.7	88.1	—	—
Births Adjusted for Underregistration, Race of Child															
1940	2,559,000	2,199,000	—	—	—	19.4	18.6	—	—	—	79.9	77.1	—	—	—
1945	2,858,000	2,471,000	—	—	—	20.4	19.7	—	—	—	85.9	83.4	—	—	—
1950	3,632,000	3,108,000	—	—	—	24.1	23.0	—	—	—	106.2	102.3	—	—	—
1955	4,097,000	3,485,000	—	—	—	25.0	23.8	—	—	—	118.3	113.7	—	—	—

—— = Data not available.

[1] For 1960–1991 includes births to races not shown separately. For 1992 and later years, unknown race of mother is imputed.

[2] Based on 100 percent of births in selected states and on a 50-percent sample of births in all other states.

[3] Based on a 50-percent sample of births.

[4] Figures by race exclude New Jersey.

[5] Based on a 20-to 50-percent sample of births.

Table A-2.   Live Births, Birth Rates, and Fertility Rates, by Race and Hispanic Origin of Mother, Final 2005 and Preliminary 2006

(Number, rate, percent.)

Race and Hispanic origin of mother	Number		Birth rate		Fertility rate		Total fertility rate		Percent of births to unmarried women	
	2005	2006	2005	2006	2005	2006	2005	2006	2005	2006
All races and origins[1]	4,138,349	4,265,996	14.0	14.2	66.7	68.5	2,053.5	2,101.0	36.9	38.5
Non-Hispanic White	2,279,768	2,309,833	11.5	11.6	58.3	59.5	1,839.5	1,864.0	25.3	26.6
Non-Hispanic Black	583,759	617,220	15.7	16.5	67.2	70.6	2,019.0	2,114.5	69.9	70.7
American Indian or Alaska Native total[2]	44,813	47,494	14.2	14.8	59.9	62.8	1,750.0	1,819.5	63.5	64.6
Asian or Pacific Islander total[2]	231,108	239,829	16.5	16.5	66.6	67.2	1,889.0	1,908.0	16.2	16.3
Hispanic[3]	985,505	1,039,051	23.1	23.4	99.4	101.5	2,885.0	2,958.5	48.0	49.9

[1]Includes Hispanic origin not stated.
[2]Data for persons of Hispanic origin are included in the data for each race group according to the person's reported race.
[3]Persons of Hispanic origin may be of any race.

Table A-3. Live Births by Age of Mother, Live-Birth Order, and Race of Mother, 2005

(Number of children born alive to mother.)

Live birth order and race of mother	All ages	Under 15 years	Total	15–19 years					20–54 years						
				15 years	16 years	17 years	18 years	19 years	20–24 years	25–29 years	30–34 years	35–39 years	40–44 years	45–49 years	50–54 years
All Races	4,138,349	6,722	414,593	18,249	41,064	73,878	116,476	164,926	1,040,388	1,131,596	950,691	483,156	104,667	6,119	417
1st child	1,637,953	6,592	331,486	17,499	37,947	64,202	92,998	118,840	492,754	402,493	269,639	110,628	22,787	1,453	121
2nd child	1,326,598	101	69,170	642	2,760	8,577	19,997	37,194	350,216	379,935	336,746	159,318	29,433	1,575	104
3rd child	699,661	5	10,773	34	161	759	2,683	7,136	141,174	214,667	198,404	111,535	21,969	1,065	69
4th child	278,310	1	1,272	4	11	61	264	932	39,728	85,315	84,807	53,492	12,974	668	53
5th child	101,738	–	161	1	3	10	30	117	9,627	29,570	32,405	22,715	6,798	437	25
6th child	40,585	–	22	–	1	–	7	14	2,137	9,955	13,491	10,819	3,901	247	13
7th child	17,840	–	8	–	–	1	1	6	429	3,387	6,227	5,467	2,148	165	9
8th child and over	18,171	–	4	–	–	1	–	3	186	1,740	4,935	6,801	4,030	455	20
Not stated	17,493	23	1,697	69	181	267	496	684	4,137	4,534	4,037	2,381	627	54	3
White	3,229,294	3,645	295,265	11,575	27,865	52,063	83,490	120,272	790,445	899,406	763,387	389,289	82,638	4,876	343
1st child	1,274,542	3,590	238,736	11,123	25,947	45,707	67,621	88,338	383,238	325,639	214,805	89,034	18,253	1,153	94
2nd child	1,052,133	44	48,050	399	1,733	5,743	13,750	26,425	269,614	308,616	273,114	128,002	23,331	1,275	87
3rd child	552,735	2	6,821	20	94	446	1,681	4,580	102,423	170,268	163,452	91,550	17,313	843	63
4th child	212,533	1	701	2	7	37	140	515	25,787	63,461	68,027	43,748	10,225	537	46
5th child	73,420	–	90	1	2	8	18	61	5,482	19,762	24,390	18,058	5,281	336	21
6th child	28,029	–	8	–	–	–	2	6	1,059	5,891	9,574	8,268	3,019	199	11
7th child	11,885	–	4	–	–	1	–	3	192	1,771	4,155	4,003	1,628	124	8
8th child and over	12,227	–	2	–	–	–	–	2	122	845	2,906	4,836	3,137	368	11
Not stated	11,790	8	853	30	82	121	278	342	2,528	3,153	2,964	1,790	451	41	2
Black	633,134	2,837	103,905	5,991	11,600	19,113	28,686	38,515	203,716	156,161	100,935	51,636	13,201	704	39
1st child	241,997	2,770	80,452	5,721	10,526	16,182	21,983	26,040	85,421	39,518	21,631	9,699	2,343	150	13
2nd child	181,695	52	18,544	222	922	2,490	5,491	9,419	66,790	48,538	30,047	14,450	3,123	144	7
3rd child	110,280	2	3,555	14	58	286	881	2,316	33,189	35,121	23,290	12,158	2,825	137	3
4th child	52,095	–	516	1	4	21	112	378	12,057	18,072	12,563	6,839	1,953	90	5
5th child	22,950	–	66	–	1	1	11	53	3,684	8,256	6,279	3,478	1,119	66	2
6th child	10,168	–	13	–	–	–	5	8	975	3,465	3,093	1,944	655	21	2
7th child	4,795	–	4	–	–	–	1	3	202	1,375	1,665	1,123	396	30	–
8th child and over	4,753	–	2	–	–	1	–	1	56	773	1,666	1,522	672	56	6
Not stated	4,401	13	753	33	89	132	202	297	1,342	1,043	701	423	115	10	1
American Indian or Alaska Native	44,813	136	7,807	401	894	1,460	2,142	2,910	15,333	11,189	6,619	2,969			
1st child	15,654	133	6,116	383	824	1,245	1,653	2,011	5,844	2,191	949	349	722	37	1
2nd child	12,041	2	1,417	13	64	188	408	744	5,267	3,084	1,574	592	67	4	1
3rd child	8,126	1	211	–	2	19	67	123	2,795	2,876	1,502	599	102	3	–
4th child	4,444	–	22	–	–	2	5	15	1,011	1,641	1,129	536	135	7	–
5th child	2,213	–	3	–	–	1	1	1	263	830	704	313	101	4	–
6th child	1,073	–	–	–	–	–	–	–	51	308	377	232	96	4	–
7th child	535	–	–	–	–	–	–	–	13	129	200	149	99	6	–
8th child and over	487	–	–	–	–	–	–	–	5	59	155	186	42	2	–
Not stated	240	–	38	5	4	5	8	16	84	71	29	13	76	6	–
Asian or Pacific Islander	231,108	104	7,616	282	705	1,242	2,158	3,229	30,894	64,840	79,750	39,262	8,106	502	34
1st child	105,760	99	6,182	272	650	1,068	1,741	2,451	18,251	35,145	32,254	11,546	2,124	146	13
2nd child	80,729	3	1,159	8	41	156	348	606	8,545	19,697	32,011	16,274	2,877	153	10
3rd child	28,520	–	186	–	7	8	54	117	2,767	6,402	10,160	7,228	1,696	78	3
4th child	9,238	–	33	1	–	1	7	24	873	2,141	3,088	2,369	695	37	2
5th child	3,155	–	2	–	–	–	–	2	198	722	1,032	866	302	31	2
6th child	1,315	–	1	–	1	–	–	–	52	291	447	375	128	21	–
7th child	625	–	–	–	–	–	–	–	22	112	207	192	82	9	1
8th child and over	704	–	–	–	–	–	–	–	3	63	208	257	145	25	3
Not stated	1,062	2	53	1	6	9	8	29	183	267	343	155	57	2	–

- = Quantity zero

Table A-4. Live Births and Birth Rates, by Age, Race, and Hispanic Origin of Mother, Final 2005 and Preliminary 2006

(Number, rate per 1,000 women in specified group.)

Age, race, and Hispanic origin of mother	2005		2006	
	Number	Rate	Number	Rate
All Races and Origins[1]				
Total[2]	4,138,349	66.7	4,265,996	68.5
10–14 years	6,722	0.7	6,405	0.6
15–19 years	414,593	40.5	435,427	41.9
15–17 years	133,191	21.4	138,920	22
18–19 years	281,402	69.9	296,507	73
20–24 years	1,040,388	102.2	1,080,507	105.9
25–29 years	1,131,596	115.5	1,182,187	116.8
30–34 years	950,691	95.8	950,472	97.7
35–39 years	483,156	46.3	498,566	47.3
40–44 years	104,667	9.1	105,476	9.4
45–54 years[3]	6,536	0.6	6,956	0.6
Non-Hispanic White				
Total[2]	2,279,768	58.3	2,309,833	59.5
10–14 years	1,331	0.2	1,270	0.2
15–19 years	165,005	25.9	169,837	26.6
15–17 years	43,864	11.5	45,307	11.8
18–19 years	121,141	48	124,530	49.3
20–24 years	515,518	81.4	528,596	83.4
25–29 years	642,553	109.1	665,889	109.2
30–34 years	581,645	96.9	567,103	98.1
35–39 years	305,142	45.6	309,130	46.3
40–44 years	64,352	8.3	63,546	8.4
45–54 years[3]	4,222	0.5	4,461	0.6
Non-Hispanic Black				
Total[2]	583,759	67.2	617,220	70.6
10–14 years	2,697	1.7	2,470	1.6
15–19 years	96,813	60.9	103,692	63.7
15–17 years	34,178	34.9	36,331	36.1
18–19 years	62,635	103	67,361	108.4
20–24 years	188,673	126.8	198,718	133.1
25–29 years	142,885	103	153,639	107.1
30–34 years	92,336	68.4	95,804	72.6
35–39 years	47,411	34.3	49,893	36
40–44 years	12,256	8.2	12,270	8.3
45–54 years[3]	688	0.5	733	0.5
American Indian or Alaska Native Total				
Total[2]	44,813	59.9	47,494	62.8
10–14 years	136	0.9	122	0.9
15–19 years	7,807	52.7	8,222	54.7
15–17 years	2,755	30.5	2,795	30.5
18–19 years	5,052	87.6	5,427	92.8
20–24 years	15,333	109.2	16,388	114.9
25–29 years	11,189	93.8	12,127	97.2
30–34 years	6,619	60.1	6,752	61.5
35–39 years	2,969	27	3,120	28.2
40–44 years	722	6	722	6.1
45–54 years[3]	38	0.3	41	0.4
Asian or Pacific Islander Total				
Total[2]	231,108	66.6	239,829	67.2
10–14 years	104	0.2	71	0.2
15–19 years	7,616	17.0	7,672	16.7
15–17 years	2,229	8.2	2,396	8.7
18–19 years	5,387	30.1	5,276	28.9
20–24 years	30,894	61.1	31,535	62.5
25–29 years	64,840	107.9	66,562	107.8
30–34 years	79,750	115.0	82,614	116.5
35–39 years	39,262	61.8	42,290	62.8
40–44 years	8,106	13.8	8,525	14.1
45–54 years[3]	536	1.0	560	1.0
Hispanic[4]				
Total[2]	985,505	99.4	1,039,051	101.5
10–14 years	2,466	1.3	2,455	1.3
15–19 years	136,906	81.7	145,651	83
15–17 years	50,046	48.5	51,982	47.9
18–19 years	86,860	134.6	93,669	139.7
20–24 years	287,896	170	303,443	177
25–29 years	266,590	149.2	280,630	152.4
30–34 years	186,398	106.8	194,590	108.4
35–39 years	85,739	54.2	91,562	55.6
40–44 years	18,597	13	19,697	13.3
45–54 years[3]	913	0.8	1,022	0.8

[1]Includes Hispanic origin not stated.
[2]The total number includes births to women of all ages, 10–54 years. The rate shown for all ages is the fertility rate, which is defined as the total number of births (regardless of the age of the mother) per 1,000 women aged 15–44 years.
[3]The number of births shown is the total for women aged 45–54 years. The birth rate is computed by relating the births to women aged 45–54 years to women aged 45–49 years, because most of the births in this group are to women aged 45–49.
[4]Persons of Hispanic origin may be of any race.

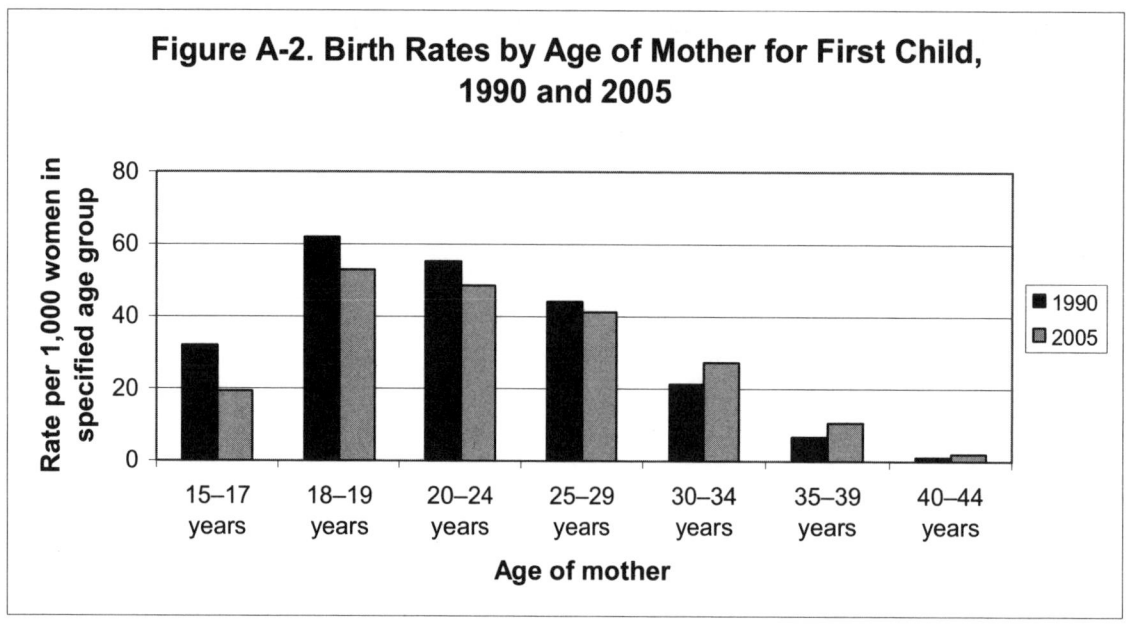

Figure A-2. Birth Rates by Age of Mother for First Child, 1990 and 2005

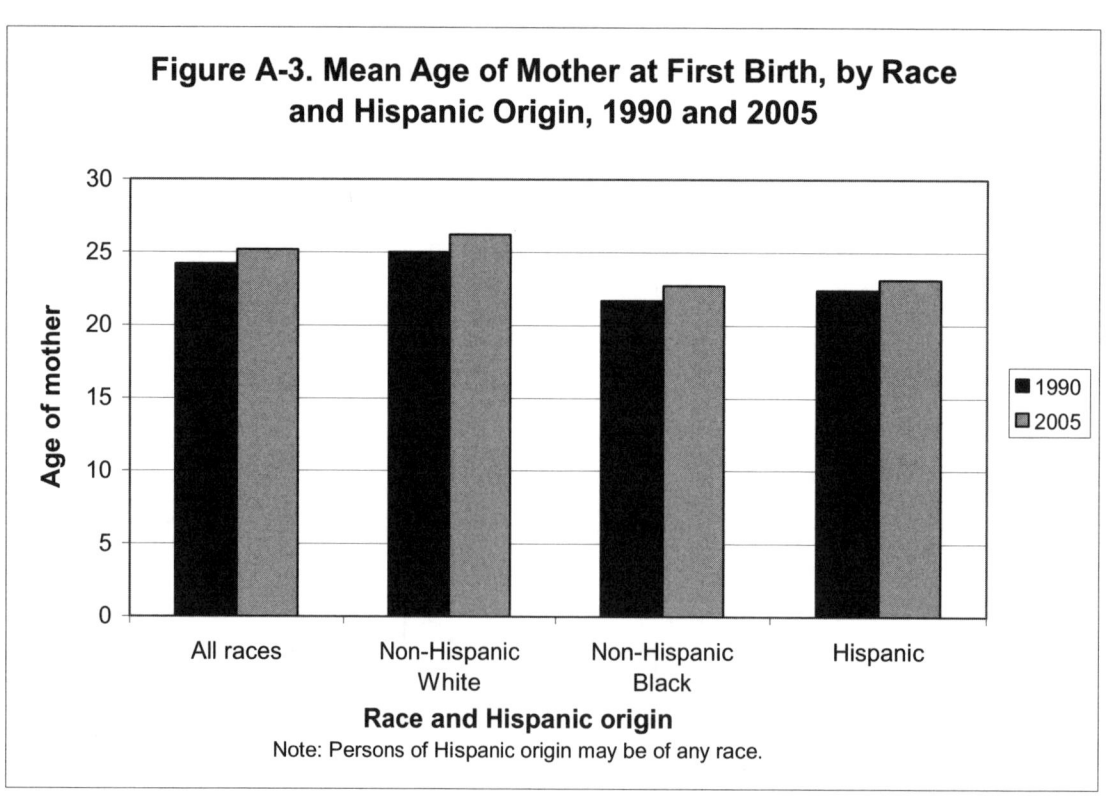

Figure A-3. Mean Age of Mother at First Birth, by Race and Hispanic Origin, 1990 and 2005

Table A-5. Fertility Rates and Birth Rates, by Age of Mother, Live-Birth Order, and Race of Mother, 2005

(Live births per 1,000 women in specified age and racial group.)

Live-birth order and race of mother	Fertility rate[1]	10–14 years	15–19 years			20–24 years	25–29 years	30–34 years	35–39 years	40–44 years	45–49 years[2]
			Total	15–17 years	18–19 years						
All Races	66.7	0.7	40.5	21.4	69.9	102.2	115.5	95.8	46.3	9.1	0.6
1st child	26.5	0.7	32.5	19.3	52.9	48.6	41.2	27.3	10.7	2.0	0.1
2nd child	21.5	0.0	6.8	1.9	14.3	34.5	38.9	34.1	15.3	2.6	0.1
3rd child	11.3	*	1.1	0.2	2.5	13.9	22.0	20.1	10.7	1.9	0.1
4th child	4.5	*	0.1	0.0	0.3	3.9	8.7	8.6	5.1	1.1	0.1
5th child	1.6	*	0.0	*	0.0	0.9	3.0	3.3	2.2	0.6	0.0
6th and 7th child	0.9	*	0.0	*	0.0	0.3	1.4	2.0	1.6	0.5	0.0
8th child and over	0.3	*	*	*	*	0.0	0.2	0.5	0.7	0.4	0.0
White	66.3	0.5	37.0	18.9	64.7	99.2	118.3	99.3	47.3	9.0	0.6
1st child	26.3	0.5	30.0	17.2	49.7	48.3	43.0	28.1	10.9	2.0	0.1
2nd child	21.7	0.0	6.0	1.6	12.8	34.0	40.7	35.7	15.6	2.5	0.1
3rd child	11.4	*	0.9	0.1	2.0	12.9	22.5	21.4	11.2	1.9	0.1
4th child	4.4	*	0.1	0.0	0.2	3.2	8.4	8.9	5.3	1.1	0.1
5th child	1.5	*	0.0	*	0.0	0.7	2.6	3.2	2.2	0.6	0.0
6th and 7th child	0.8	*	*	*	*	0.2	1.0	1.8	1.5	0.5	0.0
8th child and over	0.3	*	*	*	*	0.0	0.1	0.4	0.6	0.3	0.0
Black	69.0	1.7	62.0	35.5	104.9	129.9	105.9	70.3	35.3	8.5	0.5
1st child	26.6	1.6	48.4	31.6	75.6	54.8	27.0	15.2	6.7	1.5	0.1
2nd child	19.9	0.0	11.2	3.5	23.5	42.9	33.1	21.1	10.0	2.0	0.1
3rd child	12.1	*	2.1	0.3	5.0	21.3	24.0	16.3	8.4	1.8	0.1
4th child	5.7	*	0.3	0.0	0.8	7.7	12.3	8.8	4.7	1.3	0.1
5th child	2.5	*	0.0	*	0.1	2.4	5.6	4.4	2.4	0.7	0.0
6th and 7th child	1.6	*	*	*	*	0.8	3.3	3.3	2.1	0.7	0.0
8th child and over	0.5	*	*	*	*	0.0	0.5	1.2	1.0	0.4	0.0
American Indian or Alaska Native	59.9	0.9	52.7	30.5	87.6	109.2	93.8	60.1	27.0	6.0	0.3
1st child	21.0	0.9	41.5	27.3	63.8	41.8	18.5	8.7	3.2	0.6	*
2nd child	16.2	*	9.6	2.9	20.1	37.7	26.0	14.4	5.4	0.9	*
3rd child	10.9	*	1.4	0.2	3.3	20.0	24.3	13.7	5.5	1.1	*
4th child	6.0	*	0.1	*	0.3	7.2	13.8	10.3	4.9	0.9	*
5th child	3.0	*	*	*	*	1.9	7.0	6.4	2.9	0.8	*
6th and 7th child	2.2	*	*	*	*	0.5	3.7	5.3	3.5	1.2	*
8th child and over	0.7	*	*	*	*	*	0.5	1.4	1.7	0.6	*
Asian or Pacific Islander	66.6	0.2	17.0	8.2	30.1	61.1	107.9	115.0	61.8	13.8	1.0
1st child	30.6	0.2	13.9	7.4	23.6	36.3	58.7	46.7	18.2	3.6	0.3
2nd child	23.4	*	2.6	0.8	5.4	17.0	32.9	46.3	25.7	4.9	0.3
3rd child	8.3	*	0.4	*	1.0	5.5	10.7	14.7	11.4	2.9	0.1
4th child	2.7	*	0.1	*	0.2	1.7	3.6	4.5	3.7	1.2	0.1
5th child	0.9	*	*	*	*	0.4	1.2	1.5	1.4	0.5	0.1
6th and 7th child	0.6	*	*	*	*	0.1	0.7	0.9	0.9	0.4	0.1
8th child and over	0.2	*	*	*	*	*	0.1	0.3	0.4	0.2	0.1

* = Figure does not meet standards of reliability or precision.

0.0 = Quantity more than zero but less than 0.05.

[1]The rate shown is the fertility rate, which is defined as the total number of births, regardless of age of mother, per 1,000 women aged 15–44 years.

[2]Birth rates are computed by relating births to women aged 45–54 years to women aged 45–49 years.

Table A-6. Total Fertility Rates and Birth Rates, by Age and Race of Mother, Selected Years, 1970–2005

(Live births per 1,000 women in specified group.)

Year and race	Total fertility rate	Age of mother									
		10–14 years	15–19 years			20–24 years	25–29 years	30–34 years	35–39 years	40–44 years	45–49 years[1]
			Total	15–17 years	18–19 years						
All Races[2]											
1970[3]	2480.0	1.2	68.3	38.8	114.7	167.8	145.1	73.3	31.7	8.1	0.5
1971[3]	2266.5	1.1	64.5	38.2	105.3	150.1	134.1	67.3	28.7	7.1	0.4
1972[4]	2010.0	1.2	61.7	39.0	96.9	130.2	117.7	59.8	24.8	6.2	0.4
1973[4]	1879.0	1.2	59.3	38.5	91.2	119.7	112.2	55.6	22.1	5.4	0.3
1974[4]	1835.0	1.2	57.5	37.3	88.7	117.7	111.5	53.8	20.2	4.8	0.3
1975[4]	1774.0	1.3	55.6	36.1	85.0	113.0	108.2	52.3	19.5	4.6	0.3
1976[4]	1738.0	1.2	52.8	34.1	80.5	110.3	106.2	53.6	19.0	4.3	0.2
1977[4]	1789.5	1.2	52.8	33.9	80.9	112.9	111.0	56.4	19.2	4.2	0.2
1978[4]	1760.0	1.2	51.5	32.2	79.8	109.9	108.5	57.8	19.0	3.9	0.2
1979[4]	1808.0	1.2	52.3	32.3	81.3	112.8	111.4	60.3	19.5	3.9	0.2
1980[4]	1839.5	1.1	53.0	32.5	82.1	115.1	112.9	61.9	19.8	3.9	0.2
1981[4]	1812.0	1.1	52.2	32.0	80.0	112.2	111.5	61.4	20.0	3.8	0.2
1982[4]	1827.5	1.1	52.4	32.3	79.4	111.6	111.0	64.1	21.2	3.9	0.2
1983[4]	1799.0	1.1	51.4	31.8	77.4	107.8	108.5	64.9	22.0	3.9	0.2
1984[4]	1806.5	1.2	50.6	31.0	77.4	106.8	108.7	67.0	22.9	3.9	0.2
1985	1844.0	1.2	51.0	31.0	79.6	108.3	111.0	69.1	24.0	4.0	0.2
1986	1837.5	1.3	50.2	30.5	79.6	107.4	109.8	70.1	24.4	4.1	0.2
1987	1872.0	1.3	50.6	31.7	78.5	107.9	111.6	72.1	26.3	4.4	0.2
1988	1934.0	1.3	53.0	33.6	79.9	110.2	114.4	74.8	28.1	4.8	0.2
1989	2014.0	1.4	57.3	36.4	84.2	113.8	117.6	77.4	29.9	5.2	0.2
1990	2081.0	1.4	59.9	37.5	88.6	116.5	120.2	80.8	31.7	5.5	0.2
1991	2062.5	1.4	61.8	38.6	94.0	115.3	117.2	79.2	31.9	5.5	0.2
1992	2046.0	1.4	60.3	37.6	93.6	113.7	115.7	79.6	32.3	5.9	0.3
1993	2019.5	1.4	59.0	37.5	91.1	111.3	113.2	79.9	32.7	6.1	0.3
1994	2001.5	1.4	58.2	37.2	90.2	109.2	111.0	80.4	33.4	6.4	0.3
1995	1978.0	1.3	56.0	35.5	87.7	107.5	108.8	81.1	34.0	6.6	0.3
1996	1976.0	1.2	53.5	33.3	84.7	107.8	108.6	82.1	34.9	6.8	0.3
1997	1971.0	1.1	51.3	31.4	82.1	107.3	108.3	83.0	35.7	7.1	0.4
1998	1999.0	1.0	50.3	29.9	80.9	108.4	110.2	85.2	36.9	7.4	0.4
1999	2007.5	0.9	48.8	28.2	79.1	107.9	111.2	87.1	37.8	7.4	0.4
2000	2056.0	0.9	47.7	26.9	78.1	109.7	113.5	91.2	39.7	8.0	0.5
2001	2034.0	0.8	45.3	24.7	76.1	106.2	113.4	91.9	40.6	8.1	0.5
2002	2013.0	0.7	43.0	23.2	72.8	103.6	113.6	91.5	41.4	8.3	0.5
2003	2042.5	0.6	41.6	22.4	70.7	102.6	115.6	95.1	43.8	8.7	0.5
2004	2045.5	0.7	41.1	22.1	70.0	101.7	115.5	95.3	45.4	8.9	0.5
2005	2053.5	0.7	40.5	21.4	69.9	102.2	115.5	95.8	46.3	9.1	0.6
White											
1980[4]	1773.0	0.6	45.4	25.5	73.2	111.1	113.8	61.2	18.8	3.5	0.2
1981[4]	1748.0	0.5	44.9	25.4	71.5	108.3	112.3	61.0	19.0	3.4	0.2
1982[4]	1767.0	0.6	45.0	25.5	70.8	107.7	111.9	64.0	20.4	3.6	0.2
1983[4]	1740.5	0.6	43.9	25.0	68.8	103.8	109.4	65.3	21.3	3.6	0.2
1984[4]	1748.5	0.6	42.9	24.3	68.4	102.7	109.8	67.7	22.2	3.6	0.2
1985	1787.0	0.6	43.3	24.4	70.4	104.1	112.3	69.9	23.3	3.7	0.2
1986	1776.0	0.6	42.3	23.8	70.1	102.7	110.8	70.9	23.9	3.8	0.2
1987	1804.5	0.6	42.5	24.6	68.9	102.3	112.3	73.0	25.9	4.1	0.2
1988	1856.5	0.6	44.4	26.0	69.6	103.7	114.8	75.4	27.7	4.5	0.2
1989	1931.0	0.7	47.9	28.1	72.9	106.9	117.8	78.1	29.7	4.9	0.2
1990	2003.0	0.7	50.8	29.5	78.0	109.8	120.7	81.7	31.5	5.2	0.2
1991	1988.0	0.8	52.6	30.5	83.3	108.8	118.0	80.2	31.8	5.2	0.2
1992	1978.0	0.8	51.4	29.9	83.2	107.7	116.9	80.8	32.1	5.7	0.2
1993	1961.5	0.8	50.6	30.0	81.5	106.1	114.7	81.3	32.6	5.9	0.3
1994	1957.5	0.8	50.5	30.4	81.2	105.0	113.0	82.2	33.5	6.2	0.3
1995	1954.5	0.8	49.5	29.6	80.2	104.7	111.7	83.3	34.2	6.4	0.3
1996	1960.5	0.7	47.5	28.0	77.6	105.3	111.7	84.6	35.3	6.7	0.3
1997	1955.0	0.7	45.5	26.6	75.0	104.5	111.3	85.7	36.1	6.9	0.3
1998	1991.0	0.6	44.9	25.6	74.1	105.4	113.6	88.5	37.5	7.3	0.4
1999	2007.5	0.6	44.0	24.4	73.0	105.0	114.9	90.7	38.5	7.4	0.4

[1]Beginning 1997, rates computed by relating births to women aged 45–54 years to women aged 45–49 years.
[2]1970–1991 includes births to races not shown separately. For 1992 and later years, unknown race of mother is imputed.
[3]Based on a 50-percent sample of births.
[4]Based on 100 percent of births in selected states and on a 50-percent sample of births in all other states.

Table A-6.   Total Fertility Rates and Birth Rates, by Age and Race of Mother, Selected Years, 1970–2005—*Continued*

(Live births per 1,000 women in specified group.)

Year and race	Total fertility rate	Age of mother									
		10–14 years	15–19 years			20–24 years	25–29 years	30–34 years	35–39 years	40–44 years	45–49 years[1]
			Total	15–17 years	18–19 years						
White—Continued											
2000	2051.0	0.6	43.2	23.3	72.3	106.6	116.7	94.6	40.2	7.9	0.4
2001	2040.0	0.5	41.2	21.4	70.8	103.7	117.0	95.8	41.3	8.0	0.5
2002	2027.5	0.5	39.4	20.5	68.0	101.6	117.4	95.5	42.4	8.2	0.5
2003	2061.0	0.5	38.3	19.8	66.2	100.6	119.5	99.3	44.8	8.7	0.5
2004	2054.5	0.5	37.7	19.5	65.0	99.2	118.6	99.1	46.4	8.9	0.5
2005	2056.0	0.5	37.0	18.9	64.7	99.2	118.3	99.3	47.3	9.0	0.6
Black											
1980[4]	2176.5	4.3	97.8	72.5	135.1	140.0	103.9	59.9	23.5	5.6	0.3
1981[4]	2117.5	4.0	94.5	69.3	131.0	136.5	102.3	57.4	23.1	5.4	0.3
1982[4]	2106.5	4.0	94.3	69.7	128.9	135.4	101.3	57.5	23.3	5.1	0.4
1983[4]	2066.0	4.1	93.9	69.6	127.1	131.9	98.4	56.2	23.3	5.1	0.3
1984[4]	2070.5	4.4	94.1	69.2	128.1	132.2	98.4	56.7	23.3	4.8	0.2
1985	2109.0	4.5	95.4	69.3	132.4	135.0	100.2	57.9	23.9	4.6	0.3
1986	2135.5	4.7	95.8	69.3	135.1	137.3	101.1	59.3	23.8	4.8	0.3
1987	2198.0	4.8	97.6	72.1	135.8	142.7	104.3	60.6	24.6	4.8	0.2
1988	2298.0	4.9	102.7	75.7	142.7	149.7	108.2	63.1	25.6	5.1	0.3
1989	2432.5	5.1	111.5	81.9	151.9	156.8	114.4	66.3	26.7	5.4	0.3
1990	2480.0	4.9	112.8	82.3	152.9	160.2	115.5	68.7	28.1	5.5	0.3
1991	2462.0	4.7	114.8	83.5	157.6	159.7	112.0	67.3	28.2	5.5	0.2
1992	2416.0	4.6	111.3	80.5	156.3	156.2	109.7	67.0	28.6	5.6	0.2
1993	2351.0	4.5	107.3	78.9	150.2	150.2	106.4	66.6	29.0	5.9	0.3
1994	2258.5	4.5	102.9	75.1	146.2	142.9	101.5	65.0	28.7	5.9	0.3
1995	2127.5	4.1	94.4	68.5	135.0	133.7	95.6	63.0	28.4	6.0	0.3
1996	2088.5	3.5	89.6	63.3	130.5	133.2	94.3	62.0	28.7	6.1	0.3
1997	2091.5	3.1	86.3	59.3	127.7	135.2	95.0	62.6	29.3	6.5	0.3
1998	2111.5	2.8	83.5	55.4	124.8	138.4	97.5	63.2	30.0	6.6	0.3
1999	2082.5	2.5	79.1	50.5	120.6	137.9	97.3	62.7	30.2	6.5	0.3
2000	2129.0	2.3	77.4	49.0	118.8	141.3	100.3	65.4	31.5	7.2	0.4
2001	2051.0	2.0	71.8	43.9	114.0	133.2	99.2	64.8	31.6	7.2	0.4
2002	1991.0	1.8	66.6	40.0	107.6	127.1	99.0	64.4	31.5	7.4	0.4
2003	1999.0	1.6	63.8	38.2	103.7	126.1	100.4	66.5	33.2	7.7	0.5
2004	2032.5	1.6	63.3	37.2	104.4	127.7	103.6	67.9	34.0	7.9	0.5
2005	2070.5	1.7	62.0	35.5	104.9	129.9	105.9	70.3	35.3	8.5	0.5
American Indian or Alaska Native											
1980[4]	2165.0	1.9	82.2	51.5	129.5	143.7	106.6	61.8	28.1	8.2	*
1981[4]	2092.5	2.1	78.4	49.7	121.5	141.2	105.6	58.9	25.2	6.6	*
1982[4]	2215.0	1.4	83.5	52.6	127.6	148.1	115.8	60.9	26.9	6.0	*
1983[4]	2182.0	1.9	84.2	55.2	121.4	145.5	113.7	58.9	25.5	6.4	*
1984[4]	2137.5	1.7	81.5	50.7	124.7	142.4	109.2	60.5	26.3	5.6	*
1985	2129.5	1.7	79.2	47.7	124.1	139.1	109.6	62.6	27.4	6.0	*
1986	2083.0	1.8	78.1	48.7	125.3	138.8	107.9	60.7	23.8	5.3	*
1987	2100.5	1.7	77.2	48.8	122.2	140.0	107.9	63.0	24.4	5.6	*
1988	2155.0	1.7	77.5	49.7	121.1	145.2	110.9	64.5	25.6	5.3	*
1989	2248.5	1.5	82.7	51.6	128.9	152.4	114.2	64.8	27.4	6.4	*
1990	2184.5	1.6	81.1	48.5	129.3	148.7	110.3	61.5	27.5	5.9	*
1991	2142.5	1.6	84.1	51.9	134.2	143.8	105.6	60.8	26.4	5.8	0.4
1992	2135.5	1.6	82.4	52.3	130.5	142.3	107.0	61.0	26.7	5.9	*
1993	2048.5	1.4	79.8	51.5	126.3	134.2	103.5	59.5	25.5	5.6	*
1994	1950.0	1.8	76.4	48.4	123.7	126.5	98.2	56.6	24.8	5.4	0.3
1995	1878.5	1.6	72.9	44.6	122.2	123.1	91.6	56.5	24.3	5.5	*
1996	1855.0	1.6	68.2	42.7	113.3	123.5	91.1	56.5	24.4	5.5	*
1997	1834.5	1.5	65.2	41.0	107.1	122.5	91.6	56.0	24.4	5.4	0.3
1998	1851.0	1.5	64.7	39.7	106.9	125.1	92.0	56.8	24.6	5.3	*
1999	1783.5	1.4	59.9	36.5	98.0	120.7	90.6	53.8	24.3	5.7	0.3
2000	1772.5	1.1	58.3	34.1	97.1	117.2	91.8	55.5	24.6	5.7	0.3
2001	1746.5	1.0	56.3	31.4	94.8	115.0	90.4	55.9	24.7	5.7	0.3
2002	1735.0	0.9	53.8	30.7	89.2	112.6	91.8	56.4	25.4	5.8	0.3
2003	1731.5	1.0	53.1	30.6	87.3	110.0	93.5	57.4	25.4	5.5	0.4
2004	1734.5	0.9	52.5	30.0	87.0	109.7	92.8	58.0	26.8	6.0	0.2
2005	1750.0	0.9	52.7	30.5	87.6	109.2	93.8	60.1	27.0	6.0	0.3

* = Figure does not meet standards of reliability or precision.
[1]Beginning 1997, rates computed by relating births to women aged 45–54 years to women aged 45–49 years.
[4]Based on 100 percent of births in selected states and on a 50-percent sample of births in all other states.

Table A-6. Total Fertility Rates and Birth Rates, by Age and Race of Mother, Selected Years, 1970–2005—*Continued*

(Live births per 1,000 women in specified group.)

Year and race	Total fertility rate	10–14 years	15–19 years			20–24 years	25–29 years	30–34 years	35–39 years	40–44 years	45–49 years[1]
			Total	15–17 years	18–19 years						
Asian or Pacific Islander											
1980[4]	1953.5	0.3	26.2	12.0	46.2	93.3	127.4	96.0	38.3	8.5	0.7
1981[4]	1976.0	0.3	28.5	13.4	49.5	96.4	129.1	93.4	38.0	8.6	0.9
1982[4]	2015.5	0.4	29.4	14.0	50.8	98.9	130.9	94.4	39.2	8.8	1.1
1983[4]	1943.5	0.5	26.1	12.9	44.5	94.0	126.2	93.3	39.4	8.2	1.0
1984[4]	1892.0	0.5	24.2	12.6	40.7	86.7	124.3	92.4	40.6	8.7	1.0
1985	1885.0	0.4	23.8	12.5	40.8	83.6	123.0	93.6	42.7	8.7	1.2
1986	1836.0	0.5	22.8	12.1	38.8	79.2	119.9	92.6	41.9	9.3	1.0
1987	1886.0	0.6	22.4	12.6	37.0	79.7	122.7	97.0	44.2	9.5	1.1
1988	1983.5	0.6	24.2	13.6	39.6	80.7	128.0	104.4	47.5	10.3	1.0
1989	1947.5	0.6	25.6	15.0	40.4	78.8	124.0	102.3	47.0	10.2	1.0
1990	2002.5	0.7	26.4	16.0	40.2	79.2	126.3	106.5	49.6	10.7	1.1
1991	1928.0	0.8	27.3	16.3	42.2	73.8	118.9	103.3	49.2	11.2	1.1
1992	1894.5	0.7	26.5	15.4	41.9	71.7	114.6	102.7	50.7	11.1	0.9
1993	1841.5	0.7	26.5	16.1	41.2	68.1	110.3	101.2	49.4	11.2	0.9
1994	1834.0	0.7	26.6	16.3	41.3	66.4	108.0	102.2	50.4	11.5	1.0
1995	1795.5	0.7	25.5	15.6	40.1	64.2	103.7	102.3	50.1	11.8	0.8
1996	1787.0	0.6	23.5	14.7	36.8	63.5	102.8	104.1	50.2	11.9	0.8
1997	1757.5	0.5	22.3	14.0	34.9	61.2	101.6	102.5	51.0	11.5	0.9
1998	1731.5	0.5	22.2	13.8	34.5	59.2	98.7	101.6	51.4	11.8	0.9
1999	1754.5	0.4	21.4	12.4	33.9	58.9	100.8	104.3	52.9	11.3	0.9
2000	1892.0	0.3	20.5	11.6	32.6	60.3	108.4	116.5	59.0	12.6	0.8
2001	1840.0	0.2	19.8	10.3	32.8	59.1	106.4	112.6	56.7	12.3	0.9
2002	1819.5	0.3	18.3	9.0	31.5	60.4	105.4	109.6	56.5	12.5	0.9
2003	1873.0	0.2	17.4	8.8	29.8	59.6	108.5	114.6	59.9	13.5	0.9
2004	1897.5	0.2	17.3	8.9	29.6	59.8	108.6	116.9	62.1	13.6	1.0
2005	1889.0	0.2	17.0	8.2	30.1	61.1	107.9	115.0	61.8	13.8	1.0

[1]Beginning 1997, rates computed by relating births to women aged 45–54 years to women aged 45–49 years.
[4]Based on 100 percent of births in selected states and on a 50-percent sample of births in all other states.

Table A-7. Birth Rates for Women Under 20 Years of Age, by Age, Race, and Hispanic Origin of Mother, Selected Years, 1991–2006 and Preliminary 2006

(Rate per 1,000 in specified group, percent change.)

Age, race, and Hispanic origin of mother	1991	2004	2005	2006	Percent change 1991–2005	Percent change 2005–2006
10–14 Years						
All races and origins[1]	1.4	0.7	0.7	0.6	−50	−14
Non-Hispanic White	0.5	0.2	0.2	0.2	−60	0
Non-Hispanic Black	4.9	1.6	1.7	1.6	−65	−6
American Indian or Alaska Native total[2]	1.6	0.9	0.9	0.9	−44	0
Asian or Pacific Islander total[2]	0.8	0.2	0.2	0.2	−75	0
Hispanic[3]	2.4	1.3	1.3	1.3	−46	0
15–19 Years						
All races and origins[1]	61.8	41.1	40.5	41.9	−34	3
Non-Hispanic White	43.4	26.7	25.9	26.6	−40	3
Non-Hispanic Black	118.2	63.1	60.9	63.7	−48	5
American Indian or Alaska Native total[2]	84.1	52.5	52.7	54.7	−37	4
Asian or Pacific Islander total[2]	27.3	17.3	17.0	16.7	−38	−2
Hispanic[3]	104.6	82.6	81.7	83.0	−22	2
15–17 Years						
All races and origins[1]	38.6	22.1	21.4	22.0	−45	3
Non-Hispanic White	23.6	12.0	11.5	11.8	−51	3
Non-Hispanic Black	86.1	37.1	34.9	36.1	−59	3
American Indian or Alaska Native total[2]	51.9	30.0	30.5	30.5	−41	0
Asian or Pacific Islander total[2]	16.3	8.9	8.2	8.7	−50	6
Hispanic[3]	69.2	49.7	48.5	47.9	−30	−1
18–19 Years						
All races and origins[1]	94.0	70.0	69.9	73.0	−26	4
Non-Hispanic White	70.6	48.7	48.0	49.3	−32	3
Non-Hispanic Black	162.2	103.9	103.0	108.4	−36	5
American Indian or Alaska Native total[2]	134.2	87	87.6	92.8	−35	6
Asian or Pacific Islander total[2]	42.2	29.6	30.1	28.9	−29	−4
Hispanic[3]	155.5	133.5	134.6	139.7	−13	4

[1]Includes Hispanic origin not stated.
[2]Data for persons of Hispanic origin are included in the data for each race group according to the person's reported race.
[3]Persons of Hispanic origin may be of any race.

Table A-8. Percentage of Live Births to Mothers Under 20 Years of Age, by State and Territory, Final 2005 and Preliminary 2006

(Percent.)

Area	2005	2006
UNITED STATES[1]	10.2	10.4
Alabama	13.1	13.8
Alaska	10.0	10.1
Arizona	12.5	12.7
Arkansas	14.7	14.7
California	9.3	9.5
Colorado	9.8	9.7
Connecticut	6.8	6.9
Delaware	10.7	10.7
District of Columbia	11.0	12.0
Florida	10.8	10.9
Georgia	11.9	12.1
Hawaii	8.3	8.6
Idaho	8.8	8.9
Illinois	9.7	10.0
Indiana	11.0	10.9
Iowa	8.5	8.7
Kansas	10.3	10.2
Kentucky	12.1	12.9
Louisiana	13.7	13.8
Maine	8.0	8.1
Maryland	8.5	8.8
Massachusetts	6.0	6.2
Michigan	9.4	9.8
Minnesota	6.8	7.0
Mississippi	15.6	16.4
Missouri	11.1	11.4
Montana	10.4	10.3
Nebraska	8.3	8.0
Nevada	10.7	10.9
New Hampshire	5.9	6.1
New Jersey	6.1	6.3
New Mexico	15.8	15.7
New York	7.0	7.1
North Carolina	11.5	11.7
North Dakota	7.9	7.4
Ohio	10.6	10.7
Oklahoma	13.1	13.6
Oregon	8.8	8.9
Pennsylvania	9.0	9.3
Rhode Island	9.0	9.2
South Carolina	13.2	13.4
South Dakota	9.5	9.5
Tennessee	13.4	13.0
Texas	13.5	13.5
Utah	6.3	6.6
Vermont	6.6	7.2
Virginia	8.5	8.6
Washington	8.3	8.3
West Virginia	11.9	12.5
Wisconsin	8.6	8.4
Wyoming	11.1	11.2
Puerto Rico	18.1	18.4
Virgin Islands	13.6	13.0
Guam	13.4	—
American Samoa	5.8	7.7
Northern Marianas	7.0	7.5

— = Data not available.
[1]Excludes data for the territories.

Table A-9. Live Births, Births and Fertility Rates by Specified Hispanic Origin and Race of Mother, 1989–2005

(Number, live births per 1,000 population in specified group, live births per 1,000 women age 15–44 years in specified group.)

Measure and year	All origins[2]	Hispanic[1]							Non-Hispanic	
		Total	Mexican	Puerto Rico	Cuban	Central and South American	Other and unknown Hispanic	Total[3]	White	Black
Number										
1989[4]	3,903,012	532,249	327,233	56,229	10,842	72,443	65,502	3,297,493	2,526,367	611,269
1990[5]	4,092,994	595,073	385,640	58,807	11,311	83,008	56,307	3,457,417	2,626,500	661,701
1991[6]	4,094,566	623,085	411,233	59,833	11,058	86,908	54,053	3,434,464	2,589,878	666,758
1992[6]	4,049,024	643,271	432,047	59,569	11,472	89,031	51,152	3,365,862	2,527,207	657,450
1993	4,000,240	654,418	443,733	58,102	11,916	92,371	48,296	3,295,345	2,472,031	641,273
1994	3,952,767	665,026	454,536	57,240	11,889	93,485	47,876	3,245,115	2,438,855	619,198
1995	3,899,589	679,768	469,615	54,824	12,473	94,996	47,860	3,160,495	2,382,638	587,781
1996	3,891,494	701,339	489,666	54,863	12,613	97,888	46,309	3,133,484	2,358,989	578,099
1997	3,880,894	709,767	499,024	55,450	12,887	97,405	45,001	3,115,174	2,333,363	581,431
1998	3,941,553	734,661	516,011	57,349	13,226	98,226	49,849	3,158,975	2,361,462	593,127
1999	3,959,417	764,339	540,674	57,138	13,088	103,307	50,132	3,147,580	2,346,450	588,981
2000	4,058,814	815,868	581,915	58,124	13,429	113,344	49,056	3,199,994	2,362,968	604,346
2001	4,025,933	851,851	611,000	57,568	14,017	121,365	47,901	3,149,572	2,326,578	589,917
2002	4,021,726	876,642	627,505	57,465	14,232	125,981	51,459	3,119,944	2,298,156	578,335
2003	4,089,950	912,329	654,504	58,400	14,867	135,586	48,972	3,149,034	2,321,904	576,033
2004	4,112,052	946,349	677,621	61,221	14,943	143,520	49,044	3,133,125	2,296,683	578,772
2005	4,138,349	985,505	693,197	63,340	16,064	151,201	61,703	3,123,005	2,279,768	583,759
Birth Rate										
1989[4,7]	16.3	26.2	25.7	23.7	10.0	28.3	(7)	15.4	14.2	22.8
1990[5,7]	16.7	26.7	28.7	21.6	10.9	27.5	(7)	15.7	14.4	23.0
1991[7,8]	16.2	26.5	27.6	23.3	9.8	28.3	(7)	15.2	13.9	22.4
1992[7,8]	15.8	26.1	27.4	22.9	10.1	27.5	(7)	14.8	13.4	21.6
1993[7]	15.4	25.4	26.8	21.5	10.5	26.3	(7)	14.3	13.1	20.7
1994[7]	15.0	24.7	26.1	20.8	10.7	24.9	(7)	13.9	12.8	19.5
1995[7]	14.6	24.1	25.8	19.0	10.8	24.2	(7)	13.5	12.5	18.2
1996[7]	14.4	23.8	26.2	17.2	10.6	22.5	(7)	13.3	12.3	17.6
1997[7]	14.2	23.0	25.3	17.2	10.0	21.3	(7)	13.1	12.2	17.4
1998[7]	14.3	22.7	24.6	17.9	9.7	21.7	(7)	13.2	12.2	17.5
1999[7]	14.2	22.5	24.2	18.0	9.4	21.7	(7)	13.0	12.1	17.1
2000[7]	14.4	23.1	25.0	18.1	9.7	21.8	(7)	13.2	12.2	17.3
2001[7]	14.1	23.0	24.8	17.8	10.3	21.8	(7)	12.8	11.8	16.6
2002[7]	13.9	22.6	24.2	16.5	10.0	22.4	(7)	12.6	11.7	16.1
2003[7]	14.1	22.9	24.7	15.1	9.9	23.0	(7)	12.7	11.8	15.9
2004[7]	14.0	22.9	24.9	16.1	9.3	22.2	(7)	12.5	11.6	15.8
2005[7]	14.0	23.1	24.7	17.2	10.2	22.8	(7)	12.4	11.5	15.7
Fertility Rate										
1989[4,7]	69.2	104.9	106.6	86.6	49.8	95.8	(7)	65.7	60.5	84.8
1990[5,7]	71.0	107.7	118.9	82.9	52.6	102.7	(7)	67.1	62.8	89.0
1991[7,8]	69.3	106.9	114.9	87.9	47.6	105.5	(7)	65.2	60.9	87.0
1992[7,8]	68.4	106.1	113.3	87.9	49.4	104.7	(7)	64.2	60.0	84.5
1993[7]	67.0	103.3	110.9	79.8	53.9	101.5	(7)	62.7	58.9	81.5
1994[7]	65.9	100.7	109.9	78.2	53.6	93.2	(7)	61.6	58.2	77.5
1995[7]	64.6	98.8	109.9	71.3	52.2	89.1	(7)	60.2	57.5	72.8
1996[7]	64.1	97.5	110.7	66.5	55.1	84.2	(7)	59.6	57.1	70.7
1997[7]	63.6	94.2	106.6	65.8	53.1	80.6	(7)	59.3	56.8	70.3
1998[7]	64.3	93.2	103.2	69.7	46.5	83.5	(7)	60.0	57.6	70.9
1999[7]	64.4	93.0	101.5	71.1	47.0	84.8	(7)	60.0	57.7	69.9
2000[7]	65.9	95.9	105.1	73.5	49.3	85.1	(7)	61.1	58.5	71.4
2001[7]	65.3	96.0	105.7	72.2	56.7	82.7	(7)	60.1	57.7	69.1
2002[7]	64.8	94.4	102.8	65.4	59.0	86.1	(7)	59.6	57.4	67.4
2003[7]	66.1	96.9	105.5	61.6	61.7	91.2	(7)	60.5	58.5	67.1
2004[7]	66.3	97.8	106.8	68.4	53.2	89.3	(7)	60.5	58.4	67.0
2005[7]	66.7	99.4	107.7	72.1	50.4	93.2	(7)	60.4	58.3	67.2

[1]Persons of Hispanic origin may be of any race.
[2]Includes origin not stated.
[3]Includes races other than White and Black.
[4]Excludes data for Louisiana, New Hampshire, and Oklahoma, which did not report Hispanic origin.
[5]Excludes data for New Hampshire and Oklahoma, which did not report Hispanic origin.
[6]Excludes data for New Hampshire, which did not report Hispanic origin.
[7]Rates for the Central and South American population includes other and unknown Hispanic.
[8]Rates are estimated for the United States based on birth data for 49 states and the District of Columbia. Births for New Hampshire that did not report Hispanic origin are included in the rates for non-Hispanic women.

Table A-10. Birth Rates by Age of Mother, Live-Birth Order, Race and Hispanic Origin of Mother, Preliminary 2006

(Rate per 1,000 women in specified group.)

Live-birth order, race, and Hispanic origin of mother	Fertility rate[1]	Age of mother							
		10–14 years	15–19 years	20–24 years	25–29 years	30–34 years	35–39 years	40–44 years	45–49 years[2]
All Races and Origins[3]	68.5	0.6	41.9	105.9	116.8	97.7	47.3	9.4	0.6
1st child	27.4	0.6	33.7	51.1	41.6	27.6	10.8	2.0	0.2
2nd child	21.9	0.0	7.0	35.4	39.2	34.4	15.6	2.7	0.2
3rd child	11.6	*	1.1	14.1	22.4	20.5	11.0	2.0	0.1
4th child and over	7.7	*	0.1	5.2	13.6	15.2	9.9	2.7	0.2
Non-Hispanic White	59.5	2.0	26.6	83.4	109.2	98.1	46.3	8.4	0.6
1st child	24.8	2.0	22.3	43.8	44.4	30.5	11.6	2.0	0.1
2nd child	19.8	*	3.8	27.3	37.3	36.9	16.4	2.6	0.2
3rd child	9.5	*	0.5	9.5	18.3	19.1	10.5	1.7	0.1
4th child and over	5.4	*	0.1	2.8	9.2	11.6	7.8	2.1	0.2
Non-Hispanic Black	70.6	16.0	63.7	133.1	107.1	72.6	36.0	8.3	0.5
1st child	27.5	15.0	50.1	57	27.3	15.4	6.8	1.5	0.1
2nd child	20.2	0.0	11.3	43.7	33.3	21.5	10.0	2.0	0.1
3rd child	12.3	*	2.0	21.6	24.5	16.9	8.5	1.8	0.1
4th child and over	10.6	*	0.3	10.9	22.0	18.8	10.6	2.9	0.2
American Indian or Alaska Native Total	62.8	0.9	54.7	114.9	97.2	61.5	28.2	6.1	0.4
1st child	22.2	0.9	42.0	44.5	19.7	9.4	3.6	0.6	*
2nd child	172	*	10.6	39.8	27.5	13.8	5.7	1.0	*
3rd child	115	*	1.9	21.2	25.0	13.9	5.8	1.0	*
4th child and over	120	*	0.3	9.4	25.0	24.3	13.1	3.4	0.2
Asian or Pacific Islander	67.2	2.0	16.7	62.5	107.8	116.5	62.8	14.1	1.0
1st child	30.9	1.0	13.7	37.8	59.0	47.3	18.7	3.7	0.3
2nd child	23.6	*	2.6	17.0	32.9	47.5	25.7	5.2	0.3
3rd child	8.3	*	0.4	5.5	10.3	14.6	11.9	2.8	0.2
4th child and over	4.4	*	0.1	2.2	5.6	7.0	6.6	2.4	0.2
Hispanic[4]	101.5	13.0	83.0	177.0	152.4	108.4	55.6	13.3	0.8
1st child	36.3	13.0	64.5	77.1	38.3	20.1	8.4	1.8	0.1
2nd child	30.9	0.0	15.8	63.4	52.3	31.6	13.6	2.8	0.2
3rd child	19.9	*	2.4	26.8	38.1	30.2	15.0	3.0	0.1
4th child and over	14.4	*	0.3	9.8	23.6	26.5	18.7	5.6	0.4

* = Figure does not meet standards of reliability or precision.
0.0 = Quantity more than zero but less than 0.05.
[1]The rate shown is the fertility rate, which is defined as the total number of births, regardless of age of mother, per 1,000 women aged 15–44 years.
[2]The birth rate for ages 45–49 years is computed by relating births to women aged 45–54 years to women aged 45–49 years, because most of the births in this group are to women aged 45–49.
[3]Includes Hispanic origin not stated.
[4]Persons of Hispanic origin may be of any race.

Table A-11. Live Births by Age of Mother, Live-Birth Order, Hispanic Origin of Mother, and by Race for Mothers of Non-Hispanic Origin, 2005

(Number of children born alive to mother, includes births with stated origin of mother only.)

Live-birth order and origin of mother	All ages	Under 15 years	Total	15 years	16 years	17 years	18 years	19 years	20–24 years	25–29 years	30–34 years	35–39 years	40–44 years	45–49 years	50–54 years
HISPANIC[1]															
Total	985,505	2,466	136,906	7,241	15,928	26,877	38,090	48,770	287,896	266,590	186,398	85,739	18,597	891	22
1st child	350,705	2,423	106,395	6,888	14,589	22,752	29,085	33,081	123,415	67,910	34,861	12,975	2,586	135	5
2nd child	301,667	37	25,699	310	1,220	3,717	7,755	12,697	103,767	91,963	54,910	21,283	3,844	161	3
3rd child	193,217	2	3,971	18	69	326	1,041	2,517	43,902	66,002	51,835	23,130	4,206	164	5
4th child	85,290	1	436	2	5	24	90	315	12,423	27,148	27,118	14,705	3,330	127	2
5th child	31,655	–	53	1	2	5	14	31	2,899	8,965	10,512	7,152	1,958	113	3
6th child	12,118	–	6	–	–	–	2	4	574	2,739	4,093	3,395	1,242	67	2
7th child	4,650	–	2	–	–	–	–	2	110	814	1,566	1,492	618	47	1
8th child and over	3,624	–	–	–	–	–	–	–	52	376	997	1,371	754	73	1
Not stated	2,579	3	344	22	43	53	103	123	754	673	506	236	59	4	–
Mexican	693,197	1,855	101,705	5,443	11,989	20,184	28,343	35,746	209,156	187,469	126,175	54,955	11,346	525	11
1st child	236,057	1,822	78,492	5,176	10,948	17,015	21,455	23,898	86,144	42,530	19,255	6,546	1,216	51	1
2nd child	208,777	29	19,560	240	960	2,868	5,933	9,559	77,201	64,350	34,336	11,419	1,813	69	–
3rd child	141,879	1	3,073	11	51	251	821	1,939	33,249	49,688	38,036	15,299	2,438	91	4
4th child	65,158	1	342	2	3	15	75	247	9,388	20,738	21,093	11,130	2,384	81	1
5th child	24,287	–	37	1	1	3	8	24	2,199	6,838	8,099	5,578	1,458	76	2
6th child	9,309	–	4	–	–	–	–	4	413	2,047	3,157	2,666	967	54	1
7th child	3,578	–	1	–	–	–	–	1	85	630	1,189	1,146	484	42	1
8th child and over	2,731	–	–	–	–	–	–	–	39	280	729	1,062	561	59	1
Not stated	1,421	2	196	13	26	32	51	74	438	368	281	109	25	2	–
Puerto Rican	63,340	175	10,839	567	1,266	2,132	3,014	3,860	19,747	16,220	10,241	4,956	1,110	50	2
1st child	24,776	172	8,513	541	1,182	1,820	2,322	2,648	8,289	4,279	2,321	992	194	16	–
2nd child	19,442	3	1,947	21	73	281	603	969	6,884	5,444	3,294	1,532	323	15	–
3rd child	11,118	–	295	1	4	18	64	208	3,112	3,768	2,432	1,250	254	7	–
4th child	4,666	–	32	–	1	5	4	22	1,045	1,693	1,168	576	148	4	–
5th child	1,806	–	2	–	–	–	2	–	243	645	543	287	83	2	1
6th child	740	–	–	–	–	–	–	–	78	226	237	150	45	3	1
7th child	301	–	–	–	–	–	–	–	11	74	118	71	26	1	–
8th child and over	244	–	–	–	–	–	–	–	2	34	94	79	33	2	–
Not stated	247	–	50	4	6	8	19	13	83	57	34	19	4	–	–
Cuban	16,064	17	1,222	44	121	210	342	505	3,217	4,052	4,630	2,320	566	38	2
1st child	7,169	16	1,040	42	112	192	282	412	1,904	1,843	1,607	609	136	14	–
2nd child	5,881	1	157	1	6	16	51	83	970	1,489	2,054	991	208	10	1
3rd child	2,114	–	17	–	1	2	7	7	248	511	686	512	133	6	1
4th child	554	–	–	–	–	–	–	–	64	142	169	127	46	6	–
5th child	144	–	–	–	–	–	–	–	12	30	44	38	20	–	–
6th child	53	–	–	–	–	–	–	–	3	15	16	12	7	–	–
7th child	18	–	–	–	–	–	–	–	–	1	7	6	3	1	–
8th child and over	19	–	–	–	–	–	–	–	–	1	4	6	7	1	–
Not stated	112	–	8	1	2	–	2	3	16	20	43	19	6	–	–
Central and South American	151,201	215	12,790	563	1,270	2,360	3,610	4,987	36,805	43,417	34,869	18,447	4,446	208	4
1st child	58,902	211	10,502	534	1,180	2,073	2,959	3,756	19,372	14,949	9,211	3,796	823	36	2
2nd child	48,843	3	1,968	25	76	258	562	1,047	12,088	15,678	12,001	5,846	1,211	47	1
3rd child	26,813	–	242	2	6	21	64	149	4,056	8,467	8,107	4,766	1,128	47	–
4th child	10,122	–	20	–	–	–	2	18	931	2,953	3,400	2,197	590	30	1
5th child	3,708	–	7	–	1	1	3	2	179	902	1,304	974	314	28	–
6th child	1,377	–	–	–	–	–	–	–	26	243	484	454	163	7	–
7th child	510	–	–	–	–	–	–	–	7	50	168	201	82	2	–
8th child and over	407	–	–	–	–	–	–	–	7	33	93	148	117	9	–
Not stated	519	1	51	2	7	7	20	15	139	142	101	65	18	2	–
Other and Unknown Hispanic	61,703	204	10,350	624	1,282	1,991	2,781	3,672	18,971	15,432	10,483	5,061	1,129	70	3
1st child	23,801	202	7,848	595	1,167	1,652	2,067	2,367	7,706	4,309	2,467	1,032	217	18	2
2nd child	18,724	1	2,067	23	105	294	606	1,039	6,624	5,002	3,225	1,495	289	20	1
3rd child	11,293	1	344	4	7	34	85	214	3,237	3,568	2,574	1,303	253	13	–
4th child	4,790	–	42	–	1	4	9	28	995	1,622	1,288	675	162	6	–
5th child	1,710	–	7	–	–	1	1	5	266	550	522	275	83	7	–
6th child	639	–	2	–	–	–	2	–	54	208	199	113	60	3	–
7th child	243	–	1	–	–	–	–	1	7	59	84	68	23	1	–
8th child and over	223	–	–	–	–	–	–	–	4	28	77	76	36	2	–
Not stated	280	–	39	2	2	6	11	18	78	86	47	24	6	–	–

– = Quantity zero
[1]Persons of Hispanic origin may be of any race.

Table A-11. Live Births by Age of Mother, Live-Birth Order, Hispanic Origin of Mother, and by Race for Mothers of Non-Hispanic Origin, 2005—*Continued*

(Number of children born alive to mother, includes births with stated origin of mother only.)

Live-birth order and origin of mother	Age of mother														
	All ages	Under 15 years	Total	15 years	16 years	17 years	18 years	19 years	20–24 years	25–29 years	30–34 years	35–39 years	40–44 years	45–49 years	50–54 years
NON-HISPANIC															
Total[2]	3,123,005	4,220	275,042	10,879	24,864	46,527	77,655	115,117	745,697	857,101	757,138	393,277	85,079	5,088	363
1st child	1,275,532	4,134	223,069	10,496	23,119	41,066	63,350	85,038	366,179	331,746	232,448	96,584	19,962	1,296	114
2nd child	1,016,338	64	43,045	325	1,520	4,810	12,125	24,265	244,417	285,712	279,564	136,726	25,324	1,388	98
3rd child	502,067	3	6,739	15	90	424	1,627	4,583	96,392	147,374	145,374	87,658	17,592	878	57
4th child	191,105	–	830	2	6	36	174	612	27,034	57,572	57,121	38,435	9,556	519	38
5th child	69,266	–	108	–	1	5	16	86	6,646	20,347	21,678	15,378	4,774	316	19
6th child	28,107	–	16	–	1	–	5	10	1,549	7,132	9,277	7,333	2,616	173	11
7th child	13,035	–	6	–	–	1	1	4	314	2,546	4,612	3,931	1,510	109	7
8th child and over	14,377	–	4	–	–	1	–	3	132	1,345	3,899	5,357	3,252	371	17
Not stated	13,178	19	1,225	41	127	184	357	516	3,034	3,327	3,165	1,875	493	38	2
White	2,279,768	1,331	165,005	4,702	12,675	26,487	47,329	73,812	515,518	642,553	581,645	305,142	64,352	3,931	291
1st child	937,836	1,313	137,652	4,585	12,045	24,096	40,082	56,844	266,007	259,923	180,173	76,020	15,643	1,016	89
2nd child	761,662	14	23,516	105	558	2,182	6,337	14,334	170,327	220,382	219,692	106,999	19,550	1,101	81
3rd child	366,578	–	3,018	2	31	133	687	2,165	60,198	106,844	113,310	69,223	13,262	672	51
4th child	130,155	–	285	–	2	13	52	218	13,956	37,342	41,710	29,454	6,984	393	31
5th child	42,834	–	41	–	–	3	6	32	2,701	11,146	14,266	11,077	3,362	226	15
6th child	16,296	–	3	–	–	–	1	2	515	3,277	5,622	4,948	1,794	128	9
7th child	7,389	–	2	–	–	1	–	1	94	988	2,651	2,555	1,020	73	6
8th child and over	8,731	–	2	–	–	–	–	2	73	486	1,980	3,495	2,396	291	8
Not stated	8,287	4	48	610	39	59	164	214	1,647	2,165	2,241	1,371	341	31	1
Black	583,759	2,697	96,813	5,602	10,829	17,747	26,627	36,008	188,673	142,885	92,336	47,411	12,256	651	37
1st child	222,633	2,635	74,868	5,356	9,816	15,005	20,370	24,321	78,150	35,773	19,864	8,996	2,196	140	11
2nd child	166,631	47	17,314	203	870	2,337	5,122	8,782	61,834	43,839	27,316	13,261	2,875	138	7
3rd child	101,797	2	3,372	13	54	266	831	2,208	31,353	32,283	21,102	10,964	2,595	123	3
4th child	48,505	–	497	1	4	20	110	362	11,422	16,881	11,531	6,266	1,816	87	5
5th child	21,592	–	63	–	1	1	9	52	3,539	7,819	5,834	3,233	1,044	58	2
6th child	9,654	–	12	–	–	–	4	8	945	3,320	2,916	1,827	612	20	2
7th child	4,578	–	4	–	–	–	1	3	191	1,335	1,593	1,054	374	27	–
8th child and over	4,542	–	2	–	–	1	–	1	53	748	1,587	1,451	643	52	6
Not stated	3,827	13	681	29	84	117	180	271	1,186	887	593	359	101	6	1

– = Quantity zero
[2]Includes races other than White and Black.

Table A-12. Live Births by Age of Mother, Live-Birth Order, and Race and Hispanic Origin of Mother, Preliminary 2006

(Number of children born alive to mother.)

Live-birth order, race, and Hispanic origin of mother	All ages	Under 15 years	15–19 years	20–24 years	25–29 years	30–34 years	35–39 years	40–44 years	45–54 years
All Races and Origins[1]	4,265,996	6,405	435,427	1,080,507	1,182,187	950,472	498,566	105,476	6,956
1st child	1,697,281	6,253	348,469	518,608	419,023	267,253	113,390	22,557	1,727
2nd child	1,354,637	101	72,537	359,749	394,403	332,794	163,456	29,855	1,741
3rd child	716,756	5	10,921	143,515	225,457	198,189	115,339	22,147	1,183
4th child and over	473,685	–	1,430	53,014	136,931	146,715	103,182	30,161	2,252
Not stated	23,638	46	2,069	5,621	6,373	5,521	3,198	756	54
Non-Hispanic White	2,309,833	1,270	169,837	528,596	665,889	567,103	309,130	63,546	4,461
1st child	957,979	1,250	142,032	276,424	269,785	175,400	76,721	15,176	1,192
2nd child	763,648	14	23,896	172,106	226,482	211,960	108,663	19,311	1,216
3rd child	367,119	–	2,938	59,929	110,792	109,727	69,948	13,044	741
4th child and over	209,020	–	335	17,746	55,524	66,751	51,821	15,563	1,281
Not stated	12,067	6	636	2,392	3,307	3,266	1,977	452	32
Non-Hispanic Black	617,220	2,470	103,692	198,718	153,639	95,804	49,893	12,270	733
1st child	237,818	2,395	80,720	84,164	38,702	20,058	9,376	2,243	161
2nd child	175,184	42	18,242	64,610	47,355	28,062	13,763	2,960	148
3rd child	106,509	2	3,281	31,851	34,803	22,055	11,712	2,677	128
4th child and over	91,316	–	500	16,072	31,140	24,577	14,502	4,242	284
Not stated	6,392	31	949	2,022	1,638	1,052	540	149	11
American Indian or Alaska Native	47,494	122	8,222	16,388	12,127	6,752	3,120	722	41
1st child	16,677	119	6,291	6,321	2,447	1,027	396	72	4
2nd child	12,901	–	1,584	5,648	3,413	1,507	619	120	9
3rd child	8,674	–	283	3,010	3,099	1,517	639	119	8
4th child and over	9,001	–	39	1,339	3,109	2,652	1,439	404	20
Not stated	240	3	25	71	59	48	28	6	–
Asian or Pacific Islander	239,829	71	7,672	31,535	66,562	82,614	42,290	8,525	560
1st child	109,881	69	6,237	18,994	36,245	33,401	12,529	2,226	180
2nd child	83,988	1	1,164	8,512	20,225	33,568	17,225	3,151	142
3rd child	29,398	1	190	2,781	6,339	10,332	7,966	1,691	98
4th child and over	15,480	–	26	1,109	3,447	4,949	4,395	1,419	135
Not stated	1,081	–	55	139	306	362	175	38	5
Hispanic[2]	1,039,051	2,455	145,651	303,443	280,630	194,590	91,562	19,697	1,022
1st child	370,153	2,404	112,916	131,813	70,405	36,045	13,735	2,672	163
2nd child	315,302	42	27,636	108,373	96,048	56,516	22,356	4,128	202
3rd child	203,288	2	4,226	45,751	69,991	54,067	24,572	4,502	178
4th child and over	147,424	–	522	16,692	43,389	47,372	30,642	8,331	476
Not stated	2,884	7	350	814	797	591	257	63	3

– = Quantity zero.
[1]Includes Hispanic origin not stated.
[2]Persons of Hispanic origin of any race.

Table A-13. Fertility Rates and Birth Rates, by Age, Live-Birth Order, Specified Hispanic Origin, and Race of Mother, 2005

(Live births per 1,000 women in specified age and racial group.)

Live-birth order and race of mother	Fertility rate[1]	10–14 years	15–19 years Total	15–17 years	18–19 years	20–24 years	25–29 years	30–34 years	35–39 years	40–44 years	45–49 years[2]
HISPANIC[3]											
Total	99.4	1.3	81.7	48.5	134.6	170.0	149.2	106.8	54.2	13.0	0.8
1st child	35.5	1.3	63.6	43.0	96.6	73.1	38.1	20.0	8.2	1.8	0.1
2nd child	30.5	0.0	15.4	5.1	31.8	61.4	51.6	31.5	13.5	2.7	0.1
3rd child	19.5	*	2.4	0.4	5.5	26.0	37.0	29.8	14.7	2.9	0.1
4th child	8.6	*	0.3	0.0	0.6	7.4	15.2	15.6	9.3	2.3	0.1
5th child	3.2	*	0.0	*	0.1	1.7	5.0	6.0	4.5	1.4	0.1
6th and 7th child	1.7	*	*	*	*	0.4	2.0	3.3	3.1	1.3	0.1
8th child and over	0.4	*	*	*	*	0.0	0.2	0.6	0.9	0.5	0.1
Mexican	107.7	1.4	93.4	55.4	156.3	183.2	154.4	108.3	56.3	13.3	0.8
1st child	36.8	1.4	72.2	48.9	110.8	75.6	35.1	16.6	6.7	1.4	0.1
2nd child	32.5	0.0	18.0	6.0	37.9	67.7	53.1	29.5	11.7	2.1	0.1
3rd child	22.1	*	2.8	0.5	6.7	29.2	41.0	32.7	15.7	2.9	0.1
4th child	10.1	*	0.3	0.0	0.8	8.2	17.1	18.1	11.4	2.8	0.1
5th child	3.8	*	0.0	*	0.1	1.9	5.6	7.0	5.7	1.7	0.1
6th and 7th child	2.0	*	*	*	*	0.4	2.2	3.7	3.9	1.7	0.1
8th child and over	0.4	*	*	*	*	0.0	0.2	0.6	1.1	0.7	0.1
Puerto Rican	72.1	1.0	63.3	37.2	*	131.0	110.4	77.5	36.0	7.9	0.4
1st child	28.3	0.9	49.9	33.4	*	55.2	29.2	17.6	7.2	1.4	*
2nd child	22.2	*	11.4	3.5	*	45.9	37.2	25.0	11.2	2.3	*
3rd child	12.7	*	1.7	0.2	*	20.7	25.7	18.5	9.1	1.8	*
4th child	5.3	*	0.2	*	*	7.0	11.6	8.9	4.2	1.1	*
5th child	2.1	*	*	*	*	1.6	4.4	4.1	2.1	0.6	*
6th and 7th child	1.2	*	*	*	*	0.6	2.0	2.7	1.6	0.5	*
8th child and over	0.3	*	*	*	*	*	0.2	0.7	0.6	0.2	*
Cuban	50.4	*	*	*	*	*	*	*	*	*	*
1st child	22.7	*	*	*	*	*	*	*	*	*	*
2nd child	18.6	*	*	*	*	*	*	*	*	*	*
3rd child	6.7	*	*	*	*	*	*	*	*	*	*
4th child	1.8	*	*	*	*	*	*	*	*	*	*
5th child	0.5	*	*	*	*	*	*	*	*	*	*
6th and 7th child	0.2	*	*	*	*	*	*	*	*	*	*
8th child and over	*	*	*	*	*	*	*	*	*	*	*
Other Hispanic[4]	93.2	1.1	62.2	37.1	97.6	156.3	154.6	116.3	58.7	14.5	0.8
1st child	36.3	1.1	49.5	33.1	72.6	76.2	50.8	30.0	12.1	2.7	0.2
2nd child	29.7	*	10.9	3.6	21.2	52.6	54.5	39.2	18.4	3.9	0.2
3rd child	16.7	*	1.6	0.3	3.3	20.5	31.7	27.5	15.2	3.6	0.2
4th child	6.6	*	0.2	*	0.4	5.4	12.1	12.1	7.2	2.0	0.1
5th child	2.4	*	*	*	*	1.3	3.8	4.7	3.1	1.0	0.1
6th and 7th child	1.2	*	*	*	*	0.3	1.5	2.4	2.1	0.9	*
8th child and over	0.3	*	*	*	*	*	0.2	0.4	0.6	0.4	*

* = Figure does not meet standards of reliability or precision.
0.0 = Quantity more than zero but less than 0.05.
[1]Fertility rates computed by relating total births, regardless of age of mother, to women aged 15–44 years.
[2]Birth rates computed by relating births to women aged 45–54 years to women aged 45–49 years.
[3]Persons of Hispanic origin may be of any race.
[4]Includes Central and South American and other and unknown Hispanic.

Table A-13. Fertility Rates and Birth Rates, by Age, Live-Birth Order, Specified Hispanic Origin, and Race of Mother, 2005—Continued

(Live births per 1,000 women in specified age and racial group.)

Live-birth order and race of mother	Fertility rate[1]	10–14 years	15–19 years Total	15–17 years	18–19 years	20–24 years	25–29 years	30–34 years	35–39 years	40–44 years	45–49 years[2]
NON-HISPANIC[5]											
Total[6]	60.4	0.5	32.4	16.0	57.6	88.7	108.0	93.4	44.9	8.6	0.6
1st child	24.8	0.5	26.4	14.6	44.5	43.7	42.0	28.8	11.1	2.0	0.1
2nd child	19.7	0.0	5.1	1.3	10.9	29.2	36.1	34.6	15.7	2.6	0.2
3rd child	9.8	*	0.8	0.1	1.9	11.5	18.6	18.0	10.0	1.8	0.1
4th child	3.7	*	0.1	0.0	0.2	3.2	7.3	7.1	4.4	1.0	0.1
5th child	1.4	*	0.0	*	0.0	0.8	2.6	2.7	1.8	0.5	0.0
6th and 7th child	0.8	*	0.0	*	0.0	0.2	1.2	1.7	1.3	0.4	0.0
8th child and over	0.3	*	*	*	*	0.0	0.2	0.5	0.6	0.3	0.0
White	58.3	0.2	25.9	11.5	48.0	81.4	109.1	96.9	45.6	8.3	0.5
1st child	24.1	0.2	21.7	10.7	38.5	42.1	44.3	30.2	11.4	2.0	0.1
2nd child	19.5	*	3.7	0.7	8.2	27.0	37.5	36.7	16.1	2.5	0.1
3rd child	9.4	*	0.5	0.0	1.1	9.5	18.2	18.9	10.4	1.7	0.1
4th child	3.3	*	0.0	*	0.1	2.2	6.4	7.0	4.4	0.9	0.1
5th child	1.1	*	0.0	*	0.0	0.4	1.9	2.4	1.7	0.4	0.0
6th and 7th child	0.6	*	*	*	*	0.1	0.7	1.4	1.1	0.4	0.0
8th child and over	0.2	*	*	*	*	0.0	0.1	0.3	0.5	0.3	0.0
Black	67.2	1.7	60.9	34.9	103.0	126.8	103.0	68.4	34.3	8.2	0.5
1st child	25.8	1.6	47.4	31.0	74.0	52.9	26.0	14.8	6.6	1.5	0.1
2nd child	19.3	0.0	11.0	3.5	23.0	41.8	31.8	20.3	9.7	1.9	0.1
3rd child	11.8	*	2.1	0.3	5.0	21.2	23.4	15.7	8.0	1.8	0.1
4th child	5.6	*	0.3	0.0	0.8	7.7	12.2	8.6	4.6	1.2	0.1
5th child	2.5	*	0.0	*	0.1	2.4	5.7	4.4	2.4	0.7	0.0
6th and 7th child	1.7	*	*	*	*	0.8	3.4	3.4	2.1	0.7	0.0
8th child and over	0.5	*	*	*	*	0.0	0.5	1.2	1.1	0.4	0.0

* = Figure does not meet standards of reliability or precision.
0.0 = Quantity more than zero but less than 0.05.
[1]Fertility rates computed by relating total births, regardless of age of mother, to women aged 15–44 years.
[2]Birth rates computed by relating births to women aged 45–54 years to women aged 45–49 years.
[5]Includes origin not stated. ..
[6]Includes races other than White and Black.

Table A-14. Total Fertility Rates, Fertility Rates, and Birth Rates, by Age, Specified Hispanic Origin, and Race of Mother, 1989–2005

(Live births per 1,000 women in specified age and racial group.)

Year, origin, and race of mother	Total fertility rate	Fertility rate[1]	Age of mother 10–14 years	15–19 years Total	15–17 years	18–19 years	20–24 years	25–29 years	30–34 years	35–39 years	40–44 years	45–49 years[2]
ALL ORIGINS												
Total												
1989	2014.0	69.2	1.4	57.3	36.4	84.2	113.8	117.6	77.4	29.9	5.2	0.2
1990	2081.0	70.9	1.4	59.9	37.5	88.6	116.5	120.2	80.8	31.7	5.5	0.2
1991	2062.5	69.3	1.4	61.8	38.6	94.0	115.3	117.2	79.2	31.9	5.5	0.2
1992	2046.0	68.4	1.4	60.3	37.6	93.6	113.7	115.7	79.6	32.3	5.9	0.3
1993	2019.5	67.0	1.4	59.0	37.5	91.1	111.3	113.2	79.9	32.7	6.1	0.3
1994	2001.5	65.9	1.4	58.2	37.2	90.2	109.2	111.0	80.4	33.4	6.4	0.3
1995	1978.0	64.6	1.3	56.0	35.5	87.7	107.5	108.8	81.1	34.0	6.6	0.3
1996	1976.0	64.1	1.2	53.5	33.3	84.7	107.8	108.6	82.1	34.9	6.8	0.3
1997	1971.0	63.6	1.1	51.3	31.4	82.1	107.3	108.3	83.0	34.9	7.1	0.4
1998	1999.0	64.3	1.0	50.3	29.9	80.9	108.4	110.2	85.2	36.9	7.4	0.4
1999	2007.5	64.4	0.9	48.8	28.2	79.1	107.9	111.2	87.1	37.8	7.4	0.4
2000	2056.0	65.9	0.9	47.7	26.9	78.1	109.7	113.5	91.2	39.7	8.0	0.5
2001	2034.0	65.3	0.8	45.3	24.7	76.1	106.2	113.4	91.9	40.6	8.1	0.5
2002	2013.0	64.8	0.7	43.0	23.2	72.8	103.6	113.6	91.5	41.4	8.3	0.5
2003	2042.5	66.1	0.6	41.6	22.4	70.7	102.6	115.6	95.1	43.8	8.7	0.5
2004	2045.5	66.3	0.7	41.1	22.1	70.0	101.7	115.5	95.3	45.4	8.9	0.5
2005	2053.5	66.7	0.7	40.5	21.4	69.9	102.2	115.5	95.8	46.3	9.1	0.6
HISPANIC[3]												
Total												
1989[4]	2,903.5	104.9	2.3	100.8	—	—	184.4	146.6	92.1	43.5	10.4	0.6
1990[5]	2,959.5	107.7	2.4	100.3	65.9	147.7	181.0	153.0	98.3	45.3	10.9	0.7
1991[6]	2,963.5	106.9	2.4	104.6	69.2	155.5	184.6	150.0	95.1	44.7	10.7	0.6
1992[6]	2,957.5	106.1	2.5	103.3	68.9	153.9	185.2	148.8	94.8	45.3	11.0	0.6
1993	2,894.5	103.3	2.6	101.8	68.5	151.1	180.0	146.0	93.2	44.1	10.6	0.6
1994	2,839.0	100.7	2.6	101.3	69.9	147.5	175.7	142.4	91.1	43.4	10.7	0.6
1995	2,798.5	98.8	2.6	99.3	68.3	145.4	171.9	140.4	90.5	43.7	10.7	0.6
1996	2,772.0	97.5	2.4	94.6	64.2	140.0	170.2	140.7	91.3	43.9	10.7	0.6
1997	2,680.5	94.2	2.1	89.6	61.1	132.4	162.6	137.5	89.6	43.4	10.7	0.6
1998	2,652.5	93.2	1.9	87.9	58.5	131.5	159.3	136.1	90.5	43.4	10.8	0.6
1999	2,649.0	93.0	1.9	86.8	56.9	129.5	157.3	135.8	92.3	44.5	10.6	0.6
2000	2,730.0	95.9	1.7	87.3	55.5	132.6	161.3	139.9	97.1	46.6	11.5	0.6
2001	2,748.5	96.0	1.6	86.4	52.8	135.5	163.5	140.4	97.6	47.9	11.6	0.7
2002	2,718.0	94.4	1.4	83.4	50.7	133.0	164.3	139.4	95.1	47.8	11.5	0.7
2003	2,785.5	96.9	1.3	82.3	49.7	132.0	163.4	144.4	102.0	50.8	12.2	0.7
2004	2,824.5	97.8	1.3	82.6	49.7	133.5	165.3	145.6	104.1	52.9	12.4	0.7
2005	2,885.0	99.4	1.3	81.7	48.5	134.6	170.0	149.2	106.8	54.2	13.0	0.8
Mexican												
1989[4]	2,916.5	106.6	2.0	94.5	—	—	184.3	153.7	96.1	41.0	11.1	0.6
1990[5]	3,214.0	118.9	2.5	108.0	69.7	162.2	200.3	165.3	104.4	49.1	12.4	0.8
1991[6]	3,103.5	114.9	2.5	108.3	70.0	164.7	192.4	156.1	99.7	49.1	11.9	0.7
1992[6]	3,107.0	113.3	2.4	105.1	—	—	196.6	160.2	97.1	47.4	11.8	0.8
1993	3,041.5	110.9	2.5	103.6	68.4	156.6	187.9	159.5	97.2	45.5	11.3	0.8
1994	3,024.0	109.9	2.7	109.2	73.6	163.3	189.1	153.6	92.5	45.3	11.7	0.7
1995	3,033.5	109.9	2.7	115.9	79.1	170.7	190.4	146.6	93.0	45.5	11.9	0.7
1996	3,052.0	110.7	2.6	112.2	77.7	161.6	185.3	154.7	96.5	46.4	12.0	0.7
1997	2,957.0	106.6	2.3	103.4	71.3	151.6	180.9	150.0	95.3	47.4	11.5	0.7
1998	2,878.0	103.2	2.1	96.4	62.9	149.2	176.5	147.4	94.9	46.9	10.8	0.6
1999	2,823.0	101.5	2.1	94.3	60.8	145.6	170.8	141.4	97.4	47.2	10.7	0.7
2000	2,906.5	105.1	1.9	95.4	60.6	146.7	174.9	144.7	102.3	49.2	12.2	0.7
2001	2,928.5	105.7	1.7	95.4	59.3	147.0	177.0	146.4	101.9	50.0	12.6	0.7
2002	2,879.5	102.8	1.5	94.5	58.6	147.5	176.9	144.5	97.9	47.5	12.3	0.8
2003	2,957.5	105.5	1.5	93.2	56.9	148.8	176.9	151.5	104.7	50.2	12.8	0.7
2004	3,021.0	106.8	1.4	95.5	58.4	152.4	180.0	153.5	106.2	54.3	12.6	0.7
2005	3,055.5	107.7	1.4	93.4	55.4	156.3	183.2	154.4	108.3	56.3	13.3	0.8

— = Data not available.

[1] Fertility rates computed by relating total births, regardless of age of mother, to women 15–44 years.

[2] Beginning 1997, rates computed by relating births to women aged 45–54 years to women aged 45–49 years.

[3] Persons of Hispanic origin may be of any race.

[4] Excludes data for Louisiana, New Hampshire, and Oklahoma, which did not report Hispanic origin.

[5] Excludes data for New Hampshire and Oklahoma, which did not report Hispanic origin.

[6] Excludes data for New Hampshire, which did not report Hispanic origin.

Table A-14. Total Fertility Rates, Fertility Rates, and Birth Rates, by Age, Specified Hispanic Origin, and Race of Mother, 1989–2005—Continued

(Live births per 1,000 women in specified age and racial group.)

Year, origin, and race of mother	Total fertility rate	Fertility rate[1]	10–14 years	15–19 years Total	15–17 years	18–19 years	20–24 years	25–29 years	30–34 years	35–39 years	40–44 years	45–49 years[2]
Puerto Rican												
1989[4]	2,421.0	86.6	3.8	112.7	—	—	171.0	98.0	65.2	26.9	6.3	*
1990[5]	2,301.0	82.9	2.9	101.6	71.6	141.6	150.1	109.9	62.8	26.2	6.2	0.5
1991[6]	2,573.5	87.9	2.7	111.0	*	*	193.3	108.9	68.1	23.9	6.5	*
1992[6]	2,568.5	87.9	3.4	106.5	—	—	199.1	102.6	65.3	29.9	6.6	*
1993	2,416.0	79.8	3.1	104.9	70.1	*	184.6	102.8	54.4	26.7	6.2	0.2
1994	2,341.5	78.2	3.1	99.6	68.8	*	169.0	103.8	59.5	27.5	5.6	
1995	2,078.0	71.3	2.9	82.8	57.3	*	138.1	97.9	61.2	26.9	5.5	0.3
1996	1,965.0	66.5	1.9	76.5	48.6	*	133.7	95.6	54.3	25.2	5.6	*
1997	1,931.5	65.8	1.7	68.9	45.0	*	136.0	92.9	54.1	26.1	6.2	0.4
1998	2,043.5	69.7	1.8	76.2	51.7	*	146.7	88.7	61.9	25.8	7.2	0.4
1999	2,104.5	71.1	1.6	74.0	49.4	*	146.0	106.5	58.0	27.3	7.2	0.3
2000	2,178.5	73.5	1.7	82.9	54.7	120.4	149.5	101.6	61.1	32.0	6.6	0.3
2001	2,165.0	72.2	1.7	82.2	*	*	147.2	93.6	70.5	30.7	6.7	0.4
2002	1,947.5	65.4	1.4	61.4	39.7	*	136.5	90.6	61.5	31.3	6.3	0.5
2003	1,841.0	61.6	1.0	60.8	35.9	*	127.9	86.6	55.6	29.5	6.4	0.4
2004	2,056.5	68.4	0.9	62.6	38.9	*	139.1	102.2	66.4	32.8	6.8	0.5
2005	2,137.5	72.1	1.0	63.3	37.2	*	131.0	110.4	77.5	36.0	7.9	0.4
Cuban												
1989[4]	1,479.0	49.8	*	*	—	—	*	*	*	*	*	*
1990[5]	1,459.5	52.6	*	30.3	18.2	46.1	64.6	95.4	67.6	28.2	4.9	*
1991[6]	1,352.5	47.6	*	*	*	*	*	*	*	*	*	*
1992[6]	1,453.5	49.4	*	*	—	—	*	*	*	*	*	*
1993	1,570.0	53.9	*	*	*	*	*	*	*	*	*	*
1994	1,587.0	53.6	*	*	*	*	*	*	*	*	*	*
1995	1,584.0	52.2	*	*	*	*	*	*	*	*	*	*
1996	1,617.0	55.1	*	*	*	*	*	*	*	*	*	*
1997	1,619.5	53.1	*	*	*	*	*	*	*	*	*	*
1998	1,402.5	46.5	*	*	*	*	*	*	*	*	*	*
1999	1,388.5	47.0	*	*	*	*	*	*	*	*	*	*
2000	1,528.0	49.3	*	23.5	14.2	43.4	64.2	104.0	68.1	37.3	7.9	*
2001	1,792.5	56.7	*	*	*	*	*	*	*	*	*	*
2002	1,940.5	59.0	*	*	*	*	*	*	*	*	*	*
2003	2,059.5	61.7	*	*	*	*	*	*	*	*	*	*
2004	1,732.5	53.2	*	*	*	*	*	*	*	*	*	*
2005	1,583.0	50.4	*	*	*	*	*	*	*	*	*	*
Other Hispanic[7]												
1989[4]	2,683.0	95.8	1.7	66.4	—	—	159.2	150.4	85.1	60.3	12.7	0.8
1990[5]	2,877.0	102.7	2.1	86.0	57.2	123.8	162.9	155.8	106.9	49.4	11.6	0.7
1991[6]	3,064.5	105.5	2.2	100.7	67.3	145.6	184.1	164.5	100.2	49.2	11.4	0.6
1992[6]	2,989.0	104.7	2.4	108.2	—	—	168.0	151.9	104.4	49.9	12.5	0.5
1993	2,914.5	101.5	2.6	102.0	74.7	134.6	167.5	139.4	106.7	51.7	12.5	0.5
1994	2,693.0	93.2	2.5	82.6	62.7	105.0	151.2	137.0	104.4	48.4	11.9	0.6
1995	2,629.5	89.1	2.3	72.1	51.3	99.4	144.3	147.7	97.9	49.4	11.6	0.6
1996	2,516.5	84.2	2.2	64.8	43.4	95.6	149.6	127.9	98.0	49.1	11.0	0.7
1997	2,376.5	80.6	1.8	66.4	44.5	98.0	129.3	125.8	95.6	43.9	11.8	0.7
1998	2,448.5	83.5	1.8	75.0	53.3	100.3	122.7	133.6	97.8	45.4	12.8	0.6
1999	2,517.0	84.8	1.5	75.5	53.1	100.5	130.2	138.4	98.3	46.5	12.3	0.7
2000	2,563.5	85.1	1.2	69.9	44.4	102.0	133.2	143.9	103.6	47.7	12.5	0.7
2001	2,519.5	82.7	1.1	65.3	35.6	115.2	136.0	143.3	95.4	50.3	11.6	0.9
2002	2,610.5	86.1	1.1	63.0	34.7	110.3	143.3	147.2	98.4	56.1	12.2	0.8
2003	2,733.0	91.2	1.0	60.4	36.4	93.1	142.2	152.8	112.3	63.2	13.9	0.8
2004	2,648.0	89.3	1.1	57.7	32.7	96.4	136.2	144.4	114.2	60.0	15.2	0.8
2005	2,822.5	93.2	1.1	62.2	37.1	97.6	156.3	154.6	116.3	58.7	14.5	0.8

—— = Data not available.

* = Figure does not meet standards of reliability or precision.

[1]Fertility rates computed by relating total births, regardless of age of mother, to women 15–44 years.

[2]Beginning 1997, rates computed by relating births to women aged 45–54 years to women aged 45–49 years.

[4]Excludes data for Louisiana, New Hampshire, and Oklahoma, which did not report Hispanic origin.

[5]Excludes data for New Hampshire and Oklahoma, which did not report Hispanic origin.

[6]Excludes data for New Hampshire, which did not report Hispanic origin.

[7]Includes Central and South American and other and unknown Hispanic.

Table A-14. Total Fertility Rates, Fertility Rates, and Birth Rates, by Age, Specified Hispanic Origin, and Race of Mother, 1989–2005—Continued

(Live births per 1,000 women in specified age and racial group.)

Year, origin, and race of mother	Total fertility rate	Fertility rate[1]	10–14 years	15–19 years Total	15–17 years	18–19 years	20–24 years	25–29 years	30–34 years	35–39 years	40–44 years	45–49 years[2]
NON-HISPANIC[8,9]												
Total												
1989[4]	1,921.0	65.7	1.3	53.4	—	—	107.8	113.4	74.7	28.6	4.8	0.2
1990[5]	1,979.5	67.1	1.3	54.8	33.8	81.4	108.1	116.5	79.2	30.7	5.1	0.2
1991[6]	1,953.0	65.2	1.3	56.1	34.4	86.1	106.5	113.1	77.5	30.8	5.1	0.2
1992[6]	1,929.0	64.2	1.2	54.3	33.2	85.3	104.3	111.4	77.9	31.1	5.4	0.2
1993	1,901.5	62.7	1.2	52.7	32.9	82.3	101.7	108.7	78.4	31.6	5.7	0.3
1994	1,883.5	61.6	1.2	51.7	32.3	81.4	99.5	106.5	79.1	32.4	6.0	0.3
1995	1,856.5	60.2	1.1	49.3	30.5	78.6	97.4	104.1	79.9	33.0	6.2	0.3
1996	1,852.0	59.6	1.0	47.0	28.4	75.8	97.3	103.6	80.8	33.9	6.5	0.3
1997	1,853.0	59.3	0.9	45.0	26.7	73.7	97.4	103.5	82.0	34.8	6.7	0.3
1998	1,887.5	60.0	0.8	44.0	25.2	72.4	98.9	105.8	84.4	36.2	7.0	0.4
1999	1,894.0	60.0	0.8	42.2	23.3	70.2	98.4	106.7	86.2	37.0	7.1	0.4
2000	1,931.5	61.1	0.7	40.7	21.9	68.2	99.5	108.4	90.2	38.8	7.6	0.4
2001	1,898.5	60.1	0.6	37.9	19.6	65.2	94.9	107.7	90.9	39.5	7.7	0.5
2002	1,877.0	59.6	0.6	35.5	18.2	61.8	91.8	107.9	90.8	40.4	7.9	0.5
2003	1,897.5	60.5	0.5	34.1	17.3	59.4	90.5	109.2	93.8	42.6	8.3	0.5
2004	1,891.0	60.5	0.5	33.3	16.7	58.1	89.0	108.7	93.6	44.1	8.5	0.5
2005	1,885.5	60.4	0.5	32.4	16.0	57.6	88.7	108.0	93.4	44.9	8.6	0.6
White												
1989[4]	1,770.0	60.5	0.4	39.9	—	—	94.7	111.7	75.0	27.8	4.3	0.2
1990[5]	1,850.5	62.8	0.5	42.5	23.2	66.6	97.5	115.3	79.4	30.0	4.7	0.2
1991[6]	1,822.5	60.9	0.5	43.4	23.6	70.6	95.7	112.1	77.7	30.2	4.7	0.2
1992[6]	1,803.5	60.0	0.5	41.7	22.7	69.8	93.9	110.6	78.3	30.4	5.1	0.2
1993	1,786.0	58.9	0.5	40.7	22.7	67.7	92.2	108.2	79.0	31.0	5.4	0.2
1994	1,782.5	58.2	0.5	40.4	22.7	67.6	90.9	106.6	80.2	32.0	5.7	0.2
1995	1,777.5	57.5	0.4	39.3	22.0	66.2	90.2	105.1	81.5	32.8	5.9	0.3
1996	1,781.0	57.1	0.4	37.6	20.6	64.0	90.1	104.9	82.8	33.9	6.2	0.3
1997	1,785.5	56.8	0.4	36.0	19.3	62.1	90.0	104.8	84.3	34.8	6.5	0.3
1998	1,825.0	57.6	0.3	35.3	18.3	60.9	91.2	107.4	87.2	36.4	6.8	0.4
1999	1,838.5	57.7	0.3	34.1	17.1	59.4	90.6	108.6	89.5	37.3	6.9	0.4
2000	1,866.0	58.5	0.3	32.6	15.8	57.5	91.2	109.4	93.2	38.8	7.3	0.4
2001	1,843.0	57.7	0.3	30.3	14.0	54.8	87.1	108.9	94.3	39.8	7.5	0.4
2002	1,828.5	57.4	0.2	28.5	13.1	51.9	84.3	109.3	94.4	40.9	7.6	0.5
2003	1,856.5	58.5	0.2	27.4	12.4	50.0	83.5	110.8	97.6	43.2	8.1	0.5
2004	1,847.0	58.4	0.2	26.7	12.0	48.7	81.9	110.0	97.1	44.8	8.2	0.5
2005	1,839.5	58.3	0.2	25.9	11.5	48.0	81.4	109.1	96.9	45.6	8.3	0.5
Black												
1989[4]	2,424.0	84.8	5.2	111.9	—	—	156.3	113.8	65.7	26.3	5.3	0.3
1990[5]	2,547.5	89.0	5.0	116.2	84.9	157.5	165.1	118.4	70.2	28.7	5.6	0.3
1991[6]	2,532.0	87.0	4.9	118.2	86.1	162.2	164.8	115.1	68.9	28.7	5.6	0.2
1992[6]	2,482.5	84.5	4.8	114.7	82.9	161.1	160.8	112.8	68.4	29.1	5.7	0.2
1993	2,412.5	81.5	4.6	110.5	81.1	154.6	154.5	109.2	68.1	29.4	5.9	0.3
1994	2,314.5	77.5	4.6	105.7	77.0	150.4	146.8	104.1	66.3	29.1	6.0	0.3
1995	2,186.5	72.8	4.2	97.2	70.4	139.2	137.8	98.5	64.4	28.8	6.1	0.3
1996	2,140.0	70.7	3.6	91.9	64.8	134.1	137.0	96.7	63.2	29.1	6.2	0.3
1997	2,137.5	70.3	3.2	88.3	60.7	131.0	138.8	97.2	63.6	29.6	6.5	0.3
1998	2,164.0	70.9	2.9	85.7	56.8	128.2	142.5	99.9	64.4	30.4	6.7	0.3
1999	2,134.0	69.9	2.6	81.0	51.7	123.9	142.1	99.8	63.9	30.6	6.5	0.3
2000	2,178.5	71.4	2.4	79.2	50.1	121.9	145.4	102.8	66.5	31.8	7.2	0.4
2001	2,104.5	69.1	2.1	73.5	44.9	116.7	137.2	102.1	66.2	32.1	7.3	0.4
2002	2,047.0	67.4	1.9	68.3	41.0	110.3	131.0	102.1	66.1	32.1	7.5	0.4
2003	2,027.5	67.1	1.6	64.7	38.7	105.3	128.1	102.1	67.4	33.4	7.7	0.5
2004	2,020.0	67.0	1.6	63.1	37.1	103.9	126.9	103.0	67.4	33.7	7.8	0.5
2005	2,019.0	67.2	1.7	60.9	34.9	103.0	126.8	103.0	68.4	34.3	8.2	0.5

—— = Data not available.

* = Figure does not meet standards of reliability or precision.

[1]Fertility rates computed by relating total births, regardless of age of mother, to women 15–44 years.

[2]Beginning 1997, rates computed by relating births to women aged 45–54 years to women aged 45–49 years.

[4]Excludes data for Louisiana, New Hampshire, and Oklahoma, which did not report Hispanic origin.

[5]Excludes data for New Hampshire and Oklahoma, which did not report Hispanic origin.

[6]Excludes data for New Hampshire, which did not report Hispanic origin.

[8]Includes origin not stated.

[9]Includes races other than White and Black.

Table A-15. Fertility Rates and Birth Rates by Live-Birth Order and by Race and Hispanic Origin of Mother, 1980–2005

(Live births per 1,000 women aged 15–44 years.)

Year, race, and Hispanic origin of mother	Fertility rate	Live-birth order						
		1	2	3	4	5	6 and 7	8 and over
All Races[1,2]								
1980[3]	68.4	29.5	21.8	10.3	3.9	1.5	1.0	0.4
1981[3]	67.3	29.0	21.6	10.1	3.8	1.5	0.9	0.4
1982[3]	67.3	28.6	22.0	10.2	3.8	1.4	0.9	0.3
1983[3]	65.7	27.8	21.5	10.1	3.7	1.4	0.9	0.3
1984[3]	65.5	27.4	21.7	10.1	3.7	1.4	0.9	0.3
1985	66.3	27.6	22.0	10.4	3.8	1.4	0.8	0.3
1986	65.4	27.2	21.6	10.3	3.8	1.4	0.8	0.3
1987	65.8	27.2	21.6	10.5	3.9	1.4	0.8	0.3
1988	67.3	27.6	22.0	10.9	4.1	1.5	0.9	0.3
1989	69.2	28.4	22.4	11.3	4.3	1.6	0.9	0.3
1990	70.9	29.0	22.8	11.7	4.5	1.7	1.0	0.3
1991	69.3	28.2	22.3	11.4	4.4	1.7	1.0	0.3
1992	68.4	27.6	22.2	11.2	4.4	1.7	1.0	0.3
1993	67.0	27.3	21.7	10.9	4.3	1.6	1.0	0.3
1994	65.9	27.1	21.2	10.6	4.1	1.6	0.9	0.3
1995	64.6	26.9	20.7	10.3	4.0	1.5	0.9	0.3
1996	64.1	26.3	20.7	10.4	4.0	1.5	0.9	0.3
1997	63.6	25.9	20.7	10.4	4.0	1.5	0.9	0.3
1998	64.3	25.9	21.0	10.6	4.1	1.5	0.9	0.3
1999	64.4	26.0	21.0	10.7	4.1	1.5	0.9	0.3
2000	65.9	26.5	21.4	11.0	4.2	1.6	0.9	0.3
2001	65.3	26.0	21.3	11.0	4.3	1.6	0.9	0.3
2002	64.8	25.8	21.1	10.9	4.3	1.5	0.9	0.3
2003	66.1	26.5	21.4	11.1	4.3	1.6	0.9	0.3
2004	66.3	26.4	21.4	11.2	4.4	1.6	0.9	0.3
2005	66.7	26.5	21.5	11.3	4.5	1.6	0.9	0.3
Non-Hispanic White[2]								
1990[4]	62.8	26.7	21.2	9.9	3.3	1.1	0.5	0.2
1991[5]	60.9	25.8	20.6	9.6	3.2	1.0	0.5	0.2
1992[5]	60.0	25.1	20.5	9.5	3.2	1.0	0.5	0.2
1993	58.9	24.8	20.1	9.2	3.1	1.0	0.5	0.2
1994	58.2	24.6	19.7	9.1	3.1	1.0	0.5	0.2
1995	57.5	24.5	19.3	8.9	3.0	1.0	0.5	0.2
1996	57.1	24.1	19.3	8.9	3.0	1.0	0.5	0.2
1997	56.8	23.8	19.3	8.9	3.0	1.0	0.5	0.2
1998	57.6	23.8	19.7	9.2	3.1	1.0	0.6	0.2
1999	57.7	24.0	19.6	9.2	3.2	1.0	0.6	0.2
2000	58.5	24.2	19.8	9.4	3.3	1.1	0.6	0.2
2001	57.7	23.6	19.7	9.3	3.3	1.1	0.6	0.2
2002	57.4	23.5	19.5	9.3	3.3	1.1	0.6	0.2
2003	58.5	24.3	19.7	9.4	3.3	1.1	0.6	0.2
2004	58.4	24.1	19.6	9.4	3.3	1.1	0.6	0.2
2005	58.3	24.1	19.5	9.4	3.3	1.1	0.6	0.2
Non-Hispanic Black[2]								
1990[4]	89.0	33.2	26.3	16.0	7.6	3.3	2.0	0.6
1991[5]	87.0	32.1	25.5	15.7	7.5	3.4	2.2	0.6
1992[5]	84.5	31.1	24.8	15.2	7.3	3.4	2.2	0.6
1993	81.5	30.5	23.6	14.3	7.0	3.2	2.2	0.7
1994	77.5	30.0	22.4	13.2	6.3	2.9	2.0	0.6
1995	72.8	28.9	20.9	12.1	5.8	2.7	1.9	0.6
1996	70.7	27.6	20.5	12.0	5.6	2.6	1.8	0.6
1997	70.3	27.2	20.6	12.0	5.7	2.5	1.8	0.6
1998	70.9	27.0	21.0	12.3	5.7	2.6	1.8	0.6
1999	69.9	26.4	20.8	12.3	5.7	2.5	1.7	0.6
2000	71.4	26.7	21.2	12.8	5.9	2.6	1.8	0.6
2001	69.1	25.9	20.4	12.4	5.8	2.5	1.7	0.6
2002	67.4	25.3	19.7	12.0	5.6	2.5	1.7	0.5
2003	67.1	25.4	19.6	11.9	5.6	2.5	1.6	0.5
2004	67.0	25.5	19.4	11.9	5.6	2.5	1.7	0.5
2005	67.2	25.8	19.3	11.8	5.6	2.5	1.7	0.5

[1]Includes races other than White and Black.
[2]Includes origin not stated.
[3]Based on 100 percent of births in selected states and on a 50-percent sample of births in all other states.
[4]Excludes data for New Hampshire and Oklahoma, which did not report Hispanic origin.
[5]Excludes data for New Hampshire, which did not report Hispanic origin.

Table A-15. Fertility Rates and Birth Rates by Live-Birth Order and by Race and Hispanic Origin of Mother, 1980–2005—*Continued*

(Live births per 1,000 women aged 15–44 years.)

Year, race, and Hispanic origin of mother	Fertility rate	Live-birth order						
		1	2	3	4	5	6 and 7	8 and over
Hispanic[6]								
1990[4]	107.7	40.7	30.9	19.5	9.3	4.0	2.6	0.8
1991[5]	106.9	40.8	30.6	19.2	9.2	3.9	2.5	0.7
1992[5]	106.1	40.1	30.9	19.0	9.1	3.9	2.5	0.7
1993	103.3	39.3	30.4	18.3	8.6	3.7	2.3	0.6
1994	100.7	39.0	29.7	17.6	8.2	3.4	2.1	0.6
1995	98.8	38.4	29.3	17.4	7.8	3.3	2.0	0.6
1996	97.5	37.2	29.4	17.4	7.8	3.2	1.9	0.5
1997	94.2	35.6	28.6	17.1	7.6	3.0	1.8	0.5
1998	93.2	34.8	28.5	17.2	7.6	3.0	1.7	0.4
1999	93.0	34.6	28.5	17.3	7.5	2.9	1.7	0.4
2000	95.9	35.8	29.2	18.0	7.7	3.0	1.7	0.4
2001	96.0	35.4	29.5	18.1	7.9	3.0	1.7	0.4
2002	94.4	34.6	29.0	17.9	7.9	3.0	1.6	0.4
2003	96.9	35.2	29.9	18.7	8.1	3.1	1.6	0.4
2004	97.8	35.1	29.9	19.1	8.4	3.2	1.7	0.4
2005	99.4	35.5	30.5	19.5	8.6	3.2	1.7	0.4

[4]Excludes data for New Hampshire and Oklahoma, which did not report Hispanic origin.
[5]Excludes data for New Hampshire, which did not report Hispanic origin.
[6]Persons of Hispanic origin may be of any race.

Table A-16. Mean Age of Mother, by Live-Birth Order, Race, and Hispanic Origin of Mother, Selected Years, 1980–2005

(Mean age at birth is the arithmetic average of the age of mothers at the time of the birth.)

Year, race, and Hispanic origin of mother	Total	Live-birth order								
		1	2	3	4	5	6 and 7	8 and over	Unknown or not stated
All Races[1]									
1980[2]	25.0	22.7	25.4	27.3	29.0	30.6	32.7	36.0	23.9
1985	25.8	23.7	26.3	27.9	29.3	30.6	32.5	35.7	26.1
1990	26.4	24.2	26.9	28.3	29.4	30.6	32.1	35.1	27.4
1995	26.9	24.5	27.5	29.1	30.1	31.2	32.6	35.4	27.1
2000	27.2	24.9	27.7	29.2	30.3	31.4	32.9	35.8	27.4
2001	27.3	25.0	27.8	29.2	30.3	31.4	32.9	35.9	27.0
2002	27.3	25.1	27.9	29.2	30.3	31.4	32.9	35.9	27.7
2003	27.4	25.2	28.0	29.3	30.4	31.4	33.0	35.8	27.9
2004	27.5	25.2	28.0	29.4	30.4	31.4	32.9	35.9	27.6
2005	27.4	25.2	28.0	29.4	30.4	31.4	32.9	35.9	28.0
Non-Hispanic White									
1990[3]	27.1	25.0	27.6	29.1	30.3	31.6	33.2	36.2	28.5
1995	27.6	25.4	28.3	29.9	31.2	32.4	33.9	36.7	28.5
2000	28.0	25.9	28.6	30.0	31.3	32.4	34.0	37.0	28.9
2001	28.1	26.0	28.6	30.1	31.3	32.4	33.9	37.0	28.2
2002	28.2	26.1	28.7	30.1	31.2	32.3	33.9	37.1	28.6
2003	28.2	26.2	28.8	30.1	31.2	32.3	33.9	37.0	28.8
2004	28.2	26.2	28.8	30.2	31.2	32.2	33.8	36.9	28.7
2005	28.2	26.2	28.8	30.1	31.2	32.2	33.8	36.9	29.1
Non-Hispanic Black									
1990[3]	24.4	21.7	24.6	26.3	27.4	28.7	30.3	33.3	26.0
1995	24.8	21.9	25.3	27.0	28.0	29.3	30.8	33.2	25.4
2000	25.2	22.3	25.5	27.1	28.2	29.5	31.0	33.9	26.0
2001	25.3	22.4	25.7	27.2	28.3	29.6	31.2	34.1	26.4
2002	25.4	22.6	25.8	27.3	28.5	29.6	31.2	34.1	26.5
2003	25.6	22.7	25.9	27.5	28.6	29.7	31.3	34.0	26.3
2004	25.6	22.7	25.9	27.5	28.6	29.8	31.2	34.1	25.7
2005	25.6	22.7	26.0	27.6	28.8	29.8	31.3	34.2	25.8
Hispanic[4]									
1990[3]	25.3	22.4	25.2	27.4	29.1	30.6	32.3	35.3	26.1
1995	25.4	22.4	25.5	27.8	29.6	31.1	32.8	35.5	24.2
2000	25.7	22.7	25.8	28.1	29.8	31.3	33.0	35.5	24.2
2001	25.9	22.8	25.9	28.2	29.9	31.4	33.1	35.7	24.4
2002	26.0	23.0	26.0	28.3	29.9	31.4	33.1	35.7	25.7
2003	26.1	23.1	26.1	28.4	30.0	31.4	33.1	35.4	25.8
2004	26.2	23.1	26.2	28.5	30.1	31.5	33.1	35.5	25.8
2005	26.2	23.1	26.2	28.5	30.1	31.4	33.2	35.6	26.5

[1]Includes races other than White and Black and origin not stated.
[2]Based on 100 percent of births in selected states and on a 50-percent sample of births in all other states.
[3]Excludes data for New Hampshire and Oklahoma, which did not report Hispanic origin.
[4]Persons of Hispanic origin may be of any race.

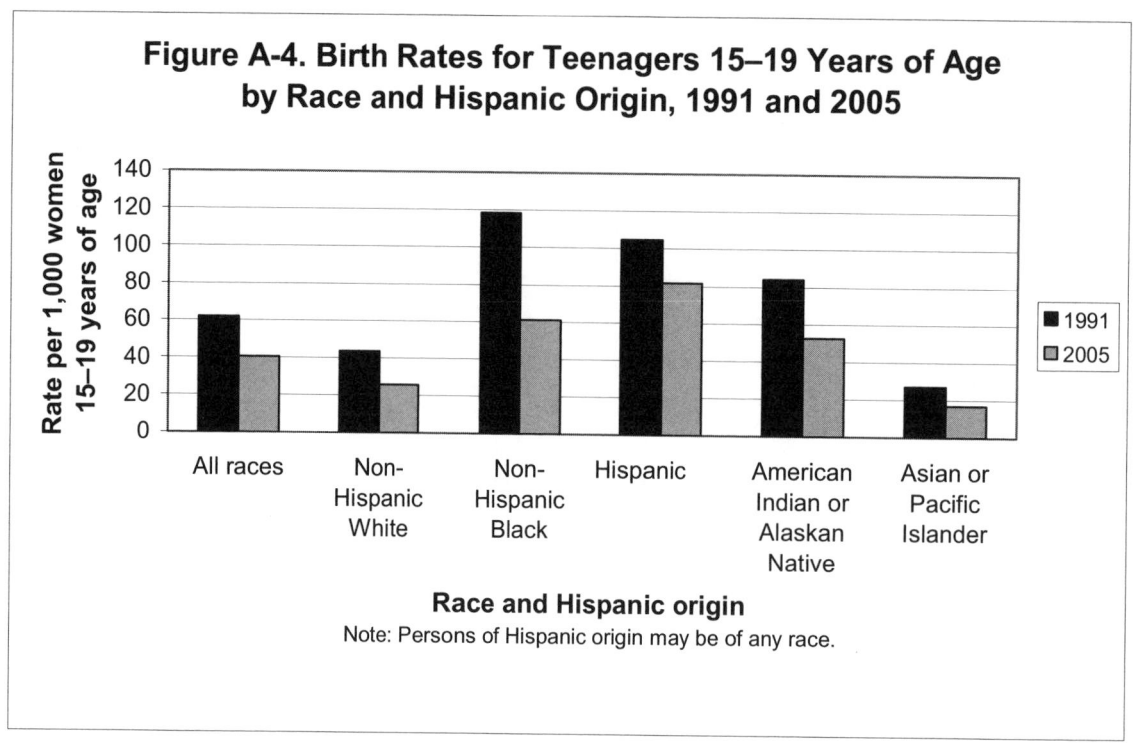

Figure A-4. Birth Rates for Teenagers 15–19 Years of Age by Race and Hispanic Origin, 1991 and 2005

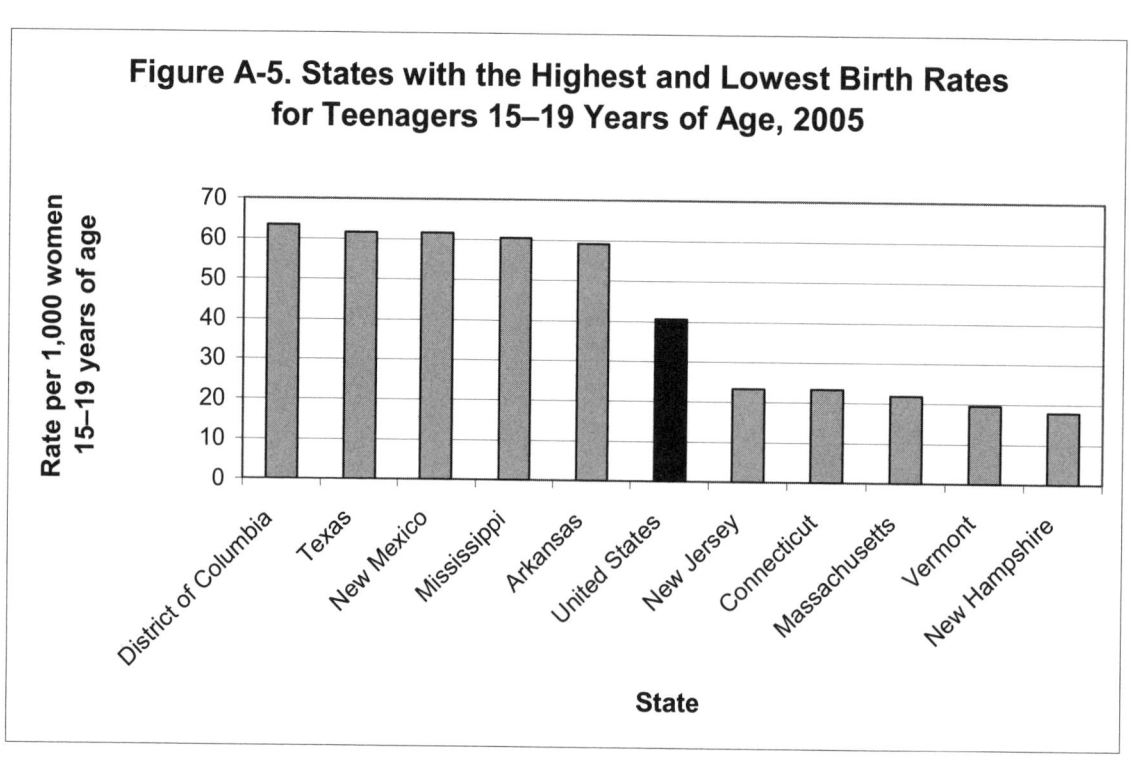

Figure A-5. States with the Highest and Lowest Birth Rates for Teenagers 15–19 Years of Age, 2005

Table A-17. Number of Births, Birth Rates, Fertility Rates, Total Fertility Rates, and Birth Rates for Teenagers 15–19 Years, by Age of Mother, by State and Territory, 2005

(Number, rate.)

Area	Number of births	Birth rate	Fertility rate	Total fertility rate	Teenage birth rate 15–19 years		
					Total	16–17 years	18–19 years
UNITED STATES[1]	4,138,349	14.0	66.7	2,053.5	40.5	21.4	69.9
Alabama..	60,453	13.3	63.5	1,934.5	49.7	26.6	84.6
Alaska...	10,459	15.8	75.4	2,442.5	37.3	17.1	69.0
Arizona...	96,199	16.2	79.2	2,368.5	58.2	33.8	96.7
Arkansas...	39,208	14.1	69.1	2,092.0	59.1	29.1	103.9
California	548,882	15.2	71.3	2,183.0	38.8	21.0	67.6
Colorado	68,944	14.8	68.8	2,078.0	42.6	24.0	71.8
Connecticut.....................................	41,718	11.9	58.7	1,912.5	23.3	12.2	41.0
Delaware...	11,643	13.8	65.1	2,010.0	44.0	22.8	76.0
District of Columbia........................	7,971	14.5	59.8	1,787.0	63.4	39.9	99.8
Florida	226,240	12.7	65.6	2,060.0	42.4	21.7	75.1
Georgia	142,200	15.7	70.0	2,143.5	52.7	27.7	91.7
Hawaii	17,924	14.1	72.9	2,276.0	36.2	19.0	61.8
Idaho..	23,062	16.1	77.4	2,319.0	37.7	16.7	68.5
Illinois..	179,020	14.0	66.4	2,027.0	38.6	21.5	65.5
Indiana...	87,193	13.9	67.3	2,059.0	43.2	20.5	78.9
Iowa...	39,311	13.3	65.4	2,005.0	32.6	16.1	56.1
Kansas..	39,888	14.5	70.4	2,136.0	41.4	20.0	72.4
Kentucky...	56,444	13.5	64.7	1,992.0	49.1	24.4	86.4
Louisiana	60,937	13.5	62.6	1,868.5	49.1	25.6	83.5
Maine..	14,112	10.7	53.6	1,780.0	24.4	10.7	44.8
Maryland...	74,980	13.4	62.8	1,995.5	31.8	16.9	55.9
Massachusetts	76,865	12.0	56.1	1,714.5	21.8	11.4	38.1
Michigan...	127,706	12.6	61.0	1,908.5	32.5	16.8	57.4
Minnesota	70,919	13.8	64.9	2,024.0	26.1	12.5	46.0
Mississippi	42,395	14.5	67.8	2,016.0	60.5	33.1	101.9
Missouri..	78,618	13.6	65.0	1,993.0	42.5	21.1	74.2
Montana	11,583	12.4	63.2	1,983.5	35.2	17.6	60.3
Nebraska...	26,145	14.9	72.1	2,188.5	34.2	18.9	56.1
Nevada	37,268	15.4	74.5	2,268.5	50.1	27.8	87.0
New Hampshire...............................	14,420	11.0	53.3	1,782.5	17.9	7.0	35.2
New Jersey	113,776	13.1	63.9	2,049.5	23.4	12.0	42.0
New Mexico	28,835	15.0	72.8	2,208.0	61.6	37.4	97.1
New York	246,351	12.8	60.3	1,856.5	26.5	13.7	46.4
North Carolina................................	123,096	14.2	67.2	2,064.0	48.5	25.7	84.8
North Dakota	8,390	13.2	65.3	1,979.0	29.7	13.9	50.4
Ohio...	148,388	12.9	63.0	1,957.5	38.9	19.6	68.5
Oklahoma	51,801	14.6	70.9	2,109.5	54.2	27.8	92.2
Oregon	45,922	12.6	61.6	1,853.5	33.0	15.7	59.8
Pennsylvania...................................	145,383	11.7	58.7	1,861.5	30.4	16.2	52.3
Rhode Island...................................	12,697	11.8	55.7	1,730.5	31.4	16.6	54.3
South Carolina	57,711	13.6	64.5	1,971.0	51.0	27.6	87.9
South Dakota	11,462	14.8	73.4	2,258.5	37.5	19.5	63.4
Tennessee	81,747	13.7	64.9	1,999.0	54.9	27.7	95.6
Texas..	385,915	16.9	77.6	2,339.0	61.6	36.0	100.7
Utah...	51,556	20.9	90.4	2,472.5	33.4	16.4	57.2
Vermont..	6,473	10.4	51.0	1,661.5	19.5	8.2	36.2
Virginia...	104,555	13.8	65.1	2,030.5	34.4	16.3	62.2
Washington	82,703	13.2	62.1	1,911.0	31.1	15.2	54.8
West Virginia...................................	20,836	11.5	58.8	1,803.5	43.4	21.0	76.7
Wisconsin	70,984	12.8	61.7	1,944.0	30.3	15.1	52.7
Wyoming	7,239	14.2	71.3	2,164.0	43.2	19.1	75.7
Puerto Rico.....................................	50,564	12.9	59.4	1,759.0	61.2	40.8	92.2
Virgin Islands	1,605	14.8	71.8	2,341.5	50.0	22.2	112.5
Guam..	3,187	18.9	85.0	2,576.0	59.2	33.5	100.5
American Samoa	1,720	27.6	125.5	3,922.0	34.2	11.7	74.6
Northern Marianas	1,335	16.6	41.4	1,163.0	30.4	22.2	40.1

[1]Excludes data for the territories.

Table A-18. Live Births by Race of Mother, by State and Territory, 2005

(Number.)

Area	All races	White	Black	American Indian or Alaska Native	Asian or Pacific Islander
UNITED STATES[1]	4,138,349	3,229,294	633,134	44,813	231,108
Alabama	60,453	41,252	18,136	190	875
Alaska	10,459	6,536	422	2,723	778
Arizona	96,199	83,147	3,645	6,454	2,953
Arkansas	39,208	30,807	7,473	241	687
California	548,882	445,277	32,252	3,121	68,232
Colorado	68,944	62,856	3,123	575	2,390
Connecticut	41,718	33,988	5,280	213	2,237
Delaware	11,643	8,192	2,912	38	501
District of Columbia	7,971	2,401	5,368	7	195
Florida	226,240	161,478	56,503	694	7,565
Georgia	142,200	90,958	46,027	262	4,953
Hawaii	17,924	5,115	487	117	12,205
Idaho	23,062	22,112	146	412	392
Illinois	179,020	138,884	30,710	287	9,139
Indiana	87,193	75,733	9,878	147	1,435
Iowa	39,311	36,603	1,508	254	946
Kansas	39,888	35,116	3,127	431	1,214
Kentucky	56,444	50,445	5,094	82	823
Louisiana	60,937	35,374	24,145	378	1,040
Maine	14,112	13,508	264	114	226
Maryland	74,980	43,285	26,526	189	4,980
Massachusetts	76,865	62,406	8,800	177	5,482
Michigan	127,706	100,039	22,509	729	4,429
Minnesota	70,919	57,776	6,898	1,468	4,777
Mississippi	42,395	23,045	18,659	283	408
Missouri	78,618	64,729	11,686	443	1,760
Montana	11,583	9,914	63	1,487	119
Nebraska	26,145	23,233	1,718	497	697
Nevada	37,268	30,664	3,219	479	2,906
New Hampshire	14,420	13,572	232	29	587
New Jersey	113,776	82,659	19,990	178	10,949
New Mexico	28,835	24,119	540	3,716	460
New York	246,351	170,021	54,360	673	21,297
North Carolina	123,096	89,636	28,433	1,685	3,342
North Dakota	8,390	7,195	129	960	106
Ohio	148,388	120,507	24,120	293	3,468
Oklahoma	51,801	40,036	4,821	5,854	1,090
Oregon	45,922	41,561	1,011	848	2,502
Pennsylvania	145,383	115,899	23,294	361	5,829
Rhode Island	12,697	10,705	1,288	149	555
South Carolina	57,711	36,098	20,369	216	1,028
South Dakota	11,462	9,267	145	1,939	111
Tennessee	81,747	61,409	18,484	157	1,697
Texas	385,915	327,298	44,076	896	13,645
Utah	51,556	48,934	482	640	1,500
Vermont	6,473	6,271	78	14	110
Virginia	104,555	74,323	22,911	162	7,159
Washington	82,703	67,917	4,230	2,083	8,473
West Virginia	20,836	19,935	707	16	178
Wisconsin	70,984	60,461	6,794	1,117	2,612
Wyoming	7,239	6,770	63	336	70
Puerto Rico	50,564	45,556	4,991	—	—
Virgin Islands	1,605	415	1,168	10	12
Guam	3,187	279	31	5	2,872
American Samoa	1,720	2	–	–	1,718
Northern Marianas	1,335	19	1	–	1,315

– = Quantity zero.
— = Data not available.
[1]Excludes data for the territories.

Table A-19. Live Births by Hispanic Origin and Race of Mothers, by State and Territory, 2005

(Number.)

Area	All origins	Total	Hispanic[1]					Non-Hispanic			Not stated
			Mexican	Puerto Rican	Cuban	Central and South American	Other and unknown Hispanic	Total[2]	White	Black	
UNITED STATES[3]................	4,138,349	985,505	693,197	63,340	16,064	151,201	61,703	3,123,005	2,279,768	583,759	29,839
Alabama............................	60,453	4,020	2,957	102	21	596	344	56,382	37,302	18,057	51
Alaska................................	10,459	779	360	68	11	54	286	9,584	5,947	374	96
Arizona..............................	96,199	42,852	40,069	324	66	1,019	1,374	51,513	40,065	3,019	1,834
Arkansas............................	39,208	4,038	3,323	49	12	604	50	35,019	26,717	7,406	151
California..........................	548,882	282,842	246,526	2,118	755	27,675	5,768	258,702	159,723	30,520	7,338
Colorado............................	68,944	21,785	17,469	291	72	852	3,101	47,153	41,454	2,959	6
Connecticut........................	41,718	8,004	1,035	4,364	79	2,299	227	33,647	26,369	4,872	67
Delaware............................	11,643	1,652	1,002	256	6	379	9	9,886	6,479	2,875	105
District of Columbia.............	7,971	1,111	140	13	1	902	55	6,835	2,062	4,604	25
Florida...............................	226,240	63,756	16,882	10,985	11,409	23,341	1,139	161,815	106,530	48,266	669
Georgia..............................	142,200	21,891	16,981	617	140	3,981	172	118,381	68,123	45,327	1,928
Hawaii................................	17,924	2,789	534	754	22	131	1,348	15,091	4,194	409	44
Idaho.................................	23,062	3,488	2,981	25	8	92	382	19,455	18,627	120	119
Illinois...............................	179,020	43,441	36,942	2,629	175	1,759	1,936	135,473	95,694	30,411	106
Indiana..............................	87,193	8,039	6,992	325	19	625	78	78,816	67,491	9,796	338
Iowa	39,311	3,115	2,486	63	8	466	92	36,081	33,452	1,479	115
Kansas...............................	39,888	6,121	4,698	99	19	438	867	33,608	29,296	2,819	159
Kentucky............................	56,444	2,509	1,741	133	100	223	312	53,901	48,209	4,841	34
Louisiana...........................	60,937	1,897	883	120	77	472	345	58,972	33,656	23,964	68
Maine	14,112	181	38	31	6	30	76	13,908	13,315	256	23
Maryland	74,980	8,681	1,961	423	57	5,902	338	66,150	37,072	24,321	149
Massachusetts.....................	76,865	10,125	534	4,439	63	4,859	230	66,252	53,922	6,754	488
Michigan............................	127,706	8,611	6,932	470	94	615	500	115,124	88,214	22,133	3,971
Minnesota...........................	70,919	5,509	4,087	100	25	875	422	64,387	52,967	5,795	1,023
Mississippi..........................	42,395	1,170	742	30	10	87	301	41,180	21,859	18,633	45
Missouri.............................	78,618	4,271	3,231	147	51	318	524	74,246	60,650	11,479	101
Montana............................	11,583	396	197	14	5	27	153	10,908	9,281	58	279
Nebraska............................	26,145	3,854	2,911	44	11	554	334	22,284	19,751	1,523	7
Nevada	37,268	14,090	11,777	267	199	1,393	454	22,645	16,506	2,998	533
New Hampshire	14,420	522	129	136	17	166	74	13,674	12,908	187	224
New Jersey..........................	113,776	27,959	6,479	6,620	803	13,855	202	85,681	58,014	16,730	136
New Mexico........................	28,835	15,823	7,800	81	47	133	7,762	13,005	8,480	482	7
New York............................	246,351	57,419	11,115	14,251	500	27,099	4,454	188,313	125,158	41,901	619
North Carolina	123,096	19,519	14,524	843	138	3,847	167	103,451	70,288	28,195	126
North Dakota......................	8,390	179	100	9	1	11	58	7,910	6,731	122	301
Ohio	148,388	6,070	3,270	1,143	81	941	635	141,092	114,997	22,566	1,226
Oklahoma...........................	51,801	6,275	5,722	122	14	367	50	45,359	33,955	4,718	167
Oregon...............................	45,922	9,165	8,404	106	54	404	197	36,515	32,349	958	242
Pennsylvania	145,383	12,208	2,751	6,208	173	1,880	1,196	131,825	106,486	19,816	1,350
Rhode Island	12,697	2,559	196	694	26	1,576	67	8,437	6,616	1,149	1,701
South Carolina	57,711	4,990	3,529	295	46	815	305	52,608	32,818	18,696	113
South Dakota......................	11,462	392	249	25	2	72	44	11,054	8,925	143	16
Tennessee	81,747	7,000	4,720	266	63	1,084	867	74,592	56,488	16,496	155
Texas.................................	385,915	191,445	160,503	1,402	346	8,888	20,306	193,616	137,524	42,152	854
Utah	51,556	7,566	5,749	109	15	669	1,024	43,696	41,202	435	294
Vermont.............................	6,473	73	20	18	1	18	16	6,336	6,139	77	64
Virginia..............................	104,555	13,058	3,521	695	88	7,798	956	91,337	62,177	22,163	160
Washington........................	82,703	15,013	12,217	318	81	677	1,720	65,583	53,733	3,239	2,107
West Virginia	20,836	174	78	13	3	34	46	20,608	19,723	696	54
Wisconsin...........................	70,984	6,252	4,957	675	39	287	294	64,703	54,342	6,719	29
Wyoming............................	7,239	828	753	11	5	12	47	6,389	5,960	52	22
Puerto Rico	50,564	47,457	68	45,634	48	1,675	32	3,098	2,922	160	9
Virgin Islands......................	1,605	377	3	88	–	135	151	1,154	134	1,000	74
Guam	3,187	56	23	17	1	4	11	3,110	249	29	21
American Samoa.................	1,720	—-	—-	—-	—-	—-	—-	—-	—-	—-	1,720
Northern Marianas..............	1,335	—-	—-	—-	—-	—-	—-	—-	—-	—-	1,335

– = Quantity zero.

—- = Data not available.

[1]Persons of Hispanic origin may be of any race.

[2]Includes races other than White and Black.

[3]Excludes data for the territories.

Table A-20. Live Births, Birth Rates, and Fertility Rates by Hispanic Origin and Race of Mothers, by State and Territory, Preliminary 2006

(Birth rates are total births per 1,000 total population; fertility rates are total births per 1,000 women aged 15–44 years.)

Area	All races and origins[1]	Non-Hispanic White	American Indian or Alaska Native total	Asian or Pacific Islander total	Hispanic[2]	Birth rate All races	Fertility rate All races
UNITED STATES[3]	4,265,996	2,309,833	47,494	239,829	1,039,051	14.2	68.5
Alabama	63,235	38,144	192	829	4,695	13.7	67.0
Alaska	10,991	6,285	2,716	897	752	16.4	76.7
Arizona	102,475	43,378	6,605	3,221	45,534	16.6	81.6
Arkansas	40,973	27,686	272	647	4,400	14.6	72.3
California	562,431	158,424	3,425	70,812	293,320	15.4	71.8
Colorado	70,750	42,127	612	2,421	22,813	14.9	70.2
Connecticut	41,807	25,648	227	2,223	8,482	11.9	58.8
Delaware	11,988	6,579	30	489	1,882	14.0	67.3
District of Columbia	8,529	2,142	7	184	1,327	14.7	58.5
Florida	236,882	107,503	789	7,531	70,060	13.1	67.3
Georgia	148,619	69,491	319	5,129	23,675	15.9	72.4
Hawaii	18,982	4,585	75	12,764	3,039	14.8	73.9
Idaho	24,184	19,496	416	349	3,792	16.5	80.9
Illinois	180,583	95,327	309	9,315	44,341	14.1	66.8
Indiana	88,674	67,983	152	1,561	8,458	14.0	68.3
Iowa	40,610	34,516	240	962	3,227	13.6	69.1
Kansas	40,964	29,670	400	1,364	6,586	14.8	73.3
Kentucky	58,291	49,256	87	980	2,777	13.9	67.2
Louisiana	63,399	35,544	426	996	2,233	14.8	70.6
Maine	14,151	13,298	84	241	218	10.7	54.5
Maryland	77,478	37,000	176	4,735	10,086	13.8	64.2
Massachusetts	77,769	53,712	173	5,654	10,755	12.1	57.0
Michigan	127,476	87,151	722	4,656	8,682	12.6	61.7
Minnesota	73,559	54,075	1,732	5,036	6,038	14.2	68.7
Mississippi	46,069	22,628	323	439	1,555	15.8	75.8
Missouri	81,388	62,116	402	1,915	4,556	13.9	67.9
Montana	12,506	9,820	1,620	121	401	13.2	69.5
Nebraska	26,733	19,980	574	699	4,000	15.1	75.1
Nevada	40,085	17,284	435	2,954	15,621	16.1	78.0
New Hampshire	14,380	12,835	18	536	585	10.9	53.4
New Jersey	115,006	56,943	192	11,151	29,202	13.2	64.4
New Mexico	29,937	8,590	3,974	548	16,514	15.3	74.7
New York	250,091	125,297	636	22,036	59,331	13.0	61.1
North Carolina	127,841	71,361	1,731	3,737	21,214	14.4	69.0
North Dakota	8,622	7,110	1,026	105	249	13.6	68.7
Ohio	150,590	115,912	329	3,216	6,736	13.1	64.7
Oklahoma	54,018	34,911	6,054	1,105	7,065	15.1	74.7
Oregon	48,717	33,876	922	2,720	9,947	13.2	65.5
Pennsylvania	149,082	107,610	457	5,953	13,294	12.0	60.6
Rhode Island	12,379	6,123	154	576	2,558	11.6	54.6
South Carolina	62,271	34,492	256	1,278	5,888	14.4	69.7
South Dakota	11,917	9,169	2,048	141	401	15.2	78.4
Tennessee	84,345	57,166	270	2,012	7,938	14.0	67.5
Texas	399,612	139,913	1,134	14,748	198,291	17.0	78.8
Utah	53,499	42,222	709	1,660	8,224	21.0	94.1
Vermont	6,509	6,198	17	108	74	10.4	52.2
Virginia	107,817	62,492	156	7,423	14,463	14.1	66.3
Washington	86,848	56,242	2,268	8,634	15,785	13.6	65.2
West Virginia	20,928	19,757	22	177	219	11.5	59.4
Wisconsin	72,335	54,541	1,233	2,735	6,870	13.0	64.0
Wyoming	7,670	6,224	347	104	897	14.9	75.9
Puerto Rico	48,590	1,328	–	–	47,143	12.4	57.2
Virgin Islands	1,431	101	51	–	253	13.2	64.6
Guam	—	—	—	—	—	—	—
American Samoa	1,442	—	–	1,440	—	25.0	110.4
Northern Marianas	1,422	—	–	1,403	—	17.2	42.4

– = Quantity zero.

— = Data not available.

[1]Includes Hispanic origin not stated.

[2]Persons of Hispanic origin may be of any race.

[3]Excludes data for the territories.

Table A-21. Total Number of Births, Rates (Birth, Fertility, and Total Fertility), and Percentage of Births with Selected Demographic Characteristics, by Race of Mother, 2005

(Number, live births per 1,000 population, percent.)

Characteristic	All races	White	Black	American Indian or Alaska Native	Asian or Pacific Islander
Number					
Births	4,138,349	3,229,294	633,134	44,813	231,108
Rate					
Birth rate	14.0	13.4	16.2	14.2	16.5
Fertility rate	66.7	66.3	69.0	59.9	66.6
Total fertility rate	2,053.5	2,056.0	2,070.5	1,750.0	1,889.0
Sex ratio[1]	1,049	1,052	1,030	1,024	1,066
Percent of All Births					
Births to mothers under 20 years	10.2	9.3	16.9	17.7	3.3
4th-and higher-order births	11.1	10.5	15.1	19.6	6.5
Births to unmarried mothers	36.9	31.7	69.3	63.5	16.2
Mothers born in the 50 states and D.C.	75.4	77.6	83.3	95.1	18.1
Mean					
Age of mother at first birth	25.2	25.4	22.8	21.7	28.5

[1]Male live births per 1,000 female live births.

Table A-22. Total Number of Births, Rates (Birth, Fertility, and Total Fertility), and Percentage of Births with Selected Demographic Characteristics, by Hispanic Origin of Mother and by Race for Mothers of Non-Hispanic Origin, 2005

(Number, live births per 1,000 population, percent.)

Characteristic	All origins[2]	Hispanic[1]						Non-Hispanic		
		Total	Mexican	Puerto Rican	Cuban	Central and South American	Other and unknown Hispanic	Total[3]	White	Black
Number										
Births	4,138,349	985,505	693,197	63,340	16,064	151,201	61,703	3,123,005	2,279,768	583,759
Rate										
Birth rate[4]	14.0	23.1	24.7	17.2	10.2	22.8	(4)	12.4	11.5	15.7
Fertility rate[4]	66.7	99.4	107.7	72.1	50.4	93.2	(4)	60.4	58.3	67.2
Total fertility rate[4]	2053.5	2885.0	3055.5	2137.5	1583.0	2822.5	(4)	1885.5	1839.5	2019.0
Sex ratio[5]	1,049	1,045	1,045	1,032	1,071	1,051	1,030	1,051	1,055	1,030
Percent of All Births										
Births to mothers under 20 years	10.2	14.1	14.9	17.4	7.7	8.6	17.1	8.9	7.3	17.0
4th-and higher-order births	11.1	14.0	15.2	12.3	4.9	10.7	12.4	10.2	9.0	15.3
Births to unmarried mothers	36.9	48.0	46.7	61.7	36.4	49.2	48.6	33.4	25.3	69.9
Mothers born in the 50 states and D.C.	75.4	37.0	35.4	68.6	47.9	13.2	77.9	87.5	94.1	87.3
Mean										
Age of mother at first birth	25.2	23.1	22.5	22.8	26.5	25.2	23.1	25.7	26.2	22.7

[1]Persons of Hispanic origin may be of any race.
[2]Includes origin not stated.
[3]Includes races other than White and Black.
[4]Rates for Central and South American include other and unknown Hispanic.
[5]Male live births per 1,000 female live births.

Table A-23. Live Births and Observed and Seasonally Adjusted Birth and Fertility Rates, by Month, 2005

(Number, rates on an annual basis per 1,000 population for specified month.)

Month	Number	Observed		Seasonally adjusted[1]	
		Birth rate	Fertility rate	Birth rate	Fertility rate
Total..	4,138,349	14.0	66.7	. . .	. . .
January..	331,478	13.2	62.9	13.9	65.9
February..	309,620	13.7	65.1	14.0	66.5
March	349,321	13.9	66.3	14.1	67.2
April	332,477	13.7	65.2	13.9	66.3
May..	346,276	13.8	65.7	14.0	66.6
June	350,879	14.4	68.8	14.2	68.5
July..	357,053	14.2	67.7	13.7	65.2
August	369,316	14.7	70.1	14.1	67.6
September..	363,369	14.9	71.2	14.1	67.2
October..	344,639	13.7	65.4	13.6	65.0
November	335,667	13.7	65.8	14.0	67.1
December..	348,254	13.8	66.1	14.0	67.2

... = Not applicable.
[1]The method of seasonal adjustment, developed by the U.S. Census Bureau, is described in The X11 Variant of the Census Method II Seasonal Adjustment Program, Technical Paper No. 15 (1967 revision).

Table A-24. Live Births by Day of Week and Index of Occurrence by Method of Delivery, 2005

(Number, ratio.)

Day of the week	Average number of births	Index of occurrence[1]		
		Total[2]	Method of delivery	
			Vaginal	Cesarean
Total..	11,338	100.0	100.0	100.0
Sunday..	7,374	65.0	73.0	47.0
Monday	11,704	103.2	100.7	108.9
Tuesday..	13,169	116.2	112.6	124.2
Wednesday	13,038	115.0	112.2	121.3
Thursday	13,013	114.8	112.0	121.0
Friday..	12,664	111.7	107.2	121.8
Saturday..	8,459	74.6	82.5	56.6

[1]Index is the ratio of the average number of births by a specified method of delivery on a given day of the week to the average daily number of births by a specified method of delivery for the year, multiplied by 100.
[2]Includes method of delivery not stated.

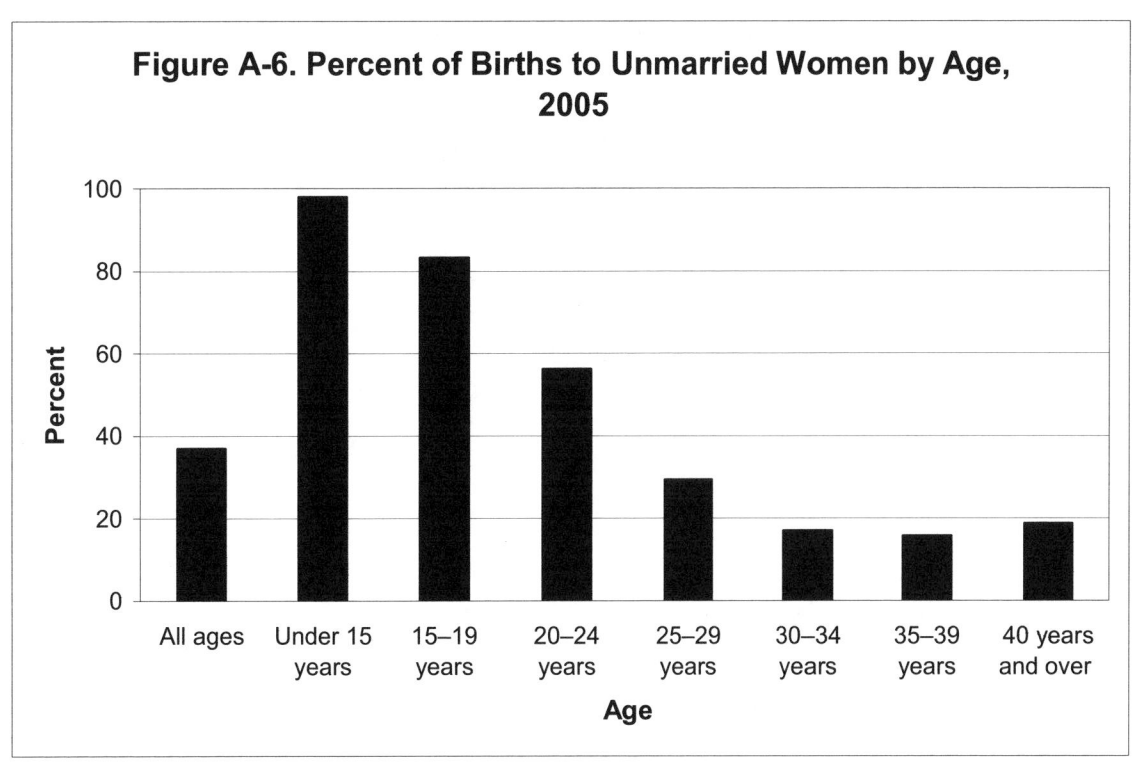

Figure A-6. Percent of Births to Unmarried Women by Age, 2005

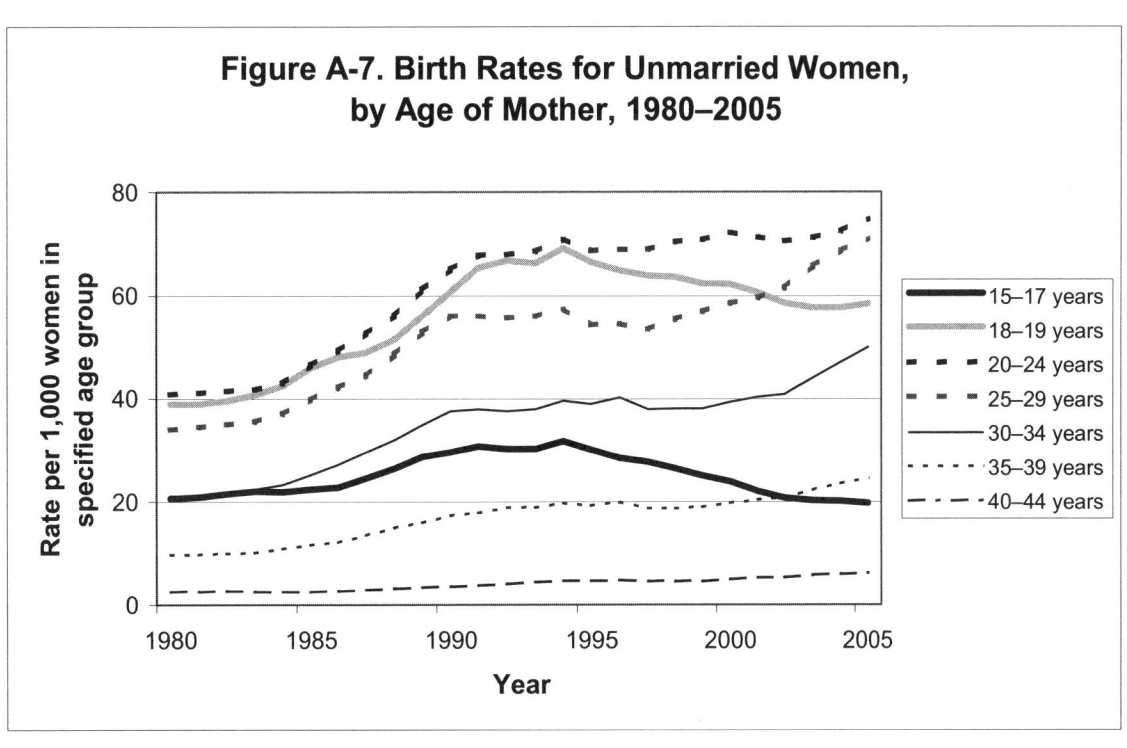

Figure A-7. Birth Rates for Unmarried Women, by Age of Mother, 1980–2005

Table A-25. Number, Birth Rate, and Percentage of Births to Unmarried Women by Age, Race, and Hispanic Origin of Mother, 2005

(Number, rate, percent.)

Measure and age of mother	All races[1]	White		Black		American Indian or Alaska Native	Asian or Pacific Islander	Hispanic[2]
		Total	Non-Hispanic	Total	Non-Hispanic			
Number								
All ages	1,527,034	1,022,560	577,617	438,614	407,756	28,461	37,399	472,649
Under 15 years	6,590	3,520	1,304	2,833	2,694	136	101	2,365
15–19 years	345,413	232,747	130,155	99,904	93,604	6,996	5,766	108,457
15 years	17,458	10,846	4,469	5,961	5,588	389	262	6,728
16 years	37,936	24,971	11,598	11,486	10,752	858	621	14,070
17 years	65,718	44,533	23,080	18,767	17,515	1,357	1,061	22,638
18 years	97,363	66,126	37,978	27,680	25,855	1,923	1,634	29,846
19 years	126,938	86,271	53,030	36,010	33,894	2,469	2,188	35,175
20–24 years	584,792	393,403	237,500	168,183	157,361	10,885	12,321	165,600
25–29 years	331,820	219,861	118,275	96,528	89,079	5,982	9,449	108,316
30–34 years	161,752	107,832	53,759	45,111	41,219	2,888	5,921	57,506
35–39 years	75,717	51,046	28,030	20,506	18,688	1,236	2,929	24,514
40 years and over	20,950	14,151	8,594	5,549	5,111	338	912	5,891
Rate per 1,000 Unmarried Women in Specified Group								
15–44 years[3]	47.5	43.0	30.1	67.8	—	—	24.9	100.3
15–19 years	34.5	29.9	20.9	60.6	—	—	13.1	68.0
15–17 years	19.7	16.8	10.3	35.4	—	—	7.3	42.7
18–19 years	58.4	50.9	37.4	101.6	—	—	22.1	112.4
20–24 years	74.9	66.6	49.1	120.7	—	—	29.7	150.4
25–29 years	71.1	66.3	45.0	93.8	—	—	35.1	153.5
30–34 years	50.0	49.1	31.2	54.0	—	—	36.6	118.1
35–39 years	24.5	23.8	16.0	26.1	—	—	24.7	59.2
40–44 years[4]	6.2	5.8	4.2	7.1	—	—	9.4	14.3
Percent of Births to Unmarried Women								
All ages	36.9	31.7	25.3	69.3	69.9	63.5	16.2	48.0
Under 15 years	98.0	96.6	98.0	99.9	99.9	100.0	97.1	95.9
15–19 years	83.3	78.8	78.9	96.1	96.7	89.6	75.7	79.2
15 years	95.7	93.7	95.0	99.5	99.8	97.0	92.9	92.9
16 years	92.4	89.6	91.5	99.0	99.3	96.0	88.1	88.3
17 years	89.0	85.5	87.1	98.2	98.7	92.9	85.4	84.2
18 years	83.6	79.2	80.2	96.5	97.1	89.8	75.7	78.4
19 years	77.0	71.7	71.8	93.5	94.1	84.8	67.8	72.1
20–24 years	56.2	49.8	46.1	82.6	83.4	71.0	39.9	57.5
25–29 years	29.3	24.4	18.4	61.8	62.3	53.5	14.6	40.6
30–34 years	17.0	14.1	9.2	44.7	44.6	43.6	7.4	30.9
35–39 years	15.7	13.1	9.2	39.7	39.4	41.6	7.5	28.6
40 years and over	18.8	16.1	12.5	39.8	39.5	44.5	10.6	30.2

— =Data not available.
[1]Includes races other than White and Black and origin not stated.
[2]Persons of Hispanic origin may be of any race.
[3]Birth rates computed by relating total births to unmarried mothers, regardless of age of mother, to unmarried women aged 15–44 years.
[4]Birth rates computed by relating births to unmarried mothers aged 40 years and over to unmarried women aged 40–44 years.

NOTE: For 48 states and the District of Columbia, marital status is reported in the birth registration process; for Michigan and New York, mother's marital status is inferred. Rates cannot be computed for unmarried non-Hispanic black women or for American Indian women because the necessary populations are not available.

Table A-26. Birth Rates for Unmarried Women by Age of Mother, 1970, 1975, and 1980–2005, and by Age, Race, and Hispanic Origin of Mother, 1980–2005

(Live births to unmarried women per 1,000 unmarried women.)

Year and race and Hispanic origin	15–44 years[1]	Age of mother			20–24 years	25–29 years	30–34 years	35–39 years	40–44 years[2]
		15–19 years							
		Total	15–17 years	18–19 years					
All Races[3]									
1970[4,5]	26.4	22.4	17.1	32.9	38.4	37.0	27.1	13.6	3.5
1975[4,6]	24.5	23.9	19.3	32.5	31.2	27.5	17.9	9.1	2.6
1980[4,6]	29.4	27.6	20.6	39.0	40.9	34.0	21.1	9.7	2.6
1980[6,7]	28.4	27.5	20.7	38.7	39.7	31.4	18.5	8.4	2.3
1981[6,7]	29.5	27.9	20.9	39.0	41.1	34.5	20.8	9.8	2.6
1982[6,7]	30.0	28.7	21.5	39.6	41.5	35.1	21.9	10.0	2.7
1983[6,7]	30.3	29.5	22.0	40.7	41.8	35.5	22.4	10.2	2.6
1984[6,7]	31.0	30.0	21.9	42.5	43.0	37.1	23.3	10.9	2.5
1985[7]	32.8	31.4	22.4	45.9	46.5	39.9	25.2	11.6	2.5
1986[7]	34.2	32.3	22.8	48.0	49.3	42.2	27.2	12.2	2.7
1987[7]	36.0	33.8	24.5	48.9	52.6	44.5	29.6	13.5	2.9
1988[7]	38.5	36.4	26.4	51.5	56.0	48.5	32.0	15.0	3.2
1989[7]	41.6	40.1	28.7	56.0	61.2	52.8	34.9	16.0	3.4
1990[7]	43.8	42.5	29.6	60.7	65.1	56.0	37.6	17.3	3.6
1991[7]	45.0	44.6	30.8	65.4	67.8	56.0	37.9	17.9	3.8
1992[7]	44.9	44.2	30.2	66.7	67.9	55.6	37.6	18.8	4.1
1993[7]	44.8	44.0	30.3	66.2	68.5	55.9	38.0	18.9	4.4
1994[7]	46.2	45.8	31.7	69.1	70.9	57.4	39.6	19.7	4.7
1995[7]	44.3	43.8	30.1	66.5	68.7	54.3	38.9	19.3	4.7
1996[7]	43.8	42.2	28.5	64.9	68.9	54.5	40.2	19.9	4.8
1997[7]	42.9	41.4	27.7	63.9	68.9	53.4	37.9	18.7	4.6
1998[7]	43.3	40.9	26.5	63.6	70.4	55.4	38.1	18.7	4.6
1999[7]	43.3	39.7	25.0	62.3	70.8	56.9	38.1	19.0	4.6
2000[7]	44.1	39.0	23.9	62.2	72.2	58.5	39.3	19.7	5.0
2001[7]	43.8	37.0	22.0	60.6	71.3	59.5	40.4	20.4	5.3
2002[7]	43.7	35.4	20.8	58.6	70.5	61.5	40.8	20.8	5.4
2003[7]	44.9	34.8	20.3	57.6	71.2	65.7	44.0	22.3	5.8
2004[7]	46.1	34.7	20.1	57.7	72.5	68.6	47.0	23.5	6.0
2005[7]	47.5	34.5	19.7	58.4	74.9	71.1	50.0	24.5	6.2
White									
1980[6,7]	18.1	16.5	12.0	24.1	25.1	21.5	14.1	7.1	1.8
1981[6,7]	18.6	17.2	12.6	24.6	25.8	22.3	14.2	7.2	1.9
1982[6,7]	19.3	18.0	13.1	25.3	26.5	23.1	15.3	7.4	2.1
1983[6,7]	19.8	18.7	13.6	26.4	27.1	23.8	15.9	7.8	2.0
1984[6,7]	20.6	19.3	13.7	27.9	28.5	25.5	16.8	8.4	2.0
1985[7]	22.5	20.8	14.5	31.2	31.7	28.5	18.4	9.0	2.0
1986[7]	23.9	21.8	14.9	33.5	34.2	30.5	20.1	9.7	2.2
1987[7]	25.3	23.2	16.2	34.5	36.6	32.0	22.3	10.7	2.4
1988[7]	27.4	25.3	17.6	36.8	39.2	35.4	24.2	12.1	2.7
1989[7]	30.2	28.0	19.3	40.2	43.8	39.1	26.8	13.1	2.9
1990[7]	32.9	30.6	20.4	44.9	48.2	43.0	29.9	14.5	3.2
1991[7]	34.5	32.7	21.7	49.4	51.4	44.3	30.9	15.2	3.2
1992[7]	35.0	32.7	21.4	51.2	52.4	44.8	31.3	16.1	3.6
1993[7]	35.6	33.3	21.9	52.0	53.8	46.0	31.9	16.3	3.9
1994[7]	37.8	35.8	23.9	55.8	57.5	48.6	33.8	17.2	4.3
1995[7]	37.0	35.0	23.3	54.7	57.2	47.4	33.7	16.8	4.2
1996[7]	37.0	34.0	22.3	53.5	57.9	48.1	35.4	17.7	4.3
1997[7]	36.3	33.6	22.0	52.9	57.9	47.0	33.6	16.6	3.9
1998[7]	36.9	33.6	21.5	53.1	59.5	48.6	34.1	16.9	4.1
1999[7]	37.4	33.2	20.6	52.9	60.2	50.8	34.9	17.4	4.1
2000[7]	38.2	32.7	19.7	53.1	61.7	52.9	35.9	17.9	4.5
2001[7]	38.5	31.3	18.1	52.1	61.8	54.6	37.2	18.6	4.9
2002[7]	38.9	30.4	17.5	51.0	61.6	56.8	38.3	19.4	5.0
2003[7]	40.4	30.1	17.2	50.4	63.0	60.8	42.0	21.2	5.5
2004[7]	41.6	30.1	17.1	50.4	64.1	63.9	45.7	22.6	5.6
2005[7]	43.0	29.9	16.8	50.9	66.6	66.3	49.1	23.8	5.8

[1]Rates computed by relating total births to unmarried mothers, regardless of age of mother, to unmarried women aged 15–44 years.
[2]Rates computed by relating births to unmarried mothers aged 40 years and over to unmarried women aged 40–44 years.
[3]Includes races other than White, Black, and Asian or Pacific Islander.
[4]Births to unmarried women are estimated for the United States from data for registration areas in which marital status of mother was reported.
[5]Based on a 50-percent sample of births.
[6]Based on 100 percent of births in selected states and on a 50-percent sample of births in all other states.
[7]Data for states in which marital status was not reported have been inferred and included with data from the remaining states.

Table A-26. Birth Rates for Unmarried Women by Age of Mother, 1970, 1975, and 1980–2005, and by Age, Race, and Hispanic Origin of Mother, 1980–2005—*Continued*

(Live births to unmarried women per 1,000 unmarried women.)

Year and race and Hispanic origin	15–44 years[1]	Age of mother							
		15–19 years			20–24 years	25–29 years	30–34 years	35–39 years	40–44 years[2]
		Total	15–17 years	18–19 years					
Non-Hispanic White									
1990[7,8]	24.4	25.0	16.2	37.0	36.4	30.3	20.5	6.1	—
1991[7]	—	—	—	—	—	—	—	—	—
1992[7]	—	—	—	—	—	—	—	—	—
1993[7]	—	—	—	—	—	—	—	—	—
1994[7]	28.4	28.1	17.9	45.0	43.8	34.7	24.6	12.8	3.1
1995[7]	28.1	27.7	17.6	44.6	43.9	34.4	25.1	12.9	3.2
1996[7]	28.2	27.0	16.9	43.9	44.5	35.0	26.4	13.8	3.3
1997[7]	27.5	26.4	16.2	43.3	44.8	34.4	24.9	12.7	2.9
1998[7]	27.9	26.2	15.5	43.1	46.3	35.4	25.0	13.1	3.1
1999[7]	27.9	25.6	14.6	42.7	46.3	36.2	24.8	13.0	3.1
2000[7]	28.0	24.7	13.6	42.1	47.0	36.9	24.8	12.9	3.3
2001[7]	27.8	23.1	12.1	40.3	46.4	37.5	25.4	13.2	3.6
2002[7]	27.8	22.1	11.5	38.8	46.1	38.5	26.0	13.5	3.7
2003[7]	28.6	21.5	11.0	37.9	47.2	40.8	27.8	14.7	4.1
2004[7]	29.4	21.2	10.7	37.5	48.0	43.3	29.6	15.6	4.1
2005[7]	30.1	20.9	10.3	37.4	49.1	45.0	31.2	16.0	4.2
Black									
1980[6,7]	81.1	87.9	68.8	118.2	112.3	81.4	46.7	19.0	5.5
1981[6,7]	79.4	85.0	65.9	114.2	110.7	83.1	45.5	19.6	5.6
1982[6,7]	77.9	85.1	66.3	112.7	109.3	82.7	44.1	19.5	5.2
1983[6,7]	76.2	85.5	66.8	111.9	107.2	79.7	43.8	19.4	4.8
1984[6,7]	75.2	86.1	66.5	113.6	107.9	77.8	43.8	19.4	4.3
1985[7]	77.0	87.6	66.8	117.9	113.1	79.3	47.5	20.4	4.3
1986[7]	79.0	88.5	67.0	121.1	118.0	84.6	50.0	20.6	4.4
1987[7]	82.6	90.9	69.9	123.0	126.1	91.6	53.1	22.4	4.7
1988[7]	86.5	96.1	73.5	130.5	133.6	97.2	57.4	24.1	5.0
1989[7]	90.7	104.5	78.9	140.9	142.4	102.9	60.5	24.9	5.0
1990[7]	90.5	106.0	78.8	143.7	144.8	105.3	61.5	25.5	5.1
1991[7]	89.0	107.8	79.9	147.7	146.4	100.0	59.8	25.5	5.4
1992[7]	85.7	104.8	77.2	146.4	142.6	96.8	57.3	25.6	5.4
1993[7]	83.0	101.2	75.9	140.0	139.9	92.8	56.7	25.7	5.8
1997[7]	80.8	99.3	73.9	139.6	135.2	91.3	56.5	26.0	5.9
1995[7]	74.5	91.2	67.4	129.2	124.6	82.3	53.3	25.3	6.0
1996[7]	72.8	87.5	62.6	127.2	122.6	81.2	53.4	25.2	6.1
1997[7]	71.5	84.5	59.0	124.8	124.2	81.4	51.0	24.3	6.5
1998[7]	71.6	81.5	55.0	121.5	127.8	86.5	50.5	24.3	6.0
1999[7]	69.7	76.5	50.0	115.8	126.8	85.5	49.0	24.2	5.8
2000[7]	70.5	75.0	48.3	115.0	129.0	85.9	50.2	25.4	6.3
2001[7]	68.1	69.9	43.8	110.2	122.8	84.1	51.1	25.4	6.3
2002[7]	66.2	64.8	39.9	104.1	119.2	85.9	49.9	24.9	6.3
2003[4]	66.3	62.2	38.1	100.4	118.0	90.4	51.2	25.3	6.5
2004[7]	67.2	61.7	37.0	100.9	119.8	91.8	52.0	25.8	6.8
2005[7]	67.8	60.6	35.4	101.6	120.7	93.8	54.0	26.1	7.1
Asian or Pacific Islander									
2000[7]	20.9	15.2	9.6	23.2	24.2	25.4	29.7	18.4	6.9
2001[7]	21.2	14.6	8.7	23.0	25.2	26.7	29.4	19.7	6.3
2002[7]	21.3	13.4	7.5	22.2	26.5	27.5	28.6	18.7	6.8
2003[7]	22.2	13.1	7.5	21.4	26.6	30.7	31.5	19.8	7.9
2004[7]	23.6	13.3	7.7	21.6	27.9	33.2	35.4	20.7	8.6
2005[7]	24.9	13.1	7.3	22.1	29.7	35.1	36.6	24.7	9.4

—— = Data not available.

[1]Rates computed by relating total births to unmarried mothers, regardless of age of mother, to unmarried women aged 15–44 years.
[2]Rates computed by relating births to unmarried mothers aged 40 years and over to unmarried women aged 40–44 years.
[7]Data for states in which marital status was not reported have been inferred and included with data from the remaining states.
[8]Rates for 1990 based on data for 48 states and the District of Columbia that reported Hispanic origin on the birth certificate. Rate shown for 1990 for ages 35–39 years are based on births to unmarried women aged 35–44 years.

Table A-26. Birth Rates for Unmarried Women by Age of Mother, 1970, 1975, and 1980–2005, and by Age, Race, and Hispanic Origin of Mother, 1980–2005—*Continued*

(Live births to unmarried women per 1,000 unmarried women.)

Year and race and Hispanic origin	Age of mother								
	15–44 years[1]	15–19 years			20–24 years	25–29 years	30–34 years	35–39 years	40–44 years[2]
		Total	15–17 years	18–19 years					
Hispanic[9]									
1990[7,8]...............	89.6	65.9	45.9	98.9	129.8	131.7	88.1	50.8	13.7
1991[7].................	92.5	71.0	49.5	107.5	134.2	135.1	88.2	47.6	14.1
1992[7].................	92.8	70.3	49.2	106.6	138.2	133.4	89.9	47.8	14.6
1993[7].................	91.4	71.1	49.6	108.8	134.3	130.4	87.8	47.1	14.1
1994[7].................	95.8	77.7	55.7	115.4	144.5	131.7	91.2	47.4	13.9
1995[7].................	88.8	73.2	52.8	108.6	135.8	122.3	84.1	42.2	12.1
1996[7].................	86.2	69.3	49.7	102.3	131.6	122.0	84.6	41.2	12.3
1997[7].................	83.2	69.2	50.7	100.6	122.8	114.8	78.8	40.5	12.1
1998[7].................	82.8	69.3	49.8	101.2	120.6	115.9	78.2	38.8	12.0
1999[7].................	84.9	68.6	48.7	99.9	126.1	119.6	84.2	42.4	11.2
2000[7].................	87.3	68.5	47.0	102.2	130.5	121.6	89.4	46.1	12.2
2001[7].................	87.8	67.1	44.2	104.3	132.3	120.7	91.4	49.7	12.2
2002[7].................	87.9	66.1	43.0	105.3	131.4	123.1	88.1	51.3	12.6
2003[7].................	92.2	66.6	43.0	107.0	133.7	136.0	99.2	54.7	13.3
2004[7].................	95.7	67.9	43.3	110.1	138.6	143.4	109.6	56.8	13.8
2005[7].................	100.3	68.0	42.7	112.4	150.4	153.5	118.1	59.2	14.3

[1]Rates computed by relating total births to unmarried mothers, regardless of age of mother, to unmarried women aged 15–44 years.

[2]Rates computed by relating births to unmarried mothers aged 40 years and over to unmarried women aged 40–44 years.

[7]Data for states in which marital status was not reported have been inferred and included with data from the remaining states.

[8]Rates for 1990 based on data for 48 states and the District of Columbia that reported Hispanic origin on the birth certificate. Rate shown for 1990 for ages 35–39 years are based on births to unmarried women aged 35–44 years.

[9]Persons of Hispanic origin of any race.

Table A-27. Number and Percentage of Births to Unmarried Women, by Race and Hispanic Origin of Mother, by State and Territory, 2005

(Number, percent.)

Area	Births to unmarried women				Percent unmarried			
	All races[1]	Non-Hispanic		Hispanic[2]	All races[1]	Non-Hispanic		Hispanic[2]
		White	Black			White	Black	
UNITED STATES[3]	1,527,034	577,617	407,756	472,649	36.9	25.3	69.9	48.0
Alabama	21,579	7,813	12,717	863	35.7	20.9	70.4	21.5
Alaska	3,768	1,392	194	294	36.0	23.4	51.9	37.7
Arizona	41,442	10,599	1,843	23,327	43.1	26.5	61.0	54.4
Arkansas	15,768	7,978	5,709	1,799	40.2	29.9	77.1	44.6
California	195,982	33,960	19,518	129,641	35.7	21.3	64.0	45.8
Colorado	18,657	7,578	1,555	8,979	27.1	18.3	52.6	41.2
Connecticut	13,425	4,909	3,286	5,009	32.2	18.6	67.4	62.6
Delaware	5,156	1,963	2,029	1,025	44.3	30.3	70.6	62.0
District of Columbia	4,464	121	3,556	750	56.0	5.9	77.2	67.5
Florida	96,809	33,558	32,992	28,797	42.8	31.5	68.4	45.2
Georgia	57,707	15,989	30,440	10,256	40.6	23.5	67.2	46.9
Hawaii	6,504	1,030	111	1,321	36.3	24.6	27.1	47.4
Idaho	5,290	3,641	32	1,322	22.9	19.5	26.7	37.9
Illinois	66,333	21,513	23,754	20,271	37.1	22.5	78.1	46.7
Indiana	35,009	22,647	7,622	4,376	40.2	33.6	77.8	54.4
Iowa	12,775	9,832	1,081	1,481	32.5	29.4	73.1	47.5
Kansas	13,647	8,192	2,041	2,986	34.2	28.0	72.4	48.8
Kentucky	20,049	15,055	3,597	1,242	35.5	31.2	74.3	49.5
Louisiana	29,230	9,746	18,390	711	48.0	29.0	76.7	37.5
Maine	4,941	4,659	91	78	35.0	35.0	35.5	43.1
Maryland	27,807	8,283	14,581	4,445	37.1	22.3	60.0	51.2
Massachusetts	23,182	11,750	3,941	6,457	30.2	21.8	58.4	63.8
Michigan	46,750	23,943	16,744	4,006	36.6	27.1	75.7	46.5
Minnesota	21,106	12,256	3,442	2,803	29.8	23.1	59.4	50.9
Mississippi	20,964	5,737	14,357	590	49.4	26.2	77.1	50.4
Missouri	29,712	18,339	8,826	2,071	37.8	30.2	76.9	48.5
Montana	4,002	2,603	25	173	34.6	28.0	43.1	43.7
Nebraska	8,077	4,802	1,061	1,817	30.9	24.3	69.7	47.1
Nevada	15,232	4,959	2,085	6,923	40.9	30.0	69.5	49.1
New Hampshire	3,939	3,498	70	245	27.3	27.1	37.4	46.9
New Jersey	35,780	8,424	11,084	15,590	31.4	14.5	66.3	55.8
New Mexico	14,642	2,581	279	8,963	50.8	30.4	57.9	56.6
New York	95,410	26,651	28,390	36,092	38.7	21.3	67.8	62.9
North Carolina	47,300	16,150	19,474	10,131	38.4	23.0	69.1	51.9
North Dakota	2,698	1,713	31	63	32.2	25.4	25.4	35.2
Ohio	57,756	35,989	17,205	3,407	38.9	31.3	76.2	56.1
Oklahoma	20,245	10,632	3,464	2,897	39.1	31.3	73.4	46.2
Oregon	15,276	9,540	620	4,190	33.3	29.5	64.7	45.7
Pennsylvania	53,128	28,904	15,090	7,484	36.5	27.1	76.2	61.3
Rhode Island	4,892	1,873	764	1,554	38.5	28.3	66.5	60.7
South Carolina	24,997	8,645	13,853	2,230	43.3	26.3	74.1	44.7
South Dakota	4,147	2,340	55	194	36.2	26.2	38.5	49.5
Tennessee	32,824	16,550	12,372	3,530	40.2	29.3	75.0	50.4
Texas	145,197	33,419	27,253	82,611	37.6	24.3	64.7	43.2
Utah	9,108	5,198	193	3,041	17.7	12.6	44.4	40.2
Vermont	2,091	1,988	32	25	32.3	32.4	41.6	34.2
Virginia	33,674	12,822	14,112	6,149	32.2	20.6	63.7	47.1
Washington	25,579	13,938	1,713	6,909	30.9	25.9	52.9	46.0
West Virginia	7,610	6,949	525	76	36.5	35.2	75.4	43.7
Wisconsin	23,056	13,318	5,526	3,055	32.5	24.5	82.2	48.9
Wyoming	2,376	1,705	32	400	32.8	28.6	61.5	48.3
Puerto Rico	28,555	1,611	116	26,815	56.5	55.1	72.5	56.5
Virgin Islands	1,138	36	772	277	70.9	26.9	77.2	73.5
Guam	1,901	40	6	21	59.6	16.1	*	37.5
American Samoa	587	—	—	—	34.1	—	—	—
Northern Marianas	747	—	—	—	56.0	—	—	—

* = Figure does not meet standards of reliability or precision.
—— = Data not available.
[1]Includes races other than White and Black and origin not stated.
[2]Persons of Hispanic origin may be of any race.
[3]Excludes data for territories.

Table A-28. Number and Percentage of Births to Unmarried Women, by Age, Final 2005 and Preliminary 2006

(Number, percent.)

Age of mother	Number		Percent	
	2005	2006	2005	2006
All ages	1,527,034	1,641,700	36.9	38.5
Under 20 years	352,003	372,826	83.5	84.4
Under 15 years	6,590	6,297	98.0	98.3
15–19 years	345,413	366,529	83.3	84.2
15–17 years	121,112	127,718	90.9	91.9
18–19 years	224,301	238,811	79.7	80.5
20–24 years	584,792	625,701	56.2	57.9
25–29 years	331,820	366,056	29.3	31.0
30–34 years	161,752	173,538	17.0	18.3
35–39 years	75,717	81,786	15.7	16.4
40–54 years	20,950	21,792	18.8	19.4

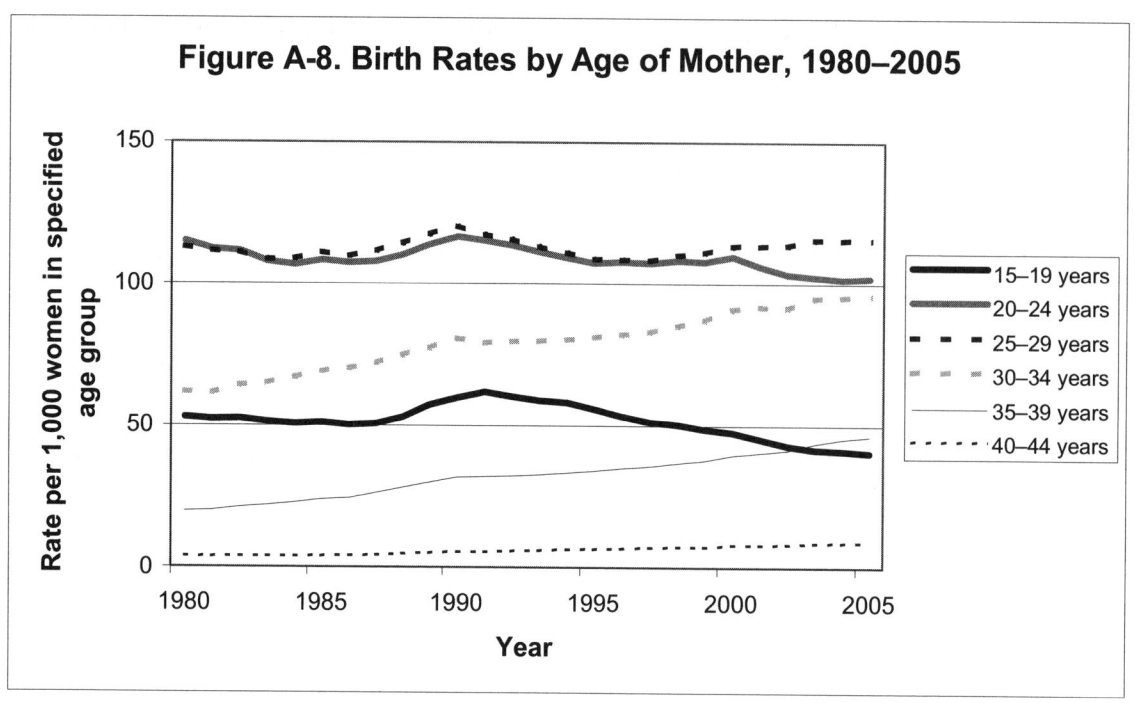

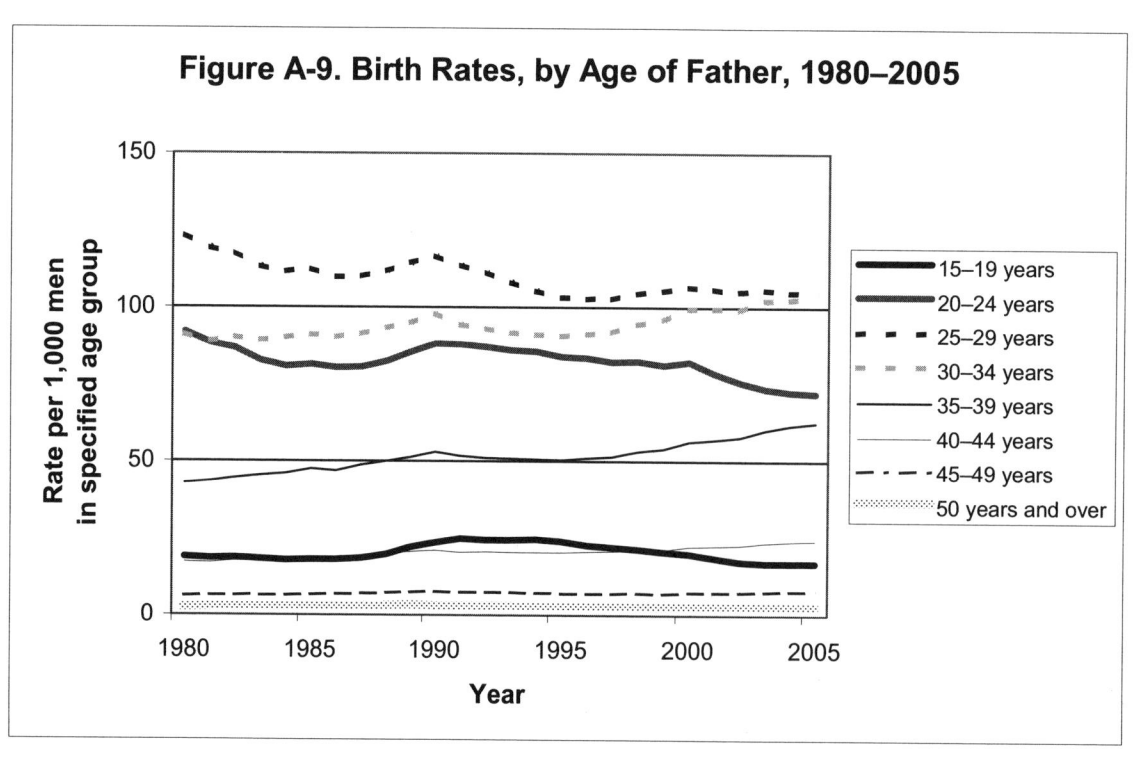

Table A-29. Birth Rates by Age and Race of Father, 1980–2005

(Live births per 1,000 men in specified group.)

Year and race of father	Age of father									
	15–54 years[1]	15–19 years[2]	20–24 years	25–29 years	30–34 years	35–39 years	40–44 years	45–49 years	50–54 years	55 years and over
All Races[3]										
1980[4]	57.0	18.8	92.0	123.1	91.0	42.8	17.1	6.1	2.2	0.3
1981[4]	56.3	18.4	88.4	119.1	88.7	43.3	17.0	6.2	2.3	0.4
1982[4]	56.4	18.6	86.5	117.3	90.3	44.5	17.5	6.4	2.3	0.4
1983[4]	55.1	18.2	82.6	113.0	89.1	45.2	17.4	6.4	2.3	0.4
1984[4]	55.0	17.8	80.7	111.4	89.9	46.0	17.8	6.3	2.4	0.4
1985	55.6	18.0	81.2	112.3	91.1	47.3	18.1	6.6	2.5	0.4
1986	54.8	17.9	80.3	109.6	90.3	46.8	18.3	6.7	2.6	0.4
1987	55.0	18.3	80.5	109.9	91.2	48.6	19.0	6.9	2.6	0.4
1988	55.8	19.6	82.4	111.6	93.2	49.9	19.9	7.1	2.7	0.4
1989	57.2	21.9	85.4	114.3	94.8	51.3	20.4	7.4	2.7	0.6
1990	58.4	23.5	88.0	116.4	97.8	53.0	21.0	7.5	2.8	0.4
1991	56.8	24.7	87.9	113.5	94.3	51.6	20.2	7.4	2.7	0.4
1992	55.3	24.4	87.1	111.1	93.0	51.1	20.4	7.3	2.7	0.4
1993	53.7	24.4	86.0	108.1	91.7	50.7	20.2	7.3	2.7	0.4
1994	52.4	24.6	85.6	105.3	91.1	50.5	20.3	7.2	2.6	0.3
1995	51.0	23.9	83.9	103.2	90.7	50.4	20.3	7.0	2.5	0.3
1996	50.2	22.7	83.4	102.8	91.3	51.1	20.5	6.9	2.5	0.3
1997	49.4	21.9	82.1	102.6	92.0	51.5	20.7	7.0	2.5	0.3
1998	49.6	21.3	82.3	104.4	94.4	53.1	21.0	7.1	2.5	0.3
1999	49.2	20.6	81.1	105.3	95.9	53.9	21.1	7.0	2.4	0.3
2000	50.0	19.8	82.1	106.5	99.5	56.3	22.2	7.3	2.5	0.3
2001	49.0	18.5	78.5	105.8	99.6	57.0	22.3	7.3	2.4	0.3
2002	48.4	17.4	75.6	105.0	99.1	57.7	22.6	7.4	2.4	0.3
2003	48.9	16.9	73.5	105.7	102.2	60.2	23.4	7.6	2.5	0.3
2004	48.8	17.0	72.4	104.9	102.5	61.7	23.9	7.7	2.4	0.3
2005	48.7	16.8	71.9	104.7	103.1	62.4	24.2	7.9	2.5	0.3
White										
1980[4]	53.4	15.4	84.9	119.4	87.8	39.7	15.0	5.1	1.8	0.3
1981[4]	52.9	15.0	81.7	115.8	85.8	40.3	15.0	5.2	1.8	0.3
1982[4]	53.1	14.9	80.1	114.2	87.5	41.7	15.6	5.3	1.9	0.3
1983[4]	52.0	14.4	76.3	110.2	86.8	42.6	15.5	5.3	1.8	0.3
1984[4]	51.8	14.0	74.3	108.8	87.9	43.5	16.0	5.3	1.9	0.3
1985	52.6	14.0	74.7	109.9	89.5	44.8	16.3	5.6	1.9	0.3
1986	51.7	13.8	73.3	107.0	88.7	44.4	16.6	5.7	2.0	0.3
1987	51.6	13.9	72.8	107.0	89.5	46.2	17.3	5.9	2.0	0.3
1988	52.2	14.8	73.7	108.3	91.2	47.6	18.1	6.1	2.1	0.3
1989	53.3	16.7	75.9	110.8	93.0	49.1	18.7	6.3	2.1	0.4
1990	54.6	18.1	78.3	113.2	96.1	50.9	19.2	6.5	2.2	0.3
1991	53.1	19.0	78.4	110.2	92.8	49.6	18.5	6.5	2.2	0.3
1992	51.8	18.8	77.8	108.2	91.9	49.1	18.8	6.4	2.2	0.3
1993	50.3	18.9	77.2	105.5	90.7	48.9	18.7	6.4	2.2	0.2
1994	49.3	19.5	77.4	103.1	90.4	48.9	18.9	6.3	2.2	0.3
1995	48.4	19.4	77.0	101.7	90.4	49.1	19.1	6.2	2.1	0.2
1996	47.7	18.7	76.7	101.4	91.1	49.9	19.2	6.1	2.1	0.2
1997	46.8	18.0	75.3	100.9	91.7	50.2	19.3	6.2	2.1	0.3
1998	47.1	17.7	75.6	102.7	94.3	51.9	19.6	6.3	2.1	0.3
1999	46.9	17.3	74.7	104.1	96.2	52.7	19.8	6.3	2.1	0.3
2000	47.6	16.6	75.8	105.4	99.5	54.7	20.7	6.5	2.1	0.3
2001	46.9	15.5	73.1	105.4	99.9	55.7	20.8	6.5	2.0	0.3
2002	46.4	14.8	70.8	104.8	99.4	56.4	21.0	6.6	2.0	0.3
2003	47.1	14.3	69.2	106.1	102.8	58.9	21.9	6.7	2.1	0.3
2004	46.7	14.3	67.7	105.0	102.5	60.2	22.2	6.8	2.0	0.2
2005	46.6	14.2	66.9	104.6	103.1	60.7	22.5	6.8	2.1	0.2

[1]Rates computed by relating total births, regardless of age of father, to men aged 15–54 years.
[2]Rates computed by relating births of fathers under 20 years of age to men aged 15–19 years.
[3]Includes races other than White and Black.
[4]Based on 100 percent of births in selected states and on a 50-percent sample of births in all other states.

Table A-29. Birth Rates by Age and Race of Father, 1980–2005—*Continued*

(Live births per 1,000 men in specified group.)

Year and race of father	Age of father									
	15–54 years[1]	15–19 years[2]	20–24 years	25–29 years	30–34 years	35–39 years	40–44 years	45–49 years	50–54 years	55 years and over
Black										
1980[4]	83.0	40.1	145.3	152.8	109.6	62.0	31.2	13.6	5.9	1.1
1981[4]	80.4	38.9	138.4	145.6	104.3	61.3	29.7	13.3	5.7	1.2
1982[4]	79.5	40.3	133.4	141.2	103.6	61.1	29.6	13.9	6.0	1.2
1983[4]	77.2	40.7	129.1	134.4	99.0	59.6	29.6	13.5	6.0	1.2
1984[4]	76.7	40.9	128.0	132.2	98.3	58.4	29.3	13.3	6.1	1.2
1985	77.2	41.8	129.5	132.7	97.3	59.4	29.5	13.3	6.5	1.2
1986	77.2	42.6	131.4	131.6	97.4	58.0	29.1	13.5	6.7	1.3
1987	78.3	44.6	136.1	133.9	97.4	58.0	30.0	13.8	6.6	1.3
1988	80.7	48.1	144.1	137.9	100.0	58.0	30.6	14.3	6.9	1.4
1989	84.1	52.9	153.4	143.5	101.4	59.9	31.1	14.9	6.9	2.7
1990	84.9	55.2	158.2	144.9	103.2	60.4	31.1	15.0	7.1	1.4
1991	83.0	57.8	158.5	142.0	99.2	58.5	29.4	14.1	6.7	1.4
1992	80.4	57.0	157.1	138.6	95.8	56.7	28.4	13.7	6.1	1.4
1993	77.6	56.2	152.7	134.2	94.0	56.3	27.7	13.4	6.3	1.3
1994	74.0	54.1	149.1	129.6	91.4	53.8	26.4	12.8	5.8	1.1
1995	69.1	49.9	139.2	123.9	87.7	52.0	25.7	11.9	5.4	1.1
1996	67.2	46.7	137.6	123.9	87.0	51.8	25.7	11.3	5.3	1.1
1997	66.7	45.1	136.3	126.3	88.8	52.6	26.1	11.4	5.2	1.0
1998	66.8	42.8	137.0	130.3	90.9	54.0	26.7	11.6	5.0	1.0
1999	65.4	41.0	133.8	129.6	91.6	54.3	26.5	11.2	4.9	1.0
2000	66.2	39.6	135.5	131.0	95.2	56.9	28.4	11.7	5.0	1.0
2001	63.3	36.5	124.5	125.9	95.6	57.1	28.2	11.8	4.7	1.0
2002	61.2	33.3	116.2	123.6	94.0	57.8	28.5	12.0	4.7	0.9
2003	61.0	32.5	111.9	122.3	96.2	59.9	29.6	12.4	4.9	0.9
2004	61.7	32.7	111.6	122.7	98.7	61.8	30.4	12.7	4.9	0.8
2005	62.5	32.2	112.1	123.6	101.0	64.1	31.5	13.6	5.2	0.7

[1]Rates computed by relating total births, regardless of age of father, to men aged 15–54 years.
[2]Rates computed by relating births of fathers under 20 years of age to men aged 15–19 years.
[3]Includes races other than White and Black.
[4]Based on 100 percent of births in selected states and on a 50-percent sample of births in all other states.

Table A-30. Number of Live Births and Percent Distribution, by Weight Gain of Mother During Pregnancy, According to Period of Gestation, Race, and Hispanic Origin of Mother: Total of 49 Reporting States and the District of Columbia, 2005

(Number, percent distribution.)

Period of gestation[1], race, and Hispanic origin of mother	All births	Less than 16 pounds	16–20 pounds	21–25 pounds	26–30 pounds	31–35 pounds	36–40 pounds	41–45 pounds	46 pounds or more	Not stated
NUMBER										
All Gestation Periods[2]										
All races[3]	3,589,467	443,454	369,024	450,359	569,903	457,238	415,240	242,280	458,047	183,922
Non-Hispanic White	2,120,045	218,632	186,346	258,886	344,988	293,641	268,035	160,389	302,017	87,111
Non-Hispanic Black	553,239	97,263	64,673	65,988	77,820	55,216	53,912	30,710	68,982	38,675
Hispanic[4]	702,663	104,391	95,262	95,577	110,183	80,089	69,500	38,628	67,986	41,047
Under 34 Weeks										
All races[3]	133,938	33,486	19,035	16,229	16,578	10,798	9,571	5,280	11,196	11,765
Non-Hispanic White	65,539	13,874	8,681	8,229	8,709	6,079	5,474	3,140	6,720	4,633
Non-Hispanic Black	36,882	11,437	5,412	4,016	4,019	2,287	2,195	1,096	2,507	3,913
Hispanic[4]	24,804	6,631	3,991	3,158	3,019	1,884	1,481	794	1,621	2,225
34–36 Weeks										
All races[3]	332,612	48,908	38,779	43,142	50,387	37,445	33,781	19,840	41,608	18,722
Non-Hispanic White	184,546	22,514	18,715	23,688	28,722	22,674	20,707	12,587	26,642	8,297
Non-Hispanic Black	65,701	12,896	8,543	8,110	9,057	5,980	5,752	3,184	7,480	4,699
Hispanic[4]	63,995	11,067	9,266	8,644	9,625	6,704	5,582	3,084	5,850	4,173
37–39 Weeks										
All races[3]	1,925,669	231,296	197,497	248,222	314,113	251,576	224,286	129,158	237,013	92,508
Non-Hispanic White	1,153,420	117,265	102,413	144,705	192,424	162,932	145,771	85,895	156,898	45,117
Non-Hispanic Black	286,882	47,991	32,995	35,140	41,722	29,757	28,803	16,327	35,599	18,548
Hispanic[4]	369,474	53,878	49,621	51,419	59,190	43,123	36,894	20,329	34,784	20,236
40 Weeks and Over										
All races[3]	1,191,727	129,122	113,409	142,510	188,478	157,171	147,358	87,873	167,889	57,917
Non-Hispanic White	714,100	64,706	56,413	82,127	114,950	101,800	95,948	58,695	111,547	27,914
Non-Hispanic Black	162,570	24,740	17,640	18,684	22,967	17,155	17,122	10,073	23,326	10,863
Hispanic[4]	243,326	32,682	32,309	32,289	38,277	28,339	25,496	14,402	25,686	13,846
PERCENT DISTRIBUTION										
All Gestation Periods[2]										
All races[3]	100.0	13.0	10.8	13.2	16.7	13.4	12.2	7.1	13.5	. . .
Non-Hispanic White	100.0	10.8	9.2	12.7	17.0	14.4	13.2	7.9	14.9	. . .
Non-Hispanic Black	100.0	18.9	12.6	12.8	15.1	10.7	10.5	6.0	13.4	. . .
Hispanic[4]	100.0	15.8	14.4	14.4	16.7	12.1	10.5	5.8	10.3	. . .
Under 34 Weeks										
All races[3]	100.0	27.4	15.6	13.3	13.6	8.8	7.8	4.3	9.2	. . .
Non-Hispanic White	100.0	22.8	14.3	13.5	14.3	10.0	9.0	5.2	11.0	. . .
Non-Hispanic Black	100.0	34.7	16.4	12.2	12.2	6.9	6.7	3.3	7.6	. . .
Hispanic[4]	100.0	29.4	17.7	14.0	13.4	8.3	6.6	3.5	7.2	. . .
34–36 Weeks										
All races[3]	100.0	15.6	12.4	13.7	16.1	11.9	10.8	6.3	13.3	. . .
Non-Hispanic White	100.0	12.8	10.6	13.4	16.3	12.9	11.7	7.1	15.1	. . .
Non-Hispanic Black	100.0	21.1	14.0	13.3	14.8	9.8	9.4	5.2	12.3	. . .
Hispanic[4]	100.0	18.5	15.5	14.4	16.1	11.2	9.3	5.2	9.8	. . .
37–39 Weeks										
All races[3]	100.0	12.6	10.8	13.5	17.1	13.7	12.2	7.0	12.9	. . .
Non-Hispanic White	100.0	10.6	9.2	13.1	17.4	14.7	13.2	7.8	14.2	. . .
Non-Hispanic Black	100.0	17.9	12.3	13.1	15.5	11.1	10.7	6.1	13.3	. .
Hispanic[4]	100.0	15.4	14.2	14.7	16.9	12.3	10.6	5.8	10.0	. . .
40 Weeks and Over										
All races[3]	100.0	11.4	10.0	12.6	16.6	13.9	13.0	7.8	14.8	. . .
Non-Hispanic White	100.0	9.4	8.2	12.0	16.8	14.8	14.0	8.6	16.3	. . .
Non-Hispanic Black	100.0	16.3	11.6	12.3	15.1	11.3	11.3	6.6	15.4	. . .
Hispanic[4]	100.0	14.2	14.1	14.1	16.7	12.3	11.1	6.3	11.2	. . .

. . . = Not applicable.
[1]Expressed in completed weeks.
[2]Includes births with period of gestation not stated.
[3]Includes races other than White and Black and origin not stated.
[4]Persons of Hispanic origin of any race.

NOTE: Excludes data for California, which did not require reporting of weight gain during pregnancy.

Table A-31. Percentage of Births with Selected Medical or Health Characteristics, by Race of Mother, 2005

(Percent.)

Characteristic	All races	White	Black	American Indian or Alaska Native	Asian or Pacific Islander
ALL BIRTHS					
Mother					
Diabetes during pregnancy............................	3.8	3.7	3.6	6.2	6.3
Weight gain of less than 16 lbs[1]	13.0	11.9	18.6	17.6	10.1
CNM delivery[2]	7.4	7.4	7.1	18.0	6.0
Cesarean delivery	30.3	30.0	32.3	25.9	29.7
Infant					
Gestational age					
Very preterm[3]	2.0	1.7	4.0	2.1	1.5
Preterm[4]	12.7	11.8	18.1	14.1	10.8
Birthweight					
Very low birthweight[5]	1.5	1.2	3.2	1.2	1.1
Low birthweight[6]	8.2	7.2	13.6	7.4	8.0
4,000 grams or more[7]	8.1	9.0	4.6	10.4	5.0
Twin birth[8]	32.2	32.0	35.7	24.2	26.3
Triplet or higher birth[9]	161.8	178.2	102.0	55.8	116.8

[1]Excludes data for California, which did not report weight gain on the birth certificate.
[2]Births delivered by certified midwives.
[3]Born prior to 32 completed weeks of gestation.
[4]Born prior to 37 completed weeks of gestation.
[5]Birthweight of less than 1,500 grams (3 lb 4 oz).
[6]Birthweight of less than 2,500 grams (5 lb 8 oz).
[7]Equivalent to 8 lb 14 oz.
[8]Live births in twin deliveries per 1,000 live births.
[9]Live births in triplet and other higher order multiple deliveries per 100,000 live births.

Table A-32. Percentage of Births with Selected Medical or Health Characteristics, by Hispanic Origin of Mother and by Race for Mothers of Non-Hispanic Origin, 2005

(Percent.)

Characteristic	All origins[2]	Hispanic[1]						Non-Hispanic		
		Total	Mexican	Puerto Rican	Cuban	Central and South American	Other and unknown Hispanic	Total[3]	White	Black
ALL BIRTHS										
Mother										
Diabetes during pregnancy...........................	3.8	3.8	3.8	4.7	3.9	3.6	3.7	3.9	3.7	3.5
Weight gain of less than 16 lbs[4]	13.0	15.8	17.0	13.6	9.2	13.6	14.9	12.3	10.8	18.9
CNM delivery[5]...	7.4	8.3	8.0	10.2	4.2	9.5	8.4	7.1	7.1	6.9
Cesarean deliver...	30.3	29.0	28.0	31.1	45.0	30.9	29.6	30.7	30.4	32.6
Infant										
Gestational age										
Very preterm[6]	2.0	1.8	1.7	2.5	2.1	1.7	2.0	2.1	1.6	4.2
Preterm[7]	12.7	12.1	11.8	14.3	13.2	12.0	13.6	12.9	11.7	18.4
Birthweight										
Very low birth weight[8]	1.5	1.2	1.1	1.9	1.5	1.2	1.4	1.6	1.2	3.3
Low birth weight[9]	8.2	6.9	6.5	9.9	7.6	6.8	8.3	8.6	7.3	14.0
4,000 grams or more[10]	8.1	7.6	8.0	6.1	8.0	7.3	6.1	8.3	9.6	4.4
Twin births[11]	32.2	22.0	20.3	31.1	32.2	23.4	26.1	35.3	36.1	36.4
Triple or higher births [12]	161.8	77.2	64.1	124.7	180.5	100.5	92.4	187.7	217.8	105.5

[1]Persons of Hispanic origin may be of any race.
[2]Includes origin not stated.
[3]Includes races other than White and Black.
[4]Excludes data for California, which did not report weight gain on the birth certificate.
[5]Births delivered by certified nurse midwives.
[6]Born prior to 32 completed weeks of gestation.
[7]Born prior to 37 completed weeks of gestation.
[8]Birthweight of less than 1,500 grams (3 lb 4 oz).
[9]Birthweight of less than 2,500 grams (5 lb 8 oz).
[10]Equivalent to 8 lb 14 oz.
[11]Live births in twin deliveries per 1,000 live births.
[12]Live births in triplet and other higher order multiple deliveries per 100,000 live births.

Table A-33. Number and Rate of Live Births to Mothers with Selected Risk Factors During Pregnancy, Obstetric Procedures, Characteristics of Labor and Delivery, and Congenital Anomalies, by Age, Race, and Hispanic Origin of Mother, 2005

(Number of live births with specified risk factor, procedure, or anomaly per 1,00 live births. Congenital anomalies are per 100,000 live births.)

Risk factor, characteristic, procedure, and anomaly	All births[1]	Factor reported	All ages	Under 20 years	20–24 years	25–29 years	30–34 years	35–39 years	40–54 years	Not stated[2]
ALL RACES[3]										
Risk Factors in this Pregnancy										
Diabetes	4,138,349	158,705	38.5	11.9	22.0	36.2	50.8	67.0	86.9	11,278
Hypertension, pregnancy-associated	4,138,349	164,864	39.9	43.3	39.5	39.5	38.0	40.4	50.8	11,278
Hypertension, chronic	4,138,349	42,744	10.4	3.7	6.1	9.3	12.8	18.7	29.2	11,278
Obstetric Procedures and Characteristics of Labor or Delivery										
Induction of labor	4,138,349	919,835	222.7	227.4	229.4	231.4	217.0	201.6	193.7	7,784
Tocolysis	4,138,349	82,818	20.1	21.9	20.9	20.4	19.2	18.0	17.8	9,929
Meconium, moderate/heavy	4,138,349	190,164	46.0	53.0	47.4	45.3	43.9	43.6	43.1	8,787
Breech/Malpresentation	4,138,349	193,151	47.1	36.5	38.9	45.3	53.3	60.2	71.0	34,095
Precipitous labor	4,138,349	82,633	20.0	13.7	18.8	20.6	21.7	23.1	22.1	13,067
Congenital Anomalies[4]										
Anencephaly	4,109,514	462	11.3	12.1	12.9	10.6	11.5	9.4	*	21,871
Meningomyelocele/Spina bifida	4,109,514	734	18.0	18.1	18.1	17.8	18.6	17.2	*	21,871
Omphalocele/Gastroschisis	4,109,514	1,340	32.8	93.3	43.9	23.4	14.8	16.5	20.0	21,871
Cleft lip/palate	4,109,514	3,233	79.1	77.9	91.0	78.3	73.2	65.7	88.3	21,871
Down syndrome	4,109,514	2,003	49.0	24.6	28.2	26.7	40.8	118.0	332.4	21,871
NON-HISPANIC WHITE										
Risk Factors in this Pregnancy										
Diabetes	2,279,768	83,053	36.5	13.6	22.7	33.7	43.7	56.7	72.3	6,166
Hypertension, pregnancy-associated	2,279,768	102,928	45.3	49.6	47.0	46.4	42.1	42.0	51.9	6,166
Hypertension, chronic	2,279,768	23,677	10.4	3.7	6.3	9.5	12.2	16.7	23.8	6,166
Obstetric Procedures and Characteristics of Labor or Delivery										
Induction of labor	2,279,768	604,618	265.8	295.5	287.5	278.1	250.3	227.7	215.3	4,668
Tocolysis	2,279,768	51,236	22.5	27.3	24.3	23.0	21.2	19.3	18.8	6,126
Meconium, moderate/heavy	2,279,768	91,998	40.4	44.8	41.2	40.0	39.4	40.1	39.0	5,057
Breech/Malpresentation	2,279,768	115,175	50.8	39.4	41.2	48.7	56.3	62.3	73.2	14,046
Precipitous labor	2,279,768	47,661	21.0	13.2	18.9	20.8	22.8	24.9	23.9	7,714
Congenital Anomalies[4]										
Anencephaly	2,271,288	234	10.4	12.7	11.6	10.1	9.9	9.9	*	12,001
Meningomyelocele/Spina bifida	2,271,288	436	19.3	19.4	18.2	19.6	21.3	18.5	*	12,001
Omphalocele/Gastroschisis	2,271,288	826	36.6	132.2	57.0	26.4	14.4	16.5	*	12,001
Cleft lip/palate	2,271,288	2,124	94.0	103.1	120.8	90.1	82.2	75.1	91.4	12,001
Down syndrome	2,271,288	1,256	55.6	30.9	30.9	28.9	45.6	120.7	346.4	12,001
NON-HISPANIC BLACK										
Risk Factors in this Pregnancy										
Diabetes	583,759	20,501	35.2	10.3	20.6	37.3	57.8	78.3	97.9	1,662
Hypertension, pregnancy-associated	583,759	26,546	45.6	48.4	42.0	42.8	48.0	53.0	63.4	1,662
Hypertension, chronic	583,759	11,794	20.3	5.6	10.8	19.4	34.0	51.0	70.8	1,662
Obstetric Procedures and Characteristics of Labor or Delivery										
Induction of labor	583,759	114,988	197.2	207.8	197.5	198.3	195.5	180.2	174.8	741
Tocolysis	583,759	12,898	22.1	22.2	22.4	22.3	22.2	20.7	19.6	829
Meconium, moderate/heavy	583,759	34,305	58.9	62.7	57.5	56.5	61.0	59.8	57.4	1,220
Breech/Malpresentation	583,759	23,590	40.7	29.7	35.1	41.0	49.6	59.0	70.6	3,461
Precipitous labor	583,759	12,424	21.3	16.7	21.0	23.4	23.2	22.5	21.1	1,620
Congenital Anomalies[4]										
Anencephaly	583,277	64	11.0	*	12.3	*	*	*	*	2,907
Meningomyelocele/Spina bifida	583,277	90	15.5	*	16.0	14.8	*	*	*	2,907
Omphalocele/Gastroschisis	583,277	185	31.9	53.5	24.5	32.4	25.1	*	*	2,907
Cleft lip/palate	583,277	242	41.7	43.4	50.1	39.4	29.4	*	*	2,907
Down syndrome	583,277	186	32.0	*	19.2	19.7	21.8	102.0	295.9	2,907

* = Figure does not meet standards of reliability or precision; based on fewer than 20 births in the numerator.
[1]Total number of births to residents of areas reporting specified risk factor, procedure or anomaly.
[2]No response reported for specific item.
[3]Includes races not shown.
[4]Excludes data for New Mexico which did not report congenital anomalies.

Table A-33. Number and Rate of Live Births to Mothers with Selected Risk Factors During Pregnancy, Obstetric Procedures, Characteristics of Labor and Delivery, and Congenital Anomalies, by Age, Race, and Hispanic Origin of Mother, 2005—*Continued*

(Number of live births with specified risk factor, procedure, or anomaly per 1,00 live births. Congenital anomalies are per 100,000 live births.)

Risk factor, characteristic, procedure, and anomaly	All births[1]	Factor reported	All ages	Under 20 years	20–24 years	25–29 years	30–34 years	35–39 years	40–54 years	Not stated[2]
HISPANIC[5]										
Risk Factors in this Pregnancy										
Diabetes	985,505	37,742	38.4	10.7	20.2	37.1	60.0	83.8	115.5	2,022
Hypertension, pregnancy-associated	985,505	27,640	28.1	32.5	25.9	25.2	28.0	33.9	44.9	2,022
Hypertension, chronic	985,505	5,204	5.3	2.5	3.0	4.5	7.2	11.7	22.5	2,022
Obstetric Procedures and Characteristics of Labor or Delivery										
Induction of labor	985,505	152,573	155.0	165.8	155.8	153.8	150.8	148.2	152.9	1,199
Tocolysis	985,505	14,069	14.3	14.9	14.1	14.5	14.0	14.0	14.5	1,459
Meconium, moderate/heavy	985,505	50,055	50.9	55.5	51.5	50.6	48.9	46.9	47.9	1,276
Breech/Malpresentation	985,505	42,734	44.0	39.3	38.4	41.5	50.7	58.0	68.6	14,269
Precipitous labor	985,505	16,524	16.8	11.8	16.8	18.7	17.7	17.3	16.5	2,087
Congenital Anomalies[4]										
Anencephaly	969,682	129	13.4	*	15.3	12.2	14.7	*	*	4,003
Meningomyelocele/Spina bifida	969,682	175	18.1	16.2	21.0	16.8	14.2	*	*	4,003
Omphalocele/Gastroschisis	969,682	251	26.0	67.1	31.6	13.8	12.5	*	*	4,003
Cleft lip/palate	969,682	658	68.1	69.3	66.8	71.1	69.8	52.1	*	4,003
Down syndrome	969,682	455	47.1	24.3	31.3	26.0	42.5	136.3	380.3	4,003

* = Figure does not meet standards of reliability or precision; based on fewer than 20 births in the numerator.
[1]Total number of births to residents of areas reporting specified risk factor, procedure or anomaly.
[2]No response reported for specific item.
[4]Excludes data for New Mexico which did not report congenital anomalies.
[5]Persons of Hispanic origin may be of any race.

Table A-34. Percentage of Mothers Beginning Prenatal Care in the First Trimester and Percentage of Mothers with Late or No Prenatal Care, by Race and Hispanic Origin of Mother: 49 States and the Territories, 2005

(Percent.)

Area	Percent beginning care in first trimester				Percent late or no care[1]			
		Non-Hispanic				Non-Hispanic		
	All races[2]	White	Black	Hispanic[3]	All races[2]	White	Black	Hispanic[3]
Alabama	83.1	89.3	77.0	51.5	4.1	1.9	4.6	21.9
Alaska	80.2	85.6	82.1	78.4	4.9	3.3	6.0	8.2
Arizona	77.7	87.5	77.4	69.5	6.2	2.8	5.8	8.9
Arkansas	80.6	84.2	74.6	68.1	4.7	3.4	7.1	8.4
California	86.6	90.1	82.8	84.5	2.7	2.1	3.5	3.1
Colorado	80.1	85.6	75.5	70.0	4.5	2.8	6.4	7.5
Connecticut	86.8	92.0	75.5	76.0	1.9	1.2	3.6	3.0
Delaware	81.9	88.2	77.9	62.6	4.9	2.3	5.0	15.3
District of Columbia	77.5	92.0	73.8	62.3	5.1	1.3	6.3	8.0
Florida[4]	72.2	77.5	63.4	69.7	6.7	4.9	9.8	7.6
Georgia	83.6	89.6	79.1	72.9	3.8	2.1	4.7	7.6
Hawaii	81.5	85.2	82.4	81.4	3.6	2.4	*	3.1
Idaho[4]	71.2	74.1	58.8	57.7	5.9	5.0	*	9.8
Illinois	86.0	90.8	75.7	82.2	2.6	1.5	5.8	2.8
Indiana	79.9	83.8	66.0	63.6	4.2	3.1	8.4	8.6
Iowa	87.6	89.6	76.0	74.2	2.2	1.7	5.5	5.2
Kansas[4]	76.6	80.8	67.8	59.8	4.8	3.5	8.3	9.4
Kentucky[4]	73.8	75.4	68.4	54.8	5.3	4.7	7.6	10.6
Louisiana	87.2	92.9	79.0	85.6	2.7	1.2	4.9	3.1
Maine	88.1	88.3	79.1	85.0	1.7	1.6	*	*
Maryland	81.3	89.2	75.1	63.1	4.3	2.1	6.4	8.1
Massachusetts	89.3	92.1	80.5	82.5	2.2	1.6	5.1	3.4
Michigan	85.6	89.6	71.7	79.0	3.0	2.0	6.9	3.8
Minnesota	86.2	90.0	75.3	71.2	2.3	1.4	4.7	5.3
Mississippi	84.2	90.5	77.7	73.7	3.0	1.6	4.3	8.4
Missouri	87.8	89.9	80.3	77.5	2.3	1.8	4.4	3.7
Montana	84.0	87.1	81.0	77.4	2.7	1.6	*	*
Nebraska[4]	75.3	78.6	66.5	62.4	4.5	3.8	6.7	7.0
Nevada	74.0	82.4	68.9	64.0	8.2	5.3	10.6	11.3
New Hampshire[4]	82.4	83.7	52.2	70.1	3.3	3.0	12.4	4.9
New Jersey	78.7	88.1	62.9	66.6	4.8	2.4	10.3	7.0
New Mexico	71.2	79.1	70.8	69.4	7.7	4.5	5.5	8.2
New York (excluding New York City)[4]	77.2	82.2	61.5	63.0	4.3	3.0	9.4	7.0
New York City	80.2	88.1	75.3	77.9	4.9	2.3	7.2	5.5
North Carolina	83.5	90.2	76.7	68.8	2.9	1.6	4.7	5.5
North Dakota	85.9	88.7	83.2	79	2.7	1.7	*	*
Ohio	87.1	89.2	78.3	78.2	2.9	2.2	5.8	5.3
Oklahoma	77.3	81.5	71.8	65.6	5.5	4.6	7	7.2
Oregon	80.9	84.4	71.3	70.1	4.1	3.3	5.9	6.1
Pennsylvania[4]	73.2	78.4	56.6	55.8	6.2	4.6	12.1	10.1
Rhode Island	89.3	92.4	83.3	85.4	2.2	1.4	4.6	3.1
South Carolina[4]	69.0	76.3	62.0	49.1	7.4	5.0	9.2	15.7
South Dakota	79.5	85.0	58.2	62.4	3.6	1.9	*	6.1
Tennessee[4]	68.8	76.3	53.2	41.3	8.0	4.8	13.9	22.1
Texas[4]	64.1	74.1	57.2	57.9	11.1	6.7	14.1	13.8
Utah	80.2	84.0	54.9	65.3	4.3	3.0	15.7	8.3
Virginia	85.0	90.5	79.9	68.6	3.8	2.1	5.2	8.4
Washington[4]	71.2	74.9	65.3	60.9	6.3	5.1	8.0	9.3
West Virginia	84.4	85.0	71.7	75.3	2.7	2.6	5.9	*
Wisconsin	85.5	88.8	76.8	72.8	2.9	2.3	5.4	4.9
Wyoming	84.9	87.0	90.2	77.4	3.3	2.7	*	4.8
Puerto Rico	74.2	72.9	64.2	74.3	3.0	3.5	*	3.0
Virgin Islands	65.9	83.3	63.6	66.6	8.3	*	9.1	7.8
Guam	62.3	85.5	75.9	75.0	11.2	*	*	*
American Samoa	—	—	—	—	—	—	—	—
Northern Marianas	31.6	—	—	—	26.7	—	—	—

* = Figure does not meet standards of reliability or precision.

—— = Data not available.

[1]Care beginning in 3rd trimester.

[2]Includes races other than White and Black and origin not stated.

[3]Persons of Hispanic origin may be of any race.

[4]Data are based on the 2003 Revision of the U.S. Certificate of Live Birth. All other states are based on the 1989 Revision of the U.S. Certificate of Live Birth. These two sets of data are not comparable.

NOTE: Excludes data for Vermont.

Table A-35. Number of Live Births by Attendant, Place of Delivery, Race, and Hispanic Origin of Mother, 2005

(Number.)

Place of delivery, race, and Hispanic origin of mother	All births	Physician			Midwife			Other	Unspecified
		Total	Doctor of medicine	Doctor of osteopathy	Total	Certified nurse midwife	Other midwife		
All Races[1]									
Total..	4,138,349	3,789,976	3,592,476	197,500	325,094	306,377	18,717	20,230	3,049
In hospital[2]	4,100,608	3,786,315	3,589,231	197,084	300,903	295,989	4,914	11,442	1,948
Not in hospital	37,402	3,576	3,167	409	24,166	10,374	13,792	8,593	1,067
Freestanding birthing center...	10,217	969	742	227	9,050	6,094	2,956	166	32
Clinic or doctor's office..........	350	212	197	15	66	43	23	71	1
Residence...............................	24,468	1,768	1,630	138	14,677	4,034	10,643	7,233	790
Other	2,367	627	598	29	373	203	170	1,123	244
Not specified	339	85	78	7	25	14	11	195	34
Non-Hispanic White									
Total..	2,279,768	2,089,951	1,960,494	129,457	176,341	161,518	14,823	12,038	1,438
In hospital[2]	2,250,246	2,087,588	1,958,491	129,097	155,886	153,074	2,812	5,819	953
Not in hospital..........................	29,300	2,320	1,964	356	20,437	8,436	12,001	6,062	481
Freestanding birthing center...	8,031	902	676	226	6,980	4,692	2,288	129	20
Clinic or doctor's office..........	260	166	156	10	48	35	13	46	–
Residence...............................	19,706	986	877	109	13,118	3,576	9,542	5,216	386
Other	1,303	266	255	11	291	133	158	671	75
Not specified	222	43	39	4	18	8	10	157	4
Non-Hispanic Black									
Total..	583,759	539,728	520,848	18,880	40,846	39,947	899	2,539	646
In hospital[2]	581,111	539,027	520,169	18,858	40,136	39,461	675	1,522	426
Not in hospital..........................	2,607	687	667	20	709	485	224	996	215
Freestanding birthing center...	468	27	27	–	429	332	97	9	3
Clinic or doctor's office..........	15	6	6	–	6	5	1	3	–
Residence...............................	1,716	470	457	13	257	132	125	832	157
Other	408	184	177	7	17	16	1	152	55
Not specified	41	14	12	2	1	1	–	21	5
Hispanic[3]									
Total..	985,505	896,394	857,623	38,771	84,221	82,042	2,179	4,230	660
In hospital[2]	981,791	896,001	857,253	38,748	82,061	81,000	1,061	3,321	408
Not in hospital..........................	3,696	383	361	22	2,157	1,039	1,118	904	252
Freestanding birthing center...	1,414	35	34	1	1,352	850	502	19	8
Clinic or doctor's office..........	36	17	15	2	11	2	9	7	1
Residence...............................	1,815	210	199	11	760	156	604	670	175
Other	431	121	113	8	34	31	3	208	68
Not specified	18	10	9	1	3	3	–	5	–

– = Quantity zero.
[1]Includes races other than White and Black and origin not stated.
[2]Includes births occurring en route to or on arrival at hospital.
[3]Persons of Hispanic origin may be of any race.

Table A-36. Live Births by Method of Delivery and Rates of Cesarean Delivery by Race and Hispanic Origin of Mother, 1989–2005

(Number, percent.)

Year	All births	Vaginal				Cesarean							
		Number				Number				Rate[1]			
		Total[2]	Non-Hispanic White	Non-Hispanic Black	Hispanic[3]	Total[2]	Non-Hispanic White	Non-Hispanic Black	Hispanic[3]	Total[2]	Non-Hispanic White	Non-Hispanic Black	Hispanic[3]
1989[4]	3,798,734	2,793,463	1,806,753	440,310	385,462	826,955	556,585	125,290	105,268	22.8	23.6	22.2	21.5
1990[5]	4,110,563	3,111,421	1,972,754	503,720	458,242	914,096	603,467	142,838	122,969	22.7	23.4	22.1	21.2
1991[6]	4,110,907	3,100,891	1,941,726	507,522	472,126	905,077	587,802	142,417	129,752	22.6	23.2	21.9	21.6
1992[6]	4,065,014	3,100,710	1,916,414	502,669	494,338	888,622	566,788	143,153	133,369	22.3	22.8	22.2	21.2
1993	4,000,240	3,098,796	1,902,433	496,333	514,493	861,987	542,013	139,702	136,279	21.8	22.2	22.0	20.9
1994	3,952,767	3,087,576	1,896,609	480,551	525,928	830,517	518,021	134,526	135,569	21.2	21.5	21.9	20.5
1995	3,899,589	3,063,724	1,867,024	457,104	539,731	806,722	496,103	127,171	136,640	20.8	21.0	21.8	20.2
1996	3,891,494	3,061,092	1,851,058	449,544	558,105	797,119	485,530	124,836	139,554	20.7	20.8	21.7	20.0
1997	3,880,894	3,046,621	1,829,213	451,744	563,114	799,033	481,982	126,138	142,907	20.8	20.9	21.8	20.2
1998	3,941,553	3,078,537	1,842,420	457,186	580,143	825,870	495,550	131,999	150,317	21.2	21.2	22.4	20.6
1999	3,959,417	3,063,870	1,810,682	449,580	599,118	862,086	514,051	135,508	161,035	22.0	22.1	23.2	21.2
2000	4,058,814	3,108,188	1,804,550	454,736	633,220	923,991	540,794	146,042	179,583	22.9	23.1	24.3	22.1
2001	4,025,933	3,027,993	1,746,551	435,455	648,821	978,411	567,488	151,908	199,874	24.4	24.5	25.9	23.6
2002	4,021,726	2,958,423	1,687,144	416,516	653,516	1,043,846	598,682	159,297	219,777	26.1	26.2	27.7	25.2
2003	4,089,950	2,949,853	1,671,414	405,671	667,656	1,119,388	637,482	167,506	241,159	27.5	27.6	29.2	26.5
2004	4,112,052	2,903,341	1,617,994	397,877	679,118	1,190,210	667,836	178,461	263,454	29.1	29.2	31.0	28.0
2005	4,138,349	2,873,918	1,579,613	392,064	698,089	1,248,815	690,260	189,287	285,376	30.3	30.4	32.6	29.0

[1]Percent of all live births by cesarean delivery.

[2]Includes races other than White and Black and origin not stated.

[3]Persons of Hispanic origin may be of any race.

[4]Excludes data for Louisiana, Maryland, Nebraska, Nevada, and Oklahoma, which did not report method of delivery on the birth certificate; data by Hispanic origin also excludes New Hampshire, which did not report Hispanic origin.

[5]Excludes data for Oklahoma, which did not report method of delivery; data by Hispanic origin also exclude New Hampshire which did not report Hispanic origin.

[6]Excludes data for New Hampshire which did not report Hispanic origin.

Table A-37. Number of Live Births by Method of Delivery and Rates of Cesarean Delivery by Age, Race and Hispanic Origin of Mother, 2005

(Number, percent.)

Race, age, and Hispanic origin of mother	Number				Cesarean delivery rate[1]
	All births	Vaginal	Cesarean	Not stated	
All Races[2]	4,138,349	2,873,918	1,248,815	15,616	30.3
Under 20 years	421,315	329,707	90,518	1,090	21.5
20–24 years	1,040,388	772,653	264,445	3,290	25.5
25–29 years	1,131,596	800,130	327,275	4,191	29.0
30–34 years	950,691	623,087	323,614	3,990	34.2
35–39 years	483,156	288,798	191,928	2,430	39.9
40–54 years	111,203	59,543	51,035	625	46.2
Non-Hispanic White	2,279,768	1,579,613	690,260	9,895	30.4
Under 20 years	166,336	129,850	35,949	537	21.7
20–24 years	515,518	384,020	129,580	1,918	25.2
25–29 years	642,553	458,018	181,874	2,661	28.4
30–34 years	581,645	384,862	194,066	2,717	33.5
35–39 years	305,142	185,397	118,087	1,658	38.9
40–54 years	68,574	37,466	30,704	404	45.0
Non-Hispanic Black	583,759	392,064	189,287	2,408	32.6
Under 20 years	99,510	75,417	23,808	285	24.0
20–24 years	188,673	133,431	54,582	660	29.0
25–29 years	142,885	95,119	47,157	609	33.1
30–34 years	92,336	56,261	35,582	493	38.7
35–39 years	47,411	25,537	21,595	279	45.8
40–54 years	12,944	6,299	6,563	82	51.0
Hispanic[3]	985,505	698,089	285,376	2,040	29.0
Under 20 years	139,372	111,225	27,933	214	20.1
20–24 years	287,896	217,307	70,073	516	24.4
25–29 years	266,590	188,729	77,267	594	29.0
30–34 years	186,398	120,408	65,554	436	35.3
35–39 years	85,739	50,150	35,372	217	41.4
40–54 years	19,510	10,270	9,177	63	47.2

[1]Percentage of all live births by cesarean delivery.
[2]Includes races other than White and Black and origin not stated.
[3]Persons of Hispanic origin may be of any race.

Table A-38. Rates of Cesarean Delivery, by Race and Hispanic Origin of Mother, by State, 2005

(Percent.)

Area	Total cesarean delivery rate[1]			
		Non-Hispanic		Hispanic[3]
	All races[2]	White	Black	
UNITED STATES[4]	30.3	30.4	32.6	29.0
Alabama	31.8	32.8	31.7	24.2
Alaska	21.9	24.7	29.9	23.0
Arizona	24.7	26.8	27.8	23.1
Arkansas	31.5	31.9	33.6	25.6
California	30.7	31.1	35.6	30.0
Colorado	24.6	25.9	26.2	21.9
Connecticut	32.4	32.8	34.0	30.6
Delaware	30.0	29.9	31.6	27.8
District of Columbia	30.5	30.9	31.8	25.2
Florida	34.9	33.6	35.0	37.2
Georgia	30.5	31.6	32.4	23.4
Hawaii	25.6	24.0	21.9	26.2
Idaho	22.6	22.3	21.7	23.2
Illinois	28.8	29.7	29.9	25.9
Indiana	28.2	28.1	29.8	26.8
Iowa	26.7	26.8	25.1	26.9
Kansas	28.9	29.3	29.9	26.7
Kentucky	33.9	34.0	34.0	30.9
Louisiana	36.8	37.9	35.8	36.1
Maine	28.3	28.4	29.4	22.1
Maryland	31.1	30.9	33.5	25.9
Massachusetts	32.2	33.3	33.3	27.1
Michigan	28.8	28.9	29.2	27.1
Minnesota	25.3	26.0	27.2	21.9
Mississippi	35.1	35.8	34.9	25.7
Missouri	29.7	30.0	29.8	26.4
Montana	25.8	25.2	*	29.3
Nebraska	28.6	29.2	30.0	25.4
Nevada	31.0	33.6	36.7	26.4
New Hampshire	28.0	28.0	25.3	28.8
New Jersey	36.3	36.8	37.6	34.5
New Mexico	22.2	23.6	29.6	22.2
New York	31.5	32.0	33.6	29.9
North Carolina	29.3	30.3	31.1	23.3
North Dakota	26.4	26.4	23.1	26.9
Ohio	28.1	28.2	28.8	26.0
Oklahoma	32.5	32.9	34.0	28.0
Oregon	27.6	27.8	30.5	25.7
Pennsylvania	28.9	29.2	28.2	27.7
Rhode Island	30.3	32.4	29.0	27.2
South Carolina	32.7	33.0	32.9	29.7
South Dakota	25.1	25.2	28.7	20.7
Tennessee	31.1	31.9	30.5	26.4
Texas	32.6	34.1	35.9	30.8
Utah	21.6	20.9	27.6	24.4
Vermont	25.9	25.8	32.5	*
Virginia	31.4	31.5	32.3	27.1
Washington	27.8	27.8	30.3	26.1
West Virginia	34.2	34.2	37.6	26.2
Wisconsin	23.7	24.4	21.8	23.1
Wyoming	24.6	24.2	*	27.7
Puerto Rico	48.1	46.3	45.6	48.2
Virgin Islands	27.5	27.5	26.9	29.2
Guam	27.5	23.4	*	*
American Samoa	—	—	—	—
Northern Marianas	22.8	—	—	—

* = Figure does not meet standards of reliability or precision.

— = Data not available.

[1] Percentage of all live births by cesarean delivery.

[2] Includes races other than White and Black and origin not stated.

[3] Persons of Hispanic origin may be of any race.

[4] Excludes data for the territories.

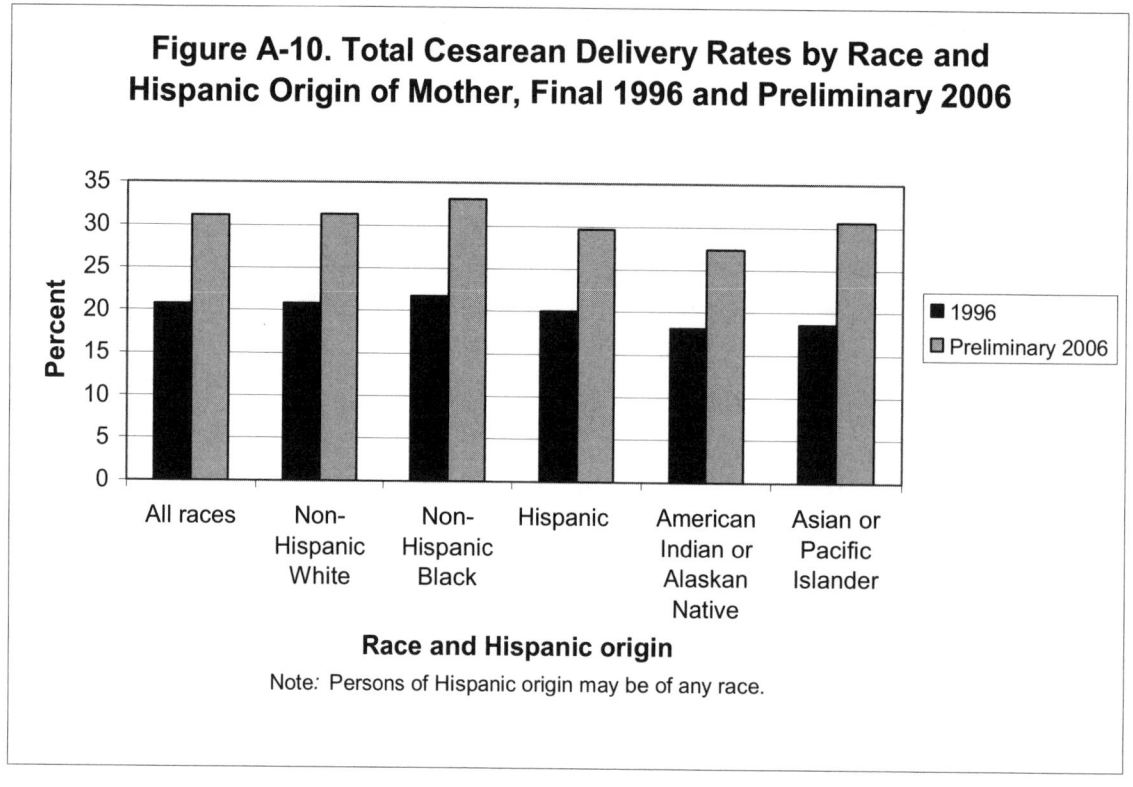

Figure A-10. Total Cesarean Delivery Rates by Race and Hispanic Origin of Mother, Final 1996 and Preliminary 2006

Note: Persons of Hispanic origin may be of any race.

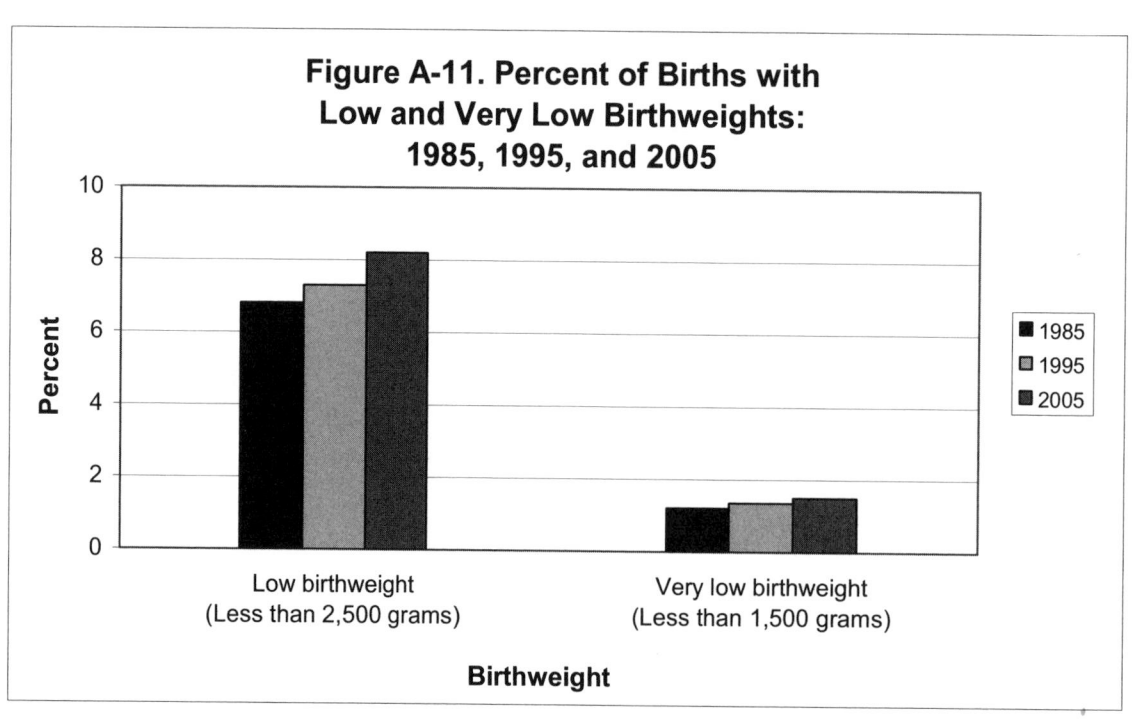

Figure A-11. Percent of Births with Low and Very Low Birthweights: 1985, 1995, and 2005

Table A-39. Total Births, Total Cesarean Delivery Rate, Percentage of Live Births Preterm and Very Preterm, and Percentage of Live Births Low and Very Low Birthweight, by Race and Hispanic Origin of Mother, Final 2005 and Preliminary 2006

(Number, rate, percent.)

Race and Hispanic origin of mother	Number		Cesarean rate[1]		Total[2]		Very preterm[3]		Total[4]		Very low birthweight[5]	
	2005	2006	2005	2006	2005	2006	2005	2006	2005	2006	2005	2006
All races and origins[6]	4,138,349	4,265,996	30.3	31.1	12.7	12.8	2.0	2.0	8.2	8.3	1.5	1.5
Non-Hispanic White	2,279,768	2,309,833	30.4	31.3	11.7	11.7	1.6	1.7	7.3	7.3	1.2	1.2
Non-Hispanic Black	583,759	617,220	32.6	33.1	18.4	18.4	4.2	4.1	14.0	14.0	3.3	3.1
American Indian or Alaska Native total[7]	44,813	47,494	25.9	27.4	14.1	14.2	2.1	2.1	7.4	7.5	1.2	1.3
Asian or Pacific Islander total[7]	231,108	239,829	29.7	30.6	10.8	10.9	1.5	1.5	8.0	8.1	1.1	1.1
Hispanic[8]	985,505	1,039,051	29.0	29.7	12.1	12.2	1.8	1.8	6.9	7.0	1.2	1.2

[1]All births by cesarean delivery per 100 live births.
[2]Less than 37 completed weeks of gestation.
[3]Less than 32 completed weeks of gestation.
[4]Less than 2,500 grams (5lb 8oz).
[5]Less than 1,500 grams (3lb 4oz).
[6]Includes Hispanic origin not stated.
[7]Data for persons of Hispanic origin are included in the data for each race group according to the person's reported race.
[8]Persons of Hispanic origin may be of any race.

Table A-40. Rates of Vaginal Birth After Cesarean Delivery (VBAC), by Race and Hispanic Origin of Mother: 49 States and the Territories, 2005

(Percent.)

Area	Rate of vaginal births after previous cesarean[1]			
	All races[2]	White	Black	Hispanic[3]
Alabama	5.9	5.3	6.3	9.7
Alaska	18.6	12.7	*	*
Arizona	6.0	5.8	*	5.0
Arkansas	6.0	5.0	7.1	10.3
California	5.5	6.2	5.3	5.0
Colorado	11.7	10.7	12.0	12.9
Connecticut	6.7	6.8	6.6	6.7
Delaware	10.3	7.8	12.2	14.8
District of Columbia	7.0	*	5.8	*
Florida[4]	5.7	5.7	6.8	4.8
Georgia	5.8	4.8	5.5	9.1
Hawaii	12.4	16.3	*	11.4
Idaho[4]	17.3	16.4	*	22.3
Illinois	9.5	8.5	9.6	11.4
Indiana	6.9	6.6	6.6	9.0
Iowa	8.4	8.2	13.3	6.9
Kansas[4]	11.3	10.7	14.2	11.7
Kentucky[4]	6.9	6.2	10.7	11.1
Louisiana	3.6	2.9	4.5	*
Maine	6.0	5.8	*	*
Maryland	9.8	9.1	10.0	12.2
Massachusetts	9.7	8.7	11.5	12.2
Michigan	8.3	7.9	8.2	11.2
Minnesota	10.6	9.3	15.2	15.7
Mississippi	3.8	2.9	4.4	*
Missouri	7.6	7.5	7.5	9.1
Montana	11.4	12.6	*	*
Nebraska[4]	9.5	8.4	19.2	12.3
Nevada[4]	4.9	3.9	*	6.8
New Hampshire[4]	16.6	17.0	*	*
New Jersey	9.6	9.1	12.6	9.1
New Mexico	13.0	13.1	*	10.1
New York (excluding New York City)[4]	10.8	10.2	14.9	10.8
New York City	13.5	17.4	11.6	13.1
North Carolina	8.9	7.5	8.3	14.3
North Dakota	10.3	10.2	*	*
Ohio	8.9	8.2	11.9	9.9
Oklahoma	2.8	2.2	3.0	5.9
Oregon	10.3	9.3	*	13.5
Pennsylvania[4]	15.2	14.3	19.6	16.0
Rhode Island	9.4	8.7	*	9.6
South Carolina[4]	10.0	8.9	11.1	11.9
South Dakota	13.7	13.7	*	*
Tennessee[4]	11.1	9.8	15.0	12.1
Texas[4]	10.0	7.8	8.1	11.9
Utah	18.2	18.1	*	19.1
Virginia	6.6	6.3	6.6	7.9
Washington[4]	13.2	12.4	17.6	15.0
West Virginia	4.8	4.6	*	*
Wisconsin	11.8	11.2	13.7	12.1
Wyoming	8.0	9.0	*	*
Puerto Rico[4]	7.4	5.4	*	7.5
Virgin Islands	19.3	*	21.7	*
Guam	9.9	*	*	*
American Samoa	—	—	—	—
Northern Marianas	—	—	—	—

* = Figure does not meet standards of reliability or precision.

—— = Data not available.

[1]Number of vaginal births after previous cesarean delivery per 100 live births to women with a previous cesarean delivery.

[2]Includes races other than White and Black and origin not stated.

[3]Persons of Hispanic origin may be of any race.

[4]Data are based on the 2003 Revision of the U.S. Certificate of Live Birth. All other states are based on the 1989 Revision of the U.S. Certificate of Live Birth. These two sets of data are not comparable.

NOTE: Excludes data for Vermont.

Table A-41. Live Births by Birthweight and Percentage Very Low and Low Birthweight, by Period of Gestation, Race, and Hispanic Origin of Mother, 2005

(Number, percent.)

Birthweight, race, and Hispanic origin of mother	All births	Period of gestation[1]									Post-term	Not stated
		Pre-term					Term				(42 weeks and over)	
		Total under 37 weeks	Under 28 weeks	28–31 weeks	32–33 weeks	34–36 weeks	Total 37–41 weeks	37–39 weeks	40 weeks	41 weeks		
ALL RACES[2]												
Total	4,138,349	522,913	31,588	51,820	65,853	373,652	3,346,066	2,199,804	790,422	355,840	239,831	29,539
Less than 500 grams	6,599	6,434	6,173	241	11	9	22	7	8	7	1	142
500–999 grams	23,864	23,330	17,405	5,335	373	217	201	147	38	16	14	319
1,000–1,499 grams	31,325	29,121	4,114	16,891	5,158	2,958	1,645	1,168	314	163	200	359
1,500–1,999 grams	66,453	55,670	981	12,742	19,449	22,498	9,365	7,782	1,072	511	774	644
2,000–2,499 grams	210,324	111,275	672	4,444	18,398	87,761	92,191	77,822	10,006	4,363	5,097	1,761
2,500–2,999 grams	748,042	140,841	1,069	4,306	9,634	125,832	569,319	443,651	89,290	36,378	32,560	5,322
3,000–3,499 grams	1,596,944	104,817	–	5,135	8,143	91,539	1,387,335	940,483	315,243	131,609	94,153	10,639
3,500–3,999 grams	1,114,887	40,689	–	2,560	3,662	34,467	988,011	575,811	280,930	131,270	78,804	7,383
4,000–4,499 grams	289,098	7,569	–	–	769	6,800	255,700	131,627	80,441	43,632	23,755	2,074
4,500–4,999 grams	42,119	1,178	–	–	90	1,088	36,766	18,087	11,624	7,055	3,865	310
5,000 grams or more	4,715	192	–	–	20	172	3,994	2,234	1,079	681	483	46
Not stated	3,979	1,797	1,174	166	146	311	1,517	985	377	155	125	540
Percent												
Very low birthweight[3]	1.5	11.3	91.1	43.5	8.4	0.9	0.1	0.1	0.0	0.1	0.1	2.8
Low birthweight[4]	8.2	43.3	96.5	76.8	66.0	30.4	3.1	4.0	1.4	1.4	2.5	11.1
NON-HISPANIC WHITE												
Total	2,279,768	265,466	12,687	24,469	32,345	195,965	1,875,177	1,231,768	443,103	200,306	130,458	8,667
Less than 500 grams	2,497	2,447	2,332	103	4	8	7	3	3	1	1	42
500–999 grams	10,015	9,836	7,113	2,442	189	92	95	70	21	4	5	79
1,000–1,499 grams	14,967	14,025	1,727	8,276	2,630	1,392	756	528	144	84	79	107
1,500–1,999 grams	33,687	28,725	373	6,581	10,302	11,469	4,426	3,701	482	243	345	191
2,000–2,499 grams	104,935	58,520	250	1,979	9,825	46,466	43,453	37,007	4,473	1,973	2,422	540
2,500–2,999 grams	364,726	73,832	431	1,637	4,108	67,656	274,173	216,907	40,482	16,784	15,288	1,433
3,000–3,499 grams	857,136	52,490	–	2,160	3,178	47,152	752,887	518,000	166,081	68,806	48,755	3,004
3,500–3,999 grams	672,270	20,293	–	1,214	1,607	17,472	604,075	355,551	169,992	78,532	45,633	2,269
4,000–4,499 grams	187,269	3,788	–	–	369	3,419	167,720	86,364	52,780	28,576	15,039	722
4,500–4,999 grams	27,541	608	–	–	43	565	24,329	11,784	7,782	4,763	2,504	100
5,000 grams or more	2,840	91	–	–	7	84	2,424	1,306	661	457	310	15
Not stated	1,885	811	461	77	83	190	832	547	202	83	77	165
Percent												
Very low birthweight[3]	1.2	9.9	91.4	44.4	8.8	0.8	0.0	0.0	0.0	0.0	0.1	2.7
Low birthweight[4]	7.3	42.9	96.5	79.5	71.1	30.4	2.6	3.4	1.2	1.2	2.2	11.3
NON-HISPANIC BLACK												
Total	583,759	107,059	11,042	13,155	14,264	68,598	442,809	301,437	98,593	42,779	31,030	2,861
Less than 500 grams	2,477	2,437	2,343	87	6	1	10	2	3	5	–	30
500–999 grams	8,014	7,879	6,057	1,661	100	61	49	32	10	7	5	81
1,000–1,499 grams	8,573	8,041	1,320	4,628	1,313	780	414	303	81	30	55	63
1,500–1,999 grams	15,764	13,165	333	2,913	4,434	5,485	2,291	1,890	287	114	189	119
2,000–2,499 grams	46,846	23,707	221	1,155	3,664	18,667	21,694	18,224	2,437	1,033	1,173	272
2,500–2,999 grams	144,803	26,859	313	1,163	2,295	23,088	110,685	85,758	17,854	7,073	6,591	668
3,000–3,499 grams	221,819	17,562	–	1,083	1,726	14,753	190,020	127,879	43,922	18,219	13,314	923
3,500–3,999 grams	108,698	5,710	–	421	586	4,703	94,869	55,246	26,974	12,649	7,644	475
4,000–4,499 grams	22,149	945	–	–	98	847	19,368	10,209	6,056	3,103	1,743	93
4,500–4,999 grams	3,203	145	–	–	13	132	2,779	1,492	820	467	260	19
5,000 grams or more	405	23	–	–	2	21	347	215	81	51	33	2
Not stated	1,008	586	455	44	27	60	283	187	68	28	23	116
Percent												
Very low birthweight[3]	3.3	17.2	91.8	48.6	10.0	1.2	0.1	0.1	0.1	0.1	0.2	6.3
Low birthweight[4]	14.0	51.9	97.0	79.7	66.8	36.5	5.5	6.8	2.9	2.8	4.6	20.6

– = Quantity zero.
0.0 = Quantity more than zero but less than 0.05.
[1]Expressed in completed weeks.
[2]Includes races other than White and Black and origin not stated.
[3]Birthweight of less than 1,500 grams (3 lb 4 oz).
[4]Birthweight of less than 2,500 grams (5 lb 8 oz).

Table A-41. Live Births by Birthweight and Percentage Very Low and Low Birthweight, by Period of Gestation, Race, and Hispanic Origin of Mother, 2005—*Continued*

(Number, percent.)

Birthweight, race, and Hispanic origin of mother	All births	Period of gestation[1]										
		Pre-term					Term				Post-term	Not stated
		Total under 37 weeks	Under 28 weeks	28–31 weeks	32–33 weeks	34–36 weeks	Total 37–41 weeks	37–39 weeks	40 weeks	41 weeks	(42 weeks and over)	
HISPANIC[5]												
Total	985,505	117,774	6,134	11,210	15,266	85,164	790,713	510,011	192,320	88,382	62,717	14,301
Less than 500 grams	1,212	1,153	1,112	40	1	–	3	1	2	–	–	56
500–999 grams	4,586	4,407	3,363	926	65	53	48	38	5	5	4	127
1,000–1,499 grams	5,988	5,411	832	3,083	896	600	377	270	71	36	46	154
1,500–1,999 grams	12,710	10,271	229	2,514	3,512	4,016	2,002	1,636	240	126	196	241
2,000–2,499 grams	43,300	21,735	161	1,057	3,893	16,624	19,652	16,254	2,347	1,051	1,185	728
2,500–2,999 grams	176,438	30,863	261	1,226	2,612	26,764	134,822	102,616	22,769	9,437	8,276	2,477
3,000–3,499 grams	399,295	28,408	–	1,557	2,736	24,115	340,012	225,106	80,365	34,541	25,544	5,331
3,500–3,999 grams	266,338	12,439	–	777	1,250	10,412	229,235	130,972	66,324	31,939	20,794	3,870
4,000–4,499 grams	64,704	2,412	–	–	249	2,163	55,557	28,467	17,464	9,626	5,672	1,063
4,500–4,999 grams	9,167	355	–	–	28	327	7,776	3,911	2,411	1,454	866	170
5,000 grams or more	1,174	58	–	–	8	50	978	572	271	135	112	26
Not stated	593	262	176	30	16	40	251	168	51	32	22	58
Percent												
Very low birthweight[3]	1.2	9.3	89.1	36.2	6.3	0.8	0.1	0.1	0.0	0.0	0.1	2.4
Low birthweight[4]	6.9	36.6	95.6	68.2	54.9	25.0	2.8	3.6	1.4	1.4	2.3	9.2

– = Quantity zero.
0.0 = Quantity more than zero but less than 0.05.
[1]Expressed in completed weeks.
[3]Birthweight of less than 1,500 grams (3 lb 4 oz).
[4]Birthweight of less than 2,500 grams (5 lb 8 oz).
[5]Persons of Hispanic origin may of any race.

Table A-42. Percentage of Live Births Very Preterm and Preterm and Percentage of Live Births of Very Low Birthweight and Low Birthweight, by Race and Hispanic Origin of Mother, 1981–2005

(Percent.)

Year	Very preterm[1]				Preterm[2]			
	All races[3]	Non-Hispanic		Hispanic[4]	All races[3]	Non-Hispanic		Hispanic[4]
		White	Black			White	Black	
1981	1.8	—	—	—	9.4	—	—	—
1982	1.8	—	—	—	9.5	—	—	—
1983	1.9	—	—	—	9.6	—	—	—
1984	1.8	—	—	—	9.4	—	—	—
1985	1.9	—	—	—	9.8	—	—	—
1986	1.9	—	—	—	10.0	—	—	—
1987	2.0	—	—	—	10.2	—	—	—
1988	2.0	—	—	—	10.2	—	—	—
1989[5]	2.0	1.3	4.7	1.8	10.6	8.4	19.0	11.1
1990[6]	1.9	1.3	4.6	1.7	10.6	8.5	18.9	11.0
1991[7]	1.9	1.4	4.7	1.7	10.8	8.7	19.0	11.0
1992[7]	1.9	1.3	4.5	1.6	10.7	8.7	18.5	10.7
1993	1.9	1.4	4.5	1.7	11.0	9.1	18.6	11.0
1994	1.9	1.4	4.4	1.7	11.0	9.3	18.2	10.9
1995	1.9	1.4	4.3	1.7	11.0	9.4	17.8	10.9
1996	1.9	1.4	4.2	1.7	11.0	9.5	17.5	10.9
1997	1.9	1.5	4.2	1.7	11.4	9.9	17.6	11.2
1998	2.0	1.5	4.2	1.7	11.6	10.2	17.6	11.4
1999	2.0	1.5	4.2	1.7	11.8	10.5	17.6	11.4
2000	1.9	1.5	4.1	1.7	11.6	10.4	17.4	11.2
2001	2.0	1.6	4.1	1.7	11.9	10.8	17.6	11.4
2002	2.0	1.6	4.0	1.7	12.1	11.0	17.7	11.6
2003	2.0	1.6	4.0	1.7	12.3	11.3	17.8	11.9
2004	2.0	1.6	4.1	1.8	12.5	11.5	17.9	12.0
2005	2.0	1.6	4.2	1.8	12.7	11.7	18.4	12.1

Year	Very low birthweight[8]				Low birthweight[9]			
	All races[3]	Non-Hispanic		Hispanic[4]	All races[3]	Non-Hispanic		Hispanic[4]
		White	Black			White	Black	
1981	1.2	—	—	—	6.8	—	—	—
1982	1.2	—	—	—	6.8	—	—	—
1983	1.2	—	—	—	6.8	—	—	—
1984	1.2	—	—	—	6.7	—	—	—
1985	1.2	—	—	—	6.8	—	—	—
1986	1.2	—	—	—	6.8	—	—	—
1987	1.2	—	—	—	6.9	—	—	—
1988	1.2	—	—	—	6.9	—	—	—
1989[5]	1.3	0.9	3.0	1.1	7.0	5.6	13.6	6.2
1990[6]	1.3	0.9	2.9	1.0	7.0	5.6	13.3	6.1
1991[7]	1.3	0.9	3.0	1.0	7.1	5.7	13.6	6.1
1992[7]	1.3	0.9	3.0	1.0	7.1	5.7	13.4	6.1
1993	1.3	1.0	3.0	1.1	7.2	5.9	13.4	6.2
1994	1.3	1.0	3.0	1.1	7.3	6.1	13.3	6.2
1995	1.4	1.0	3.0	1.1	7.3	6.2	13.2	6.3
1996	1.4	1.1	3.0	1.1	7.4	6.4	13.1	6.3
1997	1.4	1.1	3.1	1.1	7.5	6.5	13.1	6.4
1998	1.5	1.2	3.1	1.2	7.6	6.6	13.2	6.4
1999	1.5	1.2	3.2	1.1	7.6	6.6	13.2	6.4
2000	1.4	1.1	3.1	1.1	7.6	6.6	13.1	6.4
2001	1.4	1.2	3.1	1.1	7.7	6.8	13.1	6.5
2002	1.5	1.2	3.2	1.2	7.8	6.9	13.4	6.5
2003	1.5	1.2	3.1	1.2	7.9	7.0	13.6	6.7
2004	1.5	1.2	3.2	1.2	8.1	7.2	13.7	6.8
2005	1.5	1.2	3.3	1.2	8.2	7.3	14.0	6.9

—— = Data not available

[1] Births of less than 32 completed weeks of gestation.
[2] Births of less than 37 completed weeks of gestation.
[3] Includes races other than White and Black and origin not stated.
[4] Persons of Hispanic origin may be of any race.
[5] Data by Hispanic origin exclude New Hampshire, Oklahoma, and Louisiana, which did not report Hispanic origin.
[6] Data by Hispanic origin exclude New Hampshire and Oklahoma, which did not report Hispanic origin.
[7] Data by Hispanic origin exclude New Hampshire, which did not report Hispanic origin.
[8] Less than 1,500 grams (3 lb 4 oz).
[9] Less than 2,500 grams (5 lb 8 oz).

Table A-43. Number and Percentage of Births Delivered Preterm, by Race and Hispanic Origin of Mother, by State and Territory, 2005

(Number, percent.)

Area	Number				Percent			
	All races[1]	Non-Hispanic		Hispanic[2]	All races[1]	Non-Hispanic		Hispanic[2]
		White	Black			White	Black	
UNITED STATES[3]	522,913	265,466	107,059	117,774	12.7	11.7	18.4	12.1
Alabama	10,107	5,432	3,947	578	16.7	14.6	21.9	14.5
Alaska	1,111	566	63	81	10.6	9.5	16.8	10.4
Arizona	12,655	4,829	609	5,793	13.2	12.1	20.2	13.5
Arkansas	5,237	3,295	1,336	470	13.4	12.3	18.1	11.7
California	56,363	15,381	4,476	28,975	10.7	10.0	15.5	10.7
Colorado	8,485	4,843	489	2,793	12.3	11.7	16.5	12.8
Connecticut	4,355	2,533	740	882	10.4	9.6	15.2	11.0
Delaware	1,629	801	528	219	14.0	12.4	18.4	13.3
District of Columbia	1,262	193	896	149	15.9	9.4	19.5	13.4
Florida	31,188	12,938	8,930	8,323	13.8	12.2	18.5	13.1
Georgia	19,324	8,250	8,131	2,221	13.6	12.1	18.0	10.2
Hawaii	2,179	410	49	358	12.2	9.8	12.0	12.9
Idaho	2,631	2,090	15	423	11.4	11.2	*	12.1
Illinois	23,452	11,299	5,946	5,210	13.1	11.8	19.6	12.0
Indiana	11,753	8,660	1,809	1,062	13.5	12.8	18.5	13.2
Iowa	4,654	3,865	261	367	11.8	11.6	17.6	11.8
Kansas	4,860	3,494	474	727	12.2	11.9	16.9	12.0
Kentucky	8,585	7,132	957	396	15.2	14.8	19.8	15.8
Louisiana	10,036	4,477	5,134	258	16.5	13.3	21.4	13.6
Maine	1,503	1,419	30	11	10.7	10.7	11.7	*
Maryland	9,949	4,171	4,140	1,103	13.3	11.3	17.0	12.7
Massachusetts	8,697	5,787	1,067	1,186	11.3	10.7	15.8	11.7
Michigan	15,877	9,785	4,284	912	12.5	11.1	19.4	10.6
Minnesota	7,588	5,507	764	539	10.7	10.4	13.2	9.8
Mississippi	7,952	3,407	4,299	131	18.8	15.6	23.1	11.3
Missouri	10,404	7,331	2,286	526	13.3	12.1	19.9	12.3
Montana	1,323	1,007	4	48	11.4	10.9	*	12.1
Nebraska	3,181	2,290	260	510	12.2	11.6	17.1	13.2
Nevada	5,160	2,162	619	1,792	13.9	13.1	20.8	12.8
New Hampshire	1,505	1,319	39	58	10.5	10.2	20.9	11.1
New Jersey	14,219	6,418	2,914	3,634	12.5	11.1	17.4	13.0
New Mexico	3,778	1,074	84	2,047	13.1	12.7	17.5	13.0
New York	29,883	13,161	7,183	7,429	12.1	10.5	17.2	12.9
North Carolina	16,868	8,565	5,289	2,391	13.7	12.2	18.8	12.3
North Dakota	962	735	18	21	11.5	10.9	*	11.7
Ohio	19,321	13,858	4,047	819	13.0	12.1	18.0	13.5
Oklahoma	6,758	4,295	851	735	13.1	12.7	18.1	11.8
Oregon	4,674	3,225	130	942	10.2	10.0	13.6	10.3
Pennsylvania	17,123	11,428	3,257	1,639	11.9	10.8	16.7	13.5
Rhode Island	1,538	730	161	334	12.1	11.0	14.0	13.1
South Carolina	9,002	4,377	3,812	658	15.6	13.3	20.4	13.2
South Dakota	1,314	973	16	45	11.5	10.9	*	11.5
Tennessee	11,947	7,681	3,242	837	14.7	13.7	19.8	12.1
Texas	52,440	17,597	7,910	25,216	13.6	12.8	18.8	13.2
Utah	5,898	4,532	74	959	11.4	11.0	17.0	12.7
Vermont	577	544	10	4	8.9	8.9	*	*
Virginia	12,837	6,982	3,696	1,457	12.3	11.2	16.7	11.2
Washington	8,717	5,288	434	1,675	10.6	9.9	13.5	11.3
West Virginia	3,003	2,809	136	17	14.4	14.3	19.6	*
Wisconsin	8,114	5,748	1,203	722	11.4	10.6	17.9	11.6
Wyoming	944	782	10	92	13.1	13.1	*	11.1
Puerto Rico	9,961	597	52	9,309	19.7	20.4	32.5	19.6
Virgin Islands	244	10	164	52	15.3	*	16.5	13.9
Guam	542	22	4	12	17.0	8.8	*	*
American Samoa	—	—	—	—	—	—	—	—
Northern Marianas	175	—	—	—	13.1	—	—	—

* = Figure does not meet standards of reliability or precision.
—— = Data not available
[1]Includes races other than White and Black and origin not stated.
[2]Persons of Hispanic origin may be of any race.
[3]Excludes data for the territories.

Table A-44. Percentage of Preterm Births, Selected Years, 1990–2005 and Preliminary 2006

(Percent.)

Year	Total preterm[1]	Late preterm[2]	32–33 weeks	Very preterm[3]
1990	10.61	7.30	1.40	1.92
2000	11.64	8.22	1.49	1.93
2005	12.73	9.09	1.60	2.03
2006	12.80	9.14	1.62	2.04

[1]Less than 37 completed weeks of gestation.
[2]34–36 completed weeks of gestation.
[3]Less than 32 completed weeks of gestation.

Table A-45. Number and Percentage Low Birthweight and Number of Live Births by Birthweight, by Age, Race and Hispanic Origin of Mother, 2005

(Number, percent.)

Age, race, and Hispanic origin of mother	Low birthweight[1] Number	Low birthweight[1] Percent	Total	Less than 500 grams	500–999 grams	1,000–1,499 grams	1500–1900 grams	2000–2499 grams	2500–2999 grams	3000–3499 grams	3,5000–3,999 grams	4000–4,499 grams	4,500–4,999 grams	5,000 grams or more	Not stated
All Races[2]															
All ages......................	338,565	8.2	4,138,349	6,599	23,864	31,325	66,453	210,324	748,042	1,596,944	1,114,887	289,098	42,119	4,715	3,979
Under 15 years	892	13.3	6,722	25	92	103	178	494	1,866	2,592	1,162	174	19	1	16
15–19 years	41,525	10.0	414,593	867	3,209	3,707	7,710	26,032	94,910	169,715	89,144	16,745	1,876	186	492
15 years......................	2,100	11.5	18,249	61	190	215	401	1,233	4,528	7,441	3,538	563	44	5	30
16 years......................	4,484	10.9	41,064	75	406	412	849	2,742	9,911	16,837	8,218	1,405	141	14	54
17 years......................	7,597	10.3	73,878	146	586	656	1,435	4,774	17,218	30,472	15,420	2,786	266	32	87
18 years......................	11,814	10.1	116,476	275	861	1,065	2,155	7,458	26,370	47,978	25,003	4,623	501	50	137
19 years......................	15,530	9.4	164,926	310	1,166	1,359	2,870	9,825	36,883	66,987	36,965	7,368	924	85	184
20–24 years	86,321	8.3	1,040,388	1,679	5,924	7,641	16,006	55,071	208,845	418,820	258,493	58,625	7,510	791	983
25–29 years	83,247	7.4	1,131,596	1,674	5,745	7,430	16,036	52,362	194,306	438,676	318,052	83,072	11,888	1,299	1,056
30–34 years	71,707	7.5	950,691	1,397	4,996	6,919	14,743	43,652	150,671	354,909	279,330	79,465	12,364	1,374	871
35–39 years	42,140	8.7	483,156	776	3,017	4,241	8,961	25,145	77,876	173,727	139,211	42,023	6,891	848	440
40–44 years	11,354	10.8	104,667	169	813	1,143	2,441	6,788	18,217	36,525	28,150	8,603	1,503	206	109
45–54 years	1,379	21.1	6,536	12	68	141	378	780	1,351	1,980	1,345	391	68	10	12
Non-Hispanic White															
All ages......................	166,101	7.3	2,279,768	2,497	10,015	14,967	33,687	104,935	364,726	857,136	672,270	187,269	27,541	2,840	1,885
Under 15 years	147	11.0	1,331	3	12	17	29	86	302	546	280	48	6	1	1
15–19 years	14,950	9.1	165,005	288	1,056	1,335	2,839	9,432	33,650	66,161	40,392	8,589	996	97	170
15 years......................	491	10.4	4,702	13	56	46	108	268	1,001	1,908	1,078	190	22	2	10
16 years......................	1,238	9.8	12,675	23	104	126	243	742	2,692	5,078	2,996	595	51	7	18
17 years......................	2,573	9.7	26,487	48	183	225	516	1,601	5,400	10,618	6,437	1,286	137	13	23
18 years......................	4,419	9.3	47,329	104	292	399	828	2,796	9,552	19,125	11,493	2,396	274	25	45
19 years......................	6,229	8.4	73,812	100	421	539	1,144	4,025	15,005	29,432	18,388	4,122	512	50	74
20–24 years	38,062	7.4	515,518	554	2,329	3,269	7,244	24,666	93,832	203,953	140,105	34,184	4,491	456	435
25–29 years	42,408	6.6	642,553	681	2,533	3,716	8,356	27,122	98,844	243,625	195,010	53,749	7,654	778	485
30–34 years	39,512	6.8	581,645	563	2,299	3,683	8,471	24,496	82,092	211,959	183,371	54,916	8,464	834	497
35–39 years	23,812	7.8	305,142	327	1,357	2,288	5,180	14,660	44,818	107,484	93,825	29,617	4,826	526	234
40–44 years	6,320	9.8	64,352	75	388	582	1,315	3,960	10,345	22,154	18,386	5,900	1,055	139	53
45–54 years	890	21.1	4,222	6	41	77	253	513	843	1,254	901	266	49	9	10
Non-Hispanic Black															
All ages......................	81,674	14.0	583,759	2,477	8,014	8,573	15,764	46,846	144,803	221,819	108,698	22,149	3,203	405	1,008
Under 15 years	463	17.2	2,697	15	54	50	95	249	862	960	358	43	1	–	–
15–19 years	14,165	14.6	96,813	376	1,301	1,355	2,655	8,478	27,382	37,832	14,867	2,151	205	24	187
15 years......................	836	14.9	5,602	29	77	87	162	481	1,664	2,157	811	114	5	1	14
16 years......................	1,636	15.1	10,829	35	158	149	310	984	3,156	4,193	1,605	200	19	1	19
17 years......................	2,597	14.6	17,747	67	244	244	454	1,588	5,024	7,035	2,634	387	32	4	34
18 years......................	3,950	14.8	26,627	101	336	391	742	2,380	7,494	10,413	4,065	592	55	6	52
19 years......................	5,146	14.3	36,008	144	486	484	987	3,045	10,044	14,034	5,752	858	94	12	68
20–24 years	25,779	13.7	188,673	724	2,280	2,595	4,788	15,392	49,573	73,820	32,629	5,736	749	78	309
25–29 years	18,740	13.1	142,885	602	1,820	1,939	3,603	10,776	33,955	54,436	28,316	6,178	897	117	246
30–34 years	12,643	13.7	92,336	454	1,423	1,442	2,541	6,783	19,954	33,948	20,012	4,729	786	108	156
35–39 years	7,507	15.8	47,411	254	906	901	1,527	3,919	10,226	16,513	9,940	2,618	461	67	79
40–44 years	2,212	18.0	12,256	50	217	272	513	1,160	2,693	4,092	2,464	662	103	10	20
45–54 years	165	24.0	688	2	13	19	42	89	158	218	112	32	1	1	1
Hispanic[3]															
All ages......................	67,796	6.9	985,505	1,212	4,586	5,988	12,710	43,300	176,438	399,295	266,338	64,704	9,167	1,174	593
Under 15 years	252	10.2	2,466	6	22	34	48	142	642	1,000	483	75	11	–	–
15–19 years	10,980	8.0	136,906	177	752	908	1,950	7,193	30,356	59,319	30,279	5,246	570	50	106
15 years......................	714	9.9	7,241	17	53	73	118	453	1,714	3,072	1,499	223	14	1	4
16 years......................	1,453	9.1	15,928	17	136	125	275	900	3,705	6,895	3,257	540	63	5	10
17 years......................	2,154	8.0	26,877	29	136	168	401	1,420	6,133	11,744	5,741	988	80	12	25
18 years......................	3,045	8.0	38,090	60	210	249	515	2,011	8,373	16,618	8,443	1,425	140	14	32
19 years......................	3,614	7.4	48,770	54	217	293	641	2,409	10,431	20,990	11,339	2,070	273	18	35
20–24 years	18,731	6.5	287,896	319	1,095	1,494	3,377	12,446	54,868	121,320	74,552	16,127	1,910	220	168
25–29 years	16,305	6.1	266,590	291	1,133	1,365	3,060	10,456	44,209	107,357	76,211	19,248	2,770	330	160
30–34 years	12,624	6.8	186,398	267	922	1,262	2,386	7,787	29,198	71,610	54,816	15,260	2,460	333	97
35–39 years	6,967	8.1	85,739	121	521	719	1,464	4,142	13,733	31,697	24,717	7,194	1,185	199	47
40–44 years	1,799	9.7	18,597	29	131	188	388	1,063	3,250	6,678	5,070	1,497	249	42	12
45–54 years	138	15.1	913	2	10	18	37	71	182	314	210	57	12	–	–

– = Quantity zero.
[1] Less than 2,500 grams (5 lb 8 oz).
[2] Includes races other than White and Black and origin not stated.
[3] Persons of Hispanic origin may be of any race.

Table A-46. Number and Percentage of Births of Low Birthweight, by Race and Hispanic Origin of Mother, by State and Territory, 2005

(Number, percent.)

Area	Number				Percent			
	All races[1]	Non-Hispanic		Hispanic[2]	All races[1]	Non-Hispanic		Hispanic[2]
		White	Black			White	Black	
UNITED STATES[3]	338,565	166,101	81,674	67,796	8.2	7.3	14.0	6.9
Alabama	6,429	3,262	2,797	288	10.7	8.8	15.5	7.2
Alaska	635	339	58	42	6.1	5.7	15.5	5.4
Arizona	6,673	2,767	392	2,772	6.9	6.9	13.0	6.5
Arkansas	3,498	2,050	1,073	291	8.9	7.7	14.5	7.2
California	37,630	10,386	3,842	17,573	6.9	6.5	12.6	6.2
Colorado	6,325	3,705	452	1,888	9.2	8.9	15.3	8.7
Connecticut	3,317	1,786	656	664	8.0	6.8	13.5	8.3
Delaware	1,106	496	427	119	9.5	7.7	14.9	7.2
District of Columbia	888	146	646	78	11.2	7.1	14.1	7.0
Florida	19,761	8,045	6,547	4,478	8.7	7.6	13.6	7.0
Georgia	13,498	5,088	6,521	1,327	9.5	7.5	14.4	6.1
Hawaii	1,468	276	44	243	8.2	6.6	10.8	8.7
Idaho	1,538	1,243	6	225	6.7	6.7	*	6.5
Illinois	15,265	6,941	4,576	2,929	8.5	7.3	15.1	6.7
Indiana	7,232	5,226	1,313	534	8.3	7.8	13.4	6.7
Iowa	2,814	2,334	184	190	7.2	7.0	12.5	6.1
Kansas	2,860	2,014	387	357	7.2	6.9	13.7	5.8
Kentucky	5,126	4,224	654	176	9.1	8.8	13.5	7.0
Louisiana	6,987	2,911	3,821	137	11.5	8.7	16.0	7.2
Maine	957	903	23	8	6.8	6.8	9.0	*
Maryland	6,844	2,641	3,185	625	9.1	7.1	13.1	7.2
Massachusetts	6,063	3,919	804	844	7.9	7.3	11.9	8.3
Michigan	10,615	6,202	3,238	556	8.3	7.0	14.7	6.5
Minnesota	4,628	3,161	654	311	6.5	6.0	11.3	5.7
Mississippi	5,016	1,905	2,996	60	11.8	8.7	16.1	5.1
Missouri	6,347	4,270	1,642	267	8.1	7.0	14.3	6.3
Montana	767	586	9	32	6.6	6.3	*	8.1
Nebraska	1,818	1,285	200	251	7.0	6.5	13.1	6.5
Nevada	3,080	1,287	444	969	8.3	7.8	14.8	6.9
New Hampshire	1,001	873	21	39	7.0	6.8	11.3	7.5
New Jersey	9,313	4,107	2,243	2,030	8.2	7.1	13.4	7.3
New Mexico	2,460	741	69	1,334	8.5	8.8	14.4	8.4
New York	20,420	8,727	5,508	4,460	8.3	7.0	13.2	7.8
North Carolina	11,308	5,536	4,102	1,227	9.2	7.9	14.6	6.3
North Dakota	535	427	12	10	6.4	6.3	*	*
Ohio	12,882	8,908	3,131	432	8.7	7.8	13.9	7.1
Oklahoma	4,131	2,561	671	418	8.0	7.5	14.2	6.7
Oregon	2,793	1,925	109	526	6.1	6.0	11.4	5.7
Pennsylvania	12,094	7,729	2,641	1,074	8.4	7.3	13.5	8.8
Rhode Island	985	467	118	220	7.8	7.1	10.3	8.6
South Carolina	5,885	2,552	2,857	359	10.2	7.8	15.3	7.2
South Dakota	754	589	12	16	6.6	6.6	*	*
Tennessee	7,748	4,726	2,449	423	9.5	8.4	14.9	6.1
Texas	31,956	10,507	5,956	14,265	8.3	7.7	14.2	7.5
Utah	3,520	2,734	46	539	6.8	6.6	10.6	7.1
Vermont	401	378	7	1	6.2	6.2	*	*
Virginia	8,573	4,451	2,805	801	8.2	7.2	12.7	6.1
Washington	5,041	2,986	316	912	6.1	5.6	9.8	6.1
West Virginia	1,990	1,862	91	5	9.6	9.4	13.1	*
Wisconsin	4,977	3,402	910	403	7.0	6.3	13.6	6.4
Wyoming	621	523	9	68	8.6	8.8	*	8.2
Puerto Rico	6,470	384	40	6,043	12.8	13.2	25.3	12.8
Virgin Islands	178	6	128	30	11.2	*	12.9	8.0
Guam	278	11	–	5	8.8	*	——	*
American Samoa	65	——	——	——	3.8	——	——	——
Northern Marianas	99	——	——	——	7.4	——	——	——

* = Figure does not meet standards of reliability or precision.
– = Quantity zero.
—— = Data not available.
[1]Includes races other than White and Black and origin not stated.
[2]Persons of Hispanic origin may be of any race.
[3]Excludes data for the territories.

Table A-47. Number and Percentage of Births of Very Low Birthweight, by Race and Hispanic Origin of Mother, by State and Territory, 2005

(Number, percent.)

Area	Number				Percent			
	All races[1]	Non-Hispanic		Hispanic[2]	All races[1]	Non-Hispanic		Hispanic[2]
		White	Black			White	Black	
UNITED STATES[3]	61,788	27,479	19,064	11,786	1.5	1.2	3.3	1.2
Alabama	1,277	550	662	47	2.1	1.5	3.7	1.2
Alaska	98	45	13	4	0.9	0.8	*	*
Arizona	1,114	431	84	499	1.2	1.1	2.8	1.2
Arkansas	638	325	255	44	1.6	1.2	3.4	1.1
California	6,749	1,729	890	3,203	1.2	1.1	2.9	1.1
Colorado	884	487	75	291	1.3	1.2	2.5	1.3
Connecticut	668	302	186	151	1.6	1.1	3.8	1.9
Delaware	243	94	113	23	2.1	1.5	3.9	1.4
District of Columbia	208	18	175	10	2.6	*	3.8	*
Florida	3,603	1,237	1,493	767	1.6	1.2	3.4	1.1
Georgia	2,604	797	1,506	210	1.8	1.2	3.3	1.0
Hawaii	244	42	14	38	1.4	1.0	*	1.4
Idaho	251	222	–	21	1.1	1.2	*	0.6
Illinois	2,884	1,187	1,039	535	1.6	1.2	3.4	1.2
Indiana	1,311	879	320	100	1.5	1.3	3.3	1.2
Iowa	525	425	40	37	1.3	1.3	2.7	1.2
Kansas	528	356	91	67	1.3	1.2	3.2	1.1
Kentucky	900	704	151	32	16.0	15.0	31.0	13.0
Louisiana	1,368	473	845	30	2.2	1.4	3.5	1.6
Maine	177	166	5	1	1.3	1.2	*	*
Maryland	1,381	460	782	101	1.8	1.2	3.2	1.2
Massachusetts	1,078	643	193	165	1.4	1.2	2.9	1.6
Michigan	2,072	1,065	799	116	1.6	1.2	3.6	1.3
Minnesota	862	569	157	52	1.2	1.1	2.7	0.9
Mississippi	972	283	673	4	2.3	1.3	3.6	*
Missouri	1,166	706	388	51	1.5	1.2	3.4	1.2
Montana	110	85	1	6	1.0	0.9	*	*
Nebraska	307	212	37	44	1.2	1.1	2.4	1.1
Nevada	474	177	108	147	1.3	1.1	3.6	1.0
New Hampshire	181	158	5	10	1.3	1.2	*	*
New Jersey	1,751	664	602	348	1.5	1.1	3.6	1.2
New Mexico	362	96	13	202	1.3	1.1	*	1.3
New York	3,731	1,408	1,311	789	1.5	1.1	3.1	1.4
North Carolina	2,259	943	1,043	212	1.8	1.3	3.7	1.1
North Dakota	99	82	1	1	1.2	1.2	*	*
Ohio	2,380	1,528	710	68	1.6	1.3	3.2	1.1
Oklahoma	732	447	146	69	1.4	1.3	3.1	1.1
Oregon	460	336	14	81	1.0	1.0	*	0.9
Pennsylvania	2,286	1,340	613	217	1.6	1.3	3.1	1.8
Rhode Island	189	82	28	48	1.5	1.2	2.4	1.9
South Carolina	1,178	442	654	65	2.0	1.3	3.5	1.3
South Dakota	128	93	4	1	1.1	1.0	*	*
Tennessee	1,383	755	531	76	1.7	1.3	3.2	1.1
Texas	5,587	1,815	1,303	2,336	14.0	13.0	3.1	1.2
Utah	528	408	7	86	1.0	1.0	*	1.1
Vermont	76	69	2	-	1.2	1.1	*	*
Virginia	1,716	810	671	154	16.0	13.0	30.0	12.0
Washington	743	419	58	138	0.9	0.8	1.8	0.9
West Virginia	336	306	19	2	1.6	1.6	*	*
Wisconsin	904	541	230	81	1.3	1.0	3.4	1.3
Wyoming	84	69	3	6	1.2	1.2	*	*
Puerto Rico	718	42	7	668	1.4	1.4	*	1.4
Virgin Islands	38	1	28	6	2.4	*	2.8	*
Guam	44	3	–	–	1.4	*	*	*
American Samoa	5	—	—	—	*	—	—	—
Northern Marianas	13	—	—	—	*	—	—	—

* = Figure does not meet standards of reliability or precision.
– = Quantity zero.
—— = Data not available.
[1]Includes races other than White and Black and origin not stated.
[2]Includes all persons of Hispanic origin of any race.
[3]Excludes data for the territories.

Table A-48. Rate of Very Low Birthweight and Low Birthweight, and Mean Birthweight Among Singletons by Race and Hispanic Origin of Mother, Selected Years, 1990–2005

(Rate.)

Mean birthweight and rate of low birthweight by race and Hispanic origin	1990[1]	1995	2000	2004	2005
All Races and Origins[2]					
Percent very low birthweight................................	1.05	1.08	1.11	1.12	1.14
Percent low birthweight..	5.90	6.05	6.00	6.31	6.41
Mean birthweight in grams (standard deviation)	3,365 (583)	3,353 (581)	3,348 (577)	3,316 (570)	3,307 (568)
Non-Hispanic White					
Percent very low birthweight................................	0.73	0.78	0.80	0.83	0.84
Percent low birthweight..	4.56	4.87	4.88	5.22	5.32
Mean birthweight in grams (standard deviation)	3,433 (562)	3,416(563)	3,410 (560)	3,375 (554)	3364 (552)
Non-Hispanic Black					
Percent very low birthweight................................	2.54	2.55	2.62	2.61	2.71
Percent low birthweight..	11.92	11.66	11.28	11.70	11.90
Mean birthweight in grams (standard deviation)	3,128 (635)	3,132 (635)	3,141 (637)	3,115(628)	3105 (629)
Hispanic[3]					
Percent very low birthweight................................	0.87	0.93	0.94	0.98	0.97
Percent low birthweight..	5.23	5.36	5.36	5.63	5.69
Mean birthweight in grams (standard deviation)	3,351 (552)	3,343 (553)	3,344 (552)	3,316 (548)	3,309 (545)

[1]Data for 1990 by race and Hispanic origin exclude data for New Hampshire and Oklahoma, which did not require reporting of Hispanic origin of mother.
[2]Includes races other than White and Black and origin not stated.
[3]Persons of Hispanic origin may be of any race.

NOTE: Very low birthweight is less than 1,500 grams. Low birthweight is less than 2,500 grams.

Table A-49. Low-Birthweight Live Births, by Detailed Race, Hispanic Origin, and Smoking Status of Mother, Selected Years, 1970–2004

(Percent.)

Birthweight, race, Hispanic origin of mother, and smoking status of mother	1970	1975	1980	1985	1990	1995	2000	2001	2002	2003	2004
PERCENT OF LIVE BIRTHS[1]											
Low Birthweight (less Than 2,500 Grams)											
All Races	7.93	7.38	6.84	6.75	6.97	7.32	7.57	7.68	7.82	7.93	8.08
White	6.85	6.27	5.72	5.65	5.70	6.22	6.55	6.68	6.80	6.94	7.07
Black or African American	13.90	13.19	12.69	12.65	13.25	13.13	12.99	12.95	13.29	13.37	13.44
American Indian or Alaska Native	7.97	6.41	6.44	5.86	6.11	6.61	6.76	7.33	7.23	7.37	7.45
Asian or Pacific Islander[2]	—	—	6.68	6.16	6.45	6.90	7.31	7.51	7.78	7.78	7.89
Chinese	6.67	5.29	5.21	4.98	4.69	5.29	5.10	5.33	5.52	—	—
Japanese	9.03	7.47	6.60	6.21	6.16	7.26	7.14	7.28	7.57	—	—
Filipino	10.02	8.08	7.40	6.95	7.30	7.83	8.46	8.66	8.61	—	—
Hawaiian	—	—	7.23	6.49	7.24	6.84	6.76	7.91	8.14	—	—
Other Asian or Pacific Islander	—	—	6.83	6.19	6.65	7.05	7.67	7.76	8.16	—	—
Hispanic or Latino[3]	—	—	6.12	6.16	6.06	6.29	6.41	6.47	6.55	6.69	6.79
Mexican	—	—	5.62	5.77	5.55	5.81	6.01	6.08	6.16	6.28	6.44
Puerto Rican	—	—	8.95	8.69	8.99	9.41	9.30	9.34	9.68	10.01	9.82
Cuban	—	—	5.62	6.02	5.67	6.50	6.49	6.49	6.50	7.04	7.72
Central and South American	—	—	5.76	5.68	5.84	6.20	6.34	6.49	6.53	6.70	6.70
Other and unknown Hispanic or Latino	—	—	6.96	6.83	6.87	7.55	7.84	7.96	7.87	8.01	7.78
Not Hispanic or Latino[3]											
White	—	—	5.69	5.61	5.61	6.20	6.60	6.76	6.91	7.04	7.20
Black or African American	—	—	12.71	12.62	13.32	13.21	13.13	13.07	13.39	13.55	13.74
Cigarette smoker[4]	—	—	—	—	11.25	12.18	11.88	11.90	12.15	12.40	12.54
Nonsmoker[4]	—	—	—	—	6.14	6.79	7.19	7.32	7.48	7.66	7.79
Very Low Birthweight (less Than 1,500 Grams)											
All Races	1.17	1.16	1.15	1.21	1.27	1.35	1.43	1.44	1.46	1.45	1.48
White	0.95	0.92	0.90	0.94	0.95	1.06	1.14	1.16	1.17	1.17	1.20
Black or African American	2.40	2.40	2.48	2.71	2.92	2.97	3.07	3.04	3.13	3.07	3.07
American Indian or Alaska Native	0.98	0.95	0.92	1.01	1.01	1.10	1.16	1.26	1.28	1.30	1.28
Asian or Pacific Islander[2]	—	—	0.92	0.85	0.87	0.91	1.05	1.03	1.12	1.09	1.14
Chinese	0.80	0.52	0.66	0.57	0.51	0.67	0.77	0.69	0.74	—	—
Japanese	1.48	0.89	0.94	0.84	0.73	0.87	0.75	0.71	0.97	—	—
Filipino	1.08	0.93	0.99	0.86	1.05	1.13	1.38	1.23	1.31	—	—
Hawaiian	—	—	1.05	1.03	0.97	0.94	1.39	1.50	1.55	—	—
Other Asian or Pacific Islander	—	—	0.96	0.91	0.92	0.91	1.04	1.06	1.17	—	—
Hispanic or Latino[3]	—	—	0.98	1.01	1.03	1.11	1.14	1.14	1.17	1.16	1.20
Mexican	—	—	0.92	0.97	0.92	1.01	1.03	1.05	1.06	1.06	1.13
Puerto Rican	—	—	1.29	1.30	1.62	1.79	1.93	1.85	1.96	2.01	1.96
Cuban	—	—	1.02	1.18	1.20	1.19	1.21	1.27	1.15	1.37	1.30
Central and South American	—	—	0.99	1.01	1.05	1.13	1.20	1.19	1.20	1.17	1.19
Other and unknown Hispanic or Latino	—	—	1.01	0.96	1.09	1.28	1.42	1.27	1.44	1.28	1.27
Not Hispanic or Latino[3]											
White	—	—	0.87	0.91	0.93	1.04	1.14	1.17	1.17	1.18	1.20
Black or African American	—	—	2.47	2.67	2.93	2.98	3.10	3.08	3.15	3.12	3.15
Cigarette smoker[4]	—	—	—	—	1.73	1.85	1.91	1.88	1.88	1.92	1.88
Nonsmoker[4]	—	—	—	—	1.18	1.31	1.40	1.42	1.45	1.44	1.47

— = Data not available.

[1]Excludes live births with unknown birthweight. Percent based on live births with known birthweight.

[2]Starting with 2003 data, estimates are not shown for Asian or Pacific Islander subgroups during the transition from single race to multiple race reporting.

[3]Persons of Hispanic origin may be of any race. Prior to 1993, data from states lacking an Hispanic-origin item on the birth certificate were excluded. Data for non-Hispanic White and non-Hispanic Black women for years prior to 1989 are not nationally representative and are provided for comparison with Hispanic data.

[4]Percent based on live births with known smoking status of mother and known birthweight. Data from states that did not require the reporting of mother's tobacco use during pregnancy on the birth certificate are not included. Reporting area for tobacco use increased from 43 states and the District of Columbia (DC) in 1989 to 49 states and DC in 2000–2002.

Table A-50. Mothers Who Smoked Cigarettes During Pregnancy, by Detailed Race, Hispanic Origin, Age, and Education of Mother, Selected Years, 1989–2004

(Percent.)

Characteristic	1989	1990	1995	2000	2001	2002	2003[1]	42 reporting areas	
								2003[2]	2004[1]
PERCENT OF MOTHERS WHO SMOKED[3,4]									
All Races....................................	19.5	18.4	13.9	12.2	12.0	11.4	10.7	10.4	10.2
White..	20.4	19.4	15.0	13.2	13.0	12.3	11.6	11.1	11.0
Black or African American	17.1	15.9	10.6	9.1	9.0	8.7	8.1	8.3	8.2
American Indian or Alaska Native	23.0	22.4	20.9	20.0	19.9	19.7	18.1	18.2	18.2
Asian or Pacific Islander[5]................	5.7	5.5	3.4	2.8	2.8	2.5	2.2	2.2	2.2
Chinese...............................	2.7	2.0	0.8	0.6	0.7	0.5	—	—	—
Japanese..............................	8.2	8.0	5.2	4.2	3.8	4.0	—	—	—
Filipino...............................	5.1	5.3	3.4	3.2	3.2	2.9	—	—	—
Hawaiian..............................	19.3	21.0	15.9	14.4	14.8	13.7	—	—	—
Other Asian or Pacific Islander......	4.2	3.8	2.7	2.3	2.3	2.1	—	—	—
Hispanic Origin and Race of Mother									
Hispanic or Latino[6].......................	8.0	6.7	4.3	3.5	3.2	3.0	2.7	2.7	2.6
Mexican...............................	6.3	5.3	3.1	2.4	2.4	2.2	2.0	2.1	2.0
Puerto Rican..........................	14.5	13.6	10.4	10.3	9.7	9.0	7.9	8.5	8.5
Cuban.................................	6.9	6.4	4.1	3.3	3.0	2.8	2.4	5.8	6.4
Central and South American...........	3.6	3.0	1.8	1.5	1.3	1.3	1.1	1.1	1.2
Other and unknown Hispanic or Latino	12.1	10.8	8.2	7.4	6.8	6.5	6.6	6.9	6.4
Not Hispanic or Latino									
White.................................	21.7	21.0	17.1	15.6	15.5	15.0	14.3	13.8	13.8
Black or African American.............	17.2	15.9	10.6	9.2	9.1	8.8	8.3	8.4	8.4
Age of Mother[3]									
Under 15 years.............................	7.7	7.5	7.3	7.1	6.0	5.8	5.3	5.1	4.1
15–19 years................................	22.2	20.8	16.8	17.8	17.5	16.7	15.4	14.9	14.2
15–17 years............................	19.0	17.6	14.6	15.0	14.4	13.4	11.9	11.5	10.5
18–19 years............................	23.9	22.5	18.1	19.2	19.0	18.2	17.1	16.5	16.0
20–24 years................................	23.5	22.1	17.1	16.8	17.0	16.7	16.1	15.5	15.5
25–29 years................................	19.0	18.0	12.8	10.5	10.3	9.9	9.4	9.0	9.2
30–34 years................................	15.7	15.3	11.4	8.0	7.6	7.1	6.5	6.2	6.1
35–39 years................................	13.6	13.3	12.0	9.1	8.6	7.8	6.8	6.7	6.3
40–54 years[7].............................	13.2	12.3	10.1	9.5	9.3	8.4	8.0	7.8	7.2
PERCENT OF MOTHERS 20 YEARS OF AGE AND OVER WHO SMOKED[3,4]									
Education of Mother[8]									
0-8 years..................................	18.9	17.5	11.0	7.9	7.2	6.8	6.2	5.7	5.5
9-11 years.................................	42.2	40.5	32.0	28.2	27.6	26.8	25.5	24.2	23.7
12 years	22.8	21.9	18.3	16.6	16.5	16.0	15.2	14.9	14.9
13-15 years................................	13.7	12.8	10.6	9.1	9.2	8.8	8.5	8.3	8.4
16 years or more	5.0	4.5	2.7	2.0	1.9	1.7	1.6	1.5	1.5

—- = Data not available.

[1]Reporting areas that have adopted the 2003 revision of the U.S. Standard Certificate of Live Birth are excluded because maternal tobacco use and education data based on the 2003 revision are not comparable with data based on the 1989 and earlier revisions of the U.S. Standard Certificate of Live Birth. In 2003, Pennsylvania and Washington adopted the 2003 revision; in 2004 Florida, Idaho, Kentucky, New Hampshire, New York State (excluding New York City), South Carolina, and Tennessee adopted the 2003 revision. In addition, California did not require reporting of tobacco use during pregnancy.

[2]Data for 2003 are limited to the 42 reporting areas using the 1989 revision of the U.S. Standard Certificate of Live Birth in 2004 and are provided for comparison with 2004.

[3]Data from states that did not require the reporting of mother's tobacco use during pregnancy on the birth certificate are not included. Reporting area for tobacco use increased from 43 states and the District of Columbia (DC) in 1989 to 49 states and DC in 2000–2002.

[4]Excludes live births for whom smoking status of mother is unknown.

[5]Maternal tobacco use during pregnancy was not reported on the birth certificates of California, which in 2004 accounted for 30% of the births to Asian or Pacific Islander mothers. Starting with 2003 data, estimates are not shown for Asian or Pacific Islander subgroups during the transition from single race to multiple race reporting.

[6]Persons of Hispanic origin may be of any race. Data from states that did not require the reporting of Hispanic origin of mother on the birth certificate are not included. Reporting of Hispanic origin increased from 47 states in 1989 to include all 50 states and DC by 1993.

[7]Prior to 1997, data are for live births to mothers 45–49 years of age.

[8]Data from states that did not require the reporting of mother's education on the birth certificate are not included.

Table A-51. Low-Birthweight Live Births Among Mothers 20 Years of Age and Over, by Detailed Race, Hispanic Origin, and Education of Mother, Selected Years, 1989–2004

(Percent.)

Education, race, and Hispanic origin of mother	1989	1990	1995	2000	2001	2002	2003[1]	2003[2]	2004[1]
PERCENT OF LIVE BIRTHS WEIGHING LESS THAN 2,500 GRAMS[3]									
Less Than 12 Years of Education									
All Races	9.0	8.6	8.4	8.2	8.2	8.2	8.4	8.2	8.3
White	7.3	7.0	7.1	7.1	7.1	7.1	7.3	7.1	7.2
Black or African American	17.0	16.5	16.0	14.8	14.6	15.0	15.2	15.3	15.3
American Indian or Alaska Native	7.3	7.4	8.0	7.2	8.3	8.4	8.0	8.0	8.7
Asian or Pacific Islander[4]	6.6	6.4	6.7	7.2	7.5	7.4	7.5	7.6	7.7
Chinese	5.4	5.2	5.3	5.3	4.9	4.4	—	—	—
Japanese	4.0	10.6	11.0	6.8	8.4	4.7	—	—	—
Filipino	6.9	7.2	7.5	8.6	8.5	9.0	—	—	—
Hawaiian	11.0	10.7	9.8	9.4	8.9	7.8	—	—	—
Other Asian or Pacific Islander	6.8	6.4	6.7	7.5	8.1	8.1	—	—	—
Hispanic or Latino[5]	6.0	5.7	5.8	6.0	6.0	6.0	6.2	6.2	6.2
Mexican	5.3	5.2	5.4	5.6	5.7	5.7	5.9	5.9	6.0
Puerto Rican	11.3	10.3	10.5	10.9	10.4	10.4	11.2	11.0	10.5
Cuban	9.4	7.9	9.2	8.4	6.7	7.5	7.9	9.7	12.1
Central and South American	5.8	5.8	6.2	6.2	6.4	6.2	6.4	6.5	6.4
Other and unknown Hispanic or Latino	8.2	8.0	7.7	8.6	8.2	7.8	8.1	8.9	7.7
Not Hispanic or Latino[5]									
White	8.4	8.3	8.9	9.0	9.1	9.3	9.5	9.4	9.6
Black or African American	17.6	16.7	16.2	15.2	14.9	15.3	15.7	15.9	16.1
12 Years of Education									
All Races	7.1	7.1	7.6	7.9	8.1	8.2	8.4	8.3	8.4
White	5.7	5.8	6.4	6.8	7.0	7.0	7.2	7.2	7.3
Black or African American	13.4	13.1	13.3	13.0	13.1	13.4	13.5	13.5	13.7
American Indian or Alaska Native	5.6	6.1	6.5	6.7	7.2	7.1	7.2	7.2	7.2
Asian or Pacific Islander[4]	6.4	6.5	7.0	7.4	7.5	7.9	7.8	7.8	7.7
Chinese	5.1	4.9	5.7	5.6	5.4	5.2	—	—	—
Japanese	7.4	6.2	7.4	7.2	8.6	7.1	—	—	—
Filipino	6.8	7.6	7.7	8.1	9.2	8.7	—	—	—
Hawaiian	7.0	6.7	6.6	6.8	7.5	8.3	—	—	—
Other Asian or Pacific Islander	6.5	6.7	7.1	7.7	7.4	8.2	—	—	—
Hispanic or Latino[5]	5.9	6.0	6.1	6.2	6.4	6.5	6.5	6.5	6.7
Mexican	5.2	5.5	5.6	5.8	6.0	6.1	6.1	6.1	6.4
Puerto Rican	8.8	8.3	8.7	8.8	9.3	9.3	9.8	10.1	9.8
Cuban	5.3	5.2	6.7	6.5	5.8	6.0	6.4	7.2	8.3
Central and South American	5.7	5.8	5.9	6.0	6.3	6.4	6.6	6.6	6.8
Other and unknown Hispanic or Latino	6.1	6.6	7.1	7.3	7.7	7.7	7.4	7.8	7.7
Not Hispanic or Latino[5]									
White	5.7	5.7	6.5	6.9	7.2	7.3	7.5	7.5	7.6
Black or African American	13.6	13.2	13.4	13.1	13.3	13.5	13.7	13.7	13.9
13 Years or More of Education									
All Races	5.5	5.4	6.0	6.6	6.7	7.0	7.1	7.1	7.2
White	4.6	4.6	5.3	5.8	6.0	6.2	6.4	6.4	6.5
Black or African American	11.2	11.1	11.4	11.6	11.6	12.0	12.0	12.0	12.2
American Indian or Alaska Native	5.6	4.7	5.7	6.5	6.7	7.0	7.3	7.4	6.5
Asian or Pacific Islander[4]	6.1	6.0	6.6	7.0	7.3	7.6	7.6	7.6	7.8
Chinese	4.5	4.4	5.1	4.8	5.3	5.7	—	—	—
Japanese	6.6	6.0	7.1	7.0	6.9	7.7	—	—	—
Filipino	7.2	7.0	7.6	8.3	8.3	8.4	—	—	—
Hawaiian	6.3	4.7	5.0	4.5	7.7	7.2	—	—	—
Other Asian or Pacific Islander	6.1	6.2	6.7	7.4	7.6	7.9	—	—	—
Hispanic or Latino[5]	5.5	5.5	5.9	6.2	6.4	6.6	6.8	6.8	6.8
Mexican	5.1	5.2	5.6	5.8	6.0	6.2	6.3	6.3	6.6
Puerto Rican	7.4	7.4	7.9	7.9	8.0	8.9	9.1	9.3	8.9
Cuban	4.9	5.0	5.6	5.9	6.7	6.4	6.9	7.5	8.1
Central and South American	5.2	5.6	5.8	6.3	6.3	6.5	6.8	6.8	6.7
Other and unknown Hispanic or Latino	5.4	5.2	6.1	6.6	7.0	7.0	7.6	7.8	6.9
Not Hispanic or Latino[5]									
White	4.6	4.5	5.2	5.8	6.0	6.2	6.4	6.3	6.5
Black or African American	11.2	11.1	11.5	11.7	11.7	12.1	12.1	12.1	12.3

— = Data not available.

[1]Reporting areas that have adopted the 2003 revision of the U.S. Standard Certificate of Live Birth are excluded because maternal education data based on the 2003 revision are not comparable with data based on the 1989 or earlier revisions to the U.S. Standard Certificate of Live Birth. In 2003, Pennsylvania and Washington adopted the 2003 revision; in 2004, Florida, Idaho, Kentucky, New Hampshire, New York State (excluding New York City), South Carolina, and Tennessee adopted the 2003 revision.

[2]Data for 2003 are limited to the 43 reporting areas using the 1989 revision of the U.S. Standard Certificate of Live Birth in 2004, and are provided for comparison with 2004.

[3]Excludes live births with unknown birthweight. Percent based on live births with known birthweight.

[4]Starting with 2003 data, estimates are not shown for Asian or Pacific Islander subgroups during the transition from single race to multiple race reporting.

[5]Persons of Hispanic origin may be of any race. Prior to 1993, data shown only for states with an Hispanic-origin item and education of mother item on the birth certificate.

NOTE: Data are based on the 1989 or earlier revisions of the U.S. Standard Certificate of Live Birth. In 1992–2002, education of mother was reported on the birth certificate by all 50 states and the District of Columbia. Prior to 1992, data from states lacking an education of mother item were excluded. Starting with 2003 data, states adopting the 2003 revision of the U. S. Standard Certificate of Live Birth are excluded.

Table A-52. Live Births by Plurality of Birth and Ratios, by Age and Race and Hispanic Origin of Mother, 2005

(Number, ratio.)

Plurality, race, and Hispanic origin of mother	All ages	Under 15 years	15–19 years Total	15–17 years	18–19 years	20–24 years	25–29 years	30–34 years	35–39 years	40–44 years	45–54 years
NUMBER											
All Live Births											
All races[1]	4,138,349	6,722	414,593	133,191	281,402	1,040,388	1,131,596	950,691	483,156	104,667	6,536
Non-Hispanic White	2,279,768	1,331	165,005	43,864	121,141	515,518	642,553	581,645	305,142	64,352	4,222
Non-Hispanic Black	583,759	2,697	96,813	34,178	62,635	188,673	142,885	92,336	47,411	12,256	688
Hispanic[2]	985,505	2,466	136,906	50,046	86,860	287,896	266,590	186,398	85,739	18,597	913
Live Births in Single Deliveries											
All races[1]	3,998,533	6,644	407,609	131,312	276,297	1,016,594	1,095,389	910,198	458,344	98,628	5,127
Non-Hispanic White	2,192,579	1,321	162,352	43,269	119,083	504,217	620,388	553,797	287,459	59,874	3,171
Non-Hispanic Black	561,889	2,655	94,575	33,574	61,001	182,134	136,861	88,159	45,139	11,752	614
Hispanic[2]	963,021	2,444	135,012	49,427	85,585	282,769	260,466	180,860	82,675	17,983	812
Live Births in Twin Deliveries											
All races[1]	133,122	78	6,901	1,860	5,041	23,329	34,572	38,050	23,208	5,695	1,289
Non-Hispanic White	82,223	10	2,635	592	2,043	11,037	20,963	25,918	16,467	4,229	964
Non-Hispanic Black	21,254	42	2,197	591	1,606	6,406	5,862	4,055	2,164	460	68
Hispanic[2]	21,723	22	1,873	619	1,254	5,067	5,922	5,288	2,876	583	92
Live Births in Higher Order Multiple Deliveries[3]											
All races[1]	6,694	-	83	19	64	465	1,635	2,443	1,604	344	120
Non-Hispanic White	4,966	-	18	3	15	264	1,202	1,930	1,216	249	87
Non-Hispanic Black	616	-	41	13	28	133	162	122	108	44	6
Hispanic[2]	761	-	21	-	21	60	202	250	188	31	9
RATIO PER 1,000 LIVE BIRTHS											
All Multiple Births											
All races[1]	33.8	11.6	16.8	14.1	18.1	22.9	32.0	42.6	51.4	57.7	215.6
Non-Hispanic White	38.2	*	16.1	13.6	17.0	21.9	34.5	47.9	58.0	69.6	248.9
Non-Hispanic Black	37.5	15.6	23.1	17.7	26.1	34.7	42.2	45.2	47.9	41.1	107.6
Hispanic[2]	22.8	8.9	13.8	12.4	14.7	17.8	23.0	29.7	35.7	33.0	110.6
Twin Births											
All races[1]	32.2	11.6	16.6	14.0	17.9	22.4	30.6	40.0	48.0	54.4	197.2
Non-Hispanic White	36.1	*	16.0	13.5	16.9	21.4	32.6	44.6	54.0	65.7	228.3
Non-Hispanic Black	36.4	15.6	22.7	17.3	25.6	34.0	41.0	43.9	45.6	37.5	98.8
Hispanic[2]	22.0	8.9	13.7	12.4	14.4	17.6	22.2	28.4	33.5	31.3	100.8
RATIO PER 100,000 LIVE BIRTHS											
Higher Order Multiple Births											
All races[1]	161.8	*	20.0	*	22.7	44.7	144.5	257.0	332.0	328.7	1836.0
Non-Hispanic White	217.8	*	*	*	*	51.2	187.1	331.8	398.5	386.9	2060.6
Non-Hispanic Black	105.5	*	42.3	*	44.7	70.5	113.4	132.1	227.8	359.0	*
Hispanic[2]	77.2	*	15.3	*	24.2	20.8	75.8	134.1	219.3	166.7	*

* = Figure does not meet standards of reliability or precision.

– = Quantity zero.

[1]Includes races other than White and Black and origin not stated.

[2]Persons of Hispanic origin may be of any race.

[3]Births in greater than twin deliveries.

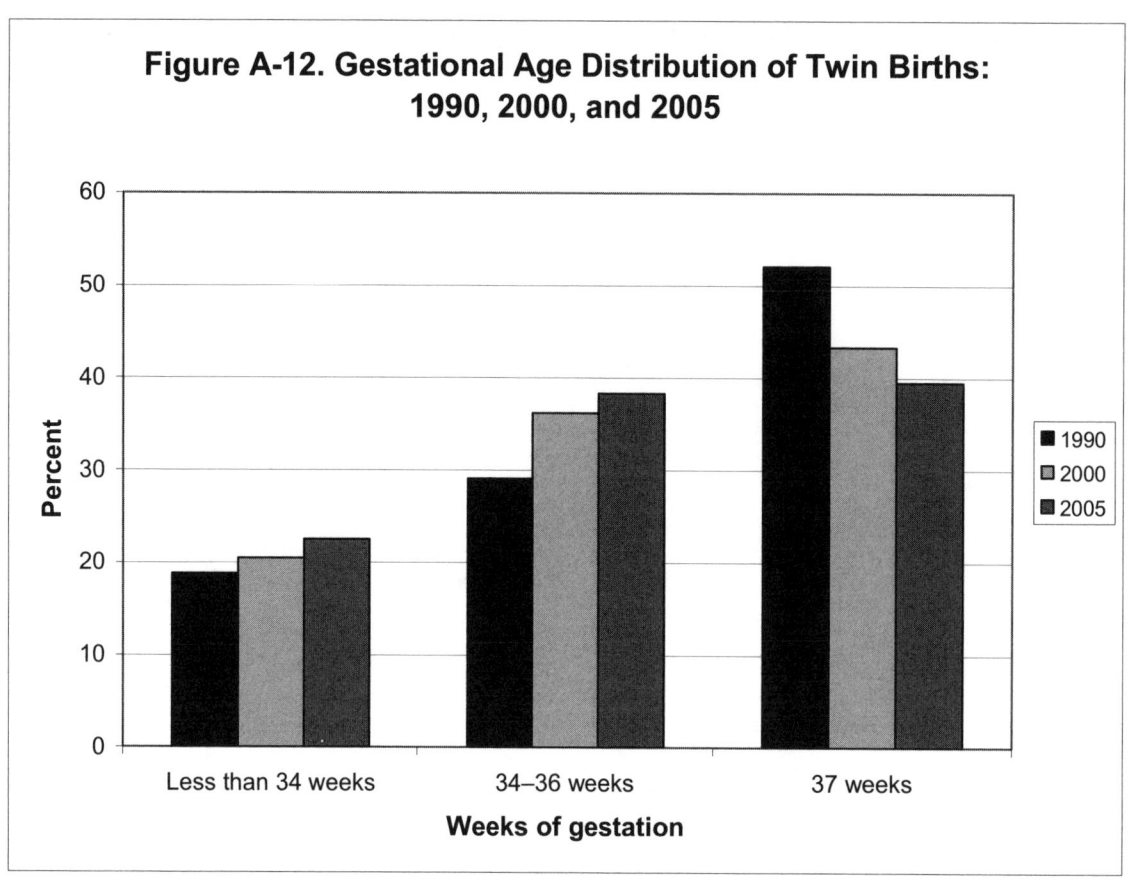

Figure A-12. Gestational Age Distribution of Twin Births: 1990, 2000, and 2005

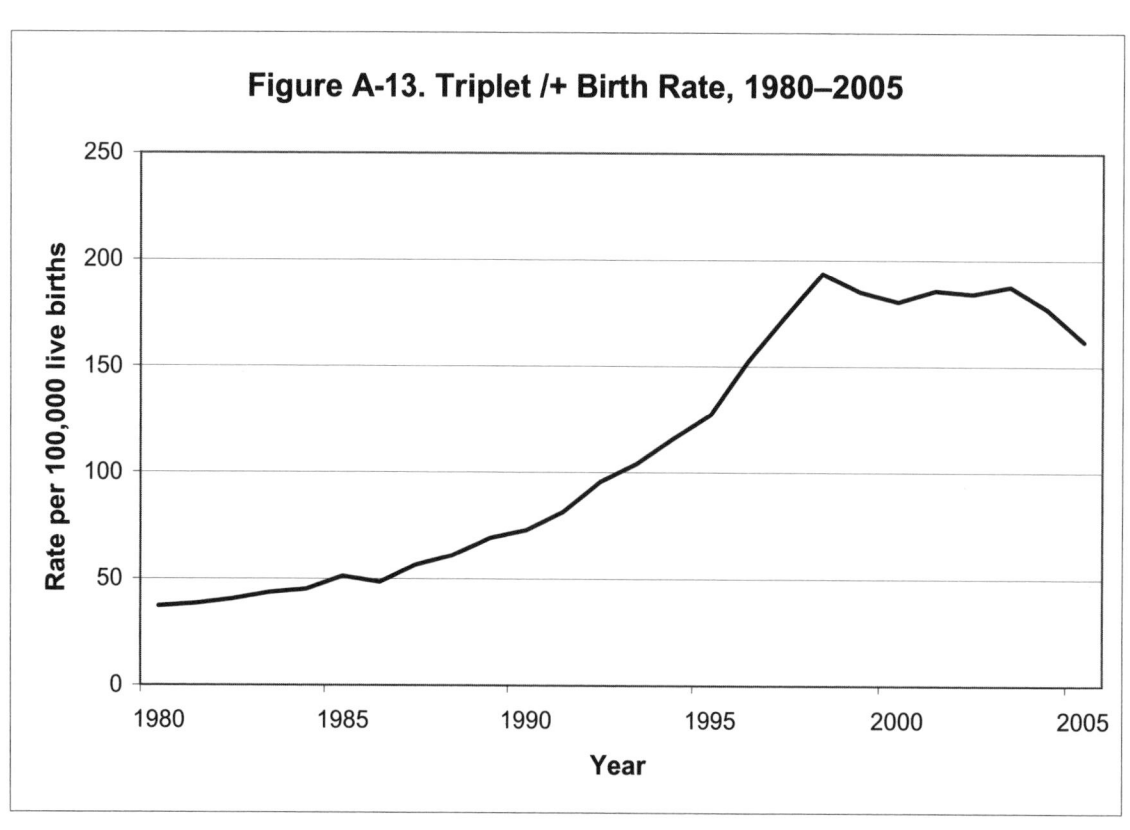

Figure A-13. Triplet /+ Birth Rate, 1980–2005

Table A-53. Numbers and Rates of Twin and Triplet and Higher Order Multiple Births, by Race and Hispanic Origin of Mother, 1980–2005

(Number, rate.)

Year, race, and Hispanic origin of mother	Total births	Twin births	Triplet/+	Twin birth rate[1]	Multiple birth rate[2]	Triplet/+ birth rate[3]
All Races[4]						
1980	3,612,258	68,339	1,337	18.9	19.3	37.0
1981	3,629,238	70,049	1,385	19.3	19.7	38.2
1982	3,680,537	71,631	1,484	19.5	19.9	40.3
1983	3,638,933	72,287	1,575	19.9	20.3	43.3
1984	3,669,141	72,949	1,653	19.9	20.3	45.1
1985	3,760,561	77,102	1,925	20.5	21.0	51.2
1986	3,756,547	79,485	1,814	21.2	21.6	48.3
1987	3,809,394	81,778	2,139	21.5	22.0	56.2
1988	3,909,510	85,315	2,385	21.8	22.4	61.0
1989	4,040,958	90,118	2,798	22.3	23.0	69.2
1990	4,158,212	93,865	3,028	22.6	23.3	72.8
1991	4,110,907	94,779	3,346	23.1	23.9	81.4
1992	4,065,014	95,372	3,883	23.5	24.4	95.5
1993	4,000,240	96,445	4,168	24.1	25.2	104.2
1994	3,952,767	97,064	4,594	24.6	25.7	116.2
1995	3,899,589	96,736	4,973	24.8	26.1	127.5
1996	3,891,494	100,750	5,939	25.9	27.4	152.6
1997	3,880,894	104,137	6,737	26.8	28.6	173.6
1998	3,941,553	110,670	7,625	28.1	30.0	193.5
1999	3,959,417	114,307	7,321	28.9	30.7	184.9
2000	4,058,814	118,916	7,325	29.3	31.1	180.5
2001	4,025,933	121,246	7,471	30.1	32.0	185.6
2002	4,021,726	125,134	7,401	31.1	33.0	184.0
2003	4,089,950	128,665	7,663	31.5	33.3	187.4
2004	4,112,052	132,219	7,275	32.2	33.9	176.9
2005	4,138,349	133,122	6,694	32.2	33.8	161.8
Non-Hispanic White						
1990[5]	2,626,500	60,210	2,358	22.9	23.8	89.8
1991[6]	2,589,878	60,904	2,612	23.5	24.5	100.9
1992[6]	2,527,207	60,640	3,115	24.0	25.2	123.3
1993	2,472,031	61,525	3,360	24.9	26.2	135.9
1994	2,438,855	62,476	3,721	25.6	27.1	152.6
1995	2,382,638	62,370	4,050	26.2	27.9	170.0
1996	2,358,989	65,523	4,885	27.8	29.8	207.1
1997	2,333,363	67,191	5,386	28.8	31.1	230.8
1998	2,283,986	71,270	6,206	30.2	32.8	262.8
1999	2,346,450	73,964	5,909	31.5	34.0	251.8
2000	2,362,968	76,018	5,821	32.2	34.6	246.3
2001	2,326,578	77,882	5,894	33.5	36.0	253.3
2002	2,298,156	79,949	5,754	34.8	37.3	250.4
2003	2,321,904	81,691	5,922	35.2	37.7	255.0
2004	2,296,683	83,346	5,590	36.3	38.7	243.4
2005	2,279,768	82,223	4,966	36.1	38.2	217.8
Non-Hispanic Black						
1990[5]	661,701	17,646	306	26.7	27.1	46.2
1991[6]	666,758	18,243	367	27.4	27.9	55.0
1992[6]	657,450	18,294	346	27.8	28.4	52.6
1993	641,273	18,115	314	28.2	28.7	49.0
1994	619,198	17,934	357	29.0	29.5	57.7
1995	587,781	16,622	340	28.3	28.9	57.8
1996	578,099	16,873	425	29.2	29.9	73.5
1997	581,431	17,472	523	30.0	30.9	90.0
1998	593,127	18,589	518	31.3	32.2	87.3
1999	588,981	18,920	561	32.1	33.1	95.2
2000	604,346	20,173	506	33.4	34.2	83.7
2001	589,917	19,974	531	33.9	34.8	90.0
2002	578,335	20,064	591	34.7	35.7	102.2
2003	576,033	20,010	631	34.7	35.8	109.5
2004	578,772	20,605	577	35.6	36.6	99.7
2005	583,759	21,254	616	36.4	37.5	105.5

[1]The number of live births in twin deliveries per 1,000 live births.
[2]The number of live births in all multiple deliveries per 1,000 live births.
[3]The number of live births in triplet and other higher-order deliveries per 100,000 live births.
[4]Includes races other than those shown.
[5]Excludes data for New Hampshire and Oklahoma, which did not report Hispanic origin.
[6]Excludes data for New Hampshire, which did not report Hispanic origin.

Table A-53. Numbers and Rates of Twin and Triplet and Higher Order Multiple Births, by Race and Hispanic Origin of Mother, 1980–2005—*Continued*

(Number, rate.)

Year, race, and Hispanic origin of mother	Total births	Twin births	Triplet/+	Twin birth rate[1]	Multiple birth rate[2]	Triplet/+ birth rate[3]
Hispanic[7]						
1990[5]	595,073	10,713	235	18.0	18.4	39.5
1991[6]	623,085	11,356	235	18.2	18.6	37.7
1992[6]	643,271	11,932	239	18.5	18.9	37.2
1993	654,418	12,294	321	18.8	19.3	49.1
1994	665,026	12,206	348	18.4	18.9	52.3
1995	679,768	12,685	355	18.7	19.2	52.2
1996	701,339	13,014	409	18.6	19.1	58.3
1997	709,767	13,821	516	19.5	20.2	72.7
1998	734,661	15,015	553	20.4	21.2	75.3
1999	764,339	15,388	583	20.1	20.9	76.3
2000	815,868	16,470	659	20.2	21.0	80.8
2001	851,851	17,257	710	20.3	21.1	83.3
2002	876,642	18,128	737	20.7	21.5	84.1
2003	912,329	19,472	784	21.3	22.2	85.9
2004	946,349	20,351	723	21.5	22.3	76.4
2005	985,505	21,723	761	22.0	22.8	77.2

[1]The number of live births in twin deliveries per 1,000 live births.
[2]The number of live births in all multiple deliveries per 1,000 live births.
[3]The number of live births in triplet and other higher-order deliveries per 100,000 live births.
[5]Excludes data for New Hampshire and Oklahoma, which did not report Hispanic origin.
[6]Excludes data for New Hampshire, which did not report Hispanic origin.
[7]Persons of Hispanic origin may be of any race.

Table A-54. Twin and Triplet and Higher Order Multiple Birth Rates by State, 2003–2005

(Number, rate per 1,000 live births.)

Area	Twin		Triplet or higher[1]	
	Number	Rate per 1,000 live births	Number	Rate per 100,000 live births
UNITED STATES	394,006	31.9	21,632	175.3
Alabama	5,774	32.2	356	198.3
Alaska	832	26.9	21	68.0
Arizona	7,451	26.5	463	164.9
Arkansas	3,393	29.4	116	100.4
California	47,394	29.0	2,445	149.6
Colorado	6,545	31.7	318	153.8
Connecticut	5,261	41.5	311	245.5
Delaware	1,223	35.6	62	180.5
District of Columbia	811	34.5		16
*				
Florida	19,643	29.9	937	142.7
Georgia	13,015	31.2	624	149.6
Hawaii	1,521	28.0	48	88.4
Idaho	1,991	29.5	120	178.1
Illinois	19,490	35.9	1,272	234.6
Indiana	8,330	31.9	611	234.3
Iowa	3,845	33.2	179	154.4
Kansas	3,608	30.3	189	158.8
Kentucky	5,119	30.6	393	234.8
Louisiana	5,981	31.3	296	154.7
Maine	1,373	32.8	58	138.4
Maryland	8,338	37.1	435	193.7
Massachusetts	10,475	44.5	684	290.4
Michigan	13,273	34.2	890	229.0
Minnesota	7,089	33.5	442	208.9
Mississippi	4,076	31.9	167	130.9
Missouri	7,592	32.5	397	170.1
Montana	952	27.6	33	95.6
Nebraska	2,519	32.1	211	269.2
Nevada	3,080	29	156	147.0
New Hampshire	1,613	37.2	93	214.4
New Jersey	14,477	41.8	999	288.7
New Mexico	2,054	24.2	56	65.9
New York	26,998	36	1,724	229.9
North Carolina	11,534	31.9	542	150.0
North Dakota	801	32.6	59	240.3
Ohio	14,950	33.4	1,065	238.2
Oklahoma	4,222	27.4	143	92.8
Oregon	4,098	29.8	143	104.0
Pennsylvania	14,708	33.7	841	192.9
Rhode Island	1,506	38.9	69	178.4
South Carolina	5,361	31.5	241	141.8
South Dakota	978	28.9	31	91.6
Tennessee	7,473	31.1	368	153.2
Texas	32,209	28.1	1,642	143.4
Utah	4,029	26.5	205	134.8
Vermont	623	31.7	21	106.8
Virginia	10,403	33.6	479	154.6
Washington	7,198	29.4	227	92.7
West Virginia	1,707	27.2	66	105.3
Wisconsin	6,505	30.8	338	160.1
Wyoming	567	27.3	30	144.6

* = Figure does not meet standards of reliability or precision.
[1]Includes triplet and quadruplet and other higher order multiple births.

Table A-55. Distribution of Triplet Births by Gestational Age, 1990, 2000, and 2005

(Percent distribution.)

Gestational age	1990	2000	2005	Percent change 1990–2005	Percent change 2000–2005
Less than 28 weeks	11.5	11.2	12.7	10	13
28–31 weeks	18.0	23.3	25.6	42	10
32–33 weeks	20.7	25.1	25.8	25	3
Less than 34 weeks	50.2	59.6	64.1	28	8
34–36 weeks	37.7	32.7	29.6	-21	-9
37 weeks or more	12.1	7.7	6.3	-48	-18

Table A-56. Birth Rates for Women Aged 10–19 Years, by Age, Race, and Hispanic Origin, Selected Years, 1991–2005 and Percent Change in Rates, 1991–2005 and 2004–2005

(Rate per 1,000 women in specified group.)

Age, race, and Hispanic origin of mother	1991	2003	2004	2005	Percent change 1991–2005	Percent change 2004–2005
10–14 Years						
All races	1.4	0.6	0.7	0.7	−50	0
White, non-Hispanic	0.5	0.2	0.2	0.2	−60	0
Black, non-Hispanic	4.9	1.6	1.6	1.7	−65	6
American Indian or Alaska Native	1.6	1.0	0.9	0.9	−44	0
Asian or Pacific Islander	0.8	0.2	0.2	0.2	−75	0
Hispanic[1]	2.4	1.3	1.3	1.3	−46	0
15–19 Years						
All races	61.8	41.6	41.1	40.5	−34	−1
White, non-Hispanic	43.4	27.4	26.7	25.9	−40	−3
Black, non-Hispanic	118.2	64.7	63.1	60.9	−48	−3
American Indian or Alaska Native	84.1	53.1	52.5	52.7	−37	0
Asian or Pacific Islander	27.3	17.4	17.3	17.0	−38	−2
Hispanic[1]	104.6	82.3	82.6	81.7	−22	−1
15–17 Years						
All races	38.6	22.4	22.1	21.4	−45	−3
White, non-Hispanic	23.6	12.4	12.0	11.5	−51	−4
Black, non-Hispanic	86.1	38.7	37.1	34.9	−59	−6
American Indian or Alaska Native	51.9	30.6	30.0	30.5	−41	2
Asian or Pacific Islander	16.3	8.8	8.9	8.2	−50	−8
Hispanic[1]	69.2	49.7	49.7	48.5	−30	−2
18–19 Years						
All races	94.0	70.7	70.0	69.9	−26	0
White, non-Hispanic	70.6	50.0	48.7	48.0	−32	−1
Black, non-Hispanic	162.2	105.3	103.9	103.0	−36	−1
American Indian or Alaska Native	134.2	87.3	87.0	87.6	−35	1
Asian or Pacific Islander	42.2	29.8	29.6	30.1	−29	2
Hispanic[1]	155.5	132.0	133.5	134.6	−13	1

[1]Persons of Hispanic origin may be of any race.

Table A-57. Birth Rates for Teenagers 15–19 Years of Age by State, 1991 and 2005, and Percentage Change, by State, 1991–2005

(Rates per 1,000 estimated female population aged 15–19 years in each area, percent.)

Area	1991	2005	Percent change, 1991–2005
UNITED STATES[1]	61.8	40.5	–34
Alabama	73.6	49.7	–32
Alaska	66.0	37.3	–43
Arizona	79.7	58.2	–27
Arkansas	79.5	59.1	–26
California	73.8	38.8	–47
Colorado	58.3	42.6	–27
Connecticut	40.1	23.3	–42
Delaware	60.4	44.0	–27
District of Columbia	109.6	63.4	–42
Florida	67.9	42.4	–38
Georgia	76.0	52.7	–31
Hawaii	59.2	36.2	–39
Idaho	53.9	37.7	–30
Illinois	64.5	38.6	–40
Indiana	60.4	43.2	–28
Iowa	42.5	32.6	–23
Kansas	55.4	41.4	–25
Kentucky	68.8	49.1	–29
Louisiana	76.0	49.1	–35
Maine	43.5	24.4	–44
Maryland	54.1	31.8	–41
Massachusetts	37.5	21.8	–42
Michigan	58.9	32.5	–45
Minnesota	37.3	26.1	–30
Mississippi	85.3	60.5	–29
Missouri	64.4	42.5	–34
Montana	46.8	35.2	–25
Nebraska	42.4	34.2	–19
Nevada	74.5	50.1	–33
New Hampshire	33.1	17.9	–46
New Jersey	41.3	23.4	–43
New Mexico	79.5	61.6	–23
New York	45.5	26.5	–42
North Carolina	70.0	48.5	–31
North Dakota	35.5	29.7	–16
Ohio	60.5	38.9	–36
Oklahoma	72.1	54.2	–25
Oregon	54.8	33.0	–40
Pennsylvania	46.7	30.4	–35
Rhode Island	44.7	31.4	–30
South Carolina	72.5	51.0	–30
South Dakota	47.6	37.5	–21
Tennessee	74.8	54.9	–27
Texas	78.4	61.6	–21
Utah	48.0	33.4	–30
Vermont	39.2	19.5	-50
Virginia	53.4	34.4	–36
Washington	53.7	31.1	–42
West Virginia	58.0	43.4	–25
Wisconsin	43.7	30.3	–31
Wyoming	54.3	43.2	–20
Puerto Rico	72.4	61.2	–15
Virgin Islands	77.9	50.0	–36
Guam	95.7	59.2	–38
American Samoa	—	34.2	—
Northern Marianas	—	30.4	—

—— = Data not available.
[1]Excludes data for the territories.

Table A-58. Educational Attainment, Smoking During Pregnancy, Timing of Prenatal Care, and Primary Cesarean and Vaginal Birth after Previous Cesarean (VBAC) by Race and Hispanic Origin of Mother: 12 and 7 States (Revised) and 37 States (Unrevised), District of Columbia, and New York City, 2004 and 2005

(Percent.)

Race and Hispanic Origin of Mother	Educational Attainment									
	Revised (12 state reporting area)[1,2]		Revised (7 state reporting area)[1,3]				Unrevised (37 state reporting area)[4]			
	High School diploma or GED or higher	Bachelor's degree or higher	High School diploma or GED or higher		Bachelor's degree or higher		12 years or more years of school		16 years or more years of school	
	2005	2005	2004	2005	2004	2005	2004	2005	2004	2005
All races and origins[5]	76.5	23.3	81.0	80.8	26.4	26.3	79.0	79.1	27.8	27.8
Non-Hispanic White	87.5	31.6	87.0	87.1	31.0	31.2	89.2	89.4	37.1	37.4
Non-Hispanic Black	75.3	10.7	73.0	73.5	10.1	10.2	76.4	77.1	13.8	14.1
Hispanic[6]	52.0	8.6	47.8	47.4	7.5	7.6	52.2	52.7	8.2	8.4

Race and Hispanic Origin of Mother	Smoking During Pregnancy					
	Revised (12 state reporting area)[1,7]	Revised (7 state reporting area)[1,3]		Unrevised (36 state reporting area)[8]	
	Smoker	Smoker		Smoker	
	2005	2004	2005	2004	2005
All races and origins[5]	12.4	16.3	16.2	10.9	10.7
Non-Hispanic White	17.7	19.0	19.2	14.0	13.9
Non-Hispanic Black	10.3	13.0	12.5	8.7	8.5
Hispanic[6]	2.7	5.7	5.4	3.1	2.9

Race and Hispanic Origin of Mother	Timing of Prenatal Care (PNC)									
	Revised (12 state reporting area)[1,2]		Revised (7 state reporting area)[1,3]				Unrevised (36 state reporting area)[4]			
	1st trimester PNC	Late or no PNC	1st trimester PNC		Late or no PNC		1st trimester PNC		Late or no PNC	
	2005	2005	2004	2005	2004	2005	2004	2005	2004	2005
All races and origins[5]	70.2	7.7	72.9	72.8	6.2	6.0	84.2	83.9	3.5	3.5
Non-Hispanic White	77.2	4.9	78.0	77.8	4.5	4.4	89.0	88.7	2.1	2.2
Non-Hispanic Black	60.1	11.3	58.9	59.3	11.4	10.8	76.3	76.5	5.7	5.6
Hispanic[6]	60.0	11.9	56.5	57.0	11.0	10.8	77.7	77.6	5.2	5.1

[1]Data are based on the 2003 Revision of the U.S. Certificate of Live Birth; these data are not comparable with those based on the 1989 Revision of the U.S. Certificate of Live Birth.
[2]Includes data from Florida, Idaho, Kansas, Kentucky, Nebraska, New Hampshire, New York State (excluding New York City), Pennsylvania, South Carolina, Tennessee, Texas, and Washington.
[3]Includes data from Idaho, Kentucky, New York State (excluding New York City), Pennsylvania, South Carolina, Tennessee and Washington. For primary cesarean and VBAC delivery, excludes births to residents of states using the 2003 Revision of the U.S. Certificate of Live birth occurring in states using the 1989 Revision of the U.S. Certificate of Live Birth.
[4]Data are based on the 1989 Revision of the U.S. Certificate of Live Birth; these data are not comparable with those based on the 2003 Revision of the U.S. Certificate of Live Birth. Excludes data from Florida, Idaho, Kansas, Kentucky, Nebraska, New Hampshire, New York State (excluding New York City), Pennsylvania, South Carolina, Tennessee, Texas, Vermont and Washington.
[5]Includes races other than White and Black and origin not stated.
[6]Persons of Hispanic origin may be of any race.
[7]Includes data from Idaho, Kansas, Kentucky, Nebraska, New Hampshire, New York State (excluding New York City), Pennsylvania, South Carolina, Tennessee, Texas, and Washington.
[8]Data are based on the 1989 Revision of the U.S. Certificate of Live Birth; these data are not comparable with those based on the 2003 Revision of the U.S. Certificate of Live Birth. Excludes data from California, Florida, Idaho, Kansas, Kentucky, Nebraska, New Hampshire, New York State (excluding New York City), Pennsylvania, South Carolina, Tennessee, Texas, Vermont and Washington.

Table A-58. Educational Attainment, Smoking During Pregnancy, Timing of Prenatal Care, and Primary Cesarean and Vaginal Birth after Previous Cesarean (VBAC) by Race and Hispanic Origin of Mother: 12 and 7 States (Revised) and 37 States (Unrevised), District of Columbia, and New York City, 2004 and 2005—_Continued_

(Percent.)

Race and Hispanic Origin of Mother	Method of Delivery									
	Revised (12 state reporting area)[1,2]		Revised (7 state reporting area)[1,3]				Unrevised (37 state reporting area)[4]			
	Primary cesarean	Vaginal birth after previous cesarean	Primary cesarean		Vaginal birth after previous cesarean	Vaginal birth after previous cesarean	Primary cesarean		previous cesarean	
	2005	2005	2004	2005	2004	2005	2004	2005	2004	2005
All races and origins[5]	24.3	10.1	23.1	23.4	14.1	12.0	19.6	20.3	9.1	7.9
Non-Hispanic White	24.5	9.6	23.4	23.7	12.9	11.1	20.0	20.8	9.0	7.7
Non-Hispanic Black	25.7	10.7	23.9	24.2	17.8	14.8	21.7	22.8	9.7	7.9
Hispanic[6]...	23.3	10.7	20.5	20.6	16.0	13.7	16.9	17.5	8.6	7.9

[1]Data are based on the 2003 Revision of the U.S. Certificate of Live Birth; these data are not comparable with those based on the 1989 Revision of the U.S. Certificate of Live Birth.
[2]Includes data from Florida, Idaho, Kansas, Kentucky, Nebraska, New Hampshire, New York State (excluding New York City), Pennsylvania, South Carolina, Tennessee, Texas, and Washington.
[3]Includes data from Idaho, Kentucky, New York State (excluding New York City), Pennsylvania, South Carolina, Tennessee and Washington. For primary cesarean and VBAC delivery, excludes births to residents of states using the 2003 Revision of the U.S. Certificate of Live birth occurring in states using the 1989 Revision of the U.S. Certificate of Live Birth.
[4]Data are based on the 1989 Revision of the U.S. Certificate of Live Birth; these data are not comparable with those based on the 2003 Revision of the U.S. Certificate of Live Birth. Excludes data from Florida, Idaho, Kansas, Kentucky, Nebraska, New Hampshire, New York State (excluding New York City), Pennsylvania, South Carolina, Tennessee, Texas, Vermont and Washington.
[5]Includes races other than White and Black and origin not stated.
[6]Persons of Hispanic origin may be of any race.

Table A-59. Percentage of Live Births Delivered by Forceps or Vacuum Extraction, 1990 and 1995–2005

(Percent.)

Year	Forceps	Vacuum extraction	Forceps or vacuum
1990[1]..	5.1	3.9	9.0
1995..	3.5	5.9	9.4
1996..	3.2	6.2	9.4
1997..	2.8	6.2	9.0
1998..	2.6	6.0	8.6
1999..	2.3	5.1	7.4
2000..	2.1	4.9	7.0
2001..	1.8	4.5	6.3
2002..	1.5	4.4	5.9
2003..	1.3	4.3	5.6
2004..	1.1	4.1	5.2
2005..	0.9	3.9	4.8

[1]Excludes data for Oklahoma, which did not report method of delivery for 1990.

Table A-60. Rates of Induction of Labor by Gestational Age, Singleton Births: 1990, 1995, 2000–2005, and Percent Change, 1990–2005 and 2000–2005

(Percent.)

Gestational age	1990	1995	2000	2001	2002	2003	2004	2005	Percent change 1990–2005	Percent change 2000–2005
All Gestations	9.6	16.2	20.2	20.8	21.1	21.1	21.7	22.8	138	13
Under 32 weeks	5.0	7.8	9.2	8.9	8.8	8.6	8.7	8.9	78	–3
32–33 weeks	6.4	10.6	13.3	12.8	12.8	12.8	13.0	13.4	109	1
34–36 weeks	7.5	12.6	16.2	16.2	16.2	16.0	16.7	17.3	131	7
Total under 37 weeks	6.9	11.6	14.8	14.7	14.7	14.5	15.1	15.6	126	5
Total 37 weeks and over	9.9	16.7	20.8	21.6	21.8	21.9	22.5	23.7	139	14
37–39 weeks	7.9	14.3	18.9	19.6	19.8	19.8	20.6	21.7	175	15
40–41 weeks	10.7	18.5	22.9	24.1	24.6	24.8	25.3	26.8	150	17
42 weeks and over	14.9	21.3	24.4	24.4	24.3	24.3	25.4	26.2	76	7

NOTE: Oklahoma did not report induction of labor in 1990.

Table A-61. Percent Distribution of Gestational Age for All Births and for Singleton Births Only, Selected Years, 1990–2005

(Percent.)

Gestational age	All births				Singleton births			
	1990	2000	2004	2005	1990	2000	2004	2005
Under 28 weeks	0.71	0.72	0.75	0.77	0.61	0.59	0.61	0.61
28–31 weeks	1.21	1.21	1.25	1.26	1.08	0.99	1.01	1.02
32–33 weeks	1.40	1.49	1.59	1.60	1.24	1.22	1.28	1.28
Total under 34 weeks	3.32	3.42	3.60	3.63	2.93	2.80	2.89	2.91
34–36 weeks	7.30	8.22	8.90	9.09	6.77	7.33	7.88	8.09
Total under 37 weeks	10.61	11.64	12.49	12.73	9.70	10.12	10.78	11.00
37–39 weeks	41.38	48.83	52.36	53.54	41.42	49.27	53.03	54.26
40 and higher weeks	48.00	39.54	35.15	33.73	48.88	40.61	36.20	34.74

Table A-62. Apgar Score at 5 Minutes, by Race and Hispanic Origin of Mother: 49 States and the District of Columbia, 2005

(Percent.)

5 minute Apgar score	All races and origins[1]	Non-Hispanic White	Non-Hispanic Black	American Indian or Alaska Native total[2]	Asian or Pacific Islander total[2]	Hispanic[3]
0–3 Poor	0.5	0.4	1.0	0.4	0.3	0.4
4–6 Intermediate	1.0	1.0	1.5	0.9	0.7	0.9
7–8 Good	10.0	10.2	10.4	9.3	7.5	9.4
9–10 Excellent	88.5	88.4	87.1	89.4	91.5	89.3
0–6 Low	1.5	1.4	2.5	1.3	1.0	1.3

[1]Includes origin not stated.
[2]Data for all persons of Hispanic origin are included in the data for each race group according to the mother's reported race.
[3]Persons of Hispanic origin may be of any race.

NOTE: An Apgar score measures five easily identifiable characteristics of newborns. A 5-minute score of 0 to 3 indicates an infant in immediate need of resuscitation; 4 to 6 is considered intermediate, and 7 to 10 is considered normal. It has been used for 50 years to asses the physical condition and the short-term prognosis of newborns. Table excludes data for California, which did not report 5-minute Apgar score on the birth certificate.

Table A-63. Total Count of Records and Percentage Complete of Preliminary File of Live Births by State and Territory, Preliminary 2005

(Number, percent.)

Area	Counts of records	Percent completeness
UNITED STATES[1]	4,273,644	99.9
Alabama	62,102	100.0
Alaska	10,895	100.0
Arizona	103,192	100.0
Arkansas	39,759	100.0
California	563,522	100.0
Colorado	71,157	100.0
Connecticut	42,178	100.0
Delaware	12,416	100.0
District of Columbia	14,602	100.0
Florida	237,491	100.0
Georgia	149,919	99.9
Hawaii	18,986	100.0
Idaho	23,719	100.0
Illinois	177,257	100.0
Indiana	89,182	100.0
Iowa	40,620	100.0
Kansas	41,946	100.0
Kentucky	56,694	99.9
Louisiana	63,499	95.1
Maine	14,009	100.0
Maryland	74,077	100.0
Massachusetts	78,618	100.0
Michigan	126,395	100.0
Minnesota	73,513	100.0
Mississippi	44,863	100.0
Missouri	82,458	100.0
Montana	12,490	100.0
Nebraska	26,898	100.0
Nevada	39,743	99.6
New Hampshire	14,070	100.0
New Jersey	111,923	100.0
New Mexico	29,337	100.0
New York	251,946	100.0
New York (excluding New York City)	126,435	100.0
New York City	125,511	100.0
North Carolina	129,002	100.0
North Dakota	9,875	100.0
Ohio	151,351	100.0
Oklahoma	53,041	100.0
Oregon	49,120	99.9
Pennsylvania	148,511	99.8
Rhode Island	13,179	100.0
South Carolina	59,624	97.5
South Dakota	12,386	100.0
Tennessee	89,429	100.0
Texas	405,880	100.0
Utah	54,528	100.0
Vermont	6,113	100.0
Virginia	105,889	100.0
Washington	86,776	99.8
West Virginia	21,137	100.0
Wisconsin	71,235	100.0
Wyoming	7,092	100.0
Puerto Rico	48,742	98.2
Virgin Islands	1,514	100.0
Guam	3,416	- - -
American Samoa	1,442	100.0
Northern Marianas	1,422	100.0

— = Data not available.

[1]Excludes data for the territories.

NOTE: Percent completeness equals the number of records in the preliminary file multiplied by 100, divided by the count of records.

Table A-64. Maternal Education for Live Births, by Detailed Race and Hispanic Origin of Mother, Selected Years, 1970–2004

(Percent.)

Education, race, and Hispanic origin of mother	1970	1975	1980	1985	1990	1995	2000	2001	2002	2003[1]	43 reporting areas	
											2003[2]	2004[1]
PERCENT OF LIVE BIRTHS[3]												
Less than 12 Years of Education												
All Races	30.8	28.6	23.7	20.6	23.8	22.6	21.7	21.7	21.5	21.6	22.1	22.2
White	27.1	25.1	20.8	17.8	22.4	21.6	21.4	21.7	21.6	21.8	22.5	22.7
Black or African American	51.2	45.3	36.4	32.6	30.2	28.7	25.5	24.9	24.4	24.0	23.9	23.8
American Indian or Alaska Native	60.5	52.7	44.2	39.0	36.4	33.0	31.6	31.0	30.8	30.5	30.2	30.1
Asian or Pacific Islander[4]	—	—	21.0	19.4	20.0	16.1	11.6	10.8	10.3	9.9	10.0	9.3
Chinese	23.0	16.5	15.2	15.5	15.8	12.9	11.7	11.9	11.3	—	—	—
Japanese	11.8	9.1	5.0	4.8	3.5	2.6	2.1	1.8	2.2	—	—	—
Filipino	26.4	22.3	16.4	13.9	10.3	8.0	6.2	6.0	5.3	—	—	—
Hawaiian	—	—	20.7	18.7	19.3	17.6	16.7	15.4	14.3	—	—	—
Other Asian or Pacific Islander	—	—	27.6	24.3	26.8	21.2	13.5	12.2	11.6	—	—	—
Hispanic or Latino[5]	—	—	51.1	44.5	53.9	52.1	48.9	48.8	48.1	47.5	48.7	48.4
Mexican	—	—	62.8	59.0	61.4	58.6	55.0	55.0	54.2	53.6	53.1	52.5
Puerto Rican	—	—	55.3	46.6	42.7	38.6	33.4	32.3	31.5	29.9	31.7	31.6
Cuban	—	—	24.1	21.1	17.8	14.4	11.9	11.8	11.8	11.5	13.4	13.0
Central and South American	—	—	41.2	37.0	44.2	41.7	37.2	36.5	35.8	35.3	38.0	39.1
Other and unknown Hispanic or Latino	—	—	40.1	36.5	33.3	33.8	31.4	30.4	31.7	30.1	28.3	29.4
Not Hispanic or Latino[5]												
White	—	—	18.1	15.7	15.2	13.3	12.2	12.0	11.7	11.5	11.0	11.0
Black or African American	—	—	37.3	33.4	30.0	28.6	25.3	24.8	24.3	23.8	23.5	23.4
16 Years or More of Education												
All Races	8.6	11.4	14.0	16.7	17.5	21.4	24.7	25.2	25.9	26.6	26.7	26.9
White	9.6	12.7	15.5	18.6	19.3	23.1	26.3	26.7	27.3	27.9	27.8	28.0
Black or African American	2.8	4.3	6.2	7.0	7.2	9.5	11.7	12.1	12.7	13.4	13.8	13.7
American Indian or Alaska Native	2.7	2.2	3.5	3.7	4.4	6.2	7.8	8.2	8.7	8.5	8.3	8.6
Asian or Pacific Islander[4]	—	—	30.8	30.3	31.0	35.0	42.8	44.0	45.7	47.1	46.8	48.6
Chinese	34.0	37.8	41.5	35.2	40.3	49.0	55.6	55.9	57.3	—	—	—
Japanese	20.7	30.6	36.8	38.1	44.1	46.2	51.1	52.0	53.5	—	—	—
Filipino	28.1	36.6	37.1	35.2	34.5	36.7	40.5	41.8	43.3	—	—	—
Hawaiian	—	—	7.9	6.5	6.8	9.7	13.5	13.2	14.6	—	—	—
Other Asian or Pacific Islander	—	—	29.2	30.2	27.3	30.5	40.7	42.6	44.4	—	—	—
Hispanic or Latino[5]	—	—	4.2	6.0	5.1	6.1	7.6	7.9	8.3	8.7	7.8	8.0
Mexican	—	—	2.2	3.0	3.3	4.0	5.1	5.3	5.5	5.9	5.9	6.1
Puerto Rican	—	—	3.0	4.6	6.5	8.7	10.4	11.1	11.8	12.9	11.7	12.0
Cuban	—	—	11.6	15.0	20.4	26.5	31.0	30.8	30.5	31.3	34.5	35.4
Central and South American	—	—	6.1	8.1	8.6	10.3	14.1	14.8	15.5	16.0	14.1	14.2
Other and unknown Hispanic or Latino	—	—	5.5	7.2	8.5	10.5	12.5	13.2	13.2	14.4	14.5	14.0
Not Hispanic or Latino[5]												
White	—	—	16.6	19.4	22.6	27.7	32.5	33.3	34.3	35.5	36.4	37.0
Black or African American	—	—	5.8	6.7	7.3	9.5	11.7	12.2	12.7	13.4	13.9	13.8

— = Data not available.

[1]Reporting areas that have adopted the 2003 revision of the U.S. Standard Certificate of Live Birth are excluded because maternal education data based on the 2003 revision are not comparable with data based on the 1989 and earlier revisions of the U.S. Standard Certificate of Live Birth. In 2003, Pennsylvania and Washington adopted the 2003 revision; in 2004, Florida, Idaho, Kentucky, New Hampshire, New York State (excluding New York City), South Carolina, and Tennessee adopted the 2003 revision.

[2]Data for 2003 are limited to the 43 reporting areas using the 1989 revision of the U.S. Standard Certificate of Live Birth in 2004 and are provided for comparison with 2004.

[3]Excludes live births for whom education of mother is unknown.

[4]Starting with 2003 data, estimates are not shown for Asian or Pacific Islander subgroups during the transition from single race to multiple race reporting.

[5]Persons of Hispanic origin may be of any race. Prior to 1993, data are shown only for states with an Hispanic-origin item and education of mother item on the birth certificate.

NOTE: Data are based on the 1989 and earlier revisions of the U.S. Standard Certificate of Live Birth. Maternal education groups shown in this table generally represent the group at highest risk for unfavorable birth outcomes (less than 12 years of education) and the group at lowest risk (16 years or more of education). In 1992–2002, education of mother was reported on the birth certificate by all 50 states and the District of Columbia. Prior to 1992, data from states lacking an education of mother item were excluded.

Table A-65. Contraceptive Use in the Past Month Among Women 15–44 Years of Age, by Age, Race, Hispanic Origin, and Method of Contraception, Selected Years, 1982–2002

(Number, percent.)

Race, Hispanic origin, and year[1]	Age				
	15–44 years	15–19 years	20–24 years	25–34 years	35–44 years
NUMBER IN THOUSANDS					
All Women[2]					
1982	54,099	9,521	10,629	19,644	14,305
1988	57,900	9,179	9,413	21,726	17,582
1995	60,201	8,961	9,041	20,758	21,440
2002	61,561	9,834	9,840	19,522	22,365
Not Hispanic or Latino					
White Only					
1982	41,279	7,010	8,081	14,945	11,243
1988	42,575	6,531	6,630	15,929	13,486
1995	42,154	5,865	6,020	14,471	15,798
2002	39,498	6,069	5,938	12,073	15,418
Black or African American Only					
1982	6,825	1,383	1,456	2,392	1,593
1988	7,408	1,362	1,322	2,760	1,965
1995	8,060	1,334	1,305	2,780	2,641
2002	8,250	1,409	1,396	2,587	2,857
Hispanic or Latino[3]					
1982	4,393	886	811	1,677	1,018
1988	5,557	999	1,003	2,104	1,451
1995	6,702	1,150	1,163	2,450	1,940
2002	9,107	1,521	1,632	3,249	2,705
PERCENT OF WOMEN USING CONTRACEPTION					
All Women[2]					
1982	55.7	24.2	55.8	66.7	61.6
1988	60.3	32.1	59.0	66.3	68.3
1995	64.2	29.8	63.5	71.1	72.3
2002	61.9	31.5	60.7	68.6	69.9
Not Hispanic or Latino					
White Only					
1982	57.3	23.6	58.7	67.8	63.5
1988	63.0	34.0	62.6	67.7	71.5
1995	66.2	30.5	65.4	72.9	73.6
2002	64.6	35.0	66.3	69.9	71.4
Black or African American Only					
1982	51.6	29.8	52.3	63.5	52.0
1988	56.8	35.7	61.8	63.5	58.7
1995	62.3	36.1	67.6	66.8	68.3
2002	57.6	32.9	50.8	67.9	63.8
Hispanic or Latino[3]					
1982	50.6	*	*36.8	67.2	59.0
1988	50.4	*18.3	40.8	67.4	54.3
1995	59.0	26.1	50.6	69.2	70.8
2002	59.0	20.4	57.4	66.2	72.9
PERCENT OF CONTRACEPTING WOMEN					
Female Sterilization					
1982	23.2	-	*4.5	22.1	43.5
1988	27.6	*	*4.6	25.0	47.6
1995	27.8	*	4.0	23.8	45.0
2002	27.0	-	3.6	21.7	45.8
Male Sterilization					
1982	10.9	*	*3.6	10.1	19.9
1988	11.7	*	*	10.2	20.8
1995	10.9	-	*	7.8	19.5
2002	10.2	-	*	7.2	18.2

* = Figure does not meet standards of reliability or precision.
- = Quantity zero.
[1]Starting with 1995 data, race-specific estimates are tabulated according to the 1997 Revisions to the Standards for the Classification of Federal Data on Race and Ethnicity and are not strictly comparable with estimates for earlier years.
[2]Includes women of other or unknown race not shown separately.
[3]Persons of Hispanic origin may be of any race.

Table A-65. Contraceptive Use in the Past Month Among Women 15–44 Years of Age, by Age, Race, Hispanic Origin, and Method of Contraception, Selected Years, 1982–2002—*Continued*

(Number, percent.)

Race, Hispanic origin, and year[1]	Age				
	15–44 years	15–19 years	20–24 years	25–34 years	35–44 years
Implant[4]					
1982	—	—	—	—	—
1988	—	—	—	—	—
1995	1.3	*	3.7	*1.3	*
2002	1.2	*	*	*1.9	*
Injectable[4]					
1982	—	—	—	—	—
1988	—	—	—	—	—
1995	3.0	9.7	6.1	2.9	*0.8
2002	5.4	13.9	10.2	5.3	*1.8
Birth Control Pill					
1982	28.0	63.9	55.1	25.7	*3.7
1988	30.8	58.8	68.2	32.6	4.3
1995	27.0	43.8	52.1	33.4	8.7
2002	31.0	53.8	52.5	34.8	15.0
Intrauterine Device					
1982	7.1	*	*4.2	9.7	6.9
1988	2.0	-	*	2.1	3.1
1995	0.8	-	*	*0.8	1.1
2002	2.2	*	1.8	3.7	*
Diaphragm					
1982	8.1	*6.0	10.2	10.3	4.0
1988	5.7	*	*3.7	7.3	6.0
1995	1.9	*	*	1.7	2.8
2002	0.6	-	*	*	*
Condom					
1982	12.0	20.8	10.7	11.4	11.3
1988	14.6	32.8	14.5	13.7	11.2
1995	23.4	45.8	33.7	23.7	15.3
2002	23.8	44.6	36.0	23.1	15.6
Periodic Abstinence-Calendar Rhythm					
1982	3.3	2.0	3.1	3.3	3.7
1988	1.7	*	1.1	1.8	2.0
1995	3.3	*	*1.5	3.7	3.9
2002	2.0	*	*2.3	*1.7	*2.4
Periodic Abstinence-Natural Family Planning					
1982	0.6	-	*	0.9	*
1988	0.6	-	*	0.7	0.7
1995	*0.5	-	*	*0.7	*
2002	*0.4	-	-	*	*
Withdrawal					
1982	2.0	2.9	3.0	1.8	1.3
1988	2.2	3.0	3.4	2.8	0.8
1995	6.1	13.2	7.1	6.0	4.5
2002	8.8	15.0	11.9	10.7	4.7
Other Methods[5]					
1982	4.9	2.6	5.4	4.8	5.3
1988	3.2	*	1.8	3.8	3.5
1995	3.2	*	3.2	3.1	3.4
2002	1.7	*	*	*1.5	*1.8

* = Figure does not meet standards of reliability or precision.

- = Quantity zero.

—— = Data not available.

[1]Starting with 1995 data, race-specific estimates are tabulated according to the 1997 Revisions to the Standards for the Classification of Federal Data on Race and Ethnicity and are not strictly comparable with estimates for earlier years.

[4]Data collected starting with the 1995 survey.

[5]In 2002, includes female condom, foam, cervical cap, Today Sponge®, suppository or insert, jelly or cream, and other methods.

Table A-65. Contraceptive Use in the Past Month Among Women 15–44 Years of Age, by Age, Race, Hispanic Origin, and Method of Contraception, Selected Years, 1982–2002—*Continued*

(Number, percent.)

Method of contraception and year	Not Hispanic or Latino[1]		Hispanic or Latino[3]
	White only	Black or African American only	
PERCENT OF CONTRACEPTING WOMEN			
Female Sterilization			
1982	22.0	30.0	23.0
1988	25.6	37.8	31.7
1995	24.5	39.9	36.6
2002	23.9	39.2	33.8
Male Sterilization			
1982	13.0	*1.5	*
1988	14.3	*0.9	*
1995	13.7	*1.8	*4.0
2002	12.9	*	4.7
Implant[4]			
1982	—	—	—
1988	—	—	—
1995	*1.0	*2.4	*2.0
2002	*0.8	*	*3.1
Injectable[4]			
1982	—	—	—
1988	—	—	—
1995	2.4	5.4	4.7
2002	4.2	9.4	7.3
Birth Control Pill			
1982	26.4	37.9	30.2
1988	29.5	38.2	33.4
1995	28.7	23.7	23.0
2002	34.9	23.1	22.1
Intrauterine Device			
1982	5.8	9.3	19.2
1988	1.5	3.2	*5.0
1995	0.7	*	*
2002	1.7	*	5.3
Diaphragm			
1982	9.2	*3.2	*
1988	6.6	*2.0	*
1995	2.3	*	*
2002	*	*	-
Condom			
1982	13.1	6.3	*6.9
1988	15.2	10.1	13.7
1995	22.5	24.9	21.2
2002	21.7	29.6	24.1
Periodic Abstinence-Calendar Rhythm			
1982	3.2	2.9	3.9
1988	1.6	1.9	*
1995	3.3	*1.7	3.2
2002	2.3	*	*
Periodic Abstinence-Natural Family Planning			
1982	0.7	0.3	-
1988	0.7	*	*
1995	0.7	*	*
2002	*	*	*
Withdrawal			
1982	2.1	1.3	2.6
1988	2.0	1.4	4.5
1995	6.4	3.3	5.7
2002	9.5	4.9	6.3

* = Figure does not meet standards of reliability or precision.

- = Quantity zero.

—— = Data not available.

[1]Starting with 1995 data, race-specific estimates are tabulated according to the 1997 Revisions to the Standards for the Classification of Federal Data on Race and Ethnicity and are not strictly comparable with estimates for earlier years.

[3]Persons of Hispanic origin may be of any race.

[4]Data collected starting with the 1995 survey.

Table A-65. Contraceptive Use in the Past Month Among Women 15–44 Years of Age, by Age, Race, Hispanic Origin, and Method of Contraception, Selected Years, 1982–2002—_Continued_

(Number, percent.)

Method of contraception and year	Not Hispanic or Latino[1]		Hispanic or Latino[3]
	White only	Black or African American only	
Other Methods[5]			
1982	4.6	7.3	5.0
1988	3.0	4.4	2.6
1995	3.3	3.8	*2.2
2002	*1.7	*1.9	*1.2

* = Figure does not meet standards of reliability or precision.

[1]Starting with 1995 data, race-specific estimates are tabulated according to the 1997 Revisions to the Standards for the Classification of Federal Data on Race and Ethnicity and are not strictly comparable with estimates for earlier years.

[3]Persons of Hispanic origin may be of any race.

[5]In 2002, includes female condom, foam, cervical cap, Today Sponge®, suppository or insert, jelly or cream, and other methods.

NOTE: Survey collects up to four methods of contraception used in the month of interview. Percents may not add to the total because more than one method could have been used in the month of interview.

Table A-66. Breastfeeding Among Mothers 15–44 Years of Age, by Year of Baby's Birth, and Selected Characteristics of Mother, Selected Annual Averages, 1972–2001

(Percent.)

Characteristic	1972–1974	1986–1988	1989–1991	1992–1994	1995–1998	1999–2001
PERCENT OF BABIES BREASTFED						
Total	30.1	54.1	53.3	57.6	64.4	66.5
Age at Baby's Birth						
Under 20 years	17.0	28.4	34.7	41.0	49.5	47.3
20–24 years	28.7	48.2	44.3	50.0	55.9	59.3
25–29 years	38.7	58.2	56.4	57.4	68.1	63.5
30–44 years	43.1	68.6	66.0	70.2	72.8	80.0
Race and Hispanic Origin						
Not Hispanic or Latino						
White	32.5	59.1	58.4	61.7	66.5	68.7
Black or African American	12.5	22.3	22.4	26.1	47.9	45.3
Hispanic or Latino[1]	33.1	55.6	57.0	63.8	71.2	76.0
Education[2]						
No high school diploma or GED	14.0	31.8	36.5	44.6	50.6	46.6
High school diploma or GED	25.0	47.4	45.5	51.1	55.9	61.6
Some college, no bachelor's degree	35.2	62.2	61.4	64.3	70.1	75.6
Bachelor's degree or higher	65.5	78.4	80.6	82.5	82.0	81.3
Geographic Region						
Northeast	29.9	51.3	53.5	56.5	61.6	66.9
Midwest	22.3	52.3	49.6	51.7	61.7	61.9
South	30.6	44.6	43.6	48.6	58.1	60.9
West	47.1	71.4	69.5	77.3	78.1	78.9
PERCENT OF BABIES WHO WERE BREASTFED 3 MONTHS OR MORE						
Total	62.3	34.6	31.8	33.6	45.8	48.4
Age at Baby's Birth						
Under 20 years	50.0	18.5	*10.5	*11.7	30.0	30.0
20–24 years	57.7	26.1	24.1	25.1	36.6	41.8
25–29 years	68.3	36.9	32.3	35.6	46.3	43.7
30–44 years	79.4	50.1	46.8	46.7	57.5	62.4
Race and Hispanic Origin						
Not Hispanic or Latino						
White	62.1	37.7	35.2	36.6	47.8	49.7
Black or African American	47.8	11.6	11.5	13.3	29.6	33.7
Hispanic or Latino[1]	64.7	38.2	33.9	35.0	49.7	54.3
Education[2]						
No high school diploma or GED	54.4	21.8	17.6	25.2	33.9	37.0
High school diploma or GED	53.7	28.2	28.0	27.4	36.9	43.1
Some college, no bachelor's degree	69.5	38.7	33.1	38.7	49.6	52.8
Bachelor's degree or higher	69.2	55.0	56.1	59.3	64.5	64.1
Geographic Region						
Northeast	64.6	29.9	37.2	36.4	48.2	48.8
Midwest	44.4	30.3	31.5	30.1	42.0	42.8
South	72.6	27.7	20.1	26.2	38.9	44.4
West	69.0	52.4	42.9	45.3	58.2	59.2

* = Figure does not meet standards of reliability or precision.
[1] Persons of Hispanic origin may be of any race.
[2] Educational attainment is presented only for women 22–44 years of age. Education is as of year of interview. GED stands for General Educational Development high school equivalency diploma.

Table A-67. Number of Pregnancies and Pregnancy Rates by Outcome of Pregnancy, and Number of Women, 1976–2004

Number in thousands, rate per 1,000 women aged 15-44 years.)

Year	All pregnancies								Women aged 15–44 years
	Total	Live births	Induced abortions	Fetal losses[1]	Total	Live births	Induced abortions	Fetal losses[1]	
	Number in thousands				Rate per 1,000 women aged 15-44 years[2]				Number in thousands
1976	5,002	3,168	1,179	655	102.7	65.0	24.2	13.4	48,721
1977	5,331	3,327	1,317	687	107.0	66.8	26.4	13.8	49,814
1978	5,433	3,333	1,410	690	106.7	65.5	27.7	13.5	50,921
1979	5,714	3,494	1,498	722	109.9	67.2	28.8	13.9	52,016
1980	5,912	3,612	1,554	746	111.9	68.4	29.4	14.1	52,833
1981	5,958	3,629	1,577	751	110.5	67.3	29.3	13.9	53,926
1982	6,024	3,681	1,574	769	110.1	67.3	28.8	14.1	54,700
1983	5,977	3,639	1,575	763	108.0	65.7	28.5	13.8	55,359
1984	6,019	3,669	1,577	773	107.4	65.5	28.1	13.8	56,031
1985	6,144	3,761	1,589	795	108.3	66.3	28.0	14.0	56,716
1986	6,129	3,757	1,574	798	106.7	65.4	27.4	13.9	57,430
1987	6,183	3,809	1,559	815	106.8	65.8	26.9	14.1	57,901
1988	6,393	3,910	1,591	893	110.0	67.3	27.4	15.4	58,120
1989	6,527	4,041	1,567	919	111.8	69.2	26.8	15.7	58,367
1990	6,786	4,158	1,609	1,019	115.8	70.9	27.4	17.4	58,619
1991	6,682	4,111	1,557	1,014	112.7	69.3	26.2	17.1	59,305
1992	6,603	4,065	1,529	1,009	111.1	68.4	25.7	17.0	59,417
1993	6,494	4,000	1,495	999	108.8	67.0	25.0	16.7	59,712
1994	6,370	3,953	1,423	994	106.1	65.9	23.7	16.6	60,020
1995	6,245	3,900	1,359	986	103.5	64.6	22.5	16.3	60,368
1996	6,240	3,891	1,360	988	102.8	64.1	22.4	16.3	60,704
1997	6,205	3,881	1,335	989	101.6	63.6	21.9	16.2	61,041
1998	6,266	3,942	1,319	1,006	102.2	64.3	21.5	16.4	61,326
1999	6,286	3,959	1,315	1,011	102.2	64.4	21.4	16.5	61,475
2000	6,410	4,059	1,313	1,038	104.1	65.9	21.3	16.9	61,577
2001	6,347	4,026	1,291	1,030	102.9	65.3	20.9	16.7	61,673
2002	6,320	4,022	1,269	1,030	101.9	64.8	20.5	16.6	62,044
2003	6,388	4,090	1,250	1,048	103.2	66.1	20.2	16.9	61,911
2004	6,390	4,112	1,222	1,056	103.0	66.3	19.7	17.0	62,033

[1]Spontaneous fetal losses from recognized pregnancies of all gestational periods as reported by women in the National Surveys of Family Growth. The rate of pregnancy loss depends on the degree to which losses at very early gestations are detected.
[2]Rates computed by relating the number of events to women of all ages to women aged 15–44 years.

NOTE: Due to rounding, figures may not add to totals.

Table A-68. Pregnancy, Live-Birth, Induced Abortion, and Fetal Loss Rates by Age, and Hispanic Origin of Women, 1990–2004

(Pregnancy outcomes per 1,000 women in specified group.)

Pregnancy outcome, race, Hispanic origin, and year	Total[1]	Under 15 years[2]	15–19 years			20–24 years	25–29 years	30–34 years	35–39 years	40–44 years[3]
			Total	15–17 years	18–19 years					
ALL RACES[4]										
All Pregnancies										
1990	115.8	3.4	116.8	77.1	167.7	198.5	179.0	118.8	56.9	11.4
1991	112.7	3.3	116.4	76.1	172.1	196.8	174.9	116.2	56.8	11.3
1992	111.1	3.3	112.3	73.5	169.3	194.3	173.1	116.6	57.4	12.0
1993	108.8	3.2	109.4	72.7	164.1	190.4	169.8	116.6	57.7	12.4
1994	106.1	3.2	106.1	71.1	159.6	184.8	166.1	116.7	58.5	12.9
1995	103.5	2.9	101.1	67.4	153.4	179.8	162.8	117.0	59.1	13.1
1996	102.8	2.7	97.0	63.4	149.0	180.5	163.2	118.4	60.6	13.5
1997	101.6	2.4	92.7	59.5	144.3	178.7	162.5	119.5	61.4	13.9
1998	102.2	2.3	90.1	56.7	140.3	178.9	164.7	122.4	63.3	14.4
1999	102.2	2.1	86.9	53.1	136.6	177.8	166.0	125.1	64.7	14.6
2000	104.1	2.0	84.8	50.8	134.5	179.9	168.6	130.6	67.4	15.4
2001	102.9	1.8	80.4	46.7	130.5	174.0	168.2	131.5	68.7	15.7
2002	101.9	1.7	76.0	44.1	124.4	169.0	168.1	130.9	70.0	16.1
2003	103.2	1.6	73.7	42.7	120.7	166.4	170.0	135.3	73.5	16.8
2004	103.0	1.6	72.2	41.5	118.6	163.7	169.1	135.2	75.8	17.1
Live Births										
1990	70.9	1.4	59.9	37.5	88.6	116.5	120.2	80.8	31.7	5.6
1991	69.3	1.4	61.8	38.6	94.0	115.3	117.2	79.2	31.9	5.7
1992	68.4	1.4	60.3	37.6	93.6	113.7	115.7	79.6	32.3	6.1
1993	67.0	1.4	59.0	37.5	91.1	111.3	113.2	79.9	32.7	6.3
1994	65.9	1.4	58.2	37.2	90.2	109.2	111.0	80.4	33.4	6.6
1995	64.6	1.3	56.0	35.5	87.7	107.5	108.8	81.1	34.0	6.8
1996	64.1	1.2	53.5	33.3	84.7	107.8	108.6	82.1	34.9	7.1
1997	63.6	1.1	51.3	31.4	82.1	107.3	108.3	83.0	35.7	7.4
1998	64.3	1.0	50.3	29.9	80.9	108.4	110.2	85.2	36.9	7.7
1999	64.4	0.9	48.8	28.2	79.1	107.9	111.2	87.1	37.8	7.8
2000	65.9	0.9	47.7	26.9	78.1	109.7	113.5	91.2	39.7	8.4
2001	65.3	0.8	45.3	24.7	76.1	106.2	113.4	91.9	40.6	8.5
2002	64.8	0.7	43.0	23.2	72.8	103.6	113.6	91.5	41.4	8.7
2003	66.1	0.6	41.6	22.4	70.7	102.6	115.6	95.1	43.8	9.2
2004	66.3	0.7	41.1	22.1	70.0	101.7	115.6	95.3	45.4	9.5
Induced Abortions										
1990	27.4	1.5	40.3	26.5	57.9	56.7	33.9	19.7	10.8	3.2
1991	26.2	1.4	37.4	24.2	55.7	56.4	33.4	19.0	10.4	3.0
1992	25.7	1.4	35.2	22.9	53.3	55.9	33.5	18.9	10.3	3.2
1993	25.0	1.4	33.9	22.2	51.2	54.9	33.2	18.6	10.2	3.2
1994	23.7	1.3	31.6	21.0	47.8	51.9	32.1	18.1	9.9	3.2
1995	22.5	1.2	29.4	19.5	44.8	49.1	31.5	17.5	9.7	3.2
1996	22.4	1.1	28.6	18.6	44.0	49.3	32.1	17.7	9.7	3.2
1997	21.9	1.0	27.1	17.2	42.6	48.1	31.9	17.7	9.5	3.1
1998	21.5	1.0	25.8	16.4	40.0	47.0	31.7	17.9	9.5	3.2
1999	21.4	0.9	24.7	15.2	38.6	46.4	31.7	18.3	9.7	3.2
2000	21.3	0.9	24.0	14.5	37.7	46.3	31.6	18.7	9.7	3.2
2001	20.9	0.8	22.6	13.5	36.3	44.7	31.4	18.7	9.7	3.3
2002	20.5	0.7	21.3	12.8	34.1	42.9	31.0	18.6	9.7	3.4
2003	20.2	0.7	20.7	12.5	33.0	41.5	30.4	18.5	9.8	3.4
2004	19.7	0.7	19.8	11.8	31.9	39.9	29.7	18.2	9.8	3.3

[1] Rates computed by relating the number of events to women of all ages to women aged 15–44 years.
[2] Rates computed by relating the number of events to women under age 15 years to women aged 10–14 years.
[3] Rates computed by relating the number of events to women aged 40 years and over to women aged 40–44 years.
[4] Includes races other than White and Black and origin not stated.

Table A-68. Pregnancy, Live-Birth, Induced Abortion, and Fetal Loss Rates by Age, and Hispanic Origin of Women, 1990–2004—*Continued*

(Pregnancy outcomes per 1,000 women in specified group.)

Pregnancy outcome, race, Hispanic origin, and year	Total[1]	Under 15 years[2]	15–19 years Total	15–17 years	18–19 years	20–24 years	25–29 years	30–34 years	35–39 years	40–44 years[3]
Fetal Losses[5]										
1990	17.4	0.5	16.6	13.0	21.2	25.3	24.9	18.3	14.4	2.6
1991	17.1	0.5	17.2	13.4	22.5	25.1	24.3	18.0	14.5	2.6
1992	17.0	0.5	16.8	13.0	22.4	24.7	24.0	18.1	14.7	2.8
1993	16.7	0.5	16.5	13.0	21.8	24.2	23.5	18.1	14.9	2.9
1994	16.6	0.5	16.3	12.9	21.6	23.7	23.0	18.2	15.2	3.0
1995	16.3	0.5	15.7	12.3	21.0	23.3	22.6	18.4	15.5	3.1
1996	16.3	0.4	15.0	11.6	20.3	23.4	22.5	18.6	15.9	3.2
1997	16.2	0.4	14.3	10.9	19.6	23.3	22.4	18.8	16.2	3.4
1998	16.4	0.3	14.0	10.4	19.4	23.6	22.8	19.3	16.8	3.5
1999	16.5	0.3	13.5	9.8	18.9	23.5	23.0	19.8	17.2	3.6
2000	16.9	0.3	13.1	9.4	18.7	23.9	23.5	20.7	18.1	3.8
2001	16.7	0.3	12.4	8.6	18.2	23.1	23.5	20.9	18.5	3.9
2002	16.6	0.2	11.8	8.1	17.4	22.5	23.5	20.8	18.8	4.0
2003	16.9	0.2	11.4	7.8	16.9	22.3	23.9	21.6	19.9	4.2
2004	17.0	0.2	11.3	7.7	16.7	22.1	23.9	21.7	20.6	4.3
NON-HISPANIC WHITE										
All Pregnancies										
1990	98.3	1.4	86.8	52.5	129.8	162.1	164.0	110.9	51.4	9.4
1991	94.4	1.3	83.8	50.1	130.4	157.6	158.9	108.2	51.3	9.3
1992	92.0	1.3	78.3	46.6	125.3	152.8	155.6	108.2	51.5	10.0
1993	90.0	1.3	75.9	46.0	120.8	149.5	152.3	108.7	52.2	10.4
1994	88.0	1.2	73.4	44.7	117.4	144.9	149.2	109.7	53.4	10.9
1995	86.6	1.2	70.6	43.0	113.7	142.4	147.4	110.9	54.4	11.2
1996	85.6	1.0	67.2	40.3	109.1	141.1	146.6	112.3	56.0	11.7
1997	84.8	1.0	64.5	37.9	106.1	140.0	146.0	114.0	57.0	12.0
1998	85.2	0.9	61.8	35.4	101.8	139.8	148.3	117.3	59.1	12.6
1999	84.8	0.8	59.0	32.4	98.2	137.7	148.9	119.9	60.3	12.9
2000	85.6	0.7	56.3	29.8	95.4	138.0	149.5	124.3	62.5	13.4
2001	84.2	0.6	52.4	27.0	90.6	131.9	148.2	125.5	63.7	13.6
2002	83.4	0.6	49.0	25.0	85.2	126.8	148.5	125.6	65.2	14.0
2003	84.8	0.6	47.1	23.9	82.2	125.7	150.1	129.3	68.7	14.6
2004	84.3	0.6	45.2	22.4	79.3	122.8	148.9	128.4	70.9	14.9
Live Births										
1990	62.8	0.5	42.6	23.3	66.9	97.9	115.3	79.2	29.9	4.8
1991	60.9	0.5	43.3	23.6	70.5	95.7	112.2	77.7	30.2	4.8
1992	60.0	0.5	41.6	22.7	69.7	93.8	110.7	78.3	30.4	5.3
1993	58.9	0.5	40.7	22.7	67.7	92.2	108.2	79.0	31.0	5.6
1994	58.2	0.5	40.4	22.7	67.6	90.9	106.6	80.2	32.0	5.9
1995	57.5	0.4	39.3	22.0	66.2	90.2	105.1	81.5	32.8	6.1
1996	57.1	0.4	37.6	20.6	64.0	90.1	104.9	82.8	33.9	6.5
1997	56.8	0.4	36.0	19.3	62.1	90.0	104.8	84.3	34.8	6.8
1998	57.6	0.3	35.3	18.3	60.9	91.2	107.4	87.2	36.4	7.1
1999	57.7	0.3	34.1	17.1	59.4	90.6	108.6	89.5	37.3	7.3
2000	58.5	0.3	32.6	15.8	57.5	91.2	109.4	93.2	38.8	7.7
2001	57.7	0.3	30.3	14.0	54.8	87.1	108.9	94.3	39.8	7.9
2002	57.4	0.2	28.5	13.1	51.9	84.3	109.3	94.4	40.9	8.1
2003	58.5	0.2	27.4	12.4	50.0	83.5	110.8	97.6	43.2	8.6
2004	58.4	0.2	26.7	12.0	48.7	81.9	110.0	97.1	44.8	8.8

[1]Rates computed by relating the number of events to women of all ages to women aged 15–44 years.
[2]Rates computed by relating the number of events to women under age 15 years to women aged 10–14 years.
[3]Rates computed by relating the number of events to women aged 40 years and over to women aged 40–44 years.
[5]Spontaneous fetal losses from recognized pregnancies of all gestational periods as estimated from reports from women in the National Surveys of Family Growth conducted by the National Center for Health Statistics. The rate of fetal loss depends on the degree to which losses at very early gestations are detected.
[6]Persons of Hispanic origin may be of any race.

Table A-68. Pregnancy, Live-Birth, Induced Abortion, and Fetal Loss Rates by Age, and Hispanic Origin of Women, 1990–2004—Continued

(Pregnancy outcomes per 1,000 women in specified group.)

Pregnancy outcome, race, Hispanic origin, and year	Total[1]	Under 15 years[2]	15–19 years			20–24 years	25–29 years	30–34 years	35–39 years	40–44 years[3]
			Total	15–17 years	18–19 years					
Induced Abortions										
1990	19.7	0.8	32.5	21.1	46.8	41.9	23.4	13.8	7.9	2.4
1991	18.1	0.7	28.7	18.3	43.0	40.0	22.2	13.0	7.5	2.2
1992	16.7	0.7	25.3	16.0	38.9	37.5	20.8	12.2	7.2	2.3
1993	16.1	0.6	24.0	15.4	36.9	36.2	20.4	11.9	7.1	2.3
1994	14.8	0.6	21.8	14.1	33.7	33.2	19.2	11.4	6.7	2.3
1995	14.2	0.6	20.5	13.4	31.6	31.6	19.3	11.1	6.7	2.3
1996	13.6	0.5	19.3	12.6	29.8	30.3	18.8	10.8	6.7	2.3
1997	13.2	0.5	18.6	11.8	29.1	29.4	18.3	10.7	6.4	2.2
1998	12.5	0.4	16.9	10.7	26.3	27.7	17.5	10.4	6.3	2.2
1999	11.9	0.4	15.5	9.4	24.6	26.3	16.6	10.2	6.1	2.2
2000	11.7	0.3	14.8	8.5	24.1	26.0	16.2	10.2	6.0	2.2
2001	11.3	0.3	13.9	8.1	22.7	24.9	15.6	9.9	5.8	2.1
2002	10.9	0.3	12.7	7.3	20.9	23.3	15.3	9.9	5.7	2.2
2003	10.8	0.3	12.4	7.2	20.2	23.1	15.0	9.7	5.8	2.2
2004	10.5	0.3	11.4	6.2	19.0	22.1	14.8	9.4	5.8	2.1
Fetal Losses[5]										
1990	15.8	0.2	11.6	8.1	16.0	22.4	25.2	17.9	13.6	2.2
1991	15.4	0.2	11.8	8.2	16.9	21.9	24.5	17.5	13.7	2.2
1992	15.2	0.2	11.4	7.9	16.7	21.5	24.2	17.7	13.8	2.4
1993	15.1	0.2	11.2	7.9	16.2	21.1	23.7	17.8	14.1	2.5
1994	15.0	0.2	11.2	7.9	16.2	20.8	23.3	18.1	14.6	2.7
1995	14.9	0.2	10.8	7.6	15.8	20.6	23.0	18.4	14.9	2.8
1996	14.9	0.1	10.3	7.2	15.3	20.6	22.9	18.7	15.4	2.9
1997	14.9	0.1	9.9	6.7	14.9	20.6	22.9	19.0	15.8	3.1
1998	15.1	0.1	9.6	6.4	14.6	20.9	23.5	19.7	16.5	3.2
1999	15.2	0.1	9.3	5.9	14.2	20.8	23.7	20.2	16.9	3.3
2000	15.4	0.1	8.8	5.5	13.8	20.9	23.9	21.0	17.7	3.5
2001	15.2	0.1	8.2	4.9	13.1	19.9	23.8	21.3	18.1	3.6
2002	15.2	0.1	7.7	4.6	12.4	19.3	23.9	21.3	18.6	3.7
2003	15.5	0.1	7.4	4.3	12.0	19.1	24.2	22.0	19.7	3.9
2004	15.5	0.1	7.2	4.2	11.6	18.8	24.0	21.9	20.4	4.0
NON-HISPANIC BLACK										
All Pregnancies										
1990	181.8	12.2	232.7	172.0	312.6	340.2	232.7	141.7	68.0	15.3
1991	177.9	11.7	231.8	170.5	316.0	342.1	228.8	139.2	67.6	15.1
1992	175.2	11.5	226.0	165.2	314.8	339.3	228.8	139.6	68.7	15.2
1993	170.6	11.1	219.0	161.9	305.1	331.5	224.7	139.3	68.9	15.8
1994	161.7	10.9	207.3	152.9	292.2	313.3	215.4	134.7	67.6	15.8
1995	151.3	9.6	189.6	139.4	268.4	291.7	205.3	130.8	66.3	15.8
1996	150.5	8.6	182.2	129.7	264.0	297.1	209.3	130.9	67.1	16.3
1997	148.9	7.6	174.7	121.3	257.3	296.7	210.2	132.0	68.0	16.7
1998	148.7	7.0	168.4	114.5	247.8	299.1	213.4	133.5	69.1	17.0
1999	148.0	6.4	161.9	106.4	242.9	298.9	214.6	134.8	70.3	16.9
2000	150.2	6.1	158.8	104.8	237.8	302.6	217.9	140.0	72.5	18.3
2001	145.5	5.5	147.2	93.9	228.0	285.1	216.5	139.9	72.8	18.4
2002	141.9	5.0	138.0	87.8	215.5	272.8	215.0	139.2	72.9	19.0
2003	140.4	4.6	131.6	83.7	206.2	264.7	212.7	141.3	74.7	19.1
2004	139.3	4.4	128.0	80.1	202.9	259.0	211.5	141.1	76.3	19.8

[1]Rates computed by relating the number of events to women of all ages to women aged 15–44 years.
[2]Rates computed by relating the number of events to women under age 15 years to women aged 10–14 years.
[3]Rates computed by relating the number of events to women aged 40 years and over to women aged 40–44 years.
[5]Spontaneous fetal losses from recognized pregnancies of all gestational periods as estimated from reports from women in the National Surveys of Family Growth conducted by the National Center for Health Statistics. The rate of fetal loss depends on the degree to which losses at very early gestations are detected.

Table A-68. Pregnancy, Live-Birth, Induced Abortion, and Fetal Loss Rates by Age, and Hispanic Origin of Women, 1990–2004—Continued

(Pregnancy outcomes per 1,000 women in specified group.)

Pregnancy outcome, race, Hispanic origin, and year	Total[1]	Under 15 years[2]	15–19 years			20–24 years	25–29 years	30–34 years	35–39 years	40–44 years[3]
			Total	15–17 years	18–19 years					
Live Births										
1990	89.0	5.0	116.2	84.9	157.5	165.2	118.3	70.2	28.6	5.8
1991	87.0	4.9	118.2	86.1	162.2	164.8	115.1	68.9	28.7	5.7
1992	84.5	4.8	114.7	82.9	161.0	160.8	112.8	68.4	29.1	5.8
1993	81.5	4.6	110.5	81.1	154.6	154.5	109.2	68.1	29.4	6.1
1994	77.5	4.6	105.7	77.0	150.4	146.8	104.1	66.3	29.1	6.2
1995	72.8	4.2	97.2	70.4	139.2	137.8	98.5	64.4	28.8	6.3
1996	70.7	3.6	91.9	64.8	134.1	137.0	96.7	63.2	29.1	6.4
1997	70.3	3.2	88.3	60.7	131.0	138.8	97.2	63.6	29.6	6.8
1998	70.9	2.9	85.7	56.8	128.2	142.5	99.9	64.4	30.4	6.9
1999	69.9	2.6	81.0	51.7	123.9	142.1	99.8	63.9	30.6	6.8
2000	71.4	2.4	79.2	50.1	121.9	145.4	102.8	66.5	31.8	7.5
2001	69.1	2.1	73.5	44.9	116.7	137.2	102.1	66.2	32.1	7.6
2002	67.4	1.9	68.3	41.0	110.3	131.0	102.1	66.1	32.1	7.9
2003	67.1	1.6	64.7	38.7	105.3	128.1	102.1	67.4	33.4	8.1
2004	67.0	1.6	63.1	37.1	103.9	126.9	103.0	67.4	33.7	8.3
Induced Abortions										
1990	67.0	5.4	83.5	57.7	117.4	133.1	85.4	47.5	23.5	6.4
1991	65.5	5.1	80.0	54.5	115.0	135.4	85.4	46.8	22.9	6.2
1992	65.9	5.1	78.6	53.5	115.2	137.6	88.4	47.7	23.4	6.2
1993	65.0	4.8	76.9	52.6	113.5	137.7	88.8	47.9	23.1	6.3
1994	61.1	4.6	71.2	49.1	105.8	129.2	85.9	45.7	22.3	6.2
1995	56.7	3.9	64.6	44.6	96.0	118.9	82.8	44.3	21.4	6.1
1996	58.6	3.8	64.1	42.4	97.9	125.3	88.9	46.1	21.9	6.4
1997	57.5	3.2	61.3	39.5	95.0	122.7	89.3	46.6	22.0	6.2
1998	56.5	3.2	58.6	38.0	89.0	120.3	89.0	47.0	21.9	6.2
1999	57.2	3.0	58.1	36.7	89.4	120.8	90.3	49.0	22.7	6.3
2000	57.4	2.9	57.4	37.3	86.8	120.2	89.9	50.7	23.0	6.6
2001	55.5	2.7	53.2	33.4	83.3	112.9	89.4	51.0	22.9	6.5
2002	54.2	2.5	50.7	32.5	78.7	108.5	87.9	50.5	23.0	6.8
2003	53.1	2.4	48.8	31.6	75.7	104.0	85.7	50.8	22.7	6.5
2004	52.1	2.2	47.3	30.2	74.2	99.9	83.4	50.5	23.9	7.0
Fetal Losses[5]										
1990	25.8	1.7	33.0	29.5	37.7	42.0	29.0	24.0	15.9	3.2
1991	25.4	1.7	33.7	29.9	38.8	41.9	28.2	23.6	16.0	3.2
1992	24.8	1.7	32.7	28.8	38.5	40.9	27.6	23.4	16.2	3.2
1993	24.1	1.6	31.7	28.2	37.0	39.3	26.7	23.3	16.4	3.4
1994	23.1	1.6	30.4	26.8	36.0	37.3	25.5	22.7	16.2	3.4
1995	21.8	1.5	27.9	24.4	33.3	35.0	24.1	22.0	16.0	3.5
1996	21.2	1.3	26.2	22.5	32.1	34.8	23.7	21.6	16.2	3.5
1997	21.1	1.1	25.1	21.1	31.3	35.3	23.8	21.8	16.4	3.8
1998	21.3	1.0	24.1	19.7	30.7	36.2	24.5	22.1	16.9	3.9
1999	20.9	0.9	22.7	18.0	29.6	36.1	24.4	21.9	17.0	3.8
2000	21.4	0.8	22.2	17.4	29.1	37.0	25.2	22.8	17.7	4.2
2001	20.8	0.7	20.5	15.6	27.9	34.9	25.0	22.7	17.8	4.2
2002	20.3	0.7	19.0	14.2	26.4	33.3	25.0	22.6	17.8	4.4
2003	20.3	0.6	18.0	13.4	25.2	32.6	25.0	23.1	18.6	4.5
2004	20.2	0.6	17.5	12.9	24.8	32.3	25.2	23.1	18.7	4.6

[1]Rates computed by relating the number of events to women of all ages to women aged 15–44 years.
[2]Rates computed by relating the number of events to women under age 15 years to women aged 10–14 years.
[3]Rates computed by relating the number of events to women aged 40 years and over to women aged 40–44 years.
[5]Spontaneous fetal losses from recognized pregnancies of all gestational periods as estimated from reports from women in the National Surveys of Family Growth conducted by the National Center for Health Statistics. The rate of fetal loss depends on the degree to which losses at very early gestations are detected.

Table A-68. Pregnancy, Live-Birth, Induced Abortion, and Fetal Loss Rates by Age, and Hispanic Origin of Women, 1990–2004—*Continued*

(Pregnancy outcomes per 1,000 women in specified group.)

Pregnancy outcome, race, Hispanic origin, and year	Total[1]	Under 15 years[2]	15–19 years			20–24 years	25–29 years	30–34 years	35–39 years	40–44 years[3]
			Total	15–17 years	18–19 years					
HISPANIC[6]										
All Pregnancies										
1990	164.2	4.4	167.4	113.0	242.4	271.2	219.3	145.4	78.1	21.0
1991	164.1	4.6	173.7	117.4	254.3	279.5	217.0	141.3	77.3	20.6
1992	166.2	4.9	174.0	119.7	253.9	286.6	219.3	144.1	80.1	21.7
1993	160.6	4.9	170.3	117.8	247.9	277.3	213.8	139.9	76.6	20.8
1994	156.6	4.9	169.0	120.3	240.7	270.1	208.8	136.5	75.8	21.1
1995	151.2	4.7	163.3	115.5	234.2	259.6	203.2	133.4	74.8	20.5
1996	149.4	4.4	157.1	109.4	228.4	256.5	204.4	134.0	74.9	20.3
1997	144.3	4.0	147.7	102.6	215.5	245.8	199.9	131.6	73.6	20.5
1998	143.9	3.8	146.3	100.3	214.5	243.2	199.1	133.7	74.2	20.6
1999	143.5	3.5	143.2	97.0	209.6	241.1	198.6	136.4	75.9	20.4
2000	146.1	3.3	142.1	93.3	211.6	244.0	202.4	142.3	78.4	21.7
2001	145.4	3.0	139.2	88.1	213.6	245.7	201.6	142.6	80.3	22.1
2002	143.1	2.7	134.7	84.8	210.1	247.2	200.3	138.9	79.8	22.1
2003	145.4	2.5	132.1	82.8	207.5	243.4	205.9	146.9	83.9	23.1
2004	145.7	2.5	132.8	82.9	210.0	244.8	206.3	148.4	86.2	22.8
Live Births										
1990	107.6	2.4	100.2	65.8	147.6	180.8	152.8	98.1	45.2	11.4
1991	106.9	2.4	104.6	69.2	155.4	184.6	149.9	95.0	44.7	11.1
1992	106.1	2.5	103.3	68.9	153.8	185.1	148.7	94.7	45.3	11.4
1993	103.3	2.6	101.8	68.5	151.1	180.0	146.0	93.2	44.1	11.1
1994	100.7	2.6	101.3	69.9	147.5	175.7	142.4	91.1	43.4	11.1
1995	98.8	2.6	99.3	68.3	145.4	171.9	140.4	90.5	43.7	11.2
1996	97.5	2.4	94.6	64.2	140.0	170.2	140.7	91.3	43.9	11.2
1997	94.2	2.1	89.6	61.1	132.4	162.6	137.5	89.6	43.4	11.2
1998	93.2	1.9	87.9	58.5	131.5	159.3	136.1	90.5	43.4	11.3
1999	93.0	1.9	86.8	56.9	129.5	157.3	135.8	92.3	44.5	11.1
2000	95.9	1.7	87.3	55.5	132.6	161.3	139.9	97.1	46.6	12.0
2001	96.0	1.6	86.4	52.8	135.5	163.5	140.4	97.6	47.9	12.1
2002	94.4	1.4	83.4	50.7	133.0	164.3	139.4	95.1	47.8	12.1
2003	96.9	1.3	82.3	49.7	132.0	163.4	144.4	102.0	50.8	12.8
2004	97.8	1.3	82.6	49.7	133.5	165.3	145.6	104.1	52.9	13.0
Induced Abortions										
1990	35.1	1.1	39.1	24.3	59.5	63.4	42.6	27.2	15.4	5.2
1991	35.8	1.4	39.6	24.2	61.7	67.4	43.6	26.8	15.4	5.2
1992	38.8	1.5	41.6	26.8	63.3	73.9	47.3	29.9	17.2	5.9
1993	36.4	1.4	39.7	25.5	60.7	70.4	45.0	27.6	15.4	5.4
1994	35.4	1.4	39.0	26.1	58.0	68.2	44.1	26.8	15.6	5.7
1995	32.2	1.2	35.8	23.5	54.0	62.1	40.8	24.4	14.3	5.0
1996	31.9	1.2	35.7	22.9	54.9	60.9	41.6	24.1	14.0	4.8
1997	30.7	1.1	32.7	20.3	51.4	58.8	40.8	23.7	13.4	4.9
1998	31.6	1.1	33.7	21.5	51.6	60.1	41.6	24.6	14.0	5.0
1999	31.4	1.0	32.1	20.2	49.1	60.3	41.5	25.2	14.1	5.0
2000	30.6	1.0	30.3	18.4	47.3	58.6	40.5	25.2	13.8	5.0
2001	29.8	0.9	28.7	16.9	45.8	57.8	39.1	25.0	13.8	5.3
2002	29.3	0.8	28.0	16.5	45.3	58.4	39.0	24.2	13.6	5.4
2003	28.7	0.8	26.9	15.8	44.0	55.6	38.8	24.0	13.5	5.4
2004	27.8	0.8	27.1	15.9	44.6	54.8	37.8	23.0	12.8	4.8

[1]Rates computed by relating the number of events to women of all ages to women aged 15–44 years.
[2]Rates computed by relating the number of events to women under age 15 years to women aged 10–14 years.
[3]Rates computed by relating the number of events to women aged 40 years and over to women aged 40–44 years.
[6]Persons of Hispanic origin may be of any race.

Table A-68. Pregnancy, Live-Birth, Induced Abortion, and Fetal Loss Rates by Age, and Hispanic Origin of Women, 1990–2004—Continued

(Pregnancy outcomes per 1,000 women in specified group.)

Pregnancy outcome, race, Hispanic origin, and year	Total[1]	Under 15 years[2]	15–19 years			20–24 years	25–29 years	30–34 years	35–39 years	40–44 years[3]
			Total	15–17 years	18–19 years					
Fetal Losses[5]										
1990	21.5	0.8	28.1	22.9	35.3	27.0	24.0	20.1	17.5	4.4
1991	21.5	0.8	29.4	24.0	37.2	27.6	23.5	19.5	17.3	4.3
1992	21.4	0.9	29.1	23.9	36.8	27.7	23.3	19.4	17.5	4.4
1993	20.9	0.9	28.8	23.8	36.1	26.9	22.9	19.1	17.0	4.3
1994	20.5	0.9	28.7	24.3	35.3	26.3	22.3	18.7	16.8	4.3
1995	20.2	0.9	28.2	23.7	34.8	25.7	22.0	18.5	16.9	4.3
1996	20.0	0.8	26.8	22.3	33.5	25.4	22.1	18.7	17.0	4.3
1997	19.3	0.7	25.4	21.2	31.7	24.3	21.6	18.4	16.8	4.3
1998	19.1	0.7	24.8	20.3	31.4	23.8	21.4	18.5	16.8	4.4
1999	19.0	0.6	24.4	19.8	31.0	23.5	21.3	18.9	17.2	4.3
2000	19.6	0.6	24.4	19.3	31.7	24.1	22.0	19.9	18.0	4.7
2001	19.6	0.5	24.1	18.3	32.4	24.4	22.0	20.0	18.5	4.7
2002	19.3	0.5	23.3	17.6	31.8	24.5	21.9	19.5	18.5	4.7
2003	19.8	0.5	22.9	17.3	31.6	24.4	22.7	20.9	19.6	4.9
2004	20.1	0.4	23.0	17.3	31.9	24.7	22.8	21.3	20.4	5.0

[1]Rates computed by relating the number of events to women of all ages to women aged 15–44 years.
[2]Rates computed by relating the number of events to women under age 15 years to women aged 10–14 years.
[3]Rates computed by relating the number of events to women aged 40 years and over to women aged 40–44 years.
[5]Spontaneous fetal losses from recognized pregnancies of all gestational periods as estimated from reports from women in the National Surveys of Family Growth conducted by the National Center for Health Statistics. The rate of fetal loss depends on the degree to which losses at very early gestations are detected.

Table A-69. Number and Percent Distribution of Pregnancies by Outcome of Pregnancy by Age, Race, and Hispanic Origin of Women, 1990 and 2004

(Number in thousands.)

Pregnancy outcome, race, and Hispanic origin	Total	Under 15 years	Total	15–17 years	18–19 years	20–24 years	25–29 years	30–34 years	35–39 years	40 years and over
1990										
NUMBER OF PREGNANCIES										
All Races[1]										
All pregnancies	6,786	28	1,017	377	641	1,864	1,902	1,303	570	102
Live births	4,158	12	522	183	338	1,094	1,277	886	318	50
Induced abortions	1,609	13	351	130	221	532	360	216	108	29
Fetal losses[2]	1,019	4	145	64	81	238	265	201	145	23
Non-Hispanic White										
All pregnancies	4,242	8	527	177	350	1,082	1,265	904	390	65
Live births	2,711	3	259	79	180	653	890	646	227	33
Induced abortions	852	5	198	71	126	279	180	113	60	17
Fetal losses[2]	679	1	70	27	43	149	195	146	103	15
Non-Hispanic Black										
All pregnancies	1,377	15	301	126	174	442	325	197	83	15
Live births	674	6	150	62	88	214	165	98	35	6
Induced abortions	507	7	108	42	65	173	119	66	29	6
Fetal losses[2]	196	2	43	22	21	54	40	33	19	3
Hispanic[3]										
All pregnancies	911	4	164	64	100	285	239	143	63	13
Live births	597	2	98	37	61	190	167	96	36	7
Induced abortions	195	1	38	14	24	67	46	27	12	3
Fetal losses[2]	119	1	27	13	15	28	26	20	14	3
PERCENT DISTRIBUTION										
All Races[1]										
All pregnancies	100.0	100.0	100.0	100.0	100.0	100.0	100.0	100.0	100.0	100.0
Live births	61.3	41.2	51.3	48.7	52.8	58.7	67.2	68.0	55.7	49.4
Induced abortions	23.7	44.5	34.5	34.5	34.5	28.6	18.9	16.6	18.9	28.1
Fetal losses[2]	15.0	14.3	14.2	16.9	12.6	12.7	13.9	15.4	25.4	22.5
Non-Hispanic White										
All pregnancies	100.0	100.0	100.0	100.0	100.0	100.0	100.0	100.0	100.0	100.0
Live births	63.9	32.8	49.1	44.3	51.6	60.4	70.3	71.4	58.1	51.1
Induced abortions	20.1	55.8	37.5	40.3	36.1	25.8	14.3	12.4	15.4	25.7
Fetal losses[2]	16.0	11.4	13.4	15.4	12.3	13.8	15.4	16.1	26.4	23.2
Non-Hispanic Black										
All pregnancies	100.0	100.0	100.0	100.0	100.0	100.0	100.0	100.0	100.0	100.0
Live births	48.9	41.3	49.9	49.3	50.4	48.5	50.9	49.5	42.1	37.6
Induced abortions	36.8	44.3	35.9	33.5	37.6	39.1	36.7	33.5	34.5	41.6
Fetal losses[2]	14.2	14.4	14.2	17.1	12.1	12.3	12.4	16.9	23.4	20.9
Hispanic[3]										
All pregnancies	100.0	100.0	100.0	100.0	100.0	100.0	100.0	100.0	100.0	100.0
Live births	65.5	55.1	59.9	58.3	60.9	66.7	69.7	67.5	57.9	54.3
Induced abortions	21.4	25.8	23.4	21.5	24.5	23.4	19.4	18.7	19.7	24.7
Fetal losses[2]	13.1	19.1	16.8	20.2	14.6	10.0	10.9	13.8	22.4	21.0
2004										
NUMBER OF PREGNANCIES										
All Races[1]										
All pregnancies	6,390	16	729	252	477	1,665	1,618	1369	795	198
Live births	4,112	7	415	134	281	1,034	1104.0	966	476	110
Induced abortions	1,222	7	200	71	128	406	285.0	184	103	38
Fetal losses[2]	1,056	2	114	47	67	225	229	220	216	50
Non-Hispanic White										
All pregnancies	3,355	4	289	86	204	784	864	807	487	119
Live births	2,322	1	171	46	125	523	638	611	308	70
Induced abortions	418	2	73	24	49	141	86	59	40	17
Fetal losses[2]	615	1	46	16	30	120	140	138	140	32

[1]Includes races other than White and Black and origin not stated.
[2]Spontaneous fetal losses from recognized pregnancies of all gestational periods as estimated from reports from women in the Health Statistics.
[3]Includes all persons of Hispanic origin of any race.

Table A-69. Number and Percent Distribution of Pregnancies by Outcome of Pregnancy by Age, Race, and Hispanic Origin of Women, 1990 and 2004—*Continued*

(Number in thousands.)

Pregnancy outcome, race, and Hispanic origin	Total	Under 15 years	Total	15–17 years	18–19 years	20–24 years	25–29 years	30–34 years	35–39 years	40 years and over
Non-Hispanic Black										
All pregnancies	1,211	7	198	76	123	387	286	195	107	30
Live births	582	3	98	35	63	190	139	93	47	12
Induced abortions	453	4	73	29	45	149	113	70	34	11
Fetal losses[2]	176	1	27	12	15	48	34	32	26	7
Hispanic[3]										
All pregnancies	1,410	5	214	81	133	414	360	253	132	32
Live births	946	2	133	49	84	280	254	178	81	18
Induced abortions	269	1	44	16	28	93	66	39	20	7
Fetal losses[2]	194	1	37	17	20	42	40	36	31	7
PERCENT DISTRIBUTION										
All Races[1]										
All pregnancies	100.0	100.0	100	100	100.0	100.0	100.0	100.0	100.0	100.0
Live births	64.4	41.9	57	53.2	59.0	62.1	68.3	70.5	59.8	55.4
Induced abortions	19.1	43.6	27.4	28.3	26.9	24.4	17.6	13.4	12.9	19.4
Fetal losses[2]	16.5	14.5	15.6	18.5	14.1	13.5	14.1	16.0	27.2	25.2
Non-Hispanic White										
All pregnancies	100.0	100.0	100	100	100.0	100.0	100.0	100.0	100.0	100.0
Live births	69.2	40.3	59	53.5	61.4	66.7	73.9	75.6	63.1	59.0
Induced abortions	12.4	45.7	25.1	27.9	24.0	18.0	10.0	7.3	8.2	14.2
Fetal losses[2]	18.3	14.0	15.8	18.6	14.7	15.3	16.2	17.1	28.7	26.8
Non-Hispanic Black										
All pregnancies	100.0	100.0	100	100	100.0	100.0	100.0	100.0	100.0	100.0
Live births	48.1	37.1	49.3	46.3	51.2	49.0	48.7	47.8	44.2	40.2
Induced abortions	37.4	50.0	37	37.7	36.6	38.6	39.4	35.8	31.3	35.2
Fetal losses[2]	14.5	12.9	13.7	16.1	12.2	12.5	11.9	16.4	24.5	23.1
Hispanic[3]										
All pregnancies	100.0	100.0	100	100	100.0	100.0	100.0	100.0	100.0	100.0
Live births	67.1	51.3	62.2	60	63.6	67.5	70.6	70.2	61.4	57.1
Induced abortions	19.1	31.0	20.4	19.1	21.2	22.4	18.3	15.5	14.9	20.9
Fetal losses[2]	13.8	17.8	17.3	20.8	15.2	10.1	11.1	14.4	23.7	22.0

[1]Includes races other than White and Black and origin not stated.
[2]Spontaneous fetal losses from recognized pregnancies of all gestational periods as estimated from reports from women in the Health Statistics.
[3]Includes all persons of Hispanic origin of any race.

NOTE: Due to rounding, figures may not add to totals. Percent distributions based on unrounded frequencies. Due to sample 2003 are based on cycles 3 through 6 of the National Survey of Family Growth (conducted 1982, 1988, 1995, and 2002).

Table A-70. Estimated Total Pregnancy, Total Fertility, and Total Induced Abortion Rates by Race and Hispanic Origin, Selected Years, 1990–2004

(Sums of rates for 5-year age groups multiplied by 5 and divided by 1,000.)

Race and Hispanic origin	Pregnancy measure				
	1990	1996	2000	2003	2004
Total Pregnancy Rate[1]					
Total[2]	3.42	3.18	3.24	3.19	3.17
Non-Hispanic White	2.93	2.68	2.72	2.68	2.66
Non-Hispanic Black	5.21	4.56	4.58	4.24	4.20
Hispanic[3]	4.53	4.26	4.17	4.19	4.22
Total[2]	2.08	1.98	2.06	2.04	2.05
Non-Hispanic White	1.85	1.78	1.87	1.86	1.85
Non-Hispanic Black	2.50	2.14	2.18	2.03	2.02
Hispanic[3]	2.95	2.77	2.73	2.79	2.82
Total[2]	0.83	0.71	0.67	0.63	0.61
Non-Hispanic White	0.61	0.44	0.38	0.34	0.33
Non-Hispanic Black	1.92	1.78	1.75	1.60	1.57
Hispanic[3]	0.97	0.91	0.87	0.83	0.81

[1]Includes estimates of fetal losses not shown separately.
[2]Includes races other than White and Black.
[3]Persons of Hispanic origin may be of any race.

NOTE: Total pregnancy rates are estimates of the number of pregnancies a woman would have if she experiences the age-specific pregnancy rates observed in reproductive years. Total fertility rates are estimates of the number of live births a woman would have if she experiences the age-specific birth rates observed in a reproductive years. Total abortion rates are estimates of the number of abortions a woman would have if she experiences the age-specific abortion rates observed reproductive years.

Table A-71. Number and Rate by Age and Race and Hispanic Origin of Mother: Total of 12 Reporting States, 2005

(Number of live births with specified risk factor per 1,000 live births in specified group.)

Risk factor, race, and Hispanic origin of mother	All births[1]	Factor reported	All ages	Under 20 years	20–24 years	25–29 years	30–34 years	35–39 years	40–54 years	Not stated[2]
All Races[3]										
Diabetes	1,268,502	57,143	46.1	15.5	28.2	44.3	61.8	80.7	103.8	29,907
Prepregnancy (diagnosis prior to this pregnancy)	1,268,502	8,500	6.9	2.6	4.5	6.7	8.4	12.2	16.5	29,907
Gestational (diagnosis in this pregnancy)	1,268,502	48,643	39.3	12.9	23.7	37.6	53.4	68.5	87.3	29,907
Hypertension	1,268,502	72,388	58.4	56.2	52.8	56.4	59.9	69.5	89.4	29,907
Prepregnancy (chronic)	1,268,502	15,109	12.2	4.8	7.6	11.3	15.3	22.1	33.7	29,907
Gestational (PIH, preeclampsia)	1,268,502	57,279	46.2	51.4	45.3	45.1	44.6	47.5	55.7	29,907
Previous preterm birth	1,268,502	25,094	20.3	7.1	19.6	22.5	22.1	24.8	25.9	29,907
Other previous poor pregnancy outcome	1,268,502	27,181	21.9	6.8	17.7	22.7	26.2	32.6	42.1	29,907
Mother had a previous cesarean delivery	1,268,502	142,347	114.5	29.0	85.6	114.0	150.1	183.1	195.3	25,499
Non-Hispanic White										
Diabetes	714,257	31,468	45.4	18.4	29.5	43.0	55.2	69.9	89.0	21,610
Prepregnancy (diagnosis prior to this pregnancy)	714,257	4,349	6.3	3.1	4.6	6.1	6.9	9.2	12.5	21,610
Gestational (diagnosis in this pregnancy)	714,257	27,119	39.2	15.2	25.0	36.9	48.3	60.6	76.5	21,610
Hypertension	714,257	43,145	62.3	60.5	58.8	62.3	61.6	67.2	81.6	21,610
Prepregnancy (chronic)	714,257	8,562	12.4	4.7	7.9	11.5	14.6	20.0	27.2	21,610
Gestational (PIH, preeclampsia)	714,257	34,583	49.9	55.8	50.9	50.8	47.0	47.2	54.3	21,610
Previous preterm birth	714,257	15,020	21.7	7.6	20.9	23.0	22.7	26.1	27.4	21,610
Other previous poor pregnancy outcome	714,257	17,706	25.6	8.7	20.2	24.5	29.3	36.8	48.4	21,610
Mother had a previous cesarean delivery	714,257	76,220	109.6	22.9	75.1	100.7	140.2	173.7	189.7	19,064
Non-Hispanic Black										
Diabetes	171,054	7,524	44.7	14.6	28.4	46.9	74.5	100.3	121.7	2,889
Prepregnancy (diagnosis prior to this pregnancy)	171,054	1,652	9.8	3.2	6.0	10.0	16.0	24.6	27.3	2,889
Gestational (diagnosis in this pregnancy)	171,054	5,872	34.9	11.4	22.5	36.9	58.4	75.6	94.4	2,889
Hypertension	171,054	12,841	76.4	65.5	61.4	72.6	95.9	120.0	152.3	2,889
Prepregnancy (chronic)	171,054	3,802	22.6	6.8	12.7	22.4	38.4	57.0	80.3	2,889
Gestational (PIH, preeclampsia)	171,054	9,039	53.8	58.7	48.8	50.2	57.4	63.0	72.0	2,889
Previous preterm birth	171,054	4,956	29.5	9.1	27.3	39.0	38.3	36.6	36.5	2,889
Other previous poor pregnancy outcome	171,054	4,672	27.8	8.3	23.9	35.5	38.5	40.7	40.6	2,889
Mother had a previous cesarean delivery	171,054	20,571	121.9	34.1	105.3	143.1	173.5	205.4	213.1	2,357
Hispanic[4]										
Diabetes	329,276	14,401	44.2	12.7	25.2	43.6	69.2	96.1	131.4	3,246
Prepregnancy (diagnosis prior to this pregnancy)	329,276	2,102	6.4	1.7	3.5	6.4	9.4	15.7	23.0	3,246
Gestational (diagnosis in this pregnancy)	329,276	12,299	37.7	11.1	21.7	37.2	59.8	80.4	108.4	3,246
Hypertension	329,276	14,447	44.3	46.5	38.9	39.2	47.2	60.6	85.2	3,246
Prepregnancy (chronic)	329,276	2,343	7.2	3.9	4.3	6.4	9.7	15.5	28.6	3,246
Gestational (PIH, preeclampsia)	329,276	12,104	37.1	42.6	34.5	32.8	37.4	45.1	56.6	3,246
Previous preterm birth	329,276	4,336	13.3	5.3	13.1	15.3	15.0	17.4	17.4	3,246
Other previous poor pregnancy outcome	329,276	3,919	12.0	3.9	9.9	13.8	14.8	19.3	25.6	3,246
Mother had a previous cesarean delivery	329,276	40,179	122.9	33.0	94.3	136.2	176.1	209.7	209.8	2,421

[1]Total number of births to residents of areas reporting specified pregnancy risk factor.

[2]No response reported for pregnancy risk factor item; includes births to residents of states using the 2003 Standard Certificate of Live Birth occurring in states using the 1989 Standard Certificate of Live Birth.

[3]Includes other races not shown.

[4]Persons of Hispanic origin may be of any race.

NOTE: Includes Florida, Idaho, Kansas, Kentucky, Nebraska, New Hampshire, New York (excluding New York City), Pennsylvania, South Carolina, Tennessee, Texas, and Washington.

Table A-72. Rates of Obstetric Procedures by Age and Race and Hispanic Origin of Mother: Total of 12 Reporting States, 2005

(Number of live births with specified obstetric procedure per 1,000 live births in specified group.)

Obstetric procedures, race, and Hispanic origin of mother	All births[1]	Factor reported	All ages	Under 20 years	20–24 years	25–29 years	30–34 years	35–39 years	40–54 years	Not stated[2]
All Races[3]										
Cervical cerclage	1,268,502	4,549	3.7	1.6	2.7	3.6	4.7	5.7	6.5	30,552
Tocolysis	1,268,502	18,994	15.3	17.2	16.1	15.1	14.7	14	13.7	30,552
External cephalic version	1,268,502	6,660	5.4	6.0	5.6	5.3	5.2	4.9	5.1	30,552
Percent successful[4]	1,268,502	5,417	81.3	85.3	83.4	80.9	77.8	79.7	78.8	30,552
Non-Hispanic White										
Cervical cerclage	714,257	2,453	3.5	1.4	2.5	3.3	4.4	5.4	5.9	22,194
Tocolysis	714,257	12,284	17.7	22.9	19.8	17.3	16.4	14.8	14.4	22,194
External cephalic version	714,257	3,261	4.7	5.1	4.6	4.7	4.8	4.6	4.4	22,194
Percent successful[4]	714,257	2,375	72.8	74.6	72.4	72.5	71.5	76.1	72.3	22,194
Non-Hispanic Black										
Cervical cerclage	171,054	1,123	6.7	2.1	4.4	7.9	11.1	13.1	12.3	2,726
Tocolysis	171,054	2,669	15.9	16.3	16.1	16.1	15.9	13.4	12.9	2,726
External cephalic version	171,054	1,681	10.0	10.3	10.9	10.2	8.9	7.9	5.9	2,726
Percent successful[4]	171,054	1,594	94.8	93.2	95.6	95.0	93.4	97	100	2,726
Hispanic[5]										
Cervical cerclage	329,276	809	2.5	1.4	2.1	2.7	3.0	3.3	4.1	3,250
Tocolysis	329,276	3,359	10.3	11.1	9.9	9.9	10.1	11.7	10.4	3,250
External cephalic version	329,276	1,399	4.3	4.6	4.2	4.4	3.9	4.1	5.6	3,250
Percent successful[4]	329,276	1,183	84.6	87.7	86.4	85.1	81.2	77.5	81.8	3,250

[1]Total number of births to residents of areas reporting specified obstetric procedure.

[2]No response reported for obstetric procedure item; includes births to residents of states using the 2003 Standard Certificate of Live Birth occurring in states using the 1989 Standard Certificate of Live Birth.

[3]Includes other races not shown.

[4]Percentage successful external cephalic version (ECV) is the number of successful ECVs per 100 live births to women with an attempted ECV in specified group.

[5]Persons of Hispanic origin may be of any race.

NOTE: Includes Florida, Idaho, Kansas, Kentucky, Nebraska, New Hampshire, New York (excluding New York City), Pennsylvania, South Carolina, Tennessee, Texas, and Washington.

Table A-73. Number and Rate of Live Births by Characteristics of Labor and Delivery, by Age, Race, and Hispanic Origin of Mother: Total of 12 Reporting States, 2005

(Number of live births with specified obstetric procedure per 1,000 live births in specified group.)

Labor and delivery characteristic, race, and Hispanic origin of mother	All births[1]	Factor reported	All ages	Under 20 years	20–24 years	25–29 years	30–34 years	35–39 years	40–54 years	Not stated[2]
All Races[3]										
Induction of labor	1,268,502	322,247	259.9	267.8	266.0	267.6	252.7	239.2	227.8	28,462
Augmentation of labor	1,268,502	267,743	215.9	266.5	235.8	216.8	193.1	173.9	154.5	28,462
Nonvertex presentation	1,268,502	22,497	18.1	11.5	13.8	17.4	22.3	26.2	30.7	28,462
Steroids (glucocorticoids) for fetal lung maturation	1,268,502	12,245	9.9	10.8	9.2	9.5	9.8	10.8	14.4	28,462
Antibiotics received by mother during labor	1,268,502	211,544	170.6	192.1	173.0	166.5	163.6	167.0	170.7	28,462
Clinical chorioamnionitis during labor	1,268,502	13,669	11.0	17.2	12.6	10.4	8.9	7.5	7.3	28,462
Moderate or heavy meconium staining of amniotic fluid	1,268,502	52,536	42.4	48.0	43.5	41.6	40.1	40.5	41.1	28,462
Fetal intolerance of labor	1,268,502	62,040	50.0	56.2	49.8	48.7	48.3	50.3	53.0	28,462
Epidural or spinal anesthesia during labor	1,268,502	827,498	667.3	664.6	651.1	662.1	684.3	687.7	668.4	28,462
Non-Hispanic White										
Induction of labor	714,257	206,411	297.6	325.2	315.8	308.5	282.1	262.8	246.6	20,760
Augmentation of labor	714,257	150,383	216.8	272.9	240.4	222.5	195.5	177.9	157.8	20,760
Nonvertex presentation	714,257	15,036	21.7	15.0	16.3	20.5	25.4	28.8	34.5	20,760
Steroids (glucocorticoids) for fetal lung maturation	714,257	7,477	10.8	12.1	10.3	10.5	10.5	11.1	14.6	20,760
Antibiotics received by mother during labor	714,257	121,782	175.6	197.0	176.0	174.0	171.9	172.4	173.9	20,760
Clinical chorioamnionitis during labor	714,257	6,378	9.2	13.6	10.4	9.3	7.9	6.9	6.7	20,760
Moderate or heavy meconium staining of amniotic fluid	714,257	27,138	39.1	42.4	40.2	38.8	37.7	38.8	38.4	20,760
Fetal intolerance of labor	714,257	37,372	53.9	63.7	54.9	53.2	51.1	52.5	53.8	20,760
Epidural or spinal anesthesia during labor	714,257	495,705	714.8	728.6	701.9	711.7	726.0	719.8	694.6	20,760
Non-Hispanic Black										
Induction of labor	171,054	37,550	223.0	236.2	221.7	222.1	223.2	206.7	196.2	2,655
Augmentation of labor	171,054	37,059	220.1	269.2	235.5	211.8	182.5	158.6	144.6	2,655
Nonvertex presentation	171,054	2,767	16.4	10.8	14.1	16.2	21.5	26.6	30.5	2,655
Steroids (glucocorticoids) for fetal lung maturation	171,054	2,430	14.4	15.0	12.9	14.3	14.4	17.9	22.0	2,655
Antibiotics received by mother during labor	171,054	37,402	221.1	251.4	228.5	211.7	201.7	205.2	201.2	2,655
Clinical chorioamnionitis during labor	171,054	1,970	11.7	17.6	12.5	10.1	8.3	7.2	7.9	2,655
Moderate or heavy meconium staining of amniotic fluid	171,054	9,013	53.5	59.2	52.2	51.0	53.4	55.5	49.0	2,655
Fetal intolerance of labor	171,054	10,716	63.6	72.9	62.4	60.6	60.8	62.4	66.0	2,655
Epidural or spinal anesthesia during labor	171,054	109,636	651.0	671.6	650.7	638.5	647.9	652.7	644.8	2,655
Hispanic[4]										
Induction of labor	329,276	67,473	206.8	224.4	210.8	204.9	195.0	194.9	196.4	2,998
Augmentation of labor	329,276	67,875	208.0	257.8	225.5	199.3	179.0	162.1	140.1	2,998
Nonvertex presentation	329,276	3,678	11.3	7.9	9.1	10.8	14.5	17.8	19.4	2,998
Steroids (glucocorticoids) for fetal lung maturation	329,276	1,950	6.0	6.9	5.3	5.2	6.3	7.6	9.4	2,998
Antibiotics received by mother during labor	329,276	43,794	134.2	151.0	135.6	127.5	126.4	135	145.7	2,998
Clinical chorioamnionitis during labor	329,276	4,356	13.4	20.8	15.8	11.3	9.4	7.2	7.8	2,998
Moderate or heavy meconium staining of amniotic fluid	329,276	14,059	43.1	47.4	43.8	42.7	40.6	38.8	44.7	2,998
Fetal intolerance of labor	329,276	11,049	33.9	37.3	33.3	31.1	33.6	37.4	41.3	2,998
Epidural or spinal anesthesia during labor	329,276	188,046	576.3	589.3	566.0	561.5	585.9	609	604.6	2,998

[1]Total number of births to residents of areas reporting specified labor and delivery characteristic.

[2]No response reported for characteristic of labor and delivery item; includes births to residents of states using the 2003 Standard Certificate of Live Birth occurring in states using the 1989 Standard Certificate of Live Birth.

[3]Includes other races not shown.

[4]Persons of Hispanic origin may be of any race.

NOTE: Includes Florida, Idaho, Kansas, Kentucky, Nebraska, New Hampshire, New York (excluding New York City), Pennsylvania, South Carolina, Tennessee, Texas, and Washington.

Table A-74. Live Births by Method of Delivery, by Age, Race, and Hispanic Origin of Mother: Total of 12 Reporting States, 2005

(Percent of live births with specified method of delivery.)

Method of delivery, race, and Hispanic orign of mother	All births	Factor reported	All ages[1]	Under 20 years	20–24 years	25–29 years	30–34 years	35–39 years	40–54 years	Not stated[2]
All Races[3]										
Attempted forceps/unsuccessful	1,268,502	7,165	0.6	0.7	0.6	0.6	0.5	0.5	0.5	60,764
Attempted vacuum extraction/unsuccessful	1,268,502	13,141	1.1	1.5	1.2	1.0	1.0	0.9	1.0	64,046
Fetal presentation at birth										
Cephalic..	1,268,502	1,129,245	92.9	94.3	94.0	93.1	92.0	91.2	89.9	53,433
Breech..	1,268,502	48,608	4.0	2.9	3.2	3.9	4.7	5.2	6.1	53,433
Other..	1,268,502	37,216	3.1	2.8	2.8	2.9	3.3	3.6	4.0	53,433
Final route and method of delivery										
Vaginal/spontaneous	1,268,502	787,723	63.4	70.1	67.9	64.6	59.5	54.3	48.8	26,632
Vaginal/forceps...	1,268,502	12,094	1.0	1.3	1.0	1.0	0.9	0.8	0.8	26,632
Vaginal/vacuum..	1,268,502	46,650	3.8	5.4	3.9	3.6	3.3	3.2	3.1	26,632
Cesarean..	1,268,502	395,403	31.8	23.2	27.2	30.9	36.3	41.8	47.4	26,632
Cesarean/trial of labor attempted[4].......................	395,403	117,119	30.8	50.0	36.3	30.5	25.6	23.1	22.7	15,029
Non-Hispanic White										
Attempted forceps/unsuccessful	714,257	3,784	0.6	0.7	0.6	0.6	0.5	0.5	0.5	30,504
Attempted vacuum extraction/unsuccessful	714,257	7,035	1.0	1.5	1.2	1.0	0.9	0.9	0.9	32,902
Fetal presentation at birth										
Cephalic..	714,257	637,768	93.1	94.9	94.4	93.4	92.2	91.4	90.2	29,515
Breech..	714,257	29,304	4.3	3.2	3.5	4.2	4.8	5.3	6.0	29,515
Other..	714,257	17,670	2.6	1.9	2.1	2.4	2.9	3.3	3.7	29,515
Final route and method of delivery										
Vaginal/spontaneous	714,257	437,940	63.1	69.2	67.6	64.8	60.0	55.4	49.9	19,747
Vaginal/forceps...	714,257	7,664	1.1	1.7	1.2	1.1	1.0	0.8	0.9	19,747
Vaginal/vacuum..	714,257	28,818	4.1	6.2	4.6	4.1	3.6	3.4	3.3	19,747
Cesarean..	714,257	220,088	31.7	22.9	26.6	30.0	35.4	40.4	45.9	19,747
Cesarean/trial of labor attempted[4].......................	220,088	65,882	30.8	52.5	38.2	31.6	25.8	22.8	22.6	6,201
Non-Hispanic Black										
Attempted forceps/unsuccessful	171,054	885	0.5	0.6	0.5	0.5	0.5	0.5	0.7	5,640
Attempted vacuum extraction/unsuccessful	171,054	1,456	0.9	1.0	0.9	0.9	0.8	0.8	0.9	5,916
Fetal presentation at birth										
Cephalic..	171,054	155,640	93.7	95.3	94.3	93.5	92.3	91.3	89.5	4,866
Breech..	171,054	5,611	3.4	2.4	2.8	3.5	4.3	5.1	7.0	4,866
Other..	171,054	4,937	3.0	2.4	2.9	3.0	3.4	3.6	3.5	4,866
Final route and method of delivery										
Vaginal/spontaneous	171,054	105,709	62.7	69.1	66.0	62.6	56.9	50.2	44.9	2,462
Vaginal/forceps...	171,054	1,227	0.7	1.1	0.8	0.6	0.6	0.5	*	2,462
Vaginal/vacuum..	171,054	5,254	3.1	5.0	3.1	2.5	2.4	2.3	2.2	2,462
Cesarean..	171,054	56,402	33.5	24.9	30.2	34.2	40.1	47.1	52.5	2,462
Cesarean/trial of labor attempted[4].......................	56,402	17,006	31.7	49.4	34.3	28.7	25.9	22.7	21.7	2,777
Hispanic[5]										
Attempted forceps/unsuccessful	329,276	2,199	0.7	0.9	0.7	0.7	0.6	0.5	0.7	20,670
Attempted vacuum extraction/unsuccessful	329,276	4,052	1.3	1.7	1.4	1.2	1.2	1.1	1.1	21,063
Fetal presentation at birth										
Cephalic..	329,276	288,435	92.0	92.8	92.9	92.3	91.0	90.0	88.6	15,928
Breech..	329,276	11,617	3.7	3.0	3.1	3.6	4.5	5.3	6.1	15,928
Other..	329,276	13,296	4.2	4.2	4.1	4.1	4.5	4.7	5.3	15,928
Final route and method of delivery										
Vaginal/spontaneous	329,276	211,814	64.8	71.7	69.2	65.2	58.9	52.8	47.2	2,596
Vaginal/forceps...	329,276	2,519	0.8	1.2	0.8	0.7	0.6	0.6	0.5	2,596
Vaginal/vacuum..	329,276	9,633	2.9	4.6	3.2	2.5	2.3	2.3	2.2	2,596
Cesarean..	329,276	102,714	31.4	22.6	26.8	31.6	38.2	44.4	50.1	2,596
Cesarean/trial of labor attempted[4].......................	102,714	28,949	29.8	47.1	34.0	27.5	23.8	23.1	22.8	5,536

* = Figure does not meet standards of reliability or precision.

[1]Total number of births to residents of areas reporting the specified item.

[2]No response reported for method of delivery item; includes births to residents of states using the 2003 Standard Certificate of Live Birth occurring in states using the 1989 Standard Certificate of Live Birth.

[3]Includes other races not shown.

[4]Cesarean/trial of labor attempted is number of women who attempted a trial of labor prior to cesarean delivery per 100 cesarean births.

[5]Persons of Hispanic origin may be of any race.

NOTE: Includes Florida, Idaho, Kansas, Kentucky, Nebraska, New Hampshire, New York (excluding New York City), Pennsylvania, South Carolina, Tennessee, Texas, and Washington.

Table A-75. Abnormal Conditions of the Newborn, by Age, Race, and Hispanic Origin of Mother: Total of 12 Reporting States, 2005

(Number of live births with specified obstetric procedure per 1,000 live births in specified group.)

Abnormal condition, race, and Hispanic origin of mother	All births[1]	Condition reported	All ages	Under 20 years	20–24 years	25–29 years	30–34 years	35–39 years	40–54 years	Not stated[2]
All Races[3]										
Assisted ventilation required immediately following delivery	1,268,502	64,649	52.3	53.9	49.6	50.9	53.2	56.4	62.5	31,612
Assisted ventilation required for more than six hours	1,268,502	12,916	10.4	11.4	10.3	10.0	9.8	11.6	13.7	31,612
NICU admission	1,268,502	81,202	65.7	66.5	60.5	62.5	66.5	77.2	93.9	31,612
Surfactant replacement therapy given to newborn	1,268,502	4,546	3.7	4.0	3.6	3.6	3.3	3.9	4.8	31,612
Antibiotics received by newborn for suspected neonatal sepsis	1,268,502	23,876	19.3	23.4	19.9	18.5	17.6	18.8	21.6	31,612
Seizure or serious neurologic dysfunction	1,268,502	407	0.3	0.4	0.3	0.4	0.2	0.3	*	31,612
Significant birth injury	1,268,502	756	0.6	0.7	0.7	0.6	0.5	0.6	1.0	31,612
Non-Hispanic White										
Assisted ventilation required immediately following delivery	714,257	38,715	56.0	56.6	53.6	54.4	56.9	59.4	66.2	22,432
Assisted ventilation required for more than six hours	714,257	7,621	11.0	11.8	11.3	10.7	10.0	12.0	13.8	22,432
NICU admission	714,257	45,318	65.5	64.6	60.8	62.4	66.4	74.8	90.1	22,432
Surfactant replacement therapy given to newborn	714,257	2,750	4.0	4.4	4.1	4.0	3.5	4.1	5.2	22,432
Antibiotics received by newborn for suspected neonatal sepsis	714,257	13,800	19.9	24.0	21.1	19.4	18.3	19.3	21.9	22,432
Seizure or serious neurologic dysfunction	714,257	272	0.4	0.6	0.4	0.4	0.3	0.4	*	22,432
Significant birth injury	714,257	470	0.7	0.9	0.7	0.7	0.6	0.6	*	22,432
Non-Hispanic Black										
Assisted ventilation required immediately following delivery	171,054	9,954	59.2	58.1	55.3	59.4	63.3	68.8	63.5	2,908
Assisted ventilation required for more than six hours	171,054	2,308	13.7	13.7	13.3	13.1	14.5	16.1	15.9	2,908
NICU admission	171,054	14,673	87.3	82.8	79.3	85.3	93.5	115.6	129.7	2,908
Surfactant replacement therapy given to newborn	171,054	766	4.6	4.8	3.9	5.0	4.7	4.8	*	2,908
Antibiotics received by newborn for suspected neonatal sepsis	171,054	3,355	20.0	22.1	19.3	18.9	19.1	21.9	22.7	2,908
Seizure or serious neurologic dysfunction	171,054	57	0.3	*	*	*	*	*	*	2,908
Significant birth injury	171,054	73	0.4	*	0.5	*	*	*	*	2,908
Hispanic[4]										
Assisted ventilation required immediately following delivery	329,276	13,449	41.3	48.5	39.6	39.0	39.8	43	50.2	3,913
Assisted ventilation required for more than six hours	329,276	2,516	7.7	9.7	6.8	7.1	7.6	8.8	11.8	3,913
NICU admission	329,276	17,954	55.2	58.3	49.5	51.7	57	69.4	88.2	3,913
Surfactant replacement therapy given to newborn	329,276	894	2.7	3.3	2.6	2.4	2.7	3.4	3.8	3,913
Antibiotics received by newborn for suspected neonatal sepsis	329,276	5,825	17.9	23.6	18.3	16.4	15.1	16.5	20.8	3,913
Seizure or serious neurologic dysfunction	329,276	64	0.2	*	*	0.3	*	*	*	3,913
Significant birth injury	329,276	190	0.6	0.6	0.6	0.5	0.5	*	*	3,913

* = Figure does not meet standards of reliability or precision.

[1]Total number of births to residents of areas reporting specified abnormal condition.

[2]No response reported for abnormal condition of the newborn item. Includes births to residents of states using the 2003 Standard Certificate of Live Birth occurring in states using the 1989 Standard Certificate of Live Birth.

[3]Includes other races not shown.

[4]Persons of Hispanic origin may be of any race.

NOTE: Includes Florida, Idaho, Kansas, Kentucky, Nebraska, New Hampshire, New York (excluding New York City), Pennsylvania, South Carolina, Tennessee, Texas, and Washington.

Table A-76. Number and Rate of Live Births by Congenital Anomaly of the Newborn, by Age of Mother: Total of 12 Reporting States, 2005

(Number of live births with specified anomaly per 100,000 live births in specified group.)

Congenital anomaly	All births[1]	Congenital anomaly reported	All ages	Under 20 years	20–24 years	25–29 years	30–34 years	35–39 years	40–54 years	Not stated[2]
Anencephaly	1,268,502	158.0	12.8	*	17.0	9.8	13.2	*	*	33,842
Menigomyelocele or spina bifida	1,268,502	216.0	17.5	17.4	14.8	19.1	15.8	23.8	*	33,842
Cyanotic congenital heart disease	1,268,502	702.0	56.9	59.4	48.7	54.0	57.5	68.5	107.6	33,842
Congenital diaphragmatic hernia	1,268,502	190.0	15.4	*	15.4	13.4	17.6	20.1	*	33,842
Omphalocele	1,268,502	119.0	9.6	*	7.7	8.9	9.9	*	*	33,842
Gastroschisis	1,268,502	349.0	28.3	105.1	37.3	15.2	7.3	*	*	33,842
Limb reduction defect	1,268,502	282.0	22.8	26.8	25.0	23.0	20.5	17.9	*	33,842
Cleft lip with or without cleft palate	1,268,502	779.0	63.1	74.6	72.1	62.3	55.7	41.7	84	33,842
Cleft palate alone	1,268,502	319.0	25.8	24.6	30.8	26.0	21.6	22.3	*	33,842
Down syndrome	1,268,502	695.0	56.3	35.5	32.1	30.7	48.0	140	403.4	33,842
Suspected chromosomal disorder	1,268,502	529.0	42.8	31.2	36.7	40.3	35.9	61.8	171.4	33,842
Hypospadias[3]	1,268,502	798.0	64.6	61.6	59.5	67.4	67.4	67.8	*	33,842
Males only[4]	649,802	798.0	126.2	120.2	116.1	131.4	131.9	132.3	*	17,422

* = Figure does not meet standards of reliability or precision
[1]Total number of births to residents of areas reporting specified congenital anomaly.
[2]No response reported for congenital anomaly of the newborn item; includes births to residents of states using the 2003 Standard Certificate of live Birth occurring in states using the 1989 Standard Certificate of Live Birth.
[3]Denominator includes both male and female births.
[4]Denominator includes males only.

NOTE: Includes Florida, Idaho, Kansas, Kentucky, Nebraska, New Hampshire, New York (excluding New York City), Pennsylvania, South Carolina, Tennessee, Texas, and Washington.

NOTES AND DEFINITIONS

SOURCES OF DATA

All of the tables in Part A are from the National Center for Health Statistics (NCHS), a component of the Centers for Disease Control and Prevention (CDC). Five different publications were used to obtain the data.

Most of the tables found in Part A were obtained from: Martin, Joyce A., Brady E. Hamilton, et al. *Births: Final Data for 2005*. National Vital Statistics Reports: Volume 56, No 6. Hyattsville, MD: National Center for Health Statistics. 2007.

Data for Tables A-2, A-4, A-7, A-8, A-10, A-12, A-20, A-28, A-39, and A-44 were obtained from: Hamilton, Brady E., Joyce A. Martin, et al. *Births: Preliminary Data for 2006*. National Vital Statistics Reports: Volume 56, No 7. Hyattsville, MD: National Center for Health Statistics. 2007.

The data for Tables A-49, A-50, A-51, A-64, A-65 and A-66 were obtained from: *Health, United States, 2007 With Chartbook on Trends in the Health of Americans*. Hyattsville, MD: National Center for Health Statistics. 2007.

Tables A-67 through A-70 were obtained from: Ventura, Stephanie J., Joyce C. Abma, et al. *Estimated Pregnancy Rates by Outcome for the United States, 1990–2004*. National Vital Statistics Reports: Volume 56, No 15. Hyattsville, MD: National Center for Health Statistics. 2008.

Finally, data for Tables A-71 through A-76 were from: Menacker, Fay and Joyce A. Martin. *Expanded Health Data from the New Birth Certificate, 2005*. National Vital Statistics Reports: Volume 56, No 13. Hyattsville, MD: National Center for Health Statistics. 2008.

NOTES ON THE DATA

Since 1980, tabulations of birth data have been by race of mother; for earlier years, they were by race of child. Race and Hispanic origin are reported independently on the birth certificate. While Hispanics can belong to any race, the majority of Hispanic origin births have been reported as White; the bulk of the remainder have been reported as Black. The tables in Part A usually show data for these categories: White, non-Hispanic White, Black, non-Hispanic Black, and Hispanic. Data for American Indians and Asian or Pacific Islanders (API) are also included. Some data are presented for Hispanic and API subgroups by country of origin.

CONCEPTS AND DEFINITIONS

Anencephaly—a congenital anomaly that consists of a partial or complete absence of the brain and skull.

Apgar score—has been employed for over 50 years to assess the physical condition and short term prognosis of newborns. Historically, the score has been measured at 1 minute, 5 minutes, and if needed, at additional 5-minute intervals after delivery. Information on the 5 minute score is included in national birth certificate data. The Apgar score measures five easily identifiable characteristics of newborns. A 5-minute score of 0 to 3 indicates an infant in immediate need of resuscitation; 4 to 6 is considered intermediate, and 7 to 10 is considered normal. The Apgar score is a useful clinical indicator for reporting overall status of the neonate and need for, and response to resuscitation efforts.

Birth cohort—consists of all persons born within a given period of time, such as a calendar year.

Birthweight—the first weight of the newborn obtained after birth. Low birthweight is defined as less than 2,500 grams or 5 pounds 8 ounces. Very low birthweight is defined as less than 1,500 grams or 3 pounds 4 ounces.

Birth rate—calculated by dividing the number of live births in a population in a year by the midyear resident population. Birth rates are expressed as the number of live births per 1,000 population. The rate may be restricted to births to women of specific age, race, marital status, or geographic location (specific rate), or it may be related to the entire population (crude rate).

Cervical cerclage—circumferential banding or suture of the cervix to prevent or treat early dilation of the cervix (e.g., incompetent cervix) in an attempt to avoid premature delivery.

Cleft lip/palate—incomplete closure of the lip. May be unilateral, bilateral, or median. Cleft palate is incomplete fusion of the palatal shelves. May be limited to the soft palate, or may extend into the hard palate.

Cyanotic heart disease—congenital heart defects resulting in lack of oxygen that cause cyanosis.

Down syndrome—the most common chromosomal defect (trisomy 21).

Fertility rate—total number of live births per 1,000 women of reproductive age (defined as women age 15–44 years).

Gestation—the time period between the first day of the last normal menstrual period and the day of birth or day of termination of pregnancy according to the National Vital Statistics System and the CDC's Abortion Surveillance.

Hispanic origin—includes persons of Mexican, Puerto Rican, Cuban, Central and South American, and other or unknown Latin American or Spanish origins. Persons of Hispanic origin may be of any race.

Hypertension, chronic—diagnosis prior to the onset of this pregnancy of elevated blood pressure above normal for age, gender, and physiological condition.

Hypertension, pregnancy-associated—diagnosis in pregnancy of elevated blood pressure above normal for age, gender, and physiological condition.

Induction of labor—initiation of uterine contractions by medical and/or surgical means for the purpose of delivery before the spontaneous onset of labor.

Meningomyelocele/Spina bifida—meningomyelocele is herniation of meninges and spinal cord tissue. Meningocele (herniation of meninges without spinal cord tissue) should also be included in this category. Both open and closed (covered with skin) lesions should be included. Spina bifida is herniation of the meninges and/or spinal cord tissue through a bony defect of spine closure.

Nonvertex presentation—includes any nonvertex fetal presentation, that is, presentation of a part of the infant's body other than the upper and back part of the infant's head.

Omphalocele/Gastroschisis—omphalocele is a defect in the anterior abdominal wall, accompanied by herniation of some abdominal organs through a widened umbilical ring into the umbilical stalk. Gastroschisis is an abnormality of the anterior abdominal wall, lateral to the umbilicus, resulting in herniation of the abdominal contents directly into the amniotic cavity

Precipitous labor—labor lasting less than 3 hours.

Prenatal care—medical care provided to a pregnant woman to prevent complications and decrease the incidence of maternal and prenatal mortality. Information on when pregnancy care began is recorded on the birth certificate. Between 1970 and 1980, the reporting area for prenatal care expanded. In 1970, 39 states and the District of Columbia (D.C.) reported prenatal care on the birth certificate. Data were not available from Alabama, Alaska, Arkansas, Connecticut, Delaware, Georgia, Idaho, Massachusetts, New Mexico, Pennsylvania, and Virginia. In 1975, these data were available from three additional states—Connecticut, Delaware, and Georgia—increasing the number of states reporting prenatal care to 42 and D.C. During 1980–2002, prenatal care information was available for the entire United States.

Suspected chromosomal disorder—includes any constellation of congenital malformations resulting from, or compatible with, known syndromes caused by detectable defects in chromosome structure.

Tocolysis—administration of any agent with the intent to inhibit preterm uterine contractions to extend the length of the pregnancy.

PART B:
MORTALITY

MORTALITY

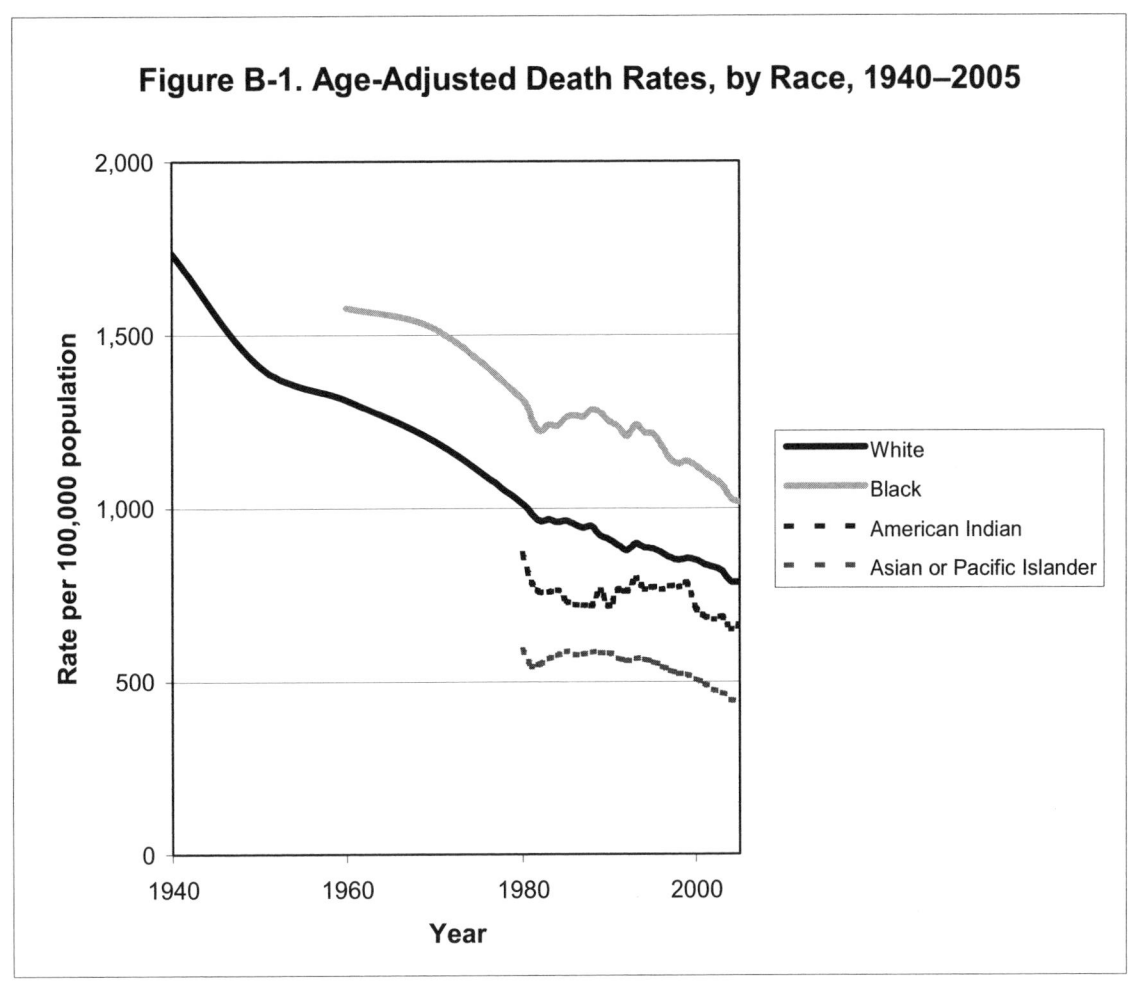

HIGHLIGHTS

- While the number of deaths increased in 2005 to 2,448,017—an increase of 2.1 percent from 2004—the age-adjusted death rate reached a record low of 798.8 per 100,000 people in 2005. The age-adjusted death rate declined for Blacks, but remained 1.3 times greater than for Whites. (Table B-1)

- In 2005, life expectancy was 77.8 years for the total population. As expected, the life expectancy of women was longer than the life expectancy of men. The difference varied by race; for all races the difference was 5.2 years, for Whites it was 5.1 years, and for Blacks it was 7.0 years. (Table B-11)

- Heart disease and cancer accounted for nearly 50 percent of all deaths in 2005. However, the age-adjusted death rates for both heart disease and cancer declined in 2005. The age-adjusted death rates increased sub-

stantially between 2004 and 2005 for chronic lower respiratory diseases, Alzheimer's disease, Parkinson's disease, and hypertensive renal disease. (Table B-15)

- There were 5,113 deaths in 2005 due to injury at work. The risk of work-related death and injury was much greater for men than for women. The age adjusted death rate for men was 4.1 per 100,000 people compared to only 0.4 per 100,000 people for women. (Table B-35)

- The infant mortality rate increased in 2005 to 6.87 per 1,000 live births. Although the increase was small, this was only the second time since 1980 that the infant mortality rate had risen from the previous year. The 2004 rate of 6.79 per 1,000 live births was the lowest ever recorded in the United States. In 1940, the infant mortality rate was 47.02 per 1,000 live births. (Table B-48)

Table B-1. Number of Deaths, Death Rates, and Age-Adjusted Death Rates, by Race and Sex, Selected Years, 1940–2005

(Number, rate per 100,000 population.)

Year	All races[1] Both sexes	Male	Female	White Both sexes	Male	Female	Black Both sexes	Male	Female	American Indian[2] or Alaskan native Both sexes	Male	Female	Asian or Pacific Islander[3] Both sexes	Male	Female
Number															
1940	1,417,269	791,003	626,266	1,231,223	690,901	540,322	178,743	95,517	83,226	4,791	2,527	2,264	—	—	—
1950	1,452,454	827,749	624,705	1,276,085	731,366	544,719	169,606	92,004	77,602	4,440	2,497	1,943	—	—	—
1960	1,711,982	975,648	736,334	1,505,335	860,857	644,478	196,010	107,701	88,309	4,528	2,658	1,870	—	—	—
1970	1,921,031	1,078,478	842,553	1,682,096	942,437	739,659	225,647	127,540	98,107	5,675	3,391	2,284	—	—	—
1980	1,989,841	1,075,078	914,763	1,738,607	933,878	804,729	233,135	130,138	102,997	6,923	4,193	2,730	11,071	6,809	4,262
1981	1,977,981	1,063,772	914,209	1,731,233	925,490	805,743	228,560	127,296	101,264	6,608	4,016	2,592	11,475	6,908	4,567
1982	1,974,797	1,056,440	918,357	1,729,085	919,239	809,846	226,513	125,610	100,903	6,679	3,974	2,705	12,430	7,564	4,866
1983	2,019,201	1,071,923	947,278	1,765,582	931,779	833,803	233,124	127,911	105,213	6,839	4,064	2,775	13,554	8,126	5,428
1984	2,039,369	1,076,514	962,855	1,781,897	934,529	847,368	235,884	129,147	106,737	6,949	4,117	2,832	14,483	8,627	5,856
1985	2,086,440	1,097,758	988,682	1,819,054	950,455	868,599	244,207	133,610	110,597	7,154	4,181	2,973	15,887	9,441	6,446
1986	2,105,361	1,104,005	1,001,356	1,831,083	952,554	878,529	250,326	137,214	113,112	7,301	4,365	2,936	16,514	9,795	6,719
1987	2,123,323	1,107,958	1,015,365	1,843,067	953,382	889,685	254,814	139,551	115,263	7,602	4,432	3,170	17,689	10,496	7,193
1988	2,167,999	1,125,540	1,042,459	1,876,906	965,419	911,487	264,019	144,228	119,791	7,917	4,617	3,300	18,963	11,155	7,808
1989	2,150,466	1,114,190	1,036,276	1,853,841	950,852	902,989	267,642	146,393	121,249	8,614	5,066	3,548	20,042	11,688	8,354
1990	2,148,463	1,113,417	1,035,046	1,853,254	950,812	902,442	265,498	145,359	120,139	8,316	4,877	3,439	21,127	12,211	8,916
1991	2,169,518	1,121,665	1,047,853	1,868,904	956,497	912,407	269,525	147,331	122,194	8,621	4,948	3,673	22,173	12,727	9,446
1992	2,175,613	1,122,336	1,053,277	1,873,781	956,957	916,824	269,219	146,630	122,589	8,953	5,181	3,772	23,660	13,568	10,092
1993	2,268,553	1,161,797	1,106,756	1,951,437	988,329	963,108	282,151	153,502	128,649	9,579	5,434	4,145	25,386	14,532	10,854
1994	2,278,994	1,162,747	1,116,247	1,959,875	988,823	971,052	282,379	153,019	129,360	9,637	5,497	4,140	27,103	15,408	11,695
1995	2,312,132	1,172,959	1,139,173	1,987,437	997,277	990,160	286,401	154,175	132,226	9,997	5,574	4,423	28,297	15,933	12,364
1996	2,314,690	1,163,569	1,151,121	1,992,966	991,984	1,000,982	282,089	149,472	132,617	10,127	5,563	4,564	29,508	16,550	12,958
1997	2,314,245	1,154,039	1,160,206	1,996,393	986,884	1,009,509	276,520	144,110	132,410	10,576	5,985	4,591	30,756	17,060	13,696
1998	2,337,256	1,157,260	1,179,996	2,015,984	990,190	1,025,794	278,440	143,417	135,023	10,845	5,994	4,851	31,987	17,659	14,328
1999	2,391,399	1,175,460	1,215,939	2,061,348	1,005,335	1,056,013	285,064	145,703	139,361	11,312	6,092	5,220	33,675	18,330	15,345
2000	2,403,351	1,177,578	1,225,773	2,071,287	1,007,191	1,064,096	285,826	145,184	140,642	11,363	6,185	5,178	34,875	19,018	15,857
2001	2,416,425	1,183,421	1,233,004	2,079,691	1,011,218	1,068,473	287,709	145,908	141,801	11,977	6,466	5,511	37,048	19,829	17,219
2002	2,443,387	1,199,264	1,244,123	2,102,589	1,025,196	1,077,393	290,051	146,835	143,216	12,415	6,750	5,665	38,332	20,483	17,849
2003	2,448,288	1,201,964	1,246,324	2,103,714	1,025,650	1,078,064	291,300	148,022	143,278	13,147	7,106	6,041	40,127	21,186	18,941
2004	2,397,615	1,181,668	1,215,947	2,056,643	1,007,266	1,049,377	287,315	145,970	141,345	13,124	7,134	5,990	40,533	21,298	19,235
2005	2,448,017	1,207,675	1,240,342	2,098,097	1,028,152	1,069,945	292,808	149,108	143,700	13,918	7,607	6,311	43,194	22,808	20,386
Death Rate															
1940	1,076.4	1,197.4	954.6	1,041.5	1,162.2	919.4	—	—	—	—	—	—	—	—	—
1950	963.8	1,106.1	823.5	945.7	1,089.5	803.3	—	—	—	—	—	—	—	—	—
1960	954.7	1,104.5	809.2	947.8	1,098.5	800.9	1,038.6	1,181.7	905.0	—	—	—	—	—	—
1970	945.3	1,090.3	807.8	946.3	1,086.7	812.6	999.3	1,186.6	829.2	—	—	—	—	—	—
1980	878.3	976.9	785.3	892.5	983.3	806.1	875.4	1,034.1	733.3	487.4	597.1	380.1	296.9	375.3	222.5
1981	862.0	954.0	775.0	880.4	965.2	799.8	842.4	992.6	707.7	445.6	547.9	345.6	272.3	336.2	211.5
1982	852.4	938.4	771.2	873.1	951.8	798.2	823.4	966.2	695.5	434.5	522.9	348.1	271.3	338.3	207.4
1983	863.7	943.2	788.4	885.4	957.7	816.4	836.6	971.2	715.9	428.5	515.1	343.9	276.1	339.1	216.1
1984	864.8	938.8	794.7	887.8	954.1	824.6	836.1	968.5	717.4	419.6	502.7	338.4	275.9	336.5	218.1
1985	876.9	948.6	809.1	900.4	963.6	840.1	854.8	989.3	734.2	416.4	492.5	342.5	283.4	344.6	224.9
1986	876.7	944.7	812.3	900.1	958.6	844.3	864.9	1,002.6	741.5	409.5	494.9	325.9	276.2	335.1	219.9
1987	876.4	939.3	816.7	900.1	952.7	849.8	868.9	1,006.2	745.7	410.7	483.8	339.0	278.9	338.3	222.0
1988	886.7	945.1	831.2	910.5	957.9	865.3	888.3	1,026.1	764.6	411.7	485.0	339.9	282.0	339.0	227.4
1989	871.3	926.3	818.9	893.2	936.5	851.8	887.9	1,026.7	763.2	430.5	510.7	351.3	280.9	334.5	229.4
1990	863.8	918.4	812.0	888.0	930.9	846.9	871.0	1,008.0	747.9	402.8	476.4	330.4	283.3	334.3	234.3
1991	857.6	908.8	808.7	883.2	922.7	845.2	861.4	994.8	741.4	405.3	468.9	342.7	278.7	326.9	232.4
1992	848.1	896.1	802.4	875.8	912.2	840.8	841.8	967.6	728.6	406.6	474.1	340.0	282.1	331.1	235.3
1993	872.8	915.0	832.5	902.7	931.8	874.6	864.6	992.2	749.6	419.8	479.6	360.7	288.0	338.1	240.3
1994	866.1	904.2	829.7	897.8	922.6	873.8	849.0	970.2	739.7	408.2	468.8	348.3	294.6	344.0	247.7
1995	868.3	900.8	837.2	901.8	921.0	883.2	846.2	960.2	743.2	409.4	459.4	360.1	294.6	341.4	250.4
1996	859.2	882.8	836.7	896.0	907.1	885.3	819.7	915.3	733.3	399.5	441.5	358.0	294.4	340.2	251.1
1997	848.8	864.6	833.6	889.1	893.3	885.0	789.9	867.1	720.1	402.7	458.2	347.7	294.1	336.8	253.9
1998	847.3	856.4	838.5	889.5	887.3	891.6	782.3	848.2	722.6	397.8	441.9	354.2	293.8	335.4	254.9
1999	857.0	859.2	854.9	901.4	892.1	910.4	788.1	847.4	734.3	399.3	431.8	367.1	296.8	333.2	262.5
2000	854.0	853.0	855.0	900.2	887.8	912.3	781.1	834.1	733.0	380.8	415.6	346.1	296.6	332.9	262.3
2001	848.5	846.4	850.4	895.1	881.9	907.9	773.5	823.9	727.7	392.1	424.2	360.2	303.8	335.0	274.4
2002	847.3	846.6	848.0	895.7	884.0	907.0	768.4	816.7	724.4	403.6	439.6	367.7	299.5	331.4	269.7
2003	841.9	840.3	843.4	890.1	877.6	902.3	763.6	813.7	717.9	422.6	457.6	387.7	303.9	330.0	279.2
2004	816.5	817.6	815.4	863.2	854.2	871.9	744.3	792.6	700.3	416.8	453.8	380.0	297.2	321.1	274.6
2005	825.9	827.2	824.6	873.7	864.5	882.8	749.4	799.2	703.9	440.3	481.9	398.8	307.7	333.9	282.8

— = Data not available.

[1]For 1940–1991, data includes steaths among races not shown separately; beginning in 1992, records coded as other races and records for which race was unknown, not stated, or not classifiable were assigned to the race of previous record.

[2]Includes Aleuts and Eskimos.

[3]Includes Chinese, Filipino, Hawaiian, Japanese, and Other Asian or Pacific Islander.

Table B-1. Number of Deaths, Death Rates, and Age-Adjusted Death Rates, by Race and Sex, Selected Years, 1940–2005—*Continued*

(Number, rate per 100,000 population.)

Year	All races[1]			White			Black			American Indian[2]			Asian or Pacific Islander[3]		
	Both sexes	Male	Female	Both sexes	Male	Female	Both sexes	Male	Female	Both sexes	Male	Female	Both sexes	Male	Female
Age-Adjusted Death Rate															
1940	1,785.0	1,976.0	1,599.4	1,735.3	1,925.2	1,550.4	—	—	—	—	—	—	—	—	—
1950	1,446.0	1,674.2	1,236.0	1,410.8	1,642.5	1,198.0	—	—	—	—	—	—	—	—	—
1960	1,339.2	1,609.0	1,105.3	1,311.3	1,586.0	1,074.4	1,577.5	1,811.1	1,369.7	—	—	—	—	—	—
1970	1,222.6	1,542.1	971.4	1,193.3	1,513.7	944.0	1,518.1	1,873.9	1,228.7	—	—	—	—	—	—
1980	1,039.1	1,348.1	817.9	1,012.7	1,317.6	796.1	1,314.8	1,697.8	1,033.3	867.0	1,111.5	662.4	589.9	786.5	425.9
1981	1,007.1	1,308.2	792.7	984.0	1,282.2	773.6	1,258.4	1,626.6	986.6	784.6	1,030.2	588.0	544.7	710.3	405.3
1982	985.0	1,279.9	776.6	963.6	1,255.9	758.7	1,221.3	1,580.4	960.1	757.0	940.1	604.4	550.4	738.2	410.3
1983	990.0	1,284.5	783.3	967.3	1,259.4	763.9	1,240.5	1,600.7	980.7	757.3	945.0	605.5	565.1	718.8	428.8
1984	982.5	1,271.4	779.8	959.7	1,245.9	760.7	1,236.7	1,600.8	976.9	761.7	946.0	567.9	574.4	724.7	443.1
1985	988.1	1,278.1	784.5	963.6	1,249.8	764.3	1,261.2	1,634.5	994.4	731.7	926.1	577.2	586.5	755.4	456.7
1986	978.6	1,261.7	778.7	952.8	1,230.5	758.1	1,266.7	1,650.1	994.4	720.8	926.7	549.3	576.4	730.5	445.4
1987	970.0	1,246.1	774.2	943.4	1,213.4	753.3	1,263.1	1,650.3	989.7	719.8	899.3	583.7	577.3	732.4	448.1
1988	975.7	1,250.7	781.0	947.6	1,215.9	759.1	1,284.3	1,677.6	1,006.8	718.6	917.4	563.6	584.2	732.0	451.0
1989	950.5	1,215.0	761.8	920.2	1,176.6	738.8	1,275.5	1,670.1	998.1	761.6	999.8	586.3	581.3	729.6	458.4
1990	938.7	1,202.8	750.9	909.8	1,165.9	728.8	1,250.3	1,644.5	975.1	716.3	916.2	561.8	582.0	716.4	469.3
1991	922.3	1,180.5	738.2	893.2	1,143.1	716.1	1,235.4	1,626.1	963.3	763.9	970.6	608.3	566.2	703.4	453.2
1992	905.6	1,158.3	725.5	877.7	1,122.4	704.1	1,206.7	1,587.8	942.5	759.0	970.4	599.4	558.5	697.3	445.8
1993	926.1	1,177.3	745.9	897.0	1,138.9	724.1	1,241.2	1,632.2	969.5	796.4	1,006.3	641.6	565.8	709.9	450.4
1994	913.5	1,155.5	738.6	885.6	1,118.7	717.5	1,216.9	1,592.8	954.6	764.8	953.3	618.8	562.7	702.5	452.1
1995	909.8	1,143.9	739.4	882.3	1,107.5	718.7	1,213.9	1,585.7	955.9	771.2	932.0	643.9	554.8	693.4	446.7
1996	894.1	1,115.7	733.0	869.0	1,082.9	713.6	1,178.4	1,524.2	940.3	763.6	924.8	641.7	543.2	676.1	439.6
1997	878.1	1,088.1	725.6	855.7	1,059.1	707.8	1,139.8	1,458.8	922.1	774.0	974.8	625.3	531.8	660.2	432.6
1998	870.6	1,069.4	724.7	849.3	1,042.0	707.3	1,127.8	1,430.5	921.6	770.4	943.9	640.5	522.4	646.9	426.7
1999	875.6	1,067.0	734.0	854.6	1,040.0	716.6	1,135.7	1,432.6	933.6	780.9	925.9	668.2	519.7	641.2	427.5
2000	869.0	1,053.8	731.4	849.8	1,029.4	715.3	1,121.4	1,403.5	927.6	709.3	841.5	604.5	506.4	624.2	416.8
2001	854.5	1,029.1	721.8	836.5	1,006.1	706.7	1,101.2	1,375.0	912.5	686.7	798.9	594.0	492.1	597.4	412.0
2002	845.3	1,013.7	715.2	829.0	992.9	701.3	1,083.3	1,341.4	901.8	677.4	794.2	581.1	474.4	578.4	395.9
2003	832.7	994.3	706.2	817.0	973.9	693.1	1,065.9	1,319.1	885.6	685.0	797.0	592.1	465.7	562.7	392.7
2004	800.8	955.7	679.2	786.3	936.9	666.9	1,027.3	1,269.4	855.3	650.0	758.1	557.9	443.9	534.7	375.5
2005	798.8	951.1	677.6	785.3	933.2	666.5	1,016.5	1,252.9	845.7	663.4	775.3	567.7	440.2	534.4	369.3

— = Data not available.

[1]For 1940–1991, data includes deaths among races not shown separately; beginning in 1992, records coded as other races and records for which race was unknown, not stated, or not classifiable were assigned to the race of previous record.

[2]Includes Aleuts and Eskimos.

[3]Includes Chinese, Filipino, Hawaiian, Japanese, and Other Asian or Pacific Islander.

Table B-2.   Deaths, Age-Adjusted Death Rates, and Life Expectancy at Birth, by Race and Sex, and Infant Deaths and Mortality Rates, by Race, Final 2005 and Preliminary 2006

(Number, death rate per 100,000 population.)

Measure and sex	All races[1]		White		Black	
	2005	2006	2005	2006	2005	2006
All deaths..	2,448,017	2,425,900	2,098,097	2,077,384	292,808	289,692
Male	1,207,675	1,201,574	1,028,152	1,022,084	149,108	148,430
Female...	1,240,342	1,224,326	1,069,945	1,055,299	143,700	141,262
Age-adjusted death rate[2]	798.8	776.4	785.3	764.4	1016.5	981.2
Male	951.1	924.6	933.2	908.0	1252.9	1214.6
Female...	677.6	657.8	666.5	648.3	845.7	812.4
Life expectancy at birth (in years)	77.8	78.1	78.3	78.5	73.2	73.6
Male	75.2	75.4	75.7	76.0	69.5	70.0
Female...	80.4	80.7	80.8	81.0	76.5	76.9
All infant deaths	28,440	28,609	18,514	18,496	8,695	8,824
Infant mortality rate[3].......................	6.87	6.71	5.73	5.58	13.73	13.33

[1]Includes races other than White and Black.
[2]Age-adjusted death rates are per 100,000 U.S. standard population based on the year 2000 standard.
[3]Infant mortality rates are deaths under 1 year per 1,000 live births in specified group.

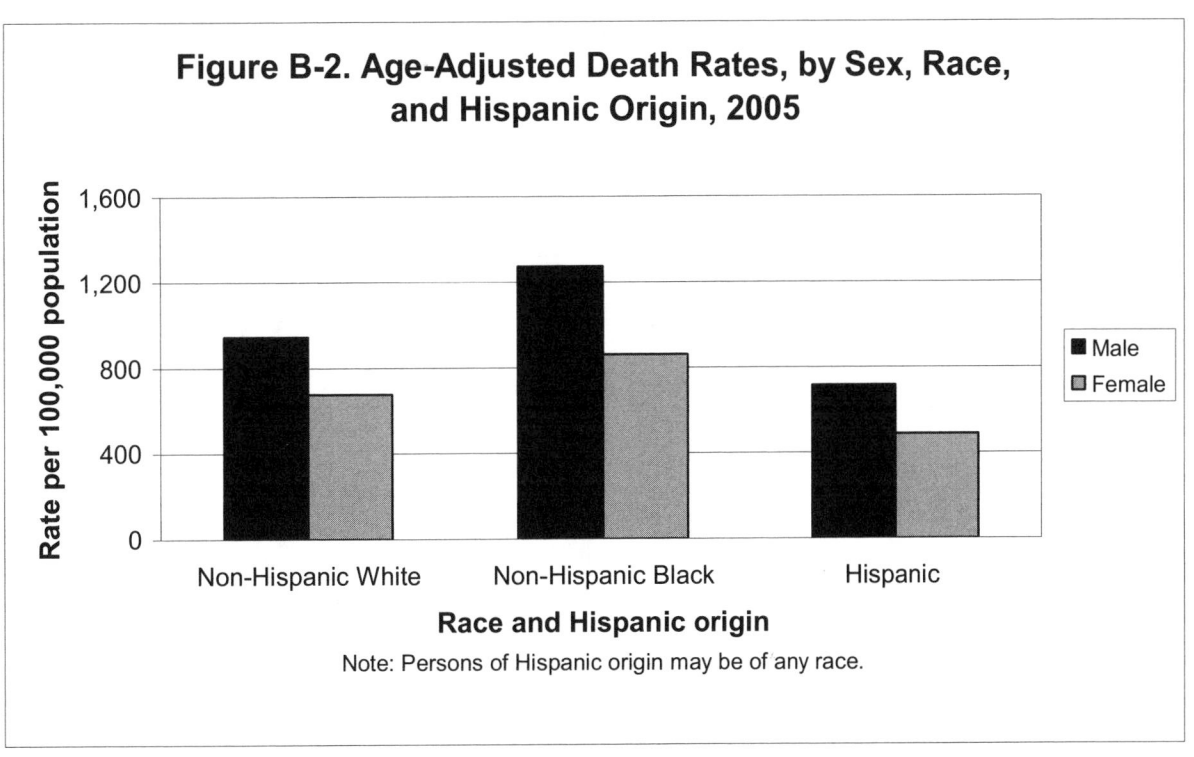

Figure B-2. Age-Adjusted Death Rates, by Sex, Race, and Hispanic Origin, 2005

Rate per 100,000 population
1,600
1,200
800
400
0
Male
Female
Non-Hispanic White
Non-Hispanic Black
Hispanic
Race and Hispanic origin

Note: Persons of Hispanic origin may be of any race.

Figure B-3. Percent Distribution of Total Deaths by Cause of Death, 2005

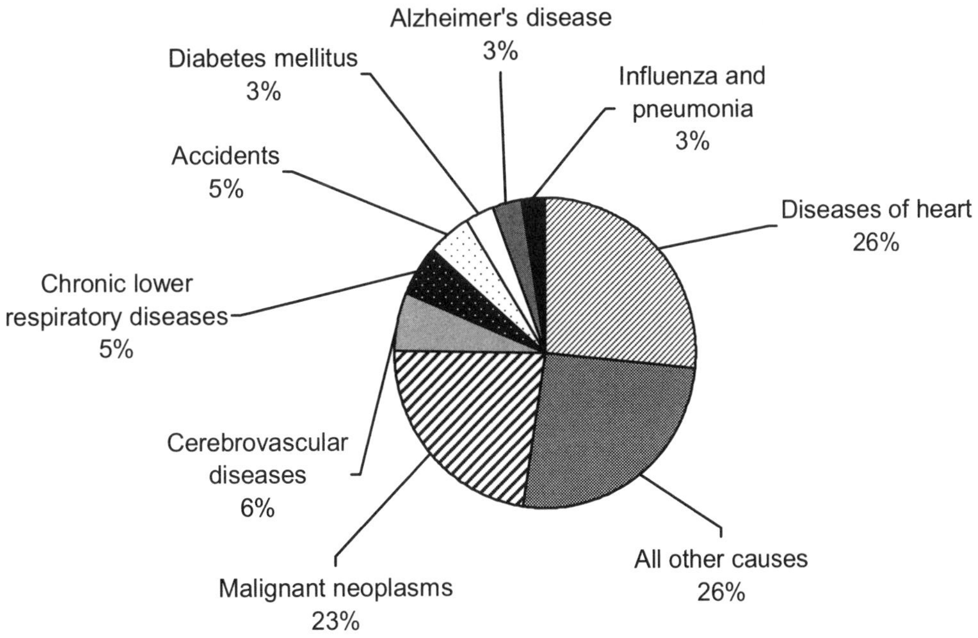

Alzheimer's disease 3%
Diabetes mellitus 3%
Influenza and pneumonia 3%
Accidents 5%
Diseases of heart 26%
Chronic lower respiratory diseases 5%
Cerebrovascular diseases 6%
All other causes 26%
Malignant neoplasms 23%

Table B-3. Number of Deaths, Death Rates, and Age-Adjusted Death Rates, by Hispanic Origin, Race for Non-Hispanic Population, and Sex, 1997–2005

(Number, rate per 100,000 population.)

Year	All origins[1]			Hispanic[2]			Non-Hispanic[3]			Non-Hispanic White			Non-Hispanic Black		
	Both sexes	Male	Female	Both sexes	Male	Female	Both sexes	Male	Female	Both sexes	Male	Female	Both sexes	Male	Female
Number															
1997	2,314,245	1,154,039	1,160,206	95,460	54,348	41,112	2,209,450	1,094,541	1,114,909	1,895,461	929,703	965,758	273,381	142,241	131,140
1998	2,337,256	1,157,260	1,179,996	98,406	55,821	42,585	2,230,127	1,096,677	1,133,450	1,912,802	931,844	980,958	275,264	141,627	133,637
1999	2,391,399	1,175,460	1,215,939	103,740	57,991	45,749	2,279,325	1,112,718	1,166,607	1,953,197	944,913	1,008,284	281,979	143,883	138,096
2000	2,403,351	1,177,578	1,225,773	107,254	60,172	47,082	2,287,846	1,112,704	1,175,142	1,959,919	944,781	1,015,138	282,676	143,297	139,379
2001	2,416,425	1,183,421	1,233,004	113,413	63,317	50,096	2,295,244	1,115,683	1,179,561	1,962,810	945,967	1,016,843	284,343	143,971	140,372
2002	2,443,387	1,199,264	1,244,123	117,135	65,703	51,432	2,318,269	1,129,090	1,189,179	1,981,973	957,645	1,024,328	286,573	144,802	141,771
2003	2,448,288	1,201,964	1,246,324	122,026	68,119	53,907	2,319,476	1,129,927	1,189,549	1,979,465	956,194	1,023,271	287,968	146,136	141,832
2004	2,397,615	1,181,668	1,215,947	122,416	68,544	53,872	2,269,583	1,109,848	1,159,735	1,933,382	938,143	995,239	283,859	144,022	139,837
2005	2,448,017	1,207,675	1,240,342	131,161	73,788	57,373	2,312,028	1,131,013	1,181,015	1,967,142	954,402	1,012,740	289,163	147,010	142,153
Death Rate															
1997	848.8	864.6	833.6	309.0	343.2	272.9	913.9	930.4	898.3	967.4	970.6	964.3	813.5	892.9	741.9
1998	847.3	856.4	838.5	303.9	336.0	270.0	916.0	925.3	907.1	972.9	969.2	976.5	805.6	873.7	744.1
1999	857.0	859.2	854.9	305.7	332.6	277.2	929.9	932.2	927.8	990.7	979.6	1,001.3	812.1	872.8	757.3
2000	854.0	853.0	855.0	303.8	331.3	274.6	929.6	928.1	931.0	993.2	978.5	1,007.3	805.5	859.5	756.7
2001	848.5	846.4	850.4	306.8	332.9	279.0	926.2	923.6	928.6	991.1	975.6	1,006.1	798.1	849.7	751.2
2002	847.3	846.6	848.0	302.2	328.7	274.0	928.8	928.0	929.5	997.5	983.9	1,010.6	792.8	842.3	748.0
2003	841.9	840.3	843.4	305.8	330.7	279.3	924.4	922.9	925.9	993.6	979.1	1,007.6	788.8	840.6	741.6
2004	816.5	817.6	815.4	296.2	321.1	269.7	899.4	900.9	898.0	967.8	957.4	977.7	768.8	818.7	723.4
2005	825.9	827.2	824.6	307.3	334.4	278.2	911.2	912.6	910.0	981.8	970.6	992.6	774.4	825.7	727.6
Age-Adjusted Death Rate															
1997	878.1	1,088.1	725.6	669.3	840.5	538.8	885.3	1,096.4	732.6	859.7	1,063.2	712.5	1,154.3	1,476.7	934.2
1998	870.6	1,069.4	724.7	665.4	833.6	536.9	878.4	1,078.2	732.4	854.1	1,046.7	712.8	1,141.8	1,448.2	932.9
1999	875.6	1,067.0	734.0	676.4	830.5	555.9	883.9	1,076.4	741.9	859.8	1,045.5	722.3	1,150.1	1,449.4	946.0
2000	869.0	1,053.8	731.4	665.7	818.1	546.0	877.9	1,063.8	740.0	855.5	1,035.4	721.5	1,137.0	1,422.0	941.2
2001	854.5	1,029.1	721.8	658.7	802.5	544.2	864.0	1,039.8	730.9	842.9	1,012.8	713.5	1,116.5	1,393.7	925.5
2002	845.3	1,013.7	715.2	629.3	766.7	518.3	856.5	1,026.5	725.8	837.5	1,002.2	709.9	1,099.2	1,360.6	915.3
2003	832.7	994.3	706.2	621.2	748.1	515.8	844.5	1,008.0	717.2	826.1	984.0	702.1	1,083.2	1,341.1	899.8
2004	800.8	955.7	679.2	586.7	706.8	485.9	814.1	971.1	691.4	797.1	949.0	677.5	1,044.7	1,291.5	869.4
2005	798.8	951.1	677.6	590.7	717.0	485.3	812.5	966.7	690.3	796.6	945.4	677.7	1,034.5	1,275.3	860.5

[1]Figures for origin not stated are included in all origins but are not distributed among specified origins.

[2]Persons of Hispanic origin may be of any race.

[3]Includes races other than White and Black.

Table B-4. Deaths and Death Rates by Age, Sex, Race, and Hispanic Origin, and Age-Adjusted Death Rates by Sex, Race, and Hispanic Origin, Final 2005 and Preliminary 2006

(Number, rate per 100,000 population.)

Age, race, sex, and Hispanic origin	2005		2006	
	Number	Rate	Number	Rate
ALL RACES, BOTH SEXES				
All Ages	2,448,017	825.9	2,425,900	810.3
Under 1 year[1]	28,440	692.5	28,609	692.7
1–4 years	4,756	29.4	4,631	28.4
5–14 years	6,602	16.3	6,153	15.3
15–24 years	34,234	81.4	34,829	82.1
25–34 years	41,925	104.4	42,860	106.0
35–44 years	84,785	193.3	82,972	190.0
45–54 years	183,530	432.0	184,822	427.1
55–64 years	275,301	906.9	281,118	890.0
65–74 years	398,355	2137.1	390,107	2062.2
75–84 years	686,665	5260.0	667,608	5117.1
85 years and over	703,169	13798.6	701,923	13251.8
Not stated	255	...	266	...
Age-adjusted rate	. . .	798.8	...	776.4
ALL RACES, MALE				
All Ages	1,207,675	827.2	1,201,574	814.6
Under 1 year[1]	16,018	762.3	16,008	757.6
1–4 years	2,765	33.4	2,542	30.5
5–14 years	3,853	18.6	3,617	17.5
15–24 years	25,509	117.8	26,015	119.1
25–34 years	29,283	143.4	30,134	146.5
35–44 years	53,309	243.0	52,091	238.4
45–54 years	114,472	547.8	115,048	540.4
55–64 years	165,429	1131.0	168,794	1108.7
65–74 years	222,807	2612.2	218,082	2515.3
75–84 years	335,235	6349.8	327,421	6179.7
85 years and over	238,796	14889.4	241,625	14311.9
Not stated	199	...	198	...
Age-adjusted rate	. . .	951.1	...	924.6
ALL RACES, FEMALE				
All Ages	1,240,342	824.6	1,224,326	806.1
Under 1 year[1]	12,422	619.4	12,601	624.7
1–4 years	1,991	25.1	2,089	26.2
5–14 years	2,749	13.9	2,536	12.9
15–24 years	8,725	42.7	8,814	42.8
25–34 years	12,642	64.1	12,726	64.1
35–44 years	31,476	143.6	30,881	141.5
45–54 years	69,058	319.9	69,775	317.4
55–64 years	109,872	698.5	112,324	86.5
65–74 years	175,548	1736.3	172,025	1678.9
75–84 years	351,430	4520.0	340,188	4390.5
85 years and over	464,373	13297.7	460,298	12755.8
Not stated	56	...	68	...
Age-adjusted rate	. . .	677.6	...	657.8
WHITE, BOTH SEXES				
All Ages	2,098,097	873.7	2,077,384	858.1
Under 1 year[1]	18,514	579.1	18,496	578.9
1–4 years	3,408	27.0	3,232	25.5
5–14 years	4,710	15.0	4,464	14.3
15–24 years	25,410	77.1	25,843	77.9
25–34 years	30,103	95.5	31,075	98.1
35–44 years	63,584	180.1	62,058	177.3
45–54 years	140,224	399.6	141,830	397.5
55–64 years	222,218	860.7	226,914	846.8
65–74 years	336,362	2094.5	328,578	2021.1
75–84 years	610,820	5263.2	593,246	5129.4
85 years and over	642,539	14021.1	641,431	13478.0
Not stated	205	. . .	218	. . .
Age-adjusted rate	. . .	785.3	. . .	764.4

[1]Death rates for "Under 1 year" (based on population estimates) differ from infant mortality rates (based on live births).

Table B-4.   Deaths and Death Rates by Age, Sex, Race, and Hispanic Origin, and Age-Adjusted Death Rates by Sex, Race, and Hispanic Origin, Final 2005 and Preliminary 2006—*Continued*

(Number, rate per 100,000 population.)

Age, race, sex, and Hispanic origin	2005		2006	
	Number	Rate	Number	Rate
WHITE, MALE				
All Ages............................	1,028,152	864.5	1,022,084	852.1
Under 1 year[1].......................	10,471	640.0	10,397	635.9
1–4 years............................	1,996	30.9	1,784	27.5
5–14 years...........................	2,749	17.1	2,630	16.4
15–24 years..........................	18,792	110.4	19,146	111.7
25–34 years..........................	21,232	130.8	22,055	135.2
35–44 years..........................	40,824	228.5	39,761	224.3
45–54 years..........................	88,882	509.3	89,575	504.6
55–64 years..........................	134,272	1068.1	137,017	1049.5
65–74 years..........................	189,550	2552.7	184,865	2455.0
75–84 years..........................	300,228	6343.2	293,052	6183.2
85 years and over....................	218,990	15156.5	221,637	14577.8
Not stated	166	. . .	163	. . .
Age-adjusted rate....................	. . .	933.2	. . .	908.0
WHITE, FEMALE				
All ages	1,069,945	882.8	1,055,299	864.0
Under 1 year[1].......................	8,043	515.3	8,099	519.1
1–4 years............................	1,412	22.9	1,448	23.4
5–14 years...........................	1,961	12.8	1,833	12.0
15–24 years..........................	6,618	41.5	6,698	41.8
25–34 years..........................	8,871	58.0	9,020	58.7
35–44 years..........................	22,760	130.4	22,296	129.0
45–54 years..........................	51,342	291.1	52,255	291.5
55–64 years..........................	87,946	663.9	89,897	654.2
65–74 years..........................	146,812	1700.4	143,712	1646.7
75–84 years..........................	310,592	4519.4	300,193	4397.7
85 years and over....................	423,549	13498.3	419,793	12961.7
Not stated	39	. . .	54	. . .
Age-adjusted rate....................	. . .	666.5	. . .	648.3
NON-HISPANIC WHITE, BOTH SEXES				
All Ages.............................	1,967,142	981.8	1,947,467	969.9
Under 1 year[1].......................	13,026	562.6	12,970	567.0
1–4 years............................	2,404	26.2	2,284	25.0
5–14 years...........................	3,681	15.2	3,370	14.1
15–24 years..........................	19,683	74.8	20,127	76.3
25–34 years..........................	23,826	98.4	24,683	102.4
35–44 years..........................	54,786	186.7	53,376	185.4
45–54 years..........................	126,669	407.1	128,124	407.1
55–64 years..........................	206,078	873.5	210,489	861.9
65–74 years..........................	314,958	2126.0	307,993	2058.4
75–84 years..........................	581,712	5330.0	565,070	5214.0
85 years and over....................	620,246	14222.4	618,868	13701.9
Not stated	73	. . .	115	. . .
Age-adjusted rate....................	. . .	796.6	. . .	778.2
NON-HISPANIC WHITE, MALE				
All Ages.............................	954,402	970.6	949,385	963.5
Under 1 year[1].......................	7,418	625.7	7,328	625.7
1–4 years............................	1,408	29.9	1,253	26.8
5–14 years...........................	2,163	17.4	1,989	16.2
15–24 years..........................	14,267	105.8	14,596	107.9
25–34 years..........................	16,366	134.1	17,175	141.6
35–44 years..........................	34,719	236.1	33,727	233.9
45–54 years..........................	79,860	517.2	80,514	515.6
55–64 years..........................	124,229	1079.6	126,865	1064.7
65–74 years..........................	177,517	2584.5	173,323	2494.2
75–84 years..........................	285,608	6420.4	279,108	6287.7
85 years and over....................	210,795	15401.3	213,425	14860.2
Not stated	52	. . .	83	. . .
Age-adjusted rate....................	. . .	945.4	. . .	924.2

... = Not applicable.
– = Quantity zero.
[1]Death rates for "Under 1 year" (based on population estimates) differ from infant mortality rates (based on live births).

Table B-4. Deaths and Death Rates by Age, Sex, Race, and Hispanic Origin, and Age-Adjusted Death Rates by Sex, Race, and Hispanic Origin, Final 2005 and Preliminary 2006—*Continued*

(Number, rate per 100,000 population.)

Age, race, sex, and Hispanic origin	2005		2006	
	Number	Rate	Number	Rate
NON-HISPANIC WHITE, FEMALE				
All Ages..	1,012,740	992.6	998,081	976.1
Under 1 year[1]................................	5,608	496.5	5,642	505.4
1–4 years...	996	22.2	1,031	23.2
5–14 years.......................................	1,518	12.9	1,381	11.9
15–24 years.....................................	5,416	42.2	5,530	43.1
25–34 years.....................................	7,460	62.1	7,507	62.7
35–44 years.....................................	20,067	137.0	19,649	136.7
45–54 years.....................................	46,809	298.7	47,610	300.2
55–64 years.....................................	81,849	677.2	83,624	668.7
65–74 years.....................................	137,441	1729.6	134,669	1680.6
75–84 years.....................................	296,104	4579.7	285,962	4469.1
85 years and over..........................	409,451	13683.1	405,443	13161.8
Not stated	21	. . .	32	. . .
Age-adjusted rate...........................	. . .	677.7	. . .	661.0
BLACK, BOTH SEXES				
All Ages..	292,808	749.4	289,692	732.3
Under 1 year[1]................................	8,695	1311.2	8,824	1298.1
1–4 years...	1,097	41.8	1,141	43.2
5–14 years.......................................	1,543	23.3	1,394	21.2
15–24 years.....................................	7,371	112.3	7,470	111.9
25–34 years.....................................	10,036	179.2	10,014	177.1
35–44 years.....................................	18,186	318.4	17,874	313.3
45–54 years.....................................	37,749	744.2	37,347	719.4
55–64 years.....................................	45,416	1483.3	46,353	1438.9
65–74 years.....................................	51,718	2928.1	51,119	2835.5
75–84 years.....................................	61,998	6134.3	59,995	5885.3
85 years and over..........................	48,952	13083.1	48,118	12483.5
Not stated	47	. . .	43	. . .
Age-adjusted rate...........................	. . .	1016.5	. . .	981.2
BLACK, MALE				
All Ages..	149,108	799.2	148,430	785.8
Under 1 year[1]................................	4,867	1437.2	4,851	1397.0
1–4 years...	623	46.7	629	46.8
5–14 years.......................................	909	27.0	832	24.9
15–24 years.....................................	5,709	172.1	5,786	171.1
25–34 years.....................................	6,843	254.3	6,897	253.4
35–44 years.....................................	10,626	395.5	10,488	391.1
45–54 years.....................................	22,248	948.6	22,081	920.6
55–64 years.....................................	26,711	1954.3	27,174	1890.6
65–74 years.....................................	27,616	3747.3	27,555	3664.9
75–84 years.....................................	28,069	7667.1	27,327	7394.6
85 years and over..........................	14,856	13809.8	14,779	13206.9
Not stated	31	. . .	30	. . .
Age-adjusted rate...........................	. . .	1252.9	. . .	1214.6
BLACK, FEMALE				
All Ages..	143,700	703.9	141,262	683.5
Under 1 year[1]................................	3,828	1179.7	3,973	1194.9
1–4 years...	474	36.7	512	39.5
5–14 years.......................................	634	19.4	562	17.3
15–24 years.....................................	1,662	51.2	1,684	51.1
25–34 years.....................................	3,193	109.8	3,117	106.3
35–44 years.....................................	7,560	250.0	7,386	244.2
45–54 years.....................................	15,501	568.4	15,265	546.6
55–64 years.....................................	18,705	1103.6	19,179	1075.2
65–74 years.....................................	24,102	2341.5	23,563	2242.0
75–84 years.....................................	33,929	5263.7	32,668	5027.1
85 years and over..........................	34,096	12789.9	33,338	12187.2
Not stated	16	. . .	13	. . .
Age-adjusted rate...........................	. . .	845.7	. . .	812.4

... = Not applicable.
[1]Death rates for "Under 1 year" (based on population estimates) differ from infant mortality rates (based on live births).

Table B-4.   Deaths and Death Rates by Age, Sex, Race, and Hispanic Origin, and Age-Adjusted Death Rates by Sex, Race, and Hispanic Origin, Final 2005 and Preliminary 2006—*Continued*

(Number, rate per 100,000 population.)

Age, race, sex, and Hispanic origin	2005		2006	
	Number	Rate	Number	Rate
NON-HISPANIC BLACK, BOTH SEXES				
All Ages..	289,163	774.4	286,294	758.4
Under 1 year[1]...............................	8,335	1323.9	8,468	1333.1
1–4 years..	1,065	42.5	1,104	44.2
5–14 years......................................	1,500	24.0	1,363	21.9
15–24 years....................................	7,244	115.8	7,335	115.4
25–34 years....................................	9,850	186.0	9,891	185.1
35–44 years....................................	17,930	328.5	17,642	324.1
45–54 years....................................	37,298	761.4	36,920	737.1
55–64 years....................................	44,937	1513.6	45,917	1471.0
65–74 years....................................	51,166	2979.6	50,560	2886.9
75–84 years....................................	61,319	6218.3	59,411	5980.3
85 years and over............................	48,481	13239.1	47,650	12648.0
Not stated......................................	38	. . .	33	. . .
Age-adjusted rate............................	. . .	1034.5	. . .	1000.5
NON-HISPANIC BLACK, MALE				
All Ages..	147,010	825.7	146,556	814.3
Under 1 year[1]...............................	4,665	1451.5	4,675	1441.3
1–4 years..	606	47.6	607	47.8
5–14 years......................................	885	27.8	816	25.8
15–24 years....................................	5,615	177.7	5,685	176.7
25–34 years....................................	6,706	264.0	6,807	265.1
35–44 years....................................	10,451	407.5	10,329	404.2
45–54 years....................................	21,946	969.9	21,802	943.0
55–64 years....................................	26,396	1993.8	26,905	1933.5
65–74 years....................................	27,303	3814.1	27,229	3731.9
75–84 years....................................	27,723	7771.1	27,052	7522.4
85 years and over............................	14,690	13978.1	14,627	13402.2
Not stated......................................	24	. . .	22	. . .
Age-adjusted rate............................	. . .	1275.3	. . .	1239.9
NON-HISPANIC BLACK, FEMALE				
All Ages..	142,153	727.6	139,739	707.4
Under 1 year[1]...............................	3,670	1190.8	3,793	1220.1
1–4 years..	459	37.2	497	40.4
5–14 years......................................	615	20.0	547	17.9
15–24 years....................................	1,629	52.6	1,650	52.6
25–34 years....................................	3,144	114.1	3,084	111.1
35–44 years....................................	7,479	258.5	7,313	253.2
45–54 years....................................	15,352	582.4	15,118	560.6
55–64 years....................................	18,541	1127.1	19,012	1099.0
65–74 years....................................	23,863	2383.1	23,331	2283.5
75–84 years....................................	33,596	5338.1	32,360	5105.5
85 years and over............................	33,791	12941.6	33,024	12340.8
Not stated......................................	14	. . .	11	. . .
Age-adjusted rate............................	. . .	860.5	. . .	827.8
AMERICAN INDIAN OR ALASKAN NATIVE, BOTH SEXES[2]				
All Ages..	13,918	440.3	13,831	432.0
Under 1 year[1]...............................	357	818.9	395	882.4
1–4 years..	100	59.2	94	54.4
5–14 years......................................	110	19.8	90	16.7
15–24 years....................................	635	107.4	654	109.2
25–34 years....................................	720	150.8	691	141.6
35–44 years....................................	1,223	265.5	1,232	267.6
45–54 years....................................	1,927	474.2	1,909	456.6
55–64 years....................................	2,240	903.8	2,191	838.1
65–74 years....................................	2,487	1999.6	2,417	1857.3
75–84 years....................................	2,433	3928.1	2,506	3883.3
85 years and over............................	1,684	7505.1	1,651	6824.0
Not stated......................................	2	. . .	1	. . .
Age-adjusted rate............................	. . .	663.4	. . .	632.8

... = Not applicable.

[1]Death rates for "Under 1 year" (based on population estimates) differ from infant mortality rates (based on live births).

[2]Includes deaths among Aleuts and Eskimos.

Table B-4. Deaths and Death Rates by Age, Sex, Race, and Hispanic Origin, and Age-Adjusted Death Rates by Sex, Race, and Hispanic Origin, Final 2005 and Preliminary 2006—*Continued*

(Number, rate per 100,000 population.)

Age, race, sex, and Hispanic origin	2005		2006	
	Number	Rate	Number	Rate
AMERICAN INDIAN OR ALASKAN NATIVE, MALE[2]				
All Ages	7,607	481.9	7,523	470.5
Under 1 year[1]	196	882.4	244	1066.6
1–4 years	62	72.4	51	58.1
5–14 years	64	22.7	46	16.8
15–24 years	439	145.1	469	153.2
25–34 years	512	206.3	480	189.3
35–44 years	777	336.6	769	332.0
45–54 years	1,160	588.9	1,186	585.5
55–64 years	1,341	1124.1	1,278	1016.8
65–74 years	1,297	2254.1	1,276	2115.2
75–84 years	1,144	4373.3	1,142	4147.1
85 years and over	614	8419.0	582	7425.4
Not stated	1	...	1	...
Age-adjusted rate	...	775.3	...	729.7
AMERICAN INDIAN OR ALASKAN NATIVE, FEMALE[2]				
All Ages	6,311	398.8	6,308	393.7
Under 1 year[1]	161	752.9	151	689.9
1–4 years	38	45.6	44	51.7
5–14 years	46	16.8	45	17.0
15–24 years	196	67.9	185	63.2
25–34 years	208	90.6	212	90.4
35–44 years	446	194.1	464	202.9
45–54 years	767	366.2	723	335.5
55–64 years	899	699.4	913	672.6
65–74 years	1,190	1780.5	1,141	1634.4
75–84 years	1,289	3602.6	1,364	3686.9
85 years and over	1,070	7065.0	1,069	6535.8
Not stated	1	...	–	...
Age-adjusted rate	...	567.7	...	547.4
ASIAN OR PACIFIC ISLANDER, BOTH SEXES				
All Ages	43,194	307.7	44,992	309.4
Under 1 year[1]	874	430.8	894	424.7
1–4 years	151	19.2	163	19.9
5–14 years	239	12.9	205	10.9
15–24 years	818	41.8	862	43.6
25–34 years	1,066	41.9	1,080	41.4
35–44 years	1,792	75.4	1,807	72.5
45–54 years	3,630	189.7	3,737	187.9
55–64 years	5,427	442.4	5,661	432.9
65–74 years	7,788	1129.1	7,994	1100.4
75–84 years	11,414	3033.4	11,862	2986.8
85 years and over	9,994	8565.5	10,724	8373.1
Not stated	1	...	4	...
Age-adjusted rate	...	440.2	...	431.6
ASIAN OR PACIFIC ISLANDER, MALE				
All Ages	22,808	333.9	23,537	332.8
Under 1 year[1]	484	464.5	516	478.0
1–4 years	84	20.8	78	18.6
5–14 years	131	14.0	109	11.4
15–24 years	569	56.9	615	60.8
25–34 years	696	55.6	702	54.8
35–44 years	1,082	93.6	1,073	88.4
45–54 years	2,182	242.4	2,206	235.2
55–64 years	3,105	545.4	3,326	549.4
65–74 years	4,344	1403.8	4,384	1337.1
75–84 years	5,794	3759.2	5,899	3647.2
85 years and over	4,336	9839.1	4,626	9605.7
Not stated	1	...	3	...
Age-adjusted rate	...	534.4	...	520.0

... = Not applicable.
– = Quantity zero.
[1]Death rates for "Under 1 year" (based on population estimates) differ from infant mortality rates (based on live births.)
[2]Includes deaths among Aleuts and Eskimos.

Table B-4.   Deaths and Death Rates by Age, Sex, Race, and Hispanic Origin, and Age-Adjusted Death Rates by Sex, Race, and Hispanic Origin, Final 2005 and Preliminary 2006—*Continued*

(Number, rate per 100,000 population.)

Age, race, sex, and Hispanic origin	2005		2006	
	Number	Rate	Number	Rate
ASIAN OR PACIFIC ISLANDER, FEMALE				
All Ages..	20,386	282.8	21,456	287.3
Under 1 year[1].................................	390	395.3	378	368.6
1–4 years..	67	17.5	85	21.3
5–14 years......................................	108	11.9	96	10.3
15–24 years....................................	249	26.1	247	25.6
25–34 years....................................	370	28.6	378	28.5
35–44 years....................................	710	58.1	735	57.5
45–54 years....................................	1,448	142.8	1,531	145.6
55–64 years....................................	2,322	353.2	2,335	332.4
65–74 years....................................	3,444	905.5	3,609	905.4
75–84 years....................................	5,620	2529.8	5,963	2533.1
85 years and over............................	5,658	7792.5	6,098	7630.3
Not stated......................................	–	. . .	1	. . .
Age-adjusted rate............................	. . .	369.3	. . .	364.9
HISPANIC, BOTH SEXES[3]				
All Ages..	131,161	307.3	130,038	293.4
Under 1 year[1].................................	5,724	614.1	5,762	593.4
1–4 years..	1,041	28.9	983	26.3
5–14 years......................................	1,068	13.7	1,121	14.0
15–24 years....................................	5,837	81.2	5,834	79.1
25–34 years....................................	6,411	81.9	6,467	79.9
35–44 years....................................	8,876	138.9	8,778	131.8
45–54 years....................................	13,569	317.8	13,751	304.4
55–64 years....................................	16,089	676.4	16,356	643.9
65–74 years....................................	21,422	1621.4	20,562	1494.8
75–84 years....................................	29,010	3977.8	28,043	3650.8
85 years and over............................	22,058	9436.7	22,338	8739.9
Not stated......................................	56	. . .	42	. . .
Age-adjusted rate............................	. . .	590.7	. . .	550.1
HISPANIC, MALE[3]				
All Ages..	73,788	334.4	72,605	316.7
Under 1 year[1].................................	3,192	670.2	3,186	642.1
1–4 years..	610	33.2	548	28.8
5–14 years......................................	612	15.3	658	16.0
15–24 years....................................	4,604	120.4	4,638	118.8
25–34 years....................................	4,960	115.5	4,934	110.7
35–44 years....................................	6,145	182.0	6,099	173.0
45–54 years....................................	8,994	417.4	9,050	395.7
55–64 years....................................	9,954	875.8	10,051	825.5
65–74 years....................................	11,984	2029.4	11,461	1858.9
75–84 years....................................	14,539	4856.8	13,840	4375.9
85 years and over............................	8,143	10140.5	8,107	9142.3
Not stated......................................	51	.	33	. . .
Age-adjusted rate............................	. . .	717.0	. . .	658.5
HISPANIC, FEMALE[3]				
All Ages..	57,373	278.2	57,432	268.4
Under 1 year[1].................................	2,532	555.4	2,576	542.5
1–4 years..	431	24.5	436	23.9
5–14 years......................................	456	12.0	463	11.8
15–24 years....................................	1,233	36.6	1,196	34.5
25–34 years....................................	1,451	41.1	1,533	42.2
35–44 years....................................	2,731	90.6	2,679	85.5
45–54 years....................................	4,575	216.4	4,701	210.8
55–64 years....................................	6,135	493.9	6,304	476.6
65–74 years....................................	9,438	1291.6	9,101	1199.0
75–84 years....................................	14,471	3365.8	14,204	3143.5
85 years and over............................	13,915	9068.4	14,231	8526.2
Not stated......................................	5	. . .	9	. . .
Age-adjusted rate............................	. . .	485.3	. . .	457.3

. . . = Not applicable.
– = Quantity zero.
[1]Death rates for "Under 1 year" (based on population estimates) differ from infant mortality rates (based on live births).
[3]Persons of Hispanic origin may be of any race. Because of a misclassification error about 3.0 percent, and statistics for Hispanic decedents under 1 year of age were underestimated by about 1.0.

NOTE: Data are subject to sampling or random variation.

Table B-5. Number of Deaths and Death Rates, by Age, Race, and Sex, 2005

(Number, rate per 100,000 population in specified group.)

Age	All races			White			Black			American Indian[1] or Alaskan native			Asian or Pacific Islander[2]		
	Both sexes	Male	Female	Both sexes	Male	Female	Both sexes	Male	Female	Both sexes	Male	Female	Both sexes	Male	Female
NUMBER															
All Ages	2,448,017	1,207,675	1,240,342	2,098,097	1,028,152	1,069,945	292,808	149,108	143,700	13,918	7,607	6,311	43,194	22,808	20,386
Under 1 year	28,440	16,018	12,422	18,514	10,471	8,043	8,695	4,867	3,828	357	196	161	874	484	390
1–4 years	4,756	2,765	1,991	3,408	1,996	1,412	1,097	623	474	100	62	38	151	84	67
5–9 years	2,837	1,556	1,281	2,018	1,109	909	663	361	302	46	27	19	110	59	51
10–14 years	3,765	2,297	1,468	2,692	1,640	1,052	880	548	332	64	37	27	129	72	57
15–19 years	13,703	9,886	3,817	10,268	7,299	2,969	2,839	2,189	650	282	180	102	314	218	96
20–24 years	20,531	15,623	4,908	15,142	11,493	3,649	4,532	3,520	1,012	353	259	94	504	351	153
25–29 years	19,568	14,242	5,326	14,079	10,323	3,756	4,647	3,334	1,313	364	264	100	478	321	157
30–34 years	22,357	15,041	7,316	16,024	10,909	5,115	5,389	3,509	1,880	356	248	108	588	375	213
35–39 years	31,420	20,011	11,409	23,177	15,031	8,146	7,048	4,247	2,801	497	306	191	698	427	271
40–44 years	53,365	33,298	20,067	40,407	25,793	14,614	11,138	6,379	4,759	726	471	255	1,094	655	439
45–49 years	79,383	49,279	30,104	60,286	38,117	22,169	16,714	9,765	6,949	874	524	350	1,509	873	636
50–54 years	104,147	65,193	38,954	79,938	50,765	29,173	21,035	12,483	8,552	1,053	636	417	2,121	1,309	812
55–59 years	127,478	77,988	49,490	101,212	62,213	38,999	22,656	13,614	9,042	1,075	678	397	2,535	1,483	1,052
60–64 years	147,823	87,441	60,382	121,006	72,059	48,947	22,760	13,097	9,663	1,165	663	502	2,892	1,622	1,270
65–69 years	172,236	98,412	73,824	143,202	82,421	60,781	24,368	13,358	11,010	1,202	624	578	3,464	2,009	1,455
70–74 years	226,119	124,395	101,724	193,160	107,129	86,031	27,350	14,258	13,092	1,285	673	612	4,324	2,335	1,989
75–79 years	307,888	159,114	148,774	270,366	141,070	129,296	30,903	14,718	16,185	1,263	611	652	5,356	2,715	2,641
80–84 years	378,777	176,121	202,656	340,454	159,158	181,296	31,095	13,351	17,744	1,170	533	637	6,058	3,079	2,979
85 years and over	703,169	238,796	464,373	642,539	218,990	423,549	48,952	14,856	34,096	1,684	614	1,070	9,994	4,336	5,658
Not stated	255	199	56	205	166	39	47	31	16	2	1	1	1	1	–
RATE															
All Ages[3]	825.9	827.2	824.6	873.7	864.5	882.8	749.4	799.2	703.9	440.3	481.9	398.8	307.7	333.9	282.8
Under 1 year[4]	692.5	762.3	619.4	579.1	640.0	515.3	1,311.2	1,437.2	1,179.7	818.9	882.4	752.9	430.8	464.5	395.3
1–4 years	29.4	33.4	25.1	27.0	30.9	22.9	41.8	46.7	36.7	59.2	72.4	45.6	19.2	20.8	17.5
5–9 years	14.5	15.6	13.4	13.3	14.2	12.3	21.1	22.6	19.6	17.4	20.1	*	12.0	12.8	11.1
10–14 years	18.1	21.5	14.4	16.7	19.8	13.4	25.2	30.9	19.3	22.0	25.1	18.7	13.9	15.2	12.6
15–19 years	65.1	91.6	37.2	62.5	86.5	37.2	83.6	127.2	38.8	93.6	117.5	68.9	33.9	45.7	21.4
20–24 years	97.6	143.9	48.2	91.5	133.8	45.8	143.1	220.4	64.5	121.8	173.4	66.9	49.0	67.1	30.2
25–29 years	97.5	138.7	54.4	89.3	126.5	49.4	162.0	239.1	89.1	145.4	201.5	83.8	40.3	54.8	26.1
30–34 years	111.4	148.1	73.7	101.7	135.1	66.6	197.3	270.7	131.0	156.6	211.7	98.0	43.2	56.3	30.7
35–39 years	149.6	189.4	109.3	138.3	176.1	99.0	254.1	323.9	191.5	222.8	270.6	173.7	56.3	70.5	42.7
40–44 years	233.4	292.7	174.7	217.8	276.4	158.6	379.3	463.8	304.8	305.7	400.1	212.9	96.2	118.9	74.9
45–49 years	353.1	443.7	264.6	326.6	413.4	239.9	602.7	755.9	469.0	394.2	486.4	307.0	146.7	179.0	117.6
50–54 years	520.8	666.0	381.6	480.7	616.6	347.5	914.9	1,184.8	686.6	570.2	712.6	437.0	239.6	317.5	171.7
55–59 years	734.6	925.7	554.3	689.7	864.0	521.9	1,254.6	1,667.1	914.1	729.8	950.2	522.7	348.9	441.1	269.5
60–64 years	1,136.9	1,410.0	887.9	1,085.7	1,341.8	847.6	1,812.2	2,380.7	1,369.2	1,158.8	1,383.0	954.4	578.2	695.8	475.6
65–69 years	1,700.0	2,084.2	1,364.7	1,649.5	2,016.7	1,322.9	2,466.3	3,174.7	1,940.8	1,662.7	1,830.6	1,513.0	889.1	1,115.6	694.4
70–74 years	2,657.6	3,267.0	2,164.0	2,618.1	3,208.8	2,129.8	3,514.3	4,509.2	2,833.5	2,467.2	2,869.6	2,137.5	1,440.6	1,805.1	1,164.6
75–79 years	4,154.0	5,103.4	3,464.7	4,128.9	5,065.8	3,435.6	5,161.7	6,579.2	4,316.0	3,372.6	3,750.3	3,081.7	2,354.3	2,918.7	1,963.8
80–84 years	6,712.9	8,147.4	5,822.0	6,731.9	8,169.0	5,831.3	7,547.7	9,376.2	6,581.9	4,777.5	5,401.8	4,356.2	4,071.9	5,038.8	3,397.9
85 years and over	13,798.6	14,889.4	13,297.7	14,021.1	15,156.5	13,498.3	13,083.1	13,809.8	12,789.9	7,505.1	8,419.0	7,065.0	8,565.5	9,839.1	7,792.5

[1]Includes Aleuts and Eskimos.
[2]Includes Chinese, Filipino, Hawaiian, Japanese, and Other Asian or Pacific Islander.
[3]Figures for age not stated are included in All ages but not distributed among age groups.
[4]Death rates for "Under 1 year" (based on population estimates) differ from infant mortality rates (based on live births).

Table B-6.   Number of Deaths and Death Rates by Hispanic Origin, Race for Non-Hispanic Population, Age, and Sex, 2005

(Number, rate per 100,000 population.)

Age	All origins[1]			Hispanic[2]			Non-Hispanic[3]			Non-Hispanic White			Non-Hispanic Black		
	Both sexes	Male	Female	Both sexes	Male	Female	Both sexes	Male	Female	Both sexes	Male	Female	Both sexes	Male	Female
NUMBER															
All Ages	2,448,017	1,207,675	1,240,342	131,161	73,788	57,373	2,312,028	1,131,013	1,181,015	1,967,142	954,402	1,012,740	289,163	147,010	142,153
Under 1 year	28,440	16,018	12,422	5,724	3,192	2,532	22,488	12,701	9,787	13,026	7,418	5,608	8,335	4,665	3,670
1–4 years	4,756	2,765	1,991	1,041	610	431	3,701	2,147	1,554	2,404	1,408	996	1,065	606	459
5–9 years	2,837	1,556	1,281	474	258	216	2,354	1,294	1,060	1,561	860	701	645	354	291
10–14 years	3,765	2,297	1,468	594	354	240	3,161	1,937	1,224	2,120	1,303	817	855	531	324
15–19 years	13,703	9,886	3,817	2,323	1,759	564	11,351	8,106	3,245	7,989	5,568	2,421	2,793	2,155	638
20–24 years	20,531	15,623	4,908	3,514	2,845	669	16,958	12,729	4,229	11,694	8,699	2,995	4,451	3,460	991
25–29 years	19,568	14,242	5,326	3,257	2,597	660	16,248	11,596	4,652	10,883	7,765	3,118	4,559	3,268	1,291
30–34 years	22,357	15,041	7,316	3,154	2,363	791	19,132	12,629	6,503	12,943	8,601	4,342	5,291	3,438	1,853
35–39 years	31,420	20,011	11,409	3,722	2,624	1,098	27,610	17,322	10,288	19,504	12,443	7,061	6,948	4,172	2,776
40–44 years	53,365	33,298	20,067	5,154	3,521	1,633	48,016	29,635	18,381	35,282	22,276	13,006	10,982	6,279	4,703
45–49 years	79,383	49,279	30,104	6,206	4,199	2,007	72,919	44,896	28,023	54,109	33,926	20,183	16,504	9,622	6,882
50–54 years	104,147	65,193	38,954	7,363	4,795	2,568	96,436	60,148	36,288	72,560	45,934	26,626	20,794	12,324	8,470
55–59 years	127,478	77,988	49,490	7,709	4,842	2,867	119,383	72,867	46,516	93,451	57,313	36,138	22,417	13,447	8,970
60–64 years	147,823	87,441	60,382	8,380	5,112	3,268	139,110	82,100	57,010	112,627	66,916	45,711	22,520	12,949	9,571
65–69 year...................	172,236	98,412	73,824	9,513	5,410	4,103	162,349	92,752	69,597	133,683	76,971	56,712	24,098	13,198	10,900
70–74 years	226,119	124,395	101,724	11,909	6,574	5,335	213,820	117,581	96,239	181,275	100,546	80,729	27,068	14,105	12,963
75–79 years	307,888	159,114	148,774	14,156	7,383	6,773	293,224	151,423	141,801	256,164	133,639	122,525	30,563	14,530	16,033
80–84 year...................	378,777	176,121	202,656	14,854	7,156	7,698	363,389	168,702	194,687	325,548	151,969	173,579	30,756	13,193	17,563
85 years and over	703,169	238,796	464,373	22,058	8,143	13,915	680,266	230,371	449,895	620,246	210,795	409,451	48,481	14,690	33,791
Not stated...................	255	199	56	56	51	5	113	77	36	73	52	21	38	24	14
RATE															
All Ages[4].......................	825.9	827.2	824.6	307.3	334.4	278.2	911.2	912.6	910.0	981.8	970.6	992.6	774.4	825.7	727.6
Under 1 year[5]................	692.5	762.3	619.4	614.1	670.2	555.4	708.4	781.7	631.6	562.6	625.7	496.5	1,323.9	1,451.5	1,190.8
1–4 years	29.4	33.4	25.1	28.9	33.2	24.5	29.4	33.3	25.3	26.2	29.9	22.2	42.5	47.6	37.2
5–9 years	14.5	15.6	13.4	12.0	12.8	11.2	15.1	16.2	13.9	13.5	14.5	12.4	21.8	23.6	20.0
10–14 years	18.1	21.5	14.4	15.4	17.9	12.7	18.6	22.2	14.8	16.8	20.1	13.3	25.9	31.6	19.9
15–19 years	65.1	91.6	37.2	67.1	98.6	33.6	64.6	90.0	37.9	60.4	82.0	37.6	86.2	131.3	39.9
20–24 years	97.6	143.9	48.2	94.2	139.6	39.5	98.0	144.3	49.8	89.3	130.1	46.8	147.6	227.8	66.2
25–29 years	97.5	138.7	54.4	80.8	115.8	36.9	101.3	144.5	58.1	90.7	128.2	52.4	168.3	248.7	92.5
30–34 years	111.4	148.1	73.7	83.0	115.1	45.3	117.5	155.9	79.5	106.0	140.0	71.6	204.6	280.3	136.3
35–39 years	149.6	189.4	109.3	109.8	145.1	69.5	156.8	197.9	116.1	143.4	182.0	104.4	263.2	334.8	199.2
40–44 years	233.4	292.7	174.7	171.7	224.7	113.8	241.8	302.1	182.9	224.0	283.2	165.0	389.7	476.2	313.6
45–49 years	353.1	443.7	264.6	256.1	339.5	169.1	363.5	454.9	275.0	333.9	420.7	248.0	616.8	772.6	481.1
50–54 years	520.8	666.0	381.6	398.8	522.2	276.8	531.3	678.1	391.0	486.6	622.6	353.5	935.4	1,211.4	702.6
55–59 years	734.6	925.7	554.3	549.3	712.8	395.9	748.5	940.7	567.0	699.3	872.9	531.6	1,281.3	1,701.2	935.2
60–64 years	1,136.9	1,410.0	887.9	859.4	1,118.0	631.0	1,156.7	1,429.2	907.5	1,101.0	1,354.3	864.3	1,846.9	2,427.3	1,395.5
65–69 years	1,700.0	2,084.2	1,364.7	1,276.5	1,596.8	1,009.5	1,729.7	2,116.2	1,391.0	1,675.1	2,042.8	1,346.2	2,511.2	3,232.7	1,977.0
70–74 years	2,657.6	3,267.0	2,164.0	2,067.5	2,611.5	1,645.2	2,695.5	3,306.7	2,199.0	2,652.5	3,242.9	2,162.2	3,572.9	4,585.9	2,880.6
75–79 years	4,154.0	5,103.4	3,464.7	3,196.2	3,987.7	2,627.7	4,207.6	5,163.4	3,513.2	4,179.8	5,122.3	3,481.1	5,236.9	6,672.3	4,382.4
80–84 years	6,712.9	8,147.4	5,822.0	5,186.4	6,265.6	4,470.5	6,784.5	8,239.6	5,884.1	6,803.0	8,261.3	5,892.3	7,641.2	9,492.7	6,664.8
85 years and over	13,798.6	14,889.4	13,297.7	9,436.7	10,140.5	9,068.4	13,990.9	15,121.2	13,475.2	14,222.4	15,401.3	13,683.1	13,239.1	13,978.1	12,941.6

[1]Figures for origin not stated are included in all origins but not distributed among specified origins.
[2]Persons of Hispanic origin may be of any race.
[3]Includes races other than White and Black.
[4]Figures for age "Under 1 year" not stated are included in All ages but not distributed among age groups.
[5]Death rates for "Under 1 year" (based on population estimates) differ from infant mortality rates (based on live births).

Table B-7. Percentage Change in Death Rates and Age-Adjusted Death Rates Between 2004 and 2005 by Age, Race, and Sex

(Percent change.)

Age	All races[1]			White			Black		
	Both sexes	Male	Female	Both sexes	Male	Female	Both sexes	Male	Female
All Ages									
Crude	1.2	1.2	1.1	1.2	1.2	1.3	0.7	0.8	0.5
Age-adjusted	-0.2	-0.5	-0.2	-0.1	-0.4	-0.1	-1.1	-1.3	-1.1
Under 1 year[2]	1.1	1.1	1.0	0.9	1.3	0.3	2.1	1.6	2.6
1–4 years.............................	-1.7	3.1	-8.1	0.0	5.1	-6.1	-6.7	-3.9	-10.3
5–14 years............................	-3.0	-3.1	-2.8	-3.2	-4.5	-1.5	-1.3	3.8	-8.1
15–24 years...........................	1.6	2.7	-2.1	0.9	1.9	-2.1	2.7	4.7	-4.7
25–34 years...........................	2.3	2.8	0.9	2.8	3.0	2.1	-0.1	0.8	-2.2
35–44 years...........................	-0.1	-0.2	0.1	0.2	-0.3	0.7	-1.2	-0.4	-2.3
45–54 years...........................	1.2	0.8	1.8	1.4	1.1	2.0	-0.1	-0.7	0.8
55–64 years...........................	-0.4	0.2	-1.3	-0.3	0.2	-1.2	-1.1	-0.3	-2.2
65–74 years...........................	-1.3	-1.2	-1.4	-1.2	-1.2	-1.3	-1.8	-1.9	-1.9
75–84 years...........................	-0.3	-0.7	0.0	-0.2	-0.7	0.1	-0.6	-0.6	-0.7
85 years and over	-0.2	-0.9	0.1	0.1	-0.6	0.4	-1.9	-4.4	-0.8

[1]Includes races other than White and Black.
[2]Death rates for "Under 1 year" (based on population estimates) differ from infant mortality rates (based on live births).

Table B-8. Percentage Change in Death Rates and Age-Adjusted Death Rates Between 2004 and 2005 by Age, Hispanic Origin, Race for Non-Hispanic Population, and Sex

(Percent change.)

Age	All origins[1]			Hispanic			Non-Hispanic[2]			Non-Hispanic White			Non-Hispanic Black		
	Both sexes	Male	Female	Both sexes	Male	Female	Both sexes	Male	Female	Both sexes	Male	Female	Both sexes	Male	Female
All Ages															
Crude..........................	1.2	1.2	1.1	3.7	4.1	3.2	1.3	1.3	1.3	1.4	1.4	1.5	0.7	0.9	0.6
Age-adjusted.................	-0.2	-0.5	-0.2	0.7	1.4	-0.1	-0.2	-0.5	-0.2	-0.1	-0.4	0.0	-1.0	-1.3	-1.0
Under 1 year[3]...............	1.1	1.1	1.0	4.6	5.3	3.8	0.4	0.4	0.4	-0.3	0.1	-0.8	2.1	1.7	2.5
1–4 years......................	-1.7	3.1	-8.1	5.9	9.9	0.8	-3.6	1.2	-10.0	-2.2	3.1	-9.0	-6.6	-3.8	-9.9
5–14 years....................	-3.0	-3.1	-2.8	-4.9	-8.4	0.0	-1.7	-1.0	-2.0	-1.9	-2.8	-0.8	-1.6	3.3	-8.3
15–24 years..................	1.6	2.7	-2.1	6.1	4.4	15.1	0.7	2.4	-4.2	-0.5	1.0	-4.7	2.7	4.9	-4.9
25–34 years..................	2.3	2.8	0.9	4.7	5.8	0.5	2.1	2.5	1.2	2.6	2.4	3.0	-0.3	0.7	-2.6
35–44 years..................	-0.1	-0.2	0.1	0.1	-1.2	2.7	0.0	0.0	0.1	0.4	0.2	0.7	-1.1	-0.4	-2.1
45–54 years..................	1.2	0.8	1.8	1.4	-0.1	3.9	1.3	1.0	1.8	1.6	1.3	2.0	0.1	-0.5	0.9
55–64 years..................	-0.4	0.2	-1.3	-1.1	0.2	-3.4	-0.2	0.3	-1.1	-0.2	0.3	-1.0	-0.9	-0.2	-2.0
65–74 years..................	-1.3	-1.2	-1.4	0.9	1.8	-0.4	-1.3	-1.3	-1.4	-1.2	-1.3	-1.3	-1.7	-1.7	-1.8
75–84 years..................	-0.3	-0.7	0.0	1.3	1.4	1.1	-0.2	-0.7	0.0	-0.1	-0.6	0.2	-0.5	-0.5	-0.6
85 years and over.........	-0.2	-0.9	0.1	-0.5	2.1	-2.0	0.0	-0.9	0.3	0.2	-0.6	0.5	-1.9	-4.6	-0.7

[1]Figures for origin not stated are included in "All origins" but not distributed among specified origins.
[2]Includes races other than White and Black.
[3]Death rates for "Under 1 year" (based on population estimates) differ from infant mortality rates (based on live births).

Table B-9.   Number of Deaths and Death Rates by Age, and Age-Adjusted Death Rates, by Specified Hispanic Origin, Race for Non-Hispanic Population, and Sex, 2005

(Number, rate per 100,000 population.)

Hispanic origin, race for non-Hispanic population, and sex	All ages	Under 1 year[1]	1–4 years	5–14 years	15–24 years	25–34 years	35–44 years	45–54 years	55–64 years	65–74 years	75–84 years	85 years and over	Age not stated	Age-adjusted rate
NUMBER														
All Origins	2,448,017	28,440	4,756	6,602	34,234	41,925	84,785	183,530	275,301	398,355	686,665	703,169	255	...
Male	1,207,675	16,018	2,765	3,853	25,509	29,283	53,309	114,472	165,429	222,807	335,235	238,796	199	...
Female	1,240,342	12,422	1,991	2,749	8,725	12,642	31,476	69,058	109,872	175,548	351,430	464,373	56	...
Hispanic[2]	131,161	5,724	1,041	1,068	5,837	6,411	8,876	13,569	16,089	21,422	29,010	22,058	56	...
Male	73,788	3,192	610	612	4,604	4,960	6,145	8,994	9,954	11,984	14,539	8,143	51	...
Female	57,373	2,532	431	456	1,233	1,451	2,731	4,575	6,135	9,438	14,471	13,915	5	...
Mexican	74,646	4,107	785	779	4,208	4,287	5,352	7,868	9,199	11,889	15,566	10,580	26	...
Male	43,409	2,295	459	448	3,378	3,365	3,749	5,246	5,703	6,678	7,923	4,141	24	...
Female	31,237	1,812	326	331	830	922	1,603	2,622	3,496	5,211	7,643	6,439	2	...
Puerto Rican	16,099	485	62	99	446	616	1,165	1,995	2,544	2,929	3,336	2,417	5	...
Male	8,912	263	38	59	324	449	785	1,355	1,549	1,635	1,605	846	4	...
Female	7,187	222	24	40	122	167	380	640	995	1,294	1,731	1,571	1	...
Cuban	12,525	61	9	9	83	120	306	620	1,059	2,173	4,049	4,034	2	...
Male	6,523	37	6	5	57	90	223	425	723	1,325	2,173	1,457	2	...
Female	6,002	24	3	4	26	30	83	195	336	848	1,876	2,577	-	...
Central and South American	13,011	453	85	96	657	888	1,119	1,537	1,576	2,099	2,469	2,032	-	...
Male	6,825	254	47	53	533	686	764	942	901	1,027	1,016	602	-	...
Female	6,186	199	38	43	124	202	355	595	675	1,072	1,453	1,430	-	...
Other and unknown Hispanic	14,880	618	100	85	443	500	934	1,549	1,711	2,332	3,590	2,995	23	...
Male	8,119	343	60	47	312	370	624	1,026	1,078	1,319	1,822	1,097	21	...
Female	6,761	275	40	38	131	130	310	523	633	1,013	1,768	1,898	2	...
Non-Hispanic[3]	2,312,028	22,488	3,701	5,515	28,309	35,380	75,626	169,355	258,493	376,169	656,613	680,266	113	...
Male	1,131,013	12,701	2,147	3,231	20,835	24,225	46,957	105,044	154,967	210,333	320,125	230,371	77	...
Female	1,181,015	9,787	1,554	2,284	7,474	11,155	28,669	64,311	103,526	165,836	336,488	449,895	36	...
White	1,967,142	13,026	2,404	3,681	19,683	23,826	54,786	126,669	206,078	314,958	581,712	620,246	73	...
Male	954,402	7,418	1,408	2,163	14,267	16,366	34,719	79,860	124,229	177,517	285,608	210,795	52	...
Female	1,012,740	5,608	996	1,518	5,416	7,460	20,067	46,809	81,849	137,441	296,104	409,451	21	...
Black	289,163	8,335	1,065	1,500	7,244	9,850	17,930	37,298	44,937	51,166	61,319	48,481	38	...
Male	147,010	4,665	606	885	5,615	6,706	10,451	21,946	26,396	27,303	27,723	14,690	24	...
Female	142,153	3,670	459	615	1,629	3,144	7,479	15,352	18,541	23,863	33,596	33,791	14	...
Origin not stated[4]	4,828	228	14	19	88	134	283	606	719	764	1,042	845	86	...
Male	2,874	125	8	10	70	98	207	434	508	490	571	282	71	...
Female	1,954	103	6	9	18	36	76	172	211	274	471	563	15	...
DEATH RATE[5]														
All Origins[6]	825.9	692.5	29.4	16.3	81.4	104.4	193.3	432.0	906.9	2,137.1	5,260.0	13,798.6	...	798.8
Male	827.2	762.3	33.4	18.6	117.8	143.4	243.0	547.8	1,131.0	2,612.2	6,349.8	14,889.4	...	951.1
Female	824.6	619.4	25.1	13.9	42.7	64.1	143.6	319.9	698.5	1,736.3	4,520.0	13,297.7	...	677.6
Hispanic	307.3	614.1	28.9	13.7	81.2	81.9	138.9	317.8	676.4	1,621.4	3,977.8	9,436.7	...	590.7
Male	334.4	670.2	33.2	15.3	120.4	115.5	182.0	417.4	875.8	2,029.4	4,856.8	10,140.5	...	717.0
Female	278.2	555.4	24.5	12.0	36.6	41.1	90.6	216.4	493.9	1,291.6	3,365.8	9,068.4	...	485.3
Mexican	265.7	591.5	30.2	14.2	86.8	80.4	134.6	306.1	664.7	1,720.4	3,920.9	8,818.1	...	582.2
Male	293.8	651.5	34.3	15.8	128.9	114.1	174.4	391.4	836.7	2,094.8	5,248.3	*	...	716.4
Female	234.5	529.8	25.8	12.5	37.2	38.7	87.8	213.1	497.7	1,399.8	3,106.4	8,613.1	...	472.7
Puerto Rican	436.6	819.9	25.9	14.0	69.8	107.5	214.7	475.0	939.4	1,841.9	5,369.5	*	...	822.5
Male	496.5	*	31.1	17.0	102.2	152.8	296.0	712.9	1,148.6	2,453.7	*	*	...	989.7
Female	379.8	*	*	11.1	37.9	59.8	136.9	278.4	731.9	1,400.6	*	*	...	690.2
Cuban	792.6	*	*	*	52.9	58.3	109.2	372.9	699.0	1,533.4	3,512.0	7,955.2	...	531.3
Male	825.9	*	*	*	*	87.4	145.8	477.1	991.1	1,854.4	4,137.3	*	...	667.1
Female	759.3	*	*	*	*	*	65.2	252.7	427.7	1,206.9	2,988.7	*	...	419.1
Central and South American	178.7	380.2	16.7	9.0	53.8	61.7	85.3	178.6	382.4	946.7	2,473.6	*	...	416.3
Male	186.0	424.9	19.2	10.2	82.9	85.1	114.5	225.1	502.7	1,243.2	*	*	...	441.7
Female	171.3	335.1	14.4	7.9	21.4	31.9	55.0	134.6	289.9	770.6	2,469.6	*	...	389.2
Other and unknown Hispanic	728.7	*	64.5	23.4	136.3	178.2	333.9	614.3	1,068.0	2,164.4	6,519.3	*	...	916.2
Male	784.5	*	71.5	23.8	178.7	260.2	443.5	877.9	1,588.0	2,583.6	*	*	...	1,081.9
Female	671.4	*	*	22.9	87.1	93.9	222.9	386.5	685.6	1,786.9	*	*	...	804.3

* = Figure does not meet standards of reliability or precision.
... = Not applicable.
- = Quantity zero.
[1]Death rates for "Under 1 year" (based on population estimates) differ from infant mortality rates (based on live births).
[2]Persons of Hispanic origin may be of any race.
[3]Includes races other than White and Black.
[4]Includes deaths for which Hispanic origin was not reported on the death certificate.
[5]Figures for age not stated are included in all ages but not distributed among age groups.
[6]Figures for origin not stated are included in all origins but not distributed among specified origins.

Table B-9.   Number of Deaths and Death Rates by Age, and Age-Adjusted Death Rates, by Specified Hispanic Origin, Race for Non-Hispanic Population, and Sex, 2005—*Continued*

(Number, rate per 100,000 population.)

Hispanic origin, race for non-Hispanic population, and sex	All ages	Under 1 year[1]	1–4 years	5–14 years	15–24 years	25–34 years	35–44 years	45–54 years	55–64 years	65–74 years	75–84 years	85 years and over	Age not stated	Age-adjusted rate
Non-Hispanic[3]	911.2	708.4	29.4	16.9	81.2	109.5	201.8	443.2	924.0	2,172.1	5,327.5	13,990.9	...	812.5
Male	912.6	781.7	33.3	19.4	116.9	150.2	252.9	560.5	1,148.7	2,649.4	6,428.1	15,121.2	...	966.7
Female	910.0	631.6	25.3	14.4	43.8	68.9	151.6	330.3	714.6	1,768.0	4,581.2	13,475.2	...	690.3
White	981.8	562.6	26.2	15.2	74.8	98.4	186.7	407.1	873.5	2,126.0	5,330.0	14,222.4	...	796.6
Male	970.6	625.7	29.9	17.4	105.8	134.1	236.1	517.2	1,079.6	2,584.5	6,420.4	15,401.3	...	945.4
Female	992.6	496.5	22.2	12.9	42.2	62.1	137.0	298.7	677.2	1,729.6	4,579.7	13,683.1	...	677.7
Black	774.4	1,323.9	42.5	24.0	115.8	186.0	328.5	761.4	1,513.6	2,979.6	6,218.3	13,239.1	...	1,034.5
Male	825.7	1,451.5	47.6	27.8	177.7	264.0	407.5	969.9	1,993.8	3,814.1	7,771.1	13,978.1	...	1,275.3
Female	727.6	1,190.8	37.2	20.0	52.6	114.1	258.5	582.4	1,127.1	2,383.1	5,338.1	12,941.6	...	860.5

... = Not applicable.
[1]Death rates for "Under 1 year" (based on population estimates) differ from infant mortality rates (based on live births).
[3]Includes races other than White and Black.

Table B–10. Abridged Life Table for the Total Population, 2005

(Number.)

Age	Probability of dying between ages x to x + n $_nq_x$	Number surviving to age x l_x	Number dying between ages x to x + n $_nd_x$	Person-years lived between ages x to x + n $_nL_x$	Total number of person-years lived above age x T_x	Expectancy of life at age x e_x
0–1	0.006879	100,000	688	99,398	7,784,998	77.8
1–5	0.001174	99,312	117	396,970	7,685,600	77.4
5–10	0.000727	99,196	72	495,784	7,288,630	73.5
10–15	0.000898	99,124	89	495,452	6,792,846	68.5
15–20	0.003251	99,035	322	494,460	6,297,395	63.6
20–25	0.004869	98,713	481	492,387	5,802,935	58.8
25–30	0.004865	98,232	478	489,966	5,310,547	54.1
30–35	0.005551	97,754	543	487,457	4,820,581	49.3
35–40	0.007433	97,211	723	484,370	4,333,124	44.6
40–45	0.011588	96,489	1,118	479,837	3,848,755	39.9
45–50	0.017540	95,371	1,673	472,927	3,368,918	35.3
50–55	0.025802	93,698	2,418	462,770	2,895,990	30.9
55–60	0.036299	91,280	3,313	448,575	2,433,221	26.7
60–65	0.055819	87,967	4,910	428,282	1,984,646	22.6
65–70	0.082066	83,057	6,816	399,173	1,556,364	18.7
70–75	0.125036	76,241	9,533	358,595	1,157,191	15.2
75–80	0.188740	66,708	12,590	303,365	798,596	12.0
80–85	0.288884	54,117	15,634	232,350	495,231	9.2
85–90	0.420212	38,484	16,171	151,473	262,881	6.8
90–95	0.575974	22,312	12,851	77,357	111,408	5.0
95–100	0.733375	9,461	6,938	27,543	34,051	3.6
100 and over	1.000000	2,523	2,523	6,508	6,508	2.6

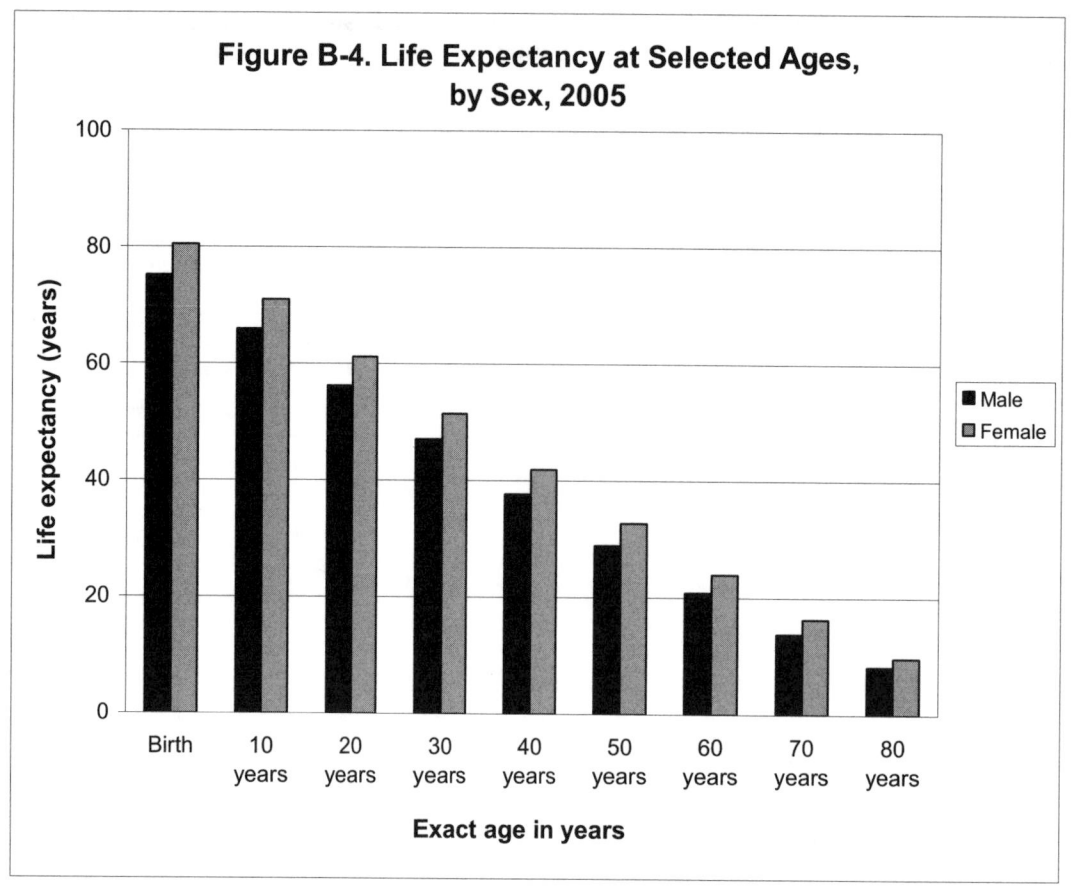

Figure B-4. Life Expectancy at Selected Ages, by Sex, 2005

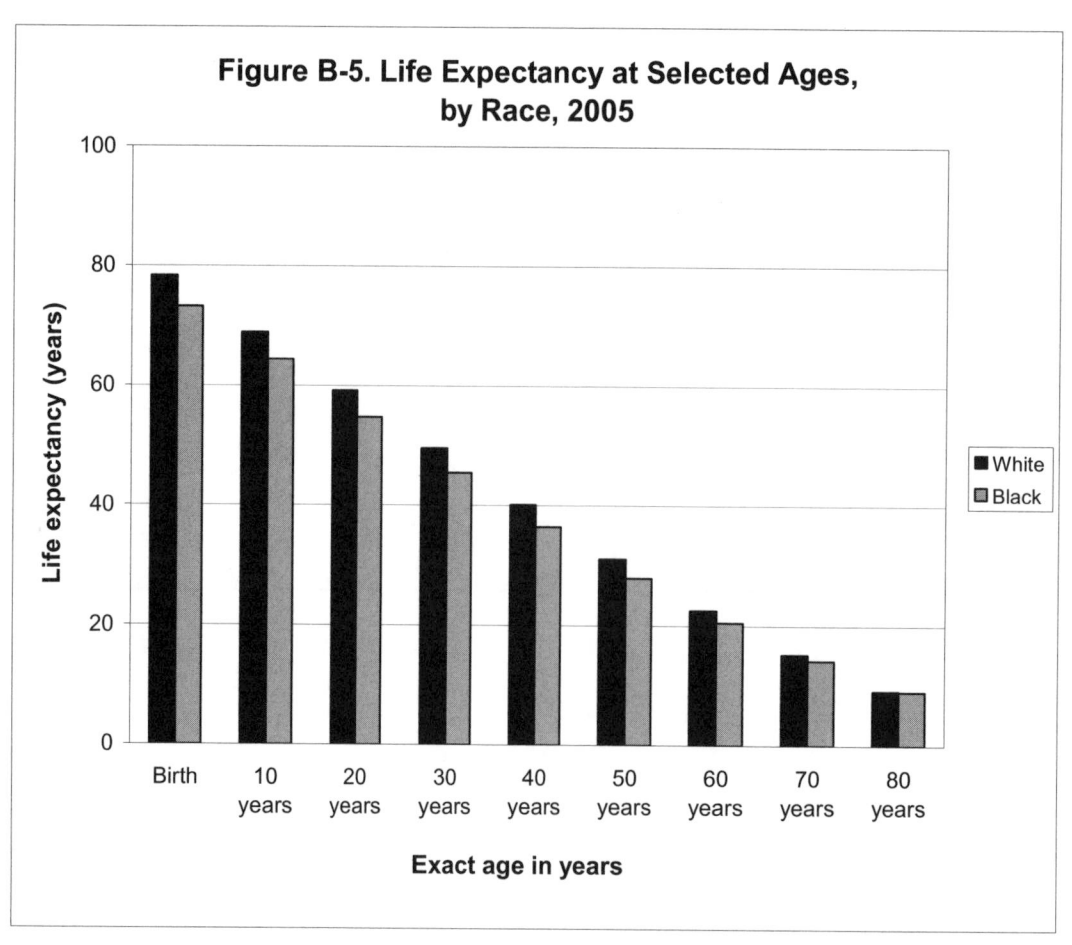

Figure B-5. Life Expectancy at Selected Ages, by Race, 2005

Table B-11. Life Expectancy at Selected Ages by Race and Sex, 2005

(Number of years.)

Exact age in years	All races[1]			White			Black		
	Both sexes	Male	Female	Both sexes	Male	Female	Both sexes	Male	Female
0	77.8	75.2	80.4	78.3	75.7	80.8	73.2	69.5	76.5
1	77.4	74.7	79.9	77.7	75.2	80.2	73.2	69.6	76.4
5	73.5	70.8	76.0	73.8	71.3	76.3	69.3	65.7	72.5
10	68.5	65.9	71.0	68.9	66.3	71.3	64.4	60.8	67.6
15	63.6	61.0	66.1	63.9	61.4	66.4	59.5	55.9	62.7
20	58.8	56.2	61.2	59.1	56.6	61.5	54.7	51.2	57.8
25	54.1	51.6	56.4	54.4	52.0	56.6	50.1	46.8	53.0
30	49.3	47.0	51.5	49.6	47.3	51.8	45.5	42.3	48.2
35	44.6	42.3	46.7	44.9	42.6	46.9	40.9	37.9	43.5
40	39.9	37.7	41.9	40.1	38.0	42.2	36.4	33.4	38.9
45	35.3	33.2	37.3	35.6	33.5	37.5	32.0	29.2	34.4
50	30.9	28.9	32.7	31.1	29.1	32.9	27.9	25.2	30.2
55	26.7	24.8	28.3	26.8	24.9	28.4	24.1	21.6	26.2
60	22.6	20.8	24.0	22.6	20.9	24.1	20.5	18.2	22.3
65	18.7	17.2	20.0	18.8	17.2	20.0	17.2	15.2	18.7
70	15.2	13.8	16.3	15.2	13.8	16.2	14.2	12.4	15.3
75	12.0	10.8	12.8	11.9	10.7	12.8	11.4	10.0	12.3
80	9.2	8.2	9.7	9.1	8.1	9.7	9.0	7.9	9.7
85	6.8	6.1	7.2	6.7	6.0	7.1	7.1	6.2	7.5
90	5.0	4.4	5.2	4.9	4.4	5.1	5.5	4.8	5.7
95	3.6	3.2	3.7	3.5	3.1	3.6	4.2	3.7	4.3
100	2.6	2.3	2.6	2.5	2.3	2.5	3.2	2.9	3.2

[1]Includes races other than White and Black.

Table B-12. Life Expectancy by Age, Race, and Sex, Final 2005 and Preliminary 2006

(Number of years.)

Race and age	Both sexes		Male		Female	
	2005	2006	2005	2006	2005	2006
All Races[1]						
0..	77.8	78.1	75.2	75.4	80.4	80.7
1..	77.4	77.7	74.7	75.0	79.9	80.2
5..	73.5	73.7	70.8	71.1	76.0	76.3
10..	68.5	68.8	65.9	66.2	71.0	71.3
15..	63.6	63.8	61.0	61.2	66.1	66.4
20..	58.8	59.0	56.2	56.5	61.2	61.5
25..	54.1	54.3	51.6	51.9	56.4	56.6
30..	49.3	49.6	47.0	47.2	51.5	51.8
35..	44.6	44.8	42.3	42.6	46.7	46.9
40..	39.9	40.2	37.7	37.9	41.9	42.2
45..	35.3	35.6	33.2	33.5	37.3	37.5
50..	30.9	31.2	28.9	29.1	32.7	33.0
55..	26.7	26.9	24.8	25.0	28.3	28.6
60..	22.6	22.8	20.8	21.1	24.0	24.3
65..	18.7	19.0	17.2	17.4	20.0	20.3
70..	15.2	15.4	13.8	14.0	16.3	16.5
75..	12.0	12.2	10.8	10.9	12.8	13.0
80..	9.2	9.3	8.2	8.3	9.7	9.9
85..	6.8	7.0	6.1	6.2	7.2	7.4
90..	5.0	5.1	4.4	4.5	5.2	5.3
95..	3.6	3.7	3.2	3.3	3.7	3.8
100......................................	2.6	2.7	2.3	2.4	2.6	2.7
White						
0	78.3	78.5	75.7	76.0	80.8	81.0
1	77.7	78.0	75.2	75.4	80.2	80.5
5	73.8	74.1	71.3	71.5	76.3	76.5
10..	68.9	69.1	66.3	66.6	71.3	71.6
15..	63.9	64.2	61.4	61.6	66.4	66.6
20..	59.1	59.3	56.6	56.9	61.5	61.7
25..	54.4	54.6	52.0	52.2	56.6	56.9
30..	49.6	49.9	47.3	47.6	51.8	52.0
35..	44.9	45.1	42.6	42.9	46.9	47.2
40..	40.1	40.4	38.0	38.2	42.2	42.4
45..	35.6	35.8	33.5	33.7	37.5	37.7
50..	31.1	31.3	29.1	29.4	32.9	33.1
55..	26.8	27.0	24.9	25.2	28.4	28.7
60..	22.6	22.9	20.9	21.2	24.1	24.3
65..	18.8	19.0	17.2	17.5	20.0	20.3
70..	15.2	15.4	13.8	14.0	16.2	16.5
75..	11.9	12.1	10.7	10.9	12.8	13.0
80..	9.1	9.2	8.1	8.2	9.7	9.9
85..	6.7	6.9	6.0	6.1	7.1	7.3
90..	4.9	5.0	4.4	4.4	5.1	5.2
95..	3.5	3.6	3.1	3.2	3.6	3.7
100......................................	2.5	2.6	2.3	2.3	2.5	2.6
Black						
0	73.2	73.6	69.5	70.0	76.5	76.9
1	73.2	73.6	69.6	70.0	76.4	76.9
5	69.3	69.7	65.7	66.1	72.5	73.0
10..	64.4	64.8	60.8	61.2	67.6	68.1
15..	59.5	59.9	55.9	56.3	62.7	63.1
20..	54.7	55.1	51.2	51.6	57.8	58.3
25..	50.1	50.5	46.8	47.1	53.0	53.4
30..	45.5	45.9	42.3	42.7	48.2	48.7
35..	40.9	41.3	37.9	38.2	43.5	44.0
40..	36.4	36.8	33.4	33.8	38.9	39.3
45..	32.0	32.4	29.2	29.5	34.4	34.9
50..	27.9	28.3	25.2	25.5	30.2	30.6
55..	24.1	24.5	21.6	21.9	26.2	26.6
60..	20.5	20.9	18.2	18.5	22.3	22.7
65..	17.2	17.6	15.2	15.5	18.7	19.1

[1]Includes races other than White and Black

Table B-12. Life Expectancy by Age, Race, and Sex, Final 2005 and Preliminary 2006—*Continued*

(Number of years.)

Race and age	Both sexes		Male		Female	
	2005	2006	2005	2006	2005	2006
Black—Continued						
70..................................	14.2	14.5	12.4	12.7	15.3	15.7
75..................................	11.4	11.7	10.0	10.2	12.3	12.6
80..................................	9.0	9.3	7.9	8.1	9.7	9.9
85..................................	7.1	7.3	6.2	6.4	7.5	7.7
90..................................	5.5	5.7	4.8	5.0	5.7	5.9
95..................................	4.2	4.4	3.7	3.9	4.3	4.4
100................................	3.2	3.3	2.9	3.0	3.2	3.3

Table B-13. Life Expectancy at Birth by Race and Sex, Selected Years, 1940–2005

(percent.)

Year	All races[1]			White			Black		
	Both sexes	Male	Female	Both sexes	Male	Female	Both sexes	Male	Female
1940..............	62.9	60.8	65.2	64.2	62.1	66.6	—	—	—
1950..............	68.2	65.6	71.1	69.1	66.5	72.2	—	—	—
1960..............	69.7	66.6	73.1	70.6	67.4	74.1	—	—	—
1970..............	70.8	67.1	74.7	71.7	68.0	75.6	64.1	60.0	68.3
1975..............	72.6	68.8	76.6	73.4	69.5	77.3	66.8	62.4	71.3
1976..............	72.9	69.1	76.8	73.6	69.9	77.5	67.2	62.9	71.6
1977..............	73.3	69.5	77.2	74.0	70.2	77.9	67.7	63.4	72.0
1978..............	73.5	69.6	77.3	74.1	70.4	78.0	68.1	63.7	72.4
1979..............	73.9	70.0	77.8	74.6	70.8	78.4	68.5	64.0	72.9
1980..............	73.7	70.0	77.4	74.4	70.7	78.1	68.1	63.8	72.5
1981..............	74.1	70.4	77.8	74.8	71.1	78.4	68.9	64.5	73.2
1982..............	74.5	70.8	78.1	75.1	71.5	78.7	69.4	65.1	73.6
1983..............	74.6	71.0	78.1	75.2	71.6	78.7	69.4	65.2	73.5
1984..............	74.7	71.1	78.2	75.3	71.8	78.7	69.5	65.3	73.6
1985..............	74.7	71.1	78.2	75.3	71.8	78.7	69.3	65.0	73.4
1986..............	74.7	71.2	78.2	75.4	71.9	78.8	69.1	64.8	73.4
1987..............	74.9	71.4	78.3	75.6	72.1	78.9	69.1	64.7	73.4
1988..............	74.9	71.4	78.3	75.6	72.2	78.9	68.9	64.4	73.2
1989..............	75.1	71.7	78.5	75.9	72.5	79.2	68.8	64.3	73.3
1990..............	75.4	71.8	78.8	76.1	72.7	79.4	69.1	64.5	73.6
1991..............	75.5	72.0	78.9	76.3	72.9	79.6	69.3	64.6	73.8
1992..............	75.8	72.3	79.1	76.5	73.2	79.8	69.6	65.0	73.9
1993..............	75.5	72.2	78.8	76.3	73.1	79.5	69.2	64.6	73.7
1994..............	75.7	72.4	79.0	76.5	73.3	79.6	69.5	64.9	73.9
1995..............	75.8	72.5	78.9	76.5	73.4	79.6	69.6	65.2	73.9
1996..............	76.1	73.1	79.1	76.8	73.9	79.7	70.2	66.1	74.2
1997..............	76.5	73.6	79.4	77.1	74.3	79.9	71.1	67.2	74.7
1998..............	76.7	73.8	79.5	77.3	74.5	80.0	71.3	67.6	74.8
1999..............	76.7	73.9	79.4	77.3	74.6	79.9	71.4	67.8	74.7
2000..............	77.0	74.3	79.7	77.6	74.9	80.1	71.9	68.3	75.2
2001..............	77.2	74.4	79.8	77.7	75.0	80.2	72.2	68.6	75.5
2002..............	77.3	74.5	79.9	77.7	75.1	80.3	72.3	68.8	75.6
2003..............	77.4	74.7	80.0	77.9	75.3	80.4	72.6	68.9	75.9
2004..............	77.8	75.2	80.4	78.3	75.7	80.8	73.1	69.5	76.3
2005..............	77.8	75.2	80.4	78.3	75.7	80.8	73.2	69.5	76.5

— = Data not available.
[1]Includes races other than White and Black.

Table B-14. Death Rates by Age and Age-Adjusted Death Rates for the 15 Leading Causes of Death, 1999–2005

(Rate per 100,000 population in specified group; age-adjusted rates per 100,000 U.S. standard population.)

Cause of death and year[1]	All ages[2]	Under 1 year[3]	1–4 years	5–14 years	15–24 years	25–34 years	35–44 years	45–54 years	55–64 years	65–74 years	75–84 years	85 years and over	Age-adjusted rate
All Causes													
1999	857.0	736.0	34.2	18.6	79.3	102.2	198.0	418.2	1,005.0	2,457.3	5,714.5	15,554.6	875.6
2000	854.0	736.7	32.4	18.0	79.9	101.4	198.9	425.6	992.2	2,399.1	5,666.5	15,524.4	869.0
2001	848.5	683.4	33.3	17.3	80.7	105.2	203.6	428.9	964.6	2,353.3	5,582.4	15,112.8	854.5
2002	847.3	695.0	31.2	17.4	81.4	103.6	202.9	430.1	952.4	2,314.7	5,556.9	14,828.3	845.3
2003	841.9	700.0	31.5	17.0	81.5	103.6	201.6	433.2	940.9	2,255.0	5,463.1	14,593.3	832.7
2004	816.5	685.2	29.9	16.8	80.1	102.1	193.5	427.0	910.3	2,164.6	5,275.1	13,823.5	800.8
2005	825.9	692.5	29.4	16.3	81.4	104.4	193.3	432.0	906.9	2,137.1	5,260.0	13,798.6	798.8
Diseases of Heart (I00-I09, I11, I13, I20-I51)													
1999	259.9	13.8	1.2	0.7	2.8	7.6	30.2	95.7	269.9	701.7	1,849.9	6,063.0	266.5
2000	252.6	13.0	1.2	0.7	2.6	7.4	29.2	94.2	261.2	665.6	1,780.3	5,926.1	257.6
2001	245.8	11.9	1.5	0.7	2.5	8.0	29.6	92.9	246.9	635.1	1,725.7	5,664.2	247.8
2002	241.7	12.4	1.1	0.6	2.5	7.9	30.5	93.7	241.5	615.9	1,677.2	5,466.8	240.8
2003	235.6	11.0	1.2	0.6	2.7	8.2	30.7	92.5	233.2	585.0	1,611.1	5,278.4	232.3
2004	222.2	10.3	1.2	0.6	2.5	7.9	29.3	90.2	218.8	541.6	1,506.3	4,895.9	217.0
2005	220.0	8.7	0.9	0.6	2.7	8.1	28.9	89.7	214.8	518.9	1,460.8	4,778.4	211.1
Malignant Neoplasms (C00-C97)													
1999	197.0	1.8	2.7	2.5	4.5	10.0	37.1	127.6	374.6	827.1	1,331.5	1,805.8	200.8
2000	196.5	2.4	2.7	2.5	4.4	9.8	36.6	127.5	366.7	816.3	1,335.6	1,819.4	199.6
2001	194.4	1.6	2.7	2.5	4.3	10.1	36.8	126.5	356.5	802.8	1,315.8	1,765.6	196.0
2002	193.2	1.8	2.6	2.6	4.3	9.7	35.8	123.8	351.1	792.1	1,311.9	1,723.9	193.5
2003	191.5	1.9	2.5	2.6	4.0	9.4	35.0	122.2	343.0	770.3	1,302.5	1,698.2	190.1
2004	188.6	1.8	2.5	2.5	4.1	9.1	33.4	119.0	333.4	755.1	1,280.4	1,653.3	185.8
2005	188.7	1.8	2.3	2.5	4.1	9.0	33.2	118.6	326.9	742.7	1,274.8	1,637.7	183.8
Cerebrovascular Diseases (I60-I69)													
1999	60.0	2.7	0.3	0.2	0.5	1.4	5.7	15.2	40.6	130.8	469.8	1,614.8	61.6
2000	59.6	3.3	0.3	0.2	0.5	1.5	5.8	16.0	41.0	128.6	461.3	1,589.2	60.9
2001	57.4	2.7	0.4	0.2	0.5	1.5	5.5	15.1	38.0	123.4	443.9	1,500.2	57.9
2002	56.4	2.9	0.3	0.2	0.4	1.4	5.4	15.1	37.2	120.3	431.0	1,445.9	56.2
2003	54.2	2.5	0.3	0.2	0.5	1.5	5.5	15.0	35.6	112.9	410.7	1,370.1	53.5
2004	51.1	3.1	0.3	0.2	0.5	1.4	5.4	14.9	34.3	107.8	386.2	1,245.9	50.0
2005	48.4	3.1	0.4	0.2	0.5	1.4	5.2	15.0	33.0	101.1	359.0	1,141.8	46.6
Chronic Lower Respiratory Diseases (J40-J47)													
1999	44.5	0.9	0.4	0.3	0.5	0.8	2.0	8.5	47.5	177.2	397.8	646.0	45.4
2000	43.4	0.9	0.3	0.3	0.5	0.7	2.1	8.6	44.2	169.4	386.1	648.6	44.2
2001	43.2	1.0	0.3	0.3	0.4	0.7	2.2	8.5	44.1	167.9	379.8	644.7	43.7
2002	43.3	1.0	0.4	0.3	0.5	0.8	2.2	8.7	42.4	163.0	386.7	637.6	43.5
2003	43.5	0.8	0.3	0.3	0.5	0.7	2.1	8.7	43.3	163.2	383.0	635.1	43.3
2004	41.5	0.9	0.3	0.3	0.4	0.6	2.0	8.4	40.4	153.8	366.7	601.7	41.1
2005	44.2	0.8	0.3	0.3	0.4	0.6	2.0	9.4	42.0	160.5	385.6	637.2	43.2
Accidents (Unintentional Injuries) (V01-X59, Y85-Y86)													
1999	35.1	22.3	12.4	7.6	35.3	29.6	33.8	31.8	30.6	44.6	100.5	282.4	35.3
2000	34.8	23.1	11.9	7.3	36.0	29.5	34.1	32.6	30.9	41.9	95.1	273.5	34.9
2001	35.7	24.2	11.2	6.9	36.1	29.9	35.4	34.1	30.3	42.8	100.9	276.4	35.7
2002	37.0	23.5	10.5	6.6	38.0	31.5	37.2	36.6	31.4	44.2	101.3	275.4	36.9
2003	37.6	23.6	10.9	6.4	37.1	31.5	37.8	38.8	32.9	44.1	101.9	278.9	37.3
2004	38.1	25.8	10.3	6.5	37.0	32.6	37.3	40.7	33.2	44.0	103.7	276.7	37.7
2005	39.7	26.4	10.3	6.0	37.4	34.9	38.6	43.2	35.8	46.3	106.1	279.5	39.1
Diabetes Mellitus (E10-E14)													
1999	24.5	*	*	0.1	0.4	1.4	4.3	12.9	38.3	91.8	178.0	317.2	25.0
2000	24.6	*	*	0.1	0.4	1.6	4.3	13.1	37.8	90.7	179.5	319.7	25.0
2001	25.1	*	*	0.1	0.4	1.5	4.3	13.6	37.8	91.4	181.4	321.8	25.3
2002	25.4	*	*	0.1	0.4	1.6	4.8	13.7	37.7	91.4	182.8	320.6	25.4
2003	25.5	*	*	0.1	0.4	1.6	4.6	13.9	38.5	90.8	181.1	317.5	25.3
2004	24.9	*	*	0.1	0.4	1.5	4.6	13.4	37.1	87.2	176.9	307.0	24.5
2005	25.3	*	*	0.1	0.5	1.5	4.7	13.4	37.2	86.8	177.2	312.1	24.6

* = Figure does not meet standards of reliability or precision.
... = Not applicable.
[1]Based on codes from the *International Classification of Diseases, Tenth Revision* (1992), except where (*) precedes the cause of death code.
[2]Figures for age not stated included in All ages but not distributed among age groups.
[3]Death rates for "Under 1 year" (based on population estimates) differ from infant mortality rates (based on live births).

Table B-14. Death Rates by Age and Age-Adjusted Death Rates for the 15 Leading Causes of Death, 1999–2005—*Continued*

(Rate per 100,000 population in specified group; age-adjusted rates per 100,000 U.S. standard population.)

Cause of death and year[1]	Age												Age-adjusted rate
	All ages[2]	Under 1 year[3]	1–4 years	5–14 years	15–24 years	25–34 years	35–44 years	45–54 years	55–64 years	65–74 years	75–84 years	85 years and over	
Alzheimer's Disease (G30)													
1999	16.0	*	*	*	*	*	*	0.2	1.9	17.4	129.5	601.3	16.5
2000	17.6	*	*	*	*	*	*	0.2	2.0	18.7	139.6	667.7	18.1
2001	18.9	*	*	*	*	*	*	0.2	2.1	18.7	147.5	710.3	19.1
2002	20.4	*	*	*	*	*	*	0.1	1.9	19.7	158.1	752.3	20.2
2003	21.8	*	*	*	*	*	*	0.2	2.0	20.9	164.4	802.4	21.4
2004	22.5	*	*	*	*	*	*	0.2	1.9	19.7	168.7	818.8	21.8
2005	24.2	*	*	*	*	*	*	0.2	2.1	20.5	177.3	861.6	22.9
Influenza and Pneumonia (J10-J18)													
1999	22.8	8.4	0.8	0.2	0.5	0.8	2.4	4.6	11.0	37.2	157.0	751.8	23.5
2000	23.2	7.6	0.7	0.2	0.5	0.9	2.4	4.7	11.9	39.1	160.3	744.1	23.7
2001	21.8	7.4	0.7	0.2	0.5	0.9	2.2	4.6	10.7	36.3	148.5	685.6	22.0
2002	22.8	6.5	0.7	0.2	0.4	0.9	2.2	4.8	11.2	37.5	156.9	696.6	22.6
2003	22.4	8.0	1.0	0.4	0.5	0.9	2.2	5.2	11.2	37.3	151.1	666.1	22.0
2004	20.3	6.7	0.7	0.2	0.4	0.8	2.0	4.6	10.8	34.6	139.3	582.6	19.8
2005	21.3	6.5	0.7	0.3	0.4	0.9	2.1	5.1	11.3	35.5	142.2	593.9	20.3
Nephritis, Nephrotic Syndrome and Nephrosis (N00-N07, N17-N19, N25-N27)													
1999	12.7	4.4	*	0.1	0.2	0.6	1.6	4.0	12.0	37.1	97.6	268.9	13.0
2000	13.2	4.3	*	0.1	0.2	0.6	1.6	4.4	12.8	38.0	100.8	277.8	13.5
2001	13.9	3.3	*	0.0	0.2	0.6	1.7	4.6	13.0	40.2	104.2	287.7	14.0
2002	14.2	4.3	*	0.1	0.2	0.7	1.7	4.7	13.0	39.2	109.1	288.6	14.2
2003	14.6	4.5	*	0.1	0.2	0.7	1.8	4.9	13.6	40.1	109.5	293.1	14.4
2004	14.5	4.3	*	0.1	0.2	0.6	1.8	5.0	13.6	38.6	108.4	286.6	14.2
2005	14.8	3.9	*	0.1	0.2	0.7	1.7	4.8	13.6	39.3	110.3	288.3	14.3
Septicemia (A40-A41)													
1999	11.0	7.5	0.6	0.2	0.3	0.7	1.8	4.6	11.4	31.2	79.4	220.7	11.3
2000	11.1	7.2	0.6	0.2	0.3	0.7	1.9	4.9	11.9	31.0	80.4	215.7	11.3
2001	11.3	7.7	0.7	0.2	0.3	0.7	1.8	5.0	12.3	32.8	82.3	205.9	11.4
2002	11.7	7.3	0.5	0.2	0.3	0.8	1.9	5.2	12.6	34.7	86.5	203.0	11.7
2003	11.7	6.9	0.5	0.2	0.4	0.8	2.1	5.3	13.1	32.6	85.0	202.5	11.6
2004	11.4	6.6	0.5	0.2	0.3	0.8	1.9	5.4	12.9	32.4	81.6	186.7	11.2
2005	11.5	7.4	0.5	0.2	0.4	0.8	1.9	5.2	12.9	32.6	81.4	187.3	11.2
Intentional Self-Harm (suicide) (*U03, X60-X84, Y87.0)													
1999	10.5	…	…	0.6	10.1	12.7	14.3	13.9	12.2	13.4	18.1	19.3	10.5
2000	10.4	…	…	0.7	10.2	12.0	14.5	14.4	12.1	12.5	17.6	19.6	10.4
2001	10.8	…	…	0.7	9.9	12.8	14.7	15.2	13.1	13.3	17.4	17.5	10.7
2002	11.0	…	…	0.6	9.9	12.6	15.3	15.7	13.6	13.5	17.7	18.0	10.9
2003	10.8	…	…	0.6	9.7	12.7	14.9	15.9	13.8	12.7	16.4	16.9	10.8
2004	11.0	…	…	0.7	10.3	12.7	15.0	16.6	13.8	12.3	16.3	16.4	10.9
2005	11.0	…	…	0.7	10.0	12.4	14.9	16.5	13.9	12.6	16.9	16.9	10.9
Chronic Liver Disease and Cirrhosis (K70, K73-K74)													
1999	9.4	*	*	*	0.1	1.0	7.3	17.4	23.7	30.6	31.9	23.2	9.6
2000	9.4	*	*	*	0.1	1.0	7.5	17.7	23.8	29.8	31.0	23.1	9.5
2001	9.5	*	*	*	0.1	1.0	7.4	18.5	22.7	30.0	30.2	22.2	9.5
2002	9.5	*	*	*	0.1	0.9	7.0	18.0	22.9	29.4	31.4	21.4	9.4
2003	9.5	*	*	*	*	0.9	6.8	18.3	23.0	29.5	30.0	20.1	9.3
2004	9.2	*	*	*	*	0.8	6.3	18.0	22.6	27.7	28.8	19.7	9.0
2005	9.3	*	*	*	0.1	0.8	6.1	17.7	23.5	27.2	29.0	19.7	9.0
Essential (Primary) Hypertension and Hypertensive Renal Disease (I10, I12)													
1999	6.1	*	*	*	*	0.2	0.7	2.2	5.5	15.2	43.6	152.1	6.2
2000	6.4	*	*	*	*	0.2	0.8	2.3	5.9	15.1	45.5	162.9	6.5
2001	6.8	*	*	*	0.1	0.3	0.7	2.4	5.8	15.5	47.7	171.9	6.8
2002	7.0	*	*	*	0.1	0.2	0.8	2.3	5.7	16.0	48.2	180.4	7.0
2003	7.5	*	*	*	0.1	0.2	0.8	2.5	6.3	16.9	51.7	188.9	7.4
2004	7.9	*	*	*	0.1	0.3	0.8	2.7	6.3	17.1	52.6	198.5	7.7
2005	8.4	*	*	*	0.1	0.2	0.9	2.7	6.4	17.7	55.6	210.0	8.0

* = Figure does not meet standards of reliability or precision.

… = Not applicable.

[1]Based on codes from the *International Classification of Diseases, Tenth Revision* (1992), except where (*) precedes the cause of death code.

[2]Figures for age not stated included in All ages but not distributed among age groups.

[3]Death rates for "Under 1 year" (based on population estimates) differ from infant mortality rates (based on live births).

Table B-14. Death Rates by Age and Age-Adjusted Death Rates for the 15 Leading Causes of Death, 1999–2005—*Continued*

(Rate per 100,000 population in specified group; age-adjusted rates per 100,000 U.S. standard population.)

Cause of death and year[1]	Age												Age-adjusted rate
	All ages[2]	Under 1 year[3]	1–4 years	5–14 years	15–24 years	25–34 years	35–44 years	45–54 years	55–64 years	65–74 years	75–84 years	85 years and over	
Parkinson's Disease (G20-G21)													
1999	5.2	*	*	*	*	*	*	0.1	1.0	11.0	58.2	124.4	5.4
2000	5.6	*	*	*	*	*	*	0.1	1.1	11.5	61.9	131.9	5.7
2001	5.8	*	*	*	*	*	*	0.1	1.2	11.7	64.6	134.2	5.9
2002	5.9	*	*	*	*	*	*	0.1	1.2	12.2	63.9	135.2	5.9
2003	6.2	*	*	*	*	*	*	0.2	1.3	12.7	67.8	138.2	6.2
2004	6.1	*	*	*	*	*	*	0.2	1.2	12.0	67.5	135.8	6.1
2005	6.6	*	*	*	*	*	*	0.2	1.4	13.0	71.2	143.7	6.4
Assault (Homicide) (*U01-*U02, X85-Y09, Y87.1)													
1999	6.1	8.7	2.5	1.1	12.9	10.5	7.1	4.6	3.0	2.6	2.5	2.4	6.0
2000	6.0	9.2	2.3	0.9	12.6	10.4	7.1	4.7	3.0	2.4	2.4	2.4	5.9
2001[4]	7.1	8.2	2.7	0.8	13.3	13.1	9.5	6.3	4.0	2.9	2.5	2.4	7.1
2002	6.1	7.5	2.7	0.9	12.9	11.2	7.2	4.8	3.2	2.3	2.3	2.1	6.1
2003	6.1	8.5	2.4	0.8	13.0	11.3	7.0	4.9	2.8	2.4	2.5	2.2	6.0
2004	5.9	8.0	2.4	0.8	12.2	11.2	6.8	4.8	3.0	2.4	2.2	2.1	5.9
2005	6.1	7.5	2.3	0.8	13.0	11.8	7.1	4.8	2.8	2.4	2.2	2.1	6.1

* = Figure does not meet standards of reliability or precision.
[1]Based on codes from the *International Classification of Diseases, Tenth Revision* (1992), except where (*) precedes the cause of death code.
[2]Figures for age not stated included in All ages but not distributed among age groups.
[3]Death rates for "Under 1 year" (based on population estimates) differ from infant mortality rates (based on live births).
[4]Figures include September 11, 2001 related deaths for which death certificates were filed as of October 24, 2002.

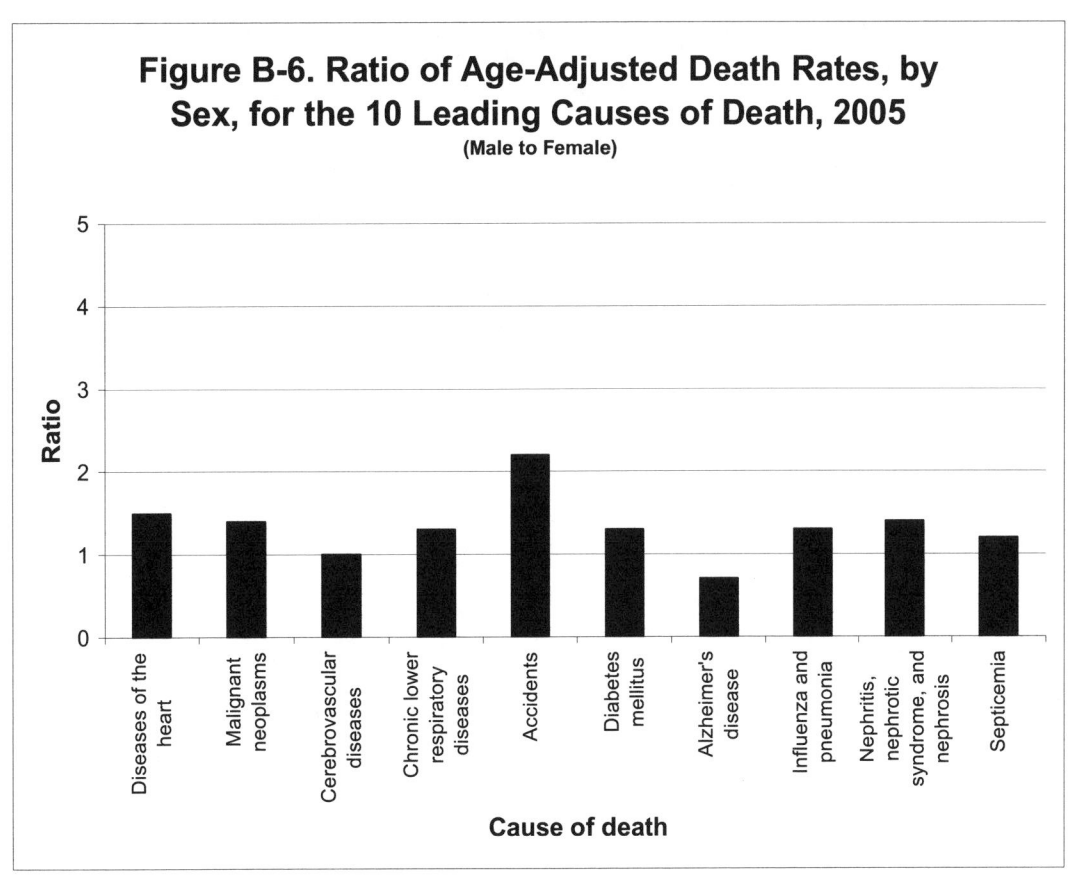

Figure B-6. Ratio of Age-Adjusted Death Rates, by Sex, for the 10 Leading Causes of Death, 2005
(Male to Female)

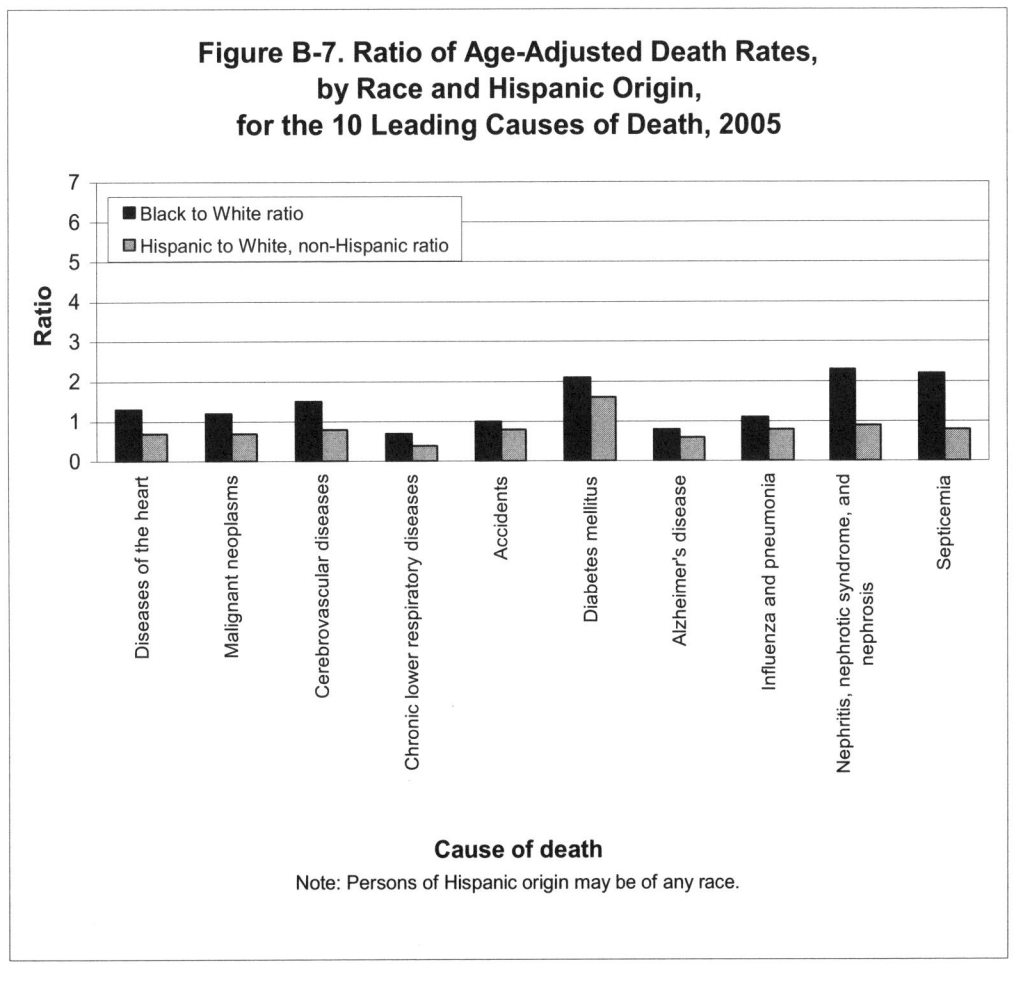

Figure B-7. Ratio of Age-Adjusted Death Rates, by Race and Hispanic Origin, for the 10 Leading Causes of Death, 2005

Note: Persons of Hispanic origin may be of any race.

Table B-15. Percentage of Total Deaths, Death Rates, Age-Adjusted Death Rates for 2005, Percentage Change in Age-Adjusted Death Rates From 2004 to 2005, and Ratio of Age-Adjusted Death Rates by Race and Sex for the 15 Leading Causes of Death for the Total Population in 2005

(Number, percent, death rate per 100,000 population.)

Rank[1]	Cause of death[2]	Number	Percent of total deaths	2005 crude death rate	Age-adjusted death rate				
					2005	Percent change 2004 to 2005	Ratio Male to female	Ratio Black to white	Ratio Hispanic[3] to non-Hispanic white
	All Causes	2,448,017	100.0	825.9	798.8	-0.2	1.4	1.3	0.7
1	Diseases of heart (I00-I09, I11, I13, I20-I51).................	652,091	26.6	220.0	211.1	-2.7	1.5	1.3	0.7
2	Malignant neoplasms (C00-C97)	559,312	22.8	188.7	183.8	-1.1	1.4	1.2	0.7
3	Cerebrovascular diseases (I60-I69)..............................	143,579	5.9	48.4	46.6	-6.8	1.0	1.5	0.8
4	Chronic lower respiratory diseases (J40-J47)	130,933	5.3	44.2	43.2	5.1	1.3	0.7	0.4
5	Accidents (unintentional injuries) (V01-X59, Y85-Y86)	117,809	4.8	39.7	39.1	3.7	2.2	1.0	0.8
6	Diabetes mellitus (E10-E14)	75,119	3.1	25.3	24.6	0.4	1.3	2.1	1.6
7	Alzheimer's disease (G30)	71,599	2.9	24.2	22.9	5.0	0.7	0.8	0.6
8	Influenza and pneumonia (J10-J18)	63,001	2.6	21.3	20.3	2.5	1.3	1.1	0.8
9	Nephritis, nephrotic syndrome and nephrosis (N00-N07, N17-N19, N25-N27)	43,901	1.8	14.8	14.3	0.7	1.4	2.3	0.9
10	Septicemia (A40-A41)..	34,136	1.4	11.5	11.2	0.0	1.2	2.2	0.8
11	Intentional self-harm (suicide) (*U03, X60-X84, Y87.0)	32,637	1.3	11.0	10.9	0.0	4.1	0.4	0.4
12	Chronic liver disease and cirrhosis (K70, K73-K74).......	27,530	1.1	9.3	9.0	0.0	2.1	0.8	1.6
13	Essential (primary) hypertension and hypertensive renal disease (I10, I12)...........................	24,902	1.0	8.4	8.0	3.9	1.0	2.6	1.0
14	Parkinson's disease (G20-G21)	19,544	0.8	6.6	6.4	4.9	2.2	0.4	0.6
15	Assault (homicide) (*U01-*U02, X85-Y09, Y87.1)	18,124	0.7	6.1	6.1	3.4	3.8	5.7	2.8
...	All other causes (Residual)	433,800	17.7	146.4	...	...	...	...	...

... = Not applicable.

[1]Rank based on number of deaths.

[2]Based on codes from the *International Classification of Diseases, Tenth Revision* (1992), except where (*) precedes the cause of death code.

[3]Data for Hispanic origin should be interpreted with caution because of inconsistencies between reporting Hispanic origin on death certificates and on censuses and surveys. Persons of Hispanic origin may be of any race.

Table B-16. Deaths, Death Rates, Age-Adjusted Death Rates and Percentage Changes in Age-Adjusted Rates from 2005 to 2006 for the 15 Leading Causes of Death, Final 2005 and Preliminary 2006

(Number, death rate per 100,000 population, percent.)

Rank[1]	Cause of death[2]	Number	Age-adjusted age rate			Percent change
			Death rate	2005	2006	
	All Causes.................................	2,425,901	810.3	798.8	776.4	–2.8
1	Diseases of heart (I00-I09, I11, I13, I20-I51)	629,191	210.2	211.1	199.4	–5.5
2	Malignant neoplasms (C00-C97)	560,102	187.1	183.8	180.8	–1.6
3	Cerebrovascular diseases (I60-I69)	137,265	45.8	46.6	43.6	–6.4
4	Chronic lower respiratory diseases (J40-J47)	124,614	41.6	43.2	40.4	–6.5
5	Accidents (unintentional injuries)					
	(V01-X59, Y85-Y86)3	117,748	39.3	39.1	38.5	–1.5
6	Alzheimer's disease (G30)	72,914	24.4	22.9	22.7	–0.9
7	Diabetes mellitus (E10-E14)	72,507	24.2	24.6	23.3	–5.3
8	Influenza and pneumonia (J10-J18)	56,247	18.8	20.3	17.7	–12.8
9	Nephritis, nephrotic syndrome and nephrosis					
	(N00-N07, N17-N19, N25-N27)	44,791	15.0	14.3	14.3	–
10	Septicemia (A40-A41).....................................	34,031	11.4	11.2	10.9	–2.7
11	Intentional self-harm (suicide)					
	(*U03, X60-X84, Y87.0)3	32,185	10.7	10.9	10.6	–2.8
12	Chronic liver disease and cirrhosis (K70, K73-K74).........	27,299	9.1	9.0	8.7	–3.3
13	Essential (primary) hypertension and					
	hypertensive renal disease (I10, I12)4	23,985	8.0	8.0	7.6	–5.0
14	Parkinson's disease (G20-G21)............................	19,660	6.6	6.4	6.3	–1.6
15	Assault (homicide)					
	(*U01-*U02, X85-Y09, Y87.1)	18,029	6.0	6.1	6.0	–1.6
	All other causes (residual)...............................	455,333	152.1	...	...	...

... = Not applicable

– = Quantity zero.

[1]Rank based on number of deaths.

[2]Based on codes from the *International Classification of Diseases, Tenth Revision* (1992), except where (*) precedes the cause of death code.

[3]For unintentional injuries, homicides, and suicides, preliminary and final data may differ significantly because of the truncated nature of the preliminary file.

[4]Cause-of-death title has been changed in 2006 to reflect the addition of secondary hypertension (*ICD–10* code I15).

NOTE: Data are subject to sampling and random variation.

Table B-17. Leading Causes of Death and Numbers of Deaths, by Sex, Race, and Hispanic Origin, 1980 and 2005

(Number.)

Sex, race, Hispanic origin, and rank order	1980		2005	
	Cause of death[1]	Deaths	Cause of death[1]	Deaths
All Persons				
	All Causes	1,989,841	**All Causes**	2,448,017
1	Diseases of heart	761,085	Diseases of heart	652,091
2	Malignant neoplasms	416,509	Malignant neoplasms	559,312
3	Cerebrovascular diseases	170,225	Cerebrovascular diseases	143,579
4	Unintentional injuries	105,718	Chronic lower respiratory diseases	130,933
5	Chronic obstructive pulmonary diseases	56,050	Unintentional injuries	117,809
6	Pneumonia and influenza	54,619	Diabetes mellitus	75,119
7	Diabetes mellitus	34,851	Alzheimer's disease	71,599
8	Chronic liver disease and cirrhosis	30,583	Influenza and pneumonia	63,001
9	Atherosclerosis	29,449	Nephritis, nephrotic syndrome and nephrosis	43,901
10	Suicide	26,869	Septicemia	34,136
Male				
	All Causes	1,075,078	**All Causes**	1,207,675
1	Diseases of heart	405,661	Diseases of heart	322,841
2	Malignant neoplasms	225,948	Malignant neoplasms	290,422
3	Unintentional injuries	74,180	Unintentional injuries	76,375
4	Cerebrovascular diseases	69,973	Chronic lower respiratory diseases	62,435
5	Chronic obstructive pulmonary diseases	38,625	Cerebrovascular diseases	56,586
6	Pneumonia and influenza	27,574	Diabetes mellitus	36,538
7	Suicide	20,505	Influenza and pneumonia	28,052
8	Chronic liver disease and cirrhosis	19,768	Suicide	25,907
9	Homicide	18,779	Nephritis, nephrotic syndrome and nephrosis	21,268
10	Diabetes mellitus	14,325	Alzheimer's disease	20,559
Female				
	All Causes	914,763	**All Causes**	1,240,342
1	Diseases of heart	355,424	Diseases of heart	329,250
2	Malignant neoplasms	190,561	Malignant neoplasms	268,890
3	Cerebrovascular diseases	100,252	Cerebrovascular diseases	86,993
4	Unintentional injuries	31,538	Chronic lower respiratory diseases	68,498
5	Pneumonia and influenza	27,045	Alzheimer's disease	51,040
6	Diabetes mellitus	20,526	Unintentional injuries	41,434
7	Atherosclerosis	17,848	Diabetes mellitus	38,581
8	Chronic obstructive pulmonary diseases	17,425	Influenza and pneumonia	34,949
9	Chronic liver disease and cirrhosis	10,815	Nephritis, nephrotic syndrome and nephrosis	22,633
10	Certain conditions originating in the perinatal period	9,815	Septicemia	18,814
White				
	All Causes	1,738,607	**All Causes**	2,098,097
1	Diseases of heart	683,347	Diseases of heart	564,796
2	Malignant neoplasms	368,162	Malignant neoplasms	482,132
3	Cerebrovascular diseases	148,734	Cerebrovascular diseases	121,868
4	Unintentional injuries	90,122	Chronic lower respiratory diseases	120,884
5	Chronic obstructive pulmonary diseases	52,375	Unintentional injuries	100,406
6	Pneumonia and influenza	48,369	Alzheimer's disease	66,191
7	Diabetes mellitus	28,868	Diabetes mellitus	59,755
8	Atherosclerosis	27,069	Influenza and pneumonia	55,540
9	Chronic liver disease and cirrhosis	25,240	Nephritis, nephrotic syndrome and nephrosis	34,806
10	Suicide	24,829	Suicide	29,527
Black or African American				
	All Causes	233,135	**All Causes**	292,808
1	Diseases of heart	72,956	Diseases of heart	74,159
2	Malignant neoplasms	45,037	Malignant neoplasms	63,165
3	Cerebrovascular diseases	20,135	Cerebrovascular diseases	17,541
4	Unintentional injuries	13,480	Unintentional injuries	13,652
5	Homicide	10,172	Diabetes mellitus	12,970
6	Certain conditions originating in the perinatal period	6,961	Homicide	8,669
7	Pneumonia and influenza	5,648	Chronic lower respiratory diseases	8,229
8	Diabetes mellitus	5,544	Nephritis, nephrotic syndrome and nephrosis	8,075
9	Chronic liver disease and cirrhosis	4,790	Human immunodeficiency virus (HIV) disease	7,022
10	Nephritis, nephrotic syndrome, and nephrosis	3,416	Septicemia	6,221

[1]Based on codes from the *International Classification of Diseases, Ninth Revision* in 1980 and *International Classification of Diseases, Tenth Revision* in 2002.

Table B-17. Leading Causes of Death and Numbers of Deaths, by Sex, Race, and Hispanic Origin, 1980 and 2005—*Continued*

(Number.)

Sex, race, Hispanic origin, and rank order	1980		2005	
	Cause of death[1]	Deaths	Cause of death[1]	Deaths
American Indian or Alaska Native				
	All Causes	6,923	**All Causes**	13,918
1	Diseases of heart	1,494	Diseases of heart	2,659
2	Unintentional injuries	1,290	Malignant neoplasms	2,465
3	Malignant neoplasms	770	Unintentional injuries	1,626
4	Chronic liver disease and cirrhosis	410	Diabetes mellitus	818
5	Cerebrovascular diseases	322	Cerebrovascular diseases	627
6	Pneumonia and influenza	257	Chronic liver disease and cirrhosis	596
7	Homicide	217	Chronic lower respiratory diseases	518
8	Diabetes mellitus	210	Suicide	392
9	Certain conditions originating in the perinatal period	199	Influenza and pneumonia	354
10	Suicide	181	Nephritis, nephrotic syndrome, and nephrosis	265
Asian or Pacific Islander				
	All Causes	11,071	**All Causes**	43,194
1	Diseases of heart	3,265	Malignant neoplasms	11,550
2	Malignant neoplasms	2,522	Diseases of heart	10,477
3	Cerebrovascular diseases	1,028	Cerebrovascular diseases	3,543
4	Unintentional injuries	810	Unintentional injuries	2,125
5	Pneumonia and influenza	342	Diabetes mellitus	1,576
6	Suicide	249	Influenza and pneumonia	1,327
7	Certain conditions originating in the perinatal period	246	Chronic lower respiratory diseases	1,302
8	Diabetes mellitus	227	Nephritis, nephrotic syndrome and nephrosis	755
9	Homicide	211	Suicide	726
10	Chronic obstructive pulmonary diseases	207	Alzheimer's disease	615
Hispanic or Latino				
	—	—	**All Causes**	131,161
1	—	—	Diseases of heart	29,555
2	—	—	Malignant neoplasms	26,156
3	—	—	Unintentional injuries	11,464
4	—	—	Cerebrovascular diseases	6,830
5	—	—	Diabetes mellitus	6,665
6	—	—	Chronic liver disease and cirrhosis	3,555
7	—	—	Homicide	3,520
8	—	—	Chronic lower respiratory diseases	3,457
9	—	—	Influenza and pneumonia	3,085
10	—	—	Certain conditions originating in the perinatal period	2,816
White Male				
	All Causes	933,878	**All Causes**	1,028,152
1	Diseases of heart	364,679	Diseases of heart	279,324
2	Malignant neoplasms	198,188	Malignant neoplasms	250,478
3	Unintentional injuries	62,963	Unintentional injuries	64,600
4	Cerebrovascular diseases	60,095	Chronic lower respiratory diseases	56,911
5	Chronic obstructive pulmonary diseases	35,977	Cerebrovascular diseases	47,194
6	Pneumonia and influenza	23,810	Diabetes mellitus	29,628
7	Suicide	18,901	Influenza and pneumonia	24,425
8	Chronic liver disease and cirrhosis	16,407	Suicide	23,478
9	Diabetes mellitus	12,125	Alzheimer's disease	18,990
10	Atherosclerosis	10,543	Nephritis, nephrotic syndrome, and nephrosis	17,137
Black or African American male				
	All Causes	130,138	**All Causes**	149,108
1	Diseases of heart	37,877	Diseases of heart	36,343
2	Malignant neoplasms	25,861	Malignant neoplasms	32,726
3	Unintentional injuries	9,701	Unintentional injuries	9,329
4	Cerebrovascular diseases	9,194	Cerebrovascular diseases	7,519
5	Homicide	8,274	Homicide	7,412
6	Certain conditions originating in the perinatal period	3,869	Diabetes mellitus	5,730
7	Pneumonia and influenza	3,386	Human immunodeficiency virus (HIV) disease	4,684
8	Chronic liver disease and cirrhosis	3,020	Chronic lower respiratory diseases	4,464
9	Chronic obstructive pulmonary diseases	2,429	Nephritis, nephrotic syndrome, and nephrosis	3,645
10	Diabetes mellitus	2,010	Certain conditions originating in the perinatal period	2,828

—- = Data not available
[1]Based on codes from the *International Classification of Diseases, Ninth Revision* in 1980 and *International Classification of Diseases, Tenth Revision* in 2002.

Table B-17. Leading Causes of Death and Numbers of Deaths, by Sex, Race, and Hispanic Origin, 1980 and 2005—*Continued*

(Number.)

Sex, race, Hispanic origin, and rank order	1980		2005	
	Cause of death[1]	Deaths	Cause of death[1]	Deaths
American Indian or Alaska Native Male				
	All Causes	4,193	All Causes	7,607
1	Unintentional injuries	946	Diseases of heart	1,471
2	Diseases of heart	917	Malignant neoplasms	1,297
3	Malignant neoplasms	408	Unintentional injuries	1,118
4	Chronic liver disease and cirrhosis	239	Diabetes mellitus	412
5	Cerebrovascular diseases	163	Chronic liver disease and cirrhosis	348
6	Homicide	162	Suicide	313
7	Pneumonia and influenza	148	Chronic lower respiratory diseases	257
8	Suicide	147	Cerebrovascular diseases	249
9	Certain conditions originating in the perinatal period	107	Homicide	193
10	Diabetes mellitus	86	Influenza and pneumonia	180
Asian or Pacific Islander Male				
	All Causes	6,809	All Causes	22,808
1	Diseases of heart	2,174	Malignant neoplasms	5,921
2	Malignant neoplasms	1,485	Diseases of heart	5,703
3	Unintentional injuries	556	Cerebrovascular diseases	1,624
4	Cerebrovascular diseases	521	Unintentional injuries	1,328
5	Pneumonia and influenza	227	Chronic lower respiratory diseases	803
6	Suicide	159	Diabetes mellitus	768
7	Chronic obstructive pulmonary diseases	158	Influenza and pneumonia	718
8	Homicide	151	Suicide	495
9	Certain conditions originating in the perinatal period	128	Nephritis, nephrotic syndrome, and nephrosis	381
10	Diabetes mellitus	103	Homicide	314
Hispanic or Latino Male[2]				
	All Causes	—	All Causes	73,788
1	—	—	Diseases of heart	15,900
2	—	—	Malignant neoplasms	13,896
3	—	—	Unintentional injuries	8,612
4	—	—	Diabetes mellitus	3,296
5	—	—	Cerebrovascular diseases	3,188
6	—	—	Homicide	3,008
7	—	—	Chronic liver disease and cirrhosis	2,561
8	—	—	Suicide	1,841
9	—	—	Chronic lower respiratory diseases	1,839
10	—	—	Certain conditions originating in the perinatal period	1,612
White Female				
	All Causes	804,729	All Causes	1,069,945
1	Diseases of heart	318,668	Diseases of heart	285,472
2	Malignant neoplasms	169,974	Malignant neoplasms	231,654
3	Cerebrovascular diseases	88,639	Cerebrovascular diseases	74,674
4	Unintentional injuries	27,159	Chronic lower respiratory diseases	63,973
5	Pneumonia and influenza	24,559	Alzheimer's disease	47,201
6	Diabetes mellitus	16,743	Unintentional injuries	35,806
7	Atherosclerosis	16,526	Influenza and pneumonia	31,115
8	Chronic obstructive pulmonary diseases	16,398	Diabetes mellitus	30,127
9	Chronic liver disease and cirrhosis	8,833	Nephritis, nephrotic syndrome, and nephrosis	17,669
10	Certain conditions originating in the perinatal period	6,512	Septicemia	15,022
Black or African American Female				
	All Causes	102,997	All Causes	143,700
1	Diseases of heart	35,079	Diseases of heart	37,816
2	Malignant neoplasms	19,176	Malignant neoplasms	30,439
3	Cerebrovascular diseases	10,941	Cerebrovascular diseases	10,022
4	Unintentional injuries	3,779	Diabetes mellitus	7,240
5	Diabetes mellitus	3,534	Nephritis, nephrotic syndrome, and nephrosis	4,430
6	Certain conditions originating in the perinatal period	3,092	Unintentional injuries	4,323
7	Pneumonia and influenza	2,262	Chronic lower respiratory diseases	3,765
8	Homicide	1,898	Septicemia	3,435
9	Chronic liver disease and cirrhosis	1,770	Alzheimer's disease	3,328
10	Nephritis, nephrotic syndrome, and nephrosis	1,722	Influenza and pneumonia	3,051

— = Data not available

[1]Based on codes from the *International Classification of Diseases, Ninth Revision* in 1980 and *International Classification of Diseases, Tenth Revision* in 2002.

[2]Persons of Hispanic origin may be of any race.

Table B-17. Leading Causes of Death and Numbers of Deaths, by Sex, Race, and Hispanic Origin, 1980 and 2005—*Continued*

(Number.)

Sex, race, Hispanic origin, and rank order	1980		2005	
	Cause of death[1]	Deaths	Cause of death[1]	Deaths
American Indian or Alaska Native Female				
	All Causes	2,730	All Causes	6,311
1	Diseases of heart	577	Diseases of heart	1,188
2	Malignant neoplasms	362	Malignant neoplasms	1,168
3	Unintentional injuries	344	Unintentional injuries	508
4	Chronic liver disease and cirrhosis	171	Diabetes mellitus	406
5	Cerebrovascular diseases	159	Cerebrovascular diseases	378
6	Diabetes mellitus	124	Chronic lower respiratory diseases	261
7	Pneumonia and influenza	109	Chronic liver disease and cirrhosis	248
8	Certain conditions originating in the perinatal period	92	Influenza and pneumonia	174
9	Nephritis, nephrotic syndrome, and nephrosis	56	Nephritis, nephrotic syndrome, and nephrosis	160
10	Homicide	55	Alzheimer's disease	125
Asian or Pacific Islander Female				
	All Causes	4,262	All Causes	20,386
1	Diseases of heart	1,091	Malignant neoplasms	5,629
2	Malignant neoplasms	1,037	Diseases of heart	4,774
3	Cerebrovascular diseases	507	Cerebrovascular diseases	1,919
4	Unintentional injuries	254	Diabetes mellitus	808
5	Diabetes mellitus	124	Unintentional injuries	797
6	Certain conditions originating in the perinatal period	118	Influenza and pneumonia	609
7	Pneumonia and influenza	115	Chronic lower respiratory diseases	499
8	Congenital anomalies	104	Alzheimer's disease	386
9	Suicide	90	Nephritis, nephrotic syndrome, and nephrosis	374
10	Homicide	60	Essential (primary) hypertension and hypertensive renal disease	326
Hispanic or Latina Female[2]				
		—	All Causes	57,373
1	—	—	Diseases of heart	13,655
2	—	—	Malignant neoplasms	12,260
3	—	—	Cerebrovascular diseases	3,642
4	—	—	Diabetes mellitus	3,369
5	—	—	Unintentional injuries	2,852
6	—	—	Chronic lower respiratory diseases	1,618
7	—	—	Influenza and pneumonia	1,579
8	—	—	Alzheimer's disease	1,437
9	—	—	Certain conditions originating in the perinatal period	1,204
10	—	—	Nephritis, nephrotic syndrome, and nephrosis	1,143

—— = Data not available

[1]Based on codes from the *International Classification of Diseases, Ninth Revision* in 1980 and *International Classification of Diseases, Tenth Revision* in 2002.

[2]Persons of Hispanic origin may be of any race.

Table B-18. Number of Deaths from 113 Selected Causes by Age, 2005

(Number.)

Cause of death[1]	All ages	Under 1 year	1–4 years	5–14 years	15–24 years	25–34 years	35–44 years	45–54 years	55–64 years	65–74 years	75–84 years	85 years and over	Not stated
ALL CAUSES	2,448,017	28,440	4,756	6,602	34,234	41,925	84,785	183,530	275,301	398,355	686,665	703,169	255
Salmonella infections (A01-A02)	30	-	-	-	1	2	2	2	6	3	9	5	-
Shigellosis and amebiasis (A03, A06)	10	-	1	2	-	-	-	1	2	2	2	-	-
Certain other intestinal infections (A04, A07-A09)	5,667	10	12	10	3	11	32	104	253	829	2,070	2,333	-
Tuberculosis (A16-A19)	648	2	3	1	18	21	38	79	91	116	165	114	-
Respiratory tuberculosis (A16)	480	2	1	-	9	11	28	62	62	81	129	95	-
Other tuberculosis (A17-A19)	168	-	2	1	9	10	10	17	29	35	36	19	-
Whooping cough (A37)	31	28	-	1	-	-	-	-	-	1	1	-	-
Scarlet fever and erysipelas (A38, A46)	3	-	1	-	-	-	-	-	-	-	-	2	-
Meningococcal infection (A39)	123	17	11	7	29	8	8	18	10	4	6	5	-
Septicemia (A40-A41)	34,136	302	85	81	148	311	840	2,211	3,912	6,073	10,626	9,544	3
Syphilis (A50-A53)	47	-	-	1	-	4	5	6	8	4	13	6	-
Acute poliomyelitis (A80)	-	-	-	-	-	-	-	-	-	-	-	-	-
Arthropod-borne viral encephalitis (A83-A84, A85.2)	6	-	1	1	-	1	-	-	2	-	1	-	-
Measles (B05)	1	-	1	-	-	-	-	-	-	-	-	-	-
Viral hepatitis (B15-B19)	5,529	-	-	1	14	61	509	2,314	1,377	648	482	123	-
Human immunodeficiency virus (HIV) disease (B20-B24)	12,543	2	2	13	159	1,318	4,363	4,516	1,612	438	104	15	1
Malaria (B50-B54)	6	-	-	-	2	1	1	1	-	1	-	-	-
Other and unspecified infectious and parasitic diseases and their sequelae (A00, A05, A20-A36, A42-A44 ,A48-A49, A54-A79, A81-A82, A85.0-A85.1, A85.8, A86-B04, B06-B09, B25-B49, B55-B99)	7,727	169	63	64	86	130	403	1,364	1,273	1,309	1,785	1,081	-
Malignant neoplasms (C00-C97)	559,312	75	377	1,000	1,717	3,601	14,566	50,405	99,240	138,446	166,421	83,455	9
Malignant neoplasms of lip, oral cavity and pharynx (C00-C14)	7,773	-	1	2	24	54	258	1,123	1,936	1,835	1,673	867	-
Malignant neoplasm of esophagus (C15)	13,499	-	-	1	3	35	316	1,510	3,100	3,682	3,581	1,271	-
Malignant neoplasm of stomach (C16)	11,514	-	-	-	20	115	448	1,103	1,783	2,615	3,470	1,960	-
Malignant neoplasms of colon, rectum and anus (C18-C21)	53,252	1	-	4	47	305	1,297	4,343	8,153	11,792	16,254	11,054	2
Malignant neoplasms of liver and intrahepatic bile ducts (C22)	16,076	8	21	16	30	89	380	2,515	3,438	3,747	4,176	1,655	1
Malignant neoplasm of pancreas (C25)	32,760	-	-	2	3	64	565	2,744	5,984	8,288	10,147	4,962	1
Malignant neoplasm of larynx (C32)	3,797	-	-	-	-	3	64	423	916	1,156	914	320	1
Malignant neoplasms of trachea, bronchus and lung (C33-C34)	159,292	-	3	1	16	133	2,323	12,624	31,363	48,390	49,032	15,404	3
Malignant melanoma of skin (C43)	8,345	-	1	3	40	216	524	1,197	1,575	1,748	2,031	1,010	-
Malignant neoplasm of breast (C50)	41,491	1	-	-	12	356	2,497	6,232	8,646	8,113	9,382	6,252	-
Malignant neoplasm of cervix uteri (C53)	3,924	-	-	-	14	168	622	958	796	575	518	273	-
Malignant neoplasms of corpus uteri and uterus, part unspecified (C54-C55)	7,096	-	-	-	4	22	146	568	1,468	1,808	1,955	1,125	-
Malignant neoplasm of ovary (C56)	14,787	-	-	3	18	83	413	1,682	3,048	3,569	4,031	1,940	-
Malignant neoplasm of prostate (C61)	28,905	-	1	-	1	3	24	395	2,154	5,764	11,666	8,897	-
Malignant neoplasms of kidney and renal pelvis (C64-C65)	12,517	8	16	30	17	49	294	1,277	2,514	3,143	3,510	1,659	-
Malignant neoplasm of bladder (C67)	13,253	-	-	-	-	15	122	523	1,482	2,772	4,859	3,480	-
Malignant neoplasms of meninges, brain and other parts of central nervous system (C70-C72)	13,152	18	84	324	234	379	948	1,943	2,839	2,943	2,633	807	-
Malignant neoplasms of lymphoid, hematopoietic and related tissue (C81-C96)	55,028	24	128	335	655	811	1,498	3,687	7,623	12,487	18,109	9,671	-
Hodgkin's disease (C81)	1,272	-	-	11	61	116	118	168	184	205	304	105	-
Non-Hodgkin's lymphoma (C82-C85)	20,873	1	6	48	127	222	566	1,410	2,925	4,626	7,111	3,831	-
Leukemia (C91-C95)	21,623	22	120	275	466	461	680	1,419	2,662	4,673	6,832	4,013	-
Multiple myeloma and immunoproliferative neoplasms (C88, C90)	11,200	-	-	-	1	11	131	688	1,842	2,969	3,846	1,712	-
Other and unspecified malignant neoplasms of lymphoid, hematopoietic and related tissue (C96)	60	1	2	1	-	1	3	2	10	14	16	10	-
All other and unspecified malignant neoplasms (C17, C23-C24, C26-C31, C37-C41 ,C44-C49, C51-C52, C57-C60, C62-C63, C66, C68-C69, C73-C80, C97)	62,851	15	122	279	579	701	1,827	5,558	10,422	14,019	18,480	10,848	1
In situ neoplasms, benign neoplasms and neoplasms of uncertain or unknown behavior (D00-D48)	13,710	59	52	76	93	162	368	729	1,318	2,350	4,594	3,909	-
Anemias (D50-D64)	4,624	19	23	26	103	157	189	253	304	494	1,193	1,863	-
Diabetes mellitus (E10-E14)	75,119	1	2	38	202	617	2,045	5,691	11,301	16,183	23,136	15,903	-
Nutritional deficiencies (E40-E64)	3,183	5	3	4	3	19	38	118	157	353	915	1,568	-
Malnutrition (E40-E46)	3,003	5	2	3	3	18	36	113	149	333	866	1,475	-
Other nutritional deficiencies (E50-E64)	180	-	1	1	-	1	2	5	8	20	49	93	-
Meningitis (G00, G03)	669	57	32	26	28	32	74	118	106	74	76	45	1
Parkinson's disease (G20-G21)	19,544	-	-	-	3	4	7	66	434	2,414	9,294	7,322	-
Alzheimer's disease (G30)	71,599	-	-	-	-	2	10	80	648	3,813	23,139	43,906	1

… = Not applicable.
- = Quantity zero.
[1]Based on codes from the *International Classification of Diseases, Tenth Revision* (1992), except where (*) precedes the cause of death code.

Table B-18. Number of Deaths from 113 Selected Causes by Age, 2005—*Continued*

(Number.)

Cause of death[1]	All ages	Under 1 year	1–4 years	5–14 years	15–24 years	25–34 years	35–44 years	45–54 years	55–64 years	65–74 years	75–84 years	85 years and over	Not stated
Major cardiovascular diseases (I00-I78)	856,030	503	217	367	1,391	4,041	15,852	46,928	79,896	124,366	256,362	326,066	41
Diseases of heart (I00-I09, I11, I13, I20-I51)	652,091	358	151	252	1,119	3,249	12,688	38,103	65,208	96,729	190,693	243,504	37
Acute rheumatic fever and chronic rheumatic heart diseases (I00-I09)	3,365	1	1	4	9	27	82	191	354	613	1,114	969	-
Hypertensive heart disease (I11)	29,282	2	-	3	36	328	1,368	3,293	3,954	3,806	6,370	10,119	3
Hypertensive heart and renal disease (I13)	3,172	-	-	-	5	33	83	189	240	426	908	1,288	-
Ischemic heart diseases (I20-I25)	445,687	13	7	14	151	1,014	6,860	25,310	46,799	70,121	134,435	160,935	28
Acute myocardial infarction (I21-I22)	151,004	11	2	7	68	392	2,734	10,070	18,553	26,674	45,449	47,041	3
Other acute ischemic heart diseases (I24)	3,565	-	1	1	3	11	82	351	515	606	935	1,060	-
Other forms of chronic ischemic heart disease (I20, I25)	291,118	2	4	6	80	611	4,044	14,889	27,731	42,841	88,051	112,834	25
Atherosclerotic cardiovascular disease, so described (I25.0)	62,799	1	-	-	16	182	1,420	5,884	9,565	10,246	16,286	19,182	17
All other forms of chronic ischemic heart disease (I20, I25.1-I25.9)	228,319	1	4	6	64	429	2,624	9,005	18,166	32,595	71,765	93,652	8
Other heart diseases (I26-I51)	170,585	342	143	231	918	1,847	4,295	9,120	13,861	21,763	47,866	70,193	6
Acute and subacute endocarditis (I33)	1,209	4	-	3	8	28	78	173	198	234	328	155	-
Diseases of pericardium and acute myocarditis (I30-I31, I40)	864	21	17	30	34	53	84	132	110	132	155	96	-
Heart failure (I50)	58,933	27	6	11	42	94	316	1,087	2,610	5,888	17,331	31,521	-
All other forms of heart disease (I26-I28, I34-I38, I42-I49, I51)	109,579	290	120	187	834	1,672	3,817	7,728	10,943	15,509	30,052	38,421	6
Essential (primary) hypertension and hypertensive renal disease (I10, I12)	24,902	2	-	3	22	84	406	1,166	1,954	3,306	7,256	10,703	-
Cerebrovascular diseases (I60-I69)	143,579	126	62	95	196	546	2,260	6,381	10,028	18,839	46,859	58,183	4
Atherosclerosis (I70)	11,841	-	1	-	2	6	31	193	440	1,008	3,387	6,773	-
Other diseases of circulatory system (I71-I78)	23,617	17	3	17	52	156	467	1,085	2,266	4,484	8,167	6,903	-
Aortic aneurysm and dissection (I71)	13,843	1	-	4	34	114	329	758	1,456	2,870	4,971	3,306	-
Other diseases of arteries, arterioles and capillaries (I72-I78)	9,774	16	3	13	18	42	138	327	810	1,614	3,196	3,597	-
Other disorders of circulatory system (I80-I99)	4,813	26	6	5	36	132	332	620	641	713	1,128	1,174	-
Influenza and pneumonia (J10-J18)	63,001	265	110	106	172	354	934	2,183	3,422	6,623	18,563	30,267	2
Influenza (J10-J11)	1,812	19	19	20	12	11	19	45	66	137	482	982	-
Pneumonia (J12-J18)	61,189	246	91	86	160	343	915	2,138	3,356	6,486	18,081	29,285	2
Other acute lower respiratory infections (J20-J22)	404	51	16	4	4	6	15	15	19	26	78	170	-
Acute bronchitis and bronchiolitis (J20-J21)	283	50	14	4	3	3	13	15	13	17	53	98	-
Unspecified acute lower respiratory infection (J22)	121	1	2	-	1	3	2	-	6	9	25	72	-
Chronic lower respiratory diseases (J40-J47)	130,933	33	56	104	148	258	890	3,977	12,747	29,910	50,333	32,473	4
Bronchitis, chronic and unspecified (J40-J42)	866	25	12	3	5	6	15	27	73	119	205	376	-
Emphysema (J43)	14,002	2	1	-	-	8	77	444	1,677	3,749	5,400	2,643	1
Asthma (J45-J46)	3,884	4	37	97	131	207	369	595	520	475	709	740	-
Other chronic lower respiratory diseases (J44, J47)	112,181	2	6	4	12	37	429	2,911	10,477	25,567	44,019	28,714	3
Pneumoconioses and chemical effects (J60-J66, J68)	1,007	-	1	1	-	-	3	22	69	175	447	288	1
Pneumonitis due to solids and liquids (J69)	17,219	17	8	13	43	66	172	476	833	1,741	5,558	8,352	-
Other diseases of respiratory system (J00-J06, J30-J39, J67, J70-J98)	27,056	303	94	61	110	181	474	1,360	2,676	5,373	9,466	6,955	3
Peptic ulcer (K25-K28)	3,478	2	1	1	8	25	108	281	376	544	1,040	1,092	-
Diseases of appendix (K35-K38)	439	2	4	12	9	9	19	33	57	76	110	108	-
Hernia (K40-K46)	1,639	43	4	2	2	5	39	83	181	210	454	616	-
Chronic liver disease and cirrhosis (K70, K73-K74)	27,530	10	1	2	23	311	2,688	7,517	7,126	5,066	3,781	1,002	3
Alcoholic liver disease (K70)	12,928	-	-	-	7	217	1,806	4,490	3,721	1,844	747	94	2
Other chronic liver disease and cirrhosis (K73-K74)	14,602	10	1	2	16	94	882	3,027	3,405	3,222	3,034	908	1
Cholelithiasis and other disorders of gallbladder (K80-K82)	3,072	-	-	4	8	16	42	113	217	448	1,055	1,169	-
Nephritis, nephrotic syndrome and nephrosis (N00-N07, N17-N19, N25-N27)	43,901	159	16	23	91	285	742	2,028	4,141	7,320	14,403	14,693	-
Acute and rapidly progressive nephritic and nephrotic syndrome (N00-N01, N04)	137	6	2	2	-	3	4	6	15	17	43	39	-
Chronic glomerulonephritis, nephritis and nephropathy not specified as acute or chronic, and renal sclerosis unspecified (N02-N03, N05-N07, N26)	867	2	1	2	11	21	30	48	93	132	252	275	-
Renal failure (N17-N19)	42,868	151	13	19	79	261	705	1,973	4,025	7,165	14,102	14,375	-
Other disorders of kidney (N25, N27)	29	-	-	-	1	-	3	1	8	6	6	4	-
Infections of kidney (N10-N12, N13.6, N15.1)	767	6	4	2	9	14	26	51	53	100	239	263	-
Hyperplasia of prostate (N40)	525	-	-	-	-	-	-	-	10	52	171	292	-
Inflammatory diseases of female pelvic organs (N70-N76)	120	-	-	-	1	5	7	13	9	23	33	29	-
Pregnancy, childbirth and the puerperium (O00-O99)	760	...	...	-	183	312	207	54	3	1	-	-	-
Pregnancy with abortive outcome (O00-O07)	33	...	...	-	6	14	11	2	-	-	-	-	-
Other complications of pregnancy, childbirth and the puerperium (O10-O99)	727	...	...	-	177	298	196	52	3	1	-	-	-
Certain conditions originating in the perinatal period (P00-P96)	14,549	14,423	58	26	18	6	6	6	2	-	1	-	3
Congenital malformations, deformations and chromosomal abnormalities (Q00-Q99)	10,410	5,552	522	396	504	436	517	693	716	338	408	327	1

... = Not applicable.

- = Quantity zero.

[1]Based on codes from the *International Classification of Diseases, Tenth Revision* (1992), except where (*) precedes the cause of death code.

Table B-18. Number of Deaths from 113 Selected Causes by Age, 2005—*Continued*

(Number.)

Cause of death[1]	All ages	Under 1 year	1–4 years	5–14 years	15–24 years	25–34 years	35–44 years	45–54 years	55–64 years	65–74 years	75–84 years	85 years and over	Not stated
Symptoms, signs and abnormal clinical and laboratory findings, not elsewhere classified (R00-R99)	31,999	3,589	233	155	775	1,178	2,052	2,831	2,199	2,390	5,088	11,436	73
All other diseases (residual)	217,632	1,198	612	857	2,060	3,159	8,118	17,122	21,108	27,236	56,700	79,449	13
Accidents (unintentional injuries) (V01-X59, Y85-Y86)	117,809	1,083	1,664	2,415	15,753	13,997	16,919	18,339	10,853	8,632	13,854	14,243	57
Transport accidents (V01-V99, Y85)	48,441	147	646	1,547	11,288	7,638	7,295	7,101	4,918	3,353	3,168	1,329	11
Motor vehicle accidents (V02-V04, V09.0, V09.2, V12-V14, V19.0-V19.2, V19.4-V19.6, V20-V79, V80.3-V80.5, V81.0-V81.1, V82.0-V82.1, V83-V86, V87.0-V87.8, V88.0-V88.8, V89.0,V89.2)	45,343	146	617	1,447	10,908	7,239	6,748	6,397	4,454	3,110	2,991	1,280	6
Other land transport accidents (V01, V05-V06, V09.1, V09.3-V09.9, V10-V11, V15-V18, V19.3, V19.8-V19.9, V80.0-V80.2, V80.6-V80.9, V81.2-V81.9, V82.2-V82.9, V87.9, V88.9, V89.1,V89.3, V89.9)	1,241	1	27	50	192	162	210	267	138	81	84	25	4
Water, air and space, and other and unspecified transport accidents and their sequelae (V90-V99, Y85)	1,857	-	2	50	188	237	337	437	326	162	93	24	1
Nontransport accidents (W00-X59, Y86)	69,368	936	1,018	868	4,465	6,359	9,624	11,238	5,935	5,279	10,686	12,914	46
Falls (W00-W19)	19,656	16	34	32	236	295	607	1,181	1,451	2,319	5,957	7,526	2
Accidental discharge of firearms (W32-W34)	789	1	22	52	203	130	114	108	67	44	33	15	-
Accidental drowning and submersion (W65-W74)	3,582	64	493	253	649	385	497	492	266	193	180	92	18
Accidental exposure to smoke, fire and flames (X00-X09)	3,197	34	204	222	168	224	334	497	398	390	468	254	4
Accidental poisoning and exposure to noxious substances (X40-X49)	23,618	20	21	51	2,484	4,386	6,729	6,983	2,007	435	317	179	6
Other and unspecified nontransport accidents and their sequelae (W20-W31, W35-W64, W75-W99 ,X10-X39, X50-X59, Y86)	18,526	801	244	258	725	939	1,343	1,977	1,746	1,898	3,731	4,848	16
Intentional self-harm (suicide) (*U03, X60-X84, Y87.0)	32,637	...	...	272	4,212	4,990	6,550	6,991	4,210	2,344	2,200	860	8
Intentional self-harm (suicide) by discharge of firearms (X72-X74)	17,002	...	...	84	1,962	2,269	2,855	3,472	2,470	1,669	1,649	571	1
Intentional self-harm (suicide) by other and unspecified means and their sequelae (*U03, X60-X71, X75-X84, Y87.0)	15,635	...	...	188	2,250	2,721	3,695	3,519	1,740	675	551	289	7
Assault (homicide) (*U01-*U02, X85-Y09, Y87.1)	18,124	306	375	341	5,466	4,752	3,109	2,060	862	440	283	109	21
Assault (homicide) by discharge of firearms (*U01.4, X93-X95)	12,352	6	37	187	4,499	3,780	2,010	1,097	405	201	97	24	9
Assault (homicide) by other and unspecified means and their sequelae (*U01.0-*U01.3, *U01.5-*U01.9, *U02, X85-X92, X96-Y09, Y87.1)	5,772	300	338	154	967	972	1,099	963	457	239	186	85	12
Legal intervention (Y35,Y89.0)	414	-	-	1	83	110	124	56	30	7	3	-	-
Events of undetermined intent (Y10-Y34, Y87.2, Y89.9)	4,742	104	69	64	484	742	1,194	1,314	424	157	106	74	10
Discharge of firearms, undetermined intent (Y22-Y24)	221	-	3	12	77	35	28	28	23	10	3	2	-
Other and unspecified events of undetermined intent and their sequelae (Y10-Y21,Y25-Y34, Y87.2,Y89.9)	4,521	104	66	52	407	707	1,166	1,286	401	147	103	72	10
Operations of war and their sequelae (Y36, Y89.1)	27	-	-	-	3	3	4	1	3	2	10	1	-
Complications of medical and surgical care (Y40-Y84, Y88)	2,653	19	16	16	29	70	144	287	364	487	759	462	-

... = Not applicable

- = Quantity zero.

[1]Based on codes from the *International Classification of Diseases, Tenth Revision* (1992), except where (*) precedes the cause of death code.

NOTE: Complete confirmation of deaths from selected causes of death, considered to be of public health concern, were not provided by the following states–Alabama, California, Connecticut, Florida, Illinois, Indiana, Kentucky, Louisiana, Maryland, Michigan, Missouri, Montana, Nevada, New Hampshire, New Jersey, New York, North Carolina, Ohio, Oklahoma, Pennsylvania, Rhode Island, Texas, Utah, Virginia, Washington, and West Virginia.

Table B-18A. Deaths, Death Rates, and Age-Adjusted Rates for 113 Selected Causes, Injury by Firearms, Drug-Induced Deaths, Alcohol-Induced Deaths, and Injury at Work, Final 2005 and Preliminary 2006

(Number, rate per 100,000 population.)

Cause of death[1]	2005			2006		
	Number	Rate	Age-adjusted rate	Number	Rate	Age-adjusted rate
ALL CAUSES	2,448,017	825.9	798.8	2,425,901	810.3	776.4
Salmonella infections (A01-A02)	30	0.0	0	33	0.0	0.0
Shigellosis and amebiasis (A03, A06)	10	*	*	4	*	*
Certain other intestinal infections (A04, A07-A09)	5,667	1.9	1.8	6,671	2.2	2.1
Tuberculosis (A16-A19)	648	0.2	0.2	644	0.2	0.2
Respiratory tuberculosis (A16)	480	0.2	0.1	485	0.2	0.1
Other tuberculosis (A17-A19)	168	0.1	0	159	0.1	0.1
Whooping cough (A37)	31	0.0	0	9	*	*
Scarlet fever and erysipelas (A38, A46)	3	*	*	2	*	*
Meningococcal infection (A39)	123	0.0	0	103	0.0	0.0
Septicemia (A40-A41)	34,136	11.5	11.2	34,031	11.4	10.9
Syphilis (A50-A53)	47	0.0	0	35	0.0	0.0
Acute poliomyelitis (A80)	-	*	*	-	*	*
Arthropod-borne viral encephalitis (A83-A84, A85.2)	6	*	*	5	*	*
Measles (B05)	1	*	*	-	*	*
Viral hepatitis (B15-B19)	5,529	1.9	1.8	6,021	2.0	1.9
Human immunodeficiency virus (HIV) disease (B20-B24)	12,543	4.2	4.2	12,045	4.0	4.0
Malaria (B50-B54)	6	*	*	9	*	*
Other and unspecified infectious and parasitic diseases and their sequelae (A00, A05, A20-A36, A42-A44, A48-A49, A54-A79, A81-A82, A85.0-A85.1, A85.8, A86-B04, B06-B09, B25-B49, B55-B99)	7,727	2.6	2.5	7,110	2.4	2.3
Malignant neoplasms (C00-C97)	559,312	188.7	183.8	560,102	187.1	180.8
Malignant neoplasms of lip, oral cavity and pharynx (C00-C14)	7,773	2.6	2.5	7,727	2.6	2.5
Malignant neoplasm of esophagus (C15)	13,499	4.6	4.4	13,674	4.6	4.4
Malignant neoplasm of stomach (C16)	11,514	3.9	3.8	11,354	3.8	3.7
Malignant neoplasms of colon, rectum and anus (C18-C21)	53,252	18.0	17.5	53,465	17.9	17.2
Malignant neoplasms of liver and intrahepatic bile ducts (C22)	16,076	5.4	5.2	16,447	5.5	5.2
Malignant neoplasm of pancreas (C25)	32,760	11.1	10.8	33,437	11.2	10.8
Malignant neoplasm of larynx (C32)	3,797	1.3	1.2	3,824	1.3	1.2
Malignant neoplasms of trachea, bronchus and lung (C33-C34)	159,292	53.7	52.6	158,525	52.9	51.5
Malignant melanoma of skin (C43)	8,345	2.8	2.7	8,487	2.8	2.7
Malignant neoplasm of breast (C50)	41,491	14.0	13.5	41,223	13.8	13.2
Malignant neoplasm of cervix uteri (C53)	3,924	1.3	1.3	3,926	1.3	1.3
Malignant neoplasms of corpus uteri and uterus, part unspecified (C54-C55)	7,096	2.4	2.3	7,374	2.5	2.4
Malignant neoplasm of ovary (C56)	14,787	5.0	4.8	14,906	5.0	4.8
Malignant neoplasm of prostate (C61)	28,905	9.8	9.5	28,331	9.5	9.1
Malignant neoplasms of kidney and renal pelvis (C64-C65)	12,517	4.2	4.1	12,376	4.1	4.0
Malignant neoplasm of bladder (C67)	13,253	4.5	4.3	13,492	4.5	4.3
Malignant neoplasms of meninges, brain and other parts of central nervous system (C70-C72)	13,152	4.4	4.3	12,853	4.3	4.2
Malignant neoplasms of lymphoid, hematopoietic and related tissue (C81-C96)	55,028	18.6	18.2	55,241	18.5	17.9
Hodgkin's disease (C81)	1,272	0.4	0.4	1,331	0.4	0.4
Non-Hodgkin's lymphoma (C82-C85)	20,873	7.0	6.9	20,663	6.9	6.7
Leukemia (C91-C95)	21,623	7.3	7.1	22,022	7.4	7.2
Multiple myeloma and immunoproliferative neoplasms (C88, C90)	11,200	3.8	3.7	11,153	3.7	3.6
Other and unspecified malignant neoplasms of lymphoid, hematopoietic and related tissue (C96)	60	0.0	0.0	71	0.0	0.0
All other and unspecified malignant neoplasms (C17, C23-C24, C26-C31, C37-C41, C44-C49, C51-C52, C57-C60, C62-C63, C66, C68-C69, C73-C80, C97)	62,851	21.2	20.6	63,441	21.2	20.4
In situ neoplasms, benign neoplasms and neoplasms of uncertain or unknown behavior (D00-D48)	13,710	4.6	4.5	14,101	4.7	4.5
Anemias (D50-D64)	4,624	1.6	1.5	4,007	1.3	1.3
Diabetes mellitus (E10-E14)	75,119	25.3	24.6	72,507	24.2	23.3
Nutritional deficiencies (E40-E64)	3,183	1.1	1.0	2,568	0.9	0.8
Malnutrition (E40-E46)	3,003	1.0	1.0	2,383	0.8	0.7
Other nutritional deficiencies (E50-E64)	180	0.1	0.1	185	0.1	0.1
Meningitis (G00, G03)	669	0.2	0.2	632	0.2	0.2
Parkinson's disease (G20-G21)	19,544	6.6	6.4	19,660	6.6	6.3
Alzheimer's disease (G30)	71,599	24.2	22.9	72,914	24.4	22.7
Major cardiovascular diseases (I00-I78)	856,030	288.8	277.3	821,494	274.4	260.5
Diseases of heart (I00-I09, I11, I13, I20-I51)	652,091	220.0	211.1	629,191	210.2	199.4
Acute rheumatic fever and chronic rheumatic heart diseases (I00-I09)	3,365	1.1	1.1	3,257	1.1	1.0
Hypertensive heart disease (I11)	29,282	9.9	9.4	29,217	9.8	9.2
Hypertensive heart and renal disease (I13)	3,172	1.1	1.0	2,919	1.0	0.9
Ischemic heart diseases (I20-I25)	445,687	150.4	144.4	424,892	141.9	134.8
Acute myocardial infarction (I21-I22)	151,004	50.9	49.1	141,961	47.4	45.2
Other acute ischemic heart diseases (I24)	3,565	1.2	1.2	3,938	1.3	1.2
Other forms of chronic ischemic heart disease (I20, I25)	291,118	98.2	94.2	278,988	93.2	88.3
Atherosclerotic cardiovascular disease, so described (I25.0)	62,799	21.2	20.3	59,734	20.0	18.9
All other forms of chronic ischemic heart disease (I20, I25.1-I25.9)	228,319	77.0	73.9	219,254	73.2	69.5

* = Figure does not meet standards of reliability or precision.
- = Quantity zero.
0.0 = Quantity more than zero but less than 0.05.
[1]Based on codes from the *International Classification of Diseases, Tenth Revision* (1992), except where (*) precedes the cause of death code.

Table B-18A. Deaths, Death Rates, and Age-Adjusted Rates for 113 Selected Causes, Injury by Firearms, Drug-Induced Deaths, Alcohol-Induced Deaths, and Injury at Work, Final 2005 and Preliminary 2006— *Continued*

(Number, rate per 100,000 population.)

Cause of death[1]	2005			2006		
	Number	Rate	Age-adjusted rate	Number	Rate	Age-adjusted rate
Other heart diseases (I26-I51)	170,585	57.6	55.2	168,906	56.4	53.4
Acute and subacute endocarditis (I33)	1,209	0.4	0.4	1,209	0.4	0.4
Diseases of pericardium and acute myocarditis (I30-I31, I40)	864	0.3	0.3	784	0.3	0.3
Heart failure (I50)	58,933	19.9	18.9	60,315	20.1	18.9
All other forms of heart disease (I26-I28, I34-I38, I42-I49, I51)	109,579	37.0	35.6	106,598	35.6	33.9
Essential hypertension and hypertensive renal disease (I10, I12, I15)[2]	24,902	8.4	8.0	23,985	8.0	7.6
Cerebrovascular diseases (I60-I69)	143,579	48.4	46.6	137,265	45.8	43.6
Atherosclerosis (I70)	11,841	4.0	3.8	8,619	2.9	2.7
Other diseases of circulatory system (I71-I78)	23,617	8.0	7.8	22,435	7.5	7.2
Aortic aneurysm and dissection (I71)	13,843	4.7	4.6	13,178	4.4	4.3
Other diseases of arteries, arterioles and capillaries (I72-I78)	9,774	3.3	3.2	9,258	3.1	2.9
Other disorders of circulatory system (I80-I99)	4,813	1.6	1.6	3,941	1.3	1.3
Influenza and pneumonia (J10-J18)	63,001	21.3	20.3	56,247	18.8	17.7
Influenza (J10-J11)	1,812	0.6	0.6	860	0.3	0.3
Pneumonia (J12-J18)	61,189	2.6	19.7	55,387	18.5	17.5
Other acute lower respiratory infections (J20-J22)	404	0.1	0.1	289	0.1	0.1
Acute bronchitis and bronchiolitis (J20-J21)	283	0.1	0.1	203	0.1	0.1
Unspecified acute lower respiratory infection (J22)	121	0.0	0.0	86	0.0	0.0
Chronic lower respiratory diseases (J40-J47)	130,933	44.2	43.2	124,614	41.6	40.4
Bronchitis, chronic and unspecified (J40-J42)	866	0.3	0.3	740	0.2	0.2
Emphysema (J43)	14,002	4.7	4.6	12,570	4.2	4.1
Asthma (J45-J46)	3,884	1.3	1.3	3,563	1.2	1.1
Other chronic lower respiratory diseases (J44, J47)	112,181	37.8	37.0	107,741	36.0	34.9
Pneumoconioses and chemical effects (J60-J66, J68)	1,007	0.3	0.3	923	0.3	0.3
Pneumonitis due to solids and liquids (J69)	17,279	5.8	5.6	16,961	5.7	5.4
Other diseases of respiratory system (J00-J06, J30-J39, J67, J70-J98)	27,056	9.1	8.9	27,676	9.2	9.0
Peptic ulcer (K25-K28)	3,478	1.2	1.1	3,286	1.1	1.0
Diseases of appendix (K35-K38)	439	0.1	0.1	429	0.1	0.1
Hernia (K40-K46)	1,639	0.6	0.5	1,738	0.6	0.5
Chronic liver disease and cirrhosis (K70, K73-K74)	27,530	9.3	9.0	27,299	9.1	8.7
Alcoholic liver disease (K70)	12,928	4.4	4.2	12,925	4.3	4.1
Other chronic liver disease and cirrhosis (K73-K74)	14,602	4.9	4.7	14,374	4.8	4.6
Cholelithiasis and other disorders of gall bladder (K80-K82)	3,072	1.0	1.0	3,123	1.0	1.0
Nephritis, nephrotic syndrome and nephrosis (N00-N07, N17-N19, N25-N27)	43,901	14.8	14.3	44,791	15.0	14.3
Acute and rapidly progressive nephritic and nephrotic syndrome (N00-N01,N04)	137	0.0	0.0	135	0.0	0.0
Chronic glomerulonephritis, nephrosis and nephropathy not specified as acute or chronic, and renal sclerosis unspecified (N02-N03,N05-N07,N26)	867	0.3	0.3	1,365	0.5	0.4
Renal failure (N17-N19)	42,868	14.5	14.0	43,270	14.5	13.8
Other disorders of kidney (N25, N27)	29	0.0	0.0	20	0.0	0.0
Infections of kidney (N10-N12, N13.6, N15.1)	767	0.3	0.2	661	0.2	0.2
Hyperplasia of prostate (N40)	525	0.2	0.2	518	0.2	0.2
Inflammatory diseases of female pelvic organs (N70-N76)	120	0.0	0.0	113	0.0	0.0
Pregnancy, childbirth and the puerperium (O00-O99)	760	0.3	0.3	787	0.3	0.3
Pregnancy with abortive outcome (O00-O07)	33	0.0	0.0	21	0.0	0.0
Other complications of pregnancy, childbirth and the puerperium (O10-O99)	727	0.2	0.2	765	0.3	0.2
Certain conditions originating in the perinatal period (P00-P96)	14,549	4.9	4.9	14,384	4.8	4.8
Congenital malformations, deformations and chromosomal abnormalities (Q00-Q99)	10,410	3.5	3.5	10,434	3.5	3.4
Symptoms, signs and abnormal clinical and laboratory findings, not elsewhere classified (R00-R99)	31,999	10.8	10.4	40,759	13.6	13.0
All other diseases (residual)	217,632	73.4	70.5	236,614	79.0	74.9
Accidents (unintentional injuries) (V01-X59, Y85-Y86)	117,809	39.7	39.1	117,748	39.3	38.5
Transport accidents (V01-V99, Y85)	48,441	16.3	16.2	47,601	15.9	15.7
Motor vehicle accidents (V02-V04, V09.0, V09.2, V12-V14, V19.0-V19.2, V19.4-V19.6, V20-V79, V80.3-V80.5, V81.0-V81.1, V82.0-V82.1, V83-V86, V87.0-V87.8, V88.0-V88.8, V89.0, V89.2)	45,343	15.3	15.2	44,572	14.9	14.7
Other land transport accidents (V01, V05-V06, V09.1, V09.3-V09.9, V10-V11, V15-V18, V19.3, V19.8-V19.9, V80.0-V80.2, V80.6-V80.9, V81.2-V81.9, V82.2-V82.9, V87.9, V88.9, V89.1, V89.3, V89.9)	1,241	0.4	0.4	1,177	0.4	0.4
Water, air and space, and other and unspecified transport accidents and their sequelae (V90-V99, Y85)	1,857	0.6	0.6	1,852	0.6	0.6
Nontransport accidents (W00-X59, Y86)	69,368	23.4	22.9	70,147	23.4	22.8
Falls (W00-W19)	19,656	6.6	6.4	20,533	6.9	6.5
Accidental discharge of firearms (W32-W34)	789	0.3	0.3	777	0.3	0.2

0.0 = Quantity more than zero but less than 0.05.
[1]Based on codes from the *International Classification of Diseases, Tenth Revision* (1992), except where (*) precedes the cause of death code.
[2]Cause-of-death title has been changed in 2006 to reflect the addition of secondary hypertension.

Table B-18A. Deaths, Death Rates, and Age-Adjusted Rates for 113 Selected Causes, Injury by Firearms, Drug-Induced Deaths, Alcohol-Induced Deaths, and Injury at Work, Final 2005 and Preliminary 2006— *Continued*

(Number, rate per 100,000 population.)

Cause of death[1]	2005			2006		
	Number	Rate	Age-adjusted rate	Number	Rate	Age-adjusted rate
Accidental drowning and submersion (W65-W74)..	3,582	1.2	1.2	3,483	1.2	1.2
Accidental exposure to smoke, fire and flames (X00-X09)...	3,197	1.1	1.1	3,066	1.0	1.0
Accidental poisoning and exposure to noxious substances (X40-X49)	23,618	8.0	7.9	24,702	8.3	8.2
Other and unspecified non-transport accidents and their sequelae (W20-W31, W35-W64, W75-W99, X10-X39, X50-X59, Y86)	18,526	6.3	6.1	17,586	5.9	5.7
Intentional self-harm (suicide) (*U03, X60-X84,Y87.0)...	32,637	11.0	10.9	32,185	10.7	10.6
Intentional self-harm (suicide) by discharge of firearms (X72-X74)	17,002	5.7	5.7	16,650	5.6	5.4
Intentional self-harm (suicide) by other and unspecified means and their sequelae (*U03, X60-X71, X75-X84, Y87.0)...	15,635	5.3	5.2	15,535	5.2	5.1
Assault (homicide) (*U01-*U02, X85-Y09, Y87.1)	18,124	6.1	6.1	18,029	6.0	6.0
Assault (homicide) by discharge of fire arms (*U014, X93-X95)...................................	12,352	4.2	4.2	12,509	4.2	4.2
Assault (homicide) by other and unspecified means and their sequelae (*U010-*U013, *U015-*U019, *U02, X85-X92, X96-Y09, Y87.1)............................	5,772	1.9	1.9	5,520	1.8	1.8
Legal intervention (Y35, Y89.0)	414	0.1	0.1	411	0.1	0.1
Events of undetermined intent (Y10-Y34, Y87.2, Y89.9)	4,742	1.6	1.6	4,706	1.6	1.6
Discharge of fire arms, undetermined intent (Y22-Y24)	221	0.1	0.1	214	0.1	0.1
Other and unspecified events of undetermined intent and their sequelae (Y10-Y21, Y25-Y34, Y87.2, Y89.9)	4,521	1.5	1.5	4,492	1.5	1.5
Operations of war and their sequelae (Y36,Y89.1)	27	0.0	0	30	0.0	0.0
Complications of medical and surgical care (Y40-Y84,Y88)..	2,653	0.9	0.9	2,492	0.8	0.8
Injury by fire arms (*U01.4, W32-W34, X72-X74, X93-X95, Y22-Y24, Y35.0)[3]	30,694	10.4	10.2	30,493	10.2	10.1
Drug-induced deaths (D52.1, D59.0, D59.2, D61.1, D64.2, E06.4, E16.0, E23.1, E24.2 ,E27.3, E66.1, F11.0-F11.5, F11.7-F11.9, F12.0-F12.5, F12.7-F12.9, F13.0-F13.5, F13.7-F13.9, F14.0-F14.5, F14.7-F14.9, F15.0-F15.5, F15.7-F15.9, F16.0-F16.5, F16.7-F16.9, F17.0, F17.3-F17.5, F17.7-F17.9, F18.0-F18.5, F18.7-18.9, F19.0-F19.5, F19.7-F19.9, G21.1, G24.0, G25.1, G25.4, G25.6, G44.4, G62.0, G72.0, I95.2, J70.2-J70.4, K85.3, L10.5, L27.0-L27.1, M10.2, M32.0, M80.4, M81.4, M83.5, M87.1, R50.2 ,R78.1-R78.5, X40-X44, X60-X64, X85, Y10-14)[3,4]..	33,541	11.3	11.3	34,679	11.6	11.5
Alcohol-induced deaths (E24.4, F10, G31.2, G62.1, G72.1, I42.6, K29.2, K70, K85.2, K86.0, R78.0, X45, X65, Y15)[3,5]...	21,634	7.3	7	21,513	7.2	6.8
Injury at work	5,113	2.2	2.1	5,189	2.2	2.2

* = Figure does not meet standards of reliability or precision.

- = Quantity zero.

0.0 = Quantity more than zero but less than 0.05.

[1]Based on codes from the *International Classification of Diseases, Tenth Revision* (1992), except where (*) precedes the cause of death code.

[3]Included in selected categories above.

[4]In 2006, drug-induced acute pancreatitis and drug-induced fever were added to the list of drug-induced codes.

[5]In 2006, alcohol-induced acute pancreatitis was added to the list of alcohol-induced codes.

NOTE: For certain causes of death such as unintentional injuries, homicides, and suicides, preliminary and final data may differ because of the truncated nature of the preliminary file. Data are subject to sampling or random variation.

Table B-19. Death Rates for 113 Selected Causes by Age, 2005

(Rate per 100,000 population in specified group.)

Cause of death[1]	All ages[2]	Under 1 year[3]	1–4 years	5–14 years	15–24 years	25–34 years	35–44 years	45–54 years	55–64 years	65–74 years	75–84 years	85 years and over
ALL CAUSES	825.9	692.5	29.4	16.3	81.4	104.4	193.3	432.0	906.9	2,137.1	5,260.0	13,798.6
Salmonella infections (A01-A02)	0.0	*	*	*	*	*	*	*	*	*	*	*
Shigellosis and amebiasis (A03, A06)	*	*	*	*	*	*	*	*	*	*	*	*
Certain other intestinal infections (A04, A07-A09)	1.9	*	*	*	*	*	0.1	0.2	0.8	4.4	15.9	45.8
Tuberculosis (A16-A19)	0.2	*	*	*	*	0.1	0.1	0.2	0.3	0.6	1.3	2.2
Respiratory tuberculosis (A16)	0.2	*	*	*	*	*	0.1	0.1	0.2	0.4	1.0	1.9
Other tuberculosis (A17-A19)	0.1	*	*	*	*	*	*	*	0.1	0.2	0.3	*
Whooping cough (A37)	0.0	0.7	*	*	*	*	*	*	*	*	*	*
Scarlet fever and erysipelas (A38, A46)	*	*	*	*	*	*	*	*	*	*	*	*
Meningococcal infection (A39)	0.0	*	*	*	0.1	*	*	*	*	*	*	*
Septicemia (A40-A41)	11.5	7.4	0.5	0.2	0.4	0.8	1.9	5.2	12.9	32.6	81.4	187.3
Syphilis (A50-A53)	0.0	*	*	*	*	*	*	*	*	*	*	*
Acute poliomyelitis (A80)	*	*	*	*	*	*	*	*	*	*	*	*
Arthropod-borne viral encephalitis (A83-A84, A85.2)..........	*	*	*	*	*	*	*	*	*	*	*	*
Measles (B05)...	*	*	*	*	*	*	*	*	*	*	*	*
Viral hepatitis (B15-B19)	1.9	*	*	*	*	0.2	1.2	5.4	4.5	3.5	3.7	2.4
Human immunodeficiency virus (HIV) disease (B20-B24)	4.2	*	*	*	0.4	3.3	9.9	10.6	5.3	2.3	0.8	*
Malaria (B50-B54)	*	*	*	*	*	*	*	*	*	*	*	*
Other and unspecified infectious and parasitic diseases and their sequelae (A00, A05, A20-A36, A42-A44, A48-A49, A54-A79, A81-A82, A85.0-A85.1, A85.8, A86-B04, B06-B09, B25-B49, B55-B99)	2.6	4.1	0.4	0.2	0.2	0.3	0.9	3.2	4.2	7.0	13.7	21.2
Malignant neoplasms (C00-C97)......................	188.7	1.8	2.3	2.5	4.1	9.0	33.2	118.6	326.9	742.7	1,274.8	1,637.7
Malignant neoplasms of lip, oral cavity and pharynx (C00-C14)	2.6	*	*	*	0.1	0.1	0.6	2.6	6.4	9.8	12.8	17.0
Malignant neoplasm of esophagus (C15)...........	4.6	*	*	*	*	0.1	0.7	3.6	10.2	19.8	27.4	24.9
Malignant neoplasm of stomach (C16)	3.9	*	*	*	0.0	0.3	1.0	2.6	5.9	14.0	26.6	38.5
Malignant neoplasms of colon, rectum and anus (C18-C21)	18.0	*	*	*	0.1	0.8	3.0	10.2	26.9	63.3	124.5	216.9
Malignant neoplasms of liver and intrahepatic bile ducts (C22)...............	5.4	*	0.1	*	0.1	0.2	0.9	5.9	11.3	20.1	32.0	32.5
Malignant neoplasm of pancreas (C25)...........	11.1	*	*	*	*	0.2	1.3	6.5	19.7	44.5	77.7	97.4
Malignant neoplasm of larynx (C32)	1.3	*	*	*	*	*	0.1	1.0	3.0	6.2	7.0	6.3
Malignant neoplasms of trachea, bronchus and lung (C33-C34)	53.7	*	*	*	*	0.3	5.3	29.7	103.3	259.6	375.6	302.3
Malignant melanoma of skin (C43)...................	2.8	*	*	*	0.1	0.5	1.2	2.8	5.2	9.4	15.6	19.8
Malignant neoplasm of breast (C50).................	14.0	*	*	*	*	0.9	5.7	14.7	28.5	43.5	71.9	122.7
Malignant neoplasm of cervix uteri (C53)	1.3	*	*	*	*	0.4	1.4	2.3	2.6	3.1	4.0	5.4
Malignant neoplasms of corpus uteri and uterus, part unspecified (C54-C55)	2.4	*	*	*	*	0.1	0.3	1.3	4.8	9.7	15.0	22.1
Malignant neoplasm of ovary (C56)..............	5.0	*	*	*	*	0.2	0.9	4.0	10.0	19.1	30.9	38.1
Malignant neoplasm of prostate (C61).............	9.8	*	*	*	*	*	0.1	0.9	7.1	30.9	89.4	174.6
Malignant neoplasms of kidney and renal pelvis (C64-C65)	4.2	*	*	0.1	*	0.1	0.7	3.0	8.3	16.9	26.9	32.6
Malignant neoplasm of bladder (C67)	4.5	*	*	*	*	*	0.3	1.2	4.9	14.9	37.2	68.3
Malignant neoplasms of meninges, brain and other parts of central nervous system (C70-C72)	4.4	*	0.5	0.8	0.6	0.9	2.2	4.6	9.4	15.8	20.2	15.8
Malignant neoplasms of lymphoid, hematopoietic and related tissue (C81-C96)	18.6	0.6	0.8	0.8	1.6	2.0	3.4	8.7	25.1	67.0	138.7	189.8
Hodgkin's disease (C81)	0.4	*	*	*	0.1	0.3	0.3	0.4	0.6	1.1	2.3	2.1
Non-Hodgkin's lymphoma (C82-C85)..........	7.0	*	*	0.1	0.3	0.6	1.3	3.3	9.6	24.8	54.5	75.2
Leukemia (C91-C95)...............................	7.3	0.5	0.7	0.7	1.1	1.1	1.6	3.3	8.8	25.1	52.3	78.7
Multiple myeloma and immunoproliferative neoplasms (C88, C90)...............	3.8	*	*	*	*	*	0.3	1.6	6.1	15.9	29.5	33.6
Other and unspecified malignant neoplasms of lymphoid, hematopoietic and related tissue (C96).....	0.0	*	*	*	*	*	*	*	*	*	*	*
All other and unspecified malignant neoplasms (C17, C23-C24, C26-C31, C37-C41, C44-C49, C51-C52, C57-C60, C62-C63, C66, C68-C69, C73-C80, C97)	21.2	*	0.8	0.7	1.4	1.7	4.2	13.1	34.3	75.2	141.6	212.9
In situ neoplasms, benign neoplasms and neoplasms of uncertain or unknown behavior (D00-D48)......................	4.6	1.4	0.3	0.2	0.2	0.4	0.8	1.7	4.3	12.6	35.2	76.7
Anemias (D50-D64)..	1.6	*	0.1	0.1	0.2	0.4	0.4	0.6	1.0	2.7	9.1	36.6
Diabetes mellitus (E10-E14).............................	25.3	*	*	0.1	0.5	1.5	4.7	13.4	37.2	86.8	177.2	312.1
Nutritional deficiencies (E40-E64)	1.1	*	*	*	*	*	0.1	0.3	0.5	1.9	7.0	30.8
Malnutrition (E40-E46)	1.0	*	*	*	*	*	0.1	0.3	0.5	1.8	6.6	28.9
Other nutritional deficiencies (E50-E64)	0.1	*	*	*	*	*	*	*	*	0.1	0.4	1.8
Meningitis (G00, G03)....................................	0.2	1.4	0.2	0.1	0.1	0.1	0.2	0.3	0.3	0.4	0.6	0.9
Parkinson's disease (G20-G21)	6.6	*	*	*	*	*	*	0.2	1.4	13.0	71.2	143.7
Alzheimer's disease (G30).................................	24.2	*	*	*	*	*	*	0.2	2.1	20.5	177.3	861.6

* = Figure does not meet standards of reliability or precision.
0.0 = Quantity more than zero but less than 0.05.
[1]Based on codes from the *International Classification of Diseases, Tenth Revision* (1992), except where (*) precedes the cause of death code.
[2]Figures for age not stated included in All ages but not distributed among age groups.
[3]Death rates for "Under 1 year" (based on population estimates) differ from infant mortality rates (based on live births).

Table B-19. Death Rates for 113 Selected Causes by Age, 2005—*Continued*

(Rate per 100,000 population in specified group.)

Cause of death[1]	All ages[2]	Under 1 year[3]	1–4 years	5–14 years	15–24 years	25–34 years	35–44 years	45–54 years	55–64 years	65–74 years	75–84 years	85 years and over
Major cardiovascular diseases (I00-I78)	288.8	12.2	1.3	0.9	3.3	10.1	36.1	110.5	263.2	667.2	1,963.8	6,398.5
Diseases of heart (I00-I09, I11, I13, I20-I51)	220.0	8.7	0.9	0.6	2.7	8.1	28.9	89.7	214.8	518.9	1,460.8	4,778.4
Acute rheumatic fever and chronic rheumatic heart diseases (I00-I09)	1.1	*	*	*	*	0.1	0.2	0.4	1.2	3.3	8.5	19.0
Hypertensive heart disease (I11)	9.9	*	*	*	0.1	0.8	3.1	7.8	13.0	20.4	48.8	198.6
Hypertensive heart and renal disease (I13)	1.1	*	*	*	*	0.1	0.2	0.4	0.8	2.3	7.0	25.3
Ischemic heart diseases (I20-I25)	150.4	*	*	*	0.4	2.5	15.6	59.6	154.2	376.2	1,029.8	3,158.1
Acute myocardial infarction (I21-I22)	50.9	*	*	*	0.2	1.0	6.2	23.7	61.1	143.1	348.2	923.1
Other acute ischemic heart diseases (I24)	1.2	*	*	*	*	*	0.2	0.8	1.7	3.3	7.2	20.8
Other forms of chronic ischemic heart disease (I20, I25)	98.2	*	*	*	0.2	1.5	9.2	35.0	91.4	229.8	674.5	2,214.2
Atherosclerotic cardiovascular disease, so described (I25.0)	21.2	*	*	*	*	0.5	3.2	13.9	31.5	55.0	124.8	376.4
All other forms of chronic ischemic heart disease (I20, I25.1-I25.9)	77.0	*	*	*	0.2	1.1	6.0	21.2	59.8	174.9	549.7	1,837.8
Other heart diseases (I26-I51)	57.6	8.3	0.9	0.6	2.2	4.6	9.8	21.5	45.7	116.8	366.7	1,377.4
Acute and subacute endocarditis (I33)	0.4	*	*	*	*	0.1	0.2	0.4	0.7	1.3	2.5	3.0
Diseases of pericardium and acute myocarditis (I30-I31, I40)	0.3	0.5	*	0.1	0.1	0.1	0.2	0.3	0.4	0.7	1.2	1.9
Heart failure (I50)	19.9	0.7	*	*	0.1	0.2	0.7	2.6	8.6	31.6	132.8	618.6
All other forms of heart disease (I26-I28, I34-I38, I42-I49, I51)	37.0	7.1	0.7	0.5	2.0	4.2	8.7	18.2	36.0	83.2	230.2	754.0
Essential (primary) hypertension and hypertensive renal disease (I10, I12)	8.4	*	*	*	0.1	0.2	0.9	2.7	6.4	17.7	55.6	210.0
Cerebrovascular diseases (I60-I69)	48.4	3.1	0.4	0.2	0.5	1.4	5.2	15.0	33.0	101.1	359.0	1,141.8
Atherosclerosis (I70)	4.0	*	*	*	*	*	0.1	0.5	1.4	5.4	25.9	132.9
Other diseases of circulatory system (I71-I78)	8.0	*	*	*	0.1	0.4	1.1	2.6	7.5	24.1	62.6	135.5
Aortic aneurysm and dissection (I71)	4.7	*	*	*	0.1	0.3	0.8	1.8	4.8	15.4	38.1	64.9
Other diseases of arteries, arterioles and capillaries (I72-I78)	3.3	*	*	*	*	0.1	0.3	0.8	2.7	8.7	24.5	70.6
Other disorders of circulatory system (I80-I99)	1.6	0.6	*	*	0.1	0.3	0.8	1.5	2.1	3.8	8.6	23.0
Influenza and pneumonia (J10-J18)	21.3	6.5	0.7	0.3	0.4	0.9	2.1	5.1	11.3	35.5	142.2	593.9
Influenza (J10-J11)	0.6	*	*	0.0	*	*	*	0.1	0.2	0.7	3.7	19.3
Pneumonia (J12-J18)	20.6	6.0	0.6	0.2	0.4	0.9	2.1	5.0	11.1	34.8	138.5	574.7
Other acute lower respiratory infections (J20-J22)	0.1	1.2	*	*	*	*	*	*	*	0.1	0.6	3.3
Acute bronchitis and bronchiolitis (J20-J21)	0.1	1.2	*	*	*	*	*	*	*	*	0.4	1.9
Unspecified acute lower respiratory infection (J22)	0.0	*	*	*	*	*	*	*	*	*	0.2	1.4
Chronic lower respiratory diseases (J40-J47)	44.2	0.8	0.3	0.3	0.4	0.6	2.0	9.4	42.0	160.5	385.6	637.2
Bronchitis, chronic and unspecified (J40-J42)	0.3	0.6	*	*	*	*	*	0.1	0.2	0.6	1.6	7.4
Emphysema (J43)	4.7	*	*	*	*	*	0.2	1.0	5.5	20.1	41.4	51.9
Asthma (J45-J46)	1.3	*	0.2	0.2	0.3	0.5	0.8	1.4	1.7	2.5	5.4	14.5
Other chronic lower respiratory diseases (J44, J47)	37.8	*	*	*	*	0.1	1.0	6.9	34.5	137.2	337.2	563.5
Pneumoconioses and chemical effects (J60-J66, J68)	0.3	*	*	*	*	*	*	0.1	0.2	0.9	3.4	5.7
Pneumonitis due to solids and liquids (J69)	5.8	*	*	*	0.1	0.2	0.4	1.1	2.7	9.3	42.6	163.9
Other diseases of respiratory system (J00-J06, J30-J39, J67, J70-J98)	9.1	7.4	0.6	0.2	0.3	0.5	1.1	3.2	8.8	28.8	72.5	136.5
Peptic ulcer (K25-K28)	1.2	*	*	*	*	0.1	0.2	0.7	1.2	2.9	8.0	21.4
Diseases of appendix (K35-K38)	0.1	*	*	*	*	*	*	0.1	0.2	0.4	0.8	2.1
Hernia (K40-K46)	0.6	1.0	*	*	*	*	0.1	0.2	0.6	1.1	3.5	12.1
Chronic liver disease and cirrhosis (K70, K73-K74)	9.3	*	*	*	0.1	0.8	6.1	17.7	23.5	27.2	29.0	19.7
Alcoholic liver disease (K70)	4.4	*	*	*	*	0.5	4.1	10.6	12.3	9.9	5.7	1.8
Other chronic liver disease and cirrhosis (K73-K74)	4.9	*	*	*	*	0.2	2.0	7.1	11.2	17.3	23.2	17.8
Cholelithiasis and other disorders of gallbladder (K80-K82)	1.0	*	*	*	*	*	0.1	0.3	0.7	2.4	8.1	22.9
Nephritis, nephrotic syndrome and nephrosis (N00-N07, N17-N19, N25-N27)	14.8	3.9	*	0.1	0.2	0.7	1.7	4.8	13.6	39.3	110.3	288.3
Acute and rapidly progressive nephritic and nephrotic syndrome (N00-N01, N04)	0.0	*	*	*	*	*	*	*	*	*	0.3	0.8
Chronic glomerulonephritis, nephritis and nephropathy not specified as acute or chronic, and renal sclerosis unspecified (N02-N03, N05-N07, N26)	0.3	*	*	*	*	0.1	0.1	0.1	0.3	0.7	1.9	5.4
Renal failure (N17-N19)	14.5	3.7	*	*	0.2	0.7	1.6	4.6	13.3	38.4	108.0	282.1
Other disorders of kidney (N25, N27)	0.0	*	*	*	*	*	*	*	*	*	*	*
Infections of kidney (N10-N12, N13.6, N15.1)	0.3	*	*	*	*	*	0.1	0.1	0.2	0.5	1.8	5.2
Hyperplasia of prostate (N40)	0.2	*	*	*	*	*	*	*	*	0.3	1.3	5.7
Inflammatory diseases of female pelvic organs (N70-N76)	0.0	*	*	*	*	*	*	*	*	0.1	0.3	0.6
Pregnancy, childbirth and the puerperium (O00-O99)	0.3	...	...	*	0.4	0.8	0.5	0.1	*	*	*	*
Pregnancy with abortive outcome (O00-O07)	0.0	...	...	*	*	*	*	*	*	*	*	*
Other complications of pregnancy, childbirth and the puerperium (O10-O99)	0.2	...	...	*	0.4	0.7	0.4	0.1	*	*	*	*
Certain conditions originating in the perinatal period (P00-P96)	4.9	351.2	0.4	0.1	*	*	*	*	*	*	*	*

* = Figure does not meet standards of reliability or precision.
… = Not applicable.
0.0 = Quantity more than zero but less than 0.05.
[1]Based on codes from the *International Classification of Diseases, Tenth Revision* (1992), except where (*) precedes the cause of death code.
[2]Figures for age not stated included in all ages but not distributed among age groups.
[3]Death rates for "Under 1 year" (based on population estimates) differ from infant mortality rates (based on live births).

Table B-19. Death Rates for 113 Selected Causes by Age, 2005—*Continued*

(Rate per 100,000 population in specified group.)

Cause of death[1]	All ages[2]	Under 1 year[3]	1–4 years	5–14 years	15–24 years	25–34 years	35–44 years	45–54 years	55–64 years	65–74 years	75–84 years	85 years and over
Congenital malformations, deformations and chromosomal abnormalities (Q00-Q99)	3.5	135.2	3.2	1.0	1.2	1.1	1.2	1.6	2.4	1.8	3.1	6.4
Symptoms, signs and abnormal clinical and laboratory findings, not elsewhere classified (R00-R99)	10.8	87.4	1.4	0.4	1.8	2.9	4.7	6.7	7.2	12.8	39.0	224.4
All other diseases (residual)	73.4	29.2	3.8	2.1	4.9	7.9	18.5	40.3	69.5	146.1	434.3	1,559.1
Accidents (unintentional injuries) (V01-X59, Y85-Y86)	39.7	26.4	10.3	6.0	37.4	34.9	38.6	43.2	35.8	46.3	106.1	279.5
Transport accidents (V01-V99, Y85)	16.3	3.6	4.0	3.8	26.8	19.0	16.6	16.7	16.2	18.0	24.3	26.1
Motor vehicle accidents (V02-V04, V09.0, V09.2, V12-V14, V19.0-V19.2, V19.4-V19.6, V20-V79, V80.3-V80.5, V81.0-V81.1, V82.0-V82.1, V83-V86, V87.0-V87.8, V88.0-V88.8, V89.0, V89.2)	15.3	3.6	3.8	3.6	25.9	18.0	15.4	15.1	14.7	16.7	22.9	25.1
Other land transport accidents (V01, V05-V06, V09.1, V09.3-V09.9, V10-V11, V15-V18, V19.3, V19.8-V19.9, V80.0-V80.2, V80.6-V80.9, V81.2-V81.9, V82.2-V82.9, V87.9, V88.9, V89.1, V89.3, V89.9)	0.4	*	0.2	0.1	0.5	0.4	0.5	0.6	0.5	0.4	0.6	0.5
Water, air and space, and other and unspecified transport accidents and their sequelae (V90-V99, Y85)	0.6	*	*	0.1	0.4	0.6	0.8	1.0	1.1	0.9	0.7	0.5
Nontransport accidents (W00-X59, Y86)	23.4	22.8	6.3	2.1	10.6	15.8	21.9	26.5	19.6	28.3	81.9	253.4
Falls (W00-W19)	6.6	*	0.2	0.1	0.6	0.7	1.4	2.8	4.8	12.4	45.6	147.7
Accidental discharge of firearms (W32-W34)	0.3	*	0.1	0.1	0.5	0.3	0.3	0.3	0.2	0.2	0.3	*
Accidental drowning and submersion (W65-W74)	1.2	1.6	3.0	0.6	1.5	1.0	1.1	1.2	0.9	1.0	1.4	1.8
Accidental exposure to smoke, fire and flames (X00-X09)	1.1	0.8	1.3	0.5	0.4	0.6	0.8	1.2	1.3	2.1	3.6	5.0
Accidental poisoning and exposure to noxious substances (X40-X49)	8.0	0.5	0.1	0.1	5.9	10.9	15.3	16.4	6.6	2.3	2.4	3.5
Other and unspecified nontransport accidents and their sequelae (W20-W31, W35-W64, W75-W99, X10-X39, X50-X59, Y86)	6.3	19.5	1.5	0.6	1.7	2.3	3.1	4.7	5.8	10.2	28.6	95.1
Intentional self-harm (suicide) (*U03, X60-X84, Y87.0)	11.0	...	...	0.7	10.0	12.4	14.9	16.5	13.9	12.6	16.9	16.9
Intentional self-harm (suicide) by discharge of firearms (X72-X74)	5.7	...	...	0.2	4.7	5.7	6.5	8.2	8.1	9.0	12.6	11.2
Intentional self-harm (suicide) by other and unspecified means and their sequelae (*U03, X60-X71, X75-X84, Y87.0)	5.3	...	...	0.5	5.3	6.8	8.4	8.3	5.7	3.6	4.2	5.7
Assault (homicide) (*U01-*U02, X85-Y09, Y87.1)	6.1	7.5	2.3	0.8	13.0	11.8	7.1	4.8	2.8	2.4	2.2	2.1
Assault (homicide) by discharge of firearms (*U01.4, X93-X95)	4.2	*	0.2	0.5	10.7	9.4	4.6	2.6	1.3	1.1	0.7	0.5
Assault (homicide) by other and unspecified means and their sequelae (*U01.0-*U01.3, *U01.5-*U01.9, *U02, X85-X92, X96-Y09, Y87.1)	1.9	7.3	2.1	0.4	2.3	2.4	2.5	2.3	1.5	1.3	1.4	1.7
Legal intervention (Y35, Y89.0)	0.1	*	*	*	0.2	0.3	0.3	0.1	0.1	*	*	*
Events of undetermined intent (Y10-Y34, Y87.2, Y89.9)	1.6	2.5	0.4	0.2	1.2	1.8	2.7	3.1	1.4	0.8	0.8	1.5
Discharge of firearms, undetermined intent (Y22-Y24)	0.1	*	*	*	0.2	0.1	0.1	0.1	0.1	*	*	*
Other and unspecified events of undetermined intent and their sequelae (Y10-Y21, Y25-Y34, Y87.2, Y89.9)	1.5	2.5	0.4	0.1	1.0	1.8	2.7	3.0	1.3	0.8	0.8	1.4
Operations of war and their sequelae (Y36, Y89.1)	0.0	*	*	*	*	*	*	*	*	*	*	*
Complications of medical and surgical care (Y40-Y84, Y88)	0.9	*	*	*	0.1	0.2	0.3	0.7	1.2	2.6	5.8	9.1

* = Figure does not meet standards of reliability or precision.

... = Not applicable.

0.0 = Quantity more than zero but less than 0.05.

[1]Based on codes from the *International Classification of Diseases, Tenth Revision* (1992), except where (*) precedes the cause of death code.

[2]Figures for age not stated included in All ages but not distributed among age groups.

[3]Death rates for "Under 1 year" (based on population estimates) differ from infant mortality rates (based on live births).

NOTE: Complete confirmation of deaths from selected causes of death, considered to be of public health concern, were not provided by the following states–Alabama, California, Connecticut, Florida, Illinois, Indiana, Kentucky, Louisiana, Maryland, Michigan, Missouri, Montana, Nevada, New Hampshire, New Jersey, New York, North Carolina, Ohio, Oklahoma, Pennsylvania, Rhode Island, Texas, Utah, Virginia, Washington, and West Virginia.

Table B-20. Number of Deaths from 113 Selected Causes by Race and Sex, 2005

(Number.)

Cause of death[1]	All races			White			All other					
							Total			Black		
	Both sexes	Male	Female	Both sexes	Male	Female	Both sexes	Male	Female	Both sexes	Male	Female
ALL CAUSES	2,448,017	1,207,675	1,240,342	2,098,097	1,028,152	1,069,945	349,920	179,523	170,397	292,808	149,108	143,700
Salmonella infections (A01-A02)	30	11	19	24	9	15	6	2	4	5	2	3
Shigellosis and amebiasis (A03, A06)	10	3	7	10	3	7	-	-	-	-	-	-
Certain other intestinal infections (A04, A07-A09)	5,667	2,209	3,458	5,271	2,044	3,227	396	165	231	324	131	193
Tuberculosis (A16-A19)	648	392	256	376	226	150	272	166	106	153	94	59
Respiratory tuberculosis (A16)	480	291	189	273	160	113	207	131	76	115	73	42
Other tuberculosis (A17-A19)	168	101	67	103	66	37	65	35	30	38	21	17
Whooping cough (A37)	31	19	12	23	13	10	8	6	2	5	4	1
Scarlet fever and erysipelas (A38, A46)	3	2	1	3	2	1	-	-	-	-	-	-
Meningococcal infection (A39)	123	68	55	101	53	48	22	15	7	17	11	6
Septicemia (A40-A41)	34,136	15,322	18,814	27,194	12,172	15,022	6,942	3,150	3,792	6,221	2,786	3,435
Syphilis (A50-A53)	47	32	15	16	10	6	31	22	9	30	21	9
Acute poliomyelitis (A80)	-	-	-	-	-	-	-	-	-	-	-	-
Arthropod-borne viral encephalitis (A83-A84, A85.2)	6	4	2	6	4	2	-	-	-	-	-	-
Measles (B05)	1	1	-	1	1	-	-	-	-	-	-	-
Viral hepatitis (B15-B19)	5,529	3,612	1,917	4,395	2,934	1,461	1,134	678	456	872	530	342
Human immunodeficiency virus (HIV) disease (B20-B24)	12,543	9,189	3,354	5,361	4,379	982	7,182	4,810	2,372	7,022	4,684	2,338
Malaria (B50-B54)	6	4	2	2	1	1	4	3	1	3	2	1
Other and unspecified infectious and parasitic diseases and their sequelae (A00, A05, A20-A36, A42-A44, A48-A49, A54-A79, A81-A82, A85.0-A85.1, A85.8, A86-B04, B06-B09, B25-B49, B55-B99)	7,727	4,216	3,511	6,427	3,519	2,908	1,300	697	603	976	524	452
Malignant neoplasms (C00-C97)	559,312	290,422	268,890	482,132	250,478	231,654	77,180	39,944	37,236	63,165	32,726	30,439
Malignant neoplasms of lip, oral cavity and pharynx (C00-C14)	7,773	5,273	2,500	6,409	4,247	2,162	1,364	1,026	338	1,080	841	239
Malignant neoplasm of esophagus (C15)	13,499	10,611	2,888	11,783	9,364	2,419	1,716	1,247	469	1,468	1,075	393
Malignant neoplasm of stomach (C16)	11,514	6,752	4,762	8,711	5,107	3,604	2,803	1,645	1,158	1,973	1,162	811
Malignant neoplasms of colon, rectum and anus (C18-C21)	53,252	26,843	26,409	44,994	22,782	22,212	8,258	4,061	4,197	6,884	3,344	3,540
Malignant neoplasms of liver and intrahepatic bile ducts (C22)	16,076	10,548	5,528	12,735	8,278	4,457	3,341	2,270	1,071	2,118	1,483	635
Malignant neoplasm of pancreas (C25)	32,760	16,147	16,613	28,092	13,958	14,134	4,668	2,189	2,479	3,783	1,756	2,027
Malignant neoplasm of larynx (C32)	3,797	2,983	814	3,060	2,388	672	737	595	142	680	548	132
Malignant neoplasms of trachea, bronchus and lung (C33-C34)	159,292	90,187	69,105	139,442	78,379	61,063	19,850	11,808	8,042	16,567	9,887	6,680
Malignant melanoma of skin (C43)	8,345	5,283	3,062	8,146	5,184	2,962	199	99	100	124	57	67
Malignant neoplasm of breast (C50)	41,491	375	41,116	34,663	311	34,352	6,828	64	6,764	5,858	56	5,802
Malignant neoplasm of cervix uteri (C53)	3,924	...	3,924	2,982	...	2,982	942	...	942	783	...	783
Malignant neoplasm of corpus uteri and uterus, part unspecified (C54-C55)	7,096	...	7,096	5,742	...	5,742	1,354	...	1,354	1,180	...	1,180
Malignant neoplasm of ovary (C56)	14,787		14,787	13,199	...	13,199	1,588	...	1,588	1,217	...	1,217
Malignant neoplasm of prostate (C61)	28,905	28,905	...	23,597	23,597	...	5,308	5,308	...	4,823	4,823	...
Malignant neoplasms of kidney and renal pelvis (C64-C65)	12,517	7,783	4,734	11,091	6,888	4,203	1,426	895	531	1,155	723	432
Malignant neoplasm of bladder (C67)	13,253	9,190	4,063	12,100	8,523	3,577	1,153	667	486	961	546	415
Malignant neoplasms of meninges, brain and other parts of central nervous system (C70-C72)	13,152	7,317	5,835	12,079	6,715	5,364	1,073	602	471	793	440	353
Malignant neoplasms of lymphoid, hematopoietic and related tissue (C81-C96)	55,028	30,031	24,997	48,703	26,707	21,996	6,325	3,324	3,001	5,046	2,633	2,413
Hodgkin's disease (C81)	1,272	684	588	1,095	582	513	177	102	75	145	85	60
Non-Hodgkin's lymphoma (C82-C85)	20,873	11,131	9,742	18,970	10,118	8,852	1,903	1,013	890	1,392	752	640
Leukemia (C91-C95)	21,623	12,231	9,392	19,414	11,034	8,380	2,209	1,197	1,012	1,718	911	807
Multiple myeloma and immunoproliferative neoplasms (C88, C90)	11,200	5,945	5,255	9,171	4,937	4,234	2,029	1,008	1,021	1,785	882	903
Other and unspecified malignant neoplasms of lymphoid, hematopoietic and related tissue (C96)	60	40	20	53	36	17	7	4	3	6	3	3
All other and unspecified malignant neoplasms (C17, C23-C24, C26-C31, C37-C41, C44-C49, C51-C52, C57-C60, C62-C63, C66, C68-C69, C73-C80, C97)	62,851	32,194	30,657	54,604	28,050	26,554	8,247	4,144	4,103	6,672	3,352	3,320
In situ neoplasms, benign neoplasms and neoplasms of uncertain or unknown behavior (D00-D48)	13,710	6,820	6,890	12,249	6,161	6,088	1,461	659	802	1,151	499	652
Anemias (D50-D64)	4,624	1,787	2,837	3,499	1,288	2,211	1,125	499	626	1,032	456	576
Diabetes mellitus (E10-E14)	75,119	36,538	38,581	59,755	29,628	30,127	15,364	6,910	8,454	12,970	5,730	7,240
Nutritional deficiencies (E40-E64)	3,183	1,116	2,067	2,677	924	1,753	506	192	314	430	156	274
Malnutrition (E40-E46)	3,003	1,059	1,944	2,518	875	1,643	485	184	301	412	149	263
Other nutritional deficiencies (E50-E64)	180	57	123	159	49	110	21	8	13	18	7	11
Meningitis (G00,G03)	669	353	316	496	262	234	173	91	82	143	76	67
Parkinson's disease (G20-G21)	19,544	11,247	8,297	18,496	10,649	7,847	1,048	598	450	711	412	299
Alzheimer's disease (G30)	71,599	20,559	51,040	66,191	18,990	47,201	5,408	1,569	3,839	4,620	1,292	3,328

... = Not applicable.
- = Quantity zero.
[1]Based on codes from the *International Classification of Diseases, Tenth Revision* (1992), except where (*) precedes the cause of death code.

Table B-20. Number of Deaths from 113 Selected Causes by Race and Sex, 2005—*Continued*

(Number.)

Cause of death[1]	All races			White			All other					
							Total			Black		
	Both sexes	Male	Female	Both sexes	Male	Female	Both sexes	Male	Female	Both sexes	Male	Female
Major cardiovascular diseases (I00-I78)	856,030	405,780	450,250	737,248	348,454	388,794	118,782	57,326	61,456	100,099	47,584	52,515
Diseases of heart (I00-I09, I11, I13, I20-I51)	652,091	322,841	329,250	564,796	279,324	285,472	87,295	43,517	43,778	74,159	36,343	37,816
Acute rheumatic fever and chronic rheumatic heart diseases (I00-I09)	3,365	1,044	2,321	3,029	926	2,103	336	118	218	227	81	146
Hypertensive heart disease (I11)	29,282	13,219	16,063	21,686	9,408	12,278	7,596	3,811	3,785	6,923	3,459	3,464
Hypertensive heart and renal disease (I13)	3,172	1,369	1,803	2,186	886	1,300	986	483	503	889	432	457
Ischemic heart diseases (I20-I25)	445,687	232,115	213,572	390,421	203,924	186,497	55,266	28,191	27,075	46,027	22,933	23,094
Acute myocardial infarction (I21-I22)	151,004	80,079	70,925	132,364	70,791	61,573	18,640	9,288	9,352	15,536	7,527	8,009
Other acute ischemic heart diseases (I24)	3,565	1,823	1,742	2,924	1,480	1,444	641	343	298	558	296	262
Other forms of chronic ischemic heart disease (I20, I25)	291,118	150,213	140,905	255,133	131,653	123,480	35,985	18,560	17,425	29,933	15,110	14,823
Atherosclerotic cardiovascular disease, so described (I25.0)	62,799	34,453	28,346	51,717	28,155	23,562	11,082	6,298	4,784	9,576	5,372	4,204
All other forms of chronic ischemic heart disease (I20, I25.1-I25.9)	228,319	115,760	112,559	203,416	103,498	99,918	24,903	12,262	12,641	20,357	9,738	10,619
Other heart diseases (I26-I51)	170,585	75,094	95,491	147,474	64,180	83,294	23,111	10,914	12,197	20,093	9,438	10,655
Acute and subacute endocarditis (I33)	1,209	695	514	949	553	396	260	142	118	229	124	105
Diseases of pericardium and acute myocarditis (I30-I31, I40)	864	439	425	661	344	317	203	95	108	164	73	91
Heart failure (I50)	58,933	23,026	35,907	52,570	20,414	32,156	6,363	2,612	3,751	5,609	2,275	3,334
All other forms of heart disease (I26-I28, I34-I38, I42-I49, I51)	109,579	50,934	58,645	93,294	42,869	50,425	16,285	8,065	8,220	14,091	6,966	7,125
Essential (primary) hypertension and hypertensive renal disease (I10, I12)	24,902	9,458	15,444	19,254	7,018	12,236	5,648	2,440	3,208	4,953	2,128	2,825
Cerebrovascular diseases (I60-I69)	143,579	56,586	86,993	121,868	47,194	74,674	21,711	9,392	12,319	17,541	7,519	10,022
Atherosclerosis (I70)	11,841	4,472	7,369	10,845	4,093	6,752	996	379	617	844	312	532
Other diseases of circulatory system (I71-I78)	23,617	12,423	11,194	20,485	10,825	9,660	3,132	1,598	1,534	2,602	1,282	1,320
Aortic aneurysm and dissection (I71)	13,843	8,168	5,675	12,156	7,203	4,953	1,687	965	722	1,304	719	585
Other diseases of arteries, arterioles and capillaries (I72-I78)	9,774	4,255	5,519	8,329	3,622	4,707	1,445	633	812	1,298	563	735
Other disorders of circulatory system (I80-I99)	4,813	2,156	2,657	3,936	1,723	2,213	877	433	444	796	388	408
Influenza and pneumonia (J10-J18)	63,001	28,052	34,949	55,540	24,425	31,115	7,461	3,627	3,834	5,780	2,729	3,051
Influenza (J10-J11)	1,812	657	1,155	1,710	609	1,101	102	48	54	69	32	37
Pneumonia (J12-J18)	61,189	27,395	33,794	53,830	23,816	30,014	7,359	3,579	3,780	5,711	2,697	3,014
Other acute lower respiratory infections (J20-J22)	404	172	232	351	147	204	53	25	28	41	17	24
Acute bronchitis and bronchiolitis (J20-J21)	283	123	160	240	101	139	43	22	21	32	15	17
Unspecified acute lower respiratory infection (J22)	121	49	72	111	46	65	10	3	7	9	2	7
Chronic lower respiratory diseases (J40-J47)	130,933	62,435	68,498	120,884	56,911	63,973	10,049	5,524	4,525	8,229	4,464	3,765
Bronchitis, chronic and unspecified (J40-J42)	866	361	505	784	315	469	82	46	36	54	33	21
Emphysema (J43)	14,002	7,264	6,738	12,987	6,618	6,369	1,015	646	369	815	509	306
Asthma (J45-J46)	3,884	1,315	2,569	2,714	843	1,871	1,170	472	698	1,016	411	605
Other chronic lower respiratory diseases (J44, J47)	112,181	53,495	58,686	104,399	49,135	55,264	7,782	4,360	3,422	6,344	3,511	2,833
Pneumoconioses and chemical effects (J60-J66, J68)	1,007	965	42	953	915	38	54	50	4	47	43	4
Pneumonitis due to solids and liquids (J69)	17,279	8,760	8,519	15,338	7,759	7,579	1,941	1,001	940	1,620	825	795
Other diseases of respiratory system (J00-J06, J30-J39, J67, J70-J98)	27,056	13,168	13,888	23,860	11,574	12,286	3,196	1,594	1,602	2,481	1,209	1,272
Peptic ulcer (K25-K28)	3,478	1,722	1,756	2,995	1,453	1,542	483	269	214	363	211	152
Diseases of appendix (K35-K38)	439	247	192	373	208	165	66	39	27	55	33	22
Hernia (K40-K46)	1,639	646	993	1,456	568	888	183	78	105	152	66	86
Chronic liver disease and cirrhosis (K70, K73-K74)	27,530	17,937	9,593	24,003	15,679	8,324	3,527	2,258	1,269	2,530	1,656	874
Alcoholic liver disease (K70)	12,928	9,425	3,503	11,205	8,250	2,955	1,723	1,175	548	1,169	801	368
Other chronic liver disease and cirrhosis (K73-K74)	14,602	8,512	6,090	12,798	7,429	5,369	1,804	1,083	721	1,361	855	506
Cholelithiasis and other disorders of gallbladder (K80-K82)	3,072	1,363	1,709	2,655	1,193	1,462	417	170	247	325	135	190
Nephritis, nephrotic syndrome and nephrosis (N00-N07, N17-N19, N25-N27)	43,901	21,268	22,633	34,806	17,137	17,669	9,095	4,131	4,964	8,075	3,645	4,430
Acute and rapidly progressive nephritic and nephrotic syndrome (N00-N01, N04)	137	67	70	114	60	54	23	7	16	18	6	12
Chronic glomerulonephritis, nephritis and nephropathy not specified as acute or chronic, and renal sclerosis unspecified (N02-N03, N05-N07, N26)	867	444	423	686	350	336	181	94	87	161	81	80
Renal failure (N17-N19)	42,868	20,745	22,123	33,983	16,715	17,268	8,885	4,030	4,855	7,891	3,558	4,333
Other disorders of kidney (N25, N27)	29	12	17	23	12	11	6	-	6	5	-	5
Infections of kidney (N10-N12, N13.6, N15.1)	767	236	531	660	204	456	107	32	75	89	27	62
Hyperplasia of prostate (N40)	525	525	…	483	483	…	42	42	…	30	30	…
Inflammatory diseases of female pelvic organs (N70-N76)	120	…	120	98	…	98	22	…	22	19	…	19
Pregnancy, childbirth and the puerperium (O00-O99)	760	…	760	453	…	453	307	…	307	267	…	267
Pregnancy with abortive outcome (O00-O07)	33	…	33	15	…	15	18	…	18	13	…	13
Other complications of pregnancy, childbirth and the puerperium (O10-O99)	727	…	727	438	…	438	289	…	289	254	…	254

… = Not applicable.

- = Quantity zero.

[1]Based on codes from the *International Classification of Diseases, Tenth Revision* (1992), except where (*) precedes the cause of death code.

Table B-20. Number of Deaths from 113 Selected Causes by Race and Sex, 2005—*Continued*

(Number.)

Cause of death[1]	All races			White			All other					
							Total			Black		
	Both sexes	Male	Female	Both sexes	Male	Female	Both sexes	Male	Female	Both sexes	Male	Female
Certain conditions originating in the perinatal period (P00-P96)	14,549	8,187	6,362	8,906	5,026	3,880	5,643	3,161	2,482	5,050	2,828	2,222
Congenital malformations, deformations and chromosomal abnormalities (Q00-Q99)	10,410	5,447	4,963	8,254	4,321	3,933	2,156	1,126	1,030	1,719	891	828
Symptoms, signs and abnormal clinical and laboratory findings, not elsewhere classified (R00-R99)	31,999	14,647	17,352	26,595	11,861	14,734	5,404	2,786	2,618	4,798	2,475	2,323
All other diseases (residual)	217,632	88,869	128,763	188,445	76,187	112,258	29,187	12,682	16,505	24,843	10,603	14,240
Accidents (unintentional injuries) (V01-X59, Y85-Y86)	117,809	76,375	41,434	100,406	64,600	35,806	17,403	11,775	5,628	13,652	9,329	4,323
Transport accidents (V01-V99, Y85)	48,441	34,086	14,355	40,647	28,568	12,079	7,794	5,518	2,276	5,842	4,237	1,605
Motor vehicle accidents (V02-V04, V09.0, V09.2, V12-V14, V19.0-V19.2, V19.4-V19.6, V20-V79, V80.3-V80.5, V81.0-V81.1, V82.0-V82.1, V83-V86, V87.0-V87.8, V88.0-V88.8, V89.0, V89.2)	45,343	31,631	13,712	38,041	26,508	11,533	7,302	5,123	2,179	5,491	3,957	1,534
Other land transport accidents (V01,V05-V06, V09.1, V09.3-V09.9, V10-V11, V15-V18, V19.3, V19.8-V19.9, V80.0-V80.2, V80.6-V80.9, V81.2-V81.9, V82.2-V82.9, V87.9,V88.9, V89.1, V89.3, V89.9)	1,241	957	284	970	738	232	271	219	52	204	163	41
Water, air and space, and other and unspecified transport accidents and their sequelae (V90-V99, Y85)	1,857	1,498	359	1,636	1,322	314	221	176	45	147	117	30
Nontransport accidents (W00-X59, Y86)	69,368	42,289	27,079	59,759	36,032	23,727	9,609	6,257	3,352	7,810	5,092	2,718
Falls (W00-W19)	19,656	10,154	9,502	18,113	9,246	8,867	1,543	908	635	1,027	602	425
Accidental discharge of firearms (W32-W34)	789	683	106	601	516	85	188	167	21	154	138	16
Accidental drowning and submersion (W65-W74)	3,582	2,818	764	2,819	2,191	628	763	627	136	556	471	85
Accidental exposure to smoke, fire and flames (X00-X09)	3,197	1,886	1,311	2,351	1,392	959	846	494	352	746	442	304
Accidental poisoning and exposure to noxious substances (X40-X49)	23,618	15,884	7,734	20,163	13,561	6,602	3,455	2,323	1,132	2,986	2,015	971
Other and unspecified nontransport accidents and their sequelae (W20-W31, W35-W64, W75-W99 ,X10-X39, X50-X59, Y86)	18,526	10,864	7,662	15,712	9,126	6,586	2,814	1,738	1,076	2,341	1,424	917
Intentional self-harm (suicide) (*U03, X60-X84, Y87.0)	32,637	25,907	6,730	29,527	23,478	6,049	3,110	2,429	681	1,992	1,621	371
Intentional self-harm (suicide) by discharge of firearms (X72-X74)	17,002	14,916	2,086	15,681	13,730	1,951	1,321	1,186	135	1,009	911	98
Intentional self-harm (suicide) by other and unspecified means and their sequelae (*U03, X60-X71, X75-X84, Y87.0)	15,635	10,991	4,644	13,846	9,748	4,098	1,789	1,243	546	983	710	273
Assault (homicide) (*U01-*U02, X85-Y09, Y87.1)	18,124	14,376	3,748	8,770	6,457	2,313	9,354	7,919	1,435	8,669	7,412	1,257
Assault (homicide) by discharge of firearms (*U01.4, X93-X95)	12,352	10,561	1,791	5,266	4,177	1,089	7,086	6,384	702	6,703	6,067	636
Assault (homicide) by other and unspecified means and their sequelae (*U01.0-*U01.3, *U01.5-*U01.9, *U02, X85-X92, X96-Y09, Y87.1)	5,772	3,815	1,957	3,504	2,280	1,224	2,268	1,535	733	1,966	1,345	621
Legal intervention (Y35, Y89.0)	414	401	13	289	277	12	125	124	1	112	111	1
Events of undetermined intent (Y10-Y34, Y87.2, Y89.9)	4,742	2,861	1,881	3,917	2,327	1,590	825	534	291	685	453	232
Discharge of firearms, undetermined intent (Y22-Y24)	221	178	43	175	141	34	46	37	9	36	28	8
Other and unspecified events of undetermined intent and their sequelae (Y10-Y21, Y25-Y34, Y87.2, Y89.9)	4,521	2,683	1,838	3,742	2,186	1,556	779	497	282	649	425	224
Operations of war and their sequelae (Y36, Y89.1)	27	27	-	21	21	-	6	6	-	6	6	-
Complications of medical and surgical care (Y40-Y84, Y88)	2,653	1,220	1,433	2,170	1,014	1,156	483	206	277	434	181	253

... = Not applicable.

- = Quantity zero.

[1]Based on codes from the *International Classification of Diseases, Tenth Revision* (1992), except where (*) precedes the cause of death code.

NOTE: Complete confirmation of deaths from selected causes of death, considered to be of public health concern, were not provided by the following states–Alabama, California, Connecticut, Florida, Illinois, Indiana, Kentucky, Louisiana, Maryland, Michigan, Missouri, Montana, Nevada, New Hampshire, New Jersey, New York, North Carolina, Ohio, Oklahoma, Pennsylvania, Rhode Island, Texas, Utah, Virginia, Washington, and West Virginia.

Table B-21. Number of Deaths from 113 Selected Causes by Hispanic Origin, Race for Non-Hispanic Population, and Sex, 2005

(Number.)

Cause of death[1]	All origins			Hispanic[2]			Non-Hispanic[3]		
	Both sexes	Male	Female	Both sexes	Male	Female	Both sexes	Male	Female
ALL CAUSES	2,448,017	1,207,675	1,240,342	131,161	73,788	57,373	2,312,028	1,131,013	1,181,015
Salmonella infections (A01-A02)	30	11	19	4	3	1	26	8	18
Shigellosis and amebiasis (A03, A06)	10	3	7	4	1	3	6	2	4
Certain other intestinal infections (A04, A07-A09)	5,667	2,209	3,458	190	65	125	5,469	2,141	3,328
Tuberculosis (A16-A19)	648	392	256	94	66	28	551	325	226
Respiratory tuberculosis (A16)	480	291	189	56	36	20	423	255	168
Other tuberculosis (A17-A19)	168	101	67	38	30	8	128	70	58
Whooping cough (A37)	31	19	12	12	8	4	19	11	8
Scarlet fever and erysipelas (A38, A46)	3	2	1	1	1	-	2	1	1
Meningococcal infection (A39)	123	68	55	16	12	4	107	56	51
Septicemia (A40-A41)	34,136	15,322	18,814	1,704	838	866	32,354	14,442	17,912
Syphilis (A50-A53)	47	32	15	1	1	-	46	31	15
Acute poliomyelitis (A80)	-	-	-	-	-	-	-	-	-
Arthropod-borne viral encephalitis (A83-A84, A85.2)	6	4	2	1	1	-	5	3	2
Measles (B05)	1	1	-	-	-	-	1	1	-
Viral hepatitis (B15-B19)	5,529	3,612	1,917	795	521	274	4,714	3,076	1,638
Human immunodeficiency virus (HIV) disease (B20-B24)	12,543	9,189	3,354	1,645	1,309	336	10,813	7,811	3,002
Malaria (B50-B54)	6	4	2	-	-	-	6	4	2
Other and unspecified infectious and parasitic diseases and their sequelae (A00, A05, A20-A36, A42-A44, A48-A49, A54-A79, A81-A82, A85.0-A85.1, A85.8, A86-B04, B06-B09, B25-B49, B55-B99)	7,727	4,216	3,511	773	452	321	6,938	3,753	3,185
Malignant neoplasms (C00-C97)	559,312	290,422	268,890	26,156	13,896	12,260	532,383	276,084	256,299
Malignant neoplasms of lip, oral cavity and pharynx (C00-C14)	7,773	5,273	2,500	314	236	78	7,445	5,026	2,419
Malignant neoplasm of esophagus (C15)	13,499	10,611	2,888	481	391	90	12,997	10,203	2,794
Malignant neoplasm of stomach (C16)	11,514	6,752	4,762	1,272	744	528	10,223	5,997	4,226
Malignant neoplasms of colon, rectum and anus (C18-C21)	53,252	26,843	26,409	2,542	1,350	1,192	50,629	25,445	25,184
Malignant neoplasms of liver and intrahepatic bile ducts (C22)	16,076	10,548	5,528	1,807	1,185	622	14,236	9,339	4,897
Malignant neoplasm of pancreas (C25)	32,760	16,147	16,613	1,748	872	876	30,976	15,262	15,714
Malignant neoplasm of larynx (C32)	3,797	2,983	814	183	165	18	3,605	2,811	794
Malignant neoplasms of trachea, bronchus and lung (C33-C34)	159,292	90,187	69,105	4,490	2,878	1,612	154,578	87,168	67,410
Malignant melanoma of skin (C43)	8,345	5,283	3,062	168	105	63	8,169	5,171	2,998
Malignant neoplasm of breast (C50)	41,491	375	41,116	1,942	6	1,936	39,490	369	39,121
Malignant neoplasm of cervix uteri (C53)	3,924	...	3,924	447	...	447	3,469	...	3,469
Malignant neoplasms of corpus uteri and uterus, part unspecified (C54-C55)	7,096	...	7,096	389	...	389	6,693	...	6,693
Malignant neoplasm of ovary (C56)	14,787	...	14,787	739	...	739	14,041	...	14,041
Malignant neoplasm of prostate (C61)	28,905	28,905	...	1,300	1,300	...	27,566	27,566	...
Malignant neoplasms of kidney and renal pelvis (C64-C65)	12,517	7,783	4,734	780	482	298	11,719	7,286	4,433
Malignant neoplasm of bladder (C67)	13,253	9,190	4,063	435	317	118	12,803	8,861	3,942
Malignant neoplasms of meninges, brain and other parts of central nervous system (C70-C72)	13,152	7,317	5,835	771	431	340	12,364	6,877	5,487
Malignant neoplasms of lymphoid, hematopoietic and related tissue (C81-C96)	55,028	30,031	24,997	3,110	1,719	1,391	51,861	28,283	23,578
Hodgkin's disease (C81)	1,272	684	588	126	78	48	1,141	602	539
Non-Hodgkin's lymphoma (C82-C85)	20,873	11,131	9,742	1,118	593	525	19,734	10,529	9,205
Leukemia (C91-C95)	21,623	12,231	9,392	1,272	747	525	20,329	11,471	8,858
Multiple myeloma and immunoproliferative neoplasms (C88, C90)	11,200	5,945	5,255	588	296	292	10,603	5,646	4,957
Other and unspecified malignant neoplasms of lymphoid, hematopoietic and related tissue (C96)	60	40	20	6	5	1	54	35	19
All other and unspecified malignant neoplasms (C17, C23-C24, C26-C31, C37-C41, C44-C49, C51-C52, C57-C60, C62-C63, C66, C68-C69, C73-C80, C97)	62,851	32,194	30,657	3,238	1,715	1,523	59,519	30,420	29,099

... = Not applicable.
- = Quantity zero.
[1]Based on codes from the *International Classification of Diseases, Tenth Revision* (1992), except where (*) precedes the cause of death code.
[2]Persons of Hispanic origin may be of any race.
[3]Includes races other than White and Black.

Table B-21. Number of Deaths from 113 Selected Causes by Hispanic Origin, Race for Non-Hispanic Population, and Sex, 2005—*Continued*

(Number.)

Cause of death[1]	All origins			Hispanic[2]			Non-Hispanic[3]		
	Both sexes	Male	Female	Both sexes	Male	Female	Both sexes	Male	Female
In situ neoplasms, benign neoplasms and neoplasms of uncertain or unknown behavior (D00-D48)	13,710	6,820	6,890	572	306	266	13,118	6,501	6,617
Anemias (D50-D64)	4,624	1,787	2,837	184	81	103	4,431	1,703	2,728
Diabetes mellitus (E10-E14)	75,119	36,538	38,581	6,665	3,296	3,369	68,325	33,178	35,147
Nutritional deficiencies (E40-E64)	3,183	1,116	2,067	139	59	80	3,034	1,052	1,982
Malnutrition (E40-E46)	3,003	1,059	1,944	132	57	75	2,861	997	1,864
Other nutritional deficiencies (E50-E64)	180	57	123	7	2	5	173	55	118
Meningitis (G00, G03)	669	353	316	63	33	30	602	317	285
Parkinson's disease (G20-G21)	19,544	11,247	8,297	726	418	308	18,804	10,823	7,981
Alzheimer's disease (G30)	71,599	20,559	51,040	2,201	764	1,437	69,315	19,764	49,551
Major cardiovascular diseases (I00-I78)	856,030	405,780	450,250	39,010	20,368	18,642	815,443	384,533	430,910
Diseases of heart (I00-I09, I11, I13, I20-I51)	652,091	322,841	329,250	29,555	15,900	13,655	621,260	306,197	315,063
Acute rheumatic fever and chronic rheumatic heart diseases (I00-I09)	3,365	1,044	2,321	162	47	115	3,200	995	2,205
Hypertensive heart disease (I11)	29,282	13,219	16,063	1,483	772	711	27,701	12,389	15,312
Hypertensive heart and renal disease (I13)	3,172	1,369	1,803	199	96	103	2,963	1,266	1,697
Ischemic heart diseases (I20-I25)	445,687	232,115	213,572	21,774	11,953	9,821	423,007	219,626	203,381
Acute myocardial infarction (I21-I22)	151,004	80,079	70,925	7,529	4,145	3,384	143,235	75,793	67,442
Other acute ischemic heart diseases (I24)	3,565	1,823	1,742	90	46	44	3,461	1,769	1,692
Other forms of chronic ischemic heart disease (I20, I25)	291,118	150,213	140,905	14,155	7,762	6,393	276,311	142,064	134,247
Atherosclerotic cardiovascular disease, so described (I25.0)	62,799	34,453	28,346	3,491	2,246	1,245	59,053	32,029	27,024
All other forms of chronic ischemic heart disease (I20, I25.1-I25.9)	228,319	115,760	112,559	10,664	5,516	5,148	217,258	110,035	107,223
Other heart diseases (I26-I51)	170,585	75,094	95,491	5,937	3,032	2,905	164,389	71,921	92,468
Acute and subacute endocarditis (I33)	1,209	695	514	80	58	22	1,127	636	491
Diseases of pericardium and acute myocarditis (I30-I31, I40)	864	439	425	74	40	34	789	399	390
Heart failure (I50)	58,933	23,026	35,907	1,721	735	986	57,140	22,255	34,885
All other forms of heart disease (I26-I28, I34-I38, I42-I49, I51)	109,579	50,934	58,645	4,062	2,199	1,863	105,333	48,631	56,702
Essential (primary) hypertension and hypertensive renal disease (I10, I12)	24,902	9,458	15,444	1,314	547	767	23,543	8,890	14,653
Cerebrovascular diseases (I60-I69)	143,579	56,586	86,993	6,830	3,188	3,642	136,548	53,319	83,229
Atherosclerosis (I70)	11,841	4,472	7,369	397	175	222	11,431	4,295	7,136
Other diseases of circulatory system (I71-I78)	23,617	12,423	11,194	914	558	356	22,661	11,832	10,829
Aortic aneurysm and dissection (I71)	13,843	8,168	5,675	477	328	149	13,344	7,822	5,522
Other diseases of arteries, arterioles and capillaries (I72-I78)	9,774	4,255	5,519	437	230	207	9,317	4,010	5,307
Other disorders of circulatory system (I80-I99)	4,813	2,156	2,657	281	126	155	4,520	2,024	2,496
Influenza and pneumonia (J10-J18)	63,001	28,052	34,949	3,085	1,506	1,579	59,804	26,482	33,322
Influenza (J10-J11)	1,812	657	1,155	55	26	29	1,752	631	1,121
Pneumonia (J12-J18)	61,189	27,395	33,794	3,030	1,480	1,550	58,052	25,851	32,201
Other acute lower respiratory infections (J20-J22)	404	172	232	19	7	12	385	165	220
Acute bronchitis and bronchiolitis (J20-J21)	283	123	160	17	6	11	266	117	149
Unspecified acute lower respiratory infection (J22)	121	49	72	2	1	1	119	48	71
Chronic lower respiratory diseases (J40-J47)	130,933	62,435	68,498	3,457	1,839	1,618	127,253	60,462	66,791
Bronchitis, chronic and unspecified (J40-J42)	866	361	505	44	19	25	820	342	478
Emphysema (J43)	14,002	7,264	6,738	301	181	120	13,678	7,067	6,611
Asthma (J45-J46)	3,884	1,315	2,569	248	106	142	3,626	1,205	2,421
Other chronic lower respiratory diseases (J44, J47)	112,181	53,495	58,686	2,864	1,533	1,331	109,129	51,848	57,281
Pneumoconioses and chemical effects (J60-J66, J68)	1,007	965	42	21	19	2	985	945	40
Pneumonitis due to solids and liquids (J69)	17,279	8,760	8,519	591	317	274	16,660	8,423	8,237
Other diseases of respiratory system (J00-J06, J30-J39, J67, J70-J98)	27,056	13,168	13,888	1,591	779	812	25,434	12,369	13,065

[1]Based on codes from the *International Classification of Diseases, Tenth Revision* (1992), except where (*) precedes the cause of death code.
[2]Persons of Hispanic origin may be of any race.
[3]Includes races other than White and Black.

Table B-21. Number of Deaths from 113 Selected Causes by Hispanic Origin, Race for Non-Hispanic Population, and Sex, 2005—Continued

(Number.)

Cause of death[1]	All origins			Hispanic[2]			Non-Hispanic[3]		
	Both sexes	Male	Female	Both sexes	Male	Female	Both sexes	Male	Female
Peptic ulcer (K25-K28)	3,478	1,722	1,756	175	92	83	3,293	1,624	1,669
Diseases of appendix (K35-K38)	439	247	192	25	12	13	413	234	179
Hernia (K40-K46)	1,639	646	993	86	28	58	1,553	618	935
Chronic liver disease and cirrhosis (K70, K73-K74)	27,530	17,937	9,593	3,555	2,561	994	23,882	15,302	8,580
Alcoholic liver disease (K70)	12,928	9,425	3,503	1,805	1,508	297	11,067	7,870	3,197
Other chronic liver disease and cirrhosis (K73-K74)	14,602	8,512	6,090	1,750	1,053	697	12,815	7,432	5,383
Cholelithiasis and other disorders of gallbladder (K80-K82)	3,072	1,363	1,709	225	102	123	2,841	1,257	1,584
Nephritis, nephrotic syndrome and nephrosis (N00-N07, N17-N19, N25-N27)	43,901	21,268	22,633	2,329	1,186	1,143	41,510	20,045	21,465
Acute and rapidly progressive nephritic and nephrotic syndrome (N00-N01, N04)	137	67	70	11	8	3	126	59	67
Chronic glomerulonephritis, nephritis and nephropathy not specified as acute or chronic, and renal sclerosis unspecified (N02-N03, N05-N07, N26)	867	444	423	63	27	36	804	417	387
Renal failure (N17-N19)	42,868	20,745	22,123	2,254	1,151	1,103	40,552	19,557	20,995
Other disorders of kidney (N25, N27)	29	12	17	1	-	1	28	12	16
Infections of kidney (N10-N12, N13.6, N15.1)	767	236	531	50	20	30	716	215	501
Hyperplasia of prostate (N40)	525	525	...	18	18	...	506	506	...
Inflammatory diseases of female pelvic organs (N70-N76)	120	...	120	9	...	9	111	...	111
Pregnancy, childbirth and the puerperium (O00-O99)	760	...	760	129	...	129	630	...	630
Pregnancy with abortive outcome (O00-O07)	33	...	33	2	...	2	31	...	31
Other complications of pregnancy, childbirth and the puerperium (O10-O99)	727	...	727	127	...	127	599	...	599
Certain conditions originating in the perinatal period (P00-P96)	14,549	8,187	6,362	2,816	1,612	1,204	11,594	6,503	5,091
Congenital malformations, deformations and chromosomal abnormalities (Q00-Q99)	10,410	5,447	4,963	1,896	996	900	8,479	4,431	4,048
Symptoms, signs and abnormal clinical and laboratory findings, not elsewhere classified (R00-R99)	31,999	14,647	17,352	1,857	1,135	722	29,884	13,353	16,531
All other diseases (residual)	217,632	88,869	128,763	10,250	5,110	5,140	207,024	83,561	123,463
Accidents (unintentional injuries) (V01-X59, Y85-Y86)	117,809	76,375	41,434	11,464	8,612	2,852	105,967	67,494	38,473
Transport accidents (V01-V99, Y85)	48,441	34,086	14,355	6,358	4,787	1,571	41,957	29,209	12,748
Motor vehicle accidents (V02-V04, V09.0, V09.2, V12-V14, V19.0-V19.2, V19.4-V19.6, V20-V79, V80.3-V80.5, V81.0-V81.1, V82.0-V82.1, V83-V86, V87.0-V87.8, V88.0-V88.8, V89.0, V89.2)	45,343	31,631	13,712	6,103	4,570	1,533	39,125	26,982	12,143
Other land transport accidents (V01, V05-V06, V09.1, V09.3-V09.9, V10-V11, V15-V18, V19.3,V19.8-V19.9, V80.0-V80.2, V80.6-V80.9, V81.2-V81.9, V82.2-V82.9, V87.9, V88.9,V89.1, V89.3-V89.9)	1,241	957	284	153	134	19	1,081	816	265
Water, air and space, and other and unspecified transport accidents and their sequelae (V90-V99, Y85)	1,857	1,498	359	102	83	19	1,751	1,411	340
Nontransport accidents (W00-X59, Y86)	69,368	42,289	27,079	5,106	3,825	1,281	64,010	38,285	25,725
Falls (W00-W19)	19,656	10,154	9,502	1,064	689	375	18,551	9,442	9,109
Accidental discharge of firearms (W32-W34)	789	683	106	95	86	9	692	595	97
Accidental drowning and submersion (W65-W74)	3,582	2,818	764	518	430	88	3,047	2,375	672
Accidental exposure to smoke, fire and flames (X00-X09)	3,197	1,886	1,311	211	125	86	2,971	1,751	1,220
Accidental poisoning and exposure to noxious substances (X40-X49)	23,618	15,884	7,734	2,018	1,603	415	21,488	14,198	7,290
Other and unspecified nontransport accidents and their sequelae (W20-W31, W35-W64, W75-W99, X10-X39, X50-X59, Y86)	18,526	10,864	7,662	1,200	892	308	17,261	9,924	7,337

... = Not applicable.

- = Quantity zero.

[1]Based on codes from the *International Classification of Diseases, Tenth Revision* (1992), except where (*) precedes the cause of death code.

[2]Persons of Hispanic origin may be of any race.

[3]Includes races other than White and Black.

Table B-21. Number of Deaths from 113 Selected Causes by Hispanic Origin, Race for Non-Hispanic Population, and Sex, 2005—*Continued*

(Number.)

Cause of death[1]	All origins			Hispanic[2]			Non-Hispanic[3]		
	Both sexes	Male	Female	Both sexes	Male	Female	Both sexes	Male	Female
Intentional self-harm (suicide) (*U03, X60-X84, Y87.0)	32,637	25,907	6,730	2,188	1,841	347	30,338	23,974	6,364
Intentional self-harm (suicide) by discharge of firearms (X72-X74)	17,002	14,916	2,086	824	756	68	16,124	14,110	2,014
Intentional self-harm (suicide) by other and unspecified means and their sequelae (*U03, X60-X71, X75-X84, Y87.0)	15,635	10,991	4,644	1,364	1,085	279	14,214	9,864	4,350
Assault (homicide) (*U01-*U02, X85-Y09, Y87.1)	18,124	14,376	3,748	3,520	3,008	512	14,504	11,288	3,216
Assault (homicide) by discharge of firearms (*U01.4, X93-X95)	12,352	10,561	1,791	2,453	2,211	242	9,835	8,296	1,539
Assault (homicide) by other and unspecified means and their sequelae (*U01.0-*U01.3, *U01.5-*U01.9, *U02, X85-X92, X96-Y09, Y87.1)	5,772	3,815	1,957	1,067	797	270	4,669	2,992	1,677
Legal intervention (Y35, Y89.0)	414	401	13	81	81	-	333	320	13
Events of undetermined intent (Y10-Y34, Y87.2, Y89.9)	4,742	2,861	1,881	325	219	106	4,388	2,621	1,767
Discharge of firearms, undetermined intent (Y22-Y24)	221	178	43	27	21	6	192	156	36
Other and unspecified events of undetermined intent and their sequelae (Y10-Y21 ,Y25-Y34, Y87.2, Y89.9)	4,521	2,683	1,838	298	198	100	4,196	2,465	1,731
Operations of war and their sequelae (Y36, Y89.1)	27	27	-	2	2	-	25	25	-
Complications of medical and surgical care (Y40-Y84, Y88)	2,653	1,220	1,433	160	61	99	2,484	1,152	1,332

Cause of death[1]	Non-Hispanic White[3]			Non-Hispanic Black			Origin not stated[4]		
	Both sexes	Male	Female	Both sexes	Male	Female	Both sexes	Male	Female
ALL CAUSES	1,967,142	954,402	1,012,740	289,163	147,010	142,153	4,828	2,874	1,954
Salmonella infections (A01-A02)	20	6	14	5	2	3	-	-	-
Shigellosis and amebiasis (A03, A06)	6	2	4	-	-	-	-	-	-
Certain other intestinal infections (A04, A07-A09)	5,082	1,978	3,104	318	129	189	8	3	5
Tuberculosis (A16-A19)	283	162	121	150	92	58	3	1	2
Respiratory tuberculosis (A16)	219	127	92	113	71	42	1	-	1
Other tuberculosis (A17-A19)	64	35	29	37	21	16	2	1	1
Whooping cough (A37)	11	5	6	5	4	1	-	-	-
Scarlet fever and erysipelas (A38, A46)	2	1	1	-	-	-	-	-	-
Meningococcal infection (A39)	86	42	44	17	11	6	-	-	-
Septicemia (A40-A41)	25,496	11,337	14,159	6,159	2,755	3,404	78	42	36
Syphilis (A50-A53)	15	9	6	30	21	9	-	-	-
Acute poliomyelitis (A80)	-	-	-	-	-	-	-	-	-
Arthropod-borne viral encephalitis (A83-A84, A85.2)	5	3	2	-	-	-	-	-	-
Measles (B05)	1	1	-	-	-	-	-	-	-
Viral hepatitis (B15-B19)	3,603	2,413	1,190	856	518	338	20	15	5
Human immunodeficiency virus (HIV) disease (B20-B24)	3,755	3,095	660	6,908	4,600	2,308	85	69	16
Malaria (B50-B54)	2	1	1	3	2	1	-	-	-
Other and unspecified infectious and parasitic diseases and their sequelae (A00, A05, A20-A36, A42-A44, A48-A49, A54-A79, A81-A82, A85.0-A85.1, A85.8, A86-B04, B06-B09, B25-B49, B55-B99)	5,662	3,071	2,591	960	514	446	16	11	5
Malignant neoplasms (C00-C97)	456,133	236,659	219,474	62,510	32,363	30,147	773	442	331
Malignant neoplasms of lip, oral cavity and pharynx (C00-C14)	6,096	4,012	2,084	1,068	832	236	14	11	3
Malignant neoplasm of esophagus (C15)	11,295	8,969	2,326	1,458	1,065	393	21	17	4
Malignant neoplasm of stomach (C16)	7,455	4,372	3,083	1,949	1,147	802	19	11	8
Malignant neoplasms of colon, rectum and anus (C18-C21)	42,479	21,443	21,036	6,804	3,301	3,503	81	48	33

- = Quantity zero.
[1]Based on codes from the *International Classification of Diseases, Tenth Revision* (1992), except where (*) precedes the cause of death code.
[2]Persons of Hispanic origin may be of any race.
[3]Includes races other than White and Black.
[4]Includes deaths for which Hispanic origin was not reported on the death certificate.

Table B-21. Number of Deaths from 113 Selected Causes by Hispanic Origin, Race for Non-Hispanic Population, and Sex, 2005—*Continued*

(Number.)

Cause of death[1]	Non-Hispanic White[3]			Non-Hispanic Black			Origin not stated[4]		
	Both sexes	Male	Female	Both sexes	Male	Female	Both sexes	Male	Female
Malignant neoplasms of liver and intrahepatic bile ducts (C22)	10,950	7,107	3,843	2,087	1,460	627	33	24	9
Malignant neoplasm of pancreas (C25)	26,366	13,102	13,264	3,743	1,740	2,003	36	13	23
Malignant neoplasm of larynx (C32)	2,877	2,224	653	673	542	131	9	7	2
Malignant neoplasms of trachea, bronchus and lung (C33-C34)	134,924	75,500	59,424	16,437	9,794	6,643	224	141	83
Malignant melanoma of skin (C43)	7,973	5,074	2,899	123	57	66	8	7	1
Malignant neoplasm of breast (C50)	32,736	305	32,431	5,804	56	5,748	59	-	59
Malignant neoplasm of cervix uteri (C53)	2,538	...	2,538	776	...	776	8	...	8
Malignant neoplasms of corpus uteri and uterus, part unspecified (C54-C55)	5,360	...	5,360	1,165	...	1,165	14	...	14
Malignant neoplasm of ovary (C56)	12,472	...	12,472	1,204	...	1,204	7	...	7
Malignant neoplasm of prostate (C61)	22,319	22,319	...	4,771	4,771	...	39	39	...
Malignant neoplasms of kidney and renal pelvis (C64-C65)	10,312	6,404	3,908	1,141	713	428	18	15	3
Malignant neoplasm of bladder (C67)	11,669	8,207	3,462	947	536	411	15	12	3
Malignant neoplasms of meninges, brain and other parts of central nervous system (C70-C72)	11,313	6,289	5,024	781	434	347	17	9	8
Malignant neoplasms of lymphoid, hematopoietic and related tissue (C81-C96)	45,619	25,000	20,619	4,988	2,604	2,384	57	29	28
Hodgkin's disease (C81)	968	504	464	141	81	60	5	4	1
Non-Hodgkin's lymphoma (C82-C85)	17,852	9,527	8,325	1,379	744	635	21	9	12
Leukemia (C91-C95)	18,152	10,289	7,863	1,697	902	795	22	13	9
Multiple myeloma and immunoproliferative neoplasms (C88, C90)	8,599	4,649	3,950	1,766	874	892	9	3	6
Other and unspecified malignant neoplasms of lymphoid, hematopoietic and related tissue (C96)	48	31	17	5	3	2	-	-	-
All other and unspecified malignant neoplasms (C17, C23-C24, C26-C31, C37-C41, C44-C49, C51-C52, C57-C60, C62-C63, C66, C68-C69, C73-C80, C97)	51,380	26,332	25,048	6,591	3,311	3,280	94	59	35
In situ neoplasms, benign neoplasms and neoplasms of uncertain or unknown behavior (D00-D48)	11,670	5,850	5,820	1,142	493	649	20	13	7
Anemias (D50-D64)	3,314	1,208	2,106	1,024	452	572	9	3	6
Diabetes mellitus (E10-E14)	53,159	26,365	26,794	12,835	5,666	7,169	129	64	65
Nutritional deficiencies (E40-E64)	2,537	865	1,672	426	153	273	10	5	5
Malnutrition (E40-E46)	2,385	818	1,567	408	146	262	10	5	5
Other nutritional deficiencies (E50-E64)	152	47	105	18	7	11	-	-	-
Meningitis (G00,G03)	433	228	205	141	75	66	4	3	1
Parkinson's disease (G20-G21)	17,767	10,232	7,535	705	409	296	14	6	8
Alzheimer's disease (G30)	63,958	18,208	45,750	4,579	1,283	3,296	83	31	52
Major cardiovascular diseases (I00-I78)	698,139	328,004	370,135	99,000	47,004	51,996	1,577	879	698
Diseases of heart (I00-I09, I11, I13, I20-I51)	535,101	263,311	271,790	73,302	35,874	37,428	1,276	744	532
Acute rheumatic fever and chronic rheumatic heart diseases (I00-I09)	2,866	878	1,988	225	80	145	3	2	1
Hypertensive heart disease (I11)	20,219	8,644	11,575	6,825	3,402	3,423	98	58	40
Hypertensive heart and renal disease (I13)	1,989	791	1,198	879	426	453	10	7	3
Ischemic heart diseases (I20-I25)	368,505	191,862	176,643	45,435	22,608	22,827	906	536	370
Acute myocardial infarction (I21-I22)	124,831	66,629	58,202	15,359	7,437	7,922	240	141	99
Other acute ischemic heart diseases (I24)	2,829	1,431	1,398	551	292	259	14	8	6
Other forms of chronic ischemic heart disease (I20, I25)	240,845	123,802	117,043	29,525	14,879	14,646	652	387	265
Atherosclerotic cardiovascular disease, so described (I25.0)	48,146	25,849	22,297	9,442	5,281	4,161	255	178	77
All other forms of chronic ischemic heart disease (I20, I25.1-I25.9)	192,699	97,953	94,746	20,083	9,598	10,485	397	209	188
Other heart diseases (I26-I51)	141,522	61,136	80,386	19,938	9,358	10,580	259	141	118
Acute and subacute endocarditis (I33)	870	496	374	226	122	104	2	1	1
Diseases of pericardium and acute myocarditis (I30-I31, I40)	591	306	285	161	72	89	1	-	1
Heart failure (I50)	50,835	19,666	31,169	5,570	2,261	3,309	72	36	36

... = Not applicable.

- = Quantity zero.

[1]Based on codes from the *International Classification of Diseases, Tenth Revision* (1992), except where (*) precedes the cause of death code.

[3]Includes races other than White and Black.

[4]Includes deaths for which Hispanic origin was not reported on the death certificate.

Table B-21. Number of Deaths from 113 Selected Causes by Hispanic Origin, Race for Non-Hispanic Population, and Sex, 2005—*Continued*

(Number.)

Cause of death[1]	Non-Hispanic White[3]			Non-Hispanic Black			Origin not stated[4]		
	Both sexes	Male	Female	Both sexes	Male	Female	Both sexes	Male	Female
All other forms of heart disease (I26-I28 ,I34-I38, I42-I49, I51)........................	89,226	40,668	48,558	13,981	6,903	7,078	184	104	80
Essential (primary) hypertension and hypertensive renal disease (I10, I12)...........................	17,949	6,474	11,475	4,906	2,108	2,798	45	21	24
Cerebrovascular diseases (I60-I69)........................	115,074	44,038	71,036	17,378	7,448	9,930	201	79	122
Atherosclerosis (I70)........................	10,443	3,920	6,523	840	310	530	13	2	11
Other diseases of circulatory system (I71-I78)........................	19,572	10,261	9,311	2,574	1,264	1,310	42	33	9
Aortic aneurysm and dissection (I71)........................	11,684	6,877	4,807	1,288	707	581	22	18	4
Other diseases of arteries, arterioles and capillaries (I72-I78)........................	7,888	3,384	4,504	1,286	557	729	20	15	5
Other disorders of circulatory system (I80-I99)........................	3,659	1,603	2,056	785	380	405	12	6	6
Influenza and pneumonia (J10-J18)........................	52,431	22,903	29,528	5,716	2,697	3,019	112	64	48
Influenza (J10-J11)........................	1,654	585	1,069	67	31	36	5	-	5
Pneumonia (J12-J18)........................	50,777	22,318	28,459	5,649	2,666	2,983	107	64	43
Other acute lower respiratory infections (J20-J22)........................	334	141	193	40	17	23	-	-	-
Acute bronchitis and bronchiolitis (J20-J21)........................	225	96	129	31	15	16	-	-	-
Unspecified acute lower respiratory infection (J22)........................	109	45	64	9	2	7	-	-	-
Chronic lower respiratory diseases (J40-J47)........................	117,337	55,015	62,322	8,136	4,406	3,730	223	134	89
Bronchitis, chronic and unspecified (J40-J42)........................	738	296	442	54	33	21	2	-	2
Emphysema (J43)........................	12,675	6,430	6,245	810	505	305	23	16	7
Asthma (J45-J46)........................	2,475	743	1,732	1,002	403	599	10	4	6
Other chronic lower respiratory diseases (J44, J47)........................	101,449	47,546	53,903	6,270	3,465	2,805	188	114	74
Pneumoconioses and chemical effects (J60-J66, J68)........................	931	895	36	47	43	4	1	1	-
Pneumonitis due to solids and liquids (J69)........................	14,739	7,430	7,309	1,606	819	787	28	20	8
Other diseases of respiratory system (J00-J06, J30-J39, J67, J70-J98)........................	22,272	10,794	11,478	2,459	1,195	1,264	31	20	11
Peptic ulcer (K25-K28)........................	2,818	1,361	1,457	358	207	151	10	6	4
Diseases of appendix (K35-K38)........................	348	196	152	55	33	22	1	1	-
Hernia (K40-K46)........................	1,372	540	832	151	66	85	-	-	-
Chronic liver disease and cirrhosis (K70,K73-K74)........................	20,428	13,088	7,340	2,495	1,634	861	93	74	19
Alcoholic liver disease (K70)........................	9,372	6,714	2,658	1,154	790	364	56	47	9
Other chronic liver disease and cirrhosis (K73-K74)........................	11,056	6,374	4,682	1,341	844	497	37	27	10
Cholelithiasis and other disorders of gallbladder (K80-K82)........................	2,427	1,087	1,340	324	135	189	6	4	2
Nephritis, nephrotic syndrome and nephrosis (N00-N07, N17-N19, N25-N27)........................	32,492	15,953	16,539	8,017	3,612	4,405	62	37	25
Acute and rapidly progressive nephritic and nephrotic syndrome (N00-N01, N04)........................	103	52	51	18	6	12	-	-	-
Chronic glomerulonephritis, nephritis and nephropathy not specified as acute or chronic, and renal sclerosis unspecified (N02-N03, N05-N07, N26)........................	623	323	300	161	81	80	-	-	-
Renal failure (N17-N19)........................	31,743	15,566	16,177	7,834	3,525	4,309	62	37	25
Other disorders of kidney (N25, N27)........................	23	12	11	4	-	4	-	-	-
Infections of kidney (N10-N12, N13.6, N15.1)........................	610	184	426	89	27	62	1	1	-
Hyperplasia of prostate (N40)........................	464	464	...	30	30	...	1	1	...
Inflammatory diseases of female pelvic organs (N70-N76)........................	89	...	89	19	...	19	-	...	-
Pregnancy, childbirth and the puerperium (O00-O99)........................	327	...	327	265	...	265	1	...	1
Pregnancy with abortive outcome (O00-O07)........................	14	...	14	13	...	13	-	...	-
Other complications of pregnancy, childbirth and the puerperium (O10-O99)........................	313	...	313	252	...	252	1	...	1
Certain conditions originating in the perinatal period (P00-P96)........................	6,216	3,495	2,721	4,837	2,712	2,125	139	72	67
Congenital malformations, deformations and chromosomal abnormalities (Q00-Q99)........................	6,412	3,352	3,060	1,656	856	800	35	20	15

... = Not applicable.

- = Quantity zero.

[1]Based on codes from the *International Classification of Diseases, Tenth Revision* (1992), except where (*) precedes the cause of death code.

[3]Includes races other than White and Black.

[4]Includes deaths for which Hispanic origin was not reported on the death certificate.

Table B-21. Number of Deaths from 113 Selected Causes by Hispanic Origin, Race for Non-Hispanic Population, and Sex, 2005—Continued

(Number.)

Cause of death[1]	Non-Hispanic white[3]			Non-Hispanic black			Origin not stated[4]		
	Both sexes	Male	Female	Both sexes	Male	Female	Both sexes	Male	Female
Symptoms, signs and abnormal clinical and laboratory findings, not elsewhere classified (R00-R99)............................	24,697	10,691	14,006	4,612	2,366	2,246	258	159	99
All other diseases (residual)	178,181	71,058	107,123	24,604	10,478	14,126	358	198	160
Accidents (unintentional injuries) (V01-X59,Y85-Y86)..	88,970	56,021	32,949	13,393	9,130	4,263	378	269	109
Transport accidents (V01-V99, Y85)........................	34,349	23,830	10,519	5,739	4,158	1,581	126	90	36
Motor vehicle accidents (V02-V04, V09.0, V09.2, V12-V14, V19.0-V19.2, V19.4-V19.6 ,V20-V79, V80.3-V80.5, V81.0-V81.1, V82.0-V82.1, V83-V86, V87.0-V87.8, V88.0-V88.8, V89.0, V89.2)..	32,002	21,992	10,010	5,394	3,883	1,511	115	79	36
Other land transport accidents (V01, V05-V06, V09.1, V09.3-V09.9, V10-V11, V15-V18, V19.3,V19.8-V19.9, V80.0-V80.2, V80.6-V80.9, V81.2-V81.9, V82.2-V82.9, V87.9, V88.9, V89.1, V89.3, V89.9).......	815	601	214	200	160	40	7	7	-
Water, air and space, and other and unspecified transport accidents and their sequelae (V90-V99, Y85)	1,532	1,237	295	145	115	30	4	4	-
Nontransport accidents (W00-X59, Y86)........................	54,621	32,191	22,430	7,654	4,972	2,682	252	179	73
Falls (W00-W19).............................	17,042	8,560	8,482	1,001	583	418	41	23	18
Accidental discharge of firearms (W32-W34).............................	508	432	76	150	134	16	2	2	-
Accidental drowning and submersion (W65-W74).............................	2,305	1,763	542	543	463	80	17	13	4
Accidental exposure to smoke, fire and flames (X00-X09)	2,147	1,270	877	731	433	298	15	10	5
Accidental poisoning and exposure to noxious substances (X40-X49).............	18,126	11,949	6,177	2,920	1,959	961	112	83	29
Other and unspecified nontransport accidents and their sequelae (W20-W31, W35-W64, W75-W99, X10-X39, X50-X59, Y86)...........................	14,493	8,217	6,276	2,309	1,400	909	65	48	17
Intentional self-harm (suicide) (*U03, X60-X84, Y87.0)	27,305	21,605	5,700	1,953	1,592	361	111	92	19
Intentional self-harm (suicide) by discharge of firearms (X72-X74)	14,829	12,947	1,882	997	901	96	54	50	4
Intentional self-harm (suicide) by other and unspecified means and their sequelae (*U03, X60-X71, X75-X84, Y87.0)	12,476	8,658	3,818	956	691	265	57	42	15
Assault (homicide) (*U01-*U02, X85-Y09, Y87.1)...........................	5,325	3,515	1,810	8,522	7,288	1,234	100	80	20
Assault (homicide) by discharge of firearms (*U01.4, X93-X95)........................	2,871	2,018	853	6,600	5,977	623	64	54	10
Assault (homicide) by other and unspecified means and their sequelae (*U01.0-*U01.3, *U01.5-*U01.9, *U02, X85-X92, X96-Y09, Y87.1)	2,454	1,497	957	1,922	1,311	611	36	26	10
Legal intervention (Y35, Y89.0)........................	208	196	12	112	111	1	-	-	-
Events of undetermined intent (Y10-Y34, Y87.2, Y89.9)	3,583	2,099	1,484	675	447	228	29	21	8
Discharge of firearms, undetermined intent (Y22-Y24)...........................	148	121	27	36	28	8	2	1	1
Other and unspecified events of undetermined intent and their sequelae (Y10-Y21, Y25-Y34, Y87.2, Y89.9)	3,435	1,978	1,457	639	419	220	27	20	7
Operations of war and their sequelae (Y36, Y89.1).............................	19	19	-	6	6	-	-	-	-
Complications of medical and surgical care (Y40-Y84, Y88).............................	2,009	952	1,057	428	177	251	9	7	2

- = Quantity zero.

[1]Based on codes from the *International Classification of Diseases, Tenth Revision* (1992), except where (*) precedes the cause of death code.
[3]Includes races other than White and Black.
[4]Includes deaths for which Hispanic origin was not reported on the death certificate.

NOTE: Complete confirmation of deaths from selected causes of death, considered to be of public health concern, were not provided by the following states—Alabama, California, Connecticut, Florida, Illinois, Indiana, Kentucky, Louisiana, Maryland, Michigan, Missouri, Montana, Nevada, New Hampshire, New Jersey, New York, North Carolina, Ohio, Oklahoma, Pennsylvania, Rhode Island, Texas, Utah, Virginia, Washington, and West Virginia.

Table B-22. Death Rates for 113 Selected Causes by Race and Sex, 2005

(Rate per 100,000 population in specified group.)

Cause of death[1]	All races			White			All other					
							Total			Black		
	Both sexes	Male	Female	Both sexes	Male	Female	Both sexes	Male	Female	Both sexes	Male	Female
ALL CAUSES	825.9	827.2	824.6	873.7	864.5	882.8	621.8	663.2	583.4	749.4	799.2	703.9
Salmonella infections (A01-A02)	0.0	*	*	0.0	*	*	*	*	*	*	*	*
Shigellosis and amebiasis (A03, A06)	*	*	*	*	*	*	*	*	*	*	*	*
Certain other intestinal infections (A04, A07-A09)	1.9	1.5	2.3	2.2	1.7	2.7	0.7	0.6	0.8	0.8	0.7	0.9
Tuberculosis (A16-A19)	0.2	0.3	0.2	0.2	0.2	0.1	0.5	0.6	0.4	0.4	0.5	0.3
Respiratory tuberculosis (A16)	0.2	0.2	0.1	0.1	0.1	0.1	0.4	0.5	0.3	0.3	0.4	0.2
Other tuberculosis (A17-A19)	0.1	0.1	0.0	0.0	0.1	0.0	0.1	0.1	0.1	0.1	0.1	*
Whooping cough (A37)	0.0	*	*	0.0	*	*	*	*	*	*	*	*
Scarlet fever and erysipelas (A38, A46)	*	*	*	*	*	*	*	*	*	*	*	*
Meningococcal infection (A39).................................	0.0	0.0	0.0	0.0	0.0	0.0	0.0	*	*	*	*	*
Septicemia (A40-A41)	11.5	10.5	12.5	11.3	10.2	12.4	12.3	11.6	13.0	15.9	14.9	16.8
Syphilis (A50-A53)..	0.0	0.0	*	*	*	*	0.1	0.1	*	0.1	0.1	*
Acute poliomyelitis (A80)	*	*	*	*	*	*	*	*	*	*	*	*
Arthropod-borne viral encephalitis (A83-A84, A85.2)..........	*	*	*	*	*	*	*	*	*	*	*	*
Measles (B05)...	*	*	*	*	*	*	*	*	*	*	*	*
Viral hepatitis (B15-B19)......................................	1.9	2.5	1.3	1.8	2.5	1.2	2.0	2.5	1.6	2.2	2.8	1.7
Human immunodeficiency virus (HIV) disease (B20-B24)..	4.2	6.3	2.2	2.2	3.7	0.8	12.8	17.8	8.1	18.0	25.1	11.5
Malaria (B50-B54)	*	*	*	*	*	*	*	*	*	*	*	*
Other and unspecified infectious and parasitic diseases and their sequelae (A00, A05, A20-A36, A42-A44, A48-A49, A54-A79, A81-A82, A85.0-A85.1, A85.8, A86-B04, B06-B09, B25-B49, B55-B99).............................	2.6	2.9	2.3	2.7	3.0	2.4	2.3	2.6	2.1	2.5	2.8	2.2
Malignant neoplasms (C00-C97)...............................	188.7	198.9	178.8	200.8	210.6	191.1	137.1	147.6	127.5	161.7	175.4	149.1
Malignant neoplasms of lip, oral cavity and pharynx (C00-C14)	2.6	3.6	1.7	2.7	3.6	1.8	2.4	3.8	1.2	2.8	4.5	1.2
Malignant neoplasm of esophagus (C15)........................	4.6	7.3	1.9	4.9	7.9	2.0	3.0	4.6	1.6	3.8	5.8	1.9
Malignant neoplasm of stomach (C16)	3.9	4.6	3.2	3.6	4.3	3.0	5.0	6.1	4.0	5.0	6.2	4.0
Malignant neoplasms of colon, rectum and anus (C18-C21)	18.0	18.4	17.6	18.7	19.2	18.3	14.7	15.0	14.4	17.6	17.9	17.3
Malignant neoplasms of liver and intrahepatic bile ducts (C22)	5.4	7.2	3.7	5.3	7.0	3.7	5.9	8.4	3.7	5.4	7.9	3.1
Malignant neoplasm of pancreas (C25)........................	11.1	11.1	11.0	11.7	11.7	11.7	8.3	8.1	8.5	9.7	9.4	9.9
Malignant neoplasm of larynx (C32)	1.3	2.0	0.5	1.3	2.0	0.6	1.3	2.2	0.5	1.7	2.9	0.6
Malignant neoplasm of trachea, bronchus and lung (C33-C34)	53.7	61.8	45.9	58.1	65.9	50.4	35.3	43.6	27.5	42.4	53.0	32.7
Malignant melanoma of skin (C43)............................	2.8	3.6	2.0	3.4	4.4	2.4	0.4	0.4	0.3	0.3	0.3	0.3
Malignant neoplasm of breast (C50)...........................	14.0	0.3	27.3	14.4	0.3	28.3	12.1	0.2	23.2	15.0	0.3	28.4
Malignant neoplasm of cervix uteri (C53)	1.3	...	2.6	1.2	...	2.5	1.7	...	3.2	2.0	...	3.8
Malignant neoplasms of corpus uteri and uterus, part unspecified (C54-C55).....................................	2.4	...	4.7	2.4	...	4.7	2.4	...	4.6	3.0	...	5.8
Malignant neoplasm of ovary (C56)...........................	5.0	...	9.8	5.5	...	10.9	2.8	...	5.4	3.1	...	6.0
Malignant neoplasm of prostate (C61).........................	9.8	19.8	...	9.8	19.8	...	9.4	19.6	...	12.3	25.8	...
Malignant neoplasms of kidney and renal pelvis (C64-C65)	4.2	5.3	3.1	4.6	5.8	3.5	2.5	3.3	1.8	3.0	3.9	2.1
Malignant neoplasm of bladder (C67)	4.5	6.3	2.7	5.0	7.2	3.0	2.0	2.5	1.7	2.5	2.9	2.0
Malignant neoplasms of meninges, brain and other parts of central nervous system (C70-C72)	4.4	5.0	3.9	5.0	5.6	4.4	1.9	2.2	1.6	2.0	2.4	1.7
Malignant neoplasms of lymphoid, hematopoietic and related tissue (C81-C96)...................................	18.6	20.6	16.6	20.3	22.5	18.1	11.2	12.3	10.3	12.9	14.1	11.8
Hodgkin's disease (C81)	0.4	0.5	0.4	0.5	0.5	0.4	0.3	0.4	0.3	0.4	0.5	0.3
Non-Hodgkin's lymphoma (C82-C85)	7.0	7.6	6.5	7.9	8.5	7.3	3.4	3.7	3.0	3.6	4.0	3.1
Leukemia (C91-C95)......................................	7.3	8.4	6.2	8.1	9.3	6.9	3.9	4.4	3.5	4.4	4.9	4.0
Multiple myeloma and immunoproliferative neoplasms (C88, C90).....................................	3.8	4.1	3.5	3.8	4.2	3.5	3.6	3.7	3.5	4.6	4.7	4.4
Other and unspecified malignant neoplasms of lymphoid, hematopoietic and related tissue (C96).....	0.0	0.0	0.0	0.0	0.0	*	*	*	*	*	*	*
All other and unspecified malignant neoplasms (C17, C23-C24, C26-C31, C37-C41, C44-C49, C51-C52, C57-C60, C62-C63, C66, C68-C69, C73-C80, C97)..	21.2	22.1	20.4	22.7	23.6	21.9	14.7	15.3	14.0	17.1	18.0	16.3
In situ neoplasms, benign neoplasms and neoplasms of uncertain or unknown behavior (D00-D48).......................	4.6	4.7	4.6	5.1	5.2	5.0	2.6	2.4	2.7	2.9	2.7	3.2
Anemias (D50-D64)..	1.6	1.2	1.9	1.5	1.1	1.8	2.0	1.8	2.1	2.6	2.4	2.8
Diabetes mellitus (E10-E14)..................................	25.3	25.0	25.7	24.9	24.9	24.9	27.3	25.5	28.9	33.2	30.7	35.5
Nutritional deficiencies (E40-E64)	1.1	0.8	1.4	1.1	0.8	1.4	0.9	0.7	1.1	1.1	0.8	1.3
Malnutrition (E40-E46).....................................	1.0	0.7	1.3	1.0	0.7	1.4	0.9	0.7	1.0	1.1	0.8	1.3
Other nutritional deficiencies (E50-E64)	0.1	0.0	0.1	0.1	0.0	0.1	0.0	*	*	*	*	*

* = Figure does not meet standards of reliability or precision.
... = Not applicable.
0.0 = Quantity more than zero but less than 0.05.
[1]Based on codes from the *International Classification of Diseases, Tenth Revision* (1992), except where (*) precedes the cause of death code.

Table B-22. Death Rates for 113 Selected Causes by Race and Sex, 2005—*Continued*

(Rate per 100,000 population in specified group.)

Cause of death[1]	All races			White			All other					
							Total			Black		
	Both sexes	Male	Female	Both sexes	Male	Female	Both sexes	Male	Female	Both sexes	Male	Female
Meningitis (G00,G03)...	0.2	0.2	0.2	0.2	0.2	0.2	0.3	0.3	0.3	0.4	0.4	0.3
Parkinson's disease (G20-G21)	6.6	7.7	5.5	7.7	9.0	6.5	1.9	2.2	1.5	1.8	2.2	1.5
Alzheimer's disease (G30)...................................	24.2	14.1	33.9	27.6	16.0	38.9	9.6	5.8	13.1	11.8	6.9	16.3
Major cardiovascular diseases (I00-I78)...............	288.8	277.9	299.3	307.0	293.0	320.8	211.1	211.8	210.4	256.2	255.0	257.2
Diseases of heart (I00-I09, I11, I13, I20-I51)......	220.0	221.1	218.9	235.2	234.9	235.5	155.1	160.8	149.9	189.8	194.8	185.2
Acute rheumatic fever and chronic rheumatic heart diseases (I00-I09)....................................	1.1	0.7	1.5	1.3	0.8	1.7	0.6	0.4	0.7	0.6	0.4	0.7
Hypertensive heart disease (I11)	9.9	9.1	10.7	9.0	7.9	10.1	13.5	14.1	13.0	17.7	18.5	17.0
Hypertensive heart and renal disease (I13)........	1.1	0.9	1.2	0.9	0.7	1.1	1.8	1.8	1.7	2.3	2.3	2.2
Ischemic heart diseases (I20-I25).....................	150.4	159.0	142.0	162.6	171.5	153.9	98.2	104.1	92.7	117.8	122.9	113.1
Acute myocardial infarction (I21-I22).............	50.9	54.8	47.2	55.1	59.5	50.8	33.1	34.3	32.0	39.8	40.3	39.2
Other acute ischemic heart diseases (I24).......	1.2	1.2	1.2	1.2	1.2	1.2	1.1	1.3	1.0	1.4	1.6	1.3
Other forms of chronic ischemic heart disease (I20, I25)...	98.2	102.9	93.7	106.2	110.7	101.9	63.9	68.6	59.7	76.6	81.0	72.6
Atherosclerotic cardiovascular disease, so described (I25.0)..	21.2	23.6	18.8	21.5	23.7	19.4	19.7	23.3	16.4	24.5	28.8	20.6
All other forms of chronic ischemic heart disease (I20, I25.1-I25.9)...........................	77.0	79.3	74.8	84.7	87.0	82.4	44.3	45.3	43.3	52.1	52.2	52.0
Other heart diseases (I26-I51).........................	57.6	51.4	63.5	61.4	54.0	68.7	41.1	40.3	41.8	51.4	50.6	52.2
Acute and subacute endocarditis (I33)	0.4	0.5	0.3	0.4	0.5	0.3	0.5	0.5	0.4	0.6	0.7	0.5
Diseases of pericardium and acute myocarditis (I30-I31, I40)...........................	0.3	0.3	0.3	0.3	0.3	0.3	0.4	0.4	0.4	0.4	0.4	0.4
Heart failure (I50)...	19.9	15.8	23.9	21.9	17.2	26.5	11.3	9.6	12.8	14.4	12.2	16.3
All other forms of heart disease (I26-I28, I34-I38, I42-I49, I51)......................	37.0	34.9	39.0	38.9	36.0	41.6	28.9	29.8	28.1	36.1	37.3	34.9
Essential (primary) hypertension and hypertensive renal disease (I10, I12)......................................	8.4	6.5	10.3	8.0	5.9	10.1	10.0	9.0	11.0	12.7	11.4	13.8
Cerebrovascular diseases (I60-I69).....................	48.4	38.8	57.8	50.7	39.7	61.6	38.6	34.7	42.2	44.9	40.3	49.1
Atherosclerosis (I70)...	4.0	3.1	4.9	4.5	3.4	5.6	1.8	1.4	2.1	2.2	1.7	2.6
Other diseases of circulatory system (I71-I78).....	8.0	8.5	7.4	8.5	9.1	8.0	5.6	5.9	5.3	6.7	6.9	6.5
Aortic aneurysm and dissection (I71)...............	4.7	5.6	3.8	5.1	6.1	4.1	3.0	3.6	2.5	3.3	3.9	2.9
Other diseases of arteries, arterioles and capillaries (I72-I78)......................................	3.3	2.9	3.7	3.5	3.0	3.9	2.6	2.3	2.8	3.3	3.0	3.6
Other disorders of circulatory system (I80-I99).....	1.6	1.5	1.8	1.6	1.4	1.8	1.6	1.6	1.5	2.0	2.1	2.0
Influenza and pneumonia (J10-J18)....................	21.3	19.2	23.2	23.1	20.5	25.7	13.3	13.4	13.1	14.8	14.6	14.9
Influenza (J10-J11)...	0.6	0.5	0.8	0.7	0.5	0.9	0.2	0.2	0.2	0.2	0.2	0.2
Pneumonia (J12-J18)......................................	20.6	18.8	22.5	22.4	20.0	24.8	13.1	13.2	12.9	14.6	14.5	14.8
Other acute lower respiratory infections (J20-J22)	0.1	0.1	0.2	0.1	0.1	0.2	0.1	0.1	0.1	0.1	*	0.1
Acute bronchitis and bronchiolitis (J20-J21)	0.1	0.1	0.1	0.1	0.1	0.1	0.1	0.1	0.1	0.1	*	*
Unspecified acute lower respiratory infection (J22)........	0.0	0.0	0.0	0.0	0.0	0.1	*	*	*	*	*	*
Chronic lower respiratory diseases (J40-J47)........	44.2	42.8	45.5	50.3	47.9	52.8	17.9	20.4	15.5	21.1	23.9	18.4
Bronchitis, chronic and unspecified (J40-J42)	0.3	0.2	0.3	0.3	0.3	0.4	0.1	0.2	0.1	0.1	0.2	0.1
Emphysema (J43)..	4.7	5.0	4.5	5.4	5.6	5.3	1.8	2.4	1.3	2.1	2.7	1.5
Asthma (J45-J46)..	1.3	0.9	1.7	1.1	0.7	1.5	2.1	1.7	2.4	2.6	2.2	3.0
Other chronic lower respiratory diseases (J44, J47)	37.8	36.6	39.0	43.5	41.3	45.6	13.8	16.1	11.7	16.2	18.8	13.9
Pneumoconioses and chemical effects (J60-J66, J68)...........	0.3	0.7	0.0	0.4	0.8	0.0	0.1	0.2	*	0.1	0.2	*
Pneumonitis due to solids and liquids (J69)	5.8	6.0	5.7	6.4	6.5	6.3	3.4	3.7	3.2	4.1	4.4	3.9
Other diseases of respiratory system (J00-J06, J30-J39, J67, J70-J98)........	9.1	9.0	9.2	9.9	9.7	10.1	5.7	5.9	5.5	6.3	6.5	6.2
Peptic ulcer (K25-K28)	1.2	1.2	1.2	1.2	1.2	1.3	0.9	1.0	0.7	0.9	1.1	0.7
Diseases of appendix (K35-K38).........................	0.1	0.2	0.1	0.2	0.2	0.1	0.1	0.1	0.1	0.1	0.2	0.1
Hernia (K40-K46)..	0.6	0.4	0.7	0.6	0.5	0.7	0.3	0.3	0.4	0.4	0.4	0.4
Chronic liver disease and cirrhosis (K70, K73-K74)	9.3	12.3	6.4	10.0	13.2	6.9	6.3	8.3	4.3	6.5	8.9	4.3
Alcoholic liver disease (K70)..........................	4.4	6.5	2.3	4.7	6.9	2.4	3.1	4.3	1.9	3.0	4.3	1.8
Other chronic liver disease and cirrhosis (K73-K74)	4.9	5.8	4.0	5.3	6.2	4.4	3.2	4.0	2.5	3.5	4.6	2.5
Cholelithiasis and other disorders of gallbladder (K80-K82)	1.0	0.9	1.1	1.1	1.0	1.2	0.7	0.6	0.8	0.8	0.7	0.9
Nephritis, nephrotic syndrome and nephrosis (N00-N07, N17-N19, N25-N27).......................	14.8	14.6	15.0	14.5	14.4	14.6	16.2	15.3	17.0	20.7	19.5	21.7
Acute and rapidly progressive nephritic and nephrotic syndrome (N00-N01, N04)	0.0	0.0	0.0	0.0	0.1	0.0	0.0	*	*	*	*	*
Chronic glomerulonephritis, nephritis and nephropathy not specified as acute or chronic, and renal sclerosis unspecified (N02-N03, N05-N07, N26).............................	0.3	0.3	0.3	0.3	0.3	0.3	0.3	0.3	0.3	0.4	0.4	0.4
Renal failure (N17-N19)...................................	14.5	14.2	14.7	14.2	14.1	14.2	15.8	14.9	16.6	20.2	19.1	21.2
Other disorders of kidney (N25, N27)	0.0	*	*	0.0	*	*	*	*	*	*	*	*
Infections of kidney (N10-N12, N13.6, N15.1).....	0.3	0.2	0.4	0.3	0.2	0.4	0.2	0.1	0.3	0.2	0.1	0.3
Hyperplasia of prostate (N40)............................	0.2	0.4	...	0.2	0.4	...	0.1	0.2	...	0.1	0.2	...
Inflammatory diseases of female pelvic organs (N70-N76)...	0.0	...	0.1	0.0	...	0.1	0.0	...	0.1	*	...	*

* = Figure does not meet standards of reliability or precision.

... = Not applicable.

0.0 = Quantity more than zero but less than 0.05.

[1]Based on codes from the *International Classification of Diseases, Tenth Revision* (1992), except where (*) precedes the cause of death code.

Table B-22. Death Rates for 113 Selected Causes by Race and Sex, 2005—*Continued*

(Rate per 100,000 population in specified group.)

Cause of death[1]	All races			White			All other					
							Total			Black		
	Both sexes	Male	Female	Both sexes	Male	Female	Both sexes	Male	Female	Both sexes	Male	Female
Pregnancy, childbirth and the puerperium (O00-O99)	0.3	...	0.5	0.2	...	0.4	0.5	...	1.1	0.7	...	1.3
Pregnancy with abortive outcome (O00-O07)	0.0	...	0.0	*	...	*	*	...	*	*	...	*
Other complications of pregnancy, childbirth and the puerperium (O10-O99)	0.2	...	0.5	0.2	...	0.4	0.5	...	1.0	0.7	...	1.2
Certain conditions originating in the perinatal period (P00-P96)	4.9	5.6	4.2	3.7	4.2	3.2	10.0	11.7	8.5	12.9	15.2	10.9
Congenital malformations, deformations and chromosomal abnormalities (Q00-Q99)	3.5	3.7	3.3	3.4	3.6	3.2	3.8	4.2	3.5	4.4	4.8	4.1
Symptoms, signs and abnormal clinical and laboratory findings, not elsewhere classified (R00-R99)	10.8	10.0	11.5	11.1	10.0	12.2	9.6	10.3	9.0	12.3	13.3	11.4
All other diseases (Residual)	73.4	60.9	85.6	78.5	64.1	92.6	51.9	46.9	56.5	63.6	56.8	69.7
Accidents (unintentional injuries) (V01-X59, Y85-Y86)	39.7	52.3	27.5	41.8	54.3	29.5	30.9	43.5	19.3	34.9	50.0	21.2
Transport accidents (V01-V99, Y85)	16.3	23.3	9.5	16.9	24.0	10.0	13.8	20.4	7.8	15.0	22.7	7.9
Motor vehicle accidents (V02-V04, V09.0, V09.2, V12-V14, V19.0-V19.2, V19.4-V19.6, V20-V79, V80.3-V80.5, V81.0-V81.1, V82.0-V82.1, V83-V86, V87.0-V87.8, V88.0-V88.8, V89.0, V89.2)	15.3	21.7	9.1	15.8	22.3	9.5	13.0	18.9	7.5	14.1	21.2	7.5
Other land transport accidents (V01, V05-V06, V09.1, V09.3-V09.9, V10-V11, V15-V18, V19.3,V19.8-V19.9, V80.0-V80.2, V80.6-V80.9, V81.2-V81.9, V82.2-V82.9, V87.9, V88.9,V89.1, V89.3,V89.9)	0.4	0.7	0.2	0.4	0.6	0.2	0.5	0.8	0.2	0.5	0.9	0.2
Water, air and space, and other and unspecified transport accidents and their sequelae (V90-V99, Y85)	0.6	1.0	0.2	0.7	1.1	0.3	0.4	0.7	0.2	0.4	0.6	0.1
Nontransport accidents (W00-X59, Y86)	23.4	29.0	18.0	24.9	30.3	19.6	17.1	23.1	11.5	20.0	27.3	13.3
Falls (W00-W19)	6.6	7.0	6.3	7.5	7.8	7.3	2.7	3.4	2.2	2.6	3.2	2.1
Accidental discharge of firearms (W32-W34)	0.3	0.5	0.1	0.3	0.4	0.1	0.3	0.6	0.1	0.4	0.7	*
Accidental drowning and submersion (W65-W74)	1.2	1.9	0.5	1.2	1.8	0.5	1.4	2.3	0.5	1.4	2.5	0.4
Accidental exposure to smoke, fire and flames (X00-X09)	1.1	1.3	0.9	1.0	1.2	0.8	1.5	1.8	1.2	1.9	2.4	1.5
Accidental poisoning and exposure to noxious substances (X40-X49)	8.0	10.9	5.1	8.4	11.4	5.4	6.1	8.6	3.9	7.6	10.8	4.8
Other and unspecified nontransport accidents and their sequelae (W20-W31, W35-W64, W75-W99, X10-X39, X50-X59, Y86)	6.3	7.4	5.1	6.5	7.7	5.4	5.0	6.4	3.7	6.0	7.6	4.5
Intentional self-harm (suicide) (*U03, X60-X84, Y87.0)	11.0	17.7	4.5	12.3	19.7	5.0	5.5	9.0	2.3	5.1	8.7	1.8
Intentional self-harm (suicide) by discharge of firearms (X72-X74)	5.7	10.2	1.4	6.5	11.5	1.6	2.3	4.4	0.5	2.6	4.9	0.5
Intentional self-harm (suicide) by other and unspecified means and their sequelae (*U03, X60-X71, X75-X84, Y87.0)	5.3	7.5	3.1	5.8	8.2	3.4	3.2	4.6	1.9	2.5	3.8	1.3
Assault (homicide) (*U01-*U02, X85-Y09, Y87.1)	6.1	9.8	2.5	3.7	5.4	1.9	16.6	29.3	4.9	22.2	39.7	6.2
Assault (homicide) by discharge of firearms (*U01.4, X93-X95)	4.2	7.2	1.2	2.2	3.5	0.9	12.6	23.6	2.4	17.2	32.5	3.1
Assault (homicide) by other and unspecified means and their sequelae (*U01.0-*U01.3, *U01.5-*U01.9, *U02, X85-X92, X96-Y09, Y87.1)	1.9	2.6	1.3	1.5	1.9	1.0	4.0	5.7	2.5	5.0	7.2	3.0
Legal intervention (Y35,Y89.0)	0.1	0.3	*	0.1	0.2	*	0.2	0.5	*	0.3	0.6	*
Events of undetermined intent (Y10-Y34, Y87.2, Y89.9)	1.6	2.0	1.3	1.6	2.0	1.3	1.5	2.0	1.0	1.8	2.4	1.1
Discharge of firearms, undetermined intent (Y22-Y24)	0.1	0.1	0.0	0.1	0.1	0.0	0.1	0.1	*	0.1	0.2	*
Other and unspecified events of undetermined intent and their sequelae (Y10-Y21, Y25-Y34, Y87.2, Y89.9)	1.5	1.8	1.2	1.6	1.8	1.3	1.4	1.8	1.0	1.7	2.3	1.1
Operations of war and their sequelae (Y36, Y89.1)	0.0	0.0	*	0.0	0.0	*	*	*	*	*	*	*
Complications of medical and surgical care (Y40-Y84, Y88)	0.9	0.8	1.0	0.9	0.9	1.0	0.9	0.8	0.9	1.1	1.0	1.2

* = Figure does not meet standards of reliability or precision.
... = Not applicable.
0.0 = Quantity more than zero but less than 0.05.
[1]Based on codes from the *International Classification of Diseases, Tenth Revision* (1992), except where (*) precedes the cause of death code.

NOTE: Complete confirmation of deaths from selected causes of death, considered to be of public health concern, were not provided by the following states–Alabama, California, Connecticut, Florida, Illinois, Indiana, Kentucky, Louisiana, Maryland, Michigan, Missouri, Montana, Nevada, New Hampshire, New Jersey, New York, North Carolina, Ohio, Oklahoma, Pennsylvania, Rhode Island, Texas, Utah, Virginia, Washington, and West Virginia.

Table B-23. Death Rates for 113 Selected Causes by Hispanic Origin, Race for Non-Hispanic Population, and Sex, 2005

(Rate per 100,000 population.)

Cause of death[1]	All origins[2]			Hispanic[3]			Non-Hispanic[4]		
	Both sexes	Male	Female	Both sexes	Male	Female	Both sexes	Male	Female
ALL CAUSES	825.9	827.2	824.6	307.3	334.4	278.2	911.2	912.6	910.0
Salmonella infections (A01-A02)	0.0	*	*	*	*	*	0.0	*	*
Shigellosis and amebiasis (A03, A06)	*	*	*	*	*	*	*	*	*
Certain other intestinal infections (A04, A07-A09)	1.9	1.5	2.3	0.4	0.3	0.6	2.2	1.7	2.6
Tuberculosis (A16-A19)	0.2	0.3	0.2	0.2	0.3	0.1	0.2	0.3	0.2
Respiratory tuberculosis (A16)	0.2	0.2	0.1	0.1	0.2	0.1	0.2	0.2	0.1
Other tuberculosis (A17-A19)	0.1	0.1	0.0	0.1	0.1	*	0.1	0.1	0.0
Whooping cough (A37)	0.0	*	*	*	*	*	*	*	*
Scarlet fever and erysipelas (A38, A46)	*	*	*	*	*	*	*	*	*
Meningococcal infection (A39)	0.0	0.0	0.0	*	*	*	0.0	0.0	0.0
Septicemia (A40-A41)	11.5	10.5	12.5	4.0	3.8	4.2	12.8	11.7	13.8
Syphilis (A50-A53)	0.0	0.0	*	*	*	*	0.0	0.0	*
Acute poliomyelitis (A80)	*	*	*	*	*	*	*	*	*
Arthropod-borne viral encephalitis (A83-A84, A85.2)	*	*	*	*	*	*	*	*	*
Measles (B05)	*	*	*	*	*	*	*	*	*
Viral hepatitis (B15-B19)	1.9	2.5	1.3	1.9	2.4	1.3	1.9	2.5	1.3
Human immunodeficiency virus (HIV) disease (B20-B24)	4.2	6.3	2.2	3.9	5.9	1.6	4.3	6.3	2.3
Malaria (B50-B54)	*	*	*	*	*	*	*	*	*
Other and unspecified infectious and parasitic diseases and their sequelae (A00, A05, A20-A36, A42-A44, A48-A49, A54-A79, A81-A82, A85.0-A85.1, A85.8, A86-B04, B06-B09, B25-B49, B55-B99)	2.6	2.9	2.3	1.8	2.0	1.6	2.7	3.0	2.5
Malignant neoplasms (C00-C97)	188.7	198.9	178.8	61.3	63.0	59.5	209.8	222.8	197.5
Malignant neoplasms of lip, oral cavity and pharynx (C00-C14)	2.6	3.6	1.7	0.7	1.1	0.4	2.9	4.1	1.9
Malignant neoplasm of esophagus (C15)	4.6	7.3	1.9	1.1	1.8	0.4	5.1	8.2	2.2
Malignant neoplasm of stomach (C16)	3.9	4.6	3.2	3.0	3.4	2.6	4.0	4.8	3.3
Malignant neoplasms of colon, rectum and anus (C18-C21)	18.0	18.4	17.6	6.0	6.1	5.8	20.0	20.5	19.4
Malignant neoplasms of liver and intrahepatic bile ducts (C22)	5.4	7.2	3.7	4.2	5.4	3.0	5.6	7.5	3.8
Malignant neoplasm of pancreas (C25)	11.1	11.1	11.0	4.1	4.0	4.2	12.2	12.3	12.1
Malignant neoplasm of larynx (C32)	1.3	2.0	0.5	0.4	0.7	*	1.4	2.3	0.6
Malignant neoplasms of trachea, bronchus and lung (C33-C34)	53.7	61.8	45.9	10.5	13.0	7.8	60.9	70.3	51.9
Malignant melanoma of skin (C43)	2.8	3.6	2.0	0.4	0.5	0.3	3.2	4.2	2.3
Malignant neoplasm of breast (C50)	14.0	0.3	27.3	4.5	*	9.4	15.6	0.3	30.1
Malignant neoplasm of cervix uteri (C53)	1.3	...	2.6	1.0	...	2.2	1.4	...	2.7
Malignant neoplasms of corpus uteri and uterus, part unspecified (C54-C55)	2.4	...	4.7	0.9	...	1.9	2.6	...	5.2
Malignant neoplasm of ovary (C56)	5.0	...	9.8	1.7	...	3.6	5.5	...	10.8
Malignant neoplasm of prostate (C61)	9.8	19.8	...	3.0	5.9	...	10.9	22.2	...
Malignant neoplasms of kidney and renal pelvis (C64-C65)	4.2	5.3	3.1	1.8	2.2	1.4	4.6	5.9	3.4
Malignant neoplasm of bladder (C67)	4.5	6.3	2.7	1.0	1.4	0.6	5.0	7.1	3.0
Malignant neoplasms of meninges, brain and other parts of central nervous system (C70-C72)	4.4	5.0	3.9	1.8	2.0	1.6	4.9	5.5	4.2
Malignant neoplasms of lymphoid, hematopoietic and related tissue (C81-C96)	18.6	20.6	16.6	7.3	7.8	6.7	20.4	22.8	18.2
Hodgkin's disease (C81)	0.4	0.5	0.4	0.3	0.4	0.2	0.4	0.5	0.4
Non-Hodgkin's lymphoma (C82-C85)	7.0	7.6	6.5	2.6	2.7	2.5	7.8	8.5	7.1
Leukemia (C91-C95)	7.3	8.4	6.2	3.0	3.4	2.5	8.0	9.3	6.8
Multiple myeloma and immunoproliferative neoplasms (C88, C90)	3.8	4.1	3.5	1.4	1.3	1.4	4.2	4.6	3.8
Other and unspecified malignant neoplasms of lymphoid, hematopoietic and related tissue (C96)	0.0	0.0	0.0	*	*	*	0.0	0.0	*
All other and unspecified malignant neoplasms (C17, C23-C24, C26-C31, C37-C41, C44-C49, C51-C52, C57-C60, C62-C63, C66, C68-C69, C73-C80, C97)	21.2	22.1	20.4	7.6	7.8	7.4	23.5	24.5	22.4

* = Figure does not meet standards of reliability or precision.
... = Category not applicable.
0.0 = Quantity more than zero but less than 0.05.
[1]Based on codes from the *International Classification of Diseases, Tenth Revision* (1992), except where (*) precedes the cause of death code.
[2]Figures for origin not stated are included in all origins but not distributed among specified origins.
[3]Persons of Hispanic origin may be of any race.
[4]Includes races other than White and Black.

Table B-23. Death Rates for 113 Selected Causes by Hispanic Origin, Race for Non-Hispanic Population, and Sex, 2005—*Continued*

(Rate per 100,000 population.)

Cause of death[1]	All origins[2]			Hispanic[3]			Non-Hispanic[4]		
	Both sexes	Male	Female	Both sexes	Male	Female	Both sexes	Male	Female
In situ neoplasms, benign neoplasms and neoplasms of uncertain or unknown behavior (D00-D48).............	4.6	4.7	4.6	1.3	1.4	1.3	5.2	5.2	5.1
Anemias (D50-D64)............................	1.6	1.2	1.9	0.4	0.4	0.5	1.7	1.4	2.1
Diabetes mellitus (E10-E14)...................	25.3	25.0	25.7	15.6	14.9	16.3	26.9	26.8	27.1
Nutritional deficiencies (E40-E64)............	1.1	0.8	1.4	0.3	0.3	0.4	1.2	0.8	1.5
Malnutrition (E40-E46)......................	1.0	0.7	1.3	0.3	0.3	0.4	1.1	0.8	1.4
Other nutritional deficiencies (E50-E64)	0.1	0.0	0.1	*	*	*	0.1	0.0	0.1
Meningitis (G00,G03).........................	0.2	0.2	0.2	0.1	0.1	0.1	0.2	0.3	0.2
Parkinson's disease (G20-G21)	6.6	7.7	5.5	1.7	1.9	1.5	7.4	8.7	6.1
Alzheimer's disease (G30)....................	24.2	14.1	33.9	5.2	3.5	7.0	27.3	15.9	38.2
Major cardiovascular diseases (I00-I78)........	288.8	277.9	299.3	91.4	92.3	90.4	321.4	310.3	332.0
Diseases of heart (I00-I09, I11, I13, I20-I51)....	220.0	221.1	218.9	69.2	72.1	66.2	244.9	247.1	242.8
Acute rheumatic fever and chronic rheumatic heart diseases (I00-I09)......	1.1	0.7	1.5	0.4	0.2	0.6	1.3	0.8	1.7
Hypertensive heart disease (I11)............	9.9	9.1	10.7	3.5	3.5	3.4	10.9	10.0	11.8
Hypertensive heart and renal disease (I13).....	1.1	0.9	1.2	0.5	0.4	0.5	1.2	1.0	1.3
Ischemic heart diseases (I20-I25).............	150.4	159.0	142.0	51.0	54.2	47.6	166.7	177.2	156.7
Acute myocardial infarction (I21-I22).........	50.9	54.8	47.2	17.6	18.8	16.4	56.5	61.2	52.0
Other acute ischemic heart diseases (I24).....	1.2	1.2	1.2	0.2	0.2	0.2	1.4	1.4	1.3
Other forms of chronic ischemic heart disease (I20, I25)...............	98.2	102.9	93.7	33.2	35.2	31.0	108.9	114.6	103.4
Atherosclerotic cardiovascular disease, so described (I25.0)..........	21.2	23.6	18.8	8.2	10.2	6.0	23.3	25.8	20.8
All other forms of chronic ischemic heart disease (I20, I25.1-I25.9)........	77.0	79.3	74.8	25.0	25.0	25.0	85.6	88.8	82.6
Other heart diseases (I26-I51)...............	57.6	51.4	63.5	13.9	13.7	14.1	64.8	58.0	71.2
Acute and subacute endocarditis (I33).....	0.4	0.5	0.3	0.2	0.3	0.1	0.4	0.5	0.4
Diseases of pericardium and acute myocarditis (I30-I31, I40)	0.3	0.3	0.3	0.2	0.2	0.2	0.3	0.3	0.3
Heart failure (I50).......................	19.9	15.8	23.9	4.0	3.3	4.8	22.5	18.0	26.9
All other forms of heart disease (I26-I28, I34-I38, I42-I49, I51)......	37.0	34.9	39.0	9.5	10.0	9.0	41.5	39.2	43.7
Essential (primary) hypertension and hypertensive renal disease (I10, I12)............	8.4	6.5	10.3	3.1	2.5	3.7	9.3	7.2	11.3
Cerebrovascular diseases (I60-I69)............	48.4	38.8	57.8	16.0	14.4	17.7	53.8	43.0	64.1
Atherosclerosis (I70).......................	4.0	3.1	4.9	0.9	0.8	1.1	4.5	3.5	5.5
Other diseases of circulatory system (I71-I78)	8.0	8.5	7.4	2.1	2.5	1.7	8.9	9.5	8.3
Aortic aneurysm and dissection (I71)........	4.7	5.6	3.8	1.1	1.5	0.7	5.3	6.3	4.3
Other diseases of arteries, arterioles and capillaries (I72-I78)........	3.3	2.9	3.7	1.0	1.0	1.0	3.7	3.2	4.1
Other disorders of circulatory system (I80-I99).................................	1.6	1.5	1.8	0.7	0.6	0.8	1.8	1.6	1.9
Influenza and pneumonia (J10-J18)............	21.3	19.2	23.2	7.2	6.8	7.7	23.6	21.4	25.7
Influenza (J10-J11).........................	0.6	0.5	0.8	0.1	0.1	0.1	0.7	0.5	0.9
Pneumonia (J12-J18).......................	20.6	18.8	22.5	7.1	6.7	7.5	22.9	20.9	24.8
Other acute lower respiratory infections (J20-J22).................................	0.1	0.1	0.2	*	*	*	0.2	0.1	0.2
Acute bronchitis and bronchiolitis (J20-J21).................................	0.1	0.1	0.1	*	*	*	0.1	0.1	0.1
Unspecified acute lower respiratory infection (J22)...........................	0.0	0.0	0.0	*	*	*	0.0	0.0	0.1
Chronic lower respiratory diseases (J40-J47).................................	44.2	42.8	45.5	8.1	8.3	7.8	50.2	48.8	51.5
Bronchitis, chronic and unspecified (J40-J42).................................	0.3	0.2	0.3	0.1	*	0.1	0.3	0.3	0.4
Emphysema (J43)...........................	4.7	5.0	4.5	0.7	0.8	0.6	5.4	5.7	5.1
Asthma (J45-J46)...........................	1.3	0.9	1.7	0.6	0.5	0.7	1.4	1.0	1.9
Other chronic lower respiratory diseases (J44, J47).................................	37.8	36.6	39.0	6.7	6.9	6.5	43.0	41.8	44.1
Pneumoconioses and chemical effects (J60-J66, J68)...........................	0.3	0.7	0.0	0.0	*	*	0.4	0.8	0.0
Pneumonitis due to solids and liquids (J69)	5.8	6.0	5.7	1.4	1.4	1.3	6.6	6.8	6.3

* = Figure does not meet standards of reliability or precision.
0.0 = Quantity more than zero but less than 0.05.
[1]Based on codes from the *International Classification of Diseases, Tenth Revision* (1992), except where (*) precedes the cause of death code.
[2]Figures for origin not stated are included in all origins but not distributed among specified origins.
[3]Persons of Hispanic origin may be of any race.
[4]Includes races other than White and Black.

Table B-23. Death Rates for 113 Selected Causes by Hispanic Origin, Race for Non-Hispanic Population, and Sex, 2005—*Continued*

(Rate per 100,000 population.)

Cause of death[1]	All origins[2]			Hispanic[3]			Non-Hispanic[4]		
	Both sexes	Male	Female	Both sexes	Male	Female	Both sexes	Male	Female
Other diseases of respiratory system (J00-J06, J30-J39, J67, J70-J98)	9.1	9.0	9.2	3.7	3.5	3.9	10.0	10.0	10.1
Peptic ulcer (K25-K28)	1.2	1.2	1.2	0.4	0.4	0.4	1.3	1.3	1.3
Diseases of appendix (K35-K38)	0.1	0.2	0.1	0.1	0.1	*	0.2	0.2	0.1
Hernia (K40-K46)	0.6	0.4	0.7	0.2	0.1	0.3	0.6	0.5	0.7
Chronic liver disease and cirrhosis (K70, K73-K74)	9.3	12.3	6.4	8.3	11.6	4.8	9.4	12.3	6.6
Alcoholic liver disease (K70)	4.4	6.5	2.3	4.2	6.8	1.4	4.4	6.4	2.5
Other chronic liver disease and cirrhosis (K73-K74)	4.9	5.8	4.0	4.1	4.8	3.4	5.1	6.0	4.1
Cholelithiasis and other disorders of gallbladder (K80-K82)	1.0	0.9	1.1	0.5	0.5	0.6	1.1	1.0	1.2
Nephritis, nephrotic syndrome and nephrosis (N00-N07, N17-N19, N25-N27).........................	14.8	14.6	15.0	5.5	5.4	5.5	16.4	16.2	16.5
Acute and rapidly progressive nephritic and nephrotic syndrome (N00-N01, N04)	0.0	0.0	0.0	*	*	*	0.0	0.0	0.1
Chronic glomerulonephritis, nephritis and nephropathy not specified as acute or chronic, and renal sclerosis unspecified (N02-N03, N05-N07, N26)	0.3	0.3	0.3	0.1	0.1	0.2	0.3	0.3	0.3
Renal failure (N17-N19)	14.5	14.2	14.7	5.3	5.2	5.3	16.0	15.8	16.2
Other disorders of kidney (N25, N27)	0.0	*	*	*	*	*	0.0	*	*
Infections of kidney (N10-N12, N13.6, N15.1)..............	0.3	0.2	0.4	0.1	0.1	0.1	0.3	0.2	0.4
Hyperplasia of prostate (N40)....................................	0.2	0.4	...	*	*	...	0.2	0.4	...
Inflammatory diseases of female pelvic organs (N70-N76)	0.0	...	0.1	*	...	*	0.0	...	0.1
Pregnancy, childbirth and the puerperium (O00-O99)	0.3	...	0.5	0.3	...	0.6	0.2	...	0.5
Pregnancy with abortive outcome (O00-O07)	0.0	...	0.0	*	...	*	0.0	...	0.0
Other complications of pregnancy, childbirth and the puerperium (O10-O99)	0.2	...	0.5	0.3	...	0.6	0.2	...	0.5
Certain conditions originating in the perinatal period (P00-P96)	4.9	5.6	4.2	6.6	7.3	5.8	4.6	5.2	3.9
Congenital malformations, deformations and chromosomal abnormalities (Q00-Q99)	3.5	3.7	3.3	4.4	4.5	4.4	3.3	3.6	3.1
Symptoms, signs and abnormal clinical and laboratory findings, not elsewhere classified (R00-R99)	10.8	10.0	11.5	4.4	5.1	3.5	11.8	10.8	12.7
All other diseases (residual)	73.4	60.9	85.6	24.0	23.2	24.9	81.6	67.4	95.1
Accidents (unintentional injuries) (V01-X59,Y85-Y86)	39.7	52.3	27.5	26.9	39.0	13.8	41.8	54.5	29.6
Transport accidents (V01-V99,Y85).............................	16.3	23.3	9.5	14.9	21.7	7.6	16.5	23.6	9.8
Motor vehicle accidents (V02-V04, V09.0, V09.2, V12-V14, V19.0-V19.2, V19.4-V19.6, V20-V79, V80.3-V80.5, V81.0-V81.1, V82.0-V82.1, V83-V86, V87.0-V87.8, V88.0-V88.8, V89.0, V89.2)...	15.3	21.7	9.1	14.3	20.7	7.4	15.4	21.8	9.4
Other land transport accidents (V01, V05-V06, V09.1, V09.3-V09.9, V10-V11, V15-V18, V19.3,V19.8-V19.9, V80.0-V80.2, V80.6-V80.9, V81.2-V81.9, V82.2-V82.9, V87.9, V88.9,V89.1, V89.3,V89.9)	0.4	0.7	0.2	0.4	0.6	*	0.4	0.7	0.2
Water, air and space, and other and unspecified transport accidents and their sequelae (V90-V99,Y85)	0.6	1.0	0.2	0.2	0.4	*	0.7	1.1	0.3
Nontransport accidents (W00-X59,Y86)..........................	23.4	29.0	18.0	12.0	17.3	6.2	25.2	30.9	19.8
Falls (W00-W19)...	6.6	7.0	6.3	2.5	3.1	1.8	7.3	7.6	7.0
Accidental discharge of firearms (W32-W34)...	0.3	0.5	0.1	0.2	0.4	*	0.3	0.5	0.1
Accidental drowning and submersion (W65-W74)..	1.2	1.9	0.5	1.2	1.9	0.4	1.2	1.9	0.5
Accidental exposure to smoke, fire and flames (X00-X09)	1.1	1.3	0.9	0.5	0.6	0.4	1.2	1.4	0.9
Accidental poisoning and exposure to noxious substances (X40-X49)..........................	8.0	10.9	5.1	4.7	7.3	2.0	8.5	11.5	5.6
Other and unspecified nontransport accidents and their sequelae (W20-W31, W35-W64, W75-W99, X10-X39, X50-X59, Y86)	6.3	7.4	5.1	2.8	4.0	1.5	6.8	8.0	5.7

* = Figure does not meet standards of reliability or precision.
... = Not applicable.
0.0 = Quantity more than zero but less than 0.05.
[1]Based on codes from the *International Classification of Diseases, Tenth Revision* (1992), except where (*) precedes the cause of death code.
[2]Figures for origin not stated are included in all origins but not distributed among specified origins.
[3]Persons of Hispanic origin may be of any race.
[4]Includes races other than White and Black.

Table B-23. Death Rates for 113 Selected Causes by Hispanic Origin, Race for Non-Hispanic Population, and Sex, 2005—Continued

(Rate per 100,000 population.)

Cause of death[1]	All origins[2]			Hispanic[3]			Non-Hispanic[4]		
	Both sexes	Male	Female	Both sexes	Male	Female	Both sexes	Male	Female
Intentional self-harm (suicide) (*U03, X60-X84, Y87.0)	11.0	17.7	4.5	5.1	8.3	1.7	12.0	19.3	4.9
Intentional self-harm (suicide) by discharge of firearms (X72-X74)	5.7	10.2	1.4	1.9	3.4	0.3	6.4	11.4	1.6
Intentional self-harm (suicide) by other and unspecified means and their sequelae (*U03, X60-X71, X75-X84, Y87.0)	5.3	7.5	3.1	3.2	4.9	1.4	5.6	8.0	3.4
Assault (homicide) (*U01-*U02, X85-Y09, Y87.1)	6.1	9.8	2.5	8.2	13.6	2.5	5.7	9.1	2.5
Assault (homicide) by discharge of firearms (*U01.4, X93-X95)	4.2	7.2	1.2	5.7	10.0	1.2	3.9	6.7	1.2
Assault (homicide) by other and unspecified means and their sequelae (*U01.0-*U01.3, *U01.5-*U01.9, *U02, X85-X92, X96-Y09, Y87.1)	1.9	2.6	1.3	2.5	3.6	1.3	1.8	2.4	1.3
Legal intervention (Y35, Y89.0)	0.1	0.3	*	0.2	0.4	*	0.1	0.3	*
Events of undetermined intent (Y10-Y34, Y87.2, Y89.9)	1.6	2.0	1.3	0.8	1.0	0.5	1.7	2.1	1.4
Discharge of firearms, undetermined intent (Y22-Y24)	0.1	0.1	0.0	0.1	0.1	*	0.1	0.1	0.0
Other and unspecified events of undetermined intent and their sequelae (Y10-Y21, Y25-Y34, Y87.2, Y89.9)	1.5	1.8	1.2	0.7	0.9	0.5	1.7	2.0	1.3
Operations of war and their sequelae (Y36, Y89.1)	0.0	0.0	*	*	*	*	0.0	0.0	*
Complications of medical and surgical care (Y40-Y84, Y88)	0.9	0.8	1.0	0.4	0.3	0.5	1.0	0.9	1.0

Cause of death[1]	Non-Hispanic White			Non-Hispanic Black		
	Both sexes	Male	Female	Both sexes	Male	Female
ALL CAUSES	981.8	970.6	992.6	774.4	825.7	727.6
Salmonella infections (A01-A02)	0.0	*	*	*	*	*
Shigellosis and amebiasis (A03, A06)	*	*	*	*	*	*
Certain other intestinal infections (A04, A07-A09)	2.5	2.0	3.0	0.9	0.7	1.0
Tuberculosis (A16-A19)	0.1	0.2	0.1	0.4	0.5	0.3
Respiratory tuberculosis (A16)	0.1	0.1	0.1	0.3	0.4	0.2
Other tuberculosis (A17-A19)	0.0	0.0	0.0	0.1	0.1	*
Whooping cough (A37)	*	*	*	*	*	*
Scarlet fever and erysipelas (A38, A46)	*	*	*	*	*	*
Meningococcal infection (A39)	0.0	0.0	0.0	*	*	*
Septicemia (A40-A41)	12.7	11.5	13.9	16.5	15.5	17.4
Syphilis (A50-A53)	*	*	*	*	0.1	*
Acute poliomyelitis (A80)	*	*	*	*	0.1	*
Arthropod-borne viral encephalitis (A83-A84, A85.2)	*	*	*	*	*	*
Measles (B05)	*	*	*	*	*	*
Viral hepatitis (B15-B19)	1.8	2.5	1.2	2.3	2.9	1.7
Human immunodeficiency virus (HIV) disease (B20-B24)	1.9	3.1	0.6	18.5	25.8	11.8
Malaria (B50-B54)	*	*	*	*	*	*
Other and unspecified infectious and parasitic diseases and their sequelae (A00, A05, A20-A36, A42-A44, A48-A49, A54-A79, A81-A82, A85.0-A85.1, A85.8, A86-B04, B06-B09, B25-B49, B55-B99)	2.8	3.1	2.5	2.6	2.9	2.3
Malignant neoplasms (C00-C97)	227.7	240.7	215.1	167.4	181.8	154.3
Malignant neoplasms of lip, oral cavity and pharynx (C00-C14)	3.0	4.1	2.0	2.9	4.7	1.2
Malignant neoplasm of esophagus (C15)	5.6	9.1	2.3	3.9	6.0	2.0
Malignant neoplasm of stomach (C16)	3.7	4.4	3.0	5.2	6.4	4.1
Malignant neoplasms of colon, rectum and anus (C18-C21)	21.2	21.8	20.6	18.2	18.5	17.9
Malignant neoplasms of liver and intrahepatic bile ducts (C22)	5.5	7.2	3.8	5.6	8.2	3.2

* = Figure does not meet standards of reliability or precision.
0.0 = Quantity more than zero but less than 0.05.
[1] Based on codes from the *International Classification of Diseases, Tenth Revision* (1992), except where (*) precedes the cause of death code.
[2] Figures for origin not stated are included in all origins but not distributed among specified origins.
[3] Persons of Hispanic origin may be of any race.
[4] Includes races other than White and Black.

Table B-23. Death Rates for 113 Selected Causes by Hispanic Origin, Race for Non-Hispanic Population, and Sex, 2005—*Continued*

(Rate per 100,000 population.)

Cause of death[1]	Non-Hispanic White			Non-Hispanic Black		
	Both sexes	Male	Female	Both sexes	Male	Female
Malignant neoplasm of pancreas (C25)............................	13.2	13.3	13.0	10.0	9.8	10.3
Malignant neoplasm of larynx (C32)	1.4	2.3	0.6	1.8	3.0	0.7
Malignant neoplasms of trachea, bronchus and lung (C33-C34)	67.3	76.8	58.2	44.0	55.0	34.0
Malignant melanoma of skin (C43)................................	4.0	5.2	2.8	0.3	0.3	0.3
Malignant neoplasm of breast (C50)............................	16.3	0.3	31.8	15.5	0.3	29.4
Malignant neoplasm of cervix uteri (C53)	1.3	...	2.5	2.1	...	4.0
Malignant neoplasms of corpus uteri and uterus, part unspecified (C54-C55)..........................	2.7	...	5.3	3.1	...	6.0
Malignant neoplasm of ovary (C56)............................	6.2	...	12.2	3.2	...	6.2
Malignant neoplasm of prostate (C61)............................	11.1	22.7	...	12.8	26.8	...
Malignant neoplasms of kidney and renal pelvis (C64-C65)...	5.1	6.5	3.8	3.1	4.0	2.2
Malignant neoplasm of bladder (C67)	5.8	8.3	3.4	2.5	3.0	2.1
Malignant neoplasms of meninges, brain and other parts of central nervous system (C70-C72)...	5.6	6.4	4.9	2.1	2.4	1.8
Malignant neoplasms of lymphoid, hematopoietic and related tissue (C81-C96)	22.8	25.4	20.2	13.4	14.6	12.2
Hodgkin's disease (C81)	0.5	0.5	0.5	0.4	0.5	0.3
Non-Hodgkin's lymphoma (C82-C85)	8.9	9.7	8.2	3.7	4.2	3.3
Leukemia (C91-C95)..	9.1	10.5	7.7	4.5	5.1	4.1
Multiple myeloma and immunoproliferative neoplasms (C88, C90)	4.3	4.7	3.9	4.7	4.9	4.6
Other and unspecified malignant neoplasms of lymphoid, hematopoietic and related tissue (C96)	0.0	0.0	*	*	*	*
All other and unspecified malignant neoplasms (C17, C23-C24, C26-C31, C37-C41, C44-C49, C51-C52, C57-C60, C62-C63, C66, C68-C69, C73-C80, C97)...	25.6	26.8	24.5	17.7	18.6	16.8
In situ neoplasms, benign neoplasms and neoplasms of uncertain or unknown behavior (D00-D48)	5.8	5.9	5.7	3.1	2.8	3.3
Anemias (D50-D64)	1.7	1.2	2.1	2.7	2.5	2.9
Diabetes mellitus (E10-E14)	26.5	26.8	26.3	34.4	31.8	36.7
Nutritional deficiencies (E40-E64)	1.3	0.9	1.6	1.1	0.9	1.4
Malnutrition (E40-E46)..	1.2	0.8	1.5	1.1	0.8	1.3
Other nutritional deficiencies (E50-E64)	0.1	0.0	0.1	*	*	*
Meningitis (G00,G03)...	0.2	0.2	0.2	0.4	0.4	0.3
Parkinson's disease (G20-G21)	8.9	10.4	7.4	1.9	2.3	1.5
Alzheimer's disease (G30)......................................	31.9	18.5	44.8	12.3	7.2	16.9
Major cardiovascular diseases (I00-I78)......................	348.4	333.6	362.8	265.1	264.0	266.1
Diseases of heart (I00-I09, I11, I13, I20-I51).................................	267.1	267.8	266.4	196.3	201.5	191.6
Acute rheumatic fever and chronic rheumatic heart diseases (I00-I09).........................	1.4	0.9	1.9	0.6	0.4	0.7
Hypertensive heart disease (I11)	10.1	8.8	11.3	18.3	19.1	17.5
Hypertensive heart and renal disease (I13)	1.0	0.8	1.2	2.4	2.4	2.3
Ischemic heart diseases (I20-I25).............................	183.9	195.1	173.1	121.7	127.0	116.8
Acute myocardial infarction (I21-I22)...	62.3	67.8	57.0	41.1	41.8	40.5
Other acute ischemic heart diseases (I24)	1.4	1.5	1.4	1.5	1.6	1.3
Other forms of chronic ischemic heart disease (I20, I25).....................................	120.2	125.9	114.7	79.1	83.6	75.0
Atherosclerotic cardiovascular disease, so described (I25.0)...........................	24.0	26.3	21.9	25.3	29.7	21.3
All other forms of chronic ischemic heart disease (I20, I25.1-I25.9)...................................	96.2	99.6	92.9	53.8	53.9	53.7
Other heart diseases (I26-I51).................................	70.6	62.2	78.8	53.4	52.6	54.2
Acute and subacute endocarditis (I33)...	0.4	0.5	0.4	0.6	0.7	0.5
Diseases of pericardium and acute myocarditis (I30-I31, I40)	0.3	0.3	0.3	0.4	0.4	0.5
Heart failure (I50)..	25.4	20.0	30.5	14.9	12.7	16.9
All other forms of heart disease (I26-I28, I34-I38, I42-I49, 51).............................	44.5	41.4	47.6	37.4	38.8	36.2

* = Figure does not meet standards of reliability or precision.
... = Not applicable.
0.0 = Quantity more than zero but less than 0.05.
[1]Based on codes from the *International Classification of Diseases, Tenth Revision* (1992), except where (*) precedes the cause of death code.

Table B-23. Death Rates for 113 Selected Causes by Hispanic Origin, Race for Non-Hispanic Population, and Sex, 2005—*Continued*

(Rate per 100,000 population.)

Cause of death[1]	Non-Hispanic White			Non-Hispanic Black		
	Both sexes	Male	Female	Both sexes	Male	Female
Essential (primary) hypertension and hypertensive renal disease (I10, I12)............................	9.0	6.6	11.2	13.1	11.8	14.3
Cerebrovascular diseases (I60-I69).......................................	57.4	44.8	69.6	46.5	41.8	50.8
Atherosclerosis (I70).......................................	5.2	4.0	6.4	2.2	1.7	2.7
Other diseases of circulatory system (I71-I78)	9.8	10.4	9.1	6.9	7.1	6.7
Aortic aneurysm and dissection (I71)	5.8	7.0	4.7	3.4	4.0	3.0
Other diseases of arteries, arterioles and capillaries (I72-I78)	3.9	3.4	4.4	3.4	3.1	3.7
Other disorders of circulatory system (I80-I99)	1.8	1.6	2.0	2.1	2.1	2.1
Influenza and pneumonia (J10-J18).......................	26.2	23.3	28.9	15.3	15.1	15.5
Influenza (J10-J11).......................	0.8	0.6	1.0	0.2	0.2	0.2
Pneumonia (J12-J18).......................	25.3	22.7	27.9	15.1	15.0	15.3
Other acute lower respiratory infections (J20-J22)	0.2	0.1	0.2	0.1	*	0.1
Acute bronchitis and bronchiolitis (J20-J21)	0.1	0.1	0.1	0.1	*	*
Unspecified acute lower respiratory infection (J22)	0.1	0.0	0.1	*	*	*
Chronic lower respiratory diseases (J40-J47)	58.6	56.0	61.1	21.8	24.7	19.1
Bronchitis, chronic and unspecified (J40-J42)	0.4	0.3	0.4	0.1	0.2	0.1
Emphysema (J43).......................	6.3	6.5	6.1	2.2	2.8	1.6
Asthma (J45-J46).......................	1.2	0.8	1.7	2.7	2.3	3.1
Other chronic lower respiratory diseases (J44, J47)	50.6	48.4	52.8	16.8	19.5	14.4
Pneumoconioses and chemical effects (J60-J66, J68)	0.5	0.9	0.0	0.1	0.2	*
Pneumonitis due to solids and liquids (J69)	7.4	7.6	7.2	4.3	4.6	4.0
Other diseases of respiratory system (J00-J06, J30-J39, J67, J70-J98)	11.1	11.0	11.2	6.6	6.7	6.5
Peptic ulcer (K25-K28)	1.4	1.4	1.4	1.0	1.2	0.8
Diseases of appendix (K35-K38).......................	0.2	0.2	0.1	0.1	0.2	0.1
Hernia (K40-K46).......................	0.7	0.5	0.8	0.4	0.4	0.4
Chronic liver disease and cirrhosis (K70, K73-K74).......................	10.2	13.3	7.2	6.7	9.2	4.4
Alcoholic liver disease (K70).......................	4.7	6.8	2.6	3.1	4.4	1.9
Other chronic liver disease and cirrhosis (K73-K74).......................	5.5	6.5	4.6	3.6	4.7	2.5
Cholelithiasis and other disorders of gallbladder (K80-K82).......................	1.2	1.1	1.3	0.9	0.8	1.0
Nephritis, nephrotic syndrome and nephrosis (N00-N07, N17-N19, N25-N27).......................	16.2	16.2	16.2	21.5	20.3	22.5
Acute and rapidly progressive nephritic and nephrotic syndrome (N00-N01, N04)	0.1	0.1	0.0	*	*	*
Chronic glomerulonephritis, nephritis and nephropathy not specified as acute or chronic, and renal sclerosis unspecified (N02-N03, N05-N07, N26)	0.3	0.3	0.3	0.4	0.5	0.4
Renal failure (N17-N19)	15.8	15.8	15.9	21.0	19.8	22.1
Other disorders of kidney (N25, N27)	0.0	*	*	*	*	*
Infections of kidney (N10-N12, N13.6, N15.1).......................	0.3	0.2	0.4	0.2	0.2	0.3
Hyperplasia of prostate (N40).......................	0.2	0.5	...	0.1	0.2	...
Inflammatory diseases of female pelvic organs (N70-N76)	0.0	...	0.1	*	...	*
Pregnancy, childbirth and the puerperium (O00-O99)	0.2	...	0.3	0.7	...	1.4
Pregnancy with abortive outcome (O00-O07).......................	*	...	*	*	...	*
Other complications of pregnancy, childbirth and the puerperium (O10-O99).......................	0.2	...	0.3	0.7	...	1.3
Certain conditions originating in the perinatal period (P00-P96)	3.1	3.6	2.7	13.0	15.2	10.9
Congenital malformations, deformations and chromosomal abnormalities (Q00-Q99).......................	3.2	3.4	3.0	4.4	4.8	4.1
Symptoms, signs and abnormal clinical and laboratory findings, not elsewhere classified (R00-R99)	12.3	10.9	13.7	12.4	13.3	11.5
All other diseases (residual)	88.9	72.3	105.0	65.9	58.9	72.3

* = Figure does not meet standards of reliability or precision.

... = Not applicable.

0.0 = Quantity more than zero but less than 0.05.

[1]Based on codes from the *International Classification of Diseases, Tenth Revision* (1992), except where (*) precedes the cause of death code.

Table B-23. Death Rates for 113 Selected Causes by Hispanic Origin, Race for Non-Hispanic Population, and Sex, 2005—*Continued*

(Rate per 100,000 population.)

Cause of death[1]	Non-Hispanic White			Non-Hispanic Black		
	Both sexes	Male	Female	Both sexes	Male	Female
Accidents (unintentional injuries) (V01-X59, Y85-Y86)	44.4	57.0	32.3	35.9	51.3	21.8
Transport accidents (V01-V99, Y85)	17.1	24.2	10.3	15.4	23.4	8.1
Motor vehicle accidents (V02-V04, V09.0, V09.2, V12-V14, V19.0-V19.2, V19.4-V19.6, V20-V79, V80.3-V80.5, V81.0-V81.1, V82.0-V82.1, V83-V86, V87.0-V87.8, V88.0-V88.8, V89.0, V89.2)	16.0	22.4	9.8	14.4	21.8	7.7
Other land transport accidents (V01, V05-V06, V09.1, V09.3-V09.9, V10-V11, V15-V18, V19.3,V19.8-V19.9, V80.0-V80.2, V80.6-V80.9, V81.2-V81.9, V82.2-V82.9, V87.9, V88.9,V89.1, V89.3,V89.9)	0.4	0.6	0.2	0.5	0.9	0.2
Water, air and space, and other and unspecified transport accidents and their sequelae (V90-V99, Y85)	0.8	1.3	0.3	0.4	0.6	0.2
Nontransport accidents (W00-X59, Y86)	27.3	32.7	22.0	20.5	27.9	13.7
Falls (W00-W19)	8.5	8.7	8.3	2.7	3.3	2.1
Accidental discharge of firearms (W32-W34)	0.3	0.4	0.1	0.4	0.8	*
Accidental drowning and submersion (W65-W74)	1.2	1.8	0.5	1.5	2.6	0.4
Accidental exposure to smoke, fire and flames (X00-X09)	1.1	1.3	0.9	2.0	2.4	1.5
Accidental poisoning and exposure to noxious substances (X40-X49)	9.0	12.2	6.1	7.8	11.0	4.9
Other and unspecified nontransport accidents and their sequelae (W20-W31, W35-W64, W75-W99, X10-X39, X50-X59, Y86)	7.2	8.4	6.2	6.2	7.9	4.7
Intentional self-harm (suicide) (*U03, X60-X84, Y87.0)	13.6	22.0	5.6	5.2	8.9	1.8
Intentional self-harm (suicide) by discharge of firearms (X72-X74)	7.4	13.2	1.8	2.7	5.1	0.5
Intentional self-harm (suicide) by other and unspecified means and their sequelae (*U03, X60-X71, X75-X84, Y87.0)	6.2	8.8	3.7	2.6	3.9	1.4
Assault (homicide) (*U01-*U02, X85-Y09, Y87.1)	2.7	3.6	1.8	22.8	40.9	6.3
Assault (homicide) by discharge of firearms (*U01.4, X93-X95)	1.4	2.1	0.8	17.7	33.6	3.2
Assault (homicide) by other and unspecified means and their sequelae (*U01.0-*U01.3, *U01.5-*U01.9, *U02, X85-X92, X96-Y09, Y87.1)	1.2	1.5	0.9	5.1	7.4	3.1
Legal intervention (Y35, Y89.0)	0.1	0.2	*	0.3	0.6	*
Events of undetermined intent (Y10-Y34, Y87.2, Y89.9)	1.8	2.1	1.5	1.8	2.5	1.2
Discharge of firearms, undetermined intent (Y22-Y24)	0.1	0.1	0.0	0.1	0.2	*
Other and unspecified events of undetermined intent and their sequelae (Y10-Y21, Y25-Y34, Y87.2, Y89.9)	1.7	2.0	1.4	1.7	2.4	1.1
Operations of war and their sequelae (Y36, Y89.1)	*	*	*	*	*	*
Complications of medical and surgical care (Y40-Y84, Y88)	1.0	1.0	1.0	1.1	1.0	1.3

* = Figure does not meet standards of reliability or precision.

0.0 = Quantity more than zero but less than 0.05.

[1]Based on codes from the *International Classification of Diseases, Tenth Revision* (1992), except where (*) precedes the cause of death code.

NOTE: Complete confirmation of deaths from selected causes of death, considered to be of public health concern, were not provided by the following states–Alabama, California, Connecticut, Florida, Illinois, Indiana, Kentucky, Louisiana, Maryland, Michigan, Missouri, Montana, Nevada, New Hampshire, New Jersey, New York, North Carolina, Ohio, Oklahoma, Pennsylvania, Rhode Island, Texas, Utah, Virginia, Washington, and West Virginia.

Table B-24. Age-Adjusted Death Rates for 113 Selected Causes by Race and Sex, 2005

(Rate per 100,000 U.S. standard population.)

Cause of death[1]	All races			White			All other — Total			All other — Black		
	Both sexes	Male	Female	Both sexes	Male	Female	Both sexes	Male	Female	Both sexes	Male	Female
ALL CAUSES	798.8	951.1	677.6	785.3	933.2	666.5	850.2	1,030.4	715.4	1,016.5	1,252.9	845.7
Salmonella infections (A01-A02)	0.0	*	*	0.0	*	*	*	*	*	*	*	*
Shigellosis and amebiasis (A03, A06)	*	*	*	*	*	*	*	*	*	*	*	*
Certain other intestinal infections (A04, A07-A09)	1.8	1.9	1.8	1.9	2.0	1.9	1.1	1.1	1.0	1.2	1.3	1.2
Tuberculosis (A16-A19)	0.2	0.3	0.1	0.1	0.2	0.1	0.7	1.0	0.4	0.5	0.8	0.3
Respiratory tuberculosis (A16)	0.1	0.2	0.1	0.1	0.1	0.1	0.5	0.8	0.3	0.4	0.6	0.2
Other tuberculosis (A17-A19)	0.0	0.1	0.0	0.0	0.0	0.0	0.1	0.2	0.1	0.1	0.2	*
Whooping cough (A37)	0.0	*	*	0.0	*	*	*	*	*	*	*	*
Scarlet fever and erysipelas (A38, A46)	*	*	*	*	*	*	*	*	*	*	*	*
Meningococcal infection (A39)	0.0	0.0	0.0	0.0	0.0	0.0	0.0	*	*	*	*	*
Septicemia (A40-A41)	11.2	12.3	10.4	10.2	11.2	9.4	17.6	19.8	16.2	22.6	25.8	20.5
Syphilis (A50-A53)	0.0	0.0	*	*	*	*	0.1	0.1	*	0.1	0.2	*
Acute poliomyelitis (A80)	*	*	*	*	*	*	*	*	*	*	*	*
Arthropod-borne viral encephalitis (A83-A84, A85.2)	*	*	*	*	*	*	*	*	*	*	*	*
Measles (B05)	*	*	*	*	*	*	*	*	*	*	*	*
Viral hepatitis (B15-B19)	1.8	2.4	1.2	1.7	2.3	1.1	2.4	3.0	1.8	2.6	3.4	1.9
Human immunodeficiency virus (HIV) disease (B20-B24)	4.2	6.2	2.3	2.2	3.6	0.8	13.4	19.4	8.3	19.4	28.2	12.0
Malaria (B50-B54)	*	*	*	*	*	*	*	*	*	*	*	*
Other and unspecified infectious and parasitic diseases and their sequelae (A00, A05, A20-A36, A42-A44, A48-A49, A54-A79, A81-A82, A85.0-A85.1, A85.8, A86-B04, B06-B09, B25-B49, B55-B99)	2.5	3.1	2.0	2.5	3.0	1.9	2.9	3.6	2.4	3.1	3.9	2.5
Malignant neoplasms (C00-C97)	183.8	225.1	155.6	182.6	222.3	155.2	188.5	241.5	154.6	222.7	293.7	179.6
Malignant neoplasms of lip, oral cavity and pharynx (C00-C14)	2.5	3.9	1.4	2.4	3.6	1.4	3.1	5.3	1.4	3.5	6.5	1.4
Malignant neoplasm of esophagus (C15)	4.4	7.9	1.7	4.5	8.0	1.6	4.0	6.9	1.9	5.0	8.8	2.3
Malignant neoplasm of stomach (C16)	3.8	5.2	2.7	3.3	4.5	2.4	7.1	10.2	5.0	7.2	10.6	4.9
Malignant neoplasms of colon, rectum and anus (C18-C21)	17.5	20.9	14.8	16.9	20.3	14.3	20.7	24.7	17.8	24.8	30.2	21.2
Malignant neoplasms of liver and intrahepatic bile ducts (C22)	5.2	7.7	3.2	4.8	7.1	3.0	7.8	11.9	4.5	7.0	11.3	3.8
Malignant neoplasm of pancreas (C25)	10.8	12.3	9.5	10.6	12.2	9.3	11.7	13.0	10.6	13.6	15.3	12.3
Malignant neoplasm of larynx (C32)	1.2	2.2	0.5	1.2	2.1	0.5	1.7	3.3	0.6	2.3	4.6	0.8
Malignant neoplasms of trachea, bronchus and lung (C33-C34)	52.6	69.0	40.5	53.1	68.7	41.5	48.6	69.9	33.9	58.4	86.4	40.0
Malignant melanoma of skin (C43)	2.7	4.0	1.8	3.1	4.5	2.1	0.5	0.5	0.4	0.4	0.5	0.4
Malignant neoplasm of breast (C50)	13.5	0.3	24.1	13.1	0.3	23.4	15.5	0.4	26.7	19.3	0.5	32.8
Malignant neoplasm of cervix uteri (C53)	1.3	...	2.4	1.1	...	2.2	2.0	...	3.6	2.5	...	4.4
Malignant neoplasms of corpus uteri and uterus, part unspecified (C54-C55)	2.3	...	4.1	2.2	...	3.8	3.3	...	5.7	4.2	...	7.1
Malignant neoplasm of ovary (C56)	4.8	...	8.6	5.0	...	9.0	3.8	...	6.6	4.3	...	7.2
Malignant neoplasm of prostate (C61)	9.5	24.5	...	8.8	22.6	...	14.7	39.5	...	19.1	53.3	...
Malignant neoplasms of kidney and renal pelvis (C64-C65)	4.1	5.9	2.7	4.2	6.0	2.8	3.4	5.1	2.3	4.0	6.0	2.6
Malignant neoplasm of bladder (C67)	4.3	7.5	2.2	4.5	7.9	2.2	3.1	4.7	2.1	3.7	5.7	2.6
Malignant neoplasms of meninges, brain and other parts of central nervous system (C70-C72)	4.3	5.3	3.5	4.7	5.7	3.8	2.3	3.0	1.9	2.5	3.2	2.0
Malignant neoplasms of lymphoid, hematopoietic and related tissue (C81-C96)	18.2	23.5	14.3	18.5	24.0	14.5	15.3	19.2	12.5	17.6	22.5	14.3
Hodgkin's disease (C81)	0.4	0.5	0.4	0.4	0.5	0.4	0.4	0.4	0.3	0.4	0.5	0.3
Non-Hodgkin's lymphoma (C82-C85)	6.9	8.7	5.5	7.2	9.1	5.8	4.5	5.6	3.7	4.7	6.0	3.8
Leukemia (C91-C95)	7.1	9.6	5.4	7.4	10.0	5.6	5.3	6.9	4.1	5.9	7.8	4.7
Multiple myeloma and immunoproliferative neoplasms (C88, C90)	3.7	4.7	3.0	3.5	4.4	2.8	5.1	6.2	4.4	6.5	8.1	5.5
Other and unspecified malignant neoplasms of lymphoid, hematopoietic and related tissue (C96)	0.0	0.0	0.0	0.0	0.0	*	*	*	*	*	*	*
All other and unspecified malignant neoplasms (C17, C23-C24, C26-C31, C37-C41, C44-C49, C51-C52, C57-C60, C62-C63, C66, C68-C69, C73-C80, C97)	20.6	24.8	17.5	20.7	24.9	17.5	19.9	23.8	17.1	23.2	28.4	19.6
In situ neoplasms, benign neoplasms and neoplasms of uncertain or unknown behavior (D00-D48)	4.5	5.5	3.8	4.6	5.7	3.8	3.7	4.1	3.4	4.1	4.6	3.9
Anemias (D50-D64)	1.5	1.5	1.5	1.3	1.2	1.3	2.5	2.6	2.5	3.3	3.4	3.2
Diabetes mellitus (E10-E14)	24.6	28.4	21.6	22.5	26.5	19.3	38.8	41.5	36.4	46.9	50.8	43.8
Nutritional deficiencies (E40-E64)	1.0	1.0	1.1	1.0	0.9	1.0	1.4	1.4	1.4	1.7	1.6	1.7
Malnutrition (E40-E46)	1.0	0.9	1.0	0.9	0.8	1.0	1.3	1.3	1.3	1.6	1.5	1.6
Other nutritional deficiencies (E50-E64)	0.1	0.0	0.1	0.1	0.0	0.1	0.0	*	*	*	*	*

* = Figure does not meet standards of reliability or precision.
... = Not applicable.
0.0 = Quantity more than zero but less than 0.05.
[1]Based on codes from the *International Classification of Diseases, Tenth Revision* (1992), except where (*) precedes the cause of death code.

Table B-24. Age-Adjusted Death Rates for 113 Selected Causes by Race and Sex, 2005—*Continued*

(Rate per 100,000 U.S. standard population.)

| Cause of death[1] | All races | | | White | | | All other | | | | | |
| | | | | | | | Total | | | Black | | |
	Both sexes	Male	Female	Both sexes	Male	Female	Both sexes	Male	Female	Both sexes	Male	Female
Meningitis (G00, G03)	0.2	0.3	0.2	0.2	0.2	0.2	0.3	0.3	0.3	0.4	0.5	0.4
Parkinson's disease (G20-G21)	6.4	9.8	4.4	6.8	10.4	4.6	3.1	4.8	2.1	3.0	4.9	1.9
Alzheimer's disease (G30)	22.9	18.5	25.1	23.7	19.0	26.1	16.2	13.5	17.5	19.4	16.4	20.7
Major cardiovascular diseases (I00-I78)	277.3	329.5	235.6	271.0	323.2	229.0	306.9	358.2	267.0	367.9	435.3	317.4
Diseases of heart (I00-I09, I11, I13, I20-I51)	211.1	260.9	172.3	207.8	258.0	168.2	224.2	269.4	189.9	271.3	329.8	228.3
Acute rheumatic fever and chronic rheumatic heart diseases (I00-I09)	1.1	0.8	1.3	1.1	0.8	1.3	0.8	0.7	0.9	0.8	0.7	0.8
Hypertensive heart disease (I11)	9.4	10.1	8.5	7.9	8.3	7.2	18.5	21.2	16.0	24.1	28.4	20.4
Hypertensive heart and renal disease (I13)	1.0	1.1	0.9	0.8	0.9	0.8	2.5	2.9	2.2	3.2	3.8	2.8
Ischemic heart diseases (I20-I25)	144.4	187.4	111.7	143.8	187.7	110.0	144.5	179.0	118.9	171.3	213.9	140.9
Acute myocardial infarction (I21-I22)	49.1	63.6	37.8	49.1	64.1	37.2	48.4	58.5	41.0	57.6	69.7	48.8
Other acute ischemic heart diseases (I24)	1.2	1.4	0.9	1.1	1.3	0.9	1.6	2.0	1.3	2.0	2.6	1.5
Other forms of chronic ischemic heart disease (I20,I25)	94.2	122.4	73.0	93.6	122.3	72.0	94.4	118.5	76.7	111.8	141.6	90.5
Atherosclerotic cardiovascular disease, so described (I25.0)	20.3	26.6	15.0	19.1	25.0	14.0	27.8	37.0	20.7	34.5	46.9	25.3
All other forms of chronic ischemic heart disease (I20, I25.1-I25.9)	73.9	95.8	58.0	74.5	97.3	57.9	66.6	81.4	56.0	77.3	94.7	65.2
Other heart diseases (I26-I51)	55.2	61.5	49.9	54.1	60.2	49.0	58.0	65.5	52.0	71.9	83.0	63.4
Acute and subacute endocarditis (I33)	0.4	0.5	0.3	0.4	0.5	0.3	0.6	0.7	0.5	0.7	0.9	0.6
Diseases of pericardium and acute myocarditis (I30-I31, I40)	0.3	0.3	0.3	0.3	0.3	0.2	0.4	0.4	0.4	0.5	0.5	0.5
Heart failure (I50)	18.9	19.9	18.0	18.9	20.0	18.1	17.4	18.1	16.6	21.7	23.0	20.4
All other forms of heart disease (I26-I28, I34-I38, I42-I49, I51)	35.6	40.7	31.3	34.5	39.5	30.4	39.7	46.4	34.5	49.0	58.6	41.9
Essential (primary) hypertension and hypertensive renal disease (I10, I12)	8.0	7.8	8.0	7.0	6.6	7.1	14.8	15.7	14.0	18.4	19.9	17.1
Cerebrovascular diseases (I60-I69)	46.6	46.9	45.6	44.7	44.7	44.0	56.9	60.4	53.6	65.2	70.5	60.7
Atherosclerosis (I70)	3.8	3.9	3.7	3.9	4.0	3.7	2.8	2.8	2.8	3.4	3.4	3.3
Other diseases of circulatory system (I71-I78)	7.8	10.0	6.1	7.6	10.0	5.9	8.1	10.0	6.7	9.6	11.7	8.0
Aortic aneurysm and dissection (I71)	4.6	6.5	3.1	4.6	6.6	3.1	4.2	5.7	3.1	4.6	6.0	3.6
Other diseases of arteries, arterioles and capillaries (I72-I78)	3.2	3.5	2.9	3.1	3.4	2.8	3.9	4.3	3.6	5.0	5.6	4.5
Other disorders of circulatory system (I80-I99)	1.6	1.6	1.5	1.5	1.5	1.4	2.0	2.3	1.8	2.7	3.1	2.3
Influenza and pneumonia (J10-J18)	20.3	23.9	17.9	20.2	23.6	18.0	20.0	25.1	16.8	21.7	26.9	18.4
Influenza (J10-J11)	0.6	0.6	0.6	0.6	0.6	0.6	0.3	0.3	0.2	0.2	0.3	0.2
Pneumonia (J12-J18)	19.7	23.3	17.3	19.6	23.0	17.3	19.7	24.8	16.5	21.5	26.6	18.2
Other acute lower respiratory infections (J20-J22)	0.1	0.1	0.1	0.1	0.1	0.1	0.1	0.1	0.1	0.1	*	0.1
Acute bronchitis and bronchiolitis (J20-J21)	0.1	0.1	0.1	0.1	0.1	0.1	0.1	0.1	0.1	0.1	*	*
Unspecified acute lower respiratory infection (J22)	0.0	0.0	0.0	0.0	0.0	0.0	*	*	*	*	*	*
Chronic lower respiratory diseases (J40-J47)	43.2	51.2	38.1	45.4	52.8	40.7	26.3	37.6	19.6	30.6	44.1	22.8
Bronchitis, chronic and unspecified (J40-J42)	0.3	0.3	0.3	0.3	0.3	0.3	0.2	0.3	0.1	0.2	0.3	0.1
Emphysema (J43)	4.6	5.8	3.8	4.9	6.0	4.1	2.7	4.3	1.6	3.1	4.9	1.9
Asthma (J45-J46)	1.3	1.0	1.5	1.0	0.7	1.3	2.5	2.2	2.7	3.0	2.7	3.3
Other chronic lower respiratory diseases (J44, J47)	37.0	44.1	32.5	39.2	45.8	35.0	21.0	30.8	15.1	24.3	36.3	17.5
Pneumoconioses and chemical effects (J60-J66, J68)	0.3	0.8	0.0	0.4	0.9	0.0	0.1	0.4	*	0.2	0.5	*
Pneumonitis due to solids and liquids (J69)	5.6	7.6	4.4	5.6	7.6	4.4	5.4	7.5	4.2	6.4	9.0	4.9
Other diseases of respiratory system (J00-J06, J30-J39, J67, J70-J98)	8.9	10.6	7.7	9.0	10.7	7.8	7.9	9.9	6.8	8.7	10.7	7.5
Peptic ulcer (K25-K28)	1.1	1.4	0.9	1.1	1.3	0.9	1.2	1.6	0.9	1.3	1.8	0.9
Diseases of appendix (K35-K38)	0.1	0.2	0.1	0.1	0.2	0.1	0.2	0.2	0.1	0.2	0.2	0.1
Hernia (K40-K46)	0.5	0.5	0.5	0.5	0.5	0.5	0.4	0.5	0.4	0.5	0.6	0.5
Chronic liver disease and cirrhosis (K70, K73-K74)	9.0	12.4	5.8	9.2	12.7	6.0	7.4	10.5	4.8	7.7	11.5	4.8
Alcoholic liver disease (K70)	4.2	6.4	2.2	4.3	6.6	2.3	3.4	5.2	2.0	3.5	5.4	1.9
Other chronic liver disease and cirrhosis (K73-K74)	4.7	6.0	3.6	4.9	6.2	3.7	3.9	5.3	2.8	4.2	6.1	2.8
Cholelithiasis and other disorders of gallbladder (K80-K82)	1.0	1.1	0.9	1.0	1.1	0.9	1.1	1.1	1.1	1.2	1.3	1.2
Nephritis, nephrotic syndrome and nephrosis (N00-N07, N17-N19, N25-N27)	14.3	17.5	12.3	12.9	16.2	10.8	23.4	26.3	21.5	29.7	34.1	26.9
Acute and rapidly progressive nephritic and nephrotic syndrome (N00-N01, N04)	0.0	0.0	0.0	0.0	0.1	0.0	0.0	*	*	*	*	*
Chronic glomerulonephritis, nephritis and nephropathy not specified as acute or chronic, and renal sclerosis unspecified (N02-N03, N05-N07, N26)	0.3	0.4	0.2	0.3	0.3	0.2	0.4	0.6	0.4	0.6	0.7	0.5
Renal failure (N17-N19)	14.0	17.1	12.0	12.6	15.8	10.5	22.9	25.7	21.0	29.0	33.3	26.3
Other disorders of kidney (N25, N27)	0.0	*	*	0.0	*	*	*	*	*	*	*	*
Infections of kidney (N10-N12, N13.6, N15.1)	0.2	0.2	0.3	0.2	0.2	0.3	0.3	0.2	0.3	0.3	0.2	0.4
Hyperplasia of prostate (N40)	0.2	0.5	…	0.2	0.5	…	0.1	0.3	…	0.1	0.4	…
Inflammatory diseases of female pelvic organs (N70-N76)	0.0	…	0.1	0.0	…	0.1	0.0	…	0.1	*	…	*

* = Figure does not meet standards of reliability or precision.
…= Not applicable.
0.0 = Quantity more than zero but less than 0.05.
[1]Based on codes from the *International Classification of Diseases, Tenth Revision* (1992), except where (*) precedes the cause of death code.

Table B-24. Age-Adjusted Death Rates for 113 Selected Causes by Race and Sex, 2005—*Continued*

(Rate per 100,000 U.S. standard population.)

Cause of death[1]	All races			White			All other Total			All other Black		
	Both sexes	Male	Female	Both sexes	Male	Female	Both sexes	Male	Female	Both sexes	Male	Female
Pregnancy, childbirth and the puerperium (O00-O99)	0.3	...	0.5	0.2	...	0.4	0.5	...	1.0	0.7	...	1.3
Pregnancy with abortive outcome (O00-O07)	0.0	...	0.0	*	...	*	*	...	*	*	...	*
Other complications of pregnancy, childbirth and the puerperium (O10-O99)	0.2	...	0.5	0.2	...	0.4	0.5	...	0.9	0.6	...	1.2
Certain conditions originating in the perinatal period (P00-P96)	4.9	5.4	4.4	3.8	4.2	3.4	8.6	9.4	7.7	10.5	11.5	9.5
Congenital malformations, deformations and chromosomal abnormalities (Q00-Q99)	3.5	3.7	3.3	3.5	3.6	3.3	3.5	3.7	3.3	3.9	4.1	3.7
Symptoms, signs and abnormal clinical and laboratory findings, not elsewhere classified (R00-R99)	10.4	11.1	9.4	10.0	10.6	9.1	11.6	13.2	10.1	14.6	17.1	12.5
All other diseases (residual)	70.5	70.5	68.6	69.7	69.5	67.9	72.2	74.5	69.3	87.7	91.5	83.5
Accidents (unintentional injuries) (V01-X59, Y85-Y86)	39.1	54.2	25.0	40.1	55.2	25.8	34.1	49.9	20.9	38.7	58.1	22.8
Transport accidents (V01-V99, Y85)	16.2	23.4	9.3	16.7	23.9	9.7	14.2	21.3	7.9	15.4	24.1	8.0
Motor vehicle accidents (V02-V04, V09.0, V09.2, V12-V14, V19.0-V19.2, V19.4-V19.6, V20-V79, V80.3-V80.5, V81.0-V81.1, V82.0-V82.1, V83-V86, V87.0-V87.8, V88.0-V88.8, V89.0, V89.2)	15.2	21.7	8.9	15.6	22.2	9.2	13.3	19.7	7.6	14.5	22.5	7.6
Other land transport accidents (V01, V05-V06, V09.1, V09.3-V09.9, V10-V11, V15-V18, V19.3,V19.8-V19.9, V80.0-V80.2, V80.6-V80.9, V81.2-V81.9, V82.2-V82.9, V87.9, V88.9, V89.1, V89.3,V89.9)	0.4	0.7	0.2	0.4	0.6	0.2	0.5	0.9	0.2	0.5	1.0	0.2
Water, air and space, and other and unspecified transport accidents and their sequelae (V90-V99, Y85)	0.6	1.0	0.2	0.7	1.1	0.2	0.4	0.7	0.2	0.4	0.7	0.1
Nontransport accidents (W00-X59, Y86)	22.9	30.9	15.7	23.4	31.4	16.1	19.9	28.6	12.9	23.3	34.0	14.8
Falls (W00-W19)	6.4	8.3	4.9	6.7	8.6	5.2	3.9	5.6	2.8	3.7	5.2	2.6
Accidental discharge of firearms (W32-W34)	0.3	0.5	0.1	0.3	0.4	0.1	0.3	0.6	0.1	0.4	0.7	*
Accidental drowning and submersion (W65-W74)	1.2	1.9	0.5	1.2	1.8	0.5	1.4	2.3	0.5	1.4	2.5	0.4
Accidental exposure to smoke, fire and flames (X00-X09)	1.1	1.4	0.8	0.9	1.2	0.7	1.7	2.3	1.3	2.2	3.1	1.6
Accidental poisoning and exposure to noxious substances (X40-X49)	7.9	10.7	5.1	8.4	11.3	5.5	6.4	9.2	3.9	8.2	11.9	4.9
Other and unspecified nontransport accidents and their sequelae (W20-W31, W35-W64, W75-W99, X10-X39, X50-X59, Y86)	6.1	8.2	4.2	6.0	8.1	4.1	6.3	8.6	4.3	7.5	10.6	5.2
Intentional self-harm (suicide) (*U03, X60-X84, Y87.0)	10.9	18.0	4.4	12.0	19.6	4.9	5.6	9.3	2.4	5.2	9.2	1.9
Intentional self-harm (suicide) by discharge of firearms (X72-X74)	5.7	10.5	1.4	6.3	11.5	1.6	2.4	4.6	0.4	2.7	5.3	0.5
Intentional self-harm (suicide) by other and unspecified means and their sequelae (*U03, X60-X71, X75-X84, Y87.0)	5.2	7.5	3.0	5.7	8.1	3.3	3.2	4.7	1.9	2.5	3.9	1.4
Assault (homicide) (*U01-*U02, X85-Y09, Y87.1)	6.1	9.6	2.5	3.7	5.3	1.9	15.6	27.1	4.8	21.1	37.3	6.1
Assault (homicide) by discharge of firearms (*U01.4, X93-X95)	4.2	7.0	1.2	2.2	3.5	0.9	11.6	21.3	2.3	16.0	29.8	3.0
Assault (homicide) by other and unspecified means and their sequelae (*U01.0-*U01.3, *U01.5-*U01.9, *U02, X85-X92, X96-Y09, Y87.1)	1.9	2.6	1.3	1.5	1.9	1.0	4.0	5.8	2.5	5.1	7.5	3.1
Legal intervention (Y35, Y89.0)	0.1	0.3	*	0.1	0.2	*	0.2	0.4	*	0.3	0.6	*
Events of undetermined intent (Y10-Y34, Y87.2, Y89.9)	1.6	1.9	1.2	1.6	1.9	1.3	1.5	2.0	1.0	1.8	2.5	1.2
Discharge of firearms, undetermined intent (Y22-Y24)	0.1	0.1	0.0	0.1	0.1	0.0	0.1	0.1	*	0.1	0.1	*
Other and unspecified events of undetermined intent and their sequelae (Y10-Y21, Y25-Y34, Y87.2, Y89.9)	1.5	1.8	1.2	1.5	1.8	1.3	1.4	1.9	1.0	1.7	2.4	1.1
Operations of war and their sequelae (Y36, Y89.1)	0.0	0.0	*	0.0	0.0	*	*	*	*	*	*	*
Complications of medical and surgical care (Y40-Y84, Y88)	0.9	0.9	0.8	0.8	0.9	0.8	1.1	1.2	1.1	1.5	1.5	1.5

* = Figure does not meet standards of reliability or precision.
...= Not applicable.
0.0 = Quantity more than zero but less than 0.05.
[1]Based on codes from the *International Classification of Diseases, Tenth Revision* (1992), except where (*) precedes the cause of death code.

NOTE: Complete confirmation of deaths from selected causes of death, considered to be of public health concern, were not provided by the following states–Alabama, California, Connecticut, Florida, Illinois, Indiana, Kentucky, Louisiana, Maryland, Michigan, Missouri, Montana, Nevada, New Hampshire, New Jersey, New York, North Carolina, Ohio, Oklahoma, Pennsylvania, Rhode Island, Texas, Utah, Virginia, Washington, and West Virginia.

Table B-25. Age-Adjusted Death Rates for 113 Selected Causes by Hispanic Origin, Race for Non-Hispanic Population, and Sex, 2005

(Rate per 100,000 population.)

Cause of death[1]	All origins[2]			Hispanic[3]			Non-Hispanic[4]		
	Both sexes	Male	Female	Both sexes	Male	Female	Both sexes	Male	Female
ALL CAUSES	798.8	951.1	677.6	590.7	717.0	485.3	812.5	966.7	690.3
Salmonella infections (A01-A02)	0.0	*	*	*	*	*	0.0	*	*
Shigellosis and amebiasis (A03, A06)	*	*	*	*	*	*	*	*	*
Certain other intestinal infections (A04, A07-A09)	1.8	1.9	1.8	1.1	0.9	1.2	1.9	1.9	1.9
Tuberculosis (A16-A19)	0.2	0.3	0.1	0.4	0.6	0.2	0.2	0.3	0.1
Respiratory tuberculosis (A16)...................	0.1	0.2	0.1	0.2	0.3	0.2	0.1	0.2	0.1
Other tuberculosis (A17-A19)	0.0	0.1	0.0	0.1	0.2	*	0.0	0.0	0.0
Whooping cough (A37)	0.0	*	*	*	*	*	*	*	*
Scarlet fever and erysipelas (A38, A46)	*	*	*	*	*	*	*	*	*
Meningococcal infection (A39)........................	0.0	0.0	0.0	*	*	*	0.0	0.0	0.0
Septicemia (A40-A41)..	11.2	12.3	10.4	8.3	9.3	7.5	11.3	12.5	10.6
Syphilis (A50-A53)...	0.0	0.0	*	*	*	*	0.0	0.0	*
Acute poliomyelitis (A80)	*	*	*	*	*	*	*	*	*
Arthropod-borne viral encephalitis (A83-A84, A85.2)	*	*	*	*	*	*	*	*	*
Measles (B05)..	*	*	*	*	*	*	*	*	*
Viral hepatitis (B15-B19)..................................	1.8	2.4	1.2	2.9	3.8	2.1	1.7	2.3	1.1
Human immunodeficiency virus (HIV) disease (B20-B24)	4.2	6.2	2.3	4.7	7.5	1.9	4.2	6.1	2.3
Malaria (B50-B54)	*	*	*	*	*	*	*	*	*
Other and unspecified infectious and parasitic diseases and their sequelae (A00, A05, A20-A36, A42-A44, A48-A49, A54-A79, A81-A82, A85.0-A85.1, A85.8, A86-B04, B06-B09, B25-B49, B55-B99)	2.5	3.1	2.0	2.9	3.4	2.4	2.5	3.0	2.0
Malignant neoplasms (C00-C97)....................	183.8	225.1	155.6	122.8	152.7	101.9	188.2	230.2	159.4
Malignant neoplasms of lip, oral cavity and pharynx (C00-C14)	2.5	3.9	1.4	1.4	2.3	0.7	2.6	4.0	1.5
Malignant neoplasm of esophagus (C15)........................	4.4	7.9	1.7	2.3	4.2	0.8	4.6	8.2	1.7
Malignant neoplasm of stomach (C16)	3.8	5.2	2.7	5.9	8.0	4.3	3.6	5.0	2.6
Malignant neoplasms of colon, rectum and anus (C18-C21)	17.5	20.9	14.8	12.4	15.2	10.4	17.8	21.3	15.1
Malignant neoplasms of liver and intrahepatic bile ducts (C22)....................	5.2	7.7	3.2	8.3	11.7	5.4	5.0	7.4	3.0
Malignant neoplasm of pancreas (C25)........................	10.8	12.3	9.5	8.6	9.4	7.8	10.9	12.5	9.6
Malignant neoplasm of larynx (C32)	1.2	2.2	0.5	0.9	1.9	*	1.3	2.3	0.5
Malignant neoplasms of trachea, bronchus and lung (C33-C34).................	52.6	69.0	40.5	22.4	33.3	14.4	54.8	71.6	42.5
Malignant melanoma of skin (C43)...................	2.7	4.0	1.8	0.7	1.0	0.5	2.9	4.2	1.9
Malignant neoplasm of breast (C50)....................	13.5	0.3	24.1	8.2	*	15.0	13.9	0.3	24.8
Malignant neoplasm of cervix uteri (C53)	1.3	...	2.4	1.6	...	3.1	1.3	...	2.4
Malignant neoplasms of corpus uteri and uterus, part unspecified (C54-C55)...........................	2.3	...	4.1	1.8	...	3.2	2.3	...	4.1
Malignant neoplasm of ovary (C56)...........................	4.8	...	8.6	3.3	...	6.0	4.9	...	8.8
Malignant neoplasm of prostate (C61)..........................	9.5	24.5	...	7.4	18.5	...	9.6	24.9	...
Malignant neoplasms of kidney and renal pelvis (C64-C65)	4.1	5.9	2.7	3.7	5.1	2.6	4.1	5.9	2.7
Malignant neoplasm of bladder (C67)	4.3	7.5	2.2	2.4	4.2	1.1	4.5	7.7	2.3
Malignant neoplasms of meninges, brain and other parts of central nervous system (C70-C72)......................................	4.3	5.3	3.5	2.9	3.5	2.4	4.5	5.5	3.6
Malignant neoplasms of lymphoid, hematopoietic and related tissue (C81-C96)..	18.2	23.5	14.3	13.7	16.9	11.3	18.4	23.9	14.4
Hodgkin's disease (C81)	0.4	0.5	0.4	0.5	0.7	0.4	0.4	0.5	0.4
Non-Hodgkin's lymphoma (C82-C85)	6.9	8.7	5.5	5.3	6.3	4.6	7.0	8.9	5.6
Leukemia (C91-C95)..................................	7.1	9.6	5.4	4.9	6.5	3.8	7.2	9.8	5.5
Multiple myeloma and immunoproliferative neoplasms (C88, C90)..	3.7	4.7	3.0	2.9	3.4	2.5	3.7	4.7	3.0
Other and unspecified malignant neoplasms of lymphoid, hematopoietic and related tissue (C96)	0.0	0.0	0.0	*	*	*	0.0	0.0	*
All other and unspecified malignant neoplasms (C17, C23-C24, C26-C31, C37-C41, C44-C49, C51-C52, C57-C60, C62-C63, C66, C68-C69, C73-C80, C97)...	20.6	24.8	17.5	14.8	17.5	12.8	21.0	25.3	17.9

* = Figure does not meet standards of reliability or precision.
... = Category not applicable.
0.0 = Quantity more than zero but less than 0.05.
[1]Based on codes from the *International Classification of Diseases, Tenth Revision* (1992), except where (*) precedes the cause of death code.
[2]Figures for origin not stated are included in All origins but not distributed among specified origins.
[3]Persons of Hispanic origin may be of any race.
[4]Includes races other than White and Black.

Table B-25. Age-Adjusted Death Rates for 113 Selected Causes by Hispanic Origin, Race for Non-Hispanic Population, and Sex, 2005—*Continued*

(Rate per 100,000 population.)

Cause of death[1]	All origins[2]			Hispanic[3]			Non-Hispanic[4]		
	Both sexes	Male	Female	Both sexes	Male	Female	Both sexes	Male	Female
In situ neoplasms, benign neoplasms and neoplasms of uncertain or unknown behavior (D00-D48)	4.5	5.5	3.8	2.6	3.2	2.2	4.6	5.7	3.9
Anemias (D50-D64)	1.5	1.5	1.5	0.9	0.9	0.9	1.6	1.5	1.6
Diabetes mellitus (E10-E14)	24.6	28.4	21.6	33.6	37.3	30.5	24.0	27.9	21.1
Nutritional deficiencies (E40-E64)	1.0	1.0	1.1	0.8	0.8	0.8	1.0	1.0	1.1
Malnutrition (E40-E46)	1.0	0.9	1.0	0.8	0.8	0.7	1.0	0.9	1.0
Other nutritional deficiencies (E50-E64)	0.1	0.0	0.1	*	*	*	0.1	0.0	0.1
Meningitis (G00,G03)	0.2	0.3	0.2	0.2	0.2	0.2	0.2	0.3	0.2
Parkinson's disease (G20-G21)	6.4	9.8	4.4	4.3	6.3	3.1	6.5	10.0	4.4
Alzheimer's disease (G30)	22.9	18.5	25.1	13.8	12.5	14.5	23.3	18.8	25.7
Major cardiovascular diseases (I00-I78)	277.3	329.5	235.6	207.2	246.6	175.4	281.5	334.8	239.0
Diseases of heart (I00-I09, I11, I13, I20-I51)	211.1	260.9	172.3	157.3	192.4	129.1	214.5	265.5	174.8
Acute rheumatic fever and chronic rheumatic heart diseases (I00-I09)	1.1	0.8	1.3	0.8	0.4	1.0	1.1	0.9	1.3
Hypertensive heart disease (I11)	9.4	10.1	8.5	7.2	7.9	6.4	9.6	10.2	8.6
Hypertensive heart and renal disease (I13)	1.0	1.1	0.9	1.0	1.1	1.0	1.0	1.1	1.0
Ischemic heart diseases (I20-I25)	144.4	187.4	111.7	118.0	148.4	94.1	146.0	189.9	112.7
Acute myocardial infarction (I21-I22)	49.1	63.6	37.8	40.4	51.1	32.1	49.7	64.5	38.1
Other acute ischemic heart diseases (I24)	1.2	1.4	0.9	0.5	0.5	0.4	1.2	1.5	1.0
Other forms of chronic ischemic heart disease (I20, I25)	94.2	122.4	73.0	77.2	96.7	61.6	95.1	123.9	73.6
Atherosclerotic cardiovascular disease, so described (I25.0)	20.3	26.6	15.0	17.3	24.4	11.6	20.4	26.6	15.1
All other forms of chronic ischemic heart disease (I20, I25.1-I25.9)	73.9	95.8	58.0	59.9	72.4	50.1	74.7	97.3	58.4
Other heart diseases (I26-I51)	55.2	61.5	49.9	30.2	34.5	26.6	56.8	63.3	51.3
Acute and subacute endocarditis (I33)	0.4	0.5	0.3	0.3	0.5	0.2	0.4	0.5	0.3
Diseases of pericardium and acute myocarditis (I30-I31, I40)	0.3	0.3	0.3	0.3	0.3	0.2	0.3	0.3	0.3
Heart failure (I50)	18.9	19.9	18.0	10.1	10.7	9.6	19.4	20.4	18.5
All other forms of heart disease (I26-I28, I34-I38, I42-I49, I51)	35.6	40.7	31.3	19.6	23.1	16.6	36.7	42.0	32.3
Essential (primary) hypertension and hypertensive renal disease (I10, I12)	8.0	7.8	8.0	7.1	6.9	7.2	8.1	7.8	8.0
Cerebrovascular diseases (I60-I69)	46.6	46.9	45.6	35.7	38.0	33.5	47.1	47.3	46.2
Atherosclerosis (I70)	3.8	3.9	3.7	2.4	2.7	2.2	3.9	4.0	3.7
Other diseases of circulatory system (I71-I78)	7.8	10.0	6.1	4.7	6.6	3.3	7.9	10.3	6.2
Aortic aneurysm and dissection (I71)	4.6	6.5	3.1	2.3	3.6	1.4	4.7	6.7	3.2
Other diseases of arteries, arterioles and capillaries (I72-I78)	3.2	3.5	2.9	2.4	3.0	1.9	3.2	3.5	3.0
Other disorders of circulatory system (I80-I99)	1.6	1.6	1.5	1.2	1.2	1.3	1.6	1.7	1.5
Influenza and pneumonia (J10-J18)	20.3	23.9	17.9	16.8	19.6	14.8	20.5	24.1	18.1
Influenza (J10-J11)	0.6	0.6	0.6	0.2	0.3	0.2	0.6	0.6	0.6
Pneumonia (J12-J18)	19.7	23.3	17.3	16.6	19.3	14.5	19.9	23.5	17.5
Other acute lower respiratory infections (J20-J22)	0.1	0.1	0.1	*	*	*	0.1	0.1	0.1
Acute bronchitis and bronchiolitis (J20-J21)	0.1	0.1	0.1	*	*	*	0.1	0.1	0.1
Unspecified acute lower respiratory infection (J22)	0.0	0.0	0.0	*	*	*	0.0	0.0	0.0
Chronic lower respiratory diseases (J40-J47)	43.2	51.2	38.1	19.3	25.1	15.4	44.8	52.9	39.6
Bronchitis, chronic and unspecified (J40-J42)	0.3	0.3	0.3	0.2	*	0.2	0.3	0.3	0.3
Emphysema (J43)	4.6	5.8	3.8	1.7	2.4	1.1	4.8	6.1	4.0
Asthma (J45-J46)	1.3	1.0	1.5	1.0	0.9	1.1	1.3	1.0	1.6
Other chronic lower respiratory diseases (J44, J47)	37.0	44.1	32.5	16.4	21.6	12.9	38.4	45.5	33.8
Pneumoconioses and chemical effects (J60-J66, J68)	0.3	0.8	0.0	0.1	*	*	0.3	0.9	0.0
Pneumonitis due to solids and liquids (J69)	5.6	7.6	4.4	3.4	4.6	2.6	5.7	7.8	4.5
Other diseases of respiratory system (J00-J06, J30-J39, J67, J70-J98)	8.9	10.6	7.7	7.9	9.0	7.1	9.0	10.7	7.7
Peptic ulcer (K25-K28)	1.1	1.4	0.9	0.9	1.0	0.8	1.2	1.4	1.0
Diseases of appendix (K35-K38)	0.1	0.2	0.1	0.1	*	*	0.1	0.2	0.1

* = Figure does not meet standards of reliability or precision.
0.0 = Quantity more than zero but less than 0.05.
[1]Based on codes from the *International Classification of Diseases, Tenth Revision* (1992), except where (*) precedes the cause of death code.
[2]Figures for origin not stated are included in All origins but not distributed among specified origins.
[3]Persons of Hispanic origin may be of any race.
[4]Includes races other than White and Black.

Table B-25. Age-Adjusted Death Rates for 113 Selected Causes by Hispanic Origin, Race for Non-Hispanic Population, and Sex, 2005—*Continued*

(Rate per 100,000 population.)

Cause of death[1]	All origins[2]			Hispanic[3]			Non-Hispanic[4]		
	Both sexes	Male	Female	Both sexes	Male	Female	Both sexes	Male	Female
Hernia (K40-K46)	0.5	0.5	0.5	0.4	0.3	0.5	0.5	0.5	0.5
Chronic liver disease and cirrhosis (K70, K73-K74)..........................	9.0	12.4	5.8	13.9	20.4	7.9	8.5	11.7	5.7
Alcoholic liver disease (K70)............................	4.2	6.4	2.2	6.4	11.3	2.0	3.9	5.9	2.2
Other chronic liver disease and cirrhosis (K73-K74)............................	4.7	6.0	3.6	7.5	9.1	5.9	4.5	5.8	3.5
Cholelithiasis and other disorders of gallbladder (K80-K82)............................	1.0	1.1	0.9	1.2	1.3	1.1	1.0	1.1	0.9
Nephritis, nephrotic syndrome and nephrosis (N00-N07, N17-N19, N25-N27).........................	14.3	17.5	12.3	12.0	14.4	10.3	14.5	17.7	12.4
Acute and rapidly progressive nephritic and nephrotic syndrome (N00-N01, N04)	0.0	0.0	0.0	*	*	*	0.0	0.0	0.0
Chronic glomerulonephritis, nephritis and nephropathy not specified as acute or chronic, and renal sclerosis unspecified (N02-N03, N05-N07, N26)............	0.3	0.4	0.2	0.3	0.3	0.3	0.3	0.4	0.2
Renal failure (N17-N19)	14.0	17.1	12.0	11.6	14.0	10.0	14.1	17.3	12.1
Other disorders of kidney (N25, N27)	0.0	*	*	*	*	*	0.0	*	*
Infections of kidney (N10-N12, N13.6, N15.1)......................	0.2	0.2	0.3	0.2	0.3	0.2	0.2	0.2	0.3
Hyperplasia of prostate (N40)...................	0.2	0.5	...	*	*	...	0.2	0.5	...
Inflammatory diseases of female pelvic organs (N70-N76)	0.0	...	0.1	*	...	*	0.0	...	0.1
Pregnancy, childbirth and the puerperium (O00-O99)	0.3	...	0.5	0.3	...	0.6	0.3	...	0.5
Pregnancy with abortive outcome (O00-O07)	0.0	...	0.0	*	...	*	0.0	...	0.0
Other complications of pregnancy, childbirth and the puerperium (O10-O99)	0.2	...	0.5	0.3	...	0.6	0.2	...	0.5
Certain conditions originating in the perinatal period (P00-P96)	4.9	5.4	4.4	4.2	4.7	3.6	5.0	5.5	4.5
Congenital malformations, deformations and chromosomal abnormalities (Q00-Q99)........................	3.5	3.7	3.3	3.3	3.4	3.2	3.5	3.7	3.3
Symptoms, signs and abnormal clinical and laboratory findings, not elsewhere classified (R00-R99)........................	10.4	11.1	9.4	5.7	6.9	4.6	10.7	11.4	9.7
All other diseases (residual)	70.5	70.5	68.6	46.8	49.2	43.7	72.0	71.9	70.1
Accidents (unintentional injuries) (V01-X59, Y85-Y86)	39.1	54.2	25.0	31.3	45.3	17.0	39.8	55.1	25.9
Transport accidents (V01-V99,Y85)........................	16.2	23.4	9.3	15.4	22.4	8.1	16.2	23.3	9.5
Motor vehicle accidents (V02-V04, V09.0, V09.2, V12-V14, V19.0-V19.2, V19.4-V19.6, V20-V79, V80.3-V80.5, V81.0-V81.1, V82.0-V82.1, V83-V86, V87.0-V87.8, V88.0-V88.8, V89.0, V89.2)........................	15.2	21.7	8.9	14.7	21.3	7.8	15.1	21.6	9.0
Other land transport accidents (V01, V05-V06, V09.1, V09.3-V09.9, V10-V11, V15-V18, V19.3,V19.8-V19.9, V80.0-V80.2, V80.6-V80.9, V81.2-V81.9, V82.2-V82.9, V87.9, V88.9,V89.1, V89.3,V89.9)........................	0.4	0.7	0.2	0.4	0.7	*	0.4	0.6	0.2
Water, air and space, and other and unspecified transport accidents and their sequelae (V90-V99, Y85)	0.6	1.0	0.2	0.3	0.5	*	0.7	1.1	0.2
Nontransport accidents (W00-X59, Y86)........................	22.9	30.9	15.7	16.0	23.0	8.9	23.6	31.7	16.4
Falls (W00-W19)........................	6.4	8.3	4.9	5.0	6.6	3.5	6.4	8.3	5.1
Accidental discharge of firearms (W32-W34)	0.3	0.5	0.1	0.2	0.4	*	0.3	0.5	0.1
Accidental drowning and submersion (W65-W74)	1.2	1.9	0.5	1.1	1.8	0.4	1.2	1.9	0.5
Accidental exposure to smoke, fire and flames (X00-X09)	1.1	1.4	0.8	0.7	0.8	0.6	1.1	1.4	0.8
Accidental poisoning and exposure to noxious substances (X40-X49)........................	7.9	10.7	5.1	5.2	7.9	2.3	8.4	11.3	5.5
Other and unspecified nontransport accidents and their sequelae (W20-W31, W35-W64, W75-W99, X10-X39, X50-X59, Y86)	6.1	8.2	4.2	3.8	5.6	2.2	6.2	8.4	4.4

* = Figure does not meet standards of reliability or precision.
... = Not applicable.
0.0 = Quantity more than zero but less than 0.05.
[1]Based on codes from the *International Classification of Diseases, Tenth Revision* (1992), except where (*) precedes the cause of death code.
[2]Figures for origin not stated are included in All origins but not distributed among specified origins.
[3]Persons of Hispanic origin may be of any race.
[4]Includes races other than White and Black.

Table B-25. Age-Adjusted Death Rates for 113 Selected Causes by Hispanic Origin, Race for Non-Hispanic Population, and Sex, 2005—Continued

(Rate per 100,000 population.)

Cause of death[1]	All origins[2]			Hispanic[3]			Non-Hispanic[4]		
	Both sexes	Male	Female	Both sexes	Male	Female	Both sexes	Male	Female
Intentional self-harm (suicide) (*U03, X60-X84,Y87.0)	10.9	18.0	4.4	5.6	9.4	1.8	11.6	19.1	4.7
Intentional self-harm (suicide) by discharge of firearms (X72-X74)	5.7	10.5	1.4	2.2	4.0	0.3	6.1	11.3	1.5
Intentional self-harm (suicide) by other and unspecified means and their sequelae (*U03, X60-X71, X75-X84, Y87.0)	5.2	7.5	3.0	3.5	5.4	1.5	5.5	7.9	3.2
Assault (homicide) (*U01-*U02, X85-Y09, Y87.1)	6.1	9.6	2.5	7.5	12.1	2.4	5.8	9.1	2.5
Assault (homicide) by discharge of firearms (*U01.4, X93-X95)	4.2	7.0	1.2	5.1	8.5	1.2	4.0	6.7	1.2
Assault (homicide) by other and unspecified means and their sequelae (*U01.0-*U01.3, *U01.5-*U01.9, *U02, X85-X92, X96-Y09, Y87.1)	1.9	2.6	1.3	2.4	3.6	1.2	1.8	2.4	1.3
Legal intervention (Y35, Y89.0)	0.1	0.3	*	0.2	0.3	*	0.1	0.3	*
Events of undetermined intent (Y10-Y34, Y87.2, Y89.9)	1.6	1.9	1.2	0.8	1.1	0.6	1.7	2.1	1.3
Discharge of firearms, undetermined intent (Y22-Y24)	0.1	0.1	0.0	0.0	0.1	*	0.1	0.1	0.0
Other and unspecified events of undetermined intent and their sequelae (Y10-Y21, Y25-Y34, Y87.2, Y89.9)	1.5	1.8	1.2	0.8	1.0	0.5	1.6	2.0	1.3
Operations of war and their sequelae (Y36, Y89.1)	0.0	0.0	*	*	*	*	0.0	0.0	*
Complications of medical and surgical care (Y40-Y84, Y88)	0.9	0.9	0.8	0.7	0.5	0.8	0.9	1.0	0.8

Cause of death[1]	Non-Hispanic White			Non-Hispanic Black		
	Both sexes	Male	Female	Both sexes	Male	Female
ALL CAUSES	796.6	945.4	677.7	1,034.5	1,275.3	860.5
Salmonella infections (A01-A02)	0.0	*	*	*	*	*
Shigellosis and amebiasis (A03, A06)	*	*	*	*	*	*
Certain other intestinal infections (A04,A07-A09)	2.0	2.0	2.0	1.2	1.3	1.2
Tuberculosis (A16-A19)	0.1	0.1	0.1	0.5	0.8	0.3
Respiratory tuberculosis (A16)	0.1	0.1	0.1	0.4	0.6	0.2
Other tuberculosis (A17-A19)	0.0	0.0	0.0	0.1	0.2	*
Whooping cough (A37)	*	*	*	*	*	*
Scarlet fever and erysipelas (A38, A46)	*	*	*	*	*	*
Meningococcal infection (A39)	0.0	0.0	0.0	*	*	*
Septicemia (A40-A41)	10.2	11.2	9.5	23.0	26.3	20.9
Syphilis (A50-A53)	*	*	*	0.1	0.2	*
Acute poliomyelitis (A80)	*	*	*	*	*	*
Arthropod-borne viral encephalitis (A83-A84, A85.2)	*	*	*	*	*	*
Measles (B05)	*	*	*	*	*	*
Viral hepatitis (B15-B19)	1.5	2.1	1.0	2.6	3.5	1.9
Human immunodeficiency virus (HIV) disease (B20-B24)	1.8	3.0	0.6	19.8	28.8	12.3
Malaria (B50-B54)	*	*	*	*	*	*
Other and unspecified infectious and parasitic diseases and their sequelae (A00, A05, A20-A36, A42-A44, A48-A49, A54-A79, A81-A82, A85.0-A85.1, A85.8, A86-B04, B06-B09, B25-B49, B55-B99)	2.4	2.9	1.9	3.2	4.0	2.6

* = Figure does not meet standards of reliability or precision.
0.0 = Quantity more than zero but less than 0.05.
[1]Based on codes from the *International Classification of Diseases, Tenth Revision* (1992), except where (*) precedes the cause of death code.
[2]Figures for origin not stated are included in All origins but not distributed among specified origins.
[3]Persons of Hispanic origin may be of any race.
[4]Includes races other than White and Black.

Table B-25. Age-Adjusted Death Rates for 113 Selected Causes by Hispanic Origin, Race for Non-Hispanic Population, and Sex, 2005—*Continued*

(Rate per 100,000 population.)

Cause of death[1]	Non-Hispanic White			Non-Hispanic Black		
	Both sexes	Male	Female	Both sexes	Male	Female
Malignant neoplasms (C00-C97)..............................	187.0	227.3	159.1	226.8	299.0	183.0
Malignant neoplasms of lip, oral cavity and pharynx (C00-C14)..	2.5	3.7	1.5	3.6	6.6	1.4
Malignant neoplasm of esophagus (C15)......................	4.6	8.3	1.6	5.1	9.0	2.4
Malignant neoplasm of stomach (C16)............................	3.0	4.2	2.2	7.3	10.8	5.0
Malignant neoplasms of colon, rectum and anus (C18-C21)..	17.2	20.7	14.5	25.2	30.7	21.6
Malignant neoplasms of liver and intrahepatic bile ducts (C22)............................	4.5	6.6	2.8	7.1	11.4	3.8
Malignant neoplasm of pancreas (C25).........................	10.7	12.4	9.4	13.9	15.6	12.5
Malignant neoplasm of larynx (C32)............................	1.2	2.1	0.5	2.3	4.6	0.8
Malignant neoplasms of trachea, bronchus and lung (C33-C34)............................	55.5	71.4	43.7	59.6	88.1	40.9
Malignant melanoma of skin (C43)............................	3.3	4.8	2.2	0.5	0.5	0.4
Malignant neoplasm of breast (C50)............................	13.5	0.3	24.0	19.7	0.5	33.5
Malignant neoplasm of cervix uteri (C53)......................	1.1	...	2.1	2.6	...	4.5
Malignant neoplasms of corpus uteri and uterus, part unspecified (C54-C55)......................	2.2	...	3.9	4.3	...	7.2
Malignant neoplasm of ovary (C56)............................	5.1	...	9.2	4.4	...	7.4
Malignant neoplasm of prostate (C61).........................	8.9	22.8	...	19.4	54.1	...
Malignant neoplasms of kidney and renal pelvis (C64-C65)..	4.2	6.0	2.8	4.1	6.1	2.6
Malignant neoplasm of bladder (C67).........................	4.7	8.2	2.3	3.7	5.7	2.6
Malignant neoplasms of meninges, brain and other parts of central nervous system (C70-C72)..	4.9	5.9	4.0	2.6	3.3	2.0
Malignant neoplasms of lymphoid, hematopoietic and related tissue (C81-C96)..	18.7	24.4	14.6	17.9	23.0	14.5
Hodgkin's disease (C81)..	0.4	0.5	0.4	0.4	0.5	0.3
Non-Hodgkin's lymphoma (C82-C85)........................	7.3	9.3	5.8	4.8	6.1	3.8
Leukemia (C91-C95)..	7.5	10.1	5.6	6.0	8.0	4.8
Multiple myeloma and immunoproliferative neoplasms (C88, C90)..	3.5	4.5	2.8	6.6	8.2	5.6
Other and unspecified malignant neoplasms of lymphoid,hematopoietic and related tissue (C96)............................	0.0	0.0	*	*	*	*
All other and unspecified malignant neoplasms (C17, C23-C24, C26-C31, C37-C41, C44-C49, C51-C52, C57-C60, C62-C63, C66, C68-C69, C73-C80, C97)..	21.1	25.3	17.9	23.6	28.9	20.0
In situ neoplasms, benign neoplasms and neoplasms of uncertain or unknown behavior (D00-D48)..	4.7	5.9	3.9	4.2	4.6	4.0
Anemias (D50-D64)..	1.3	1.2	1.3	3.4	3.5	3.3
Diabetes mellitus (E10-E14)............................	21.5	25.6	18.4	47.7	51.7	44.6
Nutritional deficiencies (E40-E64).........................	1.0	0.9	1.0	1.7	1.6	1.7
Malnutrition (E40-E46)............................	0.9	0.8	1.0	1.6	1.5	1.7
Other nutritional deficiencies (E50-E64).................	0.1	0.0	0.1	*	*	*
Meningitis (G00,G03)..	0.2	0.2	0.2	0.4	0.5	0.3
Parkinson's disease (G20-G21)............................	7.0	10.6	4.7	3.0	5.0	1.9
Alzheimer's disease (G30)............................	24.2	19.4	26.7	19.7	16.7	20.9
Major cardiovascular diseases (I00-I78)............................	274.5	327.8	231.7	373.9	442.6	322.5
Diseases of heart (I00-I09,I11,I13,I20-I51)............................	210.7	262.2	170.3	275.6	335.1	231.9
Acute rheumatic fever and chronic rheumatic heart diseases (I00-I09)............	1.1	0.9	1.3	0.8	0.7	0.9
Hypertensive heart disease (I11)............................	8.0	8.4	7.2	24.4	28.9	20.8
Hypertensive heart and renal disease (I13)..	0.8	0.8	0.7	3.3	3.9	2.8

* = Figure does not meet standards of reliability or precision.
... = Not applicable.
0.0 = Quantity more than zero but less than 0.05.
[1]Based on codes from the *International Classification of Diseases, Tenth Revision* (1992), except where (*) precedes the cause of death code.

Table B-25. Age-Adjusted Death Rates for 113 Selected Causes by Hispanic Origin, Race for Non-Hispanic Population, and Sex, 2005—*Continued*

(Rate per 100,000 population.)

Cause of death[1]	Non-Hispanic White			Non-Hispanic Black		
	Both sexes	Male	Female	Both sexes	Male	Female
Ischemic heart diseases (I20-I25)................................	145.2	190.2	110.7	173.7	216.9	142.8
Acute myocardial infarction (I21-I22)................................	49.7	65.1	37.4	58.5	70.9	49.5
Other acute ischemic heart diseases (I24)	1.1	1.4	0.9	2.0	2.6	1.6
Other forms of chronic ischemic heart disease (I20, I25)	94.4	123.7	72.4	113.2	143.4	91.7
Atherosclerotic cardiovascular disease, so described (I25.0)	19.1	24.9	14.1	34.9	47.5	25.7
All other forms of chronic ischemic heart disease (I20, I25.1-I25.9)	75.3	98.7	58.2	78.3	95.9	66.0
Other heart diseases (I26-I51)...................	55.6	61.9	50.3	73.4	84.8	64.7
Acute and subacute endocarditis (I33)...................................	0.4	0.5	0.3	0.7	0.9	0.6
Diseases of pericardium and acute myocarditis (I30-I31, I40)	0.3	0.3	0.2	0.5	0.5	0.5
Heart failure (I50)...............................	19.4	20.5	18.5	22.1	23.5	20.7
All other forms of heart disease (I26-I28, I34-I38, I42-I49, I51)	35.5	40.6	31.3	50.1	59.9	42.8
Essential (primary) hypertension and hypertensive renal disease (I10, I12)................	7.0	6.6	7.0	18.8	20.3	17.4
Cerebrovascular diseases (I60-I69)................	45.0	44.8	44.4	66.3	71.8	61.7
Atherosclerosis (I70)................................	4.0	4.1	3.8	3.4	3.4	3.3
Other diseases of circulatory system (I71-I78)...............................	7.8	10.2	6.1	9.8	11.8	8.2
Aortic aneurysm and dissection (I71)	4.7	6.8	3.2	4.7	6.1	3.6
Other diseases of arteries, arterioles and capillaries (I72-I78)	3.1	3.4	2.9	5.1	5.7	4.6
Other disorders of circulatory system (I80-I99)...............................	1.5	1.6	1.4	2.7	3.1	2.4
Influenza and pneumonia (J10-J18).................	20.4	23.8	18.1	22.1	27.3	18.7
Influenza (J10-J11)...........................	0.6	0.6	0.6	0.2	0.3	0.2
Pneumonia (J12-J18)..........................	19.7	23.1	17.5	21.8	27.0	18.5
Other acute lower respiratory infections (J20-J22)...................................	0.1	0.1	0.1	0.1	*	0.1
Acute bronchitis and bronchiolitis (J20-J21)................................	0.1	0.1	0.1	0.1	*	*
Unspecified acute lower respiratory infection (J22)................................	0.0	0.0	0.0	*	*	*
Chronic lower respiratory diseases (J40-J47)...............................	47.2	54.7	42.5	31.1	44.8	23.2
Bronchitis, chronic and unspecified (J40-J42)...............................	0.3	0.3	0.3	0.2	0.3	0.1
Emphysema (J43).............................	5.1	6.3	4.4	3.1	5.0	1.9
Asthma (J45-J46)..........................	1.0	0.7	1.3	3.1	2.7	3.4
Other chronic lower respiratory diseases (J44, J47)........................	40.8	47.4	36.6	24.7	36.7	17.7
Pneumoconioses and chemical effects (J60-J66, J68).............................	0.4	0.9	0.0	0.2	0.5	*
Pneumonitis due to solids and liquids (J69)	5.7	7.7	4.5	6.5	9.2	4.9
Other diseases of respiratory system (J00-J06, J30-J39, J67, J70-J98)	9.0	10.8	7.8	8.9	10.9	7.6
Peptic ulcer (K25-K28)	1.1	1.3	1.0	1.3	1.8	0.9
Diseases of appendix (K35-K38)	0.1	0.2	0.1	0.2	0.2	0.1
Hernia (K40-K46)	0.5	0.5	0.5	0.5	0.6	0.5
Chronic liver disease and cirrhosis (K70, K73-K74).............................	8.7	11.8	5.8	7.8	11.7	4.9
Alcoholic liver disease (K70)...............	4.0	5.9	2.3	3.5	5.5	2.0
Other chronic liver disease and cirrhosis (K73-K74)........................	4.6	5.8	3.6	4.3	6.2	2.9
Cholelithiasis and other disorders of gallbladder (K80-K82)........................	0.9	1.1	0.8	1.3	1.4	1.2

* = Figure does not meet standards of reliability or precision.
... = Not applicable.
0.0 = Quantity more than zero but less than 0.05.
[1]Based on codes from the *International Classification of Diseases, Tenth Revision* (1992), except where (*) precedes the cause of death code.

Table B-25. Age-Adjusted Death Rates for 113 Selected Causes by Hispanic Origin, Race for Non-Hispanic Population, and Sex, 2005—*Continued*

(Rate per 100,000 population.)

Cause of death[1]	Non-Hispanic White			Non-Hispanic Black		
	Both sexes	Male	Female	Both sexes	Male	Female
Nephritis, nephrotic syndrome and nephrosis (N00-N07, N17-N19, N25-N27)	12.9	16.2	10.7	30.3	34.8	27.4
Acute and rapidly progressive nephritic and nephrotic syndrome (N00-N01, N04)	0.0	0.0	0.0	*	*	*
Chronic glomerulonephritis, nephritis and nephropathy not specified as acute or chronic, and renal sclerosis unspecified (N02-N03, N05-N07, N26)	0.2	0.3	0.2	0.6	0.8	0.5
Renal failure (N17-N19)	12.6	15.8	10.5	29.6	33.9	26.8
Other disorders of kidney (N25, N27)	0.0	*	*	*	*	*
Infections of kidney (N10-N12, N13.6, N15.1)	0.2	0.2	0.3	0.3	0.3	0.4
Hyperplasia of prostate (N40)	0.2	0.5	...	0.1	0.4	...
Inflammatory diseases of female pelvic organs (N70-N76)	0.0	...	0.1	*	...	*
Pregnancy, childbirth and the puerperium (O00-O99)	0.2	...	0.3	0.7	...	1.3
Pregnancy with abortive outcome (O00-O07)	*	...	*	*	...	*
Other complications of pregnancy, childbirth and the puerperium (O10-O99)	0.2	...	0.3	0.6	...	1.3
Certain conditions originating in the perinatal period (P00-P96)	3.7	4.1	3.3	10.6	11.7	9.5
Congenital malformations, deformations and chromosomal abnormalities (Q00-Q99)	3.4	3.6	3.2	3.9	4.2	3.8
Symptoms, signs and abnormal clinical and laboratory findings, not elsewhere classified (R00-R99)	10.4	10.9	9.4	14.6	16.9	12.5
All other diseases (residual)	71.1	70.8	69.3	89.4	93.3	85.2
Accidents (unintentional injuries) (V01-X59, Y85-Y86)	41.0	56.2	26.8	39.5	59.2	23.3
Transport accidents (V01-V99, Y85)	16.6	23.8	9.8	15.8	24.7	8.2
Motor vehicle accidents (V02-V04, V09.0, V09.2, V12-V14, V19.0-V19.2, V19.4-V19.6, V20-V79, V80.3-V80.5, V81.0-V81.1, V82.0-V82.1, V83-V86, V87.0-V87.8, V88.0-V88.8, V89.0, V89.2)	15.5	22.0	9.4	14.8	23.1	7.8
Other land transport accidents (V01, V05-V06, V09.1, V09.3-V09.9, V10-V11, V15-V18, V19.3,V19.8-V19.9, V80.0-V80.2, V80.6-V80.9, V81.2-V81.9, V82.2-V82.9, V87.9, V88.9,V89.1, V89.3,V89.9)	0.4	0.6	0.2	0.6	1.0	0.2
Water, air and space, and other and unspecified transport accidents and their sequelae (V90-V99, Y85)	0.7	1.2	0.3	0.4	0.7	0.1
Nontransport accidents (W00-X59, Y86)	24.3	32.4	17.0	23.7	34.5	15.1
Falls (W00-W19)	6.8	8.7	5.3	3.7	5.2	2.6
Accidental discharge of firearms (W32-W34)	0.3	0.4	0.1	0.4	0.7	*
Accidental drowning and submersion (W65-W74)	1.2	1.8	0.5	1.4	2.6	0.4
Accidental exposure to smoke, fire and flames (X00-X09)	1.0	1.3	0.7	2.3	3.1	1.6
Accidental poisoning and exposure to noxious substances (X40-X49)	9.0	12.0	6.0	8.3	12.1	5.1
Other and unspecified nontransport accidents and their sequelae (W20-W31, W35-W64, W75-W99, X10-X39, X50-X59, Y86)	6.2	8.3	4.3	7.6	10.7	5.3

* = Figure does not meet standards of reliability or precision.
... = Not applicable.
0.0 = Quantity more than zero but less than 0.05.
[1]Based on codes from the *International Classification of Diseases, Tenth Revision* (1992), except where (*) precedes the cause of death code.

Table B-25. Age-Adjusted Death Rates for 113 Selected Causes by Hispanic Origin, Race for Non-Hispanic Population, and Sex, 2005—*Continued*

(Rate per 100,000 population.)

Cause of death[1]	Non-Hispanic White			Non-Hispanic Black		
	Both sexes	Male	Female	Both sexes	Male	Female
Intentional self-harm (suicide) (*U03,X60-X84,Y87.0)	12.9	21.2	5.3	5.4	9.4	1.9
Intentional self-harm (suicide) by discharge of firearms (X72-X74)	6.9	12.6	1.7	2.8	5.4	0.5
Intentional self-harm (suicide) by other and unspecified means and their sequelae (*U03, X60-X71, X75-X84, Y87.0)	6.1	8.6	3.6	2.6	4.0	1.4
Assault (homicide) (*U01-*U02, X85-Y09, Y87.1)	2.7	3.5	1.8	21.8	38.5	6.2
Assault (homicide) by discharge of firearms (*U01.4, X93-X95)	1.4	2.1	0.9	16.6	30.9	3.1
Assault (homicide) by other and unspecified means and their sequelae (*U01.0-*U01.3, *U01.5-*U01.9, *U02, X85-X92, X96-Y09, Y87.1)	1.2	1.5	0.9	5.2	7.6	3.1
Legal intervention (Y35, Y89.0)	0.1	0.2	*	0.3	0.6	*
Events of undetermined intent (Y10-Y34, Y87.2, Y89.9)	1.8	2.1	1.4	1.9	2.6	1.2
Discharge of firearms, undetermined intent (Y22-Y24)	0.1	0.1	0.0	0.1	0.1	*
Other and unspecified events of undetermined intent and their sequelae (Y10-Y21, Y25-Y34, Y87.2, Y89.9)	1.7	2.0	1.4	1.8	2.5	1.2
Operations of war and their sequelae (Y36, Y89.1)	*	*	*	*	*	*
Complications of medical and surgical care (Y40-Y84, Y88)	0.8	1.0	0.8	1.5	1.5	1.5

* = Figure does not meet standards of reliability or precision.
[1]Based on codes from the *International Classification of Diseases, Tenth Revision* (1992), except where (*) precedes the cause of death code.

NOTE: Complete confirmation of deaths from selected causes of death, considered to be of public health concern, were not provided by the following states–Alabama, California, Connecticut, Florida, Illinois, Indiana, Kentucky, Louisiana, Maryland, Michigan, Missouri, Montana, Nevada, New Hampshire, New Jersey, New York, North Carolina, Ohio, Oklahoma, Pennsylvania, Rhode Island, Texas, Utah, Virginia, Washington, and West Virginia.

Table B-26. Number of Deaths, Death Rates, and Age-Adjusted Death Rates for Injury Deaths According to Mechanism and Intent of Death, 2005

(Number, rate per 100,000 population.)

Mechanism and intent of death[1]	Number	Rate	Age-adjusted rate
ALL INJURY (*U01-*U03, V01-Y36, Y85-Y87, Y89)	173,753	58.6	57.8
Unintentional (V01-X59, Y85-Y86)	117,809	39.7	39.1
Suicide (*U03, X60-X84, Y87.0)	32,637	11.0	10.9
Homicide (*U01-*U02, X85-Y09, Y87.1)	18,124	6.1	6.1
Undetermined (Y10-Y34, Y87.2, Y89.9)	4,742	1.6	1.6
Legal intervention/war (Y35-Y36, Y89[.0,.1])	441	0.1	0.1
Cut/Pierce (W25-W29, W45, X78, X99,Y28, Y35.4)	2,795	0.9	0.9
Unintentional (W25-W29, W45)	90	0.0	0.0
Suicide (X78)	590	0.2	0.2
Homicide (X99)	2,097	0.7	0.7
Undetermined (Y28)	18	*	*
Legal intervention/war (Y35.4)	-	*	*
Drowning (W65-W74, X71, X92, Y21)	4,248	1.4	1.4
Unintentional (W65-W74)	3,582	1.2	1.2
Suicide (X71)	375	0.1	0.1
Homicide (X92)	49	0.0	0.0
Undetermined (Y21)	242	0.1	0.1
Fall (W00-W19, X80, Y01, Y30)	20,426	6.9	6.6
Unintentional (W00-W19)	19,656	6.6	6.4
Suicide (X80)	683	0.2	0.2
Homicide (Y01)	18	*	*
Undetermined (Y30)	69	0.0	0.0
Fire/Hot Object or Substance (*U01.3, X00-X19, X76-X77, X97-X98, Y26-Y27, Y36.3)[2]	3,736	1.3	1.2
Unintentional (X00-X19)	3,299	1.1	1.1
Suicide (X76-X77)	160	0.1	0.0
Homicide (*U01.3, X97-X98)	157	0.1	0.1
Undetermined (Y26-Y27)	120	0.0	0.0
Legal intervention/war (Y36.3)	-	*	*
Fire/Flame (X00-X09, X76, X97, Y26)	3,626	1.2	1.2
Unintentional (X00-X09)	3,197	1.1	1.1
Suicide (X76)	160	0.1	0.0
Homicide (X97)	149	0.1	0.1
Undetermined (Y26)	120	0.0	0.0
Hot Object/Substance (X10-X19, X77, X98, Y27)	110	0.0	0.0
Unintentional (X10-X19)	102	0.0	0.0
Suicide (X77)	-	*	*
Homicide (X98)	8	*	*
Undetermined (Y27)	-	*	*
Firearm (*U01.4, W32-W34, X72-X74, X93-X95, Y22-Y24, Y35.0)	30,694	10.4	10.2
Unintentional (W32-W34)	789	0.3	0.3
Suicide (X72-X74)	17,002	5.7	5.7
Homicide (*U01.4, X93-X95)	12,352	4.2	4.2
Undetermined (Y22-Y24)	221	0.1	0.1
Legal intervention/war (Y35.0)	330	0.1	0.1
Machinery (W24, W30-W31)[3]	755	0.3	0.2
All Transport (*U01.1, V01-V99, X82, Y03, Y32, Y36.1)	47,894	16.2	16.0
Unintentional (V01-V99)	47,717	16.1	15.9
Suicide (X82)	113	0.0	0.0
Homicide (*U01.1, Y03)	38	0.0	0.0
Undetermined (Y32)	26	0.0	0.0
Legal intervention/war (Y36.1)	-	*	*
Motor vehicle traffic (V02-V04[.1, .9], V09.2, V12-V14[.3-.9], V19[.4-.6], V20-V28[.3-.9], V29-V79[.4-.9], V80[.3-.5], V81.1, V82.1, V83-V86[.0-.3], V87[.0-.8], V89.2)[3]	43,667	14.7	14.6
Occupant (V30-V79[.4-.9], V83-V86[.0-.3])[3]	19,125	6.5	6.4
Motorcyclist (V20-V28[.3-.9], V29[.4-.9])[3]	4,296	1.4	1.5
Pedal cyclist (V12-V14[.3-.9], V19[.4-.6])[3]	700	0.2	0.2
Pedestrian (V02-V04[.1, .9], V09.2)[3]	4,917	1.7	1.6
Other (V80[.3-.5], V81.1, V82.1)[3]	12	*	*
Unspecified (V87[.0-.8], V89.2)[3]	14,617	4.9	4.9
Pedal cyclist, other (V10-V11, V12-V14[.0-.2], V15-V18, V19[.0-.3, .8, .9])[3]	227	0.1	0.1
Pedestrian, other (V01, V02-V04[.0], V05, V06, V09[.0, .1, .3, .9])[3]	1,157	0.4	0.4

* = Figure does not meet standards of reliability or precision.
- = Quantity zero.
0.0 = Quantity more than zero but less than 0.05.
[1]Based on codes from the *International Classification of Diseases, Tenth Revision* (1992), except where (*) precedes the cause of death code.
[2]Codes *U01.3 and Y36.3 cannot be divided separately into the subcategories shown below; therefore, subcategories may not add to the total.
[3]Intent of death is unintentional.

Table B-26. Number of Deaths, Death Rates, and Age-Adjusted Death Rates for Injury Deaths According to Mechanism and Intent of Death, 2005—*Continued*

(Number, rate per 100,000 population.)

Mechanism and intent of death[1]	Number	Rate	Age-adjusted rate
Other land transport (V20-V28[.0-.2], V29-V79[.0-.3], V80[.0-.2, .6-.9], V81-V82[.0, .2-.9], V83-V86[.4-.9], V87.9, V88[.0-.9], V89[.0, .1, .3, .9], X82, Y03, Y32)	1,710	0.6	0.6
Unintentional (V20-V28[.0-.2], V29-V79[.0-.3], V80(.0-.2, .6-.9), V81-V82[.0, .2-.9], V83-V86[.4-.9], V87.9, V88[.0-.9], V89[.0, .1, .3, .9])	1,533	0.5	0.5
Suicide (X82)	113	0.0	0.0
Homicide (Y03)	38	0.0	0.0
Undetermined (Y32)	26	0.0	0.0
Other transport (*U01.1, V90-V99, Y36.1)	1,133	0.4	0.4
Unintentional (V90-V99)	1,133	0.4	0.4
Homicide (*U01.1)	-	*	*
Legal intervention/war (Y36.1)	-	*	*
Natural/Environmental (W42-W43, W53-W64, W92-W99, X20-X39, X51-X57)[3]	2,462	0.8	0.8
Overexertion (X50)[3]	11	*	*
Poisoning (*U01[.6-.7], X40-X49, X60-X69, X85-X90, Y10-Y19, Y35.2)	32,691	11.0	11.0
Unintentional (X40-X49)	23,618	8.0	7.9
Suicide (X60-X69)	5,744	1.9	1.9
Homicide (*U01[.6-.7], X85-X90)	89	0.0	0.0
Undetermined (Y10-Y19)	3,240	1.1	1.1
Legal intervention/war (Y35.2)	-	*	*
Struck By or Against (W20-W22, W50-W52, X79, Y00, Y04, Y29, Y35.3)	1,095	0.4	0.4
Unintentional (W20-W22, W50-W52)	880	0.3	0.3
Suicide (X79)	-	*	*
Homicide (Y00, Y04)	209	0.1	0.1
Undetermined (Y29)	5	*	*
Legal intervention/war (Y35.3)	1	*	*
Suffocation (W75-W84, X70, X91, Y20)	13,920	4.7	4.6
Unintentional (W75-W84)	5,900	2.0	1.9
Suicide (X70)	7,248	2.4	2.4
Homicide (X91)	633	0.2	0.2
Undetermined (Y20)	139	0.0	0.0
Other Specified, Classifiable (*U01[.0, .2, .5], *U03.0, W23, W35-W41, W44, W49, W85-W91, X75, X81, X96, Y02,Y05-Y07, Y25, Y31, Y35[.1, .5], Y36[.0, .2, .4-.8], Y85)	2,108	0.7	0.7
Unintentional (W23, W35-W41, W44, W49, W85-W91, Y85)	1,479	0.5	0.5
Suicide (*U03.0, X75, X81)	328	0.1	0.1
Homicide (*U01[.0, .2, .5], X96, Y02, Y05-Y07)	220	0.1	0.1
Undetermined (Y25, Y31)	16	*	*
Legal intervention/war (Y35[.1, .5], Y36[.0, .2, .4-.8])	65	0.0	0.0
Other Specified, Not Elsewhere Classified (*U01.8, *U02, X58, X83, Y08, Y33, Y35.6, Y86-Y87, Y89[.0-.1])	2,023	0.7	0.7
Unintentional (X58, Y86)	1,020	0.3	0.3
Suicide (X83, Y87.0)	228	0.1	0.1
Homicide (*U01.8, *U02, Y08, Y87.1)	548	0.2	0.2
Undetermined (Y33, Y87.2)	185	0.1	0.1
Legal intervention/war (Y35.6, Y89[.0, .1])	42	0.0	0.0
Unspecified (*U01.9, *U03.9, X59, X84, Y09, Y34, Y35.7, Y36.9, Y89.9)	8,895	3.0	2.9
Unintentional (X59)	6,551	2.2	2.1
Suicide (*U03.9, X84)	166	0.1	0.1
Homicide (*U01.9, Y09)	1,714	0.6	0.6
Undetermined (Y34, Y89.9)	461	0.2	0.2
Legal intervention/war (Y35.7, Y36.9)	3	*	*

* = Figure does not meet standards of reliability or precision.

- = Quantity zero.

0.0 = Quantity more than zero but less than 0.05.

[1]Based on codes from the *International Classification of Diseases, Tenth Revision* (1992), except where (*) precedes the cause of death code.

[3]Intent of death is unintentional.

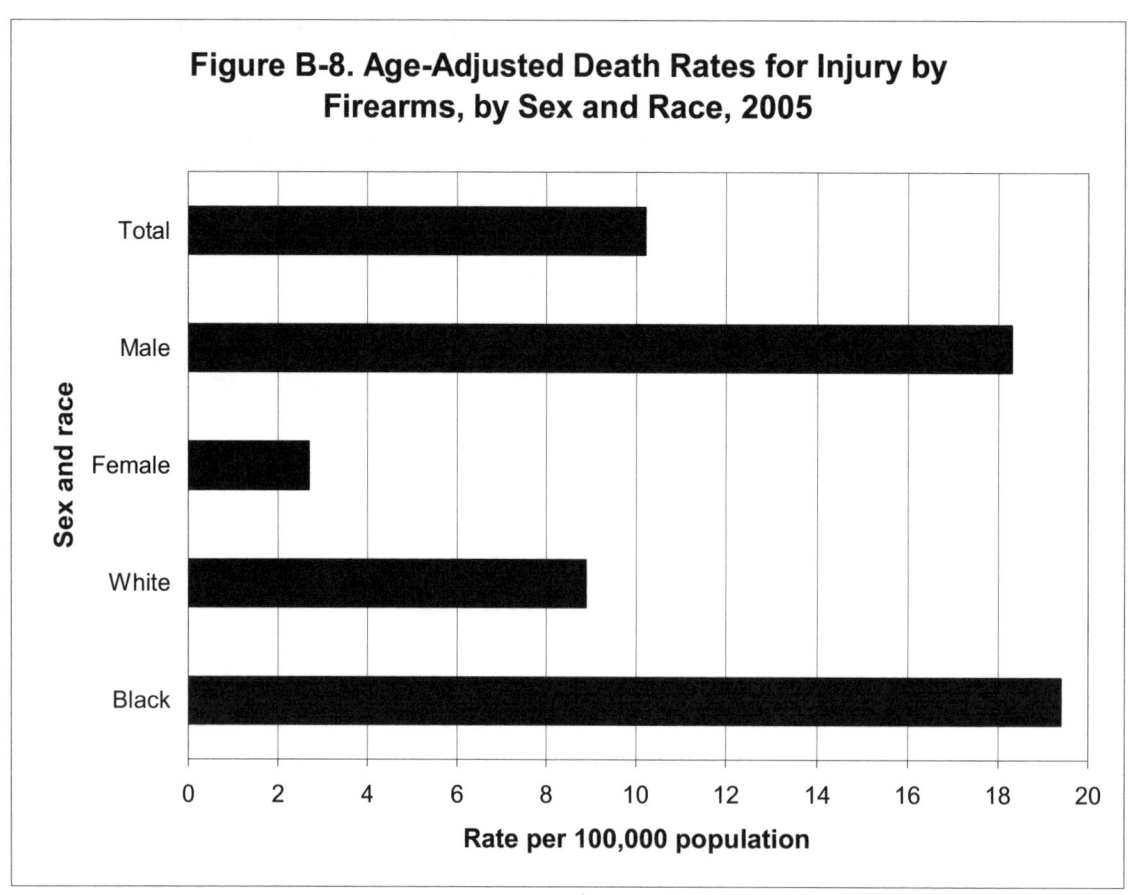

Figure B-8. Age-Adjusted Death Rates for Injury by Firearms, by Sex and Race, 2005

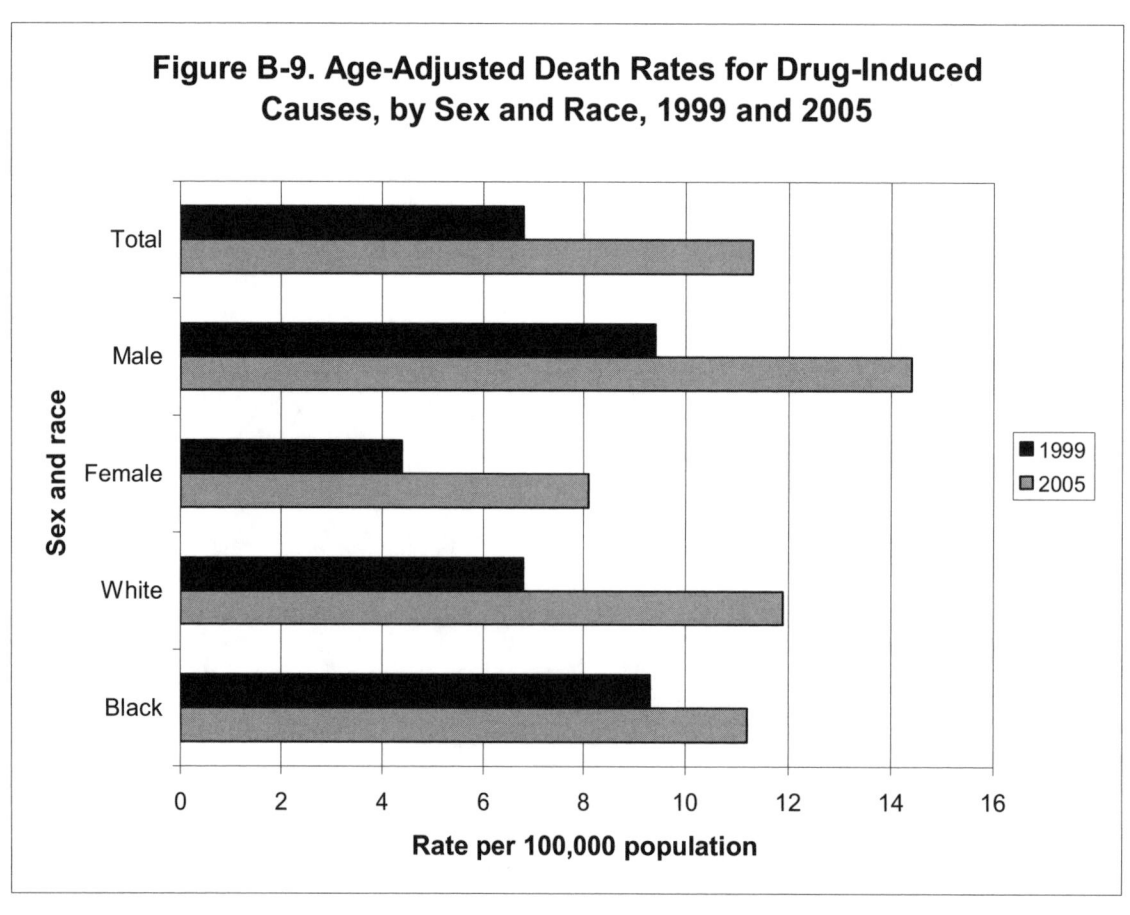

Figure B-9. Age-Adjusted Death Rates for Drug-Induced Causes, by Sex and Race, 1999 and 2005

Table B-27. Number of Deaths, Death Rates, and Age-Adjusted Death Rates for Injury by Firearms, by Race and Sex, 1999–2005

(Number, rate per 100,000 population.)

| Year | All races | | | White | | | All other | | | | | |
| | | | | | | | Total | | | Black | | |
	Both sexes	Male	Female	Both sexes	Male	Female	Both sexes	Male	Female	Both sexes	Male	Female
Number												
1999	28,874	24,700	4,174	21,143	17,942	3,201	7,731	6,758	973	7,017	6,184	833
2000	28,663	24,582	4,081	20,945	17,750	3,195	7,718	6,832	886	7,054	6,284	770
2001	29,573	25,480	4,093	21,760	18,527	3,233	7,813	6,953	860	7,184	6,438	746
2002	30,242	26,098	4,144	21,902	18,714	3,188	8,340	7,384	956	7,623	6,798	825
2003	30,136	26,124	4,012	21,763	18,647	3,116	8,373	7,477	896	7,659	6,882	777
2004	29,569	25,498	4,071	21,442	18,223	3,219	8,127	7,275	852	7,448	6,709	739
2005	30,694	26,657	4,037	21,958	18,788	3,170	8,736	7,869	867	7,984	7,226	758
Rate												
1999	10.3	18.1	2.9	9.2	15.9	2.8	15.4	28.0	3.7	19.4	36.0	4.4
2000	10.2	17.8	2.8	9.1	15.6	2.7	15.0	27.8	3.3	19.3	36.1	4.0
2001	10.4	18.2	2.8	9.4	16.2	2.7	14.9	27.6	3.2	19.3	36.4	3.8
2002	10.5	18.4	2.8	9.3	16.1	2.7	15.6	28.7	3.4	20.2	37.8	4.2
2003	10.4	18.3	2.7	9.2	16.0	2.6	15.4	28.6	3.2	20.1	37.8	3.9
2004	10.1	17.6	2.7	9.0	15.5	2.7	14.7	27.3	3.0	19.3	36.4	3.7
2005	10.4	18.3	2.7	9.1	15.8	2.6	15.5	29.1	3.0	20.4	38.7	3.7
Age Adjusted Rate												
1999	10.3	18.4	2.9	9.1	16.2	2.7	14.4	26.3	3.6	18.4	34.1	4.3
2000	10.2	18.1	2.8	9.0	15.9	2.7	14.1	26.0	3.2	18.4	34.2	3.9
2001	10.3	18.5	2.8	9.2	16.3	2.7	14.0	25.9	3.1	18.4	34.5	3.8
2002	10.4	18.6	2.8	9.2	16.2	2.7	14.6	26.9	3.3	19.3	36.0	4.1
2003	10.3	18.4	2.7	9.0	16.0	2.6	14.4	26.4	3.1	19.0	35.6	3.8
2004	10.0	17.7	2.7	8.8	15.4	2.7	13.8	25.5	2.9	18.4	34.5	3.6
2005	10.2	18.3	2.7	8.9	15.7	2.6	14.5	26.9	2.9	19.4	36.4	3.6

NOTE: Causes of death attributable to injury by firearms include *ICD-10* codes *U01.4, W32-W34, X72-X74, X93-X95, Y22-Y24, and Y35.0.

Table B-28. Number of Deaths, Death Rates, and Age-Adjusted Death Rates for Injury by Firearms, by Hispanic Origin, Race for Non-Hispanic Population, and Sex, 1999–2005

(Number, rate per 100,000 population.)

Year	All origins[1] Both sexes	Male	Female	Hispanic[2] Both sexes	Male	Female	Non-Hispanic[3] Both sexes	Male	Female	Non-Hispanic White Both sexes	Male	Female	Non-Hispanic Black Both sexes	Male	Female
Number															
1999	28,874	24,700	4,174	2,878	2,549	329	25,877	22,050	3,827	18,260	15,384	2,876	6,933	6,114	819
2000	28,663	24,582	4,081	2,891	2,582	309	25,637	21,881	3,756	18,042	15,160	2,882	6,958	6,193	765
2001	29,573	25,480	4,093	3,087	2,774	313	26,341	22,573	3,768	18,676	15,760	2,916	7,063	6,323	740
2002	30,242	26,098	4,144	3,143	2,834	309	26,944	23,127	3,817	18,762	15,881	2,881	7,494	6,681	813
2003	30,136	26,124	4,012	3,319	2,998	321	26,710	23,036	3,674	18,457	15,670	2,787	7,566	6,794	772
2004	29,569	25,498	4,071	3,278	2,973	305	26,189	22,436	3,753	18,200	15,283	2,917	7,347	6,620	727
2005	30,694	26,657	4,037	3,469	3,144	325	27,103	23,406	3,697	18,521	15,672	2,849	7,865	7,122	743
Rate															
1999	10.3	18.1	2.9	8.5	14.6	2.0	10.6	18.5	3.0	9.3	15.9	2.9	20.0	37.1	4.5
2000	10.2	17.8	2.8	8.2	14.2	1.8	10.4	18.3	3.0	9.1	15.7	2.9	19.8	37.1	4.2
2001	10.4	18.2	2.8	8.3	14.6	1.7	10.6	18.7	3.0	9.4	16.3	2.9	19.8	37.3	4.0
2002	10.5	18.4	2.8	8.1	14.2	1.6	10.8	19.0	3.0	9.4	16.3	2.8	20.7	38.9	4.3
2003	10.4	18.3	2.7	8.3	14.6	1.7	10.6	18.8	2.9	9.3	16.0	2.7	20.7	39.1	4.0
2004	10.1	17.6	2.7	7.9	13.9	1.5	10.4	18.2	2.9	9.1	15.6	2.9	19.9	37.6	3.8
2005	10.4	18.3	2.7	8.1	14.2	1.6	10.7	18.9	2.8	9.2	15.9	2.8	21.1	40.0	3.8
Age-Adjusted Rate															
1999	10.3	18.4	2.9	8.2	14.2	2.0	10.5	18.7	3.0	8.9	15.8	2.8	19.0	35.2	4.4
2000	10.2	18.1	2.8	7.8	13.6	1.8	10.3	18.4	3.0	8.8	15.5	2.8	18.9	35.2	4.1
2001	10.3	18.5	2.8	7.8	13.7	1.7	10.5	18.8	3.0	9.1	16.0	2.8	18.9	35.4	3.9
2002	10.4	18.6	2.8	7.6	13.4	1.6	10.7	19.1	3.0	9.0	16.0	2.8	19.8	37.0	4.2
2003	10.3	18.4	2.7	7.8	13.6	1.6	10.5	18.8	2.8	8.8	15.6	2.7	19.7	36.8	3.9
2004	10.0	17.7	2.7	7.5	13.1	1.5	10.2	18.2	2.9	8.7	15.1	2.8	19.0	35.7	3.7
2005	10.2	18.3	2.7	7.6	13.3	1.6	10.5	18.8	2.8	8.8	15.3	2.7	20.0	37.7	3.7

[1]Figures for origin not stated are included in all origins but not distributed among specified origins.
[2]Persons of Hispanic origin may be of any race.
[3]Includes races other than White and Black.

NOTE: Causes of death attributable to injury by firearms include *ICD-10* codes *U01.4, W32-W34, X72-X74, X93-X95, Y22-Y24, and Y35.0.

Table B-29. Number of Deaths, Death Rates, and Age-Adjusted Death Rates for Drug-Induced Causes, by Race and Sex, 1999–2005

(Number, rate per 100,000 population.)

Year	All races Both sexes	Male	Female	White Both sexes	Male	Female	All other Total Both sexes	Male	Female	All other Black Both sexes	Male	Female
Number												
1999	19,128	12,885	6,243	15,714	10,506	5,208	3,414	2,379	1,035	3,100	2,191	909
2000	19,720	13,137	6,583	16,388	10,857	5,531	3,332	2,280	1,052	3,034	2,094	940
2001	21,705	14,253	7,452	18,195	11,882	6,313	3,510	2,371	1,139	3,165	2,163	1,002
2002	26,040	16,734	9,306	22,146	14,170	7,976	3,894	2,564	1,330	3,463	2,307	1,156
2003	28,723	18,426	10,297	24,683	15,824	8,859	4,040	2,602	1,438	3,527	2,303	1,224
2004	30,711	19,362	11,349	26,474	16,634	9,840	4,237	2,728	1,509	3,633	2,352	1,281
2005	33,541	21,208	12,333	28,804	18,152	10,652	4,737	3,056	1,681	4,098	2,677	1,421
Rate												
1999	6.9	9.4	4.4	6.9	9.3	4.5	6.8	9.9	3.9	8.6	12.7	4.8
2000	7.0	9.5	4.6	7.1	9.6	4.7	6.5	9.3	3.9	8.3	12.0	4.9
2001	7.6	10.2	5.1	7.8	10.4	5.4	6.7	9.4	4.2	8.5	12.2	5.1
2002	9.0	11.8	6.3	9.4	12.2	6.7	7.3	10.0	4.8	9.2	12.8	5.8
2003	9.9	12.9	7.0	10.4	13.5	7.4	7.4	9.9	5.1	9.2	12.7	6.1
2004	10.5	13.4	7.6	11.1	14.1	8.2	7.6	10.2	5.2	9.4	12.8	6.3
2005	11.3	14.5	8.2	12.0	15.3	8.8	8.4	11.3	5.8	10.5	14.3	7.0
Age-Adjusted Rate												
1999	6.8	9.4	4.4	6.8	9.2	4.4	7.2	10.8	4.1	9.3	14.3	5.1
2000	7.0	9.5	4.6	7.1	9.4	4.7	6.9	10.1	4.1	9.0	13.5	5.2
2001	7.6	10.1	5.1	7.8	10.2	5.3	7.1	10.3	4.3	9.2	13.6	5.4
2002	9.0	11.7	6.3	9.4	12.1	6.7	7.6	10.8	4.9	9.9	14.2	6.1
2003	9.9	12.8	7.0	10.4	13.4	7.4	7.8	10.7	5.2	9.9	14.1	6.4
2004	10.4	13.3	7.6	11.1	13.9	8.1	8.0	11.1	5.3	10.1	14.3	6.6
2005	11.3	14.4	8.1	11.9	15.1	8.7	8.7	12.1	5.8	11.2	15.8	7.2

Table B-30. Number of Deaths, Death Rates, and Age-Adjusted Death Rates for Drug-Induced Causes, by Hispanic Origin, Race for Non-Hispanic Population, and Sex, 1999–2005

(Number, rate per 100,000 population.)

Year	All origins[1]			Hispanic[2]			Non-Hispanic[3]			Non-Hispanic White			Non-Hispanic Black		
	Both sexes	Male	Female	Both sexes	Male	Female	Both sexes	Male	Female	Both sexes	Male	Female	Both sexes	Male	Female
Number															
1999	19,128	12,885	6,243	1,965	1,605	360	16,966	11,136	5,830	13,644	8,831	4,813	3,030	2,134	896
2000	19,720	13,137	6,583	1,700	1,348	352	17,835	11,656	6,179	14,585	9,439	5,146	2,977	2,050	927
2001	21,705	14,253	7,452	1,731	1,335	396	19,799	12,778	7,021	16,367	10,465	5,902	3,099	2,113	986
2002	26,040	16,734	9,306	2,137	1,647	490	23,756	14,978	8,778	19,949	12,478	7,471	3,404	2,264	1,140
2003	28,723	18,426	10,297	2,358	1,800	558	26,199	16,497	9,702	22,245	13,959	8,286	3,466	2,256	1,210
2004	30,711	19,362	11,349	2,257	1,671	586	28,339	17,605	10,734	24,201	14,952	9,249	3,577	2,309	1,268
2005	33,541	21,208	12,333	2,596	1,969	627	30,809	19,140	11,669	26,186	16,170	10,016	4,019	2,612	1,407
Rate															
1999	6.9	9.4	4.4	5.8	9.2	2.2	6.9	9.3	4.6	6.9	9.2	4.8	8.7	12.9	4.9
2000	7.0	9.5	4.6	4.8	7.4	2.1	7.2	9.7	4.9	7.4	9.8	5.1	8.5	12.3	5.0
2001	7.6	10.2	5.1	4.7	7.0	2.2	8.0	10.6	5.5	8.3	10.8	5.8	8.7	12.5	5.3
2002	9.0	11.8	6.3	5.5	8.2	2.6	9.5	12.3	6.9	10.0	12.8	7.4	9.4	13.2	6.0
2003	9.9	12.9	7.0	5.9	8.7	2.9	10.4	13.5	7.6	11.2	14.3	8.2	9.5	13.0	6.3
2004	10.5	13.4	7.6	5.5	7.8	2.9	11.2	14.3	8.3	12.1	15.3	9.1	9.7	13.1	6.6
2005	11.3	14.5	8.2	6.1	8.9	3.0	12.1	15.4	9.0	13.1	16.4	9.8	10.8	14.7	7.2
Age-Adjusted Rate															
1999	6.8	9.4	4.4	6.4	10.3	2.5	6.8	9.2	4.6	6.8	8.9	4.6	9.4	14.4	5.2
2000	7.0	9.5	4.6	5.4	8.3	2.4	7.1	9.5	4.8	7.2	9.6	4.9	9.1	13.6	5.3
2001	7.6	10.1	5.1	5.3	8.0	2.5	7.9	10.4	5.4	8.1	10.6	5.7	9.3	13.8	5.5
2002	9.0	11.7	6.3	6.2	9.3	3.0	9.4	12.1	6.8	9.9	12.6	7.2	10.1	14.5	6.3
2003	9.9	12.8	7.0	6.7	9.9	3.3	10.3	13.3	7.4	11.0	14.1	8.0	10.1	14.4	6.6
2004	10.4	13.3	7.6	6.2	8.9	3.4	11.1	14.1	8.2	12.0	15.0	8.9	10.4	14.6	6.8
2005	11.3	14.4	8.1	6.8	10.0	3.5	11.9	15.2	8.8	12.8	16.2	9.6	11.4	16.1	7.4

[1]Figures for origin not stated are included in all origins but not distributed among specified origins.
[2]Persons of Hispanic origin may be of any race.
[3]Includes races other than White and Black.

Table B-31. Number of Deaths, Death Rates, and Age-Adjusted Death Rates for Alcohol-Induced Causes, by Race and Sex, 1999–2005

(Number, rate per 100,000 population.)

Year	All races			White			All other					
							Total			Black		
	Both sexes	Male	Female	Both sexes	Male	Female	Both sexes	Male	Female	Both sexes	Male	Female
Number												
1999	19,469	14,894	4,575	15,903	12,277	3,626	3,566	2,617	949	2,832	2,100	732
2000	19,643	14,993	4,650	16,223	12,509	3,714	3,420	2,484	936	2,712	1,993	719
2001	20,114	15,149	4,965	16,640	12,588	4,052	3,474	2,561	913	2,723	2,048	675
2002	20,218	15,272	4,946	16,988	12,926	4,062	3,230	2,346	884	2,434	1,798	636
2003	20,687	15,630	5,057	17,437	13,218	4,219	3,250	2,412	838	2,406	1,824	582
2004	21,081	15,906	5,175	17,875	13,525	4,350	3,206	2,381	825	2,351	1,784	567
2005	21,634	16,238	5,396	18,432	13,917	4,515	3,202	2,321	881	2,316	1,698	618
Rate												
1999	7.0	10.9	3.2	7.0	10.9	3.1	7.1	10.9	3.6	7.8	12.2	3.9
2000	7.0	10.9	3.2	7.1	11.0	3.2	6.7	10.1	3.5	7.4	11.4	3.7
2001	7.1	10.8	3.4	7.2	11.0	3.4	6.6	10.2	3.3	7.3	11.6	3.5
2002	7.0	10.8	3.4	7.2	11.1	3.4	6.0	9.1	3.2	6.4	10.0	3.2
2003	7.1	10.9	3.4	7.4	11.3	3.5	6.0	9.2	3.0	6.3	10.0	2.9
2004	7.2	11.0	3.5	7.5	11.5	3.6	5.8	8.9	2.9	6.1	9.7	2.8
2005	7.3	11.1	3.6	7.7	11.7	3.7	5.7	8.6	3.0	5.9	9.1	3.0
Age-Adjusted Rate												
1999	7.1	11.5	3.2	6.8	11.0	3.0	8.7	14.4	4.1	9.8	16.7	4.5
2000	7.0	11.4	3.2	6.9	11.1	3.0	8.0	13.1	4.0	9.1	15.3	4.3
2001	7.0	11.2	3.3	6.9	10.9	3.3	7.8	13.0	3.7	8.9	15.1	3.9
2002	6.9	11.0	3.3	6.9	10.9	3.2	7.1	11.6	3.5	7.8	13.1	3.6
2003	7.0	11.0	3.3	7.0	11.0	3.3	6.8	11.3	3.2	7.4	12.8	3.3
2004	7.0	11.0	3.3	7.1	11.0	3.3	6.6	11.0	3.1	7.2	12.3	3.1
2005	7.0	11.0	3.4	7.2	11.1	3.4	6.4	10.3	3.2	6.8	11.4	3.3

Table B-32. Number of Deaths, Death Rates, and Age-Adjusted Death Rates for Alcohol-Induced Causes, by Hispanic Origin, Race for Non-Hispanic Population, and Sex, 1999–2005

(Number, rate per 100,000.)

Year	All origins[1] Both sexes	Male	Female	Hispanic[2] Both sexes	Male	Female	Non-Hispanic[3] Both sexes	Male	Female	Non-Hispanic White Both sexes	Male	Female	Non-Hispanic Black Both sexes	Male	Female
Number															
1999	19,469	14,894	4,575	2,184	1,864	320	17,143	12,905	4,238	13,633	10,337	3,296	2,794	2,066	728
2000	19,643	14,993	4,650	2,323	2,024	299	17,177	12,843	4,334	13,815	10,408	3,407	2,672	1,959	713
2001	20,114	15,149	4,965	2,381	2,026	355	17,593	13,009	4,584	14,186	10,497	3,689	2,677	2,016	661
2002	20,218	15,272	4,946	2,408	2,065	343	17,661	13,078	4,583	14,494	10,783	3,711	2,396	1,768	628
2003	20,687	15,630	5,057	2,422	2,048	374	18,160	13,490	4,670	14,977	11,133	3,844	2,367	1,787	580
2004	21,081	15,906	5,175	2,406	2,056	350	18,567	13,761	4,806	15,418	11,428	3,990	2,318	1,754	564
2005	21,634	16,238	5,396	2,658	2,265	393	18,877	13,890	4,987	15,729	11,610	4,119	2,282	1,670	612
Rate															
1999	7.0	10.9	3.2	6.4	10.7	1.9	7.0	10.8	3.4	6.9	10.7	3.3	8.0	12.5	4.0
2000	7.0	10.9	3.2	6.6	11.1	1.7	7.0	10.7	3.4	7.0	10.8	3.4	7.6	11.7	3.9
2001	7.1	10.8	3.4	6.4	10.7	2.0	7.1	10.8	3.6	7.2	10.8	3.6	7.5	11.9	3.5
2002	7.0	10.8	3.4	6.2	10.3	1.8	7.1	10.7	3.6	7.3	11.1	3.7	6.6	10.3	3.3
2003	7.1	10.9	3.4	6.1	9.9	1.9	7.2	11.0	3.6	7.5	11.4	3.8	6.5	10.3	3.0
2004	7.2	11.0	3.5	5.8	9.6	1.8	7.4	11.2	3.7	7.7	11.7	3.9	6.3	10.0	2.9
2005	7.3	11.1	3.6	6.2	10.3	1.9	7.4	11.2	3.8	7.9	11.8	4.0	6.1	9.4	3.1
Age-Adjusted Rate															
1999	7.1	11.5	3.2	10.3	18.6	3.0	6.8	10.8	3.2	6.4	10.2	3.0	10.0	16.9	4.6
2000	7.0	11.4	3.2	10.5	19.4	2.6	6.7	10.6	3.2	6.4	10.1	3.1	9.3	15.5	4.4
2001	7.0	11.2	3.3	10.1	18.1	2.9	6.7	10.5	3.4	6.5	10.1	3.3	9.0	15.4	4.0
2002	6.9	11.0	3.3	9.5	17.0	2.7	6.7	10.4	3.3	6.6	10.2	3.3	7.9	13.3	3.7
2003	7.0	11.0	3.3	9.2	16.2	2.8	6.8	10.5	3.3	6.7	10.4	3.4	7.6	12.9	3.3
2004	7.0	11.0	3.3	8.6	15.1	2.5	6.8	10.6	3.4	6.8	10.5	3.4	7.3	12.5	3.2
2005	7.0	11.0	3.4	9.1	16.2	2.6	6.8	10.4	3.5	6.8	10.4	3.5	7.0	11.6	3.4

[1]Figures for origin not stated are included in all origins but not distributed among specified origins.
[2]Persons of Hispanic origin may be of any race.
[3]Includes races other than White and Black.

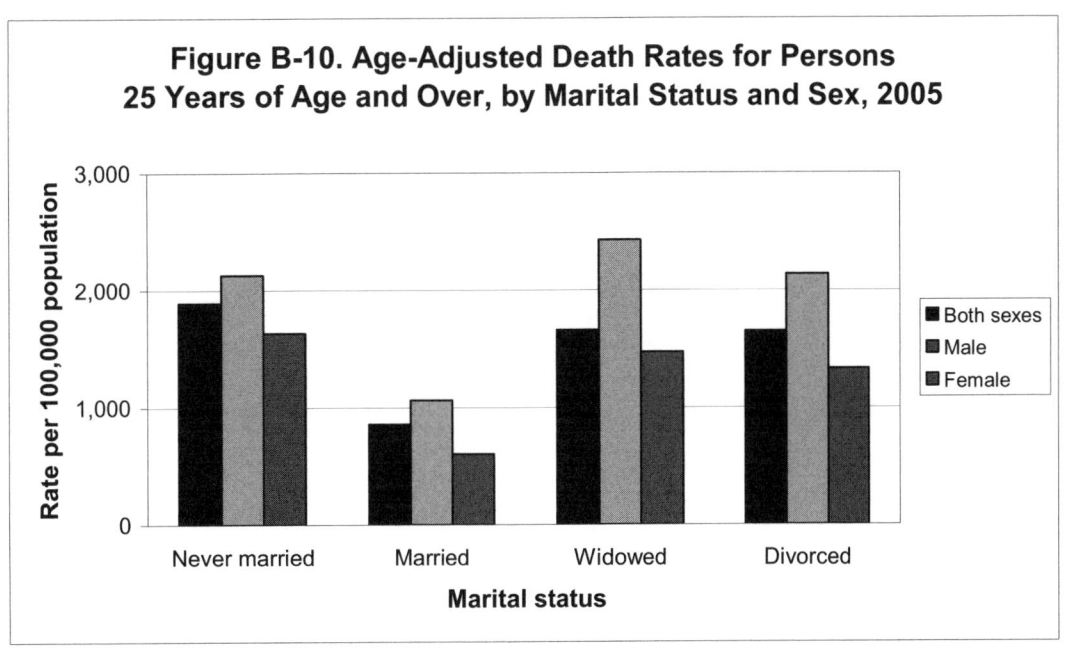

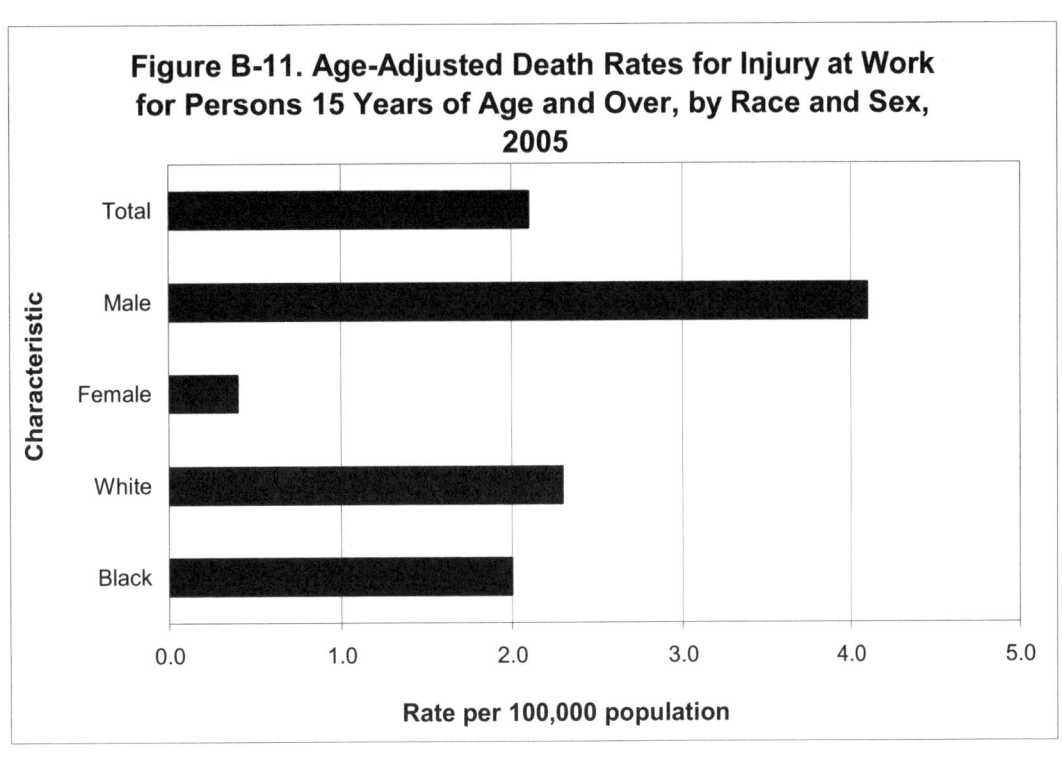

Table B-33. Number of Deaths, Death Rates, and Age-Adjusted Death Rates for Those Aged 15 Years and Over, by Marital Status and Sex, 2005

(Number, rate per 100,000 population.)

Marital status and sex	15 years and over[1]	15–24 years	25–34 years	35–44 years	45–54 years	55–64 years	65–74 years	75 years and over	Age-adjusted rate[2]
NUMBER									
Both Sexes	2,407,964	34,234	41,925	84,785	183,530	275,301	398,355	1,389,834	...
Never married	257,695	31,590	24,231	30,385	41,513	31,935	27,244	70,797	...
Ever married	2,138,926	2,521	17,415	53,544	139,876	240,886	368,914	1,315,770	...
Married	929,991	2,151	12,915	33,802	82,966	145,005	213,767	439,385	...
Widowed	908,645	46	277	1,418	6,971	25,121	88,826	785,986	...
Divorced	300,290	324	4,223	18,324	49,939	70,760	66,321	90,399	...
Not stated	11,343	123	279	856	2,141	2,480	2,197	3,267	...
Male	1,184,840	25,509	29,283	53,309	114,472	165,429	222,807	574,031	...
Never married	157,583	23,903	18,093	21,329	28,758	20,749	16,714	28,037	...
Ever married	1,019,139	1,512	10,972	31,354	84,008	142,690	204,435	544,168	...
Married	629,498	1,309	8,201	19,742	49,585	91,963	142,260	316,438	...
Widowed	227,537	18	121	527	2,527	7,733	25,439	191,172	...
Divorced	162,104	185	2,650	11,085	31,896	42,994	36,736	36,558	...
Not stated	8,118	94	218	626	1,706	1,990	1,658	1,826	...
Female	1,223,124	8,725	12,642	31,476	69,058	109,872	175,548	815,803	...
Never married	100,112	7,687	6,138	9,056	12,755	11,186	10,530	42,760	...
Ever married	1,119,787	1,009	6,443	22,190	55,868	98,196	164,479	771,602	...
Married	300,493	842	4,714	14,060	33,381	53,042	71,507	122,947	...
Widowed	681,108	28	156	891	4,444	17,388	63,387	594,814	...
Divorced	138,186	139	1,573	7,239	18,043	27,766	29,585	53,841	...
Not stated	3,225	29	61	230	435	490	539	1,441	...
RATE[3]									
Both Sexes	1,021.6	81.4	104.4	193.3	432.0	906.9	2,137.1	7,657.4	1,215.8
Never married	373.7	84.0	156.0	401.1	858.2	1,630.4	3,402.2	10,803.2	1,888.1
Ever married	1,282.7	56.3	70.8	147.6	371.6	848.3	2,068.0	7,520.9	1,157.0
Married	720.0	52.4	58.4	111.3	276.8	664.7	1,714.2	5,284.2	855.8
Widowed	6,119.9	*	245.0	366.7	807.9	1,363.4	2,575.4	9,639.1	1,658.6
Divorced	1,321.0	97.7	177.9	331.3	733.2	1,492.9	3,454.4	8,813.4	1,650.2
Male	1,030.8	117.8	143.4	243.0	547.8	1,131.0	2,612.2	8,339.6	1,403.0
Never married	416.4	119.4	200.0	477.6	1,069.0	2,132.4	4,280.4	10,944.3	2,131.1
Ever married	1,321.8	92.9	96.5	179.4	461.5	1,045.1	2,511.8	8,211.3	1,325.4
Married	972.8	87.9	79.2	131.9	329.6	809.7	2,125.9	6,585.6	1,059.4
Widowed	8,108.3	*	*	535.6	1,350.7	2,261.8	3,755.9	13,057.7	2,425.4
Divorced	1,691.4	148.5	267.4	459.3	1,072.9	2,200.3	4,771.4	10,212.3	2,132.5
Female	1,012.8	42.7	64.1	143.6	319.9	698.5	1,736.3	7,240.6	1,063.5
Never married	321.7	43.7	94.6	291.2	594.0	1,134.8	2,566.4	10,712.6	1,631.9
Ever married	1,249.1	35.4	48.7	118.0	287.4	666.0	1,695.6	7,099.8	1,025.4
Married	466.2	32.2	40.1	91.3	223.6	507.2	1,237.5	3,502.7	599.7
Widowed	5,656.5	*	177.0	309.0	657.6	1,158.7	2,286.9	8,891.0	1,471.6
Divorced	1,051.1	67.2	113.8	232.2	470.1	996.8	2,572.7	8,063.4	1,330.0

* = Figure does not meet standards of reliability or precision.
... = Not applicable.
[1] Excludes figures for age not stated.
[2] Calculated based on ages 25 years and over.
[3] Figures for marital status not stated are included in totals for both sexes, male, and female but are not distributed among specified marital status groups.

Table B-34. Number of Deaths, Death Rates, and Age-Adjusted Death Rates for Ages 25–64 Years, by Educational Attainment and Sex, Total of 31 Reporting States, 2005

(Number, rate per 100,000 population.)

Years of school completed and sex	25–64 years[1]	25–34 years	35–44 years	45–54 years	55–64 years	Age-adjusted rate[2]
NUMBER						
Both Sexes...	338,073	24,510	48,633	105,597	159,333	...
Under 12 years...	73,090	5,667	10,767	20,863	35,793	...
12 years	148,051	11,008	22,254	47,267	67,522	...
13 years or more...	103,913	6,835	13,697	33,355	50,026	...
Not stated[3]...	13,019	1,000	1,915	4,112	5,992	...
Male..	209,218	17,067	30,507	65,816	95,828	...
Under 12 years...	46,960	4,168	7,085	13,715	21,992	...
12 years	91,838	7,973	14,350	30,096	39,419	...
13 years or more...	61,605	4,216	7,758	19,223	30,408	...
Not stated[3]...	8,815	710	1,314	2,782	4,009	...
Female	128,855	7,443	18,126	39,781	63,505	...
Under 12 years...	26,130	1,499	3,682	7,148	13,801	...
12 years	56,213	3,035	7,904	17,171	28,103	...
13 years or more...	42,308	2,619	5,939	14,132	19,618	...
Not stated[3]...	4,204	290	601	1,330	1,983	...
RATE[4]						
Both Sexes...	389.4	110.3	203.2	447.9	931.9	364.6
Under 12 years...	704.6	199.8	402.9	808.6	1,567.4	650.4
12 years	521.5	166.2	280.8	593.4	1,149.1	477.6
13 years or more...	216.2	53.6	102.7	256.0	559.7	206.3
Male..	486.2	151.8	256.5	567.5	1,154.5	460.4
Under 12 years...	853.6	263.7	470.9	1,040.7	2,002.1	821.4
12 years	631.5	215.8	344.0	752.3	1,473.1	605.8
13 years or more...	268.0	70.6	124.8	306.2	671.9	249.4
Female	294.2	67.8	150.5	332.1	721.9	271.8
Under 12 years...	536.4	119.4	315.2	566.2	1,164.5	471.7
12 years	405.9	103.6	210.6	433.1	878.2	352.3
13 years or more...	168.7	38.6	83.4	209.3	444.7	164.9

... = Not applicable.

[1]Excludes figures for age not stated.

[2]Calculated based on ages 25–64 years.

[3]Includes deaths that occurred in states that reported the revised education attainment item on the death certificate and in states that did not have an education item on the death certificate.

[4]Figures for education not stated are included in totals for both sexes, male, and female but are not distributed among specified years of education.

Table B-35. Number of Deaths, Death Rates, and Age-Adjusted Death Rates for Ages 15 Years and Over, by Injury at Work, Race, and Sex, 2005

(Number, rate per 100,000 population.)

Race and sex	15 years and over[1]	15–24 years	25–34 years	35–44 years	45–54 years	55–64 years	65 years and over	Age-adjusted rate[2]
NUMBER								
All Races, Both Sexes[3]	5,113	483	846	1,089	1,231	860	604	...
Male	4,670	449	785	1,001	1,127	783	525	...
Female	443	34	61	88	104	77	79	...
White, Both Sexes	4,351	414	725	905	1,020	744	543	...
Male	3,991	386	676	840	937	677	475	...
Female	360	28	49	65	83	67	68	...
Black, Both Sexes	573	46	92	142	162	83	48	...
Male	512	42	83	124	149	73	41	...
Female	61	4	9	18	13	10	7	...
RATE								
All Races, Both Sexes[3]	2.2	1.1	2.1	2.5	2.9	2.8	1.6	2.1
Male	4.1	2.1	3.8	4.6	5.4	5.4	3.4	4.1
Female	0.4	0.2	0.3	0.4	0.5	0.5	0.4	0.4
White, Both Sexes	2.3	1.3	2.3	2.6	2.9	2.9	1.7	2.3
Male	4.2	2.3	4.2	4.7	5.4	5.4	3.5	4.2
Female	0.4	0.2	0.3	0.4	0.5	0.5	0.4	0.4
Black, Both Sexes	2.0	0.7	1.6	2.5	3.2	2.7	1.5	2.0
Male	3.8	1.3	3.1	4.6	6.4	5.3	3.4	4.0
Female	0.4	*	*	*	*	*	*	0.4

* = Figure does not meet standards of reliability or precision.
... = Not applicable.
[1]Excludes figures for age not stated.
[2]Calculated based on ages 15 years and over.
[3]Includes races other than White and Black.

Table B-36. Number of Deaths, Death Rates, and Age-Adjusted Death Rates for Injury at Work, by Race and Sex, 1993–2005

(Number, rate per 100,000 population.)

Year	All races			White			All other					
							Total			Black		
	Both sexes	Male	Female	Both sexes	Male	Female	Both sexes	Male	Female	Both sexes	Male	Female
Number												
1993	5,847	5,352	495	4,979	4,581	398	868	771	97	677	608	69
1994	5,987	5,425	562	5,103	4,642	461	884	783	101	710	632	78
1995	5,872	5,334	538	5,007	4,550	457	865	784	81	692	627	65
1996	5,778	5,280	498	4,940	4,535	405	838	745	93	649	582	67
1997	5,666	5,144	522	4,785	4,352	433	881	792	89	684	626	58
1998	5,543	5,036	507	4,804	4,366	438	739	670	69	587	535	52
1999	5,651	5,152	499	4,805	4,385	420	846	767	79	659	598	61
2000	5,430	4,969	461	4,657	4,270	387	773	699	74	591	536	55
2001[1]	8,303	7,181	1,122	7,093	6,211	882	1,210	970	240	849	680	169
2002	5,305	4,859	446	4,568	4,199	369	737	660	77	559	500	59
2003	5,025	4,609	416	4,272	3,929	343	753	680	73	577	530	47
2004	5,157	4,729	428	4,458	4,111	347	699	618	81	545	482	63
2005	5,113	4,670	443	4,351	3,991	360	762	679	83	573	512	61
Rate												
1993	2.9	5.5	0.5	2.9	5.5	0.5	2.7	5.2	0.6	2.9	5.6	0.5
1994	2.9	5.5	0.5	3.0	5.5	0.5	2.7	5.1	0.6	3.0	5.7	0.6
1995	2.8	5.3	0.5	2.9	5.4	0.5	2.6	5.0	0.5	2.8	5.5	0.5
1996	2.7	5.2	0.5	2.8	5.3	0.4	2.4	4.6	0.5	2.6	5.1	0.5
1997	2.7	5.0	0.5	2.7	5.0	0.5	2.5	4.8	0.5	2.7	5.3	0.4
1998	2.6	4.8	0.5	2.7	5.0	0.5	2.0	3.9	0.4	2.3	4.5	0.4
1999	2.6	4.9	0.4	2.6	4.9	0.5	2.3	4.4	0.4	2.5	4.9	0.4
2000	2.5	4.6	0.4	2.5	4.8	0.4	2.0	3.7	0.4	2.2	4.3	0.4
2001[1]	3.7	6.6	1.0	3.8	6.9	0.9	3.1	5.3	1.2	3.1	5.4	1.2
2002	2.3	4.4	0.4	2.4	4.6	0.4	1.8	3.5	0.4	2.0	3.9	0.4
2003	2.2	4.1	0.4	2.3	4.2	0.4	1.8	3.5	0.3	2.1	4.0	0.3
2004	2.2	4.2	0.4	2.3	4.4	0.4	1.7	3.1	0.4	1.9	3.6	0.4
2005	2.2	4.1	0.4	2.3	4.2	0.4	1.8	3.4	0.4	2.0	3.8	0.4
Age-Adjusted Rate												
1993	2.9	5.5	0.5	2.9	5.5	0.5	2.8	5.4	0.6	3.0	6.0	0.5
1994	2.9	5.5	0.5	3.0	5.6	0.5	2.8	5.4	0.6	3.1	6.0	0.6
1995	2.8	5.3	0.5	2.9	5.4	0.5	2.7	5.3	0.5	3.0	6.0	0.5
1996	2.8	5.2	0.5	2.8	5.3	0.4	2.5	4.8	0.5	2.6	5.3	0.5
1997	2.7	5.0	0.5	2.7	5.0	0.5	2.6	5.0	0.5	2.8	5.5	0.4
1998	2.6	4.8	0.5	2.7	5.0	0.5	2.1	4.1	0.4	2.3	4.7	0.4
1999	2.6	4.9	0.4	2.6	4.9	0.4	2.3	4.5	0.4	2.6	5.1	0.4
2000	2.5	4.6	0.4	2.5	4.8	0.4	2.1	3.9	0.4	2.3	4.6	0.4
2001[1]	3.7	6.6	1.0	3.8	6.8	0.9	3.1	5.3	1.1	3.1	5.5	1.1
2002	2.3	4.4	0.4	2.4	4.5	0.4	1.9	3.7	0.4	2.1	4.1	0.4
2003	2.2	4.1	0.3	2.2	4.2	0.3	1.9	3.7	0.4	2.1	4.3	0.3
2004	2.2	4.2	0.4	2.3	4.4	0.3	1.7	3.3	0.4	2.0	3.8	0.4
2005	2.1	4.1	0.4	2.3	4.2	0.4	1.8	3.5	0.4	2.0	4.0	0.4

[1]Figures include September 11, 2001, terrorism-related deaths for which death certificates were filed as of October 24, 2002.

Table B-37. Deaths From Selected Occupational Diseases Among Persons 15 Years of Age and Over, Selected Years, 1980–2005

(Number.)

Cause of death[1]	1980[2]	1985[2,3]	1990[2]	1995[2]	2000[3]	2001	200[2]	2003	2004	2005
UNDERLYING AND NONUNDERLYING CAUSE OF DEATH										
Number of Death Certificates with Cause of Death Code(s) Mentioned										
Angiosarcoma of liver[4]	—	—	—	—	16	25	23	24	21	26
Malignant mesothelioma[5]	699	715	874	897	2,531	2,508	2,573	2,625	2,657	2,704
Pneumoconiosis[6]	4,151	3,783	3,644	3,151	2,859	2,743	2,715	2,635	2,524	2,425
Coal workers' pneumoconiosis	2,576	2,615	1,990	1,413	949	886	858	772	703	652
Asbestosis	339	534	948	1,169	1,486	1,449	1,467	1,464	1,460	1,416
Silicosis	448	334	308	242	151	163	146	177	165	160
Other (including unspecified)	814	321	413	343	290	260	263	236	214	222
UNDERLYING CAUSE OF DEATH										
Number of Deaths										
Angiosarcoma of liver[4]	—	—	—	—	15	22	20	20	21	23
Malignant mesothelioma[5]	531	573	725	780	2,384	2,371	2,429	2,476	2,504	2,553
Pneumoconiosis	1,581	1,355	1,335	1,117	1,142	1,110	1,094	1,101	1,013	983
Coal workers' pneumoconiosis	982	958	734	533	389	367	354	318	292	270
Asbestosis	101	139	302	355	558	550	529	583	542	532
Silicosis	207	143	150	114	71	82	89	102	76	74
Other (including unspecified)	291	115	149	115	124	111	122	98	103	107

— = Data not available.

[1]Cause of death titles for selected occupational diseases and corresponding code numbers according to the *International Classification of Diseases (ICD), Ninth and Tenth Revisions.*

Cause of death	ICD-9 code	ICD-10 code
Angiosarcoma of liver.	—	C22.3
Malignant mesothelioma	158.8, 158.9, 163	C45
Pneumoconiosis	500-505	J60-J66
Coal workers' pneumoconiosis	500	J60
Asbestosis	501	J61
Silicosis	502	J62
Other (including unspecified)	503-505	J63-J66

[2]For the period 1980–1998, underlying cause of death was coded according to the *International Classification of Diseases, Ninth Revision.*

[3]Starting with 1999 data, the *International Classification of Diseases, Tenth Edition* was introduced for coding cause of death. Discontinuities exist between 1998 and 1999 due to coding and classification changes. Caution should be exercised in interpreting trends for the causes of death in this table, especially for those with major changes (e.g., malignant mesothelioma).

[4]Prior to 1999, there was no discrete code for this condition.

[5]Prior to 1999, the combined *International Classification of Diseases, Ninth Edition,* categories of malignant neoplasm of peritoneum and malignant neoplasm of pleura served as a crude surrogate for malignant mesothelioma category under *International Classification of Disease, Tenth Edition.*

[6]For underlying and nonunderlying cause of death, counts for pneumoconiosis subgroups may sum to slightly more than total pneumoconiosis due to the reporting of more than one type of pneumoconiosis on some death certificates.

Table B-38. Number of Deaths, Death Rates, and Age-Adjusted Death Rates for Major Causes of Death by State and Territory, 2005

(Number, rate per 100,000 population.)

State and territory	All causes			Human immunodeficiency virus (HIV) disease (B20-B24)			Malignant neoplasms (C00-C97)			Diabetes mellitus (E10-E14)		
	Number	Rate	Age-adjusted rate[1]	Number	Rate	Age-adjusted rate[1]	Number	Rate	Age-adjusted rate[1]	Number	Rate	Age-adjusted rate[1]
UNITED STATES[2]	2,448,017	825.9	798.8	12,543	4.2	4.2	559,312	188.7	183.8	75,119	25.3	24.6
Alabama	47,090	1,033.2	998.0	172	3.8	3.8	9,913	217.5	204.1	1,429	31.4	29.8
Alaska	3,168	477.4	750.5	7	*	*	732	110.3	169.2	93	14.0	22.2
Arizona	45,827	771.6	771.7	138	2.3	2.5	9,820	165.3	163.7	1,208	20.3	20.2
Arkansas	28,055	1,009.5	930.2	86	3.1	3.2	6,361	228.9	208.3	824	29.6	27.1
California	237,037	656.0	713.0	1,291	3.6	3.7	54,732	151.5	167.0	7,697	21.3	23.5
Colorado	29,627	635.1	742.8	93	2.0	2.0	6,395	137.1	159.6	753	16.1	19.2
Connecticut	29,467	839.4	696.2	148	4.2	4.0	7,052	200.9	175.7	811	23.1	19.7
Delaware	7,472	885.8	830.5	63	7.5	7.3	1,799	213.3	197.8	233	27.6	25.9
District of Columbia	5,483	996.0	971.4	204	37.1	37.1	1,151	209.1	206.0	192	34.9	34.6
Florida	170,791	960.0	749.4	1,718	9.7	9.8	40,592	228.2	178.1	5,193	29.2	22.6
Georgia	66,736	735.6	905.8	666	7.3	7.3	14,358	158.3	190.4	1,742	19.2	23.3
Hawaii	9,136	716.4	609.0	18	*	*	2,169	170.1	148.9	218	17.1	14.7
Idaho	10,556	738.6	766.7	8	*	*	2,368	165.7	174.1	299	20.9	22.1
Illinois	103,974	814.6	798.2	410	3.2	3.2	24,250	190.0	190.1	3,034	23.8	23.6
Indiana	55,675	887.7	858.7	102	1.6	1.7	12,796	204.0	199.3	1,719	27.4	26.7
Iowa	27,811	937.6	742.0	16	*	*	6,453	217.5	182.5	727	24.5	19.8
Kansas	24,682	899.3	806.8	32	1.2	1.2	5,428	197.8	185.4	710	25.9	23.6
Kentucky	40,223	963.8	958.4	62	1.5	1.5	9,505	227.8	219.9	1,187	28.4	27.9
Louisiana	44,355	980.5	1,020.8	403	8.9	9.2	9,249	204.5	209.3	1,695	37.5	38.7
Maine	12,868	973.7	813.0	11	*	*	3,218	243.5	201.9	385	29.1	24.2
Maryland	43,892	783.7	796.4	528	9.4	9.0	10,371	185.2	188.3	1,388	24.8	25.5
Massachusetts	53,874	841.9	722.0	184	2.9	2.7	13,182	206.0	185.2	1,271	19.9	17.4
Michigan	86,867	858.3	812.3	224	2.2	2.2	20,094	198.5	190.8	2,842	28.1	26.7
Minnesota	37,535	731.3	683.9	53	1.0	1.0	8,823	171.9	167.8	1,258	24.5	23.2
Mississippi	29,196	999.5	1,026.9	191	6.5	6.8	6,065	207.6	208.4	677	23.2	23.5
Missouri	54,656	942.3	869.4	130	2.2	2.2	12,419	214.1	197.7	1,549	26.7	24.7
Montana	8,528	911.4	798.4	7	*	*	1,956	209.0	184.4	285	30.5	26.5
Nebraska	14,963	850.8	749.5	26	1.5	1.6	3,355	190.8	174.8	449	25.5	23.2
Nevada	19,029	788.0	892.0	86	3.6	3.6	4,238	175.5	191.0	336	13.9	15.3
New Hampshire	10,194	778.2	732.4	13	*	*	2,549	194.6	183.7	310	23.7	22.5
New Jersey	71,963	825.5	745.9	604	6.9	6.6	17,171	197.0	182.1	2,540	29.1	26.7
New Mexico	14,983	777.0	795.0	34	1.8	1.8	3,141	162.9	162.6	595	30.9	31.2
New York	152,427	791.6	718.0	1,644	8.5	8.2	35,556	184.7	170.8	4,051	21.0	19.3
North Carolina	74,638	859.6	876.0	416	4.8	4.8	16,724	192.6	192.8	2,261	26.0	26.3
North Dakota	5,744	902.2	699.1	3	*	*	1,302	204.5	168.9	204	32.0	25.8
Ohio	109,031	951.1	856.8	223	1.9	1.9	24,702	215.5	196.5	3,794	33.1	30.0
Oklahoma	36,180	1,019.8	980.8	93	2.6	2.7	7,446	209.9	197.6	1,217	34.3	32.6
Oregon	31,091	853.9	773.5	57	1.6	1.6	7,326	201.2	186.9	1,149	31.6	29.0
Pennsylvania	129,532	1,042.1	814.7	360	2.9	2.8	29,616	238.3	193.3	3,553	28.6	22.6
Rhode Island	10,007	929.9	747.3	23	2.1	2.0	2,292	213.0	184.1	282	26.2	21.6
South Carolina	38,707	909.7	904.4	249	5.9	5.9	8,652	203.3	197.3	1,187	27.9	27.2
South Dakota	7,086	913.2	757.0	6	*	*	1,612	207.7	180.9	241	31.1	25.8
Tennessee	57,260	960.3	959.8	281	4.7	4.6	12,995	217.9	211.5	1,844	30.9	30.4
Texas	156,457	684.4	828.7	980	4.3	4.5	34,291	150.0	178.5	5,605	24.5	29.6
Utah	13,432	543.9	731.2	15	*	*	2,520	102.0	139.4	541	21.9	30.4
Vermont	5,066	813.1	728.4	7	*	*	1,202	192.9	172.9	173	27.8	25.1
Virginia	57,855	764.5	801.5	233	3.1	3.0	13,877	183.4	188.8	1,642	21.7	22.6
Washington	46,203	734.8	738.1	138	2.2	2.1	11,048	175.7	179.5	1,554	24.7	25.1
West Virginia	20,780	1,143.7	960.4	22	1.2	1.2	4,617	254.1	207.7	766	42.2	34.4
Wisconsin	46,709	843.7	752.2	60	1.1	1.0	10,943	197.7	182.3	1,276	23.0	20.8
Wyoming	4,099	804.8	801.4	5	*	*	886	174.0	167.7	130	25.5	25.7
Puerto Rico[3]	29,531	754.9	777.9	519	13.3	14.4	4,837	123.6	125.0	2,790	71.3	72.4
Virgin Islands[3]	663	609.9	724.7	7	*	*	124	114.1	130.9	42	38.6	46.4
Guam[3]	677	401.6	657.4	1	*	*	95	56.4	92.3	34	20.2	40.0
American Samoa[3]	272	436.1	1,224.8	-	*	*	36	57.7	152.2	32	51.3	165.9
Northern Marianas[3]	186	231.5	1,061.0	-	*	*	27	33.6	147.7	15	*	*

* = Figure does not meet standards of reliability or precision.
- = Quantity zero.
[1]Death rates are affected by the population composition of the area. Age-adjusted death rates should be used for comparisons between areas.
[2]Excludes data for Puerto Rico, Virgin Islands, Guam, American Samoa and Northern Marianas.
[3]Age-adjusted death rates for Puerto Rico, Virgin Islands, Guam, American Samoa, and Northern Marianas are calculated using different age groups in the weighting procedures.

Table B-38. Number of Deaths, Death Rates, and Age-Adjusted Death Rates for Major Causes of Death by State and Territory, 2005—*Continued*

(Number, rate per 100,000 population.)

State and territory	Alzheimer's disease (G30)			Diseases of heart (I00-I09, I11, I13, I20-I51)			Cerebrovascular diseases (I60-I69)			Influenza and pneumonia (J10-J18)		
	Number	Rate	Age-adjusted rate[1]	Number	Rate	Age-adjusted rate[1]	Number	Rate	Age-adjusted rate[1]	Number	Rate	Age-adjusted rate[1]
UNITED STATES[2]	71,599	24.2	22.9	652,091	220.0	211.1	143,579	48.4	46.6	63,001	21.3	20.3
Alabama	1,501	32.9	33.2	12,869	282.4	273.5	2,952	64.8	63.1	1,011	22.2	21.9
Alaska	61	9.2	21.3	627	94.5	162.6	178	26.8	53.2	44	6.6	12.3
Arizona	1,831	30.8	31.3	10,966	184.6	185.0	2,364	39.8	40.1	1,297	21.8	21.9
Arkansas	686	24.7	22.6	7,575	272.6	249.5	1,847	66.5	61.0	886	31.9	29.2
California	7,706	21.3	23.2	64,916	179.7	196.3	15,585	43.1	47.4	7,553	20.9	22.8
Colorado	1,064	22.8	28.5	6,307	135.2	162.0	1,599	34.3	41.7	666	14.3	17.2
Connecticut	777	22.1	16.1	7,650	217.9	172.9	1,528	43.5	34.7	956	27.2	20.5
Delaware	180	21.3	20.0	2,031	240.8	224.3	384	45.5	42.5	162	19.2	18.0
District of Columbia	112	20.3	19.1	1,518	275.7	268.2	231	42.0	40.9	98	17.8	17.0
Florida	4,608	25.9	18.4	46,279	260.1	194.6	9,361	52.6	39.2	2,802	15.8	11.8
Georgia	1,745	19.2	27.0	16,781	185.0	234.8	3,854	42.5	55.2	1,596	17.6	23.3
Hawaii	192	15.1	11.4	2,319	181.9	152.0	688	54.0	44.1	241	18.9	15.0
Idaho	407	28.5	29.4	2,450	171.4	177.9	718	50.2	52.2	289	20.2	20.5
Illinois	2,827	22.1	20.8	28,226	221.1	214.3	6,252	49.0	47.5	2,949	23.1	22.0
Indiana	1,651	26.3	24.7	14,542	231.9	222.3	3,296	52.6	50.4	1,317	21.0	20.0
Iowa	1,082	36.5	25.4	7,437	250.7	191.4	1,902	64.1	47.7	896	30.2	21.4
Kansas	912	33.2	27.2	5,960	217.1	189.2	1,571	57.2	49.4	730	26.6	22.5
Kentucky	1,147	27.5	28.9	10,782	258.4	258.5	2,168	51.9	52.8	1,021	24.5	25.1
Louisiana	1,405	31.1	34.2	11,008	243.3	255.7	2,469	54.6	57.6	996	22.0	23.7
Maine	476	36.0	29.1	2,941	222.5	182.7	693	52.4	42.8	352	26.6	21.8
Maryland	958	17.1	17.5	11,594	207.0	210.3	2,476	44.2	45.1	1,194	21.3	21.7
Massachusetts	1,638	25.6	19.8	13,280	207.5	172.7	2,977	46.5	38.1	1,935	30.2	24.2
Michigan	2,359	23.3	21.2	25,128	248.3	231.4	5,057	50.0	46.5	1,950	19.3	17.8
Minnesota	1,320	25.7	22.5	7,926	154.4	141.5	2,379	46.3	42.2	846	16.5	14.5
Mississippi	721	24.7	26.7	8,637	295.7	306.8	1,622	55.5	58.0	645	22.1	23.5
Missouri	1,635	28.2	25.4	14,974	258.2	235.5	3,347	57.7	52.6	1,527	26.3	23.9
Montana	267	28.5	23.9	1,855	198.3	169.4	522	55.8	47.7	213	22.8	18.9
Nebraska	473	26.9	21.8	3,640	207.0	176.7	986	56.1	47.7	370	21.0	17.3
Nevada	310	12.8	17.1	5,094	210.9	242.1	945	39.1	46.8	454	18.8	22.4
New Hampshire	376	28.7	26.1	2,530	193.1	179.4	497	37.9	35.5	273	20.8	19.4
New Jersey	1,815	20.8	17.6	20,655	236.9	208.9	3,614	41.5	36.7	1,637	18.8	16.3
New Mexico	327	17.0	18.3	3,435	178.1	184.5	730	37.9	39.6	353	18.3	19.2
New York	2,065	10.7	9.2	51,985	270.0	239.6	6,622	34.4	30.6	5,521	28.7	25.3
North Carolina	2,417	27.8	29.5	17,765	204.6	209.6	4,861	56.0	58.0	1,830	21.1	22.0
North Dakota	287	45.1	29.8	1,512	237.5	175.3	368	57.8	41.5	172	27.0	18.5
Ohio	3,478	30.3	26.0	29,003	253.0	224.3	6,279	54.8	48.3	2,416	21.1	18.6
Oklahoma	1,012	28.5	28.1	10,043	283.1	272.6	2,235	63.0	61.0	948	26.7	26.1
Oregon	1,239	34.0	28.9	6,791	186.5	164.7	2,289	62.9	55.5	614	16.9	14.5
Pennsylvania	3,429	27.6	18.9	36,207	291.3	218.5	7,650	61.5	45.5	3,068	24.7	18.0
Rhode Island	298	27.7	18.8	3,005	279.2	213.8	533	49.5	37.4	253	23.5	17.2
South Carolina	1,316	30.9	32.4	9,359	219.9	218.9	2,458	57.8	58.5	771	18.1	18.4
South Dakota	290	37.4	27.3	1,776	228.9	182.1	511	65.9	51.4	241	31.1	23.4
Tennessee	2,033	34.1	36.2	14,946	250.6	252.1	3,659	61.4	63.0	1,588	26.6	27.6
Texas	4,629	20.2	27.2	40,152	175.6	219.5	9,366	41.0	52.1	3,654	16.0	20.4
Utah	368	14.9	21.5	2,872	116.3	162.6	794	32.2	45.4	333	13.5	18.8
Vermont	184	29.5	25.7	1,234	198.1	173.6	260	41.7	36.5	97	15.6	13.7
Virginia	1,550	20.5	22.5	14,192	187.5	198.0	3,675	48.6	52.1	1,464	19.3	20.9
Washington	2,309	36.7	35.9	10,985	174.7	174.3	2,895	46.0	46.3	927	14.7	14.5
West Virginia	504	27.7	23.2	5,538	304.8	251.8	1,151	63.4	52.6	458	25.2	21.0
Wisconsin	1,512	27.3	22.4	11,842	213.9	185.8	2,960	53.5	46.1	1,268	22.9	19.1
Wyoming	110	21.6	22.7	952	186.9	186.9	221	43.4	44.8	119	23.4	24.4
Puerto Rico[3]	1,397	35.7	38.5	6,112	156.2	161.1	1,525	39.0	40.9	1,081	27.6	29.1
Virgin Islands[3]	9	*	*	205	188.6	234.1	37	34.0	42.4	13	*	*
Guam[3]	3	*	*	208	123.4	223.4	62	36.8	65.2	11	*	*
American Samoa[3]	-	*	*	45	72.1	231.7	23	36.9	101.5	12	*	*
Northern Marianas[3]	1	*	*	42	52.3	266.0	6	*	*	2	*	*

* = Figure does not meet standards of reliability or precision.
- = Quantity zero.
[1]Death rates are affected by the population composition of the area. Age-adjusted death rates should be used for comparisons between areas.
[2]Excludes data for Puerto Rico, Virgin Islands, Guam, American Samoa and Northern Marianas.
[3]Age-adjusted death rates for Puerto Rico, Virgin Islands, Guam, American Samoa, and Northern Marianas are calculated using different age groups in the weighting procedures.

Table B-38. Number of Deaths, Death Rates, and Age-Adjusted Death Rates for Major Causes of Death by State and Territory, 2005—*Continued*

(Number, rate per 100,000 population.)

State and territory	Chronic lower respiratory diseases (J40-J47)			Chronic liver disease and cirrhosis (K70, K73-K74)			Nephritis, nephrotic syndrome, and nephrosis (N00-N07, N17-N19, N25-N27)			Accidents (V01-X59, Y85-Y86)		
	Number	Rate	Age-adjusted rate[1]	Number	Rate	Age-adjusted rate[1]	Number	Rate	Age-adjusted rate[1]	Number	Rate	Age-adjusted rate[1]
UNITED STATES[2]	130,933	44.2	43.2	27,530	9.3	9.0	43,901	14.8	14.3	117,809	39.7	39.1
Alabama	2,382	52.3	50.0	478	10.5	9.7	1,036	22.7	22.0	2,395	52.5	51.8
Alaska	158	23.8	42.2	52	7.8	9.0	38	5.7	10.3	313	47.2	51.3
Arizona	2,821	47.5	47.4	757	12.7	12.8	608	10.2	10.2	3,150	53.0	53.8
Arkansas	1,559	56.1	51.2	228	8.2	7.5	624	22.5	20.5	1,329	47.8	46.8
California	13,188	36.5	40.9	3,822	10.6	11.0	2,482	6.9	7.5	11,129	30.8	31.4
Colorado	1,914	41.0	50.3	436	9.3	9.7	470	10.1	12.3	1,947	41.7	43.8
Connecticut	1,471	41.9	35.3	283	8.1	7.2	580	16.5	13.1	1,134	32.3	29.8
Delaware	411	48.7	46.1	67	7.9	7.3	128	15.2	14.2	293	34.7	33.9
District of Columbia	132	24.0	23.9	67	12.2	11.9	68	12.4	12.1	207	37.6	37.0
Florida	9,482	53.3	39.8	2,139	12.0	10.2	2,416	13.6	10.2	8,868	49.8	47.1
Georgia	3,411	37.6	48.4	689	7.6	8.3	1,520	16.8	21.2	3,762	41.5	44.4
Hawaii	287	22.5	18.7	96	7.5	6.7	150	11.8	10.1	436	34.2	31.7
Idaho	717	50.2	53.9	126	8.8	8.8	110	7.7	7.9	606	42.4	43.1
Illinois	5,067	39.7	39.7	1,002	7.9	7.8	2,402	18.8	18.4	4,182	32.8	32.4
Indiana	3,471	55.3	54.1	496	7.9	7.7	1,284	20.5	19.8	2,480	39.5	38.9
Iowa	1,703	57.4	46.6	215	7.2	6.5	250	8.4	6.2	1,202	40.5	36.1
Kansas	1,567	57.1	52.4	200	7.3	7.0	517	18.8	16.7	1,149	41.9	40.2
Kentucky	2,578	61.8	61.3	380	9.1	8.5	912	21.9	22.0	2,405	57.6	57.3
Louisiana	1,906	42.1	44.5	380	8.4	8.3	1,187	26.2	27.6	3,072	67.9	68.8
Maine	830	62.8	52.3	116	8.8	7.1	250	18.9	15.5	579	43.8	41.1
Maryland	1,908	34.1	35.4	459	8.2	7.9	752	13.4	13.8	1,376	24.6	24.7
Massachusetts	2,647	41.4	35.8	505	7.9	7.3	1,410	22.0	18.4	1,907	29.8	27.7
Michigan	4,466	44.1	42.3	1,010	10.0	9.5	1,681	16.6	15.6	3,451	34.1	33.3
Minnesota	1,965	38.3	36.9	317	6.2	6.0	669	13.0	12.0	1,922	37.4	35.4
Mississippi	1,473	50.4	51.9	272	9.3	9.2	667	22.8	23.7	1,936	66.3	66.6
Missouri	3,085	53.2	49.2	419	7.2	6.7	1,156	19.9	18.3	2,848	49.1	47.4
Montana	580	62.0	55.1	120	12.8	11.5	109	11.6	10.1	524	56.0	52.4
Nebraska	949	54.0	48.3	133	7.6	7.3	245	13.9	12.2	704	40.0	37.1
Nevada	1,227	50.8	59.4	275	11.4	11.4	438	18.1	21.4	1,104	45.7	47.3
New Hampshire	630	48.1	46.2	114	8.7	8.0	173	13.2	12.4	477	36.4	35.2
New Jersey	3,148	36.1	32.9	730	8.4	7.8	1,597	18.3	16.5	2,561	29.4	28.3
New Mexico	855	44.3	46.0	285	14.8	14.4	239	12.4	12.9	1,267	65.7	66.6
New York	6,818	35.4	32.4	1,224	6.4	5.9	2,360	12.3	11.0	4,645	24.1	22.9
North Carolina	4,149	47.8	49.1	782	9.0	8.8	1,561	18.0	18.5	4,123	47.5	47.8
North Dakota	272	42.7	34.0	68	10.7	9.6	67	10.5	7.6	287	45.1	39.3
Ohio	6,580	57.4	51.7	1,105	9.6	8.8	1,902	16.6	14.8	4,438	38.7	37.1
Oklahoma	2,368	66.7	63.5	428	12.1	11.3	564	15.9	15.3	2,005	56.5	55.8
Oregon	1,837	50.5	46.9	394	10.8	10.1	295	8.1	7.2	1,469	40.3	38.1
Pennsylvania	6,149	49.5	38.1	1,058	8.5	7.3	3,108	25.0	19.0	5,446	43.8	40.3
Rhode Island	523	48.6	39.0	107	9.9	9.0	156	14.5	11.2	334	31.0	26.7
South Carolina	1,977	46.5	46.2	480	11.3	10.6	823	19.3	19.3	2,272	53.4	53.1
South Dakota	440	56.7	47.5	83	10.7	10.2	55	7.1	5.7	402	51.8	48.1
Tennessee	3,185	53.4	53.3	631	10.6	9.9	719	12.1	12.0	3,147	52.8	52.5
Texas	7,988	34.9	43.9	2,459	10.8	11.7	2,729	11.9	14.9	8,598	37.6	40.3
Utah	592	24.0	33.9	127	5.1	6.7	177	7.2	10.1	743	30.1	34.0
Vermont	381	61.2	55.6	48	7.7	6.7	52	8.3	7.4	272	43.7	41.2
Virginia	2,897	38.3	41.2	570	7.5	7.3	1,277	16.9	17.9	2,638	34.9	35.3
Washington	2,699	42.9	44.7	558	8.9	8.6	450	7.2	7.2	2,543	40.4	39.6
West Virginia	1,350	74.3	60.5	213	11.7	9.8	442	24.3	20.2	940	51.7	49.4
Wisconsin	2,449	44.2	40.4	467	8.4	7.8	930	16.8	14.7	2,490	45.0	42.2
Wyoming	291	57.1	57.2	60	11.8	10.5	66	13.0	13.5	302	59.3	58.6
Puerto Rico[3]	1,215	31.1	32.7	230	5.9	5.8	941	24.1	24.6	1,120	28.6	28.9
Virgin Islands[3]	13	*	*	12	*	*	11	*	*	24	22.1	22.6
Guam[3]	21	12.5	25.0	11	*	*	10	*	*	45	26.7	34.2
American Samoa[3]	21	33.7	133.9	-	*	*	4	*	*	16	*	*
Northern Marianas[3]	7	*	*	5	*	*	6	*	*	18	*	*

* = Figure does not meet standards of reliability or precision.

- = Quantity zero.

[1]Death rates are affected by the population composition of the area. Age-adjusted death rates should be used for comparisons between areas.

[2]Excludes data for Puerto Rico, Virgin Islands, Guam, American Samoa and Northern Marianas.

[3]Age-adjusted death rates for Puerto Rico, Virgin Islands, Guam, American Samoa, and Northern Marianas are calculated using different age groups in the weighting procedures.

Table B-38. Number of Deaths, Death Rates, and Age-Adjusted Death Rates for Major Causes of Death by State and Territory, 2005—Continued

(Number, rate per 100,000 population.)

State and territory	Motor vehicle accidents[4]			Intentional self-harm (suicide) (*U03, X60-X84, Y87.0)			Assault (homicide) (*U01-*U02, X85-Y09, Y87.1)			Injury by firearms[5]		
	Number	Rate	Age-adjusted rate[1]	Number	Rate	Age-adjusted rate[1]	Number	Rate	Age-adjusted rate[1]	Number	Rate	Age-adjusted rate[1]
UNITED STATES[2]	45,343	15.3	15.2	32,637	11.0	10.9	18,124	6.1	6.1	30,694	10.4	10.2
Alabama	1,188	26.1	25.7	535	11.7	11.5	433	9.5	9.6	736	16.1	15.9
Alaska	93	14.0	14.6	131	19.7	20.2	37	5.6	5.4	116	17.5	17.8
Arizona	1,200	20.2	20.4	945	15.9	16.2	532	9.0	8.8	934	15.7	15.8
Arkansas	696	25.0	24.6	400	14.4	14.2	219	7.9	7.9	439	15.8	15.6
California	4,427	12.3	12.3	3,206	8.9	9.1	2,540	7.0	6.9	3,453	9.6	9.6
Colorado	673	14.4	14.3	800	17.1	17.3	182	3.9	3.8	535	11.5	11.6
Connecticut	293	8.3	8.3	295	8.4	8.1	107	3.0	3.2	187	5.3	5.3
Delaware	119	14.1	13.8	83	9.8	9.6	55	6.5	6.5	75	8.9	8.8
District of Columbia	38	6.9	6.9	33	6.0	5.5	180	32.7	31.7	154	28.0	27.0
Florida	3,526	19.8	19.7	2,347	13.2	12.6	998	5.6	5.9	1,838	10.3	10.1
Georgia	1,686	18.6	18.8	924	10.2	10.5	649	7.2	7.0	1,064	11.7	11.9
Hawaii	141	11.1	11.0	107	8.4	8.3	25	2.0	2.0	28	2.2	2.2
Idaho	283	19.8	19.8	228	16.0	16.2	45	3.1	3.2	195	13.6	13.9
Illinois	1,469	11.5	11.5	1,086	8.5	8.5	866	6.8	6.7	1,019	8.0	7.9
Indiana	975	15.5	15.4	745	11.9	11.9	368	5.9	5.9	705	11.2	11.2
Iowa	468	15.8	15.2	333	11.2	10.9	44	1.5	1.5	201	6.8	6.6
Kansas	498	18.1	17.9	362	13.2	13.1	106	3.9	3.8	257	9.4	9.2
Kentucky	1,003	24.0	23.7	566	13.6	13.3	222	5.3	5.3	548	13.1	12.9
Louisiana	1,029	22.7	22.4	505	11.2	11.1	592	13.1	12.9	858	19.0	18.6
Maine	192	14.5	14.1	175	13.2	12.3	22	1.7	1.7	109	8.2	7.7
Maryland	628	11.2	11.2	472	8.4	8.4	576	10.3	10.4	657	11.7	11.9
Massachusetts	484	7.6	7.3	480	7.5	7.2	178	2.8	2.8	224	3.5	3.4
Michigan	1,231	12.2	12.1	1,108	10.9	10.8	677	6.7	6.8	1,074	10.6	10.6
Minnesota	642	12.5	12.2	547	10.7	10.3	139	2.7	2.7	361	7.0	6.9
Mississippi	965	33.0	32.9	363	12.4	12.6	254	8.7	8.8	455	15.6	15.7
Missouri	1,203	20.7	20.3	727	12.5	12.4	417	7.2	7.2	752	13.0	12.8
Montana	236	25.2	24.7	206	22.0	21.5	33	3.5	3.4	161	17.2	16.7
Nebraska	287	16.3	15.9	187	10.6	10.8	44	2.5	2.5	135	7.7	7.6
Nevada	459	19.0	19.3	480	19.9	20.1	190	7.9	7.9	390	16.2	16.3
New Hampshire	162	12.4	12.2	162	12.4	11.8	19	*	*	88	6.7	6.5
New Jersey	760	8.7	8.7	536	6.1	6.0	427	4.9	5.1	434	5.0	5.1
New Mexico	461	23.9	23.6	342	17.7	17.7	152	7.9	8.0	267	13.8	13.8
New York	1,530	7.9	7.8	1,189	6.2	6.0	901	4.7	4.7	1,019	5.3	5.2
North Carolina	1,666	19.2	19.1	1,009	11.6	11.5	661	7.6	7.5	1,119	12.9	12.8
North Dakota	130	20.4	19.6	92	14.5	13.7	11	*	*	61	9.6	8.8
Ohio	1,404	12.2	12.1	1,341	11.7	11.4	630	5.5	5.6	1,116	9.7	9.6
Oklahoma	833	23.5	23.0	522	14.7	14.7	214	6.0	6.0	468	13.2	13.0
Oregon	512	14.1	13.8	560	15.4	14.8	102	2.8	2.8	402	11.0	10.7
Pennsylvania	1,771	14.2	13.8	1,430	11.5	11.1	749	6.0	6.3	1,352	10.9	10.8
Rhode Island	87	8.1	7.9	71	6.6	6.3	32	3.0	3.0	39	3.6	3.6
South Carolina	1,071	25.2	25.0	510	12.0	11.8	337	7.9	7.9	589	13.8	13.8
South Dakota	176	22.7	22.4	121	15.6	15.3	22	2.8	2.9	82	10.6	10.1
Tennessee	1,308	21.9	21.7	856	14.4	14.0	495	8.3	8.3	976	16.4	16.0
Texas	3,780	16.5	16.8	2,418	10.6	10.9	1,501	6.6	6.5	2,490	10.9	11.1
Utah	319	12.9	13.6	348	14.1	15.1	63	2.6	2.4	227	9.2	9.9
Vermont	82	13.2	12.9	78	12.5	12.2	12	*	*	44	7.1	6.7
Virginia	969	12.8	12.7	866	11.4	11.2	490	6.5	6.4	888	11.7	11.6
Washington	762	12.1	12.0	822	13.1	12.7	231	3.7	3.6	567	9.0	8.7
West Virginia	403	22.2	21.9	255	14.0	13.2	93	5.1	5.4	261	14.4	13.7
Wisconsin	870	15.7	15.3	643	11.6	11.5	236	4.3	4.3	474	8.6	8.5
Wyoming	155	30.4	30.0	90	17.7	17.2	16	*	*	71	13.9	13.4

* = Figure does not meet standards of reliability or precision.
- = Quantity zero.

[1]Death rates are affected by the population composition of the area. Age-adjusted death rates should be used for comparisons between areas.
[2]Excludes data for Puerto Rico, Virgin Islands, Guam, American Samoa and Northern Marianas.
[4]*International Classification of Diseases, Tenth Edition* codes for motor vehicle accidents are V02-V04, V09.0, V09.2, V12-V14, V19.0-V19.2, V19.4-V19.6, V20-V79, V80.3-V80.5, V81.0-V81.1, V82.0-V82.1, V83-V86, V87.0-V87.8, V88.0-V88.8, V89.0, V89.2.
[5]*International Classification of Diseases, Tenth Edition* codes for Injury by firearms are *U01.4, W32-W34, X72-X74, X93-X95, Y22-Y24, Y35.0.

Table B-38. Number of Deaths, Death Rates, and Age-Adjusted Death Rates for Major Causes of Death by State and Territory, 2005—*Continued*

(Number, rate per 100,000 population.)

State and territory	Motor vehicle accidents[4]			Intentional self-harm (suicide) (*U03, X60-X84, Y87.0)			Assault (homicide) (*U01-*U02, X85-Y09, Y87.1)			Injury by firearms[5]		
	Number	Rate	Age-adjusted rate[1]	Number	Rate	Age-adjusted rate[1]	Number	Rate	Age-adjusted rate[1]	Number	Rate	Age-adjusted rate[1]
Puerto Rico[3]	426	10.9	10.7	290	7.4	7.5	765	19.6	19.2	730	18.7	18.3
Virgin Islands[3]	4	*	*	2	*	*	37	34.0	34.9	30	27.6	29.4
Guam[3]	25	14.8	17.3	27	16.0	15.7	7	*	*	5	*	*
American Samoa[3]	3	*	*	-	*	*	2	*	*	1	*	*
Northern Marianas[3]	11	*	*	3	*	*	5	*	*	1	*	*

* = Figure does not meet standards of reliability or precision.

- = Quantity zero.

[1]Death rates are affected by the population composition of the area. Age-adjusted death rates should be used for comparisons between areas.

[3]Age-adjusted death rates for Puerto Rico, Virgin Islands, Guam, American Samoa, and Northern Marianas are calculated using different age groups in the weighting procedures.

[4]*International Classification of Diseases, Tenth Edition* codes for motor vehicle accidents are V02-V04, V09.0, V09.2, V12-V14, V19.0-V19.2, V19.4-V19.6, V20-V79, V80.3-V80.5, V81.0-V81.1, V82.0-V82.1, V83-V86, V87.0-V87.8, V88.0-V88.8, V89.0, V89.2.

[5]*International Classification of Diseases, Tenth Edition* codes for Injury by firearms are *U01.4, W32-W34, X72-X74, X93-X95, Y22-Y24, Y35.0.

Table B-39. Deaths, Death Rates, and Age-Adjusted Death Rates, by State and Territory, Final 2005 and Preliminary 2006

(Number, rate per 100,000.)

Area	2005			2006		
	Number	Rate	Age-adjusted rate	Number	Rate	Age-adjusted rate
UNITED STATES[1]	2,448,017	825.9	798.8	2,425,900	810.3	776.4
Alabama	47,090	1033.2	998.0	46,973	1021.4	952.3
Alaska	3,168	477.4	750.5	3,344	499.1	774.4
Arizona	45,827	771.6	771.7	46,367	751.9	724.2
Arkansas	28,055	1009.5	930.2	27,891	992.3	888.5
California	237,037	656.0	713.0	237,069	650.3	700.2
Colorado	29,627	635.1	742.8	29,519	621.0	716.8
Connecticut	29,467	839.4	696.2	29,275	835.3	715.1
Delaware	7,472	885.8	830.5	7,206	844.3	783.4
District of Columbia	5,483	996.0	971.4	5,353	920.5	894.5
Florida	170,791	960.0	749.4	170,069	940.1	711.3
Georgia	66,736	735.6	905.8	67,507	720.9	855.5
Hawaii	9,136	716.4	609.0	9,451	735.2	631.0
Idaho	10,556	738.6	766.7	10,610	723.5	747.2
Illinois	103,974	814.6	798.2	102,183	796.3	781.2
Indiana	55,675	887.7	858.7	55,575	880.3	846.8
Iowa	27,811	937.6	742.0	27,360	917.5	730.2
Kansas	24,682	899.3	806.8	24,549	888.1	794.6
Kentucky	40,223	963.8	958.4	40,072	952.7	914.5
Louisiana	44,355	980.5	1020.8	39,974	932.3	928.5
Maine	12,868	973.7	813.0	12,295	930.3	774.8
Maryland	43,892	783.7	796.4	43,575	775.9	792.9
Massachusetts	53,874	841.9	722.0	53,453	830.4	719.8
Michigan	86,867	858.3	812.3	86,033	852.2	813.6
Minnesota	37,535	731.3	683.9	37,031	716.7	672.8
Mississippi	29,196	999.5	1026.9	28,562	981.3	961.1
Missouri	54,656	942.3	869.4	54,682	935.9	848.3
Montana	8,528	911.4	798.4	8,474	897.1	781.5
Nebraska	14,963	850.8	749.5	14,897	842.4	735.1
Nevada	19,029	788.0	892.0	18,448	739.2	824.0
New Hampshire	10,194	778.2	732.4	10,058	764.9	724.7
New Jersey	71,963	825.5	745.9	70,336	806.2	736.4
New Mexico	14,983	777.0	795.0	15,261	780.8	774.0
New York	152,427	791.6	718.0	148,808	770.8	701.2
North Carolina	74,638	859.6	876.0	74,714	843.6	843.6
North Dakota	5,744	902.2	699.1	5,868	922.8	726.7
Ohio	109,031	951.1	856.8	106,863	931.0	841.1
Oklahoma	36,180	1019.8	980.8	35,430	989.9	920.4
Oregon	31,091	853.9	773.5	31,566	853.0	774.7
Pennsylvania	129,532	1042.1	814.7	125,713	1010.5	801.8
Rhode Island	10,007	929.9	747.3	9,687	907.4	746.9
South Carolina	38,707	909.7	904.4	38,802	897.9	865.5
South Dakota	7,086	913.2	757.0	7,081	905.6	740.1
Tennessee	57,260	960.3	959.8	56,833	941.1	908.2
Texas	156,457	684.4	828.7	157,365	669.4	784.8
Utah	13,432	543.9	731.2	13,736	538.7	705.0
Vermont	5,066	813.1	728.4	5,042	808.1	720.7
Virginia	57,855	764.5	801.5	57,696	754.9	781.1
Washington	46,203	734.8	738.1	46,108	720.9	722.4
West Virginia	20,780	1143.7	960.4	20,676	1137.0	941.3
Wisconsin	46,709	843.7	752.2	46,153	830.6	746.6
Wyoming	4,099	804.8	801.4	4,311	837.1	822.7
Puerto Rico	29,531	754.9	777.9	28,413	723.4	730.0
Virgin Islands	663	609.9	724.7	629	579.2	651.9
Guam	677	401.6	657.4	679	397.0	615.5
American Samoa	272	436.1	1224.8	266	460.3	1312.0
Northern Marianas	186	231.5	1061.0	170	206.2	997.6

[1]Excludes data for Puerto Rico, Virgin to sampling Islands, Guam, American Samoa, and Northern Marianas.

NOTE: Data are subject to sampling or random variation.

Table B-40. Age-Adjusted Death Rates, by Race, Sex, Region, and Urbanization Level, Selected Annual Averages, 1996–1998, 1999–2001, and 2003–2005

(Deaths per 100,000 standard population.)

Sex, region, and urbanization level[1]	All races			White			Black or African American		
	1996–1998	1999–2001	2003–2005	1996–1998	1999–2001	2003–2005	1996–1998	1999–2001	2003–2005
BOTH SEXES									
All Regions									
Metropolitan counties									
Large									
Central	894.5	869.0	794.2	858.8	836.7	768.0	1,164.2	1,133.6	1,047.8
Fringe	839.3	833.0	775.7	828.0	823.7	770.5	1,059.6	1,040.8	951.6
Medium	865.6	859.0	809.7	846.5	842.2	795.9	1,152.4	1,137.3	1,054.5
Small	887.8	887.9	840.7	866.5	868.8	823.6	1,173.1	1,164.3	1,093.4
Nonmetropolitan counties									
Micropolitan	913.0	907.1	866.4	892.1	890.0	851.3	1,208.2	1,174.9	1,112.8
Nonmicropolitan	933.0	923.2	886.7	909.6	902.8	867.7	1,191.6	1,162.8	1,105.9
Northeast									
Metropolitan counties									
Large									
Central	909.6	861.7	779.9	881.4	838.6	761.5	1,052.4	1,001.1	914.0
Fringe	827.8	814.0	753.4	823.3	810.8	754.5	1,000.0	986.6	890.7
Medium	851.9	836.2	785.9	842.2	828.6	781.1	1,076.6	1,040.8	940.7
Small	852.0	849.5	802.7	847.8	846.5	799.6	1,106.9	1,072.4	1,004.3
Nonmetropolitan counties									
Micropolitan	878.4	854.4	812.7	877.9	855.7	814.7	*	*	*
Nonmicropolitan	893.6	877.4	826.8	892.0	876.3	827.4	*	*	*
Midwest									
Metropolitan counties									
Large									
Central	951.7	939.6	863.6	880.7	868.9	796.7	1,213.7	1,205.9	1,117.8
Fringe	856.4	856.1	796.6	845.9	846.3	789.0	1,121.2	1,123.1	1,052.6
Medium	876.1	873.5	822.3	857.0	856.1	806.4	1,168.9	1,151.6	1,076.1
Small	860.8	861.5	809.2	847.4	850.8	797.6	1,178.9	1,146.9	1,103.7
Nonmetropolitan counties									
Micropolitan	868.8	865.2	819.1	863.9	863.0	817.7	1,222.0	1,103.5	999.8
Nonmicropolitan	867.6	852.7	814.5	858.2	845.9	806.8	1,388.1	1,058.9	1,035.1
South									
Metropolitan counties									
Large									
Central	938.1	926.8	847.7	864.9	859.1	785.5	1,241.9	1,212.8	1,122.3
Fringe	845.3	845.6	786.2	821.9	826.2	773.0	1,071.4	1,048.4	947.1
Medium	891.8	892.4	839.5	852.1	855.8	807.5	1,172.6	1,164.4	1,082.0
Small	943.6	950.5	904.7	907.5	917.9	876.7	1,183.2	1,180.0	1,106.0
Nonmetropolitan counties									
Micropolitan	974.1	973.3	935.1	933.5	939.3	905.0	1,218.9	1,194.3	1,137.1
Nonmicropolitan	1,005.3	1,003.0	970.3	975.9	978.5	950.0	1,188.4	1,171.2	1,114.8
West									
Metropolitan counties									
Large									
Central	819.2	792.4	727.8	829.4	804.1	745.0	1,107.9	1,077.7	1,010.0
Fringe	818.6	803.6	759.2	823.2	810.1	768.9	1,060.8	1,006.2	1,009.2
Medium	814.7	800.5	761.1	826.9	815.8	778.4	1,045.4	996.3	933.7
Small	827.6	815.7	773.8	826.6	815.7	776.1	973.5	990.7	859.8
Nonmetropolitan counties									
Micropolitan	861.0	851.8	815.3	860.4	854.7	819.7	*	*	*
Nonmicropolitan	867.1	847.4	807.0	845.9	828.6	788.3	*	*	*

* = Figure does not meet standard of reliability or precision.
[1]Urbanization levels are for county of residence of decedent. The levels were developed by NCHS using information from the Office of Management and Budget, Department of Agriculture, and Census Bureau.

Table B-40. Age-Adjusted Death Rates, by Race, Sex, Region, and Urbanization Level, Selected Annual Averages, 1996–1998, 1999–2001, and 2003–2005—*Continued*

(Deaths per 100,000 standard population.)

Sex, region, and urbanization level[1]	All races			White			Black or African American		
	1996–1998	1999–2001	2003–2005	1996–1998	1999–2001	2003–2005	1996–1998	1999–2001	2003–2005
MALE									
All Regions									
Metropolitan counties									
Large									
Central	1,108.6	1,057.6	955.5	1,060.6	1,015.2	921.0	1,503.8	1,436.1	1,312.4
Fringe	1,025.2	998.7	910.4	1,010.9	987.3	903.8	1,329.0	1,281.1	1,147.7
Medium	1,069.9	1,038.5	966.0	1,045.4	1,017.7	947.9	1,469.0	1,409.2	1,294.7
Small	1,104.6	1,079.2	1,007.2	1,077.4	1,056.1	986.5	1,497.6	1,449.1	1,343.1
Nonmetropolitan counties									
Micropolitan	1,139.9	1,108.6	1,037.0	1,113.5	1,087.5	1,018.2	1,547.8	1,475.9	1,370.4
Nonmicropolitan	1,172.3	1,132.9	1,067.2	1,143.3	1,108.3	1,044.6	1,529.0	1,457.3	1,367.7
Northeast									
Metropolitan counties									
Large									
Central	1,142.0	1,065.3	946.4	1,102.8	1,034.5	921.2	1,374.4	1,280.7	1,148.2
Fringe	1,018.1	985.3	892.2	1,012.6	982.3	894.9	1,263.0	1,219.0	1,065.3
Medium	1,061.6	1,018.1	944.4	1,049.9	1,009.7	939.6	1,351.2	1,262.4	1,129.5
Small	1,062.7	1,034.1	967.7	1,057.9	1,032.3	965.1	1,376.8	1,280.7	1,186.6
Nonmetropolitan counties									
Micropolitan	1,093.5	1,042.5	979.9	1,093.7	1,045.6	984.0	*	*	*
Nonmicropolitan	1,096.9	1,056.9	981.3	1,096.1	1,056.6	984.0	*	*	*
Midwest									
Metropolitan counties									
Large									
Central	1,192.6	1,155.5	1,046.9	1,101.0	1,064.6	961.8	1,559.8	1,525.5	1,401.8
Fringe	1,051.7	1,030.0	933.7	1,038.7	1,018.7	924.6	1,399.4	1,372.7	1,267.5
Medium	1,089.0	1,063.2	985.0	1,065.3	1,043.8	967.2	1,470.0	1,394.4	1,296.9
Small	1,076.0	1,057.3	977.4	1,059.7	1,045.0	965.0	1,463.9	1,401.9	1,311.8
Nonmetropolitan counties									
Micropolitan	1,092.0	1,063.4	988.0	1,086.0	1,062.0	987.9	1,551.8	1,315.8	1,105.5
Nonmicropolitan	1,094.7	1,050.5	987.6	1,083.0	1,043.3	979.7	1,788.2	1,225.3	1,156.9
South									
Metropolitan counties									
Large									
Central	1,172.0	1,130.9	1,025.5	1,074.6	1,042.9	946.3	1,616.0	1,542.6	1,415.2
Fringe	1,030.8	1,009.7	920.4	1,000.5	984.8	903.1	1,351.1	1,297.8	1,150.4
Medium	1,106.6	1,081.2	1,003.9	1,053.0	1,033.8	962.7	1,517.1	1,466.2	1,350.9
Small	1,185.9	1,160.8	1,089.3	1,138.6	1,118.6	1,053.0	1,526.9	1,487.0	1,377.4
Nonmetropolitan counties									
Micropolitan	1,228.0	1,198.9	1,121.5	1,175.1	1,154.7	1,081.3	1,577.6	1,519.8	1,423.2
Nonmicropolitan	1,275.7	1,240.6	1,173.5	1,239.3	1,210.2	1,147.5	1,530.4	1,478.0	1,389.2
West									
Metropolitan counties									
Large									
Central	996.3	949.8	866.4	1,006.7	962.4	884.5	1,383.8	1,323.2	1,229.0
Fringe	981.1	947.0	883.0	988.0	954.5	893.2	1,228.8	1,171.2	1,165.5
Medium	987.4	952.8	897.2	1,003.1	969.3	911.4	1,230.6	1,165.1	1,069.5
Small	1,003.7	970.5	907.5	1,001.7	971.6	909.6	1,178.9	1,088.1	992.2
Nonmetropolitan counties									
Micropolitan	1,037.8	1,012.6	954.0	1,036.0	1,013.6	955.6	*	*	*
Nonmicropolitan	1,048.7	1,010.9	944.0	1,023.0	986.8	919.2	*	*	*

* = Figure does not meet standard of reliability or precision.

[1]Urbanization levels are for county of residence of decedent. The levels were developed by NCHS using information from the Office of Management and Budget, Department of Agriculture, and Census Bureau.

Table B-40. Age-Adjusted Death Rates, by Race, Sex, Region, and Urbanization Level, Selected Annual Averages, 1996–1998, 1999–2001, and 2003–2005—*Continued*

(Deaths per 100,000 standard population.)

Sex, region, and urbanization level[1]	All races			White			Black or African American		
	1996–1998	1999–2001	2003–2005	1996–1998	1999–2001	2003–2005	1996–1998	1999–2001	2003–2005
FEMALE									
All Regions									
Metropolitan counties									
Large									
Central	738.9	730.1	670.4	711.3	703.8	648.9	934.4	929.3	863.0
Fringe	705.7	711.1	670.5	696.3	702.7	665.7	875.9	876.4	810.0
Medium..............................	716.8	724.6	686.6	701.9	710.6	675.4	932.0	945.4	879.5
Small	731.2	745.7	710.5	713.7	729.1	695.8	951.9	966.5	912.3
Nonmetropolitan counties									
Micropolitan	745.9	754.8	729.0	728.8	740.2	716.0	975.6	968.3	926.9
Nonmicropolitan	750.6	759.5	736.2	731.4	741.9	719.6	951.5	953.0	911.4
Northeast									
Metropolitan counties									
Large									
Central	748.4	719.6	658.3	725.6	699.1	642.7	848.3	823.6	758.6
Fringe	696.3	692.6	649.7	692.4	689.3	649.6	827.2	828.1	763.2
Medium..............................	709.1	707.5	668.5	701.4	700.9	664.2	883.4	877.0	794.9
Small	706.7	717.3	678.9	703.2	713.8	676.1	919.9	930.0	862.3
Nonmetropolitan counties									
Micropolitan	725.0	717.5	684.5	724.3	718.1	685.5	*	*	*
Nonmicropolitan	741.8	738.5	699.4	740.1	737.4	698.7	*	*	*
Midwest									
Metropolitan counties									
Large									
Central	784.1	786.2	728.7	729.7	730.9	675.6	974.4	984.5	917.2
Fringe	722.9	733.8	692.5	714.5	725.1	686.1	924.6	948.2	895.9
Medium..............................	728.9	739.6	701.2	713.6	724.3	687.3	955.1	972.7	908.6
Small	710.8	721.4	683.8	700.0	712.2	673.4	963.1	952.5	937.2
Nonmetropolitan counties									
Micropolitan	711.2	721.2	689.8	707.3	718.6	687.8	998.7	948.8	900.4
Nonmicropolitan	696.1	700.0	672.4	688.9	693.9	665.4	1,123.8	955.4	940.6
South									
Metropolitan counties									
Large									
Central	768.6	776.3	711.5	712.1	721.7	659.8	988.2	989.8	920.6
Fringe	705.7	719.6	677.4	686.1	702.4	665.6	882.4	881.0	803.5
Medium..............................	731.2	746.6	705.9	700.1	716.0	678.8	938.9	958.2	893.9
Small	771.0	795.0	760.5	740.9	767.1	736.6	956.5	974.2	917.0
Nonmetropolitan counties									
Micropolitan	788.4	803.8	783.7	754.8	774.5	758.5	977.3	975.7	937.0
Nonmicropolitan	803.4	821.3	803.5	778.3	799.5	785.5	946.7	955.0	913.7
West									
Metropolitan counties									
Large									
Central	682.6	670.1	615.9	691.8	679.9	631.1	906.0	899.3	838.8
Fringe	696.3	693.8	659.9	699.2	699.1	668.5	920.1	876.5	877.2
Medium..............................	680.5	681.3	649.8	691.6	696.1	668.6	890.3	855.7	809.5
Small	687.3	691.3	660.8	687.2	690.7	663.3	789.8	886.6	722.0
Nonmetropolitan counties									
Micropolitan	712.6	715.1	691.0	713.8	720.0	697.0	*	*	*
Nonmicropolitan	710.4	704.0	679.2	694.2	690.7	666.3	*	*	*

* = Figure does not meet standard of reliability or precision.
[1]Urbanization levels are for county of residence of decedent. The levels were developed by NCHS using information from the Office of Management and Budget, Department of Agriculture, and Census Bureau.

NOTE: The 1997 population estimates used to compute rates for 1996–1998 are intercensal population estimates based on the 2000 census. The 2000 population estimates used to compute rates for 1999–2001 are based on the 2000 census. The 2004 population estimates used to compute rates for 2003–2005 are postcensal population estimates based on the 2000 census.

Table B-41. Deaths and Death Rates for the 10 Leading Causes of Death in Specified Age Groups, Preliminary 2006

(Number, rate per 100,000 population.)

Age and rank[1]	Cause of death[2]	Number	Rate
All Ages[3]			
	All Causes	2,425,901	810.3
1	Diseases of heart (I00-I09, I11, I13, I20-I51)	629,191	210.2
2	Malignant neoplasms (C00-C97)	560,102	187.1
3	Cerebrovascular diseases (I60-I69)	137,265	45.8
4	Chronic lower respiratory diseases (J40-J47)	124,614	41.6
5	Accidents (unintentional injuries) (V01-X59,Y85-Y86)	117,748	39.3
	Motor vehicle accidents (V02-V04, V09.0, V09.2, V12-V14, V19.0-V19.2, V19.4-V19.6, V20-V79, V80.3-V80.5, V81.0-V81.1, V82.0-V82.1, V83-V86, V87.0-V87.8, V88.0-V88.8, V89.0, V89.2)	44,572	14.9
	All other accidents (V01, V05-V06, V09.1, V09.3-V09.9, V10-V12, V15-V18, V19.3, V19.8-V19.9, V80.0-V80.2, V80.6-V80.9, V81.2-V81.9, V82.2-V82.9, V87.9, V88.9, V89.1, V89.3, V89.9, V90-V99, W00-X59, Y85-Y86)	73,177	24.4
6	Alzheimer's disease (G30)	72,914	24.4
7	Diabetes mellitus (E10-E14)	72,507	24.2
8	Influenza and pneumonia (J10-J18)	56,247	18.8
9	Nephritis, nephrotic syndrome and nephrosis (N00-N07, N17-N19, N25-N27)	44,791	15.0
10	Septicemia (A40-A41)	34,031	11.4
	All other causes (residual)	576,491	192.5
1–4 Years			
	All Causes	4,636	28.5
1	Accidents (unintentional injuries) (V01-X59, Y85-Y86)	1,591	9.8
	Motor vehicle accidents (V02-V04, V09.0, V09.2, V12-V14, V19.0-V19.2, V19.4-V19.6, V20-V79, V80.3-V80.5, V81.0-V81.1, V82.0-V82.1, V83-V86, V87.0-V87.8, V88.0-V88.8, V89.0, V89.2)	586	3.6
	All other accidents (V01, V05-V06, V09.1, V09.3-V09.9, V10-V12, V15-V18, V19.3, V19.8-V19.9, V80.0-V80.2, V80.6-V80.9, V81.2-V81.9, V82.2-V82.9, V87.9, V88.9, V89.1, V89.3, V89.9, V90-V99, W00-X59, Y85-Y86)	1,005	6.2
2	Congenital malformations, deformations and chromosomal abnormalities (Q00-Q99)	501	3.1
3	Malignant neoplasms (C00-C97)	372	2.3
4	Assault (homicide) (*U01-*U02, X85-Y09, Y87.1)	350	2.1
5	Diseases of heart (I00-I09, I11, I13, I20-I51)	160	1.0
6	Influenza and pneumonia (J10-J18)	114	0.7
7	Septicemia (A40-A41)	88	0.5
8	Certain conditions originating in the perinatal period (P00-P96)	67	0.4
9	In situ neoplasms, benign neoplasms and neoplasms of uncertain or unknown behavior (D00-D48)	63	0.4
10	Cerebrovascular diseases (I60-I69)	53	0.3
	All other causes (residual)	1,277	7.8
5–14 Years			
	All Causes	6,136	15.2
1	Accidents (unintentional injuries) (V01-X59, Y85-Y86)	2,228	5.5
	Motor vehicle accidents (V02-V04, V09.0, V09.2, V12-V14, V19.0-V19.2, V19.4-V19.6, V20-V79, V80.3-V80.5, V81.0-V81.1, V82.0-V82.1, V83-V86, V87.0-V87.8, V88.0-V88.8, V89.0, V89.2)	1,323	3.3
	All other accidents (V01, V05-V06, V09.1, V09.3-V09.9, V10-V12, V15-V18, V19.3, V19.8-V19.9, V80.0-V80.2, V80.6-V80.9, V81.2-V81.9, V82.2-V82.9, V87.9, V88.9, V89.1, V89.3, V89.9, V90-V99, W00-X59, Y85-Y86)	905	2.2
2	Malignant neoplasms (C00-C97)	916	2.3
3	Assault (homicide) (*U01-*U02, X85-Y09, Y871)	387	1
4	Congenital malformations, deformations and chromosomal abnormalities (Q00-Q99)	330	0.8
5	Diseases of heart (I00-I09, I11, I13, I20-I51)	242	0.6
6	Intentional self-harm (suicide) (*U03, X60-X84, Y870)	213	0.5
7	Chronic lower respiratory diseases (J40-J47)	113	0.3
8	Cerebrovascular diseases (I60-I69)	93	0.2
9	Septicemia (A40-A41)	78	0.2
10	In situ neoplasms, benign neoplasms and neoplasms of uncertain or unknown behavior (D00-D48)	76	0.2
	All other causes (residual)	1,460	3.6
15–24 Years			
	All Causes	34,632	81.6
1	Accidents (unintentional injuries) (V01-X59, Y85-Y86)	15,859	37.4
	Motor vehicle accidents (V02-V04, V09.0, V09.2, V12-V14, V19.0-V19.2, V19.4-V19.6, V20-V79, V80.3-V80.5, V81.0-V81.1, V82.0-V82.1, V83-V86, V87.0-V87.8, V88.0-V88.8, V89.0, V89.2)	10,845	25.6
	All other accidents (V01, V05-V06, V09.1, V09.3-V09.9, V10-V12, V15-V18, V19.3, V19.8-V19.9, V80.0-V80.2, V80.6-V80.9, V81.2-V81.9, V82.2-V82.9, V87.9, V88.9, V89.1, V89.3, V89.9, V90-V99, W00-X59, Y85-Y86)	5,014	11.8
2	Assault (homicide) (*U01-*U02, X85-Y09, Y871)	5,596	13.2
3	Intentional self-harm (suicide) (*U03, X60-X84, Y87.0)	4,097	9.7
4	Malignant neoplasms (C00-C97)	1,643	3.9
5	Diseases of heart (I00-I09, I11, I13, I20-I51)	1,021	2.4
6	Congenital malformations, deformations and chromosomal abnormalities (Q00-Q99)	456	1.1
7	Cerebrovascular diseases (I60-I69)	206	0.5
8	Human immunodeficiency virus (HIV) disease (B20-B24)	198	0.5
9	Influenza and pneumonia (J10-J18)	180	0.4
10	Pregnancy, childbirth and the puerperium (O00-O99)	172	0.4
	All other causes (residual)	5,204	12.3

[1]Rank based on the number of deaths.
[2]Based on codes from the *International Classification of Diseases, Tenth Revision* (1992), except where (*) precedes the cause of death code.
[3]Includes deaths under 1 year of age.

Table B-41. Deaths and Death Rates for the 10 Leading Causes of Death in Specified Age Groups, Preliminary 2006—Continued

(Number, rate per 100,000 population.)

Age and rank[1]	Cause of death[2]	Number	Rate
25–44 Years			
	All Causes...	125,173	148.9
1	Accidents (unintentional injuries) (V01-X59,Y85-Y86)	30,949	36.8
	Motor vehicle accidents (V02-V04, V09.0, V09.2, V12-V14, V19.0-V19.2, V19.4-V19.6, V20-V79, V80.3-V80.5, V81.0-V81.1, V82.0-V82.1, V83-V86, V87.0-V87.8, V88.0-V88.8, V89.0, V89.2)	13,779	16.4
	All other accidents (V01, V05-V06, V09.1, V09.3-V09.9, V10-V12, V15-V18, V19.3, V19.8-V19.9, V80.0-V80.2, V80.6-V80.9, V81.2-V81.9, V82.2-V82.9, V87.9, V88.9, V89.1, V89.3, V89.9, V90-V99, W00-X59, Y85-Y86)	17,170	20.4
2	Malignant neoplasms (C00-C97)	17,604	20.9
3	Diseases of heart (I00-I09, I11, I13, I20-I51)	14,873	17.7
4	Intentional self-harm (suicide) (*U03, X60-X84, Y870)	11,240	13.4
5	Assault (homicide) (*U01-*U02, X85-Y09, Y871)	7,525	8.9
6	Human immunodeficiency virus (HIV) disease (B20-B24)	5,150	6.1
7	Chronic liver disease and cirrhosis (K70, K73-K74)	2,805	3.3
8	Diabetes mellitus (E10-E14)	2,705	3.2
9	Cerebrovascular diseases (I60-I69)	2,703	3.2
10	Septicemia (A40-A41)	1,131	1.3
	All other causes (residual)..	28,488	33.9
45–64 Years			
	All Causes...	464,463	620.4
1	Malignant neoplasms (C00-C97)	151,654	202.6
2	Diseases of heart (I00-I09, I11, I13, I20-I51)	101,588	135.7
3	Accidents (unintentional injuries) (V01-X59, Y85-Y86)	29,505	39.4
	Motor vehicle accidents (V02-V04, V09.0, V09.2, V12-V14, V19.0-V19.2, V19.4-V19.6, V20-V79, V80.3-V80.5, V81.0-V81.1, V82.0-V82.1, V83-V86, V87.0-V87.8, V88.0-V88.8, V89.0, V89.2)	10,939	14.6
	All other accidents (V01, V05-V06, V09.1, V09.3-V09.9, V10-V12, V15-V18, V19.3, V19.8-V19.9, V80.0-V80.2, V80.6-V80.9, V81.2-V81.9, V82.2-V82.9, V87.9, V88.9, V89.1, V89.3, V89.9, V90-V99, W00-X59, Y85-Y86)	18,566	24.8
4	Diabetes mellitus (E10-E14)	17,012	22.7
5	Cerebrovascular diseases (I60-I69)	16,779	22.4
6	Chronic lower respiratory diseases (J40-J47)	16,181	21.6
7	Chronic liver disease and cirrhosis (K70, K73-K74)	14,725	19.7
8	Intentional self-harm (suicide) (*U03, X60-X84, Y870)	11,492	15.4
9	Nephritis, nephrotic syndrome and nephrosis (N00-N07, N17-N19, N25-N27)	6,495	8.7
10	Septicemia (A40-A41)	6,184	8.3
	All other causes (residual)..	92,848	124
65 Years and Over			
	All Causes...	1,762,004	4,728.90
1	Diseases of heart (I00-I09, I11, I13, I20-I51)	510,934	1,371.30
2	Malignant neoplasms (C00-C97)	387,828	1,040.90
3	Cerebrovascular diseases (I60-I69)	117,284	314.8
4	Chronic lower respiratory diseases (J40-J47)	107,058	287.3
5	Alzheimer's disease (G30)	72,135	193.6
6	Diabetes mellitus (E10-E14)	52,599	141.2
7	Influenza and pneumonia (J10-J18)	49,459	132.7
8	Nephritis, nephrotic syndrome and nephrosis (N00-N07, N17-N19, N25-N27)	36,960	99.2
9	Accidents (unintentional injuries) (V01-X59, Y85-Y86)	36,436	97.8
	Motor vehicle accidents (V02-V04, V09.0, V09.2, V12-V14, V19.0-V19.2, V19.4-V19.6, V20-V79, V80.3-V80.5, V81.0-V81.1, V82.0-V82.1, V83-V86, V87.0-V87.8, V88.0-V88.8, V89.0, V89.2)	6,953	18.7
	All other accidents (V01, V05-V06, V09.1, V09.3-V09.9, V10-V12, V15-V18, V19.3, V19.8-V19.9, V80.0-V80.2, V80.6-V80.9, V81.2-V81.9, V82.2-V82.9, V87.9, V88.9, V89.1, V89.3, V89.9, V90-V99, W00-X59, Y85-Y86)	29,483	79.1
10	Septicemia (A40-A41)	26,125	70.1
	All other causes (residual)..	365,186	980.1

[1]Rank based on the number of deaths.
[2]Based on codes from the *International Classification of Diseases, Tenth Revision* (1992), except where (*) precedes the cause of death code.

NOTE: For certain causes of death such as unintentional injuries, homicides, and suicides, preliminary subject to sampling or random variation.

Table B-42. Years of Potential Life Lost Before Age 75 for Selected Causes of Death, by Sex, Race, and Hispanic Origin, Selected Years, 1980–2005

(Years lost before age 75 per 100,000 population.)

Sex, race, Hispanic origin, and cause of death[2]	Crude 2005	Age-adjusted[1]								
		1980	1990	1995	2000[3]	2001	2002	2003	2004	2005
ALL PERSONS										
All Causes	7,489.8	10,448.4	9,085.5	8,626.2	7,578.1	7,531.2	7,499.6	7,466.9	7,270.6	7,299.8
Diseases of heart	1,160.3	2,238.7	1,617.7	1,475.4	1,253.0	1,221.1	1,212.7	1,187.9	1,128.9	1,110.4
Ischemic heart disease	739.2	1,729.3	1,153.6	1,013.2	841.8	809.7	792.0	765.1	720.6	701.8
Cerebrovascular diseases	200.4	357.5	259.6	246.5	223.3	211.9	208.1	203.6	198.1	193.3
Malignant neoplasms	1,602.7	2,108.8	2,003.8	1,841.6	1,674.1	1,651.7	1,622.7	1,586.9	1,543.4	1,525.2
Trachea, bronchus, and lung	418.3	548.5	561.4	497.3	443.1	431.2	423.4	412.2	402.8	392.9
Colorectal	131.1	190.0	164.7	152.0	141.9	142.4	141.0	133.8	127.3	124.7
Prostate[4]	54.8	84.9	96.8	83.5	63.6	61.8	60.1	58.6	55.8	55.1
Breast[5]	316.3	463.2	451.6	398.6	332.6	328.1	316.8	313.7	302.1	296.2
Chronic lower respiratory diseases	189.9	169.1	187.4	190.4	188.1	185.8	184.5	183.9	173.7	181.2
Influenza and pneumonia	85.6	160.2	141.5	126.9	87.1	82.3	82.7	90.8	79.1	83.6
Chronic liver disease and cirrhosis	158.8	300.3	196.9	173.7	164.1	164.7	160.5	159.6	153.9	152.6
Diabetes mellitus	188.3	134.4	155.9	174.7	178.4	180.5	184.3	184.6	178.4	179.9
Human immunodeficiency virus (HIV) disease	132.0	—	383.8	595.3	174.6	167.8	161.8	153.3	143.4	133.6
Unintentional injuries	1,132.4	1,543.5	1,162.1	1,057.2	1,026.5	1,036.8	1,079.2	1,084.6	1,098.0	1,132.7
Motor vehicle-related injuries	565.6	912.9	716.4	616.3	574.3	572.5	585.8	569.6	567.6	564.4
Suicide[6]	347.9	392.0	393.1	384.7	334.5	342.6	346.7	343.3	353.0	347.3
Homicide[6]	276.5	425.5	417.4	378.6	266.5	311.0	274.4	274.3	264.8	276.8
MALE										
All Causes	9,337.0	13,777.2	11,973.5	11,289.2	9,572.2	9,507.1	9,470.0	9,416.4	9,143.1	9,206.1
Diseases of heart	1,589.1	3,352.1	2,356.0	2,117.4	1,766.0	1,708.3	1,706.9	1,664.2	1,583.4	1,561.6
Ischemic heart disease	1,065.8	2,715.1	1,766.3	1,531.5	1,255.4	1,201.8	1,179.6	1,138.8	1,070.5	1,044.3
Cerebrovascular diseases	215.7	396.7	286.6	276.9	244.6	233.5	227.6	225.9	219.6	213.7
Malignant neoplasms	1,672.9	2,360.8	2,214.6	2,008.5	1,810.8	1,782.4	1,754.2	1,711.4	1,663.3	1,639.7
Trachea, bronchus, and lung	487.3	821.1	764.8	645.6	554.9	535.9	520.5	504.6	490.3	476.3
Colorectal	149.0	214.9	194.3	179.4	167.3	166.6	168.2	157.7	149.7	146.2
Prostate	54.8	84.9	96.8	83.5	63.6	61.8	60.1	58.6	55.8	55.1
Chronic lower respiratory diseases	196.2	235.1	224.8	213.1	206.0	200.7	200.7	199.5	188.4	195.8
Influenza and pneumonia	98.5	202.5	180.0	155.7	102.8	96.9	97.3	106.4	93.6	97.8
Chronic liver disease and cirrhosis	221.1	415.0	283.9	254.8	236.9	233.6	226.6	229.4	219.0	216.1
Diabetes mellitus	220.3	140.4	170.4	194.6	203.8	209.6	217.2	218.2	212.6	216.5
Human immunodeficiency virus (HIV) disease	189.1	—	686.2	991.2	258.9	247.7	237.0	223.7	205.1	192.0
Unintentional injuries	1,623.8	2,342.7	1,715.1	1,531.6	1,475.6	1,490.1	1,542.2	1,537.7	1,547.4	1,608.5
Motor vehicle-related injuries	808.4	1,359.7	1,018.4	851.1	796.4	803.5	817.2	795.0	789.1	795.9
Suicide[6]	552.1	605.6	634.8	628.4	539.1	552.3	555.7	548.2	553.0	548.0
Homicide[6]	447.0	675.0	658.0	589.6	410.5	480.5	425.0	430.5	414.3	439.0
Female										
All Causes	5,642.9	7,350.3	6,333.1	6,057.5	5,644.6	5,609.2	5,580.0	5,560.5	5,435.8	5,425.7
Diseases of heart	731.6	1,246.0	948.5	883.9	774.6	765.4	748.8	739.5	699.9	682.6
Ischemic heart disease	412.7	852.1	600.3	537.8	457.6	444.3	430.2	415.0	391.8	379.0
Cerebrovascular diseases	185.1	324.0	235.9	218.7	203.9	192.1	190.3	183.0	178.1	174.4
Malignant neoplasms	1,532.6	1,896.8	1,826.6	1,698.9	1,555.3	1,538.4	1,507.7	1,477.3	1,437.6	1,424.3
Trachea, bronchus, and lung	349.2	310.4	382.2	365.2	342.1	336.6	335.4	328.1	323.2	316.9
Colorectal	113.3	168.7	138.7	127.5	118.7	120.4	115.9	111.9	106.8	104.9
Breast	316.3	463.2	451.6	398.6	332.6	328.1	316.8	313.7	302.1	296.2
Chronic lower respiratory diseases	183.5	114.0	155.9	171.0	172.3	172.8	170.0	169.9	160.4	168.2
Influenza and pneumonia	72.8	122.0	106.2	100.2	72.3	68.7	69.1	76.0	65.3	70.0
Chronic liver disease and cirrhosis	96.4	194.5	115.1	96.6	94.5	98.8	97.4	92.6	91.3	91.6
Diabetes mellitus	156.3	128.5	142.3	155.9	154.4	153.0	153.1	152.9	146.0	145.1
Human immunodeficiency virus (HIV) disease	75.0	—	87.8	205.7	92.0	89.4	88.1	84.1	82.7	76.2
Unintentional injuries	641.1	755.3	607.4	580.1	573.2	578.3	610.3	624.6	641.1	648.0
Motor vehicle-related injuries	322.8	470.4	411.6	378.4	348.5	337.2	349.8	339.2	341.1	327.1
Suicide[6]	143.8	184.2	153.3	140.8	129.1	131.9	136.6	136.6	150.9	144.1
Homicide[6]	106.0	181.3	174.3	163.2	118.9	137.4	119.6	112.9	110.2	108.7

— = Data not available.

[1]Age-adjusted rates are calculated using the year 2000 standard population. Prior to 2003, age-adjusted rates were calculated using standard million proportions based on rounded population numbers. Starting with 2003 data, unrounded population numbers are used to calculate age-adjusted rates.

[2]Underlying cause of death code numbers are based on the applicable revision of the *International Classification of Diseases* for data years shown. For the period 1980–1998, causes were coded using codes from the *International Classification of Diseases, Ninth Edition* that are most nearly comparable with the 113 cause list for the *International Classification of Diseases, Tenth Edition.*

[3]Starting with 1999 data, cause of death is coded according to the *International Classification of Diseases, Tenth Edition.*

[4]Rate for male population only.

[5]Rate for female population only.

[6]Figures for 2001 include September 11-related deaths for which death certificates were filed as of October 24, 2002.

[7]The race groups, White, Black, Asian or Pacific Islander, and American Indian or Alaska Native, include persons of Hispanic and non-Hispanic origin. Persons of Hispanic origin may be of any race. Death rates for the American Indian or Alaska Native and Asian or Pacific Islander populations are known to be underestimated.

Table B-42. Years of Potential Life Lost Before Age 75 for Selected Causes of Death, by Sex, Race, and Hispanic Origin, Selected Years, 1980–2005—*Continued*

(Years lost before age 75 per 100,000 population.)

Sex, race, Hispanic origin, and cause of death[2]	Crude 2005	Age-adjusted[1]								
		1980	1990	1995	2000[3]	2001	2002	2003	2004	2005
WHITE[7]										
All Causes	7,070.6	9,554.1	8,159.5	7,744.9	6,949.5	6,941.6	6,936.6	6,910.6	6,743.7	6,775.6
Diseases of heart	1,096.1	2,100.8	1,490.3	1,353.0	1,149.4	1,115.0	1,111.8	1,081.3	1,031.0	1,011.7
Ischemic heart disease	736.3	1,682.7	1,113.4	975.2	805.3	773.0	759.5	731.5	690.4	672.0
Cerebrovascular diseases	171.8	300.7	213.1	205.2	187.1	175.6	173.5	166.7	165.4	160.4
Malignant neoplasms	1,619.0	2,035.9	1,929.3	1,780.5	1,627.8	1,610.2	1,582.8	1,546.5	1,502.0	1,485.9
Trachea, bronchus, and lung	433.8	529.9	544.2	487.1	436.3	427.5	418.5	407.9	398.3	389.4
Colorectal	128.0	186.8	157.8	145.0	134.1	135.0	134.0	125.5	120.5	117.3
Prostate[4]	49.6	74.8	86.6	73.0	54.3	53.1	51.3	50.5	48.4	47.0
Breast[5]	303.5	460.2	441.7	381.5	315.6	309.6	297.5	295.0	282.1	275.1
Chronic lower respiratory diseases	200.7	165.4	182.3	185.7	185.3	184.7	183.5	184.2	174.3	182.2
Influenza and pneumonia	80.0	130.8	116.9	108.3	77.7	72.7	75.1	82.2	71.5	76.3
Chronic liver disease and cirrhosis	167.6	257.3	175.8	164.6	162.7	164.4	162.9	162.3	157.2	156.7
Diabetes mellitus	169.7	115.7	133.7	149.4	155.6	156.2	160.3	160.3	155.2	156.3
Human immunodeficiency virus (HIV) disease	69.3	—	309.0	422.6	94.7	88.4	84.7	82.1	74.5	69.8
Unintentional injuries	1,160.5	1,520.4	1,139.7	1,040.9	1,031.8	1,049.0	1,101.6	1,117.7	1,134.9	1,170.9
Motor vehicle-related injuries	579.6	939.9	726.7	623.6	586.1	585.1	604.0	588.5	587.6	585.7
Suicide[6]	380.8	414.5	417.7	411.6	362.0	373.5	380.1	375.0	386.0	381.2
Homicide[6]	156.8	271.7	234.9	220.2	156.6	204.0	159.7	159.3	157.0	159.7
BLACK OR AFRICAN AMERICAN[7]										
All Causes	11,378.1	17,873.4	16,593.0	15,809.7	12,897.1	12,579.7	12,401.0	12,304.0	11,922.4	11,890.7
Diseases of heart	1,808.3	3,619.9	2,891.8	2,681.8	2,275.2	2,248.9	2,212.8	2,205.7	2,090.5	2,046.0
Ischemic heart disease	930.5	2,305.1	1,676.1	1,510.2	1,300.1	1,260.6	1,218.7	1,182.6	1,119.0	1,080.2
Cerebrovascular diseases	389.5	883.2	656.4	583.6	507.0	491.3	474.1	479.6	452.0	441.7
Malignant neoplasms	1,813.0	2,946.1	2,894.8	2,597.1	2,294.7	2,228.4	2,196.6	2,163.9	2,107.3	2,069.7
Trachea, bronchus, and lung	436.1	776.0	811.3	683.0	593.0	557.5	561.9	542.1	529.3	511.8
Colorectal	172.9	232.3	241.8	226.9	222.4	219.6	213.7	214.4	196.6	199.6
Prostate[4]	103.6	200.3	223.5	210.0	171.0	164.1	160.3	154.3	143.0	144.8
Breast[5]	452.3	524.2	592.9	577.4	500.0	501.7	495.9	490.6	477.7	485.7
Chronic lower respiratory diseases	187.5	203.7	240.6	244.0	232.7	220.5	222.8	212.3	201.8	211.0
Influenza and pneumonia	135.2	384.9	330.8	269.8	161.2	152.1	146.7	157.5	141.2	145.3
Chronic liver disease and cirrhosis	124.4	644.0	371.8	250.3	185.6	181.5	161.3	158.9	148.4	138.4
Diabetes mellitus	331.9	305.3	361.5	400.8	383.4	392.6	396.7	396.0	378.8	379.9
Human immunodeficiency virus (HIV) disease	550.3	—	1,014.7	1,945.4	763.3	743.5	720.6	670.1	637.8	594.4
Unintentional injuries	1,153.2	1,751.5	1,392.7	1,272.1	1,152.8	1,133.4	1,129.3	1,082.1	1,095.5	1,134.6
Motor vehicle-related injuries	553.2	750.2	699.5	621.8	580.8	571.7	558.5	536.2	543.8	532.3
Suicide[6]	198.0	238.0	261.4	254.2	208.7	201.5	196.5	199.5	200.6	194.0
Homicide[6]	1,031.5	1,580.8	1,612.9	1,352.8	941.6	963.6	962.2	965.0	918.7	967.8
AMERICAN INDIAN OR ALASKAN NATIVE[7]										
All Causes	8,116.4	13,390.9	9,506.2	9,332.5	7,758.2	7,991.8	8,278.0	8,541.6	8,405.4	8,624.4
Diseases of heart	865.1	1,819.9	1,391.0	1,296.3	1,030.1	1,027.7	959.9	1,099.3	975.8	1,010.2
Ischemic heart disease	522.3	1,208.2	901.8	877.3	709.3	695.2	648.4	708.1	628.3	625.2
Cerebrovascular diseases	174.5	269.3	223.3	255.3	198.1	193.5	201.7	190.7	171.4	209.4
Malignant neoplasms	916.1	1,101.3	1,141.1	1,099.5	995.7	1,099.5	1,066.0	997.2	1,068.4	1,084.3
Trachea, bronchus, and lung	216.8	181.1	268.1	267.7	227.8	238.7	226.3	223.9	264.1	268.2
Colorectal	93.5	78.8	82.4	103.5	93.8	87.9	115.7	85.5	92.1	109.7
Prostate[4]	26.8	66.7	42.0	51.1	44.5	35.2	36.3	34.7	37.1	37.6
Breast[5]	130.7	205.5	213.4	195.9	174.1	175.2	187.1	146.8	186.0	149.2
Chronic lower respiratory diseases	125.9	89.3	129.0	145.3	151.8	139.3	137.0	163.6	148.6	155.3
Influenza and pneumonia	99.4	307.9	206.3	199.7	124.0	141.3	100.9	171.8	116.1	113.6
Chronic liver disease and cirrhosis	448.3	1,190.3	535.1	604.8	519.4	506.0	495.8	504.6	480.5	498.9
Diabetes mellitus	291.9	305.5	292.3	360.6	305.6	297.3	344.7	355.2	323.5	347.3
Human immunodeficiency virus (HIV) disease	82.3	—	70.1	246.9	68.4	88.1	79.9	80.7	93.8	89.9
Unintentional injuries	1,968.5	3,541.0	2,183.9	1,980.9	1,700.1	1,632.0	1,764.6	1,818.4	1,732.9	1,875.6
Motor vehicle-related injuries	1,091.2	2,102.4	1,301.5	1,210.3	1,032.2	989.4	1,089.3	1,081.8	968.3	1,004.9
Suicide[6]	544.0	515.0	495.9	445.2	403.1	420.6	420.8	418.2	511.6	498.6
Homicide[6]	369.0	628.9	434.2	432.7	278.5	287.0	366.5	323.1	304.7	337.5

—- = Data not available.

[1]Age-adjusted rates are calculated using the year 2000 standard population. Prior to 2003, age-adjusted rates were calculated using standard million proportions based on rounded population numbers. Starting with 2003 data, unrounded population numbers are used to calculate age-adjusted rates.

[2]Underlying cause of death code numbers are based on the applicable revision of the *International Classification of Diseases* for data years shown. For the period 1980–1998, causes were coded using codes from the *International Classification of Diseases, Ninth Edition* that are most nearly comparable with the 113 cause list for the *International Classification of Diseases, Tenth Edition.*

[3]Starting with 1999 data, cause of death is coded according to the *International Classification of Diseases, Tenth Edition.*

[4]Rate for male population only.

[5]Rate for female population only.

[6]Figures for 2001 include September 11-related deaths for which death certificates were filed as of October 24, 2002.

[7]The race groups, White, Black, Asian or Pacific Islander, and American Indian or Alaska Native, include persons of Hispanic and non-Hispanic origin. Persons of Hispanic origin may be of any race. Death rates for the American Indian or Alaska Native and Asian or Pacific Islander populations are known to be underestimated.

Table B-42. Years of Potential Life Lost Before Age 75 for Selected Causes of Death, by Sex, Race, and Hispanic Origin, Selected Years, 1980–2005—*Continued*

(Years lost before age 75 per 100,000 population.)

Sex, race, Hispanic origin, and cause of death[2]	Crude	Age-adjusted[1]								
	2005	1980	1990	1995	2000[3]	2001	2002	2003	2004	2005
ASIAN OR PACIFIC ISLANDER[7]										
All Causes	3,458.2	5,378.4	4,705.2	4,333.2	3,811.1	3,798.7	3,635.5	3,657.5	3,452.1	3,533.2
Diseases of heart	486.1	952.8	702.2	664.9	567.9	547.1	539.4	534.3	474.9	513.8
Ischemic heart disease	304.1	697.7	486.6	440.6	381.1	369.4	352.0	354.7	303.4	326.5
Cerebrovascular diseases	152.9	266.9	233.5	220.0	199.4	198.8	186.5	192.9	167.5	162.8
Malignant neoplasms	905.3	1,218.6	1,166.4	1,122.1	1,033.8	1,029.6	990.3	959.1	949.9	945.3
Trachea, bronchus, and lung	157.0	238.2	204.7	197.0	185.8	180.8	173.8	173.9	176.0	169.2
Colorectal	74.5	115.9	105.1	99.5	91.6	97.2	92.8	94.4	87.7	78.7
Prostate[4]	16.8	17.0	32.4	25.3	18.8	13.3	20.8	14.6	15.1	20.4
Breast[5]	181.3	222.2	216.5	237.8	200.8	205.0	188.4	192.3	193.4	178.4
Chronic lower respiratory diseases	32.4	56.4	72.8	65.8	56.5	52.1	44.8	45.1	36.5	36.0
Influenza and pneumonia	37.7	79.3	74.0	64.3	48.6	45.4	38.0	47.7	36.1	40.3
Chronic liver disease and cirrhosis	43.1	85.6	72.4	48.4	44.8	44.5	40.0	36.8	38.3	43.6
Diabetes mellitus	72.5	83.1	74.0	83.5	77.0	83.8	76.4	79.9	78.3	78.1
Human immunodeficiency virus (HIV) disease	17.2	—	77.0	110.4	19.9	21.6	24.8	22.3	21.9	16.6
Unintentional injuries	421.4	742.7	636.6	525.7	425.7	431.4	431.1	429.6	415.0	413.7
Motor vehicle-related injuries	248.7	472.6	445.5	351.9	263.4	275.9	269.7	269.6	254.4	242.1
Suicide[6]	176.8	217.1	200.6	211.1	168.6	166.4	162.7	172.1	175.5	164.6
Homicide[6]	134.5	201.1	205.8	202.3	113.1	165.1	127.5	120.6	98.8	130.8
HISPANIC OR LATINO[7,8]										
All Causes	5,303.3	—	7,963.3	7,426.7	6,037.6	5,982.2	5,865.9	5,910.0	5,654.0	5,757.9
Diseases of heart	505.1	—	1,082.0	962.0	821.3	791.6	796.9	767.7	733.1	727.0
Ischemic heart disease	309.8	—	756.6	665.8	564.6	539.1	540.1	501.3	483.3	483.2
Cerebrovascular diseases	133.9	—	238.0	232.0	207.8	201.4	193.4	187.3	187.9	184.9
Malignant neoplasms	735.3	—	1,232.2	1,172.0	1,098.2	1,099.1	1,052.9	1,056.5	1,013.7	1,017.5
Trachea, bronchus, and lung	85.7	—	193.7	173.9	152.1	154.9	150.5	144.9	136.3	138.1
Colorectal	58.7	—	100.2	97.9	101.4	95.8	96.7	100.1	91.2	86.4
Prostate[4]	20.8	—	47.7	60.8	42.9	49.4	44.1	43.4	38.8	41.7
Breast[5]	147.8	—	299.3	257.7	230.7	233.6	205.1	218.4	203.4	197.3
Chronic lower respiratory diseases	42.2	—	78.8	82.1	68.5	67.6	69.0	67.1	64.1	62.2
Influenza and pneumonia	57.8	—	130.1	108.5	76.0	66.1	65.5	76.4	67.8	69.5
Chronic liver disease and cirrhosis	151.9	—	329.1	281.4	252.1	247.7	237.9	221.8	212.5	210.3
Diabetes mellitus	132.3	—	177.8	228.8	215.6	212.1	207.1	214.0	192.3	202.2
Human immunodeficiency virus (HIV) disease	119.6	—	600.1	865.0	209.4	190.3	179.1	175.4	154.9	139.3
Unintentional injuries	1,044.1	—	1,190.6	1,017.9	920.1	945.8	958.1	961.5	917.6	980.1
Motor vehicle-related injuries	625.8	—	740.8	593.0	540.2	554.0	569.6	563.6	547.7	569.2
Suicide[6]	201.9	—	256.2	245.1	188.5	185.1	185.6	188.3	200.3	193.2
Homicide[6]	389.7	—	720.8	575.4	335.1	365.2	330.2	345.0	328.8	343.0

— = Data not available.

[1]Age-adjusted rates are calculated using the year 2000 standard population. Prior to 2003, age-adjusted rates were calculated using standard million proportions based on rounded population numbers. Starting with 2003 data, unrounded population numbers are used to calculate age-adjusted rates.

[2]Underlying cause of death code numbers are based on the applicable revision of the *International Classification of Diseases* for data years shown. For the period 1980–1998, causes were coded using codes from the *International Classification of Diseases, Ninth Edition* that are most nearly comparable with the 113 cause list for the *International Classification of Diseases, Tenth Edition*

[3]Starting with 1999 data, cause of death is coded according to the *International Classification of Diseases, Tenth Edition.*

[4]Rate for male population only.

[5]Rate for female population only.

[6]Figures for 2001 include September 11-related deaths for which death certificates were filed as of October 24, 2002.

[7]The race groups, White, Black, Asian or Pacific Islander, and American Indian or Alaska Native, include persons of Hispanic and non-Hispanic origin. Persons of Hispanic origin may be of any race. Death rates for the American Indian or Alaska Native and Asian or Pacific Islander populations are known to be underestimated.

[8]Prior to 1997, excludes data from states lacking an Hispanic-origin item on the death certificate.

Table B-42. Years of Potential Life Lost Before Age 75 for Selected Causes of Death, by Sex, Race, and Hispanic Origin, Selected Years, 1980–2005—*Continued*

(Years lost before age 75 per 100,000 population.)

Sex, race, Hispanic origin, and cause of death[2]	Crude	Age-adjusted[1]								
	2005	1980	1990	1995	2000[3]	2001	2002	2003	2004	2005
WHITE, NOT HISPANIC OR LATINO[8]										
All Causes	7,380.0	—	8,022.5	7,607.5	6,960.5	6,970.9	6,997.9	6,961.6	6,832.9	6,853.3
Diseases of heart	1,213.0	—	1,504.0	1,368.2	1,175.1	1,144.4	1,143.8	1,114.7	1,064.9	1,046.4
Ischemic heart disease	820.8	—	1,127.2	988.7	824.7	794.7	781.3	755.8	713.8	694.4
Cerebrovascular diseases	178.2	—	210.1	199.6	183.0	170.6	169.4	162.8	161.1	155.5
Malignant neoplasms	1,795.3	—	1,974.1	1,814.2	1,668.4	1,652.3	1,629.7	1,590.6	1,549.7	1,534.3
Trachea, bronchus, and lung	505.7	—	566.8	507.0	460.3	451.9	443.7	433.5	425.1	416.3
Colorectal	141.9	—	162.1	147.8	136.2	138.5	137.6	127.7	123.4	120.8
Prostate[4]	55.6	—	89.2	73.6	54.9	53.2	51.7	51.0	49.2	47.3
Breast[5]	333.0	—	451.5	389.3	322.3	315.9	305.9	301.8	290.0	283.6
Chronic lower respiratory diseases	233.2	—	188.1	190.6	193.8	194.3	193.3	194.2	184.1	194.0
Influenza and pneumonia	83.9	—	112.3	105.8	76.4	72.9	75.8	82.1	71.3	76.8
Chronic liver disease and cirrhosis	168.3	—	162.4	151.4	150.9	153.0	152.1	153.2	148.3	147.8
Diabetes mellitus	175.8	—	131.2	142.8	150.2	151.0	155.8	154.9	152.0	151.5
Human immunodeficiency virus (HIV) disease	57.5	—	271.2	362.1	76.0	71.0	67.8	65.4	59.7	56.6
Unintentional injuries	1,171.6	—	1,114.7	1,026.1	1,041.4	1,057.2	1,117.4	1,135.8	1,170.6	1,199.6
Motor vehicle-related injuries	562.5	—	715.7	618.0	588.8	584.1	603.3	585.3	588.6	579.9
Suicide[6]	415.2	—	433.0	427.7	389.2	405.3	413.9	408.1	419.8	416.6
Homicide[6]	104.2	—	162.0	148.6	113.2	160.1	114.8	109.6	110.3	109.1

— = Data not available.

[1]Age-adjusted rates are calculated using the year 2000 standard population. Prior to 2003, age-adjusted rates were calculated using standard million proportions based on rounded population numbers. Starting with 2003 data, unrounded population numbers are used to calculate age-adjusted rates.

[2]Underlying cause of death code numbers are based on the applicable revision of the *International Classification of Diseases* for data years shown. For the period 1980–1998, causes were coded using codes from the *International Classification of Diseases, Ninth Edition* that are most nearly comparable with the 113 cause list for the *International Classification of Diseases, Tenth Edition*

[3]Starting with 1999 data, cause of death is coded according to the *International Classification of Diseases, Tenth Edition*.

[4]Rate for male population only.

[5]Rate for female population only.

[6]Figures for 2001 include September 11-related deaths for which death certificates were filed as of October 24, 2002.

[8]Prior to 1997, excludes data from states lacking an Hispanic-origin item on the death certificate.

Table B-43. Death Rates for Heart Disease, by Sex, Race, Hispanic Origin, and Age, Selected Years, 1950–2005

(Rate per 100,000 population.)

Sex, race, Hispanic origin, and age	1950[1,2]	1960[1,2]	1970[2]	1980[2]	1990[2]	2000[3]	2001	2002	2003	2004	2005
All Persons											
All ages, age-adjusted[4]	586.8	559.0	492.7	412.1	321.8	257.6	247.8	240.8	232.3	217.0	211.1
All ages, crude	355.5	369.0	362.0	336.0	289.5	252.6	245.8	241.7	235.6	222.2	220.0
Under 1 year	3.5	6.6	13.1	22.8	20.1	13.0	11.9	12.4	11.0	10.3	8.7
1–4 years	1.3	1.3	1.7	2.6	1.9	1.2	1.5	1.1	1.2	1.2	0.9
5–14 years	2.1	1.3	0.8	0.9	0.9	0.7	0.7	0.6	0.6	0.6	0.6
15–24 years	6.8	4.0	3.0	2.9	2.5	2.6	2.5	2.5	2.7	2.5	2.7
25–34 years	19.4	15.6	11.4	8.3	7.6	7.4	8.0	7.9	8.2	7.9	8.1
35–44 years	86.4	74.6	66.7	44.6	31.4	29.2	29.6	30.5	30.7	29.3	28.9
45–54 years	308.6	271.8	238.4	180.2	120.5	94.2	92.9	93.7	92.5	90.2	89.7
55–64 years	808.1	737.9	652.3	494.1	367.3	261.2	246.9	241.5	233.2	218.8	214.8
65–74 years	1,839.8	1,740.5	1,558.2	1,218.6	894.3	665.6	635.1	615.9	585.0	541.6	518.9
75–84 years	4,310.1	4,089.4	3,683.8	2,993.1	2,295.7	1,780.3	1,725.7	1,677.2	1,611.1	1,506.3	1,460.8
85 years and over	9,150.6	9,317.8	7,891.3	7,777.1	6,739.9	5,926.1	5,664.2	5,446.8	5,278.4	4,895.9	4,778.4
Male											
All ages, age-adjusted[4]	697.0	687.6	634.0	538.9	412.4	320.0	305.4	297.4	286.6	267.9	260.9
All ages, crude	423.4	439.5	422.5	368.6	297.6	249.8	242.5	240.7	235.0	222.8	221.1
Under 1 year	4.0	7.8	15.1	25.5	21.9	13.3	11.8	12.9	12.1	10.9	9.4
1–4 years	1.4	1.4	1.9	2.8	1.9	1.4	1.5	1.1	1.1	1.1	1.0
5–14 years	2.0	1.4	0.9	1.0	0.9	0.8	0.7	0.7	0.7	0.6	0.6
15–24 years	6.8	4.2	3.7	3.7	3.1	3.2	3.2	3.3	3.4	3.2	3.6
25–34 years	22.9	20.1	15.2	11.4	10.3	9.6	10.3	10.5	10.5	10.5	10.8
35–44 years	118.4	112.7	103.2	68.7	48.1	41.4	41.7	43.1	42.8	40.9	40.7
45–54 years	440.5	420.4	376.4	282.6	183.0	140.2	136.6	138.4	136.2	132.3	131.5
55–64 years	1,104.5	1,066.9	987.2	746.8	537.3	371.7	349.8	343.4	331.7	312.8	306.9
65–74 years	2,292.3	2,291.3	2,170.3	1,728.0	1,250.0	898.3	851.3	827.1	785.3	723.8	692.3
75–84 years	4,825.0	4,742.4	4,534.8	3,834.3	2,968.2	2,248.1	2,177.3	2,110.1	2,030.3	1,893.6	1,829.4
85 years and over	9,659.8	9,788.9	8,426.2	8,752.7	7,418.4	6,430.0	6,040.5	5,823.5	5,621.5	5,239.3	5,143.4
Female											
All ages, age-adjusted[4]	484.7	447.0	381.6	320.8	257.0	210.9	203.9	197.2	190.3	177.3	172.3
All ages, crude	288.4	300.6	304.5	305.1	281.8	255.3	249.0	242.7	236.2	221.6	218.9
Under 1 year	2.9	5.4	10.9	20.0	18.3	12.5	12.0	11.8	9.8	9.7	8.0
1–4 years	1.2	1.1	1.6	2.5	1.9	1.0	1.4	1.0	1.3	1.2	0.9
5–14 years	2.2	1.2	0.8	0.9	0.8	0.5	0.7	0.6	0.5	0.6	0.6
15–24 years	6.7	3.7	2.3	2.1	1.8	2.1	1.8	1.7	2.1	1.7	1.7
25–34 years	16.2	11.3	7.7	5.3	5.0	5.2	5.6	5.2	5.7	5.2	5.3
35–44 years	55.1	38.2	32.2	21.4	15.1	17.2	17.6	18.0	18.6	17.7	17.1
45–54 years	177.2	127.5	109.9	84.5	61.0	49.8	50.7	50.6	50.2	49.6	49.2
55–64 years	510.0	429.4	351.6	272.1	215.7	159.3	151.8	147.2	141.9	131.5	129.1
65–74 years	1,419.3	1,261.3	1,082.7	828.6	616.8	474.0	455.9	440.1	417.5	388.6	372.7
75–84 years	3,872.0	3,582.7	3,120.8	2,497.0	1,893.8	1,475.1	1,428.9	1,389.7	1,331.1	1,245.6	1,210.5
85 years and over	8,796.1	9,016.8	7,591.8	7,350.5	6,478.1	5,720.9	5,506.8	5,283.3	5,126.7	4,741.5	4,610.8
White Male[5]											
All ages, age-adjusted[4]	700.2	694.5	640.2	539.6	409.2	316.7	301.8	294.1	282.9	264.6	258.0
All ages, crude	433.0	454.6	438.3	384.0	312.7	265.8	257.8	256.0	249.5	236.5	234.9
45–54 years	423.6	413.2	365.7	269.8	170.6	130.7	127.0	128.6	125.3	122.2	121.3
55–64 years	1,081.7	1,056.0	979.3	730.6	516.7	351.8	330.8	324.0	313.2	294.4	288.2
65–74 years	2,308.3	2,297.9	2,177.2	1,729.7	1,230.5	877.8	829.1	807.8	761.1	703.2	671.9
75–84 years	4,907.3	4,839.9	4,617.6	3,883.2	2,983.4	2,247.0	2,175.8	2,112.0	2,030.1	1,897.1	1,831.8
85 years and over	9,950.5	10,135.8	8,818.0	8,958.0	7,558.7	6,560.8	6,157.2	5,939.8	5,747.2	5,348.4	5,288.4
Black or African American Male[5]											
All ages, age-adjusted[4]	639.4	615.2	607.3	561.4	485.4	392.5	384.5	371.0	364.3	342.1	329.8
All ages, crude	346.2	330.6	330.3	301.0	256.8	211.1	209.0	206.3	206.0	196.7	194.8
45–54 years	622.5	514.0	512.8	433.4	328.9	247.2	242.6	246.0	248.1	240.0	237.4
55–64 years	1,433.1	1,236.8	1,135.4	987.2	824.0	631.2	602.2	605.3	580.9	560.2	549.1
65–74 years	2,139.1	2,281.4	2,237.8	1,847.2	1,632.9	1,268.8	1,245.8	1,192.7	1,195.5	1,096.6	1,041.6
75–84 years[6]	4,106.1	3,533.6	3,783.4	3,578.8	3,107.1	2,597.6	2,569.3	2,449.6	2,426.6	2,235.5	2,204.1
85 years and over	—	6,037.9	5,367.6	6,819.5	6,479.6	5,633.5	5,459.9	5,125.7	4,850.3	4,637.3	4,230.5
American Indian or Alaska Native Male[5]											
All ages, age-adjusted[4]	—	—	—	320.5	264.1	222.2	200.7	201.2	203.2	182.7	173.2
All ages, crude	—	—	—	130.6	108.0	90.1	89.1	92.0	98.5	91.4	93.2
45–54 years	—	—	—	238.1	173.8	108.5	109.1	104.2	116.7	94.1	112.2
55–64 years	—	—	—	496.3	411.0	285.0	301.1	273.2	293.5	260.7	275.0
65–74 years	—	—	—	1,009.4	839.1	748.2	682.1	638.4	655.6	590.0	554.4
75–84 years	—	—	—	2,062.2	1,788.8	1,655.7	1,384.5	1,422.7	1,309.9	1,252.1	1,123.9
85 years and over	—	—	—	4,413.7	3,860.3	3,318.3	2,895.7	3,162.4	3,266.5	2,812.6	2,509.3

— = Data not available.

[1]Includes deaths of persons who were not residents of the 50 states and the District of Columbia.

[2]Underlying cause of death was coded according to the Sixth Revision of the *International Classification of Diseases* in 1950, Seventh Revision in 1960, Eighth Revision in 1970, and Ninth Revision in 1980–1998.

[3]Starting with 1999 data, cause of death is coded according to the *International Classification of Diseases*.

[4]Age-adjusted rates are calculated using the year 2000 standard population. Prior to 2003, age-adjusted rates were calculated using standard million proportions based on rounded population numbers. Starting with 2003 data, unrounded population numbers are used to calculate age-adjusted rates.

[5]The race groups, White, Black, Asian or Pacific Islander, and American Indian or Alaska Native, include persons of Hispanic and non-Hispanic origin. Persons of Hispanic origin may be of any race. Death rates for the American Indian or Alaska Native and Asian or Pacific Islander populations are known to be underestimated.

[6]In 1950, rate is for the age group 75 years and over.

Table B-43. Death Rates for Heart Disease, by Sex, Race, Hispanic Origin, and Age, Selected Years, 1950–2005—Continued

(Rate per 100,000 population.)

Sex, race, Hispanic origin, and age	1950[1,2]	1960[1,2]	1970[2]	1980[2]	1990[2]	2000[3]	2001	2002	2003	2004	2005
Asian or Pacific Islander Male[5]											
All ages, age-adjusted[4]	—	—	—	286.9	220.7	185.5	169.8	169.8	158.3	146.5	141.1
All ages, crude	—	—	—	119.8	88.7	90.6	87.3	89.4	86.3	81.4	83.5
45–54 years	—	—	—	112.0	70.4	61.1	60.1	60.6	62.7	56.6	58.1
55–64 years	—	—	—	306.7	226.1	182.6	162.0	154.2	152.9	138.9	145.3
65–74 years	—	—	—	852.4	623.5	482.5	439.1	422.4	398.3	347.7	374.9
75–84 years	—	—	—	2,010.9	1,642.2	1,354.7	1,273.8	1,252.4	1,145.1	1,047.0	984.3
85 years and over	—	—	—	5,923.0	4,617.8	4,154.2	3,688.1	3,841.3	3,524.6	3,416.7	3,052.0
Hispanic or Latino Male[5,7]											
All ages, age-adjusted[4]	—	—	—	—	270.0	238.2	232.6	219.8	206.8	193.9	192.4
All ages, crude	—	—	—	—	91.0	74.7	74.6	74.0	72.2	70.2	72.1
45–54 years	—	—	—	—	116.4	84.3	82.9	80.5	79.6	77.6	77.9
55–64 years	—	—	—	—	363.0	264.8	242.2	256.0	235.6	224.6	219.3
65–74 years	—	—	—	—	829.9	684.8	683.7	657.7	625.0	572.2	561.5
75–84 years	—	—	—	—	1,971.3	1,733.2	1,702.7	1,599.5	1,543.5	1,489.0	1,469.2
85 years and over	—	—	—	—	4,711.9	4,897.5	4,784.3	4,301.8	3,874.5	3,496.8	3,534.2
White, Not Hispanic or Latino Male[7]											
All ages, age-adjusted[4]	—	—	—	—	413.6	319.9	304.8	297.7	286.9	268.7	262.2
All ages, crude	—	—	—	—	336.5	297.5	289.5	289.2	282.9	269.1	267.8
45–54 years	—	—	—	—	172.8	134.3	130.7	133.1	129.8	126.9	126.2
55–64 years	—	—	—	—	521.3	356.3	335.8	327.6	317.7	298.8	293.0
65–74 years	—	—	—	—	1,243.4	885.1	834.7	813.5	767.3	709.5	677.6
75–84 years	—	—	—	—	3,007.7	2,261.9	2,190.4	2,129.9	2,049.9	1,915.1	1,849.3
85 years and over	—	—	—	—	7,663.4	6,606.6	6,195.4	5,994.1	5,821.0	5,430.9	5,374.1
White Female[5]											
All ages, age-adjusted[4]	478.0	441.7	376.7	315.9	250.9	205.6	198.7	192.1	185.4	172.9	168.2
All ages, crude	289.4	306.5	313.8	319.2	298.4	274.5	267.7	261.0	253.8	238.3	235.5
45–54 years	141.9	103.4	91.4	71.2	50.2	40.9	41.5	41.7	41.1	40.7	40.8
55–64 years	460.2	383.0	317.7	248.1	192.4	141.3	134.3	130.6	125.2	117.2	114.5
65–74 years	1,400.9	1,229.8	1,044.0	796.7	583.6	445.2	429.0	414.7	392.0	365.4	351.8
75–84 years	3,925.2	3,629.7	3,143.5	2,493.6	1,874.3	1,452.4	1,407.9	1,368.2	1,315.2	1,229.1	1,193.3
85 years and over	9,084.7	9,280.8	7,839.9	7,501.6	6,563.4	5,801.4	5,582.5	5,350.6	5,193.6	4,810.4	4,691.0
Black or African American Female[5]											
All ages, age-adjusted[4]	536.9	488.9	435.6	378.6	327.5	277.6	269.8	263.2	253.8	236.5	228.3
All ages, crude	287.6	268.5	261.0	249.7	237.0	212.6	208.6	205.0	200.0	188.3	185.2
45–54 years	525.3	360.7	290.9	202.4	155.3	125.0	125.9	124.9	124.1	121.2	115.4
55–64 years	1,210.2	952.3	710.5	530.1	442.0	332.8	323.1	312.3	304.7	276.0	272.0
65–74 years	1,659.4	1,680.5	1,553.2	1,210.3	1,017.5	815.2	768.0	734.0	712.0	656.5	614.9
75–84 years[6]	3,499.3	2,926.9	2,964.1	2,707.2	2,250.9	1,913.1	1,849.6	1,821.9	1,699.6	1,622.9	1,595.1
85 years and over	—	5,650.0	5,003.8	5,796.5	5,766.1	5,298.7	5,207.3	5,111.2	4,976.5	4,534.7	4,365.6
American Indian or Alaska Native Female[5]											
All ages, age-adjusted[4]	—	—	—	175.4	153.1	143.6	127.0	123.6	127.5	119.9	115.9
All ages, crude	—	—	—	80.3	77.5	71.9	68.2	68.5	75.9	73.6	75.1
45–54 years	—	—	—	65.2	62.0	40.2	42.7	29.7	45.4	49.5	52.0
55–64 years	—	—	—	193.5	197.0	149.4	126.5	124.3	153.4	116.9	122.1
65–74 years	—	—	—	577.2	492.8	391.8	384.2	365.8	390.3	317.4	348.6
75–84 years	—	—	—	1,364.3	1,050.3	1,044.1	934.3	1,002.5	950.3	894.1	846.8
85 years and over	—	—	—	2,893.3	2,868.7	3,146.3	2,510.3	2,372.5	2,284.1	2,449.1	2,145.9
Asian or Pacific Islander Female[5]											
All ages, age-adjusted[4]	—	—	—	132.3	149.2	115.7	112.9	108.1	104.2	96.1	91.9
All ages, crude	—	—	—	57.0	62.0	65.0	67.9	67.4	68.2	65.1	66.2
45–54 years	—	—	—	28.6	17.5	15.9	18.4	16.4	14.8	13.7	15.8
55–64 years	—	—	—	92.9	99.0	68.8	62.8	61.8	60.3	50.7	56.9
65–74 years	—	—	—	313.3	323.9	229.6	241.7	239.9	207.2	205.6	194.3
75–84 years	—	—	—	1,053.2	1,130.9	866.2	848.7	796.9	769.7	697.4	682.9
85 years and over	—	—	—	3,211.0	4,161.2	3,367.2	3,186.3	3,067.4	3,020.0	2,817.1	2,560.3

— = Data not available.

[1]Includes deaths of persons who were not residents of the 50 states and the District of Columbia.

[2]Underlying cause of death was coded according to the Sixth Revision of the *International Classification of Diseases* in 1950, Seventh Revision in 1960, Eighth Revision in 1970, and Ninth Revision in 1980–1998.

[3]Starting with 1999 data, cause of death is coded according to the *International Classification of Diseases*.

[4]Age-adjusted rates are calculated using the year 2000 standard population. Prior to 2003, age-adjusted rates were calculated using standard million proportions based on rounded population numbers. Starting with 2003 data, unrounded population numbers are used to calculate age-adjusted rates.

[5]The race groups, White, Black, Asian or Pacific Islander, and American Indian or Alaska Native, include persons of Hispanic and non-Hispanic origin. Persons of Hispanic origin may be of any race. Death rates for the American Indian or Alaska Native and Asian or Pacific Islander populations are known to be underestimated.

[7]Prior to 1997, excludes data from states lacking an Hispanic-origin item on the death certificate.

Table B-43. Death Rates for Heart Disease, by Sex, Race, Hispanic Origin, and Age, Selected Years, 1950–2005—*Continued*

(Rate per 100,000 population.)

Sex, race, Hispanic origin, and age	1950[1,2]	1960[1,2]	1970[2]	1980[2]	1990[2]	2000[3]	2001	2002	2003	2004	2005
Hispanic or Latina Female[5,7]											
All ages, age-adjusted[4]	—	—	—	—	177.2	163.7	161.0	149.7	145.8	130.0	129.1
All ages, crude	—	—	—	—	79.4	71.5	71.8	69.7	69.6	64.1	66.2
45–54 years	—	—	—	—	43.5	28.2	27.9	30.2	27.0	27.0	26.2
55–64 years	—	—	—	—	153.2	111.2	107.2	105.7	102.1	93.1	92.6
65–74 years	—	—	—	—	460.4	366.3	363.1	346.4	330.6	305.5	305.9
75–84 years	—	—	—	—	1,259.7	1,169.4	1,155.7	1,090.8	1,067.0	962.7	973.4
85 years and over	—	—	—	—	4,440.3	4,605.8	4,521.1	4,032.8	3,962.5	3,421.2	3,341.3
White, Not Hispanic or Latina Female[7]											
All ages, age-adjusted[4]	—	—	—	—	252.6	206.8	200.0	193.7	187.1	175.1	170.3
All ages, crude	—	—	—	—	320.0	304.9	298.4	292.3	285.1	269.1	266.4
45–54 years	—	—	—	—	50.2	41.9	42.7	42.6	42.4	42.2	42.4
55–64 years	—	—	—	—	193.6	142.9	136.0	132.0	126.6	118.9	116.1
65–74 years	—	—	—	—	584.7	448.5	431.8	417.4	394.8	368.6	354.6
75–84 years	—	—	—	—	1,890.2	1,458.9	1,414.7	1,377.2	1,324.0	1,241.2	1,203.6
85 years and over	—	—	—	—	6,615.2	5,822.7	5,601.6	5,384.5	5,232.2	4,862.4	4,745.1

— = Data not available.

[1]Includes deaths of persons who were not residents of the 50 states and the District of Columbia.

[2]Underlying cause of death was coded according to the Sixth Revision of the *International Classification of Diseases* in 1950, Seventh Revision in 1960, Eighth Revision in 1970, and Ninth Revision in 1980–1998.

[3]Starting with 1999 data, cause of death is coded according to the *International Classification of Diseases*.

[4]Age-adjusted rates are calculated using the year 2000 standard population. Prior to 2003, age-adjusted rates were calculated using standard million proportions based on rounded population numbers. Starting with 2003 data, unrounded population numbers are used to calculate age-adjusted rates.

[5]The race groups, White, Black, Asian or Pacific Islander, and American Indian or Alaska Native, include persons of Hispanic and non-Hispanic origin. Persons of Hispanic origin may be of any race. Death rates for the American Indian or Alaska Native and Asian or Pacific Islander populations are known to be underestimated.

[7]Prior to 1997, excludes data from states lacking an Hispanic-origin item on the death certificate.

Table B-44. Death Rates for Cerebrovascular Diseases, by Sex, Race, Hispanic Origin, and Age, Selected Years, 1950–2005

(Rate per 100,000 population.)

Sex, race, Hispanic origin, and age	1950[1,2]	1960[1,2]	1970[2]	1980[2]	1990[2]	2000[3]	2001	2002	2003	2004	2005
All Persons											
All ages, age-adjusted[4]	180.7	177.9	147.7	96.2	65.3	60.9	57.9	56.2	53.5	50.0	46.6
All ages, crude	104.0	108.0	101.9	75.0	57.8	59.6	57.4	56.4	54.2	51.1	48.4
Under 1 year	5.1	4.1	5.0	4.4	3.8	3.3	2.7	2.9	2.5	3.1	3.1
1–4 years	0.9	0.8	1.0	0.5	0.3	0.3	0.4	0.3	0.3	0.3	0.4
5–14 years	0.5	0.7	0.7	0.3	0.2	0.2	0.2	0.2	0.2	0.2	0.2
15–24 years	1.6	1.8	1.6	1.0	0.6	0.5	0.5	0.4	0.5	0.5	0.5
25–34 years	4.2	4.7	4.5	2.6	2.2	1.5	1.5	1.4	1.5	1.4	1.4
35–44 years	18.7	14.7	15.6	8.5	6.4	5.8	5.5	5.4	5.5	5.4	5.2
45–54 years	70.4	49.2	41.6	25.2	18.7	16.0	15.1	15.1	15.0	14.9	15.0
55–64 years	194.2	147.3	115.8	65.1	47.9	41.0	38.0	37.2	35.6	34.3	33.0
65–74 years	554.7	469.2	384.1	219.0	144.2	128.6	123.4	120.3	112.9	107.8	101.1
75–84 years	1,499.6	1,491.3	1,254.2	786.9	498.0	461.3	443.9	431.0	410.7	386.2	359.0
85 years and over	2,990.1	3,680.5	3,014.3	2,283.7	1,628.9	1,589.2	1,500.2	1,445.9	1,370.1	1,245.9	1,141.8
Male											
All ages, age-adjusted[4]	186.4	186.1	157.4	102.2	68.5	62.4	59.0	56.5	54.1	50.4	46.9
All ages, crude	102.5	104.5	94.5	63.4	46.7	46.9	45.2	44.2	42.9	40.7	38.8
Under 1 year	6.4	5.0	5.8	5.0	4.4	3.8	3.1	3.2	2.8	3.4	3.5
1–4 years	1.1	0.9	1.2	0.4	0.3	*	0.3	0.4	0.3	0.3	0.5
5–14 years	0.5	0.7	0.8	0.3	0.2	0.2	0.2	0.2	0.2	0.2	0.3
15–24 years	1.8	1.9	1.8	1.1	0.7	0.5	0.5	0.5	0.5	0.5	0.4
25–34 years	4.2	4.5	4.4	2.6	2.1	1.5	1.6	1.4	1.6	1.4	1.5
35–44 years	17.5	14.6	15.7	8.7	6.8	5.8	5.7	5.3	5.8	5.6	5.2
45–54 years	67.9	52.2	44.4	27.2	20.5	17.5	16.7	16.7	16.7	16.7	16.5
55–64 years	205.2	163.8	138.7	74.6	54.3	47.2	43.4	42.7	40.8	39.5	38.5
65–74 years	589.6	530.7	449.5	258.6	166.6	145.0	140.4	135.0	127.8	121.1	113.6
75–84 years	1,543.6	1,555.9	1,361.6	866.3	551.1	490.8	467.3	445.9	431.4	402.9	372.9
85 years and over	3,048.6	3,643.1	2,895.2	2,193.6	1,528.5	1,484.3	1,380.2	1,317.9	1,236.0	1,118.1	1,023.3
Female											
All ages, age-adjusted[4]	175.8	170.7	140.0	91.7	62.6	59.1	56.4	55.2	52.3	48.9	45.6
All ages, crude	105.6	111.4	109.0	85.9	68.4	71.8	69.2	68.2	65.1	61.2	57.8
Under 1 year	3.7	3.2	4.0	3.8	3.1	2.7	2.3	2.5	2.2	2.8	2.6
1–4 years	0.7	0.7	0.7	0.5	0.3	0.4	0.4	0.3	0.3	*	0.3
5–14 years	0.4	0.6	0.6	0.3	0.2	0.2	0.2	0.2	0.1	0.2	0.2
15–24 years	1.5	1.6	1.4	0.8	0.6	0.5	0.5	0.3	0.5	0.5	0.5
25–34 years	4.3	4.9	4.7	2.6	2.2	1.5	1.5	1.4	1.4	1.4	1.2
35–44 years	19.9	14.8	15.6	8.4	6.1	5.7	5.4	5.5	5.3	5.1	5.1
45–54 years	72.9	46.3	39.0	23.3	17.0	14.5	13.6	13.6	13.4	13.1	13.6
55–64 years	183.1	131.8	95.3	56.8	42.2	35.3	32.9	32.1	30.9	29.5	27.9
65–74 years	522.1	415.7	333.3	188.7	126.7	115.1	109.3	108.1	100.5	96.6	90.5
75–84 years	1,462.2	1,441.1	1,183.1	740.1	466.2	442.1	428.6	421.2	396.8	374.9	349.5
85 years and over	2,949.4	3,704.4	3,081.0	2,323.1	1,667.6	1,632.0	1,550.4	1,501.5	1,429.4	1,303.4	1,196.1
White Male[5]											
All ages, age-adjusted[4]	182.1	181.6	153.7	98.7	65.5	59.8	56.5	54.2	51.7	48.1	44.7
All ages, crude	100.5	102.7	93.5	63.1	46.9	48.4	46.6	45.7	44.2	41.8	39.7
45–54 years	53.7	40.9	35.6	21.7	15.4	13.6	12.7	12.9	12.9	12.8	12.8
55–64 years	182.2	139.0	119.9	64.0	45.7	39.7	36.1	35.6	33.3	32.4	31.7
65–74 years	569.7	501.0	420.0	239.8	152.9	133.8	128.5	123.8	117.3	110.8	103.0
75–84 years	1,556.3	1,564.8	1,361.6	852.7	539.2	480.0	458.8	437.5	422.4	393.7	364.8
85 years and over	3,127.1	3,734.8	3,018.1	2,230.8	1,545.4	1,490.7	1,386.2	1,327.4	1,247.0	1,129.3	1,033.7
Black or African American Male[5]											
All ages, age-adjusted[4]	228.8	238.5	206.4	142.0	102.2	89.6	85.4	81.7	79.5	74.9	70.5
All ages, crude	122.0	122.9	108.8	73.0	53.0	46.1	44.6	43.5	43.2	41.5	40.3
45–54 years	211.9	166.1	136.1	82.1	68.4	49.5	48.8	46.5	46.9	44.8	44.8
55–64 years	522.8	439.9	343.4	189.7	141.7	115.4	111.9	110.3	112.1	107.4	103.7
65–74 years	783.6	899.2	780.1	472.3	326.9	268.5	269.2	262.9	237.4	235.2	224.3
75–84 years[6]	1,504.9	1,475.2	1,445.7	1,066.3	721.5	659.2	613.9	587.8	588.9	551.0	503.7
85 years and over	—	2,700.0	1,963.1	1,873.2	1,421.5	1,458.8	1,349.1	1,252.2	1,180.3	1,061.0	983.5
American Indian or Alaska Native Male[5]											
All ages, age-adjusted[4]	—	—	—	66.4	44.3	46.1	37.5	37.1	34.9	35.0	31.3
All ages, crude	—	—	—	23.1	16.0	16.8	14.2	15.4	15.6	15.6	15.8
45–54 years	—	—	—	*	*	13.3	12.6	15.4	15.5	14.0	13.7
55–64 years	—	—	—	72.0	39.8	48.6	24.1	34.5	30.7	29.9	36.0
65–74 years	—	—	—	170.5	120.3	144.7	131.5	96.6	101.4	109.4	113.0
75–84 years	—	—	—	523.9	325.9	373.3	247.8	276.4	280.7	312.0	229.4
85 years and over	—	—	—	1,384.7	949.8	834.9	833.0	768.3	596.9	559.5	466.2

* = Figure does not meet standard of reliability or precision.

— = Data not available.

[1]Includes deaths of persons who were not residents of the 50 states and the District of Columbia.

[2]Underlying cause of death was coded according to the Sixth Revision of the *International Classification of Diseases* in 1950, Seventh Revision in 1960, Eighth Revision in 1970, and Ninth Revision in 1980–1998.

[3]Starting with 1999 data, cause of death is coded according to the *International Classification of Diseases, Tenth Edition.*

[4]Age-adjusted rates are calculated using the year 2000 standard population.

Prior to 2003, age-adjusted rates were calculated using standard million proportions based on rounded population numbers. Starting with 2003 data, unrounded population numbers are used to calculate age-adjusted rates.

[5]The race groups, White, Black, Asian or Pacific Islander, and American Indian or Alaska Native, include persons of Hispanic and non-Hispanic origin. Persons of Hispanic origin may be of any race. Death rates for the American Indian or Alaska Native and Asian or Pacific Islander populations are known to be underestimated.

[6]In 1950, rate is for the age group 75 years and over.

Table B-44. Death Rates for Cerebrovascular Diseases, by Sex, Race, Hispanic Origin, and Age, Selected Years, 1950–2005—Continued

(Rate per 100,000 population.)

Sex, race, Hispanic origin, and age	1950[1,2]	1960[1,2]	1970[2]	1980[2]	1990[2]	2000[3]	2001	2002	2003	2004	2005
Asian or Pacific Islander Male[5]											
All ages, age-adjusted[4]	—	—	—	71.4	59.1	58.0	55.3	50.8	48.5	44.2	41.5
All ages, crude	—	—	—	28.7	23.3	27.2	27.5	25.9	26.0	24.3	23.8
45–54 years	—	—	—	17.0	15.6	15.0	15.9	14.9	14.7	19.2	14.4
55–64 years	—	—	—	59.9	51.8	49.3	46.2	40.4	42.2	36.8	33.4
65–74 years	—	—	—	197.9	167.9	135.6	134.7	112.9	128.3	102.6	105.0
75–84 years	—	—	—	619.5	483.9	438.7	409.8	390.3	355.7	350.8	337.4
85 years and over	—	—	—	1,399.0	1,196.6	1,415.6	1,327.7	1,233.6	1,093.0	969.0	873.6
Hispanic or Latino Male[5,7]											
All ages, age-adjusted[4]	—	—	—	—	46.5	50.5	48.9	44.3	43.0	41.5	38.0
All ages, crude	—	—	—	—	15.6	15.8	15.7	15.0	14.9	15.0	14.4
45–54 years	—	—	—	—	20.0	18.1	18.7	18.6	18.1	17.5	17.8
55–64 years	—	—	—	—	49.2	48.8	43.5	45.0	43.5	42.9	40.3
65–74 years	—	—	—	—	126.4	136.1	127.2	124.6	113.9	114.4	106.2
75–84 years	—	—	—	—	356.6	392.9	386.3	338.5	337.1	323.3	294.0
85 years and over	—	—	—	—	866.3	1,029.9	1,005.6	856.7	837.4	778.9	692.4
White, Not Hispanic or Latino Male[7]											
All ages, age-adjusted[4]	—	—	—	—	66.3	59.9	56.5	54.4	51.9	48.2	44.8
All ages, crude	—	—	—	—	50.6	53.9	52.0	51.3	49.7	47.0	44.8
45–54 years	—	—	—	—	14.9	13.0	11.9	12.1	12.1	12.1	12.1
55–64 years	—	—	—	—	45.1	38.7	35.1	34.5	32.1	31.1	30.7
65–74 years	—	—	—	—	154.5	133.1	128.0	123.2	116.9	110.0	102.4
75–84 years	—	—	—	—	547.3	482.3	460.5	441.1	426.0	396.9	368.2
85 years and over	—	—	—	—	1,578.7	1,505.9	1,399.0	1,345.9	1,264.2	1,145.3	1,050.5
White Female[5]											
All ages, age-adjusted[4]	169.7	165.0	135.5	89.0	60.3	57.3	54.5	53.4	50.5	47.2	44.0
All ages, crude	103.3	110.1	109.8	88.6	71.6	76.9	74.0	73.0	69.5	65.3	61.6
45–54 years	55.0	33.8	30.5	18.6	13.5	11.2	10.2	10.4	10.0	10.1	10.5
55–64 years	156.9	103.0	78.1	48.6	35.8	30.2	27.6	27.4	25.8	25.1	23.8
65–74 years	498.1	383.3	303.2	172.5	116.1	107.3	99.9	99.5	92.1	89.0	83.2
75–84 years	1,471.3	1,444.7	1,176.8	728.8	456.5	434.2	421.6	414.1	389.9	366.8	342.9
85 years and over	3,017.9	3,795.7	3,167.6	2,362.7	1,685.9	1,646.7	1,563.5	1,516.9	1,442.1	1,315.7	1,208.5
Black or African American Female[5]											
All ages, age-adjusted[4]	238.4	232.5	189.3	119.6	84.0	76.2	73.7	71.8	69.8	65.5	60.7
All ages, crude	128.3	127.7	112.2	77.8	60.7	58.3	56.9	55.8	54.8	51.9	49.1
45–54 years	248.9	166.2	119.4	61.8	44.1	38.1	37.3	35.7	36.0	33.9	35.0
55–64 years	567.7	452.0	272.4	138.4	96.9	76.4	74.4	70.1	71.8	65.0	59.8
65–74 years	754.4	830.5	673.5	361.7	236.7	190.9	189.5	181.2	175.3	166.8	153.7
75–84 years[6]	1,496.7	1,413.1	1,338.3	917.5	595.0	549.2	530.3	532.2	498.3	489.5	450.2
85 years and over	—	2,578.9	2,210.5	1,891.6	1,495.2	1,556.5	1,491.2	1,434.3	1,414.2	1,270.7	1,156.5
American Indian or Alaska Native Female[5]											
All ages, age-adjusted[4]	—	—	—	51.2	38.4	43.7	44.0	38.0	34.2	35.1	37.1
All ages, crude	—	—	—	22.0	19.3	21.5	23.3	21.5	19.9	21.3	23.9
45–54 years	—	—	—	*	*	14.4	15.1	13.5	14.6	10.8	17.7
55–64 years	—	—	—	*	40.7	37.9	30.4	33.1	26.0	24.5	35.8
65–74 years	—	—	—	128.3	100.5	79.5	133.3	112.4	94.8	110.9	115.2
75–84 years	—	—	—	404.2	282.0	391.1	359.9	304.8	304.7	258.8	287.9
85 years and over	—	—	—	1,095.5	776.2	931.5	830.5	689.9	569.1	710.1	627.3
Asian or Pacific Islander Female[5]											
All ages, age-adjusted[4]	—	—	—	60.8	54.9	49.1	48.2	45.4	42.6	38.9	36.3
All ages, crude	—	—	—	26.4	24.3	28.7	29.8	29.2	28.8	27.0	26.6
45–54 years	—	—	—	20.3	19.7	13.3	11.3	12.6	12.6	10.5	9.9
55–64 years	—	—	—	43.7	42.1	33.3	35.2	32.1	30.8	28.1	27.2
65–74 years	—	—	—	136.1	124.0	102.8	113.2	112.5	95.6	78.1	81.0
75–84 years	—	—	—	446.6	396.6	386.0	359.6	331.7	330.2	312.5	269.2
85 years and over	—	—	—	1,545.2	1,395.0	1,246.6	1,236.8	1,149.8	1,042.4	979.9	928.3

* = Figure does not meet standard of reliability or precision.

—— = Data not available.

[1]Includes deaths of persons who were not residents of the 50 states and the District of Columbia.

[2]Underlying cause of death was coded according to the Sixth Revision of the *International Classification of Diseases* in 1950, Seventh Revision in 1960, Eighth Revision in 1970, and Ninth Revision in 1980–1998.

[3]Starting with 1999 data, cause of death is coded according to the *International Classification of Diseases, Tenth Edition*.

[4]Age-adjusted rates are calculated using the year 2000 standard population.
Prior to 2003, age-adjusted rates were calculated using standard million proportions based on rounded population numbers.
Starting with 2003 data, unrounded population numbers are used to calculate age-adjusted rates.

[5]The race groups, White, Black, Asian or Pacific Islander, and American Indian or Alaska Native, include persons of Hispanic and non-Hispanic origin. Persons of Hispanic origin may be of any race. Death rates for the American Indian or Alaska Native and Asian or Pacific Islander populations are known to be underestimated.

[7]Prior to 1997, excludes data from states lacking an Hispanic-origin item on the death certificate.

Table B-44. Death Rates for Cerebrovascular Diseases, by Sex, Race, Hispanic Origin, and Age, Selected Years, 1950–2005—*Continued*

(Rate per 100,000 population.)

Sex, race, Hispanic origin, and age	1950[1,2]	1960[1,2]	1970[2]	1980[2]	1990[2]	2000[3]	2001	2002	2003	2004	2005
Hispanic or Latina Female[5,7]											
All ages, age-adjusted[4]	—	—	—	—	43.7	43.0	41.6	38.6	38.1	35.4	33.5
All ages, crude	—	—	—	—	20.1	19.4	19.1	18.4	18.6	17.9	17.7
45–54 years	—	—	—	—	15.2	12.4	13.1	12.0	11.7	11.8	12.1
55–64 years	—	—	—	—	38.5	31.9	28.2	27.6	27.8	27.7	27.1
65–74 years	—	—	—	—	102.6	95.2	89.6	85.6	86.0	83.0	75.8
75–84 years	—	—	—	—	308.5	311.3	310.7	307.2	302.8	272.2	262.6
85 years and over	—	—	—	—	1,055.3	1,108.9	1,061.2	918.5	902.3	830.4	762.5
White, not Hispanic or Latina Female[7]											
All ages, age-adjusted[4]	—	—	—	—	61.0	57.6	54.8	53.9	50.8	47.7	44.4
All ages, crude	—	—	—	—	77.2	85.5	82.6	82.1	78.2	73.7	69.6
45–54 years	—	—	—	—	13.2	10.9	9.8	10.1	9.7	9.8	10.2
55–64 years	—	—	—	—	35.7	29.9	27.4	27.2	25.5	24.7	23.3
65–74 years	—	—	—	—	116.9	107.6	100.3	100.2	92.1	89.0	83.6
75–84 years	—	—	—	—	461.9	438.3	425.6	418.4	393.6	371.6	347.2
85 years and over	—	—	—	—	1,714.7	1,661.6	1,577.4	1,536.7	1,461.3	1,335.1	1,227.3

* = Figure does not meet standard of reliability or precision.

—— = Data not available.

[1]Includes deaths of persons who were not residents of the 50 states and the District of Columbia.

[2]Underlying cause of death was coded according to the Sixth Revision of the *International Classification of Diseases* in 1950, Seventh Revision in 1960, Eighth Revision in 1970, and Ninth Revision in 1980–1998.

[3]Starting with 1999 data, cause of death is coded according to the *International Classification of Diseases, Tenth Edition.*

[4]Age-adjusted rates are calculated using the year 2000 standard population.

Prior to 2003, age-adjusted rates were calculated using standard million proportions based on rounded population numbers.

Starting with 2003 data, unrounded population numbers are used to calculate age-adjusted rates.

[5]The race groups, White, Black, Asian or Pacific Islander, and American Indian or Alaska Native, include persons of Hispanic and non-Hispanic origin. Persons of Hispanic origin may be of any race. Death rates for the American Indian or Alaska Native and Asian or Pacific Islander populations are known to be underestimated.

[7]Prior to 1997, excludes data from states lacking an Hispanic-origin item on the death certificate.

Table B-45. Death Rates for Malignant Neoplasms, by Sex, Race, Hispanic Origin, and Age, Selected Years, 1950–2005

(Rate per 100,000 population.)

Sex, race, Hispanic origin, and age	1950[1,2]	1960[1,2]	1970[2]	1980[2]	1990[2]	2000[3]	2001	2002	2003	2004	2005
All Persons											
All ages, age-adjusted[4]	193.9	193.9	198.6	207.9	216.0	199.6	196.0	193.5	190.1	185.8	183.8
All ages, crude	139.8	149.2	162.8	183.9	203.2	196.5	194.4	193.2	191.5	188.6	188.7
Under 1 year	8.7	7.2	4.7	3.2	2.3	2.4	1.6	1.8	1.9	1.8	1.8
1–4 years	11.7	10.9	7.5	4.5	3.5	2.7	2.7	2.6	2.5	2.5	2.3
5–14 years	6.7	6.8	6.0	4.3	3.1	2.5	2.5	2.6	2.6	2.5	2.5
15–24 years	8.6	8.3	8.3	6.3	4.9	4.4	4.3	4.3	4.0	4.1	4.1
25–34 years	20.0	19.5	16.5	13.7	12.6	9.8	10.1	9.7	9.4	9.1	9.0
35–44 years	62.7	59.7	59.5	48.6	43.3	36.6	36.8	35.8	35.0	33.4	33.2
45–54 years	175.1	177.0	182.5	180.0	158.9	127.5	126.5	123.8	122.2	119.0	118.6
55–64 years	390.7	396.8	423.0	436.1	449.6	366.7	356.5	351.1	343.0	333.4	326.9
65–74 years	698.8	713.9	754.2	817.9	872.3	816.3	802.8	792.1	770.3	755.1	742.7
75–84 years	1,153.3	1,127.4	1,169.2	1,232.3	1,348.5	1,335.6	1,315.8	1,311.9	1,302.5	1,280.4	1,274.8
85 years and over	1,451.0	1,450.0	1,320.7	1,594.6	1,752.9	1,819.4	1,765.6	1,723.9	1,698.2	1,653.3	1,637.7
Male											
All ages, age-adjusted[4]	208.1	225.1	247.6	271.2	280.4	248.9	243.7	238.9	233.3	227.7	225.1
All ages, crude	142.9	162.5	182.1	205.3	221.3	207.2	205.3	203.8	201.3	198.4	198.9
Under 1 year	9.7	7.7	4.4	3.7	2.4	2.6	1.5	2.0	1.7	1.8	2.1
1–4 years	12.5	12.4	8.3	5.2	3.7	3.0	2.9	2.7	2.8	2.6	2.6
5–14 years	7.4	7.6	6.7	4.9	3.5	2.7	2.5	2.9	2.8	2.7	2.7
15–24 years	9.7	10.2	10.4	7.8	5.7	5.1	5.0	4.9	4.6	4.8	4.8
25–34 years	17.7	18.8	16.3	13.4	12.6	9.2	9.3	9.2	8.9	8.6	8.8
35–44 years	45.6	48.9	53.0	44.0	38.5	32.7	32.6	31.5	30.8	29.1	28.9
45–54 years	156.2	170.8	183.5	188.7	162.5	130.9	130.3	128.0	127.4	124.3	121.6
55–64 years	413.1	459.9	511.8	520.8	532.9	415.8	405.2	399.8	386.8	376.7	369.5
65–74 years	791.5	890.5	1,006.8	1,093.2	1,122.2	1,001.9	984.6	964.8	931.7	907.6	899.1
75–84 years	1,332.6	1,389.4	1,588.3	1,790.5	1,914.4	1,760.6	1,727.1	1,711.3	1,695.4	1,662.1	1,649.7
85 years and over	1,668.3	1,741.2	1,720.8	2,369.5	2,739.9	2,710.7	2,613.6	2,491.1	2,413.8	2,349.5	2,319.3
Female											
All ages, age-adjusted[4]	182.3	168.7	163.2	166.7	175.7	167.6	164.7	163.1	160.9	157.4	155.6
All ages, crude	136.8	136.4	144.4	163.6	186.0	186.2	183.9	183.0	182.0	179.1	178.8
Under 1 year	7.6	6.8	5.0	2.7	2.2	2.3	1.8	1.6	2.1	1.9	1.5
1–4 years	10.8	9.3	6.7	3.7	3.2	2.5	2.5	2.4	2.1	2.4	2.0
5–14 years	6.0	6.0	5.2	3.6	2.8	2.2	2.4	2.4	2.4	2.2	2.2
15–24 years	7.6	6.5	6.2	4.8	4.1	3.6	3.5	3.6	3.4	3.4	3.3
25–34 years	22.2	20.1	16.7	14.0	12.6	10.4	10.9	10.2	9.9	9.6	9.1
35–44 years	79.3	70.0	65.6	53.1	48.1	40.4	41.0	40.0	39.1	37.7	37.5
45–54 years	194.0	183.0	181.5	171.8	155.5	124.2	122.7	119.8	117.1	113.8	115.8
55–64 years	368.2	337.7	343.2	361.7	375.2	321.3	311.5	306.0	302.3	293.2	287.4
65–74 years	612.3	560.2	557.9	607.1	677.4	663.6	652.2	648.5	635.3	627.1	610.9
75–84 years	1,000.7	924.1	891.9	903.1	1,010.3	1,058.5	1,045.4	1,046.7	1,040.1	1,023.5	1,020.3
85 years and over	1,299.7	1,263.9	1,096.7	1,255.7	1,372.1	1,456.4	1,410.7	1,391.1	1,381.9	1,340.1	1,324.6
White Male[5]											
All ages, age-adjusted[4]	210.0	224.7	244.8	265.1	272.2	243.9	239.2	235.2	230.1	224.4	222.3
All ages, crude	147.2	166.1	185.1	208.7	227.7	218.1	216.4	215.5	213.1	209.9	210.6
25–34 years	17.7	18.8	16.2	13.6	12.3	9.2	9.3	9.1	8.9	8.6	8.5
35–44 years	44.5	46.3	50.1	41.1	35.8	30.9	31.3	30.5	29.9	28.2	28.4
45–54 years	150.8	164.1	172.0	175.4	149.9	123.5	123.6	121.8	119.9	117.5	115.7
55–64 years	409.4	450.9	498.1	497.4	508.2	401.9	392.1	386.0	375.6	364.9	356.5
65–74 years	798.7	887.3	997.0	1,070.7	1,090.7	984.3	969.4	954.8	922.7	896.3	889.9
75–84 years	1,367.6	1,413.7	1,592.7	1,779.7	1,883.2	1,736.0	1,704.6	1,695.3	1,683.6	1,652.7	1,646.2
85 years and over	1,732.7	1,791.4	1,772.2	2,375.6	2,715.1	2,693.7	2,597.6	2,486.8	2,412.1	2,348.9	2,322.7
Black or African American Male[5]											
All ages, age-adjusted[4]	178.9	227.6	291.9	353.4	397.9	340.3	330.9	319.6	308.8	301.2	293.7
All ages, crude	106.6	136.7	171.6	205.5	221.9	188.5	184.5	181.5	178.3	176.2	175.4
25–34 years	18.0	18.4	18.8	14.1	15.7	10.1	10.5	11.2	10.3	10.0	11.9
35–44 years	55.7	72.9	81.3	73.8	64.3	48.4	44.6	43.0	41.7	38.4	36.2
45–54 years	211.7	244.7	311.2	333.0	302.6	214.2	204.8	197.3	207.0	197.0	186.1
55–64 years	490.8	579.7	689.2	812.5	859.2	626.4	604.2	610.3	583.8	569.2	568.3
65–74 years	636.5	938.5	1,168.9	1,417.2	1,613.9	1,363.8	1,335.3	1,274.7	1,221.5	1,209.7	1,183.8
75–84 years[6]	853.5	1,053.3	1,624.8	2,029.6	2,478.3	2,351.8	2,290.0	2,223.0	2,144.2	2,087.2	2,017.5
85 years and over	—	1,155.2	1,387.0	2,393.9	3,238.3	3,264.8	3,209.9	2,976.1	2,825.5	2,748.8	2,683.7

—— = Data not available.

[1]Includes deaths of persons who were not residents of the 50 states and the District of Columbia.

[2]Underlying cause of death was coded according to the Sixth Revision of the *International Classification of Diseases* in 1950, Seventh Revision in 1960, Eighth Revision in 1970, and Ninth Revision in 1980–1998.

[3]Starting with 1999 data, cause of death is coded according to *International Classification of Diseases, Tenth Edition.*

[4]Age-adjusted rates are calculated using the year 2000 standard population. Prior to 2003, age-adjusted rates were calculated using standard million proportions based on rounded population numbers. Starting with 2003 data, unrounded population numbers are used to calculate age-adjusted rates.

[5]The race groups, White, Black, Asian or Pacific Islander, and American Indian or Alaska Native, include persons of Hispanic and non-Hispanic origin. Persons of Hispanic origin may be of any race. Death rates for the American Indian or Alaska Native and Asian or Pacific Islander populations are known to be underestimated.

[6]In 1950, rate is for the age group 75 years and over.

Table B-45. Death Rates for Malignant Neoplasms, by Sex, Race, Hispanic Origin, and Age, Selected Years, 1950–2005—Continued

(Rate per 100,000 population.)

Sex, race, Hispanic origin, and age	1950[1,2]	1960[1,2]	1970[2]	1980[2]	1990[2]	2000[3]	2001	2002	2003	2004	2005
American Indian or Alaska Native male[5]											
All ages, age-adjusted[4]	—	—	—	140.5	145.8	155.8	155.3	141.9	139.9	147.1	147.6
All ages, crude..	—	—	—	58.1	61.4	67.0	72.4	70.4	70.3	78.9	82.2
25–34 years	—	—	—	*	*	*	*	*	*	*	*
35–44 years	—	—	—	*	22.8	21.4	22.9	18.9	19.0	18.1	26.9
45–54 years	—	—	—	86.9	86.9	70.3	77.1	76.1	81.9	86.3	81.7
55–64 years	—	—	—	213.4	246.2	255.6	256.0	261.4	222.7	268.6	269.1
65–74 years	—	—	—	613.0	530.6	648.0	673.9	604.9	565.4	642.0	622.2
75–84 years	—	—	—	936.4	1,038.4	1,152.5	1,093.0	1,069.3	995.2	1,060.0	1,020.7
85 years and over	—	—	—	1,471.2	1,654.4	1,584.2	1,487.5	1,036.3	1,459.1	1,134.1	1,302.6
Asian or Pacific Islander Male[5]											
All ages, age-adjusted[4]	—	—	—	165.2	172.5	150.8	147.0	137.9	137.2	136.3	133.0
All ages, crude..	—	—	—	81.9	82.7	85.2	87.0	84.0	84.2	85.9	86.7
25–34 years	—	—	—	6.3	9.2	7.4	7.1	7.9	7.6	5.9	7.2
35–44 years	—	—	—	29.4	27.7	26.1	24.8	22.7	21.7	23.6	20.0
45–54 years	—	—	—	108.2	92.6	78.5	83.9	82.8	77.0	77.2	75.9
55–64 years	—	—	—	298.5	274.6	229.2	234.8	224.7	196.1	198.7	199.4
65–74 years	—	—	—	581.2	687.2	559.4	515.1	481.7	498.1	496.8	492.2
75–84 years	—	—	—	1,147.6	1,229.9	1,086.1	1,095.9	1,012.7	1,056.9	1,021.6	991.4
85 years and over	—	—	—	1,798.7	1,837.0	1,823.2	1,676.4	1,544.3	1,545.6	1,552.4	1,488.6
Hispanic or Latino Male[5,7]											
All ages, age-adjusted[4]	—	—	—	—	174.7	171.7	168.2	161.4	156.5	151.2	152.7
All ages, crude..	—	—	—	—	65.5	61.3	62.2	61.2	61.5	60.9	63.0
25–34 years	—	—	—	—	8.0	6.9	6.3	6.3	6.8	6.4	6.5
35–44 years	—	—	—	—	22.5	20.1	21.7	18.4	18.2	18.6	17.8
45–54 years	—	—	—	—	96.6	79.4	81.5	78.4	81.1	77.4	75.9
55–64 years	—	—	—	—	294.0	253.1	253.5	254.3	246.5	239.0	236.9
65–74 years	—	—	—	—	655.5	651.2	642.8	622.3	617.6	585.8	603.5
75–84 years	—	—	—	—	1,233.4	1,306.4	1,258.3	1,190.8	1,163.9	1,174.2	1,161.8
85 years and over	—	—	—	—	2,019.4	2,049.7	1,967.4	1,869.0	1,668.6	1,508.8	1,601.5
White, Not Hispanic or Latino male[7]											
All ages, age-adjusted[4]	—	—	—	—	276.7	247.7	243.1	239.6	234.6	229.2	227.3
All ages, crude..	—	—	—	—	246.2	244.4	243.4	243.8	241.8	239.2	240.7
25–34 years	—	—	—	—	12.8	9.7	10.0	9.8	9.4	9.3	9.0
35–44 years	—	—	—	—	36.8	32.3	32.6	32.5	31.9	29.9	30.5
45–54 years	—	—	—	—	153.9	127.2	127.3	125.9	123.8	121.9	120.3
55–64 years	—	—	—	—	520.6	412.0	401.7	395.5	384.8	374.6	366.1
65–74 years	—	—	—	—	1,109.0	1,002.1	988.2	975.3	942.0	917.5	910.4
75–84 years	—	—	—	—	1,906.6	1,750.2	1,721.8	1,716.5	1,707.8	1,677.3	1,673.7
85 years and over	—	—	—	—	2,744.4	2,714.1	2,616.8	2,507.7	2,441.7	2,387.1	2,358.3
White Female[5]											
All ages, age-adjusted[4]	182.0	167.7	162.5	165.2	174.0	166.9	163.9	162.4	160.2	157.0	155.2
All ages, crude..	139.9	139.8	149.4	170.3	196.1	199.4	196.7	195.8	194.6	191.7	191.1
25–34 years	20.9	18.8	16.3	13.5	11.9	10.1	10.4	9.9	9.4	9.0	8.6
35–44 years	74.5	66.6	62.4	50.9	46.2	38.2	39.3	38.5	37.3	35.8	36.0
45–54 years	185.8	175.7	177.3	166.4	150.9	120.1	118.9	115.3	112.1	109.2	110.7
55–64 years	362.5	329.0	338.6	355.5	368.5	319.7	308.6	303.1	299.8	290.8	284.0
65–74 years	616.5	562.1	554.7	605.2	675.1	665.6	652.9	650.4	638.9	630.8	616.2
75–84 years	1,026.6	939.3	903.5	905.4	1,011.8	1,063.4	1,049.8	1,053.1	1,046.3	1,033.1	1,030.5
85 years and over	1,348.3	1,304.9	1,126.6	1,266.8	1,372.3	1,459.1	1,416.7	1,395.1	1,386.5	1,348.9	1,333.6
Black or African American Female[5]											
All ages, age-adjusted[4]	174.1	174.3	173.4	189.5	205.9	193.8	191.3	190.3	187.7	182.5	179.6
All ages, crude..	111.8	113.8	117.3	136.5	156.1	151.8	151.3	151.7	151.4	148.9	149.1
25–34 years	34.3	31.0	20.9	18.3	18.7	13.5	15.0	13.3	13.9	13.9	12.6
35–44 years	119.8	102.4	94.6	73.5	67.4	58.9	57.3	56.2	55.4	54.2	52.5
45–54 years	277.0	254.8	228.6	230.2	209.9	173.9	166.8	168.2	167.2	160.9	166.3
55–64 years	484.6	442.7	404.8	450.4	482.4	391.0	390.9	385.4	380.4	369.4	365.4
65–74 years	477.3	541.6	615.8	662.4	773.2	753.1	748.4	741.1	714.6	706.2	679.6
75–84 years[6]	605.3	696.3	763.3	923.9	1,059.9	1,124.0	1,125.0	1,123.1	1,116.9	1,083.6	1,071.9
85 years and over	—	728.9	791.5	1,159.9	1,431.3	1,527.7	1,457.5	1,468.0	1,475.3	1,387.7	1,365.8

* = Figure does not meet standard of reliability or precision.

— = Data not available.

[1]Includes deaths of persons who were not residents of the 50 states and the District of Columbia.

[2]Underlying cause of death was coded according to the Sixth Revision of the *International Classification of Diseases* in 1950, Seventh Revision in 1960, Eighth Revision in 1970, and Ninth Revision in 1980–1998.

[3]Starting with 1999 data, cause of death is coded according to *International Classification of Diseases, Tenth Edition.*

[4]Age-adjusted rates are calculated using the year 2000 standard population. Prior to 2003, age-adjusted rates were calculated using standard million proportions based on rounded population numbers. Starting with 2003 data, unrounded population numbers are used to calculate age-adjusted rates.

[5]The race groups, White, Black, Asian or Pacific Islander, and American Indian or Alaska Native, include persons of Hispanic and non-Hispanic origin. Persons of Hispanic origin may be of any race. Death rates for the American Indian or Alaska Native and Asian or Pacific Islander populations are known to be underestimated.

[6]In 1950, rate is for the age group 75 years and over.

[7]Prior to 1997, excludes data from states lacking an Hispanic-origin item on the death certificate.

Table B-45. Death Rates for Malignant Neoplasms, by Sex, Race, Hispanic Origin, and Age, Selected Years, 1950–2005—*Continued*

(Rate per 100,000 population.)

Sex, race, Hispanic origin, and age	1950[1,2]	1960[1,2]	1970[2]	1980[2]	1990[2]	2000[3]	2001	2002	2003	2004	2005
American Indian or Alaska Native Female[5]											
All ages, age-adjusted[4]	—	—	—	94.0	106.9	108.3	114.1	112.9	105.6	108.6	105.9
All ages, crude..	—	—	—	50.4	62.1	61.3	68.8	71.0	68.2	73.0	73.8
25–34 years	—	—	—	*	*	*	*	9.4	*	*	*
35–44 years	—	—	—	36.9	31.0	23.7	25.7	23.6	24.3	27.4	23.5
45–54 years	—	—	—	96.9	104.5	59.7	79.4	80.6	75.7	72.0	85.5
55–64 years	—	—	—	198.4	213.3	200.9	221.7	202.5	195.8	211.8	201.5
65–74 years	—	—	—	350.8	438.9	458.3	463.8	473.2	411.2	480.7	475.8
75–84 years	—	—	—	446.4	554.3	714.0	752.7	703.9	784.4	707.3	701.5
85 years and over	—	—	—	786.5	843.7	983.2	905.2	1,001.2	686.0	724.6	581.0
Asian or Pacific Islander Female[5]											
All ages, age-adjusted[4]	—	—	—	93.0	103.0	100.7	99.3	95.9	96.7	92.0	94.5
All ages, crude..	—	—	—	54.1	60.5	72.1	74.0	72.6	75.6	73.8	78.1
25–34 years	—	—	—	9.5	7.3	8.1	8.0	6.4	7.2	6.6	7.7
35–44 years	—	—	—	38.7	29.8	28.9	25.6	23.6	25.8	24.2	25.1
45–54 years	—	—	—	99.8	93.9	78.2	82.5	78.5	77.6	77.0	75.4
55–64 years	—	—	—	174.7	196.2	176.5	167.7	171.2	166.7	159.1	171.3
65–74 years	—	—	—	301.9	346.2	357.4	373.3	358.1	361.5	344.2	328.1
75–84 years	—	—	—	522.1	641.4	650.1	633.1	606.4	616.9	578.4	606.8
85 years and over	—	—	—	800.0	971.7	988.5	929.2	910.1	907.9	872.9	942.0
Hispanic or Latina Female[5,7]											
All ages, age-adjusted[4]	—	—	—	—	111.9	110.8	108.6	106.1	105.9	101.4	101.9
All ages, crude..	—	—	—	—	60.7	58.5	58.7	58.1	59.1	57.7	59.5
25–34 years	—	—	—	—	9.7	7.8	8.3	7.5	7.4	7.5	7.1
35–44 years	—	—	—	—	34.8	30.7	29.8	28.4	28.0	25.4	27.0
45–54 years	—	—	—	—	100.5	84.7	84.2	78.0	80.2	73.5	79.9
55–64 years	—	—	—	—	205.4	192.5	196.7	179.8	185.9	183.0	172.5
65–74 years	—	—	—	—	404.8	410.0	394.5	395.6	379.7	380.7	382.5
75–84 years	—	—	—	—	663.0	716.5	681.2	692.2	702.1	663.6	688.5
85 years and over	—	—	—	—	1,022.7	1,056.5	1,068.6	1,031.2	1,014.8	937.0	880.4
White, Not Hispanic or Latina Female[7]											
All ages, age-adjusted[4]	—	—	—	—	177.5	170.0	167.2	165.9	163.8	160.9	159.1
All ages, crude	—	—	—	—	210.6	220.6	218.4	218.5	217.6	215.3	215.1
25–34 years	—	—	—	—	11.9	10.5	10.7	10.3	9.8	9.3	8.9
35–44 years	—	—	—	—	47.0	38.9	40.4	39.9	38.6	37.5	37.5
45–54 years	—	—	—	—	154.9	123.0	121.9	118.7	115.1	112.9	113.9
55–64 years	—	—	—	—	379.5	328.9	317.3	312.8	308.9	299.8	293.6
65–74 years	—	—	—	—	688.5	681.0	669.7	667.7	657.6	649.8	634.4
75–84 years	—	—	—	—	1,027.2	1,075.3	1,064.4	1,068.3	1,062.4	1,052.0	1,049.5
85 years and over	—	—	—	—	1,385.7	1,468.7	1,425.1	1,405.4	1,399.1	1,364.5	1,353.2

* = Figure does not meet standard of reliability or precision.

—— = Data not available.

[1]Includes deaths of persons who were not residents of the 50 states and the District of Columbia.

[2]Underlying cause of death was coded according to the Sixth Revision of the *International Classification of Diseases* in 1950, Seventh Revision in 1960, Eighth Revision in 1970, and Ninth Revision in 1980–1998.

[3]Starting with 1999 data, cause of death is coded according to *International Classification of Diseases, Tenth Edition.*

[4]Age-adjusted rates are calculated using the year 2000 standard population. Prior to 2003, age-adjusted rates were calculated using standard million proportions based on rounded population numbers. Starting with 2003 data, unrounded population numbers are used to calculate age-adjusted rates.

[5]The race groups, White, Black, Asian or Pacific Islander, and American Indian or Alaska Native, include persons of Hispanic and non-Hispanic origin. Persons of Hispanic origin may be of any race. Death rates for the American Indian or Alaska Native and Asian or Pacific Islander populations are known to be underestimated.

[7]Prior to 1997, excludes data from states lacking an Hispanic-origin item on the death certificate.

Table B-46. Death Rates for Suicide, by Sex, Race, Hispanic Origin, and Age, Selected Years, 1950–2005

(Rate per 100,000 population.)

Sex, race, Hispanic origin, and age	1950[1,2]	1960[1,2]	1970[2]	1980[2]	1990[2]	2000[3]	2001	2002	2003	2004	2005
All Persons											
All ages, age-adjusted[4]	13.2	12.5	13.1	12.2	12.5	10.4	10.7	10.9	10.8	10.9	10.9
All ages, crude	11.4	10.6	11.6	11.9	12.4	10.4	10.8	11.0	10.8	11.0	11.0
Under 1 year		...	...	...	...	...	...	...	*	*	*
1–4 years	...	...	...	...	...	...	...	...	*	*	*
5–14 years	0.2	0.3	0.3	0.4	0.8	0.7	0.7	0.6	0.6	0.7	0.7
15–24 years	4.5	5.2	8.8	12.3	13.2	10.2	9.9	9.9	9.7	10.3	10.0
15–19 years	2.7	3.6	5.9	8.5	11.1	8.0	7.9	7.4	7.3	8.2	7.7
20–24 years	6.2	7.1	12.2	16.1	15.1	12.5	12.0	12.4	12.1	12.5	12.4
25–44 years	11.6	12.2	15.4	15.6	15.2	13.4	13.8	14.0	13.8	13.9	13.7
25–34 years	9.1	10.0	14.1	16.0	15.2	12.0	12.8	12.6	12.7	12.7	12.4
35–44 years	14.3	14.2	16.9	15.4	15.3	14.5	14.7	15.3	14.9	15.0	14.9
45–64 years	23.5	22.0	20.6	15.9	15.3	13.5	14.4	14.9	15.0	15.4	15.4
45–54 years	20.9	20.7	20.0	15.9	14.8	14.4	15.2	15.7	15.9	16.6	16.5
55–64 years	26.8	23.7	21.4	15.9	16.0	12.1	13.1	13.6	13.8	13.8	13.9
65 years and over	30.0	24.5	20.8	17.6	20.5	15.2	15.3	15.6	14.6	14.3	14.7
65–74 years	29.6	23.0	20.8	16.9	17.9	12.5	13.3	13.5	12.7	12.3	12.6
75–84 years	31.1	27.9	21.2	19.1	24.9	17.6	17.4	17.7	16.4	16.3	16.9
85 years and over	28.8	26.0	19.0	19.2	22.2	19.6	17.5	18.0	16.9	16.4	16.9
Male											
All ages, age-adjusted[4]	21.2	20.0	19.8	19.9	21.5	17.7	18.2	18.4	18.0	18.0	18.0
All ages, crude	17.8	16.5	16.8	18.6	20.4	17.1	17.6	17.9	17.6	17.7	17.7
Under 1 year	...	...	...	...	...	...	*	*	*		
1–4 years	...	...	...	...	...	...	*	*	*		
5–14 years	0.3	0.4	0.5	0.6	1.1	1.2	1.0	0.9	0.9	0.9	1.0
15–24 years	6.5	8.2	13.5	20.2	22.0	17.1	16.6	16.5	16.0	16.8	16.2
15–19 years	3.5	5.6	8.8	13.8	18.1	13.0	12.9	12.2	11.6	12.6	12.1
20–24 years	9.3	11.5	19.3	26.8	25.7	21.4	20.5	20.8	20.2	20.8	20.2
25–44 years	17.2	17.9	20.9	24.0	24.4	21.3	22.1	22.2	21.9	21.7	21.6
25–34 years	13.4	14.7	19.8	25.0	24.8	19.6	21.0	20.5	20.6	20.4	19.9
35–44 years	21.3	21.0	22.1	22.5	23.9	22.8	23.1	23.7	23.2	23.0	23.1
45–64 years	37.1	34.4	30.0	23.7	24.3	21.3	22.5	23.5	23.5	23.7	24.0
45–54 years	32.0	31.6	27.9	22.9	23.2	22.4	23.4	24.4	24.4	24.8	25.2
55–64 years	43.6	38.1	32.7	24.5	25.7	19.4	21.1	22.2	22.3	22.1	22.2
65 years and over	52.8	44.0	38.4	35.0	41.6	31.1	31.5	31.8	29.8	29.0	29.5
65–74 years	50.5	39.6	36.0	30.4	32.2	22.7	24.6	24.7	23.4	22.6	22.7
75–84 years	58.3	52.5	42.8	42.3	56.1	38.6	37.8	38.1	35.1	34.8	35.8
85 years and over	58.3	57.4	42.4	50.6	65.9	57.5	51.1	50.7	47.8	45.0	45.0
Female											
All ages, age-adjusted[4]	5.6	5.6	7.4	5.7	4.8	4.0	4.0	4.2	4.2	4.5	4.4
All ages, crude	5.1	4.9	6.6	5.5	4.8	4.0	4.1	4.3	4.3	4.6	4.5
Under 1 year	...	...	...	...	...	...	*	*	*		
1–4 years	...	...	...	...	...	...	*	*	*		
5–14 years	0.1	0.1	0.2	0.2	0.4	0.3	0.3	0.3	0.3	0.5	0.3
15–24 years	2.6	2.2	4.2	4.3	3.9	3.0	2.9	2.9	3.0	3.6	3.5
15–19 years	1.8	1.6	2.9	3.0	3.7	2.7	2.7	2.4	2.7	3.5	3.0
20–24 years	3.3	2.9	5.7	5.5	4.1	3.2	3.1	3.5	3.4	3.6	4.0
25–44 years	6.2	6.6	10.2	7.7	6.2	5.4	5.5	5.8	5.7	6.0	5.8
25–34 years	4.9	5.5	8.6	7.1	5.6	4.3	4.4	4.6	4.6	4.7	4.7
35–44 years	7.5	7.7	11.9	8.5	6.8	6.4	6.4	6.9	6.6	7.1	6.8
45–64 years	9.9	10.2	12.0	8.9	7.1	6.2	6.6	6.7	7.0	7.6	7.2
45–54 years	9.9	10.2	12.6	9.4	6.9	6.7	7.2	7.4	7.7	8.6	8.0
55–64 years	9.9	10.2	11.4	8.4	7.3	5.4	5.7	5.7	5.9	6.1	6.1
65 years and over	9.4	8.4	8.1	6.1	6.4	4.0	3.9	4.1	3.8	3.8	4.0
65–74 years	10.1	8.4	9.0	6.5	6.7	4.0	3.9	4.1	3.8	3.8	4.0
75–84 years	8.1	8.9	7.0	5.5	6.3	4.0	4.0	4.2	4.0	3.9	4.0
85 years and over	8.2	6.0	5.9	5.5	5.4	4.2	3.4	3.8	3.3	3.6	4.0
White Male[5]											
All ages, age-adjusted[4]	22.3	21.1	20.8	20.9	22.8	19.1	19.6	20.0	19.6	19.6	19.6
All ages, crude	19.0	17.6	18.0	19.9	22.0	18.8	19.5	19.9	19.5	19.6	19.7
15–24 years	6.6	8.6	13.9	21.4	23.2	17.9	17.6	17.7	16.9	17.9	17.3
25–44 years	17.9	18.5	21.5	24.6	25.4	22.9	24.0	24.0	23.9	23.8	23.5
45–64 years	39.3	36.5	31.9	25.0	26.0	23.2	24.7	25.9	26.1	26.1	26.6
65 years and over	55.8	46.7	41.1	37.2	44.2	33.3	33.7	34.2	32.1	31.2	32.1
65–74 years	53.2	42.0	38.7	32.5	34.2	24.3	26.3	26.8	25.2	24.2	24.9
75–84 years	61.9	55.7	45.5	45.5	60.2	41.1	40.2	40.6	37.5	37.1	38.4
85 years and over	61.9	61.3	45.8	52.8	70.3	61.6	55.0	53.9	51.4	48.4	48.2

* = Figure does not meet standards of reliability or precision.

... = Not applicable.

[1]Includes deaths of persons who were not residents of the 50 states and the District of Columbia.

[2]Underlying cause of death was coded according to the Sixth Revision of the *International Classification of Diseases* in 1950, Seventh Revision in 1960, Eighth Revision in 1970, and Ninth Revision in 1980–1998.

[3]Starting with 1999 data, cause of death is coded according to the *International Classification of Diseases, Tenth Edition.*

[4]Age-adjusted rates are calculated using the year 2000 standard population. Prior to 2003, age-adjusted rates were calculated using standard million proportions based on rounded population numbers. Starting with 2003 data, unrounded population numbers are used to calculate age-adjusted rates.

[5]The race groups, white, black, Asian or Pacific Islander, and American Indian or Alaska Native, include persons of Hispanic and non-Hispanic origin. Persons of Hispanic origin may be of any race. Death rates for the American Indian or Alaska Native and Asian or Pacific Islander populations are known to be underestimated.

Table B-46. Death Rates for Suicide, by Sex, Race, Hispanic Origin, and Age, Selected Years, 1950–2005—Continued

(Rate per 100,000 population.)

Sex, race, Hispanic origin, and age	1950[1,2]	1960[1,2]	1970[2]	1980[2]	1990[2]	2000[3]	2001	2002	2003	2004	2005
Black or African American Male[5]											
All ages, age-adjusted[4]	7.5	8.4	10.0	11.4	12.8	10.0	9.8	9.8	9.2	9.6	9.2
All ages, crude	6.3	6.4	8.0	10.3	12.0	9.4	9.2	9.1	8.8	9.0	8.7
15–24 years	4.9	4.1	10.5	12.3	15.1	14.2	13.0	11.3	12.1	12.2	11.5
25–44 years	9.8	12.6	16.1	19.2	19.6	14.3	14.4	15.1	14.3	13.7	13.7
45–64 years	12.7	13.0	12.4	11.8	13.1	9.9	9.7	9.6	9.0	10.1	9.4
65 years and over	9.0	9.9	8.7	11.4	14.9	11.5	11.5	11.7	9.2	11.3	10.2
65–74 years	10.0	11.3	8.7	11.1	14.7	11.1	10.7	9.7	8.3	9.8	8.4
75–84 years[6]	*	*	*	10.5	14.4	12.1	13.5	13.8	11.3	15.0	12.8
85 years and over	—	*	*	*	*	*	*	*	*	*	*
American Indian or Alaska Native Male[5]											
All ages, age-adjusted[4]	—	—	—	19.3	20.1	16.0	17.4	16.4	16.6	18.7	18.9
All ages, crude	—	—	—	20.9	20.9	15.9	17.0	16.8	17.1	19.5	19.8
15–24 years	—	—	—	45.3	49.1	26.2	24.7	27.9	27.2	30.7	32.7
25–44 years	—	—	—	31.2	27.8	24.5	27.6	26.8	30.1	30.8	29.4
45–64 years	—	—	—	*	*	15.4	17.0	14.1	9.5	16.0	16.8
65 years and over	—	—	—	*	*	*	*	*	*	*	*
Asian or Pacific Islander Male[5]											
All ages, age-adjusted[4]	—	—	—	10.7	9.6	8.6	8.4	8.0	8.5	8.4	7.3
All ages, crude	—	—	—	8.8	8.7	7.9	7.7	7.6	8.0	7.9	7.2
15–24 years	—	—	—	10.8	13.5	9.1	9.1	8.7	9.0	9.3	7.2
25–44 years	—	—	—	11.0	10.6	9.9	9.3	9.3	9.2	8.4	9.5
45–64 years	—	—	—	13.0	9.7	9.7	8.2	9.1	10.0	11.1	8.9
65 years and over	—	—	—	18.6	16.8	15.4	18.3	14.4	17.5	15.1	11.0
Hispanic or Latino Male[5,7]											
All ages, age-adjusted[4]	—	—	—	—	13.7	10.3	10.1	9.9	9.7	9.8	9.4
All ages, crude	—	—	—	—	11.4	8.4	8.3	8.3	8.3	8.6	8.3
15–24 years	—	—	—	—	14.7	10.9	9.5	10.6	11.2	12.8	12.1
25–44 years	—	—	—	—	16.2	11.2	11.8	10.9	10.9	11.0	11.2
45–64 years	—	—	—	—	16.1	12.0	11.4	11.9	12.0	11.8	10.7
65 years and over	—	—	—	—	23.4	19.5	18.5	17.5	15.6	15.9	14.1
White, Not Hispanic or Latino Male[7]											
All ages, age-adjusted[4]	—	—	—	—	23.5	20.2	21.0	21.4	21.0	21.0	21.2
All ages, crude	—	—	—	—	23.1	20.4	21.4	21.9	21.6	21.6	22.0
15–24 years	—	—	—	—	24.4	19.5	19.6	19.3	18.2	19.0	18.4
25–44 years	—	—	—	—	26.4	25.1	26.4	26.9	26.8	26.8	26.6
45–64 years	—	—	—	—	26.8	24.0	25.9	27.2	27.4	27.4	28.2
65 years and over	—	—	—	—	45.4	33.9	34.4	35.1	33.1	32.1	33.2
White Female[5]											
All ages, age-adjusted[4]	6.0	5.9	7.9	6.1	5.2	4.3	4.5	4.7	4.6	5.0	4.9
All ages, crude	5.5	5.3	7.1	5.9	5.3	4.4	4.6	4.8	4.7	5.1	5.0
15–24 years	2.7	2.3	4.2	4.6	4.2	3.1	3.1	3.1	3.1	3.8	3.7
25–44 years	6.6	7.0	11.0	8.1	6.6	6.0	6.2	6.6	6.4	6.6	6.5
45–64 years	10.6	10.9	13.0	9.6	7.7	6.9	7.3	7.5	7.8	8.5	8.1
65 years and over	9.9	8.8	8.5	6.4	6.8	4.3	4.1	4.3	4.0	4.0	4.2
Black or African American Female[5]											
All ages, age-adjusted[4]	1.8	2.0	2.9	2.4	2.4	1.8	1.8	1.6	1.9	1.8	1.9
All ages, crude	1.5	1.6	2.6	2.2	2.3	1.7	1.7	1.5	1.8	1.8	1.8
15–24 years	1.8	*	3.8	2.3	2.3	2.2	1.3	1.7	2.0	2.2	1.7
25–44 years	2.3	3.0	4.8	4.3	3.8	2.6	2.6	2.4	2.8	2.9	2.8
45–64 years	2.7	3.1	2.9	2.5	2.9	2.1	2.6	2.1	2.4	2.2	2.5
65 years and over	*	*	2.6	*	1.9	1.3	1.6	1.1	1.4	*	1.4
American Indian or Alaska Native Female[5]											
All ages, age-adjusted[4]	—	—	—	4.7	3.6	3.8	4.0	4.1	3.5	5.9	4.6
All ages, crude	—	—	—	4.7	3.7	4.0	4.1	4.3	3.7	6.2	5.0
15–24 years	—	—	—	*	*	*	*	7.4	8.3	10.5	10.1
25–44 years	—	—	—	10.7	*	7.2	6.1	5.6	4.6	9.8	7.4
45–64 years	—	—	—	*	*	*	*	*	*	*	*
65 years and over	—	—	—	*	*	*	*	*	*	*	*

* = Figure does not meet standards of reliability or precision.

—— = Data not available.

[1]Includes deaths of persons who were not residents of the 50 states and the District of Columbia.

[2]Underlying cause of death was coded according to the Sixth Revision of the *International Classification of Diseases* in 1950, Seventh Revision in 1960, Eighth Revision in 1970, and Ninth Revision in 1980–1998.

[3]Starting with 1999 data, cause of death is coded according to the *International Classification of Diseases, Tenth Edition.*

[4]Age-adjusted rates are calculated using the year 2000 standard population. Prior to 2003, age-adjusted rates were calculated using standard million proportions based on rounded population numbers. Starting with 2003 data, unrounded population numbers are used to calculate age-adjusted rates.

[5]The race groups, white, black, Asian or Pacific Islander, and American Indian or Alaska Native, include persons of Hispanic and non-Hispanic origin. Persons of Hispanic origin may be of any race. Death rates for the American Indian or Alaska Native and Asian or Pacific Islander populations are known to be underestimated

[6]In 1950, rate is for the age group 75 years and over.

Table B-46. Death Rates for Suicide, by Sex, Race, Hispanic Origin, and Age, Selected Years, 1950–2005— *Continued*

(Rate per 100,000 population.)

Sex, race, Hispanic origin, and age	1950[1,2]	1960[1,2]	1970[2]	1980[2]	1990[2]	2000[3]	2001	2002	2003	2004	2005
Asian or Pacific Islander Female[5]											
All ages, age-adjusted[4]	—	—	—	5.5	4.1	2.8	2.9	3.0	3.1	3.5	3.3
All ages, crude	—	—	—	4.7	3.4	2.7	2.8	2.9	3.1	3.4	3.2
15–24 years	—	—	—	*	3.9	2.7	3.6	*	3.4	2.8	3.7
25–44 years	—	—	—	5.4	3.8	3.3	2.9	3.3	3.4	4.1	3.4
45–64 years	—	—	—	7.9	5.0	3.2	3.8	3.8	4.3	4.5	3.8
65 years and over	—	—	—	*	8.5	5.2	4.9	6.8	4.6	6.4	6.8
Hispanic or Latina Female[5,7]											
All ages, age-adjusted[4]	—	—	—	—	2.3	1.7	1.6	1.8	1.7	2.0	1.8
All ages, crude	—	—	—	—	2.2	1.5	1.5	1.6	1.5	1.8	1.7
15–24 years	—	—	—	—	3.1	2.0	2.3	2.1	2.2	2.5	2.7
25–44 years	—	—	—	—	3.1	2.1	2.0	2.0	2.0	2.3	2.2
45–64 years	—	—	—	—	2.5	2.5	2.3	2.5	2.4	3.1	2.1
65 years and over	—	—	—	—	*	*	*	1.9	*	1.8	2.0
White, not Hispanic or Latina Female[7]											
All ages, age-adjusted[4]	—	—	—	—	5.4	4.7	4.9	5.1	5.0	5.4	5.3
All ages, crude	—	—	—	—	5.6	4.9	5.0	5.3	5.3	5.7	5.6
15–24 years	—	—	—	—	4.3	3.3	3.3	3.4	3.3	4.0	3.9
25–44 years	—	—	—	—	7.0	6.7	6.9	7.5	7.2	7.5	7.4
45–64 years	—	—	—	—	8.0	7.3	7.8	8.0	8.3	9.1	8.7
65 years and over	—	—	—	—	7.0	4.4	4.3	4.5	4.2	4.1	4.3

* = Figure does not meet standards of reliability or precision.

—— = Data not available.

[1]Includes deaths of persons who were not residents of the 50 states and the District of Columbia.

[2]Underlying cause of death was coded according to the Sixth Revision of the *International Classification of Diseases* in 1950, Seventh Revision in 1960, Eighth Revision in 1970, and Ninth Revision in 1980–1998.

[3]Starting with 1999 data, cause of death is coded according to the *International Classification of Diseases, Tenth Edition*.

[4]Age-adjusted rates are calculated using the year 2000 standard population. Prior to 2003, age-adjusted rates were calculated using standard million proportions based on rounded population numbers. Starting with 2003 data, unrounded population numbers are used to calculate age-adjusted rates.

[5]The race groups, White, Black, Asian or Pacific Islander, and American Indian or Alaska Native, include persons of Hispanic and non-Hispanic origin. Persons of Hispanic origin may be of any race. Death rates for the American Indian or Alaska Native and Asian or Pacific Islander populations are known to be underestimated.

[7]Prior to 1997, excludes data from states lacking an Hispanic-origin item on the death certificate.

Table B-47. Death Rates for Human Immunodeficiency Virus (HIV) Disease, by Sex, Race, Hispanic Origin, and Age, Selected Years, 1987–2005

(Rate per 100,000 population.)

Sex, race, Hispanic origin, and age	1987[1]	1990[1]	1995[1]	2000[2]	2001	2002	2003	2004	2005
All Persons									
All ages, age-adjusted[3]	5.6	10.2	16.2	5.2	5.0	4.9	4.7	4.5	4.2
All ages, crude	5.6	10.1	16.2	5.1	5.0	4.9	4.7	4.4	4.2
Under 1 year	2.3	2.7	1.5	*	*	*	*	*	*
1–4 years	0.7	0.8	1.3	*	*	*	*	*	*
5–14 years	0.1	0.2	0.5	0.1	0.1	0.1	0.1	0.1	*
15–24 years	1.3	1.5	1.7	0.5	0.6	0.4	0.4	0.5	0.4
25–34 years	11.7	19.7	28.3	6.1	5.3	4.6	4.0	3.7	3.3
35–44 years	14.0	27.4	44.2	13.1	13.0	12.7	12.0	10.9	9.9
45–54 years	8.0	15.2	26.0	11.0	10.5	11.2	10.9	10.6	10.6
55–64 years	3.5	6.2	10.9	5.1	5.2	5.1	5.4	5.4	5.3
65–74 years	1.3	2.0	3.6	2.2	2.1	2.2	2.4	2.4	2.3
75-84 years	0.8	0.7	0.7	0.7	0.7	0.8	0.7	0.8	0.8
85 years and over	*	*	*	*	*	*	*	*	*
Male									
All ages, age-adjusted[3]	10.4	18.5	27.3	7.9	7.5	7.4	7.1	6.6	6.2
All ages, crude	10.2	18.5	27.6	7.9	7.6	7.4	7.1	6.6	6.3
Under 1 year	2.2	2.4	1.7	*	*	*	*	*	*
1–4 years	0.7	0.8	1.2	*	*	*	*	*	*
5–14 years	0.2	0.3	0.5	0.1	0.1	*	*	*	*
15–24 years	2.2	2.2	2.0	0.5	0.5	0.4	0.4	0.5	0.4
25–34 years	20.7	34.5	45.5	8.0	7.1	5.9	5.1	4.5	4.0
35–44 years	26.3	50.2	75.5	19.8	19.5	18.8	17.5	15.7	14.3
45–54 years	15.5	29.1	46.2	17.8	16.8	17.7	17.2	16.3	16.4
55–64 years	6.8	12.0	19.7	8.7	8.6	8.5	9.1	9.0	8.8
65–74 years	2.4	3.7	6.4	3.8	3.5	3.9	4.0	4.0	4.1
75-84 years	1.2	1.1	1.3	1.3	1.5	1.4	1.5	1.4	1.4
85 years and over	*	*	*	*	*	*	*	*	*
Female									
All ages, age-adjusted[3]	1.1	2.2	5.3	2.5	2.5	2.5	2.4	2.4	2.3
All ages, crude	1.1	2.2	5.3	2.5	2.5	2.5	2.4	2.4	2.2
Under 1 year	2.5	3.0	1.2	*	*	*	*	*	*
1–4 years	0.7	0.8	1.5	*	*	*	*	*	*
5–14 years	*	0.2	0.5	0.1	*	*	*	*	*
15–24 years	0.3	0.7	1.4	0.4	0.6	0.4	0.4	0.4	0.3
25–34 years	2.8	4.9	10.9	4.2	3.5	3.3	2.8	2.8	2.6
35–44 years	2.1	5.2	13.3	6.5	6.7	6.7	6.5	6.2	5.6
45–54 years	0.8	1.9	6.6	4.4	4.4	4.8	4.8	5.2	5.1
55–64 years	0.5	1.1	2.8	1.8	2.0	1.9	2.1	2.0	2.0
65–74 years	0.5	0.8	1.4	0.8	0.9	0.8	1.0	1.0	0.9
75-84 years	0.5	0.4	0.3	0.3	*	0.3	0.3	0.5	0.4
85 years and over	*	*	*	*	*	*	*	*	*
All Ages, Age-Adjusted[4]									
White male	8.7	15.7	20.4	4.6	4.4	4.3	4.2	3.8	3.6
Black or African American male	26.2	46.3	89.0	35.1	33.8	33.3	31.3	29.2	28.2
American Indian or Alaska Native male	*	3.3	10.5	3.5	4.2	3.4	3.5	4.3	4.0
Asian or Pacific Islander male	2.5	4.3	6.0	1.2	1.2	1.5	1.1	1.2	1.0
Hispanic or Latino male[4,5]	18.8	28.8	40.8	10.6	9.7	9.1	9.2	8.2	7.5
White, not Hispanic or Latino male[4,5]	10.7	14.1	17.9	3.8	3.6	3.5	3.4	3.1	3.0
White female	0.6	1.1	2.5	1.0	0.9	0.9	0.9	0.9	0.8
Black or African American female	4.6	10.1	24.4	13.2	13.4	13.4	12.8	13.0	12.0
American Indian or Alaska Native female	*	*	2.5	1.0	*	*	1.5	1.5	1.5
Asian or Pacific Islander female	*	*	0.6	0.2	*	*	*	*	*
Hispanic or Latina female[4,5]	2.1	3.8	8.8	2.9	2.7	2.6	2.7	2.4	1.9
White, not Hispanic or Latina female[4,5]	0.5	0.7	1.7	0.7	0.6	0.6	0.6	0.6	0.6

* = Figure does not meet standard of reliability or precision.

[1]Categories for the coding and classification of human immunodeficiency virus (HIV) disease were introduced in the United States in 1987. For the period 1987–1998, underlying cause of death was coded according to the the *International Classification of Diseases, Ninth Edition.*

[2]Starting with 1999 data, cause of death is coded according to the *International Classification of Diseases, Tenth Edition.* To estimate change between 1998 and 1999, compare the 1999 rate with the comparability-modified rate for 1998.

[3]Age-adjusted rates are calculated using the year 2000 standard population. Prior to 2003, age-adjusted rates were calculated using standard million proportions based on rounded population numbers. Starting with 2003 data, unrounded population numbers are used to calculate age-adjusted rates.

[4]The race groups, White, Black, Asian or Pacific Islander, and American Indian or Alaska Native, include persons of Hispanic and non-Hispanic origin. Persons of Hispanic origin may be of any race. Death rates for the American Indian or Alaska Native and Asian or Pacific Islander populations are known to be underestimated.

[5]Prior to 1997, excludes data from states lacking an Hispanic-origin item on the death certificate.

Table B-47. Death Rates for Human Immunodeficiency Virus (HIV) Disease, by Sex, Race, Hispanic Origin, and Age, Selected Years, 1987–2005—*Continued*

(Rate per 100,000 population.)

Sex, race, Hispanic origin, and age	1987[1]	1990[1]	1995[1]	2000[2]	2001	2002	2003	2004	2005
Age 25–44 Years									
All persons	12.7	23.2	36.3	9.8	9.4	8.9	8.2	7.5	6.8
White male..	19.2	35.0	46.1	8.8	8.3	7.7	7.2	6.3	5.7
Black or African American male.............	60.2	102.0	179.4	55.4	53.5	49.9	44.8	39.9	36.2
American Indian or Alaska Native male....	*	7.7	28.5	5.5	7.3	8.3	6.4	8.6	6.1
Asian or Pacific Islander male................	4.1	8.1	12.1	1.9	2.1	1.8	1.9	1.7	1.4
Hispanic or Latino male[4,5]...................	36.8	59.3	73.9	14.3	12.4	11.5	10.3	9.3	8.3
White, not Hispanic or Latino male[4,5].....	23.3	31.6	41.2	7.4	7.2	6.6	6.2	5.5	4.9
White female.....................................	1.2	2.3	5.9	2.1	1.9	1.8	1.8	1.6	1.5
Black or African American female...........	11.6	23.6	53.6	26.7	26.0	25.9	23.6	23.1	20.7
American Indian or Alaska Native female..	*	*	*	*	*	*	*	*	*
Asian or Pacific Islander female.............	*	*	1.2	*	*	*	*	*	*
Hispanic or Latina female[4,5]................	4.9	8.9	17.2	4.6	4.3	3.8	3.8	3.1	2.6
White, not Hispanic or Latina female[4,5]...	1.0	1.5	4.2	1.6	1.3	1.3	1.3	1.3	1.2
Age 45–64 Years									
All persons	5.8	11.1	19.9	8.7	8.4	8.7	8.7	8.5	8.4
White male..	9.9	18.6	26.0	8.1	7.7	7.8	7.9	7.5	7.3
Black or African American male.............	27.3	53.0	133.2	71.6	68.8	70.7	68.1	66.0	66.2
American Indian or Alaska Native male....	*	*	*	*	7.8	*	*	7.2	8.9
Asian or Pacific Islander male................	*	6.5	9.1	2.1	1.9	3.4	2.1	2.4	2.0
Hispanic or Latino male[4,5]...................	25.8	37.9	67.1	23.3	21.5	20.3	22.5	19.4	18.0
White, not Hispanic or Latino male[4,5].....	12.6	16.9	22.4	6.5	6.1	6.4	6.2	6.0	6.0
White female.....................................	0.5	0.9	2.4	1.3	1.2	1.4	1.4	1.4	1.4
Black or African American female...........	2.6	7.5	27.0	19.6	20.8	21.4	21.8	22.7	22.0
American Indian or Alaska Native female..	*	*	*	*	*	*	*	*	*
Asian or Pacific Islander female.............	*	*	*	*	*	*	*	*	*
Hispanic or Latina female[4,5]................	*	3.1	12.6	5.8	5.4	5.7	5.3	5.0	4.1
White, not Hispanic or Latina female[4,5]...	0.5	0.7	1.5	0.9	0.8	0.9	0.9	0.9	1.1

* = Figure does not meet standard of reliability or precision.

[1]Categories for the coding and classification of human immunodeficiency virus (HIV) disease were introduced in the United States in 1987.
For the period 1987–1998, underlying cause of death was coded according to the the *International Classification of Diseases, Ninth Edition.*

[2]Starting with 1999 data, cause of death is coded according to the *International Classification of Diseases, Tenth Edition.* To estimate change between 1998 and 1999, compare the 1999 rate with the comparability-modified rate for 1998.

[4]The race groups, White, Black, Asian or Pacific Islander, and American Indian or Alaska Native, include persons of Hispanic and non-Hispanic origin. Persons of Hispanic origin may be of any race.
Death rates for the American Indian or Alaska Native and Asian or Pacific Islander populations are known to be underestimated.

[5]Prior to 1997, excludes data from states lacking an Hispanic-origin item on the death certificate.

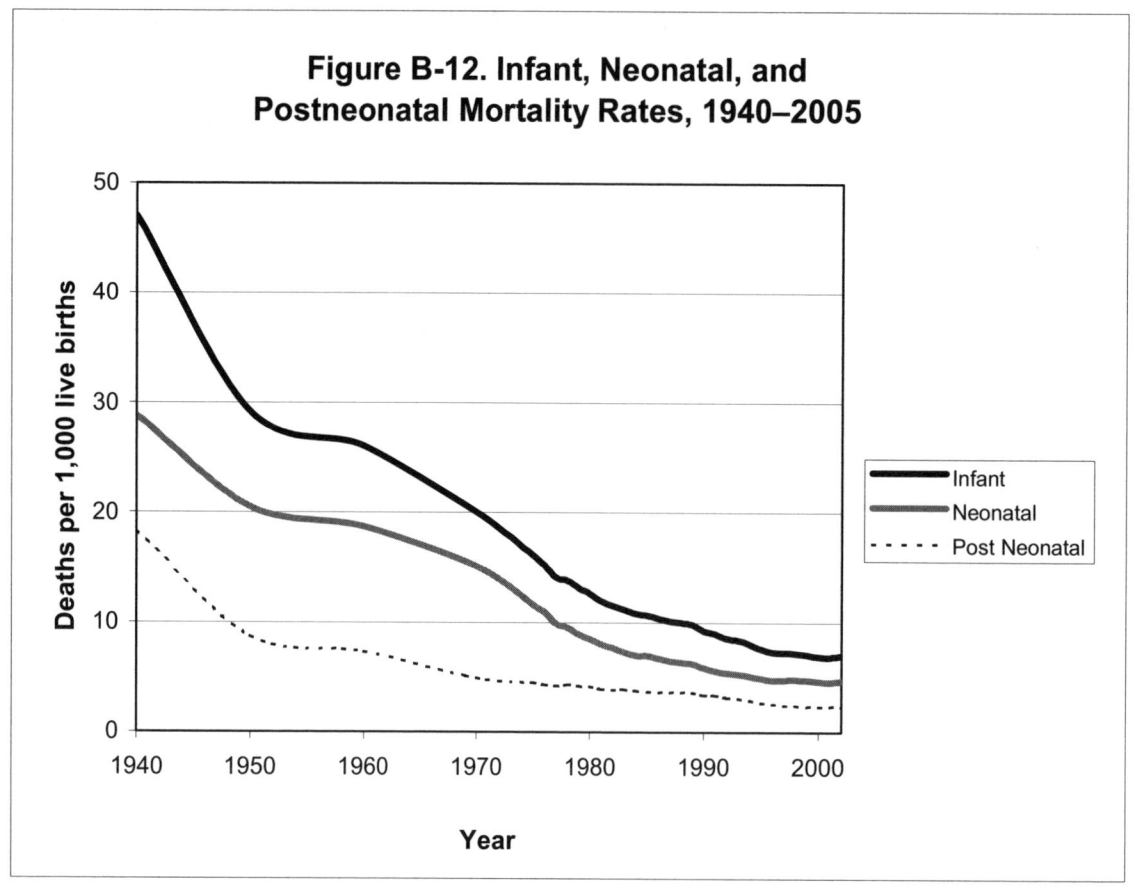

Figure B-12. Infant, Neonatal, and Postneonatal Mortality Rates, 1940–2005

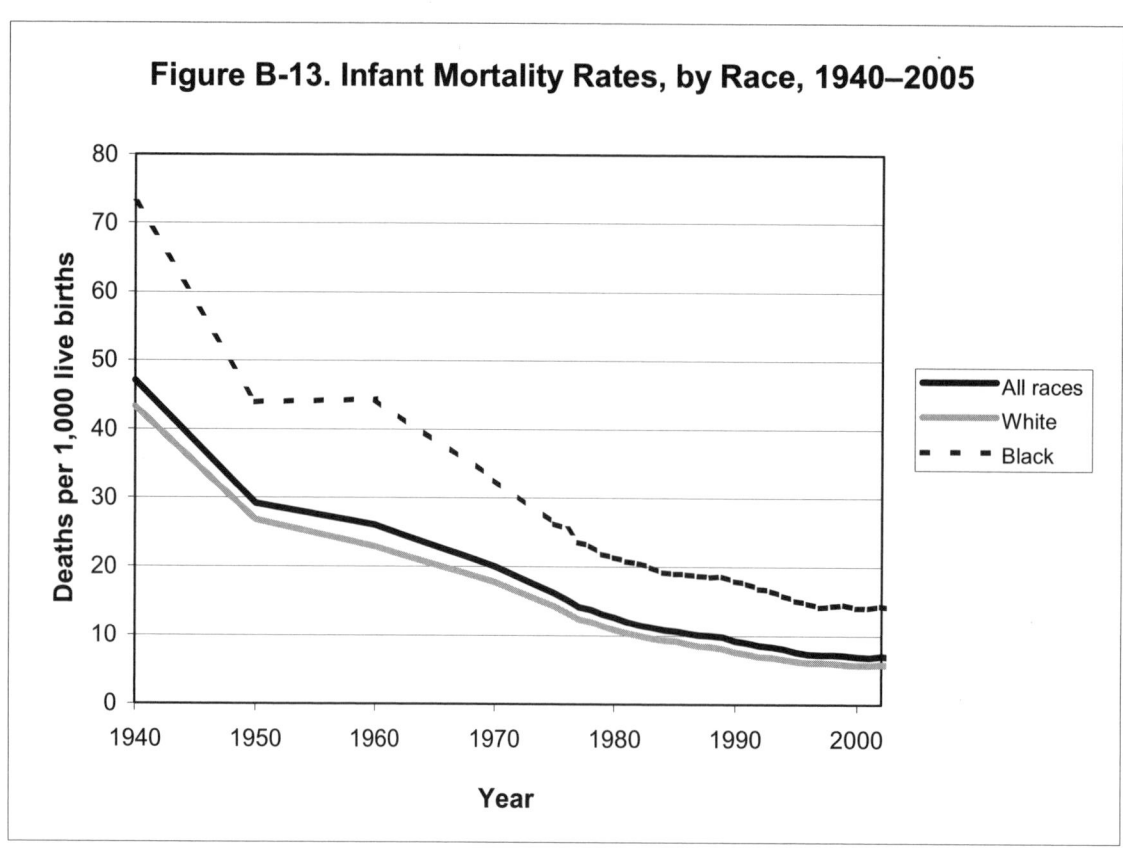

Figure B-13. Infant Mortality Rates, by Race, 1940–2005

Table B-48. Infant, Neonatal, and Postneonatal Mortality Rates by Race and Sex, Selected Years, 1940–2005

(Rate per 1,000 live births in specified group.)

Year	All races			White			All other					
							Total			Black		
	Both sexes	Male	Female	Both sexes	Male	Female	Both sexes	Male	Female	Both sexes	Male	Female
INFANT MORTALITY RATE												
Race of Mother[1]												
1980	12.60	13.93	11.21	10.86	12.12	9.52	20.19	21.89	18.43	22.19	24.16	20.15
1981	11.93	13.14	10.66	10.34	11.50	9.12	18.82	20.36	17.24	20.81	22.54	19.03
1982	11.52	12.77	10.21	9.94	11.08	8.73	18.31	20.07	16.49	20.48	22.45	18.44
1983	11.16	12.31	9.96	9.61	10.66	8.49	17.80	19.44	16.11	19.98	21.95	17.96
1984	10.79	11.90	9.62	9.30	10.38	8.17	17.05	18.37	15.69	19.15	20.67	17.58
1985	10.64	11.91	9.32	9.17	10.39	7.88	16.84	18.33	15.28	19.01	20.76	17.22
1986	10.35	11.55	9.10	8.80	9.87	7.67	16.72	18.45	14.91	18.90	20.91	16.81
1987	10.08	11.17	8.94	8.48	9.45	7.45	16.46	18.06	14.80	18.75	20.63	16.83
1988	9.95	10.99	8.86	8.36	9.35	7.31	16.08	17.33	14.79	18.54	20.04	16.99
1989	9.81	10.81	8.77	8.08	9.01	7.10	16.33	17.60	15.02	18.61	20.02	17.15
1990	9.22	10.26	8.13	7.56	8.51	6.56	15.52	16.96	14.03	17.96	19.62	16.25
1991	8.94	10.00	7.84	7.30	8.26	6.30	15.07	16.53	13.57	17.57	19.38	15.71
1992	8.52	9.39	7.61	6.92	7.69	6.12	14.44	15.72	13.10	16.85	18.38	15.26
1993	8.37	9.25	7.43	6.82	7.56	6.05	14.07	15.58	12.52	16.52	18.33	14.67
1994	8.02	8.81	7.20	6.57	7.22	5.89	13.47	14.82	12.08	15.83	17.49	14.12
1995	7.59	8.33	6.81	6.29	6.99	5.55	12.61	13.53	11.65	15.12	16.34	13.86
1996	7.32	8.02	6.59	6.07	6.67	5.44	12.18	13.31	11.01	14.68	16.04	13.27
1997	7.23	7.95	6.47	6.03	6.67	5.36	11.76	12.83	10.65	14.16	15.47	12.82
1998	7.20	7.83	6.54	5.95	6.47	5.41	11.92	13.01	10.79	14.31	15.75	12.82
1999	7.06	7.72	6.36	5.77	6.35	5.15	11.94	12.94	10.90	14.56	15.92	13.16
2000	6.91	7.57	6.21	5.68	6.22	5.11	11.44	12.57	10.26	14.09	15.50	12.63
2001	6.85	7.52	6.14	5.65	6.21	5.06	11.33	12.44	10.18	14.02	15.48	12.52
2002	6.97	7.64	6.27	5.79	6.42	5.13	11.41	12.24	10.55	14.36	15.43	13.25
2003	6.85	7.60	6.07	5.72	6.36	5.05	11.09	12.24	9.90	14.01	15.53	12.43
2004	6.79	7.47	6.09	5.66	6.22	5.07	10.92	12.01	9.77	13.79	15.19	12.33
2005	6.87	7.56	6.15	5.73	6.32	5.11	10.92	11.98	9.82	13.73	15.15	12.27
Race of Child[2]												
1940	47.02	52.45	41.29	43.23	48.32	37.84	73.78	82.21	65.19	72.94	81.07	64.61
1950	29.21	32.75	25.48	26.77	30.21	23.13	44.46	48.87	39.93	43.91	48.27	39.44
1960	26.04	29.33	22.59	22.91	26.01	19.64	43.21	47.88	38.46	44.32	49.12	39.43
1970	20.01	22.37	17.52	17.75	19.95	15.42	30.92	34.20	27.53	32.65	36.18	29.01
1975	16.07	17.86	14.18	14.17	15.94	12.30	24.23	26.24	22.17	26.21	28.32	24.03
1976	15.24	16.82	13.57	13.31	14.81	11.71	23.50	25.51	21.42	25.54	27.83	23.19
1977	14.12	15.75	12.40	12.34	13.90	10.68	21.68	23.71	19.58	23.64	25.91	21.30
1978	13.78	15.26	12.23	12.01	13.37	10.58	21.06	23.15	18.90	23.14	25.39	20.77
1979	13.07	14.50	11.56	11.42	12.82	9.94	19.81	21.47	18.09	21.78	23.66	19.85
1980	12.60	13.93	11.21	11.00	12.27	9.65	19.12	20.73	17.47	21.37	23.27	19.43
NEONATAL MORTALITY RATE												
Race of Mother[1]												
1980	8.48	9.31	7.60	7.39	8.19	6.54	13.21	14.27	12.13	14.62	15.91	13.29
1981	8.02	8.81	7.20	6.99	7.73	6.20	12.51	13.52	11.48	13.98	15.16	12.77
1982	7.70	8.48	6.88	6.69	7.39	5.94	12.04	13.15	10.88	13.62	14.86	12.34
1983	7.28	8.01	6.52	6.31	6.98	5.61	11.41	12.46	10.33	12.93	14.20	11.63
1984	7.00	7.66	6.31	6.09	6.72	5.41	10.87	11.66	10.06	12.32	13.22	11.40
1985	6.96	7.75	6.13	6.00	6.75	5.21	11.00	12.00	9.95	12.62	13.81	11.39
1986	6.71	7.42	5.97	5.72	6.34	5.05	10.79	11.83	9.70	12.31	13.59	10.98
1987	6.46	7.11	5.79	5.40	5.96	4.82	10.68	11.72	9.61	12.30	13.52	11.05
1988	6.32	6.95	5.65	5.27	5.84	4.67	10.33	11.22	9.42	12.05	13.14	10.93
1989	6.23	6.79	5.63	5.15	5.66	4.60	10.30	11.08	9.49	11.92	12.84	10.97
1990	5.85	6.50	5.16	4.79	5.38	4.17	9.86	10.79	8.89	11.55	12.69	10.38
1991	5.59	6.17	4.98	4.53	5.01	4.04	9.52	10.54	8.47	11.25	12.56	9.89
1992	5.37	5.84	4.89	4.35	4.72	3.96	9.19	10.02	8.32	10.83	11.83	9.79
1993	5.29	5.75	4.81	4.29	4.64	3.92	9.02	9.90	8.11	10.69	11.76	9.59
1994	5.12	5.58	4.64	4.20	4.55	3.83	8.60	9.51	7.65	10.21	11.32	9.07
1995	4.91	5.36	4.44	4.08	4.50	3.64	8.13	8.71	7.53	9.85	10.63	9.05
1996	4.77	5.18	4.34	3.97	4.31	3.62	7.86	8.59	7.12	9.56	10.45	8.65
1997	4.77	5.20	4.32	3.99	4.37	3.59	7.74	8.36	7.09	9.40	10.12	8.65
1998	4.80	5.21	4.37	3.98	4.31	3.63	7.91	8.63	7.17	9.55	10.51	8.56
1999	4.73	5.11	4.33	3.88	4.19	3.56	7.94	8.60	7.25	9.77	10.72	8.79

[1]Infant deaths based on race of child as stated on the death certificate; live births based on race of mother as stated on the birth certificate.
[2]Infant deaths based on race of child as stated on the death certificate; live births based on race of parents as stated on the birth certificate.

Table B-48. Infant, Neonatal, and Postneonatal Mortality Rates by Race and Sex, Selected Years, 1940–2005—
Continued

(Rate per 1,000 live births in specified group.)

Year	All races Both sexes	Male	Female	White Both sexes	Male	Female	All other Total Both sexes	Male	Female	Black Both sexes	Male	Female
Race of Mother—Continued												
2000	4.63	5.06	4.17	3.82	4.16	3.46	7.60	8.39	6.79	9.38	10.39	8.35
2001	4.54	4.97	4.08	3.78	4.15	3.39	7.37	8.06	6.65	9.21	10.15	8.25
2002	4.66	5.06	4.25	3.89	4.27	3.50	7.55	8.03	7.05	9.51	10.13	8.87
2003	4.62	5.08	4.14	3.87	4.26	3.46	7.40	8.14	6.64	9.40	10.40	8.37
2004	4.52	4.94	4.09	3.78	4.14	3.41	7.19	7.82	6.54	9.13	9.95	8.27
2005	4.54	4.93	4.12	3.79	4.10	3.46	7.18	7.88	6.47	9.07	9.96	8.14
Race of Child[2]												
1940	28.75	32.56	24.74	27.20	30.85	23.33	39.71	44.87	34.45	39.90	44.78	34.89
1950	20.50	23.34	17.50	19.37	22.18	16.40	27.54	30.76	24.23	27.80	31.09	24.44
1960	18.73	21.24	16.09	17.24	19.66	14.70	26.86	30.04	23.62	27.83	31.13	24.49
1970	15.08	16.96	13.10	13.77	15.55	11.88	21.43	23.87	18.91	22.76	25.37	20.07
1975	11.58	12.91	10.18	10.38	11.70	8.98	16.78	18.21	15.31	18.32	19.78	16.81
1976	10.92	12.03	9.75	9.66	10.73	8.52	16.31	17.68	14.90	17.92	19.47	16.32
1977	9.88	11.00	8.70	8.75	9.83	7.60	14.66	16.02	13.27	16.08	17.60	14.52
1978	9.49	10.54	8.38	8.39	9.34	7.38	14.01	15.54	12.43	15.47	17.17	13.72
1979	8.87	9.79	7.89	7.88	8.80	6.92	12.89	13.91	11.83	14.31	15.45	13.14
1980	8.48	9.31	7.60	7.48	8.29	6.62	12.52	13.51	11.49	14.08	15.32	12.81
POSTNEONATAL MORTALITY RATE												
Race of Mother[1]												
1980	4.13	4.62	3.61	3.47	3.93	2.98	6.97	7.62	6.30	7.57	8.25	6.87
1981	3.91	4.34	3.46	3.35	3.77	2.92	6.31	6.84	5.76	6.83	7.38	6.26
1982	3.82	4.29	3.33	3.25	3.68	2.79	6.28	6.92	5.61	6.86	7.59	6.10
1983	3.88	4.30	3.44	3.29	3.68	2.88	6.39	6.98	5.78	7.05	7.75	6.32
1984	3.79	4.23	3.31	3.22	3.65	2.76	6.18	6.71	5.63	6.83	7.46	6.18
1985	3.68	4.15	3.19	3.17	3.64	2.67	5.84	6.33	5.33	6.40	6.95	5.83
1986	3.64	4.13	3.13	3.08	3.53	2.62	5.93	6.62	5.21	6.59	7.33	5.83
1987	3.62	4.06	3.15	3.08	3.49	2.64	5.77	6.34	5.18	6.45	7.10	5.77
1988	3.64	4.04	3.21	3.09	3.51	2.65	5.75	6.11	5.37	6.49	6.90	6.07
1989	3.59	4.01	3.14	2.93	3.35	2.49	6.03	6.52	5.53	6.69	7.18	6.19
1990	3.38	3.76	2.97	2.78	3.14	2.39	5.66	6.16	5.13	6.41	6.93	5.87
1991	3.35	3.82	2.86	2.76	3.25	2.26	5.55	5.99	5.10	6.32	6.82	5.81
1992	3.14	3.55	2.72	2.58	2.97	2.16	5.25	5.69	4.78	6.02	6.54	5.47
1993	3.07	3.50	2.62	2.54	2.92	2.13	5.06	5.68	4.42	5.83	6.57	5.08
1994	2.90	3.22	2.56	2.37	2.67	2.06	4.88	5.32	4.42	5.61	6.17	5.04
1995	2.67	2.97	2.37	2.21	2.49	1.91	4.47	4.82	4.11	5.27	5.71	4.81
1996	2.55	2.84	2.24	2.09	2.36	1.81	4.32	4.72	3.90	5.11	5.60	4.62
1997	2.45	2.75	2.14	2.04	2.30	1.77	4.02	4.47	3.56	4.77	5.34	4.17
1998	2.40	2.62	2.16	1.97	2.16	1.78	4.01	4.38	3.62	4.76	5.24	4.26
1999	2.33	2.61	2.03	1.88	2.16	1.60	4.00	4.34	3.64	4.79	5.20	4.36
2000	2.28	2.51	2.04	1.86	2.06	1.66	3.83	4.18	3.47	4.70	5.11	4.28
2001	2.31	2.55	2.06	1.87	2.06	1.67	3.96	4.37	3.53	4.81	5.32	4.27
2002	2.31	2.58	2.03	1.89	2.15	1.63	3.86	4.21	3.50	4.85	5.30	4.38
2003	2.23	2.52	1.94	1.84	2.09	1.58	3.69	4.10	3.26	4.60	5.13	4.06
2004	2.27	2.53	2.00	1.87	2.07	1.66	3.72	4.19	3.23	4.66	5.24	4.06
2005	2.34	2.63	2.03	1.94	2.22	1.65	3.73	4.10	3.36	4.67	5.19	4.13
Race of Child[2]												
1940	18.27	19.89	16.55	16.03	17.47	14.50	34.07	37.35	30.74	33.05	36.29	29.72
1950	8.71	9.41	7.98	7.40	8.04	6.73	16.92	18.11	15.70	16.10	17.18	15.00
1960	7.31	8.10	6.49	5.66	6.35	4.94	16.35	17.84	14.84	16.48	17.99	14.95
1970	4.93	5.41	4.42	3.98	4.40	3.54	9.49	10.33	8.62	9.89	10.81	8.94
1975	4.49	4.95	4.00	3.80	4.24	3.33	7.45	8.03	6.86	7.89	8.54	7.22
1976	4.32	4.79	3.83	3.65	4.08	3.19	7.19	7.83	6.52	7.63	8.36	6.88
1977	4.24	4.75	3.71	3.59	4.07	3.08	7.01	7.69	6.31	7.56	8.32	6.78
1978	4.30	4.72	3.85	3.63	4.03	3.20	7.05	7.60	6.48	7.64	8.22	7.05
1979	4.20	4.71	3.67	3.54	4.02	3.03	6.92	7.57	6.25	7.47	8.21	6.71
1980	4.13	4.62	3.61	3.52	3.98	3.02	6.61	7.22	5.97	7.29	7.95	6.62

[1]Infant deaths based on race of child as stated on the death certificate; live births based on race of mother as stated on the birth certificate.
[2]Infant deaths based on race of child as stated on the death certificate; live births based on race of parents as stated on the birth certificate.

Table B-49. Number of Infant, Neonatal, and Postneonatal Deaths and Mortality Rates, by Sex, 2004–2005

(Number, rate per 1,000 live births.)

Infant age and sex	2004 Number	2004 Rate	2005 Number	2005 Rate	Percent change[1] from 2004 to 2005
Infant					
Total	27,936	6.79	28,440	6.87	1.2
Male	15,718	7.47	16,018	7.56	1.2
Female	12,218	6.09	12,422	6.15	1.0
Neonatal					
Total	18,593	4.52	18,770	4.54	0.4
Male	10,390	4.94	10,444	4.93	-0.2
Female	8,203	4.09	8,326	4.12	0.7
Postneonatal					
Total	9,343	2.27	9,670	2.34	3.1
Male	5,328	2.53	5,574	2.63	4.0
Female	4,015	2.00	4,096	2.03	1.5

[1]Percentage change based on a comparison of the 2005 and 2004 mortality rates.

Table B-50. Infant Deaths and Infant Mortality Rates, by Age, Race, and Hispanic Origin, Final 2005 and Preliminary 2006

(Number, rate per live births.)

Infant age and sex	2005 Number	2005 Rate	2006 Number	2006 Rate
All Races[1]				
Under 1 year	28,440	6.87	28,609	6.71
Under 28 days	18,770	4.54	19,013	4.46
28 days–11 months	9,670	2.34	9,596	2.25
White				
Under 1 year	18,514	5.73	18,496	5.58
Under 28 days	12,239	3.79	12,340	3.72
28 days–11 months	6,275	1.94	6,156	1.86
Non-Hispanic White				
Under 1 year	13,026	5.71	12,970	5.62
Under 28 days	8,515	3.74	8,543	3.70
28 days–11 months	4,511	1.98	4,427	1.92
Black				
Under 1 year	8,695	13.73	8,824	13.33
Under 28 days	5,740	9.07	5,854	8.84
28 days–11 months	2,955	4.67	2,970	4.49
Hispanic[2]				
Under 1 year	5,724	5.81	5,762	5.55
Under 28 days	3,859	3.92	3,939	3.79
28 days–11 months	1,865	1.89	1,823	1.75

[1]Includes races other than White or Black.
[2]Persons of Hispanic origin may be of any race. Because of a misclassification error in New Mexico, statistics for Hispanic decedents of all ages were underestimated by about 3.0 percent, and statistics for Hispanic decedents under 1 year of age were underestimated by about 1.0 percent.

NOTE: Data are subject to sampling or random variation. For information regarding the calculation of standard errors and further discussion of the variability of the data. Although the infant mortality rate is the preferred indicator of the risk of dying during the first year of life, another measure of infant mortality, the infant death rate, is shown elsewhere in this report. The two measures typically are similar, yet they can differ because the denominators used for these measures are different.

Table B-51. Number of Infant Deaths and Infant Mortality Rates for 130 Selected Causes by Race, 2005

(Number, rate per 100,000 live births.)

Cause of death[1]	Number			Rate		
	All races[2]	White	Black	All races[2]	White	Black
ALL CAUSES..	28,440	18,514	8,695	687.2	573.3	1,373.3
Certain infectious and parasitic diseases (A00-B99)	530	321	184	12.8	9.9	29.1
Certain intestinal infectious diseases (A00-A08)	9	5	3	*	*	*
Diarrhea and gastroenteritis of infectious origin (A09)	1	1	-	*	*	*
Tuberculosis (A16-A19)	2	2	-	*	*	*
Tetanus (A33, A35)	-	-	-	*	*	*
Diphtheria (A36)	-	-	-	*	*	*
Whooping cough (A37)	28	21	5	0.7	0.7	*
Meningococcal infection (A39)	17	13	2	*	*	*
Septicemia (A40-A41)	302	160	131	7.3	5.0	20.7
Congenital syphilis (A50)	-	-	-	*	*	*
Gonococcal infection (A54)	-	-	-	*	*	*
Viral diseases (A80-B34)	119	83	29	2.9	2.6	4.6
Acute poliomyelitis (A80)	-	-	-	*	*	*
Varicella (chickenpox) (B01)	-	-	-	*	*	*
Measles (B05)	-	-	-	*	*	*
Human immunodeficiency virus (HIV) disease (B20-B24)	2	2	-	*	*	*
Mumps (B26)	-	-	-	*	*	*
Other and unspecified viral diseases (A81-B00, B02-B04, B06-B19, B25, B27-B34).......	117	81	29	2.8	2.5	4.6
Candidiasis (B37)	20	13	6	0.5	*	*
Malaria (B50-B54)	-	-	-	*	*	*
Pneumocystosis (B59)	2	1	1	*	*	*
All other and unspecified infectious and parasitic diseases						
(A20-A32, A38, A42-A49, A51-A53, A55-A79, B35-B36, B38-B49, B55-B58, B60-B99).......	30	22	7	0.7	0.7	*
Neoplasms (C00-D48)...	134	106	25	3.2	3.3	3.9
Malignant neoplasms (C00-C97)..	75	64	10	1.8	2.0	*
Hodgkin's disease and non-Hodgkin's lymphomas (C81-C85)	1	1	-	*	*	*
Leukemia (C91-C95)	22	18	4	0.5	*	*
Other and unspecified malignant neoplasms (C00-C80, C88, C90, C96-C97)	52	45	6	1.3	1.4	*
In situ neoplasms, benign neoplasms and neoplasms of uncertain or unknown behavior						
(D00-D48)...	59	42	15	1.4	1.3	*
Diseases of the blood and blood-forming organs and certain disorders involving the						
immune mechanism (D50-D89)	94	61	25	2.3	1.9	3.9
Anemias (D50-D64)	19	9	6	*	*	*
Hemorrhagic conditions and other diseases of blood and blood-forming organs						
(D65-D76)	60	40	18	1.4	1.2	*
Certain disorders involving the immune mechanism (D80-D89).......	15	12	1	*	*	*
Endocrine, nutritional and metabolic diseases (E00-E88).................	226	161	50	5.5	5.0	7.9
Short stature, not elsewhere classified (E34.3).........................	8	5	3	*	*	*
Nutritional deficiencies (E40-E64)	5	2	3	*	*	*
Cystic fibrosis (E84)	5	4	1	*	*	*
Volume depletion, disorders of fluid, electrolyte and acid-base balance (E86-E87)............	63	37	21	1.5	1.1	3.3
All other endocrine, nutritional and metabolic diseases						
(E00-E32, E34.0-E34.2, E34.4-E34.9, E65-E83, E85, E88)	145	113	22	3.5	3.5	3.5
Diseases of the nervous system (G00-G98).....................................	354	258	71	8.6	8.0	11.2
Meningitis (G00, G03)	57	35	18	1.4	1.1	*
Infantile spinal muscular atrophy, type I (Werdnig-Hoffman) (G12.0).......	15	14	-	*	*	*
Infantile cerebral palsy (G80)...	8	3	4	*	*	*
Anoxic brain damage, not elsewhere classified (G93.1).............	42	25	15	1.0	0.8	*
Other diseases of nervous system						
(G04, G06-G11, G12.1-G12.9, G20-G72, G81-G92, G93.0, G93.2-G93.9, G95-G98)	232	181	34	5.6	5.6	5.4
Diseases of the ear and mastoid process (H60-H93)	7	3	3	*	*	*
Diseases of the circulatory system (I00-I99)	529	339	157	12.8	10.5	24.8
Pulmonary heart disease and diseases of pulmonary circulation (I26-I28)........	98	67	28	2.4	2.1	4.4
Pericarditis, endocarditis and myocarditis (I30, I33, I40)...........	13	4	8	*	*	*
Cardiomyopathy (I42)...	82	57	19	2.0	1.8	*
Cardiac arrest (I46)...	24	15	7	0.6	*	*
Cerebrovascular diseases (I60-I69)	126	79	40	3.0	2.4	6.3
All other diseases of circulatory system (I00-I25, I31, I34-I38, I44-I45, I47-I51, I70-I99)	186	117	55	4.5	3.6	8.7
Diseases of the respiratory system (J00-J98)...................................	669	412	233	16.2	12.8	36.8
Acute upper respiratory infections (J00-J06).............................	10	6	3	*	*	*
Influenza and pneumonia (J10-J18)...	265	158	98	6.4	4.9	15.5
Influenza (J10-J11)...	19	14	5	*	*	*
Pneumonia (J12-J18)..	246	144	93	5.9	4.5	14.7
Acute bronchitis and acute bronchiolitis (J20-J21)	50	29	18	1.2	0.9	*
Bronchitis, chronic and unspecified (J40-J42)...........................	25	15	9	0.6	*	*
Asthma (J45-J46)	4	2	2	*	*	*
Pneumonitis due to solids and liquids (J69)	17	13	3	*	*	*
Other and unspecified diseases of respiratory system						
(J22, J30-J39, J43-J44, J47-J68, J70-J98)...............................	298	189	100	7.2	5.9	15.8
Diseases of the digestive system (K00-K92)	626	390	213	15.1	12.1	33.6
Gastritis, duodenitis, and noninfective enteritis and colitis (K29, K50-K55)............	341	191	138	8.2	5.9	21.8
Hernia of abdominal cavity and intestinal obstruction without hernia (K40-K46, K56)	77	57	15	1.9	1.8	*
All other and unspecified diseases of digestive system (K00-K28, K30-K38, K57-K92)	208	142	60	5.0	4.4	9.5

* = Figure does not meet standard of reliability or precision.
- = Quantity zero.
[1]Based on codes from the International Classification of Diseases, Tenth Revision (1992), except where (*) precedes the cause of death code.
[2]Includes races other than White and Black.

Table B-51. Number of Infant Deaths and Infant Mortality Rates for 130 Selected Causes by Race, 2005—
Continued

(Number, rate per 100,000 live births.)

Cause of death[1]	Number			Rate		
	All races[2]	White	Black	All races[2]	White	Black
Diseases of the genitourinary system (N00-N95)	180	111	64	4.3	3.4	10.1
Renal failure and other disorders of kidney (N17-N19, N25, N27)	151	91	56	3.6	2.8	8.8
Other and unspecified diseases of genitourinary system (N00-N15, N20-N23, N26, N28-N95)	29	20	8	0.7	0.6	*
Certain conditions originating in the perinatal period (P00-P96)	14,423	8,815	5,018	348.5	273.0	792.6
Newborn affected by maternal factors and by complications of pregnancy, labor and delivery (P00-P04)	3,228	2,014	1,106	78.0	62.4	174.7
Newborn affected by maternal hypertensive disorders (P00.0)	88	42	41	2.1	1.3	6.5
Newborn affected by other maternal conditions which may be unrelated to present pregnancy (P00.1-P00.9)	70	47	22	1.7	1.5	3.5
Newborn affected by maternal complications of pregnancy (P01)	1,776	1,050	660	42.9	32.5	104.2
Newborn affected by incompetent cervix (P01.0)	496	282	194	12.0	8.7	30.6
Newborn affected by premature rupture of membranes (P01.1)	837	489	321	20.2	15.1	50.7
Newborn affected by multiple pregnancy (P01.5)	255	159	83	6.2	4.9	13.1
Newborn affected by other maternal complications of pregnancy (P01.2-P01.4, P01.6-P01.9)	188	120	62	4.5	3.7	9.8
Newborn affected by complications of placenta, cord and membranes (P02)	1,110	760	320	26.8	23.5	50.5
Newborn affected by complications involving placenta (P02.0-P02.3)	585	420	146	14.1	13.0	23.1
Newborn affected by complications involving cord (P02.4-P02.6)	50	40	10	1.2	1.2	*
Newborn affected by chorioamnionitis (P02.7)	471	297	163	11.4	9.2	25.7
Newborn affected by other and unspecified abnormalities of membranes (P02.8-P02.9)	4	3	1	*	*	*
Newborn affected by other complications of labor and delivery (P03)	134	85	44	3.2	2.6	6.9
Newborn affected by noxious influences transmitted via placenta or breast milk (P04)	50	30	19	1.2	0.9	*
Disorders related to length of gestation and fetal malnutrition (P05-P08)	4,798	2,675	1,922	115.9	82.8	303.6
Slow fetal growth and fetal malnutrition (P05)	83	52	27	2.0	1.6	4.3
Disorders related to short gestation and low birth weight, not elsewhere classified (P07)	4,714	2,623	1,894	113.9	81.2	299.1
Extremely low birth weight or extreme immaturity (P07.0, P07.2)	3,645	2,048	1,447	88.1	63.4	228.5
Other low birth weight or preterm (P07.1, P07.3)	1,069	575	447	25.8	17.8	70.6
Disorders related to long gestation and high birth weight (P08)	1	-	1	*	*	*
Birth trauma (P10-P15)	26	21	4	0.6	0.7	*
Intrauterine hypoxia and birth asphyxia (P20-P21)	529	388	121	12.8	12.0	19.1
Intrauterine hypoxia (P20)	119	79	33	2.9	2.4	5.2
Birth asphyxia (P21)	410	309	88	9.9	9.6	13.9
Respiratory distress of newborn (P22)	860	534	295	20.8	16.5	46.6
Other respiratory conditions originating in the perinatal period (P23-P28)	1,160	728	391	28.0	22.5	61.8
Congenital pneumonia (P23)	104	64	36	2.5	2.0	5.7
Neonatal aspiration syndromes (P24)	46	32	12	1.1	1.0	*
Interstitial emphysema and related conditions originating in the perinatal period (P25)	121	83	34	2.9	2.6	5.4
Pulmonary hemorrhage originating in the perinatal period (P26)	181	109	64	4.4	3.4	10.1
Chronic respiratory disease originating in the perinatal period (P27)	270	135	127	6.5	4.2	20.1
Atelectasis (P28.0-P28.1)	377	263	101	9.1	8.1	16.0
All other respiratory conditions originating in the perinatal period (P28.2-P28.9)	61	42	17	1.5	1.3	*
Infections specific to the perinatal period (P35-P39)	1,039	656	335	25.1	20.3	52.9
Bacterial sepsis of newborn (P36)	834	520	273	20.2	16.1	43.1
Omphalitis of newborn with or without mild hemorrhage (P38)	6	5	1	*	*	*
All other infections specific to the perinatal period (P35, P37, P39)	199	131	61	4.8	4.1	9.6
Hemorrhagic and hematological disorders of newborn (P50-P61)	782	552	194	18.9	17.1	30.6
Neonatal hemorrhage (P50-P52, P54)	665	466	169	16.1	14.4	26.7
Hemorrhagic disease of newborn (P53)	-	-	-	*	*	*
Hemolytic disease of newborn due to isoimmunization and other perinatal jaundice (P55-P59)	16	11	4	*	*	*
Hematological disorders (P60-P61)	101	75	21	2.4	2.3	3.3
Syndrome of infant of a diabetic mother and neonatal diabetes mellitus (P70.0-P70.2)	19	12	6	*	*	*
Necrotizing enterocolitis of newborn (P77)	546	313	207	13.2	9.7	32.7
Hydrops fetalis not due to hemolytic disease (P83.2)	165	135	17	4.0	4.2	*
Other perinatal conditions (P29, P70.3-P70.9, P71-P76, P78-P81, P83.0-P83.1, P83.3-P83.9, P90-P96)	1,271	787	420	30.7	24.4	66.3
Congenital malformations, deformations and chromosomal abnormalities (Q00-Q99)	5,552	4,187	1,080	134.2	129.7	170.6
Anencephaly and similar malformations (Q00)	313	252	46	7.6	7.8	7.3
Congenital hydrocephalus (Q03)	90	63	21	2.2	2.0	3.3
Spina bifida (Q05)	22	18	4	0.5	*	*
Other congenital malformations of nervous system (Q01-Q02, Q04, Q06-Q07)	314	248	49	7.6	7.7	7.7
Congenital malformations of heart (Q20-Q24)	1,377	1,075	241	33.3	33.3	38.1
Other congenital malformations of circulatory system (Q25-Q28)	245	172	61	5.9	5.3	9.6
Congenital malformations of respiratory system (Q30-Q34)	598	431	129	14.5	13.3	20.4
Congenital malformations of digestive system (Q35-Q45)	105	73	28	2.5	2.3	4.4
Congenital malformations of genitourinary system (Q50-Q64)	375	289	68	9.1	8.9	10.7
Congenital malformations and deformations of musculoskeletal system, limbs and integument (Q65-Q85)	558	407	119	13.5	12.6	18.8
Down's syndrome (Q90)	123	97	22	3.0	3.0	3.5

* = Figure does not meet standard of reliability or precision.
- = Quantity zero.
[1]Based on codes from the *International Classification of Diseases, Tenth Revision* (1992), except where (*) precedes the cause of death code.
[2]Includes races other than White and Black.

Table B-51. Number of Infant Deaths and Infant Mortality Rates for 130 Selected Causes by Race, 2005—
Continued

(Number, rate per 100,000 live births.)

Cause of death[1]	Number			Rate		
	All races[2]	White	Black	All races[2]	White	Black
Edward's syndrome (Q91.0-Q91.3)..	405	302	84	9.8	9.4	13.3
Patau's syndrome (Q91.4-Q91.7)...	310	234	61	7.5	7.2	9.6
Other congenital malformations and deformations (Q10-Q18, Q86-Q89)	526	378	112	12.7	11.7	17.7
Other chromosomal abnormalities, not elsewhere classified (Q92-Q99)................................	191	148	35	4.6	4.6	5.5
Symptoms, signs and abnormal clinical and laboratory findings, not elsewhere classified (R00-R99)..	3,589	2,331	1,121	86.7	72.2	177.1
Sudden infant death syndrome (R95)	2,230	1,493	663	53.9	46.2	104.7
Other symptoms, signs and abnormal clinical and laboratory findings, not elsewhere classified (R00-R53, R55-R94, R96-R99)	1,359	838	458	32.8	25.9	72.3
All other diseases (residual)...	15	11	3	*	*	*
External causes of mortality (*U01, V01-Y84)..	1,512	1,008	448	36.5	31.2	70.8
Accidents (unintentional injuries) (V01-X59)	1,083	734	314	26.2	22.7	49.6
Transport accidents (V01-V99)	147	100	38	3.6	3.1	6.0
Motor vehicle accidents (V02-V04, V09.0, V09.2, V12-V14, V19.0-V19.2, V19.4-V19.6, V20-V79, V80.3-V80.5, V81.0-V81.1, V82.0-V82.1, V83-V86, V87.0-V87.8, V88.0-V88.8, V89.0, V89.2)..	146	99	38	3.5	3.1	6.0
Other and unspecified transport accidents (V01, V05-V06, V09.1, V09.3-V09.9, V10-V11, V15-V18, V19.3,V19.8-V19.9, V80.0-V80.2, V80.6-V80.9, V81.2-V81.9, V82.2-V82.9, V87.9, V88.9,V89.1, V89.3,V89.9)............	1	1	-	*	*	*
Falls (W00-W19)..	16	13	2	*	*	*
Accidental discharge of firearms (W32-W34)..	1	-	1	*	*	*
Accidental drowning and submersion (W65-W74)...	64	56	8	1.5	1.7	*
Accidental suffocation and strangulation in bed (W75)...	514	334	167	12.4	10.3	26.4
Other accidental suffocation and strangulation (W76-W77, W81-W84)........................	186	124	54	4.5	3.8	8.5
Accidental inhalation and ingestion of food or other objects causing obstruction of respiratory tract (W78-W80)	48	38	9	1.2	1.2	*
Accidents caused by exposure to smoke, fire and flames (X00-X09)	34	23	10	0.8	0.7	*
Accidental poisoning and exposure to noxious substances (X40-X49)	20	12	7	0.5	*	*
Other and unspecified accidents (W20-W31, W35-W64, W85-W99, X10-X39, X50-X59)	53	34	18	1.3	1.1	*
Assault (homicide) (*U01, X85-Y09)..	306	195	95	7.4	6.0	15.0
Assault (homicide) by hanging, strangulation and suffocation (X91)	27	17	9	0.7	*	*
Assault (homicide) by discharge of firearms (*U01.4, X93-X95)...............................	6	4	2	*	*	*
Neglect, abandonment and other maltreatment syndromes (Y06-Y07)........................	99	66	27	2.4	2.0	4.3
Assault (homicide) by other and unspecified means (*U01.0-*U01.3, *U01.5-*U01.9, X85-X90, X92, X96-X99, Y00-Y05, Y08-Y09)	174	108	57	4.2	3.3	9.0
Complications of medical and surgical care (Y40-Y84)..	19	11	8	*	*	*
Other external causes (Y10-Y36)...	104	68	31	2.5	2.1	4.9

* = Figure does not meet standard of reliability or precision.
- = Quantity zero.
[1]Based on codes from the *International Classification of Diseases, Tenth Revision* (1992), except where (*) precedes the cause of death code.
[2]Includes races other than White and Black.

NOTE: Complete confirmation of deaths from selected causes of death, considered to be of public health concern, were not provided by the following states–Alabama, California, Connecticut, Florida, Illinois, Indiana, Kentucky, Louisiana, Maryland, Michigan, Missouri, Montana, Nevada, New Hampshire, New Jersey, New York, North Carolina, Ohio, Oklahoma, Pennsylvania, Rhode Island, Texas, Utah, Virginia, Washington, and West Virginia.

Table B-52. Number of Infant Deaths, Infant Mortality Rates, and Percent Change in Rate from Previous Year, for 10 Leading Causes of Infant Death, 2005

(Number, percent, rate per 100,000 live births)

Rank[1]	Cause of death[2]	Number	Percent of total deaths	Rate	Percent change from 2004 to 2005[3]
	ALL CAUSES	28,440	100.0	687.2	1.2
1	Congenital malformations, deformations and chromosomal abnormalities (Q00-Q99)...............................	5,552	19.5	134.2	-1.8
2	Disorders related to short gestation and low birth weight, not elsewhere classified (P07).........................	4,714	16.6	113.9	0.9
3	Sudden infant death syndrome (R95)	2,230	7.8	53.9	-1.3
4	Newborn affected by maternal complications of pregnancy (P01)	1,776	6.2	42.9	2.9
5	Newborn affected by complications of placenta, cord and membranes (P02)	1,110	3.9	26.8	5.9
6	Accidents (unintentional injuries) (V01-X59)	1,083	3.8	26.2	2.3
7	Respiratory distress of newborn (P22)..	860	3.0	20.8	-2.3
8	Bacterial sepsis of newborn (P36)..	834	2.9	20.2	0.5
9	Neonatal hemorrhage (P50-P52, P54)...	665	2.3	16.1	7.3
10	Necrotizing enterocolitis of newborn (P77)...	546	1.9	13.2	23.4
...	All other causes (residual)..	9,070	31.9	219.2	...

... = Not applicable.

[1]Rank based on number of deaths.

[2]Based on codes from the *International Classification of Diseases, Tenth Revision* (1992), except where (*) precedes the cause of death code.

[3]Percentage change based on a comparison of the 2005 infant mortality rate with the 2004 infant mortality rate.

Table B-53. Infant Deaths and Infant Mortality Rates for 130 Selected Causes, Final 2005 and Preliminary 2006

(Number, rate per 100,000 live births.)

Cause of death	2005		2006	
	Number	Rate	Number	Rate
ALL CAUSES............................	28,440	687.2	28,609	670.6
Certain infectious and parasitic diseases (A00–B99)	530	12.8	500	11.7
Certain intestinal infectious diseases (A00–A08)	9	*	15	*
Diarrhea and gastroenteritis of infectious origin (A09)	1	*	2	*
Tuberculosis (A16–A19)	2	*	1	*
Tetanus (A33, A35)	–	*	–	*
Diphtheria (A36)	–	*	–	*
Whooping cough (A37)	28	0.7	8	*
Meningococcal infection (A39)	17	*	10	*
Septicemia (A40–A41)	302	7.3	293	6.9
Congenital syphilis (A50)	–	*	–	*
Gonococcal infection (A54)	–	*	–	*
Viral diseases (A80–B34)	119	2.9	116	2.7
Acute poliomyelitis (A80)	–	*	–	*
Varicella (chickenpox) (B01)	–	*	–	*
Measles (B05)	–	*	–	*
Human immunodeficiency virus (HIV) disease (B20–B24).............	2	*	7	*
Mumps (B26)	–	*	–	*
Other and unspecified viral diseases (A81–B00, B02–B04, B06–B19, B25, B27–B34)	117	2.8	109	2.6
Candidiasis (B37)	20	0.5	15	*
Malaria (B50–B54).............	–	*	–	*
Pneumocystosis (B59)	2	*	–	*
All other and unspecified infectious and parasitic diseases (A20–A32, A38, A42–A49, A51–A53, A55–A79, B35–B36, B38–B49, B55–B58, B60–B99)	30	0.7	38	0.9
Neoplasms (C00–D48)	134	3.2	139	3.3
Malignant neoplasms (C00–C97)	75	1.8	77	1.8
Hodgkin's disease and non-Hodgkin's lymphomas (C81–C85).............	1	*	1	*
Leukemia (C91–C95)	22	0.5	31	0.7
Other and unspecified malignant neoplasms (C00–C80, C88, C90, C96–C97)	52	1.3	45	1.1
In situ neoplasms,benign neoplasms and neoplasms of uncertain or unknown behavior (D00–D48)	59	1.4	62	1.5
Diseases of the blood and blood-forming organs and certain disorders involving the immune mechanism (D50–D89).........	94	2.3	104	2.4
Anemias (D50–D64)	19	*	10	*
Hemorrhagic conditions and other diseases of blood and blood-forming organs (D65–D76).............	60	1.4	63	1.5
Certain disorders involving the immune mechanism (D80–D89)	15	*	31	0.7
Endocrine, nutritional and metabolic diseases (E00–E88)	226	5.5	200	4.7
Short stature, not elsewhere classified (E34.3)	8	*	8	*
Nutritional deficiencies (E40–E64)	5	*	7	*
Cystic fibrosis (E84)	5	*	10	*
Volume depletion, disorders of fluid, electrolyte and acid–base balance (E86–E87).............	63	1.5	56	1.3
All other endocrine, nutritional and metabolic diseases (E00–E32, E34.0–E34.2, E34.4–E34.9, E65–E83, E85, E88)	145	3.5	118	2.8
Diseases of the nervous system(G00–G98)	354	8.6	361	8.5
Diseases of the nervous system (G00–G98)	57	1.4	57	1.3
Meningitis (G00, G03)	15	*	9	*
Infantile spinal muscularatrophy, type I (Werdnig-Hoffman) (G12.0)	8	*	8	*
Infantile cerebral palsy (G80).............	42	1	55	1.3
Anoxic brain damage,not elsewhere classified (G93.1).............	232	5.6	232	5.4
Other diseases of nervous system (G04, G06–G11, G12.1–G12.9, G20–G72, G81–G92, G93.0, G93.2–G93.9, G95–G98)				
Diseases of the ear and mastoid process (H60–H93)	7	*	2	*
Diseases of the circulatory system (I00–I99)	529	12.8	539	12.6
Pulmonary heart disease and diseases of pulmonary circulation (I26–I28).............	98	2.4	81	1.9
Pericarditis,endocarditis and myocarditis (I30, I33, I40)	13	*	7	*
Cardiomyopathy (I42).............	82	2	109	2.6
Cardiac arrest (I46)	24	0.6	14	*
Cerebrovascular diseases (I60–I69).............	126	3	145	3.4
All other diseases of circulatory system (I00–I25, I31, I34–I38, I44–I45, I47–I51, I70–I99).............	186	4.5	181	4.2
Diseases of the respiratory system (J00–J98)	669	16.2	644	15.1
Acute upper respiratory infections (J00–J06)	10	*	11	*
Influenza and pneumonia (J10–J18)	265	6.4	244	5.7
Influenza (J10–J11)	19	*	17	*
Pneumonia (J12–J18)	246	5.9	228	5.3
Acute bronchitis and acute bronchiolitis (J20–J21).............	50	1.2	45	1.1
Bronchitis, chronic and unspecified (J40–J42)	25	0.6	19	*
Asthma (J45–J46).............	4	*	5	*
Pneumonitis due to solids and liquids (J69)	17	*	9	*
Other and unspecified diseases of respiratory system (J22, J30–J39, J43–J44, J47–J68, J70–J98).............	298	7.2	311	7.3
Diseases of the digestive system (K00–K92)	626	15.1	588	13.8
Gastritis, duodenitis, and noninfective enteritis and colitis (K29, K50–K55).............	341	8.2	326	7.6
Hernia of abdominal cavity and intestinal obstruction without hernia (K40–K46, K56).............	77	1.9	70	1.6
All other and unspecified diseases of digestive system (K00–K28, K30–K38, K57–K92)	208	5	192	4.5
Diseases of the genitourinary system (N00–N95)	180	4.3	181	4.2
Renal failure and other disorders of kidney (N17–N19, N25, N27).............	151	3.6	159	3.7
Other and unspecified diseases of genitourinary system (N00–N15, N20–N23, N26, N28–N95)	29	0.7	22	0.5

* = Figure does not meet standards of reliability or precision.
– = Quantity zero.

Table B-53. Infant Deaths and Infant Mortality Rates for 130 Selected Causes, Final 2005 and Preliminary 2006—*Continued*

(Number, rate per 100,000 live births.)

Cause of death	2005		2006	
	Number	Rate	Number	Rate
Certain conditions originating in the perinatal period (P00–P96).........	14,423	348.5	14,223	333.4
Newborn affected by maternal factors and by complications of pregnancy, labor and delivery (P00–P04)	3,228	78	3,125	73.3
Newborn affected by maternal hypertensive disorders (P0.00)	88	2.1	85	2
Newborn affected by other maternal conditions which may be unrelated to present pregnancy (P00.1–P00.9)	70	1.7	68	1.6
Newborn affected by maternal complications of pregnancy (P01).........	1,776	42.9	1,694	39.7
Newborn affected by incompetent cervix (P01.0)	496	12	444	10.4
Newborn affected by premature rupture of membranes (P01.1)	837	20.2	830	19.5
Newborn affected by multiple pregnancy (P01.5)	255	6.2	213	5
Newborn affected by other maternal complications of pregnancy (P01.2–P01.4, P01.6–P01.9)	188	4.5	207	4.9
Newborn affected by complications of placenta,cord and membranes (P02).........	1,110	26.8	1,123	26.3
Newborn affected by complications involving placenta (P02.0–P02.3)	585	14.1	561	13.2
Newborn affected by complications involving cord (P02.4–P02.6)	50	1.2	54	1.3
Newborn affected by chorioamnionitis (P02.7)	471	11.4	507	11.9
Newborn affected by other and unspecified abnormalities of membranes (P02.8–P02.9)	4	*	1	*
Newborn affected by other complications of labor and delivery (P03)	134	3.2	97	2.3
Newborn affected by noxious influences transmitted via placenta or breast milk (P04)	50	1.2	58	1.4
Disorders related to length of gestation and fetal malnutrition (P05–P08).........	4,798	115.9	4,943	115.9
Slow fetal growth and fetal malnutrition (P05).........	83	2.0	102	2.4
Disorders related to short gestation and low birthweight, not elsewhere classified (P07).........	4,714	113.9	4,841	113.5
Extremely low birthweight or extreme immaturity (P07.0, P07.2)	3,645	88.1	3,678	86.2
Other low birth weight or preterm (P07.1, P07.3)	1,069	25.8	1,163	27.3
Disorders related to long gestation and high birthweight (P08)	1	*	–	*
Birth trauma (P10–P15)	26	0.6	23	0.5
Intrauterine hypoxia and birth asphyxia (P20–P21)	529	12.8	344	8.1
Intrauterine hypoxia (P20)	119	2.9	109	2.6
Birth asphyxia (P21)	410	9.9	236	5.5
Respiratory distress of newborn (P22)	860	20.8	801	18.8
Other respiratory conditions originating in the perinatal period (P23–P28)	1,160	28.0	1,199	28.1
Congenital pneumonia (P23).........	104	2.5	89	2.1
Neonatal aspiration syndromes (P24).........	46	1.1	49	1.1
Interstitial emphysema and related conditions originating in the perinatal period (P25)	121	2.9	155	3.6
Pulmonary hemorrhage originating in the perinatal period (P26).........	181	4.4	179	4.2
Chronic respiratory disease originating in the perinatal period (P27).........	270	6.5	262	6.1
Atelectasis (P28.0–P28.1)	377	9.1	396	9.3
All other respiratory conditions originating in the perinatal period (P28.2–P28.9)	61	1.5	69	1.6
Infections specific to the perinatal period (P35–P39)	1,039	25.1	979	22.9
Bacterial sepsis of newborn (P36).........	834	20.2	786	18.4
Omphalitis of newborn with or without mild hemorrhage (P38)	6	*	–	*
All other infections specific to the perinatal period (P35, P37, P39)	199	4.8	193	4.5
Hemorrhagic and hematological disorders of newborn (P50–P61)	782	18.9	708	16.6
Neonatal hemorrhage (P50–P52, P54).........	665	16.1	598	14.0
Hemorrhagic disease of newborn (P53).........	–	*	1	*
Hemolytic disease of newborn due to isoimmunization and other perinatal jaundice (P55–P59)	16	*	10	*
Hematological disorders (P60–P61).........	101	2.4	99	2.3
Syndrome of infant of a diabetic mother and neonatal diabetes mellitus (P70.0–P70.2)	19	*	16	*
Necrotizing enterocolitis of newborn (P77)	546	13.2	528	12.4
Hydrops fetalis not due to hemolytic disease (P83.2)	165	4.0	171	4.0
Other perinatal conditions (P29, P70.3–P76, P78–P81, P83.0–P83.1, P83.3–P96)	1,271	30.7	1,385	32.5
Congenital malformations, deformations, and chromosomal abnormalities (Q00–Q99)	5,552	134.2	5,827	136.6
Anencephaly and similar malformations (Q00)	313	7.6	332	7.8
Congenital hydrocephalus (Q03)	90	2.2	82	1.9
Spina bifida (Q05)	22	0.5	24	0.6
Other congenital malformations of nervoussystem (Q01–Q02, Q04, Q06–Q07)	314	7.6	389	9.1
Congenital malformations of heart (Q20–Q24)	1,377	33.3	1,399	32.8
Other congenital malformations of circulatory system (Q25–Q28)	245	5.9	232	5.4
Congenital malformations of respiratory system (Q30–Q34)	598	14.5	449	10.5
Congenital malformations of digestive system (Q35–Q45)	105	2.5	109	2.6
Congenital malformations of genitourinary system (Q50–Q64)	375	9.1	523	12.3
Congenital malformations and deformations of musculoskeletal system, limbs and integument (Q65–Q85)	558	13.5	627	14.7
Downs's syndrome (Q90).........	123	3.0	93	2.2
Edward's syndrome (Q91.0–Q91.3)	405	9.8	518	12.1
Patau's syndrome (Q91.4-Q91.7).........	310	7.5	327	7.7
Other congenital malformations and deformations (Q10-Q18, Q86–Q89)	526	12.7	523	12.3
Other chromosomal abnormalities, not elsewhere classified (Q92-Q99).........	191	4.6	200	4.7
Symptoms, signs and abnormal clinical and laboratory findings, not elsewhere classified (R00-R99)	3,589	86.7	3,749	87.9
Sudden infant death syndrome (R95)	2,230	53.9	2,145	50.3
Other symptoms, signs and abnormal clinical and laboratory findings, not elsewhere classified (R00-R53, R55-R94, R96-R99)	1,359	32.8	1,604	37.6
All other diseases (residual).........	15	*	42	1

* = Figure does not meet standards of reliability or precision.

– = Quantity zero.

Table B-53. Infant Deaths and Infant Mortality Rates for 130 Selected Causes, Final 2005 and Preliminary 2006—*Continued*

(Number, rate per 100,000 live births.)

Cause of death	2005		2006	
	Number	Rate	Number	Rate
External causes of mortality (*U01, V01-Y84)..	1,512	36.5	1,510	35.4
Accidents (unintentional injuries) (V01-X59)..	1,083	26.2	1,119	26.2
Transport accidents (V01-V99)...	147	3.6	136	3.2
Motor vehicle accidents (V02-V04, V09.0, V09.2, V12-V14, V19.0-V19.2, V19.4-V19.6, V20-V79, V80.3-V80.5, V81.0-V81.1, V82.0-V82.1, V83-V86, V87.0-V87.8, V88.0-V88.8, V89.0, V89.2).........	146	3.5	133	3.1
Other and unspecified transport accidents (V01, V05-V06, V09.1, V09.3-V09.9, V10-V11, V15-V18, V19.3,V19.8-V19.9, V80.0-V80.2, V80.6-V80.9, V81.2-V81.9, V82.2-V82.9, V87.9, V88.9,V89.1, V89.3,V89.9)	1	*	22	*
Falls (W00-W19)...	16	*	2	0.5
Accidental discharge of firearms (W32-W34)..	1	*	–	*
Accidental drowning and submersion (W65-W74)...	64	1.5	51	1.2
Accidental suffocation and strangulation in bed (W75)..	514	12.4	559	13.1
Other accidental suffocation and strangulation (W76-W77, W81-W84)................	186	4.5	193	4.5
Accidental inhalation and ingestion of food or other objects causing obstruction of respiratory tract (W78-W80)...	48	1.2	64	1.5
Accidents caused by exposure to smoke, fire and flames (X00-X09)	34	0.8	27	0.6
Accidental poisoning and exposure to noxious substances (X40-X49)	20	0.5	15	*
Other and unspecified accidents (W20-W31, W35-W64, W85-W99, X10-X39, X50-X59) ...	53	1.3	51	1.2
Assault (homicide) (*U01, X85-Y09)...	306	7.4	292	6.8
Assault (homicide) by hanging, strangulation and suffocation (X91)	27	0.7	23	0.5
Assault (homicide) by discharge of firearms (*U01.4, X93-X95)........................	6	*	6	*
Neglect, abandonment and other maltreatment syndromes (Y06-Y07)...............	99	2.4	67	1.6
Assault (homicide) by other and unspecified means (*U01.0-*U01.3, *U01.5-*U01.9, X85-X90, X92, X96-X99, Y00-Y05, Y08-Y09)	174	4.2	195	4.6
Complications of medical and surgical care (Y40-Y84)	19	*	21	0.5
Other external causes (Y10-Y36)..	104	2.5	78	1.8

* = Figure does not meet standards of reliability or precision.
– = Quantity zero.

NOTE: For certain causes of death such as unintentional injuries, homicides, suicides, and respiratory diseases, preliminary and final data differ because of the truncated nature of the preliminary file. Data are subject to sampling or random variation.

Table B-54. Infant Deaths and Infant Mortality Rates for the 10 Leading Causes of Infant Death, by Race and Hispanic Origin, Preliminary 2006

(Number, rate per 100,000 live births.)

Race and Rank[1]	Cause of death[2]	Number	Rate
All Races[3]			
	All Causes	28,609	670.6
1	Congenital malformations, deformations and chromosomal abnormalities (Q00–Q99)	5,827	136.6
2	Disorders related to short gestation and low birth weight, not elsewhere classified (P07)	4,841	113.5
3	Sudden infant death syndrome (R95)	2,145	50.3
4	Newborn affected by maternal complications of pregnancy (P01)	1,694	39.7
5	Newborn affected by complications of placenta, cord and membranes (P02)	1,123	26.3
6	Accidents (unintentional injuries) (V01–X59)	1,119	26.2
7	Respiratory distress of newborn (P22)	801	18.8
8	Bacterial sepsis of newborn (P36)	786	18.4
9	Neonatal hemorrhage (P50–P52, P54)	598	14.0
10	Diseases of the circulatory system (I00–I99)	539	12.6
	All other causes (residual)	9,136	214.2
White			
	All Causes	18,486	557.4
1	Congenital malformations, deformations and chromosomal abnormalities (Q00–Q99)	4,388	132.3
2	Disorders related to short gestation and low birth weight, not elsewhere classified (P07)	2,681	80.8
3	Sudden infant death syndrome (R95)	1,406	42.4
4	Newborn affected by maternal complications of pregnancy (P01)	1,039	31.3
5	Accidents (unintentional injuries) (V01–X59)	710	21.4
6	Newborn affected by complications of placenta, cord and membranes (P02)	695	21.0
7	Respiratory distress of newborn (P22)	503	15.2
8	Bacterial sepsis of newborn (P36)	480	14.5
9	Neonatal hemorrhage (P50–P52, P54)	411	12.4
10	Diseases of the circulatory system (I00–I99)	335	10.1
	All other causes (residual)	5,838	176.0
Non-Hispanic White			
	All Causes	13,019	563.6
1	Congenital malformations, deformations and chromosomal abnormalities (Q00–Q99)	2,989	129.4
2	Disorders related to short gestation and low birth weight, not elsewhere classified (P07)	1,805	78.1
3	Sudden infant death syndrome (R95)	1,171	50.7
4	Newborn affected by maternal complications of pregnancy (P01)	751	32.5
5	Accidents (unintentional injuries) (V01–X59)	547	23.7
6	Newborn affected by complications of placenta, cord and membranes (P02)	472	20.4
7	Respiratory distress of newborn (P22)	353	15.3
8	Bacterial sepsis of newborn (P36)	331	14.3
9	Neonatal hemorrhage (P50–P52, P54)	299	12.9
10	Diseases of the circulatory system (I00–I99)	239	10.3
	All other causes (residual)	4,062	175.9
Black			
	All Causes	8,842	1335.2
1	Disorders related to short gestation and low birth weight, not elsewhere classified (P07)	1,978	298.7
2	Congenital malformations, deformations and chromosomal abnormalities (Q00–Q99)	1,157	174.7
3	Sudden infant death syndrome (R95)	656	99.1
4	Newborn affected by maternal complications of pregnancy (P01)	595	89.9
5	Newborn affected by complications of placenta, cord and membranes (P02)	378	57.1
6	Accidents (unintentional injuries) (V01–X59)	351	53.0
7	Bacterial sepsis of newborn (P36)	272	41.1
8	Respiratory distress of newborn (P22)	267	40.3
9	Necrotizing enterocolitis of newborn (P77)	204	30.8
10	Diseases of the circulatory system (I00–I99)	175	26.4
	All other causes (residual)	2,809	424.2
Hispanic[4]			
	All Causes	5,706	549.2
1	Congenital malformations, deformations and chromosomal abnormalities (Q00–Q99)	1,442	138.8
2	Disorders related to short gestation and low birth weight, not elsewhere classified (P07)	919	88.4
3	Newborn affected by maternal complications of pregnancy (P01)	299	28.8
4	Sudden infant death syndrome (R95)	244	23.5
5	Newborn affected by complications of placenta, cord and membranes (P02)	227	21.8
6	Accidents (unintentional injuries) (V01–X59)	178	17.1
7	Respiratory distress of newborn (P22)	159	15.3
8	Bacterial sepsis of newborn (P36)	152	14.6
9	Neonatal hemorrhage (P50–P52, P54)	113	10.9
10	Diseases of the circulatory system (I00–I99)	99	9.5
	All other causes (residual)	1,874	180.4

[1]Rank based on number of deaths.
[2]Based on codes from the *International Classification of Diseases, Tenth Revision* (1992), except where (*) precedes the cause of death code.
[3]Includes races other than White and Black.
[4]Persons of Hispanic origin may be of any race. Because of a misclassification error in New Mexico, statistics for Hispanic decedents of all ages were about 3.0 percent, and statistics for Hispanic decedents under 1 year of age were underestimated by about 1.0 percent.

NOTE: For certain causes of death such as unintentional injuries, homicides, suicides, and sudden infant death syndrome, preliminary and final data may differ because of the truncated nature of the preliminary file. Data are subject to sampling or random variation.

Table B-55. Number of Infant and Neonatal Deaths and Mortality Rates, by Race, State, and Territory, 2005

(Number, rate per 1,000 live births in specified group.)

Sex, state, or territory	Infant deaths					
	All races[1]		White		Black	
	Number	Rate	Number	Rate	Number	Rate
UNITED STATES[2]	28,440	6.9	18,514	5.7	8,695	13.7
Male	16,018	7.6	10,471	6.3	4,867	15.2
Female	12,422	6.2	8,043	5.1	3,828	12.3
Alabama	568	9.4	296	7.2	266	14.7
Alaska	62	5.9	31	4.7	4	*
Arizona	662	6.9	549	6.6	46	12.6
Arkansas	309	7.9	196	6.4	111	14.9
California	2,930	5.3	2,232	5.0	440	13.6
Colorado	444	6.4	379	6.0	51	16.3
Connecticut	243	5.8	167	4.9	71	13.5
Delaware	105	9.0	49	6.0	55	18.9
District of Columbia	112	14.1	21	8.8	91	17.0
Florida	1,629	7.2	916	5.7	679	12.0
Georgia	1,159	8.2	537	5.9	580	12.6
Hawaii	116	6.5	32	6.3	5	*
Idaho	141	6.1	134	6.1	1	*
Illinois	1,328	7.4	791	5.7	502	16.4
Indiana	698	8.0	526	7.0	168	17.0
Iowa	210	5.3	185	5.1	21	13.9
Kansas	294	7.4	233	6.6	55	17.6
Kentucky	375	6.6	303	6.0	67	13.2
Louisiana	613	10.1	249	7.0	359	14.9
Maine	97	6.9	93	6.9	2	*
Maryland	547	7.3	219	5.1	308	11.6
Massachusetts	396	5.2	302	4.8	72	8.2
Michigan	1,012	7.9	580	5.8	411	18.3
Minnesota	362	5.1	261	4.5	73	10.6
Mississippi	481	11.4	153	6.6	321	17.2
Missouri	590	7.5	412	6.4	171	14.6
Montana	81	7.0	66	6.7	-	*
Nebraska	147	5.6	120	5.2	18	*
Nevada	215	5.8	160	5.2	44	13.7
New Hampshire	76	5.3	68	5.0	3	*
New Jersey	595	5.2	332	4.0	220	11.0
New Mexico	177	6.1	134	5.6	9	*
New York	1,431	5.8	855	5.0	507	9.3
North Carolina	1,083	8.8	584	6.5	465	16.4
North Dakota	50	6.0	42	5.8	-	*
Ohio	1,225	8.3	809	6.7	408	16.9
Oklahoma	417	8.1	291	7.3	74	15.4
Oregon	269	5.9	243	5.9	10	*
Pennsylvania	1,061	7.3	716	6.2	329	14.1
Rhode Island	82	6.5	62	5.8	15	*
South Carolina	543	9.4	257	7.1	281	13.8
South Dakota	83	7.2	56	6.0	1	*
Tennessee	724	8.9	455	7.4	258	14.0
Texas	2,537	6.6	1,872	5.7	620	14.1
Utah	230	4.5	215	4.4	1	*
Vermont	42	6.5	39	6.2	2	*
Virginia	781	7.5	431	5.8	323	14.1
Washington	421	5.1	327	4.8	46	10.9
West Virginia	169	8.1	158	7.9	11	*
Wisconsin	469	6.6	329	5.4	120	17.7
Wyoming	49	6.8	47	6.9	-	*
Puerto Rico	466	9.2	456	10.0	10	*
Virgin Islands	11	*	1	*	10	*
Guam	34	10.7	4	*	-	*
American Samoa	12	*	-	*	-	*
Northern Marianas	6	*	-	*	-	*

* = Figure does not meet standards of reliability or precision.
- = Quantity zero.
[1]Includes races other than White and Black.
[2]Excludes data for Puerto Rico, Virgin Islands, Guam, American Samoa, and Northern Marianas.

Table B-55. Number of Infant and Neonatal Deaths and Mortality Rates, by Race, State, and Territory, 2005—Continued

(Number, rate per 1,000 live births in specified group.)

Sex, state, or territory	Neonatal deaths					
	All races[1]		White		Black	
	Number	Rate	Number	Rate	Number	Rate
UNITED STATES[2]	18,770	4.5	12,239	3.8	5,740	9.1
Male..	10,444	4.9	6,796	4.1	3,201	10.0
Female...	8,326	4.1	5,443	3.5	2,539	8.1
Alabama.......................................	347	5.7	189	4.6	155	8.6
Alaska..	31	3.0	17	*	2	*
Arizona..	433	4.5	376	4.5	21	5.8
Arkansas......................................	188	4.8	114	3.7	72	9.6
California......................................	1,991	3.6	1,545	3.5	269	8.3
Colorado......................................	329	4.8	284	4.5	38	12.2
Connecticut..................................	175	4.2	129	3.8	43	8.1
Delaware	78	6.7	37	4.5	40	13.7
District of Columbia.......................	79	9.9	15	*	64	11.9
Florida	1,024	4.5	568	3.5	436	7.7
Georgia	770	5.4	335	3.7	406	8.8
Hawaii	75	4.2	20	3.9	3	*
Idaho...	93	4.0	88	4.0	-	*
Illinois	891	5.0	537	3.9	330	10.8
Indiana	476	5.5	349	4.6	123	12.5
Iowa..	136	3.5	118	3.2	15	*
Kansas...	195	4.9	156	4.4	33	10.6
Kentucky	226	4.0	185	3.7	39	7.7
Louisiana	351	5.8	145	4.1	202	8.4
Maine	68	4.8	64	4.7	2	*
Maryland	394	5.3	151	3.5	227	8.6
Massachusetts	286	3.7	219	3.5	54	6.1
Michigan......................................	699	5.5	389	3.9	294	13.1
Minnesota	231	3.3	165	2.9	52	7.5
Mississippi....................................	284	6.7	71	3.1	209	11.2
Missouri.......................................	371	4.7	259	4.0	109	9.3
Montana.......................................	48	4.1	41	4.1	-	*
Nebraska	86	3.3	71	3.1	9	*
Nevada	130	3.5	100	3.3	24	7.5
New Hampshire	62	4.3	56	4.1	1	*
New Jersey....................................	395	3.5	229	2.8	139	7.0
New Mexico...................................	105	3.6	88	3.7	5	*
New York......................................	992	4.0	611	3.6	324	6.0
North Carolina..............................	755	6.1	387	4.3	341	12.0
North Dakota................................	36	4.3	29	4.0	-	*
Ohio..	828	5.6	539	4.5	284	11.8
Oklahoma.....................................	248	4.8	174	4.4	47	9.8
Oregon	174	3.8	158	3.8	6	*
Pennsylvania.................................	751	5.2	511	4.4	227	9.7
Rhode Island.................................	64	5.0	50	4.7	10	*
South Carolina..............................	336	5.8	158	4.4	175	8.6
South Dakota................................	52	4.5	42	4.5	1	*
Tennessee....................................	462	5.7	265	4.3	190	10.3
Texas...	1,595	4.1	1,180	3.6	389	8.8
Utah..	155	3.0	145	3.0	1	*
Vermont.......................................	26	4.0	24	3.8	1	*
Virginia..	537	5.1	298	4.0	219	9.6
Washington..................................	254	3.1	197	2.9	26	6.2
West Virginia................................	106	5.1	101	5.1	5	*
Wisconsin.....................................	318	4.5	228	3.8	78	11.5
Wyoming......................................	34	4.7	32	4.7	-	*
Puerto Rico	335	6.6	326	7.2	9	*
Virgin Islands	9	*	1	*	8	*
Guam	21	6.6	3	*	-	*
American Samoa...........................	5	*	-	*	-	*
Northern Marianas........................	5	*	-	*	-	*

* = Figure does not meet standards of reliability or precision.
- = Quantity zero.
[1]Includes races other than White and Black.
[2]Excludes data for Puerto Rico, Virgin Islands, Guam, American Samoa, and Northern Marianas.

Table B-56. Infant Mortality Rates by Birthweight, Selected Years, 1983–2004

(Deaths per 1,000 live births.)

Birthweight	1983[1]	1985[1]	1990[1]	1995[2]	2000[2]	2001[2]	2002[2]	2003[2]	2004[2]
All Birthweights....................	10.9	10.4	8.9	7.6	6.9	6.8	7.0	6.8	6.8
Less than 2,500 grams	95.9	93.9	78.1	65.3	60.2	59.4	60.3	59.4	57.9
Less than 1,500 grams..........	400.6	387.7	317.6	270.7	246.9	246.9	253.2	253.1	245.2
Less than 500 grams...........	890.3	895.9	898.2	904.9	847.9	856.8	863.6	866.2	850.1
500–999 grams	584.2	559.2	440.1	351.0	313.8	313.0	321.5	319.0	314.6
1,000–1,499 grams	162.3	145.4	97.9	69.6	60.9	59.4	57.7	56.9	55.7
1,500–1,999 grams.............	58.4	54.0	43.8	33.5	28.7	27.6	26.9	28.0	27.4
2,000–2,499 grams..............	22.5	20.9	17.8	13.7	11.9	11.4	11.7	11.0	11.1
2,500 grams or more	4.7	4.3	3.7	3.0	2.5	2.5	2.4	2.3	2.3
2,500–2,999 grams...............	8.8	7.9	6.7	5.5	4.6	4.5	4.5	4.1	4.2
3,000–3,499 grams...............	4.4	4.3	3.7	2.9	2.4	2.3	2.3	2.2	2.1
3,500–3,999 grams...............	3.2	3.0	2.6	2.0	1.7	1.7	1.6	1.6	1.5
4,000 grams or more	3.3	3.2	2.4	2.0	1.6	1.6	1.5	1.6	1.5
4,000–4,499 grams	2.9	2.9	2.2	1.8	1.5	1.5	1.4	1.3	1.4
4,500–4,999 grams	3.9	3.8	2.5	2.2	2.1	2.0	2.0	2.4	1.5
5,000 grams or more[3]	14.4	14.7	9.8	8.5	*6.1	*6.5	*5.1	*6.4	*4.9

* = Figure does not meet standards of reliability or precision.
[1]Rates based on unweighted birth cohort data.
[2]Rates based on a period file using weighted data; unknown birthweight imputed when period of gestation is known and proportionately distributed when period of gestation is unknown.
[3]In 1989, a birthweight-gestational age consistency check instituted for the natality file resulted in a decrease in the number of deaths to infants coded with birthweights of 5,000 grams or more and a discontinuity in the mortality trend for infants weighing 5,000 grams or more at birth. Starting with 1989 data, the rates are believed to be more accurate.

Table B-57. Number of Maternal Deaths and Maternal Mortality Rates for Selected Causes by Race, 2005

(Number, rate per 100,000 live births.)

Cause of death[1]	Number				Rate			
		All other				All other		
	All races	White	Total	Black	All races	White	Total	Black
Maternal causes (A34, O00-O95, O98-O99)	623	360	263	231	15.1	11.1	28.9	36.5
Pregnancy with abortive outcome (O00-O07)	33	15	18	13	0.8	*	*	*
Ectopic pregnancy (O00)...	18	7	11	9	*	*	*	*
Spontaneous abortion (O03)	4	3	1	1	*	*	*	*
Medical abortion (O04)	4	2	2	-	*	*	*	*
Other abortion (O05)...	1	-	1	-	*	*	*	*
Other and unspecified pregnancy with abortive outcome (O01-O02, O06-O07)	6	3	3	3	*	*	*	*
Other direct obstetric causes (A34, O10-O92)	389	222	167	152	9.4	6.9	18.4	24.0
Eclampsia and pre-eclampsia (O11, O13-O16)	50	27	23	23	1.2	0.8	2.5	3.6
Hemorrhage of pregnancy and childbirth and placenta previa (O20, O44-O46, O67, O72)..........................	39	23	16	14	0.9	0.7	*	*
Complications predominately related to the puerperium (A34, O85-O92)	122	72	50	45	2.9	2.2	5.5	7.1
Obstetrical tetanus (A34)	-	-	-	-	*	*	*	*
Obstetric embolism (O88)	56	35	21	18	1.4	1.1	2.3	*
Other complications predominately related to the puerperium (O85-O87, O89-O92)........................	66	37	29	27	1.6	1.1	3.2	4.3
All other direct obstetric causes (O10, O12, O21-O43, O47-O66, O68-O71, O73-O75)............................	178	100	78	70	4.3	3.1	8.6	11.1
Obstetric death of unspecified cause (O95)...............	42	29	13	12	1.0	0.9	*	*
Indirect obstetric causes (O98-O99)	159	94	65	54	3.8	2.9	7.2	8.5
Maternal causes more than 42 days after delivery or termination of pregnancy (O96-O97).......................	137	93	44	36	3.3	2.9	4.8	5.7
Death from any obstetric cause occurring more than 42 days but less than one year after delivery (O96)	130	91	39	31	3.1	2.8	4.3	4.9
Death from sequelae of direct obstetric causes (O97)	7	2	5	5	*	*	*	*

* = Figure does not meet standard of reliability or precision.
- = Quantity zero.
[1]Based on codes from the *International Classification of Diseases, Tenth Revision* (1992), except where (*) precedes the cause of death code.

Table B-58. Number of Maternal Deaths and Maternal Mortality Rates for Selected Causes, by Hispanic Origin and Race for Non-Hispanic Population, 2005

(Number, rate per 100,000 live births.)

Cause of death[1]	Number					Rate				
	All origins[2]	Hispanic[3]	Non-Hispanic[4]	Non-Hispanic White	Non-Hispanic Black	All origins[2]	Hispanic[3]	Non-Hispanic[4]	Non-Hispanic White	Non-Hispanic Black
Maternal causes (A34, O00-O95, O98-O99)	623	95	527	267	229	15.1	9.6	16.9	11.7	39.2
Pregnancy with abortive outcome (O00-O07)	33	2	31	14	13	0.8	*	1.0	*	*
Ectopic pregnancy (O00)	18	-	18	7	9	*	*	*	*	*
Spontaneous abortion (O03)	4	-	4	3	1	*	*	*	*	*
Medical abortion (O04)	4	1	3	2	-	*	*	*	*	*
Other abortion (O05)	1	-	1	-	-	*	*	*	*	*
Other and unspecified pregnancy with abortive outcome (O01-O02, O06-O07)	6	1	5	2	3	*	*	*	*	*
Other direct obstetric causes (A34, O10-O92)	389	61	327	162	150	9.4	6.2	10.5	7.1	25.7
Eclampsia and pre-eclampsia (O11, O13-O16)	50	8	42	19	23	1.2	*	1.3	*	3.9
Hemorrhage of pregnancy and childbirth and placenta previa (O20, O44-O46, O67, O72)	39	10	28	12	14	0.9	*	0.9	*	*
Complications predominately related to the puerperium (A34, O85-O92)	122	19	103	53	45	2.9	*	3.3	2.3	7.7
Obstetrical tetanus (A34)	-	-	-	-	-	*	*	*	*	*
Obstetric embolism (O88)	56	10	46	25	18	1.4	*	1.5	1.1	*
Other complications predominately related to the puerperium (O85-O87, O89-O92)	66	9	57	28	27	1.6	*	1.8	1.2	4.6
All other direct obstetric causes (O10, O12, O21-O43, O47-O066, O68-O71, O73-O75)	178	24	154	78	68	4.3	2.4	4.9	3.4	11.6
Obstetric death of unspecified cause (O95)	42	11	31	18	12	1.0	*	1.0	*	*
Indirect obstetric causes (O98-O99)	159	21	138	73	54	3.8	2.1	4.4	3.2	9.3
Maternal causes more than 42 days after delivery or termination of pregnancy (O96-O97)	137	34	103	60	36	3.3	3.5	3.3	2.6	6.2
Death from any obstetric cause occurring more than 42 days but less than one year after delivery (O96)	130	33	97	59	31	3.1	3.3	3.1	2.6	5.3
Death from sequelae of direct obstetric causes (O97)	7	1	6	1	5	*	*	*	*	*

* = Figure does not meet standard of reliability or precision.

- = Quantity zero.

[1]Based on codes from the *International Classification of Diseases, Tenth Revision* (1992), except where (*) precedes the cause of death code.

[2]All origins includes origin not stated; specified origins exclude origins not stated.

[3]Persons of Hispanic origin may be of any race.

[4]Includes races other than White and Black.

Table B-59. Maternal Mortality for Complications of Pregnancy, Childbirth, and the Puerperium, by Race, Hispanic Origin, and Age, Selected Years, 1950–2005

(Number, rate per 100,000 live births.)

Race, Hispanic origin, and age	1950[1,2]	1960[1,2]	1970[2]	1980[2]	1985	1990[2]	1991	1992	1993	1994	1995	1996	1997	1998	1999[7]	2000[7]	2001	2002	2003[8]	2004[8]	2005[8]
NUMBER OF DEATHS																					
All Persons	2,960	1,579	803	334	295	343	323	318	302	328	277	294	327	281	391	396	399	357	495	540	623
White	1,873	936	445	193	156	177	187	161	152	193	129	159	179	158	214	240	228	190	280	300	360
Black or African American	1,041	624	342	127	124	153	125	140	135	118	133	121	125	104	154	137	150	148	183	214	231
American Indian or Alaska Native	—	—	—	3	7	4	3	5	3	-	1	6	2	2	5	6	5	-	7	4	5
Asian or Pacific Islander	—	—	—	11	8	9	8	12	12	17	14	8	21	17	18	13	16	19	25	22	27
Hispanic or Latina[3]	—	—	—	—	29	47	63	48	48	64	43	39	57	42	67	81	81	62	92	80	95
White, not Hispanic or Latina[3]	—	—	—	—	60	125	120	115	104	127	84	114	121	116	149	160	151	128	188	225	267
DEATHS PER 100,000 LIVE BIRTHS																					
Age																					
All ages, age-adjusted[4]	73.7	32.1	21.5	9.4	7.6	7.6	7.2	7.3	6.7	7.9	6.3	6.4	7.6	6.1	8.3	8.2	8.8	7.6	9.7	11.3	12.4
All ages, crude	83.3	37.1	21.5	9.2	7.8	8.2	7.9	7.8	7.5	8.3	7.1	7.6	8.4	7.1	9.9	9.8	9.9	8.9	12.1	13.1	15.1
Under 20 years	70.7	22.7	18.9	7.6	6.9	7.5	6.8	7.1	4.5	6.9	3.9	*	5.7	*	6.6	*	8.8	6.7	6.2	6.6	7.4
20–24 years	47.6	20.7	13.0	5.8	5.4	6.1	5.9	6.9	5.9	7.6	5.7	5.0	6.2	5.0	6.2	7.4	6.9	5.8	7.7	10.8	10.7
25–29 years	63.5	29.8	17.0	7.7	6.4	6.0	5.9	4.8	5.9	7.1	6.0	6.6	7.9	6.7	8.2	7.9	8.5	7.5	8.7	11.0	11.8
30–34 years	107.7	50.3	31.6	13.6	8.9	9.5	8.8	9.2	7.7	6.5	7.3	7.6	8.3	7.5	10.1	10.0	10.1	9.3	10.9	11.8	12.8
35 years and over[5]	222.0	104.3	81.9	36.3	25.0	20.7	19.0	16.9	19.6	18.3	15.9	19.0	16.1	14.5	23.0	22.7	18.9	18.4	33.1	28.2	38.0
White																					
All ages, age-adjusted[4]	53.1	22.4	14.4	6.7	4.9	5.1	5.0	4.7	4.2	5.8	3.6	4.1	5.2	4.2	5.5	6.2	6.5	4.8	6.9	7.5	9.1
All ages, crude	61.1	26.0	14.3	6.6	5.1	5.4	5.8	5.0	4.8	6.2	4.2	5.1	5.8	5.1	6.8	7.5	7.2	6.0	8.7	9.3	11.1
Under 20 years	44.9	14.8	13.8	5.8	*	*	*	*	*	6.2	*	*	*	*	*	*	7.4	*	*	*	*
20–24 years	35.7	15.3	8.4	4.2	3.3	3.9	3.8	4.7	3.5	4.7	3.5	*	4.2	3.1	4.0	5.6	5.3	3.4	5.3	6.5	9.0
25–29 years	45.0	20.3	11.1	5.4	4.6	4.8	4.2	3.1	3.6	6.1	4.0	4.0	5.4	4.9	5.4	5.9	5.8	4.6	6.9	6.9	7.2
30–34 years	75.9	34.3	18.7	9.3	5.1	5.0	7.2	6.3	5.5	5.0	4.0	5.0	5.4	4.9	7.0	7.1	8.1	6.7	6.8	9.0	9.3
35 years and over[5]	174.1	73.9	59.3	25.5	17.5	12.6	14.3	9.4	11.7	12.0	9.1	14.9	11.5	11.0	16.6	18.0	11.4	13.3	23.8	22.0	28.9
Black or African American																					
All ages, age-adjusted[4]	—	92.0	65.5	24.9	22.1	21.7	18.1	20.1	20.0	18.1	20.9	19.9	20.1	16.1	23.3	20.1	22.4	22.9	25.5	32.3	31.7
All ages, crude	—	103.6	60.9	22.4	21.3	22.4	18.3	20.8	20.5	18.5	22.1	20.3	20.8	17.1	25.4	22.0	24.7	24.9	30.5	34.7	36.5
Under 20 years	—	54.8	32.3	13.1	*	*	*	13.7	*	*	*	*	*	*	*	*	*	*	*	*	*
20–24 years	—	56.9	41.9	13.9	14.6	14.7	13.2	15.3	14.4	18.2	15.3	15.1	15.3	12.7	14.0	15.3	14.6	14.9	15.8	27.9	18.2
25–29 years	—	92.8	65.2	22.4	19.4	14.9	16.6	15.8	21.1	*	21.0	25.5	24.3	17.2	26.6	21.8	24.7	27.1	20.7	38.6	37.1
30–34 years	—	150.6	117.8	44.0	38.0	44.2	23.1	30.9	25.8	*	31.2	28.6	32.9	27.7	36.1	34.8	30.6	28.4	46.1	40.4	46.6
35 years and over[5]	—	299.5	207.5	100.6	77.2	79.7	61.9	65.2	69.9	64.5	61.4	49.9	40.4	37.2	69.9	62.8	71.0	62.9	104.1	79.2	112.8
Hispanic or Latina[3,6]																					
All ages, age-adjusted[4]	—	—	—	—	7.1	7.4	9.3	7.1	6.6	9.1	5.4	4.8	7.6	5.2	7.9	9.0	8.8	6.0	8.6	7.3	8.2
All ages, crude	—	—	—	—	7.8	7.9	10.1	7.5	7.3	9.6	6.3	5.6	8.0	5.7	8.8	9.9	9.5	7.1	10.1	8.5	9.6
White, not Hispanic or Latino[3]																					
All ages, age-adjusted[4]	—	—	—	—	4.0	4.4	4.0	4.1	3.8	4.9	3.3	3.9	4.4	4.0	4.9	5.5	5.8	4.4	6.3	7.8	9.6
All ages, crude	—	—	—	—	4.3	4.8	4.6	4.6	4.2	5.2	3.5	4.8	5.2	4.9	6.4	6.8	6.5	5.6	8.1	9.8	11.7

—— = Data not available.

- = Quantity zero.

* = Figure does not meet standards of reliability or precision.

[1]Includes deaths of persons who were not residents of the 50 states and the District of Columbia.

[2]Underlying cause of death was coded according to the Sixth Revision of the *International Classification of Diseases* in 1950, Seventh Revision in 1960, Eighth Revision in 1970, and Ninth Revision in 1980–1998.

[3]Prior to 1997, excludes data from states lacking an Hispanic-origin item on the death certificate. Persons of Hispanic origin may be of any race.

[4]Rates are age-adjusted to the 1970 distribution of live births by mother's age.

[5]Rates computed by relating deaths of women 35 years and over to live births to women 35-49 years.

[6]Age-specific maternal mortality rates are not calculated because rates based on fewer than 20 deaths are considered unreliable.

[7]Starting with 1999 data, cause of death is coded according to the *International Classification of Diseases*. Major changes in the classification and coding of maternal deaths account for an increase in the number of maternal deaths.

[8]Increases are due to methodological changes in reporting and data processing.

NOTES AND DEFINITIONS

SOURCES OF DATA

Three different publications were used to obtain the mortality data in Part B. The majority of the tables came from the following source: Kung, Hsiang-Ching, Donna L. Hoyert, et al. *Deaths: Final Data for 2005*. National Vital Statistics Reports: Volume 56, No 10. Hyattsville, MD: National Center for Health Statistics. 2008.

Tables B-2, B-4, B-12, B-16, B-18A, B-39, B-41, B-50, B-53 and B-54 came from: Heron, Melonie P., Donna L. Hoyert, et al. *Deaths: Preliminary Data for 2006*. National Vital Statistics Reports: Volume 56, No 16. Hyattsville, MD: National Center for Health Statistics. 2008.

In addition, Tables B-17, B-37, B-40, B-42 through B-47, B-56, and B-59 all are derived from: *Health, United States, 2007 With Chartbook on Trends in the Health of Americans*. Hyattsville, MD: National Center for Health Statistics. 2007.

NOTES ON THE DATA

Final data in Part B are based on information from all resident death certificates filed in the 50 states and the District of Columbia. It is believed that more than 99 percent of all deaths that occur in the United States are registered. Data shown for geographic areas are by place of residence. Beginning with 1970, mortality statistics for the United States exclude deaths of non-residents of the United States. All data exclude fetal deaths.

Mortality statistics for Puerto Rico, Virgin Islands, American Samoa, and Northern Marianas exclude deaths of nonresidents of Puerto Rico, Virgin Islands, American Samoa, and Northern Marianas. For Guam, however, mortality statistics exclude deaths that occurred to a resident of any place other than Guam or the United States.

Race and Hispanic origin are reported separately on the death certificate. Therefore, data shown by race include persons of Hispanic and non-Hispanic origin, and data for Hispanic origin include persons of any race. Unless otherwise specified, deaths of Hispanic origin are included in the totals for each race group—White, Black, American Indian or Alaska Native (AIAN), and Asian or Pacific Islander (API)—according to the decedent's race as reported on the death certificate. Data shown for Hispanic persons include all persons of Hispanic origin of any race.

Cause of death statistics are classified in accordance with the *International Classification of Diseases, Tenth Revision (ICD-10)*. Data for 2005 are based on records of deaths that occurred during 2005 and were received by the

National Center for Health Statistics (NCHS) as of October 4, 2007. Preliminary data for 2006 are based on records of deaths that occurred in calendar year 2006 and were received by the NCHS as of December 19, 2007.

CONCEPTS AND DEFINITIONS

Age-adjusted death rate—the death rate used to make comparisons of relative mortality risks across groups and over time. This rate should be viewed as a construct or an index rather than as a direct or actual measure of mortality risk. Statistically, it is a weighted average of the age-specific death rates, where the weights represent the fixed population proportions by age.

Age-specific death rate—deaths per 100,000 population in a specified age group, such as 1–4 years or 5–9 years for a specified period.

Cause of death—for the purpose of national mortality statistics, every death is attributed to one underlying condition, based on information reported on the death certificate and using the international rules for selecting the underlying cause of death from the conditions stated on the death certificate. The underlying cause is defined by the World Health Organization as the disease or injury that initiated the train of events leading directly to death, or the circumstances of the accident or violence that produced the fatal injury. Generally more medical information is reported on death certificates than is directly reflected in the underlying cause of death. The conditions that are not selected as underlying cause of death constitute the nonunderlying causes of death, also known as multiple cause of death.

Cause-of-death ranking—selected causes of death of public health and medical importance comprise tabulation lists and are ranked according to the number of deaths assigned to these causes. The top-ranking causes determine the leading causes of death. Certain causes on the tabulation lists are not ranked if, for example, the category title represents a group title (such as major cardiovascular diseases and symptoms, signs, and abnormal clinical and laboratory findings, not elsewhere classified); or the category title begins with the words "other" and "all other". In addition, when one of the titles that represents a subtotal (such as malignant neoplasms) is ranked, its component parts are not ranked.

Crude death rate—total deaths per 100,000 population for a specified period. The crude death rate represents the average chance of dying during a specified period for persons in the entire population.

Infant deaths—deaths of infants under 1 year of age.

International Classification of Diseases (ICD)—used to code and classify cause-of-death data. It is developed collaboratively by the World Health Organization and 10 international centers, one of which is housed at NCHS. The purpose of it is to promote international comparability in the collection, classification, processing, and presentation of health statistics. Since 1900, it has been modified about once every 10 years, except for the 20-year interval between the ninth and tenth editions. The purpose of the revisions is to stay abreast with advances in medical science. New revisions usually introduce major disruptions in time series of mortality statistics.

Hispanic origin—includes persons of Mexican, Puerto Rican, Cuban, Central and South American, and other or unknown Latin American or Spanish origins. Persons of Hispanic origin may be of any race.

Life expectancy—the expected life span at birth–or the remaining life span at a later age–if current mortality rates in each bracket were to remain unchanged.

Neonatal deaths—deaths of infants aged 0–27 days.

Perinatal mortality rate—the sum of late fetal deaths plus infant deaths within 7 days of birth divided by the sum of live births plus late fetal deaths, per 1,000 live births plus late fetal deaths.

Perinatal mortality ratio—the sum of late fetal deaths plus infant deaths within 7 days of birth divided by the number of live births, per 1,000 live births.

Postneonatal deaths—deaths of infants aged 28 days–1 year old.

Years of potential life lost (YPLL)—a measure of premature mortality. YPLL is presented for persons under 75 years of age because the average life expectancy in the United States is over 75 years. YPLL-75 is calculated using the following eight age groups: under 1 year, 1–14 years, 15–24 years, 25–34 years, 35–44 years, 45–54 years, 55–64 years, and 65–74 years. The number of deaths for each age group is multiplied by years of life lost, calculated as the difference between age 75 years and the midpoint of the age group. For the eight age groups, the midpoints are 0.5, 7.5, 19.5, 29.5, 39.5, 49.5, 59.5, and 69.5. For example, the death of a person 15–24 years of age counts as 55.5 years of life lost. Years of potential life lost is derived by summing years of life lost over all age groups.

PART C:
HEALTH

HEALTH

DETERMINANTS AND MEASURES OF HEALTH

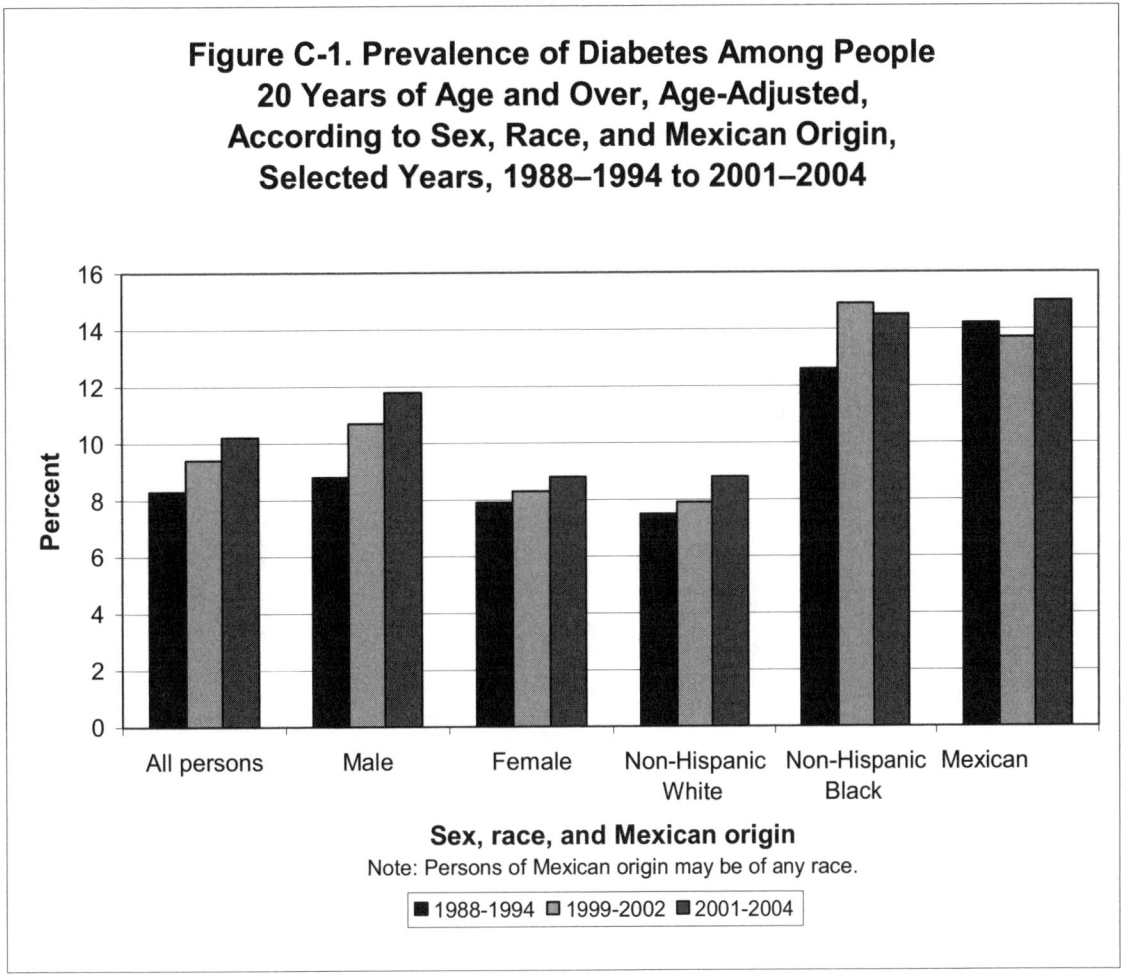

Figure C-1. Prevalence of Diabetes Among People 20 Years of Age and Over, Age-Adjusted, According to Sex, Race, and Mexican Origin, Selected Years, 1988–1994 to 2001–2004

Note: Persons of Mexican origin may be of any race.

■ 1988-1994 ▨ 1999-2002 ■ 2001-2004

HIGHLIGHTS

- The prevalence of diabetes in the total population increased from 8.3 percent in 1988–1994 to 10.2 percent in 2001–2004. Non-Hispanic Whites had a much lower rate of diabetes than either Mexicans or Non-Hispanic Blacks. In the 2001–2004 time period, 15 percent of Mexicans had diabetes compared to 14.5 percent of Non-Hispanic Blacks and 8.8 percent of Non-Hispanic Whites. (Determinants and Measures of Health, Table C-6)

- The percentage of people who smoked remained steady at 20.8 percent in 2005. Smoking declined sharply for a number of years following the first Surgeon General's Report on smoking in 1964. However, since 1990, it has declined at much slower rate. (Use of Addictive Substances, Table C-22)

- In 2006, 5.7 percent of people did not receive medical care, 7.8 percent of people experienced delayed medical

care due to costs, and 7.0 percent of people did not receive prescription drugs due to costs. (Ambulatory Care, Table C-33)

- The number of admissions to a mental health organization have increased from 1.8 million in 1986 to 2.7 million in 2004. (Inpatient Care, Table C-50)

- Employment for personal and home care aides is expected to grow faster than any other occupation in the health care industry from 2006 to 2016. (Health Personnel, Table C-61)

- National health care expenditures totaled nearly two trillion dollars in 2005, a 6.9 percent increase from 2004. (Health Expenditures, Table C-65)

- In 2007, 15.3 percent people did not have health insurance, a decline from 15.8 percent in 2006. (Health Insurance, Table C-78)

241

Table C-1. Occupational Injuries and Illnesses with Days Away from Work, Job Transfer, or Restriction, by Industry, 2003–2005

(Cases per 100 full-time workers, number.)

Industry	Injuries and illnesses with days away from work, job transfer, or restriction					
	Cases per 100 full-time workers[1]			Number of cases in thousands[2]		
	2003	2004	2005	2003	2004	2005
Total private sector[3]	2.6	2.5	2.4	2,301.9	2,225.0	2,184.8
Agriculture, forestry, fishing, and hunting[4]	3.3	3.7	3.3	29.3	31.5	29.5
Mining	2.0	2.3	2.2	11.2	12.9	13.7
Utilities	2.2	2.5	2.4	12.2	14.1	12.9
Construction	3.6	3.4	3.4	218.0	212.2	222.5
Manufacturing	3.8	3.6	3.5	538.0	519.9	490.8
Wholesale trade	2.8	2.7	2.7	147.4	146.2	146.8
Retail trade	2.7	2.7	2.6	319.6	322.8	314.2
Transportation and warehousing	5.4	4.9	4.6	204.0	190.0	185.6
Information	1.1	1.1	1.1	30.8	31.1	30.9
Finance and insurance	0.4	0.3	0.4	21.3	18.4	19.1
Real estate and rental and leasing	2.1	1.9	2.1	35.6	33.4	37.1
Professional, scientific, and technical services	0.6	0.5	0.6	36.0	32.2	38.4
Management of companies and enterprises	1.6	1.5	1.3	25.1	23.4	20.8
Administrative and support and waste management and remediation service	2.4	2.2	2.0	96.7	94.9	89.5
Educational services	1.2	1.0	1.0	17.9	14.5	14.8
Health care and social assistance	3.1	2.9	2.8	337.9	322.8	318.4
Arts, entertainment, and recreation	2.9	3.1	2.9	34.1	35.2	34.1
Accommodation and food services	2.0	1.7	1.7	135.2	122.5	120.8
Other services, except public administration	1.7	1.6	1.5	51.7	47.0	44.8

[1]Incidence rate calculated as (N/EH) x 200,000, where N = total number of injuries and illnesses, EH = total hours worked by all employees during the calendar year, and 200,000 = base for 100 full-time equivalent employees working 40 hours per week, 50 weeks per year.
[2]Because of rounding, components may not add to total number of cases in private sector.
[3]Totals include data for industries not shown separately. Excludes self-employed, private households, and employees in federal, state, and local government agencies.
[4]Excludes farms with fewer than 11 employees.

NOTE: Starting with 2003 data, the Survey of Occupational Injuries and Illnesses began using the 2002 North American Industry Classification System (NAICS) to classify establishments by industry. Prior to 2003, the survey used the Standard Industrial Classification (SIC) system. Because of substantial differences between these systems, the data measured by these surveys are not directly comparable.

Table C-2.   Selected Notifiable Disease Rates and Number of Cases, Selected Years, 1950–2005

(Cases per 100,000 population, number.)

Disease	1950	1960	1970	1980	1985	1990	1995	2000	2001	2002	2003	2004	2005
Rate													
Diphtheria	3.83	0.51	0.21	0.00	0.00	0.00	-	0.00	0.00	0.00	0.00	-	-
Haemophilus influenzae, invasive......................	—	—	—	—	—	—	0.45	0.51	0.57	0.62	0.70	0.72	0.78
Hepatitis A	—	—	27.87	12.84	10.03	12.64	12.13	4.91	3.77	3.13	2.66	1.95	1.53
Hepatitis B	—	—	4.08	8.39	11.50	8.48	4.19	2.95	2.79	2.84	2.61	2.14	1.78
Lyme disease	—	—	—	—	—	—	4.49	6.53	6.05	8.44	7.39	6.84	7.94
Meningococcal disease	—	—	1.23	1.25	1.04	0.99	1.25	0.83	0.83	0.64	0.61	0.47	0.42
Mumps	—	—	55.55	3.86	1.30	2.17	0.35	0.13	0.10	0.10	0.08	0.09	0.11
Pertussis (whooping cough)	79.82	8.23	2.08	0.76	1.50	1.84	1.97	2.88	2.69	3.47	4.04	8.88	8.72
Poliomyelitis, total	22.02	1.77	0.02	0.00	0.00	0.00	0.00	-	-	-	-	-	-
Paralytic[1]	—	1.40	0.02	0.00	0.00	0.00	0.00	-	-	-	-	-	0.00
Rocky Mountain spotted fever	—	—	0.19	0.52	0.30	0.26	0.23	0.18	0.25	0.39	0.38	0.60	0.66
Rubella (German measles)	—	—	27.75	1.72	0.26	0.45	0.05	0.06	0.01	0.01	0.00	-	-
Rubeola (measles)	211.01	245.42	23.23	5.96	1.18	11.17	0.12	0.03	0.04	0.02	0.02	0.01	0.02
Salmonellosis, excluding typhoid fever	—	3.85	10.84	14.88	27.37	19.54	17.66	14.51	14.39	15.73	15.16	14.51	15.43
Shigellosis	15.45	6.94	6.79	8.41	7.14	10.89	12.32	8.41	7.19	8.37	8.19	5.03	5.51
Tuberculosis[2]	—	30.83	18.28	12.25	9.30	10.33	8.70	6.01	5.68	5.36	5.17	4.99	4.80
Sexually transmitted diseases[3]													
Syphilis[4]	146.02	68.78	45.26	30.51	28.39	54.32	26.05	11.20	11.31	11.42	11.79	11.38	11.33
Primary and secondary	16.73	9.06	10.89	12.06	11.40	20.26	6.21	2.12	2.14	2.38	2.47	2.72	2.97
Early latent	39.71	10.11	8.08	9.00	9.11	22.19	10.01	3.35	3.05	2.92	2.88	2.65	2.78
Late and late latent[5]	70.22	45.91	24.94	9.30	7.74	10.32	9.12	5.53	5.95	5.95	6.30	5.89	5.47
Congenital[6]	8.97	2.48	0.97	0.12	0.11	1.55	0.70	0.21	0.18	0.16	0.15	0.13	0.11
Chlamydia[7]	—	—	—	—	17.42	160.19	187.84	251.38	274.52	289.41	301.74	316.51	332.51
Gonorrhea[8]	192.50	145.40	297.22	445.10	382.98	276.43	147.46	128.67	126.77	122.01	115.23	112.42	115.64
Chancroid	3.34	0.94	0.70	0.30	0.87	1.69	0.23	0.03	0.01	0.02	0.02	0.01	0.01
Number													
Diphtheria	5,796	918	435	3	3	4	-	1	2	1	1	-	-
Haemophilus influenzae, invasive......................	—	—	—	—	—	—	1,180	1,398	1,597	1,743	2,013	2,085	2,304
Hepatitis A	—	—	56,797	29,087	23,210	31,441	31,582	13,397	10,609	8,795	7,653	5,683	4,488
Hepatitis B	—	—	8,310	19,015	26,611	21,102	10,805	8,036	7,843	7,996	7,526	6,212	5,119
Lyme disease	—	—	—	—	—	—	11,700	17,730	17,029	23,763	21,273	19,804	23,305
Meningococcal disease	—	—	2,505	2,840	2,479	2,451	3,243	2,256	2,333	1,814	1,756	1,361	1,245
Mumps	—	—	104,953	8,576	2,982	5,292	906	338	266	270	231	258	314
Pertussis (whooping cough)	120,718	14,809	4,249	1,730	3,589	4,570	5,137	7,867	7,580	9,771	11,647	25,827	25,616
Poliomyelitis, total	33,300	3,190	33	9	8	6	7	-	-	-	-	-	-
Paralytic[1]	—	2,525	31	9	8	6	7	-	-	-	-	-	1
Rocky Mountain spotted fever	—	—	380	1,163	714	651	590	495	695	1,104	1,091	1,713	1,936
Rubella (German measles)	—	—	56,552	3,904	630	1,125	128	176	23	18	7	10	11
Rubeola (measles)	319,124	441,703	47,351	13,506	2,822	27,786	309	86	116	44	56	37	66
Salmonellosis, excluding typhoid fever	—	6,929	22,096	33,715	65,347	48,603	45,970	39,574	40,495	44,264	43,657	42,197	45,322
Shigellosis	23,367	12,487	13,845	19,041	17,057	27,077	32,080	22,922	20,221	23,541	23,581	14,627	16,168
Tuberculosis[2]	—	55,494	37,137	27,749	22,201	25,701	22,860	16,377	15,989	15,075	14,874	14,517	14,097
Sexually transmitted diseases[3]													
Syphilis[4]	217,558	122,538	91,382	68,832	67,563	135,590	69,358	31,618	32,283	32,918	34,289	33,419	33,278
Primary and secondary	23,939	16,145	21,982	27,204	27,131	50,578	16,543	5,979	6,103	6,862	7,177	7,980	8,724
Early latent	59,256	18,017	16,311	20,297	21,689	55,397	26,657	9,465	8,701	8,429	8,361	7,768	8,176
Late and late latent[5]	113,569	81,798	50,348	20,979	18,414	25,750	24,296	15,594	16,976	17,168	18,319	17,300	16,049
Congenital[6]	13,377	4,416	1,953	277	329	3,865	1,862	580	503	459	432	371	329
Chlamydia[7]	—	—	—	—	25,848	323,663	478,577	709,452	783,242	834,555	877,478	929,462	976,445
Gonorrhea[8]	286,746	258,933	600,072	1,004,029	911,419	690,042	392,651	363,136	361,705	351,852	335,104	330,132	339,593
Chancroid	4,977	1,680	1,416	788	2,067	4,212	607	78	38	48	54	30	17

0.00 = Rate greater than zero but less than 0.005.

- = Quantity zero.

—— = Data not available.

[1]Data for 1986 and subsequent years may be updated due to retrospective case evaluations or late reports.

[2]Case reporting for tuberculosis began in 1953. Data prior to 1975 are not comparable with subsequent years because of changes in reporting criteria effective in 1975. 2005 data were updated through the Division of Tuberculosis Elimination, NCHHSTP, as of May 12, 2005.

[3]Starting with 1991, data include both civilian and military cases.

[4]Includes stage of syphilis not stated.

[5]Includes cases of unknown duration.

[6]Starting with 1989, data reflect change in case definition introduced in 1988. All cases of congenitally acquired syphilis were reported through 1994; starting with 1995 data, only congenital syphilis for cases less than one year of age were reported. See STD Surveillance Report for congenital syphilis rates per 100,000 live births. In 2005, the rate was 8.0 congenital syphilis cases per 100,000 live births.

[7]Prior to 1994, chlamydia was not notifiable. In 1994–1999, cases for New York were exclusively reported by New York City. Starting with 2000 data, includes cases for the entire state.

[8]Data for 1994 do not include cases from Georgia.

NOTE: The total resident population was used to calculate all rates except sexually transmitted diseases (STD), which used the civilian resident population prior to 1991.

Table C-3. Acquired Immunodeficiency Syndrome (AIDS) Cases, According to Age at Diagnosis and Other Selected Characteristics, 2001–2005

(Number, percent distribution.)

Sex, race, Hispanic origin, age at diagnosis, and region of residence	Year of diagnosis					
	All years[1]	2001	2002	2003	2004	2005
ESTIMATED NUMBER OF CASES[2]						
All persons[3]	952,629	38,079	38,408	39,666	39,524	40,608
Sex						
Male, 13 years and over	761,723	27,908	28,276	28,891	28,817	29,766
Female, 13 years and over	181,802	10,049	10,027	10,704	10,656	10,774
Children, under 13 years	9,101	121	105	71	50	68
Male, 13 Years and Over						
Hispanic origin and race						
Not Hispanic or Latino						
White	346,533	9,352	9,558	9,613	9,714	10,027
Black or African American	278,917	12,696	12,769	12,940	12,843	13,048
Asian or Pacific Islander	6,545	312	352	378	373	389
American Indian or Alaska Native	2,544	126	134	142	127	137
Hispanic or Latino[4]	124,598	5,255	5,274	5,646	5,579	5,949
Age at Diagnosis						
13–14 years	615	40	32	35	48	43
15–24 years	27,413	929	1,049	1,242	1,370	1,581
25–34 years	246,054	6,445	6,236	6,048	6,076	6,060
35–44 years	305,376	11,769	11,970	11,984	11,538	11,502
45–54 years	132,339	6,378	6,589	7,005	6,982	7,716
55–64 years	38,713	1,791	1,894	1,993	2,158	2,274
65 years and over	11,207	557	506	585	644	591
Female, 13 Years and Over						
Hispanic origin and race						
Not Hispanic or Latino						
White	37,390	1,637	1,702	1,629	1,800	1,747
Black or African American	112,999	6,684	6,717	7,237	7,108	7,093
Asian or Pacific Islander	1,060	60	74	84	97	92
American Indian or Alaska Native	662	40	47	44	59	45
Hispanic or Latino[4]	28,843	1,570	1,420	1,633	1,510	1,714
Age at Diagnosis						
13–14 years	447	42	35	44	35	44
15–24 years	12,671	642	673	662	674	701
25–34 years	62,013	2,799	2,650	2,737	2,607	2,470
35–44 years	67,825	3,938	3,790	4,150	3,989	3,954
45–54 years	27,342	1,975	2,110	2,269	2,455	2,637
55–64 years	8,204	490	586	633	695	757
65 years and over	3,297	163	183	210	201	211
Children, Under 13 Years						
Hispanic origin and race						
Not Hispanic or Latino						
White	1,613	13	14	12	6	6
Black or African American	5,631	85	72	46	31	46
Asian or Pacific Islander	54	1	1	-	1	1
American Indian or Alaska Native	32	-	1	-	1	-
Hispanic or Latino[4]	1,738	23	16	11	9	13
Region of Residence						
Northeast	300,963	11,273	10,292	10,955	10,452	11,529
Midwest	97,930	3,929	4,126	4,282	4,225	4,862
South	359,725	16,571	17,301	18,014	18,761	18,115
West	194,011	6,306	6,689	6,414	6,086	6,102

0.0 = Rate greater than zero but less than 0.05.

- = Quantity zero.

[1]Based on cases reported to the Centers for Disease Control and Prevention from the beginning of the epidemic (1981) through June 30, 2006.

[2]Numbers are point estimates that result from adjustments for reporting delays to AIDS case counts. The estimates do not include adjustments for incomplete reporting. Data are provisional.

[3]Total for all years includes 3,469 persons of unknown race or multiple races, 3 persons of unknown sex, 1,136 persons of unknown state of residence, and 3 persons who were residents of other areas. All persons totals were calculated independent of values for subpopulations. Consequently, sums of subpopulations may not equal totals for all persons.

[4]Persons of Hispanic origin may be of any race.

[5]Percents may not sum to 100% due to rounding and because persons of unknown race and Hispanic origin are included in totals.

Table C-3. Acquired Immunodeficiency Syndrome (AIDS) Cases, According to Age at Diagnosis and Other Selected Characteristics, 2001–2005—*Continued*

(Number, percent distribution.)

Sex, race, Hispanic origin, age at diagnosis, and region of residence	Year of diagnosis					
	All years[1]	2001	2002	2003	2004	2005
PERCENT DISTRIBUTION[5]						
All persons[3]	100.0	100.0	100.0	100.0	100.0	100.0
Male, 13 years and over	80.0	73.3	73.6	72.8	72.9	73.3
Female, 13 years and over	19.1	26.4	26.1	27.0	27.0	26.5
Children, under 13 years	1.0	0.3	0.3	0.2	0.1	0.2
Male, 13 Years and Over						
Hispanic origin and race						
Not Hispanic or Latino						
White	36.4	24.6	24.9	24.2	24.6	24.7
Black or African American	29.3	33.3	33.2	32.6	32.5	32.1
Asian or Pacific Islander	0.7	0.8	0.9	1.0	0.9	1.0
American Indian or Alaska Native	0.3	0.3	0.3	0.4	0.3	0.3
Hispanic or Latino[4]	13.1	13.8	13.7	14.2	14.1	14.6
Age at Diagnosis						
13–14 years	0.1	0.1	0.1	0.1	0.1	0.1
15–24 years	2.9	2.4	2.7	3.1	3.5	3.9
25–34 years	25.8	16.9	16.2	15.2	15.4	14.9
35–44 years	32.1	30.9	31.2	30.2	29.2	28.3
45–54 years	13.9	16.7	17.2	17.7	17.7	19.0
55–64 years	4.1	4.7	4.9	5.0	5.5	5.6
65 years and over	1.2	1.5	1.3	1.5	1.6	1.5
Female, 13 Years and Over						
Hispanic origin and race						
Not Hispanic or Latino						
White	3.9	4.3	4.4	4.1	4.6	4.3
Black or African American	11.9	17.6	17.5	18.2	18.0	17.5
Asian or Pacific Islander	0.1	0.2	0.2	0.2	0.2	0.2
American Indian or Alaska Native	0.1	0.1	0.1	0.1	0.1	0.1
Hispanic or Latino[4]	3.0	4.1	3.7	4.1	3.8	4.2
Age at Diagnosis						
13–14 years	0.0	0.1	0.1	0.1	0.1	0.1
15–24 years	1.3	1.7	1.8	1.7	1.7	1.7
25–34 years	6.5	7.4	6.9	6.9	6.6	6.1
35–44 years	7.1	10.3	9.9	10.5	10.1	9.7
45–54 years	2.9	5.2	5.5	5.7	6.2	6.5
55–64 years	0.9	1.3	1.5	1.6	1.8	1.9
65 years and over	0.3	0.4	0.5	0.5	0.5	0.5
Children, Under 13 Years						
Hispanic origin and race						
Not Hispanic or Latino						
White	0.2	0.0	0.0	0.0	0.0	0.0
Black or African American	0.6	0.2	0.2	0.1	0.1	0.1
Asian or Pacific Islander	0.0	0.0	0.0	-	0.0	0.0
American Indian or Alaska Native	0.0	-	0.0	-	0.0	-
Hispanic or Latino[4]	0.2	0.1	0.0	0.0	0.0	0.0
Region of Residence						
Northeast	31.6	29.6	26.8	27.6	26.4	28.4
Midwest	10.3	10.3	10.7	10.8	10.7	12.0
South	37.8	43.5	45.0	45.4	47.5	44.6
West	20.4	16.6	17.4	16.2	15.4	15.0

0.0 = Rate greater than zero but less than 0.05.
- = Quantity zero.
[1]Based on cases reported to the Centers for Disease Control and Prevention from the beginning of the epidemic (1981) through June 30, 2006.

Table C-4.   Age-Adjusted Cancer Incidence Rates for Selected Cancer Sites, by Sex, Race, and Hispanic Origin, Selected Geographic Areas, Selected Years, 1990–2004

(Number of new cases per 100,000 population.)

Site, sex, race, and Hispanic origin	1990	1995	2000	2001	2002	2003	2004	1990–2004 APC[1]
NUMBER OF NEW CASES PER 100,000 POPULATION[2]								
All Sites								
All persons	475.3	470.0	471.4	472.8	465.9	452.3	446.6	-0.5
White	482.8	476.4	483.3	485.6	476.5	462.4	456.4	-0.4
Black or African American	512.2	533.1	514.6	503.2	510.3	495.4	489.8	-0.7
American Indian or Alaska Native[3]	341.6	360.9	336.2	351.2	322.7	334.2	353.5	-0.3
Asian or Pacific Islander	334.9	335.6	330.1	334.8	333.0	319.7	317.8	-0.5
Hispanic or Latino[4]	352.5	354.3	352.9	352.3	354.3	332.4	336.3	-0.5
White, not Hispanic or Latino[4]	495.1	490.7	501.8	505.3	495.4	483.1	476.4	-0.3
Male	583.7	562.9	560.5	558.9	548.3	532.5	523.0	-1.1
White	590.5	562.1	565.7	566.0	553.1	536.1	527.8	-1.1
Black or African American	685.3	731.9	692.6	670.9	671.0	645.2	628.2	-1.2
American Indian or Alaska Native[3]	388.3	414.8	348.7	397.9	343.9	390.4	351.8	-1.0
Asian or Pacific Islander	386.5	393.2	386.3	380.0	375.3	370.2	360.5	-0.8
Hispanic or Latino[4]	414.9	434.4	425.0	421.5	422.1	392.9	398.0	-0.7
White, not Hispanic or Latino[4]	606.3	576.4	585.5	586.2	572.3	557.4	548.1	-1.0
Female	410.9	409.6	411.1	413.8	409.9	397.5	394.1	-0.1
White	421.0	422.4	428.6	431.5	425.0	412.6	407.7	0.0
Black or African American	403.4	400.1	394.6	388.6	402.2	394.1	396.7	-0.2
American Indian or Alaska Native[3]	310.1	326.3	333.7	321.3	306.8	297.3	358.4	0.4
Asian or Pacific Islander	294.5	293.3	291.5	305.0	307.1	287.5	291.7	0.0
Hispanic or Latino[4]	318.3	305.0	310.3	309.4	312.3	294.9	298.0	-0.3
White, not Hispanic or Latino[4]	430.8	436.5	445.4	450.2	443.0	432.4	426.7	0.2
Lung and Bronchus								
Male	95.0	86.8	77.5	76.7	75.0	74.3	69.3	-2.1
White	94.2	85.0	76.3	75.9	74.4	73.3	68.1	-2.1
Black or African American	133.6	136.6	109.6	111.8	108.1	109.2	98.4	-2.3
Asian or Pacific Islander	64.4	59.9	62.4	56.2	56.6	56.7	57.0	-1.0
Hispanic or Latino[4]	59.2	52.1	44.3	41.8	47.7	42.9	37.1	-2.3
White, not Hispanic or Latino[4]	97.5	88.4	80.3	80.5	78.0	77.3	72.5	-1.9
Female	47.2	49.3	48.5	48.5	48.8	48.8	47.2	0.0
White	48.4	51.7	50.8	50.7	51.0	51.6	48.8	0.1
Black or African American	52.8	49.7	54.1	54.1	54.7	53.3	55.9	0.3
Asian or Pacific Islander	28.3	27.3	26.9	29.2	28.6	27.8	29.4	0.3
Hispanic or Latino[4]	25.8	24.7	23.7	23.6	23.0	22.0	23.4	-1.2
White, not Hispanic or Latino[4]	50.8	54.9	54.5	54.5	55.1	56.1	52.8	0.4
Colon and Rectum								
Male	72.2	63.1	62.4	61.2	59.2	57.3	54.8	-1.6
White	72.9	62.5	62.2	60.7	58.2	56.1	54.0	-1.7
Black or African American	72.7	74.3	72.4	70.9	70.5	74.1	70.9	-0.4
Asian or Pacific Islander	61.4	58.0	56.4	55.3	57.1	51.2	47.2	-1.2
Hispanic or Latino[4]	47.5	44.8	49.1	48.4	43.9	44.8	43.9	-0.5
White, not Hispanic or Latino[4]	75.0	64.0	63.6	62.2	59.7	57.5	55.3	-1.7
Female	50.2	45.8	45.9	45.0	44.6	42.6	40.7	-1.0
White	49.8	45.5	45.5	44.2	43.8	42.2	39.7	-1.1
Black or African American	60.9	54.9	57.3	55.6	54.5	53.2	51.6	-0.6
Asian or Pacific Islander	38.0	38.3	36.6	40.1	40.1	35.4	35.2	-0.7
Hispanic or Latino[4]	34.2	31.3	32.9	31.1	30.9	31.1	30.4	-0.6
White, not Hispanic or Latino[4]	50.9	46.8	46.8	45.8	45.3	43.5	41.0	-1.0
Prostate								
Male	166.7	165.7	177.0	177.7	174.9	162.0	159.3	-1.5
White	168.3	160.7	173.0	175.3	170.9	157.1	155.5	-1.7
Black or African American	217.9	273.0	284.2	262.2	271.9	243.2	233.9	-1.1
American Indian or Alaska Native[3]	98.4	88.0	60.9	76.7	75.2	90.9	68.6	-3.2
Asian or Pacific Islander	88.1	102.4	103.2	104.5	98.7	99.7	96.0	-0.9
Hispanic or Latino[4]	118.1	138.1	145.5	142.2	143.7	128.6	137.7	-0.3
White, not Hispanic or Latino[4]	172.1	163.3	177.0	179.9	174.7	161.4	158.4	-1.7
Breast								
Female	129.2	130.6	133.5	134.3	130.7	121.6	121.0	-0.1
White	134.2	136.1	140.6	141.7	137.1	126.5	125.4	-0.1
Black or African American	116.5	122.3	119.1	114.4	119.4	119.7	118.8	0.0
American Indian or Alaska Native[3]	65.3	92.5	88.8	80.3	70.9	81.6	85.9	-0.2
Asian or Pacific Islander	86.9	86.4	91.4	97.9	96.9	88.0	92.5	0.8
Hispanic or Latino[4]	88.2	86.7	93.6	88.0	89.0	81.9	83.9	-0.2
White, not Hispanic or Latino[4]	138.9	142.0	147.4	149.9	144.6	134.0	132.7	0.1

0.0 = Quantity is greater is than -0.05 but less than 0.05.

[1]Annual percent change (APC) has been calculated by fitting a linear regression model to the natural logarithm of the yearly rates from 1990–2004.

[2]Age adjusted by 5-year age groups to the year 2000 U.S. standard population. Age-adjusted rates are based on at least 25 cases.

[3]Estimates for American Indian or Alaska Native population are based on the Contract Health Service Delivery Area (CHSDA) counties within SEER areas. Estimates for American Indian or Alaska Native are not shown for some sites because of the small number of annual cases.

[4]Hispanic data exclude cases from Alaska. Persons of Hispanic origin may be of any race.

Table C-4.   Age-Adjusted Cancer Incidence Rates for Selected Cancer Sites, by Sex, Race, and Hispanic Origin, Selected Geographic Areas, Selected Years, 1990–2004—*Continued*

(Number of new cases per 100,000 population.)

Site, sex, race, and Hispanic origin	1990	1995	2000	2001	2002	2003	2004	1990–2004 APC[1]
Cervix Uteri								
Female..	11.9	9.9	8.8	8.7	8.2	8.1	7.7	-2.7
White	11.2	9.2	8.9	8.4	8.2	7.8	7.6	-2.4
Black or African American......................	16.4	14.6	10.6	10.6	9.7	10.3	9.5	-3.7
Asian or Pacific Islander	12.1	10.9	7.8	9.4	7.9	7.8	6.8	-4.2
Hispanic or Latino[4]...............................	21.3	17.7	17.0	14.9	14.3	13.8	12.6	-3.4
White, not Hispanic or Latino[4]	9.7	7.8	7.0	7.0	6.9	6.4	6.5	-2.5
Corpus Uteri[5]								
Female..	24.2	24.4	23.3	24.0	23.3	22.6	22.9	-0.3
White	26.0	26.0	25.2	25.6	24.2	24.0	24.2	-0.4
Black or African American......................	16.2	16.9	16.3	18.7	21.1	18.4	18.2	1.3
Asian or Pacific Islander	12.9	17.0	15.9	17.0	18.3	16.0	17.8	1.4
Hispanic or Latino[4]...............................	17.3	16.2	14.9	16.4	16.6	16.6	18.2	0.2
White, not Hispanic or Latino[4]	26.7	27.1	26.5	26.9	25.2	25.1	24.9	-0.3
Ovary								
Female..	15.5	14.5	14.1	14.0	13.6	13.1	12.6	-1.2
White	16.4	15.4	15.0	15.2	14.4	13.8	13.2	-1.1
Black or African American......................	11.2	10.8	10.5	9.3	9.7	11.1	10.1	-0.6
Asian or Pacific Islander	11.2	10.4	9.8	9.5	11.6	9.7	9.7	-0.4
Hispanic or Latino[4]...............................	12.2	11.8	10.7	13.1	13.1	10.5	10.7	-0.4
White, not Hispanic or Latino[4]	16.7	15.8	15.6	15.6	14.5	14.4	13.6	-1.1
Oral Cavity and Pharynx								
Male	18.5	16.4	15.7	14.9	15.5	14.8	14.7	-1.6
White	17.9	16.3	15.6	15.2	15.6	14.9	15.0	-1.3
Black or African American......................	25.4	22.1	19.1	18.1	17.8	16.8	15.6	-2.9
Asian or Pacific Islander	14.8	11.8	13.1	9.7	12.5	11.3	10.8	-1.7
Hispanic or Latino[4]...............................	10.8	12.1	8.9	9.2	9.3	7.9	9.5	-2.0
White, not Hispanic or Latino[4]	18.7	16.9	16.6	16.1	16.6	16.0	15.9	-1.1
Female..	7.3	7.0	6.2	6.6	6.4	5.8	5.9	-1.4
White	7.4	7.1	6.2	6.6	6.5	5.7	5.9	-1.5
Black or African American......................	6.4	6.6	5.3	6.4	6.2	6.6	5.8	-1.0
Asian or Pacific Islander	6.1	5.2	6.1	5.6	5.8	4.9	5.5	-1.0
Hispanic or Latino[4]...............................	3.9	3.7	3.6	4.2	3.7	3.4	3.2	-1.5
White, not Hispanic or Latino[4]	7.8	7.5	6.6	7.0	7.0	6.1	6.3	-1.3
Stomach								
Male	14.6	13.5	12.5	11.8	11.8	11.5	11.5	-1.9
White	12.8	11.9	10.7	10.2	10.3	10.0	10.0	-1.9
Black or African American......................	21.5	18.4	18.4	17.4	15.7	17.7	15.4	-2.5
Asian or Pacific Islander	26.9	24.1	22.2	18.9	19.9	18.4	19.1	-2.9
Hispanic or Latino[4]...............................	20.2	19.2	16.1	15.5	15.8	15.4	15.6	-2.2
White, not Hispanic or Latino[4]	12.1	11.1	10.0	9.4	9.5	9.1	9.1	-2.1
Female..	6.7	6.2	6.1	5.7	6.1	5.8	5.8	-1.0
White	5.7	5.1	5.0	4.6	5.0	4.8	4.9	-1.2
Black or African American......................	9.9	9.8	8.6	8.9	9.7	9.1	7.2	-1.2
Asian or Pacific Islander	15.3	13.0	12.8	12.0	10.9	10.7	10.6	-2.8
Hispanic or Latino[4]...............................	10.8	11.0	10.7	9.9	10.2	9.6	9.6	-0.7
White, not Hispanic or Latino[4]	5.1	4.5	4.2	3.8	4.2	4.0	4.0	-1.8
Pancreas								
Male	13.0	12.7	12.8	12.7	12.6	12.2	12.9	-0.1
White	12.7	12.4	12.6	12.9	12.9	12.1	12.7	0.1
Black or African American......................	19.3	19.1	18.1	15.3	13.7	16.6	17.1	-1.4
Asian or Pacific Islander	11.2	10.3	10.6	9.7	9.7	9.9	11.1	-1.0
Hispanic or Latino[4]...............................	10.7	12.1	12.1	9.7	10.5	9.5	10.7	-0.3
White, not Hispanic or Latino[4]	12.8	12.4	12.7	13.2	13.2	12.5	12.9	0.2
Female..	10.0	9.9	9.8	9.8	10.3	10.1	9.9	-0.1
White	9.8	9.6	9.6	9.5	10.0	10.0	9.7	0.0
Black or African American......................	12.9	15.5	12.7	13.3	15.6	14.1	13.6	-0.8
Asian or Pacific Islander	9.7	8.1	9.1	8.9	8.7	7.9	8.6	0.4
Hispanic or Latino[4]...............................	9.8	8.7	9.0	9.6	10.4	7.7	8.4	-0.9
White, not Hispanic or Latino[4]	9.7	9.7	9.7	9.5	10.0	10.4	9.9	0.2

0.0 = Quantity is greater is than -0.05 but less than 0.05.
[1]Annual percent change (APC) has been calculated by fitting a linear regression model to the natural logarithm of the yearly rates from 1990–2004.
[4]Hispanic data exclude cases from Alaska. Persons of Hispanic origin may be of any race.
[5]Includes corpus uteri only cases and not uterus, not elsewhere specified cases.

Table C-4.   Age-Adjusted Cancer Incidence Rates for Selected Cancer Sites, by Sex, Race, and Hispanic Origin, Selected Geographic Areas, Selected Years, 1990–2004—*Continued*

(Number of new cases per 100,000 population.)

Site, sex, race, and Hispanic origin	1990	1995	2000	2001	2002	2003	2004	1990–2004 APC[1]
Urinary Bladder								
Male	37.2	35.3	36.7	36.4	35.2	36.1	35.5	-0.2
White	40.7	38.8	40.7	40.5	38.7	39.9	39.3	-0.1
Black or African American	19.6	19.2	19.9	18.9	20.3	22.2	20.9	0.3
Asian or Pacific Islander	15.6	16.3	16.5	16.5	18.9	16.9	16.4	1.0
Hispanic or Latino[4]	21.9	17.6	19.7	20.4	19.3	18.6	17.5	-0.8
White, not Hispanic or Latino[4]	42.3	41.0	43.2	43.1	41.2	42.6	42.3	0.1
Female	9.5	9.3	9.0	9.0	9.1	9.0	8.9	-0.4
White	9.9	10.1	9.9	9.9	10.0	9.7	9.7	-0.1
Black or African American	8.6	7.2	7.7	7.0	8.2	7.2	8.0	-0.1
Asian or Pacific Islander	5.3	4.4	4.1	4.5	3.2	4.7	3.7	-0.9
Hispanic or Latino[4]	5.7	5.1	5.6	5.2	5.8	4.0	5.2	-0.9
White, not Hispanic or Latino[4]	10.3	10.6	10.4	10.5	10.6	10.6	10.3	0.1
Non-Hodgkin's Lymphoma								
Male	22.6	25.0	23.4	23.8	23.3	23.4	24.0	0.1
White	23.7	26.1	24.7	24.9	24.6	24.8	25.2	0.1
Black or African American	17.4	21.4	17.5	17.7	17.8	18.6	21.0	0.2
Asian or Pacific Islander	16.6	16.4	15.7	17.3	16.0	15.6	15.5	-0.3
Hispanic or Latino[4]	17.4	20.8	20.0	18.0	19.6	18.3	19.4	0.0
White, not Hispanic or Latino[4]	24.3	26.6	25.3	25.8	25.2	25.7	26.0	0.2
Female	14.5	15.1	15.8	15.9	16.1	16.7	16.6	1.1
White	15.4	15.9	16.8	16.7	17.1	17.6	17.5	1.1
Black or African American	10.2	10.1	11.8	12.1	11.4	12.8	12.7	2.1
Asian or Pacific Islander	9.1	11.7	11.1	12.6	11.6	12.2	11.5	1.4
Hispanic or Latino[4]	13.3	12.7	13.2	14.1	12.8	14.1	14.3	-0.7
White, not Hispanic or Latino[4]	15.7	16.2	17.2	17.2	17.8	18.1	18.1	1.2
Leukemia								
Male	17.1	17.5	16.3	16.8	15.9	15.8	15.0	-0.7
White	17.9	18.7	17.3	18.0	17.2	16.7	15.7	-0.6
Black or African American	16.0	13.1	13.3	12.4	11.5	13.1	13.9	-0.7
Asian or Pacific Islander	8.5	9.9	9.9	9.8	8.8	9.9	9.3	-0.2
Hispanic or Latino[4]	12.0	14.5	12.5	10.8	11.5	11.0	11.5	-0.4
White, not Hispanic or Latino[4]	18.2	19.1	17.7	18.7	17.7	17.3	16.0	-0.5
Female	9.8	10.1	9.9	9.9	9.4	9.2	9.3	-0.5
White	10.2	10.7	10.6	10.6	10.0	9.6	9.7	-0.4
Black or African American	8.4	8.0	9.2	8.6	7.0	8.0	8.3	-0.7
Asian or Pacific Islander	6.0	6.3	6.1	5.0	6.2	6.0	6.0	-0.7
Hispanic or Latino[4]	8.4	8.1	7.5	6.9	8.0	6.6	7.8	-0.8
White, not Hispanic or Latino[4]	10.2	10.9	10.6	11.0	10.0	10.0	9.8	-0.2

0.0 = Quantity is greater is than -0.05 but less than 0.05.
[1]Annual percent change (APC) has been calculated by fitting a linear regression model to the natural logarithm of the yearly rates from 1990–2004.

Table C-5.   Five-Year Relative Cancer Survival Rates for Selected Cancer Sites According to Race and Sex, for Selected Geographic Areas and Years, 1975–1977 through 1996–2003

(Percent.)

Sex and site	White						Black or African American							
	1975–1977	1981–1983	1987–1989	1990–1992	1993–1995	1996–2003	1975–1977	1978–1980	1981–1983	1984–1986	1987–1989	1990–1992	1993–1995	1996–2003
BOTH SEXES														
All Sites	51.0	52.8	57.7	62.4	63.4	67.0	39.8	39.6	39.6	40.7	43.6	48.2	52.8	57.0
Oral cavity and pharynx	54.6	55.0	56.6	58.7	60.9	62.0	36.4	35.1	31.8	35.7	34.4	33.3	38.2	40.6
Esophagus	5.6	7.6	11.0	13.6	14.3	17.5	3.1	4.3	4.3	8.2	6.4	9.4	7.5	10.9
Stomach	14.8	16.9	19.1	19.3	20.7	22.2	16.3	16.9	17.2	20.0	20.0	24.1	19.8	24.2
Colon	51.6	56.7	61.7	63.9	61.4	65.6	46.3	49.5	49.7	49.9	53.2	54.2	52.3	54.7
Rectum	49.4	53.8	59.6	61.2	61.7	66.4	44.9	35.4	40.6	46.1	53.5	52.2	54.8	58.4
Pancreas	2.5	2.8	3.4	4.6	4.2	4.9	2.3	5.9	3.7	4.9	5.7	3.7	3.7	4.6
Lung and bronchus	12.8	13.9	13.8	14.5	15.1	15.7	11.5	12.0	11.7	11.4	11.2	10.8	13.0	12.5
Urinary bladder	74.5	79.3	81.4	81.9	82.2	81.3	50.6	55.6	60.3	60.8	63.3	64.7	61.8	65.0
Non-Hodgkin's lymphoma	48.3	52.8	52.8	52.9	54.4	64.8	48.8	52.3	50.4	47.5	47.5	42.1	42.0	56.0
Leukemia	35.9	40.2	45.5	48.0	49.3	50.8	33.5	29.4	34.3	33.8	36.9	37.4	42.0	40.3
MALE														
All Sites	43.3	47.6	53.3	61.3	62.4	66.6	32.7	33.3	34.2	35.5	38.8	47.3	53.5	59.2
Oral cavity and pharynx	54.1	53.8	54.4	57.0	59.9	61.2	30.0	29.9	26.4	29.8	30.1	28.3	32.8	35.0
Esophagus	4.9	6.8	11.4	12.9	14.5	17.1	1.6	3.3	3.6	7.6	5.0	9.7	7.6	9.4
Stomach	13.7	16.0	16.0	16.4	19.3	20.4	16.4	16.0	16.8	17.5	17.2	23.1	17.6	22.1
Colon	51.1	57.5	62.5	64.4	61.2	65.8	45.3	47.8	45.9	49.6	51.6	55.8	51.2	56.1
Rectum	48.4	52.3	59.8	60.4	60.4	65.7	41.7	35.1	38.3	43.3	49.0	54.1	52.1	57.1
Pancreas	2.7	2.3	3.2	4.3	3.8	5.3	2.7	4.3	4.0	4.2	5.1	3.2	3.5	3.2
Lung and bronchus	11.5	12.3	12.5	13.0	13.1	13.6	10.7	10.0	10.5	10.6	11.1	9.6	11.5	10.8
Prostate gland	69.8	75.0	85.4	95.3	96.1	99.0	61.3	62.8	63.7	66.3	72.2	85.5	91.4	95.3
Urinary bladder	75.6	80.4	83.4	84.1	83.4	82.1	56.8	64.3	65.7	63.7	68.0	67.6	69.0	68.3
Non-Hodgkin's lymphoma	47.7	52.5	49.2	48.2	50.3	62.8	42.0	48.0	49.5	44.9	42.6	38.1	35.3	52.1
Leukemia	35.0	40.0	47.4	48.2	50.0	50.8	30.4	28.5	33.7	32.7	35.0	31.6	41.6	40.6
FEMALE														
All Sites	57.8	57.6	62.1	63.5	64.4	67.4	47.2	46.5	45.6	46.4	48.9	49.2	51.9	54.5
Colon	52.1	56.1	61.0	63.5	61.6	65.5	46.7	50.6	52.4	50.1	54.5	53.0	53.0	53.7
Rectum	50.5	55.4	59.4	62.2	63.2	67.3	47.4	35.5	42.9	48.8	58.0	49.8	57.9	59.6
Pancreas	2.3	3.3	3.5	4.9	4.6	4.4	2.0	7.4	3.3	5.4	6.1	4.0	3.9	5.8
Lung and bronchus	15.9	17.1	15.8	16.6	17.7	18.1	14.0	17.9	14.9	13.0	11.5	12.8	15.8	14.9
Melanoma of skin	86.7	87.7	91.4	92.1	92.8	94.1	*	*	*	*	90.4	*	*	77.5
Breast	75.9	77.7	85.3	86.7	87.9	90.3	62.3	63.8	64.1	65.1	71.2	71.7	72.8	77.9
Cervix uteri	70.6	69.0	73.6	71.9	74.6	74.3	64.9	61.7	61.7	58.4	58.2	58.6	64.0	65.8
Corpus uteri[1]	89.2	84.0	85.7	87.2	86.5	86.9	61.8	56.1	54.2	58.5	59.2	57.0	62.0	62.4
Ovary	36.5	40.3	39.9	42.5	42.7	44.7	43.1	40.3	39.3	40.5	35.3	37.8	42.8	37.5
Non-Hodgkin's lymphoma	48.9	53.1	57.2	58.7	59.7	67.1	56.1	58.1	51.5	51.0	53.5	47.7	54.8	61.1

* = Figure does not meet standards of reliability or precision.

[1]Includes corpus uteri only cases and not uterus, not elsewhere specified cases.

NOTE: Rates are based on follow up of patients through 2004. The rate is the ratio of the observed survival rate for the patient group to the expected survival rate for persons in the general population similar to the patient group with respect to age, sex, race, and calendar year of observation. It estimates the chance of surviving the effects of cancer. The site variable distinguishes Kaposi Sarcoma and Mesothelioma as individual cancer sites. As a result, Kaposi Sarcoma and Mesothelioma cases are excluded from each of the sites shown except all sites combined. The race groups, White and Black, include persons of Hispanic and non-Hispanic origin. Due to death certificate race-ethnicity classification and other methodological issues related to developing life tables, survival rates for race-ethnicity groups other than White and Black are not calculated.

Table C-6. Diabetes Among Adults 20 Years of Age and Over, by Sex, Age, Race and Hispanic Origin, 1988–1994 through 2001–2004

(Percent.)

Sex, age, and race and Hispanic origin[1]	Physician-diagnosed and undiagnosed diabetes [1,2]			Physician-diagnosed diabetes[1]			Undiagnosed diabetes[2]		
	1988–1994	1999–2002	2001–2004	1988–1994	1999–2002	2001–2004	1988–1994	1999–2002	2001–2004
20 Years and Over, Age-Adjusted[3]									
All persons[4]	8.3	9.4	10.2	5.4	6.6	7.3	2.9	2.8	2.9
Male	8.8	10.7	11.8	5.4	7.0	7.6	3.4	3.6	4.1
Female	7.9	8.3	8.8	5.4	6.2	7.1	2.5	2.1	1.7
Not Hispanic or Latino									
White only	7.5	7.9	8.8	5.0	5.2	6.1	2.5	2.7	2.6
Black or African American only	12.6	14.9	14.5	8.6	11.3	11.6	4.0	3.6	*2.9
Mexican[5]	14.2	13.7	15.0	9.7	10.5	11.8	4.5	3.1	*3.2
20 Years and Over, Crude									
All persons[4]	7.8	9.3	10.0	5.1	6.5	7.2	2.7	2.8	2.8
Male	7.9	10.2	11.2	4.8	6.7	7.2	3.0	3.5	3.9
Female	7.8	8.5	8.9	5.4	6.3	7.1	2.4	2.2	1.7
Not Hispanic or Latino									
White only	7.5	8.4	9.2	5.0	5.5	6.4	2.5	2.9	2.8
Black or African American only	10.4	13.4	12.7	6.9	10.1	10.1	3.4	*3.3	*2.6
Mexican[5]	9.0	8.3	9.3	5.6	6.5	7.0	3.4	1.8	*
Age									
20–39 years	1.6	*2.3	2.3	1.1	1.7	1.6	*0.6	*	*
40–59 years	8.8	9.8	10.9	5.5	6.6	7.9	3.3	3.3	3.0
60 years and over	18.9	20.9	22.5	12.8	15.1	16.2	6.1	5.8	6.3

* = Figure does not meet standards of reliability or precision.
[1]Physician-diagnosed diabetes was obtained by self-report and excludes women who reported having diabetes only during pregnancy.
[2]Undiagnosed diabetes is defined as a fasting blood glucose of at least 126 mg/dL and no reported physician diagnosis. Respondents had fasted for at least 8 hours and less than 24 hours.
[3]Estimates are age-adjusted to the year 2000 standard population using three age groups: 20-39 years, 40-59 years, and 60 years and over. Age-adjusted estimates in this table may differ from other age-adjusted estimates based on the same data and presented elsewhere if different age groups are used in the adjustment procedure.
[4]Includes all other races and Hispanic origins not shown separately.
[5]Persons of Mexican origin may be of any race.

Table C-7. Limitation of Activity Caused by Chronic Conditions, by Selected Characteristics, Selected Years, 1997–2006

(Percent.)

Characteristic	1997	1999	2000	2001	2002	2003	2004	2005	2006
PERCENT OF PERSONS WITH ANY ACTIVITY LIMITATION[1]									
Age									
All ages, age-adjusted[2,3]	13.3	12.2	11.7	12.1	12.3	12.1	11.9	11.7	11.6
All ages, crude[2]	12.8	11.9	11.5	11.9	12.2	12.1	11.9	11.8	11.8
Under 18 years	6.6	6.0	6.0	6.8	7.1	6.9	7.0	7.0	7.3
Under 5 years	3.5	3.1	3.2	3.3	3.2	3.6	3.5	4.3	3.9
5–17 years	7.8	7.0	7.0	8.0	8.5	8.1	8.4	8.0	8.6
18–44 years	7.0	6.3	5.8	6.0	6.2	6.0	6.0	5.7	5.5
18–24 years	5.1	4.4	3.6	4.6	4.3	4.1	4.4	4.2	4.1
25–44 years	7.6	6.9	6.5	6.5	6.8	6.6	6.5	6.3	6.0
45–54 years	14.2	13.1	12.5	13.1	13.8	13.0	12.5	11.9	12.5
55–64 years	22.2	21.1	19.7	20.7	21.1	21.1	19.9	19.9	20.0
65 years and over	38.7	35.6	34.8	34.6	34.5	34.6	34.1	33.8	32.6
65–74 years	30.0	27.5	26.1	26.0	25.2	26.3	25.5	25.2	24.8
75 years and over	50.2	45.6	45.2	44.7	45.2	44.0	43.9	43.5	41.6
Sex[3]									
Male	13.1	12.1	11.7	12.2	12.3	11.9	11.8	11.7	11.6
Female	13.4	12.2	11.5	11.9	12.3	12.2	11.9	11.6	11.5
Race[3,4]									
White only	13.1	12.0	11.5	11.8	12.1	11.8	11.6	11.5	11.4
Black or African American only	17.1	15.3	14.3	15.6	14.9	15.3	15.3	14.1	14.1
American Indian or Alaska Native only	23.1	18.8	20.1	18.9	19.5	21.2	17.1	16.0	18.4
Asian only	7.5	6.8	6.6	6.7	6.4	6.4	6.4	6.4	6.6
Native Hawaiian or Other Pacific Islander only	—	*	*	*	*	*	*	*	*
2 or more races	—	20.3	19.8	19.8	22.0	20.2	18.8	19.9	19.7
Black or African American; White	—	14.9	*20.3	14.8	*8.3	*16.8	*15.8	*10.9	22.2
American Indian or Alaska Native; White	—	26.0	25.3	22.0	30.0	24.8	21.5	26.3	22.7
Hispanic Origin and Race[3,4]									
Hispanic or Latino	12.8	10.4	10.3	10.5	10.7	10.2	10.2	10.5	10.0
Mexican	12.5	9.6	10.3	10.3	10.8	9.7	10.1	11.4	9.8
Not Hispanic or Latino	13.5	12.4	11.9	12.4	12.6	12.4	12.3	11.9	11.9
White only	13.2	12.2	11.7	12.1	12.4	12.2	12.1	11.8	11.8
Black or African American only	17.0	15.2	14.3	15.5	15.0	15.4	15.3	14.2	14.1
Percent of Poverty Level[3,5]									
Below 100%	25.4	23.1	22.0	22.3	22.9	23.1	23.0	22.4	22.1
100%–less than 200%	17.9	17.3	16.3	17.1	17.4	17.0	16.3	16.2	16.4
200% or more	10.1	9.5	9.0	9.5	9.5	9.2	9.2	9.0	8.7
Hispanic Origin and Race and Percent of Poverty Level[3,4,5]									
Hispanic or Latino									
Below 100%	19.2	16.0	16.0	16.2	16.3	15.5	15.5	15.9	15.7
100%–less than 200%	12.7	11.1	11.1	10.9	12.2	9.9	10.5	11.0	10.6
200% or more	9.2	7.5	7.3	7.9	7.7	8.2	7.7	7.9	7.1
Not Hispanic or Latino									
White only									
Below 100%	27.8	25.7	24.4	24.8	25.4	26.2	26.2	25.2	25.7
100%–less than 200%	19.2	19.4	18.0	18.8	19.5	19.3	18.7	18.5	18.8
200% or more	10.4	9.7	9.3	9.7	9.7	9.4	9.5	9.3	9.0
Black or African American only									
Below 100%	28.2	26.3	23.2	24.8	25.0	26.1	27.1	25.3	22.5
100%–less than 200%	19.5	17.7	17.3	20.1	17.9	19.0	16.6	15.8	16.8
200% or more	10.7	9.4	9.6	10.0	10.0	9.7	10.3	9.5	9.0
Geographic Region[3]									
Northeast	13.0	11.3	10.6	11.1	11.8	11.3	11.0	10.6	11.3
Midwest	13.1	12.9	12.3	13.3	13.1	13.3	12.7	12.8	12.5
South	13.9	12.6	11.7	12.3	12.6	12.4	12.3	12.0	11.9
West	13.0	11.7	12.1	11.5	11.5	11.1	11.4	10.9	10.5
Location of Residence[3]									
Within MSA[6]	12.7	11.4	10.9	11.3	11.4	11.2	11.2	11.0	11.1
Outside MSA[6]	15.5	15.1	14.6	15.3	15.9	15.7	14.9	14.5	14.2

* = Figure does not meet standards of reliability or precision.

—- = Data not available.

[1]Limitation of activity is assessed by asking respondents a series of questions about limitations in their ability to perform activities usual for their age group because of a physical, mental, or emotional problems. The category limitation of activity includes limitations in personal care (ADL), routine needs (IADL), and other limitations due to a chronic condition.

[2]Includes all other races not shown separately.

[3]Estimates are age-adjusted to the year 2000 standard population using six age groups: Under 18 years, 18–44 years, 45–54 years, 55–64 years, 65–74 years, and 75 years and over. Age-adjusted estimates in this table may differ from other age-adjusted estimates based on the same data and presented elsewhere if different age groups are used in the adjustment procedure.

[4]The race groups, White, Black, American Indian or Alaska Native, Asian, Native Hawaiian or Other Pacific Islander, and 2 or more races, include persons of Hispanic and non-Hispanic origin. Persons of Hispanic origin may be of any race.

[5]Percent of poverty level is based on family income and family size and composition using U.S. Census Bureau poverty thresholds.

[6]MSA is metropolitan statistical area. Starting with 2006 data, MSA status is determined using 2000 census data and the 2000 standards for defining MSAs.

Table C-7.   Limitation of Activity Caused by Chronic Conditions, by Selected Characteristics, Selected Years, 1997–2006—*Continued*

(Percent.)

Characteristic	1997	1999	2000	2001	2002	2003	2004	2005	2006
PERCENT OF PERSONS WITH ANY ADL LIMITATION[7]									
Age									
65 years and over, age-adjusted[2,8]	6.7	6.3	6.3	6.4	6.1	6.4	6.1	6.2	5.8
65 years and over, crude[2]	6.4	6.1	6.1	6.3	6.0	6.3	6.0	6.1	5.7
65–74 years	3.4	3.1	3.3	3.4	2.7	3.1	2.9	3.2	3.2
75 years and over	10.4	9.9	9.5	9.6	9.8	9.9	9.5	9.4	8.6
Sex[8]									
Male	5.2	4.9	5.1	6.0	4.7	5.2	4.8	4.6	4.6
Female	7.7	7.2	7.0	6.5	7.0	7.2	6.9	7.2	6.6
Race[4,8]									
White only	6.3	5.8	5.8	5.7	5.6	5.9	5.8	5.7	5.4
Black or African American only	11.7	12.0	10.3	11.8	10.0	10.5	8.7	10.3	11.1
American Indian or Alaska Native only	*	*	*	*	*	*	*	*	*
Asian only	*	*	*7.5	*9.2	*	*	*8.0	*7.5	*5.8
Native Hawaiian or Other Pacific Islander only	—	*	*	*	*	*	*	*	*
2 or more races	—	*	*	*	*	*	*	*	*
Hispanic Origin and Race[4,8]									
Hispanic or Latino	10.8	8.6	8.6	11.2	9.2	10.3	10.4	10.7	7.7
Mexican	11.4	8.9	9.4	10.6	10.2	9.8	10.7	12.0	7.6
Not Hispanic or Latino	6.5	6.2	6.2	6.1	5.9	6.1	5.8	5.9	5.7
White only	6.1	5.7	5.7	5.5	5.5	5.7	5.5	5.4	5.2
Black or African American only	11.7	12.0	10.2	11.9	10.1	10.4	8.7	10.1	11.1
Percent of Poverty Level[5,8]									
Below 100%	12.5	10.1	9.8	11.2	9.5	10.4	10.1	10.4	9.6
100%–less than 200%	7.4	6.9	6.9	7.5	6.9	7.0	6.7	6.5	7.1
200% or more	5.3	5.5	5.3	5.0	5.1	5.5	5.2	5.4	4.6
Hispanic Origin and Race and Percent of Poverty Level[4,5,8]									
Hispanic or Latino									
Below 100%	16.0	*9.1	12.1	13.5	12.5	*15.2	15.9	16.0	*9.7
100%–less than 200%	11.1	9.8	*7.8	11.3	10.0	*8.4	*10.3	11.3	7.5
200% or more	*6.6	*7.0	*6.8	8.8	*6.7	*8.5	*6.6	*7.3	*6.5
Not Hispanic or Latino									
White only									
Below 100%	11.8	8.9	9.1	9.9	8.2	8.9	8.2	9.3	9.1
100%–less than 200%	6.6	6.0	6.4	6.5	6.3	6.4	6.2	5.7	6.6
200% or more	5.0	5.3	5.0	4.6	4.8	5.1	4.9	5.0	4.3
Black or African American only									
Below 100%	13.5	14.7	10.4	15.9	13.8	14.0	13.9	*11.4	*12.8
100%–less than 200%	12.4	13.2	9.9	12.3	*9.8	10.4	*7.4	*8.4	12.1
200% or more	9.8	8.7	11.1	9.3	8.1	8.4	*6.3	10.8	*9.0
Geographic Region[8]									
Northeast	6.1	5.8	5.7	6.5	6.3	6.6	5.6	6.0	5.5
Midwest	5.8	5.4	5.6	4.9	5.2	4.7	5.4	5.3	5.6
South	8.2	7.1	7.4	7.5	6.3	7.2	6.8	6.8	6.5
West	5.9	6.7	5.7	6.0	6.5	6.5	6.1	6.4	5.3
Location of Residence[8]									
Within MSA[6]	6.6	6.3	6.4	6.1	6.2	6.3	6.3	6.2	5.7
Outside MSA[6]	7.2	6.4	6.0	7.3	5.6	6.7	5.3	5.8	6.1

* = Figure does not meet standards of reliability or precision.

—— = Data not available.

[4]The race groups, White, Black, American Indian or Alaska Native, Asian, Native Hawaiian or Other Pacific Islander, and 2 or more races, include persons of Hispanic and non-Hispanic origin. Persons of Hispanic origin may be of any race.

[5]Percent of poverty level is based on family income and family size and composition using U.S. Census Bureau poverty thresholds.

[6]MSA is metropolitan statistical area. Starting with 2006 data, MSA status is determined using 2000 census data and the 2000 standards for defining MSAs.

[7]These estimates are for noninstitutionalized older persons. ADL is activities of daily living and IADL is instrumental activities of daily living. Respondents were asked about needing the help of another person with personal care (ADL) and routine needs such as chores and shopping (IADL) because of a physical, mental, or emotional problem(s).

[8]Estimates are age-adjusted to the year 2000 standard population using two age groups: 65–74 years and 75 years and over.

Table C-7. Limitation of Activity Caused by Chronic Conditions, by Selected Characteristics, Selected Years, 1997–2006—*Continued*

(Percent.)

Characteristic	1997	1999	2000	2001	2002	2003	2004	2005	2006
PERCENT OF PERSONS WITH ANY IADL LIMITATION[7]									
Age									
65 years and over, age-adjusted[2,8]	13.7	12.4	12.7	12.6	12.2	12.2	11.5	12.0	11.2
65 years and over, crude[2]	13.1	12.0	12.5	12.4	12.1	12.1	11.5	12.0	11.1
65–74 years	6.9	6.2	6.6	6.7	6.0	6.5	5.5	6.4	5.6
75 years and over	21.2	19.1	19.4	18.9	19.1	18.4	18.1	18.3	17.3
Sex[8]									
Male	9.1	8.4	9.2	9.6	7.8	8.6	8.4	8.1	7.9
Female	16.9	15.1	15.1	14.6	15.2	14.6	13.6	14.8	13.6
Race[4,8]									
White only	13.1	11.6	12.2	11.8	11.5	11.5	11.0	11.5	10.3
Black or African American only	21.3	20.9	19.4	18.8	18.5	19.2	17.0	17.8	19.7
American Indian or Alaska Native only	*	*25.2	*	*	*	*	*	*	*
Asian only	*9.1	*9.1	*10.1	15.9	*11.2	*11.8	12.3	*11.3	*8.2
Native Hawaiian or Other Pacific Islander only	—	*	*	*	*	*	*	*	*
2 or more races	—	*	*	*16.0	*20.8	*20.4	*21.4	*	*21.5
Hispanic Origin and Race[4,8]									
Hispanic or Latino	16.3	14.1	13.4	17.0	13.1	13.8	14.8	16.9	12.8
Mexican	18.8	15.6	16.3	17.0	14.0	15.1	15.3	19.6	12.2
Not Hispanic or Latino	13.6	12.3	12.7	12.3	12.2	12.1	11.3	11.8	11.1
White only	13.0	11.5	12.1	11.6	11.5	11.4	10.7	11.2	10.2
Black or African American only	21.2	21.0	19.4	18.8	18.7	19.0	17.1	17.7	19.7
Percent of Poverty Level[5,8]									
Below 100%	25.3	22.2	20.8	22.9	21.1	21.6	20.9	21.8	19.7
100%–less than 200%	15.8	15.0	15.5	14.9	14.7	15.0	13.3	14.7	14.1
200% or more	10.4	9.6	9.9	9.7	9.5	9.4	9.1	9.3	8.5
Hispanic Origin and Race and Percent of Poverty Level[4,5,8]									
Hispanic or Latino									
Below 100%	25.5	19.1	18.5	24.0	17.3	20.1	24.0	26.2	15.9
100%–less than 200%	15.5	14.3	14.6	16.4	15.6	12.3	14.4	17.6	16.0
200% or more	10.2	10.5	8.4	12.2	8.7	*11.1	*8.9	11.3	*7.8
Not Hispanic or Latino									
White only									
Below 100%	24.9	21.6	20.4	23.0	20.4	20.7	19.2	20.7	17.9
100%–less than 200%	15.2	14.4	15.0	14.1	14.2	14.8	12.7	14.2	13.0
200% or more	10.3	9.2	9.7	9.2	9.2	9.0	8.8	8.9	8.3
Black or African American only									
Below 100%	27.8	26.8	22.8	25.8	26.6	28.3	26.0	24.6	28.4
100%–less than 200%	22.4	21.9	20.6	18.6	19.3	18.9	17.7	16.3	20.1
200% or more	15.1	16.1	15.9	14.9	13.4	13.9	10.5	14.9	13.5
Geographic Region[8]									
Northeast	12.2	11.2	11.6	11.3	11.0	11.4	9.9	10.9	10.1
Midwest	13.1	12.3	13.2	12.6	11.7	11.3	11.9	12.0	11.4
South	15.8	13.2	13.2	13.3	13.0	13.1	12.7	13.0	12.2
West	12.4	12.3	12.6	12.6	12.7	12.1	11.0	11.5	10.5
Location of Residence[8]									
Within MSA[6]	13.5	12.1	12.6	12.2	12.1	12.0	11.3	11.5	11.1
Outside MSA[6]	14.4	13.4	13.2	13.8	12.6	12.8	12.4	14.0	11.8

* = Figure does not meet standards of reliability or precision.

—— = Data not available.

[4]The race groups, White, Black, American Indian or Alaska Native, Asian, Native Hawaiian or Other Pacific Islander, and 2 or more races, include persons of Hispanic and non-Hispanic origin. Persons of Hispanic origin may be of any race.

[5]Percent of poverty level is based on family income and family size and composition using U.S. Census Bureau poverty thresholds.

[6]MSA is metropolitan statistical area. Starting with 2006 data, MSA status is determined using 2000 census data and the 2000 standards for defining MSAs.

[7]These estimates are for noninstitutionalized older persons. ADL is activities of daily living and IADL is instrumental activities of daily living. Respondents were asked about needing the help of another person with personal care (ADL) and routine needs such as chores and shopping (IADL) because of a physical, mental, or emotional problem(s).

[8]Estimates are age-adjusted to the year 2000 standard population using two age groups: 65–74 years and 75 years and over.

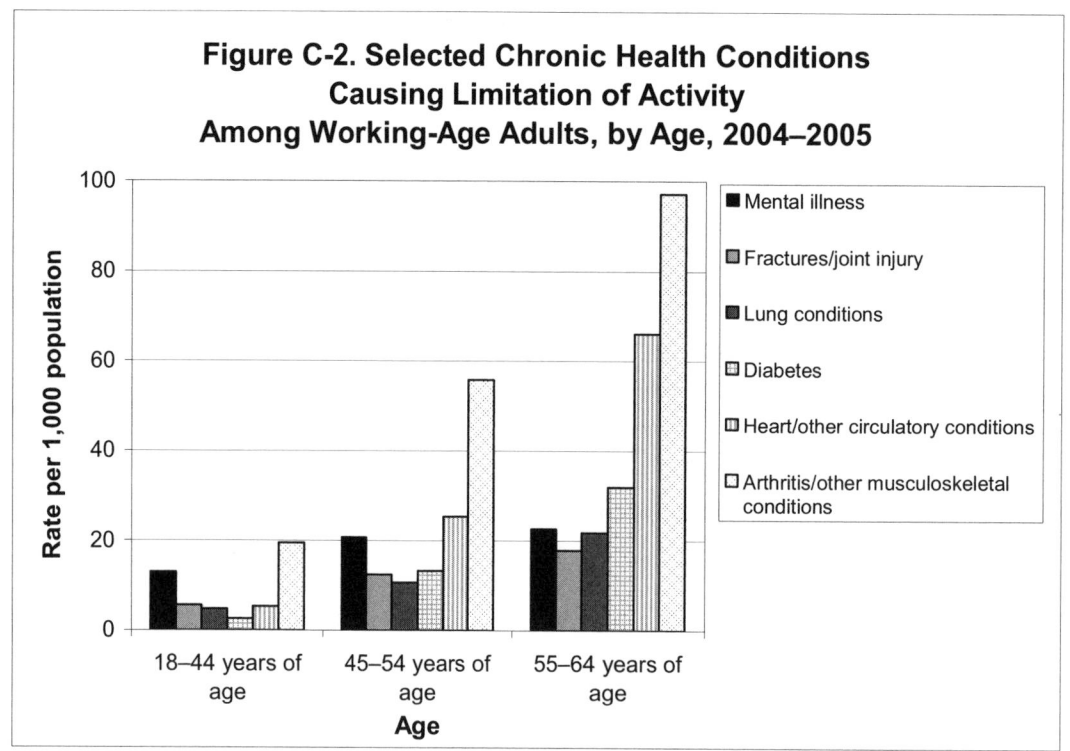

Figure C-2. Selected Chronic Health Conditions Causing Limitation of Activity Among Working-Age Adults, by Age, 2004–2005

Figure C-3. Selected Chronic Health Conditions Causing Limitation of Activity Among Older Adults, by Age, 2004–2005

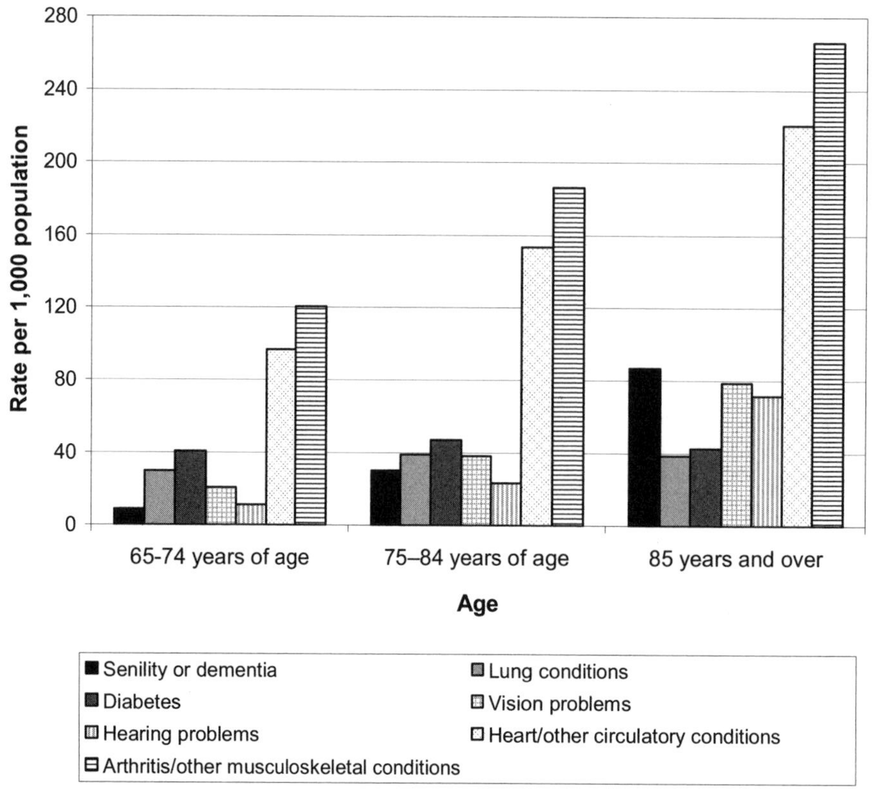

Table C-8A.   Limitation of Activity Caused by Selected Chronic Health Conditions Among Working-Age Adults, by Age, 2004–2005

(Number per 1,000 population.)

Type of chronic health condition	Number of persons with limitation of activity caused by selected chronic health conditions					
	18–44 years		45–54 years		55–64 years	
	Rate	Standard error	Rate	Standard error	Rate	Standard error
Mental illness	13.0	0.5	20.7	1.1	22.6	1.2
Fractures or joint injury	5.5	0.3	12.4	0.7	17.9	1.0
Lung	4.8	0.3	10.6	0.7	21.8	1.4
Diabetes	2.5	0.2	13.2	0.7	31.9	1.5
Heart or other circulatory	5.3	0.3	25.3	1.0	66.0	2.1
Arthritis or other musculoskeletal	19.5	0.7	55.8	1.7	97.1	2.6

NOTE: Data are for the civilian noninstitutionalized population. Conditions refer to response categories in the National Health Interview Survey; some conditions include several response categories. Mental illness includes depression, anxiety or emotional problem, and other mental conditions. Heart or other circulatory includes heart problem, stroke problem, hypertension or high blood pressure, and other circulatory system conditions. Arthritis or other musculoskeletal includes arthritis or rheumatism, back or neck problem, and other musculoskeletal system conditions. Persons may report more than one chronic health condition as the cause of their activity limitation.

Table C-8B.   Limitation of Activity Caused by Selected Chronic Health Conditions Among Older Adults, by Age, 2004–2005

(Number per 1,000 population.)

Type of chronic health condition	Number of persons with limitation of activity caused by selected chronic health conditions					
	65–74 years		75–84 years		85 years and over	
	Rate	Standard error	Rate	Standard error	Rate	Standard error
Senility or dementia	8.8	0.9	30.2	2.2	86.9	6.3
Lung	29.9	1.8	39.0	2.3	38.5	4.1
Diabetes	40.6	1.9	47.2	2.6	42.6	4.5
Vision	20.8	1.5	38.4	2.5	78.7	6.1
Hearing	11.1	1.0	23.3	2.0	71.8	5.8
Heart or other circulatory	96.7	3.2	153.5	5.0	220.7	9.8
Arthritis or other musculoskeletal	120.4	3.4	186.3	5.2	266.2	10.1

NOTE: Data are for the civilian noninstitutionalized population. Conditions refer to response categories in the National Health Interview Survey; some conditions include several response categories. Vision includes vision conditions or problems seeing and hearing includes hearing problems. Heart or other circulatory includes heart problem, stroke problem, hypertension or high blood pressure, and other circulatory system conditions. Arthritis or other musculoskeletal includes arthritis or rheumatism, back or neck problem, and other musculoskeletal system conditions. Senility is the term offered to respondents on a flashcard, but this category may include Alzheimer's disease or other types of dementia reported by the respondent. Persons may report more than one chronic health condition as the cause of their activity limitation.

Table C-9.   Respondent-Assessed Health Status, by Selected Characteristics, Selected Years, 1991–2006

(Percent.)

Characteristic	1991[1]	1995[1]	2000	2001	2002	2003	2004	2005	2006
PERCENT OF PERSONS WITH FAIR OR POOR HEALTH									
All ages, age-adjusted[2,3]	10.4	10.6	9.0	9.2	9.3	9.2	9.3	9.2	9.2
All ages, crude[3]	10.0	10.1	8.9	9.1	9.2	9.2	9.4	9.3	9.5
Age									
Under 18 years	2.6	2.6	1.7	1.8	1.9	1.8	1.8	1.8	1.9
Under 6 years	2.7	2.7	1.5	1.6	1.6	1.4	1.5	1.6	1.9
6–17 years	2.6	2.5	1.8	1.9	2.1	2.0	2.0	1.9	1.9
18–44 years	6.1	6.6	5.1	5.4	5.5	5.6	5.7	5.5	5.7
18–24 years	4.8	4.5	3.3	3.3	3.6	3.8	3.6	3.3	3.7
25–44 years	6.4	7.2	5.7	6.0	6.2	6.3	6.4	6.3	6.3
45–54 years	13.4	13.4	11.9	11.8	12.7	12.1	12.3	11.6	12.9
55–64 years	20.7	21.4	17.9	19.1	17.9	18.9	17.9	18.3	18.8
65 years and over	29.0	28.3	26.9	26.5	26.3	25.5	26.7	26.6	24.8
65–74 years	26.0	25.6	22.5	22.9	22.0	22.3	22.4	23.4	21.9
75 years and over	33.6	32.2	32.1	30.7	31.3	29.2	31.5	30.2	28.1
Sex[2]									
Male	10.0	10.1	8.8	9.0	8.9	8.8	9.0	8.8	9.0
Female	10.8	11.1	9.3	9.5	9.6	9.5	9.6	9.5	9.5
Race[2,4]									
White only	9.6	9.7	8.2	8.2	8.5	8.5	8.6	8.6	8.6
Black or African American only	16.8	17.2	14.6	15.4	14.1	14.7	14.6	14.3	14.4
American Indian or Alaska Native only	18.3	18.7	17.2	14.5	13.2	16.3	16.5	13.2	12.1
Asian only	7.8	9.3	7.4	8.1	6.7	7.4	8.6	6.8	6.9
Native Hawaiian or Other Pacific Islander only	—	—	*	*	*	*	*	*	*
2 or more races	—	—	16.2	13.9	12.5	14.7	12.6	14.5	13.1
Hispanic Origin and Race[2,4]									
Hispanic or Latino	15.6	15.1	12.8	12.6	13.1	13.9	13.3	13.3	13.0
Mexican	17.0	16.7	12.8	12.4	13.3	13.7	13.4	14.3	14.1
Not Hispanic or Latino	10.0	10.1	8.7	8.9	8.9	8.7	8.9	8.7	8.8
White only	9.1	9.1	7.9	7.9	8.2	7.9	8.0	8.0	8.0
Black or African American only	16.8	17.3	14.6	15.5	14.0	14.6	14.6	14.4	14.4
Percent of Poverty Level[2,5]									
Below 100%	22.8	23.7	19.6	20.2	20.3	20.4	21.3	20.4	20.3
100%-less than 200%	14.7	15.5	14.1	14.5	14.6	14.4	14.4	14.4	14.4
200% or more	6.8	6.7	6.3	6.4	6.4	6.1	6.3	6.2	6.1
Geographic Region[2]									
Northeast	8.3	9.1	7.6	7.4	8.1	8.2	7.6	7.5	8.2
Midwest	9.1	9.7	8.0	8.8	8.3	8.3	8.2	8.3	8.8
South	13.1	12.3	10.7	10.8	10.9	10.7	11.2	11.0	10.4
West	9.7	10.1	8.8	8.5	8.7	8.4	8.9	8.6	8.5
Location of Residence[2]									
Within MSA[6]	9.9	10.1	8.5	8.7	8.7	8.6	8.8	8.7	8.7
Outside MSA[6]	11.9	12.6	11.1	11.0	11.7	11.5	11.5	11.2	11.7

* = Figure does not meet standards of reliability or precision.

—— = Data not available.

[1]Data prior to 1997 are not strictly comparable with data for later years due to the 1997 questionnaire redesign.

[2]Estimates are age-adjusted to the year 2000 standard population using six age groups: Under 18 years, 18–44 years, 45–54 years, 55–64 years, 65–74 years, and 75 years and over.

[3]Includes all other races not shown separately.

[4]The race groups, White, Black, American Indian or Alaska Native, Asian, Native Hawaiian or Other Pacific Islander, and 2 or more races, include persons of Hispanic and non-Hispanic origin. Persons of Hispanic origin may be of any race.

[5]Percent of poverty level is based on family income and family size and composition using U.S. Census Bureau poverty thresholds.

[6]MSA = metropolitan statistical area. Starting with 2006 data, MSA status is determined using 2000 census data and the 2000 standards for defining MSAs.

Table C-10. Serious Psychological Distress in the Past 30 Days Among Adults 18 Years of Age and Over, by Selected Characteristics, Selected Annual Averages, 1997–1998 through 2005–2006

(Percent)

Characteristic	1997–1998	2000–2001	2002–2003	2004–2005	2005–2006
PERCENT OF PERSONS WITH SERIOUS PERSONAL DISTRESS[1]					
18 years and over, age-adjusted[2,3]	3.2	3.0	3.1	3.0	3.0
Age					
18–44 years	2.9	2.7	2.9	2.8	2.7
18–24 years	2.7	2.6	2.8	2.5	2.1
25–44 years	3.0	2.8	2.9	2.9	2.9
45–64 years	3.7	3.6	4.0	3.7	3.8
45–54 years	3.9	3.7	4.2	3.9	3.9
55–64 years	3.4	3.4	3.6	3.4	3.6
65 years and over	3.1	2.7	2.3	2.5	2.4
65–74 years	2.5	2.8	2.3	2.2	2.2
75 years and over	3.8	2.5	2.3	2.9	2.5
Sex[2]					
Male	2.5	2.4	2.3	2.3	2.3
Female	3.8	3.5	3.9	3.7	3.6
Race[2,4]					
White only	3.1	2.9	3.0	2.9	2.8
Black or African American only	4.0	3.1	3.4	3.6	3.7
American Indian or Alaska Native only	7.8	*7.4	*7.1	*3.5	*4.7
Asian only	2.0	*2.0	*1.9	1.7	2.3
Native Hawaiian or Other Pacific Islander only	—	*	*	*	*
2 or more races	—	5.5	7.3	7.9	5.5
Hispanic Origin and Race[2,4]					
Hispanic or Latino	5.0	4.0	3.9	3.7	3.3
Mexican	5.2	3.4	3.7	3.6	3.3
Not Hispanic or Latino	3.0	2.9	3.1	3.0	2.9
White only	2.9	2.9	3.0	2.9	2.8
Black or African American only	3.9	3.1	3.4	3.6	3.7
Percent of Poverty Level[2,5]					
Below 100%	9.1	7.7	8.6	8.6	7.6
100%–less than 200%	5.0	5.0	5.2	5.0	5.2
200% or more	1.8	1.9	1.8	1.7	1.7
Hispanic Origin and Race and Percent of Poverty Level[2,4,5]					
Hispanic or Latino					
Below 100%	8.6	6.9	7.6	6.6	5.1
100%–less than 200%	5.4	4.4	3.8	3.9	3.2
200% or more	2.9	2.5	2.7	2.4	2.6
Not Hispanic or Latino					
White only					
Below 100%	9.6	8.9	9.6	10.2	8.9
100%–less than 200%	5.2	5.5	6.1	5.6	6.1
200% or more	1.8	1.9	1.8	1.7	1.6
Black or African American only					
Below 100%	8.7	6.3	7.1	7.6	7.4
100%–less than 200%	4.3	4.3	4.5	4.8	5.0
200% or more	1.6	1.5	1.6	1.7	1.7
Geographic Region[2]					
Northeast	2.7	2.5	3.0	2.5	2.6
Midwest	2.6	2.8	2.7	2.7	2.8
South	3.8	3.2	3.5	3.7	3.4
West	3.3	3.2	3.0	2.8	2.6
Location of Residence[2]					
Within MSA[6]	3.0	2.8	2.9	2.8	2.8
Outside MSA[6]	3.9	3.6	3.9	4.0	3.9

* = Figure does not meet standards of reliability or precision.

—- = Data not available.

[1]Serious psychological distress is measured by a six-question scale that asks respondents how often they experienced each of six symptoms of psychological distress in the past 30 days.

[2]Estimates are age-adjusted to the year 2000 standard population using five age groups: 18-44 years, 45–54 years, 55–64 years, 65–74 years, and 75 years and over.

[3]Includes all other races not shown separately.

[4]The race groups, White, Black, American Indian or Alaska Native, Asian, Native Hawaiian or Other Pacific Islander, and 2 or more races, include persons of Hispanic and non-Hispanic origin. Persons of Hispanic origin may be of any race.

[5]Percent of poverty level is based on family income and family size and composition using U.S. Census Bureau poverty thresholds.

[6]MSA = metropolitan statistical area. Starting with 2005–2006 data, MSA status is determined using 2000 census data and the 2000 standards for defining MSAs.

Table C-11. Suicidal Ideation, Suicide Attempts, and Injurious Suicide Attempts Among Students in Grades 9-12, by Sex, Grade Level, Race, and Hispanic Origin, Selected Years, 1991–2005

(Percent.)

Sex, grade level, race, and Hispanic origin	1991	1993	1995	1997	1999	2001	2003	2005
PERCENT OF STUDENTS WHO SERIOUSLY CONSIDERED SUICIDE[1]								
Total	29.0	24.1	24.1	20.5	19.3	19.0	16.9	16.9
Male								
Total	20.8	18.8	18.3	15.1	13.7	14.2	12.8	12.0
9th grade	17.6	17.7	18.2	16.1	11.9	14.7	11.9	12.2
10th grade	19.5	18.0	16.7	14.5	13.7	13.8	13.2	11.9
11th grade	25.3	20.6	21.7	16.6	13.7	14.1	12.9	11.9
12th grade	20.7	18.3	16.3	13.5	15.6	13.7	13.2	11.6
Not Hispanic or Latino								
White	21.7	19.1	19.1	14.4	12.5	14.9	12.0	12.4
Black or African American	13.3	15.4	16.7	10.6	11.7	9.2	10.3	7.0
Hispanic or Latino[2]	18.0	17.9	15.7	17.1	13.6	12.2	12.9	11.9
Female								
Total	37.2	29.6	30.4	27.1	24.9	23.6	21.3	21.8
9th grade	40.3	30.9	34.4	28.9	24.4	26.2	22.2	23.9
10th grade	39.7	31.6	32.8	30.0	30.1	24.1	23.8	23.0
11th grade	38.4	28.9	31.1	26.2	23.0	23.6	20.0	21.6
12th grade	30.7	27.3	23.9	23.6	21.2	18.9	18.0	18.0
Not Hispanic or Latino								
White	38.6	29.7	31.6	26.1	23.2	24.2	21.2	21.5
Black or African American	29.4	24.5	22.2	22.0	18.8	17.2	14.7	17.1
Hispanic or Latino[2]	34.6	34.1	34.1	30.3	26.1	26.5	23.4	24.2
PERCENT OF STUDENTS WHO ATTEMPTED SUICIDE[1]								
Total	7.3	8.6	8.7	7.7	8.3	8.8	8.5	8.4
Male								
Total	3.9	5.0	5.6	4.5	5.7	6.2	5.4	6.0
9th grade	4.5	5.8	6.8	6.3	6.1	8.2	5.8	6.8
10th grade	3.3	5.9	5.4	3.8	6.2	6.7	5.5	7.6
11th grade	4.1	3.4	5.8	4.4	4.8	4.9	4.6	4.5
12th grade	3.8	4.5	4.7	3.7	5.4	4.4	5.2	4.3
Not Hispanic or Latino								
White	3.3	4.4	5.2	3.2	4.5	5.3	3.7	5.2
Black or African American	3.3	5.4	7.0	5.6	7.1	7.5	7.7	5.2
Hispanic or Latino[2]	3.7	7.4	5.8	7.2	6.6	8.0	6.1	7.8
Female								
Total	10.7	12.5	11.9	11.6	10.9	11.2	11.5	10.8
9th grade	13.8	14.4	14.9	15.1	14.0	13.2	14.7	14.1
10th grade	12.2	13.1	15.1	14.3	14.8	12.2	12.7	10.8
11th grade	8.7	13.6	11.4	11.3	7.5	11.5	10.0	11.0
12th grade	7.8	9.1	6.6	6.2	5.8	6.5	6.9	6.5
Not Hispanic or Latino								
White	10.4	11.3	10.4	10.3	9.0	10.3	10.3	9.3
Black or African American	9.4	11.2	10.8	9.0	7.5	9.8	9.0	9.8
Hispanic or Latino[2]	11.6	19.7	21.0	14.9	18.9	15.9	15.0	14.9
PERCENT OF STUDENTS WITH AN INJURIOUS SUICIDE ATTEMPT[1,3]								
Total	1.7	2.7	2.8	2.6	2.6	2.6	2.9	2.3
Male								
Total	1.0	1.6	2.2	2.0	2.1	2.1	2.4	1.8
9th grade	1.0	2.1	2.3	3.2	2.6	2.6	3.1	2.1
10th grade	0.5	1.3	2.4	1.4	1.8	2.5	2.1	2.2
11th grade	1.5	1.1	2.0	2.6	2.1	1.6	2.0	1.4
12th grade	0.9	1.5	2.2	1.0	1.7	1.5	1.8	1.0
Not Hispanic or Latino								
White	1.0	1.4	2.1	1.5	1.6	1.7	1.1	1.5
Black or African American	0.4	2.0	2.8	1.8	3.4	3.6	5.2	1.4
Hispanic or Latino[2]	0.5	2.0	2.9	2.1	1.4	2.5	4.2	2.8

[1]Response is for the 12 months preceding the survey.
[2]Persons of Hispanic origin may be of any race.
[3]A suicide attempt that required medical attention.

Table C-11. Suicidal Ideation, Suicide Attempts, and Injurious Suicide Attempts Among Students in Grades 9-12, by Sex, Grade Level, Race, and Hispanic Origin, Selected Years, 1991–2005—*Continued*

(Percent.)

Sex, grade level, race, and Hispanic origin	1991	1993	1995	1997	1999	2001	2003	2005
Female								
Total	2.5	3.8	3.4	3.3	3.1	3.1	3.2	2.9
9th grade	2.8	3.5	6.3	5.0	3.8	3.8	3.9	4.0
10th grade	2.6	5.1	3.8	3.7	4.0	3.6	3.2	2.4
11th grade	2.1	3.9	2.9	2.8	2.8	2.8	2.9	2.9
12th grade	2.4	2.9	1.3	2.0	1.3	1.7	2.2	2.2
Not Hispanic or Latino								
White	2.3	3.6	2.9	2.6	2.3	2.9	2.4	2.7
Black or African American	2.9	4.0	3.6	3.0	2.4	3.1	2.2	2.6
Hispanic or Latino[2]	2.7	5.5	6.6	3.8	4.6	4.2	5.7	3.7

[2]Persons of Hispanic origin may be of any race.

NOTE: Only youths attending school participated in the survey.

Table C-12. Severe Headache or Migraine, Low Back Pain, and Neck Pain Among Adults 18 Years of Age and Over, by Selected Characteristics, Selected Years, 1997–2006

(Percent.)

Characteristic	Severe headache or migraine[1]			Low back pain[1]			Neck pain[1]		
	1997	2000	2006	1997	2000	2006	1997	2000	2006
Percent of Adults with Pain the Past 3 Months									
18 years and over, age-adjusted[2,3]	15.8	14.7	15.1	28.2	27.3	27.3	14.7	14.4	14.3
18 years and over, crude[3]	16.0	14.8	15.1	28.1	27.2	27.6	14.6	14.4	14.6
Age									
18–44 years	18.7	17.2	17.8	26.1	24.6	23.9	13.3	12.6	11.7
18–24 years	18.7	16.1	16.5	21.9	20.9	18.6	9.8	8.7	8.1
25–44 years	18.7	17.6	18.2	27.3	25.8	25.7	14.3	13.9	13.0
45–64 years	15.8	14.8	14.7	31.3	30.4	31.1	17.0	17.7	18.6
45–54 years	17.8	16.3	16.9	31.3	29.4	30.0	17.3	17.8	18.9
55–64 years	12.7	12.3	11.8	31.2	32.0	32.7	16.6	17.6	18.1
65 years and over	7.0	7.0	7.3	29.5	30.0	31.7	15.0	14.0	14.9
65–74 years	8.2	7.9	8.5	30.2	29.6	31.2	15.0	13.9	15.8
75 years and over	5.4	6.0	5.9	28.6	30.6	32.2	15.0	14.2	13.9
Sex[2]									
Male	9.9	8.9	9.7	26.5	25.5	25.7	12.6	12.1	12.1
Female	21.4	20.3	20.4	29.6	28.8	28.9	16.6	16.5	16.5
Sex and Age									
Male									
18–44 years	11.9	10.4	11.1	24.8	23.4	22.4	11.6	10.6	9.6
45–54 years	10.3	9.1	10.6	29.4	27.4	28.9	13.9	14.8	16.0
55–64 years	8.8	7.6	7.8	30.7	29.6	29.8	14.6	15.1	15.9
65–74 years	5.0	5.1	6.3	29.0	27.5	27.6	13.6	12.0	13.1
75 years and over	*2.4	4.5	*4.8	22.5	26.3	31.9	12.6	12.4	12.2
Female									
18–44 years	25.4	23.9	24.4	27.3	25.7	25.3	14.9	14.6	13.8
45–54 years	24.9	23.2	22.9	33.1	31.3	31.0	20.6	20.7	21.6
55–64 years	16.3	16.7	15.4	31.7	34.2	35.3	18.4	19.8	20.2
65–74 years	10.7	10.1	10.3	31.1	31.2	34.3	16.1	15.5	18.1
75 years and over	7.4	6.9	6.6	32.4	33.2	32.3	16.5	15.2	15.1
Race[2,4]									
White only	15.9	15.0	15.3	28.7	28.0	28.1	15.1	15.0	15.1
Black or African American only	16.7	13.9	15.8	26.9	24.3	24.3	13.3	10.7	11.0
American Indian or Alaska Native only	18.9	21.1	19.6	33.3	31.4	34.0	16.2	19.6	15.6
Asian only	11.7	12.0	9.7	21.0	19.0	18.1	9.2	11.0	9.4
Native Hawaiian or Other Pacific Islander only	—	*	*	—	*	*	—	*	*
2 or more races	—	19.9	21.2	—	41.8	40.7	—	22.1	21.2
Hispanic Origin and Race[2,4]									
Hispanic or Latino	15.5	13.5	14.1	26.4	25.0	25.0	13.9	13.4	13.6
Mexican	14.6	12.3	13.0	25.2	21.5	23.3	12.9	11.6	12.1
Not Hispanic or Latino	15.9	15.0	15.4	28.4	27.7	27.8	14.9	14.7	14.6
White only	16.1	15.4	15.7	29.1	28.4	29.0	15.4	15.4	15.7
Black or African American only	16.8	13.8	15.8	26.9	24.2	24.2	13.3	10.6	10.9
Education[5,6]									
25 years and over									
No high school diploma or GED	19.2	17.9	17.1	33.6	32.4	31.6	16.5	15.9	16.4
High school diploma or GED	16.0	14.8	15.1	30.2	29.4	30.4	15.5	15.4	14.6
Some college or more	13.8	13.4	14.2	26.9	26.3	27.2	14.6	15.0	15.4
Percent of Poverty Level[2,7]									
Below 100%	23.3	19.9	21.2	35.4	32.4	35.3	18.6	16.5	18.4
100%–less than 200%	18.9	17.7	16.3	30.8	30.6	31.0	16.1	15.3	15.8
200% or more	13.8	13.3	13.7	26.3	25.8	25.0	13.8	13.9	13.4

* = Figure does not meet standards of reliability or precision.

—— = Data not available.

[1]In three separate questions, respondents were asked, During the past 3 months, did you have a severe headache or migraine? low back pain? neck pain? Respondents were instructed to report pain that had lasted a whole day or more, and not to report fleeting or minor aches or pains. Persons may be represented in more than one column.

[2]Estimates are age-adjusted to the year 2000 standard population using five age groups: 18-44 years, 45–54 years, 55–64 years, 65–74 years, and 75 years and over. Age-adjusted estimates in this table may differ from other age-adjusted estimates based on the same data and presented elsewhere if different age groups are used in the adjustment procedure.

[3]Includes all other races not shown separately and unknown education level.

[4]The race groups, White, Black, American Indian or Alaska Native, Asian, Native Hawaiian or Other Pacific Islander, and 2 or more races, include persons of Hispanic and non-Hispanic origin. Persons of Hispanic origin may be of any race.

[5]Estimates are for persons 25 years of age and over and are age-adjusted to the year 2000 standard population using five age groups: 25–44 years, 45–54 years, 55–64 years, 65–74 years, and 75 years and over.

[6]GED stands for General Educational Development high school equivalency diploma.

[7]Percent of poverty level is based on family income and family size and composition using U.S. Census Bureau poverty thresholds.

Table C-12. Severe Headache or Migraine, Low Back Pain, and Neck Pain Among Adults 18 Years of Age and Over, by Selected Characteristics, Selected Years, 1997–2006—*Continued*

(Percent.)

Characteristic	Severe headache or migraine[1]			Low back pain[1]			Neck pain[1]		
	1997	2000	2006	1997	2000	2006	1997	2000	2006
Geographic Region[2]									
Northeast..	14.5	12.7	14.3	27.1	26.0	28.2	14.0	13.5	14.5
Midwest..	15.6	15.1	15.1	28.7	28.2	29.0	15.3	14.5	15.3
South..	17.1	14.9	15.6	27.5	26.5	25.9	13.9	13.7	12.8
West...	15.3	15.9	14.9	30.0	28.6	27.4	16.1	16.5	15.9
Location of Residence[2]									
Within MSA[8]..	15.2	14.4	14.7	27.0	26.6	26.7	14.2	14.3	14.2
Outside MSA[8]...	18.1	16.1	17.1	32.5	29.6	30.6	16.4	14.9	15.1

* = Figure does not meet standards of reliability or precision.

— = Data not available.

[1]In three separate questions, respondents were asked, During the past 3 months, did you have a severe headache or migraine? low back pain? neck pain? Respondents were instructed to report pain that had lasted a whole day or more, and not to report fleeting or minor aches or pains. Persons may be represented in more than one column.

[2]Estimates are age-adjusted to the year 2000 standard population using five age groups: 18-44 years, 45–54 years, 55–64 years, 65–74 years, and 75 years and over. Age-adjusted estimates in this table may differ from other age-adjusted estimates based on the same data and presented elsewhere if different age groups are used in the adjustment procedure.

Table C-13. Joint Pain Among Adults 18 Years of Age and Over, by Selected Characteristics, Selected Years, 2002–2006

(Percent.)

Characteristic	Any joint pain[1]			Knee pain[1]			Shoulder pain[1]			Finger pain[1]			Hip pain[1]		
	2002	2004	2006	2002	2004	2006	2002	2004	2006	2002	2004	2006	2002	2004	2006
PERCENT OF ADULTS REPORTING JOINT PAIN IN PAST 30 DAYS															
Age															
18 years and over, age-adjusted[2,3]	29.5	30.8	29.2	16.5	18.2	17.5	8.6	9.2	8.3	7.5	7.6	7.2	6.6	7.5	6.7
18 years and over, crude[3]	29.5	31.1	29.7	16.5	18.4	17.8	8.7	9.4	8.6	7.5	7.7	7.4	6.6	7.6	6.8
18–44 years	19.3	19.2	18.0	10.5	11.4	11.0	4.9	5.0	4.4	3.4	3.1	3.2	3.2	3.5	3.0
18–24 years	14.2	12.9	11.7	8.3	8.0	6.9	3.4	2.8	1.7	2.0	1.5	1.6	1.6	*1.4	1.6
25–44 years	21.0	21.4	20.2	11.2	12.6	12.5	5.4	5.7	5.3	3.9	3.7	3.8	3.8	4.2	3.5
45–64 years	37.5	39.8	38.3	20.4	22.8	22.8	12.3	13.4	12.1	11.0	11.0	10.3	9.1	10.3	9.5
45–54 years	34.3	36.5	34.8	18.4	20.7	20.9	10.5	12.6	11.4	9.1	8.9	8.0	7.8	8.8	8.1
55–64 years	42.3	44.5	43.2	23.4	25.8	25.4	15.1	14.5	13.2	13.9	14.1	13.6	11.0	12.5	11.4
65 years and over	47.2	51.6	48.2	28.6	31.6	28.6	14.1	15.2	14.1	13.9	15.4	14.6	12.9	15.1	13.4
65–74 years	46.0	49.3	47.6	27.6	30.4	27.8	14.0	14.1	14.5	14.4	14.3	14.3	12.6	13.7	13.3
75 years and over	48.7	54.2	48.8	29.7	32.9	29.4	14.1	16.5	13.7	13.3	16.7	15.0	13.3	16.8	13.5
Sex[2]															
Male	28.0	29.3	27.8	15.2	17.1	16.4	8.4	9.4	8.7	5.8	6.0	5.8	5.1	5.5	5.5
Female	30.7	32.2	30.3	17.6	19.2	18.5	8.8	9.0	7.9	8.9	8.9	8.5	8.0	9.2	7.7
Sex and Age															
Male															
18–44 years	20.1	19.5	18.6	10.7	11.5	11.2	5.5	5.5	5.0	3.0	2.8	3.1	2.5	2.5	2.4
45–54 years	31.1	34.0	33.2	16.2	19.0	20.1	9.5	13.1	12.0	6.6	7.2	7.0	5.6	5.9	6.3
55–64 years	37.3	41.2	38.4	20.1	23.5	20.8	13.7	14.7	13.6	10.5	11.1	8.9	8.0	9.2	9.1
65–74 years	41.7	43.3	41.7	24.1	25.6	22.8	13.3	12.7	14.0	11.2	10.2	10.1	10.5	11.1	11.7
75 years and over	43.9	49.8	45.1	25.7	30.9	28.5	11.4	14.6	13.2	10.0	12.2	11.4	10.1	13.1	11.8
Female															
18–44 years	18.4	18.9	17.5	10.2	11.3	10.8	4.2	4.4	3.8	3.8	3.4	3.3	3.9	4.4	3.5
45–54 years	37.3	38.9	36.3	20.5	22.3	21.6	11.4	12.1	10.8	11.5	10.6	8.9	9.9	11.6	9.8
55–64 years	46.8	47.6	47.6	26.4	27.9	29.6	16.3	14.3	12.8	17.0	16.8	17.9	13.7	15.5	13.5
65–74 years	49.6	54.4	52.7	30.5	34.5	32.1	14.7	15.3	14.9	17.1	17.7	18.0	14.2	15.9	14.8
75 years and over	51.6	57.0	51.2	32.1	34.2	30.0	15.7	17.8	14.1	15.3	19.5	17.3	15.2	19.1	14.6
Race[2,4]															
White only	29.8	31.6	29.9	16.3	18.6	17.8	8.8	9.5	8.6	7.6	8.0	7.6	6.9	7.8	6.9
Black or African American only	30.8	28.1	28.7	20.2	18.2	18.7	8.3	7.7	7.8	6.5	5.1	5.6	5.6	6.1	6.3
American Indian or Alaska Native only	36.7	38.3	40.7	24.5	23.4	24.5	*11.3	*14.2	*10.9	*12.9	*9.1	*13.9	*10.4	*7.9	*7.2
Asian only	18.1	20.0	16.3	8.5	10.8	9.2	3.9	6.3	4.1	*3.2	*4.0	3.2	*2.3	4.0	*2.1
Native Hawaiian or Other Pacific Islander only	*	*	*	*	*	*	*	*	*	*	*	*	*	*	*
2 or more races	42.7	37.7	34.7	28.1	20.3	23.7	15.4	13.1	10.8	12.8	9.2	12.5	10.0	7.7	*8.4
Hispanic Origin and Race[2,4]															
Hispanic or Latino	23.4	23.8	23.3	13.6	14.8	13.9	7.6	7.4	7.5	6.8	6.5	5.8	3.8	4.3	4.0
Mexican	24.6	23.3	23.8	14.1	15.0	15.2	8.3	7.7	7.2	7.8	6.5	6.5	4.0	3.9	4.1
Not Hispanic or Latino	30.4	31.9	30.1	17.0	18.9	18.1	8.9	9.5	8.5	7.6	7.7	7.4	6.9	7.9	7.0
White only	30.8	33.1	31.2	16.9	19.4	18.7	9.1	9.9	9.0	7.8	8.2	7.9	7.3	8.3	7.4
Black or African American only	30.8	28.1	28.7	20.1	18.3	18.7	8.3	7.8	7.8	6.5	5.0	5.6	5.7	6.1	6.2
Education[5,6]															
25 years of age and over															
No high school diploma or GED	33.0	34.0	31.1	19.5	19.9	19.1	10.8	11.8	10.4	9.5	8.8	8.2	7.3	9.1	7.1
High school diploma or GED	32.9	34.2	32.4	18.6	20.3	19.1	10.2	10.4	9.8	8.3	8.9	8.0	7.3	8.5	7.4
Some college or more	31.1	33.2	31.8	16.9	19.3	18.9	8.8	9.5	8.9	8.2	8.1	8.2	7.5	8.2	7.6
Percent of Poverty Level[2,7]															
Below 100%	31.7	33.8	34.6	19.9	21.1	22.9	11.2	10.6	11.8	9.8	8.5	9.2	8.5	9.1	8.9
100%–less than 200%	31.7	32.2	30.4	19.0	19.9	18.9	10.4	10.8	9.1	8.9	8.1	7.8	7.5	8.4	7.3
200% or more	28.7	30.2	28.2	15.6	17.4	16.4	8.0	8.7	7.6	6.9	7.3	6.9	6.2	7.1	6.2

* = Figure does not meet standards of reliability or precision.

[1]Starting with 2002 data, respondents were asked, "During the past 30 days, have you had any symptoms of pain, aching, or stiffness in or around a joint?" Respondents were instructed not to include the back or neck. To facilitate their response, respondents were shown a card illustrating the body joints. Respondents reporting more than one type of joint pain were included in each response category. This table shows the most commonly reported joints.

[2]Estimates are age-adjusted to the year 2000 standard population using five age groups: 18–44 years, 45–54 years, 55–64 years, 65–74 years, and 75 years and over.

[3]Includes all other races not shown separately and unknown education level.

[4]The race groups, White, Black, American Indian or Alaska Native, Asian, Native Hawaiian or Other Pacific Islander, and 2 or more races, include persons of Hispanic and non-Hispanic origin. Persons of Hispanic origin may be of any race.

[5]Estimates are for persons 25 years of age and over and are age-adjusted to the year 2000 standard population using five age groups: 25–44 years, 45–54 years, 55–64 years, 65–74 years, and 75 years and over.

[6]GED stands for General Educational Development high school equivalency diploma.

[7]Percent of poverty level is based on family income and family size and composition using U.S. Census Bureau poverty thresholds.

Table C-13. Joint Pain Among Adults 18 Years of Age and Over, by Selected Characteristics, Selected Years, 2002–2006—*Continued*

(Percent.)

Characteristic	Any joint pain[1]			Knee pain[1]			Shoulder pain[1]			Finger pain[1]			Hip pain[1]		
	2002	2004	2006	2002	2004	2006	2002	2004	2006	2002	2004	2006	2002	2004	2006
Hispanic Origin and Race and Percent of Poverty Level[2,4,7]															
Hispanic or Latino															
Below 100%	26.8	25.2	27.0	16.1	15.0	18.1	11.5	7.5	9.4	8.6	7.3	8.6	5.9	4.2	4.5
100%–less than 200%	24.5	24.1	21.6	14.4	15.2	12.0	8.2	8.1	7.2	8.2	6.1	5.0	3.9	4.1	4.0
200% or more	21.4	23.3	22.9	11.7	14.6	12.9	5.4	6.7	7.4	5.5	6.8	5.0	2.5	4.6	*3.9
Not Hispanic or Latino															
White only															
Below 100%	34.2	39.4	39.3	21.3	24.3	26.2	12.4	12.6	13.5	10.9	10.5	10.5	9.9	12.1	11.0
100%–less than 200%	34.9	36.8	35.1	20.3	22.5	22.5	11.6	12.6	10.8	9.9	9.6	9.2	9.1	10.4	8.7
200% or more	29.8	31.8	29.8	15.9	18.3	17.2	8.4	9.1	8.2	7.3	7.7	7.5	6.7	7.7	6.7
Black or African American only															
Below 100%	31.6	32.5	33.6	20.8	22.4	22.5	9.1	9.4	10.7	7.9	5.8	7.5	8.1	7.6	8.8
100%–less than 200%	34.0	29.6	28.5	23.2	19.9	18.1	10.9	8.2	7.7	7.4	4.9	6.5	6.4	6.8	6.4
200% or more	29.1	25.2	26.8	18.5	15.6	17.2	7.1	7.0	6.6	5.6	4.9	4.5	4.5	5.0	5.2
Geographic Region[2]															
Northeast	27.5	29.1	27.3	15.8	16.7	16.1	7.9	7.5	7.2	6.6	6.5	6.3	5.7	6.5	5.3
Midwest	32.1	34.7	33.4	18.4	21.2	19.8	8.6	10.2	9.7	7.5	8.2	8.2	6.9	8.5	7.5
South	29.3	30.1	27.9	16.7	18.0	17.3	9.1	9.5	7.7	7.6	7.8	7.0	7.0	7.9	6.7
West	28.4	29.3	28.1	14.6	16.6	16.3	8.6	9.3	8.8	8.0	7.5	7.3	6.4	6.7	6.8
Location of Residence[2]															
Within MSA[8]	28.3	29.6	28.4	16.0	17.3	16.8	8.1	8.8	8.1	7.2	7.3	7.0	6.2	7.0	6.3
Outside MSA[8]	33.9	35.9	32.5	18.7	22.1	20.4	10.8	11.0	9.6	8.4	8.6	8.2	8.0	9.4	8.1

* = Figure does not meet standards of reliability or precision.

[1]Starting with 2002 data, respondents were asked, "During the past 30 days, have you had any symptoms of pain, aching, or stiffness in or around a joint?" Respondents were instructed not to include the back or neck. To facilitate their response, respondents were shown a card illustrating the body joints. Respondents reporting more than one type of joint pain were included in each response category. This table shows the most commonly reported joints.

[2]Estimates are age-adjusted to the year 2000 standard population using five age groups: 18–44 years, 45–54 years, 55–64 years, 65–74 years, and 75 years and over.

[4]The race groups, White, Black, American Indian or Alaska Native, Asian, Native Hawaiian or Other Pacific Islander, and 2 or more races, include persons of Hispanic and non-Hispanic origin. Persons of Hispanic origin may be of any race.

[7]Percent of poverty level is based on family income and family size and composition using U.S. Census Bureau poverty thresholds.

[8]MSA = metropolitan statistical area. Starting with 2006 data, MSA status is determined using 2000 census data and the 2000 standards for defining MSAs.

Table C-14. Vision and Hearing Limitations Among Adults 18 Years of Age and Over, by Selected Characteristics, Selected Years, 1997–2006

(Percent.)

Characteristic	Any trouble seeing, even with eye glasses or contacts[1]				A lot of trouble hearing or deaf[2]			
	1997	2000	2003	2006	1997	2000	2003	2006
18 years and over, age-adjusted[3,4]	10.0	9.0	8.8	9.5	3.2	3.2	3.1	3.4
18 years and over, crude[4]	9.8	8.9	8.7	9.6	3.1	3.1	3.0	3.4
Age								
18–44 years	6.2	5.3	5.2	5.4	1.0	0.9	0.9	0.8
18–24 years	5.4	4.2	5.1	5.0	*0.5	*0.7	*	*0.6
25–44 years	6.5	5.7	5.2	5.6	1.2	1.0	1.0	0.8
45–64 years	12.0	10.7	10.6	12.2	3.1	3.0	2.8	3.5
45–54 years	12.2	10.9	10.5	11.7	2.6	2.3	1.9	2.7
55–64 years	11.6	10.5	10.7	12.7	3.9	4.0	4.1	4.6
65 years and over	18.1	17.4	16.6	17.4	9.8	10.5	10.5	11.4
65–74 years	14.2	13.6	13.1	13.6	6.6	7.4	6.7	7.1
75 years and over	23.1	21.9	20.6	21.7	14.1	14.3	14.9	16.4
Sex[3]								
Male	8.8	7.9	7.3	8.4	4.2	4.3	4.0	4.3
Female	11.1	10.1	10.1	10.5	2.4	2.3	2.3	2.6
Sex and Age								
Male								
18–44 years	5.3	4.4	4.1	4.4	1.2	1.1	1.1	0.6
45–54 years	10.1	8.8	8.6	10.6	3.6	2.9	2.7	3.3
55–64 years	10.5	9.5	8.6	11.3	5.4	6.2	5.4	7.1
65–74 years	13.2	12.8	11.8	11.9	9.4	10.8	10.2	11.3
75 years and over	21.4	20.7	18.1	21.8	17.7	18.0	17.8	19.6
Female								
18–44 years	7.1	6.2	6.2	6.5	0.9	0.8	0.7	0.9
45–54 years	14.2	12.8	12.3	12.8	1.7	1.8	1.2	2.1
55–64 years	12.6	11.5	12.5	14.0	2.6	1.9	2.8	2.3
65–74 years	15.0	14.4	14.1	15.1	4.4	4.5	3.8	3.5
75 years and over	24.2	22.7	22.3	21.7	11.7	12.1	12.9	14.4
Race[3,5]								
White only	9.7	8.8	8.5	9.5	3.4	3.4	3.3	3.6
Black or African American only	12.8	10.6	10.8	10.4	2.0	1.6	1.7	1.4
American Indian or Alaska Native only	19.2	16.6	18.9	*16.7	14.1	*	*	*10.7
Asian only	6.2	6.3	6.1	7.0	*	*2.4	*	*2.2
Native Hawaiian or Other Pacific Islander only	—	*	*	*	—	*	*	*
2 or more races	—	16.2	11.6	15.5	—	*5.7	*	*5.1
Hispanic Origin and Race[3,5]								
Hispanic or Latino	10.0	9.7	9.1	9.9	1.5	2.3	2.0	2.0
Mexican	10.2	8.3	9.0	11.1	1.8	3.0	2.6	*2.5
Not Hispanic or Latino	10.0	9.1	8.8	9.5	3.3	3.3	3.2	3.5
White only	9.8	8.9	8.6	9.5	3.5	3.5	3.4	3.8
Black or African American only	12.8	10.6	10.7	10.3	2.0	1.6	1.8	1.3
Education[6,7]								
25 years of age and over								
No high school diploma or GED	15.0	12.2	12.6	12.9	4.8	4.6	4.9	4.8
High school diploma or GED	10.6	9.5	9.3	10.6	3.7	3.9	3.5	3.9
Some college or more	8.9	8.9	8.1	9.2	2.9	2.8	2.8	3.6
Percent of Poverty Level[3,8]								
Below 100%	17.0	12.9	13.7	14.2	4.5	3.7	3.9	4.2
100%-less than 200%	12.9	11.6	11.6	12.2	3.6	4.2	3.6	4.1
200% or more	8.2	7.8	7.3	8.1	3.0	2.8	2.8	3.1

* = Figure does not meet standards of reliability or precision.

—— = Data not available.

[1]Respondents were asked, "Do you have any trouble seeing, even when wearing glasses or contact lenses?" Respondents were also asked, "Are you blind or unable to see at all?" In this analysis, any trouble seeing and blind are combined into one category. In 2006, 0.4% of adults 18 years of age and over identified themselves as blind.

[2]Respondents were asked, "Which statement best describes your hearing without a hearing aid: good, a little trouble, a lot of trouble, or deaf?" In this analysis, a lot of trouble and deaf are combined into one category. In 2006, 0.3% of adults 18 years of age and over identified themselves as deaf.

[3]Estimates are age-adjusted to the year 2000 standard population using five age groups: 18–44 years, 45–54 years, 55–64 years, 65–74 years, and 75 years and over. Age-adjusted estimates in this table may differ from other age-adjusted estimates based on the same data and presented elsewhere if different age groups are used in the adjustment procedure.

[4]Includes all other races not shown separately and unknown education level.

[5]The race groups, White, Black, American Indian or Alaska Native, Asian, Native Hawaiian or Other Pacific Islander, and 2 or more races, include persons of Hispanic and non-Hispanic origin. Persons of Hispanic origin may be of any race.

[6]Estimates are for persons 25 years of age and over and are age-adjusted to the year 2000 standard population using five age groups: 25–44 years, 45–54 years, 55–64 years, 65–74 years, and 75 years and over.

[7]GED stands for General Educational Development high school equivalency diploma.

[8]Percent of poverty level is based on family income and family size and composition using U.S. Census Bureau poverty thresholds.

Table C-14. Vision and Hearing Limitations Among Adults 18 Years of Age and Over, by Selected Characteristics, Selected Years, 1997–2006—*Continued*

(Percent.)

Characteristic	Any trouble seeing, even with eye glasses or contacts[1]				A lot of trouble hearing or deaf[2]			
	1997	2000	2003	2006	1997	2000	2003	2006
Geographic Region[3]								
Northeast	8.6	7.4	7.5	7.3	2.2	2.4	2.9	3.0
Midwest	9.5	9.6	9.3	10.4	3.5	3.5	3.3	3.4
South	11.4	9.2	9.4	10.2	3.5	3.3	3.0	3.6
West...	9.7	9.9	8.1	9.2	3.4	3.5	3.2	3.4
Location of Residence[3]								
Within MSA[9]	9.5	8.5	8.2	9.2	2.9	3.0	2.7	3.2
Outside MSA[9]..............................	12.0	11.1	10.7	10.8	4.5	3.9	4.4	4.3

[1]Respondents were asked, "Do you have any trouble seeing, even when wearing glasses or contact lenses?" Respondents were also asked, "Are you blind or unable to see at all?" In this analysis, any trouble seeing and blind are combined into one category. In 2006, 0.4% of adults 18 years of age and over identified themselves as blind.

[2]Respondents were asked, "Which statement best describes your hearing without a hearing aid: good, a little trouble, a lot of trouble, or deaf?" In this analysis, a lot of trouble and deaf are combined into one category. In 2006, 0.3% of adults 18 years of age and over identified themselves as deaf.

[3]Estimates are age-adjusted to the year 2000 standard population using five age groups: 18–44 years, 45–54 years, 55–64 years, 65–74 years, and 75 years and over. Age-adjusted estimates in this table may differ from other age-adjusted estimates based on the same data and presented elsewhere if different age groups are used in the adjustment procedure.

Table C-15. Selected Health Conditions and Risk Factors, Selected Years, 1988–1994 through 2003–2004

(Percent.)

Health conditions	1988–1994	1999–2000	2001–2002	2003–2004
PERCENT OF PERSONS 20 YEARS OF AGE AND OVER				
Diabetes[1]				
Total, age-adjusted[2]	8.0	8.5	9.8	10.0
Total, crude	7.8	8.3	9.6	10.3
High Serum Total Cholesterol[3]				
Total, age-adjusted[4]	20.8	18.3	16.5	16.9
Total, crude	19.6	17.8	16.4	17.0
Hypertension[5]				
Total, age-adjusted[4]	25.5	30.0	29.7	32.1
Total, crude	24.1	28.9	28.9	32.5
Overweight (Includes Obesity)[6]				
Total, age-adjusted[4]	56.0	64.0	65.3	66.0
Total, crude	54.9	63.6	65.2	66.2
Obesity[7]				
Total, age-adjusted[4]	22.9	30.1	29.9	32.0
Total, crude	22.3	29.9	30.0	32.0
Untreated Dental Caries[8]				
Total, age-adjusted[4]	27.7	24.3	21.3	27.1
Total, crude	28.2	25.0	21.6	27.6
PERCENT OF PERSONS UNDER 20 YEARS OF AGE				
Overweight[9]				
2-5 years	7.2	10.3	10.6	13.9
6-11 years	11.3	15.1	16.3	18.8
12-19 years	10.5	14.8	16.7	17.4
Untreated Dental Caries[8]				
2-5 years	19.1	23.2	15.8	23.4
6-19 years	23.6	22.7	20.6	25.1

[1]Includes physician-diagnosed and undiagnosed diabetes. Physician-diagnosed diabetes was obtained by self-report and excludes women who reported having diabetes only during pregnancy. Undiagnosed diabetes is defined as a fasting blood glucose of at least 126 mg/dL and no reported physician diagnosis.

[2]Estimates are age-adjusted to the year 2000 standard population using three age groups: 20–39 years, 40–59 years, and 60 years and over. Age-adjusted estimates in this table may differ from other age-adjusted estimates based on the same data and presented elsewhere if different age groups are used in the adjustment procedure.

[3]High serum cholesterol is defined as greater than or equal to 240 mg/dL (6.20 mmol/L).

[4]Age-adjusted to the 2000 standard population using five age groups: 20–34 years, 35–44 years, 45–54 years, 55–64 years, and 65 years and over. Age-adjusted estimates may differ from other age-adjusted estimates based on the same data and presented elsewhere if different age groups are used in the adjustment procedure.

[5]Hypertension is defined as having elevated blood pressure and/or taking antihypertensive medication. Elevated blood pressure is defined as having systolic pressure of at least 140 mmHg or diastolic pressure of at least 90 mmHg. Those with elevated blood pressure may be taking prescribed medicine for high blood pressure. Respondents were asked, Are you now taking prescribed medicine for your high blood pressure?

[6]Excludes pregnant women. Overweight is defined as a body mass index (BMI) greater than or equal to 25 kilograms/meter^2.

[7]Excludes pregnant women. Obesity is defined as a BMI greater than or equal to 30 kilograms/meter^2.

[8]Untreated dental caries refers to untreated coronal caries, that is, caries on the crown or enamel surface of the tooth. Root caries are not included. Excludes edentulous persons (persons without teeth) of all ages.

[9]Overweight is defined as a BMI at or above the sex- and age-specific 95th percentile BMI cutoff points from the 2000 CDC Growth Charts.

Table C-16. Hypertension and Elevated Blood Pressure Among Persons 20 Years of Age and Over, by Sex, Age, Race, Hispanic Origin, and Poverty Level, Selected Years, 1988–1994 through 2001–2004

(Percent.)

Characteristic	Hypertension[1,2]			Elevated blood pressure[1]		
	1988–1994	1999–2002	2001–2004	1988–1994	1999–2002	2001–2004
20–74 Years, Age-Adjusted[3]						
Both sexes[4]	21.7	25.6	26.7	15.4	16.4	15.9
Male	23.4	25.2	26.9	18.2	16.3	16.1
Female	20.0	25.7	26.2	12.6	16.1	15.5
Not Hispanic or Latino						
White only, male	22.6	24.0	26.0	17.3	14.8	14.9
White only, female	18.4	23.3	24.1	11.2	14.1	14.1
Black or African American only, male	34.3	36.9	37.8	27.9	25.6	25.1
Black or African American only, female	35.0	39.5	40.3	23.5	25.7	24.0
Mexican male[5]	23.4	22.6	22.1	19.1	18.2	14.9
Mexican female[5]	21.0	23.4	25.1	16.5	17.2	16.8
Percent of Poverty Level[6]						
Below 100%	27.5	29.0	30.8	19.0	19.3	19.5
100%–less than 200%	22.6	29.3	30.1	15.8	19.5	18.7
200% or more	20.4	24.1	25.4	14.6	14.9	14.8
20 Years and Over, Age-Adjusted[3]						
Both sexes[4]	25.5	30.0	30.9	18.5	19.9	19.0
Male	26.4	28.8	30.3	20.6	19.1	18.3
Female	24.4	30.6	31.0	16.4	20.2	19.2
Not Hispanic or Latino						
White only, male	25.6	27.6	29.3	19.7	17.6	17.1
White only, female	23.0	28.5	29.0	15.1	18.5	17.9
Black or African American only, male	37.5	40.6	41.5	30.3	28.2	27.8
Black or African American only, female	38.3	43.5	44.3	26.4	28.9	26.9
Mexican male[5]	26.9	26.8	26.1	22.2	21.5	17.8
Mexican female[5]	25.0	27.9	29.7	20.4	21.2	20.5
Percent of Poverty Level[6]						
Below 100%	31.7	33.9	35.5	22.5	23.3	23.1
100%–less than 200%	26.6	33.5	34.0	19.3	23.0	21.5
200% or more	23.9	28.2	29.4	17.5	18.2	17.7
20 Years and Over, Crude						
Both sexes[4]	24.1	30.2	30.8	17.6	19.9	18.7
Male	23.8	27.6	29.0	18.7	18.2	17.6
Female	24.4	32.7	32.5	16.5	21.6	19.8
Not Hispanic or Latino						
White only, male	24.3	28.3	29.9	18.7	17.8	17.4
White only, female	24.6	32.9	32.9	16.4	21.6	20.2
Black or African American only, male	31.1	35.9	36.7	25.5	25.2	24.7
Black or African American only, female	32.5	42.1	41.6	22.2	27.3	24.4
Mexican male[5]	16.4	16.5	15.8	13.9	14.1	11.4
Mexican female[5]	15.9	18.8	19.0	12.7	13.8	12.8
Percent of Poverty Level[6]						
Below 100%	25.7	30.3	28.3	18.7	21.1	18.3
100%–less than 200%	26.7	34.8	34.6	19.8	24.1	21.6
200% or more	22.2	28.2	29.9	16.2	17.8	17.8
Male						
20–34 years	7.1	*8.1	7.0	6.6	*7.3	6.1
35–44 years	17.1	17.1	19.2	15.2	12.1	11.9
45–54 years	29.2	31.0	35.9	21.9	20.4	23.0
55–64 years	40.6	45.0	47.5	28.4	24.8	25.7
65–74 years	54.4	59.6	61.7	39.9	34.9	30.2
75 years and over	60.4	69.0	67.1	49.7	50.6	45.0
Female						
20–34 years	2.9	*2.7	*2.7	*2.4	*1.4	*
35–44 years	11.2	15.1	14.0	6.4	8.5	6.8
45–54 years	23.9	31.8	35.2	13.7	19.1	22.3
55–64 years	42.6	53.9	54.4	27.0	31.9	29.6
65–74 years	56.2	72.7	72.9	38.2	53.0	48.3
75 years and over	73.6	83.1	82.0	59.9	64.4	58.5

* = Figure does not meet standards of reliability or precision.

[1]Hypertension is defined as having elevated blood pressure and/or taking antihypertensive medication. Elevated blood pressure is defined as having systolic pressure of at least 140 mmHg or diastolic pressure of at least 90 mmHg. Those with elevated blood pressure may be taking prescribed medicine for high blood pressure.

[2]Respondents were asked, "Are you now taking prescribed medicine for your high blood pressure?"

[3]Age-adjusted to the 2000 standard population using five age groups: 20–34 years, 35–44 years, 45–54 years, 55–64 years, and 65 years and over. Age-adjusted estimates may differ from other age-adjusted estimates based on the same data and presented elsewhere if different age groups are used in the adjustment procedure.

[4]Includes persons of all races and Hispanic origins, not just those shown separately.

[5]Persons of Mexican origin may be of any race.

[6]Poverty level is based on family income and family size. Persons with unknown poverty level are excluded.

NOTE: Percents are based on the average of blood pressure measurements taken.

Table C-17. Serum Total Cholesterol Levels Among Persons 20 Years of Age and Over, by Sex, Age, Race, Hispanic Origin, and Poverty Level, Selected Years, 1960–2004

(Percent, level.)

Characteristic	1960–1962	1971–1974	1976–1980[1]	1988–1994	1999–2002	2001–2004
PERCENT OF POPULATION WITH HIGH SERUM TOTAL CHOLESTEROL						
20–74 Years, Age-Adjusted[2]						
Both sexes[3]	33.3	28.6	27.8	19.7	17.0	16.5
Male	30.6	27.9	26.4	18.8	16.9	16.6
Female	35.6	29.1	28.8	20.5	17.0	16.2
Not Hispanic or Latino						
White only, male	—	—	26.4	18.7	17.0	16.5
White only, female	—	—	29.6	20.7	17.4	16.7
Black or African American only, male	—	—	25.5	16.4	12.5	14.4
Black or African American only, female	—	—	26.3	19.9	16.6	14.3
Mexican male[4]	—	—	20.3	18.7	17.6	17.0
Mexican female[4]	—	—	20.5	17.7	12.7	12.8
Percent of Poverty Level[5]						
Below 100%	—	24.4	23.5	19.3	17.8	18.9
100%–less than 200%	—	28.9	26.5	19.4	18.8	17.5
200% or more	—	28.9	29.0	19.6	16.5	16.0
20 Years and Over, Age-Adjusted[2]						
Both sexes[3]	—	—	—	20.8	17.3	16.7
Male	—	—	—	19.0	16.4	16.1
Female	—	—	—	22.0	17.8	16.8
Not Hispanic or Latino						
White only, male	—	—	—	18.8	16.5	16.0
White only, female	—	—	—	22.2	18.1	17.4
Black or African American only, male	—	—	—	16.9	12.4	14.2
Black or African American only, female	—	—	—	21.4	17.7	14.8
Mexican male[4]	—	—	—	18.5	17.4	16.9
Mexican female[4]	—	—	—	18.7	13.8	14.0
Percent of Poverty Level[5]						
Below 100%	—	—	—	20.6	18.3	19.3
100%–less than 200%	—	—	—	20.6	19.1	17.8
200% or more	—	—	—	20.4	16.5	15.9
20 Years and Over, Crude						
Both sexes[3]	—	—	—	19.6	17.3	16.7
Male	—	—	—	17.7	16.6	16.4
Female	—	—	—	21.3	18.0	17.0
Not Hispanic or Latino						
White only, male	—	—	—	18.0	16.9	16.5
White only, female	—	—	—	22.5	19.1	18.1
Black or African American only, male	—	—	—	14.7	12.2	13.8
Black or African American only, female	—	—	—	18.2	16.1	13.5
Mexican male[4]	—	—	—	15.4	15.0	15.1
Mexican female[4]	—	—	—	14.3	10.7	10.8
Percent of Poverty Level[5]						
Below 100%	—	—	—	17.6	16.4	17.3
100%–less than 200%	—	—	—	19.8	18.2	16.4
200% or more	—	—	—	19.5	16.9	16.6
Male						
20–34 years	15.1	12.4	11.9	8.2	9.8	9.0
35–44 years	33.9	31.8	27.9	19.4	19.8	21.2
45–54 years	39.2	37.5	36.9	26.6	23.6	23.1
55–64 years	41.6	36.2	36.8	28.0	19.9	19.9
65–74 years	38.0	34.7	31.7	21.9	13.7	11.0
75 years and over	—	—	—	20.4	10.2	9.9
Female						
20–34 years	12.4	10.9	9.8	7.3	8.9	9.3
35–44 years	23.1	19.3	20.7	12.3	12.4	11.4
45–54 years	46.9	38.7	40.5	26.7	21.4	20.0
55–64 years	70.1	53.1	52.9	40.9	25.6	27.6
65–74 years	68.5	57.7	51.6	41.3	32.3	26.3
75 years and over	—	—	—	38.2	26.5	23.8

— = Data not available.

[1]Data for Mexicans are for 1982–1984.

[2]Age-adjusted to the 2000 standard population using five age groups: 20–34 years, 35–44 years, 45–54 years, 55–64 years, and 65 years and over. Age-adjusted estimates may differ from other age-adjusted estimates based on the same data and presented elsewhere if different age groups are used in the adjustment procedure.

[3]Includes persons of all races and Hispanic origins, not just those shown separately.

[4]Persons of Mexican origin may be of any race.

[5]Poverty level is based on family income and family size. Persons with unknown poverty level are excluded.

Table C-17. Serum Total Cholesterol Levels Among Persons 20 Years of Age and Over, by Sex, Age, Race and Hispanic Origin, and Poverty Level, Selected Years, 1960–2004—Continued

(Percent, level.)

Characteristic	1960–1962	1971–1974	1976–1980[1]	1988–1994	1999–2002	2001–2004
MEAN SERUM CHOLESTEROL LEVEL, MG/DL						
20–74 Years, Age-Adjusted[2]						
Both sexes[3]	222	216	215	205	203	202
Male	220	216	213	204	203	201
Female	224	217	216	205	202	201
Not Hispanic or Latino						
White only, male	—	—	213	204	202	201
White only, female	—	—	216	206	204	202
Black or African American only, male	—	—	211	201	195	198
Black or African American only, female	—	—	216	204	200	198
Mexican male[4]	—	—	209	206	205	202
Mexican female[4]	—	—	209	204	198	199
Percent of Poverty Level[5]						
Below 100%	—	211	211	203	200	202
100%–less than 200%	—	217	213	203	203	202
200% or more	—	217	216	206	203	202
20 Years and Over, Age-Adjusted[2]						
Both sexes[3]	—	—	—	206	203	202
Male	—	—	—	204	202	201
Female	—	—	—	207	204	202
Not Hispanic or Latino						
White only, male	—	—	—	205	202	201
White only, female	—	—	—	208	205	203
Black or African American only, male	—	—	—	202	195	198
Black or African American only, female	—	—	—	207	202	199
Mexican male[4]	—	—	—	206	204	201
Mexican female[4]	—	—	—	206	199	200
Percent of Poverty Level[5]						
Below 100%	—	—	—	205	201	203
100%–less than 200%	—	—	—	205	204	202
200% or more	—	—	—	207	203	202
20 Years and Over, Crude						
Both sexes[3]	—	—	—	204	203	202
Male	—	—	—	202	202	201
Female	—	—	—	206	204	203
Not Hispanic or Latino						
White only, male	—	—	—	203	203	201
White only, female	—	—	—	208	206	205
Black or African American only, male	—	—	—	198	194	197
Black or African American only, female	—	—	—	201	199	196
Mexican male[4]	—	—	—	199	200	198
Mexican female[4]	—	—	—	198	194	194
Percent of Poverty Level[5]						
Below 100%	—	—	—	200	198	199
100%–less than 200%	—	—	—	202	202	200
200% or more	—	—	—	205	204	203
Male						
20–34 years	198	194	192	186	188	186
35–44 years	227	221	217	206	207	210
45–54 years	231	229	227	216	215	213
55–64 years	233	229	229	216	212	208
65–74 years	230	226	221	212	202	194
75 years and over	—	—	—	205	195	194
Female						
20–34 years	194	191	189	184	185	186
35–44 years	214	207	207	195	198	198
45–54 years	237	232	232	217	211	209
55–64 years	262	245	249	235	221	219
65–74 years	266	250	246	233	224	219
75 years and over	—	—	—	229	217	213

— = Data not available.

[1] Data for Mexicans are for 1982–1984.

[2] Age-adjusted to the 2000 standard population using five age groups: 20–34 years, 35–44 years, 45–54 years, 55–64 years, and 65 years and over. Age-adjusted estimates may differ from other age-adjusted estimates based on the same data and presented elsewhere if different age groups are used in the adjustment procedure.

[3] Includes persons of all races and Hispanic origins, not just those shown separately.

[4] Persons of Mexican origin may be of any race.

[5] Poverty level is based on family income and family size. Persons with unknown poverty level are excluded.

NOTE: High serum cholesterol is defined as greater than or equal to 240 mg/dL (6.20 mmol/L). Borderline high serum cholesterol is defined as greater than or equal to 200 mg/dL and less than 240 mg/dL.

Table C-18. Mean Energy and Macronutrient Intake Among Persons 20–74 Years of Age, by Sex and Age, Selected Years, 1971–2004

(Number, percent)

Characteristic	1971–1974	1976–1980	1988–1994	2001–2004
Energy Intake in Kcals				
Male, age-adjusted[1]	2,450	2,439	2,664	2,693
Male, crude	2,461	2,459	2,692	2,697
20–39 years	2,784	2,753	2,964	2,949
40–59 years	2,303	2,315	2,567	2,649
60–74 years	1,918	1,906	2,104	2,117
Female, age-adjusted[1]	1,542	1,522	1,796	1,886
Female, crude	1,540	1,525	1,804	1,884
20–39 years	1,652	1,643	1,956	2,032
40–59 years	1,510	1,473	1,734	1,836
60–74 years	1,325	1,322	1,520	1,622
Percent Kcals from Carbohydrate				
Male, age-adjusted[1]	42.4	42.6	48.3	48.2
Male, crude	42.4	42.7	48.3	48.2
20–39 years	42.2	43.1	48.1	49.5
40–59 years	41.6	41.5	47.8	47.1
60–74 years	44.8	44.1	49.7	47.3
Female, age-adjusted[1]	45.4	46.0	50.7	50.6
Female, crude	45.5	46.1	50.7	50.6
20–39 years	45.8	46.0	50.6	51.4
40–59 years	44.4	45.0	50.0	49.6
60–74 years	46.8	48.6	52.6	51.1
Percent Kcals from Total Fat				
Male, age-adjusted[1]	36.9	36.7	33.9	33.4
Male, crude	36.9	36.7	33.9	33.4
20–39 years	37.0	36.2	34.0	32.1
40–59 years	36.9	37.2	34.2	34.1
60–74 years	36.4	36.8	32.9	34.9
Female, age-adjusted[1]	36.1	36.0	33.4	33.8
Female, crude	36.0	35.9	33.3	33.8
20–39 years	36.3	36.0	33.6	33.0
40–59 years	36.3	36.4	34.0	34.6
60–74 years	34.9	34.7	31.6	34.0
Percent Kcals from Saturated Fat				
Male, age-adjusted[1]	13.5	13.2	11.3	10.8
Male, crude	13.5	13.2	11.4	10.8
20–39 years	13.6	13.1	11.5	10.7
40–59 years	13.5	13.4	11.3	10.9
60–74 years	13.3	13.1	10.9	11.0
Female, age-adjusted[1]	13.0	12.5	11.2	10.9
Female, crude	12.9	12.5	11.2	10.9
20–39 years	13.0	12.6	11.4	10.9
40–59 years	13.1	12.6	11.3	11.1
60–74 years	12.4	11.8	10.4	10.6

[1]Age–adjusted to the 2000 standard population using three age groups, 20–39 years, 40–59 years, and 60–74 years. Age–adjusted estimates in this table may differ from other age–adjusted estimates based on the same data and presented elsewhere if different age groups are used in the adjustment procedure.

NOTE: Estimates of energy intake include kilocalories (kcals) from all foods and beverages, including alcoholic beverages, consumed during the preceding 24 hours. Individuals who reported no energy intake were excluded. In 2001–2004, only data collected in the Mobile Examination Center were used to calculate dietary intake.

Table C-19. Leisure-Time Physical Activity Among Adults 18 Years of Age and Over, by Selected Characteristics, Selected Years, 1998–2006

(Percent.)

Characteristic	Inactive[1]			Some leisure-time activity[1]			Regular leisure-time activity[1]		
	1998	2002	2006	1998	2002	2006	1998	2002	2006
18 years and over, age-adjusted[2,3]	40.5	38.2	39.5	30.0	30.1	29.5	29.5	31.7	31.0
18 years and over, crude[3]	40.2	38.1	39.5	30.0	30.1	29.6	29.8	31.7	30.9
Age									
18–44 years	35.2	33.1	34.9	31.4	31.0	30.4	33.5	35.9	34.6
18–24 years	32.8	32.9	34.8	30.1	28.3	27.1	37.1	38.8	38.1
25–44 years	35.9	33.2	35.0	31.8	31.9	31.6	32.4	34.9	33.4
45–64 years	41.2	38.4	39.7	30.6	31.5	30.8	28.2	30.1	29.5
45–54 years	38.9	37.5	38.2	31.4	31.2	30.7	29.8	31.3	31.1
55–64 years	44.9	39.7	41.9	29.3	32.0	30.9	25.8	28.3	27.2
65 years and over	55.4	53.6	53.4	24.7	24.8	24.5	19.9	21.6	22.0
65–74 years	49.1	46.9	48.0	26.5	27.1	25.8	24.4	26.0	26.2
75 years and over	63.3	61.3	59.6	22.4	22.2	23.1	14.3	16.6	17.3
Sex[2]									
Male	37.8	36.1	38.5	28.7	28.8	28.4	33.5	35.1	33.1
Female	42.9	40.1	40.3	31.1	31.3	30.7	26.0	28.7	29.0
Sex and Age									
Male									
18–44 years	32.0	30.6	34.2	30.7	29.7	28.8	37.2	39.7	36.9
45–54 years	37.7	37.5	39.0	29.6	29.8	28.4	32.6	32.8	32.7
55–64 years	44.5	39.1	41.1	26.9	30.9	30.6	28.6	30.0	28.2
65–74 years	45.3	44.3	46.9	23.6	26.1	25.0	31.1	29.6	28.2
75 years and over	57.4	55.6	52.1	21.6	21.0	26.6	20.9	23.5	21.4
Female									
18–44 years	38.2	35.6	35.6	32.0	32.3	32.0	29.8	32.1	32.4
45–54 years	39.9	37.5	37.5	33.0	32.6	33.0	27.1	29.9	29.5
55–64 years	45.2	40.2	42.6	31.5	33.0	31.1	23.3	26.8	26.3
65–74 years	52.2	49.0	49.0	28.7	27.9	26.5	19.0	23.1	24.5
75 years and over	67.0	64.8	64.4	22.9	22.9	20.8	10.1	12.3	14.7
Race[2,4]									
White only	38.8	36.5	38.2	30.5	30.4	29.9	30.7	33.1	31.9
Black or African American only	52.2	48.5	48.9	25.2	27.1	26.2	22.6	24.4	24.9
American Indian or Alaska Native only	49.2	45.4	32.8	19.0	28.9	37.8	31.8	25.7	29.5
Asian only	39.4	39.0	39.8	35.2	33.1	29.7	25.4	27.9	30.5
Native Hawaiian or Other Pacific Islander only	—	*	*	—	*	*	—	*	*
2 or more races	—	30.6	34.2	—	32.5	35.8	—	36.9	30.0
Hispanic Origin and Race[2,4]									
Hispanic or Latino	55.5	53.9	53.4	23.4	23.5	23.8	21.1	22.7	22.8
Mexican	56.7	54.9	53.9	23.9	23.1	24.2	19.4	22.0	22.0
Not Hispanic or Latino	38.8	36.0	37.3	30.7	30.9	30.4	30.5	33.1	32.3
White only	36.7	33.9	35.3	31.3	31.5	31.0	32.0	34.6	33.8
Black or African American only	52.2	48.6	49.0	25.1	26.9	26.4	22.6	24.6	24.7
Education[5,6]									
No high school diploma or GED	64.8	63.2	62.3	19.4	19.5	21.2	15.8	17.2	16.5
High school diploma or GED	47.6	45.4	47.5	28.7	28.5	29.0	23.7	26.2	23.5
Some college or more	30.2	28.1	29.2	34.3	34.7	33.3	35.5	37.1	37.6
Percent of Poverty Level[2,7]									
Below 100%	59.4	56.5	56.0	20.5	22.5	23.4	20.1	21.0	20.6
100%–less than 200%	52.2	50.5	50.4	26.2	25.8	25.8	21.6	23.7	23.8
200% or more	34.7	32.3	33.6	32.4	32.3	31.6	33.0	35.4	34.8

* = Figure does not meet standards of reliability or precision.

— = Data not available.

[1]All questions related to leisure-time physical activity were phrased in terms of current behavior and lack a specific reference period. Respondents were asked about the frequency and duration of vigorous and light/moderate physical activity during leisure time. Adults classified as inactive reported no sessions of light/moderate or vigorous leisure-time activity of at least 10 minutes duration; adults classified with some leisure-time activity reported at least one session of light/moderate or vigorous physical activity of at least 10 minutes duration but did not meet the definition for regular leisure-time activity; adults classified with regular leisure-time activity reported three or more sessions per week of vigorous activity lasting at least 20 minutes or five or more sessions per week of light/moderate activity lasting at least 30 minutes in duration.

[2]Estimates are age-adjusted to the year 2000 standard population using five age groups: 18–44 years, 45–54 years, 55–64 years, 65–74 years, and 75 years and over. Age-adjusted estimates in this table may differ from other age-adjusted estimates based on the same data and presented elsewhere if different age groups are used in the adjustment procedure.

[3]Includes all other races not shown separately and unknown education level.

[4]The race groups, White, Black, American Indian or Alaska Native, Asian, Native Hawaiian or Other Pacific Islander, and 2 or more races, include persons of Hispanic and non-Hispanic origin. Persons of Hispanic origin may be of any race.

[5]Estimates are for persons 25 years of age and over and are age-adjusted to the year 2000 standard population using five age groups: 25–44 years, 45–54 years, 55–64 years, 65–74 years, and 75 years and over.

[6]GED stands for General Educational Development high school equivalency diploma.

[7]Percent of poverty level is based on family income and family size and composition using U.S. Census Bureau poverty thresholds.

Table C-19. Leisure-Time Physical Activity Among Adults 18 Years of Age and Over, by Selected Characteristics, Selected Years, 1998–2006—*Continued*

(Percent.)

Characteristic	Inactive[1]			Some leisure-time activity[1]			Regular leisure-time activity[1]		
	1998	2002	2006	1998	2002	2006	1998	2002	2006
Geographic Region[2]									
Northeast............	39.4	35.0	36.1	31.3	31.5	31.1	29.4	33.5	32.8
Midwest............	37.3	35.5	34.7	31.7	32.7	32.7	31.0	31.8	32.6
South............	46.9	42.5	44.8	27.1	28.2	27.2	26.0	29.2	28.0
West............	33.9	36.5	38.1	31.6	29.0	28.9	34.6	34.5	33.0
Location of Residence[2]									
Within MSA[8]............	39.3	36.9	38.0	30.6	30.7	30.2	30.0	32.4	31.8
Outside MSA[8]............	44.7	43.5	46.4	27.5	27.7	26.6	27.8	28.9	26.9

[1]All questions related to leisure-time physical activity were phrased in terms of current behavior and lack a specific reference period. Respondents were asked about the frequency and duration of vigorous and light/moderate physical activity during leisure time. Adults classified as inactive reported no sessions of light/moderate or vigorous leisure-time activity of at least 10 minutes duration; adults classified with some leisure-time activity reported at least one session of light/moderate or vigorous physical activity of at least 10 minutes duration but did not meet the definition for regular leisure-time activity; adults classified with regular leisure-time activity reported three or more sessions per week of vigorous activity lasting at least 20 minutes or five or more sessions per week of light/moderate activity lasting at least 30 minutes in duration.
[2]Estimates are age-adjusted to the year 2000 standard population using five age groups: 18–44 years, 45–54 years, 55–64 years, 65–74 years, and 75 years and over. Age-adjusted estimates in this table may differ from other age-adjusted estimates based on the same data and presented elsewhere if different age groups are used in the adjustment procedure.
[8]MSA = metropolitan statistical area. Starting with 2006 data, MSA status is determined using 2000 census data and the 2000 standards for defining MSAs.

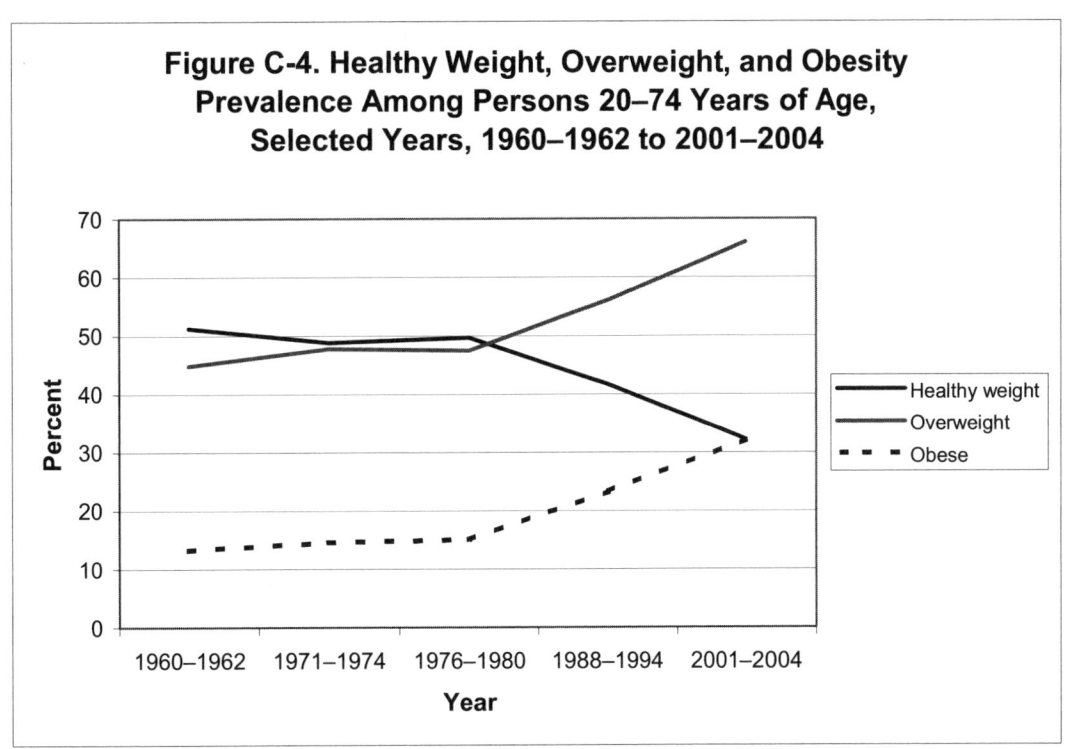

Figure C-4. Healthy Weight, Overweight, and Obesity Prevalence Among Persons 20–74 Years of Age, Selected Years, 1960–1962 to 2001–2004

Figure C-5. Overweight Children and Adolescents 6-19 Years of Age, Selected Years, 1963–1965 to 2001–2004

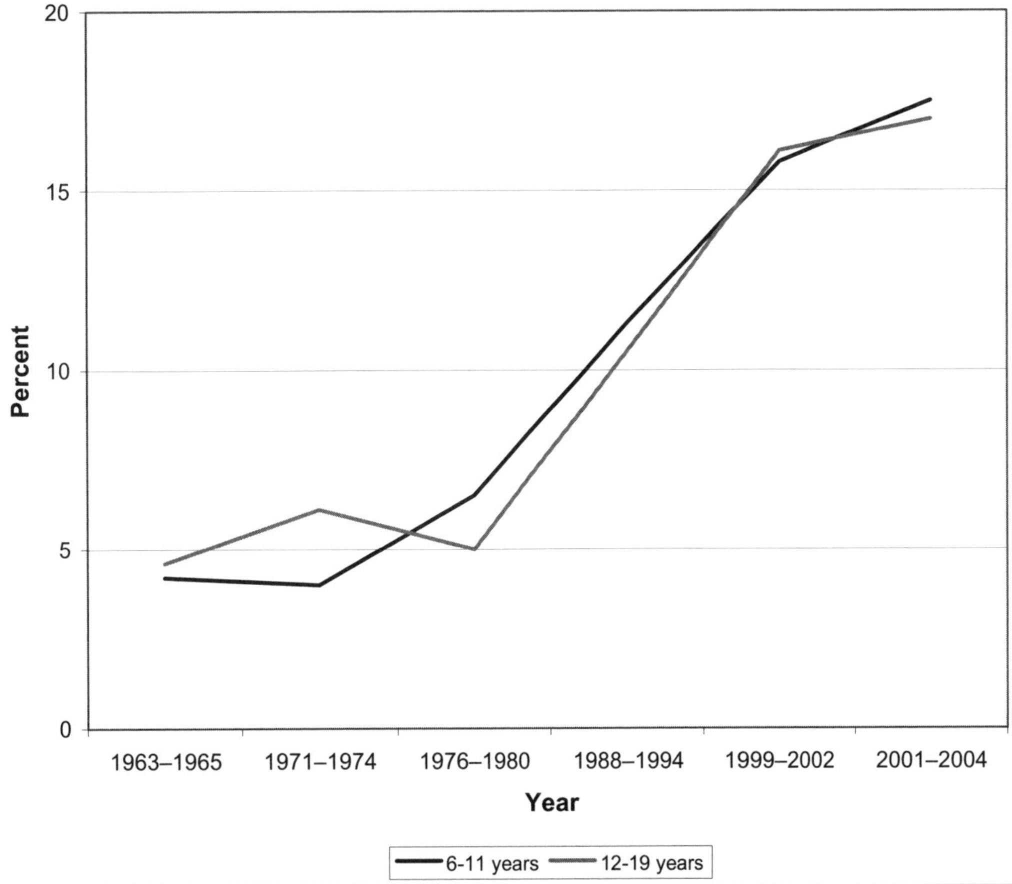

Table C-20. Overweight, Obesity, and Healthy Weight Among Persons 20 Years of Age and Over, by Sex, Age, Race, and Hispanic Origin, and Poverty Level, Selected Years, 1960–2004

(Percent.)

Characteristic	1960–1962	1971–1974	1976–1980[1]	1988–1994	1999–2002	2001–2004
PERCENT OF POPULATION OVERWEIGHT[2]						
20–74 Years, Age-Adjusted[3]						
Both sexes[4]	44.8	47.7	47.4	56.0	65.2	66.0
Male	49.5	54.7	52.9	61.0	68.8	70.7
Female	40.2	41.1	42.0	51.2	61.7	61.4
Not Hispanic or Latino						
White only, male	—	—	53.8	61.6	69.5	71.1
White only, female	—	—	38.7	47.2	57.0	57.1
Black or African American only, male	—	—	51.3	58.2	62.0	66.8
Black or African American only, female	—	—	62.6	68.5	77.5	79.5
Mexican male[5]	—	—	61.6	69.4	74.1	75.8
Mexican female[5]	—	—	61.7	69.6	71.4	73.2
Percent of Poverty Level[6]						
Below 100%	—	49.3	50.0	59.8	65.2	63.9
100%–less than 200%	—	50.9	49.0	58.2	68.0	66.2
200% or more	—	46.7	46.6	54.5	64.9	66.1
20 Years and Over, Age-Adjusted[3]						
Both sexes[4]	—	—	—	56.0	65.1	66.0
Male	—	—	—	60.9	68.8	70.5
Female	—	—	—	51.4	61.6	61.6
Not Hispanic or Latino						
White only, male	—	—	—	61.6	69.4	71.0
White only, female	—	—	—	47.5	57.2	57.6
Black or African American only, male	—	—	—	57.8	62.6	67.0
Black or African American only, female	—	—	—	68.2	77.1	79.6
Mexican male[5]	—	—	—	68.9	73.2	74.6
Mexican female[5]	—	—	—	68.9	71.2	73.0
Percent of Poverty Level[6]						
Below 100%	—	—	—	59.6	64.6	63.4
100%–less than 200%	—	—	—	58.0	67.3	66.2
200% or more	—	—	—	54.8	65.1	66.1
20 Years and Over, Crude						
Both sexes[4]	—	—	—	54.9	65.2	66.1
Male	—	—	—	59.4	68.6	70.4
Female	—	—	—	50.7	62.0	61.9
Not Hispanic or Latino						
White only, male	—	—	—	60.6	69.9	71.6
White only, female	—	—	—	47.4	58.2	58.7
Black or African American only, male	—	—	—	56.7	61.7	66.3
Black or African American only, female	—	—	—	66.0	76.8	79.1
Mexican male[5]	—	—	—	63.9	70.1	71.8
Mexican female[5]	—	—	—	65.9	69.3	71.4
Percent of Poverty Level[6]						
Below 100%	—	—	—	56.8	62.5	61.4
100%–less than 200%	—	—	—	55.7	66.2	65.3
200% or more	—	—	—	54.2	65.8	67.1
Male						
20–34 years	42.7	42.8	41.2	47.5	57.4	59.0
35–44 years	53.5	63.2	57.2	65.5	70.5	72.9
45–54 years	53.9	59.7	60.2	66.1	75.7	78.5
55–64 years	52.2	58.5	60.2	70.5	75.4	77.3
65–74 years	47.8	54.6	54.2	68.5	76.2	76.1
75 years and over	—	—	—	56.5	67.4	66.8
Female						
20–34 years	21.2	25.8	27.9	37.0	52.8	51.6
35–44 years	37.2	40.5	40.7	49.6	60.6	60.1
45–54 years	49.3	49.0	48.7	60.3	65.1	67.4
55–64 years	59.9	54.5	53.7	66.3	72.2	69.9
65-74 years	60.9	55.9	59.5	60.3	70.9	71.5
75 years and over	—	—	—	52.3	59.9	63.7

—— = Data not available.

[1]Data for Mexicans are for 1982–1984.

[2]Body mass index (BMI) greater than or equal to 25 kilograms/meter[2].

[3]Age-adjusted to the 2000 standard population using five age groups. Age-adjusted estimates in this table may differ from other age-adjusted estimates based on the same data and presented elsewhere if different age groups are used in the adjustment procedure.

[4]Includes persons of all races and Hispanic origins, not just those shown separately.

[5]Persons of Mexican origin may be of any race.

[6]Poverty level is based on family income and family size. Persons with unknown poverty level are excluded.

Table C-20. Overweight, Obesity, and Healthy Weight Among Persons 20 Years of Age and Over, by Sex, Age, Race, and Hispanic Origin, and Poverty Level, Selected Years, 1960–2004—*Continued*

(Percent.)

Characteristic	1960–1962	1971–1974	1976–1980[1]	1988–1994	1999–2002	2001–2004
PERCENT OF POPULATION OBESE[7]						
20–74 Years, Age-Adjusted[3]						
Both sexes[4]	13.3	14.6	15.1	23.3	31.1	32.1
Male	10.7	12.2	12.8	20.6	28.1	30.2
Female	15.7	16.8	17.1	26.0	34.0	34.0
Not Hispanic or Latino						
White only, male	—	—	12.4	20.7	28.7	31.0
White only, female	—	—	15.4	23.3	31.3	31.5
Black or African American only, male	—	—	16.5	21.3	27.9	31.2
Black or African American only, female	—	—	31.0	39.1	49.6	51.6
Mexican male[5]	—	—	15.7	24.4	29.0	30.5
Mexican female[5]	—	—	26.6	36.1	38.9	40.3
Percent of Poverty Level[6]						
Below 100%	—	20.7	21.9	29.2	36.0	34.9
100%–less than 200%	—	18.4	18.7	26.6	35.4	34.6
200% or more	—	12.4	12.9	21.4	29.2	30.6
20 Years and Over, Age-Adjusted[3]						
Both sexes[4]	—	—	—	22.9	30.4	31.4
Male	—	—	—	20.2	27.5	29.5
Female	—	—	—	25.5	33.2	33.2
Not Hispanic or Latino						
White only, male	—	—	—	20.3	28.0	30.2
White only, female	—	—	—	22.9	30.7	30.7
Black or African American only, male	—	—	—	20.9	27.8	30.8
Black or African American only, female	—	—	—	38.3	48.8	51.1
Mexican male[5]	—	—	—	23.8	27.8	29.1
Mexican female[5]	—	—	—	35.2	38.0	39.4
Percent of Poverty Level[6]						
Below 100%	—	—	—	28.1	34.7	33.7
100%–less than 200%	—	—	—	26.1	34.1	33.6
200% or more	—	—	—	21.1	28.7	30.0
20 Years and Over, Crude						
Both sexes[4]	—	—	—	22.3	30.5	31.5
Male	—	—	—	19.5	27.5	29.5
Female	—	—	—	25.0	33.4	33.3
Not Hispanic or Latino						
White only, male	—	—	—	19.9	28.4	30.5
White only, female	—	—	—	22.7	31.3	31.2
Black or African American only, male	—	—	—	20.7	27.5	30.7
Black or African American only, female	—	—	—	36.7	48.8	51.1
Mexican male[5]	—	—	—	20.6	26.0	27.8
Mexican female[5]	—	—	—	33.3	37.0	38.5
Percent of Poverty Level[6]						
Below 100%	—	—	—	25.9	33.0	33.0
100%–less than 200%	—	—	—	24.3	32.8	32.6
200% or more	—	—	—	20.9	29.3	30.7
Male						
20–34 years	9.2	9.7	8.9	14.1	21.7	23.2
35–44 years	12.1	13.5	13.5	21.5	28.5	33.8
45–54 years	12.5	13.7	16.7	23.2	30.6	31.8
55–64 years	9.2	14.1	14.1	27.2	35.5	36.0
65–74 years	10.4	10.9	13.2	24.1	31.9	32.1
75 years and over	—	—	—	13.2	18.0	19.9
Female						
20–34 years	7.2	9.7	11.0	18.5	28.4	28.6
35–44 years	14.7	17.7	17.8	25.5	32.1	33.3
45–54 years	20.3	18.9	19.6	32.4	36.9	38.0
55–64 years	24.4	24.1	22.9	33.7	42.1	39.0
65–74 years	23.2	22.0	21.5	26.9	39.3	37.9
75 years and over	—	—	—	19.2	23.6	23.2

— = Data not available.

[1]Data for Mexicans are for 1982–1984.

[3]Age-adjusted to the 2000 standard population using five age groups. Age-adjusted estimates in this table may differ from other age-adjusted estimates based on the same data and presented elsewhere if different age groups are used in the adjustment procedure.

[4]Includes persons of all races and Hispanic origins, not just those shown separately.

[5]Persons of Mexican origin may be of any race.

[6]Poverty level is based on family income and family size. Persons with unknown poverty level are excluded.

[7]Body mass index (BMI) greater than or equal to 30 kilograms/meter^2.

Table C-20. Overweight, Obesity, and Healthy Weight Among Persons 20 Years of Age and Over, by Sex, Age, Race, and Hispanic Origin, and Poverty Level, Selected Years, 1960–2004—*Continued*

(Percent.)

Characteristic	1960–1962	1971–1974	1976–1980[1]	1988–1994	1999–2002	2001–2004
PERCENT OF POPULATION WITH A HEALTHY WEIGHT[8]						
20–74 Years, Age-Adjusted[3]						
Both sexes[4]	51.2	48.8	49.6	41.7	32.9	32.2
Male	48.3	43.0	45.4	37.9	30.2	28.1
Female	54.1	54.3	53.7	45.3	35.6	36.2
Not Hispanic or Latino						
White only, male	—	—	45.3	37.4	29.5	27.8
White only, female	—	—	56.7	49.2	39.7	40.2
Black or African American only, male	—	—	46.6	40.0	35.5	31.3
Black or African American only, female	—	—	35.0	28.9	21.3	18.9
Mexican male[5]	—	—	37.1	29.8	25.6	24.2
Mexican female[5]	—	—	36.4	29.0	27.5	26.3
Percent of Poverty Level[6]						
Below 100%	—	45.8	45.1	37.3	32.4	33.7
100%–less than 200%	—	45.1	47.6	39.2	29.7	31.8
200% or more	—	50.2	51.0	43.4	33.5	32.4
20 Years and Over, Age-Adjusted[3]						
Both sexes[4]	—	—	—	41.6	33.0	32.3
Male	—	—	—	37.9	30.2	28.3
Female	—	—	—	45.0	35.7	36.1
Not Hispanic or Latino						
White only, male	—	—	—	37.3	29.6	28.0
White only, female	—	—	—	48.7	39.5	39.8
Black or African American only, male	—	—	—	40.1	34.7	30.8
Black or African American only, female	—	—	—	29.2	21.7	18.9
Mexican male[5]	—	—	—	30.2	26.5	25.3
Mexican female[5]	—	—	—	29.7	27.5	26.5
Percent of Poverty Level[6]						
Below 100%	—	—	—	37.5	32.7	34.3
100%–less than 200%	—	—	—	39.3	30.5	31.9
200% or more	—	—	—	43.1	33.4	32.4
20 Years and Over, Crude						
Both sexes[4]	—	—	—	42.6	32.9	32.2
Male	—	—	—	39.4	30.4	28.4
Female	—	—	—	45.7	35.4	35.8
Not Hispanic or Latino						
White only, male	—	—	—	38.2	29.2	27.4
White only, female	—	—	—	48.8	38.7	38.8
Black or African American only, male	—	—	—	41.5	35.9	31.5
Black or African American only, female	—	—	—	31.2	21.9	19.3
Mexican male[5]	—	—	—	35.2	29.4	28.1
Mexican female[5]	—	—	—	32.4	29.4	28.0
Percent of Poverty Level[6]						
Below 100%	—	—	—	39.8	34.5	36.2
100%–less than 200%	—	—	—	41.5	31.5	32.6
200% or more	—	—	—	43.6	32.8	31.6
Male						
20–34 years	55.3	54.7	57.1	51.1	40.3	38.3
35–44 years	45.2	35.2	41.3	33.4	29.0	26.5
45–54 years	44.8	38.5	38.7	33.6	24.0	21.2
55–64 years	44.9	38.3	38.7	28.6	23.8	22.2
65–74 years	46.2	42.1	42.3	30.1	22.8	23.1
75 years and over	—	—	—	40.9	32.0	32.1

—— = Data not available.

[1]Data for Mexicans are for 1982–1984.

[3]Age-adjusted to the 2000 standard population using five age groups. Age-adjusted estimates in this table may differ from other age-adjusted estimates based on the same data and presented elsewhere if different age groups are used in the adjustment procedure.

[4]Includes persons of all races and Hispanic origins, not just those shown separately.

[5]Persons of Mexican origin may be of any race.

[6]Poverty level is based on family income and family size. Persons with unknown poverty level are excluded.

[8]Body mass index (BMI) of 18.5 to less than 25 kilograms/meter^2.

Table C-20. Overweight, Obesity, and Healthy Weight Among Persons 20 Years of Age and Over, by Sex, Age, Race, and Hispanic Origin, and Poverty Level, Selected Years, 1960–2004—*Continued*

(Percent.)

Characteristic	1960–1962	1971–1974	1976–1980[1]	1988–1994	1999–2002	2001–2004
Female						
20–34 years	67.6	65.8	65.0	57.9	42.6	44.2
35–44 years	58.4	56.7	55.6	47.1	37.1	38.3
45–54 years	47.6	49.3	48.7	37.2	33.1	31.0
55–64 years	38.1	41.1	43.5	31.5	27.6	29.2
65–74 years	36.4	40.6	37.8	37.0	26.4	27.0
75 years and over	—	—	—	43.0	36.9	34.6

— = Data not available.

[1]Data for Mexicans are for 1982–1984.

NOTE: Percents do not sum to 100 because the percentage of persons with BMI less than 18.5 kilograms/meter^2 is not shown and the percentage of persons with obesity is a subset of the percent with overweight. Excludes pregnant women.

Table C-21. Overweight Children and Adolescents 6–19 Years of Age, by Age, Sex, Race, Hispanic Origin, and Poverty Level, Selected Years, 1963–2004

(Percent.)

Characteristic	1963–1965 and 1966–1970[1]	1971–1974	1976–1980[2]	1988–1994	1999–2002	2001–2004
PERCENT OF POPULATION OVERWEIGHT[3]						
6–11 Years of Age						
Both sexes[4]	4.2	4.0	6.5	11.3	15.8	17.5
Boys	4.0	*4.3	6.6	11.6	16.9	18.7
Not Hispanic or Latino						
White only	—	—	6.1	10.7	14.0	16.9
Black or African American only	—	—	6.8	12.3	17.0	17.2
Mexican[5]	—	—	13.3	17.5	26.5	25.6
Girls	4.5	*3.6	6.4	11.0	14.7	16.3
Not Hispanic or Latino						
White only	—	—	5.2	*9.8	13.1	15.6
Black or African American only	—	—	11.2	17.0	22.8	24.8
Mexican[5]	—	—	9.8	15.3	17.1	16.6
Percent of Poverty Level[6]						
Below 100%	—	—	—	11.4	19.1	20.0
100%–less than 200%	—	—	—	11.1	16.4	18.4
200% or more	—	—	—	11.1	14.3	15.4
12–19 Years of Age						
Both sexes[4]	4.6	6.1	5.0	10.5	16.1	17.0
Boys	4.5	6.1	4.8	11.3	16.7	17.9
Not Hispanic or Latino						
White only	—	—	3.8	11.6	14.6	17.9
Black or African American only	—	—	6.1	10.7	18.7	17.7
Mexican[5]	—	—	7.7	14.1	24.7	20.0
Girls	4.7	6.2	5.3	9.7	15.4	16.0
Not Hispanic or Latino						
White only	—	—	4.6	8.9	12.7	14.6
Black or African American only	—	—	10.7	16.3	23.6	23.8
Mexican[5]	—	—	8.8	*13.4	19.9	17.1
Percent of Poverty Level[6]						
Below 100%	—	—	—	15.8	19.9	18.2
100%–less than 200%	—	—	—	11.2	15.2	17.0
200% or more	—	—	—	7.9	14.9	16.3

* = Figure does not meet standards of reliability or precision.

— = Data not available.

[1]Data for 1963–1965 are for children 6–11 years of age; data for 1966–1970 are for adolescents 12–17 years of age, not 12–19 years.

[2]Data for Mexicans are for 1982–1984.

[3]Overweight is defined as body mass index (BMI) at or above the sex- and age-specific 95th percentile BMI cutoff points from the 2000 CDC Growth Charts.

[4]Includes persons of all races and Hispanic origins, not just those shown separately.

[5]Persons of Mexican origin may be of any race.

[6]Poverty level is based on family income and family size. Persons with unknown poverty level are excluded.

USE OF ADDICTIVE SUBSTANCES

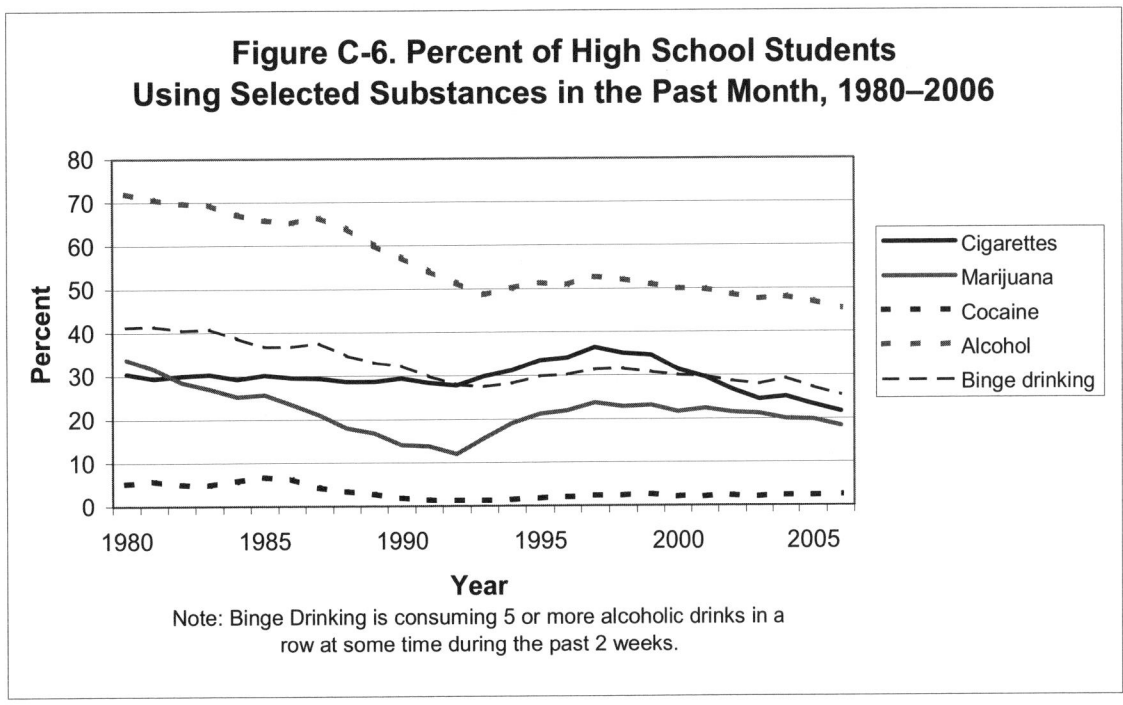

Figure C-6. Percent of High School Students Using Selected Substances in the Past Month, 1980–2006

Note: Binge Drinking is consuming 5 or more alcoholic drinks in a row at some time during the past 2 weeks.

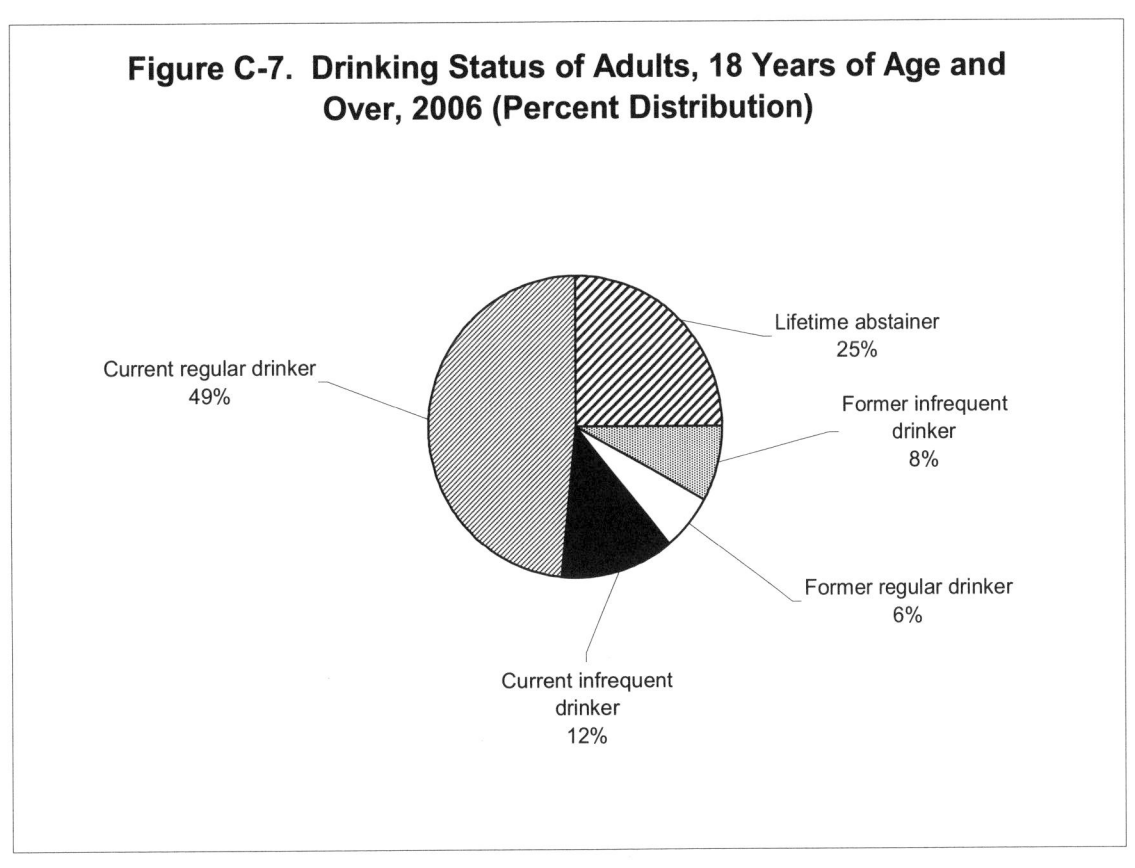

Figure C-7. Drinking Status of Adults, 18 Years of Age and Over, 2006 (Percent Distribution)

Table C-22. Current Cigarette Smoking Among Adults[1] 18 Years of Age and Over, by Sex, Race, and Age, Selected Years, 1965–2006

(Percent of people who are current cigarette smokers.)

Sex, race, and age	1965[2]	1974[2]	1985[2]	1990[2]	1995[2]	2000	2001	2002	2003	2004	2005	2006
18 Years and Over, Age-Adjusted[3]												
All persons	41.9	37.0	29.9	25.3	24.6	23.1	22.6	22.3	21.5	20.8	20.8	20.8
Male	51.2	42.8	32.2	28.0	26.5	25.2	24.6	24.6	23.7	23.0	23.4	23.6
Female	33.7	32.2	27.9	22.9	22.7	21.1	20.7	20.0	19.4	18.7	18.3	18.1
White male[4]	50.4	41.7	31.3	27.6	26.2	25.4	24.8	24.9	23.8	23.0	23.3	23.5
Black or African American male[4]	58.8	53.6	40.2	32.8	29.4	25.7	27.5	26.6	25.3	23.5	25.9	26.1
White female[4]	33.9	32.0	27.9	23.5	23.4	22.0	22.0	21.0	20.1	19.5	19.1	18.8
Black or African American female[4]	31.8	35.6	30.9	20.8	23.5	20.7	18.0	18.3	17.9	16.9	17.1	18.5
18 Years and Over, Crude												
All persons	42.4	37.1	30.1	25.5	24.7	23.2	22.7	22.4	21.6	20.9	20.9	20.8
Male	51.9	43.1	32.6	28.4	27.0	25.6	25.1	25.1	24.1	23.4	23.9	23.9
Female	33.9	32.1	27.9	22.8	22.6	20.9	20.6	19.8	19.2	18.5	18.1	18.0
White male[4]	51.1	41.9	31.7	28.0	26.6	25.7	25.0	25.0	24.0	23.2	23.6	23.6
Black or African American male[4]	60.4	54.3	39.9	32.5	28.5	26.2	27.6	27.0	25.7	23.9	26.5	27.0
White female[4]	34.0	31.7	27.7	23.4	23.1	21.4	21.5	20.6	19.7	19.1	18.7	18.4
Black or African American female[4]	33.7	36.4	31.0	21.2	23.5	20.8	18.1	18.5	18.1	17.3	17.3	18.8
All Males												
18–24 years	54.1	42.1	28.0	26.6	27.8	28.1	30.2	32.1	26.3	25.6	28.0	28.5
25–34 years	60.7	50.5	38.2	31.6	29.5	28.9	26.9	27.2	28.7	26.1	27.7	27.4
35–44 years	58.2	51.0	37.6	34.5	31.5	30.2	27.3	29.7	28.1	26.5	26.0	24.8
45–64 years	51.9	42.6	33.4	29.3	27.1	26.4	26.4	24.5	23.9	25.0	25.2	24.5
65 years and over	28.5	24.8	19.6	14.6	14.9	10.2	11.5	10.1	10.1	9.8	8.9	12.6
White Male[4]												
18–24 years	53.0	40.8	28.4	27.4	28.4	30.4	32.3	34.3	27.7	26.7	29.7	28.9
25–34 years	60.1	49.5	37.3	31.6	29.9	29.7	28.7	27.7	28.8	26.3	27.7	27.9
35–44 years	57.3	50.1	36.6	33.5	31.2	30.6	27.8	29.7	28.8	26.6	26.3	25.3
45–64 years	51.3	41.2	32.1	28.7	26.3	25.8	25.1	24.4	23.3	24.4	24.5	23.4
65 years and over	27.7	24.3	18.9	13.7	14.1	9.8	10.7	9.3	9.6	9.4	7.9	12.6
Black or African American Male[4]												
18–24 years	62.8	54.9	27.2	21.3	*14.6	20.9	21.6	22.7	18.6	18.0	21.6	31.2
25–34 years	68.4	58.5	45.6	33.8	25.1	23.2	23.8	28.9	31.0	21.2	29.8	26.3
35–44 years	67.3	61.5	45.0	42.0	36.3	30.7	29.9	28.3	23.6	28.4	23.3	22.2
45–64 years	57.9	57.8	46.1	36.7	33.9	32.2	34.3	29.8	30.1	29.2	32.4	32.6
65 years and over	36.4	29.7	27.7	21.5	28.5	14.2	21.1	19.4	18.0	14.1	16.8	16.0
All Females												
18–24 years	38.1	34.1	30.4	22.5	21.8	24.9	23.2	24.5	21.5	21.5	20.7	19.3
25–34 years	43.7	38.8	32.0	28.2	26.4	22.3	22.7	21.3	21.3	21.0	21.5	21.5
35–44 years	43.7	39.8	31.5	24.8	27.1	26.2	25.7	23.7	24.2	21.6	21.3	20.6
45–64 years	32.0	33.4	29.9	24.8	24.0	21.7	21.4	21.1	20.2	19.8	18.8	19.3
65 years and over	9.6	12.0	13.5	11.5	11.5	9.3	9.1	8.6	8.3	8.1	8.3	8.3
White Female[4]												
18–24 years	38.4	34.0	31.8	25.4	24.9	28.5	27.1	26.7	23.6	22.9	22.6	20.7
25–34 years	43.4	38.6	32.0	28.5	27.3	24.9	25.2	23.8	22.5	22.6	23.1	23.7
35–44 years	43.9	39.3	31.0	25.0	27.0	26.6	26.9	24.4	25.2	22.7	22.2	21.7
45–64 years	32.7	33.0	29.7	25.4	24.3	21.4	21.6	21.5	20.1	20.1	18.9	18.8
65 years and over	9.8	12.3	13.3	11.5	11.7	9.1	9.4	8.5	8.4	8.2	8.4	8.4
Black or African American Female[4]												
18–24 years	37.1	35.6	23.7	10.0	*8.8	14.2	10.0	17.1	10.8	15.6	14.2	14.8
25–34 years	47.8	42.2	36.2	29.1	26.7	15.5	16.8	13.9	17.0	18.3	16.9	15.4
35–44 years	42.8	46.4	40.2	25.5	31.9	30.2	24.0	24.0	23.2	18.9	19.0	21.0
45–64 years	25.7	38.9	33.4	22.6	27.5	25.6	22.6	22.2	23.3	20.9	21.0	25.5
65 years and over	7.1	*8.9	14.5	11.1	13.3	10.2	9.3	9.4	8.0	6.7	10.0	9.3

* = Figure does not meet standards of reliability or precision.
[1]Starting with 1993 data, current cigarette smokers were defined as ever smoking 100 cigarettes in their lifetime and smoking now on every day or some days.
[2]Data prior to 1997 are not strictly comparable with data for later years due to the 1997 questionnaire redesign.
[3]Estimates are age-adjusted to the year 2000 standard population using five age groups: 18–24 years, 25–34 years, 35–44 years, 45–64 years, 65 years and over. Age-adjusted estimates in this table may differ from other age-adjusted estimates based on the same data and presented elsewhere if different age groups are used in the adjustment procedure.
[4]The race groups, White and Black, include persons of Hispanic and non-Hispanic origin. Persons of Hispanic origin may be of any race.

Table C-23. Current Cigarette Smoking Among Adults[1] 25 Years of Age and Over, by Sex, Race, and Education Level, Selected Years, 1974–2006

(Percent of people who are current cigarette smokers.)

Sex, race, and education level	1974[2]	1985[2]	1990[2]	1995[2]	2000	2001	2002	2003	2004	2005	2006
25 YEARS AND OVER, AGE-ADJUSTED[3]											
All Persons[4]	36.9	30.0	25.4	24.5	22.6	22.0	21.4	21.1	20.4	20.3	20.3
No high school diploma or GED	43.7	40.8	36.7	35.6	31.6	30.5	30.5	29.7	29.1	28.2	28.8
High school diploma or GED	36.2	32.0	29.1	29.1	29.2	28.1	27.9	27.8	25.8	27.0	26.5
Some college, no bachelor's degree	35.9	29.5	23.4	22.6	21.7	22.2	21.5	21.1	21.4	21.8	22.1
Bachelor's degree or higher	27.2	18.5	13.9	13.6	10.9	10.8	10.0	10.2	10.0	9.1	8.2
All Males[4]	42.9	32.8	28.2	26.4	24.7	23.8	23.5	23.3	22.6	22.7	22.9
No high school diploma or GED	52.3	45.7	42.0	39.7	36.0	34.2	34.0	34.4	33.6	31.7	31.6
High school diploma or GED	42.4	35.5	33.1	32.7	32.1	30.2	31.0	29.9	28.2	29.9	29.7
Some college, no bachelor's degree	41.8	32.9	25.9	23.7	23.3	24.3	23.2	22.7	23.4	24.9	25.2
Bachelor's degree or higher	28.3	19.6	14.5	13.8	11.6	11.2	11.0	11.2	10.8	9.7	9.2
White Males[4,5]	41.9	31.7	27.6	25.9	24.7	23.7	23.5	23.2	22.4	22.4	22.7
No high school diploma or GED	51.5	45.0	41.8	38.7	38.2	34.8	35.6	33.6	32.6	31.6	31.4
High school diploma or GED	42.0	34.8	32.9	32.9	32.4	30.3	31.0	29.6	28.9	30.0	29.2
Some college, no bachelor's degree	41.6	32.2	25.4	23.3	23.5	24.5	23.2	23.3	22.9	24.5	25.8
Bachelor's degree or higher	27.8	19.1	14.4	13.4	11.3	11.2	11.1	11.2	10.5	9.3	8.9
Black or African American Males[4,5]	53.4	42.1	34.5	31.6	26.4	28.4	27.2	26.3	24.4	26.5	25.4
No high school diploma or GED	58.1	50.5	41.6	41.9	38.2	37.9	37.2	37.4	36.7	35.9	35.2
High school diploma or GED	*50.7	41.8	37.4	36.6	29.0	33.4	31.3	33.4	23.1	30.1	31.3
Some college, no bachelor's degree	*45.3	41.8	28.1	26.4	19.9	24.1	25.6	19.5	24.7	27.4	21.0
Bachelor's degree or higher	*41.4	*32.0	*20.8	*17.3	14.6	11.3	*10.8	*10.3	11.3	10.0	12.9
All Females[4]	32.0	27.5	22.9	22.9	20.5	20.4	19.3	19.1	18.3	18.0	17.9
No high school diploma or GED	36.6	36.5	31.8	31.7	27.1	26.9	26.9	24.9	24.5	24.6	26.0
High school diploma or GED	32.2	29.5	26.1	26.4	26.6	26.4	25.2	25.8	23.7	24.1	23.4
Some college, no bachelor's degree	30.1	26.3	21.0	21.6	20.4	20.4	20.0	19.7	19.7	19.1	19.6
Bachelor's degree or higher	25.9	17.1	13.3	13.3	10.1	10.5	9.0	9.3	9.3	8.5	7.2
White Females[4,5]	31.7	27.3	23.3	23.1	21.0	21.3	20.2	19.6	19.0	18.6	18.5
No high school diploma or GED	36.8	36.7	33.4	32.4	28.4	29.2	29.0	25.0	24.4	24.6	25.9
High school diploma or GED	31.9	29.4	26.5	26.8	27.8	28.3	26.8	26.8	24.7	25.9	24.6
Some college, no bachelor's degree	30.4	26.7	21.2	22.2	21.1	21.3	20.5	20.6	21.1	19.5	20.5
Bachelor's degree or higher	25.5	16.5	13.4	13.5	10.2	10.9	9.6	9.4	9.9	9.1	7.7
Black or African American Females[4,5]	35.6	32.0	22.4	25.7	21.6	19.1	18.4	18.9	17.1	17.5	19.1
No high school diploma or GED	36.1	39.4	26.3	32.3	31.1	26.3	27.1	26.9	29.2	27.8	31.2
High school diploma or GED	40.9	32.1	24.1	27.8	25.4	21.3	19.5	23.3	21.0	18.2	18.6
Some college, no bachelor's degree	32.3	23.9	22.7	20.8	20.4	17.4	20.7	17.0	13.9	17.5	18.9
Bachelor's degree or higher	*36.3	26.6	17.0	17.3	10.8	11.6	*7.7	11.4	*6.9	*6.6	*8.5

* = Figure does not meet standards of reliability or precision.

[1]Starting with 1993 data, current cigarette smokers were defined as ever smoking 100 cigarettes in their lifetime and smoking now on every day or some days.

[2]Data prior to 1997 are not strictly comparable with data for later years due to the 1997 questionnaire redesign.

[3]Estimates are age-adjusted to the year 2000 standard population using four age groups: 25–34 years, 35–44 years, 45–64 years, and 65 years and over. For age groups where smoking was 0% or 100%, the age-adjustment procedure was modified to substitute the percentage smoking from the next lower education group.

[4]Includes unknown education level. Education categories shown are for 1997 and subsequent years. GED stands for General Educational Development high school equivalency diploma. In 1974–1995 the following categories based on number of years of school completed were used: less than 12 years, 12 years, 13–15 years, 16 years or more.

[5]The race groups, White and Black, include persons of Hispanic and non-Hispanic origin. Persons of Hispanic origin may be of any race.

Table C-24 Current Cigarette Smoking Among Adults[1], by Sex, Race, Hispanic Origin, Age, and Education Level, Selected Annual Averages, 1990–2006

(Percent of people who are current cigarette smokers.)

Characteristic	Male			Female		
	1990–1992[2]	1995–1998[2]	2004–2006	1990–1992[2]	1995–1998[2]	2004–2006
18 Years and Over, Age-Adjusted[3]						
All persons[4]...............................	27.9	26.5	23.3	23.7	22.1	18.4
Race[5]						
White only	27.4	26.4	23.3	24.3	22.9	19.1
Black or African American only	33.9	30.7	25.2	23.1	21.8	17.5
American Indian or Alaska Native only	34.2	40.5	31.5	36.7	28.9	23.2
Asian only	24.8	18.1	18.1	6.3	11.0	5.2
Native Hawaiian or Other Pacific						
Islander only	—	—	*	—	—	*
2 or more races..............................	—	—	30.3	—	—	25.8
American Indian or Alaska Native;						
White	—	—	35.5	—	—	33.1
Hispanic Origin and Race[5]						
Hispanic or Latino	25.7	24.4	19.0	15.8	13.7	10.5
Mexican	26.2	24.5	19.2	14.8	12.0	9.5
Not Hispanic or Latino......................	28.1	26.9	24.2	24.4	23.1	19.6
White only	27.7	26.9	24.3	25.2	24.1	20.9
Black or African American only	33.9	30.7	25.5	23.2	21.9	17.6
18 Years and Over, Crude						
All persons[4]...............................	28.4	27.0	23.7	23.6	22.0	18.2
Race[5]						
White only	27.8	26.8	23.5	24.1	22.6	18.7
Black or African American only	33.2	30.6	25.8	23.3	21.8	17.8
American Indian or Alaska Native only	35.5	39.2	32.8	37.3	31.2	24.2
Asian only	24.9	20.0	19.1	6.3	11.2	5.3
Native Hawaiian or Other Pacific						
Islander only	—	—	*	—	—	*
2 or more races..............................	—	—	32.4	—	—	26.0
American Indian or Alaska Native;						
White	—	—	37.4	—	—	33.3
Age, Hispanic Origin, and Race[5]						
18–24 Years						
Hispanic or Latino............................	19.3	26.5	20.3	12.8	12.0	10.1
Not Hispanic or Latino						
White only....................................	28.9	35.5	31.0	28.7	31.6	25.1
Black or African American only	17.7	21.3	23.1	10.8	9.8	14.6
25–34 Years						
Hispanic or Latino............................	29.9	25.9	19.7	19.2	12.6	9.3
Not Hispanic or Latino						
White only....................................	32.7	30.5	29.7	30.9	28.5	27.0
Black or African American only	34.6	28.5	26.1	29.2	22.0	16.7
35–44 Years						
Hispanic or Latino............................	32.1	26.2	22.0	19.9	17.6	13.0
Not Hispanic or Latino						
White only....................................	32.3	31.5	26.9	27.3	28.1	24.0
Black or African American only	44.1	34.7	25.1	31.3	30.3	19.9
45–64 Years						
Hispanic or Latino............................	26.6	26.8	21.8	17.1	14.7	12.3
Not Hispanic or Latino						
White only....................................	28.4	26.8	24.4	26.1	22.3	20.1
Black or African American only	38.0	38.8	31.7	26.1	26.9	22.8
65 Years and Over						
Hispanic or Latino............................	16.1	14.7	8.3	6.6	9.4	5.6
Not Hispanic or Latino						
White only....................................	14.2	10.6	10.1	12.3	11.6	8.5
Black or African American only	25.2	20.9	16.0	10.7	11.2	8.7

* = Figure does not meet standards of reliability or precision.

—— = Data not available.

[1]Starting with 1993 data, current cigarette smokers were defined as ever smoking 100 cigarettes in their lifetime and smoking now on every day or some days.

[2]Data prior to 1997 are not strictly comparable with data for later years due to the 1997 questionnaire redesign. The column labeled 1995–1998 includes data for 1995, 1997, and 1998 because cigarette smoking data were not collected in 1996.

[3]Estimates are age-adjusted to the year 2000 standard population using five age groups: 18–24 years, 25–34 years, 35–44 years, 45–64 years, and 65 years and over.

[4]Includes all other races not shown separately and unknown education level.

[5]The race groups, White, Black, American Indian or Alaska Native (AI/AN), Asian, Native Hawaiian or Other Pacific Islander, and 2 or more races, include persons of Hispanic and non-Hispanic origin. Persons of Hispanic origin may be of any race.

Table C-24 Current Cigarette Smoking Among Adults[1], by Sex, Race, Hispanic Origin, Age, and Education Level, Selected Annual Averages, 1990–2006—*Continued*

(Percent of people who are current cigarette smokers.)

Characteristic	Male			Female		
	1990–1992[2]	1995–1998[2]	2004–2006	1990–1992[2]	1995–1998[2]	2004–2006
Education, Hispanic Origin, and Race[5,6]						
25 Years and Over, Age-Adjusted[7]						
No high school diploma or GED						
Hispanic or Latino	30.2	27.6	20.6	15.8	13.3	9.5
Not Hispanic or Latino						
White only	46.1	43.9	43.0	40.4	40.7	40.8
Black or African American only	45.4	44.6	37.2	31.3	30.0	30.3
High School Diploma or GED						
Hispanic or Latino	29.6	26.7	18.7	18.4	16.4	12.0
Not Hispanic or Latino						
White only	32.9	32.8	31.2	28.4	28.8	27.7
Black or African American only	38.2	35.7	28.7	25.4	26.6	19.7
Some college or more						
Hispanic or Latino	20.4	16.6	15.8	14.3	13.5	10.6
Not Hispanic or Latino						
White only	19.3	18.3	16.6	18.1	17.2	15.0
Black or African American only	25.6	23.3	19.1	22.8	18.9	13.3

[1]Starting with 1993 data, current cigarette smokers were defined as ever smoking 100 cigarettes in their lifetime and smoking now on every day or some days.
[2]Data prior to 1997 are not strictly comparable with data for later years due to the 1997 questionnaire redesign. The column labeled 1995–1998 includes data for 1995, 1997, and 1998 because cigarette smoking data were not collected in 1996.
[5]The race groups, White, Black, American Indian or Alaska Native (AI/AN), Asian, Native Hawaiian or Other Pacific Islander, and 2 or more races, include persons of Hispanic and non-Hispanic origin. Persons of Hispanic origin may be of any race.
[6]Education categories shown are for 1997 and subsequent years. GED stands for General Educational Development high school equivalency diploma. In years prior to 1997, the following categories based on number of years of school completed were used: less than 12 years, 12 years, 13 years or more.
[7]Estimates are age-adjusted to the year 2000 standard using four age groups: 25–34 years, 35–44 years, 45–64 years, and 65 years and over.

Table C-25. Use of Selected Substances in the Past Month Among Persons 12 Years of Age and Over, by Age, Sex, Race, and Hispanic Origin, Selected Years, 2002–2005

(Percent of population.)

Age, sex, race, and Hispanic origin	Any illicit drug[1]			Marijuana			Nonmedical use of any psychotherapeutic drug[2]		
	2002	2004	2005	2002	2004	2005	2002	2004	2005
12 years and over	8.3	7.9	8.1	6.2	6.1	6.0	2.6	2.5	2.6
Age									
12–13 years	4.2	3.8	3.8	1.4	1.1	0.9	1.7	1.7	1.7
14–15 years	11.2	10.9	8.9	7.6	7.3	5.9	4.0	4.1	2.8
16–17 years	19.8	17.3	17.0	15.7	14.5	13.6	6.2	5.1	5.4
18–25 years	20.2	19.4	20.1	17.3	16.1	16.6	5.4	6.1	6.3
26–34 years	10.5	11.1	11.0	7.7	8.3	8.6	3.6	3.6	3.5
35 years and over	4.6	4.2	4.5	3.1	3.1	3.0	1.6	1.3	1.5
Sex									
Male	10.3	9.9	10.2	8.1	8.0	8.2	2.7	2.6	2.8
Female	6.4	6.1	6.1	4.4	4.3	4.0	2.6	2.4	2.5
Age and Sex									
12–17 years	11.6	10.6	9.9	8.2	7.6	6.8	4.0	3.6	3.3
Male	12.3	10.6	10.1	9.1	8.1	7.5	3.6	3.2	3.1
Female	10.9	10.6	9.7	7.2	7.1	6.2	4.3	4.1	3.6
Hispanic Origin and Race[3]									
Not Hispanic or Latino									
White only	8.5	8.1	8.1	6.5	6.2	6.1	2.8	2.7	2.8
Black or African American only	9.7	8.7	9.7	7.4	7.0	7.6	2.0	1.6	1.8
American Indian or Alaska Native only	10.1	12.3	12.8	6.7	9.1	9.8	3.2	3.0	5.0
Native Hawaiian or Other Pacific Islander only	7.9	*	8.7	4.4	*	5.7	3.8	4.6	3.3
Asian only	3.5	3.1	3.1	1.8	2.0	1.6	0.7	0.9	1.5
2 or more races	11.4	13.3	12.2	9.0	9.6	10.6	3.5	5.7	2.7
Hispanic or Latino	7.2	7.2	7.6	4.3	5.0	5.1	2.9	2.4	2.5

Age, sex, race, and Hispanic origin	Alcohol use			Binge alcohol use[4]			Heavy alcohol use[5]		
	2002	2004	2005	2002	2004	2005	2002	2004	2005
12 years and over	51.0	50.3	51.8	22.9	22.8	22.7	6.7	6.9	6.6
Age									
12–13 years	4.3	4.3	4.2	1.8	2.0	2.0	0.3	0.2	0.2
14–15 years	16.6	16.4	15.1	9.2	9.1	8.0	1.9	1.6	1.7
16–17 years	32.6	32.5	30.1	21.4	22.4	19.7	5.6	6.3	5.3
18–25 years	60.5	60.5	60.9	40.9	41.2	41.9	14.9	15.1	15.3
26–34 years	61.4	60.5	62.5	33.1	32.2	32.9	9.0	9.4	9.6
35 years and over	52.1	51.2	53.3	18.6	18.5	18.3	5.2	5.3	4.7
Sex									
Male	57.4	56.9	58.1	31.2	31.1	30.5	10.8	10.6	10.3
Female	44.9	44.0	45.9	15.1	14.9	15.2	3.0	3.5	3.1
Age and Sex									
12–17 years	17.6	17.6	16.5	10.7	11.1	9.9	2.5	2.7	2.4
Male	17.4	17.2	15.9	11.4	11.6	10.4	3.1	3.2	3.0
Female	17.9	18.0	17.2	9.9	10.5	9.4	1.9	2.1	1.8
Hispanic Origin and Race[3]									
Not Hispanic or Latino									
White only	55.0	55.2	56.5	23.4	23.8	23.4	7.5	7.9	7.4
Black or African American only	39.9	37.1	40.8	21.0	18.3	20.3	4.4	4.4	4.2
American Indian or Alaska Native only	44.7	36.2	42.4	27.9	25.8	32.8	8.7	7.7	11.5
Native Hawaiian or Other Pacific Islander only	*	*	37.3	25.2	*	25.7	8.3	4.9	5.3
Asian only	37.1	37.4	38.1	12.4	12.4	12.7	2.6	2.7	2.0
2 or more races	49.9	52.4	47.3	19.8	23.5	20.8	7.5	6.9	5.6
Hispanic or Latino	42.8	40.2	42.6	24.8	24.0	23.7	5.9	5.3	5.6

* = Figure does not meet standards of reliability or precision.

[1]Any illicit drug includes marijuana/hashish, cocaine (including crack), heroin, hallucinogens (including LSD and PCP), inhalants, or any prescription-type psychotherapeutic drug used nonmedically.

[2]Nonmedical use of prescription-type psychotherapeutic drugs includes the nonmedical use of pain relievers, tranquilizers, stimulants, or sedatives; does not include over-the-counter drugs.

[3]Persons of Hispanic origin may be of any race.

[4]Binge alcohol use is defined as drinking five or more drinks on the same occasion on at least one day in the past 30 days. Occasion is defined as at the same time or within a couple of hours of each other.

[5]Heavy alcohol use is defined as drinking five or more drinks on the same occasion on each of five or more days in the past 30 days. By definition, all heavy alcohol users are also binge alcohol users.

Table C-25. Use of Selected Substances in the Past Month Among Persons 12 Years of Age and Over, by Age, Sex, Race, and Hispanic Origin, Selected Years, 2002–2005

(Percent of population.)

Age, sex, race, and Hispanic origin	Any tobacco[6]			Cigarettes			Cigars		
	2002	2004	2005	2002	2004	2005	2002	2004	2005
12 years and over	30.4	29.2	29.4	26.0	24.9	24.9	5.4	5.7	5.6
Age									
12–13 years	3.8	3.4	3.0	3.2	2.8	2.4	0.7	0.9	0.7
14–15 years	13.4	13.2	11.3	11.2	10.9	9.2	3.8	3.8	3.3
16–17 years	29.0	27.0	24.8	24.9	22.2	20.6	9.3	9.7	8.6
18–25 years	45.3	44.6	44.3	40.8	39.5	39.0	11.0	12.7	12.0
26–34 years	38.2	37.2	37.7	32.7	32.4	33.0	6.6	6.5	6.8
35 years and over	27.9	26.5	27.0	23.4	22.2	22.3	4.1	4.1	4.2
Sex									
Male	37.0	35.7	35.8	28.7	27.7	27.4	9.4	9.8	9.6
Female	24.3	23.1	23.4	23.4	22.3	22.5	1.7	1.9	1.8
Age and Sex									
12–17 years	15.2	14.4	13.1	13.0	11.9	10.8	4.5	4.8	4.2
Male	16.0	15.3	14.2	12.3	11.3	10.7	6.2	6.6	5.8
Female	14.4	13.5	11.9	13.6	12.5	10.8	2.7	2.8	2.5
Hispanic Origin and Race[3]									
Not Hispanic or Latino									
White only	32.0	31.4	31.2	26.9	26.4	26.0	5.5	6.0	5.9
Black or African American only	28.8	27.3	28.4	25.3	23.5	24.5	6.8	6.0	6.4
American Indian or Alaska Native only	44.3	33.8	41.7	37.1	31.0	36.0	5.2	4.9	10.6
Native Hawaiian or Other Pacific Islander only	28.8	*	30.3	*	*	28.8	4.1	*	3.7
Asian only	18.6	11.7	14.6	17.7	10.3	13.4	1.1	1.8	1.6
2 or more races	38.1	41.3	33.9	35.0	38.3	30.9	5.5	9.1	7.8
Hispanic or Latino	25.2	23.3	24.5	23.0	21.3	22.1	5.0	4.7	4.3

* = Figure does not meet standards of reliability or precision.
[3]Persons of Hispanic origin may be of any race.
[6]Any tobacco product includes cigarettes, smokeless tobacco (i.e., chewing tobacco or snuff), cigars, or pipe tobacco.

Table C-26. Use of Selected Substances Among High School Seniors, Tenth-, and Eighth-Graders, by Sex and Race, Selected Years, 1980–2006

(Percent.)

Substance, grade in school, sex, and race	Percent using substance in the last month								
	1980	1990	2000	2001	2002	2003	2004	2005	2006
Cigarettes									
All seniors	30.5	29.4	31.4	29.5	26.7	24.4	25.0	23.2	21.6
Male	26.8	29.1	32.8	29.7	27.4	26.2	25.3	24.8	22.4
Female	33.4	29.2	29.7	28.7	25.5	22.1	24.1	20.7	20.1
White	31.0	32.5	36.6	34.1	30.9	28.2	28.2	27.6	24.7
Black or African American	25.2	12.0	13.6	12.9	11.3	9.0	11.3	10.7	11.0
All tenth-graders	—	—	23.9	21.3	17.7	16.7	16.0	14.9	14.5
Male	—	—	23.8	20.9	16.7	16.2	16.2	14.5	13.4
Female	—	—	23.6	21.5	18.6	17.0	15.7	15.1	15.5
White	—	—	27.3	24.0	20.8	19.3	18.1	17.6	16.3
Black or African American	—	—	11.3	10.9	9.1	8.8	9.6	8.7	8.5
All eighth-graders	—	—	14.6	12.2	10.7	10.2	9.2	9.3	8.7
Male	—	—	14.3	12.2	11.0	9.6	8.3	8.7	8.1
Female	—	—	14.7	12.0	10.4	10.6	9.9	9.7	8.9
White	—	—	16.4	12.8	11.1	10.6	9.4	9.4	9.1
Black or African American	—	—	8.4	8.0	7.3	6.4	7.5	7.1	5.4
Marijuana									
All seniors	33.7	14.0	21.6	22.4	21.5	21.2	19.9	19.8	18.3
Male	37.8	16.1	24.7	25.6	25.3	24.7	23.0	23.6	19.7
Female	29.1	11.5	18.3	19.1	17.4	17.3	16.6	15.8	16.4
White	34.2	15.6	22.0	23.9	22.8	22.8	21.5	21.6	19.2
Black or African American	26.5	5.2	17.5	16.5	16.4	16.1	14.2	14.6	16.7
All tenth-graders	—	—	19.7	19.8	17.8	17.0	15.9	15.2	14.2
Male	—	—	23.3	22.7	19.3	19.0	17.4	16.7	15.7
Female	—	—	16.2	16.8	16.4	15.0	14.2	13.4	12.6
White	—	—	20.1	20.4	19.1	17.4	15.8	15.7	14.7
Black or African American	—	—	17.0	16.5	14.4	15.6	17.2	15.3	14.2
All eighth-graders	—	—	9.1	9.2	8.3	7.5	6.4	6.6	6.5
Male	—	—	10.2	11.0	9.5	8.5	6.3	7.6	6.7
Female	—	—	7.8	7.3	7.1	6.4	6.3	5.7	6.0
White	—	—	8.3	8.6	7.9	7.0	5.5	5.8	5.7
Black or African American	—	—	8.5	7.7	7.1	7.4	8.1	8.2	6.7
Cocaine									
All seniors	5.2	1.9	2.1	2.1	2.3	2.1	2.3	2.3	2.5
Male	6.0	2.3	2.7	2.5	2.7	2.6	2.9	2.6	3.0
Female	4.3	1.3	1.6	1.6	1.8	1.4	1.7	1.8	2.1
White	5.4	1.8	2.2	2.3	2.8	2.1	2.5	2.4	2.6
Black or African American	2.0	0.5	1.0	0.6	0.2	1.0	0.9	0.7	1.0
All tenth-graders	—	—	1.8	1.3	1.6	1.3	1.7	1.5	1.5
Male	—	—	2.1	1.5	1.8	1.3	1.9	1.9	1.6
Female	—	—	1.4	1.2	1.4	1.3	1.4	1.2	1.3
White	—	—	1.7	1.2	1.7	1.4	1.7	1.6	1.5
Black or African American	—	—	0.4	0.3	0.4	0.5	0.4	0.6	0.7
All eighth-graders	—	—	1.2	1.2	1.1	0.9	0.9	1.0	1.0
Male	—	—	1.3	1.1	1.1	1.0	0.8	0.9	1.0
Female	—	—	1.1	1.2	1.1	0.8	1.0	1.0	0.9
White	—	—	1.1	1.1	1.0	0.8	0.8	0.8	0.8
Black or African American	—	—	0.5	0.4	0.5	0.5	0.8	0.5	0.4
Inhalants									
All seniors	1.4	2.7	2.2	1.7	1.5	1.5	1.5	2.0	1.5
Male	1.8	3.5	2.9	2.3	2.2	2.0	1.7	2.4	1.5
Female	1.0	2.0	1.7	1.1	0.8	1.1	1.3	1.6	1.4
White	1.4	3.0	2.1	1.8	1.3	1.7	1.6	1.9	1.5
Black or African American	1.0	1.5	2.1	1.3	1.2	0.7	1.0	1.2	1.2
All tenth-graders	—	—	2.6	2.5	2.4	2.2	2.4	2.2	2.3
Male	—	—	3.0	2.5	2.3	2.3	2.4	1.9	2.2
Female	—	—	2.2	2.4	2.4	2.2	2.3	2.5	2.4
White	—	—	2.8	2.5	2.6	2.6	2.6	2.4	2.4
Black or African American	—	—	1.5	0.9	1.5	0.5	1.4	1.4	1.8
All eighth-graders	—	—	4.5	4.0	3.8	4.1	4.5	4.2	4.1
Male	—	—	4.1	3.6	3.5	3.4	4.0	3.1	3.6
Female	—	—	4.8	4.3	3.9	4.7	5.1	5.3	4.7
White	—	—	4.5	4.1	3.9	4.3	4.4	4.2	4.2
Black or African American	—	—	2.3	2.6	2.7	2.3	3.8	3.3	2.7

—— = Data not available.
0.0 = Quantity more than zero but less than 0.05.

Table C-26. Use of Selected Substances Among High School Seniors, Tenth-, and Eighth-Graders, by Sex and Race, Selected Years, 1980–2006—*Continued*

(Percent.)

Substance, grade in school, sex, and race	Percent using substance in the last month								
	1980	1990	2000	2001	2002	2003	2004	2005	2006
MDMA (Ecstasy)									
All seniors	—	—	3.6	2.8	2.4	1.3	1.2	1.0	1.3
Male	—	—	4.1	3.7	2.6	1.3	1.6	1.0	1.5
Female	—	—	3.1	2.0	2.1	1.2	0.9	1.0	1.1
White	—	—	3.9	2.8	2.5	1.3	1.2	1.1	1.4
Black or African American	—	—	1.9	0.9	0.5	0.6	1.1	1.0	0.6
All tenth-graders	—	—	2.6	2.6	1.8	1.1	0.8	1.0	1.2
Male	—	—	2.5	3.5	1.6	1.2	1.0	1.0	1.5
Female	—	—	2.5	1.6	1.8	1.1	0.6	0.9	0.8
White	—	—	2.5	2.6	2.3	1.2	0.9	0.9	1.3
Black or African American	—	—	1.8	1.0	0.5	0.7	0.1	0.2	1.0
All eighth-graders	—	—	1.4	1.8	1.4	0.7	0.8	0.6	0.7
Male	—	—	1.6	1.9	1.5	0.7	0.7	0.8	0.5
Female	—	—	1.2	1.8	1.3	0.7	0.9	0.4	0.8
White	—	—	1.4	2.0	1.0	0.7	0.6	0.6	0.5
Black or African American	—	—	0.8	1.1	0.6	0.4	1.2	1.1	0.7
Alcohol[1]									
All seniors	72.0	57.1	50.0	49.8	48.6	47.5	48.0	47.0	45.3
Male	77.4	61.3	54.0	54.7	52.3	51.7	51.1	50.7	47.3
Female	66.8	52.3	46.1	45.1	45.1	43.8	45.1	43.3	43.0
White	75.8	62.2	55.3	55.3	52.7	52.0	52.5	52.3	49.1
Black or African American	47.7	32.9	29.3	29.6	30.7	29.2	29.2	29.0	29.5
All tenth-graders	—	—	41.0	39.0	35.4	35.4	35.2	33.2	33.8
Male	—	—	43.3	41.1	35.3	35.3	36.3	32.8	33.8
Female	—	—	38.6	36.8	35.7	35.3	34.0	33.6	33.8
White	—	—	44.3	41.0	39.0	38.4	37.3	37.0	36.0
Black or African American	—	—	24.7	26.0	23.2	24.0	25.4	23.0	22.4
All eighth-graders	—	—	22.4	21.5	19.6	19.7	18.6	17.1	17.2
Male	—	—	22.5	22.3	19.1	19.4	17.9	16.2	16.3
Female	—	—	22.0	20.6	20.0	19.8	19.0	17.9	17.6
White	—	—	23.9	22.5	20.4	19.9	18.6	17.9	16.5
Black or African American	—	—	15.1	14.9	14.7	16.5	16.0	14.9	12.4
Binge Drinking[2]									
All seniors	41.2	32.2	30.0	29.7	28.6	27.9	29.2	27.1	25.4
Male	52.1	39.1	36.7	36.0	34.2	34.2	34.3	32.6	28.9
Female	30.5	24.4	23.5	23.7	23.0	22.1	24.2	21.6	21.5
White	44.6	36.2	34.4	34.5	32.9	31.9	33.1	31.8	28.9
Black or African American	17.0	11.6	11.0	12.6	10.4	11.1	11.7	10.9	11.9
All tenth-graders	—	—	26.2	24.9	22.4	22.2	22.0	21.0	21.9
Male	—	—	29.8	28.6	23.8	23.2	23.8	22.0	22.9
Female	—	—	22.5	21.4	21.0	21.2	20.2	19.9	20.9
White	—	—	28.5	26.4	24.6	24.3	23.7	23.5	23.5
Black or African American	—	—	12.9	12.3	12.4	11.7	11.5	11.0	12.2
All eighth-graders	—	—	14.1	13.2	12.4	11.9	11.4	10.5	10.9
Male	—	—	14.4	13.7	12.5	12.2	10.8	10.2	10.5
Female	—	—	13.6	12.4	12.1	11.6	11.8	10.6	10.8
White	—	—	14.6	13.1	12.3	11.4	11.2	10.8	10.1
Black or African American	—	—	9.3	8.8	9.9	10.9	8.6	8.2	8.0

—— = Data not available.

0.0 = Quantity more than zero but less than 0.05.

[1]In 1993, the alcohol question was changed to indicate that a drink meant more than a few sips. Data for 1993, available in the spreadsheet version of this table, are based on a half sample.

[2]Five or more alcoholic drinks in a row at least once in the prior 2-week period.

Table C-27. Alcohol Consumption Among Adults 18 Years of Age and Over, by Selected Characteristics, Selected Years, 1997–2006

(Percent.)

Characteristic	Both sexes			Male			Female		
	1997	2000	2006	1997	2000	2006	1997	2000	2006
DRINKING STATUS PERCENT DISTRIBUTION[1]									
18 Years and Over, Age-Adjusted[2]									
All	100.0	100.0	100.0	100.0	100.0	100.0	100.0	100.0	100.0
Lifetime abstainer	21.2	24.2	25.0	14.0	17.5	17.8	27.6	30.0	31.5
Former drinker[3]	15.7	14.4	14.1	16.2	14.8	14.9	15.3	14.2	13.5
Infrequent	9.0	8.2	7.9	7.7	7.0	7.1	10.1	9.2	8.7
Regular	6.7	6.2	6.2	8.5	7.8	7.7	5.2	5.0	4.8
Current drinker[3]	63.1	61.4	60.8	69.8	67.6	67.4	57.0	55.8	54.9
Infrequent	13.8	13.2	12.4	10.2	9.1	9.2	17.3	17.1	15.5
Regular	48.1	46.7	48.0	58.1	56.6	57.6	38.9	37.6	39.2
18 Years and Over, Crude									
All	100.0	100.0	100.0	100.0	100.0	100.0	100.0	100.0	100.0
Lifetime abstainer	21.1	24.1	24.9	14.0	17.5	17.7	27.7	30.1	31.7
Former drinker[3]	15.5	14.3	14.3	15.6	14.3	14.8	15.4	14.4	13.8
Infrequent	8.9	8.1	8.0	7.5	6.8	7.0	10.1	9.3	8.9
Regular	6.6	6.2	6.2	8.1	7.5	7.7	5.2	5.0	4.9
Current drinker[3]	63.4	61.6	60.8	70.5	68.2	67.6	57.0	55.5	54.5
Infrequent	13.9	13.2	12.4	10.1	9.1	9.2	17.3	17.0	15.4
Regular	48.4	46.8	47.9	58.8	57.2	57.7	38.8	37.4	38.9
PERCENT CURRENT DRINKERS AMONG ALL ADULTS									
All Persons									
18–44 years	69.4	67.3	65.8	74.8	73.0	71.4	64.2	61.7	60.4
18–24 years	62.2	59.1	59.3	66.7	63.6	64.2	57.7	54.6	54.5
25–44 years	71.6	69.9	68.1	77.2	76.0	73.9	66.1	64.0	62.4
45–64 years	63.3	62.0	61.5	70.8	68.1	67.3	56.2	56.4	56.1
45–54 years	67.1	65.1	64.9	73.8	70.3	69.8	60.7	60.1	60.3
55–64 years	57.3	57.3	56.8	65.8	64.5	63.8	49.4	50.7	50.4
65 years and over	43.4	42.1	43.7	52.7	50.2	54.4	36.6	36.2	35.6
65–74 years	48.6	47.0	48.2	56.7	52.7	58.5	42.0	42.3	39.4
75 years and over	36.6	36.2	38.5	46.7	46.7	48.8	30.2	29.8	31.8
Race[2,4]									
White only	66.0	64.5	63.8	71.8	69.7	69.4	60.7	59.8	58.6
Black or African American only	47.8	46.7	48.5	56.9	56.2	58.7	40.9	39.5	40.4
American Indian or Alaska Native only	53.9	54.2	52.8	66.1	62.4	57.3	45.2	47.0	48.1
Asian only	45.8	43.0	43.0	60.2	55.9	55.9	31.6	29.3	31.3
Native Hawaiian or Other Pacific Islander only	*	*	*	*	*	*	*	*	*
2 or more races	—	61.4	55.0	—	70.5	59.5	—	52.5	52.9
Hispanic Origin and Race[2,4]									
Hispanic or Latino	53.4	52.4	50.5	64.6	63.8	62.6	42.1	41.2	38.2
Mexican	53.0	51.0	49.0	66.9	64.5	61.5	38.9	36.9	35.2
Not Hispanic or Latino	64.1	62.6	62.5	70.2	68.2	68.2	58.7	57.6	57.5
White only	67.5	65.9	66.4	72.7	70.4	70.8	62.9	61.9	62.4
Black or African American only	47.8	46.7	48.4	57.1	56.4	58.8	40.7	39.3	40.3
Geographic Region[2]									
Northeast	68.7	67.9	68.5	74.4	73.1	74.5	63.8	63.7	63.6
Midwest	66.8	65.6	65.5	73.0	70.7	70.5	61.1	61.1	60.7
South	56.2	54.2	55.1	63.9	62.1	62.5	49.2	47.1	48.5
West	64.9	62.7	59.6	71.5	68.4	66.8	58.9	57.1	52.8
Location of Residence[2]									
Within MSA[5]	64.7	62.9	62.5	71.0	69.0	69.2	59.1	57.4	56.5
Outside MSA[5]	57.4	55.9	53.0	65.7	62.6	58.9	49.5	50.3	47.5
PERCENT DISTRIBUTION OF CURRENT DRINKERS									
Level of Alcohol Consumption in Past Year[6]									
18 Years and Over, Age-Adjusted[2]									
All drinking levels	100.0	100.0	100.0	100.0	100.0	100.0	100.0	100.0	100.0
Light	69.6	70.7	67.5	59.5	60.4	58.7	81.0	82.0	77.5
Moderate	22.5	22.2	24.2	31.8	31.9	33.1	12.0	11.5	14.0
Heavier	7.9	7.1	8.3	8.7	7.7	8.1	7.0	6.5	8.4

* = Figure does not meet standards of reliability or precision.
—— = Data not available.

[1]Drinking status categories are based on self-reported responses to questions about alcohol consumption. Lifetime abstainers had fewer than 12 drinks in their lifetime. Former drinkers had at least 12 drinks in their lifetime and none in the past year. Former infrequent drinkers are former drinkers who had fewer than 12 drinks in any one year. Former regular drinkers are former drinkers who had at least 12 drinks in any one year. Current drinkers had at least 12 drinks in their lifetime and at least one drink in the past year. Current infrequent drinkers are current drinkers who had fewer than 12 drinks in the past year. Current regular drinkers are current drinkers who had at least 12 drinks in the past year.

[2]Estimates are age-adjusted to the year 2000 standard population using four age groups: 18–24 years, 25–44 years, 45–64 years, and 65 years and over.

[3]The totals for current and former drinkers include a small number of adults who did not provide sufficient information on frequency or amount of drinking; therefore, infrequent or regular drinking status could not be determined for these people.

[4]The race groups, White, Black, American Indian or Alaska Native, Asian, Native Hawaiian or Other Pacific Islander, and 2 or more races, include persons of Hispanic and non-Hispanic origin. Persons of Hispanic origin may be of any race.

[5]MSA = metropolitan statistical area. Starting with 2006 data, MSA status is determined using 2000 census data and the 2000 standards for defining MSAs.

[6]Level of alcohol consumption categories are based on self-reported responses to questions about average alcohol consumption and are defined as follows: light drinkers: three drinks or fewer per week; moderate drinkers: more than three drinks and up to 14 drinks per week for men and more than three drinks and up to seven drinks per week for women; heavier drinkers: more than 14 drinks per week for men and more than seven drinks per week for women.

Table C-27. Alcohol Consumption Among Adults 18 Years of Age and Over, by Selected Characteristics, Selected Years, 1997–2006—*Continued*

(Percent.)

Characteristic	Both sexes			Male			Female		
	1997	2000	2006	1997	2000	2006	1997	2000	2006
18 Years and Over, Crude									
All drinking levels	100.0	100.0	100.0	100.0	100.0	100.0	100.0	100.0	100.0
Light	69.8	70.8	67.7	59.6	60.5	58.8	81.4	82.3	77.8
Moderate	22.3	22.1	24.0	31.7	31.8	33.0	11.7	11.3	13.9
Heavier	7.9	7.1	8.3	8.8	7.7	8.2	6.9	6.4	8.4
NUMBER OF DAYS IN THE PAST YEAR WITH FIVE OR MORE DRINKS									
18 Years and Over, Crude									
All current drinkers	100.0	100.0	100.0	100.0	100.0	100.0	100.0	100.0	100.0
No days	65.9	68.3	67.0	54.7	57.0	57.8	78.6	80.8	77.3
At least 1 day	34.1	31.7	33.0	45.3	43.0	42.2	21.4	19.2	22.7
1–11 days	18.5	17.4	17.9	22.0	21.1	20.5	14.6	13.2	15.1
12 or more days	15.6	14.3	15.1	23.4	21.9	21.7	6.8	6.0	7.6
PERCENT OF ADULTS CURRENT DRINKERS WHO DRANK 5 OR MORE DRINKS ON AT LEAST 1 DAY									
All Persons									
18 years and over, age-adjusted[2]	32.4	30.2	32.1	43.3	40.9	40.9	20.2	18.4	22.1
18 years and over, crude	34.1	31.7	33.0	45.3	43.0	42.2	21.4	19.2	22.7
18–44 years	42.4	40.3	42.1	54.6	52.3	52.2	28.7	26.9	30.6
18–24 years	51.6	52.0	53.4	61.5	60.6	62.0	40.2	42.3	43.5
25–44 years	40.0	37.2	38.8	52.8	50.0	49.2	25.7	22.9	26.8
45–64 years	25.3	23.5	26.4	36.1	34.9	35.6	12.9	10.8	16.1
45–54 years	28.5	25.5	29.9	40.1	37.8	38.9	15.3	12.0	20.1
55–64 years	19.6	19.9	20.8	28.9	29.9	30.6	8.3	8.7	9.7
65 years and over	11.2	9.1	10.3	17.8	14.9	14.5	4.4	3.3	5.5
65–74 years	13.9	11.2	13.5	21.6	18.3	18.7	5.5	4.2	7.0
75 years and over	6.7	5.7	5.6	11.0	9.5	7.7	*2.5	*	*
Race[2,4]									
White only	33.3	30.9	33.7	44.4	41.8	42.7	20.9	19.2	23.6
Black or African American only	23.6	23.9	23.6	31.7	34.2	32.5	14.9	12.6	13.5
American Indian or Alaska Native only	54.5	45.1	42.1	70.5	47.1	53.4	38.4	34.7	*28.0
Asian only	25.5	20.4	20.3	30.7	25.4	24.5	16.6	10.8	*12.8
Native Hawaiian or Other Pacific Islander only	*	*	*	*	*	*	*	*	*
Hispanic Origin and Race[2,4]									
Hispanic or Latino	36.8	32.3	32.2	46.3	43.1	40.2	22.3	16.1	19.1
Mexican	39.0	37.8	36.9	50.1	49.1	46.6	20.3	18.0	18.6
Not Hispanic or Latino	31.9	30.2	32.1	42.7	40.8	41.1	20.0	18.8	22.5
White only	33.2	31.2	34.0	44.5	42.1	43.2	21.0	19.7	24.2
Black or African American only	23.4	23.7	23.6	31.7	33.8	32.5	14.4	12.7	13.4
Geographic Region[2]									
Northeast	31.3	28.8	29.9	43.1	39.7	37.8	18.9	18.1	22.2
Midwest	33.8	33.3	37.8	44.7	44.7	46.8	21.6	21.5	27.3
South	30.9	27.4	30.3	40.5	37.2	40.0	19.2	15.6	19.2
West	33.4	32.0	30.3	44.6	43.1	37.9	20.8	18.8	21.0
Location of Residence[2]									
Within MSA[5]	31.6	30.0	32.0	42.4	40.4	40.6	19.8	18.4	22.4
Outside MSA[5]	34.8	31.2	32.4	45.7	43.1	42.8	21.2	18.5	20.2

* = Figure does not meet standards of reliability or precision.
[4]The race groups, White, Black, American Indian or Alaska Native, Asian, Native Hawaiian or Other Pacific Islander, and 2 or more races, include persons of Hispanic and non-Hispanic origin. Persons of Hispanic origin may be of any race.
[5]MSA = metropolitan statistical area. Starting with 2006 data, MSA status is determined using 2000 census data and the 2000 standards for defining MSAs.

AMBULATORY CARE

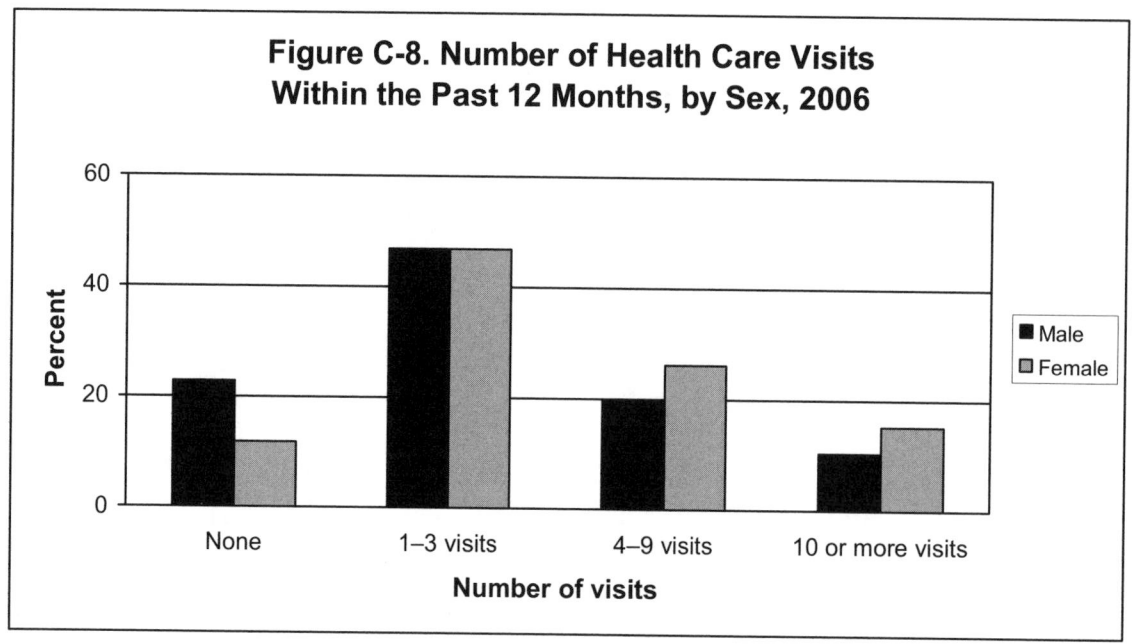

Figure C-8. Number of Health Care Visits Within the Past 12 Months, by Sex, 2006

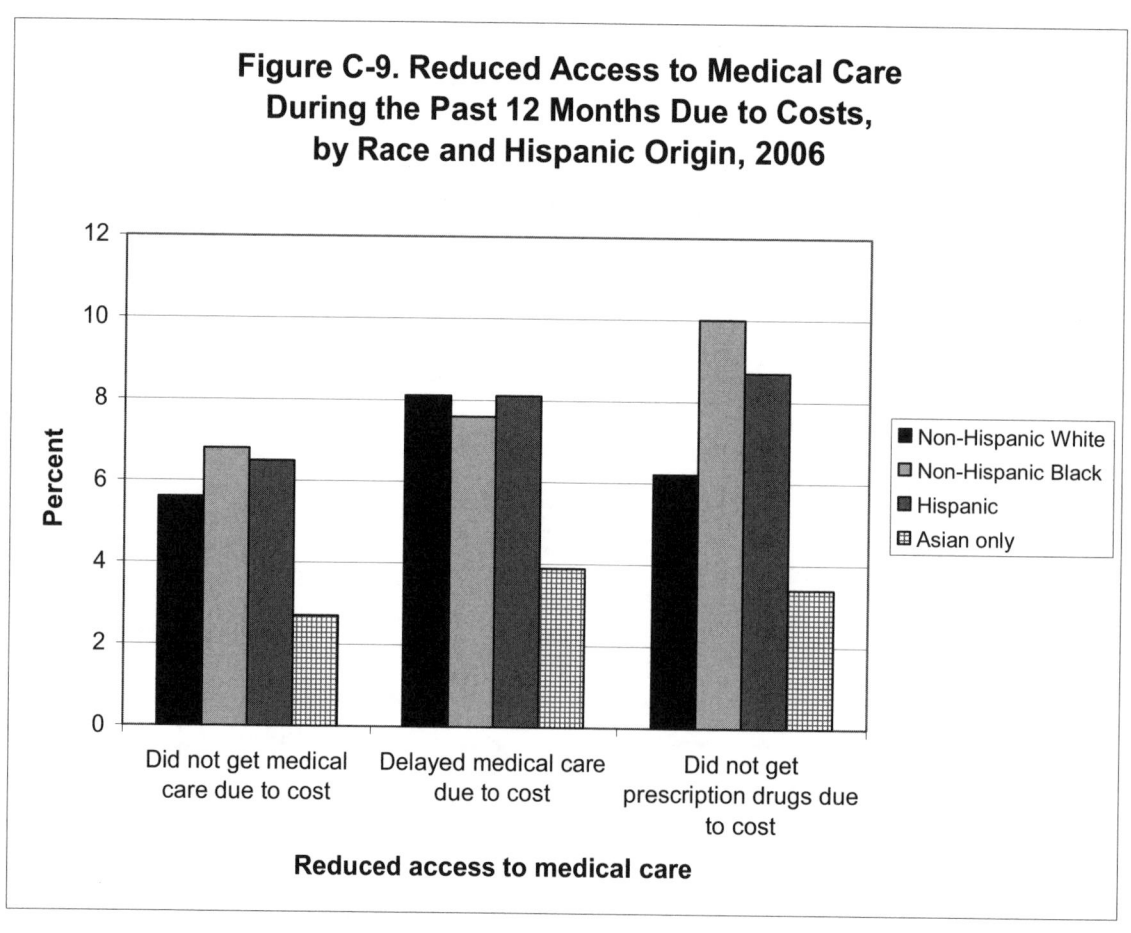

Figure C-9. Reduced Access to Medical Care During the Past 12 Months Due to Costs, by Race and Hispanic Origin, 2006

Table C-28. Health Care Visits to Doctor Offices, Emergency Departments, and Home Visits Within the Past 12 months, by Selected Characteristics, Selected Years, 1997–2006

(Percent.)

Characteristic	None				1–3 visits				4-9 visits				10 or more visits			
	1997	2000	2003	2006	1997	2000	2003	2006	1997	2000	2003	2006	1997	2000	2003	2006
18 years and over, age-adjusted[1,2]	16.5	16.7	15.8	17.2	46.2	45.4	45.8	46.9	23.6	24.6	24.8	23.1	13.7	13.3	13.6	12.8
18 years and over, crude[1]	16.5	16.8	15.8	17.2	46.5	45.5	45.8	46.8	23.5	24.5	24.8	23.1	13.5	13.2	13.5	12.9
Age																
Under 18 years	11.8	12.3	11.3	10.9	54.1	53.8	54.5	57.2	25.2	26.2	26.7	24.6	8.9	7.6	7.5	7.3
Under 6 years	5.0	6.3	5.5	4.9	44.9	44.5	46.0	50.6	37.0	38.1	39.0	34.8	13.0	11.1	9.4	9.7
6–17 years	15.3	15.2	14.0	13.8	58.7	58.2	58.7	60.5	19.3	20.6	20.8	19.6	6.8	6.0	6.6	6.1
18–44 years	21.7	23.5	22.4	25.3	46.7	45.2	46.7	45.8	19.0	19.1	19.1	17.8	12.6	12.2	11.8	11.0
18–24 years	22.0	24.8	23.6	25.3	46.8	45.3	47.2	47.2	20.0	18.7	18.2	17.4	11.2	11.2	11.0	10.2
25–44 years	21.6	23.1	22.0	25.4	46.7	45.1	46.6	45.3	18.7	19.2	19.4	17.9	13.0	12.5	12.0	11.4
45–64 years	16.9	15.0	14.7	16.4	42.9	43.4	42.2	44.3	24.7	25.7	26.6	23.6	15.5	15.9	16.5	15.7
45–54 years	17.9	16.4	16.9	18.5	43.9	45.2	44.2	46.1	23.4	23.7	24.5	21.8	14.8	14.7	14.3	13.6
55–64 years	15.3	12.8	11.4	13.5	41.3	40.6	39.2	41.9	26.7	28.8	29.8	26.1	16.7	17.8	19.6	18.5
65 years and over.	8.9	7.5	6.3	6.0	34.7	32.2	31.5	33.2	32.5	36.6	35.8	36.2	23.8	23.7	26.4	24.6
65–74 years	9.8	9.0	7.1	6.7	36.9	34.5	34.0	34.6	31.6	34.5	35.7	36.6	21.6	22.1	23.3	22.1
75 years and over	7.7	5.8	5.4	5.3	31.8	29.3	28.6	31.5	33.8	39.3	36.0	35.7	26.6	25.6	30.0	27.6
Sex[2]																
Male	21.3	21.7	20.6	22.8	47.1	45.9	46.8	46.8	20.6	22.3	21.9	20.0	11.0	10.1	10.7	10.4
Female	11.8	11.9	11.1	11.8	45.4	44.8	44.9	46.8	26.5	27.0	27.7	26.2	16.3	16.3	16.3	15.2
Race[2,3]																
White only	16.0	16.1	15.7	17.2	46.1	45.1	45.6	46.2	23.9	25.2	25.1	23.4	14.0	13.6	13.6	13.2
Black or African American only	16.8	17.2	14.7	16.0	46.1	46.7	45.8	49.2	23.2	23.4	25.2	23.3	13.9	12.6	14.3	11.5
American Indian or Alaska Native only	17.1	21.3	23.3	13.5	38.0	43.0	41.4	44.2	24.2	20.0	20.6	27.6	20.7	15.7	14.7	14.7
Asian only	22.8	20.3	22.6	21.9	49.1	49.2	47.8	51.3	19.7	20.8	20.7	18.1	8.3	9.7	8.9	8.7
Native Hawaiian or Other Pacific Islander only	—	*	*	*	—	*	*	*	—	*	*	*	—	*	*	*
2 or more races	—	12.1	11.1	16.3	—	41.7	44.9	44.8	—	28.2	23.0	21.3	—	18.0	21.0	17.6
Hispanic Origin and Race[2,3]																
Hispanic or Latino	24.9	26.8	25.3	27.1	42.3	41.8	42.9	43.0	20.3	19.8	20.3	19.6	12.5	11.6	11.5	10.3
Mexican	28.9	31.0	27.8	31.1	40.8	40.8	42.5	40.8	18.5	17.8	18.8	18.3	11.8	10.3	11.0	9.8
Not Hispanic or Latino	15.4	15.2	14.1	15.4	46.7	45.9	46.3	47.6	24.0	25.3	25.3	23.7	13.9	13.6	14.0	13.2
White only	14.7	14.5	13.5	15.0	46.6	45.4	46.2	46.9	24.4	25.9	26.1	24.2	14.3	14.1	14.2	13.9
Black or African American only	16.9	17.1	14.6	15.7	46.1	46.8	45.9	49.5	23.1	23.5	25.3	23.4	13.8	12.6	14.2	11.4
Respondent-Assessed Health Status[2]																
Fair or poor	7.8	9.0	8.7	12.2	23.3	21.9	23.2	21.2	29.0	27.4	28.8	28.1	39.9	41.7	39.3	38.6
Good to excellent	17.2	17.4	16.4	17.8	48.4	47.6	48.1	49.3	23.3	24.5	24.5	22.8	11.1	10.6	10.9	10.1
Percent of Poverty Level[2,4]																
Below 100%	20.6	22.1	20.9	21.0	37.8	37.6	37.8	39.5	22.7	22.8	23.7	22.3	18.9	17.6	17.6	17.2
100%–less than 200%	20.1	21.7	19.8	21.6	43.3	42.5	41.5	43.5	21.7	21.7	23.6	21.5	14.9	14.2	15.1	13.3
200% or more	14.5	14.4	13.7	15.2	48.7	47.3	48.4	49.3	24.2	25.7	25.4	23.7	12.6	12.6	12.6	11.9
Hispanic Origin, Race, and Percent of Poverty Level[2,3,4]																
Hispanic or Latino																
Below 100%	30.2	32.4	29.9	32.8	34.8	33.5	37.0	35.3	19.9	18.8	18.5	19.2	15.0	15.3	14.6	12.7
100%–less than 200%	28.7	30.6	28.6	29.9	39.7	40.8	40.2	42.0	20.4	17.3	20.6	19.3	11.2	11.3	10.5	8.8
200% or more	18.9	21.6	20.7	22.2	48.8	46.5	47.7	47.4	20.4	22.0	21.2	20.4	11.9	9.9	10.3	10.1
Not Hispanic or Latino																
White only																
Below 100%	17.0	18.2	17.0	16.3	38.3	37.2	37.5	38.7	23.9	24.7	25.9	24.2	20.9	19.9	19.5	20.8
100%–less than 200%	17.3	18.6	16.6	18.8	44.1	41.7	41.0	43.7	22.2	23.6	24.9	22.2	16.3	16.0	17.4	15.4
200% or more	13.8	13.4	12.5	14.0	48.2	46.9	48.1	48.6	24.9	26.5	26.3	24.6	13.1	13.3	13.1	12.7
Black or African American only																
Below 100%	17.4	18.6	15.7	18.1	38.5	40.5	38.1	45.0	23.4	23.9	26.5	21.9	20.7	17.0	19.6	15.0
100%–less than 200%	18.8	20.8	15.4	17.9	43.7	44.4	44.2	45.5	22.9	20.5	25.9	24.2	14.5	14.3	14.5	12.5
200% or more	15.6	14.7	13.7	13.5	51.7	50.6	50.6	53.6	22.7	24.1	24.3	23.5	10.0	10.6	11.4	9.3

* = Figure does not meet standards of reliability or precision.

—— = Data not available.

[1] Includes all other races not shown separately and unknown health insurance status.

[2] Estimates are age-adjusted to the year 2000 standard population using six age groups: Under 18 years, 18–44 years, 45–54 years, 55–64 years, 65–74 years, and 75 years and over.

[3] The race groups, White, Black, American Indian or Alaska Native, Asian, Native Hawaiian or Other Pacific Islander, and 2 or more races, include persons of Hispanic and non-Hispanic origin. Persons of Hispanic origin may be of any race.

[4] Percent of poverty level is based on family income and family size and composition using U.S. Census Bureau poverty thresholds.

Table C-28. Health Care Visits to Doctor Offices, Emergency Departments, and Home Visits Within the Past 12 months, by Selected Characteristics, Selected Years, 1997–2006—*Continued*

(Percent.)

Characteristic	Number of health care visits															
	None				1–3 visits				4-9 visits				10 or more visits			
	1997	2000	2003	2006	1997	2000	2003	2006	1997	2000	2003	2006	1997	2000	2003	2006
Health Insurance Status at Time of Interview[5,6]																
Under 65 years																
Insured	14.3	14.1	12.8	14.3	49.0	48.5	49.1	50.4	23.6	24.6	25.2	23.1	13.1	12.7	12.9	12.3
Private	14.7	14.4	13.2	14.7	50.6	50.2	51.1	52.6	23.1	24.3	24.6	22.4	11.6	11.1	11.1	10.3
Medicaid	9.8	10.5	9.9	11.3	35.5	32.7	35.2	37.4	26.5	26.8	28.1	25.5	28.2	30.0	26.8	25.8
Health Insurance Status Prior to Interview[5,6]																
Uninsured	33.7	36.9	38.1	39.2	42.8	42.1	42.4	42.2	15.3	13.8	13.4	12.5	8.2	7.2	6.1	6.1
Insured continuously all 12 months	14.1	14.0	12.7	14.3	49.2	48.8	49.3	50.8	23.6	24.6	25.2	23.1	13.0	12.6	12.8	11.9
Uninsured for any period up to 12 months	18.9	20.6	20.4	19.1	46.0	44.5	46.2	46.3	20.8	20.8	21.2	20.9	14.4	14.1	12.2	13.7
Uninsured more than 12 months	39.0	43.2	44.3	45.6	41.4	39.6	39.8	40.2	13.2	12.1	11.2	9.6	6.4	5.1	4.7	4.5
Percent of Poverty Level and Health Insurance Status[4,5,6]																
Under 65 years																
Below 100%																
Insured continuously all 12 month	13.8	15.2	12.7	12.6	39.7	40.3	40.9	43.1	25.2	24.3	25.8	24.2	21.4	20.1	20.5	20.1
Uninsured for any period up to 12 months	19.7	15.8	18.4	17.8	37.6	41.1	43.9	39.3	21.9	23.4	21.6	23.4	20.9	19.7	16.1	19.5
Uninsured more than 12 months	41.2	44.3	47.7	50.1	39.9	37.3	35.7	35.3	12.2	11.8	11.7	9.9	6.6	6.7	4.9	4.8
100%–less than 200%																
Insured continuously all 12 months	16.0	15.9	13.8	16.3	46.4	46.2	45.0	45.9	21.9	22.4	24.4	23.0	15.8	15.5	16.8	14.8
Uninsured for any period up to 12 months	18.8	22.1	20.2	20.6	45.1	46.0	42.0	49.8	21.0	17.4	24.8	18.7	15.0	14.5	12.9	10.9
Uninsured more than 12 months	38.7	44.4	43.4	44.3	41.0	38.3	39.1	42.1	14.0	12.2	12.1	10.2	6.3	5.1	5.4	3.4
200% or more																
Insured continuously all 12 months	13.7	13.3	12.4	14.1	51.0	50.0	51.1	52.6	23.6	25.0	25.3	22.9	11.7	11.6	11.3	10.4
Uninsured for any period up to 12 months	17.8	21.2	20.4	18.6	50.3	45.3	49.6	48.0	20.4	21.6	19.1	20.7	11.5	11.9	10.9	12.7
Uninsured more than 12 months	36.6	39.9	41.8	42.8	43.8	42.5	44.7	42.4	13.2	13.4	9.6	9.3	6.4	4.2	4.0	*5.5
Geographic Region[2]																
Northeast	13.2	12.5	10.4	12.1	45.9	46.2	47.6	47.6	26.0	27.3	27.0	25.1	14.9	14.0	15.0	15.2
Midwest	15.9	14.4	14.2	15.2	47.7	46.2	47.2	48.4	22.8	25.6	25.4	23.6	13.6	13.9	13.2	12.7
South	17.2	18.5	16.5	18.3	46.1	44.7	45.1	45.6	23.3	24.0	24.8	23.5	13.5	12.9	13.6	12.6
West..	19.1	20.3	21.0	21.7	44.8	44.9	44.2	46.7	22.8	22.1	22.2	20.2	13.3	12.8	12.6	11.3
Location of Residence[2]																
Within MSA[7]	16.2	16.7	16.0	16.8	46.4	45.8	45.9	47.5	23.7	24.4	24.8	23.1	13.7	13.1	13.3	12.6
Outside MSA[7]	17.3	16.8	15.0	19.2	45.4	43.5	45.6	43.7	23.3	25.5	24.9	23.3	13.9	14.2	14.5	13.8

* = Figure does not meet standards of reliability or precision.

—— = Data not available.

[4]Percent of poverty level is based on family income and family size and composition using U.S. Census Bureau poverty thresholds.

[5]Estimates for persons under 65 years of age are age-adjusted to the year 2000 standard population using four age groups: Under 18 years, 18–44 years, 45–54 years, and 55–64 years of age.

[6]Health insurance categories are mutually exclusive. Persons who reported both Medicaid and private coverage are classified as having private coverage.

[7]MSA = metropolitan statistical area. Starting with 2006 data, MSA status is determined using 2000 census data and the 2000 standards for defining MSAs.

Table C-29. Visits to Primary Care Generalist and Specialist Physicians, by Selected Characteristics and Type of Physician, Selected Years, 1980–2005

(Percent.)

Age, sex, and race	Type of primary care generalist physician											
	All primary care generalists				General and family practice				Internal medicine			
	1980	1990	2000	2005	1980	1990	2000	2005	1980	1990	2000	2005
PERCENT OF ALL PHYSICIANS' OFFICE VISITS												
All Persons	66.2	63.6	58.9	58.8	33.5	29.9	24.1	22.1	12.1	13.8	15.3	17.4
Under 18 years	77.8	79.5	79.7	84.0	26.1	26.5	19.9	14.2	2.0	2.9	*	*
18–44 years	65.3	65.2	62.1	63.5	34.3	31.9	28.2	27.0	8.6	11.8	12.7	18.2
45–64 years	60.2	55.5	51.2	51.9	36.3	32.1	26.4	25.4	19.5	18.6	20.1	21.9
45–54 years	60.2	55.6	52.3	54.8	37.4	32.0	27.8	26.7	17.1	17.1	18.7	22.1
55–64 years	60.2	55.5	49.9	48.8	35.4	32.1	24.7	24.1	21.8	20.0	21.7	21.6
65 years and over	61.6	52.6	46.5	43.3	37.5	28.1	20.2	19.3	22.7	23.3	24.5	22.6
65–74 years	61.2	52.7	46.6	43.9	37.4	28.1	19.7	21.7	22.1	23.0	24.5	20.4
75 years and over	62.3	52.4	46.4	42.8	37.6	28.0	20.8	17.0	23.5	23.7	24.5	24.7
Sex and Age												
Male												
Under 18 year	77.3	78.1	77.7	83.3	25.6	24.1	18.3	13.6	2.0	3.0	*	*
18–44 years	50.8	51.8	51.5	58.0	38.0	35.9	34.2	33.8	11.5	15.0	14.4	22.9
45–64 years	55.6	50.6	49.4	53.0	34.4	31.0	28.7	27.0	20.5	19.2	19.8	25.8
65 years and over	58.2	51.2	43.1	39.2	35.6	27.7	19.3	17.1	22.3	23.3	23.8	22.0
Female												
Under 18 years	78.5	81.1	82.0	84.7	26.6	29.1	21.7	14.8	2.0	2.8	*	*
18–44 years	72.1	71.3	67.2	66.5	32.5	30.0	25.3	23.3	7.3	10.3	11.9	15.7
45–64 years	63.4	58.8	52.5	51.1	37.7	32.8	24.9	24.3	18.9	18.2	20.2	19.1
65 years and over	63.9	53.5	48.9	46.1	38.7	28.3	20.9	20.8	22.9	23.3	25.0	23.0
Race and Age[1]												
White												
Under 18 years	77.6	79.2	78.5	83.8	26.4	27.1	21.2	14.1	2.0	2.3	*	*
18–44 years	64.8	64.4	61.4	62.4	34.5	31.9	29.2	28.1	8.6	10.6	11.0	17.0
45–64 years	59.6	54.2	49.3	51.5	36.0	31.5	27.3	26.1	19.2	17.6	17.1	21.0
65 years and over	61.4	51.9	45.1	42.8	36.6	27.5	20.3	19.8	23.3	23.1	23.0	21.6
Black or African American												
Under 18 years	79.9	85.5	87.3	83.6	23.7	20.2	*	*	*2.2	9.8	*	*
18–44 years	68.5	68.3	65.0	71.6	31.7	31.9	22.0	20.5	9.0	18.1	20.9	*24.7
45–64 years	66.1	61.6	61.7	51.7	38.6	31.2	23.3	17.2	22.6	26.9	35.9	*28.0
65 years and over	64.6	58.6	52.8	37.8	49.0	28.9	*18.5	*11.2	14.2	28.7	33.4	25.0

Age, sex, and race	Type of primary care generalist physician											
	Specialty care physicians				Obstetrics and gynecology				Pediatrics			
	1980	1990	2000	2005	1980	1990	2000	2005	1980	1990	2000	2005
PERCENT OF ALL PHYSICIANS' OFFICE VISITS												
All Ages	9.6	8.7	7.8	6.4	10.9	11.2	11.7	13.0	33.8	36.4	41.1	41.2
Under 18 years	1.3	1.2	*1.1	*1.1	48.5	48.9	57.3	66.2	22.2	20.5	20.3	16.0
18–44 years	21.7	20.8	20.4	17.5	0.7	0.7	*0.9	*0.8	34.7	34.8	37.9	36.5
45–64 years	4.2	4.6	4.5	4.5	*	*	*	*	39.8	44.5	48.8	48.1
45–54 years	5.6	6.3	5.6	5.9	*	*	*	*	39.8	44.4	47.7	45.2
55–64 years	2.9	3.1	3.3	3.0	*	*	*	*	39.8	44.5	50.1	51.2
65 years and over	1.4	1.1	1.5	*1.4	*	*	*	*	38.4	47.4	53.5	56.7
65–74 years	1.7	1.6	2.0	*1.7	*	*	*	*	38.8	47.3	53.4	56.1
75 years and over	1.0	*0.6	*1.0	*1.0	*	*	*	*	37.7	47.6	53.6	57.2
Sex and Age												
Male												
Under 18 years	...	...	...	...	49.4	50.7	58.0	67.1	22.7	21.9	22.3	16.7
18–44 years	...	...	...	...	1.0	0.7	*1.7	*1.2	49.2	48.2	48.5	42.0
45–64 years	...	...	...	...	*	*	*	*	44.4	49.4	50.6	47.0
65 years and over	...	...	...	...	*	*	*	*	41.8	48.8	56.9	60.8
Female												
Under 18 years	2.5	2.3	2.1	*2.4	47.4	46.9	56.5	65.2	21.5	18.9	18.0	15.3
18–44 years	31.7	30.4	29.6	26.8	0.6	0.7	*	*0.6	27.9	28.7	32.8	33.5
45–64 years	6.7	7.7	7.3	7.6	*	*	*	*	36.6	41.2	47.5	48.9
65 years and over	2.1	1.8	2.6	*2.3	*	*	*	*	36.1	46.5	51.1	53.9

* = Figure does not meet standards of reliability or precision.

... = Not applicable.

[1]Starting with 1999 data, the instruction for the race item on the Patient Record Form was changed so that more than one race could be recorded. In previous years only one racial category could be checked. Estimates for racial groups presented in this table are for visits where only one race was recorded. Because of the small number of responses with more than one racial group checked, estimates for visits with multiple races checked are unreliable and are not presented.

Table C-29. Visits to Primary Care Generalist and Specialist Physicians, by Selected Characteristics and Type of Physician, Selected Years, 1980–2005—*Continued*

(Percent.)

Age, sex, and race	Type of primary care generalist physician											
	Specialty care physicians				Obstetrics and gynecology				Pediatrics			
	1980	1990	2000	2005	1980	1990	2000	2005	1980	1990	2000	2005
Race and Age[1]												
White												
Under 18 years	1.1	1.0	*1.2	*0.9	48.2	48.8	54.7	66.0	22.4	20.8	21.5	16.2
18–44 years	21.0	21.1	20.4	16.5	0.7	0.7	*0.8	*0.8	35.2	35.6	38.6	37.6
45–64 years	4.1	4.8	4.7	4.3	*	*	*	*	40.4	45.8	50.7	48.5
65 years and over	1.4	1.2	1.5	*1.4	*	*	*	*	38.6	48.1	54.9	57.2
Black or African American												
Under 18 years	2.8	*3.4	*	*	51.2	52.1	75.0	67.2	20.1	14.5	*12.7	*16.4
18–44 years	27.1	17.9	20.7	*25.9	*	*	*	*	31.5	31.7	35.0	28.4
45–64 years	4.8	3.5	*2.4	*6.3	*	*	*	*	33.9	38.4	38.3	48.3
65 years and over	*	*	*	*	*	*	*	*	35.4	41.4	47.2	62.2

* = Figure does not meet standards of reliability or precision.

[1]Starting with 1999 data, the instruction for the race item on the Patient Record Form was changed so that more than one race could be recorded. In previous years only one racial category could be checked. Estimates for racial groups presented in this table are for visits where only one race was recorded. Because of the small number of responses with more than one racial group checked, estimates for visits with multiple races checked are unreliable and are not presented.

NOTE: This table presents data on visits to physician offices and excludes visits to other sites, such as hospital outpatient and emergency departments. In 1980 the survey excluded Alaska and Hawaii. Data for all other years include all 50 states and the District of Columbia. Visits with specialty of physician unknown are excluded.

Table C-30. No Health Care Visits to an Office or Clinic Within the Past 12 Months Among Children Under 18 Years of Age, by Selected Characteristics, Selected Annual Averages, 1997–2006

(Percent.)

Characteristic	Under 18 years			Under 6 years			6-17 years		
	1997–1998	2003–2004	2005–2006	1997–1998	2003–2004	2005–2006	1997–1998	2003–2004	2005–2006
PERCENT OF CHILDREN WITHOUT A HEALTH CARE VISIT[1]									
All children[2]	12.8	12.0	11.7	5.7	6.3	6.1	16.3	14.8	14.4
Race[3]									
White only	12.2	11.8	11.3	5.5	6.4	6.3	15.5	14.4	13.8
Black or African American only	14.3	11.9	11.7	6.5	5.5	4.6	18.1	14.8	15.1
American Indian or Alaska Native only	13.8	16.3	*15.7	*	*	*	*17.6	19.5	*17.7
Asian only	16.3	17.8	17.5	*5.6	*7.9	10.5	22.1	22.2	20.8
Native Hawaiian or Other Pacific Islander only	—	*	*	—	*	*	—	*	*
2 or more races	—	8.9	10.4	—	*	*	—	11.8	14.8
Hispanic Origin and Race[3]									
Hispanic or Latino	19.3	19.1	17.4	9.7	10.4	9.6	25.3	24.1	21.9
Not Hispanic or Latino	11.6	10.3	10.3	4.8	5.2	5.1	14.9	12.7	12.6
White only	10.7	9.5	9.4	4.3	4.9	5.0	13.7	11.6	11.4
Black or African American only	14.5	11.9	11.7	6.5	5.4	*4.4	18.3	14.9	15.1
Percent of Poverty Level[4]									
Below 100%	17.6	15.9	14.2	8.1	7.6	7.7	23.6	20.8	18.2
100%–less than 200%	16.2	15.7	14.9	7.2	8.7	8.4	20.8	19.4	18.2
200% or more	9.9	9.4	9.6	4.1	4.7	4.6	12.6	11.5	11.8
Hispanic Origin, Race and Percent of Poverty Level[3,4]									
Hispanic or Latino									
Below 100%	23.2	21.8	20.0	11.7	11.4	11.5	31.1	28.3	25.6
100%–less than 200%	20.9	20.9	19.1	9.7	11.2	10.1	28.1	26.6	24.4
200% or more	13.4	14.9	13.4	7.2	8.5	7.0	16.8	18.1	16.7
Not Hispanic or Latino									
White only									
Below 100%	14.0	12.3	9.4	*5.6	*5.3	*5.6	19.7	16.2	11.8
100%–less than 200%	14.1	12.4	13.2	6.0	7.5	8.5	18.0	15.3	15.4
200% or more	9.2	8.3	8.4	3.6	4.1	4.0	11.7	10.2	10.3
Black or African American only									
Below 100%	15.8	12.9	12.1	7.6	*5.4	*	20.5	17.0	16.4
100%–less than 200%	16.4	13.4	13.1	*7.7	*6.9	*	20.4	15.8	16.2
200% or more	11.8	10.2	10.2	*4.1	*4.6	*	14.8	12.7	13.1
Health Insurance Status at Time of Interview[5]									
Insured	10.4	9.8	9.5	4.5	5.3	4.9	13.4	12.1	11.9
Private	10.4	9.8	9.4	4.3	5.4	4.4	13.1	11.6	11.6
Medicaid	10.1	9.7	9.5	5.0	4.8	5.8	14.4	13.1	12.2
Uninsured	28.8	32.5	31.7	14.6	17.9	20.6	34.9	37.8	35.6
Health Insurance Status Prior to Interview[5]									
Insured continuously all 12 months	10.3	9.7	9.5	4.4	5.3	4.9	13.2	12.0	11.9
Uninsured for any period up to 12 months	15.9	15.6	15.8	7.7	7.0	9.3	20.9	20.2	18.8
Uninsured more than 12 months	34.9	41.7	39.0	19.9	26.0	28.0	40.2	46.0	42.2
Percent of Poverty Level and Health Insurance Status Prior to Interview[4,5]									
Below 100%									
Insured continuously all 12 months	12.6	11.7	10.4	5.7	5.5	5.8	17.6	15.6	13.5
Uninsured for any period up to 12 months	19.9	17.0	17.5	*9.9	*	*	26.1	22.0	21.6
Uninsured more than 12 months	39.9	47.4	44.6	24.9	35.3	*32.3	45.2	50.8	48.4
100%–less than 200%									
Insured continuously all 12 months	12.6	12.1	11.5	4.8	7.1	6.7	16.7	15.0	14.2
Uninsured for any period up to 12 months	15.6	18.1	17.7	*8.7	*10.3	*10.8	20.2	22.2	20.4
Uninsured more than 12 months	33.7	42.9	39.2	21.3	26.1	26.0	37.9	48.0	42.9
200% or more									
Insured continuously all 12 months	8.9	8.5	8.6	3.8	4.6	3.9	11.3	10.2	10.7
Uninsured for any period up to 12 months	12.4	12.7	12.8	*	*	*7.7	16.7	17.3	15.2
Uninsured more than 12 months	29.7	32.8	32.5	*10.5	*	*25.8	36.7	37.6	34.4

* = Figure does not meet standards of reliability or precision.

— = Data not available.

[1]Respondents were asked how many times a health professional was seen in the past 12 months at a doctor's office, clinic, or some other place. Excluded are visits to emergency rooms, hospitalizations, home visits, and telephone calls. Starting with 2000 data, dental visits were also excluded.

[2]Includes all other races not shown separately and unknown health insurance status.

[3]The race groups, White, Black, American Indian or Alaska Native, Asian, Native Hawaiian or Other Pacific Islander, and 2 or more races, include persons of Hispanic and non-Hispanic origin. Persons of Hispanic origin may be of any race.

[4]Percent of poverty level is based on family income and family size and composition using U.S. Census Bureau poverty thresholds.

[5]Health insurance categories are mutually exclusive. Persons who reported both Medicaid and private coverage are classified as having private coverage.

Table C-30. No Health Care Visits to an Office or Clinic Within the Past 12 Months Among Children Under 18 Years of Age, by Selected Characteristics, Selected Annual Averages, 1997–2006—*Continued*

(Percent.)

Characteristic	Under 18 years			Under 6 years			6-17 years		
	1997–1998	2003–2004	2005–2006	1997–1998	2003–2004	2005–2006	1997–1998	2003–2004	2005–2006
Geographic Region									
Northeast..	7.0	5.6	6.8	3.1	3.0	4.0	8.9	6.7	8.1
Midwest	12.2	10.0	9.8	5.9	4.3	5.2	15.3	12.8	12.0
South..	14.3	12.4	12.4	5.6	6.4	6.2	18.5	15.3	15.5
West...	16.3	18.4	16.5	7.9	10.5	8.8	20.7	22.2	20.3
Location of Residence									
Within MSA[6]..	12.3	11.8	11.4	5.4	6.4	5.9	15.9	14.5	14.1
Outside MSA[6]...	14.6	12.5	12.9	6.9	5.7	7.4	17.9	15.8	15.4

[6]MSA = metropolitan statistical area. Starting with 2005–2006 data, MSA status is determined using 2000 census data and the 2000 standards for defining MSAs.

Table C-31. No Usual Source of Health Care Among Children Under 18 Years of Age, by Selected Characteristics, Selected Annual Averages, 1993–2006

(Percent.)

Characteristic	Under 18 years			Under 6 years			6-17 years		
	1993– 1994[1]	2001– 2002	2005– 2006	1993– 19941	2001– 2002	2005– 2006	1993– 1994[1]	2001– 2002	2005– 2006
PERCENT OF CHILDREN WITHOUT A USUAL SOURCE OF HEALTHCARE[2]									
All children[3]	7.7	6.0	5.4	5.2	4.4	3.6	9.0	6.8	6.3
Race[4]									
White only	7.0	5.2	5.3	4.7	4.0	3.5	8.3	5.8	6.1
Black or African American only	10.3	6.6	5.7	7.6	3.6	3.5	11.9	8.0	6.7
American Indian or Alaska Native only	*9.3	*	*5.8	*	*	*	*8.7	*	*6.6
Asian only	9.7	11.2	7.7	*3.4	*	*4.2	13.5	13.2	9.4
Native Hawaiian or Other Pacific Islander only	—	*	*	—	*	*	—	*	*
2 or more races	—	7.3	*4.6	—	*7.0	*	—	*7.5	*4.9
Hispanic Origin and Race[4]									
Hispanic or Latino	14.3	13.5	11.5	9.3	9.2	7.2	17.7	16.0	14.1
Not Hispanic or Latino	6.7	4.4	3.9	4.4	3.2	2.5	7.8	4.9	4.6
White only	5.7	3.4	3.3	3.7	2.7	2.2	6.7	3.7	3.8
Black or African American only	10.2	6.6	5.4	7.7	3.6	*3.2	11.6	8.0	6.5
Percent of Poverty Level[5]									
Below 100%	13.9	11.7	8.6	9.4	8.2	5.6	16.8	13.7	10.5
100%–less than 200%	9.8	8.9	8.1	6.7	7.0	5.2	11.6	9.9	9.6
200% or more	3.7	3.3	3.3	1.8	2.1	2.1	4.6	3.8	3.9
Hispanic Origin, Race, Percent of Poverty Level[4,5]									
Hispanic or Latino									
Below 100%	19.6	18.5	14.3	12.7	12.1	8.7	24.8	22.4	18.1
100%–less than 200%	15.3	16.0	12.7	9.9	11.2	8.4	18.9	18.7	15.3
200% or more	5.0	7.1	7.9	*2.7	*4.5	*4.5	6.5	8.6	9.7
Not Hispanic or Latino									
White only									
Below 100%	10.2	7.5	5.1	6.5	*	*	12.7	8.2	6.1
100%–less than 200%	8.7	5.4	5.9	6.3	*4.8	*3.6	10.1	5.7	6.9
200% or more	3.4	2.4	2.3	1.6	1.5	*1.5	4.2	2.7	2.6
Black or African American only									
Below 100%	13.7	9.0	5.8	10.9	*4.0	*3.4	15.5	11.5	7.2
100%–less than 200%	9.1	7.3	6.9	*6.0	*5.1	*	10.8	8.4	8.1
200% or more	4.6	4.2	4.0	*	*	*	5.8	5.1	4.7
Health Insurance Status at the Time of Interview[6]									
Insured	5.0	3.3	2.8	3.3	2.2	2.0	5.9	3.8	3.2
Private	3.8	2.5	2.1	1.9	1.4	1.1	4.6	3.0	2.5
Medicaid	8.9	5.5	3.9	6.4	4.0	3.1	11.3	6.5	4.5
Uninsured	23.5	29.1	30.6	18.0	25.2	23.2	26.0	30.7	33.3
Health Insurance Status Prior to Interview[6]									
Insured continuously all 12 months	4.6	3.0	2.6	3.1	2.0	1.9	5.5	3.4	2.9
Uninsured for any period up to 12 months	15.3	16.7	14.5	10.9	13.8	10.5	18.1	18.4	16.3
Uninsured more than 12 months	27.6	36.5	39.0	21.4	32.1	29.9	30.0	38.1	41.6
Percent of Poverty Level and Health Insurance Status Prior to Interview[5,6]									
Below 100%									
Insured continuously all 12 months	8.6	5.0	3.8	5.8	*2.7	3.0	10.7	6.4	4.4
Uninsured for any period up to 12 months	21.7	21.2	16.4	18.0	18.5	*13.8	23.7	23.0	17.8
Uninsured more than 12 months	31.2	46.2	43.3	25.5	42.5	33.0	33.4	47.6	46.6
100%–less than 200%									
Insured continuously all 12 months	5.6	4.0	3.2	3.7	3.3	2.5	6.7	4.4	3.6
Uninsured for any period up to 12 months	14.5	18.7	16.9	*9.7	*15.8	*12.2	18.0	20.2	18.7
Uninsured more than 12 months	27.6	33.8	38.1	21.4	29.9	28.4	30.2	35.3	40.9
200% or more									
Insured continuously all 12 months	2.8	2.1	2.0	1.4	1.3	1.3	3.5	2.5	2.3
Uninsured for any period up to 12 months	9.1	11.9	10.8	*5.7	*8.4	*6.6	11.4	13.9	12.8
Uninsured more than 12 months	18.3	27.3	35.3	*10.6	*18.8	*28.5	20.9	29.8	37.3

* = Figure does not meet standards of reliability or precision.

— = Data not available.

[1]Data prior to 1997 are not strictly comparable with data for later years due to the 1997 questionnaire redesign.

[2]Persons who report the emergency department as the place of their usual source of care are defined as having no usual source of care.

[3]Includes all other races not shown separately and unknown health insurance status.

[4]The race groups, White, Black, American Indian or Alaska Native, Asian, Native Hawaiian or Other Pacific Islander, and 2 or more races, include persons of Hispanic and non-Hispanic origin. Persons of Hispanic origin may be of any race.

[5]Percent of poverty level is based on family income and family size and composition using U.S. Census Bureau poverty thresholds.

[6]Health insurance categories are mutually exclusive. Persons who reported both Medicaid and private coverage are classified as having private coverage.

Table C-31. No Usual Source of Health Care Among Children Under 18 Years of Age, by Selected Characteristics, Selected Annual Averages, 1993–2006—*Continued*

(Percent.)

Characteristic	Under 18 years			Under 6 years			6-17 years		
	1993–1994[1]	2001–2002	2005–2006	1993–19941	2001–2002	2005–2006	1993–19941	2001–2002	2005–2006
Geographic Region									
Northeast	4.1	2.4	2.4	2.9	*2.4	*1.6	4.8	2.4	2.8
Midwest	5.2	4.2	3.5	4.1	3.8	2.8	5.9	4.4	3.9
South	10.9	7.3	6.9	7.3	4.6	4.4	12.7	8.7	8.1
West	8.6	8.8	7.5	5.3	6.3	4.6	10.6	10.1	8.9
Location of Residence									
Within MSA[7]	7.7	6.1	5.4	5.0	4.5	3.5	9.2	6.9	6.4
Outside MSA[7]	7.8	5.7	5.5	6.0	3.9	4.1	8.7	6.5	6.2

* = Figure does not meet standards of reliability or precision.

[7]MSA = metropolitan statistical area. Starting with 2005–2006 data, MSA status is determined using 2000 census data and the 2000 standards for defining MSAs.

Table C-32. No Usual Source of Health Care Among Adults 18–64 Years of Age, by Selected Characteristics, Selected Annual Averages, 1993–2006

(Percent.)

Characteristic	1993–1994[1]	2001–2002	2003–2004	2004–2005	2005–2006
PERCENT OF ADULTS WITHOUT A USUAL SOURCE OF HEALTHCARE[2]					
18–64 years[3]	18.9	16.4	17.3	18.0	18.4
Age					
18–44 years	21.7	20.6	21.7	22.8	23.5
18–24 years	26.6	27.2	28.0	29.9	29.8
25–44 years	20.3	18.5	19.5	20.3	21.3
45–64 years	12.8	9.2	10.4	10.6	10.7
45–54 years	14.1	10.3	11.7	11.9	12.3
55–64 years	11.1	7.6	8.7	8.8	8.4
Sex					
Male	23.9	21.6	22.5	23.3	23.9
Female	14.1	11.4	12.4	12.9	13.0
Race[4]					
White only	18.4	15.4	17.0	17.7	18.1
Black or African American only	20.0	16.9	18.4	19.3	19.8
American Indian or Alaska Native only	19.7	16.3	21.5	22.8	21.9
Asian only	24.8	20.1	19.3	18.8	17.9
Native Hawaiian or Other Pacific Islander only	—	*	*	*	*
2 or more races	—	20.1	18.4	18.1	20.9
American Indian or Alaska Native; White	—	18.1	17.8	19.1	21.4
Hispanic Origin and Race[4]					
Hispanic or Latino	30.3	32.5	32.9	34.0	35.1
Mexican	32.4	36.5	36.4	37.8	39.3
Not Hispanic or Latino	17.7	14.0	14.9	15.4	15.6
White only	17.1	13.1	14.0	14.6	14.8
Black or African American only	19.7	16.8	18.1	19.0	19.2
Percent of Poverty Level[5]					
Below 100%	29.5	29.3	28.9	31.8	32.1
100%–less than 200%	25.4	25.6	26.6	27.1	27.8
200% or more	14.8	12.3	13.1	13.4	13.6
Hispanic Origin and Race and Percent of Poverty Level[4,5]					
Hispanic or Latino					
Below 100%	40.0	46.3	42.8	44.5	46.7
100%–less than 200%	36.9	40.0	39.7	40.7	41.8
200% or more	19.0	22.4	23.7	24.8	25.5
Not Hispanic or Latino					
White only					
Below 100%	28.2	23.4	23.0	26.8	26.2
100%–less than 200%	23.3	20.7	22.0	22.8	23.5
200% or more	14.3	10.8	11.7	11.9	12.0
Black or African American only					
Below 100%	24.7	22.8	24.3	28.3	29.5
100%–less than 200%	22.3	20.4	22.8	22.1	22.6
200% or more	15.1	13.2	14.0	14.2	13.5
Health Insurance Status at the Time of Interview[6]					
Insured	13.3	9.1	9.4	9.7	9.7
Private	13.1	9.0	9.5	9.5	9.6
Medicaid	16.3	11.1	9.9	12.1	11.6
Uninsured	43.1	49.1	50.2	52.5	53.0
Health Insurance Status Prior to Interview[6]					
Insured continuously all 12 months	—	8.3	8.7	8.9	8.9
Uninsured for any period up to 12 months	—	33.3	32.1	34.0	33.4
Uninsured more than 12 months	—	54.6	55.0	57.4	58.0

* = Figure does not meet standards of reliability or precision.

—— = Data not available.

[1]Data prior to 1997 are not strictly comparable with data for later years due to the 1997 questionnaire redesign.

[2]Persons who report the emergency department as the place of their usual source of care are defined as having no usual source of care.

[3]Includes all other races not shown separately and unknown health insurance status.

[4]The race groups, White, Black, American Indian or Alaska Native, Asian, Native Hawaiian or Other Pacific Islander, and 2 or more races, include persons of Hispanic and non-Hispanic origin. Persons of Hispanic origin may be of any race.

[5]Percent of poverty level is based on family income and family size and composition using U.S. Census Bureau poverty thresholds.

[6]Health insurance categories are mutually exclusive. Persons who reported both Medicaid and private coverage are classified as having private coverage.

Table C-32. No Usual Source of Health Care Among Adults 18–64 Years of Age, by Selected Characteristics, Selected Annual Averages, 1993–2006—*Continued*

(Percent.)

Characteristic	1993–1994[1]	2001–2002	2003–2004	2004–2005	2005–2006
Percent of Poverty Level and Health Insurance Status Prior to Interview[5,6]					
Below 100%					
Insured continuously all 12 months...	—	11.5	11.2	12.7	12.0
Uninsured for any period up to 12 months............................	—	36.5	36.2	39.4	36.5
Uninsured more than 12 months..	—	58.8	57.2	61.6	63.2
100%–less than 200%					
Insured continuously all 12 months...	—	11.0	10.5	10.7	10.4
Uninsured for any period up to 12 months............................	—	35.1	34.2	37.1	37.8
Uninsured more than 12 months..	—	54.5	55.1	56.0	57.0
200% or more					
Insured continuously all 12 months...	—	7.6	8.2	8.2	8.3
Uninsured for any period up to 12 months............................	—	31.5	29.5	30.6	30.2
Uninsured more than 12 months..	—	51.7	53.4	55.8	55.2
Geographic Region					
Northeast...	14.7	11.9	12.1	11.7	12.2
Midwest	16.2	14.1	14.7	15.4	15.8
South..	21.8	18.3	19.7	21.0	21.4
West..	21.1	19.9	21.0	21.2	21.1
Location of Residence					
Within MSA[7]..	19.3	16.6	17.6	18.3	18.7
Outside MSA[7]...	17.5	15.4	16.2	16.6	16.7

— = Data not available.

[1]Data prior to 1997 are not strictly comparable with data for later years due to the 1997 questionnaire redesign.

[5]Percent of poverty level is based on family income and family size and composition using U.S. Census Bureau poverty thresholds.

[6]Health insurance categories are mutually exclusive. Persons who reported both Medicaid and private coverage are classified as having private coverage.

[7]MSA = metropolitan statistical area. Starting with 2005–2006 data, MSA status is determined using 2000 census data and the 2000 standards for defining MSAs.

Table C-33. Reduced Access to Medical Care During the Past 12 Months Due to Cost, by Selected Characteristics, Selected Years, 1997–2006

(Percent.)

Characteristic	Did not get medical care due to cost[1]				Delayed medical care due to cost[2]				Did not get prescription drugs[3]			
	1997	2000	2003	2006	1997	2000	2003	2006	1997	2000	2003	2006
Total, age-adjusted[4,5]	4.5	4.5	5.2	5.7	7.3	6.4	7.1	7.8	4.7	5.1	6.2	7.0
Total, crude[5]	4.5	4.5	5.3	5.8	7.3	6.4	7.1	7.8	4.8	5.1	6.3	7.0
Age												
Under 18 years	2.2	2.5	2.2	2.4	3.7	3.9	3.6	4.0	2.2	2.4	2.7	3.0
Under 6 years	1.6	1.9	1.7	2.1	3.0	3.2	3.0	3.5	1.6	2.2	2.1	2.7
6–17 years	2.5	2.8	2.5	2.6	4.1	4.2	3.9	4.2	2.4	2.5	3.0	3.2
18–44 years	6.1	5.8	7.2	7.8	9.7	8.2	9.3	10.0	6.9	6.9	8.4	9.6
45–64 years	5.8	5.5	6.7	7.7	9.0	7.7	9.1	10.4	5.1	5.9	7.6	8.7
65 years and over	2.3	2.4	2.7	2.3	3.9	3.9	3.7	3.7	2.8	3.9	4.4	3.6
Sex												
Male	3.8	4.0	4.8	5.5	6.4	5.6	6.5	7.3	3.9	4.0	5.1	5.6
Female	5.2	5.0	5.7	6.1	8.1	7.2	7.7	8.4	5.6	6.2	7.4	8.4
Race[6]												
White only	4.4	4.3	5.2	5.8	7.5	6.5	7.3	8.0	4.5	4.9	6.0	6.7
Black or African American only	5.5	5.4	6.3	6.7	6.6	6.4	6.7	7.7	7.1	6.6	8.4	9.8
American Indian or Alaska Native only	6.7	7.1	*9.0	*6.3	10.0	8.9	11.4	*7.8	*7.5	*9.8	*10.0	*13.6
Asian only	2.6	2.4	2.3	2.7	4.0	3.6	3.4	3.9	*2.3	2.5	2.6	3.4
Native Hawaiian or Other Pacific Islander only	—	*	*	*	—	*	*	*	—	*	*	*
2 or more races	—	7.3	8.4	6.9	—	10.8	10.0	9.6	—	7.4	8.3	8.1
Hispanic Origin and Race[6]												
Hispanic or Latino	5.7	4.8	6.2	6.5	6.9	5.8	7.1	8.1	5.5	5.5	7.9	8.7
Mexican	5.5	4.5	5.8	6.2	6.6	5.3	6.7	7.8	5.5	5.5	8.8	9.0
Not Hispanic or Latino	4.4	4.4	5.1	5.7	7.3	6.5	7.1	7.8	4.7	5.1	6.0	6.7
White only	4.2	4.3	5.0	5.6	7.6	6.6	7.3	8.1	4.3	4.9	5.7	6.2
Black or African American only	5.6	5.4	6.2	6.8	6.6	6.5	6.7	7.6	7.1	6.6	8.4	10.0
Education[7]												
No high school diploma or GED	8.5	7.8	9.6	10.1	10.9	9.4	10.7	11.4	8.9	10.2	11.3	13.1
High school diploma or GED	5.2	5.2	6.5	7.1	8.5	7.6	8.4	9.4	5.9	6.0	8.3	8.4
Some college or more	4.2	4.1	5.2	5.9	7.9	6.3	7.7	8.6	4.1	4.4	5.8	6.4
Percent of Poverty Level[8]												
Below 100%	9.8	9.6	10.0	10.6	11.6	11.1	11.0	12.2	10.3	11.2	12.7	13.7
100%–less than 200%	7.4	7.3	9.0	9.6	11.2	10.1	11.1	11.8	7.9	8.8	10.5	11.1
200% or more	2.5	2.7	3.2	3.6	5.1	4.5	5.2	5.7	2.6	3.0	3.7	4.2
Age and Percent of Poverty Level[8]												
Under 18 years of age												
Below 100%	4.5	5.0	3.5	3.5	5.5	5.9	4.8	4.8	4.6	5.2	5.8	5.5
100%–less than 200%	3.0	3.9	3.7	4.2	5.9	6.2	5.5	6.6	3.4	4.1	3.7	3.9
200% or more	1.1	1.3	1.3	1.4	2.2	2.4	2.6	2.7	0.8	1.0	1.3	1.8
18–44 years												
Below 100%	12.7	11.6	13.3	14.2	14.8	13.4	14.0	16.0	13.8	14.4	15.6	17.2
100%–less than 200%	10.1	9.4	12.7	12.6	14.9	12.7	14.8	14.7	11.6	11.3	13.9	15.4
200% or more	3.5	3.8	4.4	4.9	7.1	6.0	6.8	7.2	4.0	4.3	5.2	6.0
45–64 years												
Below 100%	18.3	18.4	18.7	21.1	21.9	19.6	19.5	22.7	17.7	20.1	21.6	26.2
100%–less than 200%	13.8	12.8	14.3	16.9	18.5	16.1	18.1	19.4	11.7	14.4	18.5	18.5
200% or more	2.8	2.9	4.0	4.4	5.8	5.1	6.3	7.3	2.4	3.0	4.1	4.8
65 years and over												
Below 100%	7.2	5.7	5.6	4.1	8.5	8.2	7.3	6.1	7.3	7.2	10.3	8.1
100%–less than 200%	3.3	3.7	4.9	4.2	5.8	5.8	6.1	5.8	4.3	6.5	7.0	6.0
200% or more	0.9	1.1	1.3	1.2	2.2	2.2	2.0	2.4	1.2	2.1	2.2	1.8

* = Figure does not meet standards of reliability or precision.
— = Data not available.
[1]Based on persons responding yes to the question, "During the past 12 months was there any time when person needed medical care but did not get it because person couldn't afford it?"
[2]Based on persons responding yes to the question, "During the past 12 months has medical care been delayed because of worry about the cost?"
[3]Based on persons responding yes to the question, "During the past 12 months was there any time when you needed prescription medicine but didn't get it because you couldn't afford it?"
[4]Estimates are age-adjusted to the year 2000 standard population using six age groups: 0–17 years, 18–44 years, 45–54 years, 55–64 years, 65–74 years, and 75 years and over.
[5]Includes all other races not shown separately, unknown health insurance status, and unknown education level.
[6]The race groups, White, Black, American Indian or Alaska Native, Asian, Native Hawaiian or Other Pacific Islander, and 2 or more races, include persons of Hispanic and non-Hispanic origin. Persons of Hispanic origin may be of any race.
[7]Estimates are for persons 25 years of age and over. GED stands for General Educational Development high school equivalency diploma.
[8]Percent of poverty level is based on family income and family size and composition using U.S. Census Bureau poverty thresholds.

Table C-33. Reduced Access to Medical Care During the Past 12 Months Due to Cost, by Selected Characteristics, Selected Years, 1997–2006—*Continued*

(Percent.)

Characteristic	Did not get medical care due to cost[1]				Delayed medical care due to cost[2]				Did not get prescription drugs[3]			
	1997	2000	2003	2006	1997	2000	2003	2006	1997	2000	2003	2006
Percent of Poverty Level and Health Insurance Status Prior to Interview for Persons under 65 Years of Age[8]												
Insured continuously all 12 months............................	1.8	1.8	2.2	2.5	3.9	3.2	3.7	4.1	2.2	2.6	3.1	3.7
Below 100%	3.6	3.6	4.1	3.5	4.8	4.9	4.8	4.8	5.2	5.8	5.7	6.3
100%–less than 200%	3.4	3.3	4.2	4.7	6.4	5.1	5.6	6.1	4.3	5.5	5.8	7.0
200% or more	1.2	1.2	1.6	1.9	3.3	2.6	3.1	3.6	1.3	1.7	2.1	2.6
Uninsured for any period												
up to 12 months	14.3	15.8	19.6	19.4	22.5	22.6	25.1	26.4	14.9	15.4	20.7	21.8
Below 100%	18.6	20.6	23.2	24.6	23.5	24.9	24.8	28.1	20.2	22.1	27.7	28.4
100%–less than 200%	15.1	15.7	21.4	21.1	24.2	23.3	26.3	27.4	15.9	14.8	21.5	21.2
200% or more	11.4	13.9	17.1	16.0	20.9	21.3	24.6	25.0	11.2	12.8	17.4	19.0
Uninsured more than 12 months	18.9	18.9	21.0	23.0	23.9	22.3	24.4	26.1	16.7	16.8	20.5	21.6
Below 100%	22.2	21.7	22.8	27.1	24.1	21.7	24.0	28.8	19.0	20.1	25.7	28.6
100%–less than 200%	18.4	18.0	21.8	23.0	23.1	21.8	25.8	25.6	16.8	17.1	21.6	21.1
200% or more	16.4	17.5	18.8	19.9	24.7	23.3	23.4	24.4	14.5	13.8	15.4	16.6
Geographic Region												
Northeast...	3.5	3.6	3.9	4.1	5.7	5.1	5.4	5.4	3.4	3.7	5.0	5.1
Midwest...	4.0	3.7	4.7	5.3	7.3	6.0	7.2	8.4	4.4	4.6	5.3	6.7
South...	5.3	5.3	6.3	7.1	8.1	7.2	7.8	8.7	5.7	6.2	7.3	8.4
West..	4.7	4.7	5.3	5.5	7.2	6.8	7.3	7.8	4.8	5.3	6.7	6.5
Location of Residence												
Within MSA[9]...	4.3	4.3	5.1	5.5	6.9	6.1	6.7	7.6	4.4	4.8	5.8	6.8
Outside MSA[9]...	5.3	5.2	6.1	7.1	8.6	7.7	8.7	9.1	6.0	6.3	8.0	7.9

[1]Based on persons responding yes to the question, "During the past 12 months was there any time when person needed medical care but did not get it because person couldn't afford it?"
[2]Based on persons responding yes to the question, "During the past 12 months has medical care been delayed because of worry about the cost?"
[3]Based on persons responding yes to the question, "During the past 12 months was there any time when you needed prescription medicine but didn't get it because you couldn't afford it?"
[8]Percent of poverty level is based on family income and family size and composition using U.S. Census Bureau poverty thresholds.
[9]MSA = metropolitan statistical area. Starting with 2006 data, MSA status is determined using 2000 census data and the 2000 standards for defining MSAs.

Table C-34. Reduced Access to Medical Care During the Past 12 Months Due to Cost, by State: 25 Largest States and the United States, Selected Annual Averages, 1997–2006

(Percent.)

State	Did not get medical care due to cost[1]			Delayed medical care due to cost[2]			Did not get prescription drugs due to cost[3]		
	1997–1998	2001–2002	2005–2006	1997–1998	2001–2002	2005–2006	1997–1998	2001–2002	2005–2006
UNITED STATES	4.4	4.7	5.5	6.9	6.6	7.7	4.5	5.8	7.1
Alabama	4.4	5.5	6.9	6.3	6.6	8.0	6.8	9.0	13.8
Arizona	5.0	4.0	6.8	7.1	6.4	9.5	4.1	5.4	7.8
California	4.2	4.2	3.8	5.8	5.5	5.3	3.9	5.0	5.2
Colorado	3.7	5.3	6.0	5.8	7.2	9.5	3.1	4.8	5.6
Florida	5.8	5.9	7.1	8.7	8.4	10.0	4.8	6.4	7.7
Georgia	4.6	4.9	5.7	7.4	6.7	5.5	4.2	3.8	5.9
Illinois	3.0	3.6	3.7	5.3	5.4	6.0	3.0	4.4	5.3
Indiana	5.2	5.6	6.7	7.8	7.6	9.5	5.1	7.2	8.1
Kentucky	6.5	7.0	9.5	10.1	9.1	10.9	6.3	9.6	11.7
Louisiana	5.8	6.9	6.3	8.6	9.0	7.9	8.7	9.6	10.8
Maryland	5.5	5.3	3.5	6.8	6.5	5.6	5.8	6.6	5.8
Massachusetts	2.4	3.5	3.2	4.3	4.6	5.0	1.7	4.8	4.5
Michigan	3.8	4.1	5.2	6.3	5.8	8.1	3.8	5.8	6.9
Minnesota	3.4	3.0	5.2	7.2	5.8	7.6	3.6	3.7	6.5
Missouri	4.0	4.4	5.8	6.5	5.4	8.8	4.3	5.4	8.9
New Jersey	3.3	3.1	4.0	6.3	4.8	5.2	3.8	4.5	3.9
New York	3.6	3.8	3.6	5.4	5.4	5.0	2.8	4.0	5.3
North Carolina	4.1	4.4	5.4	6.6	6.6	7.2	4.0	6.0	5.4
Ohio	4.6	4.2	5.7	8.2	7.3	9.0	5.0	6.3	7.5
Pennsylvania	3.4	3.7	4.9	5.1	5.3	6.2	4.3	3.8	6.7
Tennessee	4.6	5.2	6.8	9.1	7.0	8.2	8.0	6.1	8.1
Texas	4.8	6.0	8.2	6.9	7.4	10.5	4.7	8.5	11.1
Virginia	3.6	4.3	3.8	5.2	5.9	5.4	4.1	4.8	5.1
Washington	4.8	5.6	6.4	7.6	7.8	10.0	4.8	6.2	6.5
Wisconsin	2.8	3.8	2.8	5.9	5.1	5.5	*3.0	3.9	4.8

* = Figure does not meet standards of reliability or precision.
[1]Based on persons responding yes to the question, "During the past 12 months was there any time when person needed medical care but did not get it because person couldn't afford it?"
[2]Based on persons responding yes to the question, "During the past 12 months has medical care been delayed because of worry about the cost?"
[3]Based on persons responding yes to the question, "During the past 12 months was there any time when you needed prescription medicine but didn't get it because you couldn't afford it?"

Table C-35. Emergency Department Visits Within the Past 12 Months Among Children Under 18 Years of Age, by Selected Characteristics, Selected Years, 1997–2006

(Percent.)

Characteristic	Under 18 years				Under 6 years				6–17 years			
	1997	2000	2003	2006	1997	2000	2003	2006	1997	2000	2003	2006
PERCENT OF CHILDREN WITH 1 OR MORE EMERGENCY DEPARTMENT VISITS												
All children[1]	19.9	20.3	20.9	21.3	24.3	25.7	26.5	28.2	17.7	17.6	18.2	17.9
Race[2]												
White only	19.4	19.9	20.3	21.2	22.6	24.8	25.2	28.0	17.8	17.6	17.9	17.9
Black or African American only	24.0	22.7	23.9	25.0	33.1	30.8	32.0	33.6	19.4	19.0	20.2	21.0
American Indian or Alaska Native only	*24.1	38.0	*22.7	*19.7	*24.3	*	*	*	*24.0	*39.0	*21.0	*
Asian only	12.6	12.3	14.2	13.4	20.8	*16.7	*20.7	19.6	8.6	9.8	*11.0	10.2
Native Hawaiian or Other Pacific Islander only	—	*	*	*	—	*	*	*	—	*	*	*
2 or more races	—	24.2	26.1	17.1	—	31.7	34.0	19.8	—	18.3	20.3	15.2
Hispanic Origin and Race[2]												
Hispanic or Latino	21.1	18.6	20.3	19.7	25.7	23.9	27.9	28.5	18.1	15.6	16.0	14.5
Not Hispanic or Latino	19.7	20.6	21.0	21.7	24.0	26.2	26.1	28.2	17.6	18.0	18.7	18.7
White only	19.2	20.2	20.4	21.5	22.2	25.1	24.6	27.6	17.7	17.9	18.5	18.7
Black or African American only	23.6	22.7	23.8	25.3	32.7	30.9	31.9	34.0	19.2	19.0	20.1	21.3
Percent of Poverty Level[3]												
Below 100%	25.1	25.0	26.9	25.8	29.5	30.7	34.5	32.6	22.2	21.7	22.6	21.6
100%–less than 200%	22.0	22.4	22.8	22.1	28.0	27.4	28.8	30.3	19.0	19.9	19.3	17.8
200% or more	17.3	18.1	18.4	19.3	20.5	23.4	22.5	25.3	15.8	15.8	16.5	16.7
Hispanic Origin and Race and Percent of Poverty Level[2,3]												
Hispanic or Latino												
Percent of poverty level												
Below 100%	21.9	19.9	23.3	21.0	25.0	25.7	31.5	31.1	19.6	16.4	18.4	14.3
100%–less than 200%	20.8	18.2	19.6	20.5	28.8	20.8	27.0	27.3	15.6	16.6	15.0	16.3
200% or more	20.4	17.8	18.1	17.7	23.4	25.3	25.0	26.5	18.7	14.0	14.7	13.3
Not Hispanic or Latino												
White only												
Percent of poverty level												
Below 100%	25.5	26.5	28.4	27.5	27.2	35.6	33.8	32.3	24.4	21.2	25.3	24.6
100%–less than 200%	22.3	24.7	23.4	22.9	25.8	29.2	27.4	33.3	20.7	22.7	21.0	18.2
200% or more	17.2	18.2	18.5	20.0	20.1	22.4	22.1	24.9	15.9	16.4	17.0	17.9
Black or African American only												
Percent of poverty level												
Below 100%	29.3	27.8	27.2	31.1	39.5	28.9	33.5	37.7	23.0	27.3	24.2	27.3
100%–less than 200%	22.5	20.8	27.0	24.8	31.7	35.3	44.1	32.9	18.5	13.8	20.7	21.1
200% or more	17.7	19.5	19.0	19.4	22.6	29.6	24.1	29.6	15.9	15.5	16.7	15.7
Health Insurance Status at the Time of Interview[4]												
Insured	19.8	20.7	21.4	21.9	24.4	25.8	26.7	28.5	17.5	18.2	18.7	18.5
Private	17.5	18.4	18.1	19.2	20.9	22.8	21.6	24.5	15.9	16.5	16.6	17.0
Medicaid	28.2	28.6	28.9	27.2	33.0	33.2	35.1	34.2	24.1	25.5	24.5	22.3
Uninsured	20.2	17.2	17.1	16.8	23.0	24.5	23.9	25.4	18.9	13.9	14.7	13.7
Health Insurance Status Prior to Interview[4]												
Insured continuously all 12 months	19.6	20.2	21.2	21.5	24.1	25.3	26.7	27.9	17.3	17.8	18.4	18.2
Uninsured for any period up to 12 months	24.0	25.9	24.1	26.0	27.1	33.9	29.7	36.2	21.9	21.7	21.0	21.1
Uninsured more than 12 months	18.4	14.7	12.6	12.8	19.3	19.1	*16.9	*17.6	18.1	13.1	11.6	11.5
Percent of Poverty Level and Health Insurance Status Prior to Interview[3,4]												
Below 100%												
Insured continuously all 12 months	26.3	26.1	29.1	26.5	30.9	31.2	36.7	31.7	22.8	22.9	24.5	23.1
Uninsured for any period up to 12 months	26.5	30.8	28.2	32.2	29.7	34.6	32.7	41.8	24.4	28.4	25.7	*25.7
Uninsured more than 12 months	17.5	15.6	*10.7	*12.5	*16.0	*22.1	*	*	18.0	*13.2	*10.5	*9.8
100%–less than 200%												
Insured continuously all 12 months	21.8	23.8	23.8	22.4	28.0	28.2	29.5	30.8	18.6	21.4	20.4	17.6
Uninsured for any period up to 12 months	24.5	24.6	22.1	27.1	29.7	33.3	31.7	*32.9	21.0	20.3	16.7	24.8
Uninsured more than 12 months	19.5	14.3	15.5	*12.9	*22.5	*15.5	*22.9	*	18.6	13.9	13.3	*11.0
200% or more												
Insured continuously all 12 months	17.1	17.9	18.3	19.5	20.3	22.7	22.4	25.2	15.6	15.8	16.5	17.0
Uninsured for any period up to 12 months	20.7	23.8	23.1	20.0	21.3	33.9	26.1	34.4	20.4	18.7	21.5	*13.6
Uninsured more than 12 months	17.9	14.1	*11.5	*13.3	*19.2	*20.9	*	*	17.3	*11.8	*10.9	*14.5

* = Figure does not meet standards of reliability or precision.

— = Data not available.

[1]Includes all other races not shown separately and unknown health insurance status.

[2]The race groups, White, Black, American Indian or Alaska Native, Asian, Native Hawaiian or Other Pacific Islander, and 2 or more races, include persons of Hispanic and non-Hispanic origin. Persons of Hispanic origin may be of any race.

[3]Percent of poverty level is based on family income and family size and composition using U.S. Census Bureau poverty thresholds.

[4]Health insurance categories are mutually exclusive. Persons who reported both Medicaid and private coverage are classified as having private coverage.

Table C-35. Emergency Department Visits Within the Past 12 Months Among Children Under 18 Years of Age, by Selected Characteristics, Selected Years, 1997–2006—*Continued*

(Percent.)

Characteristic	Under 18 years				Under 6 years				6–17 years			
	1997	2000	2003	2006	1997	2000	2003	2006	1997	2000	2003	2006
Geographic Region												
Northeast	18.5	19.7	21.8	24.1	20.7	21.6	26.3	30.8	17.4	18.8	19.7	21.1
Midwest	19.5	20.3	21.4	22.4	26.0	25.6	27.2	28.3	16.4	17.8	18.7	19.5
South	21.8	21.9	21.7	22.8	25.6	28.6	27.8	32.5	19.9	18.7	18.6	18.0
West	18.5	18.0	18.3	15.4	23.5	24.7	23.6	19.3	15.9	14.7	15.8	13.4
Location of Residence												
Within MSA[5]	19.7	19.9	20.2	20.8	23.9	24.5	25.2	27.3	17.4	17.6	17.8	17.6
Outside MSA[5]	20.8	21.9	23.6	23.9	26.2	31.3	31.8	32.6	18.6	17.8	19.7	19.6
PERCENT OF CHILDREN WITH 2 OR MORE EMERGENCY DEPARTMENT VISITS												
All children[1]	7.1	7.0	7.0	7.7	9.6	10.0	8.7	10.6	5.8	5.6	6.2	6.3
Race[2]												
White only	6.6	6.4	6.3	7.5	8.4	8.7	7.6	10.1	5.7	5.4	5.7	6.2
Black or African American only	9.6	10.5	10.4	9.9	14.9	16.2	13.9	14.8	6.9	7.9	8.8	7.6
American Indian and Alaska Native only	*	*	*	*	*	*	*	*	*	*	*	*
Asian only	*5.7	*3.1	*6.7	5.8	*12.9	*	*	*6.7	*	*	*	*5.3
Native Hawaiian and Other Pacific Islander only	—	*	*	*	—	*	*	*	—	*	*	*
2 or more races	—	*8.7	8.7	*6.2	—	*14.3	*10.1	*	—	*	*7.6	*
Hispanic Origin and Race[2]												
Hispanic or Latino	8.9	7.0	7.4	7.7	11.8	9.4	10.8	11.2	7.0	5.6	5.5	5.6
Not Hispanic or Latino	6.8	7.0	6.9	7.7	9.2	10.1	8.2	10.4	5.7	5.6	6.4	6.4
White only	6.2	6.3	6.0	7.3	7.8	8.6	6.6	9.6	5.5	5.2	5.8	6.2
Black or African American only	9.3	10.6	10.6	9.9	14.6	16.6	14.4	14.5	6.8	7.9	8.9	7.7
Percent of Poverty Level[3]												
Below 100%	11.1	11.9	11.6	10.1	14.5	16.4	12.9	12.4	8.9	9.4	10.8	8.6
100%–less than 200%	8.3	8.0	8.6	8.8	12.2	11.8	10.6	12.6	6.3	6.1	7.4	6.9
200% or more	5.3	5.2	5.1	6.4	6.5	7.0	6.4	8.9	4.7	4.4	4.5	5.3
Hispanic Origin and Race and Percent of Poverty Level[2,3]												
Hispanic or Latino												
Percent of poverty level												
Below 100%	10.4	8.2	9.6	8.2	13.9	10.9	13.6	10.8	8.0	6.6	7.2	*6.4
100%–less than 200%	8.2	7.4	7.5	8.8	12.0	8.5	11.7	12.7	5.7	6.7	*4.9	*6.5
200% or more	7.6	5.5	5.2	6.3	8.4	8.7	6.9	*10.1	7.1	*3.9	4.5	*4.2
Not Hispanic or Latino												
White only												
Percent of poverty level												
Below 100%	10.7	12.8	10.5	10.0	12.2	18.4	*10.1	*10.5	9.8	*9.5	*10.7	*9.6
100%–less than 200%	8.0	8.0	8.5	8.6	11.2	11.8	7.7	*11.6	6.4	6.3	9.0	*7.3
200% or more	5.0	4.9	4.8	6.4	5.8	6.1	5.7	8.8	4.6	4.4	4.4	5.4
Black or African American only												
Percent of poverty level												
Below 100%	12.7	14.7	14.6	12.3	19.1	18.5	14.7	16.5	8.8	12.8	14.5	10.0
100%–less than 200%	9.2	8.9	11.7	10.4	*13.5	17.5	21.6	*17.0	*7.2	*4.8	*8.1	*7.2
200% or more	5.5	8.1	6.7	6.9	*8.2	14.1	*10.1	*9.5	*4.5	5.8	*5.1	*5.9
Health Insurance Status at the Time of Interview[4]												
Insured	7.0	7.0	7.1	7.8	9.6	9.6	8.7	10.6	5.7	5.7	6.3	6.4
Private	5.2	5.2	5.1	6.3	6.8	7.1	5.4	8.5	4.5	4.5	4.9	5.3
Medicaid	13.1	13.1	11.7	10.8	16.2	15.9	14.0	13.7	10.4	11.2	10.1	8.8
Uninsured	7.7	6.6	6.6	7.0	9.8	11.3	*8.8	*11.4	6.8	4.5	5.9	5.5
Health Insurance Status Prior to Interview[4]												
Insured continuously all 12 months	6.9	6.7	7.0	7.7	9.4	9.2	8.9	10.4	5.7	5.5	6.1	6.3
Uninsured for any period up to 12 months	8.5	10.6	9.4	9.6	11.5	16.0	*8.2	*13.3	6.6	7.7	10.1	7.8
Uninsured more than 12 months	6.8	5.8	4.0	*5.5	*8.6	8.9	*	*	6.2	4.7	*3.7	*4.4

* = Figure does not meet standards of reliability or precision.

— = Data not available.

[1]Includes all other races not shown separately and unknown health insurance status.

[2]The race groups, White, Black, American Indian or Alaska Native, Asian, Native Hawaiian or Other Pacific Islander, and 2 or more races, include persons of Hispanic and non-Hispanic origin. Persons of Hispanic origin may be of any race.

[3]Percent of poverty level is based on family income and family size and composition using U.S. Census Bureau poverty thresholds.

[4]Health insurance categories are mutually exclusive. Persons who reported both Medicaid and private coverage are classified as having private coverage.

[5]MSA = metropolitan statistical area. Starting with 2006 data, MSA status is determined using 2000 census data and the 2000 standards for defining MSAs.

Table C-35. Emergency Department Visits Within the Past 12 Months Among Children Under 18 Years of Age, by Selected Characteristics, Selected Years, 1997–2006—*Continued*

(Percent.)

Characteristic	Under 18 years				Under 6 years				6–17 years			
	1997	2000	2003	2006	1997	2000	2003	2006	1997	2000	2003	2006
Geographic Region												
Northeast..	6.2	6.4	7.8	9.6	7.6	7.9	8.0	10.8	5.4	5.6	7.6	9.1
Midwest..	6.6	6.6	6.3	7.4	10.4	9.0	8.5	10.4	4.8	5.5	5.3	6.0
South...	8.0	8.5	8.0	8.4	10.1	12.6	9.5	12.6	6.9	6.6	7.3	6.4
West..	7.1	5.4	5.5	5.1	10.0	8.5	8.1	7.3	5.6	3.9	4.2	3.9
Location of Residence												
Within MSA[5]..	7.2	6.6	6.7	7.4	9.6	8.9	8.3	10.2	5.9	5.5	6.0	6.1
Outside MSA[5]...	6.8	8.6	8.2	9.0	9.7	15.0	10.3	12.8	5.6	5.8	7.2	7.2

[5]MSA = metropolitan statistical area. Starting with 2006 data, MSA status is determined using 2000 census data and the 2000 standards for defining MSAs.

Table C-36. Emergency Department Visits Within the Past 12 Months Among Adults 18 Years of Age and Over, by Selected Characteristics, Selected Years, 1997–2006

(Percent.)

Characteristic	One or more emergency department visits				Two or more emergency department visits			
	1997	2000	2003	2006	1997	2000	2003	2006
18 years and over, age-adjusted[1,2]	19.6	20.2	20.0	20.5	6.7	6.9	7.0	7.5
18 years and over, crude[1]	19.6	20.1	20.0	20.4	6.7	6.8	7.0	7.4
Age								
18–44 years	20.7	20.5	20.0	20.5	6.8	7.0	6.8	7.3
18–24 years	26.3	25.7	23.9	24.9	9.1	8.8	8.2	9.6
25–44 years	19.0	18.8	18.6	18.9	6.2	6.4	6.4	6.5
45–64 years	16.2	17.6	18.5	18.4	5.6	5.6	6.4	6.8
45–54 years	15.7	17.9	17.8	17.9	5.5	5.8	5.9	6.3
55–64 years	16.9	17.0	19.3	18.9	5.7	5.3	7.0	7.5
65 years and over	22.0	23.7	22.9	24.5	8.1	8.6	8.7	9.0
65–74 years	20.3	21.6	19.7	20.6	7.1	7.4	7.1	6.8
75 years and over	24.3	26.2	26.6	28.9	9.3	10.0	10.4	11.6
Sex[2]								
Male	19.1	18.7	18.2	19.0	5.9	5.7	5.6	6.0
Female	20.2	21.6	21.8	22.1	7.5	7.9	8.4	8.9
Race[2,3]								
White only	19.0	19.4	19.2	20.1	6.2	6.4	6.4	7.0
Black or African American only	25.9	26.5	27.8	25.6	11.1	10.8	12.4	11.3
American Indian or Alaska Native only	24.8	30.3	22.5	21.1	13.1	*12.6	*9.1	*10.5
Asian only	11.6	13.6	12.9	13.6	*2.9	*3.8	*3.5	3.8
Native Hawaiian or Other Pacific Islander only	—	*	*	*	—	*	*	*
2 or more races	—	32.5	25.2	24.5	—	11.3	11.1	*9.4
American Indian or Alaska Native; White	—	33.9	29.7	21.9	—	*9.4	*15.1	*
Hispanic Origin and Race[2,3]								
Hispanic or Latino	19.2	18.3	18.5	17.3	7.4	7.0	7.3	5.7
Mexican	17.8	17.4	17.0	15.4	6.4	7.1	6.4	4.8
Not Hispanic or Latino	19.7	20.6	20.3	21.1	6.7	6.9	7.0	7.7
White only	19.1	19.8	19.5	20.8	6.2	6.4	6.3	7.3
Black or African American only	25.9	26.5	27.7	25.8	11.0	10.8	12.3	11.3
Percent of Poverty Level[2,4]								
Below 100%	28.1	29.0	26.3	28.2	12.8	13.3	12.6	13.0
100%–less than 200%	23.8	23.9	23.2	24.0	9.3	9.6	9.9	10.6
200% or more	17.0	18.0	18.2	18.2	4.9	5.2	5.4	5.5
Hispanic Origin and Race and Percent of Poverty Level[2,3,4]								
Hispanic or Latino								
Below 100%	22.1	22.4	21.2	20.7	9.8	9.7	9.6	6.8
100%–less than 200%	19.2	18.1	17.6	16.0	8.1	6.7	7.3	5.9
200% or more	17.6	16.8	17.9	16.5	5.4	6.1	6.4	5.2
Not Hispanic or Latino								
White only								
Below 100%	29.5	30.1	27.0	31.7	13.0	13.9	12.7	15.2
100%–less than 200%	24.3	25.5	24.0	26.3	9.1	10.4	10.0	11.7
200% or more	16.8	17.7	17.8	18.3	4.8	5.0	5.0	5.3
Black or African American only								
Below 100%	34.6	35.4	33.4	31.4	17.5	17.4	18.1	15.8
100%–less than 200%	29.2	28.5	31.2	30.3	12.8	12.2	15.7	13.6
200% or more	19.7	22.6	24.0	21.5	7.2	8.0	8.7	8.5
Health Insurance Status at the Time of Interview[5,6]								
18–64 years								
Insured	18.8	19.5	19.7	19.9	6.1	6.4	6.7	7.2
Private	16.9	17.6	17.4	17.2	4.7	5.1	5.0	5.3
Medicaid	37.6	42.2	39.7	39.0	19.7	21.0	21.6	20.7
Uninsured	20.0	19.3	18.1	18.9	7.5	6.9	6.7	6.9

* = Figure does not meet standards of reliability or precision.
—— = Data not available.
[1]Includes all other races not shown separately and unknown health insurance status.
[2]Estimates are for persons 18 years of age and over and are age-adjusted to the year 2000 standard population using five age groups: 18–44 years, 45–54 years, 55–64 years, 65–74 years, and 75 years and over.
[3]The race groups, White, Black, American Indian or Alaska Native, Asian, Native Hawaiian or Other Pacific Islander, and 2 or more races, include persons of Hispanic and non-Hispanic origin. Persons of Hispanic origin may be of any race.
[4]Percent of poverty level is based on family income and family size and composition using U.S. Census Bureau poverty thresholds.
[5]Estimates for persons 18–64 years of age are age-adjusted to the year 2000 standard population using three age groups: 18–44 years, 45–54 years, and 55–64 years of age.
[6]Health insurance categories are mutually exclusive. Persons who reported both Medicaid and private coverage are classified as having private coverage.

Table C-36. Emergency Department Visits Within the Past 12 Months Among Adults 18 Years of Age and Over, by Selected Characteristics, Selected Years, 1997–2006—*Continued*

(Percent.)

Characteristic	One or more emergency department visits				Two or more emergency department visits			
	1997	2000	2003	2006	1997	2000	2003	2006
Health Insurance Status Prior to Interview[5,6]								
18–64 years								
Insured continuously all 12 months...	18.3	19.0	19.2	19.1	5.8	6.1	6.4	6.7
Uninsured for any period up to 12 months.............................	25.5	28.2	25.7	27.4	9.4	10.3	10.0	11.8
Uninsured more than 12 months...	18.9	17.3	16.8	17.4	7.1	6.4	6.3	6.3
Percent of Poverty Level and Health Insurance Status Prior to Interview[4,5,6]								
18–64 years								
Below 100%								
Insured continuously all 12 months	30.2	31.6	29.4	29.6	14.7	15.4	14.6	14.3
Uninsured for any period up to 12 months.............................	34.1	43.7	30.8	39.5	16.1	18.1	15.0	21.9
Uninsured more than 12 months...	20.8	20.5	19.2	19.4	8.1	9.1	8.7	8.2
100%–less than 200%								
Insured continuously all 12 months	24.5	25.5	24.7	25.6	8.9	10.2	10.9	11.8
Uninsured for any period up to 12 months.............................	28.7	27.7	30.0	27.2	12.3	11.7	11.3	12.6
Uninsured more than 12 months...	19.0	17.4	16.7	16.8	8.3	6.4	6.7	5.8
200% or more								
Insured continuously all 12 months	16.0	17.0	17.2	16.8	4.4	4.7	4.8	4.9
Uninsured for any period up to 12 months.............................	20.2	22.9	22.4	22.8	5.3	7.0	7.7	7.3
Uninsured more than 12 months...	17.4	15.6	15.3	16.7	5.3	4.7	4.3	5.3
Geographic Region[2]								
Northeast..	19.5	20.0	20.3	22.4	6.9	6.2	6.9	8.9
Midwest	19.3	20.1	20.0	20.6	6.2	6.9	6.4	7.3
South..	20.9	21.2	20.9	21.0	7.3	7.6	8.1	7.7
West...	17.7	18.6	18.2	18.1	6.0	6.3	5.9	5.9
Location of Residence[2]								
Within MSA[7]..	19.1	19.6	19.5	20.1	6.4	6.6	6.6	7.3
Outside MSA[7]	21.5	22.5	22.3	22.6	7.8	7.8	8.6	8.2

[1]Includes all other races not shown separately and unknown health insurance status.
[2]Estimates are for persons 18 years of age and over and are age-adjusted to the year 2000 standard population using five age groups: 18–44 years, 45–54 years, 55–64 years, 65–74 years, and 75 years and over.
[4]Percent of poverty level is based on family income and family size and composition using U.S. Census Bureau poverty thresholds.
[5]Estimates for persons 18–64 years of age are age-adjusted to the year 2000 standard population using three age groups: 18–44 years, 45–54 years, and 55–64 years of age.
[6]Health insurance categories are mutually exclusive. Persons who reported both Medicaid and private coverage are classified as having private coverage.
[7]MSA = metropolitan statistical area. Starting with 2006 data, MSA status is determined using 2000 census data and the 2000 standards for defining MSAs.

Table C-37. Injury-Related Visits to Hospital Emergency Departments, by Sex, Age, Intent and Mechanism of Injury, Selected Annual Averages, 1995–2005

(Number in thousands, rate per 10,000 persons.)

Sex, age, and intent and mechanism of injury[1]	Injury-related visits in thousands			Injury-related visits per 10,000 persons		
	1995–1996	2000–2001	2004–2005	1995–1996	2000–2001	2004–2005
BOTH SEXES						
All Ages[2,3]	36,081	39,918	41,664	1,360.9	1,441.9	1,435.8
MALE						
All Ages[2,3]	20,030	21,852	22,139	1,530.7	1,606.2	1,556.3
Under 18 Years[2]	6,238	6,517	6,405	1,720.2	1,759.4	1,711.2
Unintentional injuries[4]	5,478	5,387	5,026	1,510.5	1,454.5	1,342.8
Falls	1,402	1,428	1,530	386.5	385.4	408.7
Struck by or against objects or persons	1,011	1,428	972	278.9	385.4	259.6
Motor vehicle traffic	453	435	401	125.0	117.5	107.1
Cut or pierce	493	403	384	136.0	108.9	102.6
Intentional injuries	290	255	219	80.0	68.8	58.4
18–24 Years[2]	2,980	3,225	3,077	2,396.9	2,418.6	2,165.5
Unintentional injuries[4]	2,423	2,347	2,130	1,948.7	1,760.3	1,499.4
Falls	299	281	358	240.8	210.5	251.7
Struck by or against objects or persons	387	443	304	311.0	332.3	213.8
Motor vehicle traffic	347	511	441	279.4	383.4	310.2
Cut or pierce	304	366	261	244.8	274.3	184.0
Intentional injuries	335	309	318	269.2	231.8	224.0
25–44 Years[2]	7,245	7,287	6,858	1,767.4	1,798.3	1,647.8
Unintentional injuries[4]	5,757	5,234	4,411	1,404.3	1,291.7	1,059.9
Falls	817	867	842	199.4	213.9	202.4
Struck by or against objects or persons	619	774	532	151.0	191.0	127.7
Motor vehicle traffic	912	793	717	222.6	195.7	172.3
Cut or pierce	860	777	582	209.8	191.8	139.8
Intentional injuries	701	458	500	171.0	113.0	120.1
45–64 Years[2]	2,240	3,218	3,852	883.4	1,066.9	1,113.3
Unintentional injuries[4]	1,845	2,314	2,458	727.6	767.0	710.5
Falls	445	542	590	175.6	179.7	170.6
Struck by or against objects or persons	186	286	232	73.3	94.6	67.1
Motor vehicle traffic	244	323	359	96.3	107.2	103.7
Cut or pierce	203	332	334	79.9	110.1	96.5
Intentional injuries	86	121	190	33.8	40.0	55.0
65 Years and Over[2]	1,327	1,605	1,947	1,000.7	1,142.8	1,312.0
Unintentional injuries[4]	1,009	1,206	1,111	760.6	858.8	748.8
Falls	505	544	653	380.9	387.5	440.2
Struck by or against objects or persons	*39	112	60	*29.4	79.8	40.5
Motor vehicle traffic	99	144	118	74.7	102.4	79.4
Cut or pierce	*81	117	62	*61.1	83.3	41.6
Intentional injuries	*	14	33	*	*	*22.1

* = Figure does not meet standards of reliability or precision.
[1]Intent and mechanism of injury are based on the first-listed external cause of injury code.
[2]Includes all injury-related visits not shown separately in table including those with undetermined intent (0.6% in 2004–2005), insufficient or no information to code cause of injury (21.8% in 2004–2005), and resulting from adverse effects of medical treatment (4.4% in 2004–2005).
[3]Rates are age adjusted to the year 2000 standard population using six age groups: under 18 years, 18–24 years, 25–44 years, 45–64 years, 65–74 years, and 75 years and over.
[4]Includes unintentional injury-related visits with mechanism of injury not shown in table.

Table C-37. Injury-Related Visits to Hospital Emergency Departments, by Sex, Age, Intent and Mechanism of Injury, Selected Annual Averages, 1995–2005

(Number in thousands, rate per 10,000 persons.)

Sex, age, and intent and mechanism of injury[1]	Injury-related visits in thousands			Injury-related visits per 10,000 persons		
	1995–1996	2000–2001	2004–2005	1995–1996	2000–2001	2004–2005
FEMALE						
All Ages[2,3]	16,051	18,066	19,524	1,186.4	1,271.4	1,313.3
Under 18 Years[2]	4,372	4,269	4,678	1,263.9	1,207.0	1,307.3
Unintentional injuries[4]	3,760	3,408	3,551	1,087.0	963.7	992.3
Falls	1,040	966	1,183	300.7	273.2	330.5
Struck by or against objects or persons	477	670	487	137.9	189.5	136.0
Motor vehicle traffic	447	437	412	129.3	123.6	115.0
Cut or pierce	253	208	210	73.0	58.9	58.6
Intentional injuries	220	166	231	63.6	46.9	64.7
18–24 Years[2]	1,900	2,338	2,440	1,523.4	1,749.3	1,732.5
Unintentional injuries[4]	1,430	1,657	1,557	1,146.7	1,239.5	1,105.7
Falls	268	296	301	214.5	221.6	214.0
Struck by or against objects or persons	134	181	161	107.4	135.1	114.4
Motor vehicle traffic	373	500	480	298.8	373.9	341.1
Cut or pierce	131	162	130	105.3	120.9	92.4
Intentional injuries	239	192	231	191.7	143.3	163.7
25–44 Years[2]	5,098	5,645	5,732	1,205.8	1,345.3	1,348.8
Unintentional injuries[4]	3,877	3,834	3,651	916.8	913.9	859.2
Falls	817	903	930	193.3	215.2	218.7
Struck by or against objects or persons	380	358	375	89.8	85.3	88.3
Motor vehicle traffic	872	849	805	206.2	202.3	189.5
Cut or pierce	338	373	326	79.8	89.0	76.7
Intentional injuries	422	406	360	99.8	96.8	84.6
45–64 Years[2]	2,369	3,098	3,833	873.7	963.9	1,045.3
Unintentional injuries[4]	1,857	2,155	2,454	685.2	670.5	669.2
Falls	600	755	927	221.5	234.8	252.7
Struck by or against objects or persons	160	186	162	58.8	57.8	44.1
Motor vehicle traffic	343	345	423	126.5	107.2	115.4
Cut or pierce	127	183	177	46.9	56.8	48.2
Intentional injuries	*64	86	143	*23.5	26.8	39.0
65 Years and Over[2]	2,313	2,716	2,842	1,256.1	1,417.4	1,416.4
Unintentional injuries[4]	1,931	2,081	1,902	1,049.0	1,086.2	947.8
Falls	1,230	1,326	1,298	667.9	691.9	647.0
Struck by or against objects or persons	82	118	116	44.8	61.5	57.6
Motor vehicle traffic	169	130	133	91.6	67.8	66.4
Cut or pierce	*42	65	61	*22.7	*34.0	30.5
Intentional injuries	*	22	12	*	*	*

* = Figure does not meet standards of reliability or precision.
[1]Intent and mechanism of injury are based on the first-listed external cause of injury code.
[2]Includes all injury-related visits not shown separately in table including those with undetermined intent (0.6% in 2004–2005), insufficient or no information to code cause of injury (21.8% in 2004–2005), and resulting from adverse effects of medical treatment (4.4% in 2004–2005).
[3]Rates are age adjusted to the year 2000 standard population using six age groups: under 18 years, 18–24 years, 25–44 years, 45–64 years, 65–74 years, and 75 years and over.
[4]Includes unintentional injury-related visits with mechanism of injury not shown in table.

Table C-38. Vaccinations of Children 19-35 Months of Age for Selected Diseases, by Race, Hispanic Origin, Poverty Level, and Residence in Metropolitan Statistical Area (MSA), Selected Years, 1995–2006

(Percent.)

Vaccination and year	Race and Hispanic origin								Poverty level		Location of residence		
		Not Hispanic or Latino									Inside MSA[1]		
	All	White	Black or African American	Native American Indian or Alaska Native	Asian[2]	Hawaiian or Other Pacific Islander[2]	2 or more races	Hispanic or Latino[3]	Below poverty level	At or above poverty level	Central city	Remaining area	Outside MSA
PERCENT													
Combined Series (4:3:1:3:3:1)[4]													
2002	66	66	62	—	74	—	61	66	62	66	64	68	61
2003	73	74	68	69	76	—	74	71	70	74	72	74	70
2004	76	77	71	67	80	—	77	76	73	77	75	78	74
2005	76	76	76	—	77	—	80	76	74	77	75	78	74
2006	77	78	74	74	76	—	75	77	74	78	77	78	75
DTP/DT/DTaP (4 doses or more)[5]													
1995	78	80	74	71	84	—	—	75	71	81	77	79	78
1996	81	83	79	85	85	—	—	77	74	84	79	83	81
1997	82	84	77	80	80	—	—	78	76	84	80	83	81
1998	84	87	77	83	89	—	—	81	80	86	82	85	85
1999	83	86	79	80	87	—	—	80	79	85	82	84	83
2000	82	84	76	75	85	—	—	79	76	84	80	83	83
2001	82	84	76	77	84	—	—	83	77	84	81	83	82
2002	82	84	76	*	88	*	78	79	75	84	79	84	80
2003	85	88	80	80	89	*	84	82	80	87	84	86	83
2004	86	88	80	77	90	*	86	84	81	87	84	87	85
2005	86	87	84	*	89	*	86	84	82	87	85	87	85
2006	85	87	81	82	86	*	84	85	81	87	84	86	85
Polio (3 doses or more)													
1995	88	89	84	86	90	—	—	87	85	89	87	88	89
1996	91	92	90	90	90	—	—	89	88	92	89	92	92
1997	91	92	89	90	89	—	—	90	89	92	90	91	92
1998	91	92	88	85	93	—	—	89	90	92	89	91	93
1999	90	90	87	88	90	—	—	89	87	91	89	90	90
2000	90	91	87	90	93	—	—	88	87	90	88	90	91
2001	89	90	85	88	90	—	—	91	87	90	88	90	91
2002	90	91	87	*	92	95	87	90	88	91	89	91	90
2003	92	93	89	91	91	90	91	90	89	93	91	92	92
2004	92	92	90	87	93	*	92	91	90	92	91	92	92
2005	92	91	91	*	93	*	94	92	90	92	91	93	92
2006	93	93	91	91	92	96	92	93	92	93	93	93	93
Measles, Mumps, Rubella													
1995	90	91	87	88	95	—	—	88	86	91	90	90	89
1996	91	91	90	89	93	—	—	88	87	92	90	91	91
1997	90	91	89	92	90	—	—	88	86	92	90	91	91
1998	92	93	89	91	92	—	—	91	90	93	92	92	93
1999	92	92	90	92	93	—	—	90	90	92	91	92	90
2000	91	92	88	87	90	—	—	90	89	91	90	91	91
2001	91	92	89	94	90	—	—	92	89	92	91	92	91
2002	92	93	90	84	95	94	89	91	90	92	90	93	90
2003	93	93	92	92	96	*	94	93	92	93	93	93	92
2004	93	94	91	89	94	*	94	93	91	94	93	94	92
2005	92	91	92	90	92	90	94	91	89	92	92	92	90
2006	92	93	91	89	95	93	91	92	91	93	93	93	92

—- = Data not available.

* = Figure does not meet standards of reliability or precision.

[1]MSA = metropolitan statistical area.

[2]Prior to data year 2002, the category Asian included Native Hawaiian and Other Pacific Islander.

[3]Persons of Hispanic origin may be of any race.

[4]The 4:3:1:3:3:1 combined series consists of 4 or more doses of diphtheria and tetanus toxoids and pertussis vaccine (DTP), diphtheria and tetanus toxoids (DT), or diphtheria and tetanus toxoids and acellular pertussis vaccine (DTaP); 3 or more doses of any poliovirus vaccine; 1 or more doses of a measles-containing vaccine (MCV); 3 or more doses of Haemophilus influenzae type b vaccine (Hib); 3 or more doses of hepatitis B vaccine; and 1 or more doses of varicella vaccine.

[5]Diphtheria and tetanus toxoids and pertussis vaccine, diphtheria and tetanus toxoids, and diphtheria and tetanus toxoids and acellular pertussis vaccine.

Table C-38. Vaccinations of Children 19-35 Months of Age for Selected Diseases, by Race, Hispanic Origin, Poverty Level, and Residence in Metropolitan Statistical Area (MSA), Selected Years, 1995–2006—*Continued*

(Percent.)

Vaccination and year	All	Race and Hispanic origin							Poverty level		Location of residence		
		Not Hispanic or Latino						Hispanic or Latino[3]	Below poverty level	At or above poverty level	Inside MSA[1]		Outside MSA
		White	Black or African American	Native American Indian or Alaska Native	Asian[2]	Hawaiian or Other Pacific Islander[2]	2 or more races				Central city	Remaining area	
Hib (3 doses or more)[6]													
1995	91	93	88	93	90	—	—	89	88	93	91	92	92
1996	91	93	89	91	92	—	—	89	87	93	90	93	92
1997	93	94	91	86	89	—	—	90	90	94	91	93	94
1998	93	95	90	90	92	—	—	92	91	95	92	94	94
1999	94	95	92	91	90	—	—	92	91	95	92	95	93
2000	93	95	93	90	92	—	—	91	90	95	92	94	95
2001	93	94	90	91	92	—	—	93	90	94	91	94	93
2002	93	94	92	*	95	93	90	92	90	94	92	94	93
2003	94	95	92	89	91	*	93	93	91	95	94	94	94
2004	94	95	91	90	92	*	96	93	92	94	93	94	94
2005	94	94	93	88	89	91	95	94	92	95	93	94	94
2006	93	94	91	94	89	96	92	94	91	94	93	94	92
Hepatitis B (3 doses or more)													
1995	68	68	66	52	80	—	—	70	65	69	69	71	59
1996	82	82	82	79	85	—	—	81	78	83	81	83	81
1997	84	85	82	83	88	—	—	81	81	85	82	85	85
1998	87	88	84	82	89	—	—	86	85	88	85	88	87
1999	88	89	87	*	88	—	—	87	87	89	87	89	88
2000	90	91	89	91	91	—	—	88	87	91	89	90	92
2001	89	90	85	86	90	—	—	90	87	90	88	90	89
2002	90	91	88	*	94	94	84	90	88	90	89	91	90
2003	92	93	92	90	94	*	93	91	91	93	92	93	93
2004	92	93	91	91	93	*	94	92	91	93	92	93	93
2005	93	93	93	90	93	*	94	93	91	94	92	94	93
2006	93	94	92	95	92	97	92	94	93	94	93	94	93
Varicella[7]													
1997	26	28	21	20	36	—	—	22	17	29	26	29	17
1998	43	42	42	28	53	—	—	47	41	44	45	45	34
1999	58	56	58	*	64	—	—	61	55	58	59	61	47
2000	68	66	67	62	77	—	—	70	64	69	69	70	60
2001	76	75	75	69	82	—	—	80	74	77	78	78	68
2002	81	79	83	71	87	*	79	82	79	81	81	83	75
2003	85	84	85	81	91	*	86	86	84	85	86	86	80
2004	88	87	86	84	91	*	89	89	86	88	88	89	85
2005	88	86	91	82	92	*	90	89	87	88	88	88	86
2006	89	89	89	85	93	90	91	90	89	90	90	90	86
PCV (3 doses or more)[8]													
2002	41	44	34	33	55	*	38	37	33	43	41	45	32
2003	68	71	62	60	71	*	66	66	62	71	68	71	61
2004	73	75	68	75	76	*	78	70	69	75	72	77	68
2005	83	83	80	*	79	*	87	84	78	84	82	85	78
2006	87	87	83	87	81	*	86	89	85	88	88	88	81

—- = Data not available.
* = Figure does not meet standards of reliability or precision.
[1]MSA = metropolitan statistical area.
[2]Prior to data year 2002, the category Asian included Native Hawaiian and Other Pacific Islander.
[3]Persons of Hispanic origin may be of any race.
[6]Haemophilus influenzae type b vaccine (Hib).
[7]Recommended in 1996. Data collection for varicella began in July 1996.
[8]Pneumococcal conjugate vaccine (PCV). Recommended in 2000. Data collection for PCV began in July 2001.

Table C-38. Vaccinations of Children 19-35 Months of Age for Selected Diseases, by Race, Hispanic Origin, Poverty Level, and Residence in Metropolitan Statistical Area (MSA), Selected Years, 1995–2006—*Continued*

(Percent.)

Vaccination and year	Not Hispanic or Latino				Hispanic or Latino[3]	
	White		Black or African American			
	Below poverty level	At or above poverty level	Below poverty level	At or above poverty level	Below poverty level	At or above poverty level
Combined series (4:3:1:3:3:1)[4]						
2002	59	67	59	62	66	66
2003	69	75	64	72	73	70
2004	72	78	68	75	75	78
2005	70	77	74	80	76	75
2006	70	79	72	77	77	79

[3]Persons of Hispanic origin may be of any race.
[4]The 4:3:1:3:3:1 combined series consists of 4 or more doses of diphtheria and tetanus toxoids and pertussis vaccine (DTP), diphtheria and tetanus toxoids (DT), or diphtheria and tetanus toxoids and acellular pertussis vaccine (DTaP); 3 or more doses of any poliovirus vaccine; 1 or more doses of a measles-containing vaccine (MCV); 3 or more doses of Haemophilus influenzae type b vaccine (Hib); 3 or more doses of hepatitis B vaccine; and 1 or more doses of varicella vaccine.

Table C-39. Vaccination Coverage Among Children 19-35 Months of Age, by Geographic Division, State, and Selected Urban Area, 2002–2006

(Percent.)

Geographic division and area	2002	2003	2004	2005	2006
PERCENT OF CHILDREN 19-35 MONTHS OF AGE WITH 4:3:1:3:3:1 SERIES[1]					
UNITED STATES	66	73	76	76	77
New England					
Connecticut	73	89	85	82	82
Maine	62	69	74	76	76
Massachusetts	78	83	84	91	84
New Hampshire	66	76	78	77	76
Rhode Island	81	80	82	80	81
Vermont	58	65	67	63	75
Middle Atlantic					
New Jersey	66	64	74	72	76
New York	67	73	78	74	79
Pennsylvania	68	79	82	77	81
East North Central					
Illinois	58	69	74	77	74
Indiana	59	62	68	70	76
Michigan	72	79	79	81	78
Ohio	64	71	71	78	75
Wisconsin	68	73	78	77	81
West North Central					
Iowa	58	63	76	76	79
Kansas	55	63	66	72	70
Minnesota	62	71	78	78	78
Missouri	60	74	75	73	81
Nebraska	64	68	73	84	75
North Dakota	56	63	71	79	80
South Dakota	62	60	73	80	74
South Atlantic					
Delaware	70	66	80	82	80
District of Columbia	68	72	80	72	78
Florida	66	74	85	78	80
Georgia	77	75	82	82	81
Maryland	71	77	76	79	78
North Carolina	70	77	78	82	82
South Carolina	74	80	77	76	80
Virginia	65	80	74	82	77
West Virginia	66	63	76	68	68
East South Central					
Alabama	73	79	80	82	79
Kentucky	64	79	77	71	79
Mississippi	64	78	80	79	73
Tennessee	67	74	79	80	77
West South Central					
Arkansas	68	75	81	64	73
Louisiana	62	65	70	74	70
Oklahoma	60	67	71	72	78
Texas	65	70	69	77	75
Mountain					
Arizona	59	68	73	75	71
Colorado	56	63	73	79	76
Idaho	53	61	70	68	69
Montana	49	65	65	65	66
Nevada	65	66	65	63	60
New Mexico	59	71	79	75	72
Utah	61	70	68	68	78
Wyoming	54	57	64	67	64
Pacific					
Alaska	56	73	66	68	67
California	67	76	79	74	79
Hawaii	69	79	80	78	79
Oregon	60	70	74	65	73
Washington	52	56	67	66	71

[1]The 4:3:1:3:3:1 combined series consists of 4 or more doses of diphtheria and tetanus toxoids and pertussis vaccine (DTP), diphtheria and tetanus toxoids (DT), or diphtheria and tetanus toxoids and acellular pertussis vaccine (DTaP); 3 or more doses of any poliovirus vaccine; 1 or more doses of a measles-containing vaccine (MCV); 3 or more doses of Haemophilus influenzae type b vaccine (Hib); 3 or more doses of hepatitis B vaccine; and 1 or more doses of varicella vaccine.

Table C-39. Vaccination Coverage Among Children 19-35 Months of Age, by Geographic Division, State, and Selected Urban Area, 2002–2006—*Continued*

(Percent.)

Geographic division and area	2002	2003	2004	2005	2006
New England					
Boston, Massachusetts	71	86	79	—	81
Middle Atlantic					
New York City, New York	71	69	77	71	72
Newark, New Jersey	50	64	64	67	68
Philadelphia, Pennsylvania	68	75	75	77	74
East North Central					
Chicago, Illinois	58	71	71	70	77
Cuyahoga County (Cleveland), Ohio	65	66	78	77	77
Detroit, Michigan	60	64	66	71	65
Franklin County (Columbus), Ohio	69	71	79	81	—
Marion County (Indianapolis), Indiana	62	66	74	—	77
Milwaukee County (Milwaukee), Wisconsin	60	71	73	74	78
South Atlantic					
Baltimore, Maryland	69	74	80	77	72
Dade County (Miami), Florida	60	73	73	—	80
District of Columbia	68	72	80	72	78
Duval County (Jacksonville), Florida	70	75	69	77	76
Fulton/DeKalb Counties (Atlanta), Georgia	75	71	81	72	75
East South Central					
Davidson County (Nashville), Tennessee	67	76	88	81	—
Shelby County (Memphis), Tennessee	61	69	71	74	74
Jefferson County (Birmingham), Alabama	74	79	81	85	—
West South Central					
Bexar County (San Antonio), Texas	72	75	73	71	75
Dallas County (Dallas), Texas	68	67	67	73	74
El Paso County (El Paso), Texas	61	72	64	69	69
Houston, Texas	56	63	62	77	70
Orleans Parish (New Orleans), Louisiana	53	68	68	—	—
Mountain					
Maricopa County (Phoenix), Arizona	62	69	72	76	68
Pacific					
King County (Seattle), Washington	56	61	74	69	69
Los Angeles County (Los Angeles), California	72	79	77	78	79
San Diego County (San Diego), California	71	75	74	—	80
Santa Clara County (Santa Clara), California	75	77	80	—	78

— = Data not available.

NOTE: Urban areas were originally selected because they were at risk for undervaccination. Final estimates from the National Immunization Survey include an adjustment for children with missing immunization provider data.

Table C-40. Influenza Vaccination Among Adults 18 Years of Age and Over, by Selected Characteristics, Selected Years, 1989–2006

(Percent.)

Characteristic	Percent receiving influenza vaccination during past 12 months[1]								
	1989	1995	2000	2001	2002	2003	2004	2005	2006
18 years and over, age-adjusted[2,3]	9.6	23.7	28.7	26.7	28.3	29.2	29.5	21.3	27.3
18 years and over, crude[3]	9.1	23.0	28.4	26.4	28.0	29.0	29.4	21.2	27.4
Age									
18–49 years	3.4	13.1	17.1	15.0	16.2	16.8	17.9	10.4	15.4
50 years and over	19.9	43.0	47.9	45.7	47.7	48.9	47.9	38.0	45.9
50–64 years	10.6	27.0	34.6	32.2	34.0	36.8	35.9	22.9	33.2
65 years and over	30.4	58.2	64.4	63.1	65.7	65.5	64.6	59.6	64.2
65–74 years	28.0	54.9	61.1	60.7	60.9	60.5	60.1	53.7	60.1
75 years and over	34.2	63.0	68.4	65.8	71.3	71.0	69.7	66.3	69.0
50 YEARS AND OVER									
Sex									
Male	19.2	40.2	45.9	44.2	45.1	46.8	45.1	34.6	43.1
Female	20.6	43.4	49.5	46.9	49.8	50.7	50.2	40.8	48.2
Race[4]									
White only	21.0	43.8	49.8	47.7	49.4	50.4	49.8	39.6	47.1
Black or African American only	12.5	28.3	33.2	32.7	36.2	35.3	32.8	26.8	34.8
American Indian or Alaska Native only	26.2	*	43.6	41.5	*37.6	44.7	51.3	*22.9	56.3
Asian only	*9.2	35.6	43.3	35.4	39.5	45.9	41.7	30.6	44.6
Native Hawaiian or Other Pacific Islander only	—	—	*	*	*	*	*	*	*
2 or more races	—	—	50.7	41.5	47.9	53.7	44.5	29.9	40.2
Hispanic Origin and Race[4]									
Hispanic or Latino	13.2	33.8	34.4	32.5	33.7	33.6	36.9	24.4	31.7
Mexican	13.0	35.4	33.0	34.3	33.9	32.8	39.2	25.4	33.5
Not Hispanic or Latino	20.3	42.4	48.8	46.6	48.7	50.1	48.8	39.1	47.0
White only	21.3	44.4	50.6	48.6	50.3	51.8	50.9	41.0	48.6
Black or African American only	12.4	28.6	33.2	32.8	36.5	35.4	32.9	26.9	35.1
Percent of Poverty Level[5]									
Below 100%	19.6	39.7	44.1	38.8	41.9	41.8	42.5	35.8	42.1
100%–less than 200%	24.0	43.2	50.7	47.2	49.8	50.9	49.9	41.0	47.4
200% or more	19.0	41.9	47.6	46.1	47.9	49.4	48.1	37.4	45.9
Hispanic Origin and Race and Percent of Poverty Level[4,5]									
Hispanic or Latino									
Below 100%	12.7	29.7	35.8	33.0	36.6	31.9	36.3	22.3	30.9
100%–less than 200%	20.4	34.7	35.6	35.2	32.6	29.9	33.1	26.4	32.0
200% or more	11.9	35.5	33.1	30.6	33.2	36.6	39.2	24.0	31.9
Not Hispanic or Latino									
White only									
Below 100%	22.3	44.7	48.6	42.7	42.7	45.9	48.1	42.2	47.8
100%–less than 200%	26.1	46.7	54.8	51.0	54.2	55.9	55.0	46.1	51.5
200% or more	19.9	43.6	49.8	48.5	50.3	51.5	50.2	39.7	47.9
Black or African American only									
Below 100%	14.7	32.0	35.5	34.7	41.8	37.4	32.0	28.9	34.8
100%–less than 200%	12.2	28.4	37.9	35.3	39.4	40.9	36.8	27.4	35.0
200% or more	12.0	26.3	29.9	30.6	33.3	32.1	31.6	25.9	35.3
Geographic Region									
Northeast	17.9	39.7	45.9	45.4	47.2	50.5	47.9	38.3	44.0
Midwest	20.0	43.2	49.3	47.9	49.6	50.2	49.9	39.8	49.4
South	20.2	41.4	46.8	43.3	46.5	48.4	47.3	37.2	43.8
West	21.8	43.8	50.1	47.7	48.1	46.4	46.5	36.7	47.2
Location of Residence									
Within MSA[6]	18.9	41.6	47.1	45.0	47.1	48.8	47.6	37.1	44.9
Outside MSA[6]	23.3	42.9	50.2	47.8	49.7	49.3	48.9	40.9	49.6

* = Figure does not meet standards of reliability or precision.
—— = Data not available.

[1]Respondents were asked, During the past 12 months, have you had a flu shot? A flu shot is usually given in the fall and protects against influenza for the flu season. Estimates exclude 1% of respondents who reported receiving Flu Mist.

[2]Estimates are age-adjusted to the year 2000 standard population using four age groups: 18–49 years, 50–64 years, 65–74 years, and 75 years and over.

[3]Includes all other races not shown separately and unknown poverty level in 1989.

[4]The race groups, White, Black, American Indian or Alaska Native, Asian, Native Hawaiian or Other Pacific Islander, and 2 or more races, include persons of Hispanic and non-Hispanic origin. Persons of Hispanic origin may be of any race.

[5]Percent of poverty level is based on family income and family size and composition using U.S. Census Bureau poverty thresholds.

[6]MSA = metropolitan statistical area. Starting with 2006 data, MSA status is determined using 2000 census data and the 2000 standards for defining MSAs.

Table C-41. Pneumococcal Vaccination Among Adults 18 Years of Age and Over, by Selected Characteristics, Selected Years, 1989–2006

(Percent.)

Characteristic	Percent ever receiving pneumococcal vaccination[1]								
	1989	1995	2000	2001	2002	2003	2004	2005	2006
18 years and over, age-adjusted[2,3]	4.6	12.0	15.4	16.1	16.4	16.4	16.8	16.7	17.0
18 years and over, crude[3]	4.4	11.7	15.1	15.7	16.0	16.0	16.5	16.5	17.0
Age									
18–49 years	2.1	6.5	5.4	5.9	5.6	5.6	5.7	5.8	5.7
50–64 years	4.4	10.0	14.7	15.4	16.3	16.7	17.2	17.1	18.2
65 years and over	14.1	34.0	53.1	54.0	56.0	55.6	56.8	56.2	57.1
65–74 years	13.1	31.4	48.2	50.3	50.2	49.8	50.4	49.4	52.0
75 years and over	15.7	37.8	59.1	58.4	62.8	62.1	64.2	63.9	63.0
65 YEARS AND OVER									
Sex									
Male	13.9	34.6	52.1	54.2	55.9	53.7	54.3	53.4	54.3
Female	14.3	33.6	53.9	53.8	56.1	57.0	58.7	58.4	59.2
Race[4]									
White only	14.9	35.3	55.6	56.7	58.7	57.9	59.1	58.4	60.0
Black or African American only	6.5	21.9	30.6	33.9	37.0	36.9	38.6	40.2	35.5
American Indian or Alaska Native only	31.2	*	70.1	*50.7	*	*	*42.0	*	*57.5
Asian only	*	*23.4	40.9	28.1	32.6	35.3	35.1	35.0	35.6
Native Hawaiian or Other Pacific Islander only	—	—	*	*	*	*	*	*	*
2 or more races	—	—	55.6	54.0	52.8	*39.3	*48.8	64.8	63.6
Hispanic Origin and Race[4]									
Hispanic or Latino	9.8	23.2	30.4	32.9	27.1	31.0	33.7	27.5	33.3
Mexican	12.9	*18.8	32.0	33.8	30.0	33.6	33.3	31.3	29.3
Not Hispanic or Latino	14.3	34.5	54.4	55.2	57.7	57.1	58.3	58.1	58.7
White only	15.1	35.9	56.8	57.8	60.4	59.6	60.9	60.6	62.0
Black or African American only	6.2	21.8	30.6	34.0	37.0	36.9	38.6	40.4	35.6
Percent of Poverty Level[5]									
Below 100%	11.2	28.7	40.6	43.2	42.6	47.7	42.5	46.7	45.4
100%–less than 200%	15.1	30.7	51.4	51.0	54.6	56.7	56.1	54.5	55.8
200% or more	15.0	37.2	56.2	57.1	59.2	56.5	59.7	58.5	59.6
Hispanic Origin and Race and Percent of Poverty Level[4,5]									
Hispanic or Latino									
Below 100%	*	*14.1	23.8	25.0	20.1	23.8	31.8	20.9	24.5
100%–less than 200%	*11.0	*15.6	32.3	32.4	25.1	26.8	29.0	26.9	30.9
200% or more	*10.4	39.4	32.9	39.4	33.5	39.5	39.1	31.7	40.7
Not Hispanic or Latino									
White only									
Below 100%	13.4	32.6	47.9	53.4	51.5	57.5	50.6	55.6	56.0
100%–less than 200%	16.0	33.5	56.1	56.0	59.9	62.1	61.9	60.5	61.6
200% or more	15.6	37.8	58.3	59.0	61.8	58.9	61.9	61.3	62.8
Black or African American only									
Below 100%	*5.0	*22.6	28.8	30.5	27.8	35.1	27.0	42.3	38.4
100%–less than 200%	7.9	*21.0	28.1	31.3	40.7	39.6	36.4	36.6	36.2
200% or more	*5.2	*21.8	34.4	39.0	39.4	35.7	49.1	42.7	33.3
Geographic Region									
Northeast	10.4	28.2	51.2	52.5	56.9	54.8	56.0	55.8	53.7
Midwest	13.7	31.0	52.6	57.3	55.8	57.1	59.5	58.5	61.5
South	14.9	35.9	51.3	52.4	54.2	55.1	57.2	57.4	55.7
West	17.9	41.1	59.7	54.6	59.3	55.7	53.7	51.4	57.2
Location of Residence									
Within MSA[6]	13.1	33.8	52.4	53.3	56.3	56.0	56.7	55.1	56.6
Outside MSA[6]	17.1	34.8	55.4	56.4	55.3	54.3	57.3	59.8	58.9

* = Figure does not meet standards of reliability or precision.

— = Data not available.

[1]Respondents were asked, "Have you ever had a pneumonia shot?" This shot is usually given only once or twice in a person's lifetime and is different from the flu shot. It is also called the pneumococcal vaccine.

[2]Estimates are age-adjusted to the year 2000 standard population using four age groups: 18–49 years, 50–64 years, 65–74 years, and 75 years and over.

[3]Includes all other races not shown separately and unknown poverty level in 1989.

[4]The race groups, White, Black, American Indian or Alaska Native, Asian, Native Hawaiian or Other Pacific Islander, and 2 or more races, include persons of Hispanic and non-Hispanic origin. Persons of Hispanic origin may be of any race.

[5]Percent of poverty level is based on family income and family size and composition using U.S. Census Bureau poverty thresholds.

[6]MSA = metropolitan statistical area.

Table C-42. Use of Mammography Among Women 40 Years of Age and Over, by Selected Characteristics, Selected Years, 1987–2005

(Percent.)

Characteristic	1987	1990	1994	1998	2000	2003	2005
PERCENT OF WOMEN HAVING A MAMMOGRAM WITHIN THE PAST 2 YEARS[1]							
40 years and over, age-adjusted[2,3]	29.0	51.7	61.0	67.0	70.4	69.5	66.6
40 years and over, crude[2]	28.7	51.4	60.9	66.9	70.4	69.7	66.8
Age							
40–49 years	31.9	55.1	61.3	63.4	64.3	64.4	63.5
50–64 years	31.7	56.0	66.5	73.7	78.7	76.2	71.8
65 years and over	22.8	43.4	55.0	63.8	67.9	67.7	63.8
65–74 years	26.6	48.7	63.0	69.4	74.0	74.6	72.5
75 years and over	17.3	35.8	44.6	57.2	61.3	60.6	54.7
Race[4]							
40 years and over, crude							
White only	29.6	52.2	60.6	67.4	71.4	70.1	67.4
Black or African American only	24.0	46.4	64.3	66.0	67.8	70.4	64.9
American Indian or Alaska Native only	*	43.2	65.8	45.2	47.4	63.1	72.8
Asian only	*	46.0	55.8	60.2	53.5	57.6	54.6
Native Hawaiian or Other Pacific Islander only	—	—	—	—	*	*	*
2 or more races	—	—	—	—	69.2	65.3	63.7
Hispanic Origin and Race[4]							
40 years and over, crude							
Hispanic or Latino	18.3	45.2	51.9	60.2	61.2	65.0	58.8
Not Hispanic or Latino	29.4	51.8	61.5	67.5	71.1	70.1	67.5
White only	30.3	52.7	61.3	68.0	72.2	70.5	68.4
Black or African American only	23.8	46.0	64.4	66.0	67.9	70.5	65.2
Age, Hispanic Origin, and Race[4]							
40–49 years							
Hispanic or Latino	*15.3	45.1	47.5	55.2	54.1	59.4	54.2
Not Hispanic or Latino							
White only	34.3	57.0	62.0	64.4	67.2	65.2	65.5
Black or African American only	27.8	48.4	67.2	65.0	60.9	68.2	62.1
50–64 years							
Hispanic or Latino	23.0	47.5	60.1	67.2	66.5	69.4	61.5
Not Hispanic or Latino							
White only	33.6	58.1	67.5	75.3	80.6	77.2	73.5
Black or African American only	26.4	48.4	63.6	71.2	77.7	76.2	71.6
65 years and over							
Hispanic or Latino	*	41.1	48.0	59.0	68.3	69.5	63.8
Not Hispanic or Latino							
White only	24.0	43.8	54.9	64.3	68.3	68.1	64.7
Black or African American only	14.1	39.7	61.0	60.6	65.5	65.4	60.5
Age and Percent of Poverty Level[5]							
40 years and over, crude							
Below 100%	14.6	30.8	43.9	50.1	54.8	55.4	48.5
100%-less than 200%	20.9	39.1	49.3	56.1	58.1	60.8	55.3
200% or more	35.2	59.2	69.6	72.6	75.9	74.3	72.5
40–49 years							
Below 100%	18.6	32.2	44.3	44.8	47.4	50.6	42.5
100%-less than 200%	18.4	39.0	50.9	46.9	43.6	54.0	49.8
200% or more	36.8	60.1	67.4	68.4	69.9	68.3	69.0
50–64 years							
Below 100%	14.6	29.9	44.7	52.7	61.7	58.3	50.4
100%-less than 200%	24.2	39.8	50.3	61.8	68.3	64.0	58.8
200% or more	37.0	63.3	75.1	78.7	82.6	80.9	76.8
65 years and over							
Below 100%	13.1	30.8	43.2	51.9	54.8	57.0	52.3
100%-less than 200%	19.9	38.6	47.9	57.8	60.3	62.8	56.2
200% or more	29.7	51.5	64.9	70.1	75.0	72.6	70.1
Health Insurance Status at the Time of Interview[6]							
40–64 years							
Insured	—	—	68.3	72.3	76.0	75.1	72.6
Private	—	—	69.4	73.4	77.1	76.3	74.6
Medicaid	—	—	54.5	59.7	61.7	63.5	55.6
Uninsured	—	—	34.0	40.1	40.7	41.5	38.1

* = Figure does not meet standards of reliability or precision.
— = Data not available.
[1]Questions concerning use of mammography differed slightly on the National Health Interview Survey across the years for which data are shown.
[2]Includes all other races not shown separately, unknown poverty level in 1987, unknown health insurance status, and unknown education level.
[3]Estimates are age-adjusted to the year 2000 standard population using four age groups: 40–49 years, 50–64 years, 65–74 years, and 75 years and over.
[4]The race groups, White, Black, American Indian or Alaska Native, Asian, Native Hawaiian or Other Pacific Islander, and 2 or more races, include persons of Hispanic and non-Hispanic origin. Persons of Hispanic origin may be of any race.
[5]Percent of poverty level is based on family income and family size and composition using U.S. Census Bureau poverty thresholds.
[6]Health insurance categories are mutually exclusive. Persons who reported both Medicaid and private coverage are classified as having private coverage.

Table C-42. Use of Mammography Among Women 40 Years of Age and Over, by Selected Characteristics, Selected Years, 1987–2005—*Continued*

(Percent.)

Characteristic	1987	1990	1994	1998	2000	2003	2005
Health Insurance Status Prior to Interview[6]							
40–64 years							
Insured continuously all 12 months	—	—	68.6	73.0	76.8	75.6	73.1
Uninsured for any period up to 12 months	—	—	49.9	47.6	53.0	56.0	51.3
Uninsured more than 12 months	—	—	26.6	36.3	34.0	37.0	32.9
Age and Education[7]							
40 years and over, crude							
No high school diploma or GED	17.8	36.4	48.2	54.5	57.7	58.1	52.8
High school diploma or GED	31.3	52.7	61.0	66.7	69.7	67.8	64.9
Some college or more	37.7	62.8	69.7	72.8	76.2	75.1	72.7
40–49 years							
No high school diploma or GED	15.1	38.5	50.4	47.3	46.8	53.3	51.2
High school diploma or GED	32.6	53.1	55.8	59.1	59.0	60.8	58.8
Some college or more	39.2	62.3	68.7	68.3	70.6	68.1	68.3
50–64 years							
No high school diploma or GED	21.2	41.0	51.6	58.8	66.5	63.4	56.9
High school diploma or GED	33.8	56.5	67.8	73.3	76.6	71.8	70.1
Some college or more	40.5	68.0	74.7	79.8	84.2	82.7	77.0
65 years and over							
No high school diploma or GED	16.5	33.0	45.6	54.7	57.4	56.9	50.7
High school diploma or GED	25.9	47.5	59.1	66.8	71.8	69.7	64.3
Some college or more	32.3	56.7	64.3	71.3	74.1	75.1	73.0

— = Data not available.

[6]Health insurance categories are mutually exclusive. Persons who reported both Medicaid and private coverage are classified as having private coverage.

[7]Education categories shown are for 1998 and subsequent years. GED stands for General Educational Development high school equivalency diploma. In years prior to 1998 the following categories based on number of years of school completed were used: less than 12 years, 12 years, 13 years or more.

Table C-43. Use of Pap Smears Among Women 18 Years of Age and Over, by Selected Characteristics, Selected Years, 1987–2005

(Percent.)

Characteristic	1987	1994	1998	1999	2000	2003	2005
PERCENT OF WOMEN HAVING A PAP SMEAR WITHIN THE PAST 3 YEARS[1]							
18 years and over, age-adjusted[2,3]	74.1	76.8	79.3	80.8	81.3	79.2	77.9
18 years and over, crude[2]	74.4	76.8	79.1	80.8	81.2	79.0	77.8
Age							
18–44 years	83.3	82.8	84.4	86.8	84.9	83.9	83.6
18–24 years	74.8	76.6	73.6	76.8	73.5	75.1	74.5
25–44 years	86.3	84.6	87.6	89.9	88.5	86.8	86.8
45–64 years	70.5	77.4	81.4	81.7	84.6	81.3	80.6
45–54 years	75.7	81.9	83.7	83.8	86.3	83.6	83.4
55–64 years	65.2	71.0	78.0	78.4	82.0	77.8	76.8
65 years and over	50.8	57.3	59.8	61.0	64.5	60.8	54.9
65–74 years	57.9	64.9	67.0	70.0	71.6	70.1	66.3
75 years and over	40.4	47.3	51.2	50.8	56.7	51.1	42.8
Race[4]							
18 years and over, crude							
White only	74.1	76.2	78.9	80.6	81.3	78.7	77.7
Black or African American only	80.7	83.5	84.2	85.7	85.1	84.0	81.1
American Indian or Alaska Native only	85.4	73.5	74.6	92.2	76.8	84.8	75.2
Asian only	51.9	66.4	68.5	64.4	66.4	68.3	64.4
Native Hawaiian or Other Pacific Islander only	—	—	—	*	*	*	*
2 or more races	—	—	—	86.9	80.0	81.6	86.3
Hispanic Origin and Race[4]							
18 years and over, crude							
Hispanic or Latino	67.6	74.4	75.2	76.3	77.0	75.4	75.5
Not Hispanic or Latino	74.9	77.0	79.6	81.3	81.7	79.5	78.1
White only	74.7	76.5	79.3	81.0	81.8	79.3	78.1
Black or African American only	80.9	83.8	84.2	86.0	85.1	83.8	81.2
Age, Hispanic Origin, and Race[4]							
18–44 years							
Hispanic or Latino	73.9	80.6	76.4	77.0	78.1	75.9	76.5
Not Hispanic or Latino							
White only	84.5	82.9	85.7	88.7	86.6	85.8	85.8
Black or African American only	89.1	89.1	88.9	90.8	88.5	88.6	86.4
45–64 years							
Hispanic or Latino	57.7	70.1	78.3	79.5	77.8	77.9	78.4
Not Hispanic or Latino:							
White only	71.2	77.5	81.7	81.9	85.9	81.4	81.4
Black or African American only	76.2	82.2	84.1	84.6	85.7	84.7	80.5
65 years and over							
Hispanic or Latino	41.7	43.8	59.8	63.7	66.8	64.6	60.0
Not Hispanic or Latino							
White only	51.8	58.2	59.7	60.5	64.2	60.7	54.1
Black or African American only	44.8	59.5	61.7	64.5	67.2	59.6	60.2
Age and Percent of Poverty Level[5]							
18 years and over, crude							
Below 100%	64.3	70.5	69.8	73.6	72.0	70.5	68.7
100%–less than 200%	68.2	70.2	70.6	72.5	73.4	71.4	69.0
200% or more	80.0	82.9	83.5	84.3	85.0	83.0	82.1
18–44 years							
Below 100%	77.1	80.2	77.1	79.7	77.1	77.1	76.2
100%–less than 200%	80.4	79.3	79.2	84.0	79.4	79.5	78.1
200% or more	86.4	86.6	87.6	89.0	88.0	86.9	87.2
45–64 years							
Below 100%	53.6	65.7	67.6	73.1	73.6	66.0	65.9
100%–less than 200%	60.4	69.1	69.9	70.4	76.1	71.4	69.7
200% or more	74.9	82.8	85.1	84.6	87.4	85.1	84.4
65 years and over							
Below 100%	33.2	43.8	48.2	51.9	53.7	52.6	44.4
100%–less than 200%	50.4	50.4	55.1	54.7	61.0	55.4	49.6
200% or more	60.0	67.4	65.3	66.4	68.8	65.4	59.7
Health Insurance Status at the Time of Interview[6]							
18–64 years, crude							
Insured	—	83.8	86.0	87.2	87.8	86.4	85.6
Private	—	83.6	86.5	87.5	88.0	87.0	86.5
Medicaid	—	86.2	83.0	84.2	85.8	82.8	80.9
Uninsured	—	68.6	69.6	73.3	70.4	66.6	67.7

* = Figure does not meet standards of reliability or precision.

— = Data not available.

[1]Questions concerning use of Pap smears differed slightly on the National Health Interview Survey across the years for which data are shown.

[2]Includes all other races not shown separately, unknown poverty level in 1987, unknown health insurance status, and unknown education level.

[3]Estimates are age-adjusted to the year 2000 standard population using five age groups: 18–44 years, 45–54 years, 55–64 years, 65–74 years, and 75 years and over. Age-adjusted estimates in this table may differ from other age-adjusted estimates based on the same data and presented elsewhere if different age groups are used in the adjustment procedure.

[4]The race groups, White, Black, American Indian or Alaska Native, Asian, Native Hawaiian or Other Pacific Islander, and 2 or more races, include persons of Hispanic and non-Hispanic origin. Persons of Hispanic origin may be of any race.

[5]Percent of poverty level is based on family income and family size and composition using U.S. Census Bureau poverty thresholds.

[6]Health insurance categories are mutually exclusive. Persons who reported both Medicaid and private coverage are classified as having private coverage.

Table C-43. Use of Pap Smears Among Women 18 Years of Age and Over, by Selected Characteristics, Selected Years, 1987–2005—*Continued*

(Percent.)

Characteristic	1987	1994	1998	1999	2000	2003	2005
Health Insurance Status Prior to Interview[6]							
18–64 years, crude							
Insured continuously all 12 months...	—	83.7	86.3	87.3	88.0	86.6	85.8
Uninsured for any period up to 12 months.............................	—	83.4	81.7	83.5	83.7	81.8	81.3
Uninsured more than 12 months	—	63.6	64.0	68.8	65.1	60.2	62.0
Age and Education[7]							
25 years and over, crude							
No high school diploma or GED...	57.1	60.9	65.0	66.1	69.9	64.9	64.2
High school diploma or GED..	76.4	76.0	77.4	79.3	79.8	75.9	73.9
Some college or more..	84.0	85.2	86.9	87.8	88.0	86.2	84.6
25–44 years							
No high school diploma or GED	75.1	73.6	76.8	79.0	79.6	71.7	75.5
High school diploma or GED	85.6	82.4	83.9	87.6	86.2	84.3	83.1
Some college or more	90.1	89.1	91.5	93.0	91.4	90.8	90.5
45–64 years							
No high school diploma or GED	58.0	66.1	69.2	71.6	75.7	71.4	69.7
High school diploma or GED	72.3	75.9	81.0	79.8	81.8	77.6	79.1
Some college or more	80.1	84.7	85.5	85.7	89.1	86.2	84.2
65 years and over							
No high school diploma or GED	44.0	47.7	52.4	51.8	56.6	52.5	46.1
High school diploma or GED	55.4	61.2	60.7	63.7	66.9	61.2	52.5
Some college or more	59.4	66.5	67.9	68.8	69.8	67.8	63.8

— = Data not available.

[6]Health insurance categories are mutually exclusive. Persons who reported both Medicaid and private coverage are classified as having private coverage.

[7]Education categories shown are for 1998 and subsequent years. GED stands for General Educational Development high school equivalency diploma. In years prior to 1998 the following categories based on number of years of school completed were used: less than 12 years, 12 years, 13 years or more.

Table C-44. Percent of Adults 50 Years of Age and Over Who Have Ever Had a Colorectal Scope Procedure, by Selected Characteristics, Annual Average from 2000, 2003, and 2005

(Percent.)

Characteristic	Total	Insured	Uninsured
Age and Sex			
50 years and over	43.8	45.7	18.6
50–64 years of age	38.2	40.8	18.5
Male...	39.3	41.9	18.4
Female..	37.2	39.9	18.5
65 years and over	51.4	51.7	*
Race and Hispanic Origin[1]			
White, not Hispanic...	40.6	42.6	21.1
Black, not Hispanic	33.8	36.7	18.1
Hispanic...	25.3	30.5	12.9
Percent of Poverty Level			
Below 200%	29.2	34.3	16.9
200% or more	40.7	42.2	20.4
Education			
Less than high school	25.8	30.2	13.2
High school	34.8	37.4	17.5
More than high school	43.6	45.1	24.5

* = Figure does not meet standards of reliability or precision.

NOTE: Data are for the civilian noninstitutionalized population. Persons of Hispanic origin may be of any race. Respondents from the National Interview Survey were asked: "Have you ever had a sigmoidoscopy, colonoscopy, or proctoscopy?" These are exams in which a health care professional inserts a tube into the rectum to look for signs of cancer or other problems. Percent of poverty level is based on family income and family size and composition using U.S. Census Bureau poverty thresholds.

[1]Persons of Hispanic origin may be of any race.

Table C-45. Prescription Drug Use in the Past Month by Sex, Age, Race and Hispanic Origin, Selected Years, 1988–2002

(Percent.)

Sex and age	All persons[1]			White only[2]			Black or African American only[2]			Mexican[2,3]		
	1988–1994	1999–2000	1999–2002	1988–1994	1999–2000	1999–2002	1988–1994	1999–2000	1999–2002	1988–1994	1999–2000	1999–2002
PERCENT OF POPULATION WITH AT LEAST ONE PRESCRIPTION DRUG IN PAST MONTH												
Both Sexes, Age-Adjusted[4]	39.1	44.3	45.3	41.1	47.4	48.9	36.9	40.1	40.1	31.7	32.0	31.7
Male	32.7	38.8	39.9	34.2	41.7	43.1	31.1	34.1	35.4	27.5	26.6	25.8
Female	45.0	49.4	50.4	47.6	52.9	54.5	41.4	44.9	43.8	36.0	37.1	37.8
Both sexes, crude	37.8	43.0	45.1	41.4	48.2	50.9	31.2	34.6	36.0	24.0	24.1	23.7
Male	30.6	36.7	38.7	33.5	41.5	43.9	25.5	28.3	30.8	20.1	19.7	18.8
Female	44.6	49.2	51.2	48.9	54.8	57.6	36.2	40.2	40.6	28.1	28.8	28.9
Under 18 years	20.5	24.1	24.2	22.9	27.2	27.6	14.8	19.2	18.6	16.1	16.4	15.9
18–44 years	31.3	34.7	35.9	34.3	39.6	41.3	27.8	26.5	28.5	21.1	19.4	19.2
45–64 years	54.8	62.1	64.1	55.5	63.5	66.1	57.5	61.7	62.3	48.1	51.2	49.3
65 years and over	73.6	83.9	84.7	74.0	84.5	85.4	74.5	86.7	81.1	67.7	69.1	72.0
Male												
Under 18 years	20.4	25.8	26.2	22.3	29.5	30.6	15.5	20.4	19.8	16.3	17.2	16.2
18–44 years	21.5	25.4	27.1	23.5	29.4	31.2	21.1	17.9	21.5	14.9	13.7	13.0
45–64 years	47.2	53.6	55.6	48.1	55.0	57.4	48.2	50.6	54.0	43.8	40.2	36.4
65 years and over	67.2	81.1	80.1	67.4	81.6	81.0	64.4	83.1	78.1	61.3	62.3	66.8
Female												
Under 18 years	20.6	22.2	22.0	23.6	24.8	24.4	14.2	17.9	17.3	16.0	15.7	15.6
18–44 years	40.7	43.8	44.6	44.7	49.6	51.7	33.4	33.8	34.2	28.1	25.7	26.2
45–64 years	62.0	69.8	72.0	62.6	72.0	74.7	64.4	70.4	69.0	52.2	60.7	62.4
65 years and over	78.3	86.0	88.1	78.8	86.6	88.8	81.3	89.4	83.1	73.0	74.7	76.3
PERCENT OF POPULATION WITH THREE OR MORE PRESCRIPTION DRUGS IN PAST MONTH												
Both Sexes, Age-Adjusted[4]	11.8	16.5	17.7	12.4	17.4	18.9	12.6	16.2	16.5	9.0	10.4	11.2
Male	9.4	13.2	14.8	9.9	14.0	15.9	10.2	15.2	14.4	7.0	8.9	9.5
Female	13.9	19.4	20.4	14.6	20.7	21.7	14.3	17.1	18.0	11.0	11.7	12.9
Both sexes, crude	11.0	15.5	17.6	12.5	18.0	20.5	9.2	12.1	13.4	4.8	5.6	6.1
Male	8.3	11.8	13.9	9.5	13.9	16.4	7.0	10.4	10.9	3.4	4.5	4.8
Female	13.6	19.2	21.1	15.4	22.0	24.5	11.1	13.6	15.6	6.4	6.7	7.5
Under 18 years	2.4	3.7	4.1	3.2	4.1	4.9	1.5	*2.5	2.5	*1.2	2.0	2.1
18–44 years	5.7	7.5	8.4	6.1	9.4	10.1	5.4	*5.0	6.5	3.0	*	2.7
45–64 years	20.0	29.5	30.8	20.9	30.1	31.6	21.9	29.9	31.1	16.0	19.5	20.7
65 years and over	35.3	47.6	51.6	35.0	47.4	52.5	41.2	55.4	50.1	31.3	37.1	39.5
Male												
Under 18 years	2.6	3.1	4.3	3.3	*3.5	5.2	1.7	*	3.0	*	2.4	1.9
18–44 years	3.6	4.9	6.7	4.1	6.3	8.4	4.2	*	4.4	*1.8	*	*1.7
45–64 years	15.1	22.4	23.5	15.8	23.4	24.0	18.7	27.1	26.3	11.6	*17.4	18.2
65 years and over	31.3	43.9	46.0	30.9	43.0	47.0	31.7	56.6	48.2	27.6	31.5	34.2
Female												
Under 18 years	2.3	4.3	3.9	3.0	*4.8	4.7	*1.2	*	*2.0	*1.5	*1.6	2.2
18–44 years	7.6	10.1	10.2	8.5	12.4	11.9	6.4	*	8.3	4.3	*	4.0
45–64 years	24.7	35.9	37.4	25.8	36.9	39.1	24.3	32.0	35.0	20.3	21.3	23.3
65 years and over	38.2	50.3	55.7	38.0	50.6	56.6	47.7	54.5	51.3	34.5	41.6	44.0

* = Figure does not meet standards of reliability or precision.
[1]Includes persons of all races and Hispanic origins, not just those shown separately.
[2]Starting with data year 1999, race-specific estimates are tabulated according to the 1997 Revisions to the Standards for the Classification of Federal Data on Race and Ethnicity and are not strictly comparable with estimates for earlier years.
[3]Persons of Mexican origin may be of any race.
[4]Age-adjusted to the 2000 standard population using four age groups: Under 18 years, 18–44 years, 45–64 years, and 65 years and over. Age-adjusted estimates in this table may differ from other age-adjusted estimates based on the same data and presented elsewhere if different age groups are used in the adjustment procedure.

Table C-46. Selected Prescription and Nonprescription Drugs Recorded During Physician Office Visits and Hospital Outpatient Department Visits, by Sex and Age, 1995–1996 and 2004–2005

(Number per 100 population.)

Age group and National Drug Code (NDC) Directory therapeutic class[1] (common reasons for use)	Total		Male		Female	
	1995–1996	2004–2005	1995–1996	2004–2005	1995–1996	2004–2005
All Ages						
Drug visits with at least one drug per 100 population[2,3]	189.8	239.4	156.5	201.9	221.5	275.2
Number of Drugs per 100 Population[4]						
Total number of drugs[5]	400.3	684.2	321.1	568.4	475.6	795.0
Antidepressants (depression and related disorders)..............	13.8	35.5	9.1	22.8	18.2	47.7
Hypertension control drugs, not otherwise specified high blood pressure)	6.0	32.1	4.1	28.1	7.8	35.9
Hyperlipidemia (high cholesterol)................................	5.4	30.8	5.4	31.0	5.4	30.6
Antiasthmatics/bronchodilators (asthma, breathing)	13.1	29.0	11.7	25.6	14.4	32.1
NSAID[6] (pain relief)	19.9	28.8	16.0	24.4	23.7	33.1
Nonnarcotic analgesics (pain relief)..............................	14.4	28.7	13.0	27.3	15.7	30.0
Acid/peptic disorders (gastrointestinal reflux, ulcers)..........	12.0	25.1	9.8	20.8	14.1	29.2
Blood glucose/sugar regulators (diabetes)........................	9.5	24.0	8.6	24.4	10.4	23.6
Antihistamines (allergies)..	13.7	23.4	10.8	18.3	16.4	28.2
Vitamins/minerals (dietary supplements).........................	9.2	21.2	3.4	12.6	14.8	29.5
Beta blockers (high blood pressure, heart disease)...............	5.9	20.0	5.1	17.7	6.7	22.3
ACE inhibitors (high blood pressure, heart disease)	9.6	19.9	9.0	19.5	10.2	20.4
Narcotic analgesics (pain relief)................................	11.2	19.7	10.3	15.9	12.2	23.3
Diuretics (high blood pressure, heart disease).....................	10.2	19.5	7.8	15.5	12.6	23.3
Estrogens/progestins (menopause, hot flashes)....................	...	...	...	...	19.8	15.1
Under 18 Years						
Drug visits with at least one drug per 100 population[2,3]	153.9	178.2	152.3	183.2	155.6	173.0
Number of Drugs per 100 Population[4]						
Total number of drugs[5]	261.3	338.4	255.6	350.2	267.3	326.1
Antiasthmatics/bronchodilators (asthma, breathing)	13.4	29.1	14.8	34.2	11.9	23.7
Penicillins (bacterial infections)	37.2	27.5	36.4	29.4	38.0	25.5
Antihistamines (allergies)	17.5	25.1	16.7	23.7	18.4	26.5
Nonnarcotic analgesics (pain relief)..............................	12.1	15.5	10.4	15.7	13.9	15.3
NSAID[6] (pain relief)	7.4	14.6	6.9	15.6	7.9	13.5
Cephalosporins (bacterial infections)	18.1	11.3	18.8	11.6	17.3	10.9
Antitussives/expectorants (cough and cold, congestion)	11.8	11.1	11.0	10.2	12.7	11.9
Erythromycins/lincosamides (infections)	10.2	10.9	11.0	10.1	9.4	11.6
Adrenal corticosteroids (anti-inflammatory)	4.3	10.5	4.7	12.4	3.9	8.6
Nasal corticosteroid inhalants (asthma, breathing, allergies) ...	3.5	10.1	3.5	10.9	3.5	9.3
Nasal decongestants (congestion)	14.0	9.9	12.4	9.9	15.7	10.0
Anorexiants/CNS stimulants (attention deficit disorder, hyperactivity) ..	3.9	8.9	5.6	13.8	2.1	3.9
Antidepressants (depression and related disorders)..............	1.9	7.5	1.9	7.9	1.9	7.0
18–44 Years						
Drug visits with at least one drug per 100 population[2,3]	136.2	159.9	90.9	109.0	180.4	210.0
Number of Drugs per 100 Population[4]						
Total number of drugs[5]	251.0	356.1	168.8	244.7	331.2	466.1
Antidepressants (depression and related disorders)..............	14.0	29.3	9.3	17.8	18.5	40.5
NSAID[6] (pain relief)	16.7	19.3	14.5	16.5	18.8	22.1
Narcotic analgesics (pain relief)................................	11.7	17.7	10.8	14.3	12.7	21.0
Antihistamines (allergies)..	10.8	17.5	7.5	11.4	14.1	23.6
Vitamins/minerals (dietary supplements).........................	11.8	15.3	1.1	3.2	22.2	27.3
Antiasthmatics/bronchodilator (asthma, breathing)...............	6.9	14.0	3.3	8.7	10.3	19.3
Acid/peptic disorders (gastrointestinal reflux, ulcers)..........	6.6	11.6	5.3	8.3	7.9	14.9
Anticonvulsants (epilepsy, seizure and related disorders).......	4.5	10.6	3.8	8.0	5.1	13.3
Nonnarcotic analgesics (pain relief)..............................	6.0	8.7	4.5	6.7	7.4	10.7
Antitussives/expectorants (cough and cold, congestion)	7.7	8.1	5.8	5.9	9.5	10.3
Nasal corticosteroid inhalants (asthma, breathing, allergies) ...	4.7	8.1	3.3	6.2	6.1	9.9
Antianxiety agents (generalized anxiety and related disorders) ...	5.8	8.0	4.5	5.3	7.1	10.6
Erythromycins/lincosamides (infections)	7.5	7.9	5.4	6.2	9.5	9.6
Hypertension control drugs, not otherwise specified (high blood pressure) ..	1.5	7.9	1.0	7.9	2.0	7.8
Contraceptive agents (prevent pregnancy)..........................	...	...	...	...	13.4	20.6

... = Not applicable.

[1]The National Drug Code (NDC) Directory therapeutic class is a general therapeutic or pharmacological classification scheme for drug products reported to the Food and Drug Administration (FDA) under the provisions of the Drug Listing Act. Drugs are classified based on the NDC Directory classifications for 2005 data.

[2]Estimated number of drug visits during the 2-year period divided by the sum of population estimates for both years times 100.

[3]Drug visits are physician office and hospital outpatient department visits in which at least one prescription or nonprescription drug was recorded on the patient record form.

[4]Estimated number of drugs recorded during visits during the 2-year period divided by the sum of population estimates for both years times 100.

[5]Until 2002, up to six prescription and nonprescription medications were recorded on the patient record form. Starting with 2003 data, up to eight prescription and nonprescription medications are recorded on the patient record form. If 2004–2005 data were restricted to six instead of eight drugs, the 2004–2005 total drug rate for all ages would be 6.4% lower.

[6]NSAID is nonsteroidal anti-inflammatory drug. Aspirin was not included as an NSAID in this analysis.

Table C-46. Selected Prescription and Nonprescription Drugs Recorded During Physician Office Visits and Hospital Outpatient Department Visits, by Sex and Age, 1995–1996 and 2004–2005—Continued

(Number per 100 population.)

Age group and National Drug Code (NDC) Directory therapeutic class[1] (common reasons for use)	Total		Male		Female	
	1995–1996	2004–2005	1995–1996	2004–2005	1995–1996	2004–2005
45–64 Years						
Drug visits with at least one drug per 100 population[2,3]	222.4	290.3	185.0	249.6	257.4	328.6
Number of Drugs per 100 Population[4]						
Total number of drugs[5]	505.1	912.0	403.2	780.7	600.4	1,035.9
Antidepressants (depression and related disorders)	23.5	59.8	14.9	39.8	31.5	78.6
Hyperlipidemia (high cholesterol)	10.4	53.4	12.0	58.1	8.8	49.0
Hypertension control drugs, not otherwise specified (high blood pressure)	9.4	52.5	6.9	50.6	11.7	54.3
Blood glucose/sugar regulators (diabetes)	17.7	44.4	16.7	49.0	18.7	40.0
NSAID[6] (pain relief)	30.3	41.2	23.9	34.8	36.4	47.3
Acid/peptic disorders (gastrointestinal reflux, ulcers)	19.8	38.4	18.3	33.6	21.3	43.0
Nonnarcotic analgesics (pain relief)	16.3	35.7	15.6	37.3	17.0	34.3
Antiasthmatics/bronchodilators (asthma, breathing)	14.4	34.0	11.4	27.3	17.1	40.3
ACE inhibitors (high blood pressure, heart disease)	16.8	33.4	17.7	35.0	16.0	31.9
Narcotic analgesics (pain relief)	17.5	31.4	17.0	27.7	18.0	34.9
Beta blockers (high blood pressure, heart disease)	10.4	28.5	9.8	27.5	11.0	29.4
Antihistamines (allergies)	13.5	27.3	9.1	19.9	17.7	34.3
Diuretics (high blood pressure, heart disease)	13.6	26.5	11.2	22.3	15.8	30.4
Vitamins/minerals (dietary supplements)	6.4	23.3	4.0	19.0	8.6	27.3
Estrogens/progestins (menopause, hot flashes)	...	...	...	...	55.7	30.4
65 Years and Over						
Drug visits with at least one drug per 100 population[2,3]	399.4	515.3	378.1	481.1	414.7	540.5
Number of Drugs per 100 Population[4]						
Total number of drugs[5]	1,047.4	1,982.0	956.9	1,820.3	1,112.5	2,101.6
Hypertension control drugs, not otherwise specified (high blood pressure)	29.1	133.3	22.7	120.7	33.8	142.6
Hyperlipidemia (high cholesterol)	24.7	128.1	25.1	135.0	24.5	123.0
Nonnarcotic analgesics (pain relief)	44.9	104.7	49.0	109.3	42.0	101.3
Diuretics (high blood pressure, heart disease)	55.2	95.4	48.5	86.0	60.0	102.4
Beta blockers (high blood pressure, heart disease)	24.9	92.7	22.8	89.5	26.4	95.0
Blood glucose/sugar regulators (diabetes)	37.5	86.4	38.0	95.7	37.1	79.6
Acid/peptic disorders (gastrointestinal reflux, ulcers)	42.2	84.2	36.0	78.8	46.6	88.2
ACE inhibitors (high blood pressure, heart disease)	42.6	81.7	41.2	84.8	43.6	79.4
Vitamins/minerals (dietary supplements)	17.1	69.8	13.1	54.4	20.0	81.2
Calcium channel blockers (high blood pressure, heart disease)	57.3	69.5	52.2	64.0	60.9	73.5
Antiasthmatics/bronchodilators (asthma, breathing)	31.3	65.7	37.1	62.7	27.0	67.9
Antidepressants (depression and related disorders)	23.5	64.7	16.7	38.9	28.5	83.7
NSAID[6] (pain relief)	41.8	63.5	31.9	51.3	49.0	72.5
Anticoagulants/thrombolytics (blood thinning, reduce or prevent blood clots)	20.7	56.8	24.0	65.5	18.3	50.4
Estrogens/progestins (menopause, hot flashes)	...	...	...	...	37.1	28.6
65–74 Years						
Drug visits with at least one drug per 100 population[2,3]	362.8	470.5	323.0	435.7	394.9	499.7
Number of Drugs per 100 Population[4]						
Total number of drugs[5]	930.5	1,747.5	804.7	1,632.9	1,032.1	1,843.9
Hyperlipidemia (high cholesterol)	27.3	127.5	27.1	141.7	27.4	115.5
Hypertension control drugs, not otherwise specified (high blood pressure)	24.8	114.6	19.2	103.8	29.3	123.6
Blood glucose/sugar regulators (diabetes)	35.7	87.9	32.4	97.2	38.4	80.1
Nonnarcotic analgesics (pain relief)	38.0	86.0	40.5	93.7	35.9	79.5
Beta blockers (high blood pressure, heart disease)	23.5	78.8	20.4	79.2	26.0	78.4
Acid/peptic disorders (gastrointestinal reflux, ulcers)	38.7	78.0	30.6	73.0	45.2	82.3
ACE inhibitors (high blood pressure, heart disease)	37.1	71.5	35.6	77.9	38.3	66.1
Diuretics (high blood pressure, heart disease)	40.1	71.4	32.4	66.7	46.4	75.3
NSAID[6] (pain relief)	42.0	64.8	31.2	53.0	50.8	74.8
Antiasthmatics/bronchodilators (asthma, breathing)	31.1	63.8	33.0	58.7	29.5	68.1
Antidepressants (depression and related disorders)	22.7	62.9	14.2	40.0	29.6	82.1
Calcium channel blockers (high blood pressure, heart disease)	48.9	61.2	46.2	58.7	51.2	63.2
Vitamins/minerals (dietary supplements)	14.1	56.4	10.1	47.5	17.4	63.9
Anticoagulants/thrombolytics (blood thinning, reduce or prevent blood clots)	14.9	42.1	17.2	50.1	12.9	35.4
Estrogens/progestins (menopause, hot flashes)	...	...	...	...	47.5	37.6

... = Not applicable.

[1]The National Drug Code (NDC) Directory therapeutic class is a general therapeutic or pharmacological classification scheme for drug products reported to the Food and Drug Administration (FDA) under the provisions of the Drug Listing Act. Drugs are classified based on the NDC Directory classifications for 2005 data.

[2]Estimated number of drug visits during the 2-year period divided by the sum of population estimates for both years times 100.

[3]Drug visits are physician office and hospital outpatient department visits in which at least one prescription or nonprescription drug was recorded on the patient record form.

[4]Estimated number of drugs recorded during visits during the 2-year period divided by the sum of population estimates for both years times 100.

[5]Until 2002, up to six prescription and nonprescription medications were recorded on the patient record form. Starting with 2003 data, up to eight prescription and nonprescription medications are recorded on the patient record form. If 2004–2005 data were restricted to six instead of eight drugs, the 2004–2005 total drug rate for all ages would be 6.4% lower.

[6]NSAID is nonsteroidal anti-inflammatory drug. Aspirin was not included as an NSAID in this analysis.

Table C-46. Selected Prescription and Nonprescription Drugs Recorded During Physician Office Visits and Hospital Outpatient Department Visits, by Sex and Age, 1995–1996 and 2004–2005—*Continued*

(Number per 100 population.)

Age group and National Drug Code (NDC) Directory therapeutic class[1] (common reasons for use)	Total		Male		Female	
	1995–1996	2004–2005	1995–1996	2004–2005	1995–1996	2004–2005
75 years and Over						
Drug visits with at least one drug per 100 population[2,3]	449.2	564.7	466.3	539.8	438.7	580.6
Number of Drugs per 100 Population[4]						
Total number of drugs[5]	1,206.8	2,240.8	1,200.9	2,062.6	1,210.4	2,354.8
Hypertension control drugs, not otherwise specified (high blood pressure)	35.1	154.0	28.4	142.6	39.2	161.3
Hyperlipidemia (high cholesterol)...........................	21.3	128.7	21.8	126.2	21.0	130.4
Nonnarcotic analgesics (pain relief).......................	54.4	125.4	62.6	129.4	49.4	122.8
Diuretics (high blood pressure, heart disease)	75.8	122.0	74.5	111.1	76.6	129.0
Beta blockers (high blood pressure, heart disease)...............	26.8	108.0	26.5	102.9	26.9	111.2
ACE inhibitors (high blood pressure, heart disease)	50.2	93.0	50.2	93.7	50.1	92.5
Acid/peptic disorders (gastrointestinal reflux, ulcers)............	47.0	91.1	44.7	86.4	48.3	94.1
Blood glucose/sugar regulators (diabetes)...........................	39.8	84.8	46.9	93.7	35.5	79.1
Vitamins/minerals (dietary supplements)............................	21.2	84.6	18.0	63.3	23.2	98.2
Calcium channel blockers (high blood pressure, heart disease)..	68.6	78.6	61.8	70.7	72.7	83.6
Anticoagulants/thrombolytics (blood thinning, reduce or prevent blood clots)	28.6	73.1	34.9	85.4	24.7	65.2
Antiasthmatics/bronchodilators (asthma, breathing)	31.5	67.7	43.7	67.8	24.0	67.7
Antidepressants (depression and related disorders)...............	24.6	66.6	20.7	37.5	27.0	85.3
NSAID[6] (pain relief)	41.5	62.0	33.1	49.1	46.7	70.2
Thyroid/antithyroid (hyper- and hypothyroidism)..................	27.1	61.0	15.1	36.3	34.4	76.7

[1]The National Drug Code (NDC) Directory therapeutic class is a general therapeutic or pharmacological classification scheme for drug products reported to the Food and Drug Administration (FDA) under the provisions of the Drug Listing Act. Drugs are classified based on the NDC Directory classifications for 2005 data.

[2]Estimated number of drug visits during the 2-year period divided by the sum of population estimates for both years times 100.

[3]Drug visits are physician office and hospital outpatient department visits in which at least one prescription or nonprescription drug was recorded on the patient record form.

[4]Estimated number of drugs recorded during visits during the 2-year period divided by the sum of population estimates for both years times 100.

[5]Until 2002, up to six prescription and nonprescription medications were recorded on the patient record form. Starting with 2003 data, up to eight prescription and nonprescription medications are recorded on the patient record form. If 2004–2005 data were restricted to six instead of eight drugs, the 2004–2005 total drug rate for all ages would be 6.4% lower.

[6]NSAID is nonsteroidal anti-inflammatory drug. Aspirin was not included as an NSAID in this analysis.

Table C-47. Adults 18 Years of Age and Over Reporting Antidepressant Drug Use in the Past Month by Sex and Race and Hispanic Origin, 1988–1994 and 1999–2002

(Percent.)

Sex, race and ethnicity	1988–1994	1999–2002
Total, Age-Adjusted..	2.5	8.0
White only, not Hispanic..	2.7	9.5
Black only, not Hispanic..	2.0	4.1
Mexican[1]..	1.5	3.1
Total, Crude..	2.4	8.1
White only, not Hispanic..	2.7	9.6
Black only, not Hispanic..	1.7	3.8
Mexican[1]..	1.3	2.3
Men, Age-Adjusted..	1.6	5.2
White only, not Hispanic..	1.7	6.1
Black only, not Hispanic..	*1.0	3.0
Mexican[1]..	0.8	*1.8
Men, Crude..	1.5	5.2
White only, not Hispanic..	1.7	6.2
Black only, not Hispanic..	*0.9	2.7
Mexican[1]..	*0.7	*
Women, Age-Adjusted..	3.3	10.6
White only, not Hispanic..	3.6	12.8
Black only, not Hispanic..	2.8	4.9
Mexican[1]..	2.2	4.5
Women, Crude..	3.2	10.7
White only, not Hispanic..	3.5	12.9
Black only, not Hispanic..	2.4	4.7
Mexican[1]..	1.8	*3.6

* = Figure does not meet standards of reliability or precision.
[1]Persons of Mexican origin may be of any race.

NOTE: Data are for the civilian noninstitutionalized population. Totals include persons of all races and Hispanic origins, not just those shown separately. Age-adjusted estimates were adjusted to the 2000 standard population using three age groups: 18–44 years, 45–64 years, and 65 years and over. Antidepressant drugs include: amitriptyline, amoxapine, bupropion, citalopram, clomipramine, desipramine, doxepin, escitalopram, fluoxetine, fluvoxamine, imipramine, isocarboxazid, maprotiline, mirtazapine, nefazodone, nortriptyline, paroxetine, phenelzine, protriptyline, sertraline, tranylcypromine, trazodone, trimipramine, venlafaxine.

Table C-48. Dental Visits in the Past Year, According to Selected Characteristics, Selected Years, 1997–2006

(Percent.)

Characteristic	2 years and over				2–17 years				18–64 years				65 years and over[1]			
	1997	2000	2003	2006	1997	2000	2003	2006	1997	2000	2003	2006	1997	2000	2003	2006
PERCENT OF PERSONS WITH A DENTAL VISIT IN THE PAST YEAR[2]																
2 years and over[3]	65.1	66.2	66.4	64.9	72.7	74.1	75.0	75.7	64.1	65.1	64.8	62.4	54.8	56.6	58.0	58.0
Sex																
Male	62.9	63.5	63.9	61.5	72.3	73.7	74.1	75.0	60.4	60.7	60.9	57.5	55.4	56.1	58.4	55.3
Female	67.1	68.8	68.8	68.2	73.0	74.6	75.9	76.5	67.7	69.4	68.6	67.1	54.4	56.9	57.7	60.0
Race[4]																
White only	66.4	67.9	67.4	65.7	74.0	75.8	76.0	76.4	65.7	67.2	65.9	63.3	56.8	58.4	59.8	59.5
Black or African American only	58.9	59.5	60.2	59.0	68.8	70.0	70.5	72.4	57.0	57.1	58.1	55.6	35.4	38.2	38.7	40.7
American Indian or Alaska Native only	55.1	58.6	62.0	55.4	66.8	71.3	69.9	72.0	49.9	55.0	58.0	51.0	*	*	*49.2	*
Asian only	62.5	67.1	65.2	69.8	69.9	72.8	72.9	75.5	60.3	65.6	63.6	68.7	53.9	60.6	57.4	66.0
Native Hawaiian or Other Pacific Islander only	—	*	*	*	—	*	*	*	—	*	*	*	—	*	*	*
2 or more races	—	65.1	66.1	65.8	—	71.4	74.5	78.1	—	60.5	59.6	54.9	—	57.4	51.0	62.9
Black or African American; White	—	63.5	69.0	72.3	—	65.7	71.3	79.5	—	60.7	60.3	59.5	—	*	*80.7	*
American Indian or Alaska Native; White	—	61.7	51.5	55.7	—	63.4	52.8	69.6	—	61.6	53.7	48.5	—	*57.8	*	62.9
Race and Hispanic Origin[4]																
Hispanic or Latino	54.0	52.3	53.3	53.0	61.0	60.6	64.5	66.3	50.8	48.6	48.3	47.2	47.8	44.5	46.0	44.2
Not Hispanic or Latino	66.4	68.2	68.5	66.9	74.7	76.8	77.3	78.1	65.7	67.5	67.4	64.9	55.2	57.2	58.7	58.9
White only	68.0	69.9	70.1	68.2	76.4	78.9	79.4	79.6	67.5	69.4	69.3	66.5	57.2	59.1	60.9	60.6
Black or African American only	58.8	59.4	60.2	59.0	68.8	70.0	70.6	72.4	56.9	57.2	58.3	55.5	35.3	38.0	38.3	40.9
Percent of Poverty Level[5]																
Below 100%	50.5	50.4	50.4	51.5	62.0	62.4	65.8	67.5	46.9	46.8	44.5	44.8	31.5	33.3	37.1	36.9
100%–less than 200%	50.8	52.2	52.9	52.0	62.5	66.1	66.6	68.4	48.3	48.4	49.1	46.8	40.8	43.0	43.6	44.5
200% or more	72.5	73.0	73.4	71.7	80.1	80.2	80.8	81.5	71.2	71.7	72.0	69.6	65.9	67.0	67.8	67.3
Hispanic Origin and Race and Percent of Poverty Level[4,5]																
Hispanic or Latino																
Below 100%	45.7	43.4	45.6	46.6	55.9	54.2	62.1	63.1	39.2	36.8	35.5	36.7	33.6	31.3	33.2	29.7
100%–less than 200%	47.2	45.5	46.7	47.5	53.8	56.9	59.1	62.2	43.5	39.2	40.8	40.7	47.9	42.9	39.4	36.5
200% or more	65.1	61.9	62.6	60.5	73.7	69.5	71.6	72.9	62.3	59.5	59.4	56.1	58.8	54.2	60.7	59.5
Not Hispanic or Latino																
White only																
Below 100%	51.7	53.6	53.2	55.1	64.4	65.0	69.1	71.6	50.6	53.3	50.4	50.6	32.0	37.2	39.9	41.4
100%–less than 200%	52.4	53.8	55.0	53.2	66.1	69.7	69.6	71.5	50.4	51.7	52.8	48.6	42.2	43.4	45.9	46.7
200% or more	73.8	75.0	75.3	73.4	81.3	82.8	83.2	83.3	72.7	73.8	74.2	71.7	67.0	68.6	69.1	68.1
Black or African American only																
Below 100%	52.8	51.8	49.6	49.3	66.1	67.1	66.7	67.1	46.2	44.4	40.8	39.9	27.7	21.7	27.6	27.8
100%–less than 200%	48.7	52.4	54.1	52.8	61.2	67.3	69.1	70.1	46.3	48.0	50.6	48.7	26.9	35.2	29.3	28.6
200% or more	67.7	66.6	67.9	67.7	77.1	74.1	74.5	79.2	66.1	65.2	67.2	65.1	49.8	52.9	51.9	58.3
Geographic Region																
Northeast	69.6	72.3	72.2	72.0	77.5	81.1	81.5	82.6	69.6	72.1	71.4	70.7	55.5	58.1	61.1	57.6
Midwest	68.4	69.9	68.8	67.0	76.4	77.2	77.6	78.2	67.4	69.2	67.6	64.5	57.6	58.6	58.8	59.9
South	60.2	61.0	61.5	60.4	68.0	69.5	70.7	72.6	59.4	59.8	59.6	57.4	49.0	50.8	53.3	54.1
West	65.0	65.3	66.8	64.6	71.5	72.0	74.1	72.6	62.9	63.0	64.7	62.0	61.9	63.1	62.8	63.1
Location of Residence																
Within MSA[6]	66.7	67.5	68.0	66.5	73.6	74.3	75.5	76.3	65.7	66.5	66.5	63.9	57.6	58.9	61.3	61.1
Outside MSA[6]	59.1	61.2	59.9	57.6	69.3	73.3	72.9	73.0	58.0	59.7	57.9	54.7	46.1	49.3	46.7	46.8

* = Figure does not meet standards of reliability or precision.

—— = Data not available.

[1]Based on the 1997–2006 National Health Interview Surveys, about 25%-30% of persons 65 years and over were edentulous (having lost all their natural teeth). In 1997–2006 about 68%–70% of older dentate persons compared with 16%-21% of older edentate persons had a dental visit in the past year.

[2]Respondents were asked, "About how long has it been since you last saw or talked to a dentist?"

[3]Includes all other races not shown separately.

[4]The race groups, White, Black, American Indian or Alaska Native, Asian, Native Hawaiian or Other Pacific Islander, and 2 or more races, include persons of Hispanic and non-Hispanic origin. Persons of Hispanic origin may be of any race.

[5]Percent of poverty level is based on family income and family size and composition using U.S. Census Bureau poverty thresholds.

[6]MSA = metropolitan statistical area. Starting with 2006 data, MSA status is determined using 2000 census data and the 2000 standards for defining MSAs.

Table C-49. Untreated Dental Caries (Cavities), by Age, Sex, Race and Hispanic Origin, and Poverty Level, Selected Annual Averages, 1971–2004

(Percent.)

Sex, race, Hispanic origin, and poverty level	2–5 years			6–19 years		
	1971–1974	1988–1994	2001–2004	1971–1974	1988–1994	2001–2004
Percent of Persons with Untreated Dental Caries						
Total[1]	25.0	19.1	19.5	54.7	23.6	22.9
Sex						
Male	26.4	19.3	20.0	54.9	22.8	23.8
Female	23.6	18.9	19.1	54.5	24.5	21.8
Race and Hispanic Origin[2]						
Not Hispanic or Latino						
White only	23.7	13.8	14.5	51.6	18.8	19.4
Black or African American only.	29.0	24.7	24.2	71.0	33.7	28.0
Mexican	—	34.9	.29.2	—	36.5	30.6
Percent of Poverty Level[3]						
Below 100%	32.0	30.2	26.1	68.0	38.3	31.5
100%–less than 200%	29.9	24.3	25.4	60.3	28.2	32.6
200% or more	17.8	9.4	12.1	46.2	15.1	14.7
Race, Hispanic Origin, and Poverty Level[2,3]						
Not Hispanic or Latino						
White only						
Below 100% of poverty level	32.1	25.7	19.6	65.9	33.5	29.3
100% or more of poverty level	22.0	11.7	13.8	49.9	16.7	17.6
Black or African American only						
Below 100% of poverty level	29.1	27.2	26.2	73.9	37.0	33.5
100% or more of poverty level	27.9	22.5	21.8	67.3	31.0	24.1
Mexican						
Below 100% of poverty level	—	38.8	35.0	—	46.4	35.9
100% or more of poverty level	—	30.3	25.1	—	26.4	27.1

Sex, race and Hispanic origin, and poverty level	20–64 years			65–74 years		
	1971–1974	1988–1994	2001–2004	1971–1974	1988–1994	2001–2004
Percent of Persons with Untreated Dental Caries						
Total[1]	48.0	28.3	25.7	29.7	25.4	16.6
Sex						
Male	50.5	31.5	28.6	32.6	29.8	16.5
Female	45.6	25.3	22.8	27.4	21.5	16.8
Race and Hispanic Origin[2]						
Not Hispanic or Latino						
White only	45.3	23.9	20.7	28.3	22.7	13.5
Black or African American only	67.3	48.5	40.7	41.5	46.7	42.2
Mexican	—	40.2	38.4	—	43.8	39.8
Percent of Poverty Level[3]						
Below 100%	63.5	48.1	44.2	34.3	46.6	44.9
100%–less than 200%	56.2	43.5	38.9	35.6	40.1	26.0
200% or more	42.7	19.6	18.2	26.2	19.2	12.1
Race, Hispanic Origin, and Poverty Level[2,3]						
Not Hispanic or Latino						
White only						
Below 100% of poverty level	60.2	43.7	40.7	33.3	*39.0	*37.6
100% or more of poverty level	44.2	21.8	18.4	28.3	22.7	13.4
Black or African American only						
Below 100% of poverty level	71.9	60.4	54.4	39.8	49.7	52.8
100% or more of poverty level	65.3	43.9	36.1	41.1	43.8	41.6
Mexican						
Below 100% of poverty level	—	52.7	47.9	—	55.5	59.2
100% or more of poverty level	—	31.8	34.4	—	35.6	33.3

* = Figure does not meet standards of reliability or precision.
—— = Data not available.
[1]Includes persons of all races and Hispanic origins, not just those shown separately, and those with unknown poverty level.
[2]Persons of Hispanic origin may be of any race.
[3]Poverty level is based on family income and family size. Persons with unknown poverty level are excluded (4% in 1971–1974, 6% in 1988–1994, and 5% in 2001–2004).

Table C-49. Untreated Dental Caries (Cavities), by Age, Sex, Race and Hispanic Origin, and Poverty Level, Selected Annual Averages, 1971–2004—*Continued*

(Percent.)

Sex, race and Hispanic origin, and poverty level	75 years and over		
	1971–1974	1988–1994	2001–2004
Percent of Persons with Untreated Dental Caries			
Total[1]	—	30.3	19.4
Sex			
Male	—	34.4	21.2
Female	—	28.1	18.2
Race and Hispanic Origin[2]			
Not Hispanic or Latino			
White only	—	27.8	17.9
Black or African American only	—	62.6	*35.2
Mexican	—	55.6	44.2
Percent of Poverty Level[3]			
Below 100%	—	47.1	31.6
100%–less than 200%	—	34.5	21.8
200% or more	—	23.2	16.4
Race, Hispanic Origin, and Poverty Level[2, 3]			
Not Hispanic or Latino			
White only			
Below 100% of poverty level	—	38.0	*32.7
100% or more of poverty level	—	26.1	16.7
Black or African American only			
Below 100% of poverty level	—	68.6	*52.2
100% or more of poverty level	—	60.2	*30.5
Mexican			
Below 100% of poverty level	—	79.4	52.9
100% or more of poverty level	—	*	42.3

* = Figure does not meet standards of reliability or precision.

—— = Data not available.

[1]Includes persons of all races and Hispanic origins, not just those shown separately, and those with unknown poverty level.

[2]Persons of Hispanic origin may be of any race.

[3]Poverty level is based on family income and family size. Persons with unknown poverty level are excluded (4% in 1971–1974, 6% in 1988–1994, and 5% in 2001–2004).

NOTE: Excludes edentulous persons (persons without teeth) of all ages. The majority of edentulous persons are 65 years of age and over. Estimates of edentulism among persons 65 years of age and over are 46% in 1971–1974, 33% in 1988–1994, and 26% in 2001–2004.

INPATIENT CARE

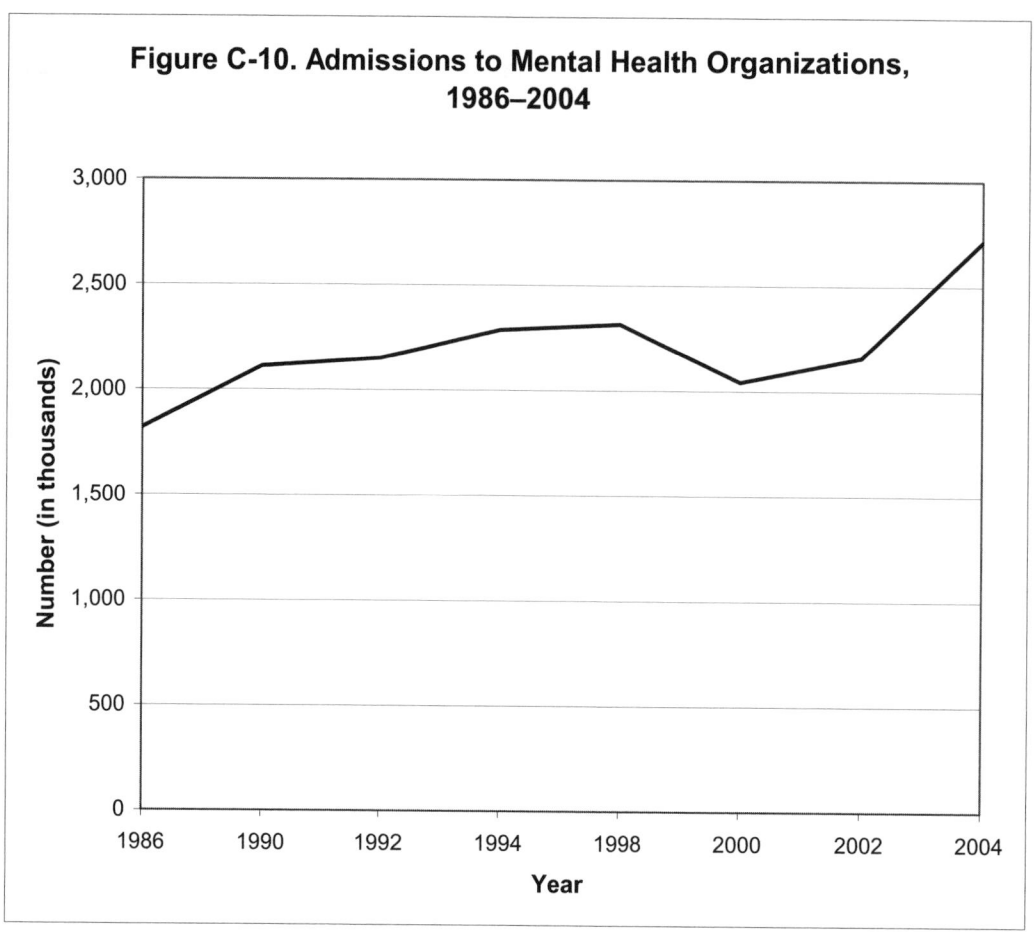

Figure C-10. Admissions to Mental Health Organizations, 1986–2004

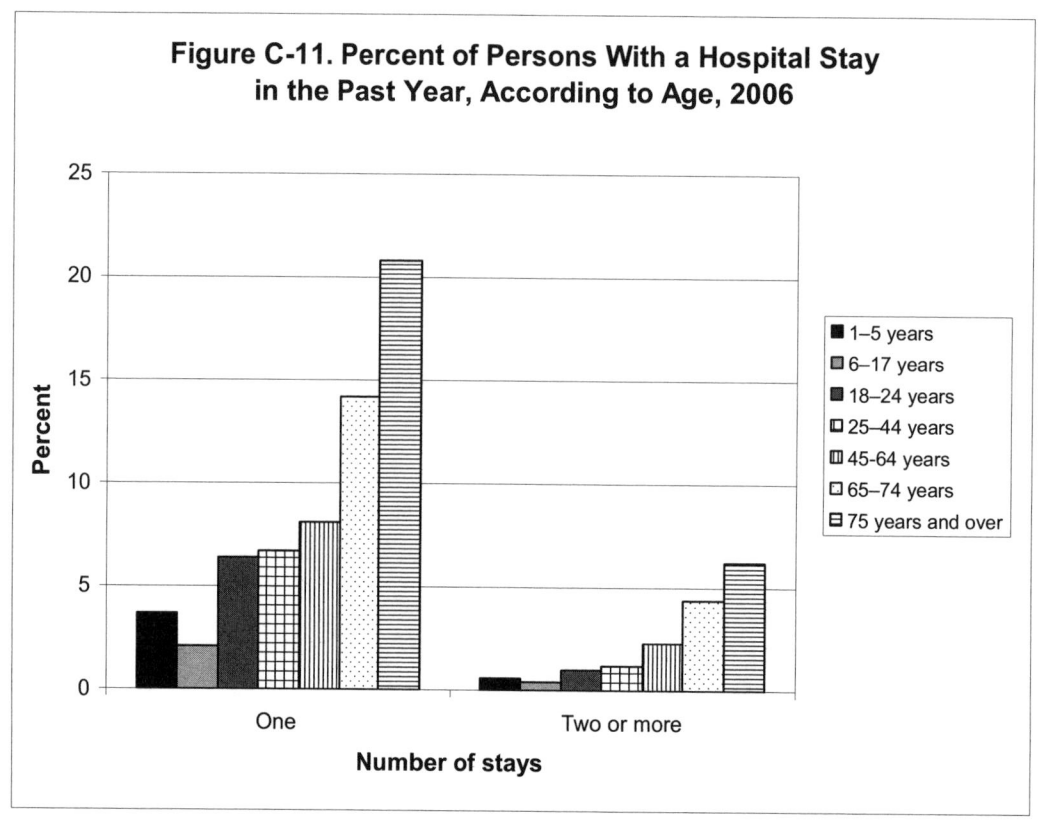

Figure C-11. Percent of Persons With a Hospital Stay in the Past Year, According to Age, 2006

Table C-50. Admissions to Mental Health Organizations, by Type of Service and Organization, Selected Years, 1986–2004

(Number in thousands, number per 100,000 civilian population.)

Service and organization	Admissions in thousands[1]					Admissions per 100,000 civilian population[2]				
	1986	1990	2000	2002	2004	1986	1990	2000	2002	2004
24-Hour Hospital and Residential Care										
All organizations	1,819	2,110	2,044	2,158	2,713	759.9	833.0	713.8	738.9	910.5
State and county mental hospitals	333	283	240	234	266	139.1	111.6	83.7	80.1	89.1
Private psychiatric hospitals	235	411	462	477	599	98.0	162.4	161.3	163.3	200.9
Nonfederal general hospital psychiatric services[3]	849	962	1,000	1,087	1,533	354.8	379.9	349.4	372.2	514.6
Department of Veterans Affairs medical centers[4]	180	203	165	158	—	75.1	80.3	57.5	54.1	—
Residential treatment centers for emotionally disturbed children	25	50	45	63	61	10.2	19.8	15.9	21.6	20.3
All other organizations[5]	198	200	132	139	255	82.7	79.0	46.0	47.6	85.5
Less than 24-Hour Care[6]										
All organizations	2,955	3,377	4,121	4,099	4,667	1,233.4	1,333.3	1,439.1	1,403.2	1,566.6
State and county mental hospitals	68	50	52	62	130	28.4	19.7	18.1	21.2	43.6
Private psychiatric hospitals	132	163	269	598	447	55.2	64.5	93.9	204.7	150.1
Nonfederal general hospital psychiatric services	533	661	1,144	681	900	222.4	260.8	399.7	233.0	302.2
Department of Veterans Affairs medical centers[4]	133	235	139	99	—	55.3	92.8	48.6	33.9	—
Residential treatment centers for emotionally disturbed children	67	100	202	222	194	28.1	39.3	70.7	75.8	65.2
All other organizations[5]	2,022	2,168	2,315	2,438	2,995	844.0	856.2	808.2	834.3	1,005.4

— = Data not available.

[1]Admissions sometimes are referred to as additions.

[2]Civilian population estimates for 2000 and beyond are based on the 2000 census as of July 1; population estimates for 1992–1998 are 1990 postcensal estimates.

[3]These data exclude mental health care provided in nonpsychiatric units of hospitals such as general medical units.

[4]Department of Veterans Affairs Medical Centers (VA general hospital psychiatric services and VA psychiatric outpatient clinics) were dropped from the survey as of 2004.

[5]Includes freestanding psychiatric outpatient clinics, partial care organizations, and multiservice mental health organizations.

[6]Formerly reported as partial care and outpatient treatment, the survey format was changed in 1994 and the reporting of these services was combined due to similarities in the care provided. These data exclude private office-based mental health care.

Table C-51. Mental Health Organizations and Beds for 24-Hour Hospital and Residential Treatment, by Type of Organization, Selected Years, 1986–2004

(Number, number per 100,000 civilian population.)

Type of organization	1986	1990	1994	1998	2000	2002	2004
Number of Mental Health Organizations							
All organizations..	3,512	3,942	3,853	3,741	3,211	3,044	2,891
State and county mental hospitals...	285	278	270	237	229	227	237
Private psychiatric hospitals..	314	464	432	347	271	255	264
Nonfederal general hospital psychiatric							
services..	1,351	1,577	1,539	1,595	1,325	1,231	1,230
Department of Veterans Affairs							
medical centers[1]...	139	131	136	124	134	132	——
Residential treatment centers for emotionally							
disturbed children..	437	501	472	462	476	510	458
All other organizations[2]	986	991	1,004	976	776	689	702
Number of Beds							
All organizations..	267,613	325,529	293,139	269,148	214,186	211,040	212,231
State and county mental hospitals...	119,033	102,307	84,063	71,266	61,833	57,314	57,034
Private psychiatric hospitals..	30,201	45,952	42,742	31,731	26,402	24,996	28,422
Nonfederal general hospital psychiatric							
services..	45,808	53,576	53,455	54,775	40,410	40,520	41,403
Department of Veterans Affairs							
medical centers[1]...	26,874	24,779	21,346	17,173	8,989	9,581	——
Residential treatment centers for emotionally							
disturbed children..	24,547	35,170	32,691	32,040	33,508	39,407	33,835
All other organizations[2]	21,150	63,745	58,842	62,163	43,044	39,222	51,536
Beds per 100,000 Civilian Population[3]							
All organizations..	111.7	128.5	110.9	94.0	74.8	72.2	71.2
State and county mental hospitals...	49.7	40.4	31.8	24.9	21.6	19.6	19.1
Private psychiatric hospitals..	12.6	18.1	16.2	11.1	9.2	8.6	9.5
Nonfederal general hospital psychiatric							
services..	19.1	21.2	20.2	19.1	14.1	13.9	13.9
Department of Veterans Affairs							
medical centers[1]...	11.2	9.9	8.1	6.0	3.1	3.3	——
Residential treatment centers for emotionally							
disturbed children..	10.3	13.9	12.4	11.2	11.7	13.5	11.4
All other organizations[2]	8.8	25.2	22.2	21.7	15.0	13.4	17.3

—— = Data not available.

[1]Department of Veterans Affairs Medical Centers (VA general hospital psychiatric services and VA psychiatric outpatient clinics) were dropped from the survey as of 2004.

[2]Includes freestanding psychiatric outpatient clinics, partial care organizations, and multiservice mental health organizations.

[3]Civilian population estimates for 2000 and beyond are based on the 2000 census as of July 1; population estimates for 1992–1998 are 1990 postcensal estimates.

Table C-52. Persons with a Hospital Stay in the Past Year, by Selected Characteristics, Selected Years, 1997–2006

(Percent.)

Characteristic	One or more hospital stays[1]				Two or more hospital stays[1]			
	1997	2000	2003	2006	1997	2000	2003	2006
1 year and over, age-adjusted[2,3]	7.8	7.6	7.7	7.3	1.8	1.8	1.8	1.8
1 year and over, crude[2]	7.7	7.5	7.7	7.3	1.7	1.8	1.8	1.8
Age								
1–17 years	2.8	2.5	2.5	2.6	0.5	0.4	0.4	0.4
1–5 years	3.9	3.8	3.7	3.7	0.7	0.7	0.7	0.6
6–17 years	2.3	1.9	2.0	2.1	0.4	0.3	0.3	0.4
18–44 years	7.4	7.0	7.1	6.6	1.2	1.1	1.1	1.2
18–24 years	7.9	7.0	7.2	6.4	1.3	1.1	1.1	1.0
25–44 years	7.3	7.0	7.1	6.7	1.2	1.2	1.1	1.2
45–64 years	8.2	8.4	8.7	8.1	2.2	2.2	2.4	2.3
45–54 years	6.9	7.3	7.4	6.8	1.7	1.8	1.9	1.9
55–64 years	10.2	10.0	10.6	9.8	2.9	2.8	3.2	2.9
65 years and over	18.0	18.2	18.2	17.3	5.4	5.8	5.6	5.3
65–74 years	16.1	16.1	15.2	14.2	4.8	4.9	4.5	4.4
75 years and over	20.4	20.7	21.6	20.8	6.2	6.8	6.9	6.2
1–64 YEARS								
Total, 1-64 years[2,4]	6.3	6.1	6.2	5.8	1.3	1.2	1.2	1.2
Sex								
Male	4.5	4.2	4.4	4.2	1.0	1.0	1.0	1.0
1–17 years	2.9	2.4	2.5	2.6	0.6	0.4	0.4	0.4
18–44 years	3.6	3.1	3.4	3.3	0.6	0.6	0.6	0.6
45–54 years	6.0	7.0	6.7	6.3	1.4	1.8	1.9	1.9
55–64 years	11.1	10.2	10.9	9.6	3.0	3.0	3.1	2.9
Female	8.0	7.8	7.9	7.4	1.6	1.4	1.5	1.5
1–17 years	2.6	2.5	2.4	2.6	0.5	0.4	0.5	0.4
18–44 years	11.2	10.8	10.8	9.8	1.8	1.7	1.6	1.7
45–54 years	7.6	7.6	8.0	7.4	2.0	1.9	1.8	1.9
55–64 years	9.4	9.8	10.3	10.0	2.9	2.7	3.3	3.0
Race[4,5]								
White only	6.2	5.9	6.1	5.8	1.2	1.1	1.2	1.2
Black or African American only	7.6	7.4	7.4	7.0	1.9	1.9	1.8	1.8
American Indian or Alaska Native only	7.6	7.0	8.2	7.0	*	*	*	*
Asian only	3.9	3.9	3.9	3.5	*0.5	*0.6	*0.4	*0.6
Native Hawaiian or Other Pacific Islander only	—	*	*	*	—	*	*	*
2 or more races	—	8.8	8.2	6.3	—	*1.6	*2.4	*1.9
Hispanic Origin and Race[4,5]								
Hispanic or Latino	6.8	5.5	5.9	5.0	1.3	0.9	1.3	1.0
Not Hispanic or Latino	6.2	6.1	6.2	5.9	1.3	1.3	1.2	1.3
White only	6.1	6.0	6.2	5.9	1.2	1.2	1.2	1.2
Black or African American only	7.5	7.4	7.4	7.0	1.9	1.9	1.8	1.8
Percent of Poverty Level[4,6]								
Below 100%	10.3	9.1	8.8	8.8	2.8	2.6	2.5	2.6
100%-less than 200%	7.3	7.3	7.4	6.7	1.7	1.9	1.8	1.7
200% or more	5.3	5.4	5.5	5.0	0.9	0.9	0.9	0.9
Hispanic Origin and Race and Percent of Poverty Level[4,5,6]								
Hispanic or Latino								
Below 100%	9.1	7.4	7.6	6.4	2.0	1.6	2.1	1.4
100%-less than 200%	5.9	5.4	6.0	5.0	1.0	0.8	1.5	*0.8
200% or more	5.8	4.7	5.1	4.2	1.1	0.7	0.8	0.8
Not Hispanic or Latino								
White only								
Below 100%	10.7	9.6	8.8	10.2	3.2	2.7	2.4	3.0
100%-less than 200%	7.7	7.8	8.1	6.9	1.8	2.2	1.9	1.8
200% or more	5.3	5.4	5.5	5.2	0.9	0.9	0.9	0.9
Black or African American only								
Below 100%	11.4	10.8	10.7	9.0	3.3	3.4	3.4	2.9
100%-less than 200%	8.0	8.5	7.7	9.2	2.1	2.3	1.7	*2.5
200% or more	5.5	5.9	6.1	5.2	1.2	1.3	1.3	1.2
Health Insurance Status at the Time of Interview[4,7]								
Insured	6.6	6.4	6.6	6.2	1.3	1.3	1.3	1.4
Private	5.6	5.5	5.6	5.1	1.0	1.0	0.9	0.9
Medicaid	16.1	15.9	15.6	13.3	4.9	4.7	4.6	4.7
Uninsured	4.8	4.5	4.4	4.4	1.0	0.9	0.9	0.8

* = Figure does not meet standards of reliability or precision.

—— = Data not available.

[1]These estimates exclude hospitalizations for institutionalized persons and those who died while hospitalized.

[2]Includes all other races not shown separately and unknown health insurance status.

[3]Estimates for persons 1 year and over are age-adjusted to the year 2000 standard population using six age groups: 1–17 years, 18–44 years, 45–54 years, 55–64 years, 65–74 years, and 75 years of age and over.

[4]Estimates are for persons 1–64 years of age and are age-adjusted to the year 2000 standard population using four age groups: 1–17 years, 18–44 years, 45–54 years, and 55–64 years of age.

[5]The race groups, White, Black, American Indian or Alaska Native, Asian, Native Hawaiian or Other Pacific Islander, and 2 or more races, include persons of Hispanic and non-Hispanic origin. Persons of Hispanic origin may be of any race.

[6]Percent of poverty level is based on family income and family size and composition using U.S. Census Bureau poverty thresholds.

[7]Health insurance categories are mutually exclusive. Persons who reported both Medicaid and private coverage are classified as having private coverage.

Table C-52. Persons with a Hospital Stay in the Past Year, by Selected Characteristics, Selected Years, 1997–2006—*Continued*

(Percent.)

Characteristic	One or more hospital stays[1]				Two or more hospital stays[1]			
	1997	2000	2003	2006	1997	2000	2003	2006
Health Insurance Status Prior to Interview[4,7]								
Insured continuously all 12 months...............	6.5	6.3	6.5	6.0	1.3	1.2	1.3	1.3
Uninsured for any period up to 12 months...............	8.5	8.4	8.0	8.3	1.8	1.9	1.7	1.9
Uninsured more than 12 months...............	3.8	3.5	3.5	3.4	0.8	0.8	0.8	0.6
Percent of Poverty Level and Health Insurance Status Prior to Interview[4,6,7]								
Below 100%								
Insured continuously all 12 months...............	12.4	10.7	10.7	10.3	3.7	3.1	3.2	3.2
Uninsured for any period up to 12 months...............	13.7	13.4	11.1	12.8	3.4	*3.4	*2.6	*3.4
Uninsured more than 12 months...............	4.9	5.0	4.3	4.4	1.0	*1.6	1.2	*1.2
100%-less than 200%								
Insured continuously all 12 months...............	8.5	8.6	8.7	7.9	2.0	2.3	2.2	2.1
Uninsured for any period up to 12 months...............	9.3	9.1	9.9	9.8	*1.9	*2.2	*1.9	*2.0
Uninsured more than 12 months...............	3.8	3.2	3.5	2.7	*0.7	*0.7	*0.7	*0.6
200% or more								
Insured continuously all 12 months...............	5.5	5.6	5.7	5.2	0.9	0.9	0.9	0.9
Uninsured for any period up to 12 months...............	5.9	6.3	5.9	5.6	*1.1	*1.3	1.2	*1.3
Uninsured more than 12 months...............	3.0	2.6	2.9	3.2	*0.6	*0.4	*0.5	*
Geographic Region[4]								
Northeast...............	6.0	5.5	5.6	5.8	1.2	1.0	1.1	1.2
Midwest...............	6.5	6.3	6.1	6.2	1.5	1.3	1.3	1.4
South...............	6.8	6.6	7.0	6.5	1.4	1.5	1.5	1.4
West...............	5.4	5.2	5.3	4.4	0.8	0.9	0.9	1.0
Location of Residence[4]								
Within MSA[8]...............	6.1	5.8	6.0	5.6	1.2	1.1	1.2	1.2
Outside MSA[8]...............	7.0	6.9	7.1	7.0	1.6	1.5	1.5	1.4
65 YEARS AND OVER								
Total 65 years and over[2,9]...............	18.1	18.3	18.3	17.3	5.4	5.8	5.6	5.3
65-74 years...............	16.1	16.1	15.2	14.2	4.8	4.9	4.5	4.4
75 years and over...............	20.4	20.7	21.6	20.8	6.2	6.8	6.9	6.2
Sex[9]								
Male...............	19.0	19.5	18.6	17.6	5.8	5.8	5.7	5.3
Female...............	17.5	17.4	18.0	17.1	5.1	5.7	5.6	5.2
Hispanic Origin and Race[5,9]								
Hispanic or Latino...............	17.3	16.6	18.2	11.8	6.2	6.4	6.5	*3.1
Not Hispanic or Latino...............	18.2	18.4	18.3	17.7	5.4	5.8	5.6	5.4
White only...............	18.3	18.4	18.3	17.8	5.4	5.7	5.4	5.4
Black or African American only...............	18.9	19.8	20.1	18.8	5.5	7.5	7.6	6.1
Percent of Poverty Level[6,9]								
Below 100%...............	20.9	20.9	21.1	18.8	6.4	7.5	7.3	5.9
100%-less than 200%...............	19.6	19.2	19.1	19.0	6.5	6.6	5.9	6.3
200% or more...............	17.1	17.4	17.5	16.4	4.9	5.2	5.3	4.7
Geographic Region[9]								
Northeast...............	17.2	16.6	17.2	18.8	5.1	4.5	5.3	5.0
Midwest...............	18.2	19.5	18.2	18.9	5.6	7.2	4.9	6.4
South...............	19.4	19.5	20.1	16.7	6.1	6.3	6.3	5.1
West...............	16.5	16.4	15.8	14.9	4.4	4.4	5.5	4.4
Location of Residence[9]								
Within MSA[8]...............	17.8	17.8	17.9	17.3	5.2	5.4	5.6	5.2
Outside MSA[8]...............	19.1	19.6	19.6	17.5	6.3	6.9	5.6	5.4

* = Figure does not meet standards of reliability or precision.

—— = Data not available.

[1]These estimates exclude hospitalizations for institutionalized persons and those who died while hospitalized.

[2]Includes all other races not shown separately and unknown health insurance status.

[4]Estimates are for persons 1–64 years of age and are age-adjusted to the year 2000 standard population using four age groups: 1–17 years, 18–44 years, 45–54 years, and 55–64 years of age.

[5]The race groups, White, Black, American Indian or Alaska Native, Asian, Native Hawaiian or Other Pacific Islander, and 2 or more races, include persons of Hispanic and non-Hispanic origin. Persons of Hispanic origin may be of any race.

[6]Percent of poverty level is based on family income and family size and composition using U.S. Census Bureau poverty thresholds.

[7]Health insurance categories are mutually exclusive. Persons who reported both Medicaid and private coverage are classified as having private coverage.

[8]MSA = metropolitan statistical area. Starting with 2006 data, MSA status is determined using 2000 census data and the 2000 standards for defining MSAs.

[9]Estimates are for persons 65 years of age and over and are age-adjusted to the year 2000 standard population using two age groups: 65–74 years and 75 years and over.

Table C-53. Discharges, Days of Care, and Average Length of Stay in Nonfederal Short-Stay Hospitals, by Selected Characteristics, Selected Years, 1980–2005

(Number per 1,000 population, number.)

Characteristic	1980[1]	1985[1]	1990	1995	2000	2001	2002	2003	2004	2005
DISCHARGES PER 1,000 POPULATION										
Total, age-adjusted[2]	173.4	151.4	125.2	118.0	113.3	115.1	117.3	119.5	118.4	116.2
Total, crude	167.7	148.4	122.3	115.7	112.8	114.9	117.5	120.0	119.2	117.4
Age										
Under 18 years	75.6	61.4	46.4	42.4	40.3	43.4	43.4	43.6	43.0	41.1
18–44 years	155.3	128.0	102.7	91.4	84.9	87.3	90.3	91.3	91.1	89.8
45–54 years	174.8	146.8	112.4	98.5	92.1	94.4	95.6	99.5	99.7	96.4
55–64 years	215.4	194.8	163.3	148.3	141.5	139.3	146.5	145.7	143.6	140.2
65 years and over	383.7	369.8	334.1	347.7	353.4	354.3	357.5	367.9	362.9	359.6
65–74 years	315.8	297.2	261.6	260.0	254.6	256.1	254.0	265.1	259.2	262.9
75 years and over	489.3	475.6	434.0	459.1	462.0	460.0	466.6	475.2	470.2	458.8
Sex[2]										
Male	153.2	137.3	113.0	104.8	99.1	100.0	102.4	104.4	102.6	101.3
Female	195.0	167.3	139.0	131.7	127.7	130.6	132.9	135.1	134.9	132.0
Geographic Region[2]										
Northeast	162.0	142.6	133.2	133.5	127.5	125.2	123.5	127.6	128.8	124.6
Midwest	192.1	158.1	128.8	113.3	110.9	113.5	113.6	117.1	114.4	117.5
South	179.7	155.5	132.5	125.2	120.9	126.3	126.7	125.8	125.6	120.2
West	150.5	145.7	100.7	96.7	89.4	88.8	99.7	103.9	101.2	100.6
DAYS OF CARE PER 1,000 POPULATION										
Total, age-adjusted[2]	1,297.0	997.5	818.9	638.6	557.7	562.2	570.9	574.6	568.7	554.2
Total, crude	1,216.7	957.7	784.0	620.2	554.6	560.9	571.7	577.8	574.1	562.1
Age										
Under 18 years	341.4	281.2	226.3	184.7	179.0	192.5	195.2	195.5	193.2	191.8
18–44 years	818.6	619.2	467.7	351.7	309.4	322.7	333.9	339.7	334.9	330.5
45–54 years	1,314.9	967.8	699.7	516.2	437.4	455.4	456.7	477.2	491.1	471.1
55–64 years	1,889.4	1,436.9	1,172.3	867.2	729.1	732.2	752.2	735.9	735.2	712.4
65 years and over	4,098.3	3,228.0	2,895.6	2,373.7	2,111.9	2,064.2	2,085.1	2,088.3	2,048.6	1,988.3
65–74 years	3,147.0	2,437.3	2,087.8	1,684.7	1,439.0	1,449.5	1,411.9	1,428.9	1,405.2	1,398.5
75 years and over	5,578.8	4,381.3	4,009.1	3,247.8	2,851.9	2,725.5	2,795.0	2,776.1	2,714.9	2,593.9
Sex[2]										
Male	1,239.7	973.3	805.8	623.9	535.9	534.5	549.5	546.7	541.1	530.1
Female	1,365.2	1,033.1	840.5	654.9	581.0	591.9	596.0	605.2	599.6	582.9
Geographic Region[2]										
Northeast	1,400.6	1,113.0	1,026.7	839.0	718.6	697.7	690.0	694.4	687.6	663.6
Midwest	1,484.8	1,078.6	830.6	590.9	500.5	491.6	502.1	507.9	498.7	495.4
South	1,262.3	957.7	820.4	666.0	592.5	623.6	618.6	609.8	614.2	583.0
West	956.9	824.7	575.5	451.1	408.2	408.3	454.7	476.4	457.5	469.0
AVERAGE LENGTH OF STAY IN DAYS										
Total, age-adjusted[2]	7.5	6.6	6.5	5.4	4.9	4.9	4.9	4.8	4.8	4.8
Total, crude	7.3	6.5	6.4	5.4	4.9	4.9	4.9	4.8	4.8	4.8
Age										
Under 18 years	4.5	4.6	4.9	4.4	4.4	4.4	4.5	4.5	4.5	4.7
18–44 years	5.3	4.8	4.6	3.8	3.6	3.7	3.7	3.7	3.7	3.7
45–54 years	7.5	6.6	6.2	5.2	4.8	4.8	4.8	4.8	4.9	4.9
55–64 years	8.8	7.4	7.2	5.8	5.2	5.3	5.1	5.1	5.1	5.1
65 years and over	10.7	8.7	8.7	6.8	6.0	5.8	5.8	5.7	5.6	5.5
65–74 years	10.0	8.2	8.0	6.5	5.7	5.7	5.6	5.4	5.4	5.3
75 years and over	11.4	9.2	9.2	7.1	6.2	5.9	6.0	5.8	5.8	5.7
Sex[2]										
Male	8.1	7.1	7.1	6.0	5.4	5.3	5.4	5.2	5.3	5.2
Female	7.0	6.2	6.0	5.0	4.6	4.5	4.5	4.5	4.4	4.4
Geographic Region[2]										
Northeast	8.6	7.8	7.7	6.3	5.6	5.6	5.6	5.4	5.3	5.3
Midwest	7.7	6.8	6.5	5.2	4.5	4.3	4.4	4.3	4.4	4.2
South	7.0	6.2	6.2	5.3	4.9	4.9	4.9	4.8	4.9	4.8
West	6.4	5.7	5.7	4.7	4.6	4.6	4.6	4.6	4.5	4.7

[1]Comparisons of data from 1980–1985 with data from later years should be made with caution as estimates of change may reflect improvements in the survey design rather than true changes in hospital use.

[2]Estimates are age-adjusted to the year 2000 standard population using six age groups: under 18 years, 18–44 years, 45–54 years, 55–64 years, 65–74 years, and 75 years and over.

NOTE: Excludes newborn infants. Rates are based on the civilian population as of July 1. Rates for 1990–1999 are not strictly comparable with rates for 2000 and beyond because population estimates for 1990–1999 have not been revised to reflect the 2000 census.

Table C-54. Discharges and Days of Care in Nonfederal Short-Stay Hospitals, by Sex, Age, and Selected First-Listed Diagnoses, Selected Years, 1990–2005

(Number per 1,000 population.)

Sex, age, and first-listed diagnosis	Discharges				Days of care			
	1990	1995	2000	2005	1990	1995	2000	2005
BOTH SEXES								
Total, age-adjusted[1,2]	125.2	118.0	113.3	116.2	818.9	638.6	557.7	554.2
Total, crude[2]	122.3	115.7	112.8	117.4	784.0	620.2	554.6	562.1
MALE								
All Ages[1,2]	113.0	104.8	99.1	101.3	805.8	623.9	535.9	530.1
Under 18 Years[2]	46.3	43.1	40.9	41.2	233.6	199.8	195.6	200.6
Pneumonia	3.7	3.9	2.6	2.9	16.7	14.7	8.5	9.0
Asthma	3.3	3.8	3.5	2.7	9.3	10.1	7.4	6.3
Injuries and poisoning	6.8	5.4	5.0	4.9	30.1	22.1	21.4	*24.0
Fracture, all sites	2.2	1.8	1.8	1.6	9.3	8.4	7.2	*6.1
18–44 Years[2]	57.9	50.7	45.0	47.1	351.7	273.0	217.5	228.3
HIV infection	*0.3	1.2	0.6	0.3	*3.0	12.6	*5.4	2.6
Alcohol and drug[3]	3.7	4.7	4.0	3.6	33.1	29.7	19.1	16.1
Serious mental illness[4]	3.4	*4.8	*5.3	6.1	47.1	*48.4	*43.6	*50.3
Diseases of heart	3.0	2.9	2.7	2.9	16.3	12.1	9.4	11.1
Intervertebral disc disorders	2.6	1.7	1.5	1.1	10.7	4.3	3.2	2.5
Injuries and poisoning	13.1	9.7	7.3	8.0	65.7	47.9	33.2	36.7
Fracture, all sites	4.0	3.2	2.5	2.7	22.7	17.8	12.8	13.4
45–64 Years[2]	140.3	121.2	112.7	114.9	943.4	682.3	570.4	577.3
HIV infection	*0.1	0.6	*0.5	0.4	*	6.4	*	4.3
Malignant neoplasms	10.6	7.6	6.2	5.9	99.1	53.4	42.1	39.2
Trachea, bronchus, lung	2.7	1.5	0.9	0.8	19.1	10.2	5.2	5.9
Diabetes	2.9	3.4	3.7	3.1	21.2	22.3	22.5	16.4
Alcohol and drug[3]	3.5	4.0	3.5	4.0	29.7	*25.7	15.8	18.6
Serious mental illness[4]	2.5	3.0	*4.0	4.7	34.8	*38.0	*34.6	41.2
Diseases of heart	31.7	29.7	26.4	22.4	185.0	143.8	101.5	85.1
Ischemic heart disease	22.6	21.3	17.7	13.3	128.2	99.1	63.8	47.0
Acute myocardial infarction	7.4	7.5	5.9	4.3	55.8	42.5	27.8	19.8
Heart failure	3.1	3.0	3.4	3.9	21.0	16.5	17.3	19.1
Cerebrovascular diseases	4.1	3.8	3.8	3.3	40.7	25.7	19.8	19.5
Pneumonia	3.4	2.9	3.4	3.5	27.1	20.5	20.3	20.0
Injuries and poisoning	11.6	10.2	8.8	10.7	82.6	56.2	49.8	59.2
Fracture, all sites	3.3	3.0	2.5	2.6	24.2	18.4	16.2	14.7
65–74 Years[2]	287.8	276.2	264.9	274.3	2,251.5	1,769.7	1,489.7	1,450.3
Malignant neoplasms	27.9	24.5	17.6	18.6	277.6	191.9	121.2	126.7
Large intestine and rectum	3.0	2.6	3.0	2.5	34.2	27.9	27.3	19.6
Trachea, bronchus, lung	6.4	5.2	2.8	2.8	55.7	40.0	19.2	21.6
Prostate	5.1	5.0	3.7	2.9	33.1	26.7	14.0	*9.7
Diabetes	4.4	5.4	4.7	5.2	39.8	47.1	29.0	29.0
Serious mental illness[4]	2.5	2.4	*3.4	2.8	43.8	*37.2	39.9	27.6
Diseases of heart	69.4	74.5	70.6	63.9	487.2	419.3	331.9	280.8
Ischemic heart disease	42.0	44.0	39.7	34.3	285.2	246.1	171.2	148.2
Acute myocardial infarction	14.0	15.5	12.5	12.0	122.4	102.3	66.5	72.8
Heart failure	11.8	15.1	13.6	13.2	93.1	88.6	77.6	64.8
Cerebrovascular diseases	13.8	17.1	13.2	12.8	114.8	112.6	59.0	58.9
Pneumonia	11.2	12.7	12.7	14.7	106.9	87.3	81.5	75.9
Hyperplasia of prostate	14.4	7.5	5.4	3.4	65.0	22.5	15.0	8.2
Osteoarthritis	5.5	6.4	10.3	12.6	48.5	37.1	48.8	48.0
Injuries and poisoning	17.6	16.1	17.9	19.4	139.0	107.0	105.7	119.1
Fracture, all sites	4.5	4.4	4.7	4.5	45.9	32.3	29.9	25.0
Fracture of neck of femur (hip)	1.5	1.8	*2.0	1.7	*18.1	14.7	*15.9	*12.0

* = Figure does not meet standards of reliability or precision.

[1]Estimates are age–adjusted to the year 2000 standard population using six age groups: under 18 years, 18–44 years, 45–54 years, 55–64 years, 65–74 years, and 75 years and over.

[2]Includes discharges with first-listed diagnoses not shown in table.

[3]Includes abuse, dependence, and withdrawal. These estimates are for nonfederal short-stay hospitals only and do not include alcohol and drug discharges from other types of facilities or programs such as the Department of Veterans Affairs or day treatment programs.

[4]These estimates are for nonfederal short-stay hospitals only and do not include serious mental illness discharges from other types of facilities or programs such as the Department of Veterans Affairs or long-term hospitals.

Table C-54. Discharges and Days of Care in Nonfederal Short-Stay Hospitals, by Sex, Age, and Selected First-Listed Diagnoses, Selected Years, 1990–2005—Continued

(Number per 1,000 population.)

Sex, age, and first-listed diagnosis	Discharges				Days of care			
	1990	1995	2000	2005	1990	1995	2000	2005
75 Years and Over[2]	478.5	474.7	467.4	476.0	4,231.6	3,261.7	2,888.0	2,745.4
Malignant neoplasms	41.0	30.2	21.9	22.7	408.3	251.2	165.2	155.8
Large intestine and rectum	5.4	4.9	4.2	3.5	80.7	53.1	44.1	33.0
Trachea, bronchus, lung	5.4	3.5	3.0	3.2	53.4	31.3	18.3	21.9
Prostate	9.7	4.3	3.2	1.9	65.6	17.6	*19.4	*10.1
Diabetes	4.6	6.9	6.5	5.3	51.2	42.0	43.2	35.4
Serious mental illness[4]	*2.6	2.5	2.9	2.0	*40.5	*29.6	*32.6	*19.3
Diseases of heart	106.2	113.9	113.3	102.6	855.7	677.2	600.9	490.8
Ischemic heart disease	49.1	51.8	53.0	41.0	398.1	321.9	276.1	201.3
Acute myocardial infarction	23.1	22.3	23.0	17.9	227.5	169.3	136.5	117.8
Heart failure	31.8	31.6	30.9	31.5	248.6	194.6	178.6	158.5
Cerebrovascular diseases	30.2	32.0	30.2	24.2	298.3	215.3	171.2	132.4
Pneumonia	38.1	40.2	36.7	35.8	391.3	323.6	228.6	208.7
Hyperplasia of prostate	17.9	9.4	6.8	5.2	109.2	32.9	21.6	17.1
Osteoarthritis	6.6	7.5	7.2	12.6	60.7	*	28.7	48.0
Injuries and poisoning	31.2	32.7	33.6	32.1	341.3	223.5	257.7	197.2
Fracture, all sites	13.7	16.1	14.4	13.4	145.1	115.0	*119.2	91.5
Fracture of neck of femur (hip)	8.5	9.0	8.4	7.8	97.8	68.9	63.3	54.1
FEMALE								
All Ages[1,2]	139.0	131.7	127.7	132.0	840.5	654.9	581.0	582.9
Under 18 Years[2]	46.4	41.6	39.6	41.0	218.7	168.8	161.5	182.6
Pneumonia	2.9	3.1	2.4	2.5	13.7	11.8	9.5	8.4
Asthma	2.2	2.6	2.4	1.7	6.8	7.2	5.5	3.8
Injuries and poisoning	4.3	3.9	3.1	3.1	16.7	13.1	*12.0	12.0
Fracture, all sites	1.3	1.1	0.9	0.9	6.4	4.5	2.3	2.6
18–44 Years[2]	146.8	131.8	124.8	133.1	582.0	429.8	401.1	434.2
HIV infection	*	0.4	0.3	*0.2	*	4.2	*2.1	*
Delivery	69.9	65.1	64.5	69.8	195.0	138.7	160.2	180.3
Alcohol and drug[3]	1.6	2.0	*2.1	2.0	14.1	12.9	*10.8	*9.9
Serious mental illness[4]	3.7	5.3	*5.4	*6.8	54.3	50.8	*41.1	*45.6
Diseases of heart	1.3	2.0	1.7	1.7	7.2	9.7	6.3	7.6
Intervertebral disc disorders	1.5	1.1	1.0	0.9	7.3	3.1	2.4	2.0
Injuries and poisoning	6.7	5.6	4.3	5.1	36.6	24.7	18.1	22.2
Fracture, all sites	1.6	1.3	1.0	1.1	10.7	5.6	4.5	5.8
45–64 Years[2]	131.0	116.0	110.2	114.5	886.5	634.2	533.6	566.4
HIV infection	*	*0.2	*	*	*	*	*	*
Malignant neoplasms	12.7	9.6	6.1	6.1	107.4	60.8	34.7	38.5
Trachea, bronchus, lung	1.7	1.5	0.5	0.7	14.8	8.0	3.4	4.3
Breast	2.8	2.1	1.3	1.1	12.1	7.6	2.6	2.7
Diabetes	2.9	3.2	2.9	2.7	25.8	19.4	15.0	13.1
Alcohol and drug[3]	1.0	1.1	1.5	1.7	8.0	*7.5	*7.1	7.1
Serious mental illness[4]	4.0	4.4	4.6	6.0	60.5	48.9	42.7	53.0
Diseases of heart	16.6	15.0	14.6	12.0	101.1	70.9	59.5	55.9
Ischemic heart disease	9.9	8.4	7.8	5.5	57.4	37.9	29.5	*24.3
Acute myocardial infarction	2.8	2.5	2.0	1.7	21.6	15.1	10.0	9.4
Heart failure	2.2	2.6	2.9	2.6	16.3	14.5	13.6	14.8
Cerebrovascular diseases	3.0	3.2	3.5	2.8	32.1	21.4	19.5	14.9
Pneumonia	3.3	3.2	3.6	3.4	26.1	21.7	20.7	18.0
Injuries and poisoning	9.4	8.4	7.7	8.7	63.3	45.4	41.2	46.0
Fracture, all sites	3.1	2.7	2.7	2.4	25.0	14.0	13.3	11.9

* = Figure does not meet standards of reliability or precision.

[1] Estimates are age–adjusted to the year 2000 standard population using six age groups: under 18 years, 18–44 years, 45–54 years, 55–64 years, 65–74 years, and 75 years and over.

[2] Includes discharges with first-listed diagnoses not shown in table.

[3] Includes abuse, dependence, and withdrawal. These estimates are for nonfederal short-stay hospitals only and do not include alcohol and drug discharges from other types of facilities or programs such as the Department of Veterans Affairs or day treatment programs.

[4] These estimates are for nonfederal short-stay hospitals only and do not include serious mental illness discharges from other types of facilities or programs such as the Department of Veterans Affairs or long-term hospitals.

Table C-54. Discharges and Days of Care in Nonfederal Short-Stay Hospitals, by Sex, Age, and Selected First-Listed Diagnoses, Selected Years, 1990–2005—*Continued*

(Number per 1,000 population.)

Sex, age, and first-listed diagnosis	Discharges				Days of care			
	1990	1995	2000	2005	1990	1995	2000	2005
65–74 Years[2]	241.1	246.9	246.1	253.3	1,959.3	1,616.2	1,397.1	1,354.9
Malignant neoplasms	20.9	20.3	14.1	12.5	189.8	148.6	101.0	82.9
Large intestine and rectum	2.4	2.3	1.7	1.8	34.9	19.9	15.2	14.0
Trachea, bronchus, lung	2.6	2.8	2.4	2.4	26.9	25.3	*17.5	17.1
Breast	3.9	3.2	2.8	1.3	17.6	10.0	*	*4.2
Diabetes	5.8	4.7	4.6	4.8	46.8	36.2	26.1	22.9
Serious mental illness[4]	3.9	5.8	4.0	4.3	62.8	82.9	46.3	47.4
Diseases of heart	45.1	48.3	52.1	43.0	316.9	276.9	256.0	191.1
Ischemic heart disease	24.4	24.3	23.3	17.5	153.8	135.4	113.9	69.5
Acute myocardial infarction	7.5	7.9	8.0	5.3	58.1	58.6	52.8	28.1
Heart failure	9.5	10.4	12.8	11.0	84.0	68.1	69.1	54.6
Cerebrovascular diseases	11.3	10.6	12.3	10.3	96.0	72.0	59.4	44.8
Pneumonia	8.5	10.4	11.3	11.8	79.6	79.5	71.4	65.8
Osteoarthritis	7.8	9.8	10.0	17.7	74.5	53.7	47.2	67.4
Injuries and poisoning	17.8	18.1	18.3	18.5	166.2	113.8	109.9	114.3
Fracture, all sites	8.4	7.0	7.7	8.0	97.3	43.9	43.8	43.8
Fracture of neck of femur (hip)	3.6	2.9	3.2	3.0	*59.6	21.5	21.1	20.8
75 Years and Over[2]	409.6	450.1	458.8	448.4	3887.1	3239.9	2830.8	2501.4
Malignant neoplasms	22.1	20.5	17.6	14.3	257.3	175.2	125.7	104.4
Large intestine and rectum	4.6	3.7	3.4	2.8	69.8	48.5	28.4	26.4
Trachea, bronchus, lung	2.1	1.9	1.9	2.0	20.6	16.2	14.0	13.6
Breast	3.9	3.1	2.5	1.6	22.0	9.0	*8.9	*
Diabetes	4.6	6.2	6.3	5.5	55.3	44.0	34.0	26.7
Serious mental illness[4]	4.2	5.0	4.7	3.1	78.4	72.7	49.2	29.7
Diseases of heart	84.6	96.1	99.1	90.5	672.8	601.3	523.4	435.8
Ischemic heart disease	33.7	37.3	35.5	26.5	253.2	220.9	185.5	119.6
Acute myocardial infarction	13.1	15.2	16.5	13.4	125.9	116.0	110.7	75.3
Heart failure	28.6	32.5	32.5	32.2	240.8	224.9	183.4	168.9
Cerebrovascular diseases	29.6	30.4	27.6	21.7	302.0	207.5	156.8	108.6
Pneumonia	23.5	28.0	30.1	28.6	255.8	227.1	206.5	168.3
Osteoarthritis	6.2	10.1	9.9	12.9	62.2	67.1	46.3	51.8
Injuries and poisoning	46.3	48.2	44.7	45.9	489.2	372.8	275.4	249.3
Fracture, all sites	31.5	31.5	30.0	27.9	352.7	251.5	190.0	150.7
Fracture of neck of femur (hip)	18.8	19.5	17.9	14.9	236.3	171.4	125.3	89.3

* = Figure does not meet standards of reliability or precision.
[2]Includes discharges with first-listed diagnoses not shown in table.
[4]These estimates are for nonfederal short-stay hospitals only and do not include serious mental illness discharges from other types of facilities or programs such as the Department of Veterans Affairs or long-term hospitals.

Table C-55. Discharges and Average Length of Stay in Nonfederal Short-Stay Hospitals, by Sex, Age, and Selected First-Listed Diagnoses, Selected Years, 1990–2005

(Number in thousands, number.)

Sex, age, and first-listed diagnosis	Discharges (in thousands)								Average length of stay							
	1990	1995	2000	2001	2002	2003	2004	2005	1990	1995	2000	2001	2002	2003	2004	2005
BOTH SEXES																
Total[1]	30,788	30,722	31,706	32,653	33,727	34,738	34,864	34,667	6.4	5.4	4.9	4.9	4.9	4.8	4.8	4.8
MALE																
All Ages[1]	12,280	12,198	12,514	12,852	13,389	13,874	13,844	13,902	6.9	5.8	5.3	5.3	5.3	5.2	5.2	5.2
Under 18 Years[1]	1,572	1,565	1,515	1,629	1,615	1,679	1,637	1,550	5.0	4.6	4.8	4.6	4.6	4.5	4.6	4.9
Pneumonia	124	143	95	114	108	115	103	108	4.6	3.7	3.3	3.5	*3.8	3.5	3.2	3.1
Asthma	111	137	129	119	123	146	127	103	2.8	2.7	2.1	2.3	2.4	2.3	2.1	2.3
Injuries and poisoning	232	196	185	192	180	207	195	183	4.4	4.1	4.3	*4.1	4.2	3.9	3.6	*4.9
Fracture, all sites	76	66	68	63	59	77	64	61	4.2	4.6	3.9	3.5	3.8	3.0	2.6	*3.8
18–44 Years[1]	3,120	2,761	2,498	2,573	2,703	2,683	2,622	2,660	6.1	5.4	4.8	4.9	4.9	4.9	4.9	4.8
HIV infection	*15	66	32	35	29	28	25	20	*10.6	10.4	*9.4	8.4	7.7	8.6	8.6	7.5
Alcohol and drug[2]	201	258	224	225	226	203	182	203	8.9	6.3	4.7	*5.1	4.5	4.1	4.4	4.5
Serious mental illness[3]	184	*262	*296	*338	361	323	319	344	13.8	*10.0	*8.2	*7.9	*7.9	8.0	7.7	*8.3
Diseases of heart	163	157	148	150	173	169	162	166	5.4	4.2	3.5	3.7	3.4	*4.5	3.5	3.8
Intervertebral disc disorders	138	94	81	74	69	69	67	60	4.2	2.5	2.2	2.2	2.3	2.3	2.0	2.3
Injuries and poisoning	704	529	408	412	445	470	453	452	5.0	4.9	4.5	4.8	4.7	4.9	5.1	4.6
Fracture, all sites	217	176	141	148	153	171	160	151	5.6	5.5	5.0	4.8	4.8	5.1	5.5	5.0
45–64 Years[1]	3,115	3,053	3,424	3,519	3,755	4,016	4,073	4,076	6.7	5.6	5.1	5.2	5.2	5.0	5.2	5.0
HIV infection	*3	15	*15	10	14	*22	15	15	*7.1	10.6	*	*13.7	8.1	*	*9.2	10.4
Malignant neoplasms	235	191	188	199	211	221	206	211	9.4	7.0	6.8	7.7	6.6	6.7	6.4	6.6
Trachea, bronchus, lung	60	37	26	28	30	30	28	29	7.1	6.9	6.0	*8.8	7.5	6.9	6.6	7.3
Diabetes	65	86	114	107	98	105	107	110	7.3	6.5	6.0	5.5	5.7	4.7	5.3	5.3
Alcohol and drug[2]	77	102	106	115	125	140	150	141	8.5	*6.4	4.5	4.7	4.2	4.5	4.5	4.7
Serious mental illness[3]	56	75	*120	148	139	147	162	167	13.7	*12.7	*8.8	*9.3	*11.1	9.1	9.0	8.8
Diseases of heart	704	749	802	768	812	827	821	795	5.8	4.8	3.8	4.0	3.9	4.0	4.0	3.8
Ischemic heart disease	502	537	539	492	515	494	507	473	5.7	4.6	3.6	3.6	3.6	3.8	3.7	3.5
Acute myocardial infarction	165	188	178	172	177	161	158	151	7.5	5.7	4.7	4.6	4.3	5.2	5.2	4.6
Heart failure	68	75	102	110	119	137	136	137	6.9	5.6	5.2	5.0	5.2	4.8	5.3	4.9
Cerebrovascular diseases	91	96	116	102	121	126	117	118	10.0	6.8	5.2	5.7	6.1	4.4	5.2	5.9
Pneumonia	75	74	102	107	102	133	126	125	8.0	7.0	6.0	5.4	5.6	6.2	5.4	5.7
Injuries and poisoning	257	257	266	307	342	369	374	380	7.2	5.5	5.7	5.1	6.0	5.5	6.3	5.5
Fracture, all sites	74	74	77	85	94	102	102	93	7.2	6.3	6.4	4.9	5.5	5.9	6.4	5.6
65–74 Years[1]	2,268	2,290	2,199	2,165	2,205	2,309	2,263	2,339	7.8	6.4	5.6	5.6	5.6	5.3	5.4	5.3
Malignant neoplasms	220	203	146	149	154	161	161	158	9.9	7.8	6.9	7.6	7.4	6.5	6.7	6.8
Large intestine and rectum	24	22	24	23	24	18	26	21	11.4	10.7	9.2	8.7	9.7	8.0	9.3	7.9
Trachea, bronchus, lung	50	44	23	23	29	30	25	24	8.7	7.6	6.8	8.4	8.1	5.8	6.4	7.6
Prostate	40	41	31	28	25	33	24	25	6.5	5.3	3.8	*4.6	*2.8	3.2	3.4	*3.3
Diabetes	34	44	39	41	43	42	47	44	9.1	8.8	6.2	5.1	6.3	5.5	5.4	5.6
Serious mental illness[3]	20	20	*28	*24	*24	24	24	24	17.4	*15.7	*11.7	*	*12.1	10.1	9.3	10.0
Diseases of heart	547	618	586	566	564	553	547	545	7.0	5.6	4.7	4.6	4.5	4.4	4.3	4.4
Ischemic heart disease	331	365	329	320	317	294	295	292	6.8	5.6	4.3	4.4	4.3	4.2	4.1	4.3
Acute myocardial infarction	110	129	104	100	110	105	91	102	8.8	6.6	5.3	5.8	6.0	5.3	5.3	6.1
Heart failure	93	126	113	107	104	118	117	113	7.9	5.9	5.7	5.8	5.3	4.9	5.1	4.9
Cerebrovascular diseases	108	141	109	109	114	112	106	109	8.3	6.6	4.5	4.7	4.1	4.3	4.5	4.6
Pneumonia	88	105	105	110	104	106	103	126	9.5	6.9	6.4	5.6	6.1	6.0	6.2	5.2
Hyperplasia of prostate	113	62	45	35	40	32	34	29	4.5	3.0	2.8	2.4	2.4	2.8	2.8	2.4
Osteoarthritis	44	53	86	74	72	81	96	108	8.8	5.8	4.7	4.6	4.2	4.1	3.8	3.8
Injuries and poisoning	139	133	149	143	153	160	146	165	7.9	6.7	5.9	7.4	6.1	5.5	6.3	6.2
Fracture, all sites	36	36	39	41	41	38	35	38	10.2	7.4	6.4	7.8	6.4	6.0	8.1	5.6
Fracture of neck of femur (hip)	12	15	*17	17	13	*12	14	14	*11.8	8.1	*7.9	*7.8	*6.4	*7.1	6.5	*7.2

* = Figure does not meet standards of reliability or precision.

[1]Includes discharges with first-listed diagnoses not shown in table.

[2]Includes abuse, dependence, and withdrawal. These estimates are for nonfederal short-stay hospitals only and do not include alcohol and drug discharges from other types of facilities or programs such as the Department of Veterans Affairs or day treatment programs.

[3]These estimates are for nonfederal short-stay hospitals only and do not include serious mental illness discharge from other types of facilities or programs such as the Department of Veterans Affairs or long-term hospitals.

VITAL STATISTICS OF THE UNITED STATES (BERNAN PRESS)

Table C-55. Discharges and Average Length of Stay in Nonfederal Short-Stay Hospitals, by Sex, Age, and Selected First-Listed Diagnoses, Selected Years, 1990–2005—Continued

(Number in thousands, number.)

Sex, age, and first-listed diagnosis	Discharges (in thousands)								Average length of stay							
	1990	1995	2000	2001	2002	2003	2004	2005	1990	1995	2000	2001	2002	2003	2004	2005
75 Years and Over[1]	2,203	2,528	2,878	2,966	3,111	3,188	3,250	3,276	8.8	6.9	6.2	5.9	6.0	5.9	5.8	5.8
Malignant neoplasms	189	161	135	156	154	159	144	156	10.0	8.3	7.6	6.9	7.5	6.9	7.0	6.9
Large intestine and rectum	25	26	26	27	24	26	26	24	15.0	10.8	10.6	9.1	9.2	9.2	8.6	9.4
Trachea, bronchus, lung	25	19	18	26	24	27	26	22	10.0	8.9	6.1	7.1	7.6	7.2	7.0	6.9
Prostate	45	23	20	*27	22	16	16	13	6.8	4.1	*6.1	*4.2	4.0	*4.4	3.7	*5.2
Diabetes	21	37	40	38	42	44	47	36	11.0	6.1	6.6	6.5	6.6	*5.5	5.4	6.7
Serious mental illness[3]	*12	13	18	19	23	17	16	14	*15.5	*11.9	*11.2	*9.1	10.3	*10.0	10.3	*9.8
Diseases of heart	489	606	697	727	759	728	761	706	8.1	5.9	5.3	5.1	5.2	5.1	5.1	4.8
Ischemic heart disease	226	276	326	311	326	311	303	282	8.1	6.2	5.2	5.0	5.2	5.1	5.3	4.9
Acute myocardial infarction	106	119	141	133	148	142	145	123	9.9	7.6	5.9	6.4	6.9	6.6	7.0	6.6
Heart failure	147	168	190	211	198	216	246	217	7.8	6.2	5.8	5.1	5.8	5.5	5.3	5.0
Cerebrovascular diseases	139	171	186	157	174	192	168	167	9.9	6.7	5.7	5.2	5.8	4.9	5.2	5.5
Pneumonia	175	214	226	248	249	260	261	247	10.3	8.1	6.2	6.4	6.2	6.2	6.0	5.8
Hyperplasia of prostate	82	50	42	45	39	36	40	36	6.1	3.5	3.2	*3.5	2.9	3.1	2.9	3.3
Osteoarthritis	30	40	44	58	75	75	79	86	10.3	*	4.5	4.6	4.4	4.5	4.0	3.8
Injuries and poisoning	144	174	207	199	211	228	225	221	10.9	6.8	7.7	6.5	6.5	6.5	6.2	6.1
Fracture, all sites	63	86	89	86	85	101	96	92	10.6	7.1	*8.3	7.3	7.2	7.1	6.4	6.8
Fracture of neck of femur (hip)	39	48	52	50	53	64	59	54	11.5	7.7	7.5	7.1	7.5	6.9	6.9	7.0
FEMALE																
All Ages[1]	18,508	18,525	19,192	19,801	20,338	20,864	21,020	20,766	6.1	5.0	4.6	4.6	4.6	4.6	4.5	4.5
Under 18 Years[1]	1,500	1,437	1,397	1,523	1,547	1,504	1,516	1,470	4.7	4.1	4.1	4.3	4.4	4.5	4.4	4.5
Pneumonia	95	106	86	89	101	88	86	91	4.7	3.8	3.9	3.9	4.1	3.2	3.3	3.3
Asthma	71	90	85	71	73	81	71	61	3.1	2.8	2.3	2.2	2.2	2.3	2.3	2.2
Injuries and poisoning	138	136	111	120	120	128	122	113	3.9	3.3	*3.8	3.6	4.2	*4.3	3.7	3.8
Fracture, all sites	42	36	32	30	29	38	30	31	5.0	4.2	2.5	2.9	2.9	3.4	3.2	3.0
18–44 Years[1]	8,018	7,235	6,941	7,178	7,411	7,537	7,597	7,410	4.0	3.3	3.2	3.3	3.3	3.3	3.3	3.3
HIV infection	*	22	15	*21	*15	19	13	*13	*	10.5	*7.5	*11.2	*9.7	7.4	7.2	*
Delivery	3,815	3,574	3,588	3,685	3,783	3,874	3,980	3,888	2.8	2.1	2.5	2.5	2.6	2.6	2.6	2.6
Alcohol and drug[2]	85	108	*116	112	105	106	109	110	9.1	6.6	*5.2	*5.2	*4.9	*5.0	*4.7	*5.0
Serious mental illness[3]	200	289	*300	338	385	333	331	*381	14.8	9.7	*7.6	7.5	*7.6	8.1	7.3	*6.7
Diseases of heart	73	108	95	99	95	102	98	96	5.4	4.9	3.7	3.5	4.1	4.1	4.8	4.4
Intervertebral disc disorders	84	62	58	55	62	60	62	51	4.7	2.7	2.3	2.7	2.6	2.4	2.5	2.2
Injuries and poisoning	366	305	237	267	268	268	298	282	5.5	4.4	4.2	3.9	3.9	3.9	4.2	4.4
Fracture, all sites	85	74	57	62	65	57	59	60	6.9	4.2	4.4	4.3	4.3	4.7	4.5	5.4
45–64 Years[1]	3,129	3,115	3,534	3,705	3,968	4,104	4,249	4,273	6.8	5.5	4.8	4.9	4.8	4.8	4.9	4.9
HIV infection	*	*5	*	5	*9	*	*11	*	*	*	*	*9.6	*8.5	*	*	*
Malignant neoplasms	303	258	195	203	198	226	211	228	8.5	6.3	5.7	6.1	5.9	5.9	6.3	6.3
Trachea, bronchus, lung	41	39	17	28	25	27	25	25	8.6	5.5	6.4	6.2	7.1	6.8	7.2	6.3
Breast	67	56	40	40	36	37	30	39	4.3	3.6	2.1	2.5	2.6	2.4	3.4	2.6
Diabetes	70	86	93	94	107	99	101	99	8.9	6.0	5.2	4.5	4.7	5.4	4.4	4.9
Alcohol and drug[2]	23	30	47	51	51	55	58	63	8.2	*6.8	*4.8	*4.5	*5.0	*5.2	4.9	4.2
Serious mental illness[3]	95	118	146	184	207	191	201	223	15.2	11.1	9.4	10.4	8.5	8.8	9.4	8.9
Diseases of heart	397	403	470	497	501	498	483	447	6.1	4.7	4.1	4.3	4.1	4.2	4.3	4.7
Ischemic heart disease	237	225	251	272	262	242	239	203	5.8	4.5	3.8	4.0	3.7	3.6	3.9	*4.5
Acute myocardial infarction	68	68	64	86	82	66	72	63	7.6	6.0	5.0	5.6	4.8	4.4	5.9	5.6
Heart failure	54	68	94	93	100	116	100	99	7.3	5.7	4.7	5.2	5.0	4.7	5.5	5.6
Cerebrovascular diseases	72	86	113	102	109	104	101	103	10.7	6.7	5.5	4.9	5.1	5.2	5.8	5.4
Pneumonia	78	87	116	112	114	132	118	126	8.0	6.7	5.7	5.4	6.3	5.6	5.8	5.3
Injuries and poisoning	225	225	248	280	279	310	335	324	6.7	5.4	5.3	5.4	5.3	5.5	5.5	5.3
Fracture, all sites	75	72	87	83	70	71	89	88	7.9	5.2	4.9	4.6	5.0	4.7	5.7	5.0
65–74 Years[1]	2,421	2,542	2,479	2,527	2,437	2,552	2,523	2,561	8.1	6.5	5.7	5.7	5.5	5.5	5.5	5.3
Malignant neoplasms	210	209	142	147	141	144	138	127	9.1	7.3	7.2	7.3	7.6	6.8	7.3	6.6
Large intestine and rectum	24	23	17	21	18	20	19	18	14.5	8.8	9.0	8.9	7.8	8.4	9.1	7.7
Trachea, bronchus, lung	26	29	25	23	30	25	22	24	10.2	8.9	*7.1	7.2	6.8	6.8	7.5	7.1
Breast	40	33	29	22	18	22	15	13	4.5	3.1	*	2.4	*3.2	*2.0	2.0	*3.3
Diabetes	59	49	47	59	52	51	50	49	8.0	7.7	5.6	6.1	5.4	5.2	5.5	4.8
Serious mental illness[3]	39	60	40	47	32	43	39	43	16.3	14.2	11.7	12.8	11.4	10.1	12.3	11.1
Diseases of heart	453	497	525	489	484	480	428	435	7.0	5.7	4.9	4.9	4.7	4.8	4.7	4.4
Ischemic heart disease	245	250	235	222	216	205	185	177	*6.3	5.6	4.9	4.9	4.6	4.2	4.2	4.0
Acute myocardial infarction	75	82	81	80	71	76	59	53	7.8	7.4	6.6	7.4	6.4	5.4	5.5	5.3
Heart failure	95	107	128	112	112	124	105	112	8.8	6.5	5.4	5.7	5.9	5.5	5.7	4.9
Cerebrovascular diseases	114	109	124	118	107	111	92	104	8.5	6.8	4.8	5.3	5.1	5.3	4.9	4.3
Pneumonia	85	107	114	115	113	116	125	119	9.4	7.6	6.3	6.5	6.1	5.6	5.8	5.6
Osteoarthritis	78	101	101	109	128	140	152	179	9.5	5.5	4.7	4.7	4.4	4.1	4.0	3.8
Injuries and poisoning	179	187	185	189	173	184	197	187	9.3	6.3	6.0	6.2	5.7	5.6	5.8	6.2
Fracture, all sites	85	72	77	79	69	73	88	81	11.5	6.2	5.7	5.3	5.7	5.4	5.4	5.5
Fracture of neck of femur (hip)	36	29	32	34	32	28	34	30	*16.7	7.5	6.7	5.9	6.5	5.9	6.9	7.0

* = Figure does not meet standards of reliability or precision.
[1] Includes discharges with first-listed diagnoses not shown in table.
[2] Includes abuse, dependence, and withdrawal. These estimates are for nonfederal short-stay hospitals only and do not include alcohol and drug discharges from other types of facilities or programs such as the Department of Veterans Affairs or day treatment programs.
[3] These estimates are for nonfederal short-stay hospitals only and do not include serious mental illness discharges from other types of facilities or programs such as the Department of Veterans Affairs or long-term hospitals.

Table C-55. Discharges and Average Length of Stay in Nonfederal Short-Stay Hospitals, by Sex, Age, and Selected First-Listed Diagnoses, Selected Years, 1990–2005—*Continued*

(Number in thousands, number.)

Sex, age, and first-listed diagnosis	Discharges (in thousands)								Average length of stay							
	1990	1995	2000	2001	2002	2003	2004	2005	1990	1995	2000	2001	2002	2003	2004	2005
75 Years and Over[1]	3,440	4,196	4,840	4,867	4,975	5,168	5,135	5,052	9.5	7.2	6.2	5.9	6.0	5.8	5.7	5.6
Malignant neoplasms	185	191	186	192	186	175	174	161	11.7	8.5	7.1	7.6	7.7	7.8	6.6	7.3
Large intestine and rectum	39	34	36	34	41	31	31	32	15.1	13.3	8.4	9.3	10.1	9.6	10.4	9.3
Trachea, bronchus, lung	18	17	20	19	17	22	24	22	9.9	8.7	7.3	7.7	8.9	*8.1	6.6	6.9
Breast	33	29	27	28	19	15	27	18	5.7	2.9	*3.5	*3.7	2.9	*3.2	2.4	*
Diabetes	39	58	67	67	56	68	68	62	11.9	7.1	5.4	5.2	5.5	4.6	5.1	4.8
Serious mental illness[3]	35	47	49	45	36	37	39	34	18.7	14.5	10.5	10.9	11.8	11.2	10.8	9.7
Diseases of heart	711	896	1,045	1,010	1,036	1,067	1,051	1,020	8.0	6.3	5.3	5.0	5.1	4.9	5.1	4.8
Ischemic heart disease	283	347	375	363	364	352	344	299	7.5	5.9	5.2	4.7	4.8	4.7	5.0	4.5
Acute myocardial infarction	110	142	174	181	172	174	165	151	9.6	7.6	6.7	6.0	6.2	6.0	6.1	5.6
Heart failure	240	303	343	337	306	343	354	363	8.4	6.9	5.6	5.6	5.3	5.4	5.4	5.2
Cerebrovascular diseases	249	283	292	301	274	269	272	244	10.2	6.8	5.7	5.2	5.2	5.6	5.3	5.0
Pneumonia	198	261	317	286	310	324	311	323	10.9	8.1	6.9	6.8	6.5	6.4	6.4	5.9
Osteoarthritis	52	94	105	117	125	134	147	146	10.1	6.6	4.7	4.6	4.5	4.4	4.1	4.0
Injuries and poisoning	389	449	472	503	526	507	501	517	10.6	7.7	6.2	6.1	5.8	5.9	6.3	5.4
Fracture, all sites	265	294	316	322	329	323	314	315	11.2	8.0	6.3	6.0	5.9	5.9	6.0	5.4
Fracture of neck of femur (hip)	158	182	189	190	183	171	181	168	12.5	8.8	7.0	6.4	6.3	6.3	6.2	6.0

* = Figure does not meet standards of reliability or precision.
[1]Includes discharges with first-listed diagnoses not shown in table.
[3]These estimates are for nonfederal short-stay hospitals only and do not include serious mental illness discharges from other types of facilities or programs such as the Department of Veterans Affairs or long-term hospitals.

Table C–56. Discharges With at Least One Procedure in Nonfederal Short–Stay Hospitals, by Sex, Age, and Selected Procedures, Selected Annual Averages, 1991–2005

(Number in thousands, number per 10,000 population.)

Age and procedure (any listed)	Both sexes			Male			Female		
	1991–1992	2001–2002	2004–2005	1991–1992	2001–2002	2004–2005	1991–1992	2001–2002	2004–2005
18 YEARS AND OVER									
Hospital discharges with at least one procedure[1] (number in thousands)	19,073	18,606	19,889	7,154	6,751	7,284	11,920	11,856	12,605
Number per 10,000 Population[2]									
Hospital discharges with at least one procedure, age–adjusted[1,3]	1,024.7	877.0	902.6	885.6	708.9	723.1	1,180.8	1,054.8	1,093.8
Hospital discharges with at least one procedure, crude[1]	1,012.9	874.1	902.3	794.9	658.2	682.9	1,212.5	1,074.9	1,108.0
Cardiac catheterization	52.4	58.9	56.1	67.0	72.9	70.2	39.0	46.0	43.0
Insertion, replacement, removal, and revision of pacemaker leads or device	8.9	10.0	9.0	9.1	10.5	9.5	8.6	9.5	8.4
Angiocardiography using contrast material	43.7	48.3	47.7	55.2	58.0	58.2	33.2	39.3	37.8
Operations on vessels of heart	32.9	42.7	41.4	47.1	59.8	58.0	19.9	26.9	25.8
Removal of coronary artery obstruction and insertion of stent(s)	18.6	28.7	30.1	25.9	39.2	41.8	11.9	18.9	19.0
Insertion of coronary artery stent(s)[4]	...	23.6	27.0	...	32.6	37.8	...	15.2	16.9
Insertion of drug–eluting coronary artery stent(s)[4]	...	...	22.4	...	...	31.1	...	...	14.2
Coronary artery bypass graft	15.2	14.3	11.6	22.7	21.0	16.5	8.4	8.2	7.0
Diagnostic procedures on small intestine	42.6	45.2	47.5	42.2	41.2	43.7	42.9	48.9	51.2
Diagnostic procedures on large intestine	29.0	26.0	25.4	24.8	22.7	20.9	32.9	29.0	29.6
Diagnostic radiology	84.8	37.0	34.7	80.9	33.5	31.8	88.5	40.3	37.3
Computerized axial tomography	60.4	27.3	28.3	59.4	25.9	26.3	61.3	28.6	30.1
Diagnostic ultrasound	68.6	32.2	33.4	57.5	29.8	31.7	78.7	34.4	35.0
Magnetic resonance imaging	11.4	9.2	10.6	11.2	8.5	9.7	11.5	9.8	11.3
Joint replacement of lower extremity	21.6	33.0	46.3	15.9	25.4	36.1	26.9	40.0	55.8
Total hip replacement	6.4	8.4	10.6	5.4	7.1	9.7	7.4	9.5	11.4
Partial hip replacement	4.7	5.3	10.3	2.4	2.8	7.9	6.8	7.7	12.6
Total knee replacement	8.3	15.9	21.9	5.9	12.7	15.6	10.6	19.0	27.8
Reduction of fracture and dislocation	26.9	24.7	24.2	25.0	21.6	21.3	28.6	27.6	27.0
Excision or destruction of intervertebral disc and spinal fusion	18.9	18.4	19.1	22.3	20.0	19.3	15.7	16.9	19.0
Excision or destruction of intervertebral disc	16.4	14.0	13.8	19.6	15.6	14.3	13.5	12.6	13.3
Cholecystectomy	28.8	20.3	18.6	18.2	13.7	12.9	38.4	26.3	23.9
Laparoscopic cholecystectomy	9.5	15.1	14.2	5.3	8.8	8.9	13.3	21.0	19.2
Lysis of peritoneal adhesions	17.7	15.1	15.3	6.6	5.9	6.5	27.9	23.6	23.4
18–44 YEARS									
Hospital discharges with at least one procedure[1] (number in thousands)	8,034	7,034	7,326	1,936	1,423	1,457	6,099	5,611	5,869
Number per 10,000 Population[2]									
Hospital discharges with at least one procedure[1]	735.7	629.1	653.2	356.6	254.2	258.1	1,110.2	1,004.8	1,053.2
Repair of hernia	5.0	4.5	4.4	5.6	2.9	3.1	4.4	6.2	5.6
Cesarean section and removal of fetus[5]	...	...	...	...	...	...	164.1	176.9	218.8
Forceps, vacuum, and breech delivery[5]	...	...	...	...	...	...	76.7	55.3	52.5
Other procedures inducing or assisting delivery[5,6]	...	...	...	...	...	...	395.0	395.4	400.8
Dilation and curettage of uterus[5]	...	...	...	...	...	...	26.0	8.0	7.4
Total abdominal hysterectomy[5]	...	...	...	...	...	...	42.3	36.9	32.6
Vaginal hysterectomy[5]	...	...	...	...	...	...	16.8	19.5	16.6
Cardiac catheterization	8.2	8.5	8.2	12.0	11.8	10.4	4.6	5.2	6.1
Angiocardiography using contrast material	7.3	7.6	7.7	10.7	10.1	9.7	4.0	5.1	5.6
Operations on vessels of heart	3.3	4.3	4.1	5.6	6.7	6.0	1.1	1.9	2.2
Removal of coronary artery obstruction and insertion of stent(s)	2.4	3.4	3.3	4.0	5.2	4.8	*0.7	1.5	1.8
Insertion of coronary artery stent(s)[4]	...	2.7	3.0	...	4.2	4.4	...	1.2	1.6
Insertion of drug–eluting coronary artery stent(s)[4]	...	...	2.3	...	...	3.4	...	...	1.3
Coronary artery bypass graft	1.0	1.0	0.8	1.7	1.6	1.2	*	*	*
Diagnostic procedures on small intestine	13.1	12.6	13.4	13.6	11.2	11.7	12.6	14.0	15.2
Diagnostic procedures on large intestine	7.2	6.1	7.1	6.4	5.3	6.1	8.0	6.9	8.2
Diagnostic radiology	38.5	15.1	15.6	37.6	12.8	12.8	39.4	17.5	18.4
Computerized axial tomography	25.1	10.6	11.7	29.2	10.9	11.2	21.2	10.3	12.2
Diagnostic ultrasound	31.7	10.4	11.4	17.3	7.3	9.2	46.1	13.4	13.6
Magnetic resonance imaging	5.8	2.9	4.0	6.3	2.8	3.8	5.2	3.0	4.2
Reduction of fracture and dislocation	16.7	13.0	12.7	22.9	17.7	17.6	10.6	8.2	7.7
Excision or destruction of intervertebral disc and spinal fusion	16.5	13.0	12.2	20.9	14.6	13.3	12.1	11.5	11.2
Excision or destruction of intervertebral disc	14.4	10.4	9.6	18.2	11.7	10.4	10.6	9.0	8.8
Cholecystectomy	16.7	12.7	12.1	6.6	4.6	5.1	26.7	20.8	19.2
Laparoscopic cholecystectomy	6.3	10.7	10.4	2.0	3.2	4.1	10.5	18.3	16.8
Lysis of peritoneal adhesions	15.0	12.2	12.0	1.9	1.9	1.8	27.9	22.5	22.4

* = Figure does not meet standards of reliability or precision.
... = Not applicable.
[1]Includes discharges for procedures not shown separately.
[2]Average annual rate.
[3]Estimates are age–adjusted to the year 2000 standard population using five age groups: 18–44 years, 45–54 years, 55–64 years, 65–74 years, and 75 years and over.
[4]The procedure code for insertion of coronary artery stents (36.06) first appears in the 1996 data. A second procedure code for the insertion of drug–eluting stents (36.07) first appears in the 2003 data.
[5]Rate for female population only.
[6]Includes artificial rupture of membranes, surgical and medical induction of labor, and episiotomy.

Table C–56. Discharges With at Least One Procedure in Nonfederal Short–Stay Hospitals, by Sex, Age, and Selected Procedures, Selected Annual Averages, 1991–2005—*Continued*

(Number in thousands, number per 10,000 population.)

Age and procedure (any listed)	Both sexes			Male			Female		
	1991–1992	2001–2002	2004–2005	1991–1992	2001–2002	2004–2005	1991–1992	2001–2002	2004–2005
45–64 YEARS									
Hospital discharges with at least one procedure[1] (number in thousands)	4,305	4,621	5,210	2,148	2,281	2,560	2,157	2,340	2,650
Number per 10,000 Population[2]									
Hospital discharges with at least one procedure[1]	908.9	704.6	726.4	939.3	714.9	732.5	880.5	694.9	720.5
Transurethral prostatectomy[7]	...	...	...	23.4	6.9	4.8	...	...	...
Repair of hernia	18.5	12.4	12.2	23.7	11.1	10.4	13.7	13.6	13.9
Total abdominal hysterectomy[5]	...	...	...	...	...	...	52.0	50.4	41.2
Vaginal hysterectomy[5]	...	...	...	...	...	...	17.6	22.4	20.0
Cardiac catheterization	91.8	80.4	73.3	127.0	104.0	99.3	59.0	58.1	48.7
Insertion, replacement, removal, and revision of pacemaker leads or device	6.7	4.3	3.7	8.3	5.4	4.8	5.3	3.3	2.6
Angiocardiography using contrast material	77.5	65.4	61.2	104.8	83.3	80.1	51.9	48.5	43.2
Operations on vessels of heart	57.6	59.4	54.5	88.6	88.0	83.8	28.7	32.3	26.7
Removal of coronary artery obstruction and insertion of stent(s)[4]	34.5	40.3	40.1	51.5	58.9	61.2	18.7	22.6	20.0
Insertion of coronary artery stent(s)[4]	...	33.0	36.4	...	49.4	56.1	...	17.5	17.7
Insertion of drug–eluting coronary artery stent(s)[4]	...	...	30.5	...	...	46.8	...	...	14.9
Coronary artery bypass graft	24.9	19.5	14.8	40.1	29.7	23.0	10.8	9.8	7.0
Diagnostic procedures on small intestine	42.9	38.9	43.7	45.9	40.3	45.6	40.1	37.7	41.9
Diagnostic procedures on large intestine	27.7	19.8	20.6	25.3	18.7	19.0	30.0	20.8	22.2
Diagnostic radiology	89.9	34.4	32.3	91.4	33.1	31.5	88.4	35.6	33.1
Computerized axial tomography	57.9	24.0	25.5	58.4	24.9	26.1	57.4	23.2	24.9
Diagnostic ultrasound	65.5	27.4	30.9	66.8	29.9	34.5	64.2	25.1	27.4
Magnetic resonance imaging	11.9	9.6	10.8	11.6	9.3	11.2	12.3	9.9	10.4
Joint replacement of lower extremity	18.3	30.2	48.0	16.9	26.0	38.8	19.7	34.2	56.6
Total hip replacement	6.7	9.2	11.3	7.1	10.0	11.9	6.2	8.4	10.7
Partial hip replacement	2.0	1.2	9.1	*1.2	*0.9	8.1	2.8	1.4	9.9
Total knee replacement	7.4	16.9	24.5	5.9	12.7	16.3	8.8	20.9	32.2
Reduction of fracture and dislocation	22.4	18.0	18.2	20.7	18.0	18.9	24.1	18.0	17.6
Excision or destruction of intervertebral disc and spinal fusion	25.6	25.4	27.1	27.7	27.0	27.3	23.6	23.8	26.9
Excision or destruction of intervertebral disc	23.1	20.6	20.1	25.4	22.0	20.8	21.0	19.2	19.4
Cholecystectomy	37.0	20.5	18.4	24.2	16.7	13.7	49.0	24.1	22.9
Laparoscopic cholecystectomy	12.4	15.0	13.8	7.7	11.2	9.1	16.8	18.7	18.3
Lysis of peritoneal adhesions	16.2	14.7	15.1	7.7	6.0	7.2	24.1	23.0	22.6
65–74 Years									
Hospital discharges with at least one procedure[1] (number in thousands)	3,288	2,856	3,036	1,662	1,381	1,482	1,626	1,475	1,554
Number per 10,000 Population[2]									
Hospital discharges with at least one procedure[2]	1,807.2	1,560.6	1,636.7	2,070.6	1,663.0	1,748.0	1,599.3	1,475.6	1,543.1
Transurethral prostatectomy[7]	...	...	...	145.3	54.4	41.1	...	...	...
Repair of hernia	37.9	26.2	22.3	52.3	28.2	21.3	26.6	24.5	23.1
Total abdominal hysterectomy[5]	...	...	...	...	...	...	24.8	19.9	15.9
Vaginal hysterectomy[5]	...	...	...	...	...	...	14.4	16.0	14.8
Cardiac catheterization	170.6	181.5	172.3	223.4	235.4	225.5	128.9	136.7	127.5
Insertion, replacement, removal, and revision of pacemaker leads or device	27.1	25.4	21.5	32.0	26.4	26.5	23.2	24.6	17.3
Angiocardiography using contrast material	139.3	147.3	143.3	178.9	182.6	185.6	108.0	118.1	107.7
Operations on vessels of heart	116.0	141.1	137.5	169.3	207.8	202.0	73.9	85.7	83.2
Removal of coronary artery obstruction and insertion of stent(s)	60.6	90.8	95.6	84.1	130.0	140.8	42.0	58.2	57.6
Insertion of coronary artery stent(s)[4]	...	74.9	85.4	...	107.7	125.8	...	47.6	51.4
Insertion of drug–eluting coronary artery stent(s)[4]	...	...	71.7	...	...	104.8	...	...	43.9
Coronary artery bypass graft	59.2	51.2	42.9	90.7	79.2	62.9	34.3	27.9	26.0
Diagnostic procedures on small intestine	106.2	106.9	108.3	116.9	107.5	110.4	97.7	106.4	106.6
Diagnostic procedures on large intestine	72.6	64.8	58.8	70.6	64.5	51.2	74.1	65.1	65.1
Diagnostic radiology	177.7	77.1	68.9	193.8	79.4	74.3	165.0	75.2	64.3
Computerized axial tomography	132.3	57.0	55.6	145.1	57.5	58.7	122.3	56.6	53.0
Diagnostic ultrasound	149.3	79.3	73.9	163.6	80.0	78.9	138.0	78.7	69.7
Magnetic resonance imaging	26.5	23.5	23.7	28.9	24.5	21.4	24.5	22.6	25.6
Joint replacement of lower extremity	79.8	110.3	161.5	59.4	92.0	133.4	95.9	125.5	185.2
Total hip replacement	25.2	25.9	36.2	20.5	21.5	32.1	28.9	29.5	39.6
Partial hip replacement	8.4	9.5	19.4	*3.9	7.7	15.0	11.9	11.1	23.1
Total knee replacement	38.9	63.4	91.4	28.1	52.5	69.8	47.4	72.4	109.6
Reduction of fracture and dislocation	36.5	39.4	41.0	28.5	28.1	27.5	42.9	48.7	52.4
Excision or destruction of intervertebral disc and spinal fusion	20.5	25.3	32.8	22.3	25.2	29.0	19.1	25.4	36.1
Excision or destruction of intervertebral disc	16.4	15.6	19.0	18.3	16.7	16.9	14.9	14.7	20.8
Cholecystectomy	59.3	40.3	36.2	54.2	36.9	33.4	63.3	43.1	38.6
Laparoscopic cholecystectomy	18.1	28.3	26.0	14.9	22.9	22.9	20.6	32.8	28.6
Lysis of peritoneal adhesions	25.3	22.4	22.7	20.3	17.4	17.7	29.3	26.6	26.9

* = Figure does not meet standards of reliability or precision.

... = Not applicable.

[1]Includes discharges for procedures not shown separately.

[2]Average annual rate.

[4]The procedure code for insertion of coronary artery stents (36.06) first appears in the 1996 data. A second procedure code for the insertion of drug–eluting stents (36.07) first appears in the 2003 data.

[5]Rate for female population only.

[7]Rate for male population only.

Table C–56. Discharges With at Least One Procedure in Nonfederal Short–Stay Hospitals, by Sex, Age, and Selected Procedures, Selected Annual Averages, 1991–2005—*Continued*

(Number in thousands, number per 10,000 population.)

Age and procedure (any listed)	Both sexes			Male			Female		
	1991–1992	2001–2002	2004–2005	1991–1992	2001–2002	2004–2005	1991–1992	2001–2002	2004–2005
75 Years and Over									
Hospital discharges with at least one procedure[1] (number in thousands)	3,446	4,096	4,317	1,409	1,667	1,785	2,037	2,430	2,532
Number per 10,000 Population[2]									
Hospital discharges with at least one procedure[1]	2,547.0	2,384.5	2,399.7	2,918.6	2,606.7	2,623.5	2,340.9	2,252.7	2,263.6
Transurethral prostatectomy[7]	...	...	...	262.6	95.3	63.7	...	...	...
Repair of hernia	43.5	27.5	28.6	67.2	36.4	34.7	30.4	22.2	24.8
Total abdominal hysterectomy[5]	...	...	...	...	...	...	14.8	13.6	8.9
Vaginal hysterectomy[5]	...	...	...	...	...	...	7.3	8.3	6.6
Cardiac catheterization	111.8	174.6	166.6	141.4	240.8	222.7	95.3	135.3	132.5
Insertion, replacement, removal, and revision of pacemaker leads or device	59.3	76.9	70.3	72.6	101.5	87.6	51.9	62.3	59.7
Angiocardiography using contrast material	91.2	142.5	144.5	114.9	190.0	189.3	78.0	114.4	117.2
Operations on vessels of heart	72.8	124.3	122.1	113.5	191.2	177.8	50.2	84.7	88.2
Removal of coronary artery obstruction and insertion of stent(s)	37.2	83.0	89.3	53.5	120.1	125.9	28.2	61.0	67.1
Insertion of coronary artery stent(s)[4]	...	69.1	79.3	...	99.6	111.6	...	50.9	59.6
Insertion of drug–eluting coronary artery stent(s)[4]	...	...	64.5	...	...	89.0	...	...	49.7
Coronary artery bypass graft	36.7	42.0	33.6	62.7	71.2	52.3	22.3	24.6	22.2
Diagnostic procedures on small intestine	193.6	215.4	212.9	222.4	222.4	215.9	177.7	211.2	211.0
Diagnostic procedures on large intestine	150.5	137.9	123.7	152.2	141.2	115.9	149.6	135.9	128.4
Diagnostic radiology	316.7	146.6	127.9	331.1	156.9	139.2	308.7	140.5	121.0
Computerized axial tomography	257.4	116.7	114.7	262.2	121.5	112.3	254.8	113.9	116.1
Diagnostic ultrasound	268.1	142.0	139.2	290.2	160.3	144.8	255.8	131.2	135.7
Magnetic resonance imaging	34.3	33.3	37.1	36.0	34.2	37.5	33.4	32.8	36.9
Joint replacement of lower extremity	117.5	160.5	175.1	95.7	135.1	153.4	129.6	175.5	188.3
Total hip replacement	25.7	34.7	38.9	21.4	27.6	36.6	28.1	38.9	40.2
Partial hip replacement	46.3	50.5	50.6	32.0	28.4	37.2	54.3	63.6	58.7
Total knee replacement	35.8	60.2	72.3	30.8	63.0	69.0	38.5	58.5	74.3
Reduction of fracture and dislocation	111.3	111.1	102.5	62.7	65.5	55.9	138.3	138.1	130.8
Excision or destruction of intervertebral disc and spinal fusion	11.4	18.0	16.2	11.8	23.4	16.2	11.2	14.6	16.2
Excision or destruction of intervertebral disc	9.4	11.0	9.1	10.5	16.0	9.7	8.7	8.1	8.7
Cholecystectomy	56.1	47.5	41.6	60.1	48.6	47.5	53.9	46.8	37.9
Laparoscopic cholecystectomy	13.4	30.0	27.5	14.1	27.5	31.0	13.0	31.5	25.4
Lysis of peritoneal adhesions	34.9	28.0	28.3	31.0	26.6	28.3	37.1	28.8	28.3

... = Not applicable.

[1]Includes discharges for procedures not shown separately.
[2]Average annual rate.
[4]The procedure code for insertion of coronary artery stents (36.06) first appears in the 1996 data. A second procedure code for the insertion of drug–eluting stents (36.07) first appears in the 2003 data.
[5]Rate for female population only.
[7]Rate for male population only.

Table C-57. Nursing Home Residents 65 Years of Age and Over, by Age, Sex, and Race, Selected Years, 1973–2004

(Number in hundreds, number per 1,000 population.)

Age, sex, and race	Number of residents in hundreds						Residents per 1,000 population[1]					
	1973–1974	1985	1995	1997	1999	2004	1973–1974	1985	1995	1997	1999	2004
All Persons												
65 years and over, age-adjusted[2]	...	...	...	...	...	...	58.5	54.0	46.4	45.4	43.3	34.8
65 years and over, crude	9,615	13,183	14,229	14,650	14,695	13,172	44.7	46.2	42.8	43.4	42.9	36.3
65–74 years	1,631	2,121	1,897	1,984	1,948	1,741	12.3	12.5	10.2	10.8	10.8	9.4
75–84 years	3,849	509	5,096	5,283	5,176	4,689	57.7	57.7	46.1	45.5	43.0	36.1
85 years and over	4,136	5,973	7,235	7,383	7,571	6,742	257.3	220.3	200.9	192.0	182.5	138.7
Male												
65 years and over, age-adjusted[2]	...	...	...	...	...	...	42.5	38.8	33.0	32.0	30.6	24.1
65 years and over, crude	2,657	3,344	3,571	3,721	3,778	3,368	30.0	29.0	26.2	26.7	26.5	22.2
65–74 years	651	806	795	808	841	754	11.3	10.8	9.6	9.8	10.3	8.9
75–84 years	1,023	1,413	1,443	1,593	1,495	1,408	39.9	43.0	33.5	34.6	30.8	27.0
85 years and over	983	1,126	1,333	1,320	1,442	1,206	182.7	145.7	131.5	119.0	116.5	80.0
Female												
65 years and over, age-adjusted[2]	...	...	...	...	...	...	67.5	61.5	52.8	52.0	49.8	40.4
65 years and over, crude	6,958	9,839	10,658	10,929	10,917	9,804	54.9	57.9	54.3	55.1	54.6	46.4
65–74 years	980	1,315	1,103	1,177	1,107	988	13.1	13.8	10.7	11.6	11.2	9.8
75–84 years	2,826	3,677	3,654	3,689	3,681	3,280	68.9	66.4	54.3	52.7	51.2	42.3
85 years and over	3,153	4,847	5,902	6,063	6,129	5,536	294.9	250.1	228.1	221.6	210.5	165.2
White[3]												
65 years and over, age-adjusted[2]	...	...	...	...	...	...	61.2	55.5	45.8	44.5	41.9	34.0
65 years and over, crude	9,206	12,274	12,715	12,949	12,796	11,488	46.9	47.7	42.7	43.0	42.1	36.2
65–74 years	1,501	1,878	1,541	1,608	1,573	1,342	12.5	12.3	9.3	10.0	10.0	8.5
75–84 years	3,697	4,736	4,513	4,644	4,406	4,060	60.3	59.1	45.0	44.2	40.5	35.2
85 years and over	4,008	5,660	6,662	6,697	6,817	6,086	270.8	228.7	203.2	192.4	181.8	139.4
Black or African American[3]												
65 years and over, age-adjusted[2]	...	...	...	...	...	...	28.2	41.5	50.8	54.4	55.5	49.9
65 years and over, crude	377	820	1,229	1,374	1,459	1,454	22.0	35.0	45.5	49.4	51.0	47.7
65–74 years	122	225	296	314	303	345	11.1	15.4	18.5	19.2	18.2	20.2
75–84 years	134	306	475	519	587	546	26.7	45.3	57.8	60.6	66.5	55.5
85 years and over	121	290	458	541	569	563	105.7	141.5	168.2	186.0	182.8	160.7

... = Not applicable.

[1]Rates are calculated using estimates of the civilian population of the United States including institutionalized persons. Population data are from unpublished tabulations provided by the U.S. Census Bureau. The 2004 population estimates are postcensal estimates as of July 1, 2004, based on the 2000 census.

[2]Age-adjusted to the year 2000 population standard using the following three age groups: 65–74 years, 75–84 years, and 85 years and over.

[3]Starting with 1999 data, the instruction for the race item on the Current Resident Questionnaire was changed so that more than one race could be recorded. In previous years, only one racial category could be checked. Estimates for racial groups presented in this table are for residents for whom only one race was recorded. Estimates for residents where multiple races were checked are unreliable due to small sample sizes and are not shown.

NOTE: Residents are persons on the roster of the nursing home as of the night before the survey. Residents for whom beds are maintained even though they may be away on overnight leave or in a hospital are included. People residing in personal care or domiciliary care homes are excluded.

Table C-58. Nursing Homes, Beds, Occupancy, and Residents, by Geographic Division and State, Selected Years, 1995–2006

(Number, percent, rate per 1,000 population 85 years and over.)

Geographic division and area	Nursing homes			Beds			Residents			Occupancy rate[1]			Resident rate[2]		
	1995	2000	2006	1995	2000	2006	1995	2000	2006	1995	2000	2006	1995	2000	2006
UNITED STATES	16,389	16,886	15,899	1,751,302	1,795,388	1,716,102	1,479,550	1,480,076	1,433,523	84.5	82.4	83.5	404.5	349.1	270.6
New England	1,140	1,137	1,021	115,488	118,562	108,027	105,792	106,308	97,511	91.6	89.7	90.3	474.2	419.5	324.6
Connecticut	267	259	245	32,827	32,433	30,100	29,948	29,657	27,364	91.2	91.4	90.9	541.7	461.4	358.2
Maine	132	126	113	9,243	8,248	7,359	8,587	7,298	6,651	92.9	88.5	90.4	417.9	313.0	246.2
Massachusetts	550	526	453	54,532	56,030	50,416	49,765	49,805	45,068	91.3	88.9	89.4	477.3	426.8	328.9
New Hampshire	74	83	82	7,412	7,837	7,829	6,877	7,158	7,052	92.8	91.3	90.1	434.1	392.6	305.0
Rhode Island	94	99	87	9,612	10,271	8,889	8,823	9,041	8,265	91.8	88.0	93.0	476.9	432.6	329.0
Vermont	23	44	41	1,862	3,743	3,434	1,792	3,349	3,111	96.2	89.5	90.6	207.0	335.0	265.6
Middle Atlantic	1,650	1,796	1,734	244,342	267,772	261,537	228,649	242,674	238,468	93.6	90.6	91.2	384.0	354.2	286.3
New Jersey	300	361	363	43,967	52,195	52,126	40,397	45,837	45,667	91.9	87.8	87.6	351.6	337.0	274.2
New York	624	665	655	107,750	120,514	120,850	103,409	112,957	112,141	96.0	93.7	92.8	371.8	362.6	301.7
Pennsylvania	726	770	716	92,625	95,063	88,561	84,843	83,880	80,660	91.6	88.2	91.1	419.2	353.1	273.6
East North Central	3,171	3,301	3,090	367,879	369,657	339,079	294,319	289,404	273,438	80.0	78.3	80.6	476.1	414.3	325.1
Illinois	827	869	799	103,230	110,766	102,941	83,696	83,604	77,204	81.1	75.5	75.0	495.3	435.4	340.0
Indiana	556	564	511	59,538	56,762	56,964	44,328	42,328	39,758	74.5	74.6	69.8	548.9	462.3	357.6
Michigan	432	439	424	49,473	50,696	47,432	43,271	42,615	41,090	87.5	84.1	86.6	345.0	299.1	235.1
Ohio	943	1,009	958	106,884	105,038	93,210	79,026	81,946	81,275	73.9	78.0	87.2	499.5	463.5	374.6
Wisconsin	413	420	398	48,754	46,395	38,532	43,998	38,911	34,111	90.2	83.9	88.5	518.9	406.9	306.9
West North Central	2,258	2,281	2,144	200,109	193,754	180,287	164,660	157,224	143,361	82.3	81.1	79.5	489.6	429.8	337.2
Iowa	419	467	455	39,959	37,034	34,532	27,506	29,204	26,866	68.8	78.9	77.8	458.0	448.5	357.4
Kansas	429	392	352	30,016	27,067	25,908	25,140	22,230	19,785	83.8	82.1	76.4	528.9	429.4	332.4
Minnesota	432	433	399	43,865	42,149	35,837	41,163	38,813	32,738	93.8	92.1	91.4	537.4	453.4	322.1
Missouri	546	551	519	52,679	54,829	54,541	39,891	38,586	38,001	75.7	70.4	69.7	432.8	391.5	334.0
Nebraska	231	236	225	18,169	17,877	16,258	16,166	14,989	13,327	89.0	83.8	82.0	501.4	441.5	340.6
North Dakota	87	88	83	7,125	6,954	6,502	6,868	6,343	5,967	96.4	91.2	91.8	522.0	430.7	355.2
South Dakota	114	114	111	8,296	7,844	6,709	7,926	7,059	6,677	95.5	90.0	99.5	543.3	438.8	350.0
South Atlantic	2,215	2,418	2,345	243,069	264,147	263,950	217,303	227,818	233,404	89.4	86.2	88.4	335.4	291.9	224.4
Delaware	42	43	44	4,739	4,906	4,754	3,819	3,900	3,855	80.6	79.5	81.1	448.7	369.7	264.9
District of Columbia	19	20	20	3,206	3,078	2,988	2,576	2,858	2,760	80.3	92.9	92.4	297.6	318.4	256.3
Florida	627	732	682	72,656	83,365	82,319	61,845	69,050	72,552	85.1	82.8	88.1	228.2	208.4	156.9
Georgia	352	363	359	38,097	39,817	39,920	35,933	36,559	35,755	94.3	91.8	89.6	496.0	416.1	315.4
Maryland	218	255	233	28,394	31,495	29,020	24,716	25,629	25,273	87.0	81.4	87.1	432.7	383.1	294.6
North Carolina	391	410	421	38,322	41,376	43,768	35,511	36,658	38,362	92.7	88.6	87.6	401.1	347.6	281.6
South Carolina	166	178	176	16,682	18,102	18,415	14,568	15,739	16,635	87.3	86.9	90.3	366.0	313.1	242.1
Virginia	271	278	279	30,070	30,595	31,830	28,119	27,091	28,380	93.5	88.5	89.2	385.2	310.4	253.1
West Virginia	129	139	131	10,903	11,413	10,936	10,216	10,334	9,832	93.7	90.5	89.9	355.2	325.2	272.6
East South Central	1,014	1,071	1,053	99,707	106,250	108,675	91,563	96,348	95,987	91.8	90.7	88.3	416.6	385.5	324.0
Alabama	221	225	231	23,353	25,248	26,836	21,691	23,089	23,488	92.9	91.4	87.5	370.1	343.1	295.3
Kentucky	288	307	293	23,221	25,341	26,041	20,696	22,730	23,261	89.1	89.7	89.3	391.9	390.1	334.9
Mississippi	183	190	203	16,059	17,068	18,323	15,247	15,815	16,419	94.9	92.7	89.6	405.3	368.7	331.1
Tennessee	322	349	326	37,074	38,593	37,475	33,929	34,714	32,819	91.5	89.9	87.6	479.6	426.1	335.9
West South Central	2,264	2,199	2,011	224,695	224,100	216,867	169,047	159,160	155,800	75.2	71.0	71.8	486.1	397.6	317.5
Arkansas	256	255	237	29,952	25,715	24,684	20,823	19,317	17,970	69.5	75.1	72.8	508.3	415.5	327.4
Louisiana	337	337	293	37,769	39,430	37,043	32,493	30,735	27,800	86.0	77.9	75.0	639.3	523.8	411.2
Oklahoma	405	392	336	33,918	33,903	30,776	26,377	23,833	20,242	77.8	70.3	65.8	499.1	416.8	308.7
Texas	1,266	1,215	1,145	123,056	125,052	124,364	89,354	85,275	89,788	72.6	68.2	72.2	439.9	358.4	296.7
Mountain	800	827	773	70,134	75,152	73,353	58,738	59,379	58,042	83.8	79.0	79.1	335.9	271.2	190.0
Arizona	152	150	135	16,162	17,458	16,508	12,382	13,253	12,775	76.6	75.9	77.4	233.3	193.4	121.5
Colorado	219	225	211	19,912	20,240	19,982	17,055	17,045	16,579	85.7	84.2	83.0	420.6	353.5	270.8
Idaho	76	84	80	5,747	6,181	6,195	4,697	4,640	4,646	81.7	75.1	75.0	321.7	257.0	198.7
Montana	100	104	97	7,210	7,667	7,338	6,415	5,973	5,405	89.0	77.9	73.7	491.4	389.5	284.5
Nevada	42	51	47	3,998	5,547	5,615	3,645	3,657	4,664	91.2	65.9	83.1	312.0	215.3	167.5
New Mexico	83	80	72	6,969	7,289	6,939	6,051	6,503	6,019	86.8	89.2	86.7	332.0	279.0	192.2
Utah	91	93	92	7,101	7,651	7,724	5,832	5,703	5,480	82.1	74.5	70.9	323.5	262.2	187.4
Wyoming	37	40	39	3,035	3,119	3,052	2,661	2,605	2,474	87.7	83.5	81.1	468.2	386.8	295.7
Pacific	1,877	1,856	1,728	185,879	175,994	164,327	149,479	141,761	137,512	80.4	80.5	83.7	302.4	241.3	179.9
Alaska	15	15	15	814	821	725	634	595	640	77.9	72.5	88.3	348.0	225.9	154.3
California	1,382	1,369	1,283	140,203	131,762	124,416	109,805	106,460	105,458	78.3	80.8	84.8	302.9	250.1	189.9
Hawaii	34	45	46	2,513	4,006	4,127	2,413	3,558	3,828	96.0	88.8	92.8	178.5	202.6	142.4
Oregon	161	150	138	13,885	13,500	12,573	11,673	9,990	8,108	84.1	74.0	64.5	244.9	173.9	114.2
Washington	285	277	246	28,464	25,905	22,486	24,954	21,158	19,478	87.7	81.7	86.6	362.5	251.6	182.0

[1]Percentage of beds occupied (number of nursing home residents per 100 nursing home beds).

[2]Number of nursing home residents (all ages) per 1,000 resident population 85 years of age and over. Resident rates for 1995–1999 are based on population estimates projected from the 1990 census. Starting with 2000 data, resident rates are based on the 2000 census and postcensal population estimates.

NOTE: Annual numbers of nursing homes, beds, and residents are based on a 15-month Online Survey Certification and Reporting Database (OSCAR) reporting cycle.

HEALTH PERSONNEL

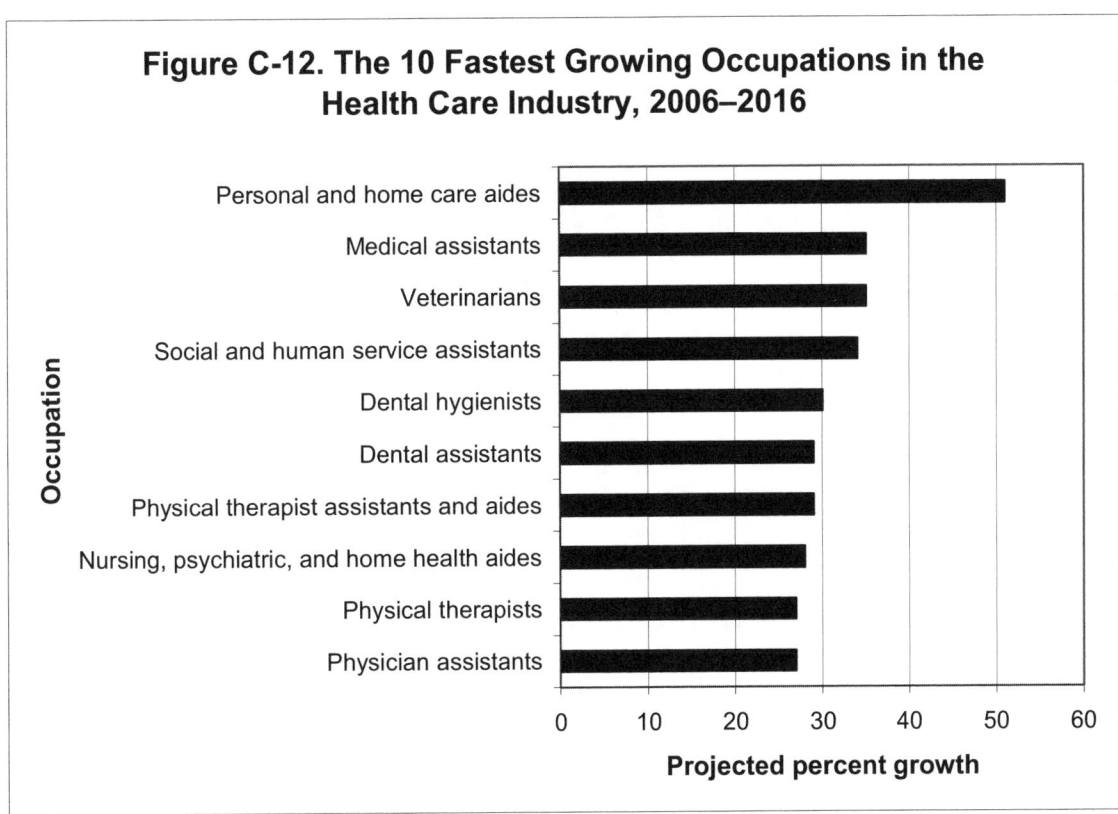

Figure C-12. The 10 Fastest Growing Occupations in the Health Care Industry, 2006–2016

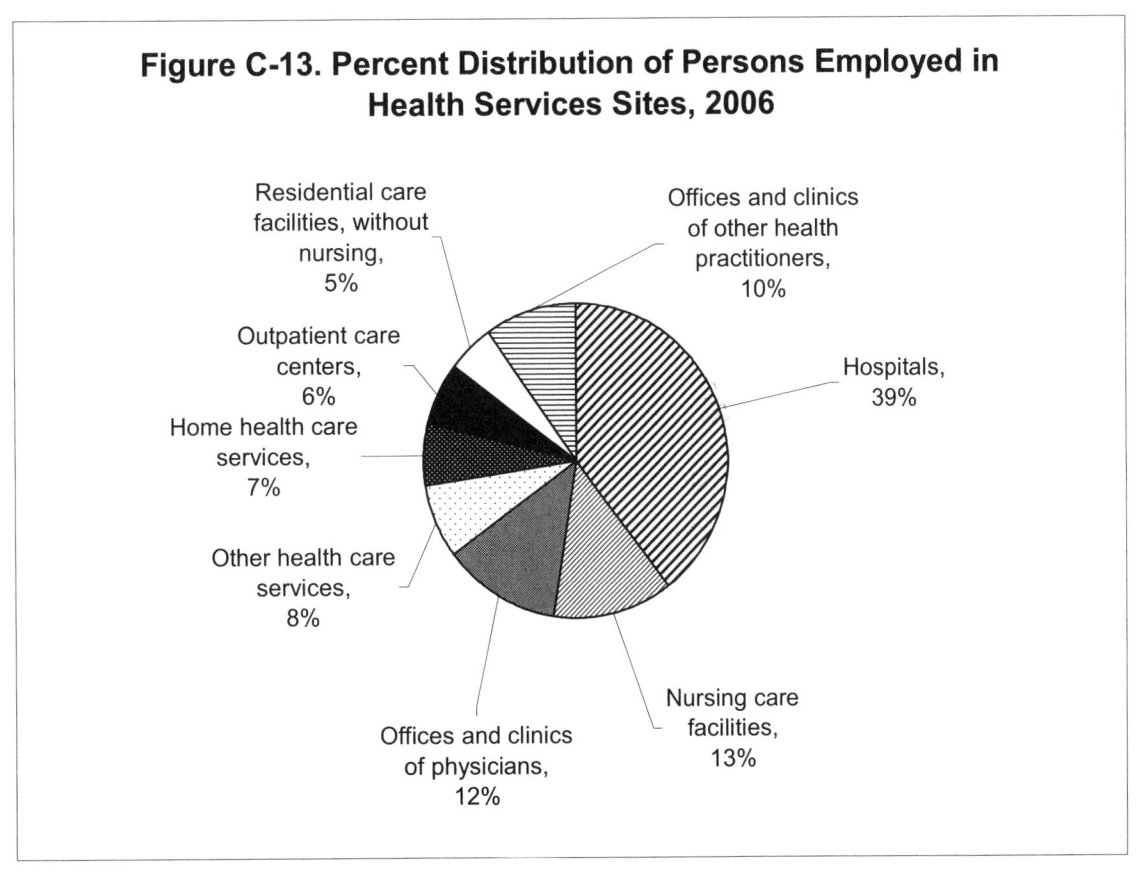

Figure C-13. Percent Distribution of Persons Employed in Health Services Sites, 2006

Table C-59. Persons Employed in Health Service Sites, by Site and Sex, 2000–2006

(Number in thousands, percent.)

Site and sex	2000	2001	2002	2003	2004	2005	2006
BOTH SEXES (NUMBER IN THOUSANDS)							
All employed civilians[1]	136,891	136,933	136,485	137,736	139,252	141,730	144,427
All Health Service Sites[2]	12,211	12,558	13,069	13,615	13,817	14,052	14,352
Offices and clinics of physicians	1,387	1,499	1,533	1,673	1,727	1,801	1,785
Offices and clinics of dentists	672	701	734	771	780	792	852
Offices and clinics of chiropractors	120	111	132	142	156	163	163
Offices and clinics of optometrists	95	102	113	92	93	98	98
Offices and clinics of other health practitioners[3]	143	140	149	250	274	275	292
Outpatient care centers	772	830	850	873	885	901	919
Home health care services	548	582	636	741	750	795	928
Other health care services[4]	1,027	1,101	1,188	943	976	1,045	1,096
Hospitals	5,202	5,256	5,330	5,652	5,700	5,719	5,712
Nursing care facilities	1,593	1,568	1,715	1,877	1,858	1,848	1,807
Residential care facilities, without nursing	652	668	689	601	618	615	700
MEN							
All Health Service Sites[2]	2,756	2,778	2,838	2,986	3,067	3,097	3,187
Offices and clinics of physicians	354	379	370	414	424	418	421
Offices and clinics of dentists	158	150	151	163	158	156	173
Offices and clinics of chiropractors	32	39	47	53	63	68	61
Offices and clinics of optometrists	26	27	29	29	24	27	29
Offices and clinics of other health practitioners[3]	38	41	42	63	69	80	80
Outpatient care centers	186	185	172	200	203	201	199
Home health care services	45	51	54	56	65	81	91
Other health care services[4]	304	345	362	297	314	311	344
Hospitals	1,241	1,187	1,195	1,263	1,333	1,347	1,337
Nursing care facilities	195	189	223	267	251	246	263
Residential care facilities, without nursing	177	185	193	181	164	162	189
WOMEN							
All Health Service Sites[2]	9,457	9,782	10,232	10,631	10,750	10,958	11,167
Offices and clinics of physicians	1,034	1,120	1,164	1,259	1,302	1,383	1,364
Offices and clinics of dentists	514	551	584	607	623	637	679
Offices and clinics of chiropractors	88	72	85	90	93	95	102
Offices and clinics of optometrists	69	75	84	64	69	71	69
Offices and clinics of other health practitioners[3]	106	99	106	186	204	195	213
Outpatient care centers	586	646	678	673	683	700	720
Home health care services	503	531	582	685	685	713	837
Other health care services[4]	723	756	826	646	662	734	752
Hospitals	3,961	4,069	4,135	4,390	4,366	4,372	4,376
Nursing care facilities	1,398	1,380	1,492	1,611	1,607	1,602	1,544
Residential care facilities, without nursing	475	483	496	420	454	453	511
BOTH SEXES (PERCENT)							
All Health Service Sites (Percent of Employed Civilians)	8.9	9.2	9.6	9.9	9.9	9.9	9.9
All Health Service Sites (Percent distribution)	100.0	100.0	100.0	100.0	100.0	100.0	100.0
Offices and clinics of physicians	11.4	11.9	11.7	12.3	12.5	12.8	12.4
Offices and clinics of dentists	5.5	5.6	5.6	5.7	5.6	5.6	5.9
Offices and clinics of chiropractors	1.0	0.9	1.0	1.0	1.1	1.2	1.1
Offices and clinics of optometrists	0.8	0.8	0.9	0.7	0.7	0.7	0.7
Offices and clinics of other health practitioners[3]	1.2	1.1	1.1	1.8	2.0	2.0	2.0
Outpatient care centers	6.3	6.6	6.5	6.4	6.4	6.4	6.4
Home health care services	4.5	4.6	4.9	5.4	5.4	5.7	6.5
Other health care services[4]	8.4	8.8	9.1	6.9	7.1	7.4	7.6
Hospitals	42.6	41.9	40.8	41.5	41.3	40.7	39.8
Nursing care facilities	13.0	12.5	13.1	13.8	13.4	13.2	12.6
Residential care facilities, without nursing	5.3	5.3	5.3	4.4	4.5	4.4	4.9

[1]Excludes workers under the age of 16 years.
[2]Data for health service sites for men and women may not sum to total for all health service sites for both sexes due to rounding.
[3]Includes health service sites such as psychologists' offices, nutritionists' offices, speech defect clinics, and other offices and clinics.
[4]Includes health service sites such as clinical laboratories, blood banks, CT-SCAN (computer tomography) centers, and other offices and clinics.

NOTE: Annual data are based on data collected each month and averaged over the year. Health service sites are based on the 2002 North American Industry Classification System.

Table C-60. Employees and Wages, by Selected Healthcare Occupations, Selected Years, 1999-2005

(Number, mean hourly wage.)

Occupation	Number of employees[1]				AAPC[2]	Mean hourly wage[3]				AAPC[2]
	1999	2000	2004	2005	1999–2005	1999	2000	2004	2005	1999–2005
Healthcare Practitioner and Technical Occupations										
Audiologists	12,950	11,530	9,810	10,030	-4.2	21.96	22.92	26.47	27.72	4.0
Cardiovascular Technologists and Technicians	41,490	40,080	43,540	43,560	0.8	16.00	16.81	19.09	19.99	3.8
Dental Hygienists	90,050	148,460	155,810	161,140	10.2	23.15	24.99	28.58	29.15	3.9
Diagnostic Medical Sonographers	29,280	31,760	41,280	43,590	6.9	21.04	22.03	25.78	26.65	4.0
Dietetic Technicians	29,190	28,010	24,630	23,780	-3.4	10.09	10.98	11.89	12.20	3.2
Dietitians and Nutritionists	41,320	43,030	46,530	48,850	2.8	17.96	18.76	21.46	22.09	3.5
Emergency Medical Technicians and Paramedics	172,360	165,530	187,900	196,880	2.2	11.19	11.89	13.30	13.68	3.4
Licensed Practical and Licensed Vocational Nurses	688,510	679,470	702,740	710,020	0.5	13.95	14.65	16.75	17.41	3.8
Nuclear Medicine Technologists	17,880	18,030	17,520	18,280	0.4	20.40	21.56	29.43	29.10	6.1
Occupational Therapists	78,950	75,150	83,560	87,430	1.7	24.96	24.10	27.19	28.41	2.2
Opticians, Dispensing	58,860	66,580	62,350	70,090	3.0	12.11	12.67	14.37	14.80	3.4
Pharmacists	226,300	212,660	222,960	229,740	0.3	30.31	33.39	40.56	42.62	5.8
Pharmacy Technicians	196,430	190,940	255,290	266,790	5.2	9.64	10.38	11.87	12.19	4.0
Physical Therapists	131,050	120,410	142,940	151,280	2.4	28.05	27.62	30.00	31.42	1.9
Physician Assistants	56,750	55,490	59,470	63,350	1.9	24.35	29.17	33.07	34.17	5.8
Psychiatric Technicians	54,560	53,350	59,010	62,040	2.2	11.30	12.53	13.43	14.04	3.7
Radiation Therapists	12,340	13,100	14,470	14,120	2.3	20.84	25.59	29.05	30.59	6.6
Radiologic Technologists and Technicians	177,850	172,080	177,220	184,580	0.6	17.07	17.93	21.41	22.60	4.8
Recreational Therapists	30,190	26,940	23,050	23,260	-4.3	14.08	14.23	16.48	16.90	3.1
Registered Nurses	2,205,430	2,189,670	2,311,970	2,368,070	1.2	21.38	22.31	26.06	27.35	4.2
Respiratory Therapists	80,230	82,670	91,350	95,320	2.9	17.72	18.37	21.24	22.24	3.9
Respiratory Therapy Technicians	33,990	28,230	24,190	22,060	-7.0	16.07	16.46	18.00	18.57	2.4
Speech-Language Pathologists	85,920	82,850	89,260	94,660	1.6	22.99	23.31	26.71	27.89	3.3
Healthcare Support Occupations										
Dental Assistants	175,160	250,870	264,820	270,720	7.5	11.60	12.86	13.97	14.41	3.7
Home Health Aides	577,530	561,120	596,330	663,280	2.3	9.04	8.71	9.13	9.34	0.5
Massage Therapists	21,910	24,620	32,200	37,670	9.5	13.82	15.51	17.63	19.33	5.8
Medical Assistants	281,480	330,830	380,340	382,720	5.3	10.89	11.46	12.21	12.58	2.4
Medical Equipment Preparers	29,070	32,760	40,380	41,790	6.2	10.20	10.68	12.14	12.42	3.3
Medical Transcriptionists	97,260	97,330	92,740	90,380	-1.2	11.86	12.37	14.01	14.36	3.2
Nursing Aides, Orderlies, and Attendants	1,308,740	1,273,460	1,384,120	1,391,430	1.0	8.59	9.18	10.39	10.67	3.7
Occupational Therapist Aides	9,250	8,890	5,240	6,220	-6.4	10.92	11.21	12.51	13.20	3.2
Occupational Therapist Assistants	17,290	15,910	20,880	22,160	4.2	15.97	16.76	18.49	19.13	3.1
Pharmacy Aides	48,270	59,890	47,720	46,610	-0.6	9.14	9.10	9.52	9.76	1.1
Physical Therapist Aides	44,340	34,620	41,910	41,930	-0.9	9.69	10.06	11.14	11.01	2.2
Physical Therapist Assistants	48,600	44,120	57,420	58,670	3.2	16.20	16.52	18.14	18.98	2.7
Psychiatric Aides	51,100	57,680	54,520	56,150	1.6	10.76	10.79	11.70	11.47	1.1

[1]Estimates do not include self-employed workers and were rounded to the nearest 10.
[2]Average annual percent change.
[3]The mean hourly wage rate for an occupation is the total wages that all workers in the occupation earn in an hour divided by the total employment of the occupation.

NOTE: This table excludes occupations such as dentists, physicians, and chiropractors, with a large percentage of workers who are self-employed and/or not employed by establishments.

Table C-61. Employment and Projected Employment of Health Care Workers by Occupation, 2006–2016

(Number, Percent.)

Occupation	Employment (2006)	Projected employment (2016)	Change (2006–2016)	
			Number	Percent
Personal and home care aides	767,000	1,156,000	389,000	51
Medical assistants	417,000	565,000	148,000	35
Veterinarians	62,000	84,000	22,000	35
Social and human service assistants	339,000	453,000	114,000	34
Dental hygienists	167,000	217,000	50,000	30
Dental assistants	280,000	362,000	82,000	29
Physical therapist assistants and aides	107,000	137,000	31,000	29
Nursing, psychiatric, and home health aides	2,296,000	2,944,000	647,000	28
Physical therapists	173,000	220,000	47,000	27
Physician assistants	66,000	83,000	18,000	27
Cardiovascular technologists and technicians	45,000	57,000	12,000	26
Occupational therapist assistants and aides	33,000	41,000	8,200	25
Surgical technologists	86,000	107,000	21,000	24
Occupational therapists	99,000	122,000	23,000	23
Registered nurses	2,505,000	3,092,000	587,000	23
Pharmacists	243,000	296,000	53,000	22
Social workers	595,000	727,000	132,000	22
Diagnostic medical sonographers	46,000	54,000	8,700	19
Emergency medical technicians and paramedics	201,000	240,000	39,000	19
Respiratory therapists	122,000	145,000	23,000	19
Medical records and health information technicians	170,000	200,000	30,000	18
Medical and health services managers	262,000	305,000	43,000	16
Nuclear medicine technologists	20,000	23,000	2,900	15
Psychologists	166,000	191,000	25,000	15
Radiologic technologists and technicians	196,000	226,000	30,000	15
Chiropractors	53,000	60,000	7,600	14
Clinical laboratory technologists and technicians	319,000	362,000	43,000	14
Licensed practical and licensed vocational nurses	749,000	854,000	105,000	14
Medical transcriptionists	98,000	112,000	13,000	14
Physicians and surgeons	633,000	633,000	90,000	14
Optometrists	33,000	36,000	3,700	11
Speech-language pathologists	110,000	121,000	12,000	11
Audiologists	12,000	13,000	1,200	10
Dentists	161,000	176,000	15,000	9
Dietitians and nutritionists	57,000	62,000	4,900	9
Opticians, dispensing	66,000	72,000	5,700	9
Podiatrists	12,000	13,000	1,100	9
Medical, dental, and ophthalmic laboratory technicians	95,000	100,000	5,000	5
Recreational therapists	25,000	26,000	1,000	4
Pharmacy aides	50,000	45,000	-5,600	-11

Table C-62. Median Hourly Earnings of the Largest Occupations in Health Care by Type of Establishment, May 2006

(Dollars.)

Occupation	Ambulatory health care services	Hospitals	Nursing and residential care services	All industries
Registered nurses	26.25	28.12	25.03	27.54
Licensed practical and licensed vocational nurses	16.78	16.89	18.35	17.57
Dental assistants	14.50	14.76	...	14.53
Medical secretaries	13.62	13.30	12.66	13.51
Medical assistants	12.58	13.14	11.60	12.64
Receptionists and information clerks	11.55	11.74	10.07	11.01
Office clerks, general	11.47	12.55	11.12	11.40
Nursing aides, orderlies, and attendants	10.76	11.06	10.30	10.67
Home health aides	9.15	10.64	9.23	9.34
Personal and home care aides	7.23	9.17	9.36	8.54

... = Not applicable.

NOTE: Earnings vary not only by type of establishment and occupation, but also by size; salaries tend to be higher in larger hospitals and group practices. Geographic location also can affect earnings.

Table C-63. Patient Care Physician Supply and Distribution Among United States Counties, by County Metropolitan Status, 2004

(Number, percent.)

Characteristic	Total	Metropolitan counties[1]	Nonmetropolitan counties
All Counties			
Number of patient care physicians..	707,380	646,571	60,809
Patient care physicians per 10,000 population	24.1	26.5	12.2
PATIENT CARE PHYSICIANS PER 10,000 POPULATION			
Number of Counties			
0	134	11	123
0.1-2.86	205	74	131
2.87-24.1	2,454	731	1,723
24.2-226	348	274	74
Percent of Counties			
0	4.3	1.0	6.0
0.1-2.86	6.5	6.8	6.4
2.87-24.1	78.1	67.1	84.0
24.2-226	11.1	25.1	3.6
Population in Counties			
0	419,773	72,270	347,503
0.1-2.86	3,199,705	1,634,433	1,565,272
2.87-24.1	164,762,304	119,992,662	44,769,642
24.2-226	125,273,622	122,257,377	3,016,245

[1]Metropolitan counties are defined using the Office of Management and Budget definition.

NOTE: Data are for active, nonfederal, patient care physicians. Doctors of medicine and doctors of osteopathy are included. Patient care physicians include physicians, full-time hospital staff, and residents or fellows.

HEALTH EXPENDITURES

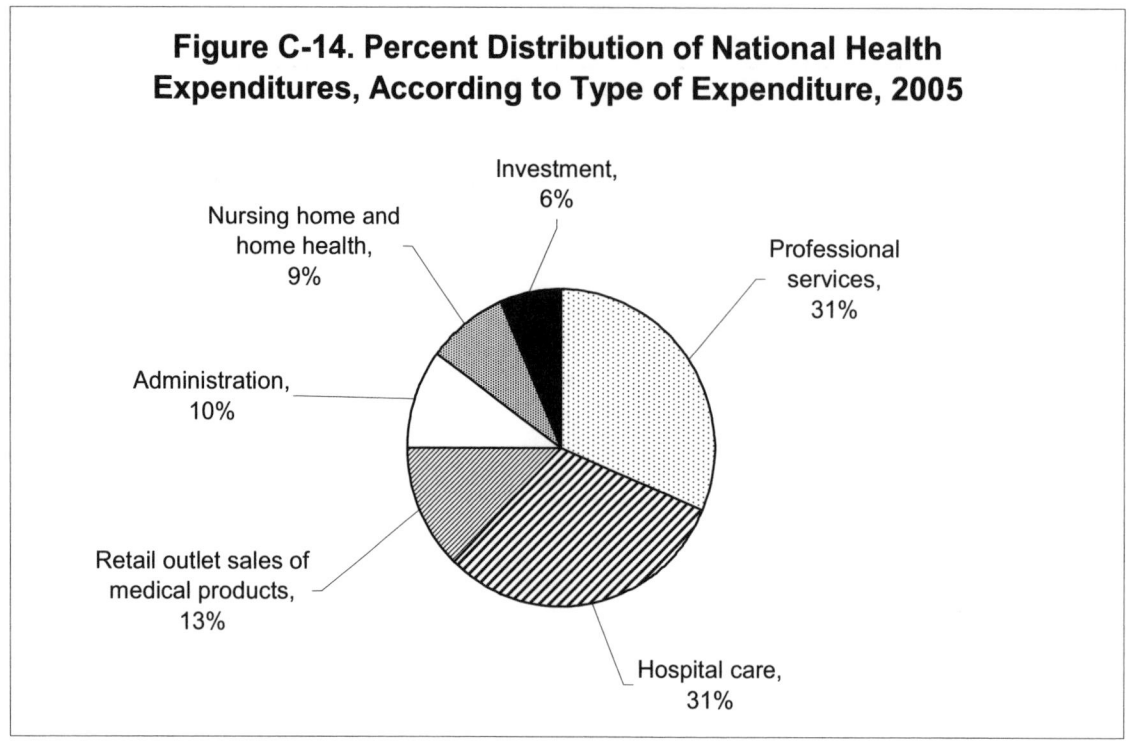

Figure C-14. Percent Distribution of National Health Expenditures, According to Type of Expenditure, 2005

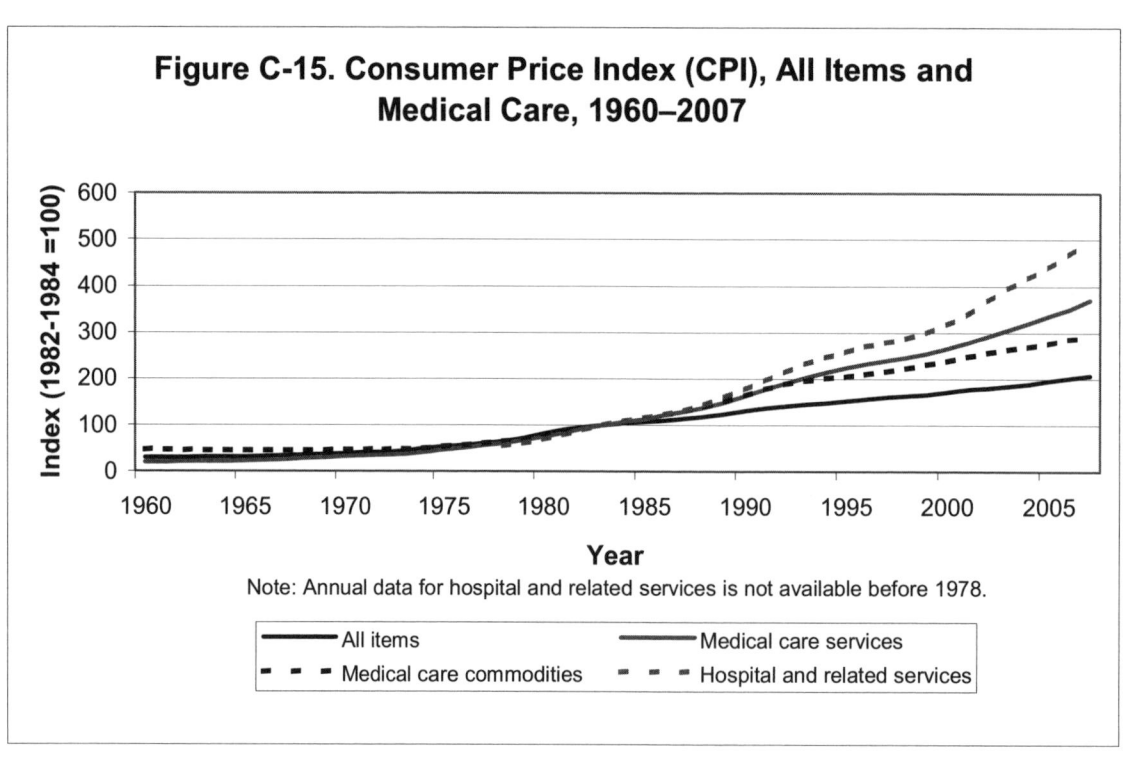

Figure C-15. Consumer Price Index (CPI), All Items and Medical Care, 1960–2007

Note: Annual data for hospital and related services is not available before 1978.

All items — Medical care services — Medical care commodities — Hospital and related services

Table C-64. Total Health Expenditures as a Percent of Gross Domestic Product and Per Capita Health Expenditures in Dollars, by Selected Countries, Selected Years, 1960–2004

(Percent, dollar.)

Country	1960	1970	1980	1990	1995	2000	2001	2002[1]	2003[1]	2004[1]
Health Expenditures as a Percent of Gross Domestic Product										
Australia	4.0	—	6.8	7.5	8.0	8.8	8.9	9.1	9.2	9.6
Austria	4.3	5.2	7.5	7.0	9.7	9.4	9.5	9.5	9.6	9.6
Belgium	—	3.9	6.3	7.2	8.2	8.6	8.7	8.9	10.1	—
Canada	5.4	7.0	7.1	9.0	9.2	8.9	9.4	9.7	9.9	9.9
Czech Republic	—	—	—	4.7	7.0	6.7	7.0	7.2	7.5	7.3
Denmark	—	—	8.9	8.3	8.1	8.3	8.6	8.8	8.9	8.9
Finland	3.8	5.6	6.3	7.8	7.4	6.7	6.9	7.2	7.4	7.5
France	3.8	5.3	7.0	8.4	9.4	9.2	9.3	10.0	10.4	10.5
Germany	—	6.2	8.7	8.5	10.1	10.3	10.4	10.6	10.8	10.6
Greece	—	6.1	6.6	7.4	9.6	9.9	10.4	10.3	10.5	10.0
Hungary	—	—	—	—	7.4	7.1	7.3	7.7	8.3	8.0
Iceland	3.0	4.7	6.2	7.9	8.4	9.2	9.3	10.0	10.5	10.2
Ireland	3.7	5.1	8.3	6.1	6.7	6.3	6.8	7.2	7.2	7.1
Italy	—	—	—	7.7	7.1	8.1	8.2	8.3	8.4	8.7
Japan	3.0	4.5	6.5	5.9	6.8	7.6	7.8	7.9	8.0	—
Korea	—	—	—	4.4	4.2	4.8	5.4	5.3	5.5	5.6
Luxembourg	—	3.1	5.2	5.4	5.6	5.8	6.4	6.8	7.7	8.0
Mexico	—	—	—	4.8	5.6	5.6	6.0	6.2	6.3	6.5
Netherlands	—	—	7.2	7.7	8.1	7.9	8.3	8.9	9.1	9.2
New Zealand	—	5.1	5.9	6.9	7.2	7.7	7.8	8.2	8.0	8.4
Norway	2.9	4.4	7.0	7.7	7.9	8.5	8.9	9.9	10.1	9.7
Poland	—	—	—	4.9	5.6	5.7	6.0	6.6	6.5	6.5
Portugal	—	2.6	5.6	6.2	8.2	9.4	9.3	9.5	9.8	10.1
Slovak Republic	—	—	—	—	—	5.5	5.5	5.6	5.9	—
Spain	1.5	3.5	5.3	6.5	7.4	7.2	7.2	7.3	7.9	8.1
Sweden	—	6.8	9.0	8.3	8.1	8.4	8.7	9.1	9.3	9.1
Switzerland	4.9	5.5	7.4	8.3	9.7	10.4	10.9	11.1	11.5	11.6
Turkey	—	—	3.3	3.6	3.4	6.6	7.5	7.4	7.6	7.7
United Kingdom	3.9	4.5	5.6	6.0	7.0	7.3	7.5	7.7	7.8	8.1
United States	5.1	7.0	8.8	11.9	13.3	13.3	14.0	14.7	15.2	15.3
Per Capita Health Expenditures[2]										
Australia	94	—	691	1306	1741	2398	2544	2724	2886	3120
Austria	77	193	770	1,328	2,229	2,667	2,748	2,857	2,958	3,124
Belgium	—	148	636	1,341	1,828	2,277	2,425	2,612	3,044	—
Canada	125	299	783	1,737	2,055	2,503	2,718	2,861	2,998	3,165
Czech Republic	—	—	—	561	902	980	1,089	1,188	1,296	1,361
Denmark	—	—	927	1,522	1,844	2,380	2,555	2,656	2,743	2,881
Finland	63	191	590	1,419	1,430	1,716	1,857	2,012	2,104	2,235
France	70	205	697	1,532	2,028	2,450	2,611	2,886	3,048	3,159
Germany	—	269	960	1,738	2,226	2,632	2,746	2,883	2,983	3,043
Greece	—	159	486	844	1,250	1,616	1,805	1,971	2,141	2,162
Hungary	—	—	—	—	685	856	975	1,115	1,249	1,276
Iceland	57	163	703	1,593	1,854	2,623	2,740	2,948	3,159	3,331
Ireland	43	117	519	794	1,216	1,809	2,099	2,395	2,455	2,596
Italy	—	—	—	1,387	1,534	2,083	2,184	2,275	2,314	2,467
Japan	30	149	580	1,116	1,541	1,967	2,082	2,138	2,249	—
Korea	—	—	—	361	540	778	938	975	1,068	1,149
Luxembourg	—	163	640	1,533	2,033	2,982	3,263	3,729	4,611	5,089
Mexico	—	—	—	306	388	506	548	578	608	662
Netherlands	—	—	755	1,435	1,822	2,257	2,519	2,775	2,909	3,041
New Zealand	—	211	506	995	1,246	1,605	1,705	1,850	1,902	2,083
Norway	49	141	665	1,393	1,893	3,080	3,286	3,616	3,769	3,966
Poland	—	—	—	300	423	590	646	734	748	805
Portugal	—	51	292	674	1,096	1,624	1,681	1,783	1,721	1,824
Slovak Republic	—	—	—	—	—	595	641	716	777	—
Spain	16	95	363	873	1,193	1,520	1,613	1,723	1,952	2,094
Sweden	—	312	944	1,589	1,734	2,271	2,404	2,593	2,745	2,825
Switzerland	166	351	1,031	2,029	2,573	3,179	3,364	3,650	3,847	4,077
Turkey	—	—	76	168	187	451	459	482	512	580
United Kingdom	84	163	480	987	1,385	1,858	2,029	2,228	2,317	2,508
United States	147	352	1,072	2,752	3,670	4,588	4,933	5,324	5,711	6,102

—— = Data not available.
[1]Preliminary figures.
[2]Per capita health expenditures for each country have been adjusted to U.S. dollars using gross domestic product purchasing power parities for each year.

Table C-65. Gross Domestic Product, Federal, and State and Local Government Expenditures, National Health Expenditures, and Average Annual Percent Change, Selected Years, 1960–2005

(Dollar, percent.)

Gross domestic product, government expenditures, and national health expenditures	1960	1970	1980	1990	1995	2000	2003	2004	2005
Amount in Billions									
Gross domestic product (GDP)	526	1,039	2,790	5,803	7,398	9,817	10,961	11,713	12,456
Federal government expenditures	87	201	586	1,254	1,604	1,864	2,252	2,383	2,556
State and local government expenditures	40	113	329	731	978	1,270	1,515	1,606	1,704
National health expenditures	28	75	254	714	1,017	1,353	1,733	1,859	1,988
Private	21	47	148	427	552	757	956	1,021	1,085
Public	7	28	106	287	465	596	778	838	903
Federal government	3	18	72	194	327	417	553	601	644
State and local government	4	10	35	93	138	179	225	237	259
Amount per Capita									
National health expenditures	148	356	1,102	2,813	3,783	4,790	5,952	6,322	6,697
Private	111	222	640	1,684	2,053	2,680	3,282	3,472	3,656
Public	36	134	462	1,130	1,730	2,110	2,670	2,850	3,041
Percent									
National health expenditures as percent of GDP	5.2	7.2	9.1	12.3	13.7	13.8	15.8	15.9	16.0
Health Expenditures as a Percent of Total Government Expenditures									
Federal government	3.3	8.8	12.2	15.5	20.4	22.4	24.6	25.2	25.2
State and local government	9.8	9.2	10.6	12.7	14.1	14.1	14.8	14.8	15.2
National Health Expenditures (Percent Distribution)	100.0	100.0	100.0	100.0	100.0	100.0	100.0	100.0	100.0
Private	75.3	62.4	58.1	59.8	54.3	55.9	55.1	54.9	54.6
Public	24.7	37.6	41.9	40.2	45.7	44.1	44.9	45.1	45.4
Average Annual Percent Change from Previous Year Shown									
Gross domestic product	...	7.0	10.4	7.6	5.0	5.8	3.7	6.9	6.3
Federal government expenditures	...	8.8	11.3	7.9	5.0	3.1	6.5	5.8	7.3
State and local government expenditures	...	10.9	11.3	8.3	6.0	5.4	6.1	6.0	6.1
National health expenditures	...	10.5	13.0	10.9	7.3	5.9	8.6	7.2	6.9
Private	...	8.5	12.2	11.2	5.2	6.5	8.1	6.8	6.3
Public	...	15.3	14.2	10.4	10.1	5.1	9.3	7.8	7.7
Federal government	...	20.0	15.0	10.5	11.0	5.0	9.8	8.6	7.2
State and local government	...	10.2	12.8	10.3	8.2	5.4	7.9	5.7	9.1
National health expenditures, per capita	...	9.2	12.0	9.8	6.1	4.8	7.5	6.2	5.9
Private	...	7.2	11.2	10.1	4.0	5.5	7.0	5.8	5.3
Public	...	13.9	13.2	9.4	8.9	4.1	8.2	6.7	6.7

… = Not applicable.

Table C-66. Consumer Price Index and Average Annual Percent Change for All Items, Selected Items, and Medical Care Components, Selected Years, 1960–2006

(Number, percent.)

Items and medical care components	1960	1970	1980	1990	1995	2000	2003	2004	2005	2006
Consumer Price Index (CPI)										
All items	29.6	38.8	82.4	130.7	152.4	172.2	184.0	188.9	195.3	201.6
All items less medical care	30.2	39.2	82.8	128.8	148.6	167.3	178.1	182.7	188.7	194.7
Services	24.1	35.0	77.9	139.2	168.7	195.3	216.5	222.8	230.1	238.9
Food	30.0	39.2	86.8	132.4	148.4	167.8	180.0	186.2	190.7	195.2
Apparel	45.7	59.2	90.9	124.1	132.0	129.6	120.9	120.4	119.5	119.5
Housing	—	36.4	81.1	128.5	148.5	169.6	184.8	189.5	195.7	203.2
Energy	22.4	25.5	86.0	102.1	105.2	124.6	136.5	151.4	177.1	196.9
Medical care	22.3	34.0	74.9	162.8	220.5	260.8	297.1	310.1	323.2	336.2
Components of Medical Care										
Medical care services	19.5	32.3	74.8	162.7	224.2	266.0	306.0	321.3	336.7	350.6
Professional services	—	37.0	77.9	156.1	201.0	237.7	261.2	271.5	281.7	289.3
Physicians' services	21.9	34.5	76.5	160.8	208.8	244.7	267.7	278.3	287.5	291.9
Dental services	27.0	39.2	78.9	155.8	206.8	258.5	292.5	306.9	324.0	340.9
Eye glasses and eye care[1]	—	—	—	117.3	137.0	149.7	155.9	159.3	163.2	168.1
Services by other medical professionals[1]	—	—	—	120.2	143.9	161.9	177.1	181.9	186.8	192.2
Hospital and related services	—	—	69.2	178.0	257.8	317.3	394.8	417.9	439.9	468.1
Hospital services[2]	—	—	—	—	—	115.9	144.7	153.4	161.6	172.1
Inpatient hospital services[2,3]	—	—	—	—	—	113.8	140.1	148.1	156.6	167.5
Outpatient hospital services[1,3]	—	—	—	138.7	204.6	263.8	337.9	356.3	373.0	395.0
Hospital rooms	9.3	23.6	68.0	175.4	251.2	—	—	—	—	—
Other inpatient services[1]	—	—	—	142.7	206.8	—	—	—	—	—
Nursing homes and adult day care[2]	—	—	—	—	—	117.0	135.2	140.4	145.0	151.0
Health insurance[4]	—	—	—	—	—	—	—	—	—	103.1
Medical care commodities	46.9	46.5	75.4	163.4	204.5	238.1	262.8	269.3	276.0	285.9
Prescription drugs and medical supplies	54.0	47.4	72.5	181.7	235.0	285.4	326.3	337.1	349.0	363.9
Nonprescription drugs and medical supplies[1]	—	—	—	120.6	140.5	149.5	152.0	152.3	151.7	154.6
Internal and respiratory over-the-counter drugs	—	42.3	74.9	145.9	167.0	176.9	181.2	180.9	179.7	183.4
Nonprescription medical equipment and supplies	—	—	79.2	138.0	166.3	178.1	178.1	179.7	180.6	183.2
Average Annual Percent Change from Previous Year Shown										
All items	...	2.7	7.8	4.7	3.1	2.5	2.2	2.7	3.4	3.2
All items excluding medical care	...	2.6	7.8	4.5	2.9	2.4	2.1	2.6	3.3	3.2
All services	...	3.8	8.3	6.0	3.9	3.0	3.5	2.9	3.3	3.8
Food	...	2.7	8.3	4.3	2.3	2.5	2.4	3.4	2.4	2.4
Apparel	...	2.6	4.4	3.2	1.2	-0.4	-2.3	-0.4	-0.7	0.0
Housing	...	—	8.3	4.7	2.9	2.7	2.9	2.5	3.3	3.8
Energy	...	1.3	12.9	1.7	0.6	3.4	3.1	10.9	17.0	11.2
Medical care	...	4.3	8.2	8.1	6.3	3.4	4.4	4.4	4.2	4.0
Components of Medical Care										
Medical care services	...	5.2	8.8	8.1	6.6	3.5	4.8	5.0	4.8	4.1
Professional services	...	—	7.7	7.2	5.2	3.4	3.2	3.9	3.8	2.7
Physicians' services	...	4.6	8.3	7.7	5.4	3.2	3.0	4.0	3.3	1.5
Dental services	...	3.8	7.2	7.0	5.8	4.6	4.2	4.9	5.6	5.2
Eye glasses and eye care[1]	...	—	—	—	3.2	1.8	1.4	2.2	2.4	3.0
Services by other medical professionals[1]	...	—	—	—	3.7	2.4	3.0	2.7	2.7	2.9
Hospital and related services	...	—	—	9.9	7.7	4.2	7.6	5.9	5.3	6.4
Hospital services[2]	...	—	—	—	—	—	7.7	6.0	5.3	6.5
Inpatient hospital services[2,3]	...	—	—	—	—	—	7.2	5.7	5.7	7.0
Outpatient hospital services[1,3]	...	—	—	—	8.1	5.2	8.6	5.4	4.7	5.9
Hospital rooms	...	9.8	11.2	9.9	7.4	—	—	—	—	—
Other inpatient services[1]	...	—	—	—	7.7	—	—	—	—	—
Nursing homes and adult day care[2]	...	—	—	—	—	—	4.9	3.8	3.3	4.1
Health insurance[4]	...	—	—	—	—	—	—	—	—	—
Medical care commodities	...	-0.1	5.0	8.0	4.6	3.1	3.3	2.5	2.5	3.6
Prescription drugs and medical supplies	...	-1.3	4.3	9.6	5.3	4.0	4.6	3.3	3.5	4.3
Nonprescription drugs and medical supplies[1]	...	—	—	—	3.1	1.2	0.6	0.2	-0.4	1.9
Internal and respiratory over-the-counter drugs	...	—	5.9	6.9	2.7	1.2	0.8	-0.2	-0.7	2.1
Nonprescription medical equipment and supplies	...	—	—	5.7	3.8	1.4	0.0	0.9	0.5	1.4

— = Data not available.
... = Not applicable.
[1]December 1986 = 100.
[2]December 1996 = 100.
[3]Special index based on a substantially smaller sample.
[4]December 2005 = 100.

NOTE: Consumer Price Index for all urban consumers (CPI-U) U.S. city average, detailed expenditure categories. 1982–1984 = 100, except where noted. Data are not seasonally adjusted.

Table C-67. Growth in Personal Health Care Expenditures and Percent Distribution of Factors Affecting Growth, 1960–2005

(Percent.)

| Period | Average annual percent increase | All factors | Factors affecting growth (percent distribution) | | | |
| | | | Inflation[2] | | Population | Intensity[3] |
			Economy-wide	Medical		
1960–2005	9.9	100	39	17	11	33
1960–1965	8.3	100	17	10	18	55
1965–1970	12.7	100	34	12	8	46
1970–1975	12.3	100	55	1	8	36
1975–1980	13.8	100	54	12	7	27
1980–1985	11.6	100	47	32	9	12
1980–1981	15.9	100	61	17	7	15
1981–1982	12.0	100	52	37	9	2
1982–1983	10.3	100	40	34	10	16
1983–1984	9.6	100	40	39	10	11
1984–1985	10.2	100	31	41	10	18
1985–1990	10.3	100	32	26	10	32
1985–1986	8.7	100	26	31	11	32
1986–1987	9.4	100	30	23	10	37
1987–1988	11.2	100	32	25	9	35
1988–1989	10.5	100	37	29	10	23
1989–1990	11.7	100	34	24	10	31
1990–1995	7.3	100	34	29	16	20
1990–1991	10.2	100	36	21	12	31
1991–1992	8.5	100	28	35	15	22
1992–1993	6.6	100	36	35	19	11
1993–1994	5.3	100	41	31	21	7
1994–1995	6.1	100	34	25	18	22
1995–2000	5.7	100	30	18	18	35
1995–1996	5.4	100	36	19	19	26
1996–1997	5.4	100	31	9	20	40
1997–1998	5.3	100	21	20	20	38
1998–1999	5.7	100	26	22	18	34
1999–2000	6.7	100	33	17	15	35
2000–2005	7.8	100	32	18	13	38
2000–2001	8.7	100	28	17	12	42
2001–2002	8.3	100	22	26	13	40
2002–2003	7.8	100	28	20	13	39
2003–2004	7.3	100	40	17	14	30
2004–2005	7.1	100	43	7	14	36

[1]Percents may not sum to 100 due to rounding.
[2]Total inflation is economy wide and medical inflation is the medical inflation above economy wide inflation.
[3]Intensity is the residual percent of growth cannot be attributed to price increases or population growth. It represents changes in use or kinds of services and supplies.

NOTE: These data include revisions in health expenditures for 1960 forward and revisions in population for 1990 forward. The implicit price deflator for gross domestic product (GDP) is used to measure economy–wide inflation for all years 1960–2005. All indexes used to calculate the factors affecting growth were rebased in 2003 with base year 2000.

Table C-68. National Health Expenditures, Average Annual Percent Change, and Percent Distribution, by Type of Expenditure, Selected Years, 1960–2005

(Dollar, percent.)

Type of national health expenditure	1960	1970	1980	1990	1995	2000	2002	2003	2004	2005
Amount in Billions										
National health expenditures	27.5	74.9	253.9	714.0	1,016.5	1,353.3	1,602.8	1,733.4	1,858.9	1,987.7
Health services and supplies	24.9	67.1	234.0	666.7	952.8	1,264.4	1,498.8	1,621.7	1,738.9	1,860.9
Personal health care	23.3	62.9	215.3	607.5	863.7	1,139.9	1,341.2	1,446.3	1,551.3	1,661.4
Hospital care	9.2	27.6	101.0	251.6	340.7	417.0	488.6	525.4	566.9	611.6
Professional services	8.3	20.6	67.3	216.8	316.5	426.7	503.1	543.0	581.1	621.7
Physician and clinical services	5.4	14.0	47.1	157.5	220.5	288.6	337.9	366.7	393.7	421.2
Other professional services	0.4	0.7	3.6	18.2	28.5	39.1	45.6	49.0	52.6	56.7
Dental services	2.0	4.7	13.3	31.5	44.5	62.0	73.3	76.9	81.5	86.6
Other personal health care	0.6	1.2	3.3	9.6	23.0	37.1	46.3	50.4	53.3	57.2
Nursing home and home health	0.9	4.3	21.4	65.2	104.6	125.8	139.9	148.5	157.7	169.3
Home health care[1]	0.1	0.2	2.4	12.6	30.5	30.5	34.2	38.0	42.7	47.5
Nursing home care[1]	0.8	4.0	19.0	52.6	74.1	95.3	105.7	110.5	115.0	121.9
Retail outlet sales of medical products	4.9	10.5	25.7	74.0	101.8	170.3	209.6	229.4	245.5	258.8
Prescription drugs	2.7	5.5	12.0	40.3	60.9	120.8	157.9	174.6	189.7	200.7
Other medical products	2.3	5.0	13.6	33.7	40.9	49.5	51.6	54.7	55.9	58.1
Government administration and net cost of private health insurance	1.2	2.8	12.2	39.2	58.1	81.2	105.2	122.6	135.2	143.0
Government public health activities[2]	0.4	1.4	6.4	20.0	31.0	43.4	52.4	52.8	52.5	56.6
Investment	2.6	7.8	19.9	47.3	63.7	88.8	104.0	111.7	119.9	126.8
Research[3]	0.7	2.0	5.4	12.7	18.3	25.6	32.5	35.8	38.3	40.0
Structures and equipment	1.9	5.8	14.5	34.7	45.4	63.2	71.5	75.9	81.7	86.8
Average Annual Percent Change from Previous Year Shown										
National health expenditures	...	10.5	13.0	10.9	7.3	5.9	8.8	8.1	7.2	6.9
Health services and supplies	...	10.4	13.3	11.0	7.4	5.8	8.9	8.2	7.2	7.0
Personal health care	...	10.4	13.1	10.9	7.3	5.7	8.5	7.8	7.3	7.1
Hospital care	...	11.6	13.9	9.6	6.3	4.1	8.2	7.5	7.9	7.9
Professional services	...	9.5	12.5	12.4	7.9	6.2	8.6	7.9	7.0	7.0
Physician and clinical services	...	10.1	12.9	12.8	7.0	5.5	8.2	8.5	7.4	7.0
Other professional services	...	6.6	17.1	17.5	9.5	6.5	8.0	7.5	7.4	7.8
Dental services	...	9.1	11.1	9.0	7.1	6.9	8.8	4.8	6.0	6.3
Other personal health care	...	7.3	10.1	11.4	19.2	10.0	11.8	8.7	5.7	7.3
Nursing home and home health	...	17.2	17.5	11.8	9.9	3.8	5.5	6.1	6.2	7.3
Home health care[1]	...	14.5	26.9	18.1	19.4	0.0	5.9	11.1	12.3	11.1
Nursing home care[1]	...	17.4	16.8	10.7	7.1	5.2	5.3	4.5	4.1	6.0
Retail outlet sales of medical products	...	7.8	9.4	11.2	6.6	10.8	10.9	9.5	7.0	5.4
Prescription drugs	...	7.5	8.2	12.8	8.6	14.7	14.3	10.6	8.6	5.8
Other medical products	...	8.1	10.6	9.5	4.0	3.9	2.1	6.1	2.1	3.9
Government administration and net cost of private health insurance	...	8.6	16.0	12.4	8.2	6.9	13.8	16.6	10.3	5.7
Government public health activities[2]	...	12.8	16.5	12.0	9.2	7.0	9.9	0.8	-0.6	7.7
Investment	...	11.7	9.9	9.0	6.1	6.9	8.2	7.4	7.3	5.7
Research[3]	...	10.9	10.8	8.9	7.7	6.9	12.8	10.1	6.7	4.6
Structures and equipment	...	11.9	9.5	9.1	5.5	6.8	6.3	6.2	7.6	6.3
Percent Distribution										
National health expenditures	100.0	100.0	100.0	100.0	100.0	100.0	100.0	100.0	100.0	100.0
Health services and supplies	90.6	89.6	92.1	93.4	93.7	93.4	93.5	93.6	93.5	93.6
Personal health care	84.7	84.0	84.8	85.1	85.0	84.2	83.7	83.4	83.5	83.6
Hospital care	33.3	36.8	39.8	35.2	33.5	30.8	30.5	30.3	30.5	30.8
Professional services	30.2	27.6	26.5	30.4	31.1	31.5	31.4	31.3	31.3	31.3
Physician and clinical services	19.4	18.7	18.5	22.1	21.7	21.3	21.1	21.2	21.2	21.2
Other professional services	1.4	1.0	1.4	2.5	2.8	2.9	2.8	2.8	2.8	2.9
Dental services	7.1	6.2	5.2	4.4	4.4	4.6	4.6	4.4	4.4	4.4
Other personal health care	2.2	1.7	1.3	1.3	2.3	2.7	2.9	2.9	2.9	2.9
Nursing home and home health	3.2	5.7	8.4	9.1	10.3	9.3	8.7	8.6	8.5	8.5
Home health care[1]	0.2	0.3	0.9	1.8	3.0	2.3	2.1	2.2	2.3	2.4
Nursing home care[1]	2.9	5.4	7.5	7.4	7.3	7.0	6.6	6.4	6.2	6.1
Retail outlet sales of medical products	18.0	14.0	10.1	10.4	10.0	12.6	13.1	13.2	13.2	13.0
Prescription drugs	9.7	7.3	4.7	5.6	6.0	8.9	9.9	10.1	10.2	10.1
Other medical products	8.2	6.6	5.4	4.7	4.0	3.7	3.2	3.2	3.0	2.9
Government administration and net cost of private health insurance	4.4	3.7	4.8	5.5	5.7	6.0	6.6	7.1	7.3	7.2
Government public health activities[2]	1.5	1.9	2.5	2.8	3.0	3.2	3.3	3.0	2.8	2.8
Investment	9.4	10.4	7.9	6.6	6.3	6.6	6.5	6.4	6.5	6.4
Research[3]	2.5	2.6	2.1	1.8	1.8	1.9	2.0	2.1	2.1	2.0
Structures and equipment	6.9	7.8	5.7	4.9	4.5	4.7	4.5	4.4	4.4	4.4

... = Not applicable.

[1]Freestanding facilities only. Additional services of this type are provided in hospital-based facilities and counted as hospital care.

[2]Includes personal care services delivered by government public health agencies.

[3]Research and development expenditures of drug companies and other manufacturers and providers of medical equipment and supplies are excluded. They are included in the expenditure class in which the product falls because these expenditures are covered by the payment received for that product.

Table C-69. Personal Health Care Expenditures, by Source of Funds and Type of Expenditure, Selected Years, 1960–2005

(Dollar, percent.)

Type of personal health care expenditures and source of funds	1960	1970	1980	1990	1995	2000	2003	2004	2005
Amount									
Per capita	125	299	935	2,394	3,214	4,034	4,966	5,276	5,598
Amount in Billions									
All personal health care expenditures[1]	23.3	62.9	215.3	607.5	863.7	1,139.9	1,446.3	1,551.3	1,661.4
Percent Distribution									
All sources of funds	100.0	100.0	100.0	100.0	100.0	100.0	100.0	100.0	100.0
Out-of-pocket payments	55.2	39.6	27.2	22.4	16.9	16.9	15.5	15.2	15.0
Private health insurance	21.4	22.3	28.4	33.7	33.2	35.4	35.9	36.0	35.9
Other private funds	2.0	2.8	4.3	5.0	5.1	5.0	4.4	4.2	4.1
Government	21.4	35.3	40.0	38.9	44.8	42.7	44.2	44.6	45.0
Federal	8.7	22.9	28.9	28.4	34.2	32.5	33.7	34.2	34.2
State and local	12.7	12.4	11.1	10.4	10.6	10.2	10.4	10.4	10.7
Amount in Billions									
Hospital care expenditures[2]	9.2	27.6	101.0	251.6	340.7	417.0	525.4	566.9	611.6
Percent Distribution									
All sources of funds	100.0	100.0	100.0	100.0	100.0	100.0	100.0	100.0	100.0
Out-of-pocket payments	20.7	9.0	5.4	4.5	3.0	3.3	3.2	3.3	3.3
Private health insurance	35.8	32.5	36.6	38.9	32.0	34.6	35.4	35.6	35.5
Other private funds	1.2	3.2	5.0	4.1	4.2	5.2	4.6	4.5	4.5
Government[3]	42.2	55.2	53.0	52.5	60.8	56.9	56.7	56.7	56.8
Medicaid[4]	...	9.6	9.1	10.6	16.7	17.0	17.2	17.1	17.3
Medicare	...	19.4	26.1	27.0	32.0	29.9	29.3	29.4	29.5
Amount in Billions									
Physician services expenditures	5.4	14.0	47.1	157.5	220.5	288.6	366.7	393.7	421.2
Percent Distribution									
All sources of funds	100.0	100.0	100.0	100.0	100.0	100.0	100.0	100.0	100.0
Out-of-pocket payments	61.7	46.2	30.4	19.2	11.8	11.2	10.2	10.1	10.1
Private health insurance	29.8	30.1	35.5	42.7	48.1	47.4	48.3	48.3	48.3
Other private funds	1.4	1.6	3.9	7.2	8.0	7.7	7.1	6.7	6.4
Government[3]	7.2	22.1	30.1	30.9	32.1	33.8	34.3	34.9	35.3
Medicaid[4]	...	4.6	5.2	4.5	6.7	6.6	6.9	7.1	7.1
Medicare	...	11.8	17.0	18.6	18.8	20.2	20.1	20.7	21.2
Amount in Billions									
Nursing home expenditures[5]	0.8	4.0	19.0	52.6	74.1	95.3	110.5	115.0	121.9
Percent Distribution									
All sources of funds	100.0	100.0	100.0	100.0	100.0	100.0	100.0	100.0	100.0
Out-of-pocket payments	77.3	52.0	37.2	36.1	28.1	30.1	27.6	26.6	26.5
Private health insurance	0.0	0.2	1.2	5.6	7.9	8.3	7.8	7.5	7.5
Other private funds	6.3	4.8	4.2	7.2	6.7	4.8	3.8	3.7	3.7
Government[3]	16.4	43.0	57.5	51.1	57.2	56.9	60.8	62.2	62.3
Medicaid[4]	...	23.3	53.8	45.8	46.0	44.1	45.0	44.8	43.9
Medicare	...	3.5	1.6	3.2	9.0	10.6	13.3	14.9	15.7
Amount in Billions									
Prescription drug expenditures	2.7	5.5	12.0	40.3	60.9	120.8	174.6	189.7	200.7
Percent Distribution									
All sources of funds	100.0	100.0	100.0	100.0	100.0	100.0	100.0	100.0	100.0
Out-of-pocket payments	96.0	82.4	70.3	55.5	38.4	27.7	25.4	25.2	25.4
Private health insurance	1.3	8.8	14.8	26.4	40.1	49.4	48.2	47.4	47.4
Other private funds	0.0	0.0	0.0	0.0	0.0	0.0	0.0	0.0	0.0
Government[3]	2.7	8.8	14.9	18.1	21.5	22.9	26.4	27.3	27.2
Medicaid[4]	...	7.6	11.7	12.6	15.9	16.7	18.6	19.1	18.6
Medicare	...	0.0	0.0	0.5	1.1	1.7	1.4	1.8	2.0
Amount in Billions									
All other personal health care expenditures[6]	5.3	11.8	36.2	105.5	167.5	218.1	269.0	285.9	306.1

... = Not applicable.

[1]Includes all expenditures for specified health services and supplies other than expenses for program administration, net cost of private health insurance, and government public health activities.

[2]Includes expenditures for hospital-based nursing home and home health agency care.

[3]Includes other government expenditures for these health care services, for example, Medicaid State Children's Health Insurance Program (SCHIP) expansions and SCHIP, care funded by the Department of Veterans Affairs, and state and locally financed subsidies to hospitals.

[4]Excludes Medicaid SCHIP expansions and SCHIP.

[5]Includes expenditures for care in freestanding nursing homes. Expenditures for care in hospital-based nursing homes are included with hospital care.

[6]Includes expenditures for dental services, other professional services, non-hospital home health care, nonprescription drugs and other medical nondurables, vision products and other medical durables, and other personal health care, not shown separately.

Table C-69. Personal Health Care Expenditures, by Source of Funds and Type of Expenditure, Selected Years, 1960–2005—*Continued*

(Dollar, percent.)

Type of personal health care expenditures and source of funds	1960	1970	1980	1990	1995	2000	2003	2004	2005
Percent Distribution									
All sources of funds	100.0	100.0	100.0	100.0	100.0	100.0	100.0	100.0	100.0
Out-of-pocket payments	84.5	78.9	64.6	50.4	39.3	39.0	35.4	34.6	33.9
Private health insurance	1.6	3.3	15.3	24.6	24.7	25.1	23.6	23.6	23.5
Other private funds	4.2	3.6	4.3	4.7	4.3	3.8	3.3	3.2	3.2
Government[3]	9.8	14.2	15.8	20.2	31.7	32.2	37.8	38.6	39.5
Medicaid[4]	...	3.3	3.9	6.5	12.5	15.9	19.7	20.1	20.6
Medicare	...	1.1	3.8	7.1	13.1	9.7	11.5	12.1	12.6

... = Not applicable.

[3]Includes other government expenditures for these health care services, for example, Medicaid State Children's Health Insurance Program (SCHIP) expansions and SCHIP, care funded by the Department of Veterans Affairs, and state and locally financed subsidies to hospitals.

[4]Excludes Medicaid SCHIP expansions and SCHIP.

Table C-70. Expenses for Health Care and Prescribed Medicine, by Selected Population Characteristics, Selected Years, 1987–2004

(Number, dollars.)

Characteristic	Population in millions[2]			Total expenses[1] Percent of persons with expense			Total expenses[1] Mean annual expense per person with expense[3]			Percent of persons with expense			Mean annual out-of-pocket expense per person with out-of-pocket expense		
	1997	2000	2004	1997	2000	2004	1997	2000	2004	1997	2000	2004	1997	2000	2004
All ages	271.3	278.4	293.5	84.1	83.5	84.7	$2,853	$2,962	$3,879	62.1	62.3	62.7	$238	$301	$437
UNDER 65 YEARS															
Total	237.1	243.6	256.5	82.5	81.8	82.9	2,163	2,333	3,028	58.7	58.5	58.5	168	218	304
Under 6 years	23.8	24.1	23.3	88.0	86.7	90.0	1,010	1,233	1,285	61.3	56.9	54.4	41	41	58
6–17 years	48.1	48.4	49.8	81.7	80.0	83.9	1,133	1,225	1,357	48.2	46.2	46.0	64	77	98
18–44 years	108.9	109.0	111.4	78.3	77.7	77.0	1,961	2,090	2,631	55.9	56.0	55.0	144	166	227
45–64 years	56.3	62.1	71.9	89.2	88.5	88.9	3,797	3,907	5,224	71.8	73.3	74.1	313	411	539
Sex															
Male	118.0	120.9	127.8	77.6	76.6	77.7	1,955	2,233	2,701	51.5	51.3	51.3	149	192	277
Female	119.1	122.7	128.7	87.4	87.0	88.0	2,347	2,420	3,316	65.8	65.6	65.7	182	239	325
Hispanic Origin and Race[4]															
Hispanic or Latino	29.4	32.0	39.9	69.5	69.0	69.3	1,801	1,590	1,903	47.7	45.0	43.6	112	160	182
Not Hispanic or Latino															
White	166.2	169.2	166.3	87.2	86.6	87.7	2,321	2,441	3,406	63.1	63.8	64.6	182	235	333
Black or African American	31.3	32.1	32.5	72.1	71.3	75.2	1,735	2,478	2,635	50.0	47.6	50.6	135	180	269
Other	10.2	10.2	17.8	75.8	76.0	82.0	1,438	1,989	2,044	44.8	47.8	49.2	146	154	247
Insurance Status[5]															
Any private insurance	174.0	181.6	180.1	86.5	85.9	87.9	2,204	2,222	3,154	61.6	61.6	62.9	160	188	275
Public insurance only	29.8	29.7	40.3	83.3	83.6	84.8	2,629	3,542	3,307	62.0	62.4	60.0	166	313	352
Uninsured all year	33.3	32.3	36.0	61.1	57.3	55.5	1,292	1,645	1,557	40.2	37.6	35.1	242	362	465
65 YEARS AND OVER															
Total	34.2	34.8	37.0	95.2	95.5	97.1	6,999	6,735	8,906	86.0	88.3	91.9	568	683	1,027
Sex															
Male	14.6	15.0	16.0	94.5	93.4	96.6	7,866	7,223	9,020	82.8	83.9	90.1	512	512	839
Female	19.6	19.8	21.0	95.7	97.1	97.5	6,361	6,381	8,819	88.3	91.5	93.3	607	802	1,166
Hispanic Origin and Race[4]															
Hispanic or Latino	1.7	1.9	2.3	94.2	92.5	91.7	7,324	6,044	7,209	87.5	83.9	86.6	464	576	759
Not Hispanic or Latino															
White	28.8	28.9	30.0	95.9	95.9	97.6	7,035	6,837	9,316	86.7	89.0	92.6	587	709	1,062
Black or African American	2.8	2.9	3.1	92.2	94.0	95.6	6,893	6,478	8,035	85.3	85.3	90.6	472	584	943
Other	*	*	1.7	*	*	97.5	*	*	5,291	*	*	89.9	*	*	883
Insurance Status[6]															
Medicare only	8.8	12.0	11.2	92.1	94.8	96.0	6,448	5,783	7,651	82.1	87.7	89.7	657	816	1,381
Medicare and private insurance	21.7	19.2	20.4	97.0	96.0	98.0	6,826	6,907	9,299	88.1	89.0	93.3	577	632	940
Medicare and other public coverage	3.2	3.2	5.0	93.2	96.3	97.3	9,865	9,242	10,329	85.0	88.5	93.7	318	541	636

* = Figure does not meet standards of reliability or precision.
[1]Includes expenses for inpatient hospital and physician services, ambulatory physician and nonphysician services, prescribed medicines, home health services, dental services, and other medical equipment, supplies, and services that were purchased or rented during the year. Excludes expenses for over-the-counter medications, alternative care services, phone contacts with health providers, and premiums for health insurance.
[2]Includes persons in the civilian noninstitutionalized population for all or part of the year. Expenditures for persons in this population for only part of the year are restricted to those incurred during periods of eligibility.
[3]Estimates of expenses have been updated to 2004 dollars using the Consumer Price Index (all items).
[4]Persons of Hispanic origin may be of any race.
[5]Any private insurance includes individuals with insurance that provided coverage for hospital and physician care at any time during the year, other than Medicare, Medicaid, or other public coverage for hospital or physician services. Public insurance only includes individuals who were not covered by private insurance at any time during the year but were covered by Medicare, Medicaid, other public coverage for hospital or physician services, and/or CHAMPUS/CHAMPVA (TRICARE) at any point during the year. Individuals with Indian Health Service coverage only are considered uninsured.
[6]Populations do not add to total because uninsured persons and persons with unknown insurance status were excluded.

Table C-71. Sources of Payment for Health Care, by Selected Population Characteristics, Selected Years, 1987–2004

(Percent.)

Characteristic	All sources	Source of payment for health care								Source of payment for health care							
		Out of pocket				Private insurance[1]				Public coverage[2]				Other[3]			
		1987	1997	2000	2004	1987	1997	2000	2004	1987	1997	2000	2004	1987	1997	2000	2004
All ages...................................	100.0	24.8	19.4	19.4	19.0	36.6	40.3	40.3	42.0	34.1	34.4	35.4	35.2	4.5	5.9	5.0	3.9
UNDER 65 YEARS																	
Total....................................	100.0	26.2	21.1	20.3	19.5	46.6	53.1	52.5	55.0	21.3	18.1	21.3	20.8	6.0	7.7	6.0	4.7
Under 6 years	100.0	18.5	14.2	10.3	10.5	39.5	49.3	51.2	57.7	35.8	25.4	33.6	28.7	6.2	11.2	4.9	3.1
6-17 years............................	100.0	35.7	29.0	27.7	25.6	47.3	53.2	48.8	47.6	11.8	14.1	20.1	23.0	5.2	3.7	3.4	3.7
18-44 years..........................	100.0	27.4	21.1	19.9	19.4	46.8	52.9	51.2	53.0	19.4	15.7	21.1	22.1	6.4	10.3	7.8	5.5
45-64 years..........................	100.0	24.0	20.1	20.2	19.3	47.8	53.6	54.5	57.3	22.4	20.3	20.2	18.8	5.8	6.0	5.2	4.5
Sex																	
Male......................................	100.0	24.5	21.3	18.1	18.8	44.6	50.3	52.2	54.8	23.9	19.5	23.5	20.6	7.1	8.9	6.3	5.8
Female...................................	100.0	27.5	21.0	22.1	20.1	48.1	55.1	52.7	55.1	19.2	17.0	19.5	20.9	5.2	6.8	5.7	3.9
Hispanic Origin and Race[4]																	
Hispanic or Latino	100.0	22.0	18.8	20.5	18.9	36.1	42.3	45.8	35.1	35.8	28.9	27.5	39.1	6.0	10.0	6.2	6.9
Not Hispanic or Latino																	
White	100.0	28.2	21.8	21.7	20.1	50.1	55.8	55.1	59.4	15.9	15.3	18.0	16.2	5.8	7.1	5.2	4.3
Black or African American..................	100.0	15.5	17.1	11.8	14.7	30.0	42.3	40.5	39.5	47.2	30.7	38.8	39.9	7.3	9.9	8.8	5.9
Other..................................	100.0	27.2	21.2	17.0	21.5	46.7	45.2	51.2	50.0	21.0	23.7	19.0	22.8	5.1	9.9	*12.8	5.8
Insurance Status																	
Any private insurance[5]	100.0	29.0	21.6	21.2	19.6	60.0	67.6	70.2	70.7	6.2	6.6	5.3	7.1	4.8	4.2	3.3	2.5
Public insurance only[6]	100.0	8.9	10.6	9.8	11.4	...	...	...	...	87.2	80.7	84.4	84.4	3.9	8.7	5.8	4.2
Uninsured all year[7]	100.0	40.6	41.3	40.4	48.0	...	...	...	...	28.6	7.5	*21.2	8.5	30.9	51.1	38.4	43.5
65 YEARS AND OVER	100.0	22.0	16.3	17.5	17.8	15.8	16.5	14.9	15.8	60.8	64.8	64.7	64.2	1.5	2.5	2.9	2.2
Sex																	
Male......................................	100.0	21.7	14.2	14.2	16.0	17.6	20.1	16.8	18.1	58.8	63.4	66.9	64.0	*1.9	2.3	2.2	1.9
Female...................................	100.0	22.2	18.1	20.2	19.2	14.4	13.2	13.3	14.0	62.3	65.9	63.0	64.4	1.1	2.7	3.5	2.4
Hispanic Origin and Race[4]																	
Hispanic or Latino	100.0	*13.5	13.6	13.9	14.3	*4.7	5.9	8.4	*12.4	80.2	77.8	75.6	69.9	*1.6	*2.7	*2.2	*3.4
Not Hispanic or Latino																	
White	100.0	23.7	17.0	18.3	18.2	16.7	17.9	15.2	16.7	58.0	62.6	64.1	63.0	1.6	2.5	2.4	2.2
Black or African American..................	100.0	11.2	11.4	13.6	14.0	*11.9	8.8	9.3	10.1	76.3	77.6	68.3	74.7	0.6	2.2	*8.9	1.2
Other..................................	100.0	*	*	*	22.1	*	*	*	*10.1	*	*	*	65.1	*	*	*	*2.8
Insurance Status																	
Medicare only	100.0	29.8	19.8	22.2	24.2	...	...	...	...	68.8	72.4	72.2	68.9	1.4	7.7	5.7	6.9
Medicare and private insurance.............	100.0	23.4	17.3	17.0	17.4	18.9	25.7	25.3	26.5	56.1	56.3	57.1	55.7	1.6	0.6	*0.6	0.4
Medicare and other public coverage	100.0	*6.2	5.2	9.1	8.5	...	...	...	...	92.9	92.7	87.3	89.7	1.0	*2.1	*3.6	0.7

... = Not applicable.

* = Figure does not meet standards of reliability or precision.

[1]Private insurance includes any type of private insurance payments reported for people with private health insurance coverage during the year.

[2]Public coverage includes payments made by Medicare, Medicaid, the Department of Veterans Affairs, other federal sources and various state and local sources.

[3]Other sources includes Workers' Compensation, unclassified sources, Medicaid payments reported for people who were not enrolled in the program at any time during the year, and any type of private insurance payments reported for people without private health insurance coverage during the year.

[4]Persons of Hispanic origin may be of any race.

[5]Includes individuals with insurance that provided coverage for hospital and physician care at any time during the year, other than Medicare, Medicaid, or other public coverage for hospital or physician services.

[6]Includes individuals who were not covered by private insurance at any time during the year but were covered by Medicare, Medicaid, other public coverage for hospital or physician services, and/or CHAMPUS/CHAMPVA (TRICARE) at any point during the year.

[7]Includes individuals not covered by either private or public insurance throughout the entire year or period of eligibility for the survey.

Table C-72. Out-of-Pocket Health Care Expenses Among Persons with Medical Expenses, by Age, Selected Years, 1987–2004

(Percent.)

Age and year	Percent of persons with expenses	Total	Amount paid out of pocket among persons with expenses[1]					
			$0	$1–124	$125–249	$250–499	$500–999	$1,000+
All Ages								
1987	84.5	100.0	10.4	29.2	16.6	17.4	13.3	13.1
1998	83.8	100.0	7.7	36.5	15.8	16.1	12.2	11.8
1999	84.3	100.0	7.4	35.9	15.5	15.6	12.8	12.7
2000	83.5	100.0	6.9	34.8	15.0	16.2	13.0	14.1
2001	85.4	100.0	7.1	31.7	14.7	16.6	13.8	16.2
2002	85.2	100.0	7.8	29.8	14.3	15.7	14.8	17.6
2003	85.6	100.0	7.6	28.0	14.0	15.8	15.2	19.5
2004	84.7	100.0	8.8	27.9	13.0	15.6	14.5	20.3
Under 6 Years								
1987	88.9	100.0	19.2	38.7	18.9	14.7	5.3	3.2
1998	87.6	100.0	17.4	60.1	12.4	6.8	2.3	0.9
1999	87.9	100.0	17.7	60.5	12.2	5.9	2.6	1.1
2000	86.7	100.0	16.7	61.0	11.1	7.5	2.4	1.3
2001	88.8	100.0	18.5	57.8	12.9	7.6	2.1	1.1
2002	88.8	100.0	21.5	51.7	14.0	7.7	3.9	1.3
2003	91.3	100.0	20.6	51.7	13.3	8.5	4.2	1.6
2004	90.0	100.0	26.0	47.9	11.9	7.9	4.2	2.1
6–17 Years								
1987	80.2	100.0	15.5	37.9	18.2	12.4	8.5	7.6
1998	80.6	100.0	16.3	47.0	15.0	11.1	5.6	5.1
1999	81.5	100.0	15.0	46.6	15.4	11.2	6.0	5.8
2000	80.0	100.0	14.7	46.5	14.5	11.2	6.5	6.6
2001	83.2	100.0	15.0	45.2	15.0	11.1	6.0	7.7
2002	83.6	100.0	16.6	43.2	14.7	12.0	6.8	6.7
2003	84.1	100.0	16.1	40.6	15.5	12.2	7.9	7.8
2004	83.9	100.0	18.7	40.9	13.0	12.0	7.7	7.7
18–44 years								
1987	81.5	100.0	10.1	32.3	17.7	18.2	11.9	9.8
1998	78.0	100.0	6.4	40.2	17.9	17.0	10.7	7.7
1999	78.9	100.0	6.4	40.2	17.6	16.6	11.1	8.1
2000	77.7	100.0	5.8	39.1	17.8	17.1	11.7	8.5
2001	79.3	100.0	6.0	34.8	17.5	18.8	13.3	9.7
2002	78.5	100.0	6.7	34.2	17.4	17.1	13.9	10.8
2003	79.0	100.0	6.4	31.6	17.4	18.3	14.0	12.3
2004	77.0	100.0	7.2	31.8	16.0	18.4	13.4	13.2
45–64 years								
1987	87.0	100.0	5.7	20.4	15.6	20.7	18.8	18.8
1998	89.2	100.0	2.9	25.6	16.2	20.1	17.7	17.5
1999	88.9	100.0	2.7	24.0	16.4	19.7	19.0	18.2
2000	88.5	100.0	2.6	22.3	15.6	19.9	18.8	20.9
2001	89.9	100.0	2.4	19.6	13.9	20.4	19.8	23.8
2002	90.0	100.0	2.3	18.8	12.8	19.1	21.3	25.8
2003	89.6	100.0	2.4	17.2	12.3	17.7	21.4	29.1
2004	88.9	100.0	2.7	17.6	12.0	18.1	21.2	28.4
65–74 Years								
1987	92.8	100.0	5.3	15.4	11.6	18.5	22.1	27.1
1998	94.3	100.0	2.0	17.8	13.3	20.7	20.6	25.6
1999	95.3	100.0	1.4	16.1	11.3	17.9	23.7	29.6
2000	94.7	100.0	1.5	14.4	10.6	20.2	20.1	33.2
2001	95.6	100.0	1.5	14.4	9.9	18.3	21.7	34.2
2002	96.1	100.0	1.8	10.1	9.9	16.4	22.5	39.3
2003	95.3	100.0	1.7	9.0	8.2	15.6	24.5	41.0
2004	96.6	100.0	1.5	11.2	9.0	13.8	19.8	44.7
75 Years or More								
1987	95.1	100.0	5.6	12.9	10.0	17.1	21.2	33.2
1998	96.3	100.0	3.0	14.3	11.6	17.7	22.2	31.3
1999	95.3	100.0	2.6	14.5	10.2	18.6	20.2	33.8
2000	96.5	100.0	2.6	14.2	8.4	18.2	22.0	34.6
2001	97.0	100.0	1.7	10.1	9.2	14.4	21.1	43.6
2002	96.5	100.0	2.2	9.0	7.7	14.4	20.4	46.2
2003	97.5	100.0	1.9	8.7	7.0	13.4	20.1	48.9
2004	97.7	100.0	1.8	8.4	8.1	11.9	18.5	51.2

[1]1987 dollars were converted to 1998 dollars using the national Consumer Price Index. Starting with 1998 data, percent distributions are based on actual dollars (nonadjusted).

NOTE: Out-of-pocket expenses include expenditures for inpatient hospital and physician services, ambulatory physician and nonphysician services, prescribed medicines, home health services, dental services, and various other medical equipment, supplies, and services that were purchased or rented during the year. Out-of-pocket expenses for over-the-counter medications, alternative care services, phone contacts with health providers, and premiums for health insurance policies are not included in these estimates. 1987 estimates are based on the National Medical Expenditure Survey (NMES), while estimates for other years are based on the Medical Expenditure Panel Survey (MEPS). Because expenditures in NMES were based primarily on charges while those for MEPS were based on payments, data for the NMES were adjusted to be more comparable to MEPS using estimated charge to payment ratios for 1987. Overall, this resulted in an approximate 11% reduction from the unadjusted 1987 NMES expenditure estimates.

Table C-73. Expenditures for Health Services and Supplies and Percent Distribution, by Type of Payer, Selected Years, 1987–2005

(Dollars, Percent.)

Type of payer	Amount in billions									Percent distribution								
	1987	1993	1997	2000	2001	2002	2003	2004	2005	1987	1993	1997	2000	2001	2002	2003	2004	2005
TOTAL[1]	477.8	853.2	1,054.3	1,264.4	1,376.2	1,498.8	1,621.7	1,738.9	1,860.9	100.0	100.0	100.0	100.0	100.0	100.0	100.0	100.0	100.0
Private	333.3	545.4	668.0	821.3	868.8	927.5	994.4	1,056.2	1,124.6	69.7	63.9	63.4	65.0	63.1	61.9	61.3	60.7	60.4
Private business	122.1	218.9	265.9	342.0	367.6	390.5	419.5	446.6	478.1	25.6	25.7	25.2	27.1	26.7	26.1	25.9	25.7	25.7
Employer contribution to private health insurance premiums	84.2	158.3	191.5	251.2	272.4	293.3	319.3	341.6	366.9	17.6	18.6	18.2	19.9	19.8	19.6	19.7	19.6	19.7
Private employer contribution to Medicare hospital insurance trust fund[2]	24.6	35.8	49.5	62.2	63.3	63.0	64.5	68.4	72.7	5.2	4.2	4.7	4.9	4.6	4.2	4.0	3.9	3.9
Workers compensation and temporary disability insurance	11.6	21.8	21.3	24.3	27.5	29.5	30.8	31.4	32.8	2.4	2.6	2.0	1.9	2.0	2.0	1.9	1.8	1.8
Industrial inplant health services	1.7	2.9	3.6	4.3	4.5	4.7	4.9	5.3	5.6	0.4	0.3	0.3	0.3	0.3	0.3	0.3	0.3	0.3
Household	188.7	290.6	353.3	425.5	448.0	482.2	515.1	548.5	582.4	39.5	34.1	33.5	33.7	32.6	32.2	31.8	31.5	31.3
Employee contribution to private health insurance premiums and individual policy premiums	43.9	89.9	112.4	133.7	147.1	167.0	182.7	196.9	207.1	9.2	10.5	10.7	10.6	10.7	11.1	11.3	11.3	11.1
Employee and self-employment contributions and voluntary premiums paid to Medicare hospital insurance trust fund[2]	29.4	43.7	63.0	82.5	82.9	84.2	86.2	91.1	96.6	6.1	5.1	6.0	6.5	6.0	5.6	5.3	5.2	5.2
Premiums paid by individuals to Medicare supplementary medical insurance trust fund	6.2	11.9	15.5	16.3	18.0	19.7	21.6	24.6	29.2	1.3	1.4	1.5	1.3	1.3	1.3	1.3	1.4	1.6
Out-of-pocket health spending	109.2	145.2	162.5	192.9	200.0	211.3	224.5	235.8	249.4	22.9	17.0	15.4	15.3	14.5	14.1	13.8	13.6	13.4
Other private revenues	22.4	36.0	48.7	53.7	53.1	54.8	59.7	61.1	64.1	4.7	4.2	4.6	4.2	3.9	3.7	3.7	3.5	3.4
Public	144.5	307.8	386.3	443.2	507.4	571.3	627.3	682.7	736.3	30.3	36.1	36.6	35.0	36.9	38.1	38.7	39.3	39.6
Federal government	74.1	176.2	220.0	235.6	277.1	317.5	354.4	389.1	416.9	15.5	20.7	20.9	18.6	20.1	21.2	21.9	22.4	22.4
Employer contributions to private health insurance premiums	4.9	11.5	11.4	14.3	15.8	17.7	19.7	21.6	23.1	1.0	1.3	1.1	1.1	1.1	1.2	1.2	1.2	1.2
Medicaid[3]	28.1	78.1	97.4	119.7	134.5	149.5	163.6	174.9	183.6	5.9	9.2	9.2	9.5	9.8	10.0	10.1	10.1	9.9
Other[4]	41.1	86.6	111.2	101.6	126.9	150.4	171.0	192.6	210.1	8.6	10.1	10.5	8.0	9.2	10.0	10.5	11.1	11.3
State and local government	70.5	131.6	166.3	207.6	230.3	253.7	273.0	293.6	319.4	14.8	15.4	15.8	16.4	16.7	16.9	16.8	16.9	17.2
Employer contributions to private health insurance premiums	16.0	35.8	43.9	56.0	63.5	73.1	82.1	91.4	97.1	3.3	4.2	4.2	4.4	4.6	4.9	5.1	5.3	5.2
Medicaid[3]	22.8	46.5	64.9	85.3	94.7	103.9	112.6	122.6	137.8	4.8	5.5	6.2	6.7	6.9	6.9	6.9	7.1	7.4
Other[5]	31.7	49.2	57.5	66.2	72.1	76.8	78.3	79.6	84.5	6.6	5.8	5.5	5.2	5.2	5.1	4.8	4.6	4.5

[1]Excludes research and construction.

[2]Includes one-half of self-employment contribution to Medicare hospital insurance trust fund.

[3]Includes Medicaid buy-in premiums for Medicare.

[4]Includes expenditures for Medicare, maternal and child health, vocational rehabilitation, Substance Abuse and Mental Health Services Administration, Indian Health Service, federal workers' compensation, other miscellaneous general hospital and medical programs, public health activities, Department of Defense, Department of Veterans Affairs, and State Children's Health Insurance Program (SCHIP).

[5]Includes other public and general assistance, maternal and child health, vocational rehabilitation, public health activities, hospital subsidies, and employer contributions to Medicare hospital insurance trust fund.

NOTE: This table disaggregates health expenditures according to four classes of payers: businesses, households (individuals), federal government, and state and local governments with a small amount of revenue coming from nonpatient revenue sources such as philanthropy. Where businesses or households pay dedicated funds into government health programs (for example, Medicare) or employers and employees share in the cost of health premiums, these costs are assigned to businesses or households accordingly. This results in a lower share of expenditures being assigned to the federal government than for tabulations of expenditures by source of funds. Estimates of national health expenditure by source of funds aim to track government-sponsored health programs over time and do not delineate the role of business employers in paying for health care. Figures may not sum to totals due to rounding.

Table C-74. Employers' Costs per Employee-Hour Worked for Total Compensation, Wages and Salaries, and Health Insurance, by Selected Characteristics, Selected Years, 1991–2006

(Dollar, percent.)

Characteristic	1991	1995	2000	2001	2002	2003	2004	2005	2006
Total Compensation per Employee-Hour Worked									
State and local government	22.31	24.86	29.05	30.06	31.29	32.62	34.21	35.50	36.96
Total private industry	15.40	17.10	19.85	20.81	21.71	22.37	23.29	24.17	25.09
Industry									
Goods producing	18.48	20.75	23.55	24.40	25.44	26.25	27.19	28.48	29.36
Service providing	14.31	15.88	18.72	19.74	20.66	21.30	22.33	23.11	24.05
Occupational Group[1]									
White collar	18.15	20.50	24.19	25.34	26.43	28.85	—	—	—
Blue collar	15.15	16.69	18.73	19.35	20.15	21.21	—	—	—
Service	7.82	8.39	9.72	10.32	10.95	13.68	—	—	—
Management, professional, and related	—	—	—	—	—	—	40.23	42.09	44.32
Sales and office	—	—	—	—	—	—	18.42	19.30	19.93
Service	—	—	—	—	—	—	11.66	12.07	12.3
Natural resources, construction, and maintenance	—	—	—	—	—	—	26.55	27.26	28.07
Production, transportation, and material moving	—	—	—	—	—	—	20.21	20.82	21.19
Census Region									
Northeast	17.56	20.09	22.67	23.91	25.00	25.70	26.29	27.09	28.75
Midwest	15.05	15.89	19.22	20.47	21.25	22.40	23.26	24.23	24.65
South	13.68	15.31	17.81	18.59	19.49	19.95	20.80	21.36	22.35
West	15.97	18.35	20.88	21.86	22.68	23.07	24.54	25.98	26.56
Union Status									
Union	19.76	22.40	25.88	27.80	29.42	30.68	31.94	33.17	34.07
Nonunion	14.54	16.28	19.07	19.98	20.79	21.36	22.28	23.09	24.03
Establishment Employment Size									
1–99 employees	13.38	14.58	17.16	17.86	18.51	18.93	19.47	20.22	20.43
100 or more	17.34	19.44	22.81	24.19	25.48	26.42	27.81	28.94	30.34
100–499	14.31	16.30	19.30	20.97	21.99	22.62	23.91	24.44	25.91
500 or more	20.60	22.85	26.93	28.17	29.79	30.94	32.54	34.59	35.94
Wages and Salaries as a Percent of Total Compensation									
State and local government	69.6	69.6	70.8	71.0	70.8	70.0	69.2	68.3	67.6
Total private industry	72.3	71.6	73.0	72.9	72.8	72.2	71.5	71.0	70.7
Industry									
Goods producing	68.7	67.3	69.0	69.1	68.7	67.7	66.7	65.5	66.2
Service providing	73.9	73.5	74.5	74.4	74.2	73.7	72.9	72.6	72.0
Occupational Group[1]									
White collar	73.8	73.1	74.0	73.8	73.7	72.9	—	—	—
Blue collar	68.4	67.6	69.4	69.7	69.5	68.5	—	—	—
Service	76.2	75.7	77.9	77.5	76.9	72.4	—	—	—
Management, professional, and related	—	—	—	—	—	—	72.1	71.5	70.9
Sales and office	—	—	—	—	—	—	73.0	72.6	72.2
Service	—	—	—	—	—	—	75.8	75.7	75.3
Natural resources, construction, and maintenance	—	—	—	—	—	—	69.1	68.0	68.0
Production, transportation, and material moving	—	—	—	—	—	—	66.9	66.2	66.7
Census Region									
Northeast	72.0	70.9	72.2	72.0	71.9	71.2	70.4	70.4	70.0
Midwest	71.1	70.7	72.4	71.8	72.0	71.6	71.1	70.1	69.4
South	73.3	72.1	73.5	73.7	73.6	73.2	72.5	72.1	72.1
West	72.8	73.0	74.0	74.1	73.5	72.6	71.6	70.9	71.0
Union Status									
Union	65.9	64.4	65.2	66.0	65.7	65.0	63.6	62.6	62.3
Nonunion	74.1	73.1	74.4	74.1	74.0	73.5	72.8	72.4	72.1
Establishment Employment Size									
1–99 employees	74.7	74.1	75.5	75.1	75.0	74.6	74.3	73.9	73.7
100 or more	70.5	69.9	71.0	71.1	70.9	70.2	69.1	68.5	68.4
100–499	72.1	71.3	72.8	72.5	72.2	71.4	70.7	70.2	70.0
500 or more	69.3	68.8	69.4	69.8	69.8	69.1	67.7	67.0	66.9

— = Data not available.

[1]Starting with 2004 data, sample establishments were classified by industry categories based on the 2000 North American Industry Classification System (NAICS).

Table C-74. Employers' Costs per Employee-Hour Worked for Total Compensation, Wages and Salaries, and Health Insurance, by Selected Characteristics, Selected Years, 1991–2006—*Continued*

(Dollar, percent.)

Characteristic	1991	1995	2000	2001	2002	2003	2004	2005	2006
Health Insurance as a Percent of Total Compensation									
State and local government..	6.9	7.8	7.8	8.5	8.6	9.2	9.8	10.2	10.6
Total private industry	6.0	6.2	5.5	6.2	5.9	6.3	6.6	6.8	6.9
Industry									
Goods producing..	6.9	7.4	6.9	7.6	7.2	7.5	7.8	8.0	8.4
Service providing..	5.5	5.7	4.9	5.6	5.5	5.9	6.2	6.4	6.4
Occupational Group[1]									
White collar	5.6	5.7	5.0	5.6	5.4	6.4	—	—	—
Blue collar..	7.0	7.5	6.8	7.5	7.3	8.0	—	—	—
Service..	4.6	5.1	4.3	5.0	5.1	7.0	—	—	—
Management, professional, and related............................	—	—	—	—	—	—	5.4	5.5	5.6
Sales and office..	—	—	—	—	—	—	7.3	7.5	7.5
Service..	—	—	—	—	—	—	6.0	6.1	6.2
Natural resources, construction, and maintenance...........................	—	—	—	—	—	—	6.9	7.5	7.7
Production, transportation, and material moving............................	—	—	—	—	—	—	8.5	8.9	9.0
Census Region									
Northeast..	6.2	6.4	5.6	6.3	5.9	6.3	6.5	6.8	6.7
Midwest	6.3	6.7	5.8	6.6	6.4	6.6	7.0	7.3	7.6
South..	5.5	6.0	5.4	6.2	5.8	6.2	6.5	6.6	6.7
West..	5.8	5.6	5.0	5.4	5.6	6.0	6.3	6.3	6.4
Union Status									
Union	8.2	9.3	8.4	8.9	8.7	9.1	9.6	10.3	10.3
Nonunion	5.4	5.5	5.0	5.7	5.4	5.8	6.1	6.2	6.3
Establishment Employment Size									
1–99 employees..	5.1	5.3	4.8	5.3	5.2	5.5	5.8	5.9	6.0
100 or more	6.6	6.9	6.0	6.9	6.6	7.0	7.2	7.5	7.5
100–499..	6.3	6.5	5.6	6.6	6.4	6.9	7.1	7.5	7.4
500 or more	6.8	7.2	6.4	7.1	6.7	7.0	7.3	7.6	7.6

—- = Data not available.
[1]Starting with 2004 data, sample establishments were classified by industry categories based on the 2000 North American Industry Classification System (NAICS).

NOTE: Costs are calculated annually from March survey data. Total compensation includes wages and salaries and benefits.

Table C-75. Nursing Home Average Monthly Charges per Resident, by Selected Facility Characteristics, Selected Years, 1985–2004

(Dollar.)

Facility characteristic	Average monthly charge				
	1985	1995	1997	1999	2004
All facilities....................................	1,508	3,132	3,638	3,531	5,690
Ownership					
Proprietary	1,436	3,044	3,530	3,266	5,356
Nonprofit and government	1,659	3,293	3,834	4,013	6,214
Certification					
Both Medicare and Medicaid	1,797	3,314	3,791	3,679	5,654
Medicare only	1,550	4,189	4,490	3,696	7,541
Medicaid only	1,267	2,167	2,448	2,396	6,206
Neither...	954	2,324	2,420	2,146	4,117
Bed Size					
Fewer than 50 beds	1,133	*4,953	3,549	3,195	5,708
50–99 beds......................................	1,394	2,688	3,207	3,071	5,446
100–199 beds...................................	1,511	3,025	3,614	3,647	5,696
200 beds or more	1,785	3,561	4,258	3,858	6,162
Geographic Region					
Northeast..	1,936	3,895	4,597	4,256	7,229
Midwest...	1,425	2,734	3,240	3,589	5,198
South...	1,294	2,743	3,236	2,902	5,005
West	1,496	3,701	3,816	3,663	5,969

* = Figure does not meet standards of reliability or precision.

NOTE: Average monthly charge is for the month prior to interview. Charges do not reflect the amount that was paid for care. Residents are persons on the roster of the nursing home as of the night before the survey. Residents for whom beds are maintained even though they may be away on overnight leave or in a hospital are included. People residing in personal care or domiciliary care homes are excluded.

Table C-76. Mental Health Expenditures, Percent Distribution, and Per Capita Expenditures, by Type of Mental Health Organization, Selected Years, 1975–2002

(Number, percent.)

Type of organization	1975	1983	1986	1990	1992	1994	1998	2000	2002
Amount in Millions									
All organizations	6,564	14,432	18,458	28,410	29,765	33,136	38,512	34,528	34,302
State and county psychiatric hospitals	3,185	5,491	6,326	7,774	7,970	7,825	7,117	7,485	7,616
Private psychiatric hospitals	467	1,712	2,629	6,101	5,302	6,468	4,106	3,885	3,929
Nonfederal general hospital psychiatric services	621	2,176	2,878	4,662	5,193	5,344	5,589	5,853	5,179
Department of Veterans Affairs medical centers[1]	699	1,316	1,338	1,480	1,530	1,386	1,690	976	1,018
Residential treatment centers for emotionally disturbed children	279	573	978	1,969	2,167	2,360	3,557	3,781	4,496
All other organizations[2]	1,313	3,164	4,310	6,424	7,603	9,753	16,454	12,549	12,063
Percent Distribution									
All organizations	100.0	100.0	100.0	100.0	100.0	100.0	100.0	100.0	100.0
State and county psychiatric hospitals	48.5	38.0	34.3	27.4	26.8	23.6	18.5	21.7	22.2
Private psychiatric hospitals	7.1	11.9	14.2	21.5	17.8	19.5	10.7	11.3	11.5
Nonfederal general hospital psychiatric services	9.5	15.1	15.6	16.4	17.4	16.1	14.5	17.0	15.1
Department of Veterans Affairs medical centers[1]	10.6	9.1	7.2	5.2	5.1	4.2	4.4	2.8	3.0
Residential treatment centers for emotionally disturbed children	4.2	4.0	5.3	6.9	7.3	7.1	9.2	11.0	13.1
All other organizations[2]	20.0	21.9	23.3	22.6	25.5	29.4	42.7	36.4	35.2
Amount per Capita[3]									
All organizations	31	62	77	116	117	128	143	122	119
State and county psychiatric hospitals	15	24	26	32	31	30	26	27	26
Private psychiatric hospitals	2	7	11	25	21	25	15	14	14
Nonfederal general hospital psychiatric services	3	9	12	19	20	21	21	21	18
Department of Veterans Affairs medical centers[1]	3	6	6	6	6	5	6	3	4
Residential treatment centers for emotionally disturbed children	1	2	4	8	9	9	13	13	16
All other organizations[2]	6	14	18	26	30	38	61	44	42

[1]Includes Department of Veterans Affairs neuropsychiatric hospitals, general hospital psychiatric services, and psychiatric outpatient clinics.
[2]Includes freestanding psychiatric outpatient clinics, partial care organizations, multiservice mental health organizations, residential treatment centers for adults, substance abuse organizations, and, in 1975 and 1979, federally-funded community mental health centers.
[3]Civilian population as of January 1 each year through 1998. The rates for 2000 and later years are based on the July 1 civilian population estimates from the Census Bureau.

NOTE: Changes in reporting procedures and definitions may affect the comparability of data prior to 1980 with those of later years. Starting with 1994 data, information on supportive residential clients (moderately staffed housing arrangements, such as supervised apartments, group homes, and halfway houses) is included in the totals and all other organizations category. This change affects the comparability of trend data prior to 1994 with data for 1994 and later years.

Table C-77. Department of Veterans Affairs Health Care Expenditures and Use, and Persons Treated, by Selected Characteristics, Selected Fiscal Years, 1970–2005

(Dollars, percent, number.)

Type of expenditure and use	1970	1980	1990	2000	2001	2002	2003	2004	2005
Amount in Millions									
All expenditures[1]	1,689	5,981	11,500	19,327	21,316	23,003	25,647	28,346	30,836
Percent Distribution									
All services	100.0	100.0	100.0	100.0	100.0	100.0	100.0	100.0	100.0
Inpatient hospital	71.3	64.3	57.5	37.3	34.7	33.6	32.2	31.1	32.0
Outpatient care	14.0	19.1	25.3	45.7	48.0	48.8	49.5	49.5	50.5
Nursing home care	5.5	7.1	9.5	8.2	8.1	8.0	8.1	7.9	7.6
All other[2]	9.1	9.6	7.7	8.8	9.2	9.6	10.2	11.5	10.0
Number in Thousands									
Inpatient hospital stays[3]	787	1,248	1,029	579	584	590	588	599	600
Outpatient visits	7,312	17,971	22,602	38,370	42,901	46,058	49,760	53,745	59,570
Nursing home stays[4]	47	57	75	91	93	87	93	93	101
Number of Inpatients[5]	—	—	598	417	426	436	443	457	587
Percent Distribution									
Total	—	—	100.0	100.0	100.0	100.0	100.0	100.0	100.0
Veterans with service-connected disability	—	—	38.9	34.4	34.6	35.2	36.2	36.5	33.6
Veterans without service-connected disability	—	—	60.3	64.7	64.5	63.9	62.9	62.6	65.8
Low income	—	—	54.8	41.7	41.4	40.9	40.8	40.9	43.7
Veterans receiving aid and attendance or housebound benefits or who are catastrophically disabled[6]	—	—	—	16.0	15.7	13.6	13.5	12.9	3.7
Veterans receiving medical care subject to copayments[7]	—	—	2.8	5.2	6.0	7.7	8.0	8.7	18.4
Other and unknown[8]	—	—	2.7	1.8	1.4	1.7	0.6	0.0	0.0
Nonveterans	—	—	0.8	0.9	0.9	0.9	0.8	0.9	0.6
Outpatients in Thousands[5]									
Total	—	—	2,564	3,657	4,072	4,456	4,715	4,894	4,603
Percent Distribution									
Total	—	—	100.0	100.0	100.0	100.0	100.0	100.0	100.0
Veterans with service-connected disability	—	—	38.3	30.7	30.0	29.5	30.3	30.8	31.7
Veterans without service-connected disability	—	—	49.8	60.8	62.5	63.9	63.4	63.1	62.6
Low income	—	—	41.1	37.6	36.6	34.1	32.7	32.8	34.4
Veterans receiving aid and attendance or housebound benefits or who are catastrophically disabled[6]	—	—	—	3.8	3.7	3.3	3.4	3.4	2.5
Veterans receiving medical care subject to copayments[7]	—	—	3.6	15.4	19.9	23.6	26.1	26.9	25.7
Other and unknown[8]	—	—	5.1	4.0	2.3	2.9	1.1	0.0	0.0
Nonveterans	—	—	11.8	8.5	7.5	6.6	6.3	6.1	5.7

— = Data not available.

[1]Health care expenditures exclude construction, medical administration, and miscellaneous operating expenses at Department of Veterans Affairs headquarters.
[2]Includes miscellaneous benefits and services, contract hospitals, education and training, subsidies to state veterans hospitals, nursing homes and residential rehabilitation treatment programs, and the Civilian Health and Medical Program of the Department of Veterans Affairs.
[3]One-day dialysis patients were included in 1980. Interfacility transfers were included starting with 1990 data.
[4]Includes Department of Veterans Affairs nursing home and residential rehabilitation treatment programs stays, and community nursing home care stays.
[5]Individuals. The inpatient and outpatient totals are not additive because most inpatients are also treated as outpatients.
[6]Includes veterans who are receiving aid and attendance or housebound benefit and veterans who have been determined by the Department of Veterans Affairs to be catastrophically disabled.
[7]Includes financial means-tested veterans who receive medical care subject to co-payments according to income level.
[8]Includes expenditures for services for veterans who were prisoner of war, exposed to Agent Orange, and other. Prior to fiscal year 1994, veterans who reported exposure to Agent Orange were classified as exempt.

NOTE: Estimates may not add to totals due to rounding.

HEALTH INSURANCE

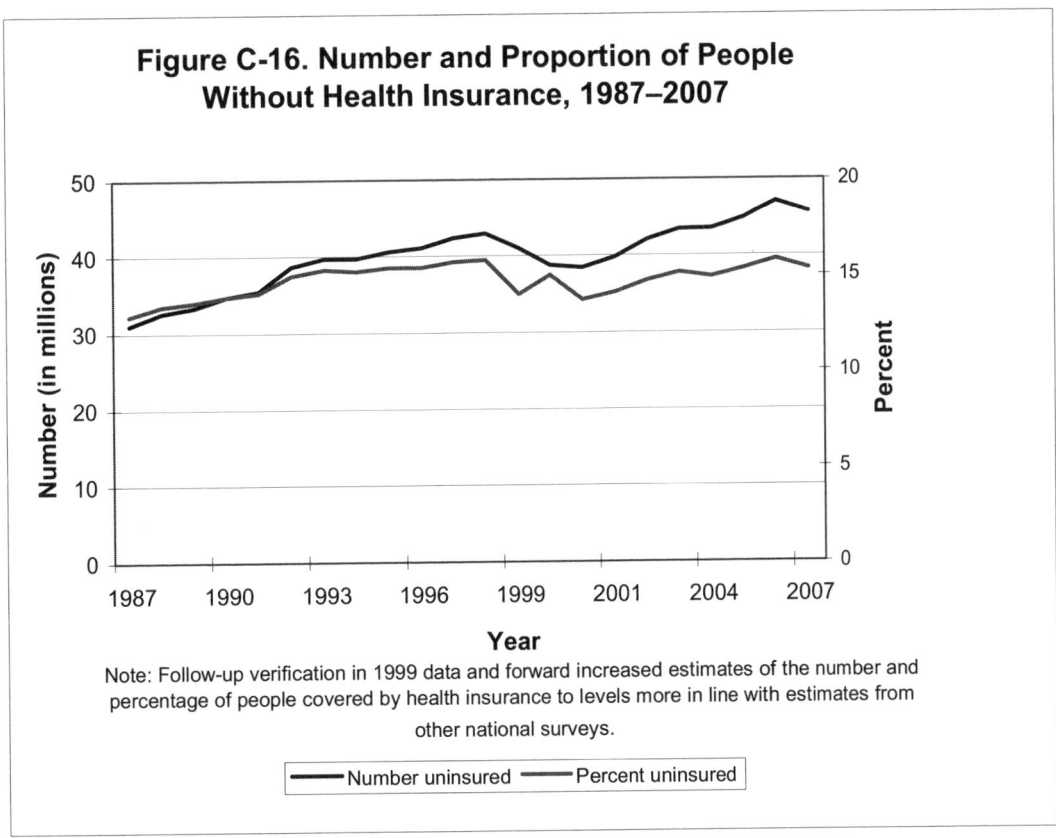

Figure C-16. Number and Proportion of People Without Health Insurance, 1987–2007

Note: Follow-up verification in 1999 data and forward increased estimates of the number and percentage of people covered by health insurance to levels more in line with estimates from other national surveys.

Number uninsured   Percent uninsured

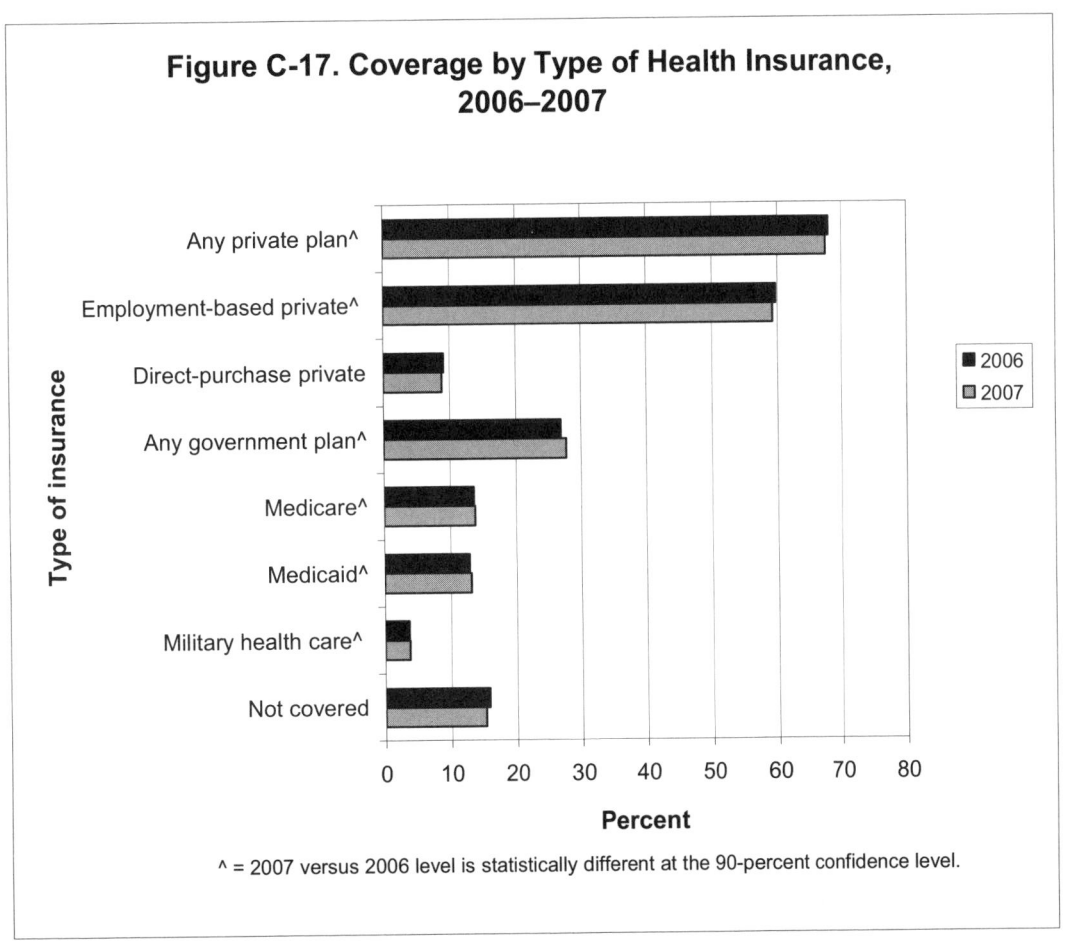

Figure C-17. Coverage by Type of Health Insurance, 2006–2007

^ = 2007 versus 2006 level is statistically different at the 90-percent confidence level.

Table C-78. Health Insurance Coverage, by Type of Coverage, 1987–2007

(Number in thousands, percent.)

Year	Total Population	Covered by private and/or government health insurance									Not covered
		Total	Private health insurance			Government health insurance					
			Total	Employment based	Direct purchase	Total	Medicaid	Medicare	Military health care[1]		
Number											
1987[2]	241,187	210,161	182,160	149,739	—	56,282	20,211	30,458	10,542		31,026
1988	243,685	211,005	182,019	150,940	—	56,850	20,728	30,925	10,105		32,680
1989	246,191	212,807	183,610	151,644	—	57,382	21,185	31,495	9,870		33,385
1990	248,886	214,167	182,135	150,215	—	60,965	24,261	32,260	9,922		34,719
1991	251,447	216,003	181,375	150,077	—	63,882	26,880	32,907	9,820		35,445
1992[3]	256,830	218,189	181,466	148,796	—	66,244	29,416	33,230	9,510		38,641
1993[4]	259,753	220,040	182,351	148,318	—	68,554	31,749	33,097	9,560		39,713
1994[5]	262,105	222,387	184,318	159,634	31,349	70,163	31,645	33,901	11,165		39,718
1995	264,314	223,733	185,881	161,453	30,188	69,776	31,877	34,655	9,375		40,582
1996[6]	266,792	225,699	188,224	164,096	28,419	69,000	31,451	35,227	8,712		41,093
1997[7]	269,094	226,735	189,955	166,419	27,431	66,685	28,956	35,590	8,527		42,359
1998	271,743	228,800	192,507	170,105	26,165	66,087	27,854	35,887	8,747		42,943
1999[8]	276,804	238,037	200,721	176,838	27,731	67,683	28,506	36,923	8,648		38,767
1999	274,087	233,073	196,536	171,692	27,298	66,176	27,890	36,066	8,530		41,014
2000[9]	279,517	241,091	202,794	179,436	26,799	69,037	29,533	37,740	9,099		38,426
2001	282,082	242,322	201,695	178,261	26,309	71,295	31,601	38,043	9,552		39,760
2002	285,933	243,914	200,891	177,095	26,846	73,624	33,246	38,448	10,063		42,019
2003	288,280	244,876	199,871	175,844	26,783	76,755	35,647	39,456	9,979		43,404
2004[10]	291,166	247,669	200,924	176,247	27,551	79,486	37,955	39,703	10,789		43,498
2005[10]	293,834	249,020	201,167	176,924	27,055	80,213	38,104	40,177	11,166		44,815
2006	296,824	249,829	201,690	177,152	27,066	80,270	38,281	40,343	10,547		46,995
2007	299,106	253,449	201,991	177,446	26,673	83,031	39,554	41,375	10,955		45,657
Percent											
1987[2]	100.0	87.1	75.5	62.1	—	23.3	8.4	12.6	4.4		12.9
1988	100.0	86.6	74.7	61.9	—	23.3	8.5	12.7	4.1		13.4
1989	100.0	86.4	74.6	61.6	—	23.3	8.6	12.8	4.0		13.6
1990	100.0	86.1	73.2	60.4	—	24.5	9.7	13.0	4.0		13.9
1991	100.0	85.9	72.1	59.7	—	25.4	10.7	13.1	3.9		14.1
1992[3]	100.0	85.0	70.7	57.9	—	25.8	11.5	12.9	3.7		15.0
1993[4]	100.0	84.7	70.2	57.1	—	26.4	12.2	12.7	3.7		15.3
1994[5]	100.0	84.8	70.3	60.9	12.0	26.8	12.1	12.9	4.3		15.2
1995	100.0	84.6	70.3	61.1	11.4	26.4	12.1	13.1	3.5		15.4
1996[6]	100.0	84.6	70.6	61.5	10.7	25.9	11.8	13.2	3.3		15.4
1997[7]	100.0	84.3	70.6	61.8	10.2	24.8	10.8	13.2	3.2		15.7
1998	100.0	84.2	70.8	62.6	9.6	24.3	10.3	13.2	3.2		15.8
1999[8]	100.0	86.0	72.5	63.9	10.0	24.5	10.3	13.3	3.1		14.0
1999	100.0	85.0	71.7	62.6	9.9	24.1	10.2	13.2	3.1		15.0
2000[9]	100.0	86.3	72.6	64.2	9.6	24.7	10.6	13.5	3.3		13.7
2001	100.0	85.9	71.5	63.2	9.3	25.3	11.2	13.5	3.4		14.1
2002	100.0	85.3	70.3	61.9	9.4	25.7	11.6	13.4	3.5		14.7
2003	100.0	84.9	69.3	61.0	9.3	26.6	12.4	13.7	3.5		15.1
2004[10]	100.0	85.1	69.0	60.5	9.5	27.3	13.0	13.6	3.7		14.9
2005[10]	100.0	84.7	68.5	60.2	9.2	27.3	13.0	13.7	3.8		15.3
2006	100.0	84.2	67.9	59.7	9.1	27.0	12.9	13.6	3.6		15.8
2007	100.0	84.7	67.5	59.3	8.9	27.8	13.2	13.8	3.7		15.3

— = Data not available.

[1]Military health care includes CHAMPUS (Comprehensive Health and Medical Plan for Uniformed Services)/Tricare and CHAMPVA (Civilian Health and Medical Program of the Department of Veterans Affairs), as well as care provided by the Health and Medical Program of the Department of Veterans Affairs and care provided by the Department of Veterans Affairs and the military.
[2]Implementation of a new CPS ASEC processing system.
[3]Implementation of 1990 census population controls.
[4]Data collection method changed from paper and pencil to computer-assisted interviewing.
[5]Health insurance questions were redesigned. Increases in estimates of employment-based and military health care coverage may be partially due to questionnaire changes. Overall coverage estimates were not affected.
[6]The data for 1996 through 2003 were constructed for consistency with the revision to the 2004 and 2005 estimates.
[7]Beginning with the 1998 CPS ASEC, people with no coverage other than access to Indian Health Service are no longer considered covered by health insurance; instead, they are considered to be uninsured. The effect of this change on the overall estimates of health insurance coverage is negligible; however, the decrease in the number of people covered by Medicaid may be partially due to this change.
[8]Estimates reflect the results of follow-up verification questions and implementation of Census 2000-based population controls.
[9]Implementation of a 28,000 household sample expansion.
[10]The 2004 and 2005 data were revised in March 2007.

Table C-79. Health Insurance Coverage by Race and Hispanic Origin, 1999–2007

(Numbers in thousands, percent.)

| Year | Total Population | Covered by private and/or government health insurance | | | | | | | | Not covered |
| | | Total | Private health insurance | | | Government health insurance | | | | |
			Total	Employment based	Direct purchase	Total	Medicaid	Medicare	Military health care[1]	
ALL RACES										
Number										
1999	276,804	238,037	200,721	176,838	27,731	67,683	28,506	36,923	8,648	38,767
2000[2]	279,517	241,091	202,794	179,436	26,799	69,037	29,533	37,740	9,099	38,426
2001	282,082	242,322	201,695	178,261	26,309	71,295	31,601	38,043	9,552	39,760
2002	285,933	243,914	200,891	177,095	26,846	73,624	33,246	38,448	10,063	42,019
2003	288,280	244,876	199,871	175,844	26,783	76,755	35,647	39,456	9,979	43,404
2004[3]	291,166	247,669	200,924	176,247	27,551	79,486	37,955	39,703	10,789	43,498
2005[3]	293,834	249,020	201,167	176,924	27,055	80,213	38,104	40,177	11,166	44,815
2006	296,824	249,829	201,690	177,152	27,066	80,270	38,281	40,343	10,547	46,995
2007	299,106	253,449	201,991	177,446	26,673	83,031	39,554	41,375	10,955	45,657
Percent										
1999	100.0	86.0	72.5	63.9	10.0	24.5	10.3	13.3	3.1	14.0
2000[2]	100.0	86.3	72.6	64.2	9.6	24.7	10.6	13.5	3.3	13.7
2001	100.0	85.9	71.5	63.2	9.3	25.3	11.2	13.5	3.4	14.1
2002	100.0	85.3	70.3	61.9	9.4	25.7	11.6	13.4	3.5	14.7
2003	100.0	84.9	69.3	61.0	9.3	26.6	12.4	13.7	3.5	15.1
2004[3]	100.0	85.1	69.0	60.5	9.5	27.3	13.0	13.6	3.7	14.9
2005[3]	100.0	84.7	68.5	60.2	9.2	27.3	13.0	13.7	3.8	15.3
2006	100.0	84.2	67.9	59.7	9.1	27.0	12.9	13.6	3.6	15.8
2007	100.0	84.7	67.5	59.3	8.9	27.8	13.2	13.8	3.7	15.3
WHITE ALONE[4]										
Number										
2002	230,809	199,392	168,745	147,706	23,686	57,072	22,171	33,135	8,065	31,417
2003	232,254	199,537	167,503	146,300	23,483	59,495	23,959	33,765	8,105	32,717
2004[3]	234,116	201,095	167,475	145,890	23,997	61,572	25,888	34,061	8,623	33,022
2005[3]	235,903	201,957	167,430	146,365	23,452	62,138	25,968	34,326	9,020	33,946
2006	237,892	202,405	167,640	146,285	23,530	62,613	26,507	34,416	8,621	35,486
2007	239,399	205,099	167,905	146,398	23,433	64,390	27,172	35,117	8,852	34,300
Percent										
2002	100.0	86.4	73.1	64.0	10.3	24.7	9.6	14.4	3.5	13.6
2003	100.0	85.9	72.1	63.0	10.1	25.6	10.3	14.5	3.5	14.1
2004[3]	100.0	85.9	71.5	62.3	10.2	26.3	11.1	14.5	3.7	14.1
2005[3]	100.0	85.6	71.0	62.0	9.9	26.3	11.0	14.6	3.8	14.4
2006	100.0	85.1	70.5	61.5	9.9	26.3	11.1	14.5	3.6	14.9
2007	100.0	85.7	70.1	61.2	9.8	26.9	11.4	14.7	3.7	14.3
WHITE[5]										
Number										
1999	225,794	197,137	170,289	149,024	24,458	53,175	18,977	32,144	6,902	28,657
2000[2]	228,208	199,280	171,543	150,708	23,722	54,287	19,889	32,695	7,158	28,928
2001	230,071	200,073	170,710	149,788	23,333	56,200	21,535	33,006	7,788	29,998
Percent										
1999	100.0	87.3	75.4	66.0	10.8	23.6	8.4	14.2	3.1	12.7
2000[2]	100.0	87.3	75.2	66.0	10.4	23.8	8.7	14.3	3.1	12.7
2001	100.0	87.0	74.2	65.1	10.1	24.4	9.4	14.3	3.4	13.0
WHITE ALONE, NOT HISPANIC										
Number										
2002	194,421	174,747	151,812	132,101	22,291	47,736	14,984	30,718	7,465	19,674
2003	194,877	174,409	150,563	130,614	22,090	49,743	16,247	31,458	7,563	20,468
2004[3]	195,347	174,793	149,882	129,766	22,346	51,002	17,462	31,624	8,005	20,554
2005[3]	195,893	174,984	149,613	130,075	21,724	51,189	17,396	31,717	8,276	20,909
2006	196,252	175,091	149,592	129,618	22,068	51,445	17,731	31,860	7,869	21,162
2007	196,768	176,220	149,122	129,138	21,717	52,512	17,786	32,436	8,131	20,548

[1]Military health care includes CHAMPUS (Comprehensive Health and Medical Plan for Uniformed Services)/Tricare and CHAMPVA (Civilian Health and Medical Program of the Department of Veterans Affairs), as well as care provided by the Health and Medical Program of the Department of Veterans Affairs and care provided by the Department of Veterans Affairs and the military.
[2]Implementation of a 28,000 household sample expansion.
[3]The 2004 and 2005 data were revised in March 2007.
[4]The 2003 CPS asked respondents to choose one or more races. White alone refers to people who reported White and did not report any other race category. The use of this single-race population does not imply that it is the preferred method of presenting or analyzing data. The Census Bureau uses a variety of approaches. About 2.6 percent of people reported more than one race in Census 2000.
[5]The 2001 CPS and earlier years asked respondents to report only one race. The reference groups for these years are White, White not Hispanic, Black, and Asian and Pacific Islander.

Table C-79. Health Insurance Coverage by Race and Hispanic Origin, 1999–2007—*Continued*

(Numbers in thousands, percent.)

Year	Total Population	Covered by private and/or government health insurance								Not covered
		Total	Private health insurance			Government health insurance				
			Total	Employment based	Direct purchase	Total	Medicaid	Medicare	Military health care[1]	
Percent										
2002	100.0	89.9	78.1	67.9	11.5	24.6	7.7	15.8	3.8	10.1
2003	100.0	89.5	77.3	67.0	11.3	25.5	8.3	16.1	3.9	10.5
2004[3]	100.0	89.5	76.7	66.4	11.4	26.1	8.9	16.2	4.1	10.5
2005[3]	100.0	89.3	76.4	66.4	11.1	26.1	8.9	16.2	4.2	10.7
2006	100.0	89.2	76.2	66.0	11.2	26.2	9.0	16.2	4.0	10.8
2007	100.0	89.6	75.8	65.6	11.0	26.7	9.0	16.5	4.1	10.4
WHITE, NOT HISPANIC										
Number										
1999	192,858	175,045	154,407	134,436	23,110	45,540	13,157	30,256	6,326	17,813
2000[2]	193,931	176,279	155,152	135,472	22,476	46,297	13,788	30,642	6,564	17,652
2001	194,822	176,488	154,218	134,586	22,009	47,661	15,035	30,811	7,144	18,333
Percent										
1999	100.0	90.8	80.1	69.7	12.0	23.6	6.8	15.7	3.3	9.2
2000[2]	100.0	90.9	80.0	69.9	11.6	23.9	7.1	15.8	3.4	9.1
2001	100.0	90.6	79.2	69.1	11.3	24.5	7.7	15.8	3.7	9.4
BLACK ALONE OR IN COMBINATION										
Number										
2002	37,350	30,093	20,440	19,038	1,638	12,624	8,744	3,851	1,342	7,257
2003	37,651	30,543	20,376	18,885	1,773	13,195	9,292	4,080	1,283	7,108
2004[3]	38,179	31,077	20,800	19,144	1,909	13,623	9,562	3,996	1,492	7,103
2005[3]	38,729	31,491	20,935	19,146	2,009	13,864	9,730	4,184	1,438	7,239
2006	39,083	31,162	20,966	19,257	1,835	13,121	9,086	4,127	1,289	7,921
2007	39,683	32,059	21,226	19,498	1,771	13,985	9,606	4,398	1,445	7,624
Percent										
2002	100.0	80.6	54.7	51.0	4.4	33.8	23.4	10.3	3.6	19.4
2003	100.0	81.1	54.1	50.2	4.7	35.0	24.7	10.8	3.4	18.9
2004[3]	100.0	81.4	54.5	50.1	5.0	35.7	25.0	10.5	3.9	18.6
2005[3]	100.0	81.3	54.1	49.4	5.2	35.8	25.1	10.8	3.7	18.7
2006	100.0	79.7	53.6	49.3	4.7	33.6	23.2	10.6	3.3	20.3
2007	100.0	80.8	53.5	49.1	4.5	35.2	24.2	11.1	3.6	19.2
BLACK ALONE[6]										
Number										
2002	35,806	28,744	19,544	18,193	1,589	12,058	8,289	3,776	1,268	7,062
2003	36,121	29,234	19,552	18,135	1,701	12,585	8,797	3,989	1,225	6,887
2004[3]	36,548	29,684	19,899	18,352	1,803	12,995	9,048	3,921	1,415	6,864
2005[3]	36,965	29,959	19,950	18,263	1,918	13,168	9,154	4,108	1,357	7,006
2006	37,369	29,717	20,034	18,401	1,766	12,454	8,531	4,059	1,216	7,652
2007	37,775	30,403	20,169	18,525	1,691	13.234	8,986	4,303	1,358	7,372
Percent										
2002	100.0	80.3	54.6	50.8	4.4	33.7	23.1	10.5	3.5	19.7
2003	100.0	80.9	54.1	50.2	4.7	34.8	24.4	11.0	3.4	19.1
2004[3]	100.0	81.2	54.4	50.2	4.9	35.6	24.8	10.7	3.9	18.8
2005[3]	100.0	81.0	54.0	49.4	5.2	35.6	24.8	11.1	3.7	19.0
2006	100.0	79.5	53.6	49.2	4.7	33.3	22.8	10.9	3.3	20.5
2007	100.0	80.5	53.4	49.0	4.5	35.0	23.8	11.4	3.6	19.5
BLACK[5]										
Number										
1999	35,893	28,918	20,638	19,039	2,118	11,361	7,652	3,615	1,216	6,975
2000[2]	35,597	29,065	20,652	19,075	1,910	11,579	7,735	3,871	1,372	6,532
2001	36,023	29,359	20,569	19,177	1,713	11,616	7,994	3,783	1,192	6,664
Percent										
1999	100.0	80.6	57.5	53.0	5.9	31.7	21.3	10.1	3.4	19.4
2000[2]	100.0	81.7	58.0	53.6	5.4	32.5	21.7	10.9	3.9	18.3
2001	100.0	81.5	57.1	53.2	4.8	32.2	22.2	10.5	3.3	18.5

[1]Military health care includes CHAMPUS (Comprehensive Health and Medical Plan for Uniformed Services)/Tricare and CHAMPVA (Civilian Health and Medical Program of the Department of Veterans Affairs), as well as care provided by the Health and Medical Program of the Department of Veterans Affairs and care provided by the Department of Veterans Affairs and the military.
[2]Implementation of a 28,000 household sample expansion.
[3]The 2004 and 2005 data were revised in March 2007.
[5]The 2001 CPS and earlier years asked respondents to report only one race. The reference groups for these years are White, White not Hispanic, Black, and Asian and Pacific Islander.
[6]Black alone refers to people who reported Black or African American and did not report any other race.

Table C-79. Health Insurance Coverage by Race and Hispanic Origin, 1999–2007—*Continued*

(Numbers in thousands, percent.)

Year	Total Population	Covered by private and/or government health insurance								Not covered
		Total	Private health insurance			Government health insurance				
			Total	Employment based	Direct purchase	Total	Medicaid	Medicare	Military health care[1]	
ASIAN ALONE OR IN COMBINATION										
Number										
2002	12,504	10,332	8,728	7,652	1,208	2,341	1,322	1,008	347	2,172
2003	12,905	10,577	8,908	7,891	1,181	2,478	1,385	1,096	355	2,329
2004[3]	13,307	11,276	9,611	8,428	1,342	2,599	1,389	1,110	440	2,031
2005[3]	13,758	11,472	9,886	8,788	1,272	2,558	1,341	1,133	461	2,286
2006	14,348	12,188	10,222	9,033	1,387	2,859	1,616	1,227	404	2,160
2007	14,444	12,122	9,995	8,951	1,216	2,888	1,659	1,238	379	2,321
Percent										
2002	100.0	82.6	69.8	61.2	9.7	18.7	10.6	8.1	2.8	17.4
2003	100.0	82.0	69.0	61.1	9.2	19.2	10.7	8.5	2.7	18.0
2004[3]	100.0	84.7	72.2	63.3	10.1	19.5	10.4	8.3	3.3	15.3
2005[3]	100.0	83.4	71.9	63.9	9.2	18.6	9.7	8.2	3.3	16.6
2006	100.0	84.9	71.2	63.0	9.7	19.9	11.3	8.6	2.8	15.1
2007	100.0	83.9	69.2	62.0	8.4	20.0	11.5	8.6	2.6	16.1
ASIAN ALONE[7]										
Number										
2002	11,558	9,499	8,024	7,004	1,151	2,132	1,202	988	270	2,060
2003	11,869	9,698	8,210	7,263	1,111	2,244	1,229	1,067	295	2,171
2004[3]	12,241	10,341	8,805	7,711	1,250	2,398	1,280	1,081	366	1,900
2005[3]	12,599	10,438	9,006	7,968	1,206	2,301	1,211	1,103	353	2,161
2006	13,194	11,149	9,339	8,201	1,323	2,636	1,480	1,187	335	2,045
2007	13,268	11,034	9,067	8,107	1,127	2,649	1,528	1,195	296	2,234
Percent										
2002	100.0	82.2	69.4	60.6	10.0	18.4	10.4	8.5	2.3	17.8
2003	100.0	81.7	69.2	61.2	9.4	18.9	10.4	9.0	2.5	18.3
2004[3]	100.0	84.5	71.9	63.0	10.2	19.6	10.5	8.8	3.0	15.5
2005[3]	100.0	82.8	71.5	63.2	9.6	18.3	9.6	8.8	2.8	17.2
2006	100.0	84.5	70.8	62.2	10.0	20.0	11.2	9.0	2.5	15.5
2007	100.0	83.2	68.3	61.1	8.5	20.0	11.5	9.0	2.2	16.8
ASIAN AND PACIFIC ISLANDER[5]										
Number										
1999	11,964	9,769	8,299	7,426	982	2,204	1,179	897	450	2,196
2000[2]	12,693	10,473	8,993	8,178	1,005	2,249	1,288	886	443	2,220
2001	12,500	10,291	8,716	7,748	1,099	2,312	1,257	949	414	2,208
Percent										
1999	100.0	81.6	69.4	62.1	8.2	18.4	9.9	7.5	3.8	18.4
2000[2]	100.0	82.5	70.9	64.4	7.9	17.7	10.1	7.0	3.5	17.5
2001	100.0	82.3	69.7	62.0	8.8	18.5	10.1	7.6	3.3	17.7
HISPANIC[8]										
Number										
1999	34,773	23,445	16,786	15,419	1,414	8,168	6,253	1,979	626	11,328
2000[2]	36,093	24,340	17,264	16,031	1,354	8,566	6,552	2,141	682	11,753
2001	37,438	25,146	17,460	16,096	1,401	9,227	7,074	2,295	704	12,292
2002	39,384	26,815	18,324	16,921	1,481	10,280	7,946	2,535	724	12,569
2003	40,425	27,355	18,372	16,970	1,559	10,716	8,505	2,462	639	13,070
2004[3]	41,840	28,527	19,090	17,499	1,788	11,530	9,205	2,614	697	13,313
2005[3]	43,168	29,214	19,252	17,597	1,856	11,958	9,357	2,771	869	13,954
2006	44,854	29,558	19,434	17,934	1,587	12,207	9,646	2,757	813	15,296
2007	46,026	31,256	20,194	18,551	1,804	13,031	10,348	2,887	801	14,770

[1]Military health care includes CHAMPUS (Comprehensive Health and Medical Plan for Uniformed Services)/Tricare and CHAMPVA (Civilian Health and Medical Program of the Department of Veterans Affairs), as well as care provided by the Health and Medical Program of the Department of Veterans Affairs and care provided by the Department of Veterans Affairs and the military.

[2]Implementation of a 28,000 household sample expansion.

[3]The 2004 and 2005 data were revised in March 2007.

[5]The 2001 CPS and earlier years asked respondents to report only one race. The reference groups for these years are White, White not Hispanic, Black, and Asian and Pacific Islander.

[7]Asian alone refers to people who reported Asian and did not report any other race.

[8]Persons of Hispanic origin may be of any race.

Table C-79. Health Insurance Coverage by Race and Hispanic Origin, 1999–2007—*Continued*

(Numbers in thousands, percent.)

| Year | Total Population | Covered by private and/or government health insurance | | | | | | | | Not covered |
| | | Total | Private health insurance | | | Government health insurance | | | | |
			Total	Employment based	Direct purchase	Total	Medicaid	Medicare	Military health care[1]	
Percent										
1999	100.0	67.4	48.3	44.3	4.1	23.5	18.0	5.7	1.8	32.6
2000[2]	100.0	67.4	47.8	44.4	3.8	23.7	18.2	5.9	1.9	32.6
2001	100.0	67.2	46.6	43.0	3.7	24.6	18.9	6.1	1.9	32.8
2002	100.0	68.1	46.5	43.0	3.8	26.1	20.2	6.4	1.8	31.9
2003	100.0	67.7	45.4	42.0	3.9	26.5	21.0	6.1	1.6	32.3
2004[3]	100.0	68.2	45.6	41.8	4.3	27.6	22.0	6.2	1.7	31.8
2005[3]	100.0	67.7	44.6	40.8	4.3	27.7	21.7	6.4	2.0	32.3
2006	100.0	65.9	43.3	40.0	3.5	27.2	21.5	6.1	1.8	34.1
2007	100.0	67.9	43.9	40.3	3.9	28.3	22.5	6.3	1.7	32.1

[1]Military health care includes CHAMPUS (Comprehensive Health and Medical Plan for Uniformed Services)/Tricare and CHAMPVA (Civilian Health and Medical Program of the Department of Veterans Affairs), as well as care provided by the Health and Medical Program of the Department of Veterans Affairs and care provided by the Department of Veterans Affairs and the military.
[2]Implementation of a 28,000 household sample expansion.
[3]The 2004 and 2005 data were revised in March 2007.

Table C-80. Health Insurance Coverage by Age, 1999–2007

(Number in thousands, percent.)

| Year | Total population | Covered by private and/or government health insurance | | | | | | | | Not covered |
| | | Total | Private health insurance | | | Government health insurance | | | | |
			Total	Employment based	Direct purchase	Total	Medicaid	Medicare	Military health care[1]	
ALL AGES										
Number										
1999[2]	276,804	238,037	200,721	176,838	27,731	67,683	28,506	36,923	8,648	38,767
2000[3]	279,517	241,091	202,794	179,436	26,799	69,037	29,533	37,740	9,099	38,426
2001	282,082	242,322	201,695	178,261	26,309	71,295	31,601	38,043	9,552	39,760
2002	285,933	243,914	200,891	177,095	26,846	73,624	33,246	38,448	10,063	42,019
2003	288,280	244,876	199,871	175,844	26,783	76,755	35,647	39,456	9,979	43,404
2004[4]	291,166	247,669	200,924	176,247	27,551	79,486	37,955	39,703	10,789	43,498
2005[4]	293,834	249,020	201,167	176,924	27,055	80,213	38,104	40,177	11,166	44,815
2006	296,824	249,829	201,690	177,152	27,066	80,270	38,281	40,343	10,547	46,995
2007	299,106	253,449	201,991	177,446	26,673	83,031	39,554	41,375	10,955	45,657
Percent										
1999[2]	100.0	86.0	72.5	63.9	10.0	24.5	10.3	13.3	3.1	14.0
2000[3]	100.0	86.3	72.6	64.2	9.6	24.7	10.6	13.5	3.3	13.7
2001	100.0	85.9	71.5	63.2	9.3	25.3	11.2	13.5	3.4	14.1
2002	100.0	85.3	70.3	61.9	9.4	25.7	11.6	13.4	3.5	14.7
2003	100.0	84.9	69.3	61.0	9.3	26.6	12.4	13.7	3.5	15.1
2004[4]	100.0	85.1	69.0	60.5	9.5	27.3	13.0	13.6	3.7	14.9
2005[4]	100.0	84.7	68.5	60.2	9.2	27.3	13.0	13.7	3.8	15.3
2006	100.0	84.2	67.9	59.7	9.1	27.0	12.9	13.6	3.6	15.8
2007	100.0	84.7	67.5	59.3	8.9	27.8	13.2	13.8	3.7	15.3
UNDER 18 YEARS										
Number										
1999[2]	72,281	63,248	50,588	47,102	4,087	16,793	14,697	364	2,076	9,033
2000[3]	72,314	63,929	50,755	47,679	3,604	17,658	15,090	518	2,563	8,385
2001	72,628	64,401	49,978	46,762	3,647	18,822	16,502	423	2,381	8,227
2002	73,312	65,082	49,807	46,510	3,876	19,662	17,526	524	2,148	8,229
2003	73,580	65,466	48,784	45,297	3,918	21,389	19,392	483	2,021	8,114
2004[4]	73,791	66,070	49,017	45,274	4,271	22,023	19,917	503	2,090	7,721
2005[4]	73,985	65,935	48,686	45,039	4,035	21,934	19,723	538	2,264	8,050
2006	74,101	65,440	47,906	44,257	3,890	22,109	20,067	411	2,058	8,661
2007	74,403	66,254	47,750	44,252	3,930	23,041	20,899	518	2,101	8,149
Percent										
1999[2]	100.0	87.5	70.0	65.2	5.7	23.2	20.3	0.5	2.9	12.5
2000[3]	100.0	88.4	70.2	65.9	5.0	24.4	20.9	0.7	3.5	11.6
2001	100.0	88.7	68.8	64.4	5.0	25.9	22.7	0.6	3.3	11.3
2002	100.0	88.8	67.9	63.4	5.3	26.8	23.9	0.7	2.9	11.2
2003	100.0	89.0	66.3	61.6	5.3	29.1	26.4	0.7	2.7	11.0
2004[4]	100.0	89.5	66.4	61.4	5.8	29.8	27.0	0.7	2.8	10.5
2005[4]	100.0	89.1	65.8	60.9	5.5	29.6	26.7	0.7	3.1	10.9
2006	100.0	88.3	64.6	59.7	5.3	29.8	27.1	0.6	2.8	11.7
2007	100.0	89.0	64.2	59.5	5.3	31.0	28.1	0.7	2.8	11.0
18 TO 24 YEARS										
Number										
1999[2]	26,326	19,245	16,817	13,836	1,591	3,485	2,684	152	787	7,081
2000[3]	26,815	19,612	17,295	14,351	1,554	3,361	2,508	207	805	7,203
2001	27,312	19,910	17,292	14,039	1,653	3,642	2,831	180	742	7,402
2002	27,438	19,575	16,834	13,691	1,582	3,738	2,909	183	779	7,863
2003	27,824	19,703	16,834	13,720	1,637	3,929	3,016	176	902	8,121
2004[4]	28,008	19,762	16,765	13,354	1,604	4,106	3,291	208	807	8,247
2005[4]	27,965	19,765	16,733	13,526	1,580	4,199	3,289	186	872	8,201
2006	28,405	20,081	17,030	13,768	1,736	4,006	3,252	154	721	8,323
2007	28,398	20,407	17,074	13,747	1,635	4,428	3,563	180	823	7,991

[1]Military health care includes CHAMPUS (Comprehensive Health and Medical Plan for Uniformed Services)/Tricare and CHAMPVA (Civilian Health and Medical Program of the Department of Veterans Affairs), as well as care provided by the Health and Medical Program of the Department of Veterans Affairs and care provided by the Department of Veterans Affairs and the military.
[2]Estimates reflect the results of follow-up verification questions and implementation of Census 2000-based population controls.
[3]Implementation of a 28,000 household sample expansion.
[4]The 2004 and 2005 data were revised in March 2007.

Table C-80. Health Insurance Coverage by Age, 1999–2007—*Continued*

(Number in thousands, percent.)

Year	Total population	Covered by private and/or government health insurance									Not covered
		Total	Private health insurance			Government health insurance					
			Total	Employment based	Direct purchase	Total	Medicaid	Medicare	Military health care[1]		
Percent											
1999[2]	100.0	73.1	63.9	52.6	6.0	13.2	10.2	0.6	3.0		26.9
2000[3]	100.0	73.1	64.5	53.5	5.8	12.5	9.4	0.8	3.0		26.9
2001	100.0	72.9	63.3	51.4	6.1	13.3	10.4	0.7	2.7		27.1
2002	100.0	71.3	61.4	49.9	5.8	13.6	10.6	0.7	2.8		28.7
2003	100.0	70.8	60.5	49.3	5.9	14.1	10.8	0.6	3.2		29.2
2004[4]	100.0	70.6	59.9	47.7	5.7	14.7	11.8	0.7	2.9		29.4
2005[4]	100.0	70.7	59.8	48.4	5.6	15.0	11.8	0.7	3.1		29.3
2006	100.0	70.7	60.0	48.5	6.1	14.1	11.4	0.5	2.5		29.3
2007	100.0	71.9	60.1	48.4	5.8	15.6	12.5	0.6	2.9		28.1
25 TO 34 YEARS											
Number											
1999[2]	39,031	30,532	27,962	26,369	2,148	3,578	2,458	332	974		8,499
2000[3]	38,865	30,547	27,951	26,388	2,056	3,551	2,480	403	922		8,318
2001	38,670	29,826	27,124	25,521	2,087	3,653	2,587	489	817		8,844
2002	39,243	29,685	26,715	25,022	2,105	3,944	2,801	455	922		9,558
2003	39,201	29,055	25,812	24,136	2,085	4,210	3,073	538	898		10,146
2004[4]	39,310	29,544	26,176	24,381	2,329	4,678	3,482	479	1,015		9,766
2005[4]	39,480	29,320	25,751	23,927	2,259	4,751	3,449	541	1,058		10,161
2006	39,868	29,154	25,814	24,009	2,160	4,460	3,374	472	890		10,713
2007	40,146	29,817	26,430	24,505	2,347	4,539	3,237	501	1,047		10,329
Percent											
1999[2]	100.0	78.2	71.6	67.6	5.5	9.2	6.3	0.8	2.5		21.8
2000[3]	100.0	78.6	71.9	67.9	5.3	9.1	6.4	1.0	2.4		21.4
2001	100.0	77.1	70.1	66.0	5.4	9.4	6.7	1.3	2.1		22.9
2002	100.0	75.6	68.1	63.8	5.4	10.1	7.1	1.2	2.3		24.4
2003	100.0	74.1	65.8	61.6	5.3	10.7	7.8	1.4	2.3		25.9
2004[4]	100.0	75.2	66.6	62.0	5.9	11.9	8.9	1.2	2.6		24.8
2005[4]	100.0	74.3	65.2	60.6	5.7	12.0	8.7	1.4	2.7		25.7
2006	100.0	73.1	64.7	60.2	5.4	11.2	8.5	1.2	2.2		26.9
2007	100.0	74.3	65.8	61.0	5.8	11.3	8.1	1.2	2.6		25.7
35 TO 44 YEARS											
Number											
1999[2]	44,474	37,894	35,074	32,776	3,170	4,028	2,390	825	1,257		6,580
2000[3]	44,566	37,820	35,186	33,135	2,747	3,920	2,390	780	1,206		6,746
2001	44,284	37,272	34,449	32,522	2,655	4,003	2,532	860	1,066		7,012
2002	44,074	36,464	33,424	31,362	2,826	4,240	2,728	881	1,121		7,610
2003	43,573	35,796	32,654	30,497	2,806	4,420	2,860	940	1,111		7,777
2004[4]	43,351	35,446	32,061	29,944	2,833	4,747	3,192	901	1,153		7,904
2005[4]	43,121	35,220	31,903	29,747	2,808	4,628	3,087	885	1,099		7,901
2006	42,762	34,744	31,531	29,463	2,788	4,409	2,977	806	1,015		8,018
2007	42,132	34,415	31,067	29,009	2,687	4,546	3,027	924	1,016		7,717
Percent											
1999[2]	100.0	85.2	78.9	73.7	7.1	9.1	5.4	1.9	2.8		14.8
2000[3]	100.0	84.9	79.0	74.4	6.2	8.8	5.4	1.8	2.7		15.1
2001	100.0	84.2	77.8	73.4	6.0	9.0	5.7	1.9	2.4		15.8
2002	100.0	82.7	75.8	71.2	6.4	9.6	6.2	2.0	2.5		17.3
2003	100.0	82.2	74.9	70.0	6.4	10.1	6.6	2.2	2.6		17.8
2004[4]	100.0	81.8	74.0	69.1	6.5	11.0	7.4	2.1	2.7		18.2
2005[4]	100.0	81.7	74.0	69.0	6.5	10.7	7.2	2.1	2.5		18.3
2006	100.0	81.2	73.7	68.9	6.5	10.3	7.0	1.9	2.4		18.8
2007	100.0	81.7	73.7	68.9	6.4	10.8	7.2	2.2	2.4		18.3

[1]Military health care includes CHAMPUS (Comprehensive Health and Medical Plan for Uniformed Services)/Tricare and CHAMPVA (Civilian Health and Medical Program of the Department of Veterans Affairs), as well as care provided by the Health and Medical Program of the Department of Veterans Affairs and care provided by the Department of Veterans Affairs and the military.
[2]Estimates reflect the results of follow-up verification questions and implementation of Census 2000-based population controls.
[3]Implementation of a 28,000 household sample expansion.
[4]The 2004 and 2005 data were revised in March 2007.

Table C-80. Health Insurance Coverage by Age, 1999–2007—*Continued*

(Number in thousands, percent.)

| Year | Total population | Covered by private and/or government health insurance | Private health insurance | | | Government health insurance | | | | Not covered |
		Total	Total	Employment based	Direct purchase	Total	Medicaid	Medicare	Military health care[1]	
45 TO 54 YEARS										
Number										
1999[2]	37,334	32,927	30,548	28,448	3,226	3,682	1,769	1,162	1,244	4,407
2000[3]	38,720	34,227	31,659	29,578	3,103	3,964	1,996	1,384	1,169	4,492
2001	39,545	34,595	31,909	29,718	3,135	3,990	2,071	1,331	1,170	4,950
2002	40,234	34,913	32,011	29,884	3,124	4,345	2,227	1,382	1,351	5,321
2003	41,068	35,443	32,368	30,053	3,255	4,569	2,359	1,569	1,369	5,625
2004[4]	41,961	36,074	32,776	30,370	3,324	4,898	2,656	1,550	1,426	5,886
2005[4]	42,797	36,570	33,114	30,651	3,396	4,956	2,837	1,591	1,355	6,227
2006	43,461	36,819	33,250	30,868	3,297	5,182	2,885	1,739	1,337	6,642
2007	43,935	37,161	33,350	30,805	3,292	5,363	3,103	1,795	1,285	6,774
Percent										
1999[2]	100.0	88.2	81.8	76.2	8.6	9.9	4.7	3.1	3.3	11.8
2000[3]	100.0	88.4	81.8	76.4	8.0	10.2	5.2	3.6	3.0	11.6
2001	100.0	87.5	80.7	75.2	7.9	10.1	5.2	3.4	3.0	12.5
2002	100.0	86.8	79.6	74.3	7.8	10.8	5.5	3.4	3.4	13.2
2003	100.0	86.3	78.8	73.2	7.9	11.1	5.7	3.8	3.3	13.7
2004[4]	100.0	86.0	78.1	72.4	7.9	11.7	6.3	3.7	3.4	14.0
2005[4]	100.0	85.5	77.4	71.6	7.9	11.6	6.6	3.7	3.2	14.5
2006	100.0	84.7	76.5	71.0	7.6	11.9	6.6	4.0	3.1	15.3
2007	100.0	84.6	75.9	70.1	7.5	12.2	7.1	4.1	2.9	15.4
55 TO 64 YEARS										
Number										
1999[2]	23,981	21,082	18,678	16,518	3,008	4,033	1,551	2,084	1,053	2,899
2000[3]	24,672	21,641	18,977	16,792	2,990	4,185	1,731	2,159	1,024	3,031
2001	25,874	22,820	19,959	17,862	2,832	4,567	1,807	2,301	1,220	3,054
2002	27,399	24,219	21,170	18,844	3,123	4,882	1,773	2,392	1,482	3,180
2003	28,375	25,039	21,963	19,692	3,051	4,893	1,757	2,494	1,471	3,335
2004[4]	29,536	26,016	22,640	20,254	3,180	5,478	2,085	2,644	1,795	3,519
2005[4]	30,981	27,154	23,543	21,092	3,194	5,886	2,325	2,708	1,908	3,826
2006	32,191	28,096	24,255	21,701	3,276	6,122	2,362	2,956	1,845	4,095
2007	33,302	29,291	25,114	22,569	3,237	6,651	2,462	3,179	2,079	4,011
Percent										
1999[2]	100.0	87.9	77.9	68.9	12.5	16.8	6.5	8.7	4.4	12.1
2000[3]	100.0	87.7	76.9	68.1	12.1	17.0	7.0	8.8	4.2	12.3
2001	100.0	88.2	77.1	69.0	10.9	17.7	7.0	8.9	4.7	11.8
2002	100.0	88.4	77.3	68.8	11.4	17.8	6.5	8.7	5.4	11.6
2003	100.0	88.2	77.4	69.4	10.8	17.2	6.2	8.8	5.2	11.8
2004[4]	100.0	88.1	76.7	68.6	10.8	18.5	7.1	9.0	6.1	11.9
2005[4]	100.0	87.6	76.0	68.1	10.3	19.0	7.5	8.7	6.2	12.4
2006	100.0	87.3	75.3	67.4	10.2	19.0	7.3	9.2	5.7	12.7
2007	100.0	88.0	75.4	67.8	9.7	20.0	7.4	9.5	6.2	12.0
65 YEARS AND OLDER										
Number										
1999[2]	33,377	33,109	21,054	11,789	10,501	32,083	2,956	32,004	1,257	268
2000[3]	33,566	33,314	20,971	11,512	10,746	32,398	3,339	32,289	1,410	251
2001	33,769	33,498	20,984	11,837	10,299	32,618	3,270	32,458	2,156	272
2002	34,234	33,976	20,929	11,782	10,210	32,813	3,283	32,631	2,259	258
2003	34,659	34,373	21,457	12,448	10,032	33,345	3,190	33,257	2,206	286
2004[4]	35,209	34,755	21,488	12,670	10,010	33,555	3,332	33,419	2,504	454
2005[4]	35,505	35,056	21,437	12,942	9,783	33,859	3,394	33,727	2,611	449
2006	36,035	35,494	21,904	13,086	9,918	33,982	3,364	33,806	2,682	541
2007	36,790	36,103	21,206	12,558	9,546	34,464	3,263	34,278	2,604	686

[1]Military health care includes CHAMPUS (Comprehensive Health and Medical Plan for Uniformed Services)/Tricare and CHAMPVA (Civilian Health and Medical Program of the Department of Veterans Affairs), as well as care provided by the Health and Medical Program of the Department of Veterans Affairs and care provided by the Department of Veterans Affairs and the military.
[2]Estimates reflect the results of follow-up verification questions and implementation of Census 2000-based population controls.
[3]Implementation of a 28,000 household sample expansion.
[4]The 2004 and 2005 data were revised in March 2007.

Table C-80. Health Insurance Coverage by Age, 1999–2007—*Continued*

(Number in thousands, percent.)

Year	Total population	Covered by private and/or government health insurance								Not covered
		Total	Private health insurance			Government health insurance				
			Total	Employment based	Direct purchase	Total	Medicaid	Medicare	Military health care[1]	
Percent										
1999[2]	100.0	99.2	63.1	35.3	31.5	96.1	8.9	95.9	3.8	0.8
2000[3]	100.0	99.3	62.5	34.3	32.0	96.5	9.9	96.2	4.2	0.7
2001	100.0	99.2	62.1	35.1	30.5	96.6	9.7	96.1	6.4	0.8
2002	100.0	99.2	61.1	34.4	29.8	95.8	9.6	95.3	6.6	0.8
2003	100.0	99.2	61.9	35.9	28.9	96.2	9.2	96.0	6.4	0.8
2004[4]	100.0	98.7	61.0	36.0	28.4	95.3	9.5	94.9	7.1	1.3
2005[4]	100.0	98.7	60.4	36.5	27.6	95.4	9.6	95.0	7.4	1.3
2006	100.0	98.5	60.8	36.3	27.5	94.3	9.3	93.8	7.4	1.5
2007	100.0	98.1	57.6	34.1	25.9	93.7	8.9	93.2	7.1	1.9

[1]Military health care includes CHAMPUS (Comprehensive Health and Medical Plan for Uniformed Services)/Tricare and CHAMPVA (Civilian Health and Medical Program of the Department of Veterans Affairs), as well as care provided by the Health and Medical Program of the Department of Veterans Affairs and care provided by the Department of Veterans Affairs and the military.
[2]Estimates reflect the results of follow-up verification questions and implementation of Census 2000-based population controls.
[3]Implementation of a 28,000 household sample expansion.
[4]The 2004 and 2005 data were revised in March 2007.

Table C-81. Number and Percentage of People Without Health Insurance Coverage by State Using 2-and 3-Year Averages, 2004–2005 and 2006–2007

(Numbers in thousands.)

Area	3-year average (2005–2007)[1]					2-year average, percentage uninsured				Change (2006–2007 average less 2004–2005 average)[3]
	Uninsured					2004–2005[1]		2006–2007		
	Total	Number	90-percent confidence interval[2] (±)	Percentage	90-percent confidence interval[2] (±)	Percentage	90-percent confidence interval[2] (±)	Percentage	90-percent confidence interval[2] (±)	
UNITED STATES	296,588	45,822	360	15.4	0.1	15.1	0.1	15.5	0.1	^0.5
Alabama	4,542	632	44	13.9	1	13.5	1.1	13.6	1.1	0.1
Alaska	664	115	8	17.3	1.1	16.9	1.3	17.4	1.3	0.5
Arizona	6,228	1,219	64	19.6	1	18.1	1.2	19.6	1.2	1.5
Arkansas	2,774	485	30	17.5	1.1	16.8	1.3	17.5	1.3	0.7
California	36,148	6,720	151	18.6	0.4	18.4	0.5	18.5	0.5	0.1
Colorado	4,773	799	52	16.7	1.1	16.3	1.3	16.8	1.3	0.5
Connecticut	3,475	344	30	9.9	0.9	10.9	1.1	9.4	1	^–1.5
Delaware	856	101	8	11.8	0.9	12.7	1.2	11.7	1.1	–1.0
District of Columbia	564	64	6	11.4	1	12.8	1.3	10.6	1.2	^–2.2
Florida	18,007	3,698	105	20.5	0.6	19.8	0.7	20.7	0.7	0.9
Georgia	9,295	1,658	70	17.8	0.8	17.6	0.9	17.6	0.9	–
Hawaii	1,267	105	10	8.3	0.8	8.5	0.9	8.2	0.9	–0.3
Idaho	1,473	216	15	14.7	1	14.7	1.2	14.6	1.2	–
Illinois	12,647	1,735	75	13.7	0.6	13.4	0.7	13.7	0.7	0.3
Indiana	6,247	766	49	12.3	0.8	13.7	1	11.6	0.9	^–2.1
Iowa	2,933	274	25	9.4	0.9	8.7	1	9.9	1	1.2
Kansas	2,713	320	26	11.8	1	10.5	1.1	12.5	1.2	^2.0
Kentucky	4,122	569	42	13.8	1	13	1.2	14.6	1.2	^1.6
Louisiana	4,166	807	48	19.4	1.1	16.9	1.3	20.2	1.4	^3.3
Maine	1,316	125	12	9.5	0.9	9.6	1.1	9.1	1.1	–0.5
Maryland	5,582	761	50	13.6	0.9	13.4	1	13.8	1.1	0.4
Massachusetts	6,334	527	41	8.3	0.7	10.3	0.8	7.9	0.7	^–2.4
Michigan	9,960	1,075	59	10.8	0.6	10.7	0.7	11	0.7	0.3
Minnesota	5,156	438	38	8.5	0.7	8.2	0.9	8.8	0.9	0.6
Mississippi	2,883	543	32	18.8	1.1	16.8	1.3	19.8	1.3	^3.0
Missouri	5,767	723	49	12.5	0.8	11.8	1	12.9	1	1.1
Montana	933	150	10	16.1	1.1	16.9	1.3	16.4	1.3	–0.5
Nebraska	1,762	212	17	12	1	10.5	1.1	12.8	1.2	^2.3
Nevada	2,517	452	29	17.9	1.1	17.7	1.4	18.4	1.4	0.7
New Hampshire	1,308	138	12	10.5	0.9	9.9	1	11	1.1	1.1
New Jersey	8,647	1,318	65	15.2	0.7	14.2	0.9	15.6	0.9	^1.4
New Mexico	1,943	425	25	21.9	1.3	20.1	1.5	22.7	1.6	^2.6
New York	19,041	2,551	93	13.4	0.5	12.8	0.6	13.6	0.6	^0.8
North Carolina	8,865	1,469	68	16.6	0.8	15.1	0.9	17.2	0.9	^2.1
North Dakota	619	68	6	11.1	0.9	10.5	1.1	11.1	1.1	0.6
Ohio	11,318	1,249	63	11	0.6	11	0.7	10.9	0.7	–0.1
Oklahoma	3,516	640	40	18.2	1.1	18.5	1.4	18.4	1.3	–0.2
Oregon	3,702	621	42	16.8	1.1	15.9	1.3	17.3	1.3	1.4
Pennsylvania	12,313	1,203	63	9.8	0.5	10.3	0.6	9.8	0.6	–0.6
Rhode Island	1,051	108	10	10.3	0.9	10.9	1.1	9.7	1.1	–1.2
South Carolina	4,264	705	46	16.5	1.1	16	1.3	16.2	1.2	0.2
South Dakota	776	87	7	11.2	0.9	11.4	1	11	1	–0.4
Tennessee	5,979	830	51	13.9	0.8	13.3	1	14	1	0.7
Texas	23,253	5,687	136	24.4	0.6	23.9	0.7	24.8	0.7	^0.9
Utah	2,573	399	25	15.6	1	14.9	1.1	15.1	1.1	0.3
Vermont	619	68	6	11	1	11	1.2	10.7	1.1	–0.3
Virginia	7,559	1,031	57	13.6	0.7	13.1	0.9	14.1	0.9	1
Washington	6,359	770	51	12.1	0.8	12.8	1	11.6	0.9	–1.3
West Virginia	1,803	268	17	14.9	1	16.5	1.2	13.8	1.1	^–2.7
Wisconsin	5,465	480	40	8.8	0.7	9.7	0.9	8.5	0.9	^–1.2
Wyoming	515	73	6	14.3	1.1	13.7	1.3	14.1	1.3	0.4

^ = Statistically different from zero at the 90-percent confidence level.

– = Represents or rounds to zero.

[1]The 2004 and 2005 data were revised in March 2007.

[2]A 90-percent confidence interval is a measure of an estimate's variability. The larger the confidence interval in relation to the size of the estimate, the less reliable the estimate.

[3]Details may not sum to totals because of rounding.

Table C-82. People Without Health Insurance Coverage by Race and Hispanic Origin Using 2-and 3-Year Averages: 2004–2005 and 2006–2007

(Number in thousands.)

Race and Hispanic origin[1]	3-year average 2005–2007[2]		2-year average				Change (2006—2007 average less 2004–2005[2] average)	
			2004–2005[2]		2006–2007[2]			
	Estimate	90-percent confidence level[3] (±)	Estimate	90-percent confidence level[3] (±)	Estimate	90-percent confidence level[3] (±)	Estimate	90-percent confidence level[3] (±)
NUMBER INSURED								
All Races...............................	45,822	360	44,156	418	46,326	427	^2,170	562
White...................................	34,578	320	33,484	372	34,893	379	^1,409	499
White, not Hispanic...................	20,873	255	20,732	300	20,855	301	123	399
Black...................................	7,343	176	6,935	202	7,512	210	^577	274
American Indian and Alaska Native.............	809	61	693	67	869	75	^176	95
Asian...................................	2,147	96	2,031	111	2,139	114	109	149
Native Hawaiian and Other Pacific Islander...................................	140	26	139	30	141	31	2	41
Hispanic...................................	14,673	233	13,633	263	15,033	274	^1,400	349
PERCENTAGE UNINSURED								
All Races...............................	15.4	0.1	15.1	0.1	15.5	0.1	^0.5	0.2
White...................................	14.5	0.1	14.2	0.2	14.6	0.2	^0.4	0.2
White, not Hispanic...................	10.6	0.1	10.6	0.2	10.6	0.2	–	0.2
Black...................................	19.6	0.5	18.9	0.5	20	0.5	^1.1	0.7
American Indian and Alaska Native.............	32.1	2	30.3	2.5	32.9	2.4	2.6	3.2
Asian...................................	16.5	0.7	16.3	0.9	16.2	0.8	–0.2	1.1
Native Hawaiian and Other Pacific Islander...................................	20.5	3.4	22.8	4.4	19.5	3.8	–3.2	5.5
Hispanic...................................	32.8	0.5	32.1	0.6	33.1	0.6	^1.0	0.8

^ = Statistically different from zero at the 90-percent confidence level.

– = Represents or rounds to zero.

[1]Federal surveys now give respondents the option of reporting more than one race. Therefore, two basic ways of defining a race group are possible. A group such as Asian may be defined as those who reported Asian and no other race (the race-alone or single-race concept) or as those who reported Asian regardless of whether they also reported another race (the race-alone-or-in-combination concept). This table shows data using the first approach (race alone). The use of the single-race population does not imply that it is the preferred method of presenting or analyzing data. About 2.6 percent of people reported more than one race in Census 2000. Persons of Hispanic origin may be of any race.

[2]The 2004 and 2005 data were revised in March 2007.

[3]A 90-percent confidence interval is a measure of an estimate's variability. The larger the confidence interval in relation to the size of the estimate, the less reliable the estimate.

Table C-83. People Without Health Insurance Coverage by Selected Characteristics, 2006 and 2007

(Number in thousands, percent.)

Characteristic	2006					2007					Change in uninsured (2007 less than 2006)[1]	
			Uninsured					Uninsured				
	Total	Number	90-percent confidence interval[2] (±)	Percentage	90-percent confidence interval[2] (±)	Total	Number	90-percent confidence interval[2] (±)	Percentage	90-percent confidence interval[2] (±)	Number	Percentage
TOTAL	296,824	46,995	532	15.8	0.2	299,106	45,657	526	15.3	0.2	^–1,337	^–0.6
Family Status												
In families	245,199	36,230	478	14.8	0.2	245,443	34,629	468	14.1	0.2	^–1,601	^–0.7
Householder	78,454	10,770	171	13.7	0.2	77,908	10,272	168	13.2	0.2	^–499	^–0.5
Related children under 18	72,609	8,303	241	11.4	0.3	72,792	7,802	233	10.7	0.3	^–501	^–0.7
Related children under 6	24,204	2,690	138	11.1	0.5	24,543	2,555	135	10.4	0.5	–135	^–0.7
In unrelated subfamilies	1,367	341	49	25.0	3.1	1,516	363	51	23.9	2.9	21	–1.0
Unrelated individuals	50,258	10,423	269	20.7	0.5	52,147	10,665	272	20.5	0.5	242	–0.3
Race and Hispanic Origin[3]												
White	237,892	35,486	473	14.9	0.2	239,399	34,300	466	14.3	0.2	^–1,186	^–0.6
White, not Hispanic	196,252	21,162	375	10.8	0.2	196,768	20,548	370	10.4	0.2	^–614	^–0.3
Black	37,369	7,652	262	20.5	0.7	37,775	7,372	258	19.5	0.7	–280	^–1.0
Asian	13,194	2,045	138	15.5	1.0	13,268	2,234	144	16.8	1.0	^188	^1.3
Hispanic	44,854	15,296	322	34.1	0.7	46,026	14,770	321	32.1	0.7	^–526	^–2.0
Age												
Under 18 years	74,101	8,661	246	11.7	0.3	74,403	8,149	238	11.0	0.3	^–512	^–0.7
18 to 24 years	28,405	8,323	241	29.3	0.7	28,398	7,991	236	28.1	0.7	^–332	^–1.2
25 to 34 years	39,868	10,713	272	26.9	0.6	40,146	10,329	267	25.7	0.6	^–384	^–1.1
35 to 44 years	42,762	8,018	237	18.8	0.5	42,132	7,717	232	18.3	0.5	^–301	–0.4
45 to 64 years	75,653	10,738	272	14.2	0.3	77,237	10,784	273	14.0	0.3	47	–0.2
65 years and older	36,035	541	62	1.5	0.2	36,790	686	70	1.9	0.2	^145	^0.4
Nativity												
Native born	259,545	34,380	467	13.2	0.2	261,842	33,269	460	12.7	0.2	^–1,111	^–0.5
Foreign born	37,279	12,615	335	33.8	0.7	37,264	12,388	333	33.2	0.7	–226	–0.6
Naturalized citizen	14,538	2,384	149	16.4	0.9	15,050	2,651	157	17.6	0.9	^267	^1.2
Not a citizen	22,741	10,231	303	45.0	1.0	22,214	9,737	296	43.8	1.0	^–494	–1.2
Region												
Northeast	54,139	6,648	209	12.3	0.4	54,031	6,143	202	11.4	0.4	^–506	^–0.9
Midwest	65,491	7,458	221	11.4	0.3	65,480	7,495	221	11.4	0.3	37	0.1
South	108,030	20,486	358	19.0	0.3	109,710	20,210	358	18.4	0.3	–276	^–0.5
West	69,163	12,403	284	17.9	0.4	69,883	11,809	278	16.9	0.4	^–593	^–1.0
Residence												
Inside metropolitan statistical areas	249,391	39,421	495	15.8	0.2	251,363	38,497	490	15.3	0.2	^–924	^–0.5
Inside principal cities	95,240	18,107	349	19.0	0.3	96,874	17,935	348	18.5	0.3	–172	^–0.5
Outside principal cities	154,151	21,314	377	13.8	0.2	154,489	20,563	370	13.3	0.2	^–751	^–0.5
Outside metropolitan statistical areas[4]	47,433	7,574	282	16.0	0.6	47,743	7,160	274	15.0	0.5	^–414	^–1.0
Household Income												
Less than $25,000	55,856	13,933	309	24.9	0.5	55,267	13,539	304	24.5	0.5	^–394	–0.4
$25,000 to $49,999	72,582	15,319	323	21.1	0.4	68,915	14,515	315	21.1	0.4	^–804	0.0
$50,000 to $74,999	58,555	8,459	243	14.4	0.4	58,355	8,488	243	14.5	0.4	29	0.1
$75,000 or more	109,831	9,283	254	8.5	0.2	116,568	9,115	252	7.8	0.2	–168	^–0.6
Work Experience												
Total, 18 to 64 years old	186,688	37,792	502	20.2	0.3	187,913	36,822	497	19.6	0.3	^–971	^–0.6
Worked during year	147,789	27,627	443	18.7	0.3	148,603	26,840	438	18.1	0.3	^–787	^–0.6
Worked full-time	123,272	22,010	402	17.9	0.3	123,882	21,060	395	17.0	0.3	^–950	^–0.9
Worked part-time	24,517	5,618	213	22.9	0.8	24,721	5,780	216	23.4	0.8	163	0.5
Did not work	38,899	10,165	284	26.1	0.6	39,310	9,981	282	25.4	0.6	–184	–0.7

– = Represents or rounds to zero.

^ = Statistically different from zero at the 90-percent confidence level.

[1]Details may not sum to totals because of rounding.

[2]A 90-percent confidence interval is a measure of an estimate's variability. The larger the confidence interval in relation to the size of the estimate, the less reliable the estimate. For more information.

[3]Federal surveys now give respondents the option of reporting more than one race. Therefore, two basic ways of defining a race group are possible. A group such as Asian may be defined as those who reported Asian and no other race (the race-alone or single-race concept) or as those who reported Asian regardless of whether they also reported another race (the race-alone-or-in combination concept). This table shows data using the first approach (race alone). The use of the single-race population does not imply that it is the preferred method of presenting or analyzing data. The Census Bureau uses a variety of approaches. About 2.6 percent of people reported more than one race in Census 2000. Data for American Indians and Alaska Natives, Native Hawaiians and Other Pacific Islanders, and those reporting two or more races are not shown separately. A person of Hispanic origin may be of any race.

[4]The "outside metropolitan statistical areas" category includes both micropolitan statistical areas and territory outside of metropolitan and micropolitan statistical areas.

Table C-84. People Without Health Insurance by Family Income, 2006 and 2007

(Numbers in thousands, percent.)

Characteristic	2006 (uninsured)					2007 (uninsured)					Change (2007 less 2006)[1]			
	Total	Number	90-percent confidence interval[2] (±)	Percent-age	90-percent confidence interval[2] (±)	Total	Number	90-percent confidence interval[2] (±)	Percent-age	90-percent confidence interval[2] (±)	Number	90-percent confidence interval[2] (±)	Percent-age	90-percent confidence interval[2] (±)
All..	296,824	46,995	532	15.8	0.2	299,106	45,657	526	15.3	0.2	^-1337	626	^-0.6	0.2
Less than $25,000.........................	66,498	18,322	351	27.6	0.5	66,017	17,802	346	27.0	0.5	^-520	413	^-0.6	0.5
$25,000 to $49,999......................	73,244	14,483	314	19.8	0.4	70,404	13,732	307	19.5	0.4	^-751	367	-0.3	0.5
$50,000 to $74,999......................	54,784	6,863	219	12.5	0.4	54,414	6,870	219	12.6	0.4	7	260	0.1	0.4
$75,000 or more...........................	102,298	7,327	226	7.2	0.2	108,271	7,253	225	6.7	0.2	-73	267	^-0.5	0.2
In Families or														
Unrelated Subfamilies...................	246,566	36,572	479	14.8	0.2	246,959	34,992	470	14.2	0.2	^-1580	562	^-0.7	0.2
Less than $25,000.........................	40,431	10,958	275	27.1	0.6	39,683	10,453	269	26.3	0.6	^-506	322	^-0.8	0.7
$25,000 to $49,999......................	58,612	12,154	289	20.7	0.4	55,004	11,208	278	20.4	0.5	^-946	336	-0.4	0.5
$50,000 to $74,999......................	49,282	6,379	212	12.9	0.4	48,407	6,367	211	13.2	0.4	-12	250	0.2	0.5
$75,000 or more...........................	98,240	7,080	223	7.2	0.2	103,865	6,965	221	6.7	0.2	-116	262	^-0.5	0.3
Unrelated Individuals														
(15 or Older)................................	50,258	10,423	269	20.7	0.5	52,147	10,665	272	20.5	0.5	242	320	-0.3	0.6
Less than $25,000.........................	26,067	7,364	227	28.2	0.7	26,334	7,349	227	27.9	0.7	-14	268	-0.3	0.9
$25,000 to $49,999......................	14,632	2,330	129	15.9	0.8	15,400	2,524	134	16.4	0.8	^195	156	0.5	1.0
$50,000 to $74,999......................	5,501	483	59	8.8	1.0	6,007	503	60	8.4	1.0	19	70	-0.4	1.2
$75,000 or more...........................	4,057	246	42	6.1	1.0	4,406	289	45	6.5	1.0	42	52	0.5	1.2

^ = Statistically different from zero at the 90-percent confidence level.

[1]Details may not sum to totals because of rounding.

[2]A 90-percent confidence interval is a measure of an estimate's variability. The larger the confidence interval in relation to the size of the estimate, the less reliable the estimate.

Table C-85. Number and Percent of Children Under 19 Years of Age, At or Below 200 Percent of Poverty, by State, Three-Year Averages for 2005, 2006, and 2007

(Numbers in thousands, percent.)

Area	Total children under 19 years, all income levels	At or below 200% of poverty				At or below 200% of poverty without health insurance			
		Number	Standard error	Percent	Standard error	Number	Standard error	Percent	Standard error
UNITED STATES	77,762	30,176	276	38.8	0.3	5,522	124	7.1	0.2
Alabama	1,165	481	36	41.2	2.5	51	12	4.4	1.0
Alaska	192	58	5	30.3	2.4	8	2	4.4	1.1
Arizona	1,735	824	50	47.5	2.2	203	26	11.7	1.4
Arkansas	727	372	25	51.1	2.6	46	9	6.4	1.3
California	10,024	4,154	114	41.4	0.9	800	53	8.0	0.5
Colorado	1,247	398	35	31.9	2.4	111	19	8.9	1.5
Connecticut	868	224	23	25.8	2.3	29	8	3.3	0.9
Delaware	214	71	6	33.0	2.5	13	3	6.0	1.3
District of Columbia	118	62	5	52.7	3.3	6	2	4.8	1.4
Florida	4,260	1,673	69	39.3	1.3	509	39	12.0	0.9
Georgia	2,552	1,049	53	41.1	1.7	210	25	8.2	1.0
Hawaii	309	89	8	29.0	2.3	8	3	2.4	0.8
Idaho	426	171	12	40.2	2.4	29	5	6.7	1.2
Illinois	3,376	1,175	58	34.8	1.5	180	24	5.3	0.7
Indiana	1,676	626	41	37.4	2.1	66	14	3.9	0.8
Iowa	737	239	22	32.4	2.5	20	7	2.7	0.9
Kansas	734	283	23	38.6	2.6	35	8	4.7	1.1
Kentucky	1,058	461	35	43.6	2.6	61	13	5.8	1.2
Louisiana	1,133	503	36	44.4	2.5	91	16	8.0	1.4
Maine	299	105	10	35.1	2.9	11	3	3.6	1.1
Maryland	1,449	380	33	26.2	2.1	74	15	5.1	1.0
Massachusetts	1,557	453	35	29.1	2.0	36	10	2.3	0.7
Michigan	2,596	953	51	36.7	1.7	83	16	3.2	0.6
Minnesota	1,313	355	32	27.0	2.1	51	12	3.9	0.9
Mississippi	813	436	27	53.6	2.5	92	13	11.3	1.6
Missouri	1,476	594	41	40.3	2.3	86	16	5.8	1.1
Montana	228	94	8	41.1	2.7	19	4	8.5	1.5
Nebraska	464	148	13	31.9	2.5	24	6	5.2	1.2
Nevada	684	257	21	37.6	2.5	64	11	9.3	1.5
New Hampshire	315	61	7	19.3	2.2	8	3	2.4	0.9
New Jersey	2,220	583	41	26.3	1.7	146	21	6.6	0.9
New Mexico	532	242	19	45.4	2.7	62	10	11.7	1.8
New York	4,741	1,924	75	40.6	1.3	233	27	4.9	0.6
North Carolina	2,320	991	53	42.7	1.8	198	25	8.5	1.0
North Dakota	154	55	5	35.6	2.6	10	2	6.2	1.3
Ohio	2,900	1,084	55	37.4	1.6	134	20	4.6	0.7
Oklahoma	940	437	31	46.5	2.6	70	13	7.4	1.4
Oregon	914	359	30	39.3	2.7	69	14	7.6	1.5
Pennsylvania	2,918	1,056	54	36.2	1.6	145	21	5.0	0.7
Rhode Island	255	85	8	33.4	2.7	9	3	3.7	1.1
South Carolina	1,087	475	36	43.7	2.6	78	15	7.1	1.3
South Dakota	203	72	6	35.5	2.3	10	2	4.8	1.0
Tennessee	1,526	669	43	43.8	2.2	76	15	5.0	0.9
Texas	6,876	3,240	100	47.1	1.1	955	58	13.9	0.8
Utah	838	302	20	36.0	2.0	63	10	7.6	1.1
Vermont	139	40	4	28.5	2.7	5	2	3.4	1.1
Virginia	1,924	622	42	32.3	1.9	113	18	5.9	0.9
Washington	1,608	516	39	32.1	2.1	61	14	3.8	0.8
West Virginia	415	189	14	45.5	2.6	14	4	3.4	0.9
Wisconsin	1,381	445	36	32.2	2.2	43	11	3.1	0.8
Wyoming	129	41	4	31.9	2.7	6	2	4.7	1.2

NOTE: Average of the three years' percentages: not average 'number' divided by average total children. Results may differ slightly based on the method used.

Table C-86. Coverage by Type for Children Under 19 Years of Age, At or Below 200 Percent of Poverty, by State, Three-Year Averages for 2005, 2006, and 2007

(Numbers in thousands, percent.)

Area	Total	Children under 19 years of age at or below 200% of poverty											
		Uninsured				Insured							
						Private Health Insurance				Government Health Insurance			
		Number	Standard error	Percent	Standard error	Number	Standard error	Percent	Standard error	Number	Standard error	Percent	Standard error
UNITED STATES	30,177	5,522	124	18.3	0.2	10,208	167	33.8	0.2	16,532	210	54.8	0.2
Alabama	481	51	12	10.8	1.6	179	22	37.3	1.8	281	28	58.4	2.1
Alaska	58	8	2	14.9	1.8	20	3	33.5	1.6	40	4	68.1	2.1
Arizona	824	203	26	24.6	1.9	247	29	30.0	1.6	414	37	50.2	1.9
Arkansas	372	46	9	12.5	1.7	120	15	32.2	1.9	239	20	64.2	2.4
California	4,154	800	53	19.3	0.7	1,194	64	28.7	0.6	2,363	88	56.9	0.8
Colorado	398	111	19	28.0	2.3	149	22	37.5	1.7	156	23	39.3	1.7
Connecticut	224	29	8	12.9	1.7	83	14	37.0	1.6	132	18	58.7	1.9
Delaware	71	13	3	18.0	2.1	27	4	38.0	1.8	35	5	50.1	2.0
District of Columbia	62	6	2	9.1	1.9	17	3	27.2	2.3	45	5	71.9	3.2
Florida	1,673	509	39	30.4	1.3	561	41	33.5	0.9	699	46	41.8	1.0
Georgia	1,049	210	25	20.0	1.4	296	30	28.2	1.1	629	42	59.9	1.5
Hawaii	89	8	3	8.4	1.4	42	6	46.5	1.8	52	6	57.7	1.9
Idaho	171	29	5	16.7	1.8	74	8	43.1	1.8	83	9	48.3	1.9
Illinois	1,175	180	24	15.4	1.1	418	36	35.6	1.0	654	44	55.7	1.2
Indiana	626	66	14	10.4	1.3	246	27	39.3	1.5	355	32	56.6	1.7
Iowa	239	20	7	8.5	1.5	106	15	44.4	1.9	144	17	60.2	2.2
Kansas	283	35	8	12.2	1.7	110	15	38.8	1.9	171	18	60.3	2.2
Kentucky	461	61	13	13.3	1.8	151	21	32.7	1.9	282	28	61.2	2.3
Louisiana	503	91	16	18.1	2.0	153	21	30.5	1.7	296	29	58.8	2.2
Maine	105	11	3	10.0	1.8	36	6	34.4	2.0	71	9	67.7	2.6
Maryland	380	74	15	19.7	1.9	138	21	36.4	1.4	205	25	53.8	1.6
Massachusetts	453	36	10	8.0	1.2	176	23	38.7	1.4	271	28	59.8	1.6
Michigan	953	83	16	8.7	1.0	411	35	43.2	1.3	552	40	57.9	1.4
Minnesota	355	51	12	14.4	1.7	151	21	42.6	1.5	179	23	50.4	1.6
Mississippi	436	92	13	21.1	2.0	112	15	25.7	1.7	260	22	59.7	2.3
Missouri	594	86	16	14.4	1.6	215	26	36.1	1.6	350	32	59.0	2.0
Montana	94	19	4	20.8	2.2	31	4	33.5	1.9	50	6	53.0	2.2
Nebraska	148	24	6	16.3	1.9	60	9	40.5	1.8	77	10	51.8	2.0
Nevada	257	64	11	24.8	2.3	124	15	48.4	2.0	81	12	31.3	1.7
New Hampshire	61	8	3	12.7	1.8	29	5	48.2	1.6	29	5	48.2	1.6
New Jersey	583	146	21	24.9	1.6	205	25	35.2	1.1	258	28	44.2	1.2
New Mexico	242	62	10	25.4	2.4	60	10	25.0	1.7	142	15	58.9	2.4
New York	1,924	233	27	12.1	0.9	705	47	36.7	0.9	1,146	59	59.6	1.1
North Carolina	991	198	25	20.0	1.5	296	30	29.8	1.2	554	40	55.9	1.6
North Dakota	55	10	2	17.4	2.1	25	3	45.3	2.0	25	3	44.8	2.0
Ohio	1,084	134	20	12.4	1.0	423	35	39.1	1.1	629	43	58.0	1.3
Oklahoma	437	70	13	15.8	1.9	138	18	31.5	1.8	269	25	61.5	2.4
Oregon	359	69	14	19.4	2.2	135	19	37.6	2.0	179	22	49.9	2.2
Pennsylvania	1,056	145	21	13.8	1.1	441	36	41.7	1.2	560	41	53.0	1.3
Rhode Island	85	9	3	11.0	1.7	32	5	37.8	1.9	54	7	62.8	2.3
South Carolina	475	78	15	16.2	1.9	166	22	35.0	1.9	267	27	56.2	2.3
South Dakota	72	10	2	13.3	1.7	29	4	40.0	1.7	42	4	58.2	2.0
Tennessee	669	76	15	11.5	1.4	238	27	35.6	1.6	406	34	60.7	2.0
Texas	3,240	955	58	29.5	1.0	778	52	24.0	0.7	1,623	74	50.1	1.0
Utah	302	63	10	20.9	1.7	145	14	48.1	1.6	115	13	38.0	1.5
Vermont	40	5	2	11.5	1.9	12	2	30.7	1.7	28	4	71.8	2.4
Virginia	622	113	18	18.1	1.5	237	26	38.2	1.3	324	31	52.1	1.5
Washington	516	61	14	11.7	1.4	191	24	37.0	1.5	316	31	61.1	1.8
West Virginia	189	14	4	7.5	1.4	64	8	33.7	1.9	128	11	67.9	2.4
Wisconsin	445	43	11	9.5	1.4	194	24	43.5	1.6	253	27	56.9	1.8
Wyoming	41	6	2	14.8	2.0	17	3	40.5	1.9	23	3	55.7	2.2

NOTE: Average of the three years' percentages: not average 'number' divided by average total children. Results may differ slightly based on the method used.

Table C-87. Medicaid Coverage Among Persons Under 65 Years of Age, by Selected Characteristics, Selected Years, 1984–2006

(Number, percent.)

Characteristic	1984[1]	1995[1]	2000	2001	2002	2003	2004(1)[2]	2004(2)[2]	2005[2]	2006[2]
Number (in millions)										
Total[3]	14.0	26.6	23.2	25.5	29.4	30.9	31.1	31.6	33.2	36.2
Percent of Population										
Total[3]	6.8	11.5	9.5	10.4	11.8	12.3	12.3	12.5	12.9	14.0
Age										
Under 18 years	11.9	21.5	19.6	21.5	24.8	26.0	25.9	26.4	27.2	29.9
Under 6 years	15.5	29.3	24.7	26.2	30.0	32.3	31.8	32.4	34.0	36.6
6–17 years	10.1	17.4	17.2	19.2	22.3	23.0	23.1	23.4	23.9	26.7
18–44 years	5.1	7.8	5.6	6.3	7.1	7.4	7.5	7.7	8.3	8.6
18–24 years	6.4	10.4	8.1	8.4	9.9	9.6	10.3	10.4	11.3	11.4
25–34 years	5.3	8.2	5.5	6.2	6.6	7.8	7.6	7.8	8.0	8.3
35–44 years	3.5	5.9	4.3	5.1	5.9	5.6	5.7	5.8	6.6	7.1
45–64 years	3.4	5.6	4.5	4.7	5.3	5.3	5.4	5.5	5.5	6.3
45–54 years	3.2	5.1	4.2	4.4	5.1	5.0	5.4	5.5	5.2	6.4
55–64 years	3.6	6.4	4.9	5.2	5.8	5.8	5.4	5.5	5.8	6.1
Sex										
Male	5.4	9.6	8.2	9.1	10.6	10.9	10.8	11.0	11.6	12.6
Female	8.1	13.4	10.8	11.6	13.0	13.6	13.7	13.9	14.3	15.5
Sex and Marital Status[4]										
Male										
Married	—	—	2.2	2.4	2.9	3.0	2.9	3.0	3.5	3.7
Divorced, separated, widowed	—	—	6.1	6.1	6.9	6.7	6.7	6.8	7.0	7.9
Never married	—	—	7.2	8.4	9.6	10.2	10.2	10.4	10.4	11.6
Female										
Married	—	—	3.1	3.4	4.1	4.3	4.2	4.3	4.7	4.6
Divorced, separated, widowed	—	—	12.7	13.9	15.8	15.3	14.9	15.2	14.6	16.2
Never married	—	—	13.2	14.0	15.3	16.0	16.9	17.1	17.3	19.0
Race[5]										
White only	4.6	8.9	7.1	8.0	9.3	10.4	10.2	10.4	11.0	11.8
Black or African American only	20.5	28.5	21.2	22.1	23.2	23.7	24.5	24.9	24.9	26.6
American Indian or Alaska Native only	*28.2	19.0	15.1	16.2	21.1	18.5	18.0	18.4	24.2	24.3
Asian only	*8.7	10.5	7.5	8.4	9.8	8.0	9.6	9.8	8.2	9.7
Native Hawaiian or Other Pacific Islander only	—	—	*	*	*	*	*	*	*	*
2 or more races	—	—	19.1	17.5	21.6	23.5	19.0	19.3	22.0	24.0
Hispanic Origin and Race[5]										
Hispanic or Latino	13.3	21.9	15.5	17.5	20.8	21.8	21.9	22.5	22.9	23.1
Mexican	12.2	21.6	14.0	16.6	20.2	21.7	21.9	22.4	23.0	23.0
Puerto Rican	31.5	33.4	29.4	30.3	29.0	31.0	28.5	29.1	31.9	35.7
Cuban	*4.8	13.4	9.2	11.1	14.9	13.8	17.9	17.9	17.7	*11.3
Other Hispanic or Latino	7.9	18.2	14.5	15.6	19.6	19.3	19.9	20.8	19.7	20.2
Not Hispanic or Latino	6.2	10.2	8.5	9.2	10.3	10.6	10.5	10.7	11.1	12.3
White only	3.7	7.1	6.1	6.7	7.7	8.0	7.8	7.9	8.5	9.5
Black or African American only	20.7	28.1	21.0	22.0	23.2	23.4	24.1	24.6	24.8	26.2
Age and Percent of Poverty Level[6]										
All ages										
Below 100%	33.0	48.4	38.4	40.0	42.8	43.2	44.2	45.0	45.7	45.8
100%–less than 150%	7.7	19.1	20.7	23.3	27.6	26.9	26.5	27.1	28.7	29.4
150%–less than 200%	3.2	8.3	11.5	14.1	16.1	17.1	16.6	16.9	18.1	18.0
200% or more	0.6	1.7	2.3	2.6	3.1	3.3	3.5	3.5	3.7	4.1
Under 18 years										
Below 100%	43.2	66.0	58.5	61.5	66.4	67.5	69.2	70.7	71.2	72.0
100%–less than 150%	9.0	27.2	35.0	38.9	47.1	49.1	46.6	47.6	49.0	52.1
150%–less than 200%	4.4	13.1	21.3	25.9	29.1	33.6	31.9	32.4	35.3	35.8
200% or more	0.8	3.3	5.1	5.7	7.2	7.6	8.0	8.0	8.3	8.9

* = Figure does not meet standards of reliability or precision.

— = Data not available.

[1]Data prior to 1997 are not strictly comparable with data for later years due to the 1997 questionnaire redesign.

[2]Beginning in the third quarter of the 2004 NHIS, persons under 65 years with no reported coverage were asked explicitly about Medicaid coverage. Estimates were calculated without and with the additional information from this question in the columns labeled 2004(1) and 2004(2), respectively, and estimates were calculated with the additional information starting with 2005 data.

[3]Includes all other races not shown separately and, in 1984 and 1989, with unknown poverty level.

[4]Includes persons 14–64 years of age.

[5]The race groups, White, Black, American Indian or Alaska Native, Asian, Native Hawaiian or Other Pacific Islander, and 2 or more races, include persons of Hispanic and non-Hispanic origin. Persons of Hispanic origin may be of any race.

[6]Percent of poverty level is based on family income and family size and composition using U.S. Census Bureau poverty thresholds.

Table C-87. Medicaid Coverage Among Persons Under 65 Years of Age, by Selected Characteristics, Selected Years, 1984–2006—Continued

(Number, percent.)

Characteristic	1984[1]	1995[1]	2000	2001	2002	2003	2004(1)[2]	2004(2)[2]	2005[2]	2006[2]
Geographic Region										
Northeast..	8.6	11.7	10.6	10.8	12.5	12.9	12.8	13.0	13.3	16.8
Midwest..	7.4	10.5	8.0	8.9	10.3	10.8	10.2	10.4	12.3	13.9
South..	5.1	11.3	9.4	10.7	12.0	12.6	12.2	12.4	12.7	12.9
West...	7.0	12.9	10.4	11.0	12.7	12.8	14.2	14.4	13.8	13.8
Location of Residence										
Within MSA[7]..	7.1	11.3	8.9	9.9	11.0	11.5	11.7	11.9	12.4	13.3
Outside MSA[7]...	6.1	12.3	11.9	12.4	15.2	15.3	14.8	15.0	15.5	17.7

[1]Data prior to 1997 are not strictly comparable with data for later years due to the 1997 questionnaire redesign.

[2]Beginning in the third quarter of the 2004 NHIS, persons under 65 years with no reported coverage were asked explicitly about Medicaid coverage. Estimates were calculated without and with the additional information from this question in the columns labeled 2004(1) and 2004(2), respectively, and estimates were calculated with the additional information starting with 2005 data.

[7]MSA = metropolitan statistical area. Starting with 2006 data, MSA status is determined using 2000 census data and the 2000 standards for defining MSAs.

Table C-88. Medicare Enrollees and Expenditures and Percent Distribution, by Medicare Program and Type of Service, Selected Years, 1970–2006

(Number, dollar, percent.)

Medicare program and type of service	1970	1980	1990	1995	2000	2001	2002	2003	2004	2005	2006[1]
ENROLLEES											
Number (in millions)											
Total Medicare[2]	20.4	28.4	34.3	37.6	39.7	40.1	40.5	41.2	41.9	42.6	43.2
Hospital insurance	20.1	28.0	33.7	37.2	39.3	39.7	40.1	40.7	41.4	42.2	42.9
Supplementary medical insurance[3]	19.5	27.3	32.6	35.6	37.3	37.7	38.0	38.6	—	—	—
Part B	19.5	27.3	32.6	35.6	37.3	37.7	38.0	38.6	39.1	39.7	40.3
Part D[4]	—	—	—	—	—	—	—	—	1.2	1.8	27.9
EXPENDITURES											
Amount (in billions)											
Total Medicare	7.5	36.8	111.0	184.2	221.7	244.8	265.8	280.8	308.9	336.4	408.3
Total hospital insurance (HI)	5.3	25.6	67.0	117.6	131.0	143.4	152.7	154.6	170.6	182.9	191.9
HI payments to managed care organizations[5]	—	0.0	2.7	6.7	21.4	20.8	19.2	19.5	20.8	24.9	32.9
HI payments for fee-for-service utilization	5.1	25.0	63.4	109.5	105.1	117.0	129.3	134.5	146.5	154.7	155.7
Inpatient hospital	4.8	24.1	56.9	82.3	87.1	96.0	104.2	108.7	116.4	121.7	121.0
Skilled nursing facility	0.2	0.4	2.5	9.1	11.1	13.1	15.2	14.7	17.1	18.5	19.9
Home health agency	0.1	0.5	3.7	16.2	4.0	4.1	5.0	4.8	5.4	5.9	6.0
Hospice	—	—	0.3	1.9	2.9	3.7	4.9	6.2	7.6	8.6	8.9
Home health agency transfer[6]	—	—	—	—	1.7	3.1	1.2	-2.2	0.0	0.0	0.0
Administrative expenses[7]	0.2	0.5	0.9	1.4	2.8	2.5	3.0	2.8	3.3	3.3	3.3
Total supplementary medical insurance (SMI)[3]	2.2	11.2	44.0	66.6	90.7	101.4	113.2	126.1	138.3	153.4	216.4
Total Part B	2.2	11.2	44.0	66.6	90.7	101.4	113.2	126.1	137.9	152.4	169.0
Part B payments to managed care organizations[5]	0.0	0.2	2.8	6.6	18.4	17.6	17.5	17.3	18.7	22.1	31.5
Part B payments for fee-for-service utilization[8]	1.9	10.4	39.6	58.4	72.2	85.1	94.5	104.3	116.2	126.9	134.1
Physician/supplies[9]	1.8	8.2	29.6	—	—	—	—	—	—	—	—
Outpatient hospital[10]	0.1	1.9	8.5	—	—	—	—	—	—	—	—
Independent laboratory[11]	0.0	0.1	1.5	—	—	—	—	—	—	—	—
Physician fee schedule	—	—	—	31.7	37.0	42.0	44.8	48.3	54.1	57.7	58.4
Durable medical equipment	—	—	—	3.7	4.7	5.4	6.5	7.5	7.8	7.9	8.4
Laboratory[12]	—	—	—	4.3	4.0	4.4	5.0	5.5	6.0	6.5	7.1
Other[13]	—	—	—	9.9	13.6	16.0	19.6	22.6	25.0	27.5	29.3
Hospital[14]	—	—	—	8.7	8.4	12.8	13.6	15.3	17.4	20.2	23.8
Home health agency	0.0	0.2	0.1	0.2	4.5	4.5	5.0	5.1	5.9	7.1	7.2
Home health agency transfer[6]	—	—	—	—	-1.7	-3.1	-1.2	2.2	0.0	0.0	0.0
Administrative expenses[7]	0.2	0.6	1.5	1.6	1.8	1.8	2.3	2.4	2.8	3.2	3.1
Part D Transitional Assistance and Start-up Costs[15]	—	—	—	—	—	—	—	—	0.2	0.7	0.0
Total Part D[4]	—	—	—	—	—	—	—	—	0.4	1.0	47.4
Premiums from enrollees	—	—	—	—	—	—	—	—	—	—	
General premium subsidy	—	—	—	—	—	—	—	—	—	—	
Reinsurance	—	—	—	—	—	—	—	—	—	—	
Employer subsidy	—	—	—	—	—	—	—	—	—	—	
Low-income subsidy	—	—	—	—	—	—	—	—	—	—	
Net risk corridor payments	—	—	—	—	—	—	—	—	—	—	
Administrative expenses	—	—	—	—	—	—	—	—	—	—	0.0

— = Data not available.

0.0 = Quantity greater than 0.0 but less than 0.05.

[1]Preliminary figures.

[2]Average number enrolled in the hospital insurance (HI) and/or supplementary medical insurance (SMI) programs for the period.

[3]Starting with 2004 data, the SMI trust fund consists of two separate accounts: Part B (which pays for a portion of the costs of physicians' services, outpatient hospital services, and other related medical and health services for voluntarily enrolled aged and disabled individuals) and Part D (Medicare Prescription Drug Account which pays private plans to provide prescription drug coverage).

[4]The Medicare Modernization Act, enacted on December 8, 2003, established within SMI two Part D accounts related to prescription drug benefits: the Medicare Prescription Drug Account and the Transitional Assistance Account. The Medicare Prescription Drug Account is used in conjunction with the broad, voluntary prescription drug benefits that began in 2006. The Transitional Assistance Account was used to provide transitional assistance benefits, beginning in 2004 and extending through 2005, for certain low-income beneficiaries prior to the start of the new prescription drug benefit.

[5]Medicare-approved managed care organizations.

[6]Starting with 1999 data, reflects annual home health HI to SMI transfer amounts.

[7]Includes research, costs of experiments and demonstration projects, fraud and abuse promotion, and peer review activity (changed to Quality Improvement Organization in 2002).

[8]Type-of-service reporting categories for fee-for-service reimbursement differ before and after 1991.

[9]Includes payment for physicians, practitioners, durable medical equipment, and all suppliers other than independent laboratory through 1990. Starting with 1991 data, physician services subject to the physician fee schedule are shown. Payments for laboratory services paid under the laboratory fee schedule and performed in a physician office are included under Laboratory beginning in 1991. Payments for durable medical equipment are shown separately beginning in 1991.

[10]Includes payments for hospital outpatient department services, skilled nursing facility outpatient services, Part B services received as an inpatient in a hospital or skilled nursing facility setting, and other types of outpatient facilities. Starting with 1991 data, payments for hospital outpatient department services, except for laboratory services, are listed under hospital.

[11]Starting with 1991 data, those independent laboratory services that were paid under the laboratory fee schedule (most of the independent lab category) are included in the laboratory line.

[12]Payments for laboratory services paid under the laboratory fee schedule performed in a physician office, independent lab, or in a hospital outpatient department.

[13]Includes payments for physician-administered drugs; freestanding ambulatory surgical center facility services; ambulance services; supplies; freestanding end-stage renal disease (ESRD) dialysis facility services; rural health clinics; outpatient rehabilitation facilities; psychiatric hospitals; and federally qualified health centers.

[14]Includes the hospital facility costs for Medicare Part B services that are predominantly in the outpatient department, with the exception of hospital outpatient laboratory services, which are included on the Laboratory line. Physician reimbursement is included on the Physician fee schedule line.

[15]Part D Administrative and Transitional Start-Up Costs were funded through the SMI Part B account.

Table C-88. Medicare Enrollees and Expenditures and Percent Distribution, by Medicare Program and Type of Service, Selected Years, 1970–2006—*Continued*

(Number, dollar, percent.)

Medicare program and type of service	1970	1980	1990	1995	2000	2001	2002	2003	2004	2005	2006[1]
PERCENT DISTRIBUTION OF EXPENDITURES											
Total hospital insurance (HI)	100.0	100.0	100.0	100.0	100.0	100.0	100.0	100.0	100.0	100.0	100.0
HI payments to managed care organizations[5]	—	0.0	4.0	5.7	16.3	14.5	12.6	12.6	12.2	13.6	17.1
HI payments for fee-for-service utilization	97.0	97.9	94.6	93.1	80.2	81.6	84.7	87.0	85.9	84.6	81.1
Inpatient hospital	91.4	94.3	85.0	70.0	66.5	67.0	68.3	70.3	68.2	66.6	63.1
Skilled nursing facility	4.7	1.5	3.7	7.8	8.5	9.1	10.0	9.5	10.0	10.1	10.4
Home health agency	1.0	2.1	5.5	13.8	3.1	2.9	3.3	3.1	3.2	3.2	3.1
Hospice	—	—	0.5	1.6	2.2	2.6	3.2	4.0	4.4	4.7	4.6
Home health agency transfer[6]	—	—	—	—	1.3	2.2	0.8	-1.4	0.0	0.0	0.0
Administrative expenses[7]	3.0	2.1	1.4	1.2	2.1	1.7	2.0	1.8	2.0	1.8	1.7
Total supplementary medical insurance (SMI)[3]	100.0	100.0	100.0	100.0	100.0	100.0	100.0	100.0	100.0	100.0	100.0
Total Part B	100.0	100.0	100.0	100.0	100.0	100.0	100.0	100.0	99.7	99.3	78.1
Part B payments to managed care organizations[4]	1.2	1.8	6.4	9.9	20.2	17.3	15.5	13.7	13.6	14.5	18.6
Part B payments for fee-for-service utilization[8]	88.1	92.8	90.1	87.6	79.6	84.0	83.5	82.7	84.0	82.7	79.3
Physician/supplies[9]	80.9	72.8	67.3	—	—	—	—	—	—	—	—
Outpatient hospital[10]	5.2	16.9	19.3	—	—	—	—	—	—	—	—
Independent laboratory[11]	0.5	1.0	3.4	—	—	—	—	—	—	—	—
Physician fee schedule	—	—	—	47.5	40.8	41.5	39.6	38.3	39.2	37.9	34.6
Durable medical equipment	—	—	—	5.5	5.2	5.4	5.8	6.0	5.6	5.3	5.0
Laboratory[12]	—	—	—	6.4	4.4	4.3	4.4	4.3	4.4	4.3	4.2
Other[13]	—	—	—	14.8	15.0	15.8	17.3	17.9	18.1	18.0	17.3
Hospital[14]	—	—	—	13.0	9.3	12.6	12.0	12.1	12.6	13.5	14.1
Home health agency	1.5	2.1	0.2	0.3	4.9	4.5	4.5	4.0	4.3	4.3	4.3
Home health agency transfer[6]	—	—	—	0.0	-1.9	-3.1	-1.0	1.7	0.0	0.0	0.0
Administrative expenses[7]	10.7	5.4	3.5	2.4	2.0	1.8	2.0	1.9	2.0	1.8	1.8
Part D Transitional Assistance and Start-up Costs[15]	—	—	—	—	—	—	—	—	0.2	0.4	0.0
Total Part D[4]	—	—	—	—	—	—	—	—	0.3	0.7	21.9

—- = Data not available.

0.0 = Quantity greater than 0.0 but less than 0.05.

[1]Preliminary figures.

[3]Starting with 2004 data, the SMI trust fund consists of two separate accounts: Part B (which pays for a portion of the costs of physicians' services, outpatient hospital services, and other related medical and health services for voluntarily enrolled aged and disabled individuals) and Part D (Medicare Prescription Drug Account which pays private plans to provide prescription drug coverage).

[4]The Medicare Modernization Act, enacted on December 8, 2003, established within SMI two Part D accounts related to prescription drug benefits: the Medicare Prescription Drug Account and the Transitional Assistance Account. The Medicare Prescription Drug Account is used in conjunction with the broad, voluntary prescription drug benefits that began in 2006. The Transitional Assistance Account was used to provide transitional assistance benefits, beginning in 2004 and extending through 2005, for certain low-income beneficiaries prior to the start of the new prescription drug benefit.

[5]Medicare-approved managed care organizations.

[6]Starting with 1999 data, reflects annual home health HI to SMI transfer amounts.

[7]Includes research, costs of experiments and demonstration projects, fraud and abuse promotion, and peer review activity (changed to Quality Improvement Organization in 2002).

[8]Type-of-service reporting categories for fee-for-service reimbursement differ before and after 1991.

[9]Includes payment for physicians, practitioners, durable medical equipment, and all suppliers other than independent laboratory through 1990. Starting with 1991 data, physician services subject to the physician fee schedule are shown. Payments for laboratory services paid under the laboratory fee schedule and performed in a physician office are included under laboratory beginning in 1991. Payments for durable medical equipment are shown separately beginning in 1991.

[10]Includes payments for hospital outpatient department services, skilled nursing facility outpatient services, Part B services received as an inpatient in a hospital or skilled nursing facility setting, and other types of outpatient facilities. Starting with 1991 data, payments for hospital outpatient department services, except for laboratory services, are listed under hospital.

[11]Starting with 1991 data, those independent laboratory services that were paid under the laboratory fee schedule (most of the independent lab category) are included in the laboratory line.

[12]Payments for laboratory services paid under the laboratory fee schedule performed in a physician office, independent lab, or in a hospital outpatient department.

[13]Includes payments for physician-administered drugs; freestanding ambulatory surgical center facility services; ambulance services; supplies; freestanding end-stage renal disease (ESRD) dialysis facility services; rural health clinics; outpatient rehabilitation facilities; psychiatric hospitals; and federally qualified health centers.

[14]Includes the hospital facility costs for Medicare Part B services that are predominantly in the outpatient department, with the exception of hospital outpatient laboratory services, which are included on the Laboratory line. Physician reimbursement is included on the Physician fee schedule line.

[15]Part D Administrative and Transitional Start-Up Costs were funded through the SMI Part B account.

NOTE: Percents are calculated using unrounded data. Totals do not necessarily equal the sum of rounded components. Estimates include service disbursements as of February 2006 for Medicare enrollees residing in the United States, Puerto Rico, Virgin Islands, Guam, other outlying areas, foreign countries, and unknown residence.

Table C-89. Medicare Enrollees and Program Payments Among Fee-for-Service Medicare Beneficiaries, by Sex and Age, Selected Years, 1994–2004

(Dollar, percent.)

Characteristic	1994	1995	2000	2001	2002	2003	2004
Fee-for-Service Enrollees in Thousands							
Total	34,076	34,062	32,740	33,860	34,977	35,815	36,345
Sex							
Male	14,533	14,563	14,195	14,746	15,314	15,736	16,040
Female	19,543	19,499	18,545	19,113	19,664	20,079	20,305
Age							
Under 65 years	4,031	4,239	4,907	5,172	5,448	5,732	6,036
65–74 years	16,713	16,373	14,230	14,689	15,107	15,390	15,528
75–84 years	9,845	9,911	9,919	10,211	10,533	10,701	10,755
85 years and over	3,486	3,540	3,684	3,787	3,889	3,991	4,026
Fee-for-Service Program Payments in Billions							
Total	146.6	159.0	174.3	197.5	215.4	232.8	255.3
Sex							
Male	63.9	68.8	76.2	86.3	94.3	102.2	111.8
Female	82.6	90.2	98.0	111.2	121.1	130.6	143.5
Age							
Under 65 years	18.8	21.0	25.8	29.7	33.2	37.3	42.3
65–74 years	55.1	58.1	57.5	64.6	70.0	75.2	81.6
75–84 years	50.7	55.3	62.7	70.9	77.1	82.5	89.9
85 years and over	21.8	24.6	28.3	32.3	35.1	37.8	41.5
Percent Distribution of Fee-for-Service Program Payments							
Total	100.0	100.0	100.0	100.0	100.0	100.0	100.0
Sex							
Male	43.6	43.2	43.7	43.7	43.8	43.9	43.8
Female	56.4	56.8	56.3	56.3	56.2	56.1	56.2
Age							
Under 65 years	12.9	13.2	14.8	15.0	15.4	16.0	16.6
65–74 years	37.6	36.5	33.0	32.7	32.5	32.3	32.0
75–84 years	34.6	34.8	36.0	35.9	35.8	35.4	35.2
85 years and over	14.9	15.5	16.2	16.4	16.3	16.2	16.3
Average Fee-for-Service Payment Per Enrollee							
Total	4,301	4,667	5,323	5,833	6,159	6,501	7,025
Sex							
Male	4,397	4,721	5,370	5,853	6,157	6,496	6,972
Female	4,229	4,627	5,286	5,818	6,159	6,505	7,067
Age							
Under 65 years	4,673	4,960	5,252	5,746	6,102	6,499	7,001
65–74 years	3,300	3,548	4,040	4,400	4,635	4,887	5,257
75–84 years	5,152	5,576	6,320	6,939	7,317	7,713	8,358
85 years and over	6,267	6,950	7,684	8,529	9,019	9,474	10,318

NOTE: Table includes data for Medicare enrollees residing in Puerto Rico, U.S. Virgin Islands, Guam, other outlying areas, foreign countries, and unknown residence. Prior to 2004, number of fee-for-service enrollees, fee-for-service program payments, and fee-for-service billing reimbursement are based on a 5% annual Denominator File derived from the Centers for Medicare & Medicaid Services' (CMS') Enrollment Database and the fee-for-service claims for a 5% sample of beneficiaries as recorded in CMS' National Claims History File. Starting with 2004 data, the 100% Denominator File was used.

Table C-90. Medicare Beneficiaries by Race, Ethnicity, and Selected Characteristics, Selected Years, 1992–2004

(Number, percent, dollar.)

Characteristic	All			Not Hispanic or Latino						Hispanic or Latino[1]		
				White			Black or African American					
	1992	2000	2004	1992	2000	2004	1992	2000	2004	1992	2000	2004
Number of Beneficiaries in Millions												
All Medicare beneficiaries	36.8	40.6	42.9	30.9	32.4	33.5	3.3	3.7	4.1	1.9	2.8	3.2
Percent Distribution of Beneficiaries												
All Medicare beneficiaries	100.0	100.0	100.0	84.2	80.1	78.2	8.9	9.1	9.6	5.2	7.0	7.5
Percent of Beneficiaries with at Least One Service												
All Medicare beneficiaries												
Long-term care facility stay	7.7	9.3	8.5	8.0	9.7	9.2	6.2	8.8	8.5	4.2	6.0	5.2
Community-Only Residents												
Inpatient hospital	17.9	19.2	17.0	18.1	19.2	16.9	18.4	22.8	18.8	16.6	16.2	15.8
Outpatient hospital	57.9	69.8	75.4	57.8	70.7	76.4	61.1	69.0	75.1	53.1	63.7	70.2
Physician/supplier[2]	92.4	94.9	96.8	93.0	95.4	97.2	89.1	92.8	95.1	87.9	92.9	95.2
Dental	40.4	43.5	46.2	43.1	46.9	49.5	23.5	24.1	27.6	29.1	33.9	38.0
Prescription medicine	85.2	91.1	93.4	85.5	91.5	93.7	83.1	89.5	90.7	84.6	90.1	91.8
Expenditures per Beneficiary												
All Medicare beneficiaries												
Total health care[3]	6,716	10,490	13,358	6,816	10,475	13,064	7,043	12,328	18,111	5,784	9,089	12,052
Long-term care facility[4]	1,581	2,310	2,371	1,674	2,406	2,466	1,255	2,438	2,983	*758	1,799	1,429
Community-Only Residents												
Total personal health care	5,054	7,911	9,689	4,988	7,814	9,537	5,530	9,419	11,419	4,938	6,934	9,593
Inpatient hospital	2,098	2,664	2,425	2,058	2,605	2,383	2,493	3,465	3,298	1,999	2,133	1,889
Outpatient hospital	504	875	1,122	478	796	1,046	668	1,523	1,777	511	915	1,126
Physician/supplier[2]	1,524	2,491	2,971	1,525	2,503	3,002	1,398	2,621	3,043	1,587	2,234	2,806
Dental	142	258	327	153	278	353	70	101	141	97	193	261
Prescription medicine	468	1,163	1,894	481	1,182	1,907	417	1,135	1,929	389	1,014	1,769
Long-Term Care Facility Residents Only												
Long-term care facility[5]	23,054	32,442	35,933	23,177	31,795	35,139	21,272	36,132	42,632	*25,026	*39,057	*36,287
Percent Distribution of Beneficiaries												
Both sexes	100.0	100.0	100.0	100.0	100.0	100.0	100.0	100.0	100.0	100.0	100.0	100.0
Male	42.9	43.4	44.1	42.7	43.3	44.2	42.0	40.0	41.8	46.7	46.9	45.8
Female	57.1	56.6	55.9	57.3	56.7	55.8	58.0	60.0	58.2	53.3	53.1	54.2
Eligibility Criteria and Age												
All Medicare beneficiaries[6]	100.0	100.0	100.0	100.0	100.0	100.0	100.0	100.0	100.0	100.0	100.0	100.0
Disabled	10.2	13.6	15.2	8.6	11.5	12.7	19.1	23.3	29.9	16.5	21.7	20.2
Under 45 years	3.5	3.9	3.8	2.9	3.2	3.1	7.6	7.5	8.1	6.9	5.5	4.8
45–64 years	6.5	9.8	11.4	5.8	8.3	9.6	11.5	15.8	21.8	9.6	16.3	15.4
Aged	89.8	86.4	84.8	91.4	88.5	87.2	81.0	76.7	70.2	83.5	78.3	79.9
65–74 years	51.5	45.4	43.8	52.0	46.7	43.8	48.0	41.7	40.2	49.4	45.5	45.0
75–84 years	28.8	30.0	29.8	29.5	31.4	31.5	24.0	25.9	21.3	27.1	22.9	26.3
85 years and over	9.7	10.9	11.2	9.9	11.5	11.9	9.0	9.0	8.7	6.9	9.9	8.6
Living Arrangement												
All living arrangements	100.0	100.0	100.0	100.0	100.0	100.0	100.0	100.0	100.0	100.0	100.0	100.0
Alone	27.0	29.3	29.0	27.5	29.8	29.8	27.7	32.5	32.2	20.2	22.9	21.4
With spouse	51.2	49.0	48.4	53.3	51.0	50.7	33.3	30.0	27.8	50.4	49.2	47.2
With children	9.1	9.5	10.5	7.7	7.6	8.5	16.8	18.6	18.8	16.6	14.8	17.8
With others	7.6	7.1	7.7	6.2	6.2	6.2	18.1	13.7	17.1	10.8	9.9	11.5
Long-term care facility	5.1	5.1	4.4	5.3	5.4	4.8	4.0	5.2	4.1	*2.0	*3.3	2.1

* = Figure does not meet standards of reliability or precision.

[1]Persons of Hispanic origin may be of any race.

[2]Physician/supplier services include medical and osteopathic doctor and health practitioner visits; diagnostic laboratory and radiology services; medical and surgical services; and durable medical equipment and nondurable medical supplies.

[3]Total health care expenditures by Medicare beneficiaries, including expenses paid by Medicare and all other sources of payment for the following services: inpatient hospital, outpatient hospital, physician/supplier, dental, prescription medicine, home health, and hospice and long-term care facility care. Does not include health insurance premiums.

[4]Expenditures for long-term care in facilities for all beneficiaries include facility room and board expenses for beneficiaries who resided in a facility for the full year, for beneficiaries who resided in a facility for part of the year and in the community for part of the year, and expenditures for short-term facility stays for full-year or part-year community residents.

[5]Expenditures for facility-based long-term care for facility-based beneficiaries include facility room and board expenses for beneficiaries who resided in a facility for the full year and for beneficiaries who resided in a facility for part of the year and in the community for part of the year. It does not include expenditures for short-term facility stays for full-year community residents.

[6]Medicare beneficiaries with end-stage renal disease (ESRD) are included within the subgroups Aged and Disabled.

Table C-90. Medicare Beneficiaries by Race, Ethnicity, and Selected Characteristics, Selected Years, 1992–2004—*Continued*

(Number, percent, dollar.)

Characteristic	All			Not Hispanic or Latino						Hispanic or Latino[1]		
				White			Black or African American					
	1992	2000	2004	1992	2000	2004	1992	2000	2004	1992	2000	2004
Percent Distribution of Beneficiaries												
Age and limitation of activity[7]												
Disabled	100.0	100.0	100.0	100.0	100.0	100.0	100.0	100.0	100.0	100.0	100.0	100.0
None	22.7	27.3	29.9	21.8	25.2	29.9	26.2	35.7	32.1	21.2	30.1	24.8
IADL only	39.0	35.1	35.1	38.9	35.5	34.5	35.8	33.2	37.1	46.1	37.3	38.7
1 or 2 ADL	21.2	21.8	21.4	21.5	23.2	21.4	21.2	17.7	20.6	*20.9	*16.8	*20.7
3–5 ADL	17.2	15.9	13.5	17.9	16.1	14.1	*16.8	*13.5	*10.2	*11.9	*15.8	*15.8
65–74 years	100.0	100.0	100.0	100.0	100.0	100.0	100.0	100.0	100.0	100.0	100.0	100.0
None	67.0	71.5	71.6	68.7	72.6	73.4	55.1	64.8	61.7	59.2	69.4	65.2
IADL only	17.8	15.4	15.8	17.0	15.1	15.3	22.9	18.0	17.2	*20.9	*13.6	18.9
1 or 2 ADL	10.4	8.6	8.7	9.6	8.2	7.9	14.4	10.8	13.0	*15.7	*13.2	*10.5
3–5 ADL	4.8	4.5	3.9	4.6	4.2	3.3	*7.6	*6.3	*8.2	*4.2	*4.0	*5.4
75–84 years	100.0	100.0	100.0	100.0	100.0	100.0	100.0	100.0	100.0	100.0	100.0	100.0
None	46.6	52.2	55.2	47.5	53.1	55.9	42.0	46.2	51.4	44.3	48.3	53.3
IADL only	23.9	23.0	21.5	23.6	22.7	21.7	26.7	20.9	*17.8	*27.8	29.9	21.3
1 or 2 ADL	16.5	14.3	13.6	16.8	13.8	13.8	15.3	17.7	*13.6	*14.9	*18.6	*11.9
3–5 ADL	13.0	10.6	9.7	12.2	10.4	8.6	*15.9	15.2	17.2	*13.0	*8.2	*13.5
85 years and over	100.0	100.0	100.0	100.0	100.0	100.0	100.0	100.0	100.0	100.0	100.0	100.0
None	19.9	24.9	27.6	20.2	25.1	28.5	*19.6	*25.9	*29.7	*19.7	*23.4	*15.2
IADL only	20.9	22.6	24.3	20.2	22.4	24.5	*22.1	*19.7	*24.1	*24.7	*24.7	*23.8
1 or 2 ADL	23.5	22.2	19.5	23.5	22.3	19.1	*24.3	*19.3	*15.0	*23.7	*28.1	*24.5
3–5 ADL	35.8	30.4	28.6	36.1	30.2	27.9	*34.0	35.1	*31.1	*31.8	*23.8	*36.5

* = Figure does not meet standards of reliability or precision.
[1]Persons of Hispanic origin may be of any race.

Table C-91. Medicare Enrollees, Enrollees in Managed Care, Payment per Enrollee, and Short-Stay Hospital Utilization by Geographic Region and State, 1994–2004

(Number, percent, dollar.)

Geographic region and area[2]	Enrollment in thousands[1]										
	1994	1995	1996	1997	1998	1999	2000	2001	2002	2003	2004
United States[3]	36,190	36,789	37,300	37,657	38,018	38,319	38,782	39,177	39,597	40,203	40,784
New England											
Connecticut	497	504	507	510	511	515	518	519	520	524	523
Maine	198	202	206	208	211	214	216	219	223	227	231
Massachusetts	924	935	946	949	950	952	961	959	958	961	965
New Hampshire	152	155	158	160	164	165	169	171	175	180	186
Rhode Island	166	167	168	168	169	168	170	170	170	171	172
Vermont	82	83	85	86	87	88	89	91	92	93	94
Mideast											
Delaware	99	102	106	108	111	112	115	117	120	122	123
District of Columbia	80	80	78	77	77	76	75	75	75	74	73
Maryland	596	606	615	621	630	635	646	655	665	676	683
New Jersey	1,158	1,171	1,182	1,191	1,197	1,201	1,212	1,215	1,219	1,224	1,220
New York	2,601	2,623	2,638	2,646	2,661	2,674	2,695	2,707	2,722	2,735	2,759
Pennsylvania	2,053	2,072	2,080	2,080	2,084	2,082	2,091	2,092	2,098	2,108	2,117
Great Lakes											
Illinois	1,605	1,620	1,626	1,625	1,626	1,622	1,626	1,633	1,641	1,657	1,673
Indiana	805	817	823	827	834	838	848	852	858	873	889
Michigan	1,331	1,347	1,359	1,364	1,378	1,385	1,402	1,412	1,420	1,438	1,462
Ohio	1,649	1,670	1,683	1,691	1,696	1,697	1,706	1,711	1,719	1,734	1,738
Wisconsin	752	758	763	766	768	770	776	780	788	798	814
Plains											
Iowa	470	473	474	477	478	475	475	475	477	479	485
Kansas	378	382	385	385	385	385	386	386	387	390	398
Minnesota	625	631	636	639	643	647	655	660	667	676	686
Missouri	821	827	837	845	847	852	859	866	875	888	897
Nebraska	247	250	251	251	252	253	254	256	258	260	259
North Dakota	101	102	102	102	102	102	102	103	103	103	103
South Dakota	114	116	117	118	118	118	118	118	119	120	123
Southeast											
Alabama	633	642	654	661	670	678	686	698	709	724	734
Arkansas	416	422	427	429	429	431	434	433	438	443	461
Florida	2,584	2,633	2,693	2,732	2,768	2,793	2,827	2,865	2,900	2,955	2,997
Georgia	819	841	860	876	891	910	928	944	963	984	1,000
Kentucky	578	589	598	601	606	612	618	627	637	647	661
Louisiana	572	581	586	591	594	595	600	605	612	621	628
Mississippi	391	398	404	408	411	414	419	424	428	438	446
North Carolina	1,001	1,025	1,049	1,071	1,091	1,112	1,131	1,157	1,180	1,208	1,240
South Carolina	497	510	523	535	545	556	570	581	592	607	627
Tennessee	754	770	784	793	805	815	830	846	861	879	894
Virginia	803	824	840	854	867	878	896	912	929	949	967
West Virginia	326	330	332	333	335	336	338	340	342	344	350
Southwest											
Arizona	578	598	617	633	649	661	676	692	707	730	763
New Mexico	205	211	217	221	225	230	234	238	243	249	258
Oklahoma	481	487	492	496	500	503	507	511	517	523	530
Texas	2,029	2,079	2,119	2,158	2,194	2,226	2,268	2,304	2,342	2,404	2,458
Rocky Mountains											
Colorado	413	425	435	445	455	462	470	480	487	499	507
Idaho	146	151	155	158	161	163	167	170	174	179	185
Montana	128	130	131	132	133	135	137	138	140	144	145
Utah	182	187	193	198	201	204	209	211	216	221	228
Wyoming	58	60	61	62	64	64	66	67	68	69	70
Far West											
Alaska	33	34	36	37	39	40	42	44	45	47	50
California	3,582	3,653	3,724	3,768	3,812	3,861	3,922	3,965	4,004	4,066	4,122
Hawaii	146	151	154	158	161	164	168	171	174	178	178
Nevada	187	197	209	219	225	235	246	258	269	282	287
Oregon	469	475	481	484	488	490	496	503	512	524	527
Washington	676	691	702	709	717	724	736	750	762	778	797

[1]Total persons enrolled in hospital insurance, supplementary medical insurance, or both, as of July 1. Includes fee-for-service and managed care enrollees.
[2]Data are shown for Bureau of Economic Analysis (BEA) regions that are constructed to show economically interdependent states.
[3]Includes residents of any of the 50 states and the District of Columbia. Excludes Puerto Rico, Guam, Virgin Islands, residence unknown, foreign countries, and other outlying areas not shown separately.

Table C-91. Medicare Enrollees, Enrollees in Managed Care, Payment per Enrollee, and Short-Stay Hospital Utilization by Geographic Region and State, 1994–2004—Continued

(Number, percent, dollar.)

Geographic region and area[2]	Percent of enrollees in managed care[4]										
	1994	1995	1996	1997	1998	1999	2000	2001	2002	2003	2004
United States[3]	7.9	9.5	11.8	14.5	17.1	18.2	17.8	15.8	13.9	13.1	13.0
New England											
Connecticut	2.6	2.8	4.1	7.8	18.9	20.9	20.3	14.4	6.2	5.9	5.5
Maine	0.1	0.1	0.1	0.2	0.3	0.7	0.9	0.2	0.1	0.1	0.2
Massachusetts	6.1	9.4	14.4	19.1	23.1	25.3	24.7	23.0	21.8	17.5	16.7
New Hampshire	0.2	0.6	1.0	4.1	9.8	9.8	1.6	1.1	1.1	1.1	1.0
Rhode Island	7.0	7.4	9.1	14.2	26.2	33.6	33.1	33.3	33.1	32.8	33.3
Vermont	0.1	0.8	1.3	1.4	1.9	2.2	0.2	0.2	0.0	0.1	0.2
Mideast											
Delaware	0.2	1.3	4.3	8.1	10.6	4.5	4.9	2.7	1.1	0.7	0.7
District of Columbia	3.9	4.8	8.7	11.1	12.2	10.8	9.2	6.4	6.6	6.9	6.6
Maryland	1.4	2.1	5.6	11.1	14.3	13.9	10.8	3.1	3.1	3.6	3.9
New Jersey	2.6	3.9	7.0	11.4	15.1	16.5	14.2	12.6	8.9	7.8	7.6
New York	6.2	7.8	10.8	14.4	17.7	18.5	18.3	17.4	17.1	17.2	18.0
Pennsylvania	3.3	6.2	13.6	20.2	24.8	27.5	28.4	24.6	24.0	24.0	24.2
Great Lakes											
Illinois	5.5	6.1	7.5	8.9	10.5	11.6	11.7	9.6	6.2	5.1	5.1
Indiana	2.6	2.6	2.8	3.2	3.7	4.1	4.1	3.5	2.7	2.1	2.2
Michigan	0.7	0.8	1.1	2.2	4.0	5.4	5.9	5.9	2.4	1.8	1.5
Ohio	2.4	2.9	4.1	9.9	15.8	17.8	17.4	15.0	14.3	13.3	12.9
Wisconsin	2.0	2.0	2.4	3.7	5.1	5.6	6.0	5.7	3.2	4.3	5.8
Plains											
Iowa	3.1	3.3	3.2	3.5	3.8	3.9	3.7	3.6	3.6	3.7	4.2
Kansas	3.3	2.9	3.8	4.8	6.4	7.5	7.9	7.9	6.1	3.6	3.4
Minnesota	19.6	18.7	17.7	17.2	16.2	13.8	13.3	12.6	12.8	13.2	14.3
Missouri	3.4	4.3	6.6	9.8	12.3	14.5	15.6	14.6	14.2	12.5	12.4
Nebraska	2.2	2.3	2.4	4.1	5.0	5.6	4.2	4.1	3.8	3.7	4.0
North Dakota	0.6	0.6	0.6	0.6	0.6	0.7	0.7	0.6	0.6	0.5	1.0
South Dakota	0.1	0.1	0.1	0.1	0.1	0.2	0.4	0.6	1.3	0.3	0.3
Southeast											
Alabama	0.8	1.9	3.5	5.0	6.9	8.0	8.7	8.0	6.8	6.4	7.4
Arkansas	0.2	0.3	1.0	2.1	3.2	4.3	4.3	4.2	0.5	0.5	0.4
Florida	13.8	16.6	19.8	23.8	27.3	28.3	26.8	23.4	19.9	18.4	18.5
Georgia	0.4	0.5	0.7	2.4	4.9	6.2	6.2	4.5	4.2	3.9	1.9
Kentucky	2.3	2.3	2.9	4.1	4.8	5.6	5.5	4.5	3.2	2.9	2.9
Louisiana	0.4	4.3	7.5	11.0	17.0	19.6	17.9	14.4	12.2	11.3	11.1
Mississippi	0.1	0.1	0.5	0.5	0.5	1.2	1.5	1.8	0.7	0.6	0.4
North Carolina	0.5	0.5	0.7	1.4	2.8	4.2	4.2	4.3	4.4	4.0	4.5
South Carolina	0.1	0.2	0.4	1.0	0.5	0.5	0.3	0.3	0.3	0.3	0.3
Tennessee	0.3	0.4	0.4	1.5	3.3	5.4	5.9	5.0	6.0	7.0	7.7
Virginia	1.5	2.1	2.9	3.5	4.9	5.6	3.9	2.1	2.0	2.0	2.0
West Virginia	8.3	7.9	7.7	7.6	7.2	7.5	7.5	7.3	7.1	6.8	6.6
Southwest											
Arizona	24.8	28.8	32.0	35.4	38.1	39.5	35.8	33.6	29.9	28.1	27.1
New Mexico	13.6	14.8	16.1	18.0	19.5	20.0	19.0	14.6	15.2	15.6	16.1
Oklahoma	2.5	3.5	4.7	6.8	8.4	10.0	10.7	10.1	8.3	7.7	7.8
Texas	4.1	6.8	9.6	11.7	14.7	17.4	17.4	11.3	8.1	6.8	7.1
Rocky Mountains											
Colorado	17.2	20.3	24.7	28.9	33.7	35.5	34.5	32.0	28.5	27.3	26.9
Idaho	2.5	2.7	2.8	4.5	6.9	9.8	10.3	9.6	9.3	9.5	10.1
Montana	0.4	0.5	0.4	0.4	1.6	2.8	0.4	0.4	0.5	0.5	0.4
Utah	9.4	9.9	10.1	13.5	12.9	3.3	3.3	3.2	3.2	3.1	3.3
Wyoming	3.3	3.2	2.9	2.7	2.6	2.3	2.6	2.6	1.7	1.5	1.7
Far West											
Alaska	0.6	0.5	0.6	0.9	1.0	0.9	0.7	0.8	0.6	0.6	0.4
California	30.0	33.9	36.6	38.9	40.1	40.7	40.4	38.8	35.1	33.2	32.2
Hawaii	29.8	30.1	31.2	32.0	32.8	33.0	32.1	33.8	33.9	33.5	33.4
Nevada	19.0	23.0	26.7	30.2	32.6	33.5	33.1	32.7	30.9	29.6	28.8
Oregon	27.7	31.3	35.3	37.2	37.8	38.0	37.5	35.6	34.3	33.7	32.5
Washington	12.5	15.4	19.8	23.8	26.0	26.3	24.8	20.6	17.8	17.0	16.0

0.0 = Quantity greater than 0.0 but less than 0.05.
[2]Data are shown for Bureau of Economic Analysis (BEA) regions that are constructed to show economically interdependent states.
[3]Includes residents of any of the 50 states and the District of Columbia. Excludes Puerto Rico, Guam, Virgin Islands, residence unknown, foreign countries, and other outlying areas not shown separately.
[4]Includes enrollees in Medicare-approved managed care organizations.

Table C-91. Medicare Enrollees, Enrollees in Managed Care, Payment per Enrollee, and Short-Stay Hospital Utilization by Geographic Region and State, 1994–2004—*Continued*

(Number, percent, dollar.)

Geographic region and area[2]	Payment per fee-for-service enrollee										
	1994	1995	1996	1997	1998	1999	2000	2001	2002	2003	2004
UNITED STATES[3]	4,375	4,750	5,048	5,416	5,299	5,280	5,423	5,942	6,271	6,618	7,148
New England											
Connecticut	4,426	5,034	5,385	5,767	5,782	5,734	5,926	6,525	6,772	7,274	7,904
Maine	3,464	3,547	3,949	4,325	4,305	4,311	4,554	4,861	5,037	5,370	5,719
Massachusetts	5,147	6,070	6,266	6,716	6,463	6,184	6,235	6,779	7,065	7,436	7,927
New Hampshire	3,414	3,619	4,021	4,524	4,430	4,185	4,382	4,918	5,030	5,756	6,138
Rhode Island	4,148	4,644	5,230	5,973	5,744	5,719	5,687	6,274	5,907	6,273	7,131
Vermont	3,182	3,751	3,962	3,771	4,142	4,226	4,533	5,059	5,070	5,356	5,809
Mideast											
Delaware	4,712	4,154	4,514	4,968	4,929	5,070	5,449	6,225	6,356	6,786	8,008
District of Columbia	5,655	5,828	6,631	7,548	7,091	7,144	6,761	7,202	7,731	7,700	8,820
Maryland	4,997	5,351	5,320	5,561	6,058	6,237	6,385	6,804	7,284	7,699	8,247
New Jersey	4,531	4,815	5,353	5,889	6,169	6,365	6,554	7,560	7,834	8,029	8,264
New York	4,855	5,322	5,541	6,117	6,124	6,230	6,392	6,883	7,180	7,449	7,995
Pennsylvania	5,212	4,987	5,333	5,831	5,819	5,733	5,883	6,306	6,781	6,900	7,263
Great Lakes											
Illinois	4,324	4,693	4,940	5,192	5,157	5,257	5,352	5,884	6,193	6,639	7,220
Indiana	3,945	4,281	4,357	4,775	4,747	4,517	4,752	5,352	5,534	5,940	6,550
Michigan	4,307	4,813	5,118	5,442	5,436	5,456	5,596	6,265	6,582	6,923	7,477
Ohio	3,982	4,320	4,614	4,989	5,021	4,979	5,228	5,697	6,037	6,480	7,189
Wisconsin	3,246	3,581	3,809	4,142	4,108	4,122	4,316	4,832	5,114	5,455	5,895
Plains											
Iowa	3,080	3,315	3,643	3,865	3,971	3,984	4,315	4,762	4,931	5,026	5,436
Kansas	3,847	4,274	4,476	4,752	4,661	4,580	4,822	5,129	5,500	6,199	6,541
Minnesota	3,394	3,731	3,856	4,131	4,191	4,076	4,195	4,756	5,213	5,487	6,070
Missouri	4,191	4,451	4,591	5,038	4,897	4,893	4,976	5,549	5,826	6,024	6,717
Nebraska	2,926	3,303	3,512	3,938	3,970	4,237	4,269	4,931	5,189	5,500	6,157
North Dakota	3,218	3,460	3,568	3,650	3,743	3,916	4,073	4,454	4,703	5,360	5,456
South Dakota	2,952	3,399	3,525	3,737	3,826	3,994	4,041	4,356	4,498	5,044	5,214
Southeast											
Alabama	4,454	4,895	5,113	5,459	4,974	4,965	5,140	5,530	5,973	6,461	6,915
Arkansas	3,719	4,026	4,303	4,517	4,555	4,500	4,774	5,193	5,466	5,680	6,236
Florida	5,027	5,477	5,901	6,152	5,903	5,944	6,190	6,685	7,055	7,507	8,243
Georgia	4,402	4,784	5,081	5,223	4,862	5,038	5,065	5,568	5,839	6,109	6,767
Kentucky	3,862	4,141	4,492	4,888	4,666	4,618	4,764	5,492	5,783	5,953	6,479
Louisiana	5,468	6,119	6,553	6,984	6,784	6,627	6,657	7,083	7,417	7,826	8,393
Mississippi	4,189	4,750	5,299	5,680	5,335	5,251	5,419	5,896	6,265	6,794	7,389
North Carolina	3,465	3,943	4,217	4,552	4,560	4,651	4,718	5,230	5,557	6,053	6,726
South Carolina	3,777	3,944	4,316	4,681	4,718	4,774	5,029	5,651	5,900	6,183	6,573
Tennessee	4,441	4,859	5,227	5,379	5,001	4,950	5,181	5,511	6,152	6,450	6,891
Virginia	3,748	4,021	4,182	4,587	4,505	4,465	4,648	5,028	5,296	5,703	6,031
West Virginia	3,798	4,224	4,593	4,896	4,778	4,846	4,853	5,344	5,585	5,940	6,408
Southwest											
Arizona	4,442	4,269	4,537	4,707	4,627	4,544	4,656	5,077	5,499	5,963	6,333
New Mexico	3,110	3,548	3,906	3,939	4,245	4,201	3,993	4,362	4,735	4,980	5,464
Oklahoma	4,098	4,625	5,201	5,557	5,105	5,121	5,266	5,774	6,112	6,606	7,241
Texas	4,703	5,416	5,905	6,531	6,147	5,856	6,003	6,382	6,736	7,295	7,915
Rocky Mountains											
Colorado	3,935	4,354	4,767	5,021	4,663	4,876	4,790	4,961	5,448	5,966	6,466
Idaho	3,045	3,341	3,683	4,044	3,903	3,937	4,251	4,696	4,867	5,195	5,255
Montana	3,114	3,532	3,532	3,808	3,738	3,790	4,097	4,572	4,653	5,014	5,335
Utah	3,443	3,996	4,197	4,334	3,980	3,864	4,072	4,514	4,752	5,234	5,862
Wyoming	3,537	3,980	4,034	4,235	3,888	4,220	4,408	4,867	4,896	5,254	5,825
Far West											
Alaska	3,687	4,775	4,538	5,487	4,476	5,447	5,003	5,563	5,642	6,036	6,737
California	5,219	5,651	5,986	6,335	6,124	6,027	5,992	6,679	6,942	7,062	7,447
Hawaii	3,069	3,419	3,565	4,043	3,555	3,544	3,771	4,017	4,454	4,553	5,139
Nevada	4,306	4,440	4,593	5,361	5,124	5,080	4,960	5,494	6,070	6,580	7,089
Oregon	3,285	3,724	3,999	4,274	4,099	4,096	4,274	4,820	4,933	5,243	5,985
Washington	3,401	3,779	4,005	4,405	4,377	4,418	4,463	4,858	5,280	5,374	5,884

[2]Data are shown for Bureau of Economic Analysis (BEA) regions that are constructed to show economically interdependent states.
[3]Includes residents of any of the 50 states and the District of Columbia. Excludes Puerto Rico, Guam, Virgin Islands, residence unknown, foreign countries, and other outlying areas not shown separately.

Table C-91. Medicare Enrollees, Enrollees in Managed Care, Payment per Enrollee, and Short-Stay Hospital Utilization by Geographic Region and State, 1994 and 2004—*Continued*

(Number, percent, dollar.)

Geographic region and area[2]	Discharges per 1,000 enrollees[5] (short-stay hospital utilization)										
	1994	1995	1996	1997	1998	1999	2000	2001	2002	2003	2004
UNITED STATES[3]	345	351	359	370	371	370	368	390	370	369	364
New England											
Connecticut	287	290	295	299	316	309	305	313	317	321	327
Maine	322	321	321	323	330	321	327	320	308	307	303
Massachusetts	350	354	365	367	367	368	357	362	363	362	365
New Hampshire	281	277	282	301	290	275	284	283	268	274	275
Rhode Island	312	328	336	355	357	337	333	352	346	349	352
Vermont	283	288	289	276	281	293	297	287	265	267	245
Mideast											
Delaware	326	315	311	326	324	338	338	344	332	334	357
District of Columbia	376	360	388	397	403	385	406	396	389	393	405
Maryland	362	369	373	353	364	378	381	387	393	401	403
New Jersey	354	357	360	369	377	379	372	375	378	381	383
New York	334	344	357	365	371	369	358	363	369	370	366
Pennsylvania	379	383	402	428	418	422	413	405	406	405	406
Great Lakes											
Illinois	374	372	379	385	386	404	409	417	420	415	421
Indiana	345	342	342	349	353	354	359	365	354	355	345
Michigan	328	339	347	353	355	357	355	368	376	376	375
Ohio	350	354	360	374	382	385	386	389	390	390	392
Wisconsin	310	311	311	319	323	328	330	329	326	327	319
Plains											
Iowa	322	332	336	346	346	356	360	364	350	333	319
Kansas	348	352	360	363	370	381	380	386	372	363	350
Minnesota	334	338	339	346	346	344	342	355	354	349	349
Missouri	349	359	359	372	372	383	391	408	406	402	399
Nebraska	281	290	299	316	320	327	313	297	287	291	286
North Dakota	327	320	326	324	327	349	335	319	295	286	285
South Dakota	356	348	351	347	352	362	354	351	324	320	297
Southeast											
Alabama	413	413	419	429	424	440	442	450	456	448	438
Arkansas	366	370	370	383	389	393	395	406	404	403	386
Florida	326	333	338	352	362	366	367	374	376	371	369
Georgia	378	377	377	379	365	369	371	373	369	367	360
Kentucky	396	391	397	404	405	414	422	422	421	411	400
Louisiana	399	421	430	449	461	470	465	465	466	461	448
Mississippi	423	432	452	472	463	459	465	464	450	446	425
North Carolina	314	331	339	349	360	366	367	366	370	372	366
South Carolina	319	329	336	346	363	373	380	385	382	378	367
Tennessee	375	376	384	384	380	381	390	395	398	403	397
Virginia	348	344	348	355	352	355	353	350	349	354	348
West Virginia	420	419	420	437	436	440	434	438	432	434	422
Southwest											
Arizona	292	320	339	358	335	311	306	307	313	313	317
New Mexico	301	308	297	314	304	299	285	280	279	279	267
Oklahoma	355	353	362	373	389	408	414	420	416	421	419
Texas	333	344	356	372	376	386	387	389	387	389	382
Rocky Mountains											
Colorado	302	309	313	315	309	320	306	305	306	305	306
Idaho	274	273	283	298	308	314	320	300	290	268	243
Montana	306	312	313	312	313	320	325	324	299	287	281
Utah	238	250	244	251	241	253	253	263	257	267	263
Wyoming	315	327	309	315	319	341	344	334	318	289	283
Far West											
Alaska	269	283	273	298	285	304	307	300	294	270	264
California	366	384	397	421	404	354	331	332	328	327	316
Hawaii	301	308	303	330	277	234	226	226	225	223	234
Nevada	291	310	315	341	332	298	287	288	302	289	302
Oregon	305	330	339	373	361	312	304	316	315	306	282
Washington	269	275	288	296	282	281	276	273	271	267	257

[2]Data are shown for Bureau of Economic Analysis (BEA) regions that are constructed to show economically interdependent states.
[3]Includes residents of any of the 50 states and the District of Columbia. Excludes Puerto Rico, Guam, Virgin Islands, residence unknown, foreign countries, and other outlying areas not shown separately.
[5]Data are for fee-for-service enrollees only.

Table C-91. Medicare Enrollees, Enrollees in Managed Care, Payment per Enrollee, and Short-Stay Hospital Utilization by Geographic Region and State, 1994–2004—*Continued*

(Number, percent, dollar.)

Geographic region and area[2]	Average length of stay in days[5] (short-stay hospital utilization)										
	1994	1995	1996	1997	1998	1999	2000	2001	2002	2003	2004
UNITED STATES[3]	7.5	7.0	6.5	6.3	6.1	6.1	6.0	5.9	5.9	5.8	5.8
New England											
Connecticut	8.1	7.3	6.9	6.4	6.2	6.2	6.2	6.2	6.1	5.9	6.0
Maine	7.6	6.7	6.1	5.9	5.7	5.6	5.6	5.6	5.6	5.4	5.4
Massachusetts	7.6	6.8	6.4	6.0	5.9	5.8	5.7	5.8	5.7	5.6	5.6
New Hampshire	7.6	7.2	6.5	6.1	5.9	5.7	5.6	5.7	5.6	5.8	5.9
Rhode Island	8.1	7.2	7.0	6.8	6.4	6.4	6.2	6.4	6.2	6.1	6.0
Vermont	7.6	7.4	6.5	5.9	5.6	6.0	5.7	5.7	5.8	5.4	5.3
Mideast											
Delaware	8.1	7.4	7.3	6.5	6.1	6.4	6.4	6.3	6.4	6.6	6.5
District of Columbia	10.1	8.5	8.1	8.1	7.9	8.0	7.9	7.7	7.5	7.1	6.9
Maryland	7.5	7.0	6.5	6.2	6.1	6.0	5.8	5.6	5.4	5.4	5.3
New Jersey	10.2	9.3	8.7	8.2	7.7	7.6	7.5	7.4	7.2	7.0	6.8
New York	11.2	10.4	9.6	9.0	8.6	8.3	8.2	7.9	7.7	7.5	7.4
Pennsylvania	8.0	7.3	6.9	6.6	6.3	6.2	6.1	6.1	6.0	5.9	5.8
Great Lakes											
Illinois	7.3	6.8	6.4	6.1	6.0	5.9	5.7	5.6	5.7	5.6	5.5
Indiana	6.9	6.5	6.0	5.8	5.8	5.8	5.7	5.6	5.6	5.6	5.5
Michigan	7.6	7.1	6.7	6.4	6.3	6.2	6.1	6.0	5.9	5.7	5.6
Ohio	7.1	6.6	6.2	6.0	5.7	5.7	5.6	5.5	5.5	5.5	5.4
Wisconsin	6.8	6.3	5.9	5.7	5.5	5.5	5.4	5.3	5.3	5.2	5.1
Plains											
Iowa	6.6	6.1	5.8	5.6	5.5	5.5	5.4	5.3	5.3	5.3	5.2
Kansas	6.5	6.2	5.9	5.7	5.7	5.6	5.5	5.4	5.4	5.3	5.2
Minnesota	5.7	5.5	5.3	5.2	5.1	5.1	5.0	5.0	4.9	4.8	4.7
Missouri	7.3	6.7	6.4	6.1	6.0	5.9	5.7	5.6	5.6	5.6	5.5
Nebraska	6.3	5.9	5.6	5.3	5.3	5.2	5.2	5.3	5.3	5.5	5.4
North Dakota	6.3	6.2	5.8	5.6	5.4	5.2	5.1	5.0	5.3	5.1	5.2
South Dakota	6.1	5.9	5.6	5.5	5.3	5.2	5.2	5.1	5.0	5.1	5.0
Southeast											
Alabama	7.0	6.5	6.1	5.9	5.8	5.6	5.5	5.5	5.5	5.4	5.4
Arkansas	7.0	6.6	6.4	6.2	6.1	5.9	5.9	5.9	5.8	5.8	5.7
Florida	7.1	6.6	6.2	6.0	5.9	5.9	5.8	5.8	5.8	5.8	5.8
Georgia	6.9	6.6	6.2	6.0	5.8	5.9	5.8	5.7	5.8	5.8	5.7
Kentucky	7.2	6.6	6.2	5.9	5.8	5.7	5.6	5.5	5.6	5.5	5.5
Louisiana	7.2	6.8	6.3	6.1	6.1	6.0	5.9	6.0	6.1	6.1	6.0
Mississippi	7.4	7.0	6.8	6.7	6.5	6.5	6.4	6.4	6.4	6.2	6.2
North Carolina	8.0	7.3	6.8	6.5	6.3	6.2	6.0	5.9	5.8	5.8	5.7
South Carolina	8.3	7.4	6.9	6.6	6.4	6.4	6.2	6.2	6.2	6.2	6.2
Tennessee	7.1	6.6	6.4	6.2	6.1	6.0	5.9	5.9	5.9	5.8	5.6
Virginia	7.3	7.0	6.6	6.4	6.2	6.1	6.1	6.0	5.8	5.9	5.8
West Virginia	7.1	6.7	6.3	6.1	6.0	5.9	5.8	5.7	5.7	5.6	5.5
Southwest											
Arizona	5.9	5.5	5.2	5.1	5.1	5.1	5.0	4.9	5.1	5.1	5.0
New Mexico	6.0	5.8	5.6	5.4	5.4	5.4	5.2	5.3	5.4	5.2	5.2
Oklahoma	7.0	6.6	6.2	6.1	6.0	5.9	5.8	5.8	5.7	5.5	5.4
Texas	7.2	6.7	6.3	6.1	6.0	5.9	5.9	5.9	5.9	5.8	5.7
Rocky Mountains											
Colorado	6.0	5.6	5.3	5.2	5.0	5.1	5.0	4.9	4.9	5.1	5.0
Idaho	5.2	5.0	4.8	4.7	4.6	4.6	4.6	4.6	4.7	4.7	4.8
Montana	5.9	5.5	5.3	5.0	5.0	5.0	4.8	4.7	4.9	4.8	4.7
Utah	5.4	5.1	4.9	4.9	4.9	4.8	4.8	4.7	4.7	4.6	4.6
Wyoming	5.6	5.7	5.1	5.2	4.9	5.1	5.0	4.9	4.9	4.8	5.3
Far West											
Alaska	6.3	6.3	6.4	6.0	5.7	5.9	5.8	6.0	5.9	5.9	6.2
California	6.1	5.8	5.6	5.5	5.6	5.8	6.0	6.1	6.1	6.1	6.0
Hawaii	9.1	9.3	8.2	7.8	7.4	7.4	8.0	8.2	7.5	7.3	6.8
Nevada	7.0	6.4	6.0	5.8	5.9	6.1	6.0	6.1	6.2	6.0	6.1
Oregon	5.2	4.9	4.7	4.6	4.7	4.7	4.6	4.6	4.6	4.6	4.8
Washington	5.3	5.2	4.9	5.0	4.9	4.9	4.9	4.9	4.9	5.0	4.8

[2]Data are shown for Bureau of Economic Analysis (BEA) regions that are constructed to show economically interdependent states.
[3]Includes residents of any of the 50 states and the District of Columbia. Excludes Puerto Rico, Guam, Virgin Islands, residence unknown, foreign countries, and other outlying areas not shown separately.
[5]Data are for fee-for-service enrollees only.

Table C-92. Number of Medicare-Certified Providers and Suppliers, Selected Years, 1975–2005

(Number.)

Providers or suppliers	1975	1980	1990	2000	2001	2002	2003	2004	2005
Home health agencies	2,242	2,924	5,730	7,857	7,099	6,813	6,928	7,519	8,090
Clinical lab improvement act facilities	—	—	—	171,018	168,333	173,807	176,947	189,340	196,296
End stage renal disease facilities	—	999	1,937	3,787	3,991	4,113	4,309	4,618	4,755
Outpatient physical therapy	117	419	1,195	2,867	2,874	2,836	2,961	2,971	2,962
Portable X-ray	132	216	443	666	675	644	641	608	553
Rural health clinics	—	391	551	3,453	3,334	3,283	3,306	3,536	3,661
Comprehensive outpatient rehabilitation facilities	—	—	186	522	518	524	587	635	634
Ambulatory surgical centers	—	—	1,197	2,894	3,147	3,371	3,597	4,136	4,445
Hospices	—	—	825	2,326	2,267	2,275	2,323	2,645	2,872

—— = Data not available.

NOTE: Provider and supplier data for 1980–1990 are as of July 1. Provider and supplier data for 1996–2005 are as of December. Providers and suppliers certified for Medicare are deemed to meet Medicaid standards.

NOTES AND DEFINITIONS

SOURCES OF DATA

The principal source for data presented in this part is from *Health, United States, 2007,* an annual report on trends in health statistics compiled by the National Center of Health Statistics (NCHS), a component of the Centers for Disease Control and Prevention (CDC). *Health, United States, 2007* contains the *Chartbook on Trends in the Health of Americans* which features a special section on access to health care. This was the source for the data in Tables C-8A, C-8B, C-44, C-47 and C-63. For more detailed information see: National Center for Health Statistics. *Health, United States, 2007 With Chartbook on Trends in the Health of Americans.* Hyattsville, MD: 2007.

The data for Tables C-61 and C-62 are derived from the *Career Guide to Industries,* a publication created by the Bureau of Labor Statistics (BLS). The *Career Guide to Industries* serves as a companion to the *Occupational Outlook Handbook,* also published by BLS, and provides detailed information on employment, working conditions, and earnings for numerous industries. For more information see: Bureau of Labor Statistics, U.S. Department of Labor, *Career Guide to Industries, 2008-09 Edition.* Washington, DC: 2008.

Tables C-79 through C-86 are from the U.S. Census Bureau. For more detailed information see: DeNavas-Walt, Carmen, Bernadette D. Proctor, and Jessica C. Smith, U.S. Census Bureau, U.S. Department of Commerce, Current Population Reports, P60-235, *Income, Poverty, and Health Insurance Coverage in the United States: 2007.* Washington, DC: 2008.

CONCEPTS AND DEFINITIONS

Activities of daily living (ADL)—activities related to personal care and include bathing or showering, dressing, getting in or out of bed or a chair, using the toilet, and eating. In the National Health Interview Survey, respondents were asked whether they or family members 3 years of age and over need the help of another person with personal care because of a physical, mental, or emotional problem. Persons are considered to have an ADL limitation if any condition(s) causing the respondent to need help with the specific activities was chronic.

Age adjustment—used to compare risks of two or more populations at one point in time or one population at two or more points in time. Age-adjusted rates are computed by the direct method by applying age-specific rates in a population of interest to a standardized age distribution, to eliminate differences in observed rates that result from age differences in population composition. Age-adjusted rates should be viewed as relative indexes rather than actual measures of risk.

Body mass index (BMI)—a measure that adjusts body-weight for height. It is calculated as weight in kilograms divided by height in meters squared. Overweight for children and adolescents is defined as BMI at or above the sex- and age-specific 95th percentile BMI cut points from the 2000 CDC Growth Charts. Healthy weight for adults is defined as a BMI of 18.5 to less than 25; overweight, as greater than or equal to a BMI of 25; and obesity, as greater than or equal to a BMI of 30.

Cholesterol, serum—a measure of the total blood cholesterol. Elevated total blood cholesterol—a combination of high-density lipoproteins (HDL), low-density lipoproteins (LDL), and very-low density lipoproteins (VLDL)—is a risk factor for cardiovascular disease. According to the National Cholesterol Education Program, high serum cholesterol is defined as greater than or equal to 240 mg/dL (6.20 mmol/L). Borderline high serum cholesterol is defined as greater than or equal to 200 mg/dL and less than 240 mg/dL. Assessments of the components of total cholesterol or lower thresholds for high total cholesterol may be used for individuals with other risk factors for cardiovascular disease.

Consumer Price Index (CPI)—prepared by the U.S. Bureau of Labor Statistics. It is a monthly measure of the average change in the prices paid by urban consumers for a fixed market basket of goods and services. The medical care component of CPI shows trends in medical care prices based on specific indicators of hospital, medical, dental, and drug prices. A revision of the definition of CPI has been in use since January 1988.

Gross domestic product (GDP)—the market value of the goods and services produced by labor and property located in the United States. As long as the labor and property are located in the United States, the suppliers (i.e., the workers and, for property, the owners) may be U.S. residents or residents of other countries.

Health expenditures, national—estimated by the Centers for Medicare & Medicaid Services (CMS) it measures spending for health care in the United States by type of service delivered (e.g., hospital care, physician services, nursing home care) and source of funding for those services (e.g., private health insurance, Medicare, Medicaid, out-of-pocket spending). CMS produces both historical and projected estimates of health expenditures by category.

Health insurance coverage—broadly defined to include both public and private payers who cover medical expenditures incurred by a defined population in a variety of settings.

Health maintenance organization (HMO)—a health care system that assumes or shares both the financial risks and the delivery risks associated with providing comprehensive medical services to a voluntarily enrolled population in a particular geographic area, usually in return for a fixed, prepaid fee. Pure HMO enrollees use only the pre-paid capitated health services of the HMO panel of medical care providers. Open-ended HMO enrollees use the prepaid HMO health services but, in addition, may receive medical care from providers who are not part of the HMO panel. There is usually a substantial deductible, co-pay-ment, or co-insurance associated with use of non-panel providers.

Hispanic origin—includes persons of Mexican, Puerto Rican, Cuban, Central and South American, and other or unknown Latin American or Spanish origins. Persons of Hispanic origin may be of any race.

Hypertension—elevated blood pressure or hypertension is defined as having an average systolic blood pressure reading of at least 140mmHg or diastolic pressure of at least 90 mmHg, which is consistent with the Seventh Report of the Joint National Committee on Prevention, Detection, Evaluation, and Treatment of High Blood Pressure. People are also considered to have hypertension if they report that they are taking a prescription medicine for high blood pressure, even if their blood pressure readings are within normal range.

Incidence—the number of cases of disease having their onset during a prescribed period of time. It is often expressed as a rate (e.g., the incidence of measles per 1,000 children 5–15 years of age during a specified year). Incidence is a measure of morbidity or other events that occur within a specified period of time. Measuring inci-dence may be complicated because the population at risk for the disease may change during the period of interest, for example, due to births, deaths, or migration. In addi-tion, determining that a case is new—that is, that its onset occurred during the prescribed period of time—may be difficult. Because of these difficulties in measuring inci-dence, many health statistics are measured using preva-lence.

Instrumental activities of daily living (IADL)—activities related to independent living and include preparing meals, managing money, shopping for groceries or personal items, performing light or heavy housework, and using a telephone. In the National Health Interview Survey (NHIS) respondents are asked whether they or family members 18 years of age and over need the help of anoth-er person for handling routine IADL needs because of a physical, mental, or emotional problem. Persons are con-sidered to have an IADL limitation in the NHIS if any causal condition is chronic.

Limitation of activity—may be defined different ways, depending on the conceptual framework. In the National Health Interview Survey, limitation of activity refers to a long-term reduction in a person's capacity to perform the usual kind or amount of activities associated with his or her age group as a result of a chronic condition. Limitation

of activity is assessed by asking persons a series of ques-tions about limitations in their or household members' ability to perform activities usual for their age group because of a physical, mental, or emotional problem. Persons are asked about limitations in activities of daily living, instrumental activities of daily living, play, school, work, difficulty walking or remembering, and any other activity limitations. For reported limitations, the causal health conditions are determined, and persons are consid-ered limited if one or more of these conditions is chronic. Children under 18 years of age who receive special educa-tion or early intervention services are considered to have a limitation of activity.

Managed care—a term originally used to refer to the pre-paid health care sector (health maintenance organizations or HMOs) where care is provided under a fixed budget and costs are therein capable of being managed. Increasingly, the term is being used to include preferred provider organ-izations (PPOs) and even forms of indemnity.

Medicare—the federal program which helps pay health care costs for people 65 and older and for certain people under 65 with long-term disabilities.

Medicaid—a program administered at the state level, which provides medical assistance to the needy. Families with dependent children, the aged, blind, and disabled who are in financial need are eligible for Medicaid. It may be known by different names in different states.

Notifiable disease—a disease, that when diagnosed, health providers are required, usually by law, to report to state or local public health officials. Notifiable diseases are those of public interest by reason of their contagiousness, sever-ity, or frequency.

Physical activity, leisure-time—starting with 1998 data, leisure-time physical activity is assessed in the National Health Interview Survey by asking adults a series of ques-tions about how often they do vigorous or light/moderate physical activity of at least 10 minutes duration and for about how long these sessions generally last. Vigorous physical activity is described as causing heavy sweating or a large increase in breathing or heart rate and light/mod-erate as causing light sweating or a slight to moderate increase in breathing or heart rate. Adults classified as inactive did not report any sessions of light/moderate or vigorous leisure-time physical activity of at least 10 min-utes duration or reported they were unable to perform leisure-time physical activity. Adults classified with some leisure-time activity reported at least one session of light/moderate or vigorous activity of at least 10 minutes duration but did not meet the requirement for regular leisure-time activity. Adults classified with regular leisure-time activity reported at least three sessions per week of vigorous leisure-time physical activity lasting at least 20 minutes in duration or at least five sessions per week of light/moderate physical activity lasting at least 30 minutes in duration.

Poverty—based on definitions originally developed by the Social Security Administration. These include a set of money income thresholds that vary by family size and composition. Families or individuals with income below their appropriate thresholds are classified as below poverty. These thresholds are updated annually by the U.S. Census Bureau to reflect changes in the Consumer Price Index for all urban consumers (CPI-U). For example, the average poverty threshold for a family of four was $19,971 in 2005, $17,603 in 2000, and $13,359 in 1990.

Preferred provider organization (PPO)—a type of medical plan where coverage is provided to participants through a network of selected health care providers (such as hospitals and physicians). The enrollees may go outside the network, but they would pay a greater percentage of the cost of coverage than within the network.

Prevalence—the number of cases of a disease, infected persons, or persons with some other attribute present during a particular interval of time. It is often expressed as a rate (e.g., the prevalence of diabetes per 1,000 persons during a year).

Short-stay hospital—hospitals that provide general (rather than specialized) care and have an average length of stay of less than 30 days.

Specialty hospital—hospitals that provide a particular type of service to the majority of their patients such as psychiatric, tuberculosis, chronic disease, rehabilitation, maternity, and alcoholic or narcotic.

State Children's Health Insurance Program (SCHIP)—Title XXI of the Social Security Act, known as the State Children's Health Insurance Program (SCHIP), is a program initiated by the Balanced Budget Act of 1997 (BBA). SCHIP provides more federal funds for states to provide health care coverage to low-income, uninsured children. SCHIP gives states broad flexibility in program design while protecting beneficiaries through federal standards. Funds from SCHIP may be used to expand Medicaid or to provide medical assistance to children during a presumptive eligibility period for Medicaid. This is one of several options from which states may select to provide health care coverage for more children, as prescribed within the BBA's Title XXI program.

Substance use—the use of selected substances including alcohol, tobacco products, drugs, inhalants, and other substances that can be consumed, inhaled, injected, or otherwise absorbed into the body with possible detrimental effects.

Suicidal ideation—having thoughts of suicide or of taking action to end one's own life. Suicidal ideation includes all thoughts of suicide, both when the thoughts include a plan to commit suicide and when they do not include a plan. Suicidal ideation is measured in the Youth Risk Behavior Survey by the question "During the past 12 months, did you ever seriously consider attempting suicide?"

Uninsured—in the Current Population Survey (CPS) persons are considered uninsured if they do not have coverage through private health insurance, Medicare, Medicaid, State Children's Health Insurance Program, military or Veterans coverage, another government program, a plan of someone outside the household, or other insurance. Persons with only Indian Health Service coverage are considered uninsured. In addition, if the respondent has missing Medicaid information but has income from certain low-income public programs, then Medicaid coverage is imputed. The questions on health insurance are administered in March and refer to the previous calendar year.

INDEX